SOCIAL WORK RESEARCH METHODS

QUALITATIVE AND QUANTITATIVE APPROACHES

with Research Navigator

LARRY W. KREUGER

University of Missouri at Columbia

W. LAWRENCE NEUMAN

University of Wisconsin at Whitewater

PEARSON

Boston   New York   San Francisco
Mexico City   Montreal   Toronto   London   Madrid   Munich   Paris
Hong Kong   Singapore   Tokyo   Cape Town   Sydney

Dedicated to

John J. Stretch,
Professor,
School of Social Services,
Saint Louis University.

Thanks for teaching.

Series Editor: Patricia M. Quinlin
Composition and Prepress Buyer: Linda Cox
Manufacturing Buyer: JoAnne Sweeney
Cover Administrator: Linda Knowles
Illustrations: Omegatype Typography, Inc.
Electronic Composition: Omegatype Typography, Inc.

For related titles and support materials, visit our online catalog at www.ablongman.com.

Originally published in 2003 under the title *Social Work Research Methods: Qualitative and Quantitative Applications.*

Screenshots in Appendix F courtesy of SPSS.

Between the time website information is gathered and then published, it is not unusual for some sites to have closed. Also, the transcription of URLs can result in unintended typographical errors. The publisher would appreciate notification where these errors occur so that they may be corrected in subsequent editions.

ISBN   0-205-47011-4

Printed in the United States of America

10   9   8   7   6   5   4   3   2   09   08

CONTENTS

PART FIVE
SOCIAL WORK RESEARCH AND
COMMUNICATION WITH OTHERS

APPENDIXES

This new book for social work students merges material from the fourth edition of a comprehensive textbook on social science research methods with up-to-date examples of research from the field of social work practice. The book covers basic content on methodology, including the roles of social workers in science and knowledge building, the interplay of social work theory and research, and positivist, interpretive, and critical perspectives. It has an extended discussion of ethics, politics, and the role of Institutional Review Boards, and examples and exercises on social work diversity and empowerment research.

The book compares and contrasts qualitative and quantitative perspectives in chapters on design, measurement, sampling, data collection, and data analysis (including SPSS). It is based on the assumption that students do not learn research and evaluation in a vacuum. Real people engage in social work research, and they do so in clinical, organizational, and community contexts that can affect their clients, interventions, and outcomes. Included are chapters on experimental research methods, field research, nonreactive research and secondary analysis, and social work evaluation. The producers and consumers of social work research need to reflect on how the larger context shapes research activities and how the social work knowledge that is created can, in turn, affect clinical and community practice and larger policy arenas. To this end the authors have developed an extensive chapter on reviewing the literature both online and via traditional sources, writing literature reviews, generating qualitative and quantitative research reports, and writing basic proposals.

Social workers need to be on guard against ethnocentric or narrow locality-specific perspectives that may constrain their own assumptions, values, and beliefs. We believe that new creative ways to do social work research lie in exploring the interplay between perspectives and research techniques that may apply to only one culture or may be more universal. With greater global communication and contact, social work students should be more sensitive to how and when the activity of social work research crosses borders and informs issues pertaining to empowerment and perhaps to strengthening differing voices. Lastly, we hope to show students not only that both qualitative and quantitative styles of social work research are of value but also that the greatest benefit may well lie in combining them. We believe that maintaining a diversity of perspectives and research techniques will best advance knowledge in the social work practice community.

Larry Kreuger would like to acknowledge the following individuals: Jan Kreuger for her understanding; Charles Cowger, Michael Kelly, and Carol Snively of the School of Social Work at the University of Missouri–Columbia for their encouragement and comments; Howard Karger at the University of Houston for bringing the authors together; Rodney Elliott at Ohio University, Jerome Rosonke at Northern State University, Roy Ruckdeschel and Buford Farris at Saint Louis University, and Roland Meinert of Columbia, Missouri, for their pedagogy; and Carrie Clark, Melissa Kleffner, Lisa Norton, Kathleen Claxton, Dawn Prough, and Jessie Miller for their assistance at various stages.

Larry Neuman extends his appreciation: "Thanks to the many students who have taught me as they learned about research over the past two decades."

The authors are also grateful to the following reviewers for their helpful suggestions and comments: Arlene K. Brown, Florida International University; Jim Hanson, University of Northern Iowa; Steve Kapp, University of Kansas; and Dr. Todd W. Rofuth, Southern Connecticut State University.

PART ONE

RESEARCH NAVIGATOR™

WHAT IS RESEARCH NAVIGATOR™?

Research Navigator™ is the easiest way for you to start a research assignment or research paper. Complete with extensive help on the research process and three exclusive databases of credible and reliable source material (including EBSCO's ContentSelect™ Academic Journal and Abstract Database, *New York Times* Search by Subject Archive, and Link Library), Research Navigator™ helps you quickly and efficiently make the most of your research time.

Research Navigator™ includes three databases of dependable source material to get your research process started:

1. EBSCO's ContentSelect™ Academic Journal and Abstract Database, organized by subject, contains fifty to one hundred of the leading academic journals per discipline. Instructors and students can search the online journals by keyword, topic, or multiple topics. Articles include abstract and citation information and can be cut, pasted, e-mailed, or saved for later use.
2. The *New York Times* Search by Subject Archive is organized by academic subject and searchable by keyword, or multiple keywords. Instructors and students can view full-text articles from the world's leading journalists from the *New York Times*. The *New York Times* Search by Subject Archive is available exclusively to instructors and students through Research Navigator.™
3. Link Library, organized by subject, offers editorially selected "Best of the Web" sites. Link libraries are continually scanned and kept up to date, providing the most relevant and accurate links for research assignments.

In addition, Research Navigator™ includes extensive online content detailing the steps in the research process, including:

— Starting the Research Process
— Finding and Evaluating Sources
— Citing Sources
— Internet Research
— Using Your Library
— Starting to Write

REGISTERING WITH RESEARCH NAVIGATOR™

www.researchnavigator.com

Research Navigator™ is simple to use and easy to navigate. The goal of Research Navigator™ is to help you complete research assignments or research papers quickly and efficiently. The site is organized around the following tabs:

— Home
— Research Process
— Finding Sources
— Using Your Library

In order to begin using Research Navigator,™ you must first register using the personal access code that appears in the front cover of this book.

To Register:

1. Go to **www.researchnavigator.com**
2. Click "Register" under "New Users" on the left side of the screen.
3. Enter the access code exactly as it appears on the inside front cover of this book. (Note: Access codes can be used only once to complete one registration. If you purchased a used guide, the access code may not work. Please go to **www.researchnavigator.com** for information on how to obtain a new access code.)
4. Follow the instructions on screen to complete your registration—you may click the Help button at any time if you are unsure how to respond.
5. Once you have successfully completed registration, write down the Login Name and Password you just created and keep them in a safe place. You will need to enter them each time you want to revisit Research Navigator.™
6. Once you register, you have access to all the resources in Research Navigator™ for twelve months.

Getting Started

From the Research Navigator™ homepage, you have easy access to all of the site's main features, including a quick route to the three exclusive databases of source content that will be discussed in greater detail on the following pages. If you are new to the research process, you may want to start by clicking the Research Process tab, located in the upper right-hand section of the page. Here you will find extensive help on all aspects of the research process, including:

— Introduction to the Research Paper
— Gathering Data
— Searching the Internet
— Evaluating Sources
— Organizing Ideas
— Writing Notes
— Drafting the Paper
— Academic Citation Styles (MLA, APA, CME, and more)
— Blending Reference Material into Your Writing
— Practicing Academic Integrity
— Revising
— Proofreading
— Editing the Final Draft

For those of you who are already familiar with the research process, you already know that the first step in completing a research assignment or research paper is to select a topic. (In some cases, your instructor may assign you a topic.) According to James D. Lester in *Writing Research Papers,* choosing a topic for the research paper can be easy (any topic will serve) yet very complicated (an informed choice is critical). He suggests selecting a person, a person's work, or a specific issue to study—President George W. Bush, John Steinbeck's *Of Mice and Men,* or learned dexterity with Nintendo games. Try to select a topic that will meet three demands.

1. It must examine a significant issue.
2. It must address a knowledgeable reader and carry that reader to another level of knowledge.
3. It must have a serious purpose, one that demands analysis of the issues, argues from a position, and explains complex details.

You can find more tips from Lester in the Research Process section of Research Navigator.™

Research Navigator™ simplifies your research efforts by giving you a convenient launching pad for gathering data on your topic. The site has aggregated three distinct types of source material commonly used in research assignments: academic journals (Content Select™); newspaper articles (*New York Times*); and World Wide Web sites (Link Library).

EBSCO'S CONTENTSELECT ACADEMIC JOURNAL AND ABSTRACT DATABASE

EBSCO's ContentSelect Academic Journal and Abstract Database contains scholarly, peer-reviewed journals (such as the *Journal of Clinical Psychology* or the *Journal of Social Work Education*). A scholarly journal is an edited collection of articles written by various authors and is published several times a year. All the issues published in one calendar year comprise a volume of that journal. For example, the *American Sociological Review* published volume 65 in the year 2000. This official journal of the American Sociological Association is published six times a year, so issues 1–6 in volume 65 are the individual issues for that year. Each issue contains between four and eight articles written by a variety of authors. Additionally, journal issues may contain letters from the editor, book reviews, and comments from authors. Each issue of a journal does not necessarily revolve around a common theme. In fact, most issues contain articles on many different topics.

Scholarly journals are similar to magazines in that they are published several times a year and contain a variety of articles in each issue; however, they are *not* magazines. What sets them apart from popular magazines like *Newsweek* or *Science News* is that the content of each issue is peer reviewed. This means that each journal has, in addition to an editor and editorial staff, a pool of reviewers. Rather than employing a staff of writers who write something on assignment, journals accept submissions from academic researchers all over the world. The editor relies on these peer reviewers both to evaluate the articles, which are submitted, and to decide if they should be accepted for publication. These published articles provide you with specialized knowledge and information about your research topic. Academic journal articles adhere to strict scientific guidelines for methodology and theoretical grounding. The information obtained in these individual articles is more scientific than information you would find in a popular magazine, in a newspaper article, or on a web page.

Using ContentSelect

Searching for articles in ContentSelect is easy! Here are some instructions and search tips to help you find articles for your research paper.

Step 1: **Select an academic subject and topic area.** When you first enter the ContentSelect Research Database, you will see a list of disciplines. To search within a single academic subject, click the name of that subject. In order to search in more than one academic subject, hold down the Alt or Command key. In the space below where all the subjects are listed, you must enter a topic area. For example if you choose Psychology as an academic subject, you might enter "Freud" as a topic area.

Step 2: Click the **GO** button to start your search.

Step 3: **Basic Search.** By clicking **GO,** you will be brought to the Basic Search tab. Basic Search lets you search for articles using a variety of methods. You can select from Standard Search, All Words, Any Words, or Exact Phrase. For more information on these options, click the **Search Tips** link at any time!

Step 4: After you have selected your method, Click **Search.**

Some ways to improve your search:

Tip 1: **Using AND, OR, and NOT** to help you search. In Standard Search, you can use AND, OR, and NOT to create a very broad or very narrow search:

- **AND** searches for articles containing all of the words. For example, typing **education AND technology** will search for articles that contain **both** education AND technology.
- **OR** searches for articles that contain at least one of the terms. For example, searching for **education OR technology** will find articles that contain either education OR technology.
- **NOT** excludes words so that the articles will not include the word that follows "NOT." For example, searching for **education NOT technology** will find articles that contain the term *education* but NOT the term *technology*.

Tip 2: **Using All Words.** When you select the "All Words" option, you do not need to use the word AND—you will automatically search for articles that contain all of the words. The order of the search words entered in does not matter. For example, typing **education technology** will search for articles that contain **both** education AND technology.

Tip 3: **Using Any Words.** After selecting the "Any Words" option, type words, a phrase, or a sentence in the window. ContentSelect will search for articles that contain any of the terms you typed (but will not search for words such as **in** and **the**). For example, type **rising medical costs in the United States** to find articles that contain *rising, medical, costs, United,* or *States.* To limit your search to find articles that contain exact terms, use quotation marks—for example, typing "United States" will search only for articles containing "United States."

Tip 4: **Using Exact Phrase.** Select this option to find articles containing an exact phrase. ContentSelect will search for articles that include all the words you entered, exactly as you entered them. For example, type **rising medical costs in the United States** to find articles that contain the exact phrase "rising medical costs in the United States."

Search by Article Number

Each and every article in EBSCO's ContentSelect Academic Journal and Abstract Database is assigned its own unique article number. In some instances, you may know the exact article number for the journal article you want to retrieve. Perhaps you noted it during a prior research session on Research Navigator.™ Such article numbers might also be found on the companion web site for your text, or in the text itself.

To retrieve a specific article, simply type that article number in the "Search by Article Number" field and click the **GO** button.

Advanced Search

The following tips will help you with an Advanced Search.

Step 1: To switch to an **Advanced Search,** from the Basic Search click the Advanced-Search tab on the navigation bar, just under the EBSCO Host logo. The Advanced-Search tab helps you focus your search using keyword searching, search history, and limiters.

Step 2: Type the words you want to search for in the **Find** field.

Step 3: Click on **Field Codes** to see a list of available field codes for limiting your search. For example, AU-Author will limit your search to an author. Enter one of these two-letter field codes before your search term. For example, if you enter AU-Smith, this will limit your results to SMITH in the Author field. For more information on field codes, click **Search Tips.**

Step 4: After you have added the appropriate field code to your topic, click **Search.**

Some ways to improve your search:

Tip 1: You can enter additional search terms in the **Find** field, and remember to use *and, or,* and *not* to connect multiple search terms (see Tip 1 under Basic Search for information on *and, or,* and *not*).

Tip 2: With Advanced Searches you can also use **Limiters** and **Expanders** to refine your search. For more information on Limiters and Expanders, click **Search Tips.**

THE *NEW YORK TIMES* SEARCH-BY-SUBJECT ARCHIVE

Newspapers, also known as periodicals because they are issued in periodic installments (e.g., daily, weekly, or monthly), provide contemporary information. Information in periodicals—journals, magazines, and newspapers—may be useful, or even critical, when you are ready to focus in on specific aspects of your topic, or to find more up-to-date information.

There are some significant differences between newspaper articles and journal articles, and you should consider the level of scholarship that is most appropriate for your research. Popular or controversial topics may not be well covered in journals, even though coverage in newspapers and "general interest" magazines such as *Newsweek* and *Science* for that same topic may be extensive.

Research Navigator™ gives you access to a one-year, "search by subject" archive of articles from one of the world's leading newspapers—the *New York Times.* To learn more about the *New York Times,* visit them on the web at **www.nytimes.com.**

Using the search-by-subject archive is easy. Simply type a word, or multiple words separated by commas, into the search box and click "go." You will see a list of articles that have appeared in the *New York Times* over the last year, sorted by most recent article first. You can further refine your search as needed. Articles can be printed or saved for later use in your research assignment. Be sure to review the citation rules for how to cite a newspaper article in endnotes or a bibliography.

"BEST OF THE WEB" LINK LIBRARY

The third database included on Research Navigator,™ Link Library, is a collection of web links, organized by academic subject and key terms. To use this database, simply select an academic subject from the dropdown list, and then find the key term for the topic you are searching. Click on the key term and see a list of five to seven editorially reviewed web sites that offer educationally relevant and reliable content. For example, if your research topic is "Allergies," you may want to select the academic subject Biology and then click on "Allergies" for links to web sites that explore this topic. Simply click on the alphabet bar to view other key terms in Biology and their corresponding links. The web links in Link Library are monitored and updated each week, reducing your incidence of finding "dead" links.

USING YOUR LIBRARY

After you have selected your topic and gathered source material from the three databases of content on Research Navigator,™ you may need to complete your research by going to your school library. Research Navigator™ does not try to replace the library, but rather helps you understand how to use library resources effectively and efficiently.

You may put off going to the library to complete research assignments or research papers because the library can seem overwhelming. Research Navigator™ provides a bridge to the library by taking you through a simple step-by-step overview of how to make the most of your library time. Written by a library scientist, the Using Your Library tab explains:

- Major types of libraries
- What the library has to offer
- How to choose the right library tools for a project
- The research process
- How to make the most of research time in the library

In addition, when you are ready to use the library to complete a research assignment or research paper, Research Navigator™ includes thirty-one discipline-specific "library guides" for you to use as a road map. Each guide includes an overview of the discipline's major subject databases, online journals, and key associations and newsgroups.

For more information and detailed walk-throughs, please visit
www.ablongman.com/researchnavigator.com

PART TWO

CONDUCTING ONLINE RESEARCH

FINDING SOURCES: SEARCH ENGINES AND SUBJECT DIRECTORIES

Your professor has just given you an assignment to give a five-minute speech on the topic "gun control." After a (hopefully brief) panic attack, you begin to think of what type of information you need before you can write the speech. To provide an interesting introduction, you decide to involve your class by taking a straw poll of their views for and against gun control, and to follow this up by giving some statistics on how many Americans favor (and oppose) gun control legislation and then by outlining the arguments on both sides of the issue. If you already know the correct URL for an authoritative web site such as Gallup Opinion Polls (www.gallup.com) or other sites, you are in great shape! However, what do you do when you don't have a clue as to which web site would have information on your topic? In these cases, many, many people routinely (and mistakenly) go to Yahoo! and type in a single term (e.g., guns). This approach is sure to bring first a smile to your face when the results offer you 101 million hits on your topic, but just as quickly make you grind your teeth in frustration when you start scrolling down the hit list and find sites that range from gun dealerships, to reviews of the video *Young Guns,* to aging fan sites for the rock group Guns n' Roses.

Finding information on a specific topic on the Web is a challenge. The more intricate your research need, the more difficult it is to find the one or two web sites among the billions that feature the information you want. This section is designed to help you avoid frustration and focus in on the right site for your research by using search engines, subject directories, and meta-sites.

Search Engines

Search engines (sometimes called search services) are becoming more numerous on the web. Originally, they were designed to help users search the web by topic. More recently, search engines have added features that enhance their usefulness, such as searching a particular part of the web (e.g., only sites of educational institutions—.edu), retrieving just one site that the search engine touts as most relevant (such as Ask Jeeves, www.ask.com), or retrieving up to ten sites that the search engine ranks as most relevant (such as Google {www.google.com}).

Search Engine Defined

According to Cohen (1999):

> *A search engine service provides a searchable database of Internet files collected by a computer program called a wanderer, crawler, robot, worm, or spider. Indexing is created from the collected*

files, and the results are presented in a schematic order. There are no selection criteria for the collection of files.

A search service therefore consists of three components: (1) a spider, a program that traverses the Web from link to link, identifying and reading pages; (2) an index, a database containing a copy of each Web page gathered by the spider; and (3) a search engine mechanism, software that enables users to query the index and then returns results in a schematic order. (p. 31)

One problem students often have in their use of search engines is that they are deceptively easy to use. Like our example of "guns," no matter what is typed into the handy box at the top, links to numerous web sites appear instantaneously, lulling students into a false sense of security. Because so much was retrieved, surely SOME of it must be useful. WRONG! Many web sites retrieved will be very light on substantive content, which is not what you need for most academic endeavors. Finding just the right web site has been likened to finding diamonds in the desert.

As you can see by the preceding definition, one reason for this is that most search engines use indexes developed by machines. Therefore they are indexing terms, not concepts. The search engine cannot tell the difference between the keyword *crack* meaning a split in the sidewalk, and *crack,* referring to crack cocaine. Using search engines properly takes some skill, and this chapter will provide tips to help you use search engines more effectively. First, however, let's look at the different types of search engines with examples:

Types of Search Engines

TYPE	DESCRIPTION	EXAMPLES
1st Generation	— Nonevaluative, do not evaluate results in terms of content or authority. — Return results ranked by relevancy alone (number of times the term[s] entered appear, usually on the first paragraph or page of the site).	AltaVista (www.altavista.com) Excite (www.excite.com) HotBot (www.hotbot.com) Ixquick Metasearch (ixquick.com) Lycos (www.lycos.com)
2nd Generation	— More creative in displaying results. — Results are ordered by characteristics such as concept, document type, web site, popularity, etc., rather than relevancy.	Ask Jeeves (www.ask.com) Direct Hit (www.directhit.com) Google (www.google.com) Simplifind (www.simpli.com) SurfWax (www.surfwax.com) Also see Meta-Search engines below. EVALUATIVE SEARCH ENGINES About.Com (www.about.com) WebCrawler (www.webcrawler.com)
Commercial Portals	— Provide additional features such as customized news, stock quotations, weather reports, shopping, etc.	GO Network (www.go.com) Google Web Directory (directory.google.com) LookSmart (www.looksmart.com)

TYPE	DESCRIPTION	EXAMPLES
	— They want to be used as a "one stop" web guide. — They profit from prominent advertisements and fees charged to featured sites.	My Starting Point (www.stpt.com) Open Directory Project (dmoz.org) Yahoo! (www.yahoo.com)
Meta-Search Engines	Run searches on multiple search engines.	There are different types of meta-search engines. Two categories are listed below.
Meta-Search Engines *Integrated Results*	— Display results for search engines in one list. — Duplicates are removed. — Only portions of results from each engine are returned.	Beaucoup.com (www.beaucoup.com) Highway 61 (www.highway61.com) Cyber411(www.cyber411. com) Mamma (www.mamma.com) MetaCrawler (www.metacrawler.com) Vivisimo (vivisimo.com) Northern Light (www.nlsearch.com) SurfWax (www.surfwax.com)
Meta-Search Engines *Nonintegrated Results*	— Comprehensive search. — Displays results from each search engine in separate results sets. — Duplicates remain. — You must sift through all the sites.	Dogpile (www.dogpile.com) GoHip (www.gohip.com) Searchalot (www.searchalot.com) ProFusion (www.profusion.com)

Quick Tips for More Effective Use of Search Engines

1. Use a search engine:
   - When you have a narrow idea to search
   - When you want to search the full text of countless web pages
   - When you want to retrieve a large number of sites
   - When the features of the search engine (such as searching particular parts of the web) help with your search

2. Always use Boolean operators to combine terms. Searching on a single term is a sure way to retrieve a very large number of web pages, few, if any, of which are on target.
   - Always check search engine's HELP feature to see what symbols are used for the operators as these vary (e.g., some engines use the & or + symbol for AND).
   - Boolean operators include:
     AND to narrow search and to make sure that **both** terms are included
       e.g., children AND violence
     OR to broaden search and to make sure that **either** term is included
       e.g., child OR children OR juveniles
     NOT to **exclude** one term
       e.g., eclipse NOT lunar

3. Use appropriate symbols to indicate important terms and to indicate phrases (Best Bet for Constructing a Search According to Cohen [1999]: Use a plus sign (+) in front of terms you want to retrieve: +solar +eclipse. Place a phrase in double quotation marks: "solar eclipse." Put together: "+solar eclipse" "+South America").

4. Use word stemming (a.k.a. truncation) to find all variations of a word (check search engine HELP for symbols).
   - If you want to retrieve child, child's, or children use child* (some engines use other symbols such as !, #, or $)
   - Some engines automatically search singular and plural terms; check HELP to see if yours does.

5. Since search engines only search a portion of the web, use several search engines or a meta-search engine to extend your reach.

6. Remember, search engines are generally mindless drones that do not evaluate. Do not rely on them to find the best web sites on your topic; use subject directories or meta-sites to enhance value (see below).

Finding Those Diamonds in the Desert: Using Subject Directories and Meta-Sites

Although some search engines, such as WebCrawler (www.webcrawler.com), do evaluate the web sites they index, most search engines do not make any judgment on the worth of the content. They just return a long—sometimes very long—list of sites that contained your keyword. However, subject directories exist that are developed by human indexers, usually librarians or subject experts, and are defined by Cohen (1999) as follows:

> A subject directory is a service that offers a collection of links to Internet resources submitted by site creators or evaluators and organized into subject categories. Directory services use selection criteria for choosing links to include, though the selectivity varies among services. (p. 27)

World Wide Web subject directories are useful when you want to see sites on your topic that have been reviewed, evaluated, and selected for their authority, accuracy, and value. They can be real time savers for students, because subject directories weed out the commercial, lightweight, or biased web sites.

Meta-sites are similar to subject directories but are more specific in nature, usually dealing with one scholarly field or discipline. Some examples of subject directories and meta-sites are found in the following table.

Smart Searching—Subject Directories and Meta-Sites

TYPES—SUBJECT DIRECTORIES	EXAMPLES
General, covers many topics	Access to Internet and Subject Resources (www2.lib.udel.edu/subj)
	Best Information on the Net (BIOTN) (library.sau.edu/bestinfo)
	Federal Web Locator (www.infoctr.edu/fwl)
	Galaxy (galaxy.einet.net)
	INFOMINE: Scholarly Internet Resource Collections (infomine.ucr.edu)

Smart Searching—Subject Directories and Meta-Sites

TYPES—SUBJECT DIRECTORIES	EXAMPLES
	InfoSurf: Help by Subject (www.library.ucsb.edu/subjects)
	Librarian's Internet Index (www.lii.org)
	Martindale's "The Reference Desk" (www.martindalecenter.com)
	PINAKES: A Subject Launchpad (www.hw.ac.uk/libWWW/irn/pinakes/pinakes.html)
	Refdesk.com (www.refdesk.com)
	Search Engines and Subject Directories [College of New Jersey] (www.tcnj.edu/~library/research/internet_search.html)
	Scout Report Archives (www.scout.cs.wisc.edu/archives)
	Selected Reference Sites (www.mnsfld.edu/depts/lib/mu~rcf.html)
	WWW Virtual Library (vlib.org)
Subject Oriented	
— Communication Studies	The Media and Communication Studies Site (www.aber.ac.uk/media)
	University of Iowa Department of Communication Studies (www.uiowa.edu/~commstud/resources)
— Cultural Studies	Sara Zupko's Cultural Studies Center (www.popcultures.com)
— Education	Educational Virtual Library (www.csu.edu.au/education/library.html)
	ERIC [Education Resources Information Center] (www.eric.ed.gov)
	Kathy Schrock's Guide for Educators (school.discovery.com/schrockguide)
— Journalism	Journalism Resources (bailiwick.lib.uiowa.edu/journalism)
	Journalism and Media Criticism page (www.chss.montclair.edu/english/furr/media.html)
— Literature	Norton Web Source to American Literature (www.wwnorton.com/naal)
	Project Gutenberg [Over 16,000 full text titles] (www.gutenberg.org)
— Medicine & Health	PubMed [National Library of Medicine's index to Medical journals, 1966 to present] (www.ncbi.nlm.nih.gov/PubMed)
	RxList: The Internet Drug Index (rxlist.com)

(continued)

Smart Searching—Subject Directories and Meta-Sites   (Continued)

	Go Ask Alice [Health and sexuality] (www.goaskalice.columbia.edu)
▬ Technology	CNET.com (www.cnet.com)

Choose subject directories to ensure that you are searching the highest quality web pages. As a bonus, subject directories periodically check web links to make sure that there are fewer dead ends and outdated links.

Another closely related group of sites are the virtual library sites, also referred to as digital library sites. Hopefully, your campus library has an outstanding web site for both on-campus and off-campus access to resources. If not, there are several virtual library sites you can use, although you should realize that some of the resources would be subscription based and not accessible unless you are a student of that particular university or college. These are useful because, like the subject directories and meta-sites, experts have organized web sites by topic and selected only those of highest quality.

You now know how to search for information and use search engines more effectively. In the next section, you will learn more tips for evaluating the information that you found.

Virtual Library Sites

PUBLIC LIBRARIES

▬ Internet Public Library	www.ipl.org
▬ Library of Congress	lcweb.loc.gov/homepage/lchp.html
▬ New York Public Library	www.nypl.org

University/College Libraries

▬ Bucknell	www.bucknell.edu/isr
▬ Case Western	www.cwru.edu/uclibraries.html
▬ Dartmouth	www.dartmouth.edu/~library
▬ Duke	www.lib.duke.edu
▬ Franklin & Marshall	www.library.fandm.edu
▬ Harvard	www.harvard.edu/museums
▬ Penn State	www.libraries.psu.edu
▬ Princeton	library.princeton.edu
▬ Stanford	www.slac.stanford.edu/FIND/spires.html
▬ ULCA	www.library.ucla.edu

Other

▬ Perseus Project [subject specific— classics, supported by grants from corporations and educational institutions]	www.perseus.tufts.edu

EVALUATING SOURCES ON THE WEB

Congratulations! You've found a great web site. Now what? The web site you found seems like the perfect web site for your research. But are you sure? Why is it perfect? What criteria are you using to determine whether this web site suits your purpose?

Think about it. Where else on earth can anyone "publish" information regardless of the accuracy, currency, or reliability of the information? The Internet has opened up a world of opportunity for posting and distributing information and ideas to virtually everyone, even those who might post misinformation for fun, or those with ulterior motives for promoting their point of view. Armed with the information provided in this guide, you can dig through the vast amount of useless information and misinformation on the World Wide Web to uncover the valuable information. Because practically anyone can post and distribute their ideas on the web, you need to develop a new set of critical thinking skills that focus on the evaluation of the quality of information, rather than be influenced and manipulated by slick graphics and flashy moving java script.

Before the existence of online sources, the validity and accuracy of a source was more easily determined. For example, in order for a book to get to the publishing stage, it must go through many critiques, validation of facts, reviews, editorial changes, and the like. Ownership of the information in the book is clear because the author's name is attached to it. The publisher's reputation is on the line too. If the book turns out to have incorrect information, reputations and money can be lost. In addition, books available in a university library are further reviewed by professional librarians and selected for library purchase because of their accuracy and value to students. Journal articles downloaded or printed from online subscription services, such as Infotrac, ProQuest, EbscoHost, or other full-text databases, are put through the same scrutiny as the paper versions of the journals.

On the World Wide Web, however, Internet service providers (ISPs) simply give web site authors a place to store information. The web site author can post information that may not be validated or tested for accuracy. One mistake students typically make is to assume that all information on the web is of equal value. Also, in the rush to get assignments in on time, students may not take the extra time to make sure that the information they are citing is accurate. It is easy just to cut and paste without really thinking about the content in a critical way. However, to make sure you are gathering accurate information and to get the best grade on your assignments, it is vital that you develop your critical ability to sift through the dirt to find the diamonds.

Web Evaluation Criteria

So, here you are, at this potentially great site. Let's go though some ways you can determine if this site is one you can cite with confidence in your research. Keep in mind, ease of use of a web site is an issue, but more important is learning how to determine the validity of data, facts, and statements for your use. The five traditional ways to verify a paper source can also be applied to your web source: *accuracy, authority, objectivity, coverage,* and *currency.*

Evaluating Web Sites Using Five Criteria to Judge Web Site Content

---

Accuracy—How reliable is the information?

Authority—Who is the author and what are his or her credentials?

Objectivity—Does the web site present a balanced or biased point of view?

Coverage—Is the information comprehensive enough for your needs?

Currency—Is the web site up to date?

Use additional criteria to judge web site content, including

- **Publisher, documentation, relevance, scope, audience, appropriateness of format,** and **navigation**
- Judging whether the site is made up of **primary (original)** or **secondary (interpretive) sources**
- Determining whether the information is **relevant** to your research

Content Evaluation

Accuracy.   Internet searches are not the same as searches of library databases because much of the information on the web has not been edited, whereas information in databases has. It is your responsibility to make sure that the information you use in a school project is accurate. When you examine the content on a web site or web page, you can ask yourself a number of questions to determine whether the information is accurate.

1. Is the information reliable?
2. Do the facts from your other research contradict the facts you find on this web page?
3. Do any misspellings and/or grammar mistakes indicate a hastily put together web site that has not been checked for accuracy?
4. Is the content on the page verifiable through some other source? Can you find similar facts elsewhere (journals, books, or other online sources) to support the facts you see on this web page?
5. Do you find links to other web sites on a similar topic? If so, check those links to ascertain whether they back up the information you see on the web page you are interested in using.
6. Is a bibliography of additional sources for research provided? Lack of a bibliography doesn't mean the page isn't accurate, but having one allows you further investigation points to check the information.
7. Does the site of a research document or study explain how the data were collected and the type of research method used to interpret the data?

If you've found a site with information that seems too good to be true, it may be. You need to verify information that you read on the web by cross-checking against other sources.

Authority.   An important question to ask when you are evaluating a web site is, "Who is the author of the information?" Do you know whether the author is a recognized authority in his or her field? Biographical information and references to publications, degrees, qualifications, and organizational affiliations can help to indicate an author's authority. For example, if you are researching the topic of laser surgery, citing a medical doctor would be better than citing a college student who has had laser surgery.

The organization sponsoring the site can also provide clues about whether the information is fact or opinion. Examine how the information was gathered and the research method used to prepare the study or report. Other questions to ask include:

1. Who is responsible for the content of the page? Although a webmaster's name is often listed, this person is not necessarily responsible for the content.
2. Is the author recognized in the subject area? Does this person cite any other publications he or she has authored?
3. Does the author list his or her background or credentials (e.g., Ph.D. degree, title such as professor, or other honorary or social distinction)?
4. Is there a way to contact the author? Does the author provide a phone number or e-mail address?
5. If the page is mounted by an organization, is it a known, reputable one?
6. How long has the organization been in existence?
7. Does the URL for the web page end in the extension .edu or .org? Such extensions indicate authority compared to dotcoms (.com), which are commercial enterprises. (For

example, www.cancer.com takes you to an online drugstore that has a cancer information page; www.cancer.org is the American Cancer Society web site.)

A good idea is to ask yourself whether the author or organization presenting the information on the Web is an authority on the subject. If the answer is no, this may not be a good source of information.

Objectivity. Every author has a point of view, and some views are more controversial than others. Journalists try to be objective by providing both sides of a story. Academics attempt to persuade readers by presenting a logical argument, which cites other scholars' work. You need to look for two-sided arguments in news and information sites. For academic papers, you need to determine how the paper fits within its discipline and whether the author is using controversial methods for reporting a conclusion.

Authoritative authors situate their work within a larger discipline. This background helps readers evaluate the author's knowledge on a particular subject. You should ascertain whether the author's approach is controversial and whether he or she acknowledges this. More important, is the information being presented as fact or opinion? Authors who argue for their position provide readers with other sources that support their arguments. If no sources are cited, the material may be an opinion piece rather than an objective presentation of information. The following questions can help you determine objectivity:

1. Is the purpose of the site clearly stated, either by the author or the organization authoring the site?
2. Does the site give a balanced viewpoint or present only one side?
3. Is the information directed toward a specific group of viewers?
4. Does the site contain advertising?
5. Does the copyright belong to a person or an organization?
6. Do you see anything to indicate who is funding the site?

Everyone has a point of view. This is important to remember when you are using web resources. A question to keep asking yourself is, What is the bias or point of view being expressed here?

Coverage. Coverage deals with the breadth and depth of information presented on a web site. Stated another way, it is about how much information is presented and how detailed the information is. Looking at the site map or index can give you an idea about how much information is contained on a site. This isn't necessarily bad. Coverage is a criteria that is tied closely to *your* research requirement. For one assignment, a given web site may be too general for your needs. For another assignment, that same site might be perfect. Some sites contain very little actual information because pages are filled with links to other sites. Coverage also relates to objectivity. You should ask the following questions about coverage:

1. Does the author present both sides of the story or is a piece of the story missing?
2. Is the information comprehensive enough for your needs?
3. Does the site cover too much too generally?
4. Do you need more specific information than the site can provide?
5. Does the site have an objective approach?

In addition to examining what is covered on a web site, equally revealing is what is not covered. Missing information can reveal a bias in the material. Keep in mind that you are evaluating the information on a web site for your research requirements.

Currency.   Currency questions deal with the timeliness of information. However, currency is more important for some topics than for others. For example, currency is essential when you are looking for technology-related topics and current events. In contrast, currency may not be relevant when you are doing research on Plato or Ancient Greece. In terms of web sites, currency also pertains to whether the site is being kept up to date and links are being maintained. Sites on the web are sometimes abandoned by their owners. When people move or change jobs, they may neglect to remove the site from the company or university server. To test currency, ask the following questions:

1. Does the site indicate when the content was created?
2. Does the site contain a last revised date? How old is the date? (In the early part of 2001, a university updated its web site with a "last updated" date of 1901! This obviously was a Y2K problem, but it does point out the need to be observant of such things!)
3. Does the author state how often he or she revises the information? Some sites are on a monthly update cycle (e.g., a government statistics page).
4. Can you tell specifically what content was revised?
5. Is the information still useful for your topic? Even if the last update is old, the site might still be worthy of use *if* the content is still valid for your research.

Relevancy to Your Research: Primary versus Secondary Sources

Some research assignments require the use of primary (original) sources. Materials such as raw data, diaries, letters, manuscripts, and original accounts of events can be considered primary material. In most cases, these historical documents are no longer copyrighted. The web is a great source for this type of resource.

Information that has been analyzed and previously interpreted is considered a secondary source. Sometimes secondary sources are more appropriate than primary sources. If, for example, you are asked to analyze a topic or to find an analysis of a topic, a secondary source of an analysis would be most appropriate. Ask yourself the following questions to determine whether the web site is relevant to your research:

1. Is it a primary or secondary source?
2. Do you need a primary source?
3. Does the assignment require you to cite different types of sources? For example, are you supposed to use at least one book, one journal article, and one web page?

You need to think critically, both visually and verbally, when evaluating web sites. Because web sites are designed as multimedia hypertexts, nonlinear texts, visual elements, and navigational tools are added to the evaluation process.

Help in Evaluating Web Sites.   One shortcut to finding high-quality web sites is using subject directories and meta-sites, which select the web sites they index by similar evaluation criteria to those just described. If you want to learn more about evaluating web sites, many colleges and universities provide sites that help you evaluate web resources. The following list contains some excellent examples of these evaluation sites:

— Evaluating Quality on the Net—Hope Tillman, Babson College
www.hopetillman.com/findqual.html

- Critical Web Evaluation—Kurt W. Wagner, William Paterson University of New Jersey
  euphrates.wpunj.edu/faculty/wagnerk/critical.html
- Evaluation Criteria—Susan Beck, New Mexico State University
  lib.nmsu.edu/instruction/evalcrit.html
- A Student's Guide to Research with the WWW
  www.slu.edu/departments/english/research
- Evaluating Web Pages: Techniques to Apply & Questions to Ask
  www.lib.berkeley.edu/TeachingLib/Guides/Internet/Evaluate.html

Critical Evaluation Web Sites

Web site and URL	Source
Critical Thinking in an Online World **www.library.ucsb.edu/untangle/jones.html**	*Paper from "Untangling the Web" (1996)*
Educom Review **www.educause.edu/apps/er/review/reviewArticles/31231.html**	*EDUCAUSE, "Literacy as a Liberal Art" (1996 article)*
Evaluating Information Found on the Internet **www.library.jhu.edu/researchhelp/general/evaluating**	*Johns Hopkins University Library*
Evaluating Web Sites **www.lib.purdue.edu/InternetEval**	*Purdue University Library*
Kathy Schrock's ABC's of Web Site Evaluation **www.kathyschrock.net/abceval**	*Author's web site*
Resource Selection and Information Evaluation **people.lis.uiuc.edu/~janicke/InfoAge.html**	*University of Illinois, Urbana–Champaign (Librarian)*
Testing the Surf: Criteria for Evaluating Internet Information Sources **info.lib.uh.edu/pr/v8/n3/smit8n3.html**	*University of Houston Libraries*
Evaluating Web Pages **www.widener.edu/Tools_Resources/Libraries/Wolfgram_Memorial_Library/Evaluate_Web_Pages/659**	*Widener University Library*
UCLA College Library Instruction: Thinking Critically about World Wide Web Resources **www.library.ucla.edu/libraries/college/help/critical**	*UCLA Library*

UG OOL: Judging Quality on the Internet   *University of Guelph*
   www.open.uoguelph.ca/resources/
   skills/judging.html

Web Evaluation Criteria   *New Mexico State University*
   lib.nmsu.edu/instruction/   *Library*
   evalcrit.html

Web Page Credibility Checklist   *Park School of Baltimore*
   www.park.pvt.k12.md.us/academics/
   research/credcheck.htm

Evaluating Web Sites for Educational   *University of North Carolina*
Uses: Bibliography and Checklist
   www.unc.edu/cit/guides/irg-49.html

Evaluating Web Sites   *Lesley University*
   www.lesley.edu/library/guides/
   research/evaluating_web.html

Tip

Can't seem to get a URL to work? If the URL doesn't begin with www, you may need to put the http:// in front of the URL. Usually, browsers can handle URLs that begin with www without the need to type in the "http://" but if you find you're having trouble, add the http://.

DOCUMENTATION GUIDELINES FOR ONLINE SOURCES

Your Citation for Exemplary Research

There's another detail left for us to handle—the formal citing of electronic sources in academic papers. The very factor that makes research on the Internet exciting is the same factor that makes referencing these sources challenging: their dynamic nature. A journal article exists, either in print or on microfilm, virtually forever. A document on the Internet can come, go, and change without warning. Because the purpose of citing sources is to allow another scholar to retrace your argument, a good citation allows a reader to obtain information from your primary sources, to the extent possible. This means you need to include not only information on when a source was posted on the Internet (if available) but also when you obtained the information.

   The two arbiters of form for academic and scholarly writing are the Modern Language Association (MLA) and the American Psychological Association (APA); both organizations have established styles for citing electronic publications.

MLA Style
   In the fifth edition of the *MLA Handbook for Writers of Research Papers,* the MLA recommends the following formats:

— **URLs:** URLs are enclosed in angle brackets (<>) and contain the access mode identifier, the formal name for such indicators as "http" or "ftp." If a URL must be split across two lines, break it only after a slash (/). Never introduce a hyphen at the end of the first line. The URL should include all the parts necessary to identify uniquely the file/document being cited.

`<http://www.csun.edu/~rtvfdept/home/index.html>`

— **An online scholarly project or reference database:** A complete online reference contains the title of the project or database (underlined); the name of the editor of the project or database (if given); electronic publication information, including version number (if relevant and if not part of the title), date of electronic publication or latest update, and name of any sponsoring institution or organization; date of access; and electronic address.

> The Perseus Project. Ed. Gregory R. Crane. Mar. 1997. De-
>   partment of Classics, Tufts University. 15 June 1998
>   <http://www.perseus.tufts.edu/>.

If you cannot find some of the information, then include the information that is available. The MLA also recommends that you print or download electronic documents, freezing them in time for future reference.

— **A document within a scholarly project or reference database:** It is much more common to use only a portion of a scholarly project or database. To cite an essay, poem, or other short work, begin this citation with the name of the author and the title of the work (in quotation marks). Then include all the information used when citing a complete online scholarly project or reference database; however, make sure you use the URL of the specific work and not the address of the general site.

> Cuthberg, Lori. "Moonwalk: Earthlings' Finest Hour." *Discov-
>   ery Channel Online.* 1999. Discovery Channel. 25 Nov. 1999
>   <http://www.discovery.com/indep/newsfeatures/moonwalk/
>   challenge.html>.

— **A professional or personal site:** Include the name of the person creating the site (reversed), followed by a period, the title of the site (underlined), or, if there is no title, a description such as homepage (such a description is neither placed in quotes nor underlined). Then specify the name of any school, organization, or other institution affiliated with the site and follow it with your date of access and the URL of the page.

> Packer, Andy. Homepage. 1Apr. 1998 <http://www.suu.edu/
>   ~students/Packer.htm>.

Some electronic references are truly unique to the online domain. These include e-mail, newsgroup postings, MUDs (multiuser domains) or MOOs (multiuser domains, object-oriented), and IRCs (Internet relay chats).

E-mail.   In citing e-mail messages, begin with the writer's name (reversed) followed by a period, then the title of the message (if any) in quotations as it appears in the subject line. Next comes a description of the message, typically "E-mail to," and the recipient (e.g., "the author"), and finally the date of the message.

> Davis, Jeffrey. "Web Writing Resources." E-mail to Nora
>   Davis. 3 Jan. 2000.

```
Sommers, Laurice. "Re: College Admissions Practices." E-
    mail to the author. 12 Aug. 1998.
```

Listservers and Newsgroups.   In citing these references, begin with the author's name (reversed) followed by a period. Next include the title of the document (in quotes) from the subject line, followed by the words "Online posting" (not in quotes). Follow this with the date of posting. For listservers, include the date of access, the name of the list (if known), and the online address of the list's moderator or administrator. For newsgroups, follow "Online posting" with the date of posting, the date of access, and the name of the newsgroup, prefixed with "news:" and enclosed in angle brackets.

```
Applebaum, Dale. "Educational Variables." Online posting.
    29 Jan. 1998. Higher Education Discussion Group. 30 Jan.
    1993 <jlucidoj@unc.edu>.
```

```
Gostl, Jack. "Re: Mr. Levitan." Online posting. 13 June
    1997. 20 June 1997 <news:alt.edu.bronxscience>.
```

MUDs, MOOs, and IRCs.   Begin with the name of the speaker(s) followed by a period. Follow with the description and date of the event, the forum in which the communication took place, the date of access, and the online address. If you accessed the MOO or MUD through telnet, your citation might appear as follows:

```
Guest. Personal interview. 13 Aug. 1998.
    <telnet://du.edu:8888>.
```

For more information on MLA documentation style for online sources, check out their web site at www.mla.org/style/sources.htm.

APA Style

The newly revised *Publication Manual of the American Psychological Association* (5th ed.) now includes guidelines for Internet resources. The manual recommends that, at a minimum, a reference of an Internet source should provide a document title or description, a date (either the date of publication or update or the date of retrieval), and an address (in Internet terms, a uniform resource locator, or URL). Whenever possible, identify the authors of a document as well. It's important to remember that, unlike the MLA, the APA does not include temporary or transient sources (e.g., letters, phone calls, etc.) in its "References" page, preferring to handle them in the text. The general suggested format is as follows:

Online periodical:

```
Author, A. A., Author, B. B., & Author, C. C. (2000).
    Title of article. Title of Periodical, xx, xxxxx. Re-
    trieved month, day, year, from source.
```

Online document:

```
Author, A. A. (2000). Title of work. Retrieved month,
    day, year, from source.
```

Some more specific examples are as follows:

FTP (File Transfer Protocol) Sites.   To cite files available for downloading via FTP, give the author's name (if known), the publication date (if available and if different from the date accessed), the full title of the paper (capitalizing only the first word and proper nouns), the date of access, and the address of the FTP site along with the full path necessary to access the file.

```
Deutsch, P. (1991) Archie: An electronic directory service
     for the Internet. Retrieved January 25, 2000 from File
     Transfer Protocol: ftp://ftp.sura.net/pub/archie/docs/
     whatis.archie
```

WWW Sites (World Wide Web).   To cite files available for viewing or downloading via the World Wide Web, give the author's name (if known), the year of publication (if known and if different from the date accessed), the full title of the article, and the title of the complete work (if applicable) in italics. Include any additional information (such as versions, editions, or revisions) in parentheses immediately following the title. Include the date of retrieval and full URL (the http address).

```
Burka, L. P. (1993). A hypertext history of multi-user dun-
     geons. MUDdex. Retrieved January 13, 1997 from the World
     Wide Web: http://www.utopia.com/talent/lpb/muddex/essay/

Tilton, J. (1995). Composing good HTML (Vers. 2.0.6). Re-
     trieved December 1, 1996 from the World Wide Web:
     http://www.cs.cmu.edu/~tilt/cgh/
```

Synchronous Communications (MOOs, MUDs, IRC, etc.).   Give the name of the speaker(s), the complete date of the conversation being referenced in parentheses, and the title of the session (if applicable). Next, list the title of the site in italics, the protocol and address (if applicable), and any directions necessary to access the work. Last, list the date of access, followed by the retrieval information. Personal interviews do not need to be listed in the References, but do need to be included in parenthetic references in the text (see the APA *Publication Manual*).

```
Cross, J. (1996, February 27). Netoric's Tuesday cafe: Why use
     MUDs in the writing classroom? MediaMoo. Retrieved March
     1, 1996 from File Transfer Protocol: ftp://daedalus
     .com/pub/ACW/NETORIC/catalog
```

Gopher Sites.   List the author's name (if applicable), the year of publication, the title of the file or paper, and the title of the complete work (if applicable). Include any print publication information (if available) followed by the protocol (i.e., gopher://). List the date that the file was accessed and the path necessary to access the file.

```
Massachusetts Higher Education Coordinating Council.
     (1994). Using coordination and collaboration to address
     change. Retrieved July 16, 1999 from the World Wide Web:
     gopher://gopher.mass.edu:170/00gopher_root%3A%5B_hecc%
     5D_plan
```

E-mail, Listservs, and Newsgroups.   Do not include personal e-mail in the list of References. Although unretrievable communication such as e-mail is not included in APA References, somewhat more public or accessible Internet postings from newsgroups or list-servs may be included. See the APA *Publication Manual* for information on in-text citations.

```
Heilke, J. (1996, May 3). Webfolios. Alliance for Comput-
    ers and Writing Discussion List. Retrieved December
    31, 1996 from the World Wide Web: http://www.ttu.edu/
    lists/acw-l/9605/0040.html
```

Other authors and educators have proposed similar extensions to the APA style. You can find links to these pages at:

```
www.psychwww.com/resource/apacrib.htm
```

Remember, "frequently referenced" does not equate to "correct" or even "desirable." Check with your professor to see if your course or school has a preference for an extended APA style.

PART THREE

WEB ACTIVITIES

WEB ACTIVITIES FOR THE HELPING PROFESSIONS

Using Usenet Newsgroups

Until a couple of years ago, Usenet newsgroups represented one of the best ways to learn about a subject area. Because of the increase in Internet traffic over the past two years, and also because of inappropriate use of Usenet to advertise commercial and often shady enterprises, it has become somewhat less useful. Still, social work and counseling students may find Usenet to be a relatively easy way to learn information about a given subject area.

Surfing the Web for Social Work and Counseling Information

Surfing the Web can be one of the most rewarding strategies for finding information, but you have to remain disciplined and try not to get lost. To beat the metaphor almost to a pulp, it's easy to find yourself bobbing in the waves with the baby sea lions and the sharks if you don't keep your information objectives in mind while you are surfing.

Using Social Work Academic Sites

Exercise

Go to the University of Southern California Social Work Information Center at **www.usc.edu/isd/libraries/locations/social_work.** Click on **E-Resources** in the menu on the left. Then, in the USC Libraries Subjects field, choose Social Work. And under Format, choose eJournals. Then examine the list of journals with full-text articles. Imagine being able to do some of your suggested reading without leaving the comfort of your computer! Now, select one of the listed journals to read.

— What happened when you tried to read from this journal? Why do you think this happened? Does your library provide such a service?

Using Government Resources

Exercise

Go to the National Library of Medicine at **www.nlm.nih.gov** and click on **Health Information** and then scroll down the page and click on **NIH Senior Health.** Click to begin. This will take you to the latest information the U.S. government has published on the topic of aging.

— How authoritative is the information presented on this site?

— How might you use information from the National Library of Medicine for your professional practice?

Using Professional Association Sites

Exercise

Visit the National Association of Social Workers (NASW) site at **www.socialworkers .org** and click on the **NASW Chapters** link under **About NASW** on the left side of the page. Does your state chapter of NASW have e-mail? Do they have a web site of their own? Visit the California Chapter of NASW at **http://naswca.org.**

— How do you think this site will be used by the chapter membership?

— What aspects of the site do you think will be most helpful to social workers?

Using Electronic Journals and Newsletters

Exercise

Go to Alcohol Alerts at **www.niaaa.nih.gov/publications/AlcoholAlerts.** This is a quarterly bulletin of the National Institute on Alcohol Abuse and Alcoholism that disseminates important research findings on a single aspect of alcohol abuse and alcoholism. Notice that you can get free copies of many of these bulletins by clicking on "ordering online" at the bottom of the page. Select a topic of interest to you and click on the link.

— How authoritative is this information?

— How useful would this information be for writing a paper on a related topic?

Using Social Work Areas of Practice Sites

Exercise

Go to the Detroit Community AIDS Library at **www.lib.wayne.edu/dcal/aids.html.** Click on the **Databases** link under Resources and then on the **PubMed** link in the list of databases. This takes you to a free Medline search page, which is a wonderful resource for finding any health-related resource.

— How useful might this resource be for you in your practice?

Exercise

Go to NetPsych.com at **http://netpsych.com.** This site explores the new uses of the Internet to deliver psychological and health care services. NetPsych is the first site to focus exclusively on online resources. Click the **HUH**? button at the bottom of the page.

— What do you think of the sites you find linked here?

— What are your impressions of online psychotherapy? Should the social work profession consider an amendment to the Code of Ethics to cover practice in such circumstances?

Exercise

Go to the Domestic Violence Handbook at **www.domesticviolence.org.** This online resource is designed to assist women who are experiencing domestic abuse. Click on **Index** at the bottom of the page and follow the link to **Personalized Safety Plan.**

— Would you be comfortable knowing that some victims of domestic violence have no other resources to help them? Why or why not?

CHAPTER 1

SCIENCE AND SOCIAL WORK RESEARCH

> *"The real problems in social work research methods and evaluation of practice effectiveness are not methodological, they're not statistical, they're not ethical. Rather, we need to learn how to succeed in the business of conceptualizing, operationalizing, and measuring success."*
> —John J. Stretch, Professor, Saint Louis University, lecture, 1982.

INTRODUCTION

Whether we are aware of it or not, we are surrounded by social work research. Educators, administrators, government officials, business leaders, human service providers, and health care professionals regularly use research findings and principles in their jobs. Social work research can be used to raise children, reduce crime, improve public health, sell products, or just understand one's life. Reports of research appear on broadcast news programs, in magazines, and in newspapers. Recently, one of the authors read in his daily newspaper about studies showing that an antiviolence course in schools re-

ally works, that the D.A.R.E. antidrug program and "boot camps" for criminal offenders are wholly ineffective, that sobriety checkpoints reduce drunk driving, that 31 percent of gay teens were physically threatened or injured while in school, and that medical doctors admitted through Affirmative Action programs are just as successful as those admitted on test scores and grades alone.

How a study was conducted or data were gathered can generate controversy. In 1998 U.S. news reports were filled with arguments and legal challenges on whether to use sampling methods

1

developed by social scientists or traditional ways in the year 2000 census. In a popular magazine, we read about advocates and opponents of single-sex schools. Each side offered supporting data, but the author said the issue hinges on the research methodology they used. Another article stated that methods used by the U.S. government to measure unemployment and poverty are flawed, making our understanding of the condition of economy and society highly inaccurate.[1]

This book is about social work research. In simple terms research is a way of going about finding answers to questions. Social work research is a type of research conducted by social workers, sociologists, social scientists, and others to seek answers to questions about the social world. You probably already have some notion of what social research entails. First, let us end possible misconceptions. When we ask students what they think research entails, the following answers are usually given:

— Based on facts alone, without theory or judgment
— Read or used only by experts or college professors
— Done only in universities by people with Ph.D. degrees
— Going to the library and finding articles on a topic
— Hanging around some exotic place and observing
— Conducting an experiment in which people are tricked into doing something
— Drawing a sample of people and giving them questionnaires
— Looking up lots of tables from government reports or books
— Using computers, statistics, charts, and graphs

The first three of these answers are wrong, and the others describe only part of what constitutes social work research. It is unwise to confuse any one part with the whole. Just as you would never mistake wearing shoes for being fully dressed, you should not mistake any one of these items for social work research.

Social work research involves many things. It is how a person finds out something new and orig-inal about the social world. To do this, a researcher needs to think logically, follow rules, and repeat steps over and over. A researcher combines theories or ideas with facts in a systematic way and uses his or her imagination and creativity. He or she quickly learns to organize and plan carefully and to select the appropriate technique to address a question. A researcher also must be sensitive to treating the people who are being studied in ethical and moral ways. In addition, a researcher must communicate to others clearly.

Social work research is a collection of methods people use systematically to produce knowledge. It is an exciting process of discovery, but it requires persistence, personal integrity, tolerance for ambiguity, interaction with others, and pride in doing quality work. You will learn more about the diversity of social research in Chapter 2.

Do not expect this book to transform you into an expert social work researcher. It can teach you to be a better consumer of research results, give you an understanding of how the research enterprise works, and prepare you to conduct small research projects yourself. After reading this textbook, you will understand research, its meaning, what it can and cannot do, and its role in the larger society.

ALTERNATIVES TO SOCIAL WORK RESEARCH

You learned most of what you know about the social world by an alternative to social work research. A great deal of what you know about the social world is based on what your parents and others have told you. You also have knowledge that you have learned from personal experience and practice. The books and magazines you have read and the movies and television you have watched also have given you information. You may also use common sense to learn about the social world.

In addition to being a collection of methods, social research is a process for producing knowledge about the social world. It is a more structured, organized, and systematic process than the alternatives.[2] Knowledge from the alternatives is often correct, but knowledge based on research is more likely to be true and has fewer potential errors. It is important to recognize that research does not always produce perfect knowledge. Nonetheless, compared to the alternatives, it is less likely to be flawed. Let us review the alternatives before examining social work research.

Authority

You gain knowledge from parents, teachers, and experts as well as from books and television and other media. When you accept something as being true just because someone in a position of authority says it is true or because it is in an authoritative publication, you are using authority as a basis of knowledge. Relying on the wisdom of authorities has advantages—it is a quick, simple, and inexpensive way to learn something. Authorities often spend time and effort to learn something, and you can benefit from their experience and work.

Relying on authorities also has limitations. It is easy to overestimate the expertise of other people. You may assume that they are right when they are not. Authorities may speak on fields they know little about; they can be plain wrong. An expert in one area may try to use his or her authority in an unrelated area. Have you ever seen television commercials wherein an expert in football uses that expertise to try to convince you to buy a car? In addition, there are these questions: Who is or is not an authority? Whom do you believe when different authorities disagree? For example, there was a time when we saw a high school teacher as being an authority on physics. Now we know that such authority does not stand up to that of a Nobel Prize winner in physics.

History is full of past experts whom we now see as being misinformed. For example, some "experts" of the past measured intelligence by counting bumps on the skull; other "experts" used bloodletting to try to cure diseases. Their errors seem obvious now, but can you be certain that today's experts will not become tomorrow's fools? Also, too much reliance on authorities can be dangerous to a democratic society. An overdependence on experts lets them keep others in the dark, and they may promote ideas that strengthen their power and position. When we have no idea of how the experts arrived at

their knowledge, we lose some of our ability to make judgments for ourselves.

Tradition

People sometimes rely on tradition for knowledge. Tradition is a special case of authority—the authority of the past. Tradition means you accept something as being true because "it's the way things have always been." For example, a father-in-law said that "drinking a shot of whiskey cures a cold." When asked about his statement, he said that he had learned it from his father when he was a child, and it had come down from past generations. Tradition was the basis of the knowledge for the cure.

Here is an example more from the social world. Many people believe that children who are raised at home by their mothers grow up to be better adjusted and have fewer personal problems than those raised in other settings. People "know" this, but how did they learn it? Most accept it because they believe (rightly or wrongly) that it was true in the past or is the way things have always been done.

Some traditional social knowledge begins as simple prejudice. A belief such as "people from that side of the tracks will never amount to anything" or "you never can trust anyone of that race" comes down from the past. Even if traditional knowledge was once true, it can become distorted as it is passed on, and soon it is no longer true. People may cling to traditional knowledge without real understanding; they assume that because something may have worked or been true in the past, it must always be true.

Common Sense

You know a lot about the social world from your ordinary reasoning or common sense. You rely on what everyone knows and what "just makes sense." For example, it "just makes sense" that murder rates are higher in nations that do not have a death penalty, because people are less likely to kill if they face execution for doing so. This and other widely held commonsense beliefs, such as that poor youth are more likely to commit deviant acts than those from the middle class, or that most Catholics do not use birth control, are false.

Common sense is valuable in daily living, but it can allow logical fallacies to slip into your thinking. For example, the "gambler's fallacy" says: "If I have a long string of losses playing a lottery, the next time I play, my chances of winning will be better." In terms of probability and the facts, this is false. Also, common sense contains contradictory ideas that go unnoticed because people use the ideas at different times—for example, "opposites attract" and "birds of a feather flock together." Common sense can originate in tradition. It is useful and sometimes correct, but it also contains errors, misinformation, contradiction, and prejudice.

Media Myths

Television shows, movies, and newspaper and magazine articles are important sources of information about social life. For example, most people who have no contact with criminals learn about crime by watching television shows and movies and by reading newspapers. However, the portrayals of crime and of many other things on television do not accurately reflect social reality. Instead, the writers who invent or "adapt" real life for television shows and movie scripts distort reality either out of ignorance or because they rely on authority, tradition, and common sense. Their primary goal is to entertain, not to present reality accurately. Although journalists who write for newspapers and newsmagazines try to present a realistic picture of the world, they must write stories in short time periods with limited information and within editorial guidelines.

Unfortunately, the media tend to perpetuate the myths of a culture. For example, the media show that most people who receive welfare are Black (actually, most are White), that most people who are mentally ill are violent and dangerous (only a small percentage actually are), and that most people who are elderly are senile and in nursing homes (a tiny minority are). Also, mass media "hype" can create a feeling that a major problem exists when it may not (see Box 1.1). People are misled by visual images more easily than by other forms of "lying"; this means that stories or stereotypes that appear on film and television can have a powerful effect on people. For example, television repeatedly shows

---

Box 1.1 _____

Is Road Rage a Media Myth?

Americans hear a lot about *road rage. Newsweek* magazine, *Time* magazine, and newspapers in most major cities have carried headlines about it. Leading national political officials have held public hearings on it, and the federal government gives millions of dollars in grants to law enforcement and transportation departments to reduce it. A California psychologist now specializes in this disorder and has appeared on several major television programs to discuss it.

The term *road rage* first appeared in 1988, and by 1997, the print media were carrying over 4,000 articles per year on it. Despite media attention about "aggressive driving" and "anger behind the wheel," there is no scientific evidence for road rage. The term is not precisely defined and can refer to such diverse things as gunshots from cars, use of hand gestures, running bicyclists off the road, tailgating, and even anger over auto repair bills! All the data on crashes and accidents show declines during the period when road rage reached an epidemic.

Perhaps media reports fueled perceptions of road rage. After hearing or reading about road rage and having a label for the behavior, people began to notice rude driving behavior and engaged in *selective observation.* We will not know for sure until it is properly studied, but the amount of such behavior may be unchanged. It may turn out that the national epidemic of road rage is a widely held myth stimulated by reports in the mass media. (For more information, see Michael Fumento, "Road Rage versus Reality," *Atlantic Monthly* (August 1998).)

---

low-income, inner-city, African American youth using illegal drugs. Eventually, most people "know" that urban Blacks use illegal drugs at a much higher rate than other groups in the United States, even though this notion is false.

Personal Experience

If something happens to you, if you personally see it or experience it, you accept it as true. Personal experience, or "seeing is believing," has a strong impact and is a forceful source of knowledge. Unfortunately, personal experience can lead you astray. Something similar to an optical illusion or mirage can occur. What appears true may actually be due to a slight error or distortion in judgment. The power of immediacy and direct personal contact is very strong. Even knowing that, people sometimes make mistakes or fall for illusions. Sometimes people believe what they see or experience rather than what is revealed by careful research designed to avoid such errors.

The four errors of personal experience reinforce each other and can occur in other areas, as well. They are a basis for misleading people through propaganda, cons or fraud, magic, stereotyping, and some advertising. The first problem, which is the most frequent, is *overgeneralization.* It occurs when you have some evidence that you believe and then assume that it applies to many other situations, too. Limited generalization may be appropriate; under certain conditions a small amount of evidence can explain a larger situation. The problem is that people often generalize well beyond limited evidence. There are many individuals, areas, and situations about which people know little or nothing, so generalizing from the little they do know might seem reasonable.

A second common error is *selective observation.* It occurs when you take special notice of some people or events and generalize from them. People often focus on or observe particular cases or situations, especially when they fit preconceived ideas. We often seek out evidence that confirms what we already know or believe and ignore the range of cases and contradictory information. We are sensitive to features that confirm our ideas—features that might otherwise go unnoticed. For example, we believe overweight people are friendly. This belief may be based on stereotypes, what our parents told us, or whatever. We observe overweight people and, without awareness, pay particular attention to their smiling, laughing, and so on. Without realizing it, we notice and remember people and situations that reinforce our preconceived ideas. Some psychologists have studied people's tendencies to "seek out" and distort their memories to make them more consistent with what they already think. We "overinterpret" gestures or smiles, pay less attention to contradictory evidence, and do not look for unfriendly behavior among overweight people.

A third error is *premature closure.* It often operates with and reinforces the first two errors. Premature closure occurs when you feel you have all the answers and do not need to listen, seek information, or raise questions any longer. Unfortunately, most of us are a little lazy or get a little sloppy in everyday experiences. We take a few pieces of evidence or look at events for a short while and then think we have things figured out. We look for evidence to confirm or reject an idea and stop when a small amount of evidence is present. We jump to conclusions, such as this: We know three people who smoked six packs of cigarettes a day and lived to be 80 years old; therefore, people who smoke lots of cigarettes will live to age 80.

The last error is the *halo effect.* It comes in many forms, but basically, it says we overgeneralize from what we interpret to be highly positive or prestigious. We give things or people we respect a halo, or a strong reputation. We let the prestige "rub off" on other things or people about which we know little. Thus, we pick up a report by a person from a prestigious university, say Harvard or Cambridge University. We assume that the author is smart and talented and that the report will be excellent. We do not make this assumption about a report by someone from Unknown University. We begin to form an opinion and prejudge the report and do not approach it by considering its own merits alone.

HOW SCIENCE WORKS

The critical factor that separates social work research from other ways of knowing about the social world is that it uses a scientific approach. *Social work research* is more than a collection of methods and a process for creating knowledge; it is a process for producing new knowledge about the social world that uses a *scientific* approach. Let us take a brief look at "science," a subject to which we will return in Chapter 4.

Science

When most people hear the word *science,* the first image that comes to mind is one of test tubes, computers, rocket ships, and people in white lab coats.

These outward trappings are a part of science. Some sciences, such as the natural sciences—biology, chemistry, physics, and zoology—deal with the physical and material world (e.g., rocks, plants, chemicals, stars, blood, electricity, etc.). The natural sciences are the basis of new technology and receive a lot of publicity. Most people first think of them when they hear the word *science*.

The social sciences, such as anthropology, psychology, political science, and sociology, involve the study of people—their beliefs, behavior, interaction, institutions, and so forth. Fewer people associate these disciplines with the word *science*. They are sometimes called *soft sciences*. This is not because their work is sloppy or lacks rigor but because their subject matter, human social life, is fluid, formidable to observe, and hard to measure precisely with laboratory instruments. The subject matter of a science (e.g., human attitudes, protoplasm, or galaxies) determines the techniques and instruments (e.g., surveys, microscopes, or telescopes) used by it.

Science is a social institution and a way to produce knowledge. It has not always been around; it

"I'm a social scientist, Michael. That means I can't explain electricity or anything like that, but if you ever want to know about people I'm your man."

is a human invention. What people now call science grew from a major shift in thinking that began with the Age of Reason or Enlightenment period in western European history, which occurred between the 1600s and the early 1800s. The Enlightenment ushered in a wave of new thinking. It included a faith in logical reasoning, an emphasis on experiences in the material world, a belief in human progress, and a questioning of traditional religious authority. It began with the study of the natural world and spread to the study of social life. The importance of science in modern society and as a basis for seeking knowledge is associated with the societal transformation called the Industrial Revolution. The advancement of science or of fields within science, such as sociology, does not just happen. It is punctuated by the triumphs and struggles of individual researchers. It is also influenced by significant social events such as war, depression, government policy, or shifts in public support.[3]

At one time, all people created new knowledge using prescientific or nonscientific methods. These included the alternatives discussed previously and other methods that are less widely accepted in modern society (e.g., oracles, mysticism, magic, astrology, or spirits). Before science became fully entrenched, such prescientific systems were generally accepted. They were an unquestioned way to produce knowledge that people took to be true. Such prescientific methods still exist but are secondary to science. Some people use nonscientific methods to study topics beyond the scope of science (e.g., religion, art, or philosophy). People in advanced modern society believe that most aspects of the social and natural world are within the scope of science. Today few people seriously question science as a legitimate way to produce knowledge about modern society.

Science refers to both *a system for producing knowledge* and *the knowledge produced from that system.* The system evolved over many years and is slowly but constantly changing. It combines assumptions about the nature of the world and knowledge; an orientation toward knowledge; and sets of procedures, techniques, and instruments for gaining knowledge. It is visible in a social institution called the scientific community.

The knowledge of science is organized in terms of theories. For now, *social theory* can be defined as a system of interconnected abstractions or ideas that condense and organize knowledge about the social world. Several types of social theory are discussed in Chapter 3. Social theory is like a map of the social world; it helps people visualize the complexity in the world and explains why things happen.

Scientists gather data by using specialized techniques and use the data to support or reject theories. *Data* are the empirical evidence or information that one gathers carefully according to rules or procedures. The data can be *quantitative* (i.e., expressed as numbers) or *qualitative* (i.e., expressed as words, pictures, or objects). *Empirical* evidence refers to observations that people experience through the senses—touch, sight, hearing, smell, and taste. This confuses people, because researchers cannot use their senses to directly observe many aspects of the social world about which they seek answers (e.g., intelligence, attitudes, opinions, feelings, emotions, power, authority, etc.). Researchers have many specialized techniques to observe and indirectly measure such aspects of the social world.

Pseudoscience

We must be cautious about *pseudoscience* posing as real natural or social science. The public faces a constant barrage of pseudoscience through television, magazines, film, newspapers, special seminars or workshops, and the like. Some individuals operating a business, or who strongly embrace a belief system, weave a mix of the outward trappings of science (e.g., technical jargon, fancy-looking machines, complex formulas and statistics, or white lab coats) and a few scientific facts with myths, fantasy, or hopes, and then add a little illogic. They then claim a "miracle cure," "new wonder treatment," "revolutionary learning program," "creationism science," "evidence of alien visitors," or "new age spiritual energy." Pseudoscience may include a few so-called experts who hold mail-order Ph.D. degrees, degrees in unrelated academic fields, or other dubious credentials. A few are applied-science practitioners (e.g., medical doctors, psychologists, etc.) who operate at the fringe of their profession.

Unfortunately, the mass media contain as much pseudoscience as (if not more than) honest science. Sometimes officials in business, government, and local schools are taken in by highly promoted "wonder cures" or "revolutionary new theories" that look like science; they mistake well-publicized fake (or pseudo) science for the real thing. Some ideas in pseudoscience are outright hoaxes or operate barely within laws against deceptive advertising. Others are modern myths held by true believers who use the cultural legitimacy of science. Pseudoscience continues because the rules are very loose about what the mass media label "scientific." Also, many people cannot distinguish between the outward trappings of science and the real thing.

Popular (or "pop") social science books sometimes cross over into pseudoscience. Some are accurate popularization of the knowledge that legitimate social researchers produced. Others appear to nonspecialists to be legitimate social science but are a distorted picture or a misuse of social science. They promote particular political or social values in the guise of social science. The information in such books is often of low quality and rarely meets the standards of the scientific community. For example, the Hite Report on female sexuality was a seriously flawed study conducted by a nonscientist that grossly distorted actual social relations. That did not prevent it from becoming a best-seller that was widely discussed in the mass media. The *Bell Curve* (Herrnstein and Murray, 1994) is a more recent example (Fischer et al., 1996).

Sadly, many people, including political and community leaders, base decisions on what they hear about or read in pseudoscience books. As an added complication, beginning in the mid-1980s in the United States, people who advocated specific ideologies donated large amounts of money to create think tanks or policy institutes. These organizations financed authors, some who held Ph.D. degrees, to write popularizations on policy issues. The think tanks then widely promoted the books to gain popular support for their political ideas. Some popularizations cross over into pseudoscience. There is no quality control on the social science books advertised on television or radio, cited in newspaper articles, or sold at local bookstores.

Books that mostly contain personal opinion or political ideology are designed to look like "real" social science texts.

The Scientific Community

Science is given life through the operation of the scientific community, which sustains the assumptions, attitudes, and techniques of science. The *scientific community* is a collection of people and a set of norms, behaviors, and attitudes that bind them together to sustain the scientific ethos. It is a community because it is a group of interacting people who share ethical principles, beliefs and values, techniques and training, and career paths. It is not a geographic community. Rather, it is a professional community whose members share an outlook on— and a commitment to—scientific research. For the most part, the scientific community includes both the natural and social sciences.[4]

Many people outside the core scientific community use scientific research techniques. A range of practitioners and technicians apply research techniques that have been developed and refined by the scientific community. They apply the knowledge and procedures originated within the scientific community. For example, many people use a research technique created by the scientific community (e.g., a survey) without possessing a deep knowledge of research, without inventing new methods of research, and without advancing science itself. Yet, those who use the techniques or results of science will be able to do so better if they also understand the principles and processes of the scientific community.

The boundaries of this community and its membership are defined loosely. There is no membership card or master roster. Many people treat a Ph.D. degree in a scientific field as an informal "entry ticket" to membership in the scientific community. The Ph.D., which stands for doctorate of philosophy, is an advanced graduate degree beyond the master's that prepares one to conduct independent research. Some researchers do not have Ph.D.'s and not all those who receive Ph.D.'s enter occupations in which they conduct research. They enter many occupations and may have other responsibilities (e.g., teaching, administration, consulting, clinical practice, advising, etc.). In fact, about one-half of the people who receive scientific Ph.D.'s do not follow careers as active researchers.

At the core of the scientific community are researchers who conduct studies on a full-time or half-time basis, usually with the help of assistants. Many research assistants are graduate students, and some are undergraduates. Working as a research assistant is the way that most scientists gain a real grasp on the details of doing research.

Colleges and universities employ most members of the scientific community's core. Some scientists work for the government or private industry in organizations such as Bell Labs, the National Opinion Research Center, or the Rand Corporation. Most are found at the approximately 200 research universities and institutes located in half a dozen advanced industrialized countries. Thus, the scientific community may be scattered geographically, but its members tend to work together in small clusters.

How big is the scientific community? This is not an easy question to answer. Using the broadest definition (including all scientists and those in science-related professions, such as engineers), about 15 percent of the labor force in advanced industrialized countries are members of the scientific community. A better way to look at the scientific community is to look at the basic unit of the larger community: the discipline (e.g., sociology, biology, psychology, etc.). Scientists are most familiar with a particular discipline because knowledge is specialized. In the United States there are about 700,000 social workers, 17,000 professional sociologists, 132,000 architects, 650,000 lawyers, and 1,257,000 accountants. Each year, about 150 people receive Ph.D.'s in social work, 16,000 receive medical degrees, and 38,000 receive law degrees.

About one-half of the Ph.D. degree holders do not conduct research for a living. Many researchers complete only one or two studies in their careers. A minority conduct dozens of studies. These numbers drop down to as few as 100 people for topic areas or specialties within disciplines (e.g., study of divorce or the death penalty). The outcomes of the scientific community affect the lives of millions of people, yet most ongoing research and new knowledge on a topic may depend on the efforts of a few hundred people.

The Norms of the Scientific Community

Behavior in any human community is regulated by social norms. The scientific community is governed by a set of professional norms and values that researchers learn and internalize during many years of schooling. The norms are mutually reinforcing and contribute to the unique role of the scientist.[5] The settings in which active researchers work and the very operation of the system of science reinforces the norms.[6] Like other social norms, professional norms are ideals of proper conduct. Because researchers are real people, their prejudices, egos, ambitions, personal lives, and the like may affect their professional behavior. The norms of science do not always work perfectly in practice and are occasionally violated.[7] Likewise, it is important to remember that the operation of science does not occur in a vacuum isolated from the real world. Diverse social, political, and economic forces affect its development and influence how it operates.

The five basic norms of science are listed in Box 1.2. They differ from those in other social institutions (e.g., business, government) and set scientists apart. Scientists largely check on each other to see that the norms are followed. For example, consistent with the norm of *universalism*, scientists will admire a brilliant, creative researcher even if he or she has strange personal habits or a disheveled appearance. Scientists may argue intensely with one another and "tear apart" a research report as part of the norm of *organized skepticism*. They usually listen to new ideas, no matter how strange. Following *disinterestedness*, scientists take results as being tentative, to be accepted only until something better comes along. They love to have other scientists read and react to their research, and some have led fights against censorship. This is consistent with the norm of *communalism*. Communalism does not always work, especially when it conflicts with the profit motive. Scientists working in the tobacco, pharmaceutical, and computer chip industries had the publication of research findings suppressed or delayed by corporate officials for whom the profit

---

Box 1.2 _____

Norms of the Scientific Community

1. *Universalism.* Irrespective of who conducts research (e.g., old or young, male or female) and regardless of where it was conducted (e.g., United States or France, Harvard or Unknown University), the research is to be judged only on the basis of scientific merit.
2. *Organized skepticism.* Scientists should not accept new ideas or evidence in a carefree, uncritical manner. They should challenge and question all evidence and subject each study to intense scrutiny. The purpose of their criticism is not to attack the individual, but to ensure that the methods used in research can stand up to close, careful examination.
3. *Disinterestedness.* Scientists must be neutral, impartial, receptive, and open to unexpected observations or new ideas. They should not be rigidly wedded to a particular idea or point of view. They should accept, even look for, evidence that runs against their positions and should honestly accept all findings based on high-quality research.
4. *Communalism.* Scientific knowledge must be shared with others; it belongs to everyone. Creating scientific knowledge is a public act, and the findings are public property, available for all to use. The way in which the research is conducted must be described in detail. New knowledge is not formally accepted until other researchers have reviewed it and it has been made publicly available in a special form and style.
5. *Honesty.* This is a general cultural norm, but it is especially strong in scientific research. Scientists demand honesty in all research; dishonesty or cheating in scientific research is a major taboo.

---

motive overrode the scientific norm of communalism.[8] Scientists expect *honesty* in the conduct and reporting of research and are aghast when anyone cheats at research.

The Scientific Method and Attitude

You have probably heard of the scientific method, and you may be wondering how it fits into all this. The *scientific method* is not one single thing. It refers to the ideas, rules, techniques, and approaches that the scientific community uses. The method arises from a loose consensus within the community of scientists. A discussion of the fundamental methods of social research is found in Chapter 4.

It is better to focus on the *scientific attitude,* or a way of looking at the world. It is an attitude that values craftsmanship, with pride in creativity, high-quality standards, and hard work. As Grinnell (1987:125) stated:

> *Most people learn about the "scientific method" rather than about the scientific attitude. While the "scientific method" is an ideal construct, the scientific attitude is the way people have of looking at the world. Doing science includes many methods; what makes them scientific is their acceptance by the scientific collective.*

Journal Articles in Science

You may be familiar with certain social work scholarly journals or specialized magazines. When the scientific community creates new knowledge, it appears in academic books or scholarly journal articles. A more detailed discussion of scholarly journals is in Chapter 16. The primary forms in which research findings or new scientific knowledge appear are *scholarly journal articles.* They are how scientists formally communicate with one another and disseminate the results of scientific research. They are also part of the much discussed explosion of knowledge. Each discipline or field has over 100 journals, each of which publishes many articles every year. For example, a leading journal in social work, published by the National Association of Social Workers, is *Social Work,* which publishes several hundred articles per year. The journal article is a crucial part of the research process and the scientific community, but it is not always well understood.[9]

Consider what happens once a researcher completes a study. First, he or she writes a description of the study and the results as a research report or a paper in a special format. Often, he or she gives an oral presentation of the paper at a meeting of a professional association, such as the American Sociological Association, and sends a copy of it to a few scientists for their comments and suggestions. Next, the researcher sends copies to the editor of a scholarly journal such as the *Sociological Quarterly* or the *Social Science Quarterly.* Each editor, a respected researcher who has been chosen by other scientists to oversee the journal, removes the title page, which is the only place the author's name appears, and sends the paper to several referees for a *blind review.* The referees are scientists who have conducted research in the same specialty area or topic. The review is "blind" because the referees do not know who conducted the research and the author does not know who were chosen as referees. This reinforces the norm of universalism, because referees judge the paper on its merits alone. They evaluate the research on the basis of its clarity, originality, standards of good research, and contribution to knowledge. Journals want to publish research that is well done and that significantly advances knowledge. The referees return their evaluations to the editor, who decides to reject the paper, ask the author for revisions, or accept it for publication.

Almost all academic fields use peer referees for publication, but not all use a blind review process. Sociology, psychology, and political science use blind reviews for almost all scholarly journals, and often three or more scholars review a study. By contrast, fields such as biology, history, and economics use a mix of review processes; sometimes reviewers know the author's identity and only one or two scholars review the study. Blind reviews with many referees slow the process and lower acceptance rates (Clemens and Powell, 1995:446). It is a very cautious method of ensuring quality control that advances the norms of organized skepticism and universalism.

Some scholarly journals are widely read and highly respected. They receive many more papers than they can publish. For example, major social science journals, such as *American Economic Review, Social Service Review, Social Work Research, American Sociological Review, American Political Science Review,* and *Social Problems* accept only 10 to 15 percent of submitted manuscripts. Even less esteemed journals regularly reject half of the submissions. Thus, researchers screen a journal article for its merits before publication, and publication represents tentative acceptance by the scientific community. Publishing a book involves a somewhat different review process that includes cost and sales considerations, but the acceptance rate is often lower, usually from 3 to 6 percent (Clemens and Powell, 1995:444).

Unlike the authors of articles for the popular magazines found at newsstands, who are paid for writing, scientists are not paid for publishing in scholarly journals. In fact, they may have to pay a small fee to help defray costs just to have their papers considered. Researchers are happy to make their research available to their peers (i.e., other scientists and researchers) through scholarly journals. Likewise, the referees are not paid for reviewing papers. They consider it an honor to be asked to conduct the reviews and a responsibility of membership in the scientific community. The scientific community imparts great respect to researchers who publish many articles in the foremost scholarly journals because the articles confirm that these researchers are leaders in advancing the primary goal of the scientific community—to contribute to the accumulation of scientific knowledge.

A researcher gains prestige and honor within the scientific community, respect from peers, and a reputation as an accomplished researcher through such publications. Researchers want to earn the respect of their peers—other highly trained scientists who are most knowledgeable about the research issues. In addition, an impressive record of respected publications helps a researcher obtain grants, fellowships, job offers, a following of students, improved working conditions, and increases in salary.[10]

You may never publish an article in a scholarly journal, but you will likely read such articles. They are a vital component of the system of scientific research. The results of most research (i.e., most new scientific knowledge) first appear in scholarly journals. Researchers read the journals to learn about the research others conducted, the methods they used, and the results they obtained.

You can participate in the process by which new knowledge is communicated.

Science as a Transformative Process

You can think of research as the use of scientific methods to transform ideas, hunches, and questions, sometimes called *hypotheses,* into scientific knowledge. This book reveals the transformative process of social work research. In the research process, a researcher starts with guesses or questions and applies specialized methods and techniques to this raw material. At the end of the process, a finished product of value appears: scientific knowledge. A highly productive researcher is one who creates a great deal of new knowledge that greatly improves people's understanding of the world.

You may be starting to feel that the research process is beyond you. After all, it involves complex technical skills and the high-powered scientific community. Yet, the fundamentals of conducting research are accessible to most people. With education and practice, you can learn to do scientific research. In addition to assimilating the scientific attitude or culture, you will need to master how and when to apply research techniques. After reading this book, you should grasp them. Soon you will be able to conduct small-scale research projects yourself.

STEPS OF THE RESEARCH PROCESS

The Steps

The research process requires a sequence of steps. Various approaches suggest somewhat different steps, but most seem to follow the seven steps discussed here. (Different types of research are covered in Chapters 2 and 4.)

The process begins with a researcher selecting a *topic*—a general area of study or issue such as divorce, crime, homelessness, or powerful elites. A topic is too broad for conducting research. This is why the next step is crucial. The researcher narrows down, or *focuses,* the topic into a specific research question that he or she can address in the study (e.g., "Do people who marry younger have a higher divorce rate?"). When learning about a topic and narrowing the focus, the researcher usually reviews past research, or the *literature,* on a topic or question. (Chapter 16 discusses how to do a literature review.) The researcher also develops a possible answer, or hypothesis. As Chapter 3 will show, theory can be important at this stage.

After specifying a research question, the researcher plans how he or she will carry out the specific study or research project. The third step involves making decisions about the many practical details of doing the research (e.g., whether to use a survey or observe in the field, how many subjects to use, which questions to ask, etc.). Now the researcher is ready to *gather the data* or evidence (e.g., ask people the questions, record answers, etc.).

Once the researcher has collected the data, the next step is to manipulate or *analyze the data* to see any patterns that emerge. The patterns or evidence help the researcher give meaning to or *interpret* the data (e.g., "People who marry young in cities have higher divorce rates, but those in rural areas do not."). Finally, the researcher *informs others* by writing a report that describes the background to the study, how he or she conducted it, and what was discovered.

The neat seven-step process shown in Figure 1.1 is oversimplified. In practice, researchers rarely complete step 1, then leave it to move to step 2, and so on. Research is more of an interactive process in which steps blend into each other. A later step may stimulate reconsideration of a previous one. The process is not strictly linear; it may flow in several directions before reaching an end. Research does not abruptly end at step 7. It is an ongoing process, and the end of one study often stimulates new thinking and fresh research questions.

The seven steps are followed for one research project. A researcher applies one cycle of the steps in a single research project or a research study on a specific topic. Each project builds on prior research and contributes to a larger body of knowledge. The larger process of scientific discovery and accumulating new knowledge requires the involvement of many researchers in numerous research projects all at the same time. A single researcher may be working on multiple research projects at once, or several researchers may collaborate on one project. Like-

wise, one project may result in one scholarly article or several, and sometimes several smaller projects are reported in a single article. It may help to look at Figure 1.1 for a summary of the steps after reading the following examples.

Examples

You can better understand the parts of the research process by seeing them in the final product of a study or a journal article. The parts of the process will be identified in four studies. The first two are quantitative studies (a survey and an experiment) and the second two are qualitative studies (a historical study and one using in-depth interviews).

Example 1. Gary Whitfield (1999), of Hopkins County Adolescent Day Treatment Program, conducted a study entitled "Validating School Social Work: An Evaluation of a Cognitive–Behavioral Approach to Reduce School Violence."

Choose a Topic. The author wanted to know whether cognitive–behavioral methods of anger management had a significant affect on school violence. He performed an extensive literature search and found that cognitive–behavioral methods were generally praised in their effectiveness in reducing violent behavior and increasing anger control.

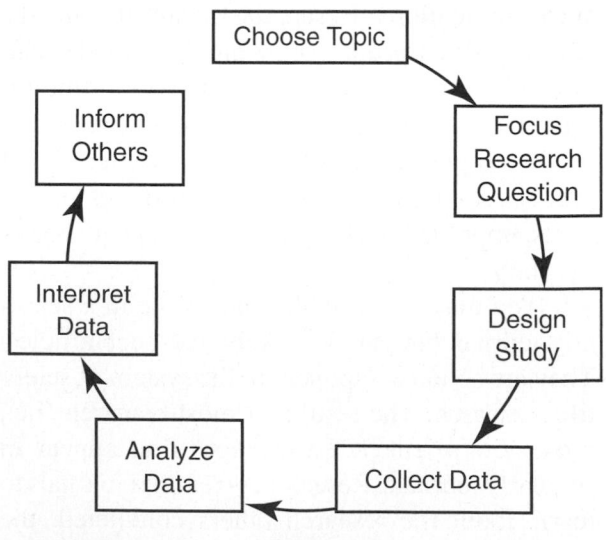

FIGURE 1.1 Steps in the Research Process

Focus the Project.   The goal of the author was to document school social work's ability to influence changes in school violence, using a theoretically based intervention. Three questions were used to focus the study further: (1) How effective was social work in using cognitive–behavioral methods to reduce school violence? (2) When trying to improve anger control, is a specific or general approach more effective? (3) Are anger control gains still apparent in subjects after six months?

Design the Study.   The researcher obtained subjects from his existing caseload of adolescent boys in the school. Each participant gave consent to participate and was paired as closely as possible with another, given existing demographics and behaviors. The members of the pairs of boys were randomly assigned to either the control or the experimental group. The control group did not receive any extra skills training beyond what they would have originally under the author's caseload. The experimental group, in addition to the typical treatments, also received skills training in relaxation techniques, anger reducers, thought-stopping techniques, and problem-solving skills.

Gather the Data.   Self-report rating scales, anger expression inventories, behavior observation scales, and staff and parent reports were all used to gather data on the subjects. The control and experimental groups were given all of the same tests and measures over multiple sessions and weeks. Sixteen subjects participated in the experiment: eight in the control group and eight in the experimental group.

Analyze the Data.   Baseline and intervention results of measures were recorded weekly for both groups of subjects. These weekly recordings were then plotted on graphs for each of the 16 subjects. All of the subjects had posttest data, but not all of them were still active in the school social work program at the 6-month follow-up measure.

Interpret the Findings.   The author found that students who had participated in the anger-control training had generally positive changes. They had fewer behavioral problems than subjects not receiving the training, as well as more positive expressions of anger. The author is quick to point out,

however, that with such a small sample there were many outside influencing factors that the study could not control for.

Inform Others.   This study was published in the July 1999 issue of *Research on Social Work Practice.*

Example 2.   Matthew Mulford, John Orbell, Catherine Shatto, and Jean Stockard (1998) from the London School of Economics, Carnegie Mellon University, and the University of Oregon conducted an experiment and published results in an article titled "Physical Attractiveness, Opportunity and Success in Everyday Exchange."

Choose a Topic.   The authors wanted to know whether perceived physical attractiveness affects daily interactions and opportunities for financial rewards. Drawing on past studies and exchange theory (see Chapter 3), the authors thought that others will believe that attractive people will act more responsibly and be more cooperative, based only on physical appearance.

Focus the Project.   The authors' goal was to extend past research that found a "halo effect" (a belief that attractive people have more of other, unrelated abilities). In particular, they examined the impact of attractiveness on decision-making situations that are widely used in economic theory. The "prisoner's dilemma" game involves making decisions to cooperate with others or to go alone to get rewards. The authors wanted to find out whether decision making was affected in ways that gave the attractive person greater financial rewards.

Design the Study.   An advertisement in the University of Oregon student newspaper was used to recruit subjects. Subjects were given $20 for participation in a first study. They could gain up to another $20 in a second study or lose the money, depending on game decisions, but they would get at least $5 in the second study. Most subjects were undergraduates but some townspeople participated. Slightly over one-half (58 percent) were women.

Gather the Data.   First, each subject had a choice to play a game with another subject. If they agreed, they could cooperate with each other, or "defect," or act alone. Playing many games meant more chances for rewards. If neither subject cooperated, rewards were very low for both; if both cooperated, the rewards were modest for both; if one cooperated but the other did not, the one who "defected" (or did not cooperate) got high rewards and the cooperating person got little. Subjects rated themselves and six subjects with whom they played on a scale from 1 to 11, where 1 = very attractive and 11 = not attractive at all.

Analyze the Data.   The authors examined the results of the decisions, the amount of rewards, and the attractiveness ratings. Women who gave themselves low attractiveness ratings (1–5) earned half as much as those who rated themselves high (9–11). Subjects who saw themselves as less attractive expected others to cooperate, whereas highly attractive people expected less cooperation from others regardless of sex.

Interpret the Findings.   The authors found that others are more likely to enter play with attractive people and, once in a game, were more willing to cooperate with them. Since attractive people were less likely to cooperate with others, they received more rewards because others overestimated their cooperativeness. Attractive people gained more by "defecting" or "going it alone" when others expected cooperation.

Inform Others.   The authors—from the fields of political science and sociology in the United States, Germany, and the United Kingdom—published the results in *American Journal of Sociology*.

Example 3.   In 1991 John Sutton of the University of California, Santa Barbara, published an article called "The Political Economy of Madness: The Expansion of the Asylum in Progressive America."

Choose a Topic.   The topic of the study was a large growth in the number of people in insane asylums and its relationship to public policy.

Focus the Project.   The study focused on a dramatic increase in the number of people in U.S. insane asylums between the 1880s and the 1920s. It built on two books on the history of mental illness in the United States written by Gerald Grob. The books documented that many criminologists, char-

ity experts, and physicians criticized prisons, mental hospitals, almshouses, and reformatories as inhumane and called for reforms in the 1880s and 1890s. Despite some reforms in the penal system and almshouses, the number of people in asylums grew from 40,000 to over 260,000 between 1880 and 1923, and people feared an "epidemic of madness." Grob had argued that the almshouses for poor people were harshly criticized and most were closed. Yet, no system of welfare was created in their place, especially for the thousands of impoverished elderly in the poorhouses. In this era prior to social welfare programs, the asylum was one of the only institutions open to them. Without alternatives, thousands of poverty-stricken people were classified as insane as a way to get food, shelter, and care.

Sutton built on Grob's work and focused his study by using a theory that says that governments try to expand, responding to public crises in ways that expand the power of government officials. Sutton noted that most government resources before the 1930s were located in state governments, in which the political party in power provided patronage and construction jobs to expand its power. He hypothesized that the growth rate in asylum inmates would vary across different states, depending on the need to expand political power and the availability of economic resources in each state.

Design the Study.   Sutton studied the details of the historical context and how mental hospitals operated in the period. He also identified statistics to measure the economic and political characteristics of each state.

Gather the Data.   Sutton examined historical studies on psychiatry, mental hospitals, and government policy in the period. He also gathered quantitative data on the size of insane populations, political competition, wealth available to states, and other state characteristics.

Analyze the Data.   Sutton could predict the size of the increase of asylum inmates in a state largely on the basis of its political and economic characteristics. The insane population grew fastest in states that had more resources, more intense competition between political parties, more older people, and more people in cities. At the time, people in some states received federal government assistance because they or a relative had fought on the Union side in the U.S. Civil War. Sutton found that asylums grew much less rapidly in states where more people were getting such federal assistance.

Interpret the Findings.   Sutton argued that asylum expansion occurred because there was no federal government solution to poverty. He agreed with Grob that many impoverished older people were classified as insane by the loose methods of early psychiatry. But he went beyond Grob to show that this did not happen equally across the country. The insane populations grew most where there was little help for impoverished people from federal government assistance, where sufficient state-level resources existed to build and staff the asylums, and where greater competition between political parties stimulated patronage jobs. At that time most of the jobs in asylums and the funds to build the asylums were given out by state-level political party officials. Thus, the state government response to the crisis of thousands of impoverished elderly people, who had no place to go when the old almshouses were shut down, was to build and staff many new asylums where there was little federal assistance. This was done when political parties sought to expand their power and stay in office by using tax revenue to swell the ranks of those who depended on the party for their jobs. Asylum expansion was a method to deal with the poor people while providing jobs controlled by the political party in power in the state government.

Inform Others.   Prior to its publication in *American Sociological Review,* this study was reported at a meeting of the American Sociological Association and at Stanford University.

Example 4.   In 2000 Jo Ann McFall and Paul Freddolino of Michigan State University published an article called "The Impact of Distance Education Programs on Community Agencies."

Choose a Topic.   Rather than study the effects that distance education has on students, as many studies in the past have done, the authors decided to study distance learning programs from a different perspective. They opted to study the impacts of distance education programs on clients, field instructors, co-operating agencies, and the networks of agencies that surround the distance education sites.

Focus the Project.   Previous research on distance education programs concluded that the presence of MSW students tended to encourage the distant agencies in which the students were placed to support the special needs populations of the community. The students of the MSW programs also were apt to incorporate unique programs into those agencies. The authors chose to study two distance MSW programs in Michigan.

Design the Study.   One year prior to the study, the authors conducted interviews on sets of focus groups to better understand the issues that impacted the distant agencies. A survey was prepared to measure the focus groups' findings. Four versions of the survey were prepared—one each for field instructors, agency directors, first-year master's students, and second-year students. The survey was composed of 14 Likert-type questions involving the following topics: student presence, new knowledge, networks, information technology, and overall impact.

Gather the Data.   Surveys with return postage paid were mailed to the agency directors, field instructors, and students participating in the distance education programs. Response rates ranged from 37.5 percent for students to 55.6 percent for field instructors. A total of 266 surveys were returned from the 362 originally sent. Data from the surveys were entered into SPSS for analysis.

Analyze the Data.   The 14 items were initially analyzed by using the five divisions originally discovered by the focus groups. After analysis, however, it was apparent that several of the items could be grouped with more than one division, making them ambiguous to the survey's divisions.

Interpret the Findings.   It was found that the presence of students in the distant agencies increased services provided to clients and also increased new programs. Less negativity than expected was found regarding the time required for supervision of the students or the need of the agency to work around each student's schedule. Respondents agreed that there was a sharing of knowledge between students and staff, but some discrepancy was found between students and field instructors when testing for application of new skills learned in the program. All respondents believed there to be a strong relationship between field instructors and students and that having students at the agency brought a new level of professionalism to their setting. The authors concluded that distance education programs had reached the goals of providing a quality education to students across the state, while improving the community's resources.

Inform Others.   This research study was published in the journal *Research on Social Work Practice.*

QUALITATIVE AND QUANTITATIVE SOCIAL WORK RESEARCH

In this book you will learn about both qualitative and quantitative styles of doing social work research. After the first several chapters, the two styles will be used to help organize most remaining chapters. Each category uses several specific research techniques (e.g., survey, interview, and historical analysis), yet there is much overlap between the type of data and the style of research. So qualitative researchers examine qualitative-type data, and vice versa. However, sometimes qualitative researchers examine quantitative data, and vice versa. Both styles are widely used, but each is rooted on a distinct logic or approach to social science (discussed in Chapter 4).

Unfortunately, there is a lot of ill will between the followers of each style of research. Some find it difficult to understand or appreciate the other style. Thus, Levine (1993:xii) wrote, "Quantitative social science," which he called "real social science," faced opposition but it "won the battle." Denzin and Lincoln (1994) argued that qualitative research expanded greatly and is rapidly displacing outdated quantitative-style research.

Although both styles share basic principles of science, the two approaches differ in significant ways (see Table 1.1). Each has its strengths and lim-

TABLE 1.1   Quantitative Style versus Qualitative Style

QUANTITATIVE STYLE	QUALITATIVE STYLE
Measure objective facts	Construct social reality, cultural meaning
Focus on variables	Focus on interactive processes, events
Reliability is key	Authenticity is key
Value free	Values are present and explicit
Independent of context	Situationally constrained
Many cases, subjects	Few cases, subjects
Statistical analysis	Thematic analysis
Researcher is detached	Researcher is involved

Sources: Cresswell (1994), Denzin and Lincoln (1994), Guba and Lincoln (1994), Mostyn (1985), and Tashakkori and Teddlie (1998).

itations, topics or issues where it glitters, and classic studies that provide remarkable insights into social life. We agree with King, Keohane, and Verba (1994:5), who stated that the best research "often combines the features of each."

No matter what style they adopt, researchers try to avoid the errors discussed earlier in this chapter, to be systematic in gathering data, and to use the idea of comparison extensively. By understanding both styles, you will know about a range of research and can use both in complementary ways. Ragin (1994:92) has explained one way the styles complement each other:

> *The key features common to all qualitative methods can be seen when they are contrasted with quantitative methods. Most quantitative data techniques are data condensers. They condense data in order to see the big picture. . . . Qualitative methods, by contrast, are best understood as data enhancers. When data are enhanced, it is possible to see key aspects of cases more clearly.*

WHY CONDUCT SOCIAL WORK RESEARCH?

Where can you find people conducting social work research? Students, professors, professional researchers, and scientists in universities, research centers, and the government, with an army of assistants and technicians, conduct much social work research. This research is not visible to the average person. Although the results may appear only in specialized publications or textbooks, the basic knowledge and research methods that professional researchers develop become the basis for all other social research.

In addition to those in universities, people who work for newspapers, television networks, market research firms, schools, hospitals, social service agencies, political parties, consulting firms, government agencies, personnel departments, public interest organizations, insurance companies, or law firms may conduct research as part of their jobs. Numerous people make use of social work research techniques. The findings from research yield better informed, less biased decisions than the guessing, hunches, intuition, and personal experience that were previously used (see Box 1.3). Unfortunately, those being studied may feel overstudied or overloaded by the research. For example, the many exit poll studies by the mass media during elections have prompted a backlash of people refusing to vote and debates over legal restrictions on such polling.

Also, some people misuse or abuse social work research—use sloppy research techniques, misinterpret findings, rig studies to find previously decided results, and so on. But the hostile reactions to such misuse may be directed at research in general instead of at the people who misuse it.

People conduct social work research for many reasons. Some want to answer practical questions (e.g., "Will the provision of health care services in shelters serving families who are homeless reduce the use of hospital emergency room care among these families?"). Others are interested in evaluating the efficacy of different types of treatment (e.g., "Will women who receive group sessions in addition to casework services differ from those who receive individual casework only, in learning to cope with their abusive partners?"). Still others want to change society (e.g., "What can be done to reduce alcoholism?"). Finally, those in the scientific community seek to build basic knowledge about society (e.g., "How can we understand the varied needs of increasing numbers of elderly clients?"). The Council on Social Work Education (CSWE) has mandated that social work education pay special attention to the diverse needs and interests of clients, practitioners, social work students, and educators. To that end we offer material throughout this book that informs diversity issues, as noted in Box 1.4.

Box 1.3 _____

The Practitioner and Social Science

Science does not, and cannot, provide people with fixed, absolute Truth. This is because science is a slow, incomplete process of reducing untruth. It is a quest for the best possible answers carried out by a collection of devoted people who labor strenuously in a careful, systematic, and open-minded manner. Many people are uneasy with the painstaking pace, hesitating progress, and incertitude of science. They demand immediate, absolute answers. Many turn to religious fanatics or political demagogues who offer final, conclusive truths in abundance.

What does this mean for diligent practitioners (e.g., human service workers, health care professionals, criminal justice officers, journalists, or policy analysts) who have to make prompt decisions in their daily work? Must they abandon scientific thinking and rely only on common sense, personal conviction, or political doctrine? No. They, too, can use social scientific thinking. Their task is difficult but possible. They must conscientiously try to locate the best knowledge currently available; use careful, independent reasoning; avoid known errors or fallacies; and be wary of any doctrine offering complete, final answers. Practitioners must always be open to new ideas, use multiple information sources, and constantly question the evidence offered to support a course of action.

Box 1.4 _____

Illustrative Sources on Diversity Issues in Science and Social Work

Appadurai, A. (1990). Disjuncture and difference in global cultural economy, *Public Culture*, 2(2):10.

Barton, J. (1998). Culturally competent research protocols, in J. Green, *Cultural awareness in the human services: A multi-ethnic approach*. Boston: Allyn & Bacon, 285–303.

Cowger, C. (1994). Assessing client strengths: Clinical assessment for client empowerment. *Social Work*, 39:262–268.

Davis, L., and J. Marsh. (1994). Is feminist research inherently qualitative, and is it a fundamentally different approach to research? In W. Hudson and P. Nurius (Eds.), *Controversial issues in social work research* (pp. 63–74). Boston: Allyn & Bacon.

Ewalt, P., and N. Mokuau. (1995). Self-determination from a Pacific perspective. *Social Work*, 40(2):168–176.

Ghali, S. B. (1977). Cultural sensitivity and the Puerto Rican client. *Social Casework*, 58:459–468.

Haj-Yakia, M. (1997). Culturally sensitive supervision of Arab social work students in western universities. *Social Work*, 42(2):166–174.

Johnson, A. and L. Kreuger. (1988). Toward a better understanding of homeless women. *Social Work*, 34(6):134–138.

Matsouka, J., and D. Ryujin. (1991). Asian American immigrants: A comparison of the Chinese, Japanese, and Filipinos. *Journal of Sociology and Social Welfare*, 18(3): 123–133.

Nakanishi, M., and B. Rittner. (1992). The inclusionary cultural model. *Journal of Social Work Education*, 28:27–35.

Rap, C., W. Shera, and W. Kisthardt. (1993). Research strategies for consumer empowerment of people with severe mental illness. *Social Work*, 38(6):727–735.

Saleebey, D. (1997). *The strengths perspective in social work practice*. New York: Longman.

CONCLUSION

In this chapter you learned what social work research is, how the research process operates, and who conducts research. You also learned about alternatives to research—ways to get fast, easy, and practical knowledge that, nonetheless, often contains error, misinformation, and false reasoning. You saw how the scientific community works, how research fits into the scientific enterprise, and how the norms of science and journal articles are crucial to the scientific community. You also learned the steps of research.

Social work research is for, about, and conducted by *people*. Despite the attention to the principles, rules, or procedures, remember that research is a human activity. Researchers are people, not unlike yourself, who became absorbed in a desire to create and discover knowledge. Many find research to be fun and exciting. They conduct it to discover new knowledge and to gain a richer understanding of the social world. Whether you become a professional researcher, someone who applies a few research techniques as part of a job, or just someone who uses the results of research, you will benefit from learning about the research process. You will be enriched if you can begin to create a personal link between yourself and the research process.

Mills offered the following valuable advice in his *Sociological Imagination* (1959:196):

> You must learn to use your life experiences in your intellectual work: to continually examine and interpret it. In this sense craftsmanship is the center of yourself and you are personally involved in every intellectual product upon which you may work.

KEY TERMS _____

blind review	overgeneralization	scientific attitude
communalism	premature closure	scientific community
data	pseudoscience	scientific method
disinterestedness	qualitative data	selective observation
empirical	quantitative data	social theory
halo effect	scholarly journal article	universalism
organized skepticism		

REVIEW QUESTIONS_____

1. What sources of knowledge are alternatives to social work research?

2. Why is social work research usually better than the alternatives?

3. Is social work research always right? Can it answer any question? Explain.

4. How did science and oracles serve similar purposes in different eras?

5. What is the scientific community? What is its role?

6. What are the norms of the scientific community? What are their effects?

7. How does a study get published in a scholarly social work journal?

8. What steps are involved in conducting a research project?

9. What does it mean to say that research steps are not rigidly fixed?

10. What types of people do research? For what reasons?

11. How might social work researchers make sure they include everyone, regardless of their diverse backgrounds, in the research process?

NOTES_____

1. See Wendy Kaminer, "The Trouble with Single Sex Schools," *Atlantic Monthly,* 281 (April 1998); John E. Schwarz, "The Hidden Side of the Clinton Economy," *Atlantic Monthly,* 282 (October 1998); Ethan Bronner, "Study of Doctors Sees Little Effect of Affirmative Action on Careers," *New York Times* (October 8, 1998); "Anti-Violence Course in Schools Does Its Job, Researchers Find," *New York Times* (May 28, 1997); Fox Butterfield, "Most Efforts to Stop Crime Fall Far Short, Study Finds," *New York Times* (April 16, 1997); "Excerpts from Ruling on Planned Use of Statistical Sampling," *New York Times* (August 25, 1998); Bob Whitby, "Truth or Dare," *Isthmus* (Madison, WI), (November 8, 1996); *Economist,* "Lies, Damned Lies, and . . . ," (July 19, 1997); "Sobriety Checkpoint Is Effective, Study Says," *New York Times,* (September 1, 1998); James Brooke, "Homophobia Often Found in Schools, Data Show," *New York Times* (October 13, 1998); and Wysong, Aniskiewicz, and Wright (1994).

2. For more on alternatives, see Babbie (1998:20–21), Kaplan (1964), and Wallace (1971).

3. The rise of science is discussed in Camic (1980), Lemert (1979), Merton (1970), Wuthnow (1979), and Ziman (1976). For more on the historical development of the social sciences, see Eastrope (1974), Laslett (1992), Ross (1991), and Turner and Turner (1991).

4. For more on the scientific community, see Bloom (1978), Cole (1983), Cole, Cole, and Simon (1981), Collins (1983), Collins and Restivo (1983), Grinnell (1999), Hagstrom (1965), Heineman-Pieper (1985), Hudson (1982), Meinert, Pardeck, and Kreuger (2000), Merton (1973), Reid (1994), Rubin and Babbie (2000), Stoner (1966), and Ziman (1968).

5. For more on the social role of the scientist, see Ben-David (1971), Camic (1980), and Tuma and Grimes (1981).

6. Norms are discussed in Hagstrom (1965), Merton (1973), and Stoner (1966).

7. Violations of norms are discussed in Blume (1974) and Mitroff (1974).

8. See Lawrence K. Altman, "Drug Firm, Relenting, Allows Unflattering Study to Appear," *New York Times* (April 16, 1997); John Markoff, "Dispute over Unauthorized Reviews Leaves Intel Embarassed," *New York Times* (March 12, 1997); and Barry Meier, "Philip Morris Censored Data About Addiction," *New York Times* (May 7, 1998).

9. The communication and publication system is described in Bakanic and colleagues (1987), Baker and Wilson (1992), Blau (1978), Cole (1983), Crane (1967), Epstein (1992), Gusfield (1976), Hargens (1988), Kreuger (1997), Lindsey (1999), Mullins (1973), Pardeck (1992), Singer (1989), Stoesz (1997), and Ziman (1968).

10. For more on the system of reward and stratification in science, see Cole and Cole (1973), Cole (1978), Fuchs and Turner (1986), Gaston (1978), Gustin (1973), Karger (1986), Long (1978), Meadows (1974), and Reskin (1977).

DIMENSIONS OF SOCIAL WORK RESEARCH

Research helps build knowledge for practice. It can generate and refine concepts, determine the evidence for generalizations and theories, and ascertain the effectiveness of practice methods.

—William Reid, *Encyclopedia of Social Work,* p. 2040.

INTRODUCTION

Three years after they graduated from college, Tim and Sharon met for lunch. Tim asked Sharon, "So, how is your new job as a researcher for Social Data, Inc.? What are you doing?" Sharon answered, "Right now I'm working on an applied research project on day care in which we're doing a cross-sectional survey to get descriptive data for an evaluation study." Sharon's description of her research project on the topic of day care touches on four dimensions of social work research. This chapter discusses those dimensions.

The picture of social work research presented in Chapter 1 was a simplified one. Research comes in several shapes and sizes. Before a researcher begins to conduct a study, he or she must decide on a specific type of research. Good researchers understand the advantages and disadvantages of each type, although most end up specializing in one.

In this chapter you will learn about the four dimensions of social work research: (1) the purpose of doing it, (2) its intended use, (3) how it treats time, and (4) the research techniques used in it. The four dimensions reinforce one another; that is, a purpose tends to go with certain techniques and particular uses. Few studies are pure types, but the dimensions simplify the complexity of conducting research.

Before conducting a research project, a researcher makes several decisions. By understanding the dimensions of research, you will be better prepared to make such decisions. In addition, an awareness of the types of research and how they fit into the research process will make it easier for you to read and understand published studies.

DIMENSIONS OF RESEARCH

The Purpose of a Study

If you ask someone why he or she is conducting a study, you might get a range of responses: "My boss told me to"; "It was a class assignment"; "I was curious"; "My roommate thought it would be a good idea." There are almost as many reasons to do research as there are researchers. Yet, the purposes of social research may be organized into three groups, based on what the researcher is trying to accomplish—explore a new topic, describe a social phenomenon, or explain why something occurs.[1] Studies may have multiple purposes (e.g., both to explore and to describe), but one purpose is usually dominant.

Exploration. Perhaps you have explored a new topic or issue to learn about it. If the issue was new or researchers had written little on it, you began at the beginning. This is called *exploratory research.* The researcher's goal is to formulate more precise questions that future research can answer. Exploratory research may be the first stage in a sequence of studies. A researcher may need to conduct an exploratory study to know enough to design and execute a second, more systematic and extensive study.

Research on AIDS (acquired immune deficiency syndrome) illustrates exploratory research. When AIDS first appeared, around 1980, no one knew what type of disease it was, or even if it was a disease. No one knew what caused it, how it spread, or why it appeared. Officials knew only that people were entering hospitals with symptoms that no one had seen before, that they failed to respond to any treatment, and that they died quickly. It took many exploratory medical and social science studies before researchers knew enough to design precise studies about the disease.

Exploratory studies often go unpublished. Instead, researchers incorporate them into more systematic research that they publish later. An example of a published exploratory study is Gaither Loewenstein's 1985 article in *Sociological Quarterly,* "The New Underclass: A Contemporary Sociological Dilemma." The purpose of the research was to explore the idea "that a new underclass is emerging in America, comprised of the previously mobile working class citizens." Because the "new" underclass in which the author was interested emerged during the 1980s, little was known about it when he began. Loewenstein wanted to learn whether a new underclass was developing. He read other studies and theories of social class, examined labor market statistics, interviewed 50 public assistance (welfare) applicants aged 18 to 30, and spent 16 months with a social group of working-class young people. The author's initial fuzzy idea, which arose from his informal social interaction with friends, became clearer and more developed during the research process.

Exploratory research rarely yields definitive answers. It addresses the "what" question: "What is this social activity really about?" It is difficult to conduct because there are few guidelines to follow. Everything about a topic is potentially important. The steps are not well defined, and the direction of inquiry changes frequently. This can be frustrating for researchers, who may feel adrift or that they are "spinning their wheels."

Exploratory researchers are creative, open minded, and flexible; adopt an investigative stance; and explore all sources of information. Researchers ask creative questions and take advantage of *serendipity,* those unexpected or chance factors that have larger implications. For example, researchers expected to find that the younger a child was at immigration to a new nation, the less the negative impact on that child when going on to college. Instead, they unexpectedly discovered that children who immigrated in a specific age group (between ages 6 and 11) were especially vulnerable to the disruption of immigration, more so than either older or younger children.[2]

Exploratory researchers frequently use qualitative data. The techniques for gathering qualitative data are less wedded to a specific theory or research question. Qualitative research tends to be more open to using a range of evidence and discovering new issues (see Box 2.1).

Box 2.1 _____

Goals of Research

EXPLORATORY	**DESCRIPTIVE**	**EXPLANATORY**
— Become familiar with the basic facts, setting, and concerns.	— Provide a detailed, highly accurate picture.	— Test a theory's predictions or principle.
— Create a general mental picture of conditions.	— Locate new data that contradict past data.	— Elaborate and enrich a theory's explanation.
— Formulate and focus questions for future research.	— Create a set of categories or classify types.	— Extend a theory to new issues or topics.
— Generate new ideas, conjectures, or hypotheses.	— Clarify a sequence of steps or stages.	— Support or refute an explanation or prediction.
— Determine the feasibility of conducting research.	— Document a causal process or mechanism.	— Link issues or topics with a general principle.
— Develop techniques for measuring and locating future data.	— Report on the background or context of a situation.	— Determine which of several explanations is best.

Description.   You may have a more highly developed idea about a social phenomenon and want to describe it. *Descriptive research* presents a picture of the specific details of a situation, social setting, or relationship. Much of the social work research found in scholarly journals or used for making policy decisions is descriptive.

Descriptive and exploratory research have many similarities. They blur together in practice. In descriptive research the researcher begins with a well-defined subject and conducts research to describe it accurately. The outcome of a descriptive study is a detailed picture of the subject. For example, results may indicate the percentage of people who hold a particular view or engage in specific behaviors—for example, that 10 percent of parents physically or sexually abuse their children.

A descriptive study presents a picture of types of people or of social activities. Donald McCabe (1992) studied cheating among U.S. college students. He was interested in how people rationalize deviance. He thought that they developed justifications that neutralized or turned back moral disapproval, in order to protect their self-images and deflect self-blame. He conducted a survey of over 6,000 students and found that two-thirds admitted to cheating on a major test or assignment at least once. Six major types of cheating appeared to be common. When McCabe asked the students why

they cheated, he discovered that they justified their behavior using four major *neutralization strategies.* The most common strategy, cited by over half of the cheaters, was a denial of responsibility. In this strategy, people claim that forces beyond their control, such as a heavy workload or peer behavior, justify the deviance. Other rationalizations given by cheating students included a denial that anyone is hurt, condemnation of the teacher, or an appeal to higher loyalties such as friendship. The example article on students' religious attitudes summarized in Chapter 1 was a descriptive study, which described how student attitudes changed over time.

Descriptive research focuses on "how" and "who" questions ("How did it happen?" "Who is involved?"). Exploring new issues or explaining why something happens (e.g., why students neutralize cheating or why students hold specific religious beliefs) is less of a concern for descriptive researchers than describing how things are.

A great deal of social work research is descriptive. Descriptive researchers use most data-gathering techniques—surveys, field research, content analysis, and historical-comparative research. Only experimental research is less effective (see Box 2.1).

Explanation.   When you encounter an issue that is already known and have a description of it, you might begin to wonder *why* things are the way they are. The desire to know "why," to explain, is the purpose of *explanatory research*. It builds on exploratory and descriptive research and goes on to identify the reason something occurs. Going beyond focusing on a topic or providing a picture of it, explanatory research looks for causes and reasons. For example, a descriptive researcher may discover that 10 percent of parents abuse their children, whereas the explanatory researcher is more interested in learning *why* parents abuse their children (see Box 2.1).

Scott South and Kim Lloyd (1995) conducted an explanatory study to explain divorce rates. They tested a theory that says the chance of a divorce increases when there is an ample supply of potential alternative partners with whom a married person comes into contact. In other words, a demographic factor (i.e., the availability of alternative spouses) has a negative impact on marriage stability. Evidence suggested that a large percent of recently divorced persons had prior involvement with someone other than their spouses. Among other results, South and Lloyd discovered that divorce rates were higher in areas where there was an imbalance in the sex ratio and where many unmarried women worked full time. The authors explained a higher divorce rate in these areas by a greater opportunity for social interaction between married men and unmarried women in the workplace. Such interaction takes place in a general social climate that emphasizes personal fulfillment and individual choice and permits divorce to end unsatisfactory marriages.

The Use of Research

For over a century, social work has had two wings. Researchers in one adopt a more detached, scientific, and academic orientation; those in the other are more activist, pragmatic, and reform oriented. This is not a rigid separation. Researchers in the two wings cooperate and maintain friendly relations. Some move from one wing to another at different stages in their careers. The difference in orientation revolves around how to use social work research. In simple terms some focus on using research to advance general knowledge, whereas others use it to solve specific problems. Those who seek an under-

standing of the fundamental nature of social reality are engaged in *basic research* (also called *academic research* or *pure research*). Applied researchers, by contrast, primarily want to apply and tailor knowledge to address a specific practical issue. They want to answer a policy question or solve a pressing social problem.

Basic Research. Basic research advances fundamental knowledge about the social world. It focuses on refuting or supporting theories that explain how the social world operates, what makes things happen, why social relations are a certain way, and why society changes. Basic research is the source of most new scientific ideas and ways of thinking about the world. It can be exploratory, descriptive, or explanatory; however, explanatory research is the most common.

Many nonscientists criticize basic research and ask, "What good is it?" They consider basic research to be a waste of time and money because it does not have a direct use or help resolve an immediate problem. It is true that knowledge produced by basic research often lacks practical applications in the short term. Yet, basic research provides a foundation for knowledge and understanding that is generalizable to many policy areas, problems, or areas of study. Basic research is the source of most of the tools—methods, theories, and ideas—that applied researchers use. Really big breakthroughs in understanding and significant advances in knowledge usually come from basic research. In contrast to applied researchers, who want quick answers to questions for use within the next month or year, basic researchers painstakingly seek answers to questions that could have an impact on thinking for over a century.

The questions asked by basic researchers seem impractical. For example, research on an unrelated topic—the causes of cancer in chickens—conducted over a decade before AIDS was discovered now provides the most promising source for advances in research on the AIDS virus. Basic research by the 1975 Nobel Prize winner Howard Temin laid the foundation for understanding how viruses work and has had major implications for questions that did not even exist when he conducted his path-breaking research years ago. Today's computers could not exist without the pure research in mathematics conducted over a century ago, for which there was no known practical application at the time.

Police officers, officials trying to prevent delinquency, or counselors of youthful offenders may see little relevance to basic research on the question, "Why does unlawful behavior occur?" Basic research rarely helps practitioners directly with their everyday concerns. Nevertheless, it stimulates new ways of thinking about deviance that have the potential to revolutionize and dramatically improve how practitioners deal with the problem. Although policymakers and service providers often feel that basic research is of little relevance, public policies and social services will be ineffective and misguided unless they are based on an understanding of actual causes.

A new idea or fundamental knowledge is not generated only by basic research. Applied research, too, can build new knowledge. Nonetheless, basic research is essential for nourishing the expansion of knowledge. Researchers at the center of the scientific community conduct most of the basic research.

Applied Research. Applied researchers try to solve specific policy problems or help practitioners accomplish tasks.[3] Theory is less central to them than seeking a solution to a specific problem for a limited setting (e.g., "Will the number of auto accidents involving drunk students decline if student governments sponsor alcohol-free parties?"). *Applied research* is frequently descriptive research, and its main strength is its immediate practical use.

People employed by businesses, government agencies, social service agencies, health organizations, and educational institutions conduct applied research. It often affects our daily lives. Decisions to market a new product, to choose one policy over another, or to continue or end a public program may be based on applied research.

The scientific community is the primary consumer of basic research. The consumers of applied research findings are practitioners such as boards of directors, teachers, counselors, and caseworkers, or decision makers such as managers, committees, and officials. Often, someone other than the researcher

who conducted the study uses the results of applied research. The use of the results may be beyond the researcher's control. This means that applied researchers have an obligation to translate findings from scientific technical language into the language of decision makers or practitioners.

The results of applied research are less likely to enter the public domain in publications. Results may be available only to a small number of decision makers or practitioners, who decide whether or how to put the research results into practice and who may or may not use the results wisely. For example, Neuberg (1988) found that the results of the famous Seattle–Denver "negative income tax" experiment of the 1960s and 1970s was seriously misinterpreted and distorted in newspaper accounts. Despite serious problems with the study and cautions from researchers, politicians used its results to justify cuts in government programs they disliked.

Because applied research has immediate implications or involves controversial issues, it often generates conflict. This is not new. For example, in 1903 Ellwood conducted an applied study of the jails and poorhouses in Missouri and documented serious deficiencies. His research report generated great public indignation, and he was accused of slandering the state that gave him employment (Turner and Turner, 1991:181).

Whyte (1984) encountered conflict over findings in his applied research on a factory in Oklahoma and on restaurants in Chicago. In the first case the management was more interested in defeating a union than in learning about employment relations; in the other, restaurant owners sought to make the industry look good rather than have findings made public on the nitty-gritty of its operations.

Merton (1973) warned that some calls for applied research on major policy issues are merely a delaying tactic by officials who want to deflect criticism for inaction or postpone a decision until after the political heat dies down.

Applied and basic researchers adopt different orientations toward research methodology (see Table 2.1). Basic researchers emphasize high scientific standards and try to conduct near-perfect research. Applied researchers make more tradeoffs. They may compromise scientific rigor to get quick,

TABLE 2.1   Basic and Applied Social Work Research Compared

BASIC	APPLIED
1. Research is intrinsically satisfying, and judgments are by other sociologists.	1. Research is part of a job and is judged by sponsors who are outside the discipline of sociology.
2. Research problems and subjects are selected with a great deal of freedom.	2. Research problems are "narrowly constrained" to the demands of employers or sponsors.
3. Research is judged by absolute norms of scientific rigor, and the highest standards of scholarship are sought.	3. The rigor and standards of scholarship depend on the uses of results. Research can be "quick and dirty" or may match high scientific standards.
4. The primary concern is with the internal logic and rigor of research design.	4. The primary concern is with the ability to generalize findings to areas of interest to sponsors.
5. The driving goal is to contribute to basic, theoretical knowledge.	5. The driving goal is to have practical payoffs or uses for results.
6. Success comes when results appear in a scholarly journal and have an impact on others in the scientific community.	6. Success comes when results are used by sponsors in decision making.

Source: Adapted from Freeman and Rossi (1984:572–573).

usable results. Compromise is no excuse for sloppy research, however. Applied researchers squeeze research into the constraints of an applied setting and balance rigor against practical needs. Such balancing requires an in-depth knowledge of research and an awareness of the consequences of compromising standards.

Types of Applied Research.   Practitioners use several types of applied research. Some of the major ones are discussed here.

Action research is applied research that treats knowledge as a form of power and abolishes the line between research and social action. There are several types of action research, but most share common characteristics: Those who are being studied participate in the research process; research incorporates ordinary or popular knowledge; research focuses on power with a goal of empowerment; research seeks to raise consciousness or increase awareness; and research is tied directly to political action.

Action researchers try to equalize power relations between themselves and research subjects, and they oppose having more control, status, and authority than those they study. These researchers try to advance a cause or improve conditions by expanding public awareness. They are explicitly political, not value neutral. Because the goal is to improve the conditions and lives of research participants, formal reports, articles, or books become secondary. Action researchers assume that knowledge develops from experience, particularly the experience of social–political action. They also assume that ordinary people can become aware of conditions and learn to take actions that can bring about improvement.

Action research is associated with the critical social science approach discussed in Chapter 4. It attracts researchers who hold specific perspectives (e.g., environmental, radical, African American, feminist, etc.). For example, most feminist research has a dual mission: to create social change by transforming gender relations and to contribute to the advancement of knowledge (Reinharz, 1992:252). A feminist researcher who studies sexual harassment might recommend policy changes both to reduce it as well as to inform potential victims so they can protect themselves and defend their rights. In one situation, action research involved working to preserve a town that was to be destroyed by a dam project. An action researcher worked together with union officials and management to redesign work to prevent layoffs. In developing nations, action researchers work among illiterate, impoverished peasants to teach literacy, study local conditions, and spread an awareness of conditions, and to attempt to improve them.[4]

Hoynes (1997) and Miller (1997) conducted action research on "Channel One," a 12-minute television program shown in 12,000 U.S. high schools to eight million students, about 40 percent of the total. Whittle Communications, the corporation that produces the program, gives schools free televisions, wiring, and satellite links, but requires that all students see the program every day, including its 2 minutes of advertising. Teachers cannot preview the programs. In a study of 36 shows from 1995 to 1996 that included 91 news stories, the researchers concluded that the programs are ahistorical, shallow, and biased. They claim students are learning to accept commercialism more than to think critically about the news. Also, the 700 commercials per year seen in class may have a larger impact than Channel One's educational content. Defenders of Channel One say that the program is highly popular with students and teachers and that it does not advertise alcohol or X-rated movies (Honan, 1997). The research appeared in media advocacy publications (Hoynes, 1997; Miller, 1997).

Gamson (1992:xviii) described a seminar on action research at Boston College that drew students from the Social Economy and Social Justice graduate program:

> *The participants in this seminar . . . are activist-scholars oriented to the concrete problems involved in mobilizing people for collective action. Participants are or have been involved in the Central American solidarity movement, the nuclear freeze movement, the movements for more equitable health care and decent housing, the labor movement. . . . Members of the seminar write papers, run workshops, and consult on media strategy for various movement organizations, as well as conduct research.*

A second type of applied research is *social impact assessment*.[5] It may be part of a larger environmental impact statement required by government agencies. Its purpose is to estimate the likely consequences of a planned change. Such an assessment can be used for planning and making choices among alternative policies—for example, to esti-

mate the ability of a local hospital to respond to an earthquake; to determine changes in housing if a major new highway is built; or to assess the impact on college admissions and long-term debt if all college students received interest-free loans to be paid back over 20 years, with payments based on the size of their incomes. Researchers conducting social impact assessment examine many outcomes and often work in an interdisciplinary research team. The impact on several areas can be measured or assessed (see Box 2.2).

Various forms of gambling have expanded rapidly in the United States. In 1980 gambling was legal in only a few states and yielded under $10 billion in profits. Just 15 years later, it was legal in most states and profits exceeded $44 billion a year. The reason is simple. Lawmakers sought new sources of revenue without raising taxes and wanted to promote economic development. The gambling industry promised them new jobs, economic revitalization, and a "cut" in the huge flow of money from gambling. This looked ideal to the lawmakers: They could help create jobs, strengthen the local economy, and get revenue without raising taxes.

Box 2.2

Areas Assessed in Social Impact Studies

- Community service (e.g., school enrollments, speed of police responses)
- Social conditions (e.g., the races of friends that children are likely to make based on play areas; crime rates; the ability of elderly people to feel that they can care for themselves)
- Economic impact (e.g., changes in income levels, business failure rate)
- Demographic consequences (e.g., changes in the mix of old and young people, population movement into or out of an area)
- Environment (e.g., changes in air quality or noise levels)
- Health outcomes (e.g., changes in occurrence of diseases or presence of harmful substances)
- Psychological well-being (e.g., changes in stress, fear, or self-esteem)

Today, most promises have gone unrealized and there is widespread disappointment. Job growth has been limited and most has been in the category of low-wage, unskilled jobs. The very high revenue estimates were not reached, as more areas offered gambling, and supply grew faster than demand. Also, money was diverted from other businesses. As people spent money on gambling, they had less for clothing and other consumer goods. In addition, few public officials anticipated extra costs for law enforcement, social services, street cleaning, and similar areas that accompanied gambling. Gambling hit lower-income people the worst, and the social problem of compulsive gambling has increased. Although only 2 to 4 percent of the population, compulsive gamblers have low work productivity, devastate their families, and often turn to crime. Of course, some come out fine—such as the nine people who invested $7 million in a casino in Joliet, Illinois. In seven months they recovered the investment and began to take in $900,000 a month in profits.

Were such results predictable? Could anyone anticipate the outcome? Yes, if the officials had first conducted high-quality social impact assessment research and followed results of the research. This rarely occurs. Most officials accept extravagant claims made by industry advocates and cling to the illusion of getting something for next to nothing, because they remain ignorant or distrustful of social science research. The few social impact studies that were conducted made accurate predictions, and the outcome was no surprise.

Evaluation research is a widely used type of applied research[6] that addresses the question, "Did it work?" Smith and Glass (1987:31) defined *evaluation* as "the process of establishing value judgments based on evidence." Example evaluation research questions are: Does a Socratic teaching technique improve learning over lecturing? Does a law enforcement program of mandatory arrest reduce spouse abuse? Does a flextime program increase employee productivity? Evaluation research measures the effectiveness of a program, policy, or way of doing something. It is frequently descriptive but can be exploratory or explanatory. Evaluation researchers use several research techniques (e.g., sur-

vey and field). If it can be used, the experimental technique is usually most effective.

Practitioners involved with a policy or program may conduct evaluation research for their own information or at the request of outside decision makers, who sometimes place limits on researchers by setting boundaries on what can be studied and determining the outcome of interest.

Ethical and political conflicts often arise in evaluation research because people have opposing interests in the findings about a program. Research results can affect getting a job, building political popularity, or promoting an alternative program. People who are personally displeased with the finding often try to attack the researcher or his or her methods as being sloppy, biased, or inadequate. In addition to creating controversy and being attacked, evaluation researchers are sometimes subjected to pressures to rig a study before they begin.

Evaluation research greatly expanded in the 1960s in the United States when many new federal social programs were created. Most researchers adopted a positivist approach (see Chapter 4) and used cost–benefit analysis. By the 1970s, evaluation research was mandated by most federal social programs. Evaluation research has limitations, however. The reports of research rarely go through a peer review process, raw data are rarely publicly available, and the focus is narrowed to select inputs and outputs more than the full process by which a program affects people's lives. In addition, policymakers can selectively use or ignore evaluation reports.

The welfare reform called *workfare* in the United States was based on evaluation research. The research focused on amounts of income earned and costs of administering programs, but failed to measure family obligations not fulfilled or harm to children because mothers were forced to work. Policymakers and politicians selectively used the evidence that showed some positive benefits on family income to justify new laws (Oliker, 1994).

Two examples illustrate how evaluation research can work. Legge and Park (1994) examined the impact of laws on alcohol-impaired driving. Unlike most nations, state governments make most public policies on alcohol-impaired driving in the United States. The laws are based on a theory of deterrence, but states place different emphases on three aspects of deterrence: certainty of being caught, severity of punishment, and celerity (i.e., speed) of punishment. For a three-year period, the authors looked at state-level data on policies and local conditions and rates of single-vehicle, late-night fatal accidents in which alcohol was suspected. The results showed that severe punishments (i.e., high fines and jail time) had no effect, but certainty (e.g., automatic guilt with a certain level of blood alcohol) and celerity (i.e., on-the-spot license suspension) reduced fatalities. The authors explain recent increases in severity by noting that politicians often quickly raise severity levels without a coordinated policy or empirical study. Many seem more interested in finding a popular issue to attract votes than in reducing the problem of alcohol-related auto fatalities.

Wysong, Aniskiewicz, and Wright (1994) evaluated the effectiveness of the D.A.R.E. (Drug Abuse Resistance Education) program found in 10,000 schools in the United States and 42 other countries. The authors note that the program is widely used, well funded, and very popular with police departments, school officials, parent groups, and others. By having police officers deliver talks in early grades, D.A.R.E. tries to reduce illicit drug use among teens by increasing knowledge of drugs, developing antidrug coping skills, and raising self-esteem. The authors examined two groups of students who were seniors in a high school in Indiana. One group had participated in the D.A.R.E. program in seventh grade and the other group had not. Consistent with past research, the authors found no lasting differences among the groups regarding age of first drug use, frequency of drug use, or self-esteem. The authors suggest that the program's popularity may be due to its political symbolic impact. The program may be effective for latent goals (i.e., helping politicians, school officials, and others feel morally good and involved in antidrug actions) but ineffective for official goals (i.e., reducing illegal drug use by teenagers).

Two types of evaluation research are formative and summative. *Formative evaluation research* is built-in monitoring or continuous feedback on a program used for program management. *Summative evaluation research* looks at final program outcomes. Both are usually necessary.

Evaluation research is a part of the administration of many organizations (e.g., schools, government agencies, businesses, etc.). One example is the *Planning, Programming, and Budgeting System (PPBS),* first used by the U.S. Department of Defense in the 1960s. PPBS is based on the idea that researchers can evaluate a program by measuring its accomplishments on the basis of its stated goals and objectives. An evaluator divides a program into components and analyzes each component with regard to its costs (staff, supplies, etc.) and accomplishments in achieving program objectives. For example, a women's health center offers pregnancy education. The program components are outreach, education, counseling, and referrals. The program objectives are to reach out to women who believe they are pregnant, provide education about pregnancy, counsel women about their health risks and concerns, and refer pregnant women to health care providers or family planning agencies. An evaluation researcher will examine the cost of each part of the program and measure how well the program meets its objectives. The researcher may ask how much staff time and how many supplies are used for outreach, how many calls or inquiries have resulted from those efforts, and whether the efforts increased the number of women from targeted groups coming to the center.[7]

Applied researchers use two tools, needs assessment and cost–benefit analysis, in social impact assessment and evaluation research. In a *needs assessment* a researcher collects data to determine major needs and their severity. It is often a preliminary step before a government agency or charity decides on a strategy to help people. Yet, it often becomes tangled in the complex relations within a community. A researcher may confront dilemmas or difficult issues.

One issue is to decide on the group to target for the assessment. Should the researcher focus on the needs of homeless people sleeping in a park, working people who lose large amounts of money betting at a race track, or executives who drink too much at the country club? The most visible need may not be the most serious one. Whom does the researcher ask or observe? Should he or she ask the executives about the needs of the homeless?

A second issue is that people may not express a need in a way that links it directly to policies or long-term solutions. A researcher may find that homeless people say they need housing. After examining the situation, however, he or she may determine that housing would be available if the homeless had jobs. The housing need is caused by a need for jobs. The need for jobs, in turn, may be caused by a need for skills and for certain types of businesses. Thus, to address the housing need, it may be necessary to attract specific types of businesses and provide job training. The apparent need may be linked to a deeper problem or condition. People may not be aware of the causes. For example, a need for health care may be caused by drinking polluted water, poor diet, and a lack of exercise. Is this a need for more health care, or is it a need for better water treatment and a public health education program?

A third issue is that people often have multiple needs. If a researcher finds that people need to reduce pollution, to eliminate gangs, and to improve transport services, which is most important? A good needs assessment identifies both the expressed and the less visible needs of a target group, as well as the more serious or widespread needs. A researcher must trace links among related needs to identify those of highest priority.

Another issue is that a needs assessment may generate political controversy or suggest solutions beyond local control. Powerful groups may not want some needs documented or publicized. The researcher who finds that a city has a lot of unreported crime may tarnish the image of a safe, well-run city promoted by the Chamber of Commerce and the city government. A needs assessment that documents racial discrimination may embarrass civic leaders who prefer to present themselves in public as unprejudiced. The needs of one group, such as people who bet too much at the race track, may be linked to the actions of another group that benefits by creating that need, such as the race track's owners and employees. Once a researcher documents needs and offers a resolution to them, he or she may be caught between opposing groups.

Social impact studies often include a *cost–benefit analysis*. Economists developed cost–benefit analysis, in which the researcher estimates the fu-

ture costs and benefits of one or several proposed actions and gives them monetary values. In brief, it works like this: A researcher identifies all the consequences of a proposed action. Next, he or she assigns each consequence a monetary value. The consequences may include intangibles such as clean air, low crime rates, political freedom, scenic beauty, low stress levels, and even human life itself. Often, the researcher assigns a probability or likelihood to the occurrence of various consequences. Next, policymakers or others identify negative consequences (costs) and positive ones (benefits). Finally, costs are compared to benefits, and policymakers decide whether they balance.

Cost–benefit analysis appears to be a neutral, rational, and technical decision-making strategy, but it can be controversial. People do not necessarily agree on what are positive and negative consequences. For example, you may see widening a nearby road as a benefit because it will let you travel to work much more rapidly. But the homeowner who lives along the road may see the same action as a cost because it will remove some of his or her lot and will generate more noise, pollution, and congestion.

There are two ways to assign monetary values to costs and benefits. *Contingency evaluation* asks people how much something is worth to them. For example, you may want to estimate the cost of air pollution that has health consequences for the average person. You might ask people: How much is it worth to you not to cough a lot and miss work two days a year due to asthma? If the average value assigned by people is $150 in a town of 20,000, then the contingency evaluation—or subjective benefit of health—would be $150 × 20,000 per year = $3 million. You might balance this against higher profits for a company or more jobs created by allowing the pollution. A problem with this estimation is that people rarely give accurate estimates, and different people may assign very different values. To an impoverished person, coughing and missing work may be worth $500, but for a wealthy person, it may be $10,000. In this example polluting companies would tend to move to towns with low-income people, worsening their living conditions.

Using the same example, *actual cost evaluation* estimates the actual medical and job loss costs.

You would estimate the health impact and then add up medical bills and costs for employers to get replacement workers. For example, if medical treatment averages $100 per person and a replacement worker costs an extra $200 per day, the cost of treating 10,000 people each year and hiring 5,000 replacement workers for two days would be $100 × 10,000 people = $1,000,000 plus $300 × 5,000 workers = $1,500,000, for a total of $2.5 million. This method ignores pain and suffering, inconvenience, and indirect costs (e.g., a parent stays home with a sick child, a child is unable to play sports because of asthma). To balance the costs with benefits by this method, the polluting factory would need to earn an extra $2.5 million in profits.

A significant issue for cost–benefit analysis is the assumption that everything has a price (learning, health, love, happiness, human dignity, chastity, etc.) and that people assign similar valuations. It also raises serious moral and political concerns. Cost–benefit calculations usually favor upper-income people over low-income or poor people. This occurs because the relative value of a cost or benefit depends on one's wealth and income. Saving 15 minutes in a commute to work is assigned a greater value or benefit for high-income people than the same 15-minute time savings for low-income people; 15 minutes of a high-income person's time is monetarily worth more. Likewise, cutting a road through an impoverished neighborhood has a lower cost, because of lower property values, than putting the road through an area of high-cost homes.

Cost–benefit analysis tends to conceal the moral–political aspect of questions. For instance, the balance between the human cost of "pulling the plug" on a life-support machine for a very ill person and the benefit of saving large expenses to keep the machines operating has both moral and economic aspects. The moral aspect stands out in decisions that involve a single identifiable person with whom the decision maker has an emotional attachment. Few of us look at this issue solely in terms of economic costs and benefits. The moral aspect can get lost in a decision that involves people who are not easily identified as individuals among a large group and for whom decision makers lack direct, personal contact. A moral aspect remains, even if the focus is on the economic costs and benefits.

Empowerment Research

The *empowerment research* approach in social work (Holmes, 1992; Lee, 1994; and Gutierrez, Parsons, and Cox, 1998) merges the concepts of four different approaches. It draws from the ecological approach (Germain and Gitterman, 1996), feminist models of research (Davis and Marsh, 1994); the constructivist approach (Rodwell, 1998), and the strengths perspective (Saleebey, 1997) into a research orientation that blends the concepts of helping others with social and economic justice (Appleby, Colon, and Hamilton, 2000). Empowerment research begins with the notion that there is no such thing as completely objective, disinterested assessment. Green (1997) explained that

> *program evaluators are inevitably on somebody's side and not on somebody else's side. The sides chosen by evaluators are most importantly expressed in whose questions are being addressed and, therefore, what criteria are used to make judgments about program quality. (p. 25)*

Empowerment research is especially well suited for social work as our clients are often marginalized from the mainstream and traditional "Euro-centered" societies. Lee (1994) suggests five concerns when working with oppressed groups: a historical understanding of oppression that locates dominant–subordinate relationships in a longitudinal framework; knowledge of the ecological perspective, which orients researchers to the adaptive capacities and stress reactions among those who are oppressed; the effects of socioeconomic class, race, and gender—factors that are often glossed over in traditional research; a feminist perspective, which stresses unique problems facing women; and a critical perspective that analyzes the link between individual pain and strategies for strength and change.

Rodgers-Farmer and Potocky-Tripodi (2001) contend that within the empowerment framework clients should be encouraged to act as co-researchers. This means that the research and evaluation tasks are ideally mutual and shared, and that more power should ultimately come to reside in the client (Lee, 1996). According to Appleby, et al. (2000), sharing responsibility evolves through three steps: (1) helping everyone to have maximal autonomy in the personal sense of self—self-esteem, self-direction, and competence; (2) improving the problem-solving potential of caseworkers and clients; and (3) obtaining resources so that goals may be reached (Gutierrez, Parsons, and Cox, 1998; Lee, 1996).

Rodwell (1998: 87–90) proposes a form of empowerment research she calls *constructivist research,* combining many of the traditional strategies found in qualitative research methods. The constructivist (empowerment-oriented) researcher, according to Rodwell, always begins in the natural setting, using the human being as the primary data-gathering instrument. The constructivist researcher relies on tacit or intuitive/felt knowledge, using qualitative methods, purposive sampling, grounded theory, emergent design, negotiated outcomes, case studies, ideographic interpretation, tentative application of findings, focus-determined boundaries, and trustworthiness and authenticity. Rodwell is particularly concerned about whether inquiry may be undertaken with due regard to the maintenance of personal rights and integrity. Can harm come to stakeholders as a result of the inquiry? In what ways might the inquiry be harmful to human functioning? Who are the potential gainers and losers for the inquiry product? What kinds of political influences can be expected in the inquiry, and from whom? What do the participants and the context have to gain or lose from the inquiry?

Researcher responsibility, according to Rodwell, includes identifying the full array of stakeholders. It involves value pluralism to ensure equal opportunity for everyone. One critical aspect of equal opportunity is equal protection. Intrinsic fairness involves the creation of an atmosphere that elicits a range of claims, concerns, and issues in a context for understanding and critiquing different perspectives. A constructivist researcher generates as much consensus as possible though valuing differences and creating a forum for negotiating distributive justice, which is central to the mediation of unresolved differences. Finally, the fostering voice for all is essential to recycling the final report.

Distinctive features of constructivist research include the idea that it is a social/political-mediated activity that is enhanced by the inquirer. The inquiry process involves continuous teaching/learning that is recursive, divergent, and never ending. It constructs a new reality based on a more sophisticated understanding of the various perspectives of the stakeholders. The inquirer is a reality shaper because when constructions emerge, the inquirer facilitates the dissemination and testing of perspectives. Inquiry designs can never be specified in advance (Rodwell 1998: 93–94).

Verbal and nonverbal data are not the only way of knowing in constructive inquiry. Intuition and other instinctive ways of knowing are central. Intuition operates when the inquirer knows what the next questions are and what next steps need to be taken to enhance co-construction. The major role of the knowledge tacit occurs in reflexivity. It is in the doing of the data collection that the understanding of the subject is achieved.

The Time Dimension in Research

Another dimension of social research is the treatment of time. An awareness of the time dimension will help you read or conduct research because different research questions or issues incorporate time in different ways.

Some studies give you a snapshot of a single, fixed time point and allow you to analyze it in detail. Other studies provide a moving picture that lets you follow events, people, or social relations over periods of time. Quantitative research is divided into two groups: a single point in time (cross-sectional research) versus multiple time points (longitudinal research). Quantitative research looks at a large group of cases, people, or units and measures a limited number of features. A case study is more distinct. It usually involves qualitative methods and focuses on one or a few cases during a limited time period.

Cross-Sectional Research.   Most social work research takes a snapshot approach to the social world. In *cross-sectional research,* researchers observe at one point in time. Cross-sectional research is usually the simplest and least costly alternative. Its disadvantage is that it cannot capture social processes or change. Cross-sectional research can be exploratory, descriptive, or explanatory, but it is most consistent with a descriptive approach to research. An example of cross-sectional research is the descriptive study by McCabe (1992) on cheating by college students.

Longitudinal Research. Researchers using *longitudinal research* examine features of people or other units at more than one time. It is usually more complex and costly than cross-sectional research, but it is also more powerful, especially when researchers seek answers to questions about social change. Descriptive and explanatory researchers use longitudinal approaches. We will now consider three types of longitudinal research: time series, panel, and cohort.

Time-series research is a longitudinal study in which the same type of information is collected on a group of people or other units across multiple time periods. Researchers can observe stability or change in the features of the units or can track conditions over time. In Chapter 1 Marvell and Moody (1995) used time series in their study on the impact of enhanced prison terms for felonies committed with guns. Their study is also a type of evaluation research, although few legislators base their actions on research, so the findings may not affect future laws or policy. The researchers examined the impact of firearm sentence-enhancement laws in the United States. The laws impose extra prison time or a minimum prison term for felonies committed with a gun. Such laws have been enacted in 49 states in the past 25 years. For 44 states that had strong sentence-enhancement laws, Marvell and Moody examined data on various features (e.g., prison population, crime rates, prison admissions, whether guns were used in specific crimes, etc.) for the years 1971 to 1993. They concluded, "We found little evidence to support the intended purposes of firearm sentencing enhancement, reducing crime rates and gun use" (1995:269).

The *panel study* is a powerful type of longitudinal research. It is more difficult to conduct than time-series research. In a panel study the researcher

observes exactly the same people, group, or organization across time periods. Panel research is formidable to conduct and very costly. Tracking people over time is often difficult because some people die or cannot be located. Nevertheless, the results of a well-designed panel study are very valuable. Even short-term panel studies can clearly show the impact of a particular life event. For example, Umberson and Chen (1994) studied 2,867 people who were interviewed twice, in 1986 and 1989. During the intervening three years, 207 experienced the death of a biological parent. Umberson and Chen found that this life event contributed to more psychological distress, increased alcohol consumption, and decreased physical health.

Another panel study (Nagin et al., 1995) looked at the impact of deviance in youth on long-term criminal activity and problems in adulthood. The reseachers examined data on 411 males from a working-class section of London who were first studied when they were about 8 years old, in 1961–62. The same men were followed until they were 32 years old, except for 8 who died. The men were interviewed at two-year intervals. Data were collected throughout the years on many personality, background, and deviant behavior measures. The men's families, teachers, and friends were also interviewed. The researchers classified the men into four groups, based on self-reported delinquency, ranging from nondelinquent to high-level chronic. The main finding was that those who were deviant only in adolescence appeared to be very similar to nonoffenders by the age of 32, except they were more likely to drink alcohol to excess and use illegal drugs.

Orbuch and Eyster (1997) conducted a panel survey to learn how Black and White couples divide household labor. Their respondents were 199 Black couples and 174 White couples who applied for marriage licenses in a Michigan county in 1986. They considered only same-race couples in a first marriage in which the woman was under 35 years old. Same-race interviewers interviewed all couples in their homes twice. The first interview was 4 to 9 months after marriage, a second was two years later. Of the original couples, 12 percent had divorced and 16 percent had moved and could not be located for the second interview. A total of 264 couples were interviewed both times. The researchers looked at couples' norms on gender equality and participation in different household tasks (e.g., meal preparation, doing dishes, doing laundry, etc.), and considered levels of education, income, and work outside the home. They assessed the impacts of gender norms, wife's resources, and race on how couples divided household labor.

The researchers found that the wife's resources (education and income) and equality norms promoted a more nearly equal division of tasks. The premarital resources that wives brought into the marriage had few long-term effects, but as wives gained more resources during marriage, the division of labor became more nearly equal. Black couples were more egalitarian than White couples, both in norms and in the division of labor. In general, White husbands were more resistant to housework and child care than Black husbands. When Black husbands participated in household tasks, the couple reported high levels of marital well-being, but this did not occur for Whites (Orbuch and Eyster, 1997).

A *cohort analysis* is similar to the panel study, but rather than observing exactly the same people, a category of people who share a similar life experience in a specified time period is studied. Cohort analysis is "explicitly macroanalytic," which means researchers examine the category as a whole for important features (Ryder, 1992:230). The focus is on the cohort, or category, not on specific individuals. Commonly used cohorts include all people born in the same year (called *birth cohorts*), all people hired at the same time, all people who retire in a one- or two-year time frame, and all people who graduate in a given year. Unlike panel studies, researchers do not have to locate exactly the same people for cohort studies. They need to identify only those who experienced a common life event.

Three examples illustrate the value of cohort studies. Forest and associates (1995) found that a U.S. woman's birth cohort affected the timing of her first pregnancy. The impact of working before marriage and education varied in four cohorts: the 1930s Depression, World War II, immediately after World War II, and the 1950s. During the Depression years, the more education she had and the longer she

worked, the later a woman began childbearing. The trend continued during World War II, although employment became more important than education. In the immediate postwar period, women were less likely to go to college and more likely to marry immediately after high school. The 1950s were unique. A woman's education or premarriage employment had little effect, and almost all women began childbearing shortly after marriage.

Morgan (1998) wanted to find out whether a "glass ceiling" of blocked career advancement or cohort caused an earnings gap between men and women engineers. She examined earnings data for male and female engineers in several college graduation cohorts, from 1971 or earlier to 1988–1992. Women's earnings were lower in past cohorts, and women in recent cohorts earn less because they have little seniority. The author found no gender gap in recent cohorts and argues that pay is affected according to when the women started working rather than their career length. A main finding is that an overall gender gap in earnings is caused more by cohort, or many female engineers in recent years, than by a glass ceiling.

Wilhelm (1998) looked at patterns of cohabitation among Americans of different cohorts. She used survey data for 1,187 adult U.S. citizens born between 1947 and 1964 and looked at three birth cohorts: 1943–1950, 1951–1957, and 1958–1964. She found three predictors of cohabitation: political activism, nonreligious beliefs, and being in recent birth cohorts. Certain factors (e.g., nonreligious and politically active) were important predictors in early cohorts, but people in later cohorts were more likely to cohabit independent of the factors. What was once a relatively rare behavior among a few parts of early cohorts has diffused and become a lifestyle option for most sectors of the population in later cohorts.

Case Studies.   In cross-sectional and longitudinal research a researcher examines features on many people or units, either at one time period or across time periods. In both, a researcher precisely measures a common set of features on many cases, usually expressed in numbers. In *case-study research,* he or she examines, in depth, many features of a few cases over a duration of time. Cases can be individuals, groups, organizations, movements, events, or geographic units. The data are usually detailed, varied, and extensive. Most involve qualitative data about a few cases. Qualitative and case-study research are not identical, but "almost all qualitative research seeks to construct representations based on in-depth, detailed knowledge of cases" (Ragin, 1994:92).[8]

In a case study a researcher may intensively investigate one or two cases or compare a limited set of cases, focusing on several factors. Case study uses the logic of analytic instead of enumerative induction. In it, the researcher carefully selects one or a few key cases to illustrate an issue and analytically studies it (or them) in detail. He or she considers the specific context of the case and examines how its parts are configured. This contrasts with longitudinal studies in which the researcher collects data on many units or cases, then looks for patterns in the mass of numbers. The researcher looks more for averages or patterns across many units or cases.[9]

Case studies help researchers connect the micro level, or the actions of individual people, to the macro level, or large-scale social structures and processes (Vaughan, 1992). "The logic of the case study is to demonstrate a causal argument about how general social forces shape and produce results in particular settings" (Walton 1992b: 122). Case-study research raises questions about the boundaries and defining characteristics of a case. Such questions help in the generation of new thinking and theory. "Case studies are likely to produce the best theory" (Walton, 1992b:129).

Researchers gather case-study data for a period of time. Data may be collected over months, years, or across many decades. Sutton's (1991) study of asylums in Chapter 1 is a case study that combined time-series research with qualitative data to study the case of asylum growth. Walton's (1992a) *Western Times and Water Wars* is a case study of one community, Owens Valley, California. Walton stated, "I have tried . . . to tell a big story through the lens of a small case" (p. xviii). The community engaged in social protest as it attempted to control its key resource (water) and destiny. The protest took different forms, on and off, for over 100 years. Walton used diverse forms of data, including direct observation, formal and informal interviews, census sta-

tistics, maps, old photos and newspapers, various historical documents, and official records.

A case study with a more narrow scope is Smith's (1995) study of Asian immigration into Flushing, New York, during the 1980s. The Asian population living in Flushing (a community in the borough of Queens of New York City) grew from 2,571 (5.6 percent of the total) in 1970 to 19,508 (35.8 percent) in 1990. Smith examined the causes of this change and described the process and its consequences. His data included census and official statistical records, maps, historical accounts, and field work.

A last example case study is Stoeker's (1993) study of a neighborhood movement in Minneapolis. He used participant observation, including participatory action research, which he supplemented with interviews, oral history, city documents, and written histories. In his conclusion Stoeker warns, "As with any case study, while we can accurately specify the causal process within the case, generalizing is more difficult" (1993:181).

DATA COLLECTION TECHNIQUES USED

Every researcher collects data using one or more techniques. This section is a brief overview of the main techniques. In later chapters you will read about these techniques in detail and learn how to use them. The techniques may be grouped into two categories: *quantitative,* collecting data in the form of numbers, and *qualitative,* collecting data in the form of words or pictures. Some techniques are more effective when addressing specific kinds of questions or topics. It takes skill, practice, and creativity to match a research question to an appropriate data collection technique.

Quantitative Data

Experiments. *Experimental research* uses the logic and principles found in natural science research. Experiments can be conducted in laboratories or in real life. They usually involve a relatively small number of people and address a well-focused question. Experiments are most effective for explanatory research. They are often limited to topics for which a researcher can manipulate the situation in which people find themselves.

In most experiments the researcher divides the people being studied into two or more groups. He or she then treats both groups identically, except that one group but not the other is given a condition the researcher is interested in: the "treatment." The researcher measures the reactions of both groups precisely. By controlling the setting for both groups and giving only one the treatment, the researcher can conclude that any differences in the reactions of the groups are due to the treatment alone. Recall reading about an experiment on physical attractiveness and financial reward (Mulford et al., 1998) in Chapter 1.

Bohm (1990) conducted an experiment to learn whether making a public commitment to an opinion prevents attitude change. In a previous experiment he gave one group of students extensive information about the death penalty issue and gave none to another group. He measured support for the death penalty with a questionnaire that students completed in private. Both groups initially showed strong support for the death penalty. After several months, however, the group receiving extensive information on the death penalty greatly lowered their support for it. The other group did not change.

In a second experiment Bohm again divided students into two groups. Subjects in the experimental group enrolled in a special class on the death penalty, whereas the control group students enrolled in other courses. This time he measured death penalty opinions by having students publicly state their opinions in each class session. In contrast to the large opinion change in the experimental group that he found in the earlier experiment, Bohm found no change during the semester and no difference between the experimental and control groups. He concluded that making their opinion public inhibits people from changing it, even when they are confronted with overwhelming factual information in support of making a change.

Surveys. Survey techniques are often used in descriptive or explanatory research. A survey researcher asks people questions in a written questionnaire (mailed or handed to people) or during an interview, then records answers. He or she manip-

ulates no situation or condition; people simply answer questions. In *survey research* the researcher asks many people numerous questions in a short time period. He or she typically summarizes answers to questions in percentages, tables, or graphs. Surveys give the researcher a picture of what many people think or report doing. A survey researcher often uses a sample or a smaller group of selected people (e.g., 150 students), but generalizes results to a larger group (e.g., 5,000 students) from which the smaller group was chosen.

Survey research is widely used. Following is an example of it in the state of Georgia, where a political controversy arose over the Confederate battle emblem on the state flag, which was added to the flag in 1956. Reingold and Wike (1998) wanted to learn whether the symbol was connected with pride in a "New South" identity, as some argued, or was an indirect expression of racism, as others claimed. In fall 1994 the Applied Research Center of Georgia State University surveyed a random sample of 826 Georgia residents by telephone in the "Georgia State Poll." The authors had three questions on New South identity and two questions on racial attitudes. They also asked about other factors (e.g., education, age, sex, race, urban or rural residence, political party, born in the South, etc.). The authors found clear racial divisions; three-fourths of Whites wanted to keep the Confederate symbol, whereas two-thirds of African Americans wanted the flag changed. Their data analysis revealed that New South identity was not related to the flag issue; if anything, it was associated with favoring a change in the flag. Younger people and urban residents also favored changing the flag. Despite public rhetoric, those most strongly in favor of keeping the Confederate symbol on the flag were Whites who had strong anti-Black attitudes.

Content Analysis. *Content analysis* is a technique for examining information, or content, in written or symbolic material (e.g., pictures, movies, song lyrics, etc.). In content analysis a researcher first identifies a body of material to analyze (e.g., books, newspapers, films, etc.) and then creates a system for recording specific aspects of it. The system might include counting how often certain words or themes occur. Finally, the researcher records what was found in the material. He or she often measures information in the content as numbers and presents it as tables or graphs. This technique lets a researcher discover features in the content of large amounts of material that might otherwise go unnoticed. Content analysis is used for exploratory and explanatory research but is most often used in descriptive research.

Three studies illustrate content analysis research. Lovdal (1989) studied gender-role stereotypes in television commercials to see whether any change occurred between the 1970s and the 1980s. She recorded all commercials on two networks between 8:00 P.M. and 10:00 P.M. during a two-week period in 1988 and coded the product advertised, setting, major actors, and sex of voice-overs. She coded a total of 353 commercials. She learned that 91 percent of commercials had voice-overs, and 90 percent of those had male voices. Research in the 1970s reported that voice-overs were used in only 69 percent of commercials, in which 90 percent had male voices. In both times men were used more for nondomestic products (e.g., cars, travel, and cameras), and women were used more for domestic products (e.g., food, shampoo, and cleaning supplies). Lovdal concluded that relatively little had changed despite a decade of publicity about gender equality. She noted other research had found that children who watched more commercials tended to have more traditional views on sex roles.

Taylor and Stern (1997) wanted to learn whether positive stereotyping of Asian Americans as a "model minority" occurs in television advertising. The authors selected one-hour segments during a week-long period in 1994 between 8:00 P.M. and 11:00 P.M. on ABC, CBS, Fox, and NBC. They found 1,313 commercials with human models. A group of six undergraduates who received 10 weeks of training coded the commercials. The authors found that Asians appeared almost three times their percentage in the U.S. population (over 8 percent of commercials) and occupied major roles in about one-half of the commercials in which they appeared. They were overrepresented in advertising products that suggest wealth and work life (e.g., banking, offices, etc.). The researchers concluded that television advertising reinforces the model minority stereotype.

Welch and Fenwick (1997) wanted to see how the mass media report and represent crime. They conducted a content analysis of statements in feature articles on crime in four major U.S. newspapers for the period from 1992 to 1995. In the 105 feature articles found, the authors identified two types of experts portrayed as making authoritative statements about crime. *Practitioner experts* (politicians, government personnel, and law enforcement officers) made 151 statements. *Academic and nongovernment experts* made a total of 116 statements. The experts were similar to others within their own group, but the two groups emphasized different topics and views. The media relied far more on practitioner experts than on academic experts, and ignored defense lawyers. The media focus was on street crime, and almost all experts were male. Compared to the academic experts, the practitioner experts were more likely to use a "moral panic" model that emphasized fear of crime, crime as threatening a valued way of life, and little on connections between social conditions and crime. The authors conclude that the media and law enforcement have a mutually rewarding relationship and represent crime in ways that advance political agendas.

Existing Statistics. In *existing statistics research* a researcher locates a source of previously collected information, often in the form of government reports or previously conducted surveys. He or she then reorganizes or combines the information in new ways to address a research question. Locating sources can be time consuming, so the researcher needs to consider carefully the meaning of what he or she finds. Frequently, a researcher does not know whether the information of interest is available when he or she begins a study. Sometimes the existing quantitative information consists of stored survey or other data that a researcher reexamines using various statistical procedures. This is called *secondary analysis research*. Existing statistics research can be used for exploratory, descriptive, or explanatory purposes but is most frequently used for descriptive research.

Two studies used existing statistics to examine the relationship between industrial restructuring (a massive departure of manufacturing jobs from central cities in the United States during the 1970s and 1980s) and violent death. The manufacturing jobs provided entry-level employment for people with low skills. Shihadeh and Ousey (1998) looked at 100 U.S. cities with over 100,000 people in 1990. They used census data on types of industries located in each city, and the prevalence of low-skill jobs by industry. They then combined the census data with data on homicides from the Uniform Crime Reports of the FBI. The authors found that a reduction in entry-level jobs was linked to greater economic deprivation for the local population, and economic deprivation was associated with higher homicide rates for both Blacks and Whites.

On the same general topic, Almgren and associates (1998) looked at homicides, suicides, and accidents in Chicago. They matched census data for 1970 and 1990 with birth and death records for 75 communities and examined the association between unemployment rates and rates of violent death in the communities. They also looked at changes in family composition and racial mix in the community areas. The authors learned that joblessness, more than racial isolation, was associated with both family disruption and violent death rates. Also, they learned that various forms of violent death are interrelated, or appear to have a common cause. The causal relationship between economic dislocation and violent death grew stronger. Thus, economically depressed areas had more violent deaths than nondepressed areas in the 1970s, but the link grew stronger over time.

Trovato (1998) used existing statistics to test a theory from Emile Durkheim about social integration. Social integration, or a feeling of belonging, may become stronger during major sports events. Thus, several studies looked at the link between suicide rates and major sports events (e.g., the Super Bowl). Trovato looked at the impact of Stanley Cup hockey games on suicide rates in Quebec. He predicted that suicide rates would drop when Montreal was engaged in the playoffs but increase when it was eliminated early. Despite minor changes in sui-

cide rates for single males, he found no evidence of a link between changes in suicide rates and the Stanley Cup tournament.

Qualitative Data

Field Research.   Most field researchers conduct case studies on a small group of people for some length of time. *Field research* begins with a loosely formulated idea or topic. Next, researchers select a social group or site for study. Once they gain access to the group or site, they adopt a social role in the setting and begin observing. The researchers observe and interact in the field setting for a period from a few months to several years. They get to know personally the people being studied and may conduct informal interviews. They take detailed notes on a daily basis. During the observation, they consider what they observe and refine or focus ideas about its significance. Finally, they leave the field site. They then reread their notes and prepare written reports. Field research is usually used for exploratory and descriptive studies; it is rarely used for explanatory research.

Fitchen used field research in *Endangered Spaces, Enduring Places* (1991). She was interested in understanding the U.S. farm crisis of the 1980s. Her study was based on several rural counties in upstate New York and on 400 interviews or periods of observation that occurred between 1985 and 1990. On many days she left home at 6:00 A.M. and spent the next 16 hours driving to or visiting people in the rural communities. Her interviews and observations took place at village cafés, feed mills, elementary schools, cow barns, town meetings, parades, social service agencies, county fairs, farm homes, and workshops for local teachers. In addition to reading research reports on the farm crisis and changes in agriculture, Fitchen read the local newspapers, statistical profiles, reports of local agencies, records of local governments, and brochures put out by local groups. She interviewed local editors and reporters, farmers, public officials, teachers, storekeepers, veterinarians, retired people, and others. She interviewed some of them several times during the five-year study. She interviewed some alone and others in small groups in many settings—over kitchen tables, on the street, in barns, in fields, in offices.

Fitchen scheduled some of the interviews, but others began by chance when she stopped to ask directions or was stuck in a small café on a rainy afternoon. The interviews were informal, tailored to the interviewee, and open ended (i.e., without a fixed set of questions or answer categories). She did not use a tape recorder but took extensive field notes during or immediately after her field visits. Fitchen discussed many themes—how rural people see themselves, rural poverty, the impact of large corporations locating plants in small towns, local results of social service cuts, and so forth. The book is peppered with lengthy quotes from Fitchen's field notes that show her complete immersion and personal involvement in the research. She reported:

> Conducting this research has been exciting and fun, and I have genuinely enjoyed listening and probing. Many of my informants have enjoyed the interaction as well: Many commented that they were pleased to have the opportunity to tell their side of the story. (Fitchen, 1991:285)

Historical–Comparative Research.   *Historical–comparative research* examines aspects of social life in a past historical era or across different cultures. The study on asylums by John Sutton, described in Chapter 1, is an example of this type of research. Researchers who use this technique may focus on one historical period or several, compare one or more cultures, or mix historical periods and cultures. This kind of research combines theory with data collection. As with field research, a researcher begins with a loosely formulated question, refining and elaborating on it during the research process. Researchers often use a mix of evidence, including existing statistics, documents (e.g., books, newspapers, diaries, photographs, and maps), observations, and interviews. Historical–comparative research can be exploratory, descriptive, or explanatory and can blend types, but it is usually descriptive.

Gordon Laxer's (1989) *Open for Business: The Roots of Foreign Ownership in Canada* uses historical–comparative research. Laxer asked why most business in Canada, the world's eighth largest manufacturing country, is under foreign control. He compared the Canadian experience since the late nineteenth century to that of the United States and European nations. Laxer studied numerous historical accounts of industrialization in several major countries. He concluded that foreign ownership in Canada is due to internal divisions that weakened a coherent national culture, failure to restrict foreign investment, slow development of markets, and a rigid system of banking. This combination of factors encouraged a reliance on large-scale foreign investment during critical periods of industrialization.

The Importance of Diversity and Cultural Awareness in Social Work Research

Social workers have a long-standing commitment to engage in research and evaluation of practice in such a way as to strengthen people from all walks of life—all cultures, ethnic groups, national origins, religions, abilities, and gender orientations. According to the Council on Social Work Education (CSWE) Policy and Accreditation Standards, social work has an obligation to prepare ". . . social workers to practice without discrimination, with respect, and with knowledge and skills related to clients' age, culture, class, disability, ethnicity, family structure, gender, national origin, race, religion, and sexual orientation." In addition, faculty in schools of social work are required to teach content on diversity, populations-at-risk, and social and economic justice. Such content emphasizes how group membership is related to access to resources so as to ensure that social services meet the needs of groups served in a culturally relevant way. As a profession we are also committed to look for ways to implement strategies to combat discrimination, oppression, and economic deprivation and to promote social and economic justice. This means that in our research and practice we are advocates for nondiscrimination. As students you will learn how to define, design, and implement strategies for effective practice with persons from diverse cultures and backgrounds, according to CSWE guidelines as noted in Box 2.3.

THE ROLE OF TECHNOLOGY IN SOCIAL WORK RESEARCH

Social workers are mastering a number of new and emerging technologies that promise a more conve-nient and efficient means of communication via electronic email, list servers, bulletin board systems (BBSs), telecommunication message systems, and Internet access. Today it is easier to communicate, to search the Internet, and to exchange informa-tion via a variety of new and emerging technolo-gies, including desktop and laptop computers, cell phones, cable communication, and a host of other

Box 2.3

Foundation Curriculum Content

All social work programs provide foundation content in the areas specified below. Content areas may be combined and delivered with a variety of instructional technologies. Content is relevant to the mission, goals, and objectives of the program and to the purposes, values, and ethics of the social work profession.

4.0 VALUES AND ETHICS

Social work education programs integrate content about values and principles of ethical decision mak-ing as presented in the National Association of Social Workers Code of Ethics. The educational experience provides students with the opportunity to be aware of personal values; develop, demonstrate, and promote the values of the profession; and analyze ethical dilemmas and the ways in which these affect practice, services, and clients.

4.1 DIVERSITY

Social work programs integrate content that promotes understanding, affirmation, and respect for people from diverse backgrounds. The content emphasizes the in-terlocking and complex nature of culture and personal identity. It ensures that social services meet the needs of groups served and are culturally relevant. Programs educate students to recognize diversity within and be-tween groups that may influence assessment, plan-ning, intervention, and research. Students learn how to define, design, and implement strategies for effective practice with persons from diverse backgrounds.

4.2 POPULATIONS-AT-RISK AND SOCIAL AND ECONOMIC JUSTICE

Social work education programs integrate content on populations-at-risk, examining the factors that con-tribute to and constitute being at risk. Programs edu-cate students to identify how group membership in-fluences access to resources, and present content on the dynamics of such risk factors and responsive and productive strategies to redress them.

Programs integrate social and economic justice content grounded in an understanding of distributive justice, human and civil rights, and the global inter-connections of oppression. Programs provide content related to implementing strategies to combat discrim-ination, oppression, and economic deprivation and to promote social and economic justice. Programs pre-pare students to advocate for nondiscriminatory so-cial and economic systems.

ACCREDITATION STANDARD 6.0 NONDISCRIMINATION AND HUMAN DIVERSITY

The program makes specific and continuous efforts to provide a learning context in which respect for all persons and understanding of diversity (including age, class, color, religion, sex, and sexual orientation) are practiced. Social work education builds upon pro-fessional purposes and values; therefore, the program provides a learning context that is nondiscriminatory and reflects the profession's fundamental tenets. The program describes how its learning context and edu-cational program (including faculty, staff, and student composition, selection of agencies and their clientele as field education settings; composition of program advisory or field committees; resource allocation; pro-gram leadership; speakers series, seminars, and special programs; research and other initiatives) and its curriculum model understanding of and respect for diversity.

mechanisms involving ever larger bandwidths, and more *synchronous* (two-way, interactive) as distinct from *asynchronous* (broadcast, one-way) communication. While these new information technologies certainly have advantages, you wonder whether they are at the same time altering relationships among caseworkers, administrators, and staff; clients; and students and teachers who traditionally interact in face-to-face (FTF) settings. These electronic regions, with varying degrees of immediacy, are interposed between two or more persons. Social workers are struggling to effectively utilize these innovations in research and practice, and they are more recently beginning to appreciate these innovations in terms of the organizational changes they are bringing about or the impacts they are likely to have on practice (Kreuger and Stretch, 2000a).

Traditionally, social workers practiced solely in closed environments, using activities, actions, and conversations contained in a physically bounded space and relying on local resources. New technology is altering these physical and resource constraints, so we need to develop a balanced view of how to best use the technology. These traditions paralleled the social and economic organization of the larger community and region. But the last quarter of the 20th century witnessed the transformation of the nearby organizational environment from industrial to information-based. The infiltration of information technologies into social work organizations and practice settings has forced practitioners to adopt many of the same practices as the larger business community—practices that stress moving products to markets involving norms of convenience and efficiency.

The use of one-way asynchronous communication has created a host of potential pitfalls for the social work practitioners (Kreuger and Stretch (b), 2000). Unlike face-to-face interaction in conventional social work settings, wherein both clinician and client share in the creation and execution of the present moment through conversation and body language, electronic technology may instead restrict the clinician's knowledge of clients to available photographic images, and likewise, clients may experience flattened and truncated two-dimensional views of their caseworkers or clinicians. Researchers

have found that a good deal of information about people with whom we are interacting is communicated primarily through nonverbal means such as gestures, facial expressions, the position of arms and legs, and tone of voice. When such information is not available, as is usually the case when using email or other electronic "post-it" note information found on most Internet providers, critical meanings may be missed, leaving both the client and the clinician less well informed.

In a national survey of distance education in schools of social work, Siegle et al. (1998) reported problems that included the limiting of instructional materials brought on solely by the demands of technology-assisted instruction; problems in developing and maintaining faculty preparation; scheduling and network synchronization demands that may disrupt the ebb and flow of learning; insufficient institutional support; and decreases in the amount of personal contact among faculty and students. Birkerts (1996) claims that while textual messages can be sent across a computer net in a few milliseconds, the conversations and other meaningful life experiences that have been the staple of social work interventive healing relationships (see, for example, [Stretch, 1967]) require much longer periods of time to unfold.

Technology in social work should be viewed as a supportive tool to further the mission, goals, and objectives of the profession (Kreuger and Stretch, 1999). To that end, better data are needed to assess how clients, caseworkers, students, and faculty adapt to temporal and spatial distance, how they relate to the emerging physical and spatial aspects of communicating from remote sites, how they manage access to sometimes costly equipment, and how they adapt to individual differences in reception of electronic messages (Wernet, Olliges and Delicath, 2000). This is especially important because the agents of transmission (electronic devices) were originally designed to mass communicate to essentially passive nonadult audiences.

Technology may not harm directly, but it may be misused when employed to mediate interpersonal relationships. Gadgets and mechanical objects cannot substitute for two streams of consciousness growing older together during face-to-face human interaction. The debate on the proper role, function, and utilities of technology is essential to support the mission of social work as continually strengthening the social environment (Kreuger, 1997).

CONCLUSION

This chapter gave you an overview of the dimensions of social work research. You saw that research can be classified in a number of different ways (e.g., by its purpose, by its research technique, etc.)

and that the dimensions of research loosely overlap with each other (see Table 2.2). The dimensions of research provide a "road map" through the terrain that is social work research.

In the next chapter we turn to social theory. You read about theory in Chapter 1, and it was mentioned again in this chapter. In Chapter 3 you will learn how theory and research methods work together and about several types of theory.

TABLE 2.2   Dimensions of Social Work Research

PURPOSE FOR STUDY	USE OF STUDY	TIME IN STUDY	DATA COLLECTION TECHNIQUE
Exploratory	Basic	Cross-sectional	Quantitative data:
Descriptive	Applied:	Longitudinal:	— Experiment
Explanatory	— Action	— Panel	— Survey
	— Impact	— Time series	— Content analysis
	— Evaluation	— Cohort analysis	— Existing statistics
		Case study	Qualitative data:
			— Field research
			— Comparative–historical

KEY TERMS

action research
applied research
basic research
case-study research
cohort analysis
constructivist research
content analysis
cost–benefit analysis
cross-sectional research
descriptive research
diversity

empowerment research
evaluation research
existing statistics research
experimental research
explanatory research
exploratory research
field research
formative evaluation research
historical–comparative research
longitudinal research
needs assessment

neutralization strategies
panel study
Planning, Programming, and
    Budgeting System
secondary analysis research
serendipity
social impact assessment
summative evaluation research
survey research
time-series research

REVIEW QUESTIONS

1. When is exploratory research used, and what can it accomplish?

2. What types of results are produced by a descriptive research study?

3. What is explanatory research? What is its primary purpose?

4. What are the major differences between basic and applied research?

5. Who is likely to conduct basic research, and where are results likely to appear?

6. Explain the differences among the three types of applied research.

7. How do time-series, panel, and cohort studies differ?

8. What are some potential problems with cost–benefit analysis?

9. What is a needs assessment? What complications can occur when conducting one?

10. Explain the differences between qualitative and quantitative research.

11. Why is empowerment research important in social work?

12. How might social work researchers assure that diversity issues are considered?

NOTES

1. Explanatory, exploratory, and descriptive research are also discussed in Babbie (1998), Bailey (1987:38–39), Churchill (1983:56–77), Grinnell (1999), Rubin and Babbie (2001), and Thyer (2001).

2. See Guy and colleagues (1987:54–55) for discussion.

3. Finsterbusch and Motz (1980), Freeman (1983), Lazarsfeld and Reitz (1975), Olsen and Micklin (1981), Rubin (1983), and Scriven (1999) discuss applied research. Also see Whyte's (1986) critique of social research that is not applied and instances in which social research affects public issues. McGrath and colleagues (1982) discuss judgment calls that are relevant in applied research.

4. See Cancian and Armstead (1992), Reason (1994), and Whyte (1989). For empowerment research see Appleby, Colon, and Hamilton (2000), Fetterman (2001), Gutierrez, Parsons, and Cox (1998), Holmes (1992), Lee (1994), Rodwell (1998), and Secret, Jordan, and Ford (1999).

5. Social impact research is discussed in Chadwick and associates (1984:313–342), Devaney and Rossi (1997), Finsterbusch and Motz (1980:75–118), Finsterbush and Wolf (1981), Ogles and Masters (1996), and Sederer and Dickey (1996). Also see Rossi and colleagues (1982) and Wright and Rossi (1981) on "natural hazards" and social science.

6. For a brief introduction to evaluation research, see Adams and Schvaneveldt (1985:315–328), Alter and Evans (1990), Bloom, Fischer, and Orme (1990), Cham-

bers, Wedel, and Rodwell (1992), Finsterbusch and Motz (1980:119–158), Fischer (1983), Gabor, Unrau, and Grinnell (1999), Jordan and Franklin (1995), Logan and Royse (2001), Smith and Glass (1987) and Tripodi (1983). A more complete discussion can be found in Alter and Evans (1990), Bloom, Fischer and Orme (1990), Burnstein and associates (1985), Freeman (1992), Rossi (1982), Rossi and Freeman (1985), Saxe and Fine (1981), and Weiss (1972).

7. PPBS and related evaluation research are discussed in Smith and Glass (1987:41–49).

8. For discussions of case-study research, see Brandell and Varkas (2001), Dixon and Thyer (1997), Gilgun (1994), Miller (1992), Mitchell (1984), Ragin (1992a, 1992b), Stake (1994), Vaughan (1992), Walton (1992b), and Yin (1988).

9. See Mitchell (1984) and Stake (1994).

10. For discussions on various aspects of diversity in social work, see Askonas and Stewart (2000), Cowger (1994), Devore and Schlesinger (1996), Ing (2001), Pinderhughes (1989), Rodgers-Farmer and Potocky-Tripodi (2001), Tran and Aroian (2000), and Weaver (1999).

11. The role of technology in social work is addressed by Cnaan and Parsloe (1989), Howard (1995), Kreuger and Stretch (2000), Saleebey (1991), and Siegel, Jennings, Conklin, and Flynn (1998).

THEORY AND RESEARCH

The primary focus of social work theory is to seek to understand the complex reality of the person-in-situation. In this odyssey, social work theory has not only developed its own body of empirically tested knowledge but has drawn on bodies of knowledge from other disciplines, particularly, but not exclusively, the behavioral and social sciences.

—F. Turner, *Encyclopedia of Social Work*, p. 2258.

INTRODUCTION

Suppose you want to make sense of the hostility between people of different races. Trying to understand it, you ask a teacher, who responds:

> *Most racially prejudiced people learn negative stereotypes about another racial group from their families, friends, and others in their immediate surroundings. If they lack sufficient intimate social contact with members of the group or intense information that contradicts those stereotypes, they remain prejudiced.*

This makes sense to you because it is consistent with what you know about how the social world works. This is an example of a small-scale social theory, a type that researchers use when conducting a study.

What do you think of when you hear the word *theory*? Theory is one of the least well-understood terms for students learning social science. Our students' eyelids droop if we begin a class by saying, "Today we are going to examine the theory of . . ." The mental picture many students have of theory is something that floats high among the clouds. Our students have called it "a tangled maze of jargon" and "abstractions that are irrelevant to the real world." The beginning of one textbook on social theory (Craib, 1984:3) echoes this perspective:

> The very word "theory" sometimes seems to scare people, and not without good reason. Much modern social theory is either unintelligible, or banal, or pointless. . . . Few people feel at home with theory or use it in a productive way.

Contrary to these views, theory has an important role in social work research and is an essential ally for the researcher. Researchers use theory differently in various types of research, but some type of theory is present in most social work research. It is less evident in applied or descriptive than in basic or explanatory research. In simple terms, researchers interweave a story about the operation of the social world (the theory) with what they observe when they examine it systematically (the data).

WHAT IS THEORY?

In Chapter 1 *social theory* was defined as a system of interconnected abstractions or ideas that condenses and organizes knowledge about the social world. It is a compact way to think of the social world. People are always creating new theories about how the world works.

Many people confuse the history of social thought, or what great thinkers said, with social theory. The classical social theorists (e.g., Durkheim, Weber, Marx, and Tonnies) played an important role in generating innovative ideas. They developed original theories that laid the foundation for subsequent generations of social thinkers. People study the classical theorists because they provided many creative and interrelated ideas at once. They radically changed the way people understood and saw the social world. We study them because geniuses who generate many original, insightful ideas and fundamentally shift how people see the social world are rare.

People often use theories without making them explicit or labeling them as such. For example, newspaper articles or television reports on social issues usually have unstated social theories embedded within them. A news report on the difficulty of implementing a school desegregation plan will contain an implicit theory about race relations. Likewise, political leaders frequently express social theories when they discuss public issues. Politicians who claim that inadequate education causes poverty or that a decline in traditional moral values causes higher crime rates are expressing theories. Compared to the theories of social scientists, such laypersons' theories are less systematic, less well formulated, and harder to test with empirical evidence.

Social science theory seems complicated compared to laypersons' theories. Luckily, a principle of good theory called *parsimony* helps. Parsimony means simpler is better. A parsimonious theory has minimal complexity, with no redundant or excess elements. Parsimony says a more powerful theory does more with less, and the less complex of two equally convincing theories is better.

Almost all research involves some theory, so the question is less *whether* you should use theory than *how* you should use it. Being explicit about the theory makes it easier to read someone else's research or to conduct your own. An awareness of how theory fits into the research process produces better-designed, easier to understand, and better-conducted studies. Most researchers disparage atheoretical or "crude empiricist" research.

Theories come in many shapes and sizes. In this chapter we provide an elementary introduction to social theory. You will encounter theory in later chapters as well.

THEORY VERSUS IDEOLOGY

Many people find the relationship between a social scientific theory and a sociopolitical ideology controversial and confusing. Few people outside the scientific community examine social theories, but most people encounter diverse ideologies in the mass media or from the champions of particular points of view. Controversy arises because the scientific community recognizes theory as essential for clarifying and building scientific knowledge, while it condemns ideology as illegitimate obfuscation that is antithetical to science. Confusion also arises because each has multiple definitions, both explain similar events in the world, and they can overlap in places.

There are similarities between theory and ideology (see Box 3.1). Both explain many events in the world: why crime occurs, why some people are poor, why divorce rates are high in some places, and so on. Social scientific theory and an ideology both contain assumptions about the nature of the social world. They both focus on what is or is not important in it, contain a system of ideas or concepts, and specify relations among the concepts. Both provide explanations of why things are the way they are and what needs to be changed to alter conditions.

An *ideology* is a type of explanation of the social world. It is a quasi-theory that lacks critical features required of a scientific theory. Many ideologies look a lot like legitimate scientific theories. One feature of ideologies is that they have fixed, strong, and unquestioned assumptions. They are full of unquestioned absolutes and normative categories (what is right/wrong, moral/immoral, good/bad, etc.). The assumptions may be founded on faith or rooted in particular social circumstances. Many ideologies advance or protect the interests of a particular group or sector of society.

Ideologies are closed belief and value systems that change very little. They are closed to contradictory evidence and use circular reasoning. Ideologies are logically "slippery" and prevent falsification (prevent assembling empirical evidence that can show them to be false). This makes them immune to significant change. Their capacity to develop is extremely limited, because they already have all the answers. In ideology, lines between assertions about what *is* the case (ideals or values) and beliefs about what *should be* the case blur together.

Ideologies selectively present and interpret empirical evidence. They often use techniques of personal experience or conviction (e.g., overgeneralization, selective observation, and premature closure) that fall short of a scientific approach. It is difficult to test ideological principles or confront them with opposing evidence. In a way, ideology cannot acknowledge contradictory evidence. Even if overwhelming evidence is amassed, the ideology will not bend or change. A true, hard-core believer in an ideology will reject or refuse to recognize

---

Box 3.1

Theory and Ideology

SIMILARITIES

- Contains a set of assumptions or a starting point
- Explains what the social world is like, how/why it changes
- Offers a system of concepts/ideas
- Specifies relationships among concepts, tells what causes what
- Provides an interconnected system of ideas

DIFFERENCES

Ideology
- Offers absolute certainty
- Has all the answers
- Fixed, closed, finished
- Avoids tests, discrepant findings
- Blind to opposing evidence
- Locked into specific moral beliefs
- Highly partial
- Has contradictions, inconsistencies
- Rooted in specific position

Theory
- Conditional, negotiated understandings
- Incomplete, recognizes uncertainty
- Growing, open, unfolding, expanding
- Welcomes tests, positive and negative evidence
- Changes based on evidence
- Detached, disconnected, strong moral stand
- Neutral, considers all sides
- Strongly seeks logical consistency, congruity
- Transcends/crosses social positions

evidence. He or she will rigidly adhere to core value premises and principles. It is a "don't confuse me with facts, I know I'm right" attitude. Supporters often react with fear and hostility to those who disagree or present carefully gathered contradictory information.

The distinction between ideology and theory has implications for how a person conducts research. A researcher can never test and show an ideology to be true or false. By contrast, a researcher can test a scientific theory or parts of it and show them to be true or false. Social scientific theories are empirically testable, and they are constantly evolving. Researchers try to directly confront a theory with evidence. They look at all relevant evidence, both that supporting and that opposing a theory, in a disinterested way. They do not know for sure whether the evidence will support a theory. If the evidence repeatedly fails to support a theory, the theory is changed or replaced.

Theories are logically consistent. If a contradiction occurs, researchers try to resolve it. Theories are also open ended, always growing or developing to higher levels. Theories that fail to develop get replaced by competing theories. Rarely do theories claim to have all the answers. Instead, they contain areas of uncertainty or incomplete knowledge and offer only partial or tentative answers. Researchers constantly test theories and are skeptical toward them. The theory itself is disinterested or detached from the position of any specific social group or sector of society. Most theories stand apart from specific social relationships. This makes them perplexing to people who are only self-interested or who operate from a particular social position.

THE PARTS OF THEORY

Concepts

Concepts are the building blocks of theory.[1] A *concept* is an idea expressed as a symbol or in words. Natural science concepts are often expressed in symbolic forms, such as Greek letters (e.g., π) or formulas (e.g., $s = d/t$; s = speed, d = distance, t = time). Most social science concepts are expressed as words. The exotic symbols of natural science theory make many people nervous, but the use of everyday

words in specialized ways in social theory can create confusion.

We do not want to exaggerate the distinction between concepts expressed as words and concepts expressed as symbols. Words, after all, are symbols, too; they are symbols we learn with language. Height is a concept with which you are already familiar. For example, we can say the word *height* or write it down; the spoken sounds and written words are part of the English language. The combination of letters in the sound symbolizes, or stands for, the idea of a *height*. Chinese or Arabic characters, the French word *hauteur,* the German word *höhe,* the Spanish word *altura*—all symbolize the same idea. In a sense, a language is merely an agreement to represent ideas by sounds or written characters that people learned at some point in their lives. Learning concepts and theory is like learning a language.[2]

Concepts are everywhere, and you use them all the time. Height is a simple concept from everyday experience. What does it mean? It is easy to *use* the concept of *height,* but describing the concept itself is difficult. It represents an abstract idea about physical relations. How would you describe it to a very young child or a creature from a distant planet who was totally unfamiliar with it? A new concept from a social theory may seem just as alien when you encounter it for the first time. Height is a characteristic of a physical object, the distance from top to bottom. Every person, building, tree, mountain, book, and so forth has a height. We can measure height and compare it with other heights. A height of zero is possible, and height can increase or decrease over time.

As with many other words, we use the word *height* in several ways. Height is used in the expressions *the height of the battle, the height of the summer,* and *the height of fashion.*

The word *height* refers to an abstract idea. We associate its sound and its written form with that idea. There is no relationship inherent between the sounds that make up the word and the idea it represents. The connection is arbitrary, but it is still useful. People can express the abstract idea to one another by using the symbol alone.

Concepts have two parts: a *symbol* (word or term) and a *definition.* We learn definitions in many ways. We learned the word *height* and its definition from our parents. We learned it as we learned to speak and were socialized to the culture. Our parents never gave us a dictionary definition. We learned it through a diffuse, nonverbal, informal process. Our parents showed us many examples; we observed and listened to others use the word; we used the word incorrectly and were corrected; and we used it correctly and were understood. Eventually, we mastered the concept.

This example shows how people learn concepts in everyday language and how we share concepts. Suppose our parents had isolated us from television and other people, then taught us that the word for the idea *height* was *zdged.* We would have had difficulty communicating with others. People must share the terms for concepts and their definitions if they are to be of value.

Everyday culture is filled with concepts, but many of them have vague and unclear definitions. Likewise, the values and experiences of people in a culture may limit everyday concepts. Everyday concepts are often rooted in misconceptions or myth. Social scientists borrow concepts from everyday culture, but they refine these concepts and add new ones. Many concepts social scientists first developed have diffused into the larger culture and become less precise. Concepts such as sexism, lifestyle, peer group, urban sprawl, and social class began as precise, technical concepts in social theory.

We create concepts from personal experience, creative thought, or observation. The classical theorists originated many concepts. The example studies in Chapters 1 and 2 contained social science concepts. Other example concepts include family system, gender role, socialization, self-worth, frustration, and displaced aggression.

Social science concepts form a specialized language, or *jargon.* Specialists use jargon as a shorthand way to communicate with one another. Most fields have their own jargon. Physicians, lawyers, engineers, accountants, plumbers, and auto mechanics all have specialized languages. They use their jargon to refer to the ideas and objects with which they work. We can read a book with the terms used by publishers and printers in order to understand their jargon—terms such as *idiot tape, fonts, cropping, halftone, galley proof, kiss impression,* *hickeys, widows,* and *kerning.* For people on the inside, jargon is a speedy, effective, and efficient way to communicate. But jargon also has negative connotations. Some people misuse it to confuse, exclude, or denigrate others. Using jargon among nonspecialists fails to communicate; it is like speaking English to people who know only Korean.

Some concepts—especially simple, concrete concepts such as *book* or *height*—can be defined through a simple, nonverbal process. Most social science concepts are more complex and abstract. They are defined by formal, dictionary-type definitions that build on other concepts. It may seem odd to use concepts to define other concepts, but we do this all the time. For example, we defined *height* as a distance between top and bottom. *Top, bottom,* and *distance* are all concepts. We often combine simple, concrete concepts from ordinary experience to create more abstract concepts. *Height* is more abstract than *top* or *bottom.* Abstract concepts refer to aspects of the world we do not directly experience. They organize thinking and extend understanding of reality.

Concepts vary in their *level of abstraction.* They are on a continuum from most concrete to most abstract. Very concrete ones refer to straightforward physical objects or familiar experiences (e.g., *height, school, age, family income,* or *housing*). More abstract concepts refer to ideas that have a diffuse, indirect expression (e.g., *family dissolution, racism, social control, political power, deviance, intelligence,* or *cognitive dissonance*). Social researchers created many of these as a way of better grasping the social world.

Researchers define scientific concepts more precisely than those we use in daily discourse. Social theory requires well-defined concepts. The definition helps to link theory with research. A valuable goal of exploratory research, and of most good research, is to clarify and refine concepts. Weak, contradictory, or unclear definitions of concepts restrict the advance of knowledge. After noting that there are many definitions of a *gang* with little consensus, Ball and Curry (1995:239) argued:

Few if any gang researchers and theorists have been sufficiently conscious of their own definition strategies, with the result that their definitions carry too many latent connotations, treated correlations or consequences as properties or causes, or contribute to similar errors of logic.

Concept Clusters.   Concepts are rarely used in isolation. Rather, they form interconnected groups, or *concept clusters*. This is true for concepts in everyday language as well as for those in social theory. Theories contain collections of associated concepts that are consistent and mutually reinforcing. Together, they form a web of meaning. For example, if we want to discuss a concept such as *urban decay*, we will need a set of associated concepts (e.g., *urban expansion, economic growth, urbanization, suburbs, center city, revitalization, mass transit,* and *racial minorities*).

Some concepts take on a range of values, quantities, or amounts. Examples of this kind of concept are *amount of income, temperature, density of population, years of schooling,* and *degree of violence.* These are called *variables,* and you will read about them in Chapter 6. Other concepts express types of nonvariable phenomena (e.g., *bureaucracy, family, revolution, homeless,* and *cold*). Theories use both kinds of concepts.

Assumptions.   Concepts contain built-in *assumptions,* statements about the nature of things that are not observable or testable. We accept them as a necessary starting point. Concepts and theories build on assumptions about the nature of human beings, social reality, or a particular phenomenon. Assumptions often remain hidden or unstated. One way for a researcher to deepen his or her understanding of a concept is to identify the assumptions on which it is based.

For example, the concept *book* assumes a system of writing, people who can read, and the existence of paper. Without such assumptions, the idea of a *book* makes little sense. A social science concept, such as *racial prejudice,* rests on several assumptions. These include people who make distinctions among individuals based on their racial heritage, attach specific motivations and characteristics to membership in a racial group, and make judgments about the goodness of specific motivations and characteristics. If race became irrelevant, people

would cease to distinguish among individuals on the basis of race, to attach specific characteristics to a racial group, and to make judgments about characteristics. If that occurred, the concept of *racial prejudice* would cease to be useful for research. Almost all concepts contain assumptions about social relations or how people behave.

Classifications.   Some concepts are simple; they have only one dimension and vary along a single continuum. Others are complex; they have multiple dimensions or many subparts. You can break complex concepts into a set of simple, or single-dimension, concepts. For example, Rueschemeyer and associates (1992:43–44) stated that democracy has three dimensions. *Democracy* means (1) regular, free elections with universal suffrage; (2) an elected legislative body that controls government; and (3) freedom of expression and association. The authors recognized that each dimension varies by degree. They classified the dimensions to create a set of types of regimes. Regimes very low on all three dimensions are totalitarian, those high on all three are democracies, and ones with other mixes are either authoritarian or liberal oligarchies.

Classifications are important in many theories. They are partway between a single, simple concept and a theory.[3] They help to organize abstract, complex concepts. To create a new classification, a researcher logically specifies and combines the characteristics of simpler concepts. You can best grasp this idea by looking at some examples.

The *ideal type* is a well-known classification. Ideal types are pure, abstract models that define the essence of the phenomenon in question. They are mental pictures that define the central aspects of a concept. Ideal types are not explanations because they do not tell why or how something occurs. They are smaller than theories, and researchers use them to build a theory. They are broader, more abstract concepts that bring together several narrower, more concrete concepts. Qualitative researchers often use ideal types to see how well observable phenomena match up to the ideal model. For example, Max Weber developed an ideal type of the concept *bureaucracy.* Many people use Weber's ideal type (see Box 3.2). It distinguishes

Box 3.2 _____

Max Weber's Ideal Type of Bureaucracy

- It is a continuous organization governed by a system of rules.
- Conduct is governed by detached, impersonal rules.
- There is division of labor, in which different offices are assigned different spheres of competence.
- Hierarchical authority relations prevail; that is, lower offices are under control of higher ones.
- Administrative actions, rules, and so on are in writing and maintained in files.
- Individuals do not own and cannot buy or sell their offices.
- Officials receive salaries rather than receiving direct payment from clients in order to ensure loyalty to the organization.
- Property of the organization is separate from personal property of officeholders.

_____

Source: Adapted from Chafetz (1978:72).

a bureaucracy from other organizational forms (e.g., social movements, kingdoms, etc.). It also clarifies critical features of a kind of organization that people once found nebulous and hard to think about. No real-life organization perfectly matches the ideal type, but the model helps us think about and study bureaucracy.

Another type of classification is the *typology,* or taxonomy,[4] in which a researcher combines two or more unidimensional, simple concepts, such that the intersection of simple concepts forms new concepts. The new concepts or types express the complex interrelation between the simple concepts.

> *One of the chief merits of a typology is parsimony. . . . A well constructed typology can work miracles in bringing order out of chaos. It can transform the overwhelming complexity of an apparent eclectic congeries of numerous apparently diverse cases into a well-ordered set of a few rather homogeneous types. (Bailey, 1992:2193)*

Robert Merton's anomie theory of deviance argues that people can understand nondeviance, or

conformity, and deviance by considering two key concepts: the goals a culture defines as worth pursuing and the means to achieve those goals that a society defines as legitimate. Merton's typology rests on two concepts: (1) whether people accept or reject the goals and (2) whether the means people use to reach the goals are legitimate or not. His typology identifies types of deviance and conformity based on the two concepts (see Table 3.1).

Conformity, or nondeviance, occurs when people accept cultural goals (e.g., obtaining a high income) and use a socially legitimate means to reach them (e.g., getting a good job and working hard). Deviance occurs when this is not the case (e.g., when someone robs a bank instead of working hard). Merton's classification of how individuals adapt to cultural goals and means to reach them summarizes his complex concept and labels each subpart. For example, *retreatism* describes a person who rejects both cultural goals and the socially legitimate means to achieve them—such as a chronic alcohol user or a religious hermit. This type of deviant rejects the cultural goal of appearing respectable and acquiring material possessions (e.g., house, car, etc.). He or she also rejects the legitimate means of reaching the goal (e.g., being honest, working at a job, etc.).

A second example comes from British sociologist Anthony Giddens (1994), who created a typology of elites using two concepts: patterns of recruitment into the elite (open versus closed) and the degree of social integration (i.e., cooperation, solidarity, etc.) within the elite (high or low). By cross-classifying these two concepts, he developed four new concepts or types of elites: solidarity, uniform, abstract, and established (see Table 3.2). He

TABLE 3.1 Robert Merton's Modes of Individual Adaptation

MODE OF ADAPTATION	SOCIETAL GOALS	INSTITUTIONAL MEANS
I. Conformity	Accept	Accept
II. Innovation	Accept	Reject
III. Ritualism	Reject	Accept
IV. Retreatism	Reject	Reject
V. Revolution	Substitute new	Substitute new

TABLE 3.2 Giddens's Types of Elites

TYPES OF SOCIAL/POLITICAL ELITES		RECRUITMENT INTO ELITE	
		Open	Closed
Social Integration	High	Solidarity Elite	Uniform Elite
	Low	Abstract Elite	Established Elite

discusses features of each type in his larger theory of elites. For example, he argues that the solidarity elite was the pattern found in state socialist nations that had a powerful communist party.

Erik O. Wright updated Karl Marx's theory of social classes in capitalism. He noted that, for Marx, inequality and exploitation are based on control over three types of resources: investments (i.e., profit-making property or capital), the organization of production, and labor power (i.e., the work of other people). Wright said that the organization of a society defines social classes. The organization of a class society creates positions that confer control over the three types of resources to those occupying the positions (see Table 3.3). People in positions that control all three resources constitute the most powerful or dominant class. In market economies this is the capitalist class. Its members include the major investors, owners, and presidents of banks or corporations. Capitalists make investment decisions (e.g., whether and where to build a new factory), determine how to organize production (e.g., use robots or low-wage workers), and give orders to others. The class near the bottom consists of workers. They occupy positions in which they have no say over investments or how to organize production. They lack authority over others and must follow orders to keep their jobs. Managers and supervisors, who assist the capitalists, are between the two major classes. They are a quasi-class that had not yet fully appeared in the 1800s when Marx developed his theory. They control some but not all of the major resources of society.

Wright's classification also points out the position of another class about which Marx wrote, the petite (small) bourgeoisie, consisting of small-scale self-employed proprietors or farmers. Members of this class own and operate their own businesses but employ no one except family members. Marx thought this class would shrink and disappear, but it is still with us today. Like Merton's and Giddens's classifications, Wright's scheme shows how to combine a set of simpler concepts (i.e., types of resources owned or not owned) into a more powerful idea (i.e., the structure of social classes in a capitalist society).

TABLE 3.3 Erik Wright's System of Social Classes

SOCIAL CLASS	CONTROL OVER SOCIETAL RESOURCE		
	Investments	Production	Labor
Capitalists	+	+	+
Managers	−	+	+
Supervisors	−	−	+
Workers	−	−	−
Petite bourgeoisie	+	+	−

+ means has control, − means no or little control

Relationships

Theories contain many concepts, their definitions, and assumptions. More significantly, theories specify how concepts relate to one another. Theories tell us whether or not concepts are related and, if they are, how they relate to each other. In addition, theories state why the relationship does or does not exist.

Beck and Tolnay (1990) presented a theory about lynching, the killing of African Americans by hanging carried out by mobs of White people in the southern United States from the late 1800s to the 1930s. They said that lynching was related to economic distress (i.e., lower prices received by Whites for the cotton grown in the area) but not to Blacks committing crimes (i.e., an increasing incidence of crimes committed by African Americans). Their theory stated connections among the three concepts—lynching, economic distress, and Black victimization.

Many theories make a causal statement, or a *proposition,* about the relationship among variables. "A proposition is a theoretical statement that specifies the connection between two or more variables, informing us how variation in one concept is accounted for by variation in another" (Turner, 1985:25). It is a relationship expressed in a theory, such as: Economic distress among the White population caused an increase in mob violence against African Americans. When a researcher empirically tests or evaluates a relationship, it is called a *hypothesis.* After many careful tests of a hypothesis confirm the proposition, the scientific community begins to develop confidence that the proposition is true.

A social theory contains concepts, a relationship among concepts, and a causal mechanism, or reason, for the relationship. A *causal mechanism* is a statement of how things work, such as: When people fear a loss, they strike out at those they believe to be their direct competitors and who have less social or political power. Reasons for a relationship are other logically connected assumptions and propositions. It could be an assumption, such as: After the Civil War, Whites in the southern United States held a deep resentment over the loss of their racially based social status. This might be combined with a proposition: The absence of strong, legitimate, and formal social control over perceived deviants or outgroup members, combined with a high level of frustration

about deviant or outgroup actions, causes an ingroup to adopt nonlegal but traditional means of asserting social control. Propositions do not exist in isolation; they are part of a web of interconnected concepts, relations, and assumptions.

Scope

Some concepts are highly abstract, some are at a middle level of abstraction, and some are at a concrete level. Theories with many abstract concepts apply to a wider range of social phenomena than those with concrete concepts. An example of an abstract theoretical relationship is: Increased size creates centralization, which in turn creates greater formalization. *Size, centralization,* and *formalization* are abstract ideas. They can refer to features of a group, organization, or society. We can translate this to say that as a social welfare organization or group gets bigger, authority and power relations within it become centralized and concentrated in a small elite. The elite will tend to rely more on written policies, rules, or laws to control and organize others in the group or organization.

By contrast, the least abstract, simplest, or lowest-level relationship is an *empirical generalization.* It is a simple relationship that is concrete and uncomplicated. A researcher creates one when he or she generalizes about an observed regularity. A theory on a topic often implies many generalizations, which can be elementary hypotheses. Here is an example of an empirical generalization: Most people who drive small Japanese-made automobiles are under 30 years of age. The generalization contains two concepts: type of car and age of driver. It states a relationship: that a type of car, defined by size and country of origin, is associated with or related to an age group. To become a full theory, it needs additional elaboration and greater breadth to explain why this occurs.

When building or extending a theory and specifying its relationships, a researcher needs to think clearly about the types of units, cases, or situations to which the theory applies:

> *Most theoretical ideas are formulated in general terms and thus applicable to some universe of cases. Sometimes these general claims are explicit (e.g., a*

theory of ethnic relations applies to all ethnic relations), and sometimes the claims are taken to be general because a theory's scope conditions have been left unspecified. (Ragin, 1992b:219)

Thinking explicitly about a theory's scope will make it stronger and allow the researcher to communicate it more clearly to others.

In a study of skin tone and social stratification among African Americans, Keith and Herring (1991) linked an empirical generalization to theory. They tested the empirical generalization that African Americans with lighter skin tones have more education and higher incomes than do those with darker tones. They found support for this generalization, but why? Their theory filled in the picture. It said that Whites were more willing to extend privileges and advantages to slaves with lighter skin tones because this indicated partial White ancestry. For 200 years under slavery, Whites' prevailing racial ideology attributed superior talents to slaves with White ancestry. Also, for aesthetic reasons, the White aristocracy preferred light-skinned slaves for personal service and sexual relationships. These relations made it easier for lighter-skinned slaves to purchase their freedom. Thus, over many years, African Americans with lighter skin tones had opportunities to obtain skills, education, and advantages that were denied their darker-skinned brethren. After slavery ended, lighter skin was still common in the social elite within the African American community. Subsequent intermarriage among people with similar amounts of education and income perpetuated the link of skin tone to economic advantage. The larger theory makes the empirical generalization richer by connecting it to other ideas about social relations under slavery, differential opportunities to obtain education, and patterns of selecting marriage partners.

FACT VERSUS THEORY

A long-standing issue in discussions of testing scientific theory is the line between fact and theory. There are two extreme positions. At one extreme is the unrefined *empiricist* position. It says that facts and theories are totally different. Theories belong to the world of soft, indistinct mental images, values, and ideas. Facts are part of the empirical world of hard, settled, observable things that are uncontaminated by theories or ideas. Ideas or theories belong to the world of thought that also contains illusions, dreams, imagination, speculation, and misconceptions. Theories can slide into speculation, illusion, or fiction. To avoid this, theory must be tested against the hard, empirical facts of "real" material reality. The extreme empiricist says that what we see is what there is. This position urges the researcher to improve measures until he or she approaches the position of a person with crystal clear, perfect vision and who is not fooled by optical illusions or visual tricks.

The opposite is the extreme *relativist* position. It says that reality is what we think it is. What we take to be reality is strongly shaped by cultural beliefs, thoughts, or mental images of it. We can never fully escape the powerful influence of our thoughts. We cannot test theories against hard, objective facts, because facts are shaped by ideas and theories. An extreme relativist says that our desires, ideas, and beliefs so strongly distort our vision that the social world we see contains mirages. We are unable to see things that our ideas and beliefs do not allow us to see.

Some researchers adopt one or the other extreme, but most fall somewhere in the middle. Those in the middle say that theories and our categories of thought influence what we take to be facts or observations of the world. Nevertheless, there is a separate reality "out there," independent of our ideas. The difficulty is that we can never get a pure, simple, direct, and unmodified measure of that reality. Our attempts to get at facts are forever clouded or tainted by our cultural beliefs, theories, and ideas. We see only a distorted image of what is really there. Our vision of reality is blurred, as if we are looking through a warped or cloudy glass. Facts we observe are always an imperfect, indirect, and distorted representation of what actually exists.

Deeper philosophical issues in the debate are further explored in Chapter 4. This debate affects how we do social research in two ways. First, it means we make allowances for the distortion. Everyone, except the most extreme empiricist, warns that our views of data might involve some distortion. The issue becomes how to control for such distortion and the degree to which such control is possible or desirable. Second, the process of research by many different people over time is likely to reduce or control distortion. Except for some postmodernists (see Chapter 4), most scholars believe that many well-conducted studies by diverse, independent, open-minded, and freely communicating researchers will get closer to the reality "out there" in the long run.

THEORIES

Theory can be baffling because it comes in so many forms. We can categorize a theory by (1) the direction of reasoning, (2) the level of social reality that it explains, (3) whether it is formal or substantive, (4) the forms of explanation it employs, and (5) the overall framework of assumptions and concepts in which it is embedded. Fortunately, not all logically possible combinations of direction, level, explanation, and framework are equally viable. There are only about half a dozen serious contenders.

Direction

Researchers approach the building and testing of theory from two directions. Some begin with abstract thinking. They logically connect the ideas in theory to concrete evidence, then test the ideas against the evidence. Others begin with specific observations of empirical evidence. On the basis of the evidence, they generalize and build toward increasingly abstract ideas. In practice, most researchers are flexible and use both approaches at various points in a study.

Deductive.   In a *deductive approach* you begin with an abstract, logical relationship among concepts, then move toward concrete empirical evidence. You may have ideas about how the world operates and want to test these ideas against "hard data." Beck and Tolnay's (1990) study on lynching, referred to earlier, used deductive logic. They began with a theory about lynching and economic distress. The theory suggested the evidence they should gather. After they had gathered and analyzed the data, they learned that the findings supported their theory.

Inductive.   If you use an *inductive approach,* you begin with detailed observations of the world and

move toward more abstract generalizations and ideas. When you begin, you may have only a topic and a few vague concepts. As you observe, you refine the concepts, develop empirical generalizations, and identify preliminary relationships. You build the theory from the ground up. Fitchen (1991) used inductive reasoning in her study of the rural crisis, described in Chapter 2. She began with a few general ideas about the farm crisis. Gradually, as she interviewed and observed, she expanded her research focus from farm issues to broader issues of rural communities. She refined concepts and generated empirical generalizations. Eventually, she developed a theory of how people adopt a self-identity as a rural community.

Another example is Schiffman's (1991) study of two antinuclear groups in the San Francisco area. Her main finding was that different groups within the same broader political movement adopt very different strategies and actions based on how they define power in society. This finding arose only during her detailed observations. It differed from her initial goal: to learn how a single-movement organization resolved internal conflicts. As she said, "My data forced me to redefine the project." Theoretical generalization generated by an inductive approach is called *grounded theory* (see Figure 3.1).

Level of Theory

Social theories can be divided into three broad groupings by the level of social reality with which they deal. Most of us devote the majority of our time to thinking about the micro level of reality, the individuals we see and interact with on a day-by-day basis. *Micro-level theory* deals with small slices of time, space, or numbers of people. The concepts are usually not very abstract.

Erving Goffman's theory of "face work" is a micro-level theory. Goffman stated that people engage in rituals during face-to-face interaction. An individual adopts a "line" in interaction that defines the type of situation and the type of person he or she is in the situation. For example, in a classroom setting, the teacher may present a line of being a friendly teacher. Others in the interaction—students—accommodate the face presented and

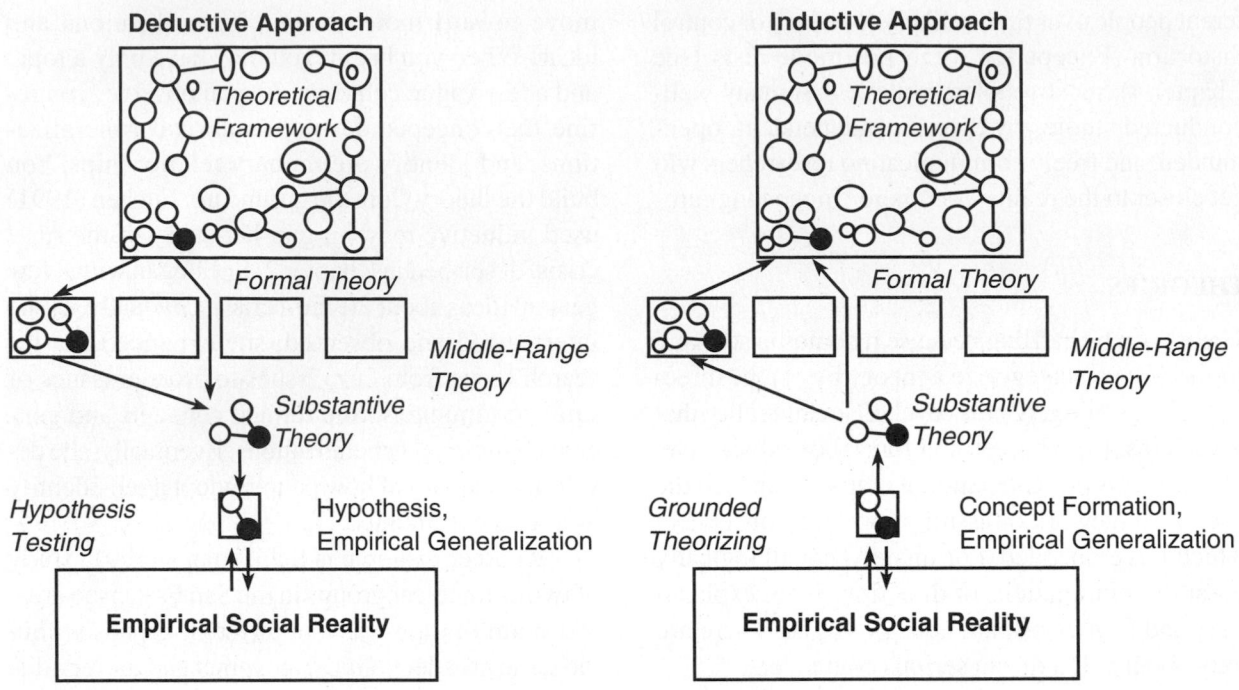

FIGURE 3.1 Deductive and Inductive Theorizing

conform to it in an unwritten code of appropriate behavior. The teacher presents the face by engaging in certain behaviors (e.g., turning on the lights, walking to the front of the room, and speaking to everyone in the room). The teacher also adopts a particular manner (e.g., stands and smiles, makes eye contact, and inquires about personal events). Others in the classroom cooperate in the ritual. This sustains the social construction of the teacher's face. Students avoid certain topics, show deference, and overlook minor errors in the teacher's presentation. This is "face work" in Goffman's theory.

Macro-level theory concerns the operation of larger aggregates such as social institutions, entire cultural systems, and whole societies. It uses more concepts that are abstract.

Lenski (1966) presented a macro-level theory of social stratification that explains overall societal inequality across thousands of years of human societies. Lenski argued that the amount of surplus a society produces (i.e., the amount beyond what people need for bare subsistence) increases with the development of human society. He argued that the

surplus grew as human society developed from a simple hunting and gathering form to an agrarian form and then to a modern industrial form. Inequality increased as a small group in society took control of the surplus. Inequality peaked historically in agrarian societies and declined in industrial society because the size and complexity of modern society diffused power across more social groups. As they gained some power, the various groups were able to get some of the surplus. Dividing the surplus among more groups reduced inequality.

Meso-level theory is relatively rare. It attempts to link macro and micro levels or to operate at an intermediate level. Theories of organizations, social movements, or communities are often at this level.

Collins (1988:451–466) offered a meso-level theory of control in organizations. This theory identifies three basic methods to control people in a large organization: coerce them (e.g., threaten them with a beating), offer them material rewards (e.g., pay increases), or use internal controls (e.g., socialization, promotion possibilities, creation of a subculture of commitment, etc.). Likewise, organizations have five administrative devices for controlling people: (1) using surveillance (e.g., watching over people), (2) inspecting outcomes (e.g., the number of products produced), (3) providing rules and written instructions, (4) controlling information, and (5) constricting the environment (e.g., enforcing when and where work is done). Each method of control and administrative device has negative side effects. For example, clients who feel watched will behave in a ritual manner and put on the appearance of working whenever they believe they are being watched. The controls are effective with different work tasks. The best controls for tasks requiring a high degree of initiative and judgment and involving a lot of uncertainty (e.g., those of a caseworker) are internal controls (e.g., professional socialization) and information control (e.g., the idea that experts are the only ones who know costs). By contrast, people doing predictable tasks with standardized products (e.g., punch-press operators) respond better to material rewards (e.g., piece rate pay) and monitoring of output (e.g., counting production units).

Formal and Substantive Theories

We can distinguish substantive from formal theory (Layder, 1993:42–43). *Substantive theory* is developed for a specific area of social concern, such as delinquent gangs, secondary classrooms, or race relations. *Formal theory* is developed for a broad conceptual area in general theory, such as homelessness, socialization, or power. If you want to test, generate, or extend a substantive theory, then you should think of cases within the same substantive area. For example, you might compare several delinquent gangs, but you do not have to theorize about deviance in general. If you want to test, generate, or extend formal theory, then you should compare cases within the same formal area. For example, you might examine various forms of homelessness. You can do this without reference to the details of substantive areas (e.g., sleeping under a bridge, living in shelters, etc.). Eventually, substantive and formal theory can be connected. There is no need to force all thinking into a single theory; in fact, "the cumulative

progress of theory is enhanced by the encouragement of multiple substantive and formal theories" (Layder, 1993:44).

Forms of Explanation

Prediction and Explanation.   A theory's primary purpose is to explain. Many people confuse prediction with explanation. There are two meanings or uses of the term *explanation.* Researchers focus on *theoretical explanation,* a logical argument that tells why something occurs. It refers to a general rule or principle. These are a researcher's theoretical argument or connections among concepts. The second type of explanation, *ordinary explanation,* makes something clear or describes something in a way that illustrates it and makes it intelligible. For example, a good teacher "explains" in the ordinary sense. The two types of explanation can blend together. This occurs when a researcher explains (i.e., makes intelligible) his or her explanation (i.e., a logical argument involving theory).

Prediction is a statement that something will occur. It is easier to predict than to explain, and an explanation has more logical power than prediction because good explanations also predict. An explanation rarely predicts more than one outcome, but the same outcome may be predicted by opposing explanations. Although it is less powerful than explanation, many people are entranced by the dramatic visibility of a prediction.

A gambling example illustrates the difference between explanation and prediction. If we enter a casino and consistently and accurately predict the next card to appear or the next number on a roulette wheel, it will be sensational. We may win a lot of money, at least until the casino officials realize we are always winning and expel us. Yet, our method of making the predictions is more interesting than the fact that we can do so. Telling you what we do to predict the next card is more fascinating than being able to predict.

Here is another example. You know that the sun "rises" each morning. You can predict that at some time, every morning, whether or not clouds obscure it, the sun will rise. But why is this so? One explanation is that the Great Turtle carries the sun across the sky on its back. Another explanation is that a god sets his arrow ablaze, which appears to us as the sun, and shoots it across the sky. Few people today believe these ancient explanations. The explanation you probably accept involves a theory about the rotation of the earth and the position of the sun, the star of our solar system. In this explanation the sun only appears to rise. The sun does not move; its apparent movement depends on the earth's rotation. We are on a planet that both spins on its axis and orbits around a star millions of miles away in space. All three explanations make the same prediction: The sun rises each morning. As you can see, a weak explanation can produce an accurate prediction. A good explanation depends on a well-developed theory and is confirmed in research by empirical observations.

Now that you have an idea of what *explanation* means, we can turn to the three ways researchers explain: causal, structural, and interpretive. The forms of explanation refer to the way in which a researcher tells others why social events occur or why social relations assume a particular pattern.

Causal Explanation. *Causal explanation,* the most common type of explanation, is used when the relationship is one of cause and effect. We use it often in everyday language, which tends to be sloppy and ambiguous. What do we mean when we say *cause?* For example, you may say that poverty causes crime or that looseness in morals causes an increase in divorce. This does not tell how or why the causal process works. Researchers try to be more precise and exact when discussing causal relations.

Philosophers have long debated the idea of cause. It has been a controversial idea since the writings of the 18th-century Scottish philosopher David Hume (1711–1776). Some people argue that causality occurs in the empirical world, but it cannot be proved. Causality is "out there" in objective reality, and researchers can only try to find evidence for it. Others argue that causality is only an idea that exists in the human mind, a mental construction, not something "real" in the world. This second position holds that causality is only a convenient way of thinking about the world. Without entering into the philosophical debate, many researchers pursue causal relationships.

You need three things to establish causality: temporal order, association, and the elimination of plausible alternatives (see Box 3.3). An implicit fourth condition is an assumption that a causal relationship makes sense or fits with broader assumptions or a theoretical framework. Let us examine the three basic conditions.

The *temporal order* condition means that a cause must come before an effect. This commonsense assumption establishes the direction of causality: from the cause toward the effect. You may ask: How can the cause come after what it is to affect? It cannot, but temporal order is only one of the conditions needed for causality. Temporal order is necessary but not sufficient to infer causality. Sometimes people make the mistake of talking about "cause" on the basis of temporal order alone. For example, a professional baseball player pitches no-hit games when he kisses his wife just before a game. The kissing occurred before the no-hit games. Does that mean the kissing is the cause of the pitching performance? It is very unlikely. As another example, race riots occurred in four separate cities in 1968, one day after an intense wave of sunspots. The temporal ordering does not establish a causal link between sunspots and race riots. After all, all prior human history occurred before some specific event. The temporal order condition simply eliminates from consideration potential causes that occurred later in time.

It is not always easy to establish temporal order. With cross-sectional research, temporal order is tricky. For example, a researcher finds that men who physically abuse female partners also consume a good deal more alcohol than men who do not abuse female partners. Does consuming more alcohol cause an increase in abuse? Or do men who physically abuse women consume more alcohol to assuage their guilt? Here is another example. Some students who get high grades say they have excellent teachers. Does getting high grades make them happy, so they return the favor by saying their professors are excellent teachers (i.e., high grades cause positive evaluations)? Or is the professor doing a great job, so students study hard and learn a lot, which the grades reflect (i.e., their learning causes

Box 3.3 _____

Three Elements of Causality

We read that several politicians visited a Catholic school in Chicago that had a record of being much more successful than public schools in educating children. The next day, the politicians called a news conference and advocated new laws and the redirection of tax money to Catholic schools. As people who want children to get a good education, we were interested in the story, but as social scientists, we critically evaluated it. The politicians' theory said Catholic schools cause more learning than public schools. They had two elements of causality: temporal order (first the children attended a Catholic school, then learning improved) and association (those attending Catholic schools performed better than those attending public school). Social work researchers know this is not enough information. They first try to eliminate alternative explanations, and then try to understand the causal mechanism (i.e., what happens in Catholic schools that helps students learn more). For example,

the politicians failed to eliminate the alternative explanation that children in the two types of schools had different family circumstances that affect learning and that this caused learning differences. If the family circumstances (e.g., parents' education and income, family religious belief and intensity of belief, two-parent vs. single-parent households, degree of parental interest in a child's education, etc.) are the same for children who attend both types of schools, then the politicians are on the right track. The focus, then, is on what Catholic schools are doing that improves learning. If the family circumstances are very different, then the politicians are making a big mistake. Unfortunately, politicians are rarely trained in social work research and most make quick, high-publicity decisions without the careful reasoning or the patience for precise empirical investigation. Luckily, sociologist James S. Coleman and others have studied this issue (see Coleman and Hoffer, 1987).

---

them to get high grades)? It is a chicken-and-egg problem. To resolve it, a researcher needs to bring in other information or design research to test for the temporal order.

Simple causal relations are unidirectional, operating in a single direction from the cause to the effect. Most studies examine unidirectional relations. More complex theories specify reciprocal-effect causal relations—that is, a mutual causal relationship or simultaneous causality. For example, studying a lot causes a student to get good grades, but getting good grades also motivates the student to continue to study. Theories often have reciprocal or feedback relationships, but these are difficult to test. Some researchers call unidirectional relations nonrecursive and reciprocal-effect relations recursive.

A researcher also needs an _association_ for causality. Two phenomena are associated if they occur together in a patterned way or appear to act together. People sometimes confuse correlation with association. Correlation has a specific technical meaning, whereas association is a more general idea. A correlation coefficient is a statistical measure that

indicates the amount of association, but there are many ways to measure association. Sometimes, researchers call association _concomitant variation_ because two variables vary together. Figure 3.2 shows 38 people from a lower-income neighborhood and 35 people from an upper-income neighborhood. Can you see an association between race and income level?

More people mistake association for causality than confuse it with temporal order. For example, it has been shown that more births occur in areas where there are more storks. This may simply be a consequence of the fact that most of the population in the U.S. lives quite close to either coast, where storks are found. Hence, there is an association between storks and births, but not a causal one.

As another example, the number of children born in India increased until the late 1960s, then slowed in the 1970s. The number of U.S.-made cars driven in the United States increased until the late 1960s, then slowed in the 1970s. The number of Indian children born and the number of U.S. cars driven are associated: They vary together or increase

Lower Income   **Upper Income**

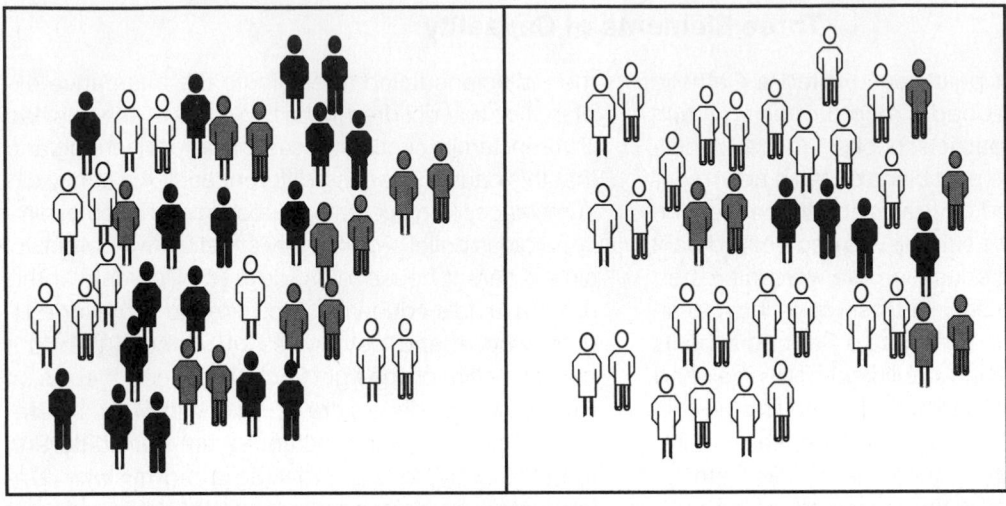

FIGURE 3.2   Association of Income and Race

and decrease at the same time. Yet there is no causal connection. By coincidence, the Indian government instituted a birth control program that slowed the number of births at the same time that Americans were buying more imported cars.

If a researcher cannot find an association, a causal relationship is unlikely. This is why researchers attempt to find correlations and other measures of association. Yet, a researcher can find an association without causality. The association eliminates potential causes that are not associated. It cannot definitely identify a cause. It is a necessary but not a sufficient condition. In other words, you need it for causality, but it is not enough alone.

An association does not have to be perfect (i.e., every time one variable is present, the other is also present) to show causality. In the stork example the correlation between number of babies born and number of storks was about .45. This means that the presence of storks was associated with about 20% of the variation in number of babies born, but it was not a perfect correlation. Storks did not account for 100% of variation in babies born, just part of it. The race and income-level association shown in Figure 3.2 is also an imperfect association.

Eliminating alternatives means that a researcher interested in causality needs to show that the effect is due to the causal variable and not to

something else. It is also called *no spuriousness* because an apparent causal relationship that is actually due to an alternative but unrecognized cause is called a spurious relationship, which is discussed in Chapter 6 (see Box 3.4).

Researchers can observe temporal order and associations. They cannot observe the elimination of alternatives. They can only demonstrate it indirectly. Eliminating alternatives is an ideal because eliminating all possible alternatives is impossible. A researcher tries to eliminate major alternative explanations in two ways: through built-in design controls and by measuring potential hidden causes. Experimental researchers build controls into the study design itself to eliminate alternative causes. They isolate an experimental situation from the influence of all variables except the main causal variable.

Researchers also try to eliminate alternatives by measuring possible alternative causes. This is common in survey research and is called *controlling for* another variable. Researchers use statistical techniques to learn whether the causal variable or something else operates on the effect variable.

Causal explanations are usually in a linear form, stating cause and effect in a straight line: *A* causes *B*, *B* causes *C*, *C* causes *D*. The foregoing explanations from the studies on skin tone and on lynching illustrate linear causal explanations. The main concepts

Box 3.4

Learning to See Causal Relations

Driving home from the university one day, one of the authors heard a radio news report about gender and racial bias in standardized tests. A person who claimed that bias was a major problem said that the tests should be changed. Since the author works in the field of education and disdains racial or gender bias, the report caught his attention. Yet, as a social scientist, he critically evaluated the news story. The evidence for a bias charge was the consistent pattern of higher scores in mathematics for male high school seniors versus female high school seniors, and for European-background students versus African American students. Was the cause of the pattern of different test scores a bias built into the tests?

When questioned by someone who had designed the tests, the person charging bias lacked a crucial piece of evidence to support a claim of test bias: the educational experience of students. It turns out that girls and boys take different numbers and types of mathematics courses in high school. Girls tend to take fewer math courses. Among the girls who complete the same mathematics curriculum as boys, the gender difference dissolves. Likewise, a large percentage of African Americans attend racially segregated, poor-quality schools in inner cities or in impoverished rural areas. For African Americans who attend high-quality suburban schools and complete the same courses, racial differences in test scores disappear. This evidence suggests that inequality in education causes test score differences. Although the tests may have problems, identifying the real cause implies that changing the tests without first improving or equalizing education could be a mistake.

---

in both theories were variables; that is, they took on a range of values. Both used one variable (e.g., amount of economic distress or darkness of skin tone) to explain a second variable (e.g., amount of lynching or differences in income and educational level). We can restate them as simple causal propositions: The higher the level of economic distress, the more lynching; or the lighter the skin tone, the greater the income and education level. They were also deductive because they developed the proposition before testing it with data. We can restate the logic of each study in a deductive causal form: If the proposition is true, then we observe certain things in the empirical evidence. Good causal explanations identify a causal relationship and specify a causal mechanism. A simple causal explanation is: X causes Y; Y occurs because of X, where X and Y are concepts (e.g., early marriage and divorce). Some researchers state causality in a predictive form: If X occurs, then Y follows. Causality can be stated in many ways: X leads to Y; X produces Y; X influences Y; X is related to Y; the greater X, the higher Y.

Here is a simple causal theory: A rise in unemployment causes an increase in child abuse. The subject to be explained is an increase in the occurrence of child abuse. What explains it is a rise in unemployment. We "explain" the increase in child abuse by identifying its cause. A complete explanation also requires elaborating the causal mechanism. This theory says that when people lose their jobs, they feel a loss of self-worth. Once they lose self-worth, they become easily frustrated, upset, and angry. Frustrated people often express their anger by directing violence toward those with whom they have close personal contact (e.g., friends, spouse, children, etc.). This is especially true if they do not understand the source of the anger or cannot direct it toward its true cause (e.g., an employer, government policy, or "economic forces").

The unemployment and child abuse example illustrates a chain of causes and a causal mechanism. Researchers can test different parts of the chain. They might test whether unemployment rates and child abuse occur together, or whether frustrated people become violent toward the people close to them. A typical research strategy is to divide a larger theory into parts and test various relationships against the data.

Diagrams of Causal Relations Among Variables.
At minimum, you need a cause and an effect for a causal relationship. Consider this hypothesis: "The

more often married people of the same religion attend religious services together, the less likely they are to be divorced." This hypothesis links "attendance at religious services" and "likelihood of divorce." It has three other elements: the group or universe it refers to (married people of the same religion), the direction of causality (from religious attendance to divorce), and the sign of the relationship (the higher or more frequent religious attendance, the less the chance of a divorce). Researchers express theories in words, pictures, or both. They often draw diagrams of the causal relations to present a simplified picture of a relationship and see it at a glance. Such symbolic representations supplement verbal descriptions of causal relations and convey complex information. They are a shorthand way to show theoretical relations.

The simplest diagram is a two-variable model, as in Figure 3.3(a). Researchers represent variables using letters, circles, or boxes. The convention is to represent a cause by an X and the effect by a Y. The arrow shows the direction of causality (e.g., from independent to dependent variable). Sometimes, researchers use subscripts when there is more than one cause (e.g., X_1, X_2), as in Figure 3.3(b). Relationships among variables are symbolized by lines with arrows. Causal relations are represented by straight lines. Associations that do not imply a causal relationship are represented by curved lines with arrows on each end. A single arrow on a line represents a unidirectional relationship. Arrows on both ends of a straight line represent reciprocal relationships.

Relationships between variables can be positive or negative. Researchers imply a positive relationship if they say nothing. A *positive relationship* means that a higher value on the causal variable goes with a higher value on the effect variable. For example, the more education a person has, the longer his or her life expectancy is. A *negative relationship* means that a higher value on the causal variable goes with a lower value on the effect variable. For example, the more frequently a couple attends religious services, the lower the chances of their divorcing each other. In diagrams, a plus sign (+) signifies a positive relationship and a negative sign (–) signifies a negative relationship.

Figure 3.3 presents some samples of relationships that can be diagrammed. Researchers would

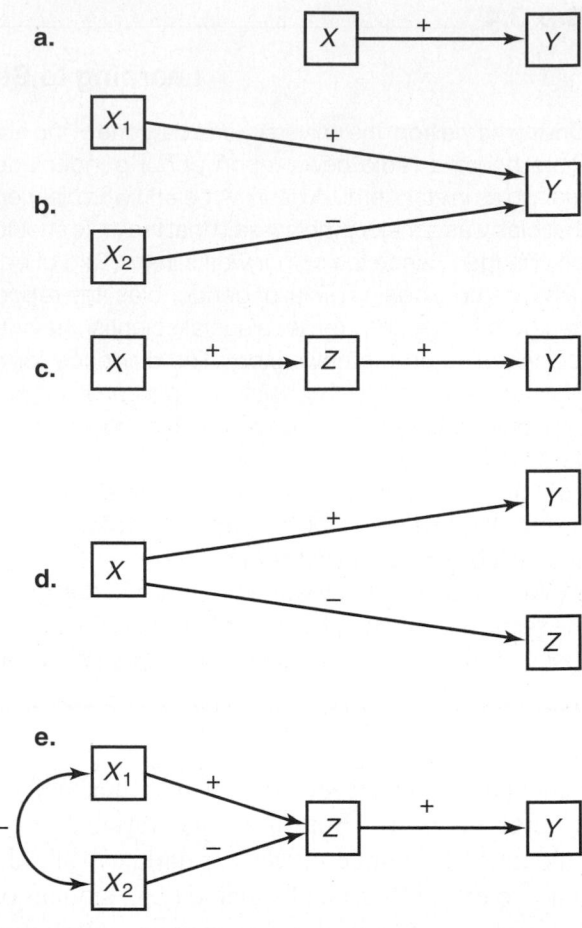

FIGURE 3.3 Causal Diagrams

not use a diagram for a very simple two-variable relationship like the one in Figure 3.3(a). As researchers add variables and increase the complexity of relationships, they find diagrams more helpful. Diagram (b) shows a slightly more complex relationship with two causal variables. It might state that the number of hours parents spend talking with a child (X_1) affects the child's sense of well-being (Y), and the number of hours a child fights with peers (X_2) has a negative effect on well-being (Y). Diagrams (c) and (d) also show three-variable relationships. The theoretical causal pattern is different in each.

Diagram (c) shows a simple linear causal chain. It says X affects Z, which in turn affects Y. For example, X represents completing a GED certificate, Z is attending job training classes, and Y is applying for jobs listed in the help wanted section of a newspaper. The theory expressed in diagram (c) says that the completion of one's GED certificate causes one to attend job training classes, which in turn causes one to apply for jobs. In (d) the theory says that X has effects on Y and Z, but that Z and Y are distinct. The theory expressed in (d) would say that completing a GED certificate increases attendance in job training classes and applications for jobs, but that those who attend job training classes don't necessarily apply for jobs. In other words, completing job training and applying for jobs are two distinct outcomes, both caused by completing the GED certificate.

Another example of the simple linear causal chain in diagram (c) would be that X represents knowledge of political events, Z is attendance at political rallies, and Y stands for making a donation to a candidate. The theory expressed by diagram (c) says that one's knowledge of politics causes one to attend political rallies, which, in turn, causes a political donation. In (d) the theory says that X has effects Y and Z, but that Y and Z are distinct. The theory expressed in (d) would say that political knowledge increases attendance at rallies and donations, but that those who attend rallies do not necessarily donate money. In other words, donations and attendance at rallies are two distinct outcomes, both caused by political knowledge.

Diagram (e) illustrates a model of a four-variable theory. In it, two causal variables are associated, but the theory states that neither is the cause of the other (e.g., they may occur at the same time). Here is an example of the relationships in diagram (e)—anxiety about grades (X_1) causes more hours of studying (Z); at the same time, spending many hours at parties (X_2) causes fewer hours of studying (Z). Grade anxiety (X_1) and hours at parties (X_2) are associated; those who party a lot begin to worry about their grades, and those who are worried party to suppress their anxiety. Many hours of studying (Z) causes higher grades (Y). The relationship between anxiety and partying is descriptive and noncausal. Diagramming relationships also helps us translate complex abstract theories into a compact picture. We will return to causal diagrams in Chapter 6.

Structural Explanation. A *structural explanation* is used with functional and pattern theories. Unlike a causal effect chain, which is similar to a string of balls lined up that hit one another in sequence, it is

more similar to a wheel with spokes from a central idea or a spider web in which each strand forms part of the whole. A researcher making a structural explanation uses a set of interconnected assumptions, concepts, and relationships. Instead of causal statements, he or she uses metaphors or analogies so that relationships "make sense." The concepts and relations within a theory form a mutually reinforcing system. In structural explanations a researcher specifies a sequence of phases or identifies essential parts that form an interlocked whole.

There are several types of structural explanations. One type is *network theory*.[5] A network theorist says that a behavior or social relationship occurs when certain patterns of interaction take place, when aspects of social relations overlap in time or space, or when relationships follow a developmental sequence.

A network theorist explains something by referring to a broader pattern, a set of syntax rules, or structures. His or her explanation shows how a specific event is just one part of a larger pattern, is one building block in a bigger structure, or is one link within a much larger system of linkages. It is a form of reasoning like that used to explain why people use language in specific ways; that is, there are syntax rules that state that X goes with Y or that sentences need a noun and a verb. The researcher explains an event by identifying the syntax rule that covers the event.

Gould's (1991) theory of the social mobilization in the Paris Commune of 1871 is an example of a structural explanation. The Paris Commune was a famous rebellion and takeover of the city of Paris—and very nearly of the government of France—by masses of poor and working people who were led by socialists, Marxists, and radicals. It was a two-month experiment in democratic socialism with free education, worker cooperatives, and radical social reforms. The Commune ended with a brutal battle in which 25,000 Parisians died, most of them shot after surrendering to the national army.

Gould said that people came from different social networks, which shaped their involvement in collective action. Thus, prior to their recruitment into the Paris Commune rebellion, people had social ties to one another. By knowing these ties, Gould predicted who was likely to join. His theory said that isolated people are unlikely to join. People join when those with whom they have intimate social relations join. In addition, a person's location within a web of social ties is important. People at the center of a dense web of ties (i.e., those who have multiple strong ties) are pulled more strongly than those on the periphery (i.e., those with only one or a few weak ties). Gould found that people from the same Paris neighborhood were recruited into a single battalion in the revolutionary defense guard. The new organization, the guard, was built on previous informal ties from the neighborhood—ties of family, neighbor, co-worker, or friend. This created intense intrabattalion loyalty. At the same time, a few people from the neighborhood, some of whom were central in it, went to other battalions. This created loyalty across guard battalions. Gould predicted the pattern of battalion behavior from the positions people held in the overlapping social networks of the neighborhood and the guard battalion. He explained the actions of battalions and their responses to events by referring to a broader pattern of social ties among people.

Structural explanation is also used in *functional theory*.[6] Functional theorists explain an event by locating it within a larger, ongoing, balanced social system. They often use biological metaphors. These researchers explain something by identifying its function within a larger system or the need it fulfills for the system. Functional explanations are in this form: "*L* occurs because it serves needs in the system *M*." Theorists assume that a system will operate to stay in equilibrium and to continue over time.

A functional theory of social change says that, over time, a social system, or society, moves through developmental stages, becoming increasingly differentiated and more complex. It evolves a specialized division of labor and develops greater individualism. These developments create greater efficiency for the system as a whole. Specialization and individualism create temporary disruptions. The traditional ways of doing things weaken, but new social relations emerge. The system generates new ways to fulfill functions or satisfy its needs.

Kalmijn (1991) used a functional explanation to explain a shift in how Americans select marriage partners. He relied on secularization theory, which holds that ongoing historical processes of industrialization and urbanization shape the development of society. During these modernization processes, people rely less on traditional ways of doing things. Religious beliefs and local community ties weaken, as does the family's control over young adults. People no longer live their entire lives in small, homogeneous communities. Young adults become more independent from their parents and from the religious organizations that formerly played a critical role in selecting marriage partners.

Society has a basic need to organize the way people select marriage partners and find partners with whom they share fundamental values. In modern society, people spend time away from small local settings in school settings. In these school settings, especially in college, they meet other unmarried people. Education is a major socialization agent in modern society. Increasingly, it affects a person's future earnings, moral beliefs and values, and ways of spending leisure time. This explains why there has been a trend in the United States for people to marry less within the same religion and increasingly to marry persons with a similar level of education. In traditional societies, the family and religious organization served the function of socializing people to moral values and linking them to potential marriage partners who held similar values. In modern society, educational institutions largely fulfill this function for the social system.

Interpretive Explanation. The purpose of *interpretive explanation* is to foster understanding. The interpretive theorist attempts to discover the meaning of an event or practice by placing it within a specific social context. He or she tries to comprehend or mentally grasp the operation of the social world, as well as get a feel for something or to see the world as another person does. Because each person's subjective world view shapes how he or she acts, the researcher attempts to discern others' reasoning and view of things. The process is similar to decoding a text or work of literature. Meaning comes from the context of a cultural symbol system.

Lachmann (1988) used an interpretive explanation in his study of the illegal art form of graffiti in New York City. He noted that the career of a graffiti artist is shaped by how others label and respond to them. He explored how graffiti mentors recruit new artists and teach the young artists that there is an audience for graffiti. Lachmann described the career of graffiti artists by placing it in the social context of low-income, inner-city neighborhoods. For example, escaping from police is part of the excitement of the career, and many artists are arrested for other crimes. Skilled artists create murals covering 60-foot subway cars and develop an independent style. Lachmann explained the search for fame and advancement in a career by referring to the culture, constraints, and values of ghetto neighborhoods. Other artists who appreciate the talent displayed by graffiti artists also shape their career paths.

Theoretical Frameworks

So far, you have learned about theory and empirical generalization. Many researchers use middle-range theory. Middle-range theories are slightly more abstract than empirical generalizations or specific hypotheses. As Merton (1967:39) stated, "Middle-range theory is principally used in sociology to guide empirical inquiry."

Middle-range theories can be formal or substantive. We can organize the terms about theory by the degree of abstraction suggested. From the most concrete to the most abstract are empirical generalizations, middle-range theories, and frameworks. A *theoretical framework* (also called a paradigm or theoretical system) is more abstract than a formal or substantive theory. Figure 3.1 shows the levels and how they are used in inductive and deductive approaches to theorizing.

Researchers do not make precise distinctions among the degrees of abstraction. When they conduct a study, they primarily use middle-range theory and empirical generalization. They rarely use a theoretical framework directly in empirical research. A researcher may test parts of a theory on a topic and occasionally contrast parts of the theories from different frameworks. Box 3.5 illustrates

Box 3.5 _____

Kalmijn's Levels of Theory in "Shifting Boundaries"

Theoretical Framework: Structural functionalism holds that the processes of industrialization and urbanization change human society from a traditional to a modern form. In this process of modernization, social institutions and practices evolve. This evolution includes those that fill the social system's basic needs, socialize people to cultural values, and regulate social behavior. Institutions that filled needs and maintained the social system in a traditional society are superseded by modern ones.

Formal Theory: Secularization theory says that during modernization, people shift away from a reliance on traditional religious beliefs and local community ties. In traditional society, institutions that conferred ascribed social status (family, church, and community) also controlled socialization and regulated social life. In modern society they are superseded by secular institutions (e.g., education, government, and media) that confer achievement-oriented status.

Middle-Range Substantive Theory: A theory of intermarriage patterns notes that young adults in modern society spend less time in small, local settings, where family, religion, and community all have a strong influence. Instead, young adults spend increasing amounts of time in school settings. In these settings, especially in college, they have opportunities to meet other unmarried people. In modern society, education has become a major socialization agent. It affects future earnings, moral beliefs and values, and leisure interests. Thus, young adults select marriage partners less on the basis of shared religious or local ties and more on the basis of common educational levels.

Empirical Generalization: Americans once married others with similar religious beliefs and affiliation. This practice is being replaced by marriage to others with similar levels of education.

the various degrees of abstraction with Kalmijn's study of changing marriage partner selection.

Social science has several major theoretical frameworks.[7] The frameworks are orientations or sweeping ways of looking at the social world. They provide collections of assumptions, concepts, and forms of explanation. Frameworks include many formal or substantive theories (e.g., theories of crime, theories of the family, etc.). Thus, there can be a structural functional theory, an exchange theory, and a conflict theory of the family. Theories within the same framework share assumptions and major concepts. Some frameworks are oriented more to the micro level; others focus on more macro-level phenomena. As you will see in Chapter 4, each is associated with an approach to research methodology. Box 3.6 shows six major frameworks in social work and briefly describes the key concepts and assumptions of each.

THEORY AND RESEARCH: THE DYNAMIC DUO

You have seen that theory and research are interrelated. Only the naive, new researcher mistakenly believes that theory is irrelevant to research or that a researcher just collects the data. Researchers who attempt to proceed without theory or fail to make it explicit may waste time collecting useless data. They easily fall into the trap of hazy and vague thinking, faulty logic, and imprecise concepts. They may find it difficult to converge onto a crisp research issue or to generate a lucid account of their study's purpose. They often find themselves adrift as they attempt to design or conduct empirical research.

The reason is simple. Theory frames how we look at and think about a topic. It gives us concepts, provides basic assumptions, directs us to the important questions, and suggests ways for us to make sense of data. Theory enables us to connect a single study to the immense base of knowledge to which other researchers contribute. To use an analogy, theory helps a researcher see the forest instead of just a single tree. Theory increases a researcher's awareness of interconnections and of the broader significance of data.

Theory has a place in virtually all research, but its prominence varies. It is generally less central in applied–descriptive research than in basic–explanatory research. Its role in applied and descriptive research may be indirect. The concepts are often more concrete, and the goal is not to create general knowledge. Nevertheless, researchers use theory in descriptive research to refine concepts, evaluate assumptions of a theory, and indirectly test hypotheses.

Theory does not remain fixed over time; it is provisional and open to revision. Theories grow into more accurate and comprehensive explanations about the makeup and operation of the social world in two ways. They advance as theorists toil to think clearly and logically, but this effort has limits. The way a theory makes significant progress is by interacting with research findings.

The scientific community expands and alters theories based on empirical results. Researchers who adopt a more deductive approach use theory to guide the design of a study and the interpretation of results. They refute, extend, or modify the theory on the basis of results. As researchers continue to conduct empirical research testing a theory, they develop confidence that some parts of it are true. Researchers may modify some propositions of a theory or reject them if several well-conducted studies have negative findings. A theory's core propositions and central tenets are more difficult to test and are refuted less often. In a slow process, researchers may decide to abandon or change a theory as the evidence against it mounts over time and cannot be logically reconciled.

Researchers adopting an inductive approach follow a slightly different process. Inductive theorizing begins with a few assumptions and broad orienting concepts. Theory develops from the ground up as the researchers gather and analyze the data. Theory emerges slowly, concept by concept and proposition by proposition in a specific area. The process is similar to a long pregnancy. Over time, the concepts and empirical generalizations emerge and mature. Soon, relationships become visible, and researchers weave together knowledge from different studies into more abstract theory.

Box 3.6 _____

Major Theoretical Frameworks in Social Work*

Psychodynamic/Functional Theory

Major Concepts: Physical needs, growth and development, meaning, conflict, the unconscious.

Key Assumptions: Human behavior is a consequence of complex relationships among drives, personality development, and conscious and unconscious mind. Individuals develop defense mechanisms that mediate relations among Id, Ego, and Superego. Treatment requires conversation between "patient" and "therapist," who functions like a blank screen (Payne, 1997), encourages insight, understanding.

Illustrative Authors

Dore, M. (1990). Functional theory: Its history and influence on contemporary social work. *Social Service Review,* 64: 358–374.

Perlman, H. (1979). *Relationship: The heart of helping people.* Chicago: University of Chicago Press.

Smalley, R. (1970). The functional approach to casework practice. In *Theories of social casework,* edited by R. Roberts and R. Nee. Chicago: University of Chicago Press.

Woods, M., and Hollis, F. (1990). *Casework: A psychosocial therapy,* 4th ed. New York: McGraw-Hill.

Behaviorist–Cognitive Theory

Major Concepts: Learning, behavior-as-action, cognition, modeling, stimulus–response.

Key Assumptions: Individual behavior is a consequence of the natural environment. Treatment requires cognitive therapies, desensitization, consistency of rewards, and token economies.

Illustrative Authors

Bandura, A. (1977). *Social learning theory.* Englewood Cliffs, NJ: Prentice Hall.

Fischer, J., and Gochros, H. (1975). *Planned behavior change: Behavior modification in social work.* New York: Free Press.

Gambrill, E. (1995). Behavioral social work: Past, present and future. *Research on Social Work Practice* 5(4): 460–484.

Kazdin, A. (1994). Critical issues and future directions. In Kazdin, A. *Behavior modification in applied settings,* 3rd ed. Pacific Grove, CA: Brooks-Cole.

Sheldon, B. (1995). *Cognitive–behavioural therapy: Research, practice and philosophy.* London: Routledge.

Thyer, B. (2000). *The philosophical legacy of behaviorism.* Boston: Kluwer Academic Publishers.

Thyer, B., and Hudson, W. (1987). Progress in behavioral social work: An introduction. *Journal of Social Services Research,* 19: 1–7.

Crisis Intervention-Task Centered Theory

Major Concepts: Crises or disturbances, hazards, tensions, stress, and trauma.

Key Assumptions: All people experience occasional disruptions to otherwise normal functioning. When they seek assistance, it is because of some crisis. Therefore, intervention typically recommends very pragmatic action to deal with and resolve disturbances in people's lives.

Illustrative Authors

Golan, N. (1978). *Treatment in crisis situations.* New York: Free Press.

Marsh, P. (1991). Task-centered practice. In *Handbook of Theory for Practice Teachers in Social Work,* edited by J. Lishman. London: Jessica Kingsley.

Reid, W. (1978). *The task-centered system.* New York: Columbia University Press.

Reid, W., and Epstein, L. (1972). *Task-centered casework.* New York: Columbia University Press.

Reid, W., and Shyne, A. (1969). *Brief and task-centered casework.* New York: Columbia University Press.

Roberts, A. (1991). *Contemporary perspectives on crisis intervention and prevention.* Englewood Cliffs, NJ: Prentice Hall.

Systems/Ecological Theory

Major Concepts: Open/closed systems, boundaries, input-throughput-output, feedback, adaptation.

Key Assumptions: Individuals operate in numerous systems—including families, neighborhoods, schools, and markets—that have capacities for action and change. Treatment involves developing, connecting, contracting, modifying interactions; collaborating and bargaining.

Illustrative Authors

Germain, C., and Gitterman, M. (1980). *The life model of social work practice.* New York: Columbia University Press.

Goldstein, H. (1973). *Social work practice: A unitary approach.* Columbia, SC: University of South Carolina Press.

Hearn, G., ed. (1969). *The general systems approach: Contributions toward an holistic conception of social work.* New York: Council on Social Work Education.

Meyer, C., ed. (1983). *Clinical social work in the eco-systems perspective.* New York: Columbia University Press.

Pincus, A., and Minahan, A. (1973). *Social work practice: Model and method.* Itasca, IL: Peacock.

Siporin, M. (1980). Ecological systems theory in social work. *Journal of Sociology and Social Welfare,* 7(4): 507–532.

(continued)

BOX 3.6 Continued

Humanist/Existential/Strengths/ Development Theory

Major Concepts: Meaning, transcendence, self-reflection, development.

Key Assumptions: Individuals are capable of continued movement toward more satisfying participation and control of their destinies by participating in groups, communities, and institutions. Treatment involves unconditional positive regard, empathy, nondirective assistance in some perspectives, active planning and prospective community development in others.

Illustrative Authors

Chapin, R. (1995). Social policy development: The strengths perspective. *Social Work,* 40(4): 506–514.

Cowger, C. (1994). Assessing client strengths: Clinical assessment for client empowerment. *Social Work,* 39(3): 262–268.

Kondrat, M. (1995). Concept, act, and interest in professional practice: Implications of an empowerment perspective. *Social Service Review,* 69(3): 405–428.

Krill, D. (1978). *Existential social work.* New York: Free Press.

Laird, J. (1993). Revisioning social work education: A social constructionist approach. *Journal of Teaching in Social Work,* 8(1/2): 1–10.

Midgley, J. (1995). *Social development: The developmental perspective in social welfare.* London: Sage.

Rogers, C. (1951). *Client-centered therapy: Its current practice, implications and theory.* London: Constable.

Saleebey, D. (1996). The strengths perspective in social work practice: Extensions and cautions. *Social Work,* 41(3): 296–305.

Stretch, J. (1967). Existentialism: A proposed philosophical orientation for social work. *Social Work,* 12(4): 94–102.

Thompson, N. (1992). *Existentialism and social work.* Aldershot, Hants: Avebury.

Truax, C., and Carkhuff, R. (1967). *Toward effective counseling and psychotherapy: Training and practice.* Chicago: Aldine.

Social Justice/Empowerment/Feminist/ Radical Theory

Major Concepts: Power, struggle, exploitation, inequality, alienation.

Key Assumptions: Society is made up of groups that have opposing interests. Coercion and attempts to gain power are ever-present aspects of human relationships. Those in power often hold on to their positions by spreading myths, co-opting others, or using violence if necessary. Intervention may involve advocacy, helping clients find, recognize, and utilize their own power bases, or by participatory and revolutionary consciousness raising and political action.

Illustrative Authors

Davis, A. (1991). A structural approach to social work. In *Handbook of Theory for Practice Teachers in Social Work,* edited by J. Lishman. London: Jessica Kingsley, pp. 64–74.

Davis, L. (1985). Female and male voices in social work. *Social Work,* 30(2): 106–113.

de Maria, W. (1992). On the trail of a radical pedagogy for social work education. *British Journal of Social Work,* 22(3): 231–252.

Fook, J. (1993). *Radical casework: A theory of practice.* St. Leonards, NSW: Allen and Unwin.

Furlong, M. (1987). A rationale for the use of empowerment as a goal in casework. *Australian Social Work,* 40(3): 25–30.

Leonard, P. (1997). Argument. In *Postmodern welfare: Reconstructing an emancipatory project.* Thousand Oaks, CA: Sage Publications, pp. 1–31.

Payne, M. (1997). *Modern social work theory,* 2nd ed. Chicago: Lyceum Books.

Rees, S. (1991). *Achieving power.* Sydney: Allen & Unwin.

Saulnier, C. (1996). *Feminist theories and social work: Approaches and applications.* New York: Haworth Press.

Solomon, B. (1976). *Black empowerment: Social work in oppressed communities.* New York: Columbia University Press.

Turner, F. (1986). *Social work treatment: Interlocking theoretical perspectives,* 3rd ed. New York: Free Press.

Turner, F. (1999). Social work practice: Theoretical base. In *Encyclopedia of Social Work,* 19th ed., Vol. 2, edited by R. Edwards (Editor-in-chief), pp. 2258–2265. Washington, DC: NASW Press.

See Turner, F. (1986, 1999) and Payne M. (1997) for excellent discussions of theory in social work.

THE ROLE OF DIVERSITY IN SOCIAL WORK THEORY

Emerging models of internationalism in various social work practice communities (Sarri, 1997) and in assorted social work educational forums (Midgley, 1990; Longres, 1997; and Asamoah, Healy, and Mayadas, 1997) have begun to point toward the need for new perspectives regarding the adequacy of social work knowledge and theory pertaining to diversity. While it may be premature to think through all of the implications emerging international developments will have for social work as a profession, it is clear that theory in social work practice will need to begin to account for the incredible diversity that exists across genders, races and ethnic groups, sexual orientations, socioeconomic statuses, places of residence, languages, education and backgrounds, and a host of other conditions. The same pressures that are at work leading toward globalization and new international markets (Drucker, 1993; Ohmae, 1995; and Thurow, 1996) suggest that social work needs to address the practicality of more-encompassing theories of human behavior that account for perspectives that are emerging across geographic, socioeconomic, and political systems.

Recent moves toward globalization in various international marketplaces suggest that barriers to cross-cultural communication will continue to be broken down by market forces that strive to provide consumers (regardless of social structure or culture) with access to a wide range of goods and services. These same forces will continually break down political barriers as well, leading inexorably toward theoretical explanations of human behavior that will seek to transcend locality-relevant restrictions. But J. Schiele (1996), among others, contends that one universal body of knowledge may not be possible in social work because Western and Euro-centric theories of human behavior reflect the conceptualizations of human behavior and practices that originated and were developed in European and Anglo cultures. These orientations paralleled larger historical movements accompanying the industrial revolution and various political agendas in European expansion and colonialization. Hence, theories derived from these value bases are more likely to be out of touch with the lives and everyday practices of most of the world's population, who are not urban or suburban consumers trying to decide what brand of cereal to purchase.

Components of Diversity

For Dixon and Taylor (1994), diversity has two manifestations, called primary and secondary diversity. *Primary diversity* manifestations are often visible and may be different for specific groups . . . but the differences are not choice driven; primary diversity issues are given traits of particular groups. Among the primary variables are race and/or ethnicity, gender, age, physical/mental abilities, sexual orientation, and size. The *secondary diversity* considerations are often invisible and may change by choice and particular circumstances. These typically would include political ideology, geography, marital/family status, socioeconomic status, religion, occupation/skills, experiences, and education.

Hoffman and Salee (1994) identify five major populations at risk and the types of problems they encounter: women (poor women and children, sexism, social problems of women, and gender relationships), ethnic minorities of color (institutional racism, individual racism, respectable racism, subtle forms that support harmful implicit policies or blame individual failure); gay men and lesbian women (AIDS crisis, homophobia, particular forms of prejudice and discrimination); the elderly (ageism, policies adverse to the elderly, care of the elderly); and the physically and mentally challenged (discrimination and adverse policies suffered).

Rounds, Weil, and Bishop (1994) offer five principles of culturally competent practice that address diversity areas: (1) Acknowledge and value diversity regarding how race, culture, and ethnicity contribute to uniqueness, and recognize the uniqueness and differences between and within; (2) conduct cultural self-assessment in terms of one's own culture and how it shapes personal and professional beliefs; (3) recognize and understand dynamics of difference in terms of behavioral expectations, interactions and degrees of self-disclosure, and the client's collective orientation; (4) acquire cultural knowledge in terms of client background, ethnic group identification, and cultural knowledge of the community; and (5) adapt social work skills to the needs and styles of the client's culture.

Finally, the *Generalist Practice* perspective from the Council on Social Work Education emphasizes the following practices in the 1994 Curriculum Policy Statement: (1) Professional relationships should be characterized by mutuality, collaboration, and respect for the client system; (2) practice assessment should examine client strengths and problems in interactions and environment; (3) knowledge, values, and skills should enhance well-being and ameliorate environmental conditions; (4) skills are needed that help in defining issues, collecting and assessing data, planning and contracting, identifying alternative interventions, selecting and implementing appropriate courses of action, using appropriate research knowledge and technological advances, and termination; and (5) includes approaches and skills for practice with clients from different social, cultural, racial, religious, spiritual, and class background and with systems of all sizes.

theory and research is an artificial one. The value of theory and its necessity for conducting good research should be clear. Researchers who proceed without theory rarely conduct top-quality research and frequently find themselves in a quandary. Likewise, theorists who proceed without linking theory to research or anchoring it to empirical reality are in jeopardy of floating off into incomprehensible speculation and conjecture. You are now familiar with the scientific community, the dimensions of research, and social theory. In the next chapter you will examine the competing approaches researchers adopt when they do social science.

CONCLUSION

In this chapter you learned about social theory—its parts, purposes, and types. The dichotomy between

KEY TERMS

association	humanist/strengths theory	positive relationship
assumption	ideal type	prediction
behaviorist–cognitive theory	inductive approach	primary diversity
causal explanation	jargon	proposition
classification	level of abstraction	psychodynamics/functional
concept cluster	macro-level theory	theory
crisis intervention theory	meso-level theory	secondary diversity
deductive approach	micro-level theory	systems/ecological theory
empirical generalization	negative relationship	temporal order
functional theory	network theory	typology
grounded theory	parsimony	

REVIEW QUESTIONS

1. How do concrete and abstract concepts differ? Give examples.
2. How do researchers use ideal types and classifications to elaborate concepts?
3. How do concepts contain built-in assumptions? Give examples.
4. What are the differences between inductive and deductive approaches to theorizing?
5. Describe how the micro, meso, and macro levels of social reality differ.
6. Discuss the differences between prediction and theoretical explanation.
7. What are the three conditions for causality? Which one is never completely demonstrated? Why?
8. Why do researchers use diagrams to show causal relationships?

9. How do structural and interpretive explanations differ from one another?

10. What is the role of the major theoretical frameworks in research?

NOTES

1. For more detailed discussions of concepts, see Chafetz (1978:45–61), Hage (1972:9–85), Kaplan (1964:34–80), Mullins (1971:7–18), Reynolds (1971), and Stinchcombe (1973).

2. Turner (1980) has provided an interesting discussion of how explanation and theorizing can be conceptualized as translation.

3. Classifications are discussed in Chafetz (1978:63–73) and Hage (1972).

4. For more on typologies and taxonomies, see Blalock (1969:30–35), Chafetz (1978:63–73), Reynolds (1971:4–5), and Stinchcombe (1968:41–47).

5. Network theory is discussed in Collins (1988:412–428) and Galaskiewicz and Wasserman (1993).

6. An introduction to functional explanation can be found in Chafetz (1978:22–25).

7. Introductions to alternative theoretical frameworks and social theories are provided in Craib (1984), Phillips (1985:44–59), and Skidmore (1979). An elementary introduction is given in Chapter 1 of Bart and Frankel (1986).

CHAPTER 4

THE MEANINGS OF METHODOLOGY

The scientific approach to social work practice offers much promise for the social work profession. Based on empirical data and scientific findings, it makes available concrete tools for effective intervention, and, most important, builds into the intervention process a problem-solving and evaluative component needed in social work.
—J. Wodarski, p. 23.

INTRODUCTION

Many people, including professionals outside the social sciences, ask, "Are social work and related social sciences real science?" They think only of the natural sciences (e.g., physics, chemistry, and biology). In this chapter we examine the meaning of *science* in the social sciences. We build on the ideas about the scientific community and the varieties of social work research and theory discussed in the previous three chapters. This chapter is concerned more with the method of inquiry—how we know— than with specific techniques for gathering and examining data. It looks at these questions: What are researchers trying to do when they conduct research? How do researchers conduct research?

The question "Where is science in social science?" is relevant to anyone wishing to learn social work research methods, because the answer is found in the methods used by researchers. Research methodology is what makes social science scientific. The question is an important one, with a long history of debate. It has been asked repeatedly since the social sciences originated. Despite two centuries of discussion and debate, the question remains with us today. Obviously, it does not have a simple answer.

A question for which there are multiple answers does not mean that anything goes; it means that social work researchers choose from *alternative approaches* to science. Each approach has its

70

own set of philosophical assumptions and principles and its own stance on how to do research. The approaches are rarely declared explicitly in research reports, and many researchers have only a vague awareness of them. Yet, the approaches play an important role and are found across the social sciences and their related applied fields.[1]

Collins (1989:134) argued that the debate over whether the social sciences are scientific comes from an overly rigid definition of *science*. He remarked, "Modern philosophy of science does not destroy sociological science; it does not say that science is impossible, but gives us a more flexible picture of what science is." The approaches in this chapter help link abstract issues in philosophy to concrete research techniques. They prescribe what good social work research involves, justify why one should do research, relate values to research, and guide ethical behavior. They are broad frameworks within which researchers conduct studies. Couch (1987:106) summarized it as follows:

> *The ontological and epistemological positions of these . . . research traditions provide the foundation of one of the more bitter quarrels in contemporary sociology. . . . Each side claims that the frame of thought they promote provides a means for acquiring knowledge about social phenomena, and each regards the efforts of the other as at best misguided. . . . They differ on what phenomena should be attended to, how one is to approach phenomena, and how the phenomena are to be analyzed.*

By the end of this chapter you should have three answers to the question, "What is scientific about social scientific research?" One answer will be for each of the three approaches to be discussed. You may find the pluralism of approaches confusing at first, but once you learn them, you will find that other aspects of research and theory become clearer. Specific research techniques are based on the general approaches discussed in this chapter. The techniques (e.g., experiments and participant observation) will make more sense to you and will be learned faster if you are aware of the logic and assumptions on which they are based. In addition, the approaches presented here will help you understand the diverse perspectives you may encounter as you read social work

research studies. Equally important, the three approaches give you an opportunity to make an informed choice among alternatives for the type of research you may want to pursue. You might feel more comfortable with one approach or another.

THE THREE APPROACHES

We need to begin by recognizing that the meaning of science was not written in stone or handed down as a sacred text; it has been an evolving human creation. Until the early 1800s, only philosophers and religious scholars who engaged in armchair speculation studied or wrote about human behavior. The classical theorists made a major contribution to modern civilization when they argued that the social world could be studied by using science. They contended that rigorous, systematic observation of the social world, combined with careful, logical thinking, could provide a new and valuable type of knowledge about human relations. In modern times science has become the accepted way to gain knowledge. So when people accepted the claim that society could be studied by using science, it was a revolutionary idea with important ramifications.

Once the idea of a science of the social world gained acceptance, the issue became: What does such a science look like, and how is it conducted? Some people went to the already accepted natural sciences (e.g., physics, biology, and chemistry) and copied their methods. Their argument was simple: The legitimacy of the natural sciences rests on the scientific method, so social scientists should adopt the same approach.

Many researchers accepted this answer, but it poses certain difficulties. First, there is a debate over what *science* means, even in the natural sciences. The scientific method is only a loose set of abstract, vague principles that provide little guidance. Scholars who specialize in the history and philosophy of science have explored multiple ways to do scientific research and have found that scientists use several methods. Second, some scholars say that human beings are qualitatively different from the objects of study in the natural sciences (stars, rocks, plants, chemical compounds, etc.). Humans think and learn, have an awareness of themselves and their past, and possess motives and reasons. These unique human characteristics mean that a special science is needed to study the social life of people.

Social work researchers did not stop while the philosophers debated. Practicing researchers developed ways to do research, based on their informal notions of science. This added to the confusion. Leading researchers used techniques to conduct social work research that sometimes deviated from the philosopher's ideal model of good science.

The three approaches in this chapter are based on a major reevaluation of social science that began in the 1960s.[2] The three alternatives to social science are the core ideas distilled from many specific arguments. They are ideal types or idealized, simplified models of more complex arguments. In practice, few social work researchers agree with all parts of an approach. Often, they mix elements from each. Yet, these approaches represent fundamental differences in outlook and alternative assumptions about social science research.[3] The approaches are different ways of looking at the world—ways to observe, measure, and understand social reality. They begin from very different positions, even when all end up looking at the same thing or saying the same thing.

To simplify the discussion, we have organized the assumptions and ideas of the approaches into answers to the following eight questions:

1. Why should one conduct social work research?
2. What is the fundamental nature of social reality? (the ontological question)
3. What is the basic nature of human beings?
4. What is the relationship between science and common sense?
5. What constitutes an explanation or theory of social reality?
6. How does one determine whether an explanation is true or false?
7. What does good evidence or factual information look like?
8. Where do sociopolitical values enter into science?

The three approaches are *positivism, interpretive social science,* and *critical social science.* Most ongoing social work research is based on the first two. Positivism is the oldest and the most widely used approach. Miller (1987:4), a philosopher of science, observed, "Positivism is the most common philosophical outlook on science. Yet there are current alternatives to it with extremely broad appeal." The interpretive approach has held a strong minority position in debates for over a century. Critical social science is less commonly seen in scholarly journals. It is included to give you the full range of debate over the meaning of social science and because it criticizes the other approaches and tries to move beyond them.

Each approach is associated with different traditions in social work theory and diverse research techniques. The linkage among the broad approaches to science, social theories, and research techniques is not strict. The approaches are similar to a research program, research tradition, or scientific paradigm. A *paradigm,* an idea made famous by Kuhn (1970), another philosopher of science, means a basic orientation to theory and research. There are many definitions of *paradigm.* In general, a scientific paradigm is a whole system of thinking. It includes basic assumptions, the important questions to be answered or puzzles to be solved, the research techniques to be used, and examples of what good scientific research looks like. For example, social work is called a multiparadigm profession because no single paradigm is all-powerful; instead, several compete with each other.[4]

POSITIVIST SOCIAL SCIENCE

Positivist social science is used widely, and *positivism,* broadly defined, is the approach of the natural sciences. In fact, most people never hear of alternative approaches. They assume that the positivist approach *is* science. There are many versions of positivism, and it has a long history within the philosophy of science and among researchers.[5] Yet, for many researchers, it has come to be a pejorative label to be avoided. Turner (1992:1511) observed, "*Positivism* no longer has a clear referent, but it is evident that, for many, being a positivist is not a good thing." The answers to the eight questions give you a picture of what a positivist approach sees as constituting social science. Varieties of positivism go by names such as logical empiricism, the accepted or conventional view, postpositivism, naturalism, the covering law model, and behaviorism.

Positivism arose from a nineteenth-century school of thought by the Frenchman who founded sociology—Auguste Comte (1798–1857). Comte's major work in six volumes, *Cours de Philosophie Positivistic (The Course of Positive Philosophy)* (1830–1842), outlined many principles of positivism still used today. British philosopher John Stuart Mill (1806–1873) elaborated and modified the principles in his *A System of Logic* (1843). Classical French sociologist Emile Durkheim (1858–1917) outlined a version of positivism in his *Rules of the Sociological Method* (1895), which became a key textbook for positivist social work researchers.

Positivism is associated with many specific social theories. Best known is its linkage to the structural–functional, rational choice, and exchange-theory frameworks. Positivist researchers prefer precise quantitative data and often use experiments, surveys, and statistics. They seek rigorous, exact measures and "objective" research, and they test hypotheses by carefully analyzing numbers from the measures. Many applied researchers (administrators, criminologists, market researchers, policy analysts, program evaluators, and planners) embrace positivism. Critics charge that positivism reduces people to numbers and that its concerns with abstract laws or formulas are not relevant to the actual lives of real people.

Positivism says that "there is only *one* logic of science, to which any intellectual activity aspiring to the title of 'science' must conform" (Keat and Urry, 1975:25, emphasis in original). Thus, the social sciences and the natural sciences must use the same method. In this view, differences between the natural and social sciences are due to the immaturity or youth of the social sciences and their subject matter. Eventually, all science, including the social sciences, will be like the most advanced science, physics. Differences among the sciences may exist as to their subject matter (e.g., geology requires techniques different from astrophysics or microbiology because of the objects being studied), but all sciences share a common set of principles and logic.

Positivism sees social science as an *organized method for combining deductive logic with precise empirical observations of individual behavior in order to discover and confirm a set of probabilistic causal laws that can be used to predict general patterns of human activity.*

The Questions

1. *Why should one conduct social work research?*

The ultimate purpose of research is scientific explanation—to discover and document universal laws of human behavior. Another important reason is to learn about how the world works so that people can control or predict events. This latter idea is sometimes called an *instrumental orientation*. It is a technical interest that assumes knowledge can be used as a tool or instrument to satisfy human wants and to control the physical and social environment.

Once we discover the laws that govern human life, we can use them to alter social relations, to improve how things are done, perhaps to solve the problem of poverty, and to better predict what will happen. For example, a positivist uses a theory of family residential mobility (e.g., family size, family buying habits, neighborhood stability, etc.) that predicts increased likelihood of a family becoming homeless. She or he conducts a study and precisely measures factors to verify causal laws in the theory. The positivist then builds knowledge that is used by a community neighborhood agency in ways that improve outcomes for clients.

This view is summarized by Turner (1985:39), a defender of the positivist approach who stated that the "social universe is amenable to the development of abstract laws that can be tested through the careful collection of data" and that researchers need to "develop abstract principles and models about invariant and timeless properties of the social universe."

Positivists say that scientists are engaged in a never-ending quest for knowledge. As more is learned, new complexities are discovered and there is still more to learn. Early versions of positivism maintained that humans can never know everything because only God possesses such knowledge; however, as creatures placed on this planet with great capacity for knowledge, humans have a duty to discover as much as they can.

2. *What is the fundamental nature of social reality?*

Modern positivists hold that social and physical reality is real. It exists "out there" and is waiting to be discovered. This idea notes that human perception and intellect may be flawed, and reality may be difficult to pin down, but it does exist. Moreover, social reality is not random; it is patterned and has order. Without this assumption (i.e., if the world were chaotic and without regularity), logic and prediction would be impossible. Science lets humans discover this order and the laws of nature. "The basic, observational laws of science are considered to be true, primary and certain, because they are built into the fabric of the natural world. Discovering a law is like discovering America, in the sense that both are already waiting to be revealed" (Mulkay, 1979:21).

Two other assumptions are that basic patterns of social reality are stable and knowledge of them is additive. The regularity in social reality does not change over time, and laws discovered today will hold in the future. We can study many parts of reality one at a time, then add the fragments together to get a picture of the whole. Some early versions of this assumption said that the order in nature was created by and is evidence of the existence of God or a supreme being.

3. *What is the basic nature of human beings?*

In positivism, humans are assumed to be self-interested, pleasure-seeking, rational individuals. People operate on the basis of external causes, with the same cause having the same effect on everyone. We can learn about people by observing their behavior, what we see in external reality. This is more important than what happens in internal, subjective reality. Sometimes this is called a *mechanical model of man* or a behaviorist approach. It means people respond to external forces that are as real as physical forces on objects. Durkheim (1938:27) stated, "Social phenomena are things and ought to be studied as things." External reality suggests that researchers may not have to examine unseen, internal motivations of an individual's behavior.

Positivists say that human behavior or social institutions do not just happen because of what a person wants. Human events can be explained with reference to *causal laws,* which describe causes and effects. They identify forces that operate in a manner similar to natural laws in the hard sciences. This suggests that the idea of free will is largely fiction and describes only aspects of human behavior that science has not yet conquered.

Few positivists believe in absolute determinism, wherein people are mere robots or puppets who must always respond exactly the same way. Rather, the causal laws are probabilistic. Laws hold for large groups of people or occur in many situations. Researchers can estimate the odds of a predicted behavior. In other words, the laws permit us to make accurate predictions of how often a social behavior will occur within a large group. The causal laws cannot predict the specific behavior of a specific person in each situation. However, they can say that under conditions X, Y, and Z, there is a 95 percent probability that one-half of the people will engage in a specified behavior.

For example, researchers cannot predict how Jane Doe will do the next time she applies for a job. However, after learning dozens of facts about Jane Doe and using laws of job-seeking behavior, researchers may be able to accurately state that there is an 85% chance that she (and people like her) will apply for a job. This does not mean that Jane Doe cannot do whatever she wants. Rather, her behavior is patterned and shaped by outside social forces.

4. *What is the relationship between science and common sense?*

Positivists see a clear separation between science and nonscience. Of the many ways to seek truth, science is special—the "best" way. Scientific knowledge is better than, and will eventually replace, the inferior ways of gaining knowledge (e.g., magic, religion, astrology, personal experience, and tradition). Science borrows some ideas from common sense, but it replaces the parts of common sense that are sloppy, logically inconsistent, unsystematic, and full of bias. The scientific community—with its special norms, scientific attitudes, and techniques—can regularly produce "Truth," whereas common sense does so only rarely and inconsistently.

A researcher working in a positivist tradition often creates a whole new vocabulary—a set of scientific ideas and associated terms. He or she wants to use ideas that are more logically consistent and carefully thought out and refined than the ideas found in everyday common sense. The positivist researcher "should formulate new concepts at the outset and not rely on lay notions. . . . There is a preference for the precision which is believed possible in a discipline-based language rather than the vague and imprecise language of everyday life" (Blaikie, 1993:206).

5. *What constitutes an explanation or theory of social reality?*

Positivist scientific explanation is *nomothetic* (*nomos* means law in Greek); it is based on a system of general laws. Science explains why social life is the way it is by discovering causal laws. Explanation takes this form: *Y* is caused by *X* because *Y* and *X* are specific instances of a causal law. In other words, a positivist explanation states the general causal law that applies to or covers specific observations about social life. This is why positivism is said to use a *covering law model* of explanation.

Positivism assumes that the laws operate according to strict, logical reasoning. Researchers connect causal laws and the specific facts observed about social life with deductive logic. Positivists believe that eventually laws and theories of social science will be expressed in formal symbolic systems, with axioms, corollaries, postulates, and theorems. Some day, social science theories will look similar to those in mathematics and the natural sciences.

The laws of human behavior should be universally valid, holding in all historical eras and in all cultures. As noted before, the laws are stated in a probabilistic form for aggregates of people. For example, a positivist explanation of a rise in the crime rate in Toronto in the 1990s refers to factors (e.g., rising divorce rate, declining commitment to traditional moral values, etc.) that could be found anywhere at any time: in Bombay in the 1890s, Chicago in the 1940s, or Singapore in the 2010s. The factors logically obey a general law (e.g., the breakdown of a traditional moral order causes an increase in the rate of criminal behavior).

6. *How does one determine whether an explanation is true or false?*

Positivism developed during the Enlightenment (post-Middle Ages) period of Western thinking (see Bernard, 1988:12–21). It includes an important Enlightenment idea: People can recognize truth and distinguish it from falsehood by applying reason, and, in the long run, over centuries, the human condition can improve through the use of reason and the pursuit of truth. As knowledge grows and ignorance declines, conditions will improve. This optimistic belief that knowledge accumulates over time plays a role in how positivists sort out true from false explanations.

In positivism, to be seriously considered, explanations must meet two conditions: they must (1) have no logical contradictions and (2) be consistent with observed facts. Yet, this is not sufficient. *Replication* is also needed (see Hegtvedt, 1992). Any researcher can replicate or reproduce the results of others. This puts a check on the whole system for creating knowledge. It ensures honesty because it repeatedly tests explanations against hard, objective facts. An open competition exists among opposing explanations, impartial rules are used, neutral facts are accurately observed, and logic is rigorously followed. Over time, scientific knowledge accumulates as different researchers conduct independent tests of a theory and add up the findings. For example, a researcher finds that rising unemployment is associated with increased child abuse in San Diego, California. A causal relationship between unemployment and child abuse is not demonstrated with just one study, however. Confirming a causal law depends on finding the same relationship in other cities with other researchers conducting independent tests using careful measures of unemployment and child abuse.

7. *What does good evidence or factual information look like?*

Positivism is dualist; it assumes that the cold, observable facts are fundamentally distinct from ideas, values, or theories. Empirical facts exist apart from personal ideas or thoughts. We can observe them by using our sense organs (eyesight, smell, hearing, and touch) or special instruments that extend the senses (e.g., telescopes, microscopes, and Geiger counters). Some researchers express this idea as a language of empirical fact and a language of abstract theory. If people disagree over facts, it must be due to the improper use of measurement instruments or to sloppy or inadequate observation. "Scientific explanation involves the accurate and precise measurement of phenomena" (Derksen and Gartrell, 1992:1714). Knowledge of observable reality obtained using our senses is superior to other knowledge (e.g., intuition, emotional feelings, etc.); it allows us to separate true from false ideas about social life.

Positivists combine this idea of the privileged status of empirical observation with the assumption that subjective understanding of the empirical world is shared. Factual knowledge is not based on just one person's observations and reasoning. It must be capable of being communicated and shared by others. Rational people who independently observe facts will agree on them. This is called *intersubjectivity,* or the shared subjective acknowledgment of the facts. Many positivists accept a version of falsification doctrine outlined by the Anglo-Austrian philosopher Sir Karl Popper (1902–1991) in his *Logic of Scientific Discovery* (1934). Popper argued that claims to knowledge "can never be proven or fully justified, they can only be refused" (Phillips, 1987:3). Good evidence for a causal law involves more than piling up supporting facts; it involves looking for evidence that contradicts the causal law. In a classic example, if I want to test the claim that all swans are white, and I find 1,000 white swans, I have not totally confirmed a causal law or pattern. All it takes is locating one black swan to refute my claim—one piece of negative evidence. This means that researchers search for disconfirming evidence, and even then, the best they can say is, "Thus far, I have not been able to locate any, so the claim might be right."

8. *Where do sociopolitical values enter into science?*

Positivists argue for a *value-free science* that is objective. There are two meanings of the term *objective:* that observers agree on what they see and that science is not based on values, opinions, attitudes, or beliefs (Derksen and Gartrell, 1992:1715). Positivists see science as a special, distinctive part of society that is free of personal, political, or religious values. It operates independently of the social and cultural forces affecting other human activity. It involves applying strict rational thinking and systematic observation in a manner that transcends personal prejudices, biases, and values. The norms and operation of the scientific community keep science objective. Scientists are socialized to unique professional norms and values. Researchers accept and internalize the norms as part of their membership in the scientific community. The scientific community has created an elaborate system of checks and balances to guard against value bias. A researcher's proper role is to be a "disinterested scientist."[6] The positivist view on values has had an immense impact on how people see ethical issues and knowledge:

> To the degree that a positivist theory of scientific knowledge has become the criterion for all knowledge, moral insights and political commitments have been delegitimized as irrational or reduced to mere subjective inclination. Ethical judgments are now thought of as personal opinion. (Brown, 1989:37)

Summary

You probably find many positivist assumptions familiar because the positivist approach is widely taught as being the same as science. Few people are aware of the origins of positivist assumptions. An early religious aspect exists in some assumptions because the scholars who developed them in western Europe during the eighteenth and nineteenth centuries had religious training and lived in a cultural–historical setting that assumed specific religious beliefs. Many positivist assumptions will reappear when you read about quantitative research techniques and measurement in later chapters. A positivist approach implies that a researcher begins with a general cause–effect relationship that he or she logically derives from a possible causal law in general theory. He or she logically links the abstract ideas of the relationship to precise measurements of the social world. The researcher remains detached, neutral, and objective as he or she measures aspects of social life, examines evidence, and replicates the research of others. These processes lead to an empirical test of, and confirmation for, the laws of social life as outlined in a theory.

When and why did positivist social science become dominant? The story is long and complicated. Many present it as a natural advance or the inevitable progress of pure knowledge. Positivist social science expanded largely due to changes in the larger political–social context. Positivism gained dominance in the United States and became the model for social work research in many nations after World War II, once the United States became the leading world power. A thrust toward objectivism—a strong version of positivism—developed in the U.S. during the 1920s. Objectivism grew as researchers shifted away from social reform-oriented studies with less formal or precise quantitative techniques toward rigorous techniques in a "value-free" manner modeled on the natural sciences. They created careful measures of the external behavior of individuals to produce quantitative data that could be subjected to statistical analysis. Objectivism displaced locally based studies that were action-oriented and largely qualitative. It grew because competition among researchers for prestige and status combined with other pressures, including funds from private foundations (e.g., Ford Foundation, Rockefeller Foundation, etc.), university administrators who wanted to avoid unconventional politics, a desire by researchers for a public image of serious professionalism, and the information needs of expanding government and corporate bureaucracies. These pressures combined to redefine social work research. The less technical, applied local studies conducted by social reformers (often women) were often overshadowed by apolitical, precise quantitative research by male professors in university departments.[7]

INTERPRETIVE SOCIAL SCIENCE

Interpretive social science can be traced to German sociologist Max Weber (1864–1920) and German philosopher Wilhem Dilthey (1833–1911). In his major work, *Einleitung in die Geisteswissenshaften (Introduction to the Human Sciences)* (1883), Dilthey argued that there were two fundamentally different types of science: *Naturwissenschaft* and *Geisteswissenschaft.* The former is based on *Erk-*

lärung, or abstract explanation. The latter is rooted in an empathetic understanding, or *Verstehen,* of the everyday lived experience of people in specific historical settings. Weber argued that social science needed to study *meaningful social action,* or social action with a purpose. He embraced *Verstehen* and felt that we must learn the personal reasons or motives that shape a person's internal feelings and guide decisions to act in particular ways.

> *We shall speak of "social action" wherever human action is subjectively related in meaning to the behavior of others. An unintended collision of two cyclists, for example, shall not be called social action. But we will define as such their possible prior attempts to dodge one another. . . . Social action is not the only kind of action significant for sociological causal explanation, but it is the primary object of an "interpretive sociology." (Weber, 1981:159)*

Interpretive social science is related to *hermeneutics,* a theory of meaning that originated in the nineteenth century. The term comes from a god in Greek mythology, Hermes, who had the job of communicating the desires of the gods to mortals. It "literally means making the obscure plain" (Blaikie, 1993:28). Hermeneutics is largely found in the humanities (philosophy, art history, religious studies, linguistics, and literary criticism). It emphasizes a detailed reading or examination of *text,* which could refer to a conversation, written words, or pictures. A researcher conducts "a reading" to discover meaning embedded within text. Each reader brings his or her subjective experience to a text. When studying the text, the researcher/reader tries to absorb or get inside the viewpoint it presents as a whole, and then develop a deep understanding of how its parts relate to the whole. In other words, true meaning is rarely simple or obvious on the surface; one reaches it only through a detailed study of the text, contemplating its many messages and seeking the connections among its parts.

There are several varieties of interpretive social science (ISS): hermeneutics, constructionism, ethnomethodology, cognitive, idealist, phenomenological, subjectivist, and qualitative sociology.[8] An interpretive approach is associated with the symbolic interactionist, or the 1920s–1930s Chicago school in sociology. It is often called a qualitative method of research.

Interpretive researchers often use participant observation and field research. These techniques require that researchers spend many hours in direct personal contact with those being studied. Other ISS researchers analyze transcripts of conversations or study videotapes of behavior in extraordinary detail, looking for subtle nonverbal communication, to understand details of interactions in their context. A positivist researcher will precisely measure selected quantitative details about thousands of people and use statistics, whereas an interpretive researcher may live a year with a dozen people and use careful methods to gather large quantities of detailed qualitative data to acquire an in-depth understanding of how they create meaning in everyday life.

In contrast to positivism's instrumental orientation, the interpretive approach adopts a *practical orientation*. It is concerned with how ordinary people manage their practical affairs in everyday life, or how they get things done. Interpretive social work is concerned with how people interact and get along with each other. In general, the interpretive approach is *the systematic analysis of socially meaningful action through the direct detailed observation of people in natural settings in order to arrive at understandings and interpretations of how people create and maintain their social worlds.*

The Questions

1. *Why should one conduct social work research?*

For interpretive researchers, the goal of social work research is to develop an understanding of social life and discover how people construct meaning in natural settings. An interpretive researcher wants to learn what is meaningful or relevant to the people being studied, or how individuals or clients experience daily life. The researcher does this by getting to know a particular social setting and seeing it from the point of view of those in it. The researcher shares the feelings and interpretations of the people he or she studies and sees things through their eyes. Summarizing the goal of his 10-year study of Willie, a repair shop owner in a rural area, interpretive researcher Harper (1987:12) said,

"The goal of the research was to share Willie's perspective."

Interpretive researchers study meaningful social action, not just the external or observable behavior of people. Social action is the action to which people attach subjective meaning; it is activity with a purpose or intent. Nonhuman species lack culture and the reasoning to plan things out and attach purpose to their behavior; therefore, social scientists should study what is unique to human social behavior. The researcher must take into account the social actor's reasons and the social context of action. For example, a physical reflex such as eye blinking is human behavior that is rarely an intentional social action (i.e., done for a reason or with human motivation), but in some situations, it can be such a social action (i.e., a wink). The activities of social actors need more than simply to have a purpose; they must also be social, and "for action to be regarded as social and to be of interest to the social scientist, the actor must attach subjective meaning to it and it must be directed towards the activities of other people" (Blaikie, 1993:37).

The interpretive approach notes that human action has little inherent meaning. It acquires meaning among people who share a meaning system that permits them to interpret the action as a socially relevant sign or action. For example, raising one finger in a situation with other people can express social meaning; the specific meaning it expresses (e.g., a direction, an expression of friendship, a vulgar sign) depends on the cultural meaning system that the social actors share.

2. *What is the fundamental nature of social reality?*

The interpretive approach sees human social life as an accomplishment. It is intentionally created out of the purposeful actions of interacting social beings. In contrast to the realist idea (shared by positivist and critical social science) that social life is "out there," independent of human consciousness, ISS says social reality is not waiting to be discovered. Instead, the social world is largely what people perceive it to be. Social life exists as people experience it and give it meaning. It is fluid and fragile. People maintain it by interacting with others in ongoing processes of communication and negotiation. They operate on the basis of untested assumptions and taken-for-granted knowledge about people and events around them.

The interpretive approach holds that social life is based on social interactions and socially constructed meaning systems. People possess an internally experienced sense of reality. This subjective sense of reality is crucial to grasp human social life. External human behavior is an indirect and often obscure indicator of true social meaning. ISS says that "access to other human beings is possible, however, only by indirect means: what we experience initially are gestures, sound, and actions and only in the process of understanding do we take the step from external signs to the underlying inner life" (Bleicher, 1980:9).

For interpretive social work researchers, social reality is based on people's definitions of it. A person's definition of a situation tells him or her how to assign meaning in constantly shifting conditions. For example, our social reality includes ways to act toward our college instructors. We generally say hello to them in the hall, raise our hands in class if we want to say something, and refer to them as Dr. Jones or Professor Smith. We learned to do this through cultural role expectations and years of experience in educational and academic environments. Yet, the social reality of the relationship is not fixed. The definition of the situation could change dramatically. The social reality could be shattered, for example, if a faculty member started behaving oddly, no longer recognized us, and never showed up for class.

Positivists assume that everyone shares the same meaning system and that we all experience the world in the same way. The interpretive approach says that people may or may not experience social or physical reality in the same way. Key questions for an interpretive researcher are: How do people experience the world? Do they create and share meaning? Interpretive social science points to numerous examples in which several people have seen, heard, or even touched the same physical object, yet come away with different meanings or interpretations of it. The interpretive social work researcher argues that positivists avoid important questions and impose one

way of experiencing the world on others. By contrast, ISS assumes that multiple interpretations of human experience, or realities, are possible. In sum, the ISS approach sees social reality as consisting of people who construct meaning and create interpretations through their daily social interaction.

3. *What is the basic nature of human beings?*

Ordinary people are engaged in a process of creating flexible systems of meaning through social interaction. They then use such meanings to interpret their social world and make sense of their lives. Human behavior may be patterned and regular, but this is not due to preexisting laws waiting to be discovered. The patterns are created out of evolving meaning systems or social conventions that people generate as they socially interact. Important questions for the interpretive researcher are, "What do people believe to be true? What do they hold to be relevant? How do they define what they are doing?"

Interpretive social work researchers want to discover what actions mean to the people who engage in them. It makes little sense to try to deduce social life from abstract, logical theories that may not relate to the feelings and experiences of ordinary people. People have their own reasons for their actions, and researchers need to learn the reasons people use. Individual motives are crucial to consider even if they are irrational, carry deep emotions, and contain false facts and prejudices.

Some interpretive social work researchers say that the laws sought by positivists may be found only after the scientific community understands how people create and use meaning systems, how common sense develops, and how people apply their common sense to situations. Other interpretive researchers say there are no such laws of human social life, so the search is futile. Schwandt (1994:130) noted, "Contemporary interpretativists and constructivists are not likely to hold that there are any unquestioned *foundations* for any interpretation" (emphasis in original). In other words, the creation of meaning and the sense of reality are only what people think they are, and no set of meanings is better or superior to another. For example, an interpretive social work researcher sees the desire to discover laws of human behavior in which unemployment causes child abuse as premature at best and dangerous at worst. Instead, he or she wants to understand how people subjectively experience unemployment and what the loss of a job means in their everyday lives. Likewise, the interpretive researcher wants to learn how child abusers account for their actions, what reasons they give for abuse, and how they feel about abusing a child. He or she explores the meaning of being unemployed and the reasons for abusing a child in order to understand what is happening to the people who are directly involved.

4. *What is the relationship between science and common sense?*

Positivists see common sense as inferior to science. By contrast, interpretive researchers argue that ordinary people use common sense to guide them in daily living; therefore, one must first grasp common sense. People use common sense all the time. It is a stockpile of everyday theories people use to organize and explain events in the world. It is critical to understand common sense because it contains the meanings that people use when they engage in routine social interactions.

An interpretive approach says that common sense and the positivist's laws are alternative ways to interpret the world; that is, they are distinct meaning systems. Neither common sense nor scientific law has all the answers. Neither is inferior or superior to the other. Instead, interpretive social work researchers see each as important in its own domain; each is created in a different way for a different purpose.

Ordinary people could not function in daily life if they based their actions on science alone. For example, in order to boil an egg, people use unsystematic experiences, habits, and guesswork. A strict application of natural science would require one to know the laws of physics that determine heating the water and the chemical laws that govern the changes in the egg's internal composition. Even natural scientists use common sense when they are not "doing science" in their area of expertise.

The interpretive approach says that common sense is a vital source of information for understanding people. A person's common sense and sense of reality emerge from a pragmatic orientation and set of assumptions about the world. People do not know that common sense is true with absolute certainty, but they must assume that it is true in order to get anything accomplished. The interpretive philosopher, Alfred Schutz (1899–1959), called this the *natural attitude.* It is the assumption that the world existed before you arrived and will continue to exist after you depart. People develop ways to maintain or reproduce a sense of reality based on systems of meaning that they create in the course of social interactions with others.

5. *What constitutes an explanation or theory of social reality?*

Positivists believe that social theory should be similar to natural science theory with deductive axioms, theorems, and interconnected causal laws. Instead of a maze of interconnected laws and propositions, theory for ISS tells a story. Interpretive social work theory describes and interprets how people conduct their daily lives. It contains concepts and limited generalizations, but it does not dramatically depart from the experience and inner reality of the people being studied.

The interpretive approach is ideographic and inductive. *Ideographic* means the approach provides a symbolic representation or "thick" description of something else. An interpretive research report may read more like a novel or a biography than like a mathematical proof. It is rich in detailed description and limited in abstraction. An interpretive analysis of a social setting, like the interpretation of a literary work, has internal coherence and is rooted in the text, which here refers to the meaningful everyday experiences of the people being studied.

Interpretive theory gives the reader a feel for another's social reality. The theory does this by revealing the meanings, values, interpretive schemes, and rules of living used by people in their daily lives. For example, it may describe major typifications people use in a setting to recognize and interpret their experiences. A *typification* is an informal model, scheme, or set of beliefs that people use to categorize and organize the flow of the daily events they experience.

Thus, interpretive theory resembles a map that outlines a social world or a tourist guidebook that describes local customs and informal norms. For example, an interpretive report on professional gamblers tells the reader about the careers and daily concerns of such people. It describes the specific individuals studied, the locations and activities observed, and the strategies used to gamble. The reader learns how professional gamblers speak, how they view others, and what their fears or ambitions are. The researcher gives a few generalizations and organizing concepts. The bulk of the report is a detailed description of the gambling world. The theory and evidence are interwoven to create a unified whole; the concepts and generalizations are wedded to their context.

6. *How does one determine whether an explanation is true or false?*

Positivists evaluate a theory by using set procedures to test hypotheses. They logically deduce from theory, collect data, and analyze facts in ways that other scientists can replicate. An explanation is considered to be true when it stands up to replication. For ISS a theory is true if it makes sense to those being studied and if it allows others to understand deeply or enter the reality of those being studied. The theory or description is accurate if the researcher conveys a deep understanding of the way others reason, feel, and see things. Prediction may be possible, but it is a type of prediction that occurs when two people are very close, as when they have been married for a long time. An interpretive explanation documents the actor's point of view and translates it into a form that is intelligible to readers. Smart (1976:100) calls this the *postulate of adequacy:*

> The postulate of adequacy asserts that if a scientific account of human action were to be presented to an individual actor as a script it must be understandable to that actor, translatable into action by the actor and furthermore comprehensible to his fellow actors in terms of a common sense interpretation of everyday life.

An interpretive researcher's description of another person's meaning system is a *secondary account.* Like a traveler telling about a foreign land, the researcher is not a native. Such an outside view never equals a primary account given by those being studied, but the closer it is to the native's primary

account, the better. For example, one way to test the truthfulness of an interpretive study of professional gambling is to have professional gamblers read it and verify its accuracy. A good report tells a reader enough about the world of professional gambling that if the reader absorbed it and then met a professional gambler, the understanding of gambling jargon, outlook, and lifestyle might lead the gambler to ask whether the reader was also a professional gambler.

7. *What does good evidence or factual information look like?*

Good evidence in positivism is observable, precise, and independent of theory and values. By contrast, ISS sees the unique features of specific contexts and meanings as essential to understand social meaning. Evidence about social action cannot be isolated from the context in which it occurs or the meanings assigned to it by the social actors involved. As Weber (1978:5) said, "Empathic or appreciative accuracy is attained when, through sympathetic participation, we can adequately grasp the emotional context in which the action took place."

Interpretive social work sees facts as fluid and embedded within a meaning system in the interpretive approach; they are not impartial, objective, and neutral. Facts are context-specific actions that depend on the interpretations of particular people in a social setting. What the positivist assumes—that neutral outsiders observe behavior and see unambiguous, objective facts—an ISS researcher takes as a question to be addressed: How do people observe ambiguities in social life and assign meaning? Interpretive researchers say that social situations contain a great deal of ambiguity. This makes it almost impossible to discover straightforward, objective facts. Most behaviors or statements can have several meanings and can be interpreted in multiple ways. In the flow of ambiguous social life, people are constantly "making sense" by reassessing clues in the situation and assigning meanings until they "know what's going on." For example, we see a woman holding her hand out, palm forward. Even this simple act carries multiple potential meanings; we do not know its meaning without knowing the social situation. It could mean that she is warding off a potential mugger, drying her nail polish, hailing a taxi, admiring a new ring, telling oncoming traffic to stop for her, or requesting five bagels at a deli counter (see Brown, 1989:34). People are able to assign appropriate meaning to an act or statement only if they take the social context in which it occurs into account.

Interpretive social work researchers rarely ask objective survey questions, aggregate the answers of many people, and claim to have something meaningful. Each person's interpretation of the survey question must be placed in a context (e.g., the individual's previous experiences or the survey interview situation), and the true meaning of a person's answer will vary according to the interview or questioning context. Moreover, because each person assigns a somewhat different meaning to the question and answer, combining answers produces only nonsense.

When studying a setting or data, interpretive researchers of the ethnomethodological school often use bracketing. *Bracketing* is a mental exercise in which the researcher identifies, then sets aside, taken-for-granted assumptions used in a social scene. The researcher questions and reexamines ordinary events that have an "obvious" meaning to those involved. For example, at an office work setting, one male coworker in his late 20s says to the male researcher, "We're getting together for softball after work tonight. Do you want to join us?" What is *not said* is that the researcher should know the rules of softball, own a softball glove, and change from a business suit into other clothing before the game. Bracketing reveals what "everyone knows"—what people assume but rarely say. It helps a researcher reveal key features of the social scene that make other events possible. It makes visible the underlying scaffolding of understandings on which actions are based.

8. *When do sociopolitical values enter into science?*

The positivist researcher calls for eliminating values and operating within an apolitical environment. The interpretive social work researcher, by contrast, argues that researchers should reflect on, reexamine, and analyze personal points of view and feelings as a part of the process of studying others.

The interpretive researcher needs, at least temporarily, to empathize with and share in the social and political commitments or values of those he or she studies.

Interpretive social work research does not try to be value free. Indeed, ISS questions the possibility of achieving it. This is because interpretive research sees values and meaning infused everywhere in everything. What the positivist calls value freedom is just another meaning system and value—the value of positivist science. The interpretive social work researcher urges making values explicit and does not assume that any one set of values is better or worse. The researcher's proper role is to be a "passionate participant" (Guba and Lincoln, 1994:115), involved with those being studied.

Summary

The interpretive approach existed for many years as the loyal opposition to positivism. Although some positivist social researchers accept the interpretive approach as useful in exploratory research (see Chapter 2), few positivists consider it to be scientific. You will read again about the interpretive outlook when you examine field research and, to a lesser degree, historical–comparative research in later chapters. The interpretive approach is the foundation of social work research techniques that are sensitive to context, that use various methods to get inside the ways others see the world, and that are more concerned with achieving an empathic understanding of feelings and world views than with testing laws of human behavior.

CRITICAL SOCIAL SCIENCE

Critical social science (CSS) offers a third alternative to the meaning of methodology. Versions of this approach are called dialectical materialism, class analysis, and structuralism.[9] Critical social science mixes nomothetic and ideographic approaches. It agrees with many of the criticisms the interpretive approach directs at positivism, but it adds some of its own and disagrees with ISS on some points. This approach is traced to Karl Marx (1818–1883) and Sigmund Freud (1856–1939), and was elaborated on by Theodor Adorno (1903–1969), Erich Fromm (1900–1980), and Herbert Marcuse (1898–1979). CSS is often associated with conflict theory, feminist analysis, and radical psychotherapy. It is also tied to critical theory, first developed by the Frankfurt School in Germany in the 1930s.[10] Critical social science criticized positivist science as being narrow, antidemocratic and nonhumanist in its use of reason. This was outlined in Adorno's essay, "The Logic of the Social Sciences" (1976). The well-known living representative of the school, Jurgen Habermas (1929–   ), advanced critical social science in his *Knowledge and Human Interests* (1971). In the field of education, Freire's *Pedagogy of the Oppressed* (1970) also falls within the CSS approach.

Another example is the French writer Pierre Bourdieu (see Schwartz, 1997). Although he has written on many topics, Bourdieu advocates a distinct approach to theory and research. Several features of his approach make it CSS. The basic approach is antipositivist and antiinterpretative. He rejects both the objective, lawlike quantitative empirical approach of positivists and the subjective, voluntarist approach of ISS. Bourdieu argues that social research must be reflexive (i.e., study and criticize itself as well as its subject matter) and is necessarily political. He also believes that a goal of research is to uncover and demystify ordinary events. Recently, a philosophical approach called *realism* has been integrated into critical social science.[11]

Interpretive social science criticizes positivism for failing to deal with the meanings of real people and their capacity to feel and think. It also believes positivism ignores the social context and is antihumanist. CSS agrees with these criticisms of positivism. It also believes that positivism defends the status quo because it assumes an unchanging social order instead of seeing current society as a particular stage in an ongoing process.

Critical researchers criticize the interpretive approach for being too subjective and relativist. The critical researcher says that ISS sees all points of view as equal. The interpretive approach treats people's ideas as more important than actual conditions and focuses on localized, micro-level, short-term settings while ignoring the broader and long-term context. ISS is overly concerned with subjective re-

ality. To critical researchers, ISS is amoral and passive. It does not take a strong value position or actively help people to see false illusions around them so that they can improve their lives. In general, CSS defines social science as a *critical process of inquiry that goes beyond surface illusions to uncover the real structures in the material world in order to help people change conditions and build a better world for themselves.*

The Questions

1. *Why should one conduct social work research?*

Critical researchers conduct research to critique and transform social relations. They do this by revealing the underlying sources of social relations and empowering people, especially less powerful people. The purpose of critical research is to change the world. More specifically, social work research should uncover myths, reveal hidden truths, and help people to change the world for themselves. In CSS the purpose is "to explain a social order in such a way that it becomes itself the catalyst which leads to the transformation of this social order" (Fay, 1987:27).

The critical social work researcher is action oriented. He or she is dissatisfied with the way things are and seeks dramatic improvements. A positivist researcher usually tries to solve problems as they are defined by government or corporate elites, without "rocking the boat." By contrast, the critical researcher may create problems by "intentionally raising and identifying more problems than the ruling elites in politics and administration are able to accommodate, much less to 'solve'" (Offe, 1981:34–35). The critical researcher asks embarrassing questions, exposes hypocrisy, and investigates conditions in order to encourage dramatic grass-roots action. "The point of all science, indeed all learning, is to change and develop out of our understandings and reduce illusion. . . . Learning is the reducing of illusion and ignorance; it can help free us from domination by hitherto unacknowledged constraints, dogmas and falsehoods" (Sayer, 1992:252).

For example, a critical social work researcher conducts a study showing that there is racial discrimination in rental housing. White landlords refuse to rent to minority tenants. A critical researcher would not just publish a report and then wait for the fair housing office of the city government to act. The researcher gives the report to newspapers and meets with grass-roots organizations to discuss the results of the study. He or she works with activists to mobilize political action in the name of social justice. When grass-roots people picket the landlords' offices, flood the landlords with racial minority applicants for apartments, or organize a march on city hall demanding action, the critical social work researcher predicts that the landlords will be forced to rent to minorities. The goal of research is to empower. Kincheloe and McLaren (1994:140) stated:

> Critical research can be best understood in the context of the empowerment of individuals. Inquiry that aspires to the name critical must be connected to an attempt to confront the injustice of a particular society or sphere within the society. Research thus becomes a transformative endeavor unembarrassed by the label "political" and unafraid to consummate a relationship with an emancipatory consciousness.

According to Cowger and Snively (2001), empowerment research and strengths-based assessment in social work must take into account the promotion of social and economic justice by asking that research and evaluation methods understand and even question existing distributions of power. Further—as noted by Saleebey (1997), Cowger and Snively (2002), and Russo (1999)—the strengths perspective recognizes that the driving force for empowerment must come from clients or client systems; this provides the fuel or energy that drives the empowerment process. Individuals or groups who are empowered have the capacity to participate in the decision-making process and not simply be accommodated or co-opted by those already in power.

Cowger and Snively identify twelve strategies for social workers assessing clients from an empowerment model or doing research based on the strengths model. These include the following: let clients decide on the facts; believe clients; discover what clients want; always move toward strengths; look for multidimensionality; discuss each client's uniqueness; use the client's own words; assessments and evaluations must always be jointly undertaken; look for areas of mutual agreement; avoid blame; avoid simplistic cause-and-effect answers; and assess, don't diagnose.

2. *What is the fundamental nature of social reality?*

Like positivism, CSS adopts a realist position (i.e., social reality is "out there" to be discovered). It differs from positivism in that it is historical realism in which reality is seen as constantly shaped by social, political, cultural, and similar factors. Social reality evolves over time. It may be misleading on the surface and have unobservable enduring real structures of power underneath. CSS assumes that social reality always changes and the change is rooted in the tensions, conflicts, or contradictions of social relations or institutions. It focuses on change and conflict, especially paradoxes or conflicts that are inherent in the very way social relations are organized. Such paradoxes or inner conflicts reveal much about the true nature of social reality.

A biological analogy illustrates such paradoxes. Death and birth appear to be opposites, yet death begins with birth. We begin to die the day we are born. This sounds strange at first, but our bodies begin to age and decay as we live. There is an inner contradiction. Birth necessarily brings about its negation, death. Thus, the inner tension between living and aging goes on all the time. In order to live, our bodies must age, or move toward death. Death and birth are less the opposites they appear to be than the interlocked parts of a single larger process of change. Sometimes this idea of a paradoxical inner conflict or contradiction that brings about change is called the *dialectic.*

Change can be uneven—extremely slow for long periods, then suddenly speed up. The critical social work researcher studies the past or different societies in order to better see change or to discover alternative ways to organize social life. CSS is interested in the development of new social relations, the evolution of social institutions or societies, and the causes of major social change.

A critical approach notes that social change and conflict are not always apparent or observable. The social world is full of illusion, myth, and distortion.

Initial observations of the world are only partial and often misleading because the human senses are limited and so is our knowledge. The appearances in surface reality do not have to be based on conscious deception. The immediately perceived characteristics of objects, events, or social relations rarely reveal everything. These illusions allow some groups in society to hold power and exploit others. Karl Marx, German sociologist and political thinker, stated this forcefully (Marx and Engels, 1947:39): "The ideas of the ruling class are in every epoch the ruling ideas; . . . The class which has the means of material production at its disposal, has control at the same time over the means of mental production, so that . . . the ideas of those who lack the means of mental production are subject to it."

The critical social work approach argues that social reality has multiple layers. Behind the immediately observable surface reality lie deep structures or unobservable mechanisms. The events and relations of superficial social reality are based on deep structures beneath the surface of casual observation. We can uncover or expose such structures with effort. Intense and directed questioning, a good theory about where to look, a clear value position, and a historical orientation help the critical social work researcher probe below the surface reality and discover the deep structures.

ISS and CSS both see social reality as changing and subject to socially created meanings. The critical science approach disagrees with the ISS emphasis on micro-level interpersonal interactions and its acceptance of any meaning system. CSS says that although subjective meaning is important, there are real, objective relations that shape social relations. The critical social work researcher questions social situations and places them into a larger, macro-level historical context.

For example, an interpretive social work researcher studies the interactions of a male boss and his female secretary and provides a colorful account of their rules of behavior, interpretive mechanisms, and systems of meaning. By contrast, the critical social work researcher begins with a point of view (e.g., feminist) and notes issues ignored in an interpretive description: Why are bosses male and secretaries female? Why do the roles of boss and

secretary have unequal power? Why are such roles created in large organizations throughout our society? How did the unequal power come about historically, and were secretaries always female? How do sex roles in society affect the relationship? Why can the boss make off-color jokes that humiliate the secretary? How are the roles of boss and secretary in conflict based on the everyday conditions faced by the boss (large salary, country club membership, new car, large home, retirement plan, stock investments, etc.) and those of the secretary (low hourly pay, children to care for, concerns about how to pay bills, television as her only recreation, etc.)? Can the secretary join with others to challenge the power of her boss and similar bosses?

3. *What is the basic nature of human beings?*

Positivism views social forces almost as if they had a life of their own and operated regardless of people's personal wishes. Such social forces have power over, and operate on, people. The critical social work approach rejects this idea as reification. *Reification* is giving the creations of your own activity a separate, alien existence. It is separating or removing yourself from what you have created, until you no longer recognize it as part of you or as something you helped to bring about. Once you no longer see your contributions and treat what you have helped to create as an outside force, you lose control over your destiny.

For example, two people meet, fall in love, and set up a household. Within two years, one begins to feel helpless and trapped by unseen forces. She or he fights with the other over household chores and spending habits. One partner's social values say it is wrong to wash dishes and empty the garbage. We understand that an agreement to adopt a particular lifestyle is the creation and personal decision of those involved. Thus, the unseen forces that make them feel trapped and helpless are their own social creations, although each will likely forget this. If people become aware of the forces that trap them (i.e., societal values, social roles, their own decisions), and take action to change them (i.e., modify their lifestyles), they may be able to find a solution and feel less trapped.

The critical social work researcher says that people have a great deal of unrealized potential.

People are creative, changeable, and adaptive. Despite their creativity and potential for change, however, people can also be misled, mistreated, and exploited by others. They become trapped in a web of social meanings, obligations, and relationships. They fail to see how change is possible and thus lose their independence, freedom, and control over their lives. This happens when people allow themselves to become isolated and detached from others in similar situations. The potential of people can be realized if they dispel their illusions and join collectively to change society. People can change the social world, but delusion, isolation, and oppressive conditions in everyday life often prevent them from realizing their dreams.

For example, for generations, most Americans believed the myth that women were inferior to men, that men had an inherent right to make major decisions, and that women were incapable of professional responsibilities. Before the 1960s most people believed that women were less capable than men. By the 1980s only a minority continued to hold such a belief. The dramatic change in belief and social relations resulted from a new consciousness and organized political action to destroy a myth that existed in laws, customs, and official policies, as well as—most importantly—in the everyday beliefs of most people.

4. *What is the relationship between science and common sense?*

The CSS position on common sense is based on the idea of *false consciousness*—that people are mistaken and act against their own true best interests as defined in objective reality. Objective reality lies behind myth and illusion. False consciousness is meaningless for ISS because it implies that a social actor uses a meaning system that is false or out of touch with objective reality. The interpretive approach says that people create and use such systems and that researchers can only describe such systems, not judge their value. The critical social work approach says that social work researchers should study subjective ideas and common sense because these shape human behavior. Yet, they are full of myth and illusion. CSS assumes that there is an objective world in which there is un-

equal control over resources and power on which common sense is based.

The structures that critical researchers talk about are not easy to see. Researchers must first demystify them and pull back the veil of their surface appearances. Careful observation is not enough. It does not tell what to observe, and observing an illusion does not dispel it. A researcher must use theory to dig beneath surface relations, to observe periods of crisis and intense conflict, to probe interconnections, to look at the past, and to consider future possibilities. Uncovering the deeper level of reality is difficult, but it is essential because surface reality is full of ideology, myth, distortion, and false appearances. "Common sense tends to naturalize social phenomena and to assume that what is, must be. A social science which builds uncritically on common sense . . . reproduces these errors" (Sayer, 1992:43).

5. *What constitutes an explanation or theory of social reality?*

Positivism is based on the idea of *determinism:* Human behavior is determined by causal laws over which humans have little control. ISS assumes *voluntarism:* People have a large amount of free will to create social meanings. The critical social work approach falls between the other two. It is partially deterministic and partially voluntaristic. CSS says that people are constrained by the material conditions, cultural context, and historical conditions in which they find themselves. The world people live in limits their options and shapes their beliefs and behavior. Yet, people are not locked into an inevitable set of social structures, relationships, or laws. People can develop new understandings or ways of seeing that enable them to change these structures, relationships, and laws. They first must develop a vision of the future and work together for change, then they can overcome those who oppose them. In a nutshell, people do shape their destiny, but not under conditions of their own choosing.

A full critical social work explanation demystifies illusion, describes the underlying structure of conditions, explains how change can be achieved, and provides a vision of a possible future. Critical theory does more than describe the unseen mechanisms that account for observable reality; it also critiques conditions and implies a plan of change.

The critical social work approach focuses less on fixed laws of human behavior because the laws are seen as changing. Human behavior is only partially governed by laws or constraints imposed by underlying social structures. People can change most of the apparent laws of society, although this is difficult and involves a long struggle. By identifying the causal mechanisms, the trigger or the levers of social relations, CSS explains how and why certain actions will bring about change.

6. *How does one determine whether an explanation is true or false?*

Positivists test theories by deducing hypotheses, testing hypotheses with replicated observations, and then combining results to support laws. Interpretive researchers support theories by seeing whether the meaning system and rules of behavior make sense to those being studied. Critical theory seeks to provide people with a resource that will help them understand and change their world. A researcher tests critical theory by accurately describing conditions generated by underlying structures, then by applying that knowledge to change social relations. A good critical social work theory teaches people about their own experiences, helps them understand their historical role, and can be used to improve conditions.

Critical theory informs practical action or suggests what to do, but theory is modified on the basis of its use. A critical theory grows and interacts with the world it seeks to explain. Because a critical approach tries to explain and change the world by penetrating hidden structures that are in constant flux, the test of an explanation is not static. Testing theory is a dynamic, ongoing process of applying theory and modifying it. Knowledge grows by an ongoing process of eroding ignorance and enlarging insights through action.

The critical approach uses praxis to separate good from bad theory. It puts the theory into practice and uses the outcome of applications to reformulate theory. *Praxis* means that explanations are valued when they help people to really understand the world and to take action that changes it. As Sayer (1992:13) argued, "Knowledge is primarily gained through activity both in attempting to change our environment (through labor or work) and through interaction with other people."

Critical social work research tries to eliminate the division between the researcher and those being researched, the distinction between science and everyday life. For example, a critical researcher develops an explanation for housing discrimination. He or she tests the explanation by using it to try to change conditions. If the explanation says that underlying economic relations cause discrimination and that landlords refuse to rent to minorities because it is profitable to rent only to nonminorities, then political actions that make it profitable to rent to minorities should change the landlords' behavior. By contrast, if the explanation says that an underlying racial hatred causes landlords to discriminate, then actions based on profit will be unsuccessful. The critical researcher would then examine race hatred as the basis of landlord behavior through new studies combined with new political action.

7. *What does good evidence or factual information look like?*

Positivism assumes that there are incontestable neutral facts on which all rational people agree. Its dualist doctrine says that social facts are like objects. They exist separately from values or theories. The interpretive approach sees the social world as made up of created meaning, with people creating and negotiating meanings. It rejects positivism's dualism, but it substitutes an emphasis on the subject. Evidence is whatever resides in the subjective understandings of those involved. The critical approach tries to bridge the object–subject gap. It says that the facts of material conditions exist independently of subjective perceptions, but that facts are not theory neutral. Instead, facts require an interpretation from within a framework of values, theory, and meaning.

For example, it is a "fact" that the United States spends a much greater percentage of its gross national product (GNP) on health care than any other advanced industrial nation, and yet it has the 14th lowest infant death rate. A critical researcher interprets the fact by noting that the United States has many people without health care and no system to cover everyone. The fact includes the way the health care is delivered to some through a complex system of for-profit insurance companies, pharmaceutical firms, hospitals, and others who benefit greatly from the current arrangement. Some powerful groups are getting rich while weaker or poor sectors of society are getting low quality or no health care. Critical researchers look at the facts and ask who benefits and who loses.

Theory helps a critical social work researcher find new facts and separate the important from the trivial ones. The theory is a type of map telling researchers where to look for facts and how to interpret them once they are uncovered. The critical approach says that theory does this in the natural sciences, as well. For example, a biologist looks into a microscope and sees red blood cells—a "fact" based on a theory about blood and cells and a biologist's education about microscopic phenomena. Without this theory and education, a biologist sees only meaningless spots. Clearly, then, facts and theories are interrelated.

For example, in *Inequality in Africa,* Nafziger (1988) used a critical perspective. He criticized "facts" on income inequality because they measured only money income in societies in which money is not widely used. He also criticized interpretations of "facts" on issues such as land distribution and infant mortality rates. Such facts ignored the number of people living on a farm and ignored those outside one group in a nation (South African Whites) that has drastically lower infant mortality rates than others in the same nation. Instead, Nafziger looked for a wide variety of facts (e.g., birth rates, urban–rural gaps, ethnic divisions, international trade, political power) and went behind the surface facts to connect them to one another. He asked, "Why is Africa the only region in the world to become more impoverished since World War II?" His theory helped him identify a number of major social groups (e.g., government leaders) and classes (e.g., peasants). Nafziger also asked whether various trends or policies served the interests of each group.

Not all theories are equally useful for finding and understanding key facts. Theories are based on beliefs and assumptions about what the world is like and on a set of moral–political values. CSS says that some values are better than others.[12] Thus, in order to interpret facts, one must understand history, adopt a set of values, and know where to look for underlying structures. Different versions of critical social work offer different value positions (e.g., Marxism versus feminism).

8. *When do sociopolitical values enter into science?*
The critical approach has an activist orientation. Social work research is a moral–political activity that requires the researcher to commit to a value position. CSS rejects positivist value freedom as a myth. It also attacks the interpretive approach for its *relativism* (the idea that everything is relative and nothing is absolute). In the interpretive approach, the reality of the genius and the reality of the idiot are equally valid and important. There is little, if any, basis for judging between alternative realities or conflicting viewpoints. For example, the interpretive social work researcher does not call a racist viewpoint wrong, because any viewpoint is true for those who believe in it. The critical approach says that there is only one, or a very few, correct points of view. Other viewpoints are plainly wrong or misleading. All social work research *necessarily* begins with a value or a moral point of view. For CSS, being objective is not being value free. Objectivity means a nondistorted, true picture of reality; "it challenges the belief that science must be protected from politics. It argues that some politics—the politics for emancipatory social change—can increase the objectivity of science" (Harding, 1986:162).

Critical social work says that to deny that a researcher has a point of view is itself a point of view. It is a technician's point of view: Conduct research and ignore the moral questions; satisfy a sponsor and follow orders. Such a view says that science is a tool or instrument anyone can use. This view was strongly criticized when Nazi scientists committed inhumane experiments and then claimed that they were blameless because they "just followed orders" and were "just scientists." Positivism adopts such an approach and produces technocratic knowledge—a form of knowledge best suited for use by the people in power to dominate or control other people.[13] For

CSS "the political use of behavioral science has made positivism into a legitimating ideology of dominant groups . . . value-freedom itself has come to provide an ethic for calculated bureaucratic control" (Brown, 1989:39).

The critical approach rejects positivism and ISS as being detached and concerned with studying the world instead of acting on it. CSS holds that knowledge is power. Social work knowledge can be used to control people, it can be hidden in ivory towers for intellectuals to play games with, or it can be given to people to help them take charge of and improve their lives. What a researcher studies, how he or she studies it, and what happens to the results involve values and morality, because knowledge has tangible effects on people's lives. The researcher who studies trivial behavior, who fails to probe beneath the surface, or who buries the results in a university library is making a moral choice. The choice is to take information from the people being studied without involving them or liberating them (see Box 4.1). Critical social work questions the morality of such a choice, even if it is not a conscious one. The researcher's proper role is to be the "transformative intellectual" (Guba and Lincoln, 1994:115).

Summary

Although few full-time researchers adopt the critical social work approach, it is often adopted by community action groups, political organizations, and social movements. It only rarely appears in scholarly journals. Critical researchers may use any research technique, but they tend to favor the historical–comparative method. This is because of its emphasis on change and because it helps researchers uncover underlying structures. Critical social work researchers differ from the others less in the research techniques they use than in how they approach a

---

Box 4.1 _____

The Extended Case Method and CSS

Michael Burawoy's (1998) extended case method is an example of critical social work. He says it applies *reflexive science* to ethnography or field research. Reflexive science is a type of CSS that says social research should be a dialogue between the researcher and the people being studied. Thus, intersubjectivity is not only among scientists, as in positivism; rather, it occurs between the researcher and people under study. Burawoy identifies four features of reflexive science:

1. The researcher interacts with subject-participants. Disruptions or disturbances that develop out of their mutual interaction help to expose and better illuminate social life.
2. The researcher adopts the subject-participant's view of the world in specific situations, but does not stop there. The researcher adds together many views from individual subjects and specific situations, aggregating them into broader social processes.
3. The researcher sees the social world simultaneously from the inside outward (i.e., from the subjective viewpoint of the people being studied) and from the outside inward (i.e., from the viewpoint of external forces that act on people).
4. The researcher constantly builds and rebuilds theory. This takes place in a dialogue with the people studied and in a dialogue with other researchers in the scientific community.

Burawoy used the extended case method to study mine workers in Zambia. He argues that positivist social science best fits situations where people are "powerless to resist wider systems of economy and polity" (p. 30)—in other words, situations in which people are dominated and have little control over their lives. The CSS approach thrives in contexts in which people try to resist or reduce power distinctions and domination. It highlights conditions of emancipation in which people come to question or challenge the external forces of power and control under which they live.

research problem, the kinds of questions they ask, and their purposes for doing research.

FEMINIST AND POSTMODERN RESEARCH

You may hear about two additional approaches that are still in a formative stage and are less well known than the three major ones. They are feminist and postmodern social work research. Both criticize positivism and offer alternatives that build on interpretive and critical social science. They are still embryonic, having gained visibility only in the late 1980s.

Feminist research is conducted by people, almost all of them women, who hold a feminist self-identity and consciously use a feminist perspective. They use multiple research techniques. Feminist methodology attempts to give a voice to women and to correct the male-oriented perspective that has predominated in the development of social science. It is inspired by works such as *Women's Ways of Knowing* (Belenky et al., 1986) that argue that women learn and express themselves differently than men.

Feminist social work research is based on a heightened awareness that the subjective experience of women differs from an ordinary interpretive perspective (Olsen, 1994). Many feminist researchers see positivism as being consistent with a male point of view; it is objective, logical, task-oriented, and instrumental. It reflects a male emphasis on individual competition, on dominating and controlling the environment, and on the hard facts and forces that act on the world. In contrast, women emphasize accommodation and gradually developing human bonds. They see the social world as a web of interconnected human relations, full of people linked together by feelings of trust and mutual obligation. Women tend to emphasize the subjective, empathetic, process-oriented, and inclusive sides of social life. Feminist social work research is also action-oriented and seeks to advance feminist values (see Box 4.2).

Feminist social work researchers argue that much nonfeminist research is sexist, largely as a result of broader cultural beliefs and a preponderance of male researchers. The research overgeneralizes from the experience of men to all people, ignores

---

Box 4.2 _____

Characteristics of Feminist Social Work Research

- Advocacy of a feminist value position and perspective
- Rejection of sexism in assumptions, concepts, and research questions
- Creation of empathic connections between the researcher and those he or she studies
- Sensitivity to how relations of gender and power permeate all spheres of social life
- Incorporation of the researcher's personal feelings and experiences into the research process
- Flexibility in choosing research techniques and crossing boundaries between academic fields
- Recognition of the emotional and mutual-dependence dimensions in human experience
- Action-oriented research that seeks to facilitate personal and societal change

---

gender as a fundamental social division, focuses on men's problems, uses males as points of reference, and assumes traditional gender roles. For example, a traditional researcher would say that a family has a problem of unemployment when the adult male in it cannot find stable work. When a woman in the same family cannot find stable work outside the home, it is not considered an equal family problem. Likewise, the concept *unwed mother* is widely used by traditional researchers, but is not a parallel of *unwed father.*

The feminist social work approach sees researchers as fundamentally gendered beings. Researchers necessarily have a gender that will shape how they experience reality, and therefore it affects their research. In addition to gender's impact on individual researchers, basic theoretical assumptions and the scientific community appear as gendered cultural contexts. Gender has a pervasive influence in culture and shapes basic beliefs and values that cannot be simply isolated and insulated in the social processes of scientific inquiry.[14]

Feminist social work researchers are not objective or detached; they interact and collaborate with the people they study. They fuse their personal and professional lives. For example, feminist researchers will attempt to comprehend an interviewee's experiences while sharing their own feelings and experiences. This process may give birth to a personal relationship between researcher and interviewee that might mature over time. Reinharz (1992:263) argued, "This blurring of the disconnection between formal and personal relations, just as the removal of the distinction . . . between the research project and the researcher's life, is a characteristic of much, if not all, feminist research."

The impact of a woman's perspective and her desire to seek and gain an intimate, profound relationship with what she studies occurs even in the biological sciences. Feminist social work researchers tend to avoid quantitative analysis and experiments. They are rarely rigidly attached to one method; rather, they use multiple methods, often qualitative research and case studies. Gorelick (1991) criticized the affinity of many feminist researchers for interpretive social science. She feels that ISS becomes limited to the consciousness of those being studied and fails to reveal hidden structures. Gorelick wants feminist researchers to adopt a more critical approach and to advocate social change more assertively.

Postmodern social work research is part of the larger postmodern movement or evolving understanding of the contemporary world that includes art, music, literature, and cultural criticism. It began in the humanities and has roots in the philosophies of existentialism, nihilism, and anarchism and in the ideas of Heidegger, Nietzsche, Sartre, and Wittgenstein. Postmodernism is a rejection of modernism. *Modernism* refers to basic assumptions, beliefs, and values that arose in the Enlightenment era. Modernism relies on logical reasoning; it is optimistic about the future and believes in progress, it has confidence in technology and science, and it embraces humanist values (i.e., judging ideas based on their effect on human welfare). Modernism holds that there are standards of beauty, truth, and morality about which most people can agree (Brannigan, 1992).

Postmodern social work research sees no separation between the arts or humanities and social sciences. It shares the critical social work goal of demystifying the social world. It seeks to deconstruct or tear apart surface appearances to reveal the internal hidden structure. Like extreme forms of ISS, postmodernism distrusts abstract explanation and holds that research can never do more than describe, with all descriptions equally valid. A researcher's description is neither superior nor inferior to anyone else's and describes only the researcher's personal experiences. Going beyond interpretive and critical social work, it attempts to radically transform or dismantle social science. Extreme postmodernists reject the possibility of a science of the social world. Postmodernists distrust all systematic empirical observation and doubt that knowledge is generalizable or accumulates over time. They see knowledge as taking numerous forms and as unique to particular people or specific locales. Rosenau (1992:77) argued, "Almost all postmodernists reject truth as even a goal or ideal because it is the very epitome of modernity. . . . Truth makes reference to order, rules, and values; depends on logic, rationality and reason, all of which the postmodernists question."

Postmodernists object to presenting research results in a detached and neutral way. The researcher or author of a report should never be hidden when someone reads it; his or her presence needs to be unambiguously evident in the report. Thus, a postmodern social work research report is similar to a work of art. Its purpose is to stimulate others, to give pleasure, to evoke a response, or to arouse curiosity. Postmodern reports often have a theatrical, expressive, or dramatic style of presentation. They may be in the form of a work of fiction, a movie, or a play. The postmodernist argues that the knowledge about social life created by a researcher may be better communicated through a skit or musical piece than by a scholarly journal article. Its value lies in telling a story that may stimulate experiences within the people who read or encounter it. Postmodernism is antielitist and rejects the use of science to predict and to make policy decisions. Postmodernists oppose those who use positivist science to reinforce power relations and bureaucratic forms of control over people (see Box 4.3).

Box 4.3 _____

Characteristics of Postmodern Social Work Research

- Rejection of all ideologies and organized belief systems, including all social theory
- Strong reliance on intuition, imagination, personal experience, and emotion
- Sense of meaninglessness and pessimism, belief that the world will never improve
- Extreme subjectivity in which there is no distinction between the mental and the external world
- Ardent relativism in which there are infinite interpretations, none superior to another
- Espousal of diversity, chaos, and complexity that is constantly changing
- Rejection of studying the past or different places since only the here and now is relevant
- Belief that causality cannot be studied because life is too complex and rapidly changing
- Assertion that research can never truly represent what occurs in the social world

CONCLUSION

You have learned two basic things in this chapter. First, there are competing approaches to social work research based on different philosophical assumptions about the purpose of science and the nature of social reality. Second, the three ideal-type approaches to social work answer basic questions about research differently (see Table 4.1). Most researchers operate primarily within one approach, but many also combine elements from the others.

Remember that you can study the same topic from any of these approaches, but each approach implies going about it differently. This can be illustrated with the topic of discrimination and job competition between minority and majority groups in four countries: aborigines in the Australian outback, Asians in western Canada, African Americans in the midwestern United States, and Pakistanis in London.

A researcher who adopts a positivist approach first deduces hypotheses from a general theory about majority–minority relations. The theory is probably in the form of causal statements or pre-

dictions. For example, Stone (1985:56) cited one theory that "seeks to explain complex patterns in terms of a few key variables. This can be useful in attempts to predict the possible development of race and ethnic relations." The researcher next gathers data from existing government statistics or conducts a survey to precisely measure the factors that the theory identifies, such as the form of initial contact, the ratio of numbers in majority versus minority groups, or the visibility of racial differences. Finally, the researcher uses statistics to formally test the theory's predictions about the degree of discrimination and the intensity of job competition.

An interpretive researcher personally talks with and observes specific people from both the minority groups and the majority groups in each of the four countries. His or her conversations and observations are used to learn what each group feels to be its major problem and whether group members feel that discrimination or job competition are everyday concerns. The researcher puts what people say into the context of their daily affairs (e.g., paying rent, getting involved in family disputes, having run-ins with the law, getting sick, etc.). After he or she sees what the minority or majority of people think about discrimination, how they get jobs, how people in the other group get jobs, and what they actually do to get or keep jobs, he or she describes findings in terms that others can understand.

A critical social work researcher begins by looking at the larger social and historical context. This includes factors such as the invasion of Australia by British colonists and the nation's history as a prison colony, the economic conditions in Asia that caused people to migrate to Canada, the legacy of slavery and civil rights struggles in the United States, and the rise and fall of Britain's colonial empire and the migration of people from its ex-colonies. He or she inquires from a moral/critical standpoint, "Does the majority group discriminate against and economically exploit the minority?" The researcher looks at many sources to document the underlying pattern of exploitation and to measure the amount of discrimination in each nation. He or she may examine statistical information on income differences between groups, personally ex-

TABLE 4.1   A Summary of Differences Among the Three Approaches to Research

	POSITIVISM	**INTERPRETIVE SOCIAL WORK**	**CRITICAL SOCIAL WORK**
1. Reason for research	To discover natural laws so people can predict and control events	To understand and describe meaningful social action	To smash myths and empower people to radically change society
2. Nature of social reality	Stable preexisting patterns or order that can be discovered	Fluid definitions of a situation created by human interaction	Conflict-filled and governed by hidden underlying structures
3. Nature of human beings	Self-interested and rational individuals who are shaped by external forces	Social beings who create meaning and who constantly make sense of their worlds	Creative, adaptive people with unrealized potential, trapped by illusion and exploitation
4. Role of common sense	Clearly distinct from and less valid than science	Powerful everyday theories used by ordinary people	False beliefs that hide power and objective conditions
5. Theory looks like	A logical, deductive system of interconnected definitions, axioms, and laws	A description of how a group's meaning system is generated and sustained	A critique that reveals true conditions and helps people see the way to a better world
6. An explanation that is true	Is logically connected to laws and based on facts	Resonates or feels right to those who are being studied	Supplies people with tools needed to change the world
7. Good evidence	Is based on precise observations that others can repeat	Is embedded in the context of fluid social interactions	Is informed by a theory that unveils illusions
8. Place for values	Science is value free, and values have no place except when choosing a topic	Values are an integral part of social life: no group's values are wrong, only different	All science must begin with a value position; some positions are right, some are wrong

amine living situations and go with people to job interviews, or conduct surveys to find out what people now think. Once the researcher finds out how discrimination keeps a minority-group from getting jobs, he or she gives results to minority-group organizations, gives public lectures on the findings, and publishes results in newspapers read by minority-group members in order to expose the true conditions and to encourage political–social action.

What does all this about three approaches mean to you in a course on social work research? First, it means that there is no single, absolutely correct approach to social work research. This does not mean

that anything goes, nor that there is no ground for tentative agreement (see Box 4.4). Rather, it means that the basis for doing social work research is not settled. In other words, more than one approach is currently "in the running." Perhaps this will always be the case. An awareness of the approaches will help you when you read research reports. Often, researchers will rely on one of these approaches, but rarely will they tell you which one they are using.

Second, it means that what you try to accomplish when you do research (i.e., discover laws, identify underlying structures, describe meaning systems) will vary with the approach you choose. The fit

Box 4.4

Common Features of the Three Approaches to Research

1. *All are empirical.* Each is rooted in the observable reality of the sights, sounds, behaviors, situations, discussions, and actions of people. Research is never based on fabrication and imagination alone.
2. *All are systematic.* Each emphasizes meticulous and careful work. All reject haphazard, shoddy, or sloppy thinking and observation.
3. *All are theoretical.* The nature of theory varies, but all emphasize using ideas and seeing patterns. None holds that social life is chaos and disorder; all hold that explanation or understanding is possible.
4. *All are public.* All say a researcher's work must be candidly expressed to other researchers; it should be made explicit and shared. All oppose keeping the research processes hidden, private, or secret.
5. *All are self-reflective.* Each approach says researchers need to think about what they do and be

self-conscious. Research is never done in a blind or unthinking manner. It involves serious contemplation and requires self-awareness.
6. *All are open-end processes.* All see research as constantly moving, evolving, changing, asking new questions, and pursuing leads. None see it as static, fixed, or closed. Current knowledge or research procedures are not "set in stone" and settled. They involve continuous change and an openness to new ways of thinking and doing things.

Thus, despite their differences, all the approaches say that social work strives to create systematically gathered, empirically based theoretical knowledge through public processes that are self-reflective and open-ended.

---

among the three approaches and types of research discussed in Chapter 2 is loose. For example, positivists are likely to conduct cost–benefit analysis, interpretive researchers are likely to do exploratory research, and critical researchers favor action-oriented research. By being aware of the approaches when you do social work research, you can make an informed decision about the type of study to conduct.

Third, the various techniques used in social work research (sampling, interviewing, participant observation, etc.) are ultimately based on the assumptions of the different approaches. Often, you will see a research technique presented without the background reasoning on which it was originally

based. By knowing about the approaches, you can better understand the principles on which the specific research techniques are based. For example, the precise measures and logic of experimental research flow directly from positivism, whereas field research is based on an interpretive approach or a more qualitative method to social inquiry.

So far, we have looked at the overall operation of the research process, different types of studies and theory, and the three fundamental approaches to social work research. By now you should have a grasp of the basic contours of social work research. In the next chapter you will see how to locate reports of specific research projects.

KEY TERMS

causal laws	ideographic	nomothetic
critical social science	instrumental orientation	paradigm
determinism	interpretive social science	positivist social science
dialectic	intersubjectivity	postmodern social work
feminist research	meaningful social action	research
hermeneutics	mechanical model of man	postulate of adequacy

practical orientation   relativism   *Verstehen*
praxis   value-free science   voluntarism

REVIEW QUESTIONS

1. What is the purpose of social work research according to each approach?

2. How does each approach define social reality?

3. What is the nature of human beings according to each approach?

4. How are science and common sense different in each approach?

5. What is social work theory according to each approach?

6. How does each approach test a social theory?

7. What does each approach say about facts and how to collect them?

8. How is value-free science possible in each approach? Explain.

9. How are the criticisms of positivism by the interpretive and critical science approaches similar?

10. How does the model of science and the scientific community presented in Chapter 1 relate to each of the three approaches?

NOTES

1. For educational research, see Bredo and Feinberg (1982) and Guba and Lincoln (1994); for psychology, see Harre and Secord (1979) and Rosnow (1981); for political science, see Sabia and Wallulis (1983); and for economics, see Hollis (1977) and Ward (1972). A general discussion of alternatives can be found in Nowotny and Rose (1979).

2. See especially Friedrichs (1970), Giddens (1976), Gouldner (1970), and Phillips (1971). General introductions are provided by Harre (1972), Suppe (1977), and Toulmin (1953).

3. Divisions of the philosophies of social science similar to the approaches discussed in this chapter can be found in Benton (1977), Blaikie (1993), Bloom (1995), Bredo and Feinberg (1982), Dean and Fenby (1989), Fay (1975), Fletcher (1974), Goldstein (1992), Guba and Lincoln (1994), Keat and Urry (1975), Lloyd (1986), Mulkay (1979), Reamer (1993), Sabia and Wallulis (1983), Smart (1976), and Wilson (1970).

4. For discussions of paradigms, see Dorfman (1996), Eckberg and Hill (1979), Hartman (1990), Haworth (1991), Kuhn (1970, 1979), Masterman (1970), Ritzer (1975), Rosnow (1981), and Thyer (1989).

5. In addition to the works listed in note 3, Halfpenny (1982), Smith (1987), Thyer (1993), and Turner (1984) have provided overviews of positivism in sociology. Also see Giddens (1978). Lenzer (1975) is an excellent introduction to Auguste Comte.

6. See Couch (1987). Also see Heineman-Pieper (1985) and Longino (1990:62–82) for an excellent analysis of objectivity in positivist research and more broadly in social science in general.

7. For a discussion, see Bannister (1987), Blumer (1991a, 1991b, 1992), Deegan (1988), Geiger (1986), Gillespie (1991), Lagemann (1989), Ross (1991), Schwendinger and Schwendinger (1974), and Silva and Slaughter (1980).

8. In addition to the works in note 3, interpretive science approaches are discussed in Berger and Luckman (1967), Bleicher (1980), Carpenter (1996), Cicourel (1973), Garfinkel (1967, 1974b), Geertz (1979), Glaser and Strauss (1967), Heineman-Pieper (1989), Holstein and Gubrium (1994), Leiter (1980), Mehan and Wood (1975), Silverman (1972), and Weber (1974, 1981).

9. In addition to the works in note 3, critical science approaches are discussed in Burawoy (1990), Cowger (1994), DeJong and Miller (1995), DePoy, Hartman, and Haslett (1999), Dickson (1984), Fay (1987), Fook (1993), Glucksmann (1974), Harding (1986), Harvey (1990), Keat (1981), Lane (1970), Lee (1994), Lemert (1981), Mayhew (1980, 1981), Rodwell (1998), Saleebey (1997), Sohn-

Rethel (1978), Veltmeyer (1978), Wardell (1979), Warner (1971), and Wilson (1982).

10. For a discussion of the Frankfurt School, see Bottomore (1984), Held (1980), Martin (1973), and Slater (1977). For more on the works of Habermas, see Holub (1991), McCarthy (1978), Pusey (1987), and Roderick (1986).

11. For discussions of realism, see Bhaskar (1975), Miller (1987), and Sayer (1992).

12. See Sprague and Zimmerman (1989) on feminists' privileged perspectives of women and Swigonski (1994), Collins (1986), and Davis and Marsh (1994) on the importance of integrating feminist perspectives into research on social work practice. The relationship between postmodernism and research is discussed by Chambron and Irving (1994), Lather (1991), Leonard (1997), and Meinert (1998); and see Rule (1978a, 1978b) on constituencies that researchers favor.

13. See Habermas (1971, 1973, 1979) for a critical science critique of positivism as being technocratic and used for domination. He has suggested an emancipatory alternative. Also see note 10.

14. See Evelyn Fox Keller's (1983) biography of Barbara McClintock and her other essays on gender and science (1985, 1990). Also see Davis (1985) and Longino (1990), Chapters 6 and 7.

CHAPTER 5

THE ETHICS AND POLITICS
OF SOCIAL WORK RESEARCH

*Many of the most important ethical debates will not be settled easily,
if at all; we firmly believe, however, that there is something of value in
encouraging professionals to distinguish between the ethical and
nonethical dimensions of their work.*

—F. Reamer & M. Abranson, p. 53.

INTRODUCTION

Thus far, you have learned about the foundations of science, different kinds of social work research, the place of theory, and alternative approaches to social work research. Before examining the details of study design, you need first to look at the relationship between the research process and morals, values, and politics. These are integral to the research process. In the preceding chapter you saw that different approaches to research treat values differently, but even the most value-free positivist recognizes that there is an ethical aspect to doing research on human beings. Although it is difficult to appreciate ethical dilemmas until doing research, one needs to consider moral–ethical issues before and while designing a study and collecting data.

The social work researcher faces many ethical dilemmas and must decide how to act. Codes of ethics (see Appendix A for the NASW Code of Ethics) and other researchers provide guidance, but ethical conduct ultimately depends on the individual researcher. The researcher has a moral and professional obligation to be ethical, even when research subjects are unaware of, or unconcerned about, ethics. Indeed, many subjects are less concerned about protecting their privacy and other rights than are researchers.[1]

The ethical issues are the concerns, dilemmas, and conflicts that arise over the proper way to conduct research. Ethics define what is or is not legitimate to do, or what "moral" research procedure involves. There are few ethical absolutes. Although there are few fixed rules, there are agreed-upon principles. These principles may conflict in practice. Many ethical issues involve a balance between two values: the pursuit of scientific knowledge and the rights of those being studied or of others in society. Potential benefits—such as advancing our understanding of social life, improving decision making, or helping research participants—must be weighed against such potential costs as a loss of dignity, self-esteem, privacy, or democratic freedoms.

The standards for ethical social work research are stricter than those in many other areas (e.g., collection agencies, police departments, advertisers, etc.). Professional social work research requires both knowledge of proper research techniques (e.g., sampling) and sensitivity to ethical concerns in research. This is not easy. As Gillespie (1999) observed, "Each decision made in research involves a potential compromise on one value for another. Researchers must try to minimize risk to participants, colleagues, and society while attempting to maximize the quality of information they produce" (p. 884).

ETHICS AND THE RESEARCHER

The Individual Researcher

Ethics begin and end with you, the researcher. A researcher's personal moral code is the best defense against unethical behavior. Before, during, and after conducting a study, a researcher has opportunities to, and *should,* reflect on research actions and consult his or her conscience. Ethical social work research depends on the integrity of the individual researcher and his or her values.

Why Be Ethical?

Given that most people who conduct social work research are genuinely concerned about others, why would a researcher act in an ethically irresponsible manner? Outside of the rare disturbed individual, most unethical behavior results from a lack of awareness and from pressures on researchers to take ethical shortcuts. Researchers face pressures to build a career, publish, advance knowledge, gain prestige, impress family and friends, hold on to a job, and so forth. Ethical social work research takes longer to complete, costs more money, is more complicated, and is more likely to be terminated before completion. Moreover, written ethical standards are in the form of vague principles. There are many places where it is possible to act unethically, and the odds of getting caught are small.

There are few rewards available for ethical social work research. The unethical researcher, if caught, faces public humiliation, a ruined career, and possible legal action, but the ethical social work researcher wins no praise. Ethical behavior arises from a sensitivity to ethical concerns that researchers internalize during their professional training, from a professional role, and from personal contact with other researchers. Moreover, the norms of the scientific community reinforce ethical behavior with an emphasis on honesty and openness.

Researchers who are oriented toward their professional role, who are committed to the scientific ethos, and who interact regularly with other researchers are likely to act ethically.

Scientific Misconduct.   The research community and agencies that fund research oppose unethical behavior called scientific misconduct, which includes research fraud and plagiarism. *Scientific misconduct* occurs when a researcher falsifies or distorts the data or the methods of data collection, or plagiarizes the work of others. It also includes significant departures from the generally accepted practices of the scientific community for doing or reporting on research. Research institutes and universities have policies and procedures to detect misconduct, report it to the scientific community and funding agencies, and penalize researchers who engage in it (e.g., through a pay cut or loss of job).

Research fraud occurs when a researcher fakes or invents data that were not really collected, or falsely reports how research was conducted. Though rare, it is treated very seriously. The most famous case of fraud was that of Sir Cyril Burt, the father of British educational psychology. Burt died in 1971 as an esteemed researcher who was famous for his studies with twins that showed a genetic basis of intelligence. In 1976, it was discovered that he had falsified data and the names of coauthors. Unfortunately, the scientific community had been misled for nearly 30 years.[2]

Plagiarism is fraud that occurs when a researcher steals the ideas or writings of another or uses them without citing the source. A special type of plagiarism is stealing the work of another researcher, an assistant, or a student, and misrepresenting it as one's own. These are serious breaches of ethical standards.[3]

Unethical but Legal.   Behavior may be unethical but not break the law. The distinction between legal and ethical behavior is illustrated in a plagiarism case. The American Sociological Association documented that a 1988 book without footnotes by a dean from Eastern New Mexico University contained large sections of a 1978 dissertation written by a sociology professor at Tufts University. The copying was not *illegal;* it did not violate copyright law because the sociologist's dissertation did not have a copyright filed with the U.S. government. Nevertheless, it was clearly *unethical* according to standards of professional behavior.[4] (See Figure 5.1 for relations between legal and moral actions.)

Power

The relationship between the researcher and subjects or employee-assistants involves power and trust. The experimenter, survey director, or research investigator has power relative to subjects or assistants. The power is legitimated by credentials, expertise, training, and the role of science in modern society. Some ethical issues involve an abuse of power and trust.

The researcher's authority to conduct research, granted by professional communities and the larger society, is accompanied by a responsibility to guide, protect, and oversee the interests of the people being studied. For example, a physician was discovered to have conducted experimental gynecological surgery on 33 women without their permission. The women had trusted the doctor, but he had abused the trust that the women, the professional community, and society placed in him.[5]

The researcher seeking ethical guidance is not alone. He or she can turn to a number of resources: professional colleagues, ethical advisory

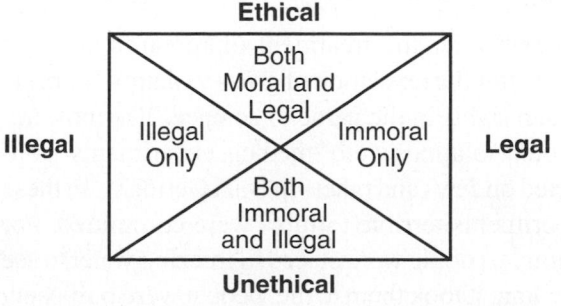

FIGURE 5.1   Typology of Legal and Moral Actions in Research

committees, institutional review boards or human subjects committees at a college or institution, codes of ethics from professional associations, and writings on ethics in research.

ETHICAL ISSUES INVOLVING RESEARCH SUBJECTS

Have you ever been a subject in a research study? If so, how were you treated? More attention is focused on the possible negative effects of research on those being studied than any other ethical issue, beginning with concerns about biomedical research. Ethical research requires balancing the value of advancing knowledge against the value of noninterference in the lives of others. Giving research subjects absolute rights of noninterference could make empirical research impossible, but giving researchers absolute rights of inquiry could nullify subjects' basic human rights. The moral question becomes, "When, if ever, are researchers justified in risking physical harm or injury to those being studied, causing them great embarrassment, or frightening them?"

The law and codes of ethics recognize some clear prohibitions: Never cause unnecessary or irreversible harm to subjects; secure prior voluntary consent when possible; and never unnecessarily humiliate, degrade, or release harmful information about specific individuals that was collected for research purposes. These are minimal standards and are subject to interpretation (e.g., What does *unnecessary* mean in a specific situation?).

Origins of Human Subject Protection

Concern over the treatment of research subjects arose after the revelation of gross violations of basic human rights in the name of science. The most notorious violations were "medical experiments" conducted on Jews and others in Nazi Germany. In these experiments terrible tortures were committed. For example, people were placed in freezing water to see how long it took them to die, people were purposely starved to death, and limbs were severed from children and transplanted onto others.[6]

Such human rights violations did not occur only in Germany, nor did they happen only long ago. A symbol of unethical research is the Tuskegee Syphilis Study, also known as *Bad Blood.* Until the 1970s, when a newspaper report caused a scandal to erupt, the U.S. Public Health Service sponsored a study in which poor, uneducated African American men in Alabama suffered and died of untreated syphilis, while researchers studied the severe physical disabilities that appear in advanced stages of the disease. The study began in 1929, before penicillin was available to treat the disease, but it continued long after treatment was available. Despite their unethical treatment of the subjects, the researchers were able to publish their results for 40 years. The study ended in 1972, but the president of the United States did not admit wrongdoing and formally apologize to the subject-victims until 1997.[7]

Unfortunately, the Bad Blood scandal is not unique. During the Cold War era, the U.S. government periodically compromised ethical research principles for military and political goals. In 1995 reports revealed that the government authorized injecting unknowing people with radioactive material in the late 1940s. In the 1950s the government warned Eastman Kodak and other film manufacturers about nuclear fallout from atomic tests to prevent fogged film, but it did not warn nearby citizens of health hazards. In the 1960s the U.S. army gave unsuspecting soldiers LSD (a hallucinogenic drug), causing serious trauma. Today these are widely recognized to be violations of two fundamental ethical principles: avoid physical harm and get informed consent.[8]

Physical Harm, Psychological Abuse, and Legal Jeopardy

Social work research can harm a research subject in several ways: physical harm, psychological harm, legal harm, and harm to a person's career or income. Physical harm is rare, even in biomedical research, where the intervention is much greater; 3 to 5 percent of studies involved any subject who suffered any harm. Different types of harm are more likely in different types of research (e.g., in experiments versus field research). Researchers need to be aware of all types of harm and minimize them at all times.[9]

Physical Harm.   A straightforward ethical principle is that researchers should not cause physical harm. An ethical researcher anticipates risks before beginning research, including basic safety concerns (safe buildings, furniture, and equipment). He or she screens out high-risk subjects (those with heart conditions, mental breakdown, or seizures) if stress is involved and anticipates the danger of injury or physical attacks on research

subjects or assistants. The researcher accepts moral and legal responsibility for injury due to participation in research and terminates a project immediately if he or she can no longer guarantee the physical safety of the people involved (see the Zimbardo study in Box 5.1).

Psychological Abuse, Stress, or Loss of Self-Esteem. The risk of physical harm is rare, but researchers

---

Box 5.1 _____

Three Cases of Ethical Controversy

Stanley *Milgram's obedience study* (Milgram, 1963, 1965, 1974) attempted to discover how the horrors of the Holocaust under the Nazis could have occurred by examining the strength of social pressure to obey authority. After signing "informed consent forms," subjects were assigned, in rigged random selection, to be a "teacher" while a confederate was the "pupil." The teacher was to test the pupil's memory of word lists and increase the electric shock level if the pupil made mistakes. The pupil was located in a nearby room, so the teacher could hear but not see the pupil. The shock apparatus was clearly labeled with increasing voltage. As the pupil made mistakes and the teacher turned switches, the pupil also made noises as if in severe pain. The researcher was present and made comments such as "You must go on" to the teacher. Milgram reported, "Subjects were observed to sweat, tremble, stutter, bite their lips, groan and dig their fingernails into their flesh. These were characteristic rather than exceptional responses to the experiment" (Milgram, 1963:375). The percentage of subjects who would shock to dangerous levels was dramatically higher than expected. Ethical concerns arose over the use of deception and the extreme emotional stress experienced by subjects.

In Laud Humphreys's (Humphreys, 1975) *Tearoom Trade study* (a study of male homosexual encounters in public restrooms), about 100 men were observed engaging in sexual acts as Humphreys pretended to be a "watchqueen" (a voyeur and lookout). Subjects were followed to their cars, and their license numbers were secretly recorded. Names and addresses were obtained from police registers when Humphreys posed as a market researcher. One year later, in dis-

guise, Humphreys used a deceptive story about a health survey to interview the subjects in their homes. Humphreys was careful to keep names in safety deposit boxes, and identifiers with subject names were burned. He significantly advanced knowledge of homosexuals who frequent "tearooms" and overturned previous false beliefs about them. There has been controversy over the study: The subjects never consented; deception was used; and the names could have been used to blackmail subjects, to end marriages, or to initiate criminal prosecution.

In the *Zimbardo prison experiment* (Zimbardo, 1972, 1973; Zimbardo et al., 1973, 1974), male students were divided into two role-playing groups: guards and prisoners. Before the experiment, volunteer students were given personality tests, and only those in the "normal" range were chosen. Volunteers signed up for two weeks, and prisoners were told that they would be under surveillance and would have some civil rights suspended, but that no physical abuse was allowed. In a simulated prison in the basement of a Stanford University building, prisoners were deindividualized (dressed in standard uniforms and called only by their numbers) and guards were militarized (with uniforms, nightsticks, and reflective sunglasses). Guards were told to maintain a reasonable degree of order and served 8-hour shifts, while prisoners were locked up 24 hours per day. Unexpectedly, the volunteers became too caught up in their roles. Prisoners became passive and disorganized, while guards became aggressive, arbitrary, and dehumanizing. By the sixth day, Zimbardo called off the experiment for ethical reasons. The risk of permanent psychological harm, and even physical harm, was too great.

may place people in stressful, embarrassing, anxiety-producing, or unpleasant situations. Researchers learn about how people respond in real-life, highly anxiety-producing situations by placing subjects in realistic situations of psychological discomfort or stress. Is it unethical to cause discomfort? The ethics of the famous Milgram obedience study are still debated (see Box 5.1). Some say that the precautions taken and the knowledge gained outweighed the stress and potential psychological harm that subjects experienced. Others believe that the extreme stress and the risk of permanent harm were too great.

Social work researchers have created high levels of anxiety or discomfort: exposing subjects to gruesome photos; falsely telling male students that they have strongly feminine personality traits; falsely telling students that they have failed; creating a situation of high fear (e.g., smoke entering a room in which the door is locked); asking subjects to harm others; placing people in a situation where they face social pressure to deny their convictions; and having subjects lie, cheat, or steal.[10] Researchers who study helping behavior often place subjects in emergency situations to see whether the subjects will lend assistance. For example, Piliavin and associates (1969) studied helping behavior in subways by faking someone's collapse onto the floor. In the field experiment the riders in the subway car were unaware of the experiment and did not volunteer to participate in it.

A sensitive social work researcher is also aware of harm to a subject's self-esteem. For example, Walster (1965) wanted to see whether changes in feelings of female self-worth affect romantic liking. In her experiment undergraduate women were given personality tests followed by phony feedback. Some subjects were told that they lacked imagination and creativity. Next, a handsome male graduate student who pretended to be another subject struck up a conversation with the women. The student acted very interested in one woman and asked her out for a dinner date. The researcher wanted to measure the woman's romantic attraction to the male. After the experiment, the subject was told of the hoax; there was no date and the man was not interested in her. Although the subjects

were debriefed, they suffered a loss of self-esteem and possible psychological harm.[11]

Only experienced researchers who take precautions before inducing anxiety or discomfort should consider conducting experiments that induce significant stress or anxiety. They should consult with others who have conducted similar studies and with mental health professionals when planning the study, screen out high-risk populations (e.g., those with emotional problems or a weak heart), and arrange for emergency interventions or termination of the research if dangerous situations arise. Researchers should always get informed consent (to be discussed) before the research and should debrief subjects immediately afterward.

Researchers should never create *unnecessary* stress, beyond the minimal amount needed to create the desired effect, or stress that has no direct, legitimate research purpose. Knowing the minimal amount comes with experience. It is better to begin with too little stress, risking finding no effect, than to create too much. If the level of stress could have long-term effects, the researcher should follow up and offer free psychological counseling.

Research that creates stress and anxiety also carries the danger that experimenters will develop a callous or manipulative attitude toward others. Researchers report guilt and regrets after conducting experiments that caused psychological harm to subjects. Experiments that place subjects in anxiety-producing situations may produce discomfort for the ethical social work researcher.

Legal Harm.   A researcher is responsible for protecting subjects from increased risk of arrest. If participation in research increases the risk of arrest, subjects will distrust researchers and be unwilling to participate in future research. Researchers may be able to secure clearance from law enforcement authorities before conducting certain types of research. For example, the U.S. Department of Justice provides written waivers for researchers studying criminal behavior.

Potential legal harm is one criticism of the 1975 study by Humphreys (see Box 5.1). In the New Jersey Negative Income Tax Experiment, those participating in the experiment received income supplements, but no explicit provision was made for monitoring whether they also received welfare checks. A local prosecuting attorney requested data on participants to identify "welfare cheats." In other words, subjects were at legal risk because they had participated in the experiment. Eventually, the conflict was resolved, but it illustrates that researchers should be aware of potential legal problems.

A related ethical issue arises when a researcher learns of illegal activity when collecting data. A researcher must weigh the value of protecting the researcher/subject relationship and the benefits to future researchers against potential harm to innocent people. A researcher bears the cost of his or her judgment. For example, in his field research on police, Van Maanen (1982:114–115) reported seeing police beat people and witnessed illegal acts and irregular procedures, but said, "On and following these troublesome incidents . . . I followed police custom: I kept my mouth shut."

Field researchers often face difficult ethical decisions. For example, when studying a psychiatric hospital, Taylor (1987) discovered the mistreatment and abuse of inmates by the staff. He had two choices: Abandon the study and call for an investigation, or keep quiet and continue with the study for several months, publicize the findings afterwards, and then advocate an end to abuse. After weighing the situation, he followed the latter course and is now an activist for the rights of mental institution inmates.

A similar ethical dilemma is illustrated by the case of a New York restaurant fire that was complicated by the issue of confidentiality. A sociology graduate student was conducting a participant observation study of waiters. During the research project, the field site, a restaurant, burned down, and arson was suspected. Local legal authorities requested the field notes and wanted to interrogate the researcher about activity in the restaurant. The researcher faced a dilemma: He could cooperate with the investigation and violate the trust, confidentiality, and integrity of ethical research, or he could uphold confidentiality and protect his subjects but face contempt of court and obstruction of justice penalties, including fines and jail. He wanted to behave ethically but he also wanted to stay out of jail. After

years of legal battles, the situation was resolved with limited cooperation by the researcher and a judicial ruling upholding the confidentiality of field notes. Nevertheless, the issue took years to resolve, and the researcher bore substantial financial and personal costs.[12]

Observing illegal behavior may be central to a research project. A researcher who covertly observes and records illegal behavior, then supplies information to law enforcement authorities, violates ethical standards regarding research subjects and undermines future research. Yet, a researcher who fails to report illegal behavior indirectly permits criminal behavior and could be charged as an accessory to a crime. Is the researcher a professional seeking knowledge or a freelance undercover informant?

Other Harm to Subjects.   Research subjects may face other types of harm. For example, a survey interview may create anxiety and discomfort among subjects who are asked to recall unpleasant events. The ethical social work researcher is sensitive to any harm to subjects, considers possible precautions, and weighs potential harm against potential benefits. Another risk of harm to subjects is that of a negative effect on their careers or incomes. For example, a researcher conducts a survey of employees and concludes that the supervisor's performance is poor. As a consequence, the supervisor loses her job. Or a researcher studies welfare recipients. As a consequence, the recipients lose their health insurance and their quality of life declines. What is the researcher's responsibility? The ethical social work researcher considers the consequences of research for those being studied. But there is no fixed answer to such questions. A researcher must evaluate each case, weigh potential harm against potential benefits, and bear the responsibility for the decision.

Deception

Has anyone ever told you a half-truth or lie to get you to do something? How did you feel about it? Social work researchers follow the ethical *principle of voluntary consent:* Never force anyone to participate in research, and do not lie. The people who participate in social work research should explicitly agree to participate. The right of a person not to participate becomes a critical issue whenever the researcher uses deception, disguises the research, or uses covert research methods.[13]

Social work researchers sometimes have deceived or lied to subjects in field and experimental research. A researcher might misrepresent his or her actions or true intentions for legitimate methodological reasons: If subjects knew the true purpose, they would modify their behavior, making it impossible to learn of their real behavior; or access to a research site might be impossible if he or she told the truth. Deception is never acceptable if the researcher could accomplish the same thing without deception.

Experimental researchers sometimes deceive subjects to prevent them from learning the true hypothesis and to reduce reactive effects. Researchers who feel they must use deception should first submit their research proposal and plan for managing deception to an *institutional review board (IRB)* or human subjects review panel. One strategy that researchers may propose to an IRB is to withhold initial disclosure of the deception by asking to conceal only a very limited procedure or piece of information temporarily. In addition, subjects should be informed that full disclosure will be forthcoming as soon as possible after the procedure has been completed. Subjects need to know in advance that something is being withheld and that they will have the opportunity to withdraw if desired and not have their data included in the planned analysis. They also have the right to be completely debriefed, or told why full disclosure was withheld.

Covert observation may be required in some field research settings to gain entry and access. If a covert stance is not essential, a researcher should never use it. If he or she does not know whether covert access is necessary, then a strategy of gradual disclosure may be best. It is better to err in the direction of disclosing one's true identity and purpose. In some situations—such as the study of cults, small extremist political sects, illegal behavior, or behavior in a large public area—it may be impossible to conduct research if a researcher discloses her or his true purpose. Researchers have studied satanic cults, UFO cults, and homosexual contacts in public restrooms with covert observation. Covert research

remains controversial, and some researchers feel that all covert research is unethical.[14] The code of ethics of the American Anthropological Association condemns it as "impractical and undesirable." Even those who accept covert research as ethical in some situations argue that it should be used only when overt observation is impossible. In addition, if possible, the researcher should inform subjects of the observation afterwards and give them an opportunity to express concerns.

Deception and covert research may increase mistrust and cynicism, and diminish public respect for social work research. Misrepresentation in field research is analogous to being an undercover agent or informer in nondemocratic societies. Deception can increase distrust by people who are frequently studied. In one case the frequent use of deception reduced helping behavior. When a student was shot at the University of Washington in Seattle in 1973, students crossing the campus made no attempt to assist. Later, it was discovered that many of the bystanders did not help because they thought that the shooting was staged as part of an experiment.[15]

Informed Consent

A fundamental ethical principle of social work research is: Never coerce anyone into participating; participation *must* be voluntary. It is not enough to get permission from subjects; they need to know what they are being asked to participate in so that they can make an informed decision. Subjects can become aware of their rights and what they are getting involved in when they read and sign a statement giving *informed consent,* a written agreement to participate given by subjects after they learn something about the research procedure.

The U.S. federal government does not require informed consent in all research involving human subjects. Nevertheless, researchers should get written consent unless there are good reasons for not obtaining it (e.g., covert field research, use of secondary data, etc.) as judged by an institutional review board (see the later discussion of IRBs and sample IRB proposal in Appendix F).

Informed consent statements provide specific information (see Box 5.2).[16] A general statement

Box 5.2 _____

Informed Consent

Informed consent statements contain the following:

1. A brief description of the purpose and procedure of the research, including the expected duration of the study
2. A statement of any risks or discomfort associated with participation
3. A guarantee of anonymity and the confidentiality of records
4. The identification of the researcher and of where to receive information about subjects' rights or questions about the study
5. A statement that participation is completely voluntary and can be terminated at any time without penalty
6. A statement of alternative procedures that may be used
7. A statement of any benefits or compensation provided to subjects and the number of subjects involved
8. An offer to provide a summary of findings

---

about the kinds of procedures or questions involved and the uses of the data are sufficient for informed consent. In a study by Singer (1978), one random group of survey respondents received a detailed informed consent statement and another did not. No significant differences were discovered. If anything, people who refused to sign such a statement were more likely to guess or answer "no response" to questions.

In their analysis of the literature, Singer and colleagues (1995) found that assuring confidentiality modestly improved responses when researchers asked about highly sensitive topics. In other situations extensive assurances of confidentiality failed to affect how or whether subjects responded.

Full disclosure with the researcher's identification helps protect subjects against fraudulent research, and also protects legitimate researchers. Informed consent lessens the chance that a con artist in the guise of a researcher will defraud or abuse subjects, and it reduces the likelihood of the bogus

use of a researcher's identity to market products or obtain information for personal advantage.

Signed informed consent statements are optional for most survey, field, and secondary data research, but are often mandated for experimental research. They are impossible to obtain in documentary research and in most telephone interview studies. The general rule is: The greater the risk of potential harm to subjects, the greater the need for a written consent statement. In sum, there are many reasons to get informed consent and few reasons not to get it.

Special Populations and New Inequalities

Special Populations and Coercion.   Some populations or groups are not capable of giving true voluntary informed consent. They may lack the necessary competency or may be indirectly coerced. Students, prison inmates, employees, military personnel, the homeless, welfare recipients, children, or the developmentally delayed may agree to participate in research. Yet, they may not be fully capable of making a decision, or may agree to participate only because some desired good—such as higher grades, early parole, promotions, or additional services—requires an agreement to participate.

It is unethical to involve "incompetent" people (e.g., children, mentally disabled, etc.) in research unless two conditions are met: A legal guardian grants written permission, and the researcher follows all ethical principles against harm to subjects. For example, a social work researcher wants to conduct a survey of smoking and drug/alcohol use among high school students. If it is conducted on school property, school officials must give permission, and written parental permission is needed for any subject who is a legal minor. It is best to ask permission from each student, as well.

It is unethical to coerce people to participate, including offering them special benefits that they cannot otherwise attain. For example, it is unethical for a commanding officer to order a soldier to participate in a study, for a professor to require a student to be a research subject in order to pass a course, or for an employer to expect an employee to complete a survey as a condition of continued employment. It is unethical even if someone other than the researcher (e.g., an employer) coerced people (e.g., employees) to participate in research.

Whether coercion to participate is involved can be a complex issue, and a social work researcher or an IRB must evaluate each case. For example, a convicted criminal is given the alternative of imprisonment or participation in an experimental rehabilitation program. The convicted criminal may not believe in the benefits of the program, but the researcher may believe that it will help the criminal. This is a case of coercion, but the researcher must judge whether the benefits to the subject and to society outweigh the ethical prohibition on coercion.

Teachers sometimes require students in social science courses to participate as subjects in research projects. This is a special case of coercion. Three arguments have been made in favor of requiring participation: (1) it would be difficult and prohibitively expensive to get subjects otherwise; (2) the knowledge created from research with students serving as subjects will benefit future students and society; (3) students will learn more about research by experiencing it directly in a realistic research setting. Of the three arguments, only the third justifies limited coercion. Limited coercion is acceptable only as long as it has a clear educational objective, the students are given a choice of research experience, and other ethical principles are upheld.[17]

Creating New Inequalities. Another type of harm occurs when one group of subjects is denied a service or benefit as a result of participation in a research project. For example, a researcher might have a new treatment for subjects with a terrible disease, such as acquired immune deficiency syndrome (AIDS). In order to determine the effects of the new treatment, some subjects receive it while others are given a placebo. The design will show whether the drug is effective, but subjects in the control group who receive the placebo may die. Of course, those receiving the drug may also die, until more is known about whether it is effective. Is it ethical to deny subjects who have been randomly assigned to the control group the potentially life-saving treatment? What if a clear, definitive test of whether the drug is effective requires a control group that receives a placebo?

A researcher can reduce new inequality among subjects in three ways. First, subjects who do not receive the "new, improved" treatment continue to receive the best previously acceptable treatment. In other words, the control group is not denied all assistance, but they receive the best treatment available prior to the new one being tested. This ensures that subjects in the control group will not suffer in absolute terms, even if they temporarily fall behind in relative terms. Second, researchers can use *crossover designs,* whereby the control group for the first phase of the experiment becomes the experimental group in the second phase, and vice versa. Finally, the researcher carefully and continuously monitors results. If it appears early in the experiment that the new treatment is highly effective, the new treatment should be offered to control group subjects. Also, in high-risk experiments with medical treatments or possible physical harm, researchers may use animal or other surrogates for humans.

Privacy, Anonymity, and Confidentiality

How would you feel if private details about your personal life were shared with the public without your knowledge? Because social work researchers transgress the privacy of subjects in order to study social behavior, they must take precautions to protect subjects' privacy.

Privacy. Survey researchers invade a person's privacy when they probe into beliefs, backgrounds, and behaviors in a way that reveals intimate private details. Experimental researchers sometimes use two-way mirrors or hidden microphones to "spy" on subjects. Even if subjects are told they are being studied, they are unaware of what the experimenter is looking for. Field researchers may observe very private aspects of another's behavior or eavesdrop on conversations. In field experimentation and ethnographic field research, privacy may be violated without advance warning. When Humphreys (1975) served as a "watchqueen" in a public restroom where homosexual contacts took place, he observed very private behavior without informing subjects. When Piliavin and colleagues (1969) had people collapse on subways to study helping behavior, those in the subway car had the privacy of their ride violated. People have been studied in public places (e.g., in waiting rooms, walking down the street, in classrooms, etc.), but some "public" places are more private than others (consider, for example, the use of periscopes to observe people who thought they were alone in a public toilet stall).[18]

Eavesdropping on conversations and observing people in quasi-private areas raises ethical concerns. The ethical social work researcher violates privacy only to the minimum degree necessary and only for legitimate research purposes. In addition, he or she protects the information on research subjects from public disclosure.

In a few situations privacy is protected by law. One case of the invasion of privacy led to the passage of a federal law. In the *Wichita Jury Study* of 1954, University of Chicago Law School researchers recorded jury discussions to examine group processes in jury deliberations. Although the findings were significant and great precautions were taken, a congressional investigation followed and a law was passed in 1956 to prohibit the "bugging" of any grand or petit jury for any purpose, even with the jurors' consent.[19]

Anonymity.   Researchers protect privacy by not disclosing a subject's identity after information is gathered. This takes two forms, both of which require separating an individual's identity from his or her responses: anonymity and confidentiality.

Anonymity means that subjects remain anonymous or nameless. For example, a field researcher provides a social picture of a particular individual, but gives a fictitious name and location, and alters some characteristics. The subject's identity is protected, and the individual is unknown or anonymous. Survey and experimental researchers discard the names or addresses of subjects as soon as possible and refer to subjects by a code number only, to protect anonymity. If a researcher using a mail survey includes a code on the questionnaire to determine which respondents failed to respond, the respondent's anonymity is not being fully protected.

In panel studies, where the same individuals are traced over time, anonymity is not possible. Likewise, historical researchers use specific names in historical or documentary research. They may do so if the original information was from public sources; if the sources were not publicly available, a researcher must obtain written permission from the owner of the documents to use specific names.

It is difficult to protect subject anonymity. In one study about a fictitious town, "Springdale," in *Small Town in Mass Society* (Vidich and Bensman, 1968), it was easy to identify the town and specific individuals in it. Town residents became upset about how the researchers portrayed them and staged a parade mocking the researchers. As in the famous Middletown study of Muncie, Indiana, people often recognize the towns studied in community research. Yet, if a researcher protects the identities of individuals with fictitious information, the gap between what was studied and what is reported to others raises questions about what was found and what was made up. A researcher may unknowingly breach a promise of anonymity in small samples. For example, let us say you conduct a survey of 100 college students and ask many questions on a questionnaire, including age, sex, religion, and hometown. The sample contains one 22-year-old Jewish male born in Stratford, Ontario. With this information, you could find out who the specific individual is and how he answered very personal questions, even though his name was not directly recorded on the questionnaire.

Confidentiality.   Even if anonymity is not possible, researchers should protect confidentiality. Anonymity protects the identity of specific individuals from being known. *Confidentiality* means that information may have names attached to it, but the researcher holds it in confidence or keeps it secret from the public. The information is not released in a way that permits linking specific individuals to responses and is publicly presented only in an aggregate form (e.g., percentages, means, etc.).

A researcher may provide anonymity without confidentiality, or vice versa, although they usually go together. Anonymity without confidentiality means that all the details about a specific individual are made public, but the individual's name is withheld. Confidentiality without anonymity means that information is not made public, but a researcher privately links individual names to specific responses.

Attempts to protect the identity of subjects from public disclosure has resulted in elaborate procedures: eliciting anonymous responses, using a third-party list custodian who holds the key to coded lists, or using the random-response technique. Past abuses suggest that such measures may be necessary. For example, Diener and Crandall (1978:70) reported that during the 1950s, the U.S. State Department and the FBI requested research records on individuals who had been involved in the famous Kinsey sex study. The Kinsey Sex Institute refused to comply with the government. The institute threatened to destroy all records rather than release any. Eventually, the government agencies backed down. The moral duty and ethical code of the researchers obligated them to destroy the records rather than give them to government officials. As Nelkin (1982b:705) remarked, "The right of researchers to protect their subjects is especially vulnerable when it conflicts with political or policy goals."

Confidentiality may protect people from physical harm. For example, one of the authors met a researcher who studied the inner workings of the secret police in a nondemocratic society. Had he released the names of informants, they would have faced certain death or imprisonment. To protect the subjects, he wrote all notes in code and kept all records secretly locked away. Although he resided in the United States, he was physically threatened by the foreign government and discovered attempts to burglarize his office. In other situations, other principles may take precedence over protecting confidentiality. For example, when studying patients in a mental hospital, a researcher discovers that a patient is preparing to kill an attendant. The researcher must weigh the benefit of confidentiality against the potential harm to the attendant.

In 1989 the U.S. government established a way to protect confidentiality. A researcher can apply for a *certificate of confidentiality,* issued by the U.S. National Institute of Health, by submitting a research proposal. The certificate guarantees the confidentiality of data on subjects from federal, state, or local government criminal or civil legal action. The research data are protected whether or not federal government funds were used to support the project. Unfortunately, the certificate protects the data on subjects, but it does not protect the researcher from legal action.

A special concern with anonymity and confidentiality arises when a researcher studies "captive" populations (e.g., students, prisoners, employees, patients, and soldiers). Gatekeepers, or those in positions of authority, may restrict access unless they receive information on subjects.[20] For example, a researcher studies drug use and sexual activity among high school students. School authorities agree to cooperate under two conditions: (1) students need parental permission to participate and (2) school officials get the names of all drug users and sexually active students in order to assist the students with counseling and inform the students' parents. An ethical social work researcher will refuse to continue rather than meet the second condition.

Subject Information as Private Property

If you freely give information about yourself for research purposes, do you lose all rights to it? Can it be used against you? People who participate in research have knowledge about them taken away and analyzed by others. The information can then be used for a number of purposes, including actions against the subject's interests.

An information industry exists in which information about people is collected, bought, sold, analyzed, and exchanged by large organizations. Information about buying habits, personal taste, spending patterns, credit ratings, voting patterns, and the like is used by many private and public organizations. Information is a form of private property. Like other "intellectual" property (copyrights, software, patents, etc.) and unlike most physical property, information continues to have value after it is exchanged.

Most people do not consider information about themselves to be their property; they freely give it away. They give a researcher their time and information for little or no compensation. Yet, concerns about privacy and the collection of more information make it reasonable to see personal information as private property. If it is private property, a subject's right to keep, sell, or give it away becomes clear. The ethical issue is strongest where the information is used against subjects or used in ways they would disapprove of if they were fully informed.

This issue is relevant for the information collected by private businesses. For example, we have filled out many forms giving information on our financial situation, health history, marital status, living habits, and the like. Others use and exchange this information; it can be used to grant or deny us a loan, refuse or grant us health insurance, permit or disallow us to rent an apartment, refuse or permit us to take a job, and target or exclude us from sales promotions and special discounts. We no longer control the information or its use. It affects us directly and is someone else's private property. For example, a group of committed nonsmokers is studied to learn about their habits and psychological profiles. A market research firm obtains the information and is hired by a tobacco company to design a campaign to promote smoking among nonsmokers. Had the nonsmokers been informed about the use of their responses, they might have chosen not to participate. A researcher can increase fairness by giving subjects a copy of the findings and—in an informed consent statement—describing the sponsor and the uses to which the information will be put.

The issue of who controls data on research subjects is relevant to the approaches to social work outlined in Chapter 4. In positivism and natural science, the description and understanding of the physical world have become the province of specialized experts. The experts control information removed from the average person, and use it to create miracle drugs, convenience items, fortunes for individuals or firms, or nightmarish weapons. Positivism implies the collection and use of information by experts separate from research subjects and the ordinary citizen. The two alternatives to positivism, each

in its own way, argue for the involvement and participation of those who are studied in the research process and in the use of research data and findings (Gustavsen, 1986).

Mandated Protections of Subjects

The U.S. federal government has regulations and laws to protect research subjects and their rights. The legal restraint is found in rules and regulations issued by the U.S. Department of Health and Human Services (HSS) Office for the Protection from Research Risks (OPRR). Although this is only one federal agency, most researchers and other government agencies look to it for guidance. Current U.S. government regulations evolved from Public Health Service policies adopted in 1966 and expanded in 1971. The National Research Act (1974) established the National Commission for the Protection of Human Subjects in Biomedical and Behavioral Research, which significantly expanded regulations, and required informed consent in most social work research. The responsibility for safeguarding ethical standards was assigned to research institutes and universities.

In 1999 the Advisory Committee to the Director of the National Institutes of Health (NIH) recommended that the role of the OPRR be expanded and that the office be elevated from NIH to HHS-wide placement. In 2000 the Office for Human Research Protections (OHRP) was established in the Office of the Secretary to elevate its stature and effective-ness. In addition, an independent National Human Research Protections Advisory Committee was established to provide broad scientific and ethical guidance to OHRP in its oversight role.

OHRP has the primary responsibility within the federal government for developing and implementing the policies, procedures, and regulations to protect human subjects involved in HHS-sponsored research. In carrying out its mission, OHRP has formal agreements with more than 4,000 federally funded universities, hospitals, and other medical and behavioral research institutions in the United States and abroad. These agreements or "assurances" outline each institution's commitment to conduct its research projects in an ethically sound manner and to protect the welfare of people involved in these projects.

Federal regulations follow a biomedical model and protect subjects from physical harm. Other rules require institutional review boards at all research institutes, colleges, and universities to review all use of human subjects. The IRB is staffed by researchers and community members. Similar committees oversee the use of animals in research. The board also oversees, monitors, and reviews the impact of all research procedures on human subjects and applies ethical guidelines. The board also reviews research procedures at the preliminary stage when first proposed. Educational tests, "normal educational practice," most surveys, most observation of public behavior, and studies of existing data in which individuals cannot be identified are exempt from the IRB.[21]

Boundaries between Research and Practice

By and large, the term *practice* refers to interventions that are designed solely to enhance the well-being of an individual client or client system and that have a reasonable expectation of success. The purpose of practice in general is to provide diagnosis or assessment, preventive treatment or therapy, or intervention to particular clients. *Research,* on the other hand, refers to activity designed to answer a question, test a hypothesis, and permit conclusions to be drawn, and thereby to develop or contribute to a generalizable body of knowledge (for example, as shown in theories, principles, and statements of relationships). Researchers usually outline their activity in a formal protocol that sets forth a scientific objective, uses a set of procedures acceptable to the scientific community, and has a good probability of reaching that objective. When clinicians or practitioners depart from the standards of generally accepted practice, the departure or innovation does not, in and of itself, constitute an experiment or research (Blaskett, 1998). The fact that an intervention or procedure is experimental, in the sense of being new, untested, or different, does not automatically place it in the category of research. The social work community agrees that radically new

interventions in practice should be made the object of formal research at an early stage in order to determine whether they are safe and effective.

Research and practice may be carried on together when research is designed to evaluate the safety and efficacy of an intervention. This need not cause any confusion regarding whether or not the activity requires ethical review; the general rule is that if there is any element of research in an activity, that activity should undergo review for the protection of human subjects.

ETHICS AND THE SCIENTIFIC COMMUNITY

Physicians, attorneys, counselors, and other professionals have a *code of ethics* and peer review boards or licensing regulations. The codes formalize professional standards and provide guidance when questions arise in practice.[22] Social work researchers do not provide a service for a fee, receive limited ethical training, and are rarely licensed. They incorporate ethical concerns into research because it is morally and socially responsible, and to protect social work research from charges of insensitivity or abusing people.

Professional social work associations have codes of ethics. The codes state proper and improper behavior and represent a consensus of professionals on ethics. Not all researchers may agree on all ethical issues, and ethical rules are subject to interpretation, but researchers are expected to uphold ethical standards as part of their membership in a professional community.

Codes of research ethics can be traced to the *Nuremberg code,* which was adopted during the Nuremberg Military Tribunal on Nazi war crimes held by the Allied Powers immediately after World War II. The code, developed as a response to the cruelty of concentration camp experiments, outlines ethical principles and rights of human subjects. These include the following:

- The principle of voluntary consent
- Avoidance of unnecessary physical and mental suffering
- Avoidance of any experiment where death or disabling injury is likely

— Termination of research if its continuation is likely to cause injury, disability, or death
— The principle that experiments should be conducted by highly qualified people using the highest levels of skill and care
— The principle that the results should be for the good of society and unattainable by any other method

The principles in the Nuremberg code dealt with the treatment of human subjects and focused on medical experimentation, but they became the basis for the ethical codes in social work research. Similar codes of human rights, such as the 1948 Universal Declaration of Human Rights by the United Nations and the 1964 Declaration of Helsinki, also have implications for social work researchers.[23] Figure 5.2 lists some of the basic principles of ethical social work research.

Professional associations have committees that review codes of ethics and hear about possible violations, but there is no strict enforcement of the codes. The penalty for a minor violation rarely goes beyond a letter. If laws have not been violated, the main penalty is the negative publicity surrounding a well-documented and serious ethical violation. The publicity may result in the loss of employment, a refusal to publish research findings in scholarly journals, and a prohibition from receiving funding for research—in other words, banishment from the community of professional researchers.

Codes of ethics do more than codify thinking and provide guidance; they also help universities and other institutions defend ethical social work research against abuses. For example, after interviewing 24 staff members and conducting observations, a researcher in 1994 documented that the staff at the Milwaukee Public Defenders Office were seriously overworked and could not effectively provide legal defense for poor people. Learning of the findings, top officials at the office contacted the university and demanded to know who on their staff had talked to the researcher, with implications that there might be reprisals. The university administration defended the researcher and refused to release the information, citing widely accepted codes that protect human research subjects.[24]

FIGURE 5.2   Basic Principles of Ethical Social Research

— Ethical responsibility rests with the individual researcher.
— Do not exploit subjects or students for personal gain.
— Some form of informed consent is highly recommended or required.
— Honor all guarantees of privacy, confidentiality, and anonymity.
— Do not coerce or humiliate subjects.
— Use deception only if needed, and always accompany it with debriefing.
— Use the research method that is appropriate to a topic.
— Detect and remove undesirable consequences to research subjects.
— Anticipate repercussions of the research or publication of results.
— Identify the sponsor who funded the research.
— Cooperate with host nations when doing comparative research.
— Release the details of the study design with the results.
— Make interpretations of results consistent with the data.
— Use high methodological standards and strive for accuracy.
— Do not conduct secret research.

ETHICS AND THE SPONSORS OF RESEARCH

Whistle-Blowing

You might find a job where you do research for a sponsor—an employer, a government agency, or a private firm that contracts with a researcher to conduct research. Special ethical problems arise when a sponsor pays for research, especially applied research. Researchers may be asked to compromise ethical or professional research standards as a condition for receiving a contract or for continued employment. Researchers need to set ethical boundaries beyond which they will refuse sponsor demands. When confronted with an illegitimate demand from a sponsor, a researcher has three basic choices: loyalty to an organization or larger group, exiting from the situation, or voicing opposition.[25] These present themselves as caving in to the sponsor, quitting, or becoming a whistle-blower. The researcher must choose his or her own course of action, but it is best to consider ethical issues early in a relationship with a sponsor and to express concerns up front.

Whistle-blowing can be strenuous and risky. Three parties are involved: the researcher who sees ethical wrongdoing, an external agency or the media, and supervisors in an employing organization. The researcher must be convinced that the breach of ethics is serious and approved of in the organization. After exhausting internal avenues to resolve the issue, he or she turns to outsiders. The outsiders may or may not be interested in the problem or able to help. Outsiders often have their own priorities (making an organization look bad, sensationalizing the problem, etc.)— ones that differ from the researcher's main concern (ending unethical behavior). Supervisors or managers may try to discredit or punish anyone who exposes problems and acts disloyal. As Frechette-Schrader (1994:78) noted, "An act of whistle blowing is a special kind of organizational disobedience or, rather, obedience to a higher principle than loyalty to an employer." Under the best of conditions, the issue may take a long time to resolve and create great emotional strain. By acting moral, a whistle-blower needs to be prepared to make sacrifices—losing a job or promotions, lowered pay or undesirable transfer, being abandoned by friends at work, or incurring legal costs. There is no guarantee that doing the right thing will change the unethical behavior or protect the researcher from retaliation.

Applied researchers in sponsored research settings need to think seriously about their professional roles. They may want to maintain some independence from an employer and affirm their membership in a community of dedicated professionals. Many find a defense against sponsor pressures by participating in professional organizations (e.g., the National Association of Social Workers), maintaining regular contacts with researchers outside the sponsoring organization, and staying current with the best research practices. The researcher least likely to uphold ethical standards in a sponsored setting is someone who is isolated and professionally insecure. Whatever the situation, unethical behav-

ior is never justified by the argument that "If I didn't do it, someone else would have."

Arriving at Particular Findings

What should you do if a sponsor tells you, directly or indirectly, what results you should come up with? An ethical social work researcher refuses to participate if he or she must arrive at specific results as a precondition for doing research. All research should be conducted without restrictions on the findings that the research yields. For example, a survey organization obtained a contract to conduct research for a shopping mall association. The association was engaged in a court battle with a political group that wanted to demonstrate at a mall. An interviewer in the survey organization objected to many survey questions that he believed were invalid and slanted to favor the shopping mall association. After he contacted a newspaper and exposed the biased questions, the interviewer was fired. Several years later, however, in a "whistle-blower lawsuit," the interviewer was awarded more than $60,000 for back pay, mental anguish, and punitive damages against the survey organization.[26]

Another example of pressure to arrive at particular findings is in the area of educational testing. Standardized tests to measure achievement by U.S. school children have come under criticism. For example, children in about 90 percent of school districts in the United States score "above average" on such tests. This was called the *Lake Wobegon effect* after the mythical town of Lake Wobegon, where, according to radio show host Garrison Keillor, "all the children are above average." The main reason for this finding was that the researchers compared current students to standards based on tests taken by students many years ago. The researchers faced pressure from teachers, school principals, superintendents, and school boards for results that would allow them to report to parents and voters that their school district was "above average."[27]

Limits on How to Conduct Studies

Can a sponsor limit research by defining what can be studied or by limiting the techniques used, either directly or indirectly (by limiting funding)? Sponsors can legitimately set conditions on research techniques used (e.g., survey versus experiment) and limit costs for research. However, the researcher must follow generally accepted research methods. Researchers should give a realistic appraisal of what can be accomplished for a given level of funding.

The issue of limits is common in *contract research*, when a firm or government agency asks for work on a particular research project. A tradeoff may develop between quality and cost in contract research. Abt (1979), the president of a major private social research firm, Abt Associates, argued that it is difficult to get a contract by bidding what the research actually costs. Once the research begins, a researcher may need to redesign the project, or costs may be higher. The contract procedure makes midstream changes difficult. A researcher may find that he or she is forced by the contract to use research procedures or methods that are less than ideal. The researcher then confronts a dilemma: Complete the contract and do low-quality research, or fail to fulfill the contract and lose money and future jobs.

A researcher should refuse to continue if he or she cannot uphold generally accepted standards of research. If a sponsor wants biased samples or leading questions, the ethical social work researcher refuses to cooperate. If legitimate research shows the sponsor's pet idea or project to be a bad course of action, a researcher may anticipate the end of employment or pressure to violate professional research standards. In the long run, the sponsor, the researcher, the scientific community, and the larger society are harmed by the violation of sound research practice. The researcher has to decide whether he or she is a "hired hand" who gives the sponsors whatever they want, even if it is ethically wrong, or a professional who is obligated to teach, guide, or even oppose sponsors in the service of higher moral principles.[28]

A researcher should ask, "Why would sponsors want the social work research conducted if they are not interested in using the findings or in the truth?" The answer is that such sponsors see social work research only as a cover they can use to legitimate a decision or practice that they could not otherwise carry out. They abuse the researcher's status as a professional to advance their own narrow goals. They are being deceitful and trying to "cash in" on the reputation of social work research for honesty and integrity. When it occurs, an ethical researcher has a moral responsibility to expose and stop the abuse.

Suppressing Findings

What happens if you conduct research and the findings make the sponsor look bad or the sponsor does not want to release the results? This is not an uncommon situation for applied researchers. For example, a sociologist conducted a study for the Wisconsin Lottery Commission on the effects of state government-sponsored gambling. After she completed the report, but before the report was released to the public, the commission asked her to remove sections that outlined many negative social effects of gambling and to eliminate her recommendations to create social services to help compulsive gamblers. The researcher was in a difficult position. Which ethical value took precedence: covering up for the sponsor that had paid for the research, or revealing the truth for all to see but then suffering the consequences?[29] A Roman Catholic priest who surveyed American bishops on their dissatisfaction with official church policy was ordered by his superiors to suppress findings and destroy the questionnaires. Instead, he resigned after 24 years in the priesthood and made his results public.[30] Researchers pay high personal and economic costs for being ethical.

Government agencies may suppress scientific information that contradicts official policy or embarrasses high officials. Retaliation against social work researchers employed by government agencies who make the information public also occurs. For example, a researcher employed by the U.S. Census Bureau who studied death caused by the 1991 Gulf War against Iraq reported that government officials suppressed findings for political reasons. The researcher, whom the agency attempted to fire, reported that findings of high death rates were delayed and underestimated by the U.S. government's agency for statistics. Before information could be released, it had to go through an office headed by a political appointee. She charged that the political appointee was most interested in protecting the administration's foreign policy. In another example, the U.S. Defense Department ordered studies destroyed that showed 10 percent of the U.S. military to be gay or lesbian and that showed no support for the banning of gays from the military.[31]

In sponsored research a researcher can negotiate conditions for releasing findings *prior to beginning* the study and sign a contract to that effect. It may be unwise to conduct the study without such a guarantee, although competing researchers who have fewer ethical scruples may do so. Alternatively, a researcher can accept the sponsor's criticism and hostility and release the findings over the sponsor's objections. Most researchers prefer the first choice, since the second one may scare away future sponsors.

Social work researchers sometimes self-censor or delay the release of findings. They do this to protect the identity of informants, to maintain access to a research site, to hold on to their jobs, or to protect the personal safety of themselves or of family members (Adler and Adler, 1993). This is a less disturbing type of censorship because it is not imposed by an outside power. It is done by someone who is close to the research and who is knowledgable about possible consequences. Researchers shoulder the ultimate responsibility for their research. Often, they can draw on many different resources, but they face many competing pressures, as well (see Box 5.3).

Concealing the True Sponsor

Is it ethical to keep the identity of a sponsor secret? For example, an abortion clinic funds a study on the attitudes of religious groups opposed to abortion. The researcher must balance the ethical value of making the sponsor's identity public to subjects and releasing results against the sponsor's desire for confidentiality and the likelihood of reduced cooperation from subjects. If the results are published, there is a clear overriding ethical mandate to reveal the true sponsor. There is less agreement on the ethical issue of revealing the true sponsor to subjects. Presser and colleagues (1992) found that the answers given by respondents may depend on the sponsor of a survey. If a respondent believes a sur-

---

Box 5.3 _____

Common Types of Misuse in Evaluation Research

1. Asking "wrong" research questions (e.g., asking summative yes/no questions when formulative questions are most appropriate or asking questions that exclude major stakeholders)
2. Requesting an evaluation study after a decision on a program has been made, using the study only as a way to delay or justify the decision already made
3. Demanding the use of a research design/data collection technique that is inappropriate for the program evaluation task
4. Interfering with the research design or data collection process to ensure that it produces desired results
5. Continuing a program when the evaluation results unambiguously show it to be ineffective, or ending a program when the results unambiguously show it to be highly effective
6. Suppressing/deleting positive results to eliminate/reduce a program, or suppressing/deleting negative results to continue/expand a program

---

Source: Adapted from Stevens and Dial (1994), who also provide examples of misuse.

---

vey is conducted by a newspaper that has taken a strong position on an issue, the respondent is less likely to contradict the newspaper's public stand on the issue. This is less of a problem if the respondent believes the survey sponsor is a neutral academic organization.

THE POLITICS OF RESEARCH

Ethics involve the morals of research practice. They primarily concern individual responsibility that is shared with others in the scientific community. The major issues are protecting subjects, being honest in doing and reporting research, and operating without interference from sponsors who might compromise the integrity of the research processes.

Politics of research is closely related. Politics can affect social work research in several ways:

what researchers can study and how they conduct research, how research findings are disseminated, and how the findings are used. The core issue is freedom of expression and the independence of science from powerful groups or institutions. No codes exist for politics similar to codes of ethics. Although it may not be perfect, the ultimate goal of social work research is to discover knowledge and seek truth. Political controversies in social work research are situations in which powerful groups or institutions want to limit the search for the truth, prevent the communication of knowledge, or misuse and selectively ignore findings. This occurs because they are advancing other, nonscientific goals.

LIMITS ON WHAT SOCIAL WORK RESEARCHERS STUDY AND HOW THEY DO RESEARCH

Direct Limits on Research

Governments or powerful groups in society may try to restrict free scientific inquiry. In nondemocratic societies control over, or the censorship of, social work research is the rule, not the exception. This is particularly the case with politically sensitive topics, including public opinion surveys. Thus, in China, eastern Europe, South Africa, Taiwan, and other places, social work researchers have been suspect, limited to "safe" topics, or forced to support official government policy.[32] In an extreme case 40 percent of German scientists were dismissed from their jobs for political reasons when the Nazis "purified" universities and research centers in 1937.[33] Another example is the purge of hundreds of professors and researchers in the United States who did not publicly swear to anticommunism and collaborate with the McCarthy investigations of the 1950s. At that time people who objected to mandatory loyalty oaths, supported racial integration, or advocated the teaching of sex education were suspected of subversion and threatened with dismissal. For instance, at the University of California alone, 25 professors were fired for refusing to sign a loyalty oath.[34]

Two possible limitations on social work research are (1) gatekeepers who control access to data

or subjects and (2) controls over how official statistics are collected. Gatekeepers can limit what is studied and may want to protect themselves or their organizations from criticism or embarrassment. They often limit access to subjects or areas with which they feel confident. For example, in 1997 the U.S. Army dropped several questions from a 153-item questionnaire on sexual harassment that was being sent to 9,000 soldiers. The reason for eliminating 6 questions was that "senior Army officials feared that the responses could be highly embarrassing to the Army" (Schmitt, 1997). Two researchers who were consultants on the project, a social anthropologist and a law professor, were upset. One said that preliminary results from an early version of the questionnaire suggested that sexual harassment at military bases was correlated with responses to the questions that asked about certain soldier behaviors (e.g., going to strip clubs, watching X-rated movies, etc.). Gatekeeper army officials did not want the potentially embarrassing information collected.

Another limitation involves official or existing statistics that government or other large organizations collect. We will examine this topic again in Chapter 11, but whether agencies collect information and how they collect it can affect research findings. Often, political factors affect how phenomena (e.g., unemployment, income, educational success, poverty level, etc.) are defined in official statistics and whether such data are collected.[35]

Hundreds of social scientists regularly rely on the data collected by the U.S. Census Bureau for conducting demographic, economic, and other studies. The original purpose of a census was to allocate elected representatives among states and districts. Later, the Census Bureau gathered information for making policy decisions, for providing social programs, and for distributing government funds based on the population size of an area. Over the years it has become a major source of social work information and a clearinghouse for official statistics on many topics. Serious distortion (e.g., systematic overcounts or undercounts of some people or areas) weakens research findings based on Census Bureau statistics, prevents full democratic representation, and undermines a fair distribution of social welfare programs or funds.

When studies documented systematic distortion, social scientists advocated getting more accurate data for the year 2000 census by using scientifically designed sampling methods. As you will see in Chapter 8, properly conducted sampling avoids the distortions created by trying to count everyone. After several years of arguments, Congress and the courts rejected sampling and determined that a method with known distortions will be used. They rejected sampling for several reasons: ignorance about social work research, valuing tradition over scientific accuracy, narrow self-interest by geographic areas that are getting more than their fair share now, and partisan fears that a political party might lose voters if electoral representation was allocated without bias.[36]

Some social work researchers, especially those who rely on existing statistics, depend on the government to supply information or documents. In the United States the Paperwork Reduction Act of 1980 created an Office of Information and Regulatory Affairs to determine whether it was necessary to collect information and maintain records. The act resulted in fewer publications from government-sponsored research. In addition, the law had been "used on occasion to restrict information not supportive of executive branch policy goals" (Shattuck and Spence, 1988:47). For example, in the health field, research projects with an environmental focus that indirectly criticized business or government policy were more likely to be rejected for publication under "paperwork reduction" justification than those with a traditional disease focus that indirectly blamed the victim.

In the name of cost cutting, federal agencies stopped collecting information, removed information from public circulation, and shifted information collection to private businesses. The number of outlets of the U.S. government publishing offices were cut and prices were raised. For example, a 67-page pamphlet titled "Infant Care," which was distributed free to mothers by public health programs, now costs $4.75.[37] Bureaucratic decisions not to collect information can have policy implications. For instance, 40 percent of the nonmoney items were eliminated from national educational statistics in the early 1980s. Information on the gender mix of teachers or administrators, which had been added

in 1974 to detect sex discrimination, was eliminated from statistical reporting. Thus, budget decisions not to collect certain information make it more difficult to show sex discrimination.[38]

Data collected by the government have been sold at low bulk rates to private business. The private businesses are then the only source of these data and charge high prices to researchers. For example, information that was once free to the public became available only through a private company that charges a $1,495 annual subscription fee. Starr and Corson (1987:447) remarked:

> The privatizing of statistical information poses some specific problems for the future of the social sciences and intellectual life. Without the capacity to make use of the new information resources in private hands, the universities and other nonprofit research centers may be left as intellectual backwaters.

In sum, there is still substantial free inquiry and independent social work research. Nevertheless, there have been politically motivated attempts to limit what social work researchers can study, as well.

Limits Due to the Influence of Politicians. Unfortunately, some people outside the scientific community attack social work research because it disagrees with their social or political values. A politician or journalist may hear about a research project in a controversial area or may misinterpret the project, then use the occasion to attract publicity. For example, Professor Harris Rubin at the University of Southern Illinois intended to investigate the effects of THC (the active agent in marijuana) on sexual arousal. Almost no scientific evidence existed, only contradictory myths. He very carefully followed all procedures and clearances, and the research project was funded by the National Institute of Mental Health in 1975. A conservative congressperson learned of the research topic from nearby newspapers and introduced an amendment in Congress to prohibit further funding. In addition, all funds for the project were to be repaid to the federal government. Despite arguments by scientists that politicians should not interfere with legitimate research, funding was cut. Politicians are afraid to support social work research if an opposing candidate could make a case to voters that the government appeared to be paying for students to "get stoned and watch porno films."[39]

Senator William Proxmire's "Golden Fleece" awards have gone to social work research projects whose scientific significance was not appreciated by the senator. He ridiculed studies of human attraction and affection, and of stress and tension as a "waste of taxpayer money." In one case a Michigan primate researcher who was attacked by the senator subsequently lost his position and funding. In a legal case that ended up in the U.S. Supreme Court, the Court ruled that the senator's statements attacking individuals on the floor of the U.S. Senate were protected, but if he mailed out newsletters and made attacks outside the Senate, he could be sued for libel or slander.[40] Another example of political pressure occurred in 1989, when funding for a major national survey on sexual behavior to combat the AIDS epidemic was blocked in Congress by members who did not believe that it was proper for researchers to inquire into human sexual behavior.[41]

A research project on teenage sex conducted by the National Institutes of Health (NIH) was canceled in 1991 after action by the U.S. Senate. The study was to survey 24,000 teens about their social activities, family life, and sexual behavior, in order to provide background for understanding AIDS and other sexually transmitted diseases. Many researchers said they did not want to speak out on the issue for fear that they would become the target of political groups. Some who spoke out said that the ability of a small minority with an extreme political ideology to kill important research was "a scandalous act" and "frightening." One sociology researcher noted that the project was not canceled because of questions about its scientific quality or importance; rather, it was an ideologically based decision that "we don't need to know this."[42]

Public attacks on social work research, even noncontroversial but misunderstood research, hurts all researchers. Politicians may "kill" research that the scientific community recognizes as legitimate, or they may promote pet projects that have little scientific value. Researchers who apply for government funds sometimes restate their project in terms that do not attract attention. The public ridicule of

unsuspecting researchers or the denial of research funds also encourages self-censorship and fosters a negative public opinion about social work research.

National Security and Limits on Social Work Research.   Military secrecy and national security became major issues during World War I and World War II. Most of the concern was with technology to create weapons, but social work researchers have been limited in their study of foreign nations, issues of military interest, and research into government itself. U.S. security agencies, such as the National Security Administration and the Central Intelligence Agency (CIA), have influenced social and natural science research into the Cold War period of the 1950s.

One government research project in the 1960s created a great controversy. The U.S. Army funded *Project Camelot,* which involved respected social work researchers who went to Chile to study political insurgency and mobilization. Several aspects of the project created controversy. First, the project's goal was to find out how to prevent peasants and disadvantaged groups in Third World countries from taking independent political action to oppose a dictator. Such counterinsurgency research is usually conducted by the Central Intelligence Agency. The researchers were accused of using their skills and knowledge to advance military interests against disadvantaged Third World people. Second, some researchers were unaware of the source of funds. Third, the people and the government of Chile were not informed about the project. Once they discovered it, they asked that it end and that all researchers leave.[43]

By the late 1960s and 1970s, freedom to conduct research expanded, restrictions on researchers were relaxed, and the government classified fewer documents. The U.S. Congress passed the *Freedom of Information Act (FOIA)* in 1966 and strengthened it in 1974. The law opened many government documents to scholars and members of the public if they file requests with government agencies. The trend toward greater openness of information and freedom of research was reversed in the 1980s. The U.S. government limited the publication of information, expanded the range of classified documents, and made less information publicly available in the name of national security and budget cutting. This has restrained academic inquiry, scientific progress, and democratic decision making.[44]

In the 1980s the definition of national security was broadened, the system for classifying government documents was expanded, and new limits were imposed on research into "sensitive areas," even if no government agency or funds are involved. It became easier to classify information and classify documents that were already in the public domain. In addition, military and security officials could restrict researchers from outside the U.S. from attending scholarly meetings or visiting U.S. classrooms, libraries, and research centers.[45]

In the past, CIA undercover agents have posed as social work researchers to get information in foreign nations. Until 1986 the CIA had a blanket rule barring researchers from disclosing CIA sponsorship of their research. At that time the rule was loosened to cover only cases where the CIA believed such disclosure "would prove damaging to the United States." For example, a Harvard professor had a contract with the CIA not to reveal that the agency paid for the research for a scholarly book on U.S. foreign policy.[46]

Cross-national research involves unique ethical issues. The research community condemns the use of undercover agents in the guise of researchers and the practice of hiding the source of funding for research. Researchers have developed ethical guidelines for conduct in other nations, which specify cooperation with host officials, the protection of subjects, and leaving information in the host nation. Nevertheless, a researcher may find interference from his or her own government; or the researcher's respect for the basic human rights of the people being studied in a nondemocratic society may lead him or her to hide information from the host government involved.[47]

Indirect Limits through Control over Research Funding

The most common way that politics shape social work research is through control over funds for doing research. In some ways this is similar to the issues involved in sponsored research. Large-scale research projects can be expensive, costing as much as a million dollars. The funds often come from private sources or governments.

There are few restrictions on research in the United States. Most officials recognize that an open and autonomous social scientific community is the best path to unbiased, valid knowledge. The peer review process promotes autonomous research because proposals for funds to conduct research submitted to a government agency are reviewed by researcher peers who evaluate the proposal on its scientific merit. Although the federal government funds most basic research, research itself is decentralized and conducted at many colleges, universities, and research centers across the nation.

The sums for social work research are tiny compared to the amounts spent by large corporations on research or to federal funding for natural science or military research. In the United States most research funding comes from the federal government, with university and private foundation funding more limited in amount, scope, and number. Thus, for large projects, researchers are forced to go to the federal government for funding.

Prior to World War II in the United States, a few private foundations set up by wealthy families (Carnegie, Ford, Rockefeller, and Sage) funded most sociological research. The foundations sought information about the serious social problems that appeared with early industrialism. They also wanted to discourage links between radicals and social work researchers and protect established social institutions. After a number of years, "The production of social science research thus becomes regularized or routinized, and its connection with sponsoring organizations becomes obscured from the public's view" (Seybold, 1987:197). Private funds redirected social work research efforts away from its early focus that was applied, action-oriented, critical, neighborhood centered, and involved participation by subjects and toward a focus that was detached, professional, positivist, and academic. After World War II, government research funding expanded. Private foundations maintained a role setting research priorities through the 1960s, when federal government funds surpassed private funds.[48]

In the United States, social work research funding is available from several federal agencies, including the National Science Foundation, Department of Defense, Agriculture Department, Commerce Department, Department of Housing and Urban Development, Department of Education, National Endowment for the Humanities, Small Business Administration, Department of Justice, Department of Labor, and the many institutes under the Department of Health and Human Services. The federal government itself employs researchers to monitor advances in knowledge and conduct research. Most social work research is conducted at colleges and universities or independent research institutes.

The primary funding source for social research in the United States (the National Science Foundation; NSF) supported only basic positivist research early in its history for political reasons. Nonpositivist social work research and applied studies were excluded to win backing from natural scientists, to counter popular perceptions that social science was "fluff," and to repel charges by ideological conservatives that social work was "left-wing." In addition, the NSF avoided supporting research on controversial topics (e.g., sex, political power, etc.). This was due to a fear, in the political climate of the 1950s and 1960s, that the study of such topics could create political problems that would jeopardize obtaining government funds for social work research (see Box 5.4).

The decision to allocate specific amounts of funds to various agencies for social work research and the applied/basic split vary from year to year and are determined by political processes. Although the scientific review committees within the NSF and NIH evaluate the scientific merit of submitted proposals, political officials decide the total amount of funds available, and whether funds must be used for applied or basic research. Useem (1976a:159) noted:

> *Since federal research policies are oriented around producing policy-relevant quantitative research, the result of responsiveness to these policies is that academic research is more oriented toward topics and techniques useful to government agencies than would be the case in the absence of federal funding. Both substantive and methodological priorities in academic social research are significantly affected by government priorities.*

Social work researchers and others can lobby for funds or programs, but the politicians set priorities. Thus, conflicts between the political parties or ideological interests affect the amount of research funding available and how it can be spent.

During the 1970s U.S. federal funding for social work research failed to keep pace with inflation. Funding for social work research in the National Science Foundation declined 24 percent between 1976 and 1980 in constant dollars. Significant conflict arose over federal funding for social work research in the early 1980s. Despite an outcry, funding dropped another 17 percent between 1980 and 1983. Social work research became a source of controversy. Political leaders thought that too many research results

---

Box 5.4 _____

U.S. Congressmen Question Research Funding

In 1998 Representative Marshall Sanford of South Carolina said he wanted to cut National Science Foundation (NSF) funding for studies of questionable "scientific value." Apparently believing he was a better judge of scientific value than the scientific community, he cited studies about automatic teller machines and billiards. NSF officials observed that in the research to which the Congressman referred, the abbreviation *ATM* stood for *asynchronous transfer modes,* a high-speed data technique, not *automatic teller machines,* and *billiards* is a term physicists use in atomic theory for a subatomic particle, not the game as the Congressman had assumed. Representative Sanford, along with a representative from California, indicated a desire to punish the NSF for supporting what they deemed unnecessary, wasteful studies. These included why people risk their resources to join social groups, differences between the social behavior of men and women, and why potential political candidates decide to run for office. Other Congressmen defended the NSF and noted that such criticisms were the result of faulty, sloppy research by the politicians, not the type of research the NSF supports through its peer review process (Lederman, 1998).

supported the policies of their opponents. Applied research was also reduced. In response, the professional associations of several social science disciplines joined together to form a lobbying organization: the *Consortium of Social Science Associations (COSSA)*. COSSA was able to reduce the size of some cuts.[49]

After dramatic shifts that followed the ebb and flow of conflicts between the White House and Congress, by the start of the 1990s, fewer inflation-adjusted federal dollars went to research than had been available 20 years earlier (D'Antonio, 1992: 122). The funding for research may be unchanged for 70 years. Funds from the private Social Science Research Council in the late 1920s, once adjusted for inflation and the size of academic profession, were probably greater than funding for social work research from the National Science Foundation at the start of the 1990s.[50]

Political values are relevant when money is allocated for research on certain questions and priorities. For example, politicians decide that money is allocated for applied research to demonstrate how "burdensome" the costs of regulation are for large corporations, but none is available to investigate the benefits of regulation for consumers. They increase funds to study crime committed by drug addicts, but eliminate funds to study crime by corporate executives. They make available new funds for research on how to promote entrepreneurship, while cutting back funds to study the human consequences of social program cutbacks.[51]

Funds for basic research can promote specific theoretical or value perspectives. For example, funds may be allocated to study how individual attributes correlate with undesirable social behaviors, while no funding exists for investigating structural and community factors. By focusing on some research questions and limiting alternatives, political groups try to shape the research that is conducted.

Many issues that social work researchers address bear directly on social beliefs, values, and policies. Political groups set priorities for these issues that are distinct from those of the scientific community. As Useem (1976b:625) noted, "These priorities are unlikely to be identical to the discipline's own priorities." This has both positive and negative effects. It ensures that the concerns of politicians or vocal public groups are addressed and that social problems that politically influential groups define as important get researched. If scientific research does not support a popular public belief (e.g., that capital punishment has a deterrent effect or that women who have abortions suffer psychological harm), funds are repeatedly allocated to try to discover evidence that will confirm popular beliefs, while scientifically central issues go unfunded.

The scientific community has some freedom to define what should be researched, but problems affecting less politically vocal groups or issues for which there is no lobby receive limited research funding. This imbalance of funding creates an imbalance in knowledge across issues. Eventually, there is substantial knowledge on the issues of interest to powerful political groups, while their opponents are weakened by a lack of knowledge.

In May 1992 members of the U.S. Congress identified 31 specific research projects to be funded by the National Science Foundation (NSF) as a waste of taxpayer money. The projects singled out to be cut included "Monogamy and Aggression," "A Systematic Study of Senate Elections," and "American Perceptions of Justice." Although the proposals had undergone a rigorous review on scientific merit, several politicians decided to overrule the scientific community. The politicians had not studied the research proposals and lacked a background in the social or natural sciences. They also criticized the NSF for supporting basic social work research. After extensive lobbying by the research community, specific research projects were no longer targeted, but still Congress cut the research budget of the NSF by the amount allocated for these research projects.[52]

A trend during the 1990s in the United States has been for universities to circumvent the peer review process for research grants and have politicians directly earmark funds for research projects at specific universities. Some states (e.g., California) received large amounts ($60 million); others got nothing. For example, politicians budgeted $12 million to study transportation injuries in the 1998 transportation bill for researchers at the State University of New York–Buffalo. The money was awarded on a noncompetitive, political basis. The total amount of earmarked funds more than doubled between 1989 and 1993, declined for a period, then reversed to rapid growth since 1996. Such "pork barrel" funding does not mean that the quality of the research suffers or that scientists are unethical. Yet, it circumvents the peer review processes, in which decisions are made solely on scientific merit; instead, it uses political deals to decide that one university or research team, as opposed to another, gets to conduct the research (Cordes, 1998).

In response to reductions in research funds from government and financial pressures, universities have increasingly turned to private donors to fund research. Yet, funding from private donors (e.g., wealthy individuals, private foundations, large corporations, foreign governments, etc.) sometimes comes with strings attached. For example, one donor foreign government withdrew $450,000 because a researcher at the university publicly endorsed a policy the government opposed (Golden, 1996). One scholar noted that such donors are not academic organizations and are trying to get across a point of view. Universities and research institutes try to avoid such controls or conditions established by private donors and try to balance donated money against the freedom to conduct and publish research without interference.

Limits on the Dissemination of Knowledge. A principle in the operation of science and a major norm of the scientific community involves the public distribution of knowledge. Powerful groups or institutions can impinge on social work research by limiting the flow of information, restricting publication, or silencing researchers.

A 1997 news report illustrates the suppression of research findings. A pharmaceutical company that had a widely used drug for thyroid problems prohibited a university research team from publishing its research results that showed the drug to be ineffective. In exchange for research funds, the researchers had signed a contract giving the company a right to veto publications. Other studies show that when drug companies fund research, 98 percent of the time the published findings show that the drugs are effective. This number is far higher than when the drug com-

panies are not the funding source. Some believe that negative findings about new products get suppressed when millions of dollars for a company are involved. Researchers may be given stock or financial incentives to show positive findings or to delay the release of findings. More than half of university researchers who received money from drug or biotechnology companies stated that private donors exerted influence on how they did their work.

Research on medicine or biotechnology is not the only area wherein profits and disseminating research findings come into conflict. In 1997 a Cornell University professor testified for 10 minutes at a town meeting about the labor practices of the largest nursing home corporation in the United States—Beverly Enterprises, which operates 700 nursing homes. The professor's testimony was backed up by years of research and documented by Congressional reports, newspaper reports, court records, interviews, and other scholars. In 1998 the company sued the professor for $225,000 for defaming it and demanded years of research documents and notes. This is called a *slap suit,* and its purpose is to stop public testimony. The practice began in the 1970s, when companies issued "strategic lawsuits" to silence opposition on a controversial issue.

In other cases a study of corporate crime was delayed and the results changed after the threat of a lawsuit by managers who had been interviewed in the study; the publication of a study of a boarding school was stopped due to a possible lawsuit after school officials wanted to change what they had said in interviews and make other changes in the book because they disagreed with the researcher's finding; and an article was changed after a researcher threatened a lawsuit over the exposure conflicts that occurred during a study conducted by a team of researchers in a book on how research actually occurs.[53]

Another issue is the use of political criteria when appointing researchers to review boards for applied research in the departments of Education and Agriculture. Executive branch officials who believed that social work researchers disapproved of their political goals and values have screened researchers on their political beliefs. Before the 1980s scientific merit, irrespective of political ideology, had been the only criterion used. Federal government officials also tried to modify funded research. For example, in 1984 a Department of Housing and Urban Development (HUD) research contract with Harvard University was dropped by researchers because HUD insisted that politically appointed officials be allowed to make "corrections" to data, findings, or methodology prior to publication.[54] In 1991 a U.S. federal court ruled that federal government agencies cannot legally require researchers to get prior approval from government officials before publishing findings from research. Such a requirement would amount to censorship and would infringe on academic freedom (discussed later).

THE DISSEMINATION AND USE OF RESEARCH FINDINGS

What do you do with your research findings? Positivist researchers recognize two areas wherein values legitimately come into play. First, researchers can select a topic area or research question. Although there are "frontier" areas of inquiry in topic areas, researchers can choose a research question on the basis of personal preference.[55] Second, once research is completed, the researchers' values shape where they disseminate their findings. They are expected to report findings to the scientific community, and funding agencies require a report, but beyond these requirements, it is up to the researcher.

Models of Relevance

What happens when the research completed involves an ethical–political concern that Rule (1978a, 1978b) has called *models of relevance?* Rule reviewed the positions that social work researchers took toward their research and its use and argued that the positions can be collapsed into five basic types (see Figure 5.3).

The models of relevance are ideal types of the positions social scientists take. Is the researcher a technician, who produces valid, reliable information about how society works, to be used by others? Or does the researcher belong to an independent community of professionals who have a say in what

research questions are asked and how results are used? On a continuum, one extreme is the amoral researcher who lacks any concern or control over research or its use. He or she supplies the knowledge that others request and nothing more. This was the stance many scientists in Nazi Germany used to justify collaboration with Nazi practices later classified as "crimes against humanity." He or she "just follows orders" and "just does the job" but asks "no questions." At the other extreme are researchers who have total control over research and its use.

The approaches to social work discussed in Chapter 4 are associated with different models of relevance, as are different political views.[56] Positivists tend to follow the "direct and positive effects" or "special constituency, the government" model. The interpretive social work researcher follows the "no net effects" or the "unco-opted" model. Critical social work researchers follow the "special constituency, the proletariat" or "special constituency, the unco-opted" models.

The models are ideal types. Specific researchers or research projects cross between models. For example, Whyte (1986) described research on employee ownership as crossing among three constituencies (the proletariat, the unco-opted, and the government) and as having direct and positive effects.

Since Rule developed models of relevance, a new model has appeared with the growth of nongovernment, private *think tanks* in the United States. This sixth model is *special constituency, wealthy individuals, and corporations.* It says social work research can reflect a researcher's personal political values and advance the political goals of wealthy groups who seek to maintain or expand their power. The think tanks are research and publicity organizations funded by wealthy individuals, corporations, and political groups. For example, the Manhattan Institute, Cato Institute, Heritage Foundation, and American Enterprise Institute grew dramatically from the early 1980s to the 1990s. They advance a political viewpoint and use social work research or pseudoscience among other means. Think tanks pay researchers, sponsor research reports, and draw public attention to results that support their political viewpoint.

FIGURE 5.3   Models of Relevance

1. *No net effects.* Social work findings produce no greater social good. Several famous social scientists who argue this are William Graham Sumner, Vilfredo Pareto, Herbert Spencer, Edward Banfield, and James Q. Wilson. These conservative social scientists see the products of research as capable of being used for anyone's self-interest and believe that, in the long run, as much harm as good has come from the greater knowledge social science yields.

2. *Direct and positive effects.* Social work knowledge results in an improvement for all. Liberal social scientists, such as Robert Merton, who adopt this stance see knowledge about social relations leading to a more rational world. Research results on social problems help us understand the social world much better, enabling us to know how we can modify it toward some greater good. For example, Lindblom and Cohen (1979) urged a redirection of social science toward what they see as social problem solving.

3. *Special constituency, the proletariat.* Social work should be used to advance the interests and position of the working class. This is the Marxist model of the appropriate use of social research. According to it, all social science falls into three categories: the trivial, that which helps the bourgeoisie, and that which aids the proletariat. Consistent with a critical science approach, research findings should be used to advocate and defend the interests of the working class and assist workers by exposing and combatting exploitation, oppression, injustice, and repression.

4. *Special constituency, the unco-opted.* Social work should be used to aid any disadvantaged or underprivileged group in society. This model, associated with Karl Mannheim and C. Wright Mills, is more general than the Marxian position. It sees many social groups as lacking power in society (women, consumers, racial minorities, gays, the poor, etc.) and argues that these groups are oppressed by the powerful in society who have access to education, wealth, and knowledge. The social researcher should defend those who lack a voice in society and who are manipulated by those in power. The powerful can use or purchase social science research for their own ends. Because they have a unique role in society and are in a position to learn about all areas of society, social researchers have an obligation to help the weak and share knowledge with them.

5. *Special constituency, the government.* Social work's proper role is to aid the decision makers of society, especially public officials. This model has been expressed by Senator Daniel Patrick Moynihan and in official NSF policy reports, and is common in nondemocratic societies. It is similar to the second model (direct and positive effects), but adds the assumption that government is in the best position to make use of social research findings and is fully committed to eradicating social problems. It is also similar to the first (no net effects) model but implies "selling" or providing findings to the highest bidder within the limits of national loyalty. It assumes that the government operates in the best interests of everyone, and that researchers have a patriotic duty to give what they learn to those with political power.

Think tank studies vary in quality, lack peer review, and are short on solid evidence but long on suggestions. The audience for this research is not the scientific community, and the primary goal is not to advance knowledge. Rather, think tank researchers conduct policy-oriented studies with an ideological viewpoint in an attempt to shape public thinking and influence political debate. Many receive significant media publicity, fame, and fortune, although their research may be inferior and lacks scientific peer review. At the same time, traditional social scientists who operate with meager funds, but who lack connections to the mass media, find that their more rigorous, careful studies of the same public issues get overlooked. The public and policy officials are often overwhelmed by the publicity of think tank research results.

After Findings Are Published

The communalism norm of the scientific community says make findings public. Once findings are part of the public domain, the researcher loses control over them. This means that others can use the findings for their own purposes. Although the researcher may have chosen a topic based on his or her values, once the findings are published, others can use them to advance opposing values.

For example, a researcher wants to increase the political rights of a Native American tribe. He or she studies the tribe's social practices, including social barriers to their achieving greater power in the community. Once the findings are published, members of the tribe can use the results to break down barriers. Yet, opponents can use the same findings to restrict the power of the tribe and to reinforce the barriers.

Findings That Influence Future Behavior

Did you ever do something differently than before because of research findings you read? If so, you are not alone. Sometimes the dissemination of findings affects social behavior. One example is the effect of political poll results. Public opinion polls affect the political preferences of voters; that is, parts of the population change their views to correspond to what opinion polls say they have found.[57] Starr (1987:54) remarked, "Official statistics count even if the methods are faulty and the data incorrect. . . . If official statistics affect social perception and cognition, so they also powerfully affect social norms."

Other social work research findings can affect behavior. In fact, the widespread dissemination of research findings may affect behavior in a way that negates or alters the original findings. For example, a study finds that professionals are likely to put a great deal of stress on the academic achievement of their children. This creates highly anxious, unhappy children. If professionals read the findings, they may alter their child-rearing behavior. Then another study, years later, might find that professionals are not likely to rear their children to achieve in academic areas any more than other groups do.

Researchers have several responses to research findings that affect social behavior:

1. They ruin predictability and regularity of human social behavior, undermining replication.
2. Only trivial behaviors are changed, so this is an issue only to researchers working in very narrow applied areas.

3. Human behavior can change because there are few unalterable laws of human behavior, and people will use knowledge in the public domain to change their lives.

In any case social work research has not uncovered the full complexity of human relations and behavior. Even if it did, and such knowledge were fully and accurately disseminated to the entire population, social work researchers would still have to study which human behaviors change and how.

Academic Freedom

Most students have heard about academic freedom, but few understand it. *Academic freedom* is the existence of an open and largely unrestricted atmosphere for the free exchange of ideas and information. In open democratic societies, many people value intellectual freedom and believe in providing scholars with freedom from interference. This idea is based on the belief that fundamental democratic institutions, the advance of unbiased knowledge, and freedom of expression require a free flow of ideas and information.

Academic freedom is related to the autonomy of research. New ideas for research topics, the interpretation of findings, the development of theories or hypotheses, and the open discussion of ideas require academic freedom.

Academic freedom in colleges, universities, and research institutes provides a context for the free discussion and open exchange of ideas that scientific research requires. For knowledge to advance, researchers, professors, and students need a setting wherein they feel free to advance or debate diverse, and sometimes unpopular, opinions or positions— a setting in which people are not afraid to explore a full range of ideas in open discussion, in classrooms, in public talks, or in publications.

The importance of academic freedom is demonstrated by the paucity of social work research in places where it is nonexistent. The major threat to academic freedom comes from social or political groups that want to restrict discussion or impose a point of view. Restrictions on academic freedom limit the growth of knowledge about society and undermine the integrity of the research process.

Academic freedom was a significant issue in the late nineteenth and early twentieth centuries, when the social sciences were institutionalized in universities. In the early years professors frequently lost their jobs because political officials or economic elites disliked the views expressed in their classrooms or publications. Famous scholars in the early period of American social science, like Thorsten Veblen, were forced out of several colleges because of what they said in the classroom or ideas they wrote about. The development of tenure, the idea that faculty could not be fired after a long probationary period without a very good reason, advanced academic freedom but did not guarantee complete academic freedom. Professors and researchers have been fired for advocating unpopular ideas.[58]

The American Association of University Professors (AAUP) maintains a "censure" list of colleges where violations of academic freedom have been documented. Most professional associations also have academic freedom committees, which censure colleges that violate standards of academic freedom. The only influence of censure lists is to embarrass the college.

Political attacks on social work are not new. They illustrate the conflict between the independent pursuit of knowledge and the views of political groups who want to impose their beliefs. These attacks raise the question, "How autonomous should social science be from the values in the larger culture?" The findings of social work research sometimes conflict with social beliefs based on nonscientific knowledge systems such as religion or political ideology. Galileo faced this issue about 400 years ago, before natural science was accepted. His astronomical findings, based on free-thinking science, contradicted official Church doctrine. Galileo was forced to recant his findings publicly, under the threat of torture. Silencing him slowed the advance of knowledge for a generation. The challenges of evolutionary theory also illustrate how scientific knowledge and popular beliefs conflict with one another.

Academic freedom is integral to good social work research. Scientific research involves more than knowing technical information (e.g., how to draw a random sample); it requires a spirit of free and open discussion, criticism on the basis of scientific merit irrespective of values, and inquiry into all areas of social life. These values are threatened when academic freedom is restricted.

OBJECTIVITY AND VALUE FREEDOM

Some argue that social science must be as objective and unbiased as the natural sciences; others maintain that value-free, objective social science is impossible. This debate cannot be resolved here, but you should understand the definitions and terminology used. The easiest way to clear up confusion is to recognize that each term has at least two alternative definitions. Sometimes, two different terms share the same definitions (see Box 5.5).

The positivist approach holds that science is value-free, unbiased, and objective. It collapses the definitions together. Value neutrality is guaranteed by logical–deductive, formal theory and a complete separation of facts from value-based concepts. The scientific community is free of prejudice and governed by free and open discussion. With complete

---

Box 5.5 _____

Objective, Value-Free, and Unbiased

1. _Objective:_
   a. Opposite of subjective; external, observable, factual, precise, quantitative
   b. Logical; created by an explicit rational procedure; absence of personal or arbitrary decisions; follows specific preestablished rules
2. _Value-Free:_
   a. Absence of any metaphysical values or assumptions; devoid of a priori philosophical elements; amoral
   b. Lack of influence from personal prejudice or cultural values; devoid of personal opinion; no room for unsupported views; neutral
3. _Unbiased:_
   a. Nonrandom error eliminated; absence of systematic error; technically correct
   b. Lack of influence from personal prejudice or cultural values; devoid of personal opinion; no room for unsupported views; neutral

value freedom and objectivity, science reveals the one and only, unified, unambiguous truth.

Max Weber, Alvin Gouldner, and Karl Mannheim are three major nonpositivist social thinkers who discussed the role of the social scientist in society. Weber (1949) argued that the fact/value separation is not clear in the social sciences. He suggested that value-laden theories define social facts or socially meaningful action. Thus, social theories necessarily contain value-based concepts, because all concepts about the social world are created by members of specific cultures. The cultural content of social concepts cannot be purged, and socially meaningful action makes sense only in a cultural context. For example, when social work researchers study racial groups, they are not interested in the biological differences between races. Race is a social concept; it is studied because the members of a culture attach social meaning to racial appearance. Race would be meaningless if people did not attach such a social meaning to observable racial differences.

Other social researchers have built on Weber's ideas. For example, Moore (1973) asked whether majority-group (e.g., Anglo, White) researchers, as "outsiders," can accurately study racial minorities, since their questions, assumptions, and interests come from a dominant, nonminority perspective. Are the culture, values, and belief system of the dominant White culture appropriate for asking important questions and really understanding the subculture of racial minorities? Similar concerns have been raised regarding gender.[59] Being from a different culture may not preclude researching a group, but it calls for extra care and sensitivity from a researcher.

Weber (1949) also argued that social scientists cannot avoid taking stands on social issues they study. Researchers *must* be unbiased (i.e., neutral and devoid of personal opinion and unsupported views) when applying accepted research techniques. They must focus on the means or mechanisms of how the social world works, not on ends, values, or normative goals. A researcher's values must be separate from the findings, and he or she should advocate positions on specific issues only when speaking as a private citizen.

Gouldner (1976) attacked the notion of value-free, objective social science. He argued that value freedom was used in the past to disguise specific value positions. In fact, value freedom is itself a value—a value in favor of "value-free." Gouldner said that complete value freedom was impossible and that scientists and other professionals use the term to hide their own values. He recommended making values explicit. A researcher can be motivated to do research by a desire to do more than dispassionately study the world. The researcher who is motivated by a strong moral desire to effect change need not invalidate good research practice.

Mannheim (1936) also questioned the ideas of *value neutrality* and *objectivity.* He saw the intellectuals of a society, especially those involved in social research, as occupying a unique social role. A person's social location in society shapes his or her ideas and viewpoints. Yet, social researchers are separate from others and are less shaped by their social position because they try to learn the viewpoints of other people and empathize with all parts of society. Social work researchers are not beholden to powerful elites, and they are also less subject to shifts in popular opinion, fads, and crazes. They can and should adopt a *relational position*—a position apart from any other specific social group, yet in touch with all groups. They should be detached or marginal in society, yet have connections with all parts of society, even parts that are often overlooked or hidden.

Can Technology Be Used to Preserve Privacy?

In the past several years many people have become increasingly concerned that public and private organizations are able to misuse technology to breach the boundaries of privacy, regulate access to services, and threaten longstanding rights of the individual to be left alone and to be secure in one's own identity. We hear almost daily about the ability of local, state, or federal governmental agencies to snoop into various aspects of our lives, and we wonder about the ability of for-profit organizations to exchange information about every detail of our private lives in order to determine what kind of marketing strategy we may be most susceptible to. Many of these concerns center on new technologies that afford such organizations easy access to otherwise confidential information. But what about the other side of the coin? Can technology be used to preserve privacy and promote the security of our identities?

One promising strategy from program evaluation research in health and human services involves combining computerized databases and statistical modeling techniques to answer what might otherwise have been ethically problematic outcome questions in ways that do not compromise the integrity of a client's rights to privacy and autonomy (Banks and Pandiani, 2002). For example, evaluation researchers may be interested in knowing how many adolescents from a particular state-run foster care program end up being admitted to a juvenile justice system the following year. Using computerized databases and statistical modeling techniques, evaluators can develop very accurate counts of the number of overlapping individuals, without being able to identify the adolescents involved. How is this possible? Ordinarily, we would pair up names or other identifying information of all the males in the foster care program and all males in the juvenile justice system one year later to determine the amount of overlap. However, this comparison of names would necessarily reveal the identity of the adolescents. And as we have learned, children, adolescents, and those who are or were institutionalized are particularly vulnerable to violation of their rights.

Program evaluators have worked out an interesting solution to this problem involving knowledge about dates of birth and gender only. They need to know only the gender and dates of birth of all adolescents in both databases in order to be able to determine the amount of overlap or case mix. Ordinarily, among any given set of people, a certain number will share the same date of birth. Among, say, 300 adolescents in a foster care program and 700 adolescents in a juvenile justice system one year later, there would be expected to be (for example) 145 shared birth dates among these cases, assuming no overlap of individuals. Now, if after comparing birth dates only, the researchers find (for

example) 185 shared birthdays, they can estimate (to within very accurate amounts) the number of adolescents (in this case 20 +/– 2) who are in both databases. The evaluators are able to determine, with great confidence, that from 18–22 of the children in the foster care system in one program year were found in the juvenile justice system the following year. All of this was accomplished without knowing or being able to determine the identity of the adolescents, thus preserving their rights to privacy and individual autonomy.

How Diversity Informs Ethical Issues

As noted in Chapter 2, social work has made a conscientious effort recently to better understand, appreciate, and integrate a number of ethical viewpoints pertaining to multicultural and diversity issues.[60] For example, the profession has worked hard to find definitions of participation that are not only inclusive of those who have been left out or forgotten in the past (Witkin, 2000), but also to more proactively seek out all voices (Rippey-Massat and Lundy, 1997) in a growing polyvocal international social work community (Midgely, 1997; Walz and Ritchie, 2000).

For example, certain cultures in the United States that have historically been subjugated, such as Native American Indians, have often been said to possess a different concept of time (Williams and Ellison, 1996). One interpretation as to why members of dominant, powerful groups in the United States have criticized minority groups' concepts of time is because the Euro-male hierarchies ordered their gender roles and divisions of labor in accordance with specific temporal requirements tied to colonialization and the power and control of access to scarce resources (Shands, 1999). Hence, representations of space and time in the United States arose out of the Euro-male social practices. According to Mitchell and Weiler (1991), colonialization was not simply the establishing of a European presence in the United States, but also it entailed the spread of a political order that inscribed in the New World new methods of controlling capital, new conceptions of space and time, and new norms regarding the proper role of various persons gaining access to scarce resources.

But according to Shands (1999), there is a dangerous hidden political significance in this perspective that needs to be examined. Academic disciplines such as social work, sociology, and psychology organize their distinctive objects of inquiry through a particular spatiotemporal framing of the world.

> *This framing is political precisely because it defines a certain and restricted set of 'self–other' relations for examination (investigator–investigated). The choice of spatiotemporality is not innocent with respect to the social relations (including domination and power) that are highlighted, or just as significantly, rendered invisible (as is often true of women's lives, sexuality, colonized subjects, and the like). Acceptance of a conventional spatiotemporal frame then amounts to acceptance of existing patterns of social relations, without even necessarily knowing it. . . .the effect is to make those disciplines complicitous with the perpetuation of those processes of domination (p. 266).*

Thus, it is difficult for social work as a profession to balance the needs of research and evaluation when the very categories available (researcher–subject, male–female, for example), have been called into question by the international social work community.

CONCLUSION

We want to end this chapter by urging you, as a consumer of social work research or a new social work researcher, to be self-aware. Be aware of the place of the researcher in society and of the societal context of social work research itself. Social work researchers, and sociologists in particular, bring a unique perspective to the larger society. Social work researchers have a responsibility and need an awareness of how the social sciences acquired their current place in society. It is easier to understand many ethical and political issues if they are seen in the context of the historical development of the social sciences.

In Chapter 1 we discussed the distinctive contribution of science to society and how social work research is a source of knowledge about the social world. The perspectives and techniques of social work research can be powerful tools for understanding the world. Nevertheless, with that power comes responsibility—a responsibility to yourself, a responsibility to your sponsors, a responsibility to the community of researchers, and a responsibility to the larger society. These responsibilities can and do come into conflict with each other at times.

Ultimately, you personally must decide to conduct research in an ethical manner, to uphold and defend the principles of the social work approach you adopt, and to demand ethical conduct by others. The truthfulness of knowledge produced by social work research and its use or misuse depend on individual researchers like you, reflecting on their actions and on how social work research fits into society. To help you with these ethical issues, we provide you with a list of websites on research ethics and human subjects issues (see Figure 5.4).

KEY TERMS

academic freedom	institutional review board (IRB)	relational position
anonymity	Milgram's obedience study	research fraud
"Bad Blood"	models of relevance	scientific misconduct
code of ethics	Nuremberg code	Tearoom Trade study
confidentiality	plagiarism	value neutrality
contract research	principle of voluntary consent	Wichita Jury Study
crossover design	Project Camelot	Zimbardo prison experiment
informed consent		

FIGURE 5.4   Websites for Research and Evaluation Ethics and Human Subjects Issues

INFORMED CONSENT

Protecting Human Research Subjects	www.hhs.gov/news/press/2000pres/20000606a.html
The Belmont Report	http://ohrp.osophs.dhhs.gov/humansubjects/guidance/belmont.htm
The Nuremberg Code	http://ohsr.od.nih.gov/nuremberg.php3
Declaration of Helsinki	www.fda.gov/oc/health/helsinki89.html
Report and Recommendations of the National Bioethics Advisory Commission (NBAC)— Executive Summary	http://bioethics.georgetown.edu/nbac/human/oversumm.pdf
An NIMH Commentary on the NBAC Report	www.nimh.nih.gov/litalert/commentary.cfm
Responsibilities of the Office of Human Subjects Research	http://ohsr.od.nih.gov/info/ainfo_1.php3
The Tuskegee Syphilis Experiment	www.infoplease.com/ipa/A0762136.html
Challenges to Human Subject Protections in U.S. Medical Research	http://jama.ama-assn.org/issues/v282n20/abs/jsc90090.html
Medical Ethics Relating to Clinical Investigations Using Human Subjects	http://archderm.ama-assn.org/issues/v135n4/ffull/ded8032.html
What Makes Clinical Research Ethical?	http://jama.ama-assn.org/issues/v283n20/abs/jsc90374.html
Ethical and Human-Rights Issues in Research on Mental Disorders	www.nejm.org/content/1999/0340/0018/1430.asp
New Office for Human Research Protections Created	www.hhs.gov/news/press/2000pres/20000606.html
Required Education in the Protection of Human Research Participants	http://grants.nih.gov/grants/guide/notice-files/NOT-OD-00-039.html
Frequently Asked Questions for the Requirement for Education on the Protection of Human Subjects	http://grants.nig.gov/grants/policy/hs_educ_faq.htm

INCLUSION/EXCLUSION

NIH Guidelines on Inclusion of Women and Minorities	http://ohrp.osophs.dhhs.gov/humansubjects/guidance/59fr14508.htm
Inclusion of Women and Minorities in Research	http://ohrp.osophs.dhhs.gov/humansubjects/guidance/hsdc94-01.htm
HHS Policy for Improving Race and Ethnicity Data	www.hhs.gov/oirm/infocollect/nclusion.html
Improving the Collection and Use of Racial and Ethnic Data in HHS	http://aspe.hhs.gov/datacncl/racerpt/index.htm
NIH Policy Guidance on the Inclusion of Children in Research	http://ohrp.osophs.dhhs.gov.humansubjects/guidance/hsdc98-03.htm
NIH Policy and Guidelines on the Inclusion of Children as Participants in Research	http://grants.nih.gov/grants/guide/notice-files/not98-024.html

CONFIDENTIALITY/PRIVACY

Privacy and Health Research	http://aspe.hhs.gov/datacncl/PHRintro.htm
Legal Issues Concerning Electronic Health Information	http://jama.ama-assn.org/issues/v282n15/abs/jlm80037.html
Privacy Protection for Research Subjects	http://ohrp.osophs.dhhs.gov/humansubjects/guidance/certconpriv.htm
The State of Health Privacy: An Uneven Terrain	www.georgetown.edu/research/ihcrp/privacy/statereport.pdf
Privacy and Security of Public Health Information	www.critpath.org/msphpa/ncshdoc.htm
Privacy and Confidentiality of Behavioral Health Care Records	www.networksplus.net/fhp/madnation/bioethics/privacy.htm
Confidentiality of Mental Health Information: Ethical, Legal, and Policy Issues	www.mentalhealth.org/features/surgeongeneralreport/chapter7/sec1.asp

(continued)

FIGURE 5.4   Continued

RISK & DISSEMINATION

Pressures in Industry-Sponsored Clinical Research	http://oig.hhs.gov/oei/reports/oei-01-97-00195.pdf
Financial Conflicts of Interest and Research Objectivity	http://grants.nih.gov/grants/guide/notice-files/ NOT-OD-00-040.html
Protection of Persons with Mental Disorders from Research Risk	http://archpsyc.ama-assn.org/issues/v56n8/abs/ yps8396.html
U.S. Government Executive Branch Policies	www.thecre.com/access/comments/1-3-1.html
Guidance on the Research Use of Stored Samples or Data	http://ohsr.od.nih.gov/info/ninfo_14.php3

GENERAL ETHICS RESOURCES

NIH Regulatory Burden–Introduction	http://grants.nih.gov/grants/policy/ regulatoryburden/intro.htm
Updating Protections for Human Subjects Involved in Research	http://jama.ama-assn.org/issues/v280n22/abs/ jpp80014.html
The Need to Revise the Declaration of Helsinki	www.nejm.org/content/1999/0341/0007/0531.asp
Proposed Revisions to the Declaration of Helsinki— Will They Weaken the Ethical Principles Underlying Human Research?	www.nejm.org/content/1999/0341/0007/0527.asp
CRE Comments to OMB on its August 11, 1999 Reproposal	www.thecre.com/access/cretoomb.html
Council on Government Relations Comment on Amendment 110	www.thecre.com/ipd/access/agency/ 1999-03-17.html
Association of American Universities Comment on Amendment 110	www.thecre.com/ipd/access/agency/ 1999-03-23.html
HHS Proposes First-Ever National Standards to Protect Patients' Personal Medical Records	http://aspe.hhs.gov/admnsimp/nprm/press4.htm
Health Privacy Project (Georgetown University)	www.healthprivacy.org/latest/ Best_Principles_Report.pdf
Shaping a Vision for 21st Century Health Statistics	http://ncvhs.hhs.gov/Vision21stReport.htm
Guidelines for Writing Research Protocols	http://ohsr.od.nih.gov//info/einfo_5.php3
A Participant's Guide to Mental Health Clinical Research	http://gopher.nimh.nih.gov/studies/clinres.cfm
Recruiting Human Subjects: Sample Guidelines for Practice	http://oig.hhs.gov/oei/reports/oei-01-97-00196.pdf

---

GOVERNMENT WEB SITES

National Bioethics Advisory Commission	www.georgetown.edu/research/nrcbl/nbac
Office of Research Integrity, U.S. Department of Health and Human Services	http://ori.dhhs.gov
Food and Drug Administration Guidance for IRBs and Clinical Investigators	www.fda.gov/oc/oha/IRB/toc.html
Department of Energy Ethics Links	www.er.doe.gov/production/ober/ humsubj/list3.html

---

REVIEW QUESTIONS _____

1. What is the primary defense against unethical conduct in research?

2. How do deception and coercion to participate in research conflict with the principle of voluntary consent?

3. Explain the ethical issues in the Milgram, Humphreys, and Zimbardo examples.

4. What is *informed consent,* and how does it protect research subjects?

5. What are the differences between *anonymity* and *confidentiality*?

6. What are the origins of codes of ethics in social work research?

7. In what ways might a sponsor attempt to influence a researcher illegitimately, and what can the researcher do about it?

8. In what ways can political groups or politicians affect social work research?

9. What would happen if research subjects treated information about themselves as their private property?

10. What is the relationship between academic freedom and research ethics?

NOTES

1. See Gillespie (1999), Klein, Bloom, and Chandler (1994), Levi (1976), Reamer (1989), Reamer and Abranson (1982), Reynolds (1979:56–57) and Sieber (1993).

2. Research fraud is discussed by Broad and Wade (1982), Diener and Crandall (1978:154–158), and Weinstein (1979). Also, see Hearnshaw (1979) and Wade (1976) on Cyril Burt. Kusserow (1989) and the September 1, 1989, issue of the National Institutes of Health weekly *Guide* summarize some recent scientific misconduct issues.

3. See "Noted Harvard Psychiatrist Resigns Post after Faculty Group Finds He Plagiarized," *Chronicle of Higher Education* (December 7, 1988).

4. See Blum (1989) and D'Antonio (1989) on this case of plagiarism. For a discussion of problems with students completing tests over the Internet, see Gibelman, Gelman, and Fast (1999).

5. See "Doctor Is Accused of 'Immoral' Tests," *New York Times* (December 9, 1988). For a more general discussion of power and trust, see Reynolds (1979:32).

6. Lifton (1986) provided an account of Nazi medical experimentation.

7. See Jones (1981) and Mitchell (1997) on the Bad Blood case.

8. Diener and Crandall (1978:128) discuss these examples.

9. See Warwick (1982) on types of harm to research subjects. See Reynolds (1979:62–68) on rates of harm in biomedical research. Kelman (1982) discusses different types of harm from different types of research.

10. College counselors report that anxiety and low self-esteem over dating are major problems among college women (Diener and Crandall, 1978:21–22). Also, see Kidder and Judd (1986:481–484).

11. See Dooley (1984:330) and Kidder and Judd (1986: 477–484).

12. See Hallowell (1985) and "Threat to Confidentiality of Fieldnotes," *ASA Footnotes,* Volume 12 (October 1984), p. 6.

13. For more on the general issue of the right not to be researched, see Barnes (1979), Boruch (1982), Moore (1973), and Sagarin (1973).

14. The debate over covert research is discussed in Denzin and Erikson (1982), Homan (1980), and Sieber (1982). Also, see the section on ethics in Chapter 13.

15. See Diener and Crandall (1978:87) and Warwick (1982:112).

16. Informed consent requirements and regulations are discussed in detail in Maloney (1984). Also, see Capron (1982) and Diener and Crandall (1978:64–66). Additional discussions may be found on websites listed in Figure 5.4.

17. See Diener and Crandall (1978:173–177) and Kidder and Judd (1986:469).

18. See Boruch (1982), Caplan (1982), Katz (1972), and Vaughan (1967) on privacy.

19. For more on the Wichita Jury Study, see Dooley (1984:338–339), Gray (1982), Robertson (1982), Tropp (1982:391), and Vaughan (1967).

20. For more on gatekeepers, see Broadhead and Rist (1976).

21. IRBs are discussed in Maloncy (1984) and Chadwick and associates (1984:20).

22. See Abbott (1988), Brint (1994), and Freidson (1986, 1994) on professionals.

23. See Beecher (1970:227–228) and Reynolds (1979: 28–31, 428–441).

24. See "UW Protects Dissertation Sources," *Capital Times* (December 19, 1994), p. 4.

25. See Hirschman (1970) on loyalty, exit, or voice. Also, see Rubin (1983:24–40) on ethical issues in applied research.

26. Additional discussion can be found in Schmeling and Miller (1988).

27. See Fiske (1989), Koretz (1988), and Weiss and Gruber (1987) on educational statistics.

28. See Staggenborg (1988) on "hired hand" research.

29. See "State Sought, Got Author's Changes in Lottery Report" *Capital Times* (July 28, 1989), p. 21.

30. See Chambers (1986).

31. See Dale W. Nelson, "Analyst: War Death Counts Falsified," *Wisconsin State Journal* (April 14, 1992),

p. 3A, and "Ex-Official Says Pentagon Dumped Findings on Gays," *Capital Times* (April 1, 1993).

32. For Russian social science research, see Keller (1988, 1989) and Swafford (1987). Also, see "Soviet Sociologist Calls Attention for Her Science," American Sociological Association *Footnotes* (April 1987), p. 2.

33. See Greenberg (1967:71).

34. For more on the decade of the 1950s and its effect on social researchers, see Caute (1978:403–430), Goldstein (1978:360–369), and Schrecker (1986).

35. See Block and Burns (1986) and Starr (1987).

36. See Steven Holmes, "Congressional Panels Move to Bar Sampling from Census," *New York Times* (September 18, 1996); David Stout, "Republicans Remain Hostile to Proposal for Census Sampling," *New York Times* (May 12, 1997); "Lies, Damned Lies and . . . ," *The Economist,* (July 19, 1997); Steven Holmes, "Tentative Pact Will Allow Census to Test Sampling Method," *New York Times* (November 11, 1997); Steven Holmes, "House Republicans Plan to Keep a Tight Reign on 2000 Census," *New York Times* (February 9, 1998).

37. See Starr and Corson (1987:435).

38. See Weiss and Gruber (1987:369).

39. See Bermant (1982:138). Nelkin (1982a) provided a general discussion of "forbidden" topics in social work research.

40. For more on the Proxmire award, see Cordes (1988).

41. "Sex Survey Is Dealt a Setback," *New York Times* (July 26, 1989), p. 7.

42. See Stephen Burd, "Scientists Fear Rise of Intrusion in Work Supported by NIH," in *Chronicle of Higher Education* (October 2, 1991), p. Alff.

43. Project Camelot is described in Horowitz (1965).

44. See Dickson (1984), Nelkin (1982b), and Shattuck and Spence (1988:2).

45. See Shattuck and Spence (1988) and Josephson (1988). Also, see "Librarians Charge Plan Would Cut Flow of Data," *New York Times* (February 21, 1989).

46. For more on the CIA and social work researchers, see Shattuck and Spence (1988:39–40) and Stephenson (1978).

47. For sensitive situations involving cross-national research, see Fuller (1988) and Van den Berge (1967).

48. For discussion, see Bannister (1987), Blumer (1991b), D'Antonio (1992), Hyman (1991), Ross (1991), and Seybold (1987).

49. See Dynes (1984) on COSSA.

50. The SSRC spent $20 million for the social sciences from 1924 to 1928 (Gieger, 1986:152) compared to $136 million allocated in 1989 by the NSF for the social sciences (D'Antonio, 1992). In the late 1920s the number of academic social scientists was about one-tenth and a dollar purchased over six times more. The number of social science doctorates—including psychology, teaching, or conducting basic research—in 1986 was about 129,000 (Science and Engineering Personnel: A National Overview, Document NSF 90-310). The size of the higher educational faculty in all academic fields in 1930 was under 83,000 (Historical Statistics of the United States, 1970, Table H696). The $20 million over four years in the 1920s, or $5 million per year, would be equivalent to roughly $300 million in 1990. The median family income before taxes in 1929 was $2,335 (Historical Statistics, Table G308).

51. For more on the effects of politics and funding cuts on social work research in the 1980s, see Cummings (1984), Himmelstein and Zald (1984), and Zuiches (1984). For more general discussion of the effect of funding on research, see Galliher and McCartney (1973) and Dickson (1984).

52. See "NIH FY 1991 Budget Rescinded by $3.1 Million, Congress Objects to 31 Research Projects Funded by NSF," *The Blue Sheet* (F-D-C Reports, Inc.) (May 27, 1992), p. 3.

53. On the issue of influence over researchers, see Punch (1986:18–19; 49–69). Also, see Lawrence Altman, "Experts See Bias in Drug Data," *New York Times* (April 29, 1997) and Sheryl Gay Stolberg, "Gifts to Science Researchers Have Strings, Study Finds," *New York Times* (April 1, 1998). On the nursing home "slap suit," see Steven Greenhouse, "Cornell Professor Fights a Slander Suit" *New York Times* (April 1, 1998) and news report of Morning Edition, National Public Radio (April 27, 1998).

54. See Shattuck and Spence (1988:35–37).

55. For more discussion on how researchers select research questions or problems, see Gieryn (1978) and Zuckerman (1978).

56. See Brym (1980) on the role of intellectuals in society.

57. Marsh (1984), Noelle-Neumann (1974, 1984), and Price (1989) discussed the effects of research results on subsequent public behavior and opinion.

58. Bartiz (1960), Schrecker (1986), Schwendinger and Schwendinger (1974), and Silva and Slaughter (1980) discuss the history of social researchers in society.

59. Committees on the Status of Women in Sociology (1986).

60. Devore and Schlesinger (1996), Green (1999), Inglehart and Becerra (1995), Kim (1995), Midgley (1990), Shands (1999), and Williams and Ellison (1996).

CHAPTER 6

QUALITATIVE AND QUANTITATIVE RESEARCH DESIGNS

Current configurations of power within the discipline make it difficult to combine different paradigms of inquiry. . . . The field of sociology has exciting possibilities, if it can remain open to a wide range of theoretical and methodological options. Sociology should become more adventurous, less clannish, more open to other disciplines. It would also be better to understand not only the limitations of each paradigm of inquiry, but also its potentialities.

—Robert R. Alford, *The Craft of Inquiry*, pp. 3–4.

INTRODUCTION

This chapter begins Part Two, in which we will look at the logic of research: strategies for designing a study, creating measures, and sampling. Differences between quantitative and qualitative styles of doing research will be more evident. Quantitative social work researchers are more concerned about issues of design, measurement, and sampling because their deductive approach emphasizes detailed planning prior to data collection and analysis. Qualitative social work researchers are more concerned about issues of the richness, texture, and feeling of raw data because their inductive approach emphasizes developing insights and generalizations out of the data collected.

QUALITATIVE AND QUANTITATIVE ORIENTATIONS TOWARD SOCIAL WORK RESEARCH

Qualitative and quantitative social work research differ in many ways, but they complement each other in many ways as well. All social work researchers systematically collect and analyze empirical data and carefully examine the patterns in them to understand and explain social life. One of the differences between the two styles comes from the nature of the data. *Soft data,* in the form of impressions, words, sentences, photos, symbols, and so forth, dictate different research strategies and data collection techniques than *hard data,* in the form of numbers. Another difference is that qualitative and quantitative social work researchers often have varying assumptions about social life and have different objectives. These differences can make tools used by the other style inappropriate or irrelevant. The differences can create confusion among students, researchers, and the readers of research reports. People who judge qualitative social work research by standards of quantitative social work research are often disappointed, and vice versa. It is best to appreciate the strengths each style offers.

To appreciate the strengths of each style, it is important to understand the distinct orientations of researchers. Almost all quantitative social work researchers rely on a positivist approach to social science. They are likely to use a technocratic perspective, apply "reconstructed logic," and follow a linear research path. They speak a language of "variables and hypotheses." Quantitative social work researchers emphasize precisely measuring vari-

ables and testing hypotheses that are linked to general causal explanations.

Qualitative social work researchers, by contrast, often rely on interpretive or critical social science. They are more likely to use a transcendent perspective, apply "logic in practice," and follow a nonlinear research path. Qualitative social work researchers speak a language of "cases and contexts." They emphasize conducting detailed examinations of cases that arise in the natural flow of social life. They usually try to present authentic interpretations that are sensitive to specific social–historical contexts. Interestingly, more female than male social work researchers adopt the qualitative approach.[1]

Researchers who use one style alone do not always communicate well with those using the other, but the languages and orientations of the styles are mutually intelligible. It takes time and effort to understand both styles and to see how they can be complementary (see Table 6.1).

Reconstructed Logic and Logic in Practice

The way social work researchers learn and discuss research usually follows one of two logics: reconstructed logic or logic in practice (Kaplan, 1964:3–11). Most researchers will mix the two logics, but the proportion of each varies. Quantitative social work researchers apply more of the reconstructed logic, whereas qualitative social work researchers tend to apply logic in practice. The differences in logic are not differences in the degree of rigor or effort. They represent differences the degree to which learning and discussions of social work research are explicit, codified, and standardized.

Reconstructed logic means that the logic of how to do research is highly organized and restated in an idealized, formal, and systematic form. It is reconstructed into logically consistent rules and terms. It is a cleansed model of how good research should proceed. This logic appears in textbooks and in published research reports. For example, the rules for conducting a simple random sample are very straightforward and follow a step-by-step procedure.

Logic in practice is the logic of how research is actually carried out. It is relatively messy, with more

TABLE 6.1   Differences between Quantitative and Qualitative Social Work Research

QUANTITATIVE	QUALITATIVE
— Tests hypothesis that the researcher begins with.	— Captures and discovers meaning once the researcher becomes immersed in the data.
— Concepts are in the form of distinct variables.	— Concepts are in the form of themes, motifs, generalizations, and taxonomies.
— Measures are systematically created before data collection and are standardized.	— Measures are created in an ad hoc manner and are often specific to the individual setting or researcher.
— Data are in the form of numbers from precise measurement.	— Data are in the form of words and images from documents, observations, and transcripts.
— Theory is largely causal and is deductive.	— Theory can be causal or noncausal and is often inductive.
— Procedures are standard, and replication is assumed.	— Research procedures are particular, and replication is very rare.
— Analysis proceeds by using statistics, tables, or charts and discussing how what they show relates to hypotheses.	— Analysis proceeds by extracting themes or generalizations from evidence and organizing data to present a coherent, consistent picture.

ambiguity, and is tied to specific cases and oriented toward the practical completion of a task. It has fewer set rules. The logic is based on judgment calls or norms shared among experienced researchers. It depends on an informal folk wisdom passed among researchers when they get together over lunch or coffee and discuss doing research.

Quantitative social work research using reconstructed logic is easier to define and learn from books or formal instruction. Quantitative social work researchers describe the technical research procedures they use (e.g., a systematic random sample of 300 drawn from a telephone directory; Likert scaling). The procedures are shared, explicit methods.

Qualitative social work research relies on the informal wisdom that has developed from the experiences of researchers. Qualitative social work research reports may not discuss method (common for historical–comparative research) or may have a personal autobiographical account tailored to a particular study (common for field research). Few procedures or terms are standardized, and there is a debate among qualitative social work researchers about whether they ever should be. Many qualitative

social work researchers learned how to do research by reading many reports, by trial and error, and by working in an apprentice role with an experienced researcher. This does not mean that qualitative social work research is less valid, but it may be more difficult for someone learning about it for the first time to grasp.

Technocratic and Transcendent Perspectives

Another way to distinguish qualitative and quantitative styles of research is the contrast between technocratic and transcendent perspectives.[2] The *technocratic perspective* fits with positivism, and quantitative social work researchers more frequently use it. In it, the researcher is the expert, and research questions often originate with the sponsors of the research (i.e., those who supply funds). The goal of research is to discover and document lawlike generalizations oriented toward increasing efficiency. It is the perspective of a technician who serves bureaucratic needs.

By contrast, the *transcendent perspective* more closely fits the interpretive and critical approaches. In it, research questions originate with the standpoint of the people being studied, not that of outsiders. Its goal is to remove false beliefs held by those being studied and to treat people as creative, compassionate living beings, not as objects. It often questions power or inequality and views social relations more as the outcome of willful actions than as laws of human nature. It tries to help people grow, take charge of their lives, and engage in social change—that is, to transcend current social conditions.

Qualitative social work research relies largely on the interpretive and critical approaches to social work. The approaches differ from each other in important ways, but both are alternatives to positivism, the foundation of quantitative social work research. Quantitative social work research is contrary to the core assumptions and goals of interpretive social work (see Chapter 4). In contrast to interpretive researchers, critical researchers use quantitative techniques. When they do so, however, critical social work researchers diverge from strict positivism. They apply theory in a different way, give the historical context a major role, critique social conditions, and reveal deep structures of social relations.

Qualitative data give quantitative social work researchers rich information about the social processes in specific settings. They may also give critical researchers the potential to break through technocratic assumptions implicit in quantitative approaches. For example, Marshall (1985) noted that qualitative social work research methods are less likely to fit into the assumptions of the dominant paradigm of educational administration. In it, educational issues are defined as managerial problems caused by ignorance, lack of motivation by students or their parents, inadequate resources, or lack of motivation by professionals or bureaucrats. A researcher using the technocratic perspective would gather data needed to resolve the problems as they have been defined by the dominant paradigm. But a qualitative social work researcher using a transcendent perspective asks critical theoretical and political questions (e.g., Who benefits?). He or she places issues in a larger socio–historical context, observes everyday processes close up, and understands the viewpoints of all involved in

schooling, including those who oppose the administrative perspective.

Linear and Nonlinear Paths

Researchers follow a path when conducting research. The path is a metaphor for the sequence of things to do: what is finished first or where a researcher has been, and what comes next or where he or she is going. The path may be one that is well worn and marked with signposts where many other researchers have trod. Alternatively, it may be a new path into unknown territory where few others have gone, and without signs marking the direction forward.

In general, quantitative social work researchers follow a more linear path than do qualitative social work researchers. A *linear research path* follows a fixed sequence of steps. It is like a staircase leading in one clear direction. It is a way of thinking and a way of looking at issues—the direct, narrow, straight path that is most common in western European and North American culture.

Qualitative social work research is more nonlinear and cyclical. Rather than moving in a straight line, a *nonlinear research path* makes successive passes through steps, sometimes moving backward and sideways before moving on. It is more of a spiral, moving slowly upward but not directly. With each cycle or repetition, a researcher collects new data and gains new insights.

People who are used to the direct, linear approach may be impatient with a less direct, cyclical path. From a strict linear perspective, a cyclical path looks inefficient and sloppy. But the diffuse cyclical approach is not merely disorganized, undefined chaos. It can be highly effective for creating a feeling for the whole, for grasping subtle shades of meaning, for pulling together divergent information, and for switching perspectives. It is not an excuse for doing poor-quality research, and it has its own discipline and rigor. It borrows devices from the humanities (e.g., metaphor, analogy, theme, motif, and irony) and is oriented toward constructing meaning. A cyclical path is suited for tasks such as translating languages, where delicate shades of meaning, subtle connotations, or contextual distinctions can be important. "Circularity is one of the strengths of the approach, because it forces the researcher to permanently reflect on the whole research process and on particular steps in light of the other steps" (Flick, 1998:43).

Triangulation

Surveyors and sailors measure distances between objects by making observations from multiple positions. By observing something from different angles or viewpoints, they get a fix on its true location (see Figure 6.1). This process, called *triangulation,* is used by quantitative and qualitative social work researchers. Applied to social research, it means it is better to look at something from several angles than to look at it in only one way.

There are several types of triangulation. The most common type is *triangulation of measures.* Researchers take multiple measures of the same phenomena. By measuring something in more than one way, researchers are more likely to see all aspects of it. For example, a teacher has students write answers to essay questions, complete a series of multiple-choice questions, give an oral presentation, and complete a term paper or applied project. The teacher's confidence in getting an accurate measure of the student's learning is greater if the student scores similarly on all four testing methods than on just one or

two. Any differences in results for the measures become interesting, informative data, as well.

Another type is *triangulation of observers.* In many studies, one researcher conducts interviews or is the sole observer of people's behavior. A single person means the limitations of the one observer become the limitations of the study. Multiple observers or researchers add alternative perspectives, backgrounds, and social characteristics and will reduce the limitations. For example, imagine a study that involves observing patient behavior in a hospital conducted by one person—a White, 55-year-old male who has substantial medical training. In addition to the single observer's background and perspective, the behaviors and conversations he notices or that could occur in his presence might differ if the observer was female, was 30 years old, was of a different race, or lacked medical training. Combining data from a variety of observers is more likely to yield a more definitive picture of the setting.

Triangulation of theory occurs when a researcher uses multiple theoretical perspectives early in the planning stages of research, or when interpreting the data. For example, the researcher plans the study by using the concepts and assumptions of both conflict theory and exchange theory, or looks at the data coming from each theoretical perspective. Using more than one theory may be difficult, but it will increase the chance of making a creative synthesis or developing new ideas.

Last, *triangulation of method* means mixing qualitative and quantitative styles of research and data. Most researchers develop an expertise in one style, but the two methods or styles have different, complementary strengths. Since there is only partial overlap, a study using both is more comprehensive. Mixing the styles can occur in several ways (see Tashakkori and Teddlie, 1998). One way is to use the methods sequentially—first one, then the other. Another way is to carry out the study by using the two methods in parallel, or both simultaneously. For example, Dressler (1991) used sequential methods. He wanted to study how various household factors, lifestyle, and family resources affected whether African Americans in a community in the U.S. South developed depression. He began using the

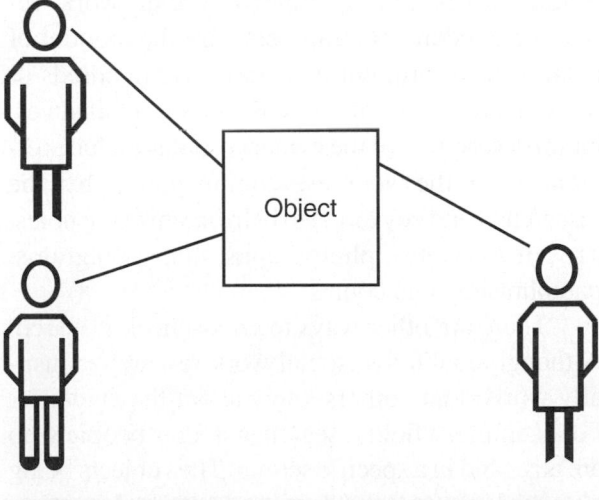

FIGURE 6.1   Triangulation: Observing from Different Viewpoints

qualitative style, with open-ended ethnographic interviews, then followed with a quantitative survey questionnaire from which he gathered data for statistical analysis.

Objectivity and Integrity

Opportunities for biased, dishonest, or unethical research exist in all research. All social work researchers want to be fair, honest, truthful, and unbiased in their research activity. Nevertheless, the qualitative and quantitative styles emphasize different ways to ensure honest, truthful research. Quantitative social work researchers stress objectivity and more "mechanical" techniques. They use the principle of replication, adhere to standardized methodological procedures, measure with numbers, and then analyze the data with statistics, an area of applied mathematics.[3] Quantitative social work research eliminates the human factor. As Porter (1995:7, 74) argues,

> *Ideally, expertise should be mechanized and objectified . . . grounded in specific techniques. . . . This ideal of objectivity is a political as well as scientific one. Objectivity means rule of law, not of men. It implies the subordination of personal interests and prejudices to public standards.*

Qualitative social work researchers emphasize the human factor and the intimate firsthand knowledge of the research setting; they avoid distancing themselves from the people or events they study. This does not mean arbitrarily interjecting personal opinion, being sloppy about data collection, or using evidence selectively to support personal prejudices. It means taking advantage of personal insight, feelings, and human perspectives to understand social life better. The researcher makes his or her presence explicit and is sensitive to prior assumptions. In place of "objective" techniques, the qualitative social work researcher is forthright and open about his or her personal involvement. Qualitative social work researchers emphasize trustworthiness as a parallel idea to objective standards in quantitative social work research design. This ensures that research activities are dependable and credible.[4]

Researcher integrity is a critical issue in qualitative social work research. Quantitative social work research addresses the issue of integrity by relying on an objective technology—such as precise statements, standard techniques, numerical measures, statistics, and replication; qualitative social work research places greater trust in the personal integrity of individual researchers, but it includes a variety of checks on how evidence is gathered.

Checks. Qualitative social work researchers ensure that their research accurately reflects the evidence and have checks on their evidence.[5] For example, the field researcher listens to and records a student who says, "Professor Smith threw an eraser at Professor Jones." The field researcher treats this evidence carefully. To strengthen the claim, the researcher considers what other people say, looks for confirming evidence, and checks for internal consistency. The researcher asks whether the student has firsthand knowledge of the event and whether the student's feelings or self-interest would lead him to lie (e.g., the student might dislike Professor Smith for other reasons). Even if the student made a false statement, it is evidence about the student's perspective. Similarly, the researcher examining historical evidence uses techniques for verifying the authenticity of sources.

Another check is the great volume of detailed written notes that qualitative social work researchers record. Researchers vary the amount of detail they record, but they may have hundreds or thousands of pages of notes. Besides a detailed verbatim description of the evidence, notes include references to the sources, commentaries by the researcher, and key terms to help organize the notes, as well as quotes, photographs, maps, diagrams, paraphrasing, and counts.

There are other ways to cross-check research. Although qualitative social work researchers usually work alone, others know about the evidence. For example, a field researcher studies people who are alive and in a specific setting. The subjects being observed can read the details of a study. Likewise, historical documents are cited, and other researchers can check references and sources.

The most important way that a qualitative social work researcher creates trust in readers is the way he or she presents evidence. A qualitative social work researcher does not present all of his or her detailed notes in a report; rather, he or she spins a web of interlocking details, providing sufficient texture and detail so that the readers feel that they are there. A qualitative social work researcher's firsthand knowledge of events, people, and situations cuts two ways. It raises questions of bias, but it also provides a sense of immediacy, direct contact, and intimate knowledge.

QUANTITATIVE DESIGN ISSUES

The Language of Variables and Hypotheses

Variation and Variables.   The *variable* is a central idea in quantitative social work research. Simply defined, a variable is a concept that varies. Quantitative social work research uses a language of variables and relationships among variables.

In Chapter 3 you learned about two types of concepts: those that refer to a fixed phenomenon (e.g., the ideal type of bureaucracy) and those that vary in quantity, intensity, or amount (e.g., amount of education). The second type of concept and measures of the concepts are variables. Variables take on two or more values. Once you begin to look for them, you will see variables everywhere. For example, gender is a variable; it can take on two values: male or female. Marital status is a variable; it can take on the values of never married single, married, divorced, or widowed. Type of crime committed is a variable; it can take on values of robbery, burglary, theft, murder, and so forth. Family income is a variable; it can take on values from zero to billions of dollars. A person's attitude toward abortion is a variable; it can range from strongly favoring legal abortion to strongly believing in antiabortion.

The values or the categories of a variable are its *attributes*. It is easy to confuse variables with attributes. Variables and attributes are related, but they have distinct purposes. The confusion arises because the attribute of one variable can itself become a separate variable with a slight change in definition. The distinction is between concepts themselves that vary and conditions within concepts that vary. For example, "male" is not a variable; it describes a category of gender and is an attribute of the variable "gender." Yet, a related idea, "degree of masculinity," is a variable. It describes the intensity or strength of attachment to attitudes, beliefs, and behaviors associated with the concept of *masculine* within a culture. "Married" is not a variable; it is an attribute of the variable "marital status." Related ideas such as "number of years married" or "depth of commitment to a marriage" are variables. Likewise, "robbery" is not a variable; it is an attribute of the variable "type of crime." "Number of robberies," "robbery rate," "amount taken during a robbery," and "type of robbery" are all variables because they vary or take on a range of values.

Quantitative social work researchers redefine concepts of interest into the language of variables. As the examples of variables and attributes illustrate, slight changes in definition change a nonvariable into a variable concept. As you saw in Chapter 3, concepts are the building blocks of theory; they organize thinking about the social world. Clear concepts with careful definitions are essential in theory.

Types of Variables.   Researchers who focus on causal relations usually begin with an effect, then search for its causes. Variables are classified into three basic types, depending on their location in a causal relationship. The cause variable, or the one that identifies forces or conditions that act on something else, is the *independent variable.* The variable that is the effect or is the result or outcome of another variable is the *dependent variable.* The independent variable is "independent of" prior causes that act on it, whereas the dependent variable "depends on" the cause.

It is not always easy to determine whether a variable is independent or dependent. Two questions help you identify the independent variable. First, does it come before other variables in time? Independent variables come before any other type. Second, if the variables occur at the same time, does the author suggest that one variable has an impact on another variable? Independent variables affect, or have an impact on, other variables. Research topics are often phrased in terms of the dependent variables because dependent variables are the phenomena to be explained. For example, suppose a researcher examines the reasons for an increase in the crime rate in Dallas, Texas; the dependent variable is the crime rate.

A basic causal relationship requires only an independent and a dependent variable. A third type of variable, the *intervening variable,* appears in more complex causal relations. It comes between the independent and dependent variables and shows the link or mechanism between them. Advances in knowledge depend not only on documenting cause-and-effect relationships but also on specifying the mechanisms that account for the causal relation. In a sense the intervening variable acts as a dependent variable with respect to the independent variable and acts as an independent variable toward the dependent variable.

For example, French sociologist Emile Durkheim developed a theory of suicide that specified a causal relationship between marital status and suicide rates. Durkheim found evidence that married people are less likely to commit suicide than single people. He believed that married people have greater social integration (i.e., feelings of belonging to a group or family). He thought that a major cause of one type of suicide was that people lacked a sense of belonging to a group. Thus, his theory can be restated as a three-variable relationship: marital status (independent variable) causes the degree of social integration (intervening variable), which affects suicide (dependent variable). Specifying the chain of causality makes the linkages in a theory clearer and helps a researcher test complex explanations.[6]

Simple theories have one dependent and one independent variable, whereas complex theories can contain dozens of variables with multiple independent, intervening, and dependent variables. For example, a theory of criminal behavior (dependent variable) identifies four independent variables: an individual's economic hardship, opportunities to commit crime easily, membership in a deviant subgroup of society that does not disapprove of crime, and lack of punishment for criminal acts. A multi-cause explanation usually specifies the independent variable that has the greatest causal effect.

A complex theoretical explanation contains a string of multiple intervening variables that are linked together. For example, family disruption causes lower self-esteem among children, which causes depression, which causes poor grades in school, which causes reduced prospects for a good job, which causes a lower adult income. The chain of variables is family disruption (independent), childhood self-esteem (intervening), depression (intervening), grades in school (intervening), job prospects (intervening), and adult income (dependent).

Two theories on the same topic may have different independent variables or predict different independent variables to be important. In addition, theories may agree about the independent and dependent variables but differ on the intervening variable or causal mechanism. For example, two theories say that family disruption causes lower adult income, but for different reasons. One theory holds that disruption encourages children to join deviant peer groups that are not socialized to norms of work and thrift. Another emphasizes the impact of the disruption on childhood depression and poor academic performance, which directly affect job performance.

A single research project usually tests only a small part of a causal chain. For example, a research project examining six variables may take the six from a large, complex theory with two dozen variables. Explicit links to a larger theory strengthen and clarify a research project. This applies especially for explanatory, basic research, which is the model for most quantitative social work research.

Causal Relationships and Hypotheses

The Hypothesis and Causality. A *hypothesis* is a proposition to be tested or a tentative statement of a relationship between two variables. Hypotheses are guesses about how the social world works; they are stated in a value-neutral form. Kerlinger (1979:35) noted that

> *hypotheses are much more important in scientific research than they would appear to be just by knowing what they are and how they are constructed. They have a deep and highly significant purpose of taking man out of himself. . . . Hypotheses are powerful tools for the advancement of knowledge, be-*

cause, although formulated by man, they can be tested and shown to be correct or incorrect apart from man's values and beliefs.

A causal hypothesis has five characteristics (see Box 6.1). The first two characteristics define the minimum elements of a hypothesis. The third restates the hypothesis. For example, the hypothesis that attending religious services reduces the probability of divorce can be restated as a prediction: Couples who frequently attend religious services have a lower divorce rate than do couples who rarely attend religious services. The prediction can be tested against empirical evidence. The fourth characteristic states that the hypothesis should be logically tied to a research question and to a theory. Researchers test hypotheses to answer the research question or to find empirical support for a theory. The last characteristic requires that a researcher use empirical data to test the hypothesis. Statements that are necessarily true as a result of logic, or questions that are impossible to answer through empirical observation (e.g., What is the "good life"? Is there a God?) cannot be scientific hypotheses.

Causal hypotheses can be stated in several ways. Sometimes the word *cause* is used, but this is not necessary. For example, a causal hypothesis between religious attendance and a reduced likelihood of divorce can be stated in 10 different ways (see Box 6.2).

Box 6.1 _____

Five Characteristics of a Causal Hypothesis

1. It has at least two variables.
2. It expresses a causal or cause–effect relationship between the variables.
3. It can be expressed as a prediction or an expected future outcome.
4. It is logically linked to a research question and a theory.
5. It is falsifiable; that is, it is capable of being tested against empirical evidence and shown to be true or false.

Box 6.2 _____

Ways to State Causal Relations

- Religious attendance *causes* reduced divorce.
- Religious attendance *leads to* reduced divorce.
- Religious attendance *is related to* reduced divorce.
- Religious attendance *influences* the reduction of divorce.
- Religious attendance *is associated with* reduced divorce.
- Religious attendance *produces* reduced divorce.
- Religious attendance *results in* reduced divorce.
- If people attend religious services, *then* the likelihood of divorce will be reduced.
- *The higher* religious attendance, *the lower* the likelihood of divorce.
- Religious attendance *reduces* the likelihood of divorce.

Researchers avoid using the term *proved* when testing hypotheses. You might hear the word *proof* used in journalism, courts of law, or advertisements, but you will rarely hear research scientists use it. A jury says that the evidence "proves" someone guilty, or a television commercial states, "Studies prove that our aspirin cures headaches the fastest." This is not the language of scientific research. In science, knowledge is tentative, and creating knowledge is an ongoing process that avoids premature closure.

Scientists do not say they have proved a hypothesis or a causal relationship. Proof implies finality, absolute certainty, or something that does not need further investigation. *Proof* is too strong a term for the cautious world of science. Evidence supports or confirms, but does not prove, the hypothesis. Even after hundreds of studies show the same results, as with the link between cigarette smoking and lung cancer, scientists do not say that they have absolute proof. They can say that overwhelming evidence, or all studies to date, support, or are consistent with, the hypothesis. Scientists do not want to close off the possibility of discovering new evidence that might contradict past findings. They do not want to cut off future inquiry or stop exploring intervening mechanisms. History contains many examples of relationships that were once thought to be proved but were later found to be in error. *Proof* is used when referring to logical or mathematical relations, as in a mathematical proof, but not in discussing empirical research.

Testing and Refining a Hypothesis. Knowledge rarely advances on the basis of one test of a single hypothesis. In fact, it is easy to get a distorted picture of the research process by focusing on a single research project that tests one hypothesis. Knowledge develops over time as researchers throughout the scientific community test many hypotheses. It grows from shifting and winnowing through many hypotheses. Each hypothesis represents an explanation of a dependent variable. If the evidence fails to support some hypotheses, they are gradually eliminated from consideration. Those that receive support remain in contention. Theorists and researchers constantly create new hypotheses to challenge those that have received support.

Figure 6.2 represents an example of the process of sifting through hypotheses over time. At a given starting point (1960), there are eight contending hypotheses. Over the years, different researchers test the hypotheses until, by 2000, two hypotheses remain as possibilities. Neither had been developed in the beginning; the others were created as researchers sorted out existing evidence and developed new theories. The process continues as the hypotheses are tested against empirical evidence.

Scientists are a skeptical group. Support for a hypothesis in one research project is not sufficient for them to accept it. The principle of replication says that a hypothesis needs several tests with consistent and repeated support to gain broad acceptance. Another way to strengthen confidence in a hypothesis is to test related causal linkages in the theory from which it comes.

The strongest contender, or the hypothesis with the greatest empirical support, is accepted as the best explanation at the time. The logic suggests that the more alternatives we test a hypothesis against, the greater our confidence in it. Some tests of hypotheses are called *crucial experiments* or crucial studies. This is a type of study where

two or more alternative explanations for some phenomenon are available, each being compatible with the empirically given data; the crucial experiment is designed to yield results that can be accounted for by only one of the alternatives, which is thereby shown to be "the correct explanation." (Kaplan, 1964:151–152)

Thus, the infrequent crucial experiment or research project is an important test of theory. Hypotheses from two different theories confront each other in crucial experiments, and one is knocked out of the competition. It is rare, but significant, when it occurs.

Types of Hypotheses. Hypotheses are links in a theoretical causal chain and can take several forms. Researchers use them to test the direction and strength of a relationship between variables. When a hypothesis defeats its competitors, or offers alternative explanations for a causal relation, it indirectly lends support to the researcher's explanation. A curious aspect of hypothesis testing is that researchers treat evidence that supports a hypothesis differently from evidence that opposes it. They give negative evidence more importance. The idea that negative evidence is critical when evaluating a hypothesis comes from the *logic of disconfirming hypotheses.*[7] It is associated with Karl Popper's idea of falsification (see Chapter 4) and with the use of null hypotheses (see later in this section).

Recall the preceding discussion of proof. A hypothesis is never proved, but it can be disproved. A researcher with supporting evidence can say only that the hypothesis remains a possibility or that it is still in the running. Negative evidence is more significant because the hypothesis becomes "tarnished" or "soiled" if the evidence fails to support it. This is because a hypothesis makes predictions. Negative and disconfirming evidence shows that the predictions are wrong. Positive or confirming evidence for a hypothesis is less critical because alternative hypotheses may make the same prediction. A researcher who finds confirming evidence for a prediction must not elevate one explanation over its alternatives.

For example, a man stands on a street corner with an umbrella and claims that his umbrella protects him from falling elephants. His hypothesis that

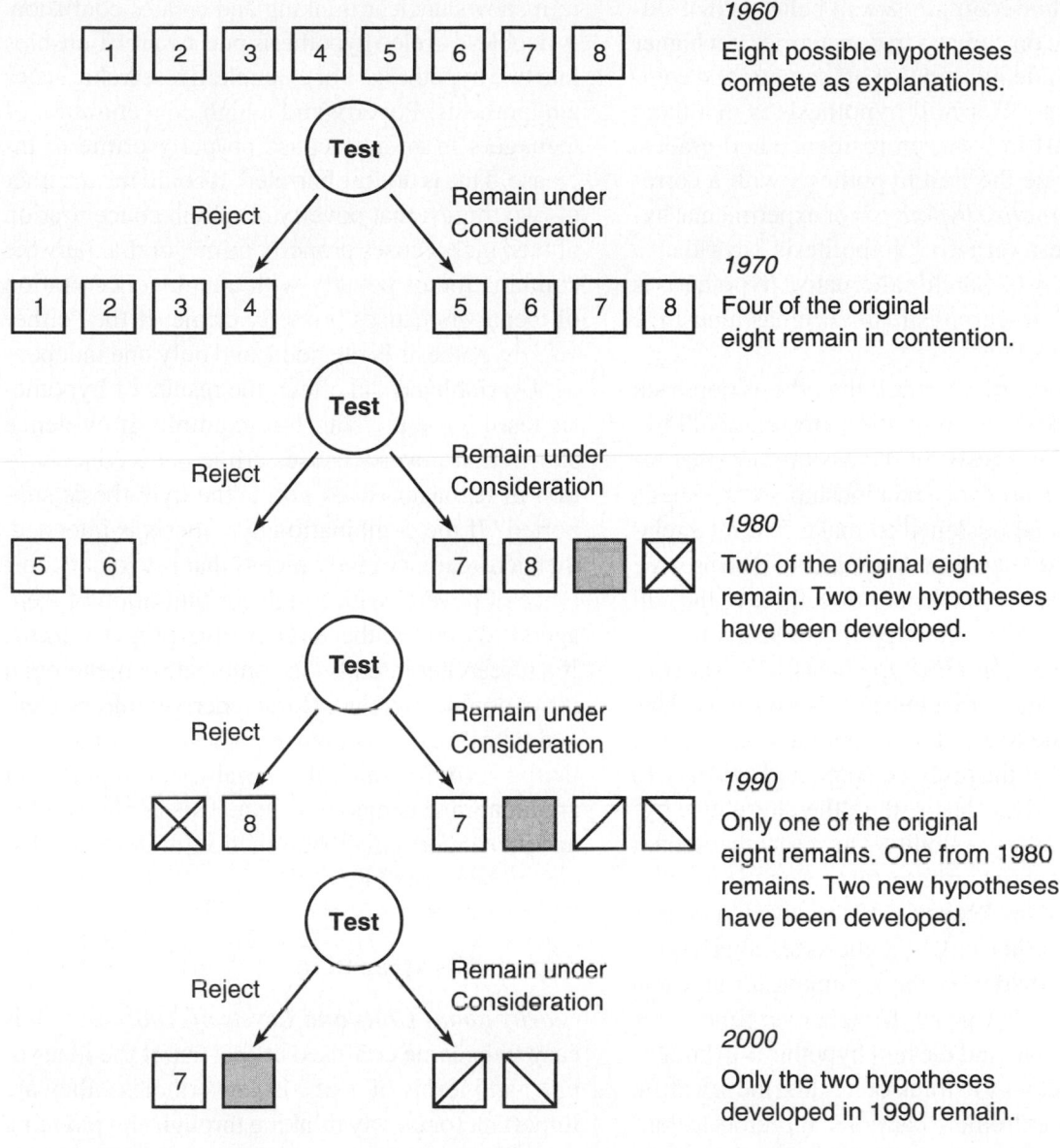

FIGURE 6.2   How the Process of Hypotheses Testing Operates over Time

the umbrella provides protection has supporting evidence. He has not had a single elephant fall on him in all the time he has had his umbrella open. Yet, such supportive evidence is weak; it also is consistent with an alternative hypothesis—that elephants do not fall from the sky. Both predict that the man will be safe from falling elephants. Negative evidence for the hypothesis—the one elephant that falls on him and his umbrella, crushing both—would destroy the hypothesis forever.

Researchers test hypotheses in two ways: a straightforward way and a null hypothesis way. Many quantitative social work researchers, especially experimenters, frame hypotheses in terms of a *null hypothesis* based on the logic of the disconfirming hypotheses. They test hypotheses by looking for evidence that will allow them to accept or reject the null hypothesis. Most people talk about a hypothesis as a way to predict a relationship. The null hypothesis does the opposite. It predicts no relationship. For example, Sarah believes that students who live on campus in dormitories get higher grades than students who live off campus and commute to college. Her null hypothesis is that there is no relationship between residence and grades. Researchers use the null hypothesis with a corresponding *alternative hypothesis* or experimental hypothesis. The alternative hypothesis says that a relationship exists. Sarah's alternative hypothesis is that students' on-campus residence has a positive effect on grades.

For most people, the null hypothesis approach is a backward way of hypothesis testing. Null hypothesis thinking rests on the assumption that researchers try to discover a relationship, so hypothesis testing should be designed to make finding a relationship more demanding. A researcher who uses the null hypothesis approach only directly tests the null hypothesis. If evidence supports or leads the researcher to accept the null hypothesis, he or she concludes that the tested relationship does not exist. This implies that the alternative hypothesis is false. On the other hand, if the researcher can find evidence to reject the null hypothesis, then the alternative hypothesis remains a possibility. The researcher cannot prove the alternative; rather, by testing the null hypothesis, he or she keeps the alternative hypothesis in contention. When null hypothesis testing is added to confirming evidence, the argument for an alterative hypothesis can grow stronger over time.

Many people find the null hypothesis to be confusing. Another way to think of it is that the scientific community is extremely cautious. It prefers to consider a causal relationship to be false until mountains of evidence show it to be true. This is similar to the Anglo-American legal idea of innocent until proven guilty. A researcher assumes, or acts as if, the null hypothesis is correct until *reasonable doubt* suggests otherwise. Researchers who use null hypotheses generally use them with specific statistical tests (e.g., t-test or F-test). Thus, a researcher may say there is reasonable doubt in a null hypothesis if a statistical test suggests that the odds of it being false are 99 in 100. This is what a researcher means when he or she says that statistical tests allow him or her to "reject the null hypothesis at the .01 level of significance."

Another type of hypothesis is the *double-barreled hypothesis*.[8] Researchers should avoid using it; it shows unclear thinking and creates confusion. A double-barreled hypothesis puts two relationships into one hypothesis. For example, a researcher states a hypothesis: Poverty and a high concentration of teenagers in an area cause property crime to increase. This is double barreled. It could mean either of two things: that poverty *or* a high concentration of teenagers causes property crime, or that *only* the combination of poverty with a high concentration of teenagers causes property crime. If the "either one" hypothesis is intended, and only one independent variable has an effect, the results of hypothesis testing are unclear. For example, if evidence shows that poverty causes crime but a concentration of teenagers does not, is the hypothesis supported? If the combination hypothesis is intended, then a researcher really means that the joint occurrence of poverty with a high concentration of teenagers only, and neither alone, causes property crime. If a researcher intends the combination meaning, it is not double barreled. Researchers should be clear and state the combination hypothesis so that the particular form in which the variables go together or are combined is made explicit. This is often called an *interaction effect* (interaction effects are discussed later; see Figure 6.3).

Aspects of Explanation

Clarity about Units and Levels of Analysis. It is easy to become confused at first about the ideas of units and levels of analysis. Nevertheless, they are important for clearly thinking through and planning a research project. All studies have both units and levels of analysis, but few researchers explicitly identify them as such. The levels and units of analysis are restricted by the topic and the research question. In other words, there is a rough match between the topic or research question and the units or levels of analysis that one can use.

A *level of analysis* is the level of social reality to which theoretical explanations refer. The level of social reality varies on a continuum from micro level (e.g., small groups or individual processes) to macro level (e.g., civilizations or structural aspects of society). The level includes a mix of the number of people, the amount of space, the scope of the activity, and the length of time. For example, an ex-

HYPOTHESIS: Poverty and a high concentration of teenagers in an area cause property crime to increase.

DOUBLE-BARRELED HYPOTHESIS: This could mean one of three things—

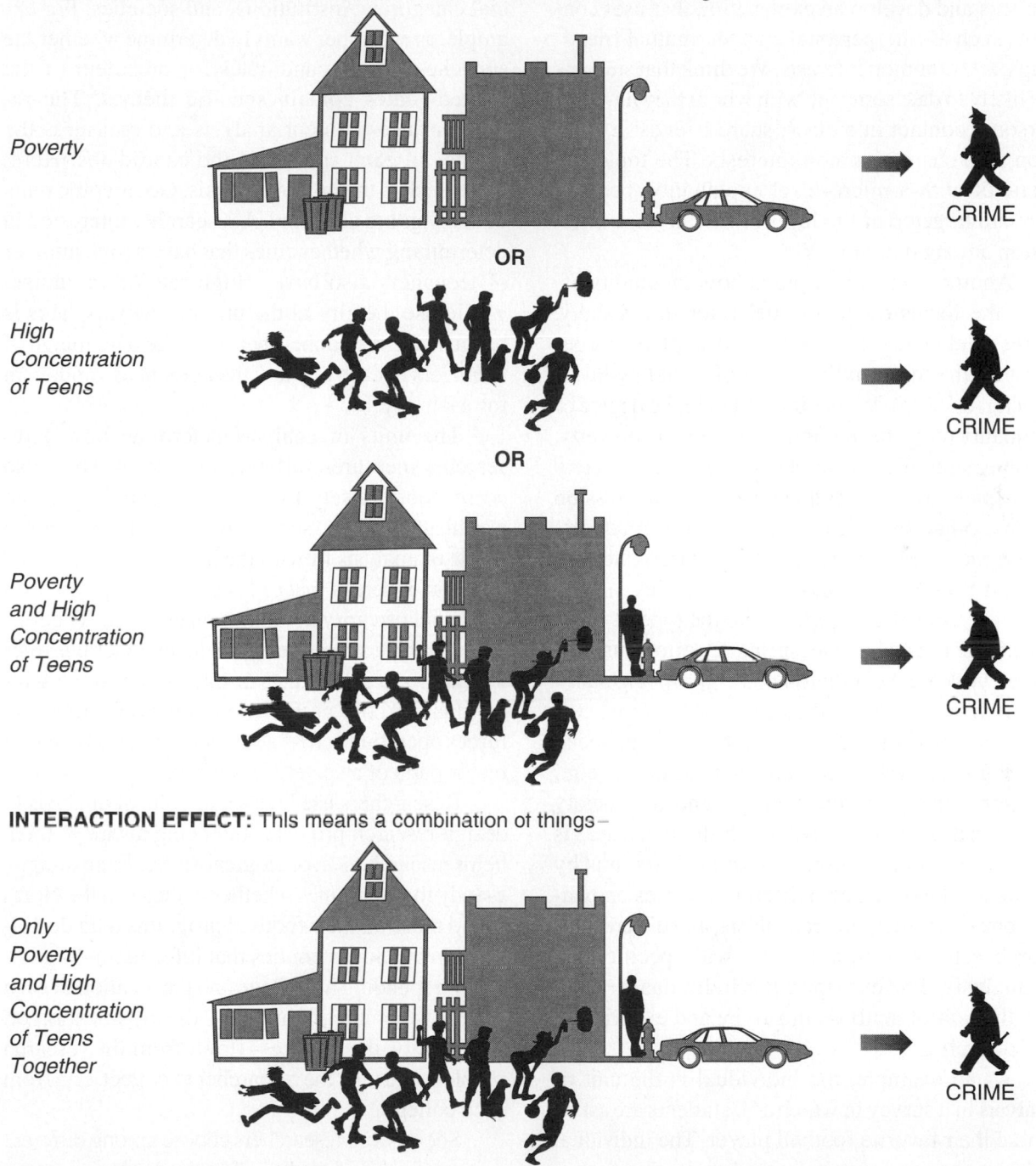

Poverty

OR

High Concentration of Teens

OR

Poverty and High Concentration of Teens

INTERACTION EFFECT: This means a combination of things—

Only Poverty and High Concentration of Teens Together

FIGURE 6.3 Double-Barreled Hypothesis versus Interaction Effect

treme micro-level analysis can involve a few seconds of interaction between two people in the same small room. An extreme macro-level analysis can involve billions of people on several continents across centuries. Most social work research uses a level of analysis that lies between these extremes.

The level of analysis delimits the kinds of assumptions, concepts, and theories that a researcher uses. For example, we want to study the topic of dating among college students. We use a micro-level analysis and develop an explanation that uses concepts such as interpersonal contact, mutual friendships, and common interests. We think that students are likely to date someone with whom they have had personal contact in a class, share friends in common, and share common interests. The topic and focus fit with a micro-level explanation because they are targeted at the level of face-to-face interaction among individuals.

Another example topic is how inequality affects the forms of violent behavior in a society. Here, we chose a more macro-level explanation because of the topic and the level of social reality at which it operates. We are interested in the degree of inequality (e.g., the distribution of wealth, property, income, and other resources) throughout a society and in patterns of societal violence (e.g., aggression against other societies, sexual assault, feuds between families). The topic and research question suggest macro-level concepts and theories.

The *unit of analysis* refers to the type of unit a researcher uses when measuring. Common units in social work are the individual, the group (e.g., family, friendship group), the organization (e.g., corporation, university), the social category (e.g., social class, gender, race), the social institution (e.g., religion, education, the family), and the society (e.g., a nation, a tribe). Although the individual is the most commonly used unit of analysis, it is by no means the only one. Different theories emphasize one or another unit of analysis, and different research techniques are associated with specific units of analysis. For example, the individual is usually the unit of analysis in survey and experimental research.

As an example, the individual is the unit of analysis in a survey in which 150 students are asked to rate their favorite football player. The individual is the unit because each individual student's response is recorded. On the other hand, a study that compares the amounts different colleges spend on their football programs would use the organization (the college) as the unit of analysis because the spending by colleges is being compared, and each college's spending is recorded.

Social work researchers use units of analysis other than individuals, groups, organizations, social categories, institutions, and societies. For example, a researcher wants to determine whether the speeches of two candidates for president of the United States contain specific themes. The researcher uses content analysis and measures the themes in each speech of the candidates. Here, the speech is the unit of analysis. Geographic units of analysis are also used. A researcher interested in determining whether cities that have a high number of teenagers also have a high rate of vandalism would use the city as the unit of analysis. This is because the researcher measures the percentage of teenagers in each city and the amount of vandalism for each city.

The units of analysis determine how a researcher measures variables or themes. They also correspond loosely to the level of analysis in an explanation. Thus, social–psychological or micro levels of analysis fit with the individual as a unit of analysis, whereas macro levels of analysis fit with the social category or institution as a unit. Theories and explanations at the micro level generally refer to features of individuals or interactions among individuals. Those at the macro level refer to social forces operating across a society or relations among major parts of a society as a whole.

Researchers use levels and units of analysis to design research projects, and being aware of them helps researchers avoid logical errors. For example, a study that examines whether colleges in the North spend more on their football programs than do colleges in the South implies that information is gathered on spending by college and the location of each college. The unit of analysis—the organization or, specifically, the college—flows from the research problem and tells the researcher to collect data from each college.

Social work researchers choose among different units or levels of analysis for similar topics or research questions. The choices are based on the theory examined and on the researcher's concerns. For example, a researcher could conduct a project on the topic of patriarchy and violence with society as the unit of analysis for the research question, "Are patriarchal societies more violent?" He or she would collect data on societies and classify each society by its degree of patriarchy and its level of violence. On the other hand, if the research question was "Is the degree of patriarchy within a family associated with violence against a spouse?" the unit of analysis could be the group or the family, and a more micro level of analysis would be appropriate. The researcher could collect data on families by measuring the degree of patriarchy within different families and the level of violence between spouses in these families. The same topic can be addressed with different levels and units of analysis because patriarchy can be a variable that describes an entire society, or it can describe social relations within one family. Likewise, violence can be defined as general behavior across a society, or as the interpersonal actions of one spouse toward the other.

Logical Errors in Causal Explanation

Developing a good explanation for any kind of theory (i.e., causal, interpretive, or network) requires avoiding common logical errors. These errors can enter at the stage of beginning research, or while interpreting and analyzing quantitative data, or while collecting and analyzing qualitative data. It is easiest to think of them as fallacies or false explanations that may appear on the surface to be legitimate.

Tautology.   A *tautology* is a form of circular reasoning in which someone appears to say something new but is really talking in circles and making a statement that is true by definition. Tautologies cannot be tested with empirical data. For example, one of the authors recently heard a news report about a representative in the U.S. Congress who argued for a new crime law that would send many more 14- and 15-year-olds to adult courts. When asked why he was interested only in harsh punishment and not prevention, the representative said that offenders would learn that crime does not pay and that would prevent crime. He believed that the only prevention that worked was harsh punishment. This sounded a bit odd when the author heard it, so he reexamined the argument and realized it was tautological (i.e., it contained a logic error). The representative essentially said punishment resulted in prevention, be-

cause he had redefined *prevention* as being the same as *punishment*. Logically, he said his punishment bill caused prevention because harsh punishment was prevention. Politicians may confuse and fool the public with circular reasoning, but social work researchers need to learn how to see through and avoid such garble.

Example.   A conservative is a person with certain attitudes, beliefs, and values (desires less government regulation, no taxes on upper-income people, a strong military, religion in public schools, an end to antidiscrimination laws, etc.). It is a tautology to say that wanting less regulation, a strong military, and so on *causes* conservatism. In sloppy everyday usage, we can say, "Sally is conservative *because* she believes that there should be less regulation." This looks like a causal statement, but it is not a causal explanation. The set of attitudes is a *reason* to label Sally as a conservative, but those attitudes cannot be the *cause* of Sally's conservatism. Her attitudes *are* conservatism, so the statement is true by definition. It would be impossible ever to come up with evidence showing that those attitudes were not associated with conservatism.

Teleology.   A *teleology* is something directed by an ultimate purpose or goal, and it takes several forms. It may be associated with events that occur because it is in "God's plan." In other words, an event occurs because God, or a deity, predetermined that it must occur. It appears when saying something occurs because it is part of the "natural unfolding" of an all-powerful inner spirit or *Geist* (German for spirit). Thus, society develops in a certain direction because of the "spirit of the nation" or a "manifest destiny." This is similar to arguments that use human nature as a cause, as in, "Crime occurs because it is just human nature." Teleology appears in theories of history in which an "ideal society" or a utopia toward which the theory says society is moving explains events occurring now. It occurs in functional arguments. Thus, the family takes a certain form (e.g., nuclear) because the family fulfills social system "needs" for continuation (i.e., functional needs of the social system's survival into the future cause the family form now).

Teleologies are not valid scientific explanations; they cannot be empirically measured. They violate the temporal order requirement of causality and they lack a true independent variable because the "causal factor" is so extremely vague. Many people confuse goal motivation (i.e., a desire for something yet to occur) with teleology. You might say a goal causes an action; for example, your goal to get an A in a class caused you to get a good grade. A person's conscious goal or desire can be a legitimate cause, and not be teleological. First, a person's mental condition (e.g., goals, desires, or aspirations) can be empirically measured. Second, the mental condition exists now. This clarifies the temporal order issue. Third, the mental condition can be compared to future events that may or may not occur and is not itself a direct cause. The mental condition can cause current behaviors, and the behaviors increase the chances that a future event will occur. Conscious human goals differ from the will of God, a society's *Geist,* or system needs—which we can never empirically measure, have no fixed existence in time, and always match what occurs.

Example.   The statement *The nuclear family is the dominant family form in Western industrial societies because it is functional for the survival of the society* is an untestable teleological statement from structural–functional theory. It is saying "society's survival" *causes* "development of family form." Yet, the only way we can observe whether or not a society survives is after the fact, or as a consequence of its having had a form of the family. Here is another example of a teleological statement: *Because it was the destiny of the United States to become a major world power, we find thousands of immigrants entering the Western frontier during the early nineteenth century.* This says that "becoming a major world power," which occurred from 1920 to 1945, caused "westward migration," which took place between 1850 and 1890. It uses the obscure term *destiny,* which, like similar terms (e.g., "in God's plan"), cannot be observed in causal relationships.

Ecological Fallacy.   The *ecological fallacy* arises from a mismatch of units of analysis. It refers to a poor fit between the units for which a researcher has empirical evidence and the units for which he or she wants to make statements. It is due to imprecise reasoning and generalizing beyond what the evidence warrants. Ecological fallacy occurs when a researcher gathers data at a *higher* or an *aggregated* unit of analysis but wants to make a statement about a *lower* or *disaggregated* unit. It is a fallacy because what happens in one unit of analysis does not always hold for a different unit of analysis.[9] Thus, if a researcher gathers data for large aggregates (e.g., organizations, entire countries, etc.) and then draws conclusions about the behavior of individuals from those data, he or she is committing the ecological fallacy. You can avoid this error by ensuring that the unit of analysis you use in an explanation is the same as, or very close to, the unit on which you collect data (see Box 6.3).

Example.   Tomsville and Joansville each have about 45,000 people living in them. Tomsville has a high percentage of upper-income people. Over half of the households in the town have family incomes of over $160,000. The town also has more motorcycles registered in it than any other town of its size. The town of Joansville has many poor people. Half its households live below the poverty line. It also has fewer motorcycles registered in it than any other town its size. But it is a *fallacy* to say, on the basis of this information alone, that rich people are more likely to own motorcycles or that the evidence shows a relationship between family income and motorcycle ownership. The reason is that we do not know which families in Tomsville or Joansville own motorcycles. We only know about the two variables—average income and number of motorcycles—for the towns as a whole. The unit of analysis for observing variables is the town as a whole. Perhaps all of the low- and middle-income families in Tomsville belong to a motorcycle club, and not a single upper-income family belongs. Or perhaps one rich family and five poor ones in Joansville each own motorcycles. In order to make a statement about the relationship between family ownership of motorcycles and family income, we have to collect information on families, not on towns as a whole.

Reductionism.   Another problem involving mismatched units of analysis and imprecise reasoning about evidence is *reductionism,* also called the *fallacy of nonequivalence* (see Box 6.4). This error occurs when a researcher explains macro-level events

Box 6.3

Ecological Fallacy

Hightop University has five sections of a course entitled Western History, each with 50 students. Last year, the dean discovered cheating in the sections and looked at the following data that included the gender composition of each section. The dean calculated a very high correlation between cheating and gender. It is plotted in Graph A.

Section	a	b	c	d	e
# Cheaters	2	4	6	8	10
% Women	80	60	40	30	20

Unfamiliar with the *ecological fallacy*, the dean concluded that men tend to be cheaters and instituted a policy to monitor male students.

You studied the *ecological fallacy* and recognize that the dean's data on characteristics on entire sections of students do not provide evidence on individual cheating behavior. You asked for data on the gender breakdown of the individual cheating students, which is shown in the following:

Section	a	b	c	d	e
Male Cheaters	1	2	3	4	5
Female Cheaters	1	2	3	4	5
Total Cheaters	2	4	6	8	10

You immediately notice that half of the cheaters are female in all sections, and there is no association between the percentage of women in a section and the percentage of male cheaters. Your plot of the data looks like Graph B. You then explain to the dean that men and women are equally likely to cheat and there is no gender difference in cheating.

The dean's chart is correct, in that it shows the data. The problem is that it is *not* evidence for a statement about gender differences in individual student behavior. Perhaps another unmeasured factor accounts for the pattern (i.e., it is a *spurious relationship*), or maybe a section with fewer women creates a social atmosphere in the classroom that supports a norm to cheat among both men and women equally. These are issues for additional study.

Despite a clear pattern of observations in Graph A, it is not the type of evidence to support a conclusion that men are more likely to cheat than women. One must have the right type of evidence (on individuals) to draw conclusions about individual cheating behavior.

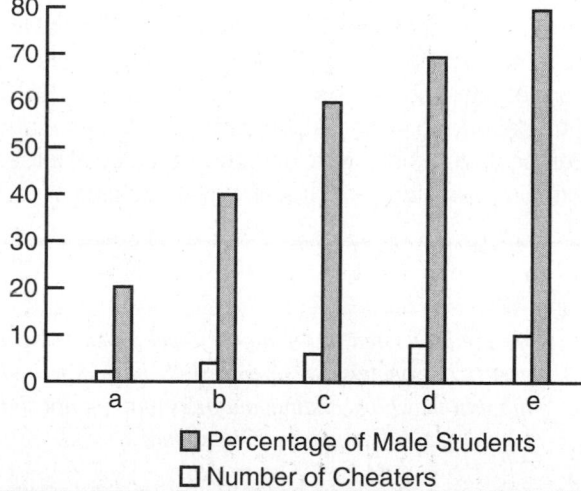

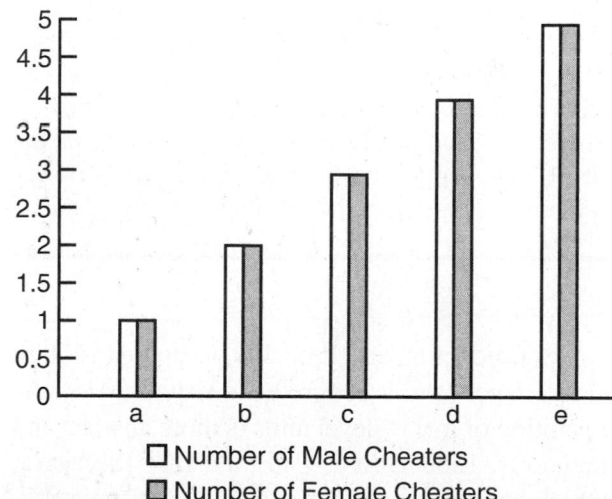

GRAPH A   Percentage of Men by Number of Cheaters in Five Sections of Western History

GRAPH B   Number of Cheaters by Gender in Five Sections of Western History

but has evidence only about specific individuals. It occurs when a researcher observes a *lower* or *disaggregated* unit of analysis but makes statements about the operations of *higher* or *aggregated* units.

It is a mirror image of the mismatch error in the ecological fallacy. A researcher who has data on how individuals behave but makes statements about the dynamics of macro-level units is committing the

Box 6.4

Error of Reductionism

Suppose you pick up a book and read the following:

American race relations changed dramatically during the Civil Rights Era of the 1960s. Attitudes among the majority, White population shifted to greater tolerance as laws and court rulings changed across the nation. Opportunities that had been legally and officially closed to all but the White population—in the areas of housing, jobs, schooling, voting rights, and so on—were opened to people of all races. From the Brown *vs.* Board of Education *decision in 1955, to the Civil Rights Act of 1964, to the War on Poverty from 1966 to 1968, a new, dramatic outlook swept the country. This was the result of the vision, dedication, and actions of America's foremost civil rights leader, Dr. Martin Luther King, Jr.*

This says: *dependent variable* = major change in U.S. race relations over a 10- to 13-year period; *independent variable* = King's vision and actions.

If you know much about the Civil Rights Era, you see a problem. The entire civil rights movement and its successes are attributed to a single individual. Yes, one individual does make a difference and helps build and guide a movement, but the *movement* is missing. The idea of a social–political movement as a causal force is reduced to its major leader. The distinct social phenomenon—a movement—is obscured. Lost are the actions of hundreds of thousands of people (marches, court cases, speeches, prayer meetings, sit-ins, rioting, petitions, beatings, etc.) involved in advancing a shared goal and the responses to them. The movement's ideology, popular mobilization, politics, organization, and strategy are absent. Related macro-level historical events and trends that may have influenced the movement (e.g., Vietnam War protest, mood shift with the killing of John F. Kennedy, African American separatist politics, African American migration to urban North) are also ignored.

This error is not unique to historical explanations. Many people think only in terms of individual actions and have an individualist bias, sometimes called *methodological individualism.* This is especially true in the extremely individualistic U.S. culture. The error is that it disregards units of analysis or forces beyond the individual. The *error of reductionism* shifts explanation to a much lower unit of analysis. One could continue to reduce from an individual's behavior to biological processes in a person, to micro-level neurochemical activities, to the subatomic level.

Most people live in "social worlds" focused on local, immediate settings and their interactions with a small set of others, so their everyday sense of reality encourages seeing social trends or events as individual actions or psychological processes. Often, they become blind to more abstract, macro-level entities—social forces, processes, organizations, institutions, movements, or structures. The idea that all social actions cannot be reduced to individuals alone is the core of sociology. In his classic work *Suicide,* Emile Durkheim fought methodological individualism and demonstrated that larger, unrecognized social forces explain even highly individual, private actions.

---

error of reductionism. It occurs because it is often easier to get data on concrete individuals. Also, the operation of macro-level units is more abstract and nebulous. Lieberson has argued that this error, which he says is common in social work research, leads to inconsistencies, contradictions, and confusion. He (1985:108, 113–114) forcefully stated:

Associations on the lower level are irrelevant for determining the validity of a proposition about processes operating on the higher level. As a matter of fact, no useful understanding of the higher-level structure can be obtained from lower-level analysis. . . . If

we are interested in the higher-level processes and events, it is because we operate with the understanding that they have distinct qualities that are not simply derived by summing up the subunits.

As with the ecological fallacy, you can avoid this error by ensuring that the unit of analysis in your explanation is very close to the one for which you have evidence.

Researchers who fail to think precisely about the units of analysis and those who do not couple data with the theory are likely to commit the ecological fallacy or reductionism. They make a mistake about the data appropriate for a research question, or they may seriously overgeneralize from the data.

You can make assumptions about units of analysis other than the ones you study empirically. Thus, research on individuals rests on assumptions that individuals act within a set of social institutions. Research on social institutions is based on assumptions about individual behavior. We know that many micro-level units form macro-level units. The danger is that it is easy to slide into using the causes or behavior of micro units, such as individuals, to explain the actions of macro units, such as social institutions. What happens among units at one level does not necessarily hold for different units of analysis. Social work is a discipline that rests on the fundamental belief that a distinct level of social reality exists beyond the individual. Explanations of this level require data and theory that go beyond the individual alone. The causes, forces, structures, or processes that exist among macro units cannot be reduced to individual behavior.

Example. Why did World War I occur? You may have heard that it was because a Serbian shot an archduke in the AustroHungarian Empire in 1914. This is reductionism. Yes, the assassination was a factor, but the macro-political event between nations—war—cannot be reduced to a specific act of one individual. If it could, we could also say that the war occurred because the assassin's alarm clock worked and woke him up that morning. If it had not worked, there would have been no assassination, so the alarm clock caused the war! The event, World War I, was much more complex and was due to many social, political, and economic forces that came together at a point in history. The actions of specific individuals had a role, but only a minor one compared to these macro forces. Individuals affect events, which eventually, in combination with larger-scale social forces and organizations, affect others and move nations, but individual actions alone are not the cause. Thus, it is likely that a war would have broken out at about that time even if the assassination had not occurred.

Spuriousness. To call a relationship between variables spurious means that it is false, a mirage. So-

cial work researchers get excited if they think they have found a spurious relationship because they can show the world to be more complex than it appears on the surface. Because any association between two variables might be spurious, researchers are cautious when they discover that two variables are associated; upon further investigation, it may not be the basis for a causal relationship. It may be an illusion, just like the mirage that resembles a pool of water on a road during a hot day.

Spuriousness occurs when two variables are associated but are not causally related because there is actually an unseen third factor that is the real cause (see Box 6.5). The third variable causes both the apparent independent and the dependent variable. It accounts for the observed association. In terms of conditions for causality, the unseen third factor represents a more powerful alternative explanation.

You now understand that you should be wary of correlations or associations, but how can you tell whether a relationship is spurious, and how do you find out what the mysterious third factor is? You will need to use statistical techniques (discussed later in this book) to test whether an association is spurious. To use them, you need a theory or at least a guess about possible third factors, based on how you think the world operates. Actually, spuriousness is based on some commonsense logic that you already use. For example, you already know that there is an association between the use of air conditioners and ice cream cone consumption. If you measured the number of air conditioners in use and the number of ice cream cones sold for each day, you would find a strong correlation, with more cones sold on the days when more air conditioners are in use. But you know that eating ice cream cones does not cause people to turn on air conditioners. Instead, both variables are caused by a third factor: hot days. The third factor is unseen until you figure it out logically. You could verify the same thing through statistics by measuring the daily temperature as well as ice cream consumption and air conditioner use. In social work research, opposing theories help people figure out which third factors are relevant for many topics (e.g., the causes of crime or the reasons for war or child abuse).

Box 6.5

Spuriousness

In their study of the news media, Neuman and colleagues (1992) found a correlation between type of news source and knowledge. People who prefer to get their news from television are less knowledgeable than those who get it from print sources. This correlation is often interpreted as the "dumbing down" of information. In other words, television news causes people to know little.

The authors found that the relationship was spurious, however, "We were able to show that the entire relationship between television news preference and lower knowledge scores is spurious" (p. 113). They found that a third variable, initially unseen, explained both a preference for television news and a level of knowledge about current events. They said, "We find

that what is really causing the television-is-the-problem effect is the preference for people with lower cognitive skill to get their news from television" (p. 98). The missing or hidden variable was "cognitive skill." The authors defined cognitive skill as a person's ability to use reason and manipulate abstract ideas. In other words, people who find it difficult to process abstract, complex information turn to television news. Others may also use the high-impact, entertaining television news sources, but they use them less and heavily supplement them with other, more demanding, information-rich print sources. People who have weak information skills also tend to be less knowledgeable about current events and about other topics that require abstract thought or dealing with complex information.

Example. Tall 15-year-olds seem to enjoy football and sports more than they enjoy shopping for clothes. Moreover, there is a strong correlation between height and preference for football. This does not mean that height *causes* a pro-football preference; the relationship is spurious because a third factor, gender, is operating. Fifteen-year-old boys are taller than 15-year-old girls, and boys prefer football. Thus, height itself may have nothing to do with liking football. Rather, a person's gender produces the height differences and is also associated with socialization to enjoy football and other sports. In fact, it could be that, among boys, the taller ones actually prefer basketball or track over football. If researchers observe height and football preference alone and ignore gender, they will be misled.

Figure 6.4 shows in graphic form the five errors discussed in this section.

REFINING RESEARCH TOPICS: QUANTITATIVE SOCIAL WORK RESEARCH

Your first step when beginning a research project is to select a topic.[10] There is no formula for this task. Whether you are an experienced researcher or just beginning, the best guide is to conduct research

on something that interests you. There are many sources of topics; Box 6.6 suggests ways to make your selection. The techniques for choosing topics are not limited to quantitative social work research but apply to all types of research.

From a Topic to a Specific Research Question

Social work researchers do not conduct research on a topic, although a topic is an essential starting point. A topic is just that—a starting point. Researchers refine and narrow down a topic into a problem or question. A common mistake of new researchers is to fail to narrow a topic sufficiently, or to try to jump from a broad topic directly into a research project without first creating a research question. In quantitative social work research, you need a narrowly focused research question before you design a research project.

Social work research projects are designed around research problems or questions. Before designing a project, focus on a specific research problem within a broad topic. For example, the personal experience example in Box 6.6 suggests labor unions as a topic. "Labor unions" is a topic, not a research question or a problem. In any large library

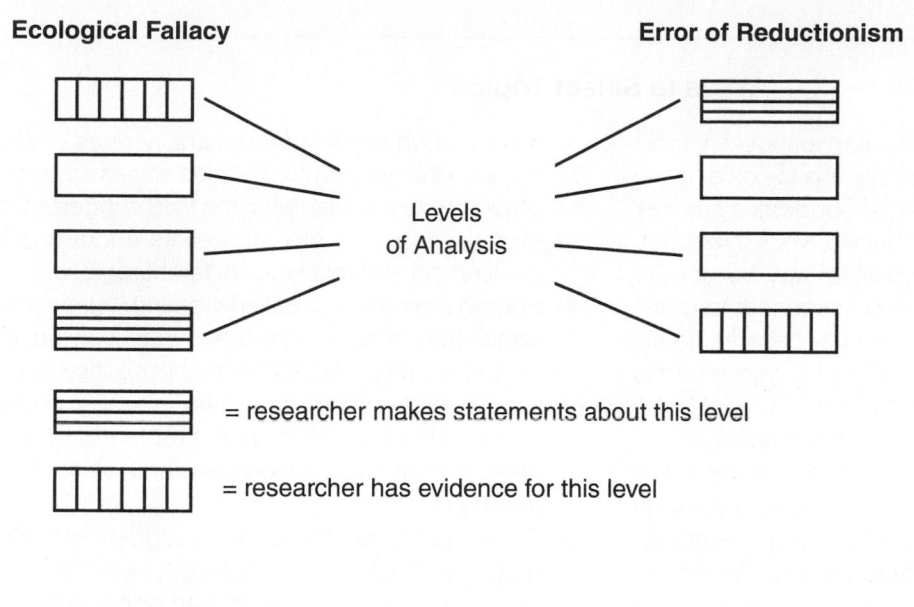

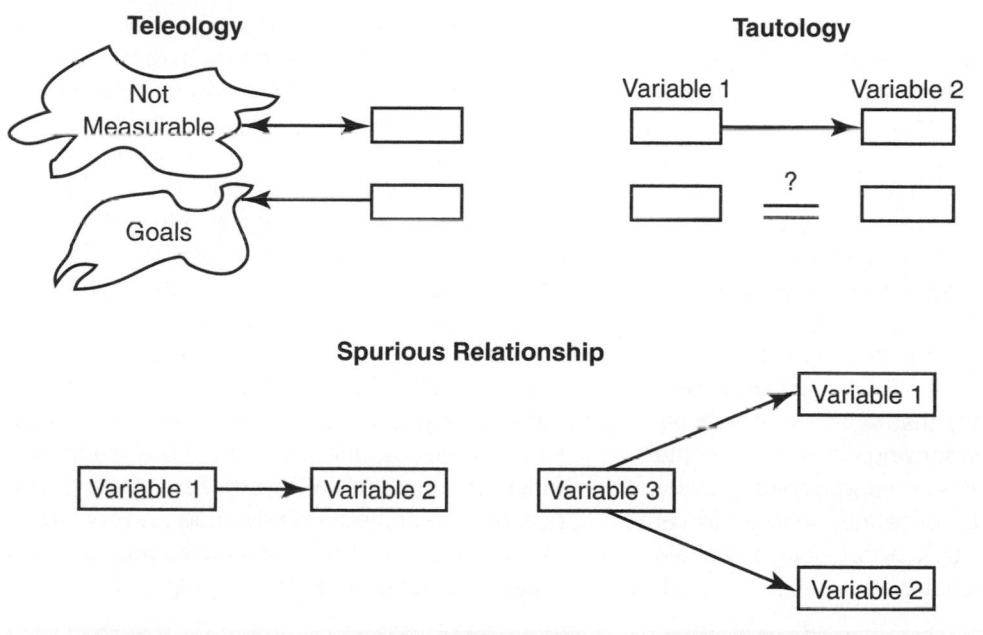

FIGURE 6.4 Five Errors in Explanation to Avoid

you will find hundreds of books and thousands of articles on unions written by sociologists, historians, economists, management officials, political scientists, and others. The books and articles focus on different aspects of the topic and adopt many perspectives on it. Before proceeding to design a social work research project, you must narrow and focus the topic. An example research question is, "How

much did U.S. labor unions contribute to racial inequality by creating barriers to skilled jobs for African Americans in the post-World War II period?"

When starting research on a topic, ask yourself, "What is it about the topic that is of greatest interest?" For a topic about which you know little, first get background knowledge by reading about it. Research questions refer to the relationships

Box 6.6

Ways to Select Topics

1. *Personal experience.* You can choose a topic based on something that happens to you or those you know. For example, while you work a summer job at a factory, the local union calls a strike. You do not have strong feelings either way, but you are forced to choose sides. You notice that tensions rise. Both management and labor become hostile toward each other. This experience suggests unions or organized labor as a topic.

2. *Curiosity based on something in the media.* Sometimes you read a newspaper or magazine article or see a television program that leaves you with questions. What you read raises questions or suggests replicating what others' research found. For example, you read a *Newsweek* article on the homeless, but you do not really know much about who they are, why they are homeless, whether this has always been a problem, and so forth. This suggests the homeless as a topic.

3. *The state of knowledge in a field.* Basic research is driven by new research findings and theories that push at the frontiers of knowledge. As theoretical explanations are elaborated and expanded, certain issues or questions need to be answered for the field to move forward. As such issues are identified and studied, knowledge advances. For example, you read about attitudes toward capital punishment and realize that most social work research points to an underlying belief in the innate wickedness of criminals among capital punishment supporters. You notice that no one has yet examined whether people who belong to certain religious groups that teach such a belief in wicked-

ness support capital punishment, nor has anyone mapped the geographic location of these religious groups. Your knowledge of the field suggests topics for a research project: beliefs about capital punishment and religion in different regions.

4. *Solving a problem.* Applied research topics often begin with a problem that needs a solution. For example, as part of your job as a dorm counselor, you want to help college freshmen establish friendships with each other. Your problem suggests friendship formation among new college students as a topic.

5. *Social premiums.* This is a term suggested by Singleton and colleagues (1988:68). It means that some topics are "hot" or offer an opportunity. For example, you read that there is a lot of money available to conduct research on nursing homes, but few people are interested in doing so. Your need of a job suggests nursing homes as a topic.

6. *Personal values.* Some people are highly committed to a set of religious, political, or social values. For example, you are strongly committed to racial equality and become morally outraged whenever you hear about racial discrimination. Your strong personal belief suggests racial discrimination as a topic.

7. *Everyday life.* Potential topics can be found throughout everyday life in old sayings, novels, songs, statistics, and what others say (especially those who disagree with you). For example, you hear that the home court advantage is very important in basketball. This statement suggests "home court advantage" as a topic for research.

---

among a small number of variables. Identify a limited number of variables and specify the relationships among them.

A research question has one or a small number of causal relationships. Box 6.7 lists some ways to focus a topic into a research question. For example, the question, "What causes divorce?" is not a good research question. A better research question is, "Is age at marriage associated with divorce?" The second question suggests two variables: age at marriage and frequency of divorce.

Another technique for focusing a research question is to specify the *universe* to which the answer to the question can be generalized. All research questions, hypotheses, and studies apply to some group or category of people, organizations, or other units. The universe is the set of all units that the research covers, or to which it can be generalized. For example, your research question is about the effects of a new attendance policy on learning by high school students. The universe is all high school students.

Box 6.7

Techniques for Narrowing a Topic into a Research Question

1. *Examine the literature.* Published articles are an excellent source of ideas for research questions. They are usually at an appropriate level of specificity and suggest research questions that focus on the following:
   a. Replicate a previous research project exactly or with slight variations.
   b. Explore unexpected findings discovered in previous research.
   c. Follow suggestions an author gives for future research at the end of an article.
   d. Extend an existing explanation or theory to a new topic or setting.
   e. Challenge findings or attempt to refute a relationship.
   f. Specify the intervening process and consider linking relations.
2. *Talk over ideas with others.*
   a. Ask people who are knowledgeable about the topic for questions about it that they have thought of.
   b. Seek out those who hold opinions that differ from yours on the topic and discuss possible research questions with them.
3. *Apply to a specific context.*
   a. Focus the topic onto a specific historical period or time period.
   b. Narrow the topic to a specific society or geographic unit.
   c. Consider which subgroups or categories of people/units are involved and whether there are differences among them.
4. *Define the aim or desired outcome of the study.*
   a. Will the research question be for an exploratory, explanatory, or descriptive study?
   b. Will the study involve applied or basic research?

When refining a topic into a research question, when designing a research project, and when formulating hypotheses, you also need to consider practical limitations. Designing a perfect social work research project is an interesting academic exercise, but if you expect to carry out a research project, practical limitations will have an impact on its design.

Major limitations include time, costs, access to resources, approval by authorities, ethical concerns, and expertise. If you have 10 hours a week for five weeks to conduct a research project, but the answer to a research question will take five years, reformulate the research question more narrowly. Estimating the amount of time required to answer a research question is difficult. The hypotheses specified, the research technique used, and the type of data collected all play significant roles. Experienced researchers are the best source of good estimates.

Cost is another limitation. As with time, there are inventive ways to answer a question within limitations, but it may be impossible to answer some questions because of the expense involved. For example, a research question about the attitudes of all sports fans toward their team mascot can be answered only with a great investment of time and money. Narrowing the research question to how students at two different colleges feel about their mascots might make it more manageable.

Access to resources is a common limitation. Resources can include the expertise of others, special equipment, or information. For example, a research question about burglary rates and family income in many different nations is almost impossible to answer because information on burglary and income is not collected or available for most countries. Some questions require the approval of authorities (e.g., to see medical records) or involve violating basic ethical principles (e.g., causing serious physical harm to a person to see the person's reaction). The expertise or background of the researcher is also a limitation. Answering some research questions involves the use of data collection techniques, statistical methods, knowledge of a foreign language, or skills that the researcher may not have. Unless the researcher can acquire the necessary training or can pay for another person's services, the research question may not be practical.

From the Research Question to Hypotheses

It is difficult to move from a broad topic to hypotheses, but the leap from a well-formulated research question to hypotheses is a short one. Hints about hypotheses are embedded within a good research

Box 6.8

Examples of Bad and Good Research Questions

BAD RESEARCH QUESTIONS

Not Empirically Testable, Nonscientific Questions
- Should abortion be legal?
- Is it right to have capital punishment?

General Topics, Not Research Questions
- Treatment of alcohol and drug abuse
- Sexuality and aging

Set of Variables, Not Questions
- Capital punishment and racial discrimination
- Urban decay and gangs

Too Vague, Ambiguous
- Do police affect delinquency?
- What can be done to prevent child abuse?

Need to Be Still More Specific
- Has the incidence of child abuse risen?
- How does poverty affect children?
- What problems do children who grow up in poverty experience that others do not?

GOOD RESEARCH QUESTIONS

Exploratory Questions
- Has the actual incidence of child abuse changed in Wisconsin in the past 10 years?

Descriptive Questions
- Is child abuse, violent or sexual, more common in families that have experienced a divorce than in intact, never-divorced families?
- Are the children raised in poverty-stricken households more likely to have medical, learning, and social-emotional adjustment difficulties than nonpoverty-stricken children?

Explanatory Questions
- Does the emotional instability created by experiencing a divorce increase the chances that divorced parents will physically abuse their children?
- Is a lack of suffcient funds for preventive treatment a major cause of more serious medical problems among children raised in families in poverty?

---

question. In addition, hypotheses are tentative answers to research questions (see Box 6.8).

Consider an example research question: "Is age at marriage associated with divorce?" The question contains two variables: "age at marriage" and "frequency of divorce." To develop a hypothesis, a researcher asks, "Which is the independent variable?" The independent variable is "age at marriage" because marriage must logically precede divorce. The researcher also asks, "What is the direction of the relationship?" The hypothesis could be: "The lower the age at time of marriage, the greater the chances that the marriage will end in divorce." This hypothesis answers the research question and makes a prediction. Notice that the research question can be reformulated and better focused now: "Are couples who marry younger more likely to divorce?"

Several hypotheses can be developed for one research question. Another hypothesis from the same research question is, "The smaller the difference between the ages of the marriage partners at the time of marriage, the less likely that the marriage will end in divorce." In this case the variable "age at marriage" is specified differently.

Hypotheses can specify that a relationship holds under some conditions but not others. As Lieberson (1985:198) remarked, "In order to evaluate the utility of a given causal proposition, it is important that there be a clear-cut statement of the conditions under which it will operate." For example, a hypothesis states, "The lower the age of the partners at time of marriage, the greater the chances that the marriage will end in divorce, unless it is a marriage between members of a tight-knit traditional religious community in which early marriage is the norm."

Formulating a research question and a hypothesis do not have to proceed in fixed stages. A researcher can formulate a tentative research question, then develop possible hypotheses; the hypothesis then helps the researcher state the research question more precisely. The process is interactive and involves creativity.

Where Is the Theory?

You may be wondering, "Where does theory fit into the process of moving from a topic to a hypothesis I can test?" Recall from Chapter 3 that theory takes many forms. Researchers use general theoretical issues and puzzles as a source of topics. Theories and theoretical frameworks provide concepts and ideas that researchers turn into variables. Theory provides the reasoning or mechanism that helps researchers connect variables into a research question. A hypothesis can both answer a research question and be an untested proposition from a theory. Researchers can express a hypothesis at an abstract, conceptual level or restate it in a more concrete, measurable form.

You first saw the steps of a social work research project in Chapter 1. Figure 6.5 gives a slightly different picture of the steps. It shows intermediate steps and the processes used to narrow a topic into a hypothesis. It also shows how the abstract theoretical level blends into the concrete empirical level as a researcher moves toward the data collection stage.

QUALITATIVE DESIGN ISSUES

The Language of Cases and Contexts

The language of qualitative social work research is one of interpretation. Researchers discuss cases in their social context and develop grounded theories that emphasize tracing the process and sequence of events in specific settings. They explain how people attach meanings to events and learn to see events from multiple perspectives. Only rarely does one hear a qualitative researcher discuss variables or hypotheses.

Quantitative social work researchers try to convert concepts about various aspects of social life into variables that can be precisely measured with numbers. Few are comfortable with qualitative data. By contrast, qualitative researchers view many aspects

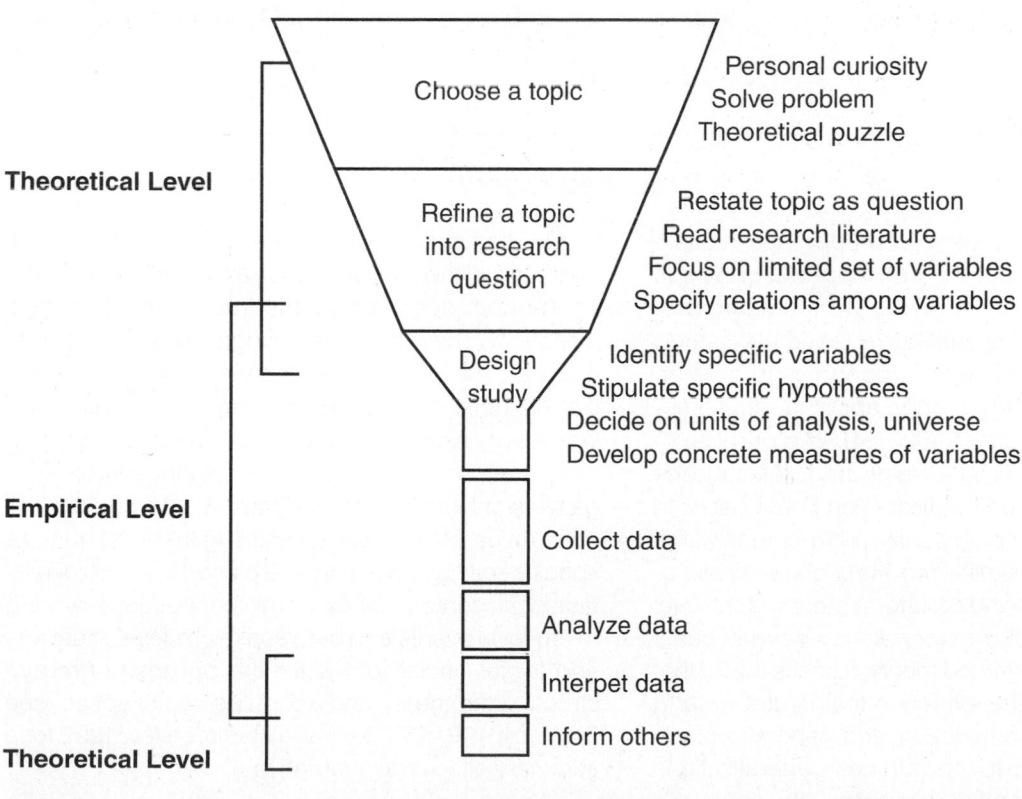

FIGURE 6.5 Steps in Research Revisited

of social life as being intrinsically qualitative. For them, qualitative data are meaningful, not deficient, and central issues are not how to turn them into variables that can be expressed with objective numbers; rather, "they concern such matters as the accessibility of other (sub)cultures, the relativity of actors' accounts of their social worlds, and the relation between sociological descriptions and actors' conceptions of their actions" (Halfpenny, 1979:803).

Some people believe that qualitative data are "soft," intangible, and immaterial. Such data are so fuzzy and elusive that researchers cannot really capture them. This is not necessarily the case. Qualitative data are empirical. They involve documenting real events, recording what people say (with words, gestures, and tone), observing specific behaviors, studying written documents, or examining visual images. These are all concrete aspects of the world. For example, some qualitative researchers take and closely scrutinize photos or videotapes of people or social events (Ball and Smith, 1992; Harper, 1994). This evidence is just as "hard" and physical as that used by quantitative researchers to measure attitudes, social pressure, intelligence, and the like.

Instead of converting ideas or aspects of the social world into general variables to form hypotheses, qualitative researchers borrow ideas from the people they study or develop new ideas as they examine a specific case in its context or particular natural setting. The theoretical categories that qualitative researchers use to understand and interpret the social world often are in the form of *grounded theory*. They are motifs, themes, distinctions, and ideas that researchers create as part of the process of gathering and analyzing qualitative data.

Grounded Theory

A qualitative social work researcher begins with a research question and little else. Theory develops during the data collection process. This more inductive method means that theory is built from data or grounded in the data. Moreover, conceptualization and operationalization occur simultaneously with data collection and preliminary data analysis. Many researchers use grounded theory. It makes qualitative research flexible and lets data and theory interact (see Box 6.9). Qualitative researchers

---

Box 6.9 _____

What Is Grounded Theory?

Grounded theory is a widely used approach in qualitative research. It is not the only approach and it is not used by all qualitative social work researchers. Grounded theory is "a qualitative research method that uses a systematic set of procedures to develop an inductively derived theory about a phenomenon" (Strauss and Corbin, 1990:24). The purpose of grounded theory is to build a theory that is faithful to the evidence. It is a method for discovering new theory. In it, the researcher compares unlike phenomena with a view toward learning similarities. He or she sees micro-level events as the foundation for a more macro-level explanation. Grounded theory shares several goals with more positivist-oriented theory. It seeks theory that is comparable with the evidence that is precise and rigorous, capable of replication, and generalizable. A grounded theory approach pursues generalizations by making comparisons across social situations.

Qualitative social work researchers use alternatives to grounded theory. Some qualitative researchers offer an in-depth depiction that is true to an informant's worldview. They excavate a single social situation to elucidate the micro processes that sustain stable social interaction. The goal of other researchers is to provide a very exacting depiction of events or a setting. They analyze specific events or settings in order to gain insight into the larger dynamics of a society. Still other researchers apply an existing theory to analyze specific settings that they have placed in a macro-level historical context. They show connections among micro-level events and between micro-level situations and larger social forces for the purpose of reconstructing the theory and informing social action (see Burawoy, 1991:271–287 and Hammersley, 1992 for a summary of several alternatives).

remain open to the unexpected, are willing to change the direction or focus of a research project, and may abandon their original research question in the middle of a project.[11]

A qualitative researcher builds theory by making comparisons. When a researcher observes an event (e.g., a police officer confronting a speeding motorist), he or she immediately ponders questions and looks for similarities and differences. When watching a police officer stop a speeder, a qualitative researcher asks, "Does the police officer always radio in the car's license number before proceeding? After radioing the car's location, does the officer ask the motorist to get out of the car sometimes, but in others casually walk up to the car and talk to the seated driver?" When data collection and theorizing are interspersed, theoretical questions arise that suggest future observations, so new data are tailored to answer theoretical questions that came from thinking about previous data.

The Context Is Critical

Qualitative social work researchers emphasize the importance of social context for understanding the social world. They hold that the meaning of a social action or statement depends, in an important way, on the context in which it appears. When a researcher removes an event, social action, answer to a question, or conversation from the social context in which it appears, or ignores the context, social meaning and significance are distorted.

Attention to social context means that a qualitative researcher notes what came before or what surrounds the focus of study. It also implies that the same events or behaviors can have different meanings in different cultures or historical eras. For example, instead of ignoring the context and counting votes across time or cultures, a qualitative researcher asks, "What does voting mean in the context?" He or she may treat the same behavior (e.g., voting for a presidential candidate) differently, depending on the social context in which it occurs (see Box 6.10). Qualitative researchers place parts of social life into a larger whole. Otherwise, the meaning of the part may be lost. For example, it is hard to understand what a baseball glove is without knowing something about the game of baseball. The whole of the game—innings, bats, curve balls, hits—gives meaning to each part, and each part without the whole has little meaning.

Bricolage

Qualitative social work researchers are *bricoleurs;* they learn to be adept at doing many things, drawing on a variety of sources, and making do with whatever is at hand (Harper, 1987:9, 74–75; Schwandt, 1997:10–11). The qualitative style emphasizes developing an ability to draw on a variety of skills, materials, and approaches as they may be needed, usually without being able to plan for them in advance. A *bricolage* technique means working with one's hands and being pragmatic at using an assortment of odds and ends in an inventive manner to accomplish a specific task. It requires having a deep knowledge of one's materials, a collection of esoteric skills, and the capacity to combine them flexibly. The mixture of using diverse materials, applying disparate approaches, and assembling bits and pieces gives qualitative researchers the aura of being similar to a skilled craftsperson who seems to be able to make or repair almost anything.

Focus on the Case and Process

In quantitative social work research, cases are usually the same as a unit of analysis, or the unit on which variables are measured. Quantitative researchers typically measure variables of their hypotheses across many cases. For example, if a researcher conducts a survey of 450 individuals, each individual is a case or unit on which he or she measures variables. Qualitative researchers tend to use a "case-oriented approach [that] places cases, not variables, center stage" (Ragin, 1992a:5). They examine a wide variety of aspects of one or a few cases. Their analyses emphasize contingencies in "messy" natural settings (i.e., the co-occurrence of many specific factors and events in one place and time). Explanations or interpretations are complex and may be in the form of an unfolding plot or a narrative story about particular people or specific events. Rich detail and astute insight into the cases

Box 6.10

Example of the Importance of Context for Meaning

"Voting in a national election" has different meanings in different contexts:

1. A one-party dictatorship with unopposed candidates, wherein people are required by law to vote. The names of nonvoters are recorded by the police. Nonvoters are suspected of being antigovernment subversives. They face fines and possible job loss for not voting.
2. A country in the midst of violent conflict between rebels and those in power. Voting is dangerous because the armed soldiers on either side may shoot voters they suspect of opposing their side. The outcome of the vote will give power to one or the other group and dramatically restructure the society. Anyone over the age of 16 can vote.
3. A context wherein people choose between a dozen political parties of roughly equal power that represent very different values and policies. Each party has a sizable organization, with its own newspapers, social clubs, and neighborhood organizers. Election days are national holidays, when no one has to work. A person votes by showing up with an identification card at any of many local voting locations. Voting itself is by secret ballot, and everyone over age 18 can vote.
4. A context in which voting is conducted in public by White males over age 21 who have regular jobs. Family, friends, and neighbors see how one another vote. Political parties do not offer distinct policies; instead, they are tied to ethnic or religious groups and are part of a person's ethnic–religious identity. Ethnic and religious group identities are very strong. They affect where one lives, where one works, whom one marries, and the like. Voting follows massive parades and week-long community events organized by ethnic and religious groups.
5. A context in which one political party is very powerful and is challenged by one or two very small, weak alternatives. The one party has held power for the past 60 years through corruption, bribery, and intimidation. It has the support of leaders throughout society (in religious organizations, educational institutions, business, unions, and the mass media). The jobs of anyone working in any government position (e.g., every police officer, post office clerk, school teacher, garbage collector, etc.) depend on the political party staying in power.
6. A context in which the choice is between two parties and there is little difference between them. People select candidates primarily on the basis of television advertising. Candidates pay for advertising with donations by wealthy people or powerful organizations. Voting is a vague civic obligation that few people take seriously. Elections are held on a workday. In order to vote, a person must meet many requirements and register to vote several weeks in advance. Recent immigrants and anyone arrested for a crime cannot vote.

---

replace the sophisticated statistical analysis of precise measures across a huge number of units or cases found in quantitative research.

The passage of time is an integral part of qualitative social work research. Qualitative researchers look at the sequence of events and pay attention to what happens first, second, third, and so on. Because qualitative researchers examine the same case or set of cases over time, they can see an issue evolve, a conflict emerge, or a social relationship develop. The researcher can detect process and causal relations.

In historical research the passage of time may involve years or decades. In field research the passage of time is shorter. Nevertheless, in both types of research a researcher notes what is occurring at different points in time and recognizes that *when* something occurs is often important.

Interpretation

The word *interpretation* means assigning significance or coherent meaning. Reports of quantitative research usually include tables and charts with numbers. Quantitative research is expressed in numbers (e.g., percentages or statistical coefficients), and a researcher gives meaning to the numbers and tells how they relate to hypotheses.

Qualitative research reports rarely include tables with numbers. The only visual presentations of data may be maps, photographs, or diagrams showing how ideas are related. A researcher weaves the data into discussions of their significance. The data are in the form of words, including quotes or descriptions of particular events. Any numerical information is supplementary to the textual evidence.

A qualitative researcher interprets data by giving them meaning, translating them, or making them understandable. However, the meaning he or she gives begins with the point of view of the people being studied. He or she interprets data by finding out how the people being studied see the world, how they define the situation, or what it means for them. As Geertz (1979:228) remarked, "The trick is to figure out what the devil they think they are up to."

Thus, the first step in qualitative interpretation—whether a researcher is examining historical documents or the text of spoken words or human behavior— is to learn about its meaning for the people being studied.[12] The people who created the social behavior have personal reasons or motives for their actions. This is *first-order interpretation.* A researcher's discovery and reconstruction of this first-order interpretation is a *second-order interpretation* because the researcher comes in from the outside to discover what occurred. In a second-order interpretation the researcher elicits an underlying coherence or sense of meaning in the data. Because meaning develops within a set of other meanings, not in a vacuum, a second-order interpretation places the human action being studied in the "stream of behavior" or events to which it is related—its context.

A researcher who adopts a strict interpretive approach may stop at a second-order interpretation—that is, once he or she understands the significance of the action for the people being studied. Many qualitative researchers go further to generalize or link the second-order interpretation to general the-

ory. They move to a broader level of interpretation, or *third-order interpretation,* wherein a researcher assigns general theoretical significance.

REFINING RESEARCH TOPICS: QUALITATIVE SOCIAL WORK RESEARCH

Both quantitative and qualitative researchers begin with a topic that must be narrowed. The quantitative style requires that a researcher quickly focus the topic. Focusing the study is an early, discrete stage, and a researcher must know the specific research question prior to collecting data. It is an essential step before hypotheses development that guides major parts of study design.

The qualitative research style is more flexible and encourages slowly focusing the topic throughout a study. In contrast to quantitative research, only a small amount of topic narrowing occurs in an early research planning stage. It is a more inductive process, and much of the narrowing occurs after a researcher has begun to collect data.

The qualitative researcher begins data gathering with a general topic and notions of what will be relevant. Focusing and refining continues after he or she has gathered some of the data and started preliminary analysis. Qualitative researchers use early data collection to guide how they adjust and sharpen the research question(s). This is because researchers rarely know the most important issues or questions until after they become fully immersed in the data. Developing a focused research question cannot occur sooner; it is a part of the data collection process, during which the researcher actively reflects on and develops preliminary interpretations. The qualitative researcher is open to unanticipated data and constantly reevaluates the focus early in a study. He or she is prepared to change the direction of research and follow new lines of evidence as they appear.

Typical research questions for qualitative researchers include, "How did a certain condition or social situation originate? How is the condition/situation maintained over time? What are the processes by which a condition/situation changes, develops, or operates?" A different type of question tries to confirm existing beliefs or assumptions. Another type of question tries to discover new ideas (see Flick, 1998:51).

EXAMPLE STUDIES: QUANTITATIVE SOCIAL WORK RESEARCH

Let us see how the ideas in this chapter—topic, research question, hypotheses, independent and dependent variables, universe, and unit of analysis—are used in three quantitative studies.

Experiment

The *topic* of Neapolitan's (1988) "The Effects of Different Types of Praise and Criticism on Performance" is the use of positive or negative feedback (praise or criticism) to affect performance. The author uses the concepts *reinforcement* and *attribution* from attribution and behavior modification theories in social psychology.

The *research question* is, "Which of four types of praise/criticism has the largest impact on improving how well people perform?" Four types of praise or criticism are considered: specific product praise (i.e., your paper is good), general actor praise (i.e., you are a good student), specific product criticism, and general actor criticism. These are taken from a typology developed by another researcher.

The main *hypothesis* is that specific product praise (SPP) has a positive effect on performance. The research project described in the method section involved 240 college students enrolled in one of seven Introduction to Sociology classes. Students were asked to write a paragraph during class time summarizing the ideas in a written passage. The students were randomly given one of four evaluations of their paragraph one week later. An equal number of students (60) received each evaluation. The four evaluations (supposedly from an English professor) corresponded to the four types of praise/criticism (e.g., the paragraph is well structured, you are a fine writer, the paragraph is poorly structured, you are a poor writer).

The *independent variable* is the type of praise or criticism in the evaluation. The researcher gave the students an evaluation of their writing and falsely told them that the evaluations came from an English professor. Students were then asked to write a second paragraph. The improvement in the second paragraph over the first represented the *dependent variable,* or performance. The improvement was measured by having the paragraphs graded by two evaluators who assigned scores from 1 (very poor) to 10 (very good) and by looking at differences between the first and second scores.

The Results section of Neapolitan's study shows the percentage of students in each of the four groups whose scores declined, did not change, or improved. The author found that 70 percent of students who received SPP improved. This was higher than for the other types of praise or criticism. There was little improvement for students who received the general actor praise or the specific product criticism. Unexpectedly, a little over half of the students who received the general actor criticism improved.

The *universe* to which the results apply includes all people. Most experimental research generalizes to everyone when no particular group is specified. The *unit of analysis* is the individual, or student, because the variables and measures are characteristics of individuals.

Survey Research

The *topic* of Bankston and Thompson's (1989) article, "Carrying Firearms for Protection," is evident in the title. The researchers discussed the research on firearms in the United States, which has largely examined the ownership of guns. They developed a focused *research question:* To what degree do people who carry firearms when away from home do so out of a fear of crime?

The authors mailed questionnaires to over 4,000 people in Louisiana, asking about their attitudes and background characteristics in addition to whether they carried a firearm. Eventually, the authors limited the study to Whites and had full data on a little over 1,000 people. The main *hypothesis* they tested was whether people who fear crime the most and who believe that a gun will protect them are most likely to carry a firearm. The authors' main *independent variable* was fear of crime, and they specified an *intervening variable:* a belief that guns provide effective protection. The *dependent variable* was how often a person carried a gun when away from home. The authors found that about one-third of the respondents carried a firearm on at least some occasions.

In the Results section the authors examined the effects of variables on how often a person carried a firearm. They found that a fear of crime did not directly affect how often a person carried a weapon, but a belief in the effectiveness of having a gun for protection had a large effect. People who thought that carrying a gun offered personal protection tended to be younger, less well-educated rural males who thought crime was a serious problem and who feared crime.

The authors noted that Louisiana is a southern state with some of the least restrictive laws on purchasing or carrying firearms. The *universe* for the results may be limited to Whites in other areas of the southern United States. The *unit of analysis* of the study was the individual.

Content Analysis

The article by Barlow, Barlow, and Chiricos (1995), "Economic Conditions and Ideologies of Crime in the Media," used content analysis. The *topic* of the study was how the media portray crime and criminals. The *hypothesis* was that the media give a distorted picture of crime, and the distortion is linked to changes in economic conditions. In particular, the authors predicted that more negative images of crime and criminals occur when unemployment is high or the economy is in a recession. Thus, the *independent variable* was the unemployment rate, and the *dependent variable* was how negatively the offender was presented. The authors also looked at overall distortion in terms of a mismatch between crime statistics and crime that gets media attention. The *research question* was, "Does the news media give a distorted picture of crime, with the distortion based on a value and belief system that condemns offenders most harshly when economic conditions are bad?"

The data for the study came from *Time* magazine. The authors sampled various years (1953, 1958, 1975, 1982) that had different economic conditions and looked at all articles during the year that

dealt with crime, criminal justice, or criminals. They found 175 articles. The *unit of analysis* was the article. The *universe* for the study was all crime-related articles that appeared in major U.S. mass circulation news magazines from the 1950s to the 1980s.

The authors also looked at the crime rate, change in the crime rate, characteristics of offenders, and types of crime as violent or nonviolent during the selected years. They rated the image of the offender in each article as to how positive or negative it appeared. A negative image showed the offender as being without remorse, as lacking a reason for the crime, as unprincipled or lying, or as unlikely to be rehabilitated. A more positive image showed the offender as confused and willing to make changes, as trying to make the best of a bad situation, as forced into crime as a result of circumstances, or as caught up in the criminal justice system.

The authors found that negative images were more common in high-unemployment periods. Specifically, 62 percent of the images in high-unemployment periods were negative versus 32 percent in low-unemployment periods. Other patterns of distortion were also found. For example, the authors discovered that 73 percent of the articles focused on violent crime, which made up about 10 percent of crimes known to police in the selected years. Some 74 percent of the articles that included a reference to the offender's race stated that the offender was non-White, whereas the percent of arrests involving non-Whites in the selected years was 28 percent. Last, despite the strong connection between employment conditions and crime, only 3 percent of the articles included information on whether the offender had a job or was unemployed.

EXAMPLE STUDIES: QUALITATIVE SOCIAL WORK RESEARCH

Examples of specific qualitative research studies show how researchers apply the principles of qualitative research in practice, how qualitative researchers do not always follow a strict interpretive approach, and how they combine a qualitative method with quantitative principles.

Field Research

Siu (1987) is a Chinese American who studied the Chinese laundryman by using the "Chicago school" style of participant observation. His father was a laundry worker, and Siu himself worked for a laundry supplier before beginning his field work. Speaking the same dialect as the Chinese laundrymen, he was adopted as a "cousin" and worked in another part of the Chinese immigrant economy—a "chop suey" house. He interviewed and spent time socializing with Chinese laundry workers and owners in the Chicago area. During his 20-year study, he developed new concepts: that of the immigrant economy (an isolated economic and social community of immigrants who specialize in a few industries) and that of sojourners (immigrants who travel without intending to stay).

Siu's book contains little analysis, but it includes many long quotes from interviews and excerpts from letters. He describes the daily life in a laundry by recounting personal events, jokes, and stories. He places his study in a context of the history of Chinese immigration to the United States and provides maps showing the spread of Chinese laundry establishments in the Chicago area over a 50-year period. He provides graphs and tables documenting the number of Chinese immigrants, the sex ratio of Chinese people in the United States, and the number of gamblers in Chinese gambling houses in Chicago. His book also contains a map of inside a typical laundry, examples of laundry tickets, personal financial accounts of laundrymen, and monthly expenditure reports of a laundry. The reader gains an in-depth feeling for and insight into the inner lives of Chinese laundrymen.

Historical–Comparative Study

Light and Bonacich (1988) studied Koreans in the Los Angeles area between 1965 and 1982. Their study traces how changes in the Korean society and economy led to an increase in Korean migration to the United States. For example, the authors show that Koreans in Korea earned between 7.5 and 27 percent of the typical American wage. The authors weave a large set of factors (e.g., role of the Korean government, changes in the Korean economy, and the history of U.S. military intervention in Korea) into a story of Korean migration.

The authors compare Koreans in Korea with those in the United States and compare Koreans with other ethnic groups in the United States. They ask, "Why do a high percentage of Koreans become small-business owners in the United States, when few were small-business owners in Korea?" They explore how small businesses owned by immigrants fit into the larger U.S. economy and how Christianity, Korean ethnic culture, and social class shaped a unique social and economic subculture at a particular juncture of history.

Many types of data were used by the authors: survey research, existing statistics, field research, government documents, international reports, and historical records. Their book contains photographs of Korean business establishments and advertisements, maps showing the spread of Korean-owned business in the Los Angeles area over 20 years, and information on the number of Koreans who migrated. They recount stories of particular people and describe in detail the responses of the Korean community to violent attacks against Asians in the Los Angeles area. The authors present limited generalizations and argue that a combination of specific circumstances (e.g., the political system in Korea, U.S. intervention, economic dislocation, U.S. wealth, cultural traditions) contributed to the formation of a community of Korean small-business owners, which concentrated in the Los Angeles area during the 1960s and 1970s.

A Look at Elite Studies

Most quantitative studies that are conducted on individuals (e.g., experiments, surveys, and existing statistics) and most field research in anthropology, sociology, education, and so on, focus on the average person or the poor and powerless. Social work researchers are aware that they also need to study powerful elites if they are to understand society. Yet, "few social researchers study elites because elites are by their very nature difficult to penetrate. Elites establish barriers that set their members apart from the rest of society" (Hertz and Imber, 1993:3). Researchers have developed special techniques to study elites. These techniques clarify general concerns and illustrate how qualitative social work research designs are valuable and distinct from quantitative research, but also complement it.

Researchers cannot study elites—people in the positions of formal or informal power—with random samples because they are too rare and because they are unlikely to participate. Quantitative researchers have studied elites, including content analyses of elite speeches (Seider, 1974), background studies of elite careers (Freitag, 1983), studies of elite networks' decision making (Knoke, 1993), and panel studies of elite survey data (Murray, 1992). This information, combined with data on the degree of social or economic inequality, provides a partial picture. Qualitative research on elites shows how elites socialize in private clubs, such as G. William Domhoff's (1974) study of Bohemian Grove, or what they discuss informally, such as Susan Ostrander's (1984) study of upper-class women. The upper class, the corporate elites, or the very wealthy belong to a distinct subculture. Some seek publicity, but most avoid it and prefer a private life away from the public intrusion and fortune seekers. It is not easy to identify or locate elites, and studying them is not for the naive researcher.

Here are some differences between interviewing elites and nonelites. First, gaining access to elites is often very difficult, and the gatekeepers are formidable. A researcher studying corporate elites may face security guards, secretaries, and others whose official job is to prevent access. Thomas (1993:83) reported, "It took me nearly two years of phone calls, screening meetings with executive assistants, and networking to interview executives." Also, time pressures are great. Elites are very busy, or give that appearance. Researchers have to schedule meetings and may have limited time. Techniques to improve access include informal settings (meals, waiting in airports, travel time, etc.) and a willingness to adjust to an elite schedule. Issues of access are more common in qualitative than quantitative research.

Second, social contacts and connections are essential for gaining access and establishing trust. A researcher's personal social background or pedigree is an important resource. If the researcher is not from a wealthy family or was not socialized under privileged conditions, he or she may need to cultivate appropriate sponsors with the so-called "right connections." He or she will need to display proper form. Elites will use whom you know, who talked to you, and who introduced whom as signs of approval or endorsement. The researcher who lacks a good sponsor or prestigious credentials or affiliations will seldom be treated seriously even if he or she gains access. Ostrander (1993) and Hunter (1993) note that elites are interested in with whom the researcher has already talked. In many types of qualitative research, personal contacts and connections are integral to the research process.

Elites are often highly educated and knowledgeable. This means that the researcher is expected to have conducted extensive library and background work prior to direct contact. It also means that the elite member may be aware of social work research techniques and may read studies. This can increase cooperation, or it can have the opposite effect. Elites may try to dominate or manipulate the research situation. Most elites are accustomed to being in charge and having others defer to them. Most are adept at detecting subtle shifts in the flow of events and are skilled at controlling social situations. This may include where people sit, the direction of a conversation, and so on. The researcher needs to gain sufficient control to accomplish his or her purpose. He or she needs refined social skills and diplomacy to get the elite member to let down his or her guard without creating tension or distress. The researcher can do this, but only with great delicacy and dexterity. Researchers may use their poise and discretion in a formal survey or when dealing with experimental subjects, but for some qualitative research, such skills are an essential research tool.

A related concern in elite studies is sensitivity to frontstage and backstage performances. *Frontstage* social settings are public, outward settings and situations in which people know others may be observing and therefore display specific social performances. *Backstage* social settings are private and intimate settings where people let their guard down and feel comfortable and trusting. Frontstage events are often intentional and highly managed to create specific impressions. Thus, a researcher may be ushered into a large plush office, with a beautiful view, original art on the walls, sofas along the wall, and a huge, clean desk. An elite member, experienced in dealing with others, may smile and give a researcher the official, public relations version of events. This "front" may not correspond to the backstage of private clubs, home, and other informal discussions of the elite member. The researcher may not get beyond the official, visible role. In backstage settings the elite member may reveal his or her true prejudices or feelings and may expose personal values or beliefs. Access to backstage situations is often very difficult. It may require developing a long-term relationship with the elite member. In quantitative studies, researchers rarely penetrate beyond the frontstage, while many qualitative studies are designed to go beyond public, surface relations.

Another set of differences involves gaining trust and handling an elite's settings or interview situations. The researcher needs to master the appropriate language and demeanor. All subcultures share ways of acting and speaking. Such informal customs and folkways contain assumptions and understandings of key events or situations. Using the proper phrases and adhering to subtle social rituals will signal that a researcher shares the outlook and assumptions of the elite subculture. The researcher who uses improper phases or who behaves unsuitably may signal that he or she is not to be trusted. For example, elite subcultures are built on an assumption of material security and inclusion. Many elites bridge the social distance between themselves and others by managing an outward appearance of composure, radiating self-confidence, and expressing social graces and manners. Some researchers find this demeanor intimidating and may feel that they are being subtly "put in their place," but in a warm, friendly, and open manner. Qualitative researchers find that they need to create trust and reduce interpersonal social distance when gathering data.

A further issue is protecting the integrity of the research process. A degree of secrecy or seclusion—for privacy, if not for physical protection—is common in elite settings. A researcher must exercise discretion. He or she needs to be sensitive to elite concerns about public exposure or fears of an exposé. Elites may be suspicious and demand a review of a research report, or may reveal things only off the record. In addition, they may detect subtle violations of agreed-upon limits or hire experts to review research reports. In addition, if a researcher violates trust, elites have the resources to bring lawsuits. At the same time, a researcher wants to learn as much as possible and uphold principles of good, unimpeded research. Qualitative researchers find that they must simultaneously balance protecting the confidentiality of subjects with ensuring the honesty of the research process itself.

CONCLUSION

In this chapter you encountered the groundwork needed to begin a study. You saw how differences in the qualitative and quantitative styles or approaches to social work research direct a researcher to prepare for a study differently. All social work researchers narrow their topic into a more specific, focused research question. The styles of research suggest different forms and sequences of decisions, and different answers to when and how to focus the research. The style that a researcher uses will depend on the topic he or she selects, the researcher's purpose and intended use of study results, the orientation toward social work that he or she adopts, and the individual researcher's own assumptions and beliefs.

Quantitative researchers take a linear path and emphasize objectivity. They are more likely to use explicit, standardized procedures and a causal explanation. Their language of variables and hypotheses is found across many areas of science that are based on a positivist tradition. The process is often deductive with a sequence of discrete steps that precede data collection: Narrow the topic to a more focused question, transform nebulous theoretical concepts into more exact variables, and develop one or more hypotheses to test. In actual practice, researchers move back and forth, but the general process flows in a single, linear direction. In addition, quantitative social work researchers take special care to avoid logical errors in hypothesis development and causal explanation.

Qualitative social work researchers follow a nonlinear path and emphasize becoming intimate with the details of a natural setting or a particular cultural–historical context. They use fewer standardized procedures or explicit steps, and often devise on-the-spot techniques for one situation or study. Their language of cases and contexts directs them to conduct detailed investigations of particular cases or processes in their search for authenticity. They rarely separate planning and design decisions into a distinct pre–data collection stage, but continue to develop the study design throughout early data collection. In fact, the more inductive qualitative style encourages a slow, flexible evolution toward a specific focus based on what the researcher is learning from the data. Grounded theory emerges from the researcher's continuous reflections on the data and the context.

The qualitative and quantitative distinction is often overdrawn and presented as a rigid dichotomy. Too often, adherents of one style of social work research judge the other style on the basis of the assumptions and standards of their own style. The quantitative researcher demands to know the variables used and the hypothesis tested. The qualitative researcher balks at turning humanity into cold numbers. The challenge for the well-versed, prudent social work researcher is to understand and appreciate each style or approach on its own terms, and to recognize the strengths and limitations of each. The ultimate goal of developing a better understanding and explanation of events in the social world comes from an appreciation of the value that each style has to offer.

KEY TERMS

alternative hypothesis	intervening variable	spuriousness
attributes	level of analysis	tautology
bricolage	linear research path	technocratic perspective
crucial experiment	logic in practice	teleology
dependent variable	logic of disconfirming	third-order interpretation
double-barreled hypothesis	hypotheses	transcendent perspective
ecological fallacy	nonlinear research path	triangulation
first-order interpretation	null hypothesis	unit of analysis
grounded theory	reconstructed logic	universe
hypothesis	reductionism	variable
independent variable	second-order interpretation	

REVIEW QUESTIONS

1. What are the implications of saying that qualitative research uses more of a logic in practice than a reconstructed logic?

2. What does it mean to say that qualitative research follows a nonlinear path? In what ways is a nonlinear path valuable?

3. Describe the differences among independent, dependent, and intervening variables.

4. Why don't we *prove* results in social work research?

5. How are units of analysis and levels of analysis related to each other?

6. What two hypotheses are used if a researcher uses the logic of disconfirming hypotheses? Why is negative evidence stronger?

7. Restate the following in terms of a hypothesis with independent and dependent variables: "The number of home visits in a year affects the number of days

without family violence, and there is a positive unidirectional relationship between the variables."

8. Compare the ways quantitative and qualitative social work researchers deal with personal bias and the issue of trusting the researcher.

9. How do qualitative and quantitative social work researchers use theory?

10. Explain how qualitative researchers approach the issue of interpreting data. Refer to first-, second-, and third-order interpretations.

NOTES

1. Ward and Grant (1985) and Grant and colleagues (1987) analyzed research in journals and suggested that journals with a higher proportion of qualitative research articles addressed gender topics, but that studies of gender are not themselves more likely to be qualitative. Also, see Davis and Marsh (1994).

2. See Lofland and Lofland (1984:118–121).

3. On the issue of using quantitative, statistical techniques as a substitute for trust, see Collins (1984) and Porter (1995).

4. For discussion, see Schwandt (1997), Swanborn (1996), and Tashakkori and Teddlie (1998:90–93).

5. For examples of checking, see Agar (1980) and Becker (1970c).

6. See Lieberson (1985:185–187) for a discussion of basic and superficial variables in a set of causal linkages. Davis (1985) and Stinchcombe (1968) provide good general introductions to making linkages among variables in social theory.

7. The logic of disconfirming hypotheses is discussed in Singleton and associates (1988:56–60).

8. See Bailey (1987:43) for a discussion of this term.

9. The general problem of aggregating observations and making causal inferences is discussed in somewhat technical terms in Blalock (1982:237–264) and in Hannan (1985). O'Brien (1992) argues that the ecological fallacy is one of a whole group of logical fallacies in which levels and units of analysis are confused and overgeneralized.

10. Problem choice and topic selection are discussed in Campbell and associates (1982) and in Zuckerman (1978). Also, see Brown (1981), Gabor, Unrau, and Grinnell (1999), Goldstein (1992), Proctor (1990), Rodwell (1998), and Royse and Thyer (1996).

11. For place of theory in qualitative social work research, see Hammersley (1995). Also, see Dean and Fenby (1989) and Hudson (1982).

12. See Blee and Billings (1986), Ricoeur (1970), and Schneider (1987) on the interpretation of text in qualitative research.

QUALITATIVE AND QUANTITATIVE MEASUREMENT

> *Measurement, in short, is not an end in itself. Its scientific worth can be appreciated only in an instrumentalist perspective, in which we ask what ends measurement is intended to serve, what role it is called upon to play in the scientific situation, and what functions it performs in inquiry.*
>
> —Abraham Kaplan, *The Conduct of Inquiry,* p. 171

INTRODUCTION

Many people look surprised when social work researchers claim to measure strange, invisible things such as affection, self-esteem, ideology, organizational power, or alienation. In this chapter you will learn about how quantitative and qualitative social work researchers approach measurement, looking at similarities and differences. Most of the chapter is devoted to measurement issues for quantitative social work research. This is because measurement is a distinct step in quantitative research with specialized terms and procedures. Measurement is a highly developed subfield in quantitative research design in which a researcher must make critical decisions that will shape subsequent steps in the research process.

By contrast, many qualitative research measurement issues are integrated into the data collection processes.

WHY MEASURE?

We use many measures in our daily lives. For example, one morning you wake up and hop onto a bathroom scale to see how well your diet is working. You glance at a thermometer to find out whether to wear a coat. Next, you get into your car and check the gas gauge to be sure you can make it to campus. As you drive, you watch the speedometer so you will not get a speeding ticket. By 8:00 A.M., you have measured weight, temperature, gasoline volume, and speed—all measures about the physical world. Such precise, well-developed measures, which we use in daily life, are fundamental in the natural sciences.

We also measure the nonphysical world in everyday life, but usually in less exact terms. We are measuring when we say that a restaurant is excellent, that Pablo is really smart, that Karen has a negative attitude toward life, that Johnson is really prejudiced, or that the movie last night had a lot of violence in it. However, such everyday judgments as "really prejudiced" or "a lot of violence" are imprecise, vague, or intuitive measures.

Measurement also extends our senses. The astronomer or biologist uses the telescope or the microscope to extend natural vision. In contrast to our senses, scientific measurement is more sensitive, varies less with the specific observer, and yields more exact information. You recognize that a thermometer gives more specific, precise information about temperature than touch can. Likewise, a good bathroom scale gives you more specific, constant, and precise information about the weight of a 5-year-old girl than you get by lifting her and calling her "heavy" or "light." Social measures provide information about social reality.

In addition, measurement helps people observe what is otherwise invisible. Measurement extends human senses. It lets us observe things that were once unseen and unknown but were predicted by theory.

Before you can measure, you need a clear idea about what you are interested in. For example, you cannot see or feel magnetism with your natural senses. Magnetism comes from a theory about the physical world. You observe its effects indirectly; for instance, metal flecks move near a magnet. The magnet allows you to "see" or measure the magnetic fields. Natural scientists have invented thousands of measures to "see" very tiny things (molecules or insect organs) or very large things (huge geological land masses or planets) that are not observable through ordinary senses. In addition, researchers are constantly creating new measures.[1]

Some of the things a social work researcher is interested in measuring are easy to see (e.g., age, sex, skin color, etc.), but most cannot be directly observed (e.g., attitudes, ideology, divorce rates, deviance, sex roles, etc.). Like the natural scientist who invents indirect measures of the "invisible" objects and forces of the physical world, the social work researcher devises measures for difficult-to-observe aspects of the social world. For example, suppose you heard a principal complain about teacher morale in a school. You can create a measure for the morale of teachers.

QUANTITATIVE AND QUALITATIVE MEASUREMENT

Both qualitative and quantitative social work researchers use careful, systematic methods to gather high-quality data. Yet, differences in the styles of research and the types of data mean they approach the measurement process differently. Designing precise ways to measure variables is a vital step in planning a study for quantitative researchers. Qualitative researchers use a wider variety of techniques to measure and create new measures while collecting data. The two approaches to measurement have three distinctions.

One difference between the two styles involves timing. Quantitative social work researchers extensively think about variables and convert them into specific actions during a planning stage that occurs before and separate from gathering or analyzing data. Measurement for qualitative researchers occurs in the data collection process, and only a little occurs in a separate, planning stage prior to data gathering.

A second difference involves the data itself. Quantitative researchers want to develop techniques that can produce quantitative data (i.e., data in the form of numbers). Thus, the researcher moves from abstract ideas, or variables, to specific data collection techniques to precise numerical information produced by the techniques. The numerical information is an empirical representation of the abstract ideas. Data for qualitative social work researchers sometimes is in the form of numbers; more often it includes written or spoken words, actions, sounds, symbols, physical objects, or visual images (e.g., maps, photographs, videos, etc.). The qualitative researcher does not convert all observation into a single, common medium such as numbers. Instead, he or she develops many flexible, ongoing processes to measure that leave the data in various shapes, sizes, and forms.

All researchers combine ideas and data to analyze the social world. In both research styles, data are empirical representations of concepts, and measurement is a process that links data to concepts.

A third difference is how the two styles make such linkages. Quantitative researchers contemplate and reflect on concepts before they gather any data. They construct measurement techniques that bridge concepts and data. The measurement techniques define what the data will be and are directions for gathering them.

Qualitative social work researchers also reflect on ideas before data collection, but they develop many, if not most, of their concepts during data collection activities. The qualitative researcher reexamines and reflects on the data and concepts simultaneously and interactively. Researchers start gathering data and creating ways to measure based on what they encounter. As they gather data, they reflect on the process and develop new ideas. The ideas give them direction and suggest new ways to measure. In turn, the new ways to measure determine how the researchers will continue to collect data. They bridge ideas and data through this type of continuing, interactive process.

PARTS OF THE MEASUREMENT PROCESS

When a researcher measures, he or she takes a concept, idea, or construct[2] and develops a measure (i.e., a technique, a process, a procedure, etc.) by which to observe the idea empirically. Quantitative re-searchers primarily follow a deductive route. They begin with the abstract idea, follow with a measurement procedure, and end with empirical data that represent the ideas. Qualitative researchers primarily follow an inductive route. They begin with empirical data, follow with abstract ideas, follow with processes relating ideas and data, and end with a mixture of ideas and data. Actually, the process is more interactive in both styles of research. As a quantitative researcher develops measures, the constructs become refined and clearer, and as the researcher applies the measures to gather data, he or she often adjusts the measurement technique. As a qualitative researcher gathers data, he or she uses some preexisting ideas to assist in data collection, and will then mix old with new ideas that are developed from the data.

Both qualitative and quantitative social work researchers use two processes: conceptualization and operationalization in measurement. *Conceptualization* is the process of taking a construct and refining it by giving it a conceptual, or theoretical, definition. A *conceptual definition* is a definition in abstract, theoretical terms. It refers to other ideas or constructs. There is no magical way to turn a construct into a precise conceptual definition. It involves thinking carefully, observing directly, consulting with others, reading what others have said, and trying possible definitions.

A good definition has one clear, explicit, and specific meaning. There is no ambiguity or vagueness. Some scholarly articles have been devoted to conceptualizing key concepts. Melbin (1978) conceptualized *night* as a frontier, Gibbs (1989) analyzed the meaning of the concept of *terrorism,* and Ball and Curry (1995) discussed ways to conceptualize what a *street gang* means. In addition to being a precondition for creating measures, as you read in Chapter 3 on theory, researchers need clear, unambiguous definitions of concepts to develop sound explanations.

A single construct can have several definitions, and people may disagree over definitions. Conceptual definitions are linked to theoretical frameworks and to value positions. For example, a conflict theorist may define *social class* as the power and property a group of people in society has or lacks. A structural functionalist defines it in terms of individuals who share a social status, lifestyle, or subjective identification. Although people disagree over definitions, the researcher should always state explicitly which definition he or she is using.

Some constructs (e.g., alienation) are highly abstract and complex. They contain lower-level concepts within them (e.g., powerlessness), which can be made even more specific (e.g., a feeling of little power over where one can live). Other constructs are concrete and simple (e.g., age). When developing definitions, a researcher needs to be aware of how complex and abstract a construct is. A concrete construct such as *age* is easier to define (e.g., number of years that have passed since birth) than is a complex, abstract concept such as *morale.*

Before you can measure, you need a concept. You also need to distinguish what you are interested in from other things. The idea that you first need a construct or concept of what is to be measured simply makes sense. How can you observe or measure something unless you know what you are looking for? For example, a biologist cannot observe a cell unless he or she first knows what a cell is, has a microscope, and has learned to distinguish it from noncell "stuff" or "junk" under the microscope. The process of measurement involves more than just having a measurement instrument (e.g., a microscope). In order to measure, the researcher needs three things: a construct, a measure, and an ability to recognize what one is looking for.[3]

For example, you want to measure teacher morale. You first define *teacher morale.* What does the construct of *morale* mean? As a variable construct, it takes on different values—high versus low or good versus bad morale. Next, you create a measure of your construct. This could take the form of survey questions, an examination of school records, or observations of teachers. Finally, you distinguish morale from other things in the answers to survey questions, school records, or observations.

A social work researcher's job is more difficult than that of the natural scientist because social measurement involves talking with people or observing their behavior. Unlike planets, cells, or chemicals, the answers people give and their actions can be ambiguous. People can react to the very fact that they are being asked questions or observed. Thus, the so-

cial work researcher has a double burden. First, he or she must have a clear construct, a good measure, and an ability to recognize what is being looked for. Second, he or she tries to measure fluid and confusing social life that may change just because of an awareness that a researcher is trying to measure.

How can you develop a conceptual definition of *teacher morale,* or at least a tentative working definition to get started? You begin with your everyday understanding of morale—something vague like "how people feel about things." You ask some of your friends how they define it. You also look at an unabridged dictionary and a thesaurus. They give definitions such as "confidence, spirit, zeal, cheerfulness, esprit de corps, mental condition towards something." You go to the library and study the research literature on morale or teacher morale to see how others have defined it. If someone else has already given an excellent definition, you might borrow it (citing the source, of course). If you do not find a definition that fits your purposes, you turn to theories of group behavior, individual mental states, and the like for ideas. As you collect various definitions, parts of definitions, and related ideas, you begin to see the boundaries of the core idea.

By now, you have a lot of definitions and need to sort them out. Most say that morale is a spirit, feeling, or mental condition toward something, or a group feeling. You separate the two extremes of your construct. This helps you turn the concept into a variable. High morale involves confidence, optimism, cheerfulness, feelings of togetherness, and willingness to endure hardship for the common good. Low morale is the opposite; it is a lack of confidence, pessimism, depression, isolation, selfishness, and an unwillingness to put forth effort for others.

You are interested in *teacher* morale, so you learn about teachers to specify the construct to them. One strategy is to make a list of examples of high or low teacher morale. High teacher morale includes saying positive things about the school, not complaining about extra work, or enjoying being with students. Low morale includes complaining a lot, not attending school events unless required to, or looking for other jobs.

Morale involves a feeling toward something else; a person has morale with regard to something. You list the various "somethings" toward which teachers have feelings (e.g., students, parents, pay, the school administration, other teachers, the profession of teaching). This raises an issue that frequently occurs when developing a definition. Are there several kinds of teacher morale, or are all these "somethings" aspects of one construct? There is no perfect answer. You have to decide whether morale means a single, general feeling with different parts or dimensions, or several distinct feelings.

What unit of analysis does your construct apply to: a group or an individual? Is morale a characteristic of an individual, of a group (e.g., a school), or of both? You decide that for your purposes morale applies only to groups of people. This tells you that the unit of analysis in your research project will be a group: all teachers in a school.

A researcher must distinguish the construct of interest from related ones. How is your construct of teacher morale similar to or different from related concepts? For example, does *morale* differ from *mood?* You decide that mood is more individual and temporary than morale. Likewise, morale differs from optimism and pessimism, which are outlooks about the future held by individuals. Morale is a group feeling that includes positive or negative feelings about the future as well as other beliefs and feelings.

Conceptualization is a process of thinking through the meanings of a construct. By now, you know that teacher morale is a mental state or feeling that ranges from high (optimistic, cheerful) to low (pessimistic, depressed); it has several dimensions (morale regarding students, morale regarding other teachers); it is a characteristic of a group; and it persists for a period of months. You have a much more specific mental picture of what you want to measure than when you began. If you had not conceptualized, you would have tried to measure what you started with—"how people feel about things."

Even with all the conceptualization about teacher morale, there is still some ambiguity. To complete the conceptualization process, you need to think about exactly what you intend to include within it. For example, what is a teacher? Does a teacher include guidance counselors, principals, athletic coaches, and librarians? What about student teachers or part-time, temporary, or substitute teachers? Does it include everyone who teaches for a liv-

ing, even if they are not employed by schools (e.g., a corporate trainer, an on-the-job supervisor who instructs an apprentice, a hospital physician who trains residents, etc.)?

Even if you restrict your definition to people in schools, what is a school? A school could include a nursery school, a training hospital, a university's Ph.D. program, a for-profit business that prepares people to take standardized tests, a dog obedience school, a summer camp that teaches students to play basketball, and a vocational school that teaches how to drive semitrailer trucks.

Some people assume "a teacher" means a full-time, professionally trained employee of a school, grades 1 through 12, who spends most of the day in a classroom with students. Others think of the legal or official government definition, which could include people who are certified to teach, even if they are not in classrooms, and exclude people who are uncertified even if they are in classrooms with students. The main point is that conceptualization means you need to be very clear in your own thinking of what you mean by *teachers* as well as by *morale* before you develop measures. You need to state what you mean very clearly and explicitly for other people to see.

Operationalization is a process of linking a conceptual definition to a specific set of measurement techniques or procedures. The specific procedures are the construct's *operational definition* (i.e., a definition in terms of the specific operations of actions a researcher carries out). An operational definition could be a survey questionnaire, a method of observing events in a field setting, a way to measure symbolic content in the mass media, or any process carried out by the researcher that reflects, documents, or represents the abstract construct as it is expressed in the conceptual definition.

There are usually multiple ways to measure a construct. Some are better or worse and more or less practical than others. The key is to fit your measure to your specific conceptual definition, to the practical constraints within which you must operate (e.g., time, money, available subjects, etc.), and to the research techniques you know or can learn. You can develop a new measure from scratch, or it can be a measure that is already being used by other researchers (see Box 7.1).

Box 7.1 _____

Five Suggestions for Coming Up with a Measure

1. *Remember the conceptual definition.* The underlying principle for any measure is to match it to the specific conceptual definition of the construct that will be used in the study.
2. *Keep an open mind.* Do not get locked into a single measure or type of measure. Be creative and constantly look for better measures. Avoid what Kaplan (1964:28) called the "law of the instrument," which means being locked into using one measurement instrument for all problems.
3. *Borrow from others.* Do not be afraid to borrow from other researchers, as long as credit is given. Good ideas for measures can be found in other studies or modified from other measures.
4. *Anticipate difficulties.* Logical and practical problems often arise when trying to measure variables of interest. Sometimes a problem can be anticipated and avoided with careful forethought and planning.
5. *Do not forget your units of analysis.* Your measure should fit with the units of analysis of the study and permit you to generalize to the universe of interest.

Operationalization links the language of theory with the language of empirical measures. Theory is full of abstract concepts, assumptions, relationships, definitions, and causality. Empirical measures describe how people concretely measure specific variables. They refer to specific operations or things people use to indicate the presence of a construct that exists in observable reality.

Quantitative Conceptualization and Operationalization

The measurement process for quantitative social work research is a straightforward sequence: first, conceptualization, followed by operationalization, followed by applying the operational definition or measuring to collect the data. Quantitative researchers developed several ways to think about rigorously linking abstract ideas to measurement procedures that will produce precise quantitative information about empirical reality.

Rules of correspondence or auxiliary theory link the conceptual definitions of constructs to concrete measures or operations for measuring constructs.[4] *Rules of correspondence* are logical statements of how an indicator corresponds to an abstract construct. For example, a rule of correspondence states that a person's verbal agreement with a set of 10 specific statements is evidence that the person holds strongly antifeminist beliefs and values. Likewise, an *auxiliary theory* explains how and why indicators and constructs connect. Such theories play a crucial role in research. Carmines and Zeller (1979:11) noted, "The auxiliary theory specifying the relationship between concepts and indicators is equally important to social work research as the substantive theory linking concepts to one another." For example, a researcher wants to measure alienation. An auxiliary theory suggests that the construct has four parts, each in a different sphere of life: family relations, work relations, relations with community, and relations with friends. The theory further specifies that certain behaviors or feelings in each sphere of life express alienation. For instance, in the sphere of work, an indicator of alienation is that a person feels a total lack of control over when, where, and with whom he or she works, what he or she does when working, or how fast he or she must work.

Figure 7.1 illustrates the measurement process for two variables that are linked together in a theory and a hypothesis. There are three levels to consider: conceptual, operational, and empirical.[5] At the most abstract level, the researcher is interested in the causal relationship between two constructs, or a *conceptual hypothesis.* At the level of operational definitions, the researcher is interested in testing an *empirical hypothesis* to determine the degree of association between indicators. This is the level at which correlations, statistics, questionnaires, and the like are used. The third level is the concrete empirical world. If the operational indicators of variables (e.g., questionnaires) are logically linked to a construct (e.g., racial discrimination), they will capture what happens in the empirical social world and relate it to the conceptual level.

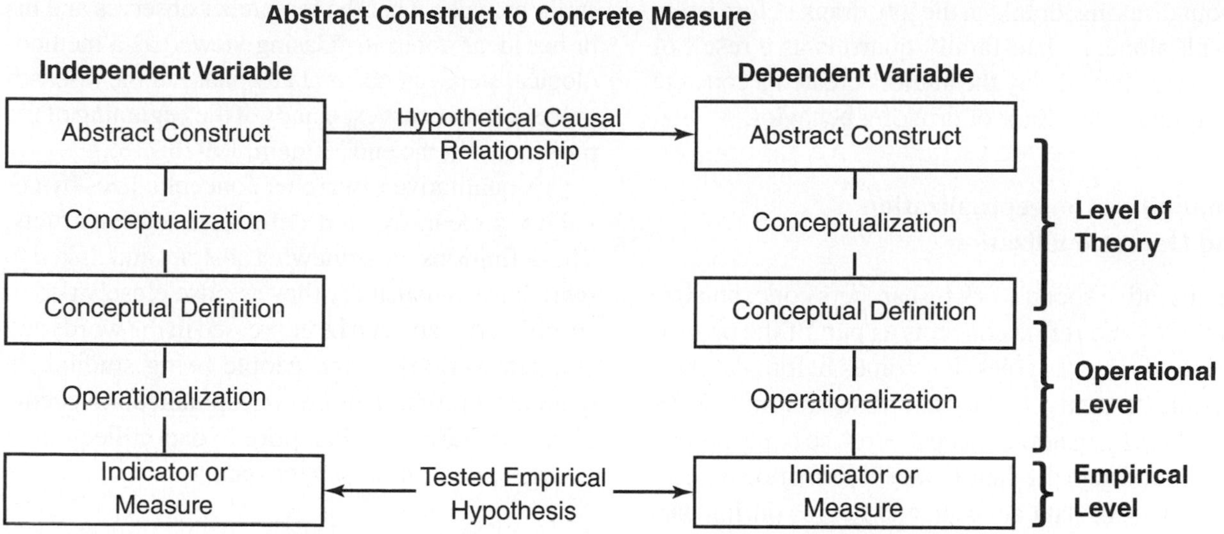

Abstract Construct to Concrete Measure

FIGURE 7.1   Conceptualization and Operationalization

The measurement process links together the three levels, moving deductively from the abstract to the concrete. A researcher first conceptualizes a variable, giving it a clear conceptual definition. Next, he or she operationalizes it by developing an operational definition or set of indicators for it. Lastly, he or she applies the indicators in the empirical world. The links from abstract constructs to empirical reality allow the researcher to test empirical hypotheses. Those tests are logically linked back to a conceptual hypothesis and causal relations in the world of theory.

How do you give your teacher morale construct an operational definition? First, you read the research reports of others and see whether a good indicator already exists. If there are no existing indicators, you must invent one from scratch. Morale is a mental state or feeling, so you measure it indirectly through people's words and actions. You might develop a questionnaire for the teachers and ask them about their feelings toward the dimensions of morale in your definition. You might go to the school and observe the teachers in the teachers' lounge, interacting with students, and at school activities. You might use school personnel records on teacher behaviors for statements that indicate morale (e.g., absences, requests for letters of recommendation for other jobs, performance reports, etc.). You

might survey students, school administrators, and others to find out what they think about teacher morale. Whichever indicator you choose, you further refine your conceptual definition as you develop it (e.g., write specific questionnaire questions).

A hypothesis has at least two variables, and the processes of conceptualization and operationalization are necessary for each variable. In the preceding example, morale is not a hypothesis. It is one variable. It could be a dependent variable caused by something else, or it could be an independent variable causing something else. It depends on your theoretical explanation.

Here is another example of measuring concepts. Seeman and Anderson (1983) tested the hypothesis that alienated people drink more alcohol. They measured alcohol drinking with a series of questions that tapped different aspects of the construct "drinking behavior." They defined the construct as having three subdimensions: frequency of drinking, quantity consumed per drinking occasion, and behavioral impairment due to drinking. They operationalized each dimension as several survey questions and combined the answers to questions to form an overall drinking measure. For example, the researchers measured the behavioral impairment subdimension by asking six questions about how often the respondent missed work because of drinking, was worried about drinking, drank on the job, drank before noon, drank alone, or had family quarrels as a result of drinking. In this way the authors created a concrete quantitative indicator of drinking behavior.

Qualitative Conceptualization and Operationalization

Quantitative social work researchers conceptualize variables and refine concepts as part of the process of measuring variables that comes before data collection or analysis. By contrast, qualitative researchers form new concepts or refine concepts that are grounded in the data. Concept formation is an integral part of data analysis and begins during data collection. Thus, conceptualization is how a qualitative researcher organizes and makes sense of data.

A qualitative social work researcher analyzes data by organizing it into categories on the basis of themes, concepts, or similar features. He or she develops new concepts, formulates conceptual definitions, and examines the relationships among concepts. Eventually, he or she links concepts to each other in terms of a sequence, as oppositional sets (X is the opposite of Y), or as sets of similar categories that he or she interweaves into theoretical statements. Qualitative researchers conceptualize or form concepts as they read through and ask critical questions of data (e.g., field notes, historical documents, secondary sources, etc.). The questions can come from the abstract vocabulary of a discipline such as sociology—for example: Is this a case of class conflict? Was role conflict present in that situation? Is this a social movement? Questions can also be logical—for example: What was the sequence of events? How does the way it happened here compare to over there? Are these the same or different, general or specific cases?

In qualitative social work research, ideas and evidence are mutually interdependent. This applies particularly to case study analysis. Cases are not given preestablished empirical units or theoretical categories apart from data; they are defined by data and theory. By analyzing a situation, the researcher organizes data and applies ideas simultaneously to create or specify a case. Making or creating a case, called *casing,* brings the data and theory together. Determining what to treat as a case resolves a tension or strain between what the researcher observes and his or her ideas about it. "Casing viewed as a methodological step, can occur at any phase of the research process, but occurs especially at the beginning of the project and at the end" (Ragin, 1992b:218).

A qualitative researcher conceptualizes by developing clear, explicit definitions of constructs. The definitions are somewhat abstract and linked to other ideas, but usually they are also closely tied to specific data, and can be expressed in the words and concrete actions of the people being studied. In qualitative research more conceptualization occurs after data collection than prior to data collection; it is largely determined by the data.

Operationalization. The operationalization process in qualitative research significantly differs from that in quantitative research. A quantitative researcher operationalizes variables by turning a conceptual definition into a set of operations or procedures that he or she later uses in data collection. It does not work the same way in qualitative research because qualitative researchers develop many conceptual definitions while or after gathering data.

Operationalization in qualitative research is a detailed description of how a researcher collected and thought about the specific data that become the basis for concepts. It is an after-the-fact description more than a before-the-fact preplanned technique. Almost in a reverse of the quantitative process, data gathering occurs with or prior to full operationalization.

Just as quantitative operationalization deviates from a rigid deductive process, the process followed by qualitative researchers is one of mutual interaction. The researcher draws on ideas from beyond the data of a specific research setting. Qualitative operationalization describes how the researcher collects data, but it includes the researcher's use of preexisting techniques and concepts that were blended with those that emerged during the data collection process.

An example of qualitative operationalization is found in Fantasia's (1988) field research on contested labor actions using the *cultures of solidarity* as the concept. A culture of solidarity is related to ideas of conflictual workplace relations and growing class consciousness among nonmanagerial workers. His conceptual definition is that it is a kind of cultural expression by workers that evolves in particular places over time. It is a process in which workers develop shared feelings and a sense of unity that are in opposition to management and business owners. It are an interactive process during which workers come to common ideas, understandings, and actions. It is "less a matter of disembodied mental attitude than a broader set of practices and repertoires available for empirical investigation" (Fantasia, 1988:14).

Fantasia operationalized the concept by describing how he gathered data, by presenting data that portray the concept, and by explaining his thinking about the data. He describes what he specificially did to collect the data (e.g., he worked in a particular factory, attended a press conference, and interviewed people), and he presents the data in detail (e.g., he describes specific events that document the concept, such as several maps showing where people stood during a confrontation with a foreman, retelling a sequence of events in a factory, recounting actions by management officials, and repeating statements individual workers made). He also provides a look into his own thinking as he reflected and tried to understand his experiences, including developing new ideas and drawing on the ideas of other scholars.

RELIABILITY AND VALIDITY

Reliability and validity are central issues in all measurement. Both concern how concrete measures are connected to constructs. Reliability and validity are salient because constructs in social theory are often ambiguous, diffuse, and not directly observable. Perfect reliability and validity are virtually impossible to achieve. Rather, they are ideals researchers strive for.

All social work researchers want their measures to be reliable and valid. Both ideas are important in establishing the truthfulness, credibility, or believability of findings. Both terms also have multiple meanings. Here, they refer to related, desirable aspects of measurement.

Reliability means dependability or consistency. It suggests that the same thing is repeated or recurs under the identical or very similar conditions. The opposite of reliability is a measurement process that yields erratic, unstable, or inconsistent results.

Validity suggests truthfulness and refers to the match between a construct—or the way a researcher conceptualizes the idea in a conceptual definition—and a measure. It refers to how well an idea about reality "fits" with actual reality. The absence of validity occurs if there is poor fit between the constructs a researcher uses to describe, theorize, or analyze the social world and what actually occurs in the social world. In simple terms, validity addresses the question of how well the social reality being measured through research matches with the constructs researchers use to understand it.

Qualitative and quantitative social work researchers want reliable and valid measurement, but beyond an agreement on the basic ideas at a general level, each style sees the specifics of reliability and validity in the research process differently.

Reliability and Validity in Quantitative Social Work Research

Reliability. As just stated, reliability means dependability. It means that the numerical results produced by an indicator do not vary because of characteristics of the measurement process or measurement instrument itself. For example, you get on your bathroom scale and read your weight. You get off and get on again and again. You have a reliable scale if it gives you the same weight each time—assuming, of course, that you are not eating, drinking, changing clothing, and so forth. An unreliable scale will register different weights each time, even though your "true" weight does not change. Another example is your car speedometer. If you are driving at a constant slow speed on a level surface, but the speedometer needle jumps from one end to the other, your speedometer is not a reliable indicator of how fast you are traveling. Actually, there are three types of reliability.[6]

Three Types of Reliability

Stability Reliability. *Stability reliability* is reliability across time. It addresses the question, "Does the measure deliver the same answer when applied in different time periods?" The weight-scale example just given is of this type of reliability. You can examine an indicator's degree of stability reliability by using the *test–retest method,* with which you retest or readminister the indicator to the same group of people. If what you are measuring is stable and the indicator has stability reliability, then you will get the same results each time. A variation of the test–retest method is to give an alternative form of the test, but the alternative form has to be very similar. For example, you have a hypothesis about gender and seating patterns in a college cafeteria. You measure your dependent variable (seating patterns) by observing and recording the number of male and female students at tables, and noting who sits down first, second, third, and so on for a three-hour period. If, as you are observing, you get tired or distracted, or you forget to record and miss more people toward the end of the three hours, then your indicator does not have a high degree of stability reliability.

Representative Reliability. *Representative reliability* is reliability across subpopulations or groups of people. It addresses the question, "Does the indicator deliver the same answer when applied to different groups?" An indicator has high representative reliability if it yields the same result for a construct when applied to different subpopulations (e.g., different classes, races, sexes, age groups, etc.). For example, you ask a question about a person's age. If people in their twenties answered your question by overstating their true age, whereas people in their fifties understated their true age, then the indicator has a low degree of representative reliability. To have representative reliability, the measure needs to give accurate information for every age group.

A *subpopulation analysis* determines whether an indicator has this type of reliability. The analysis involves comparing the indicator across different subpopulations or subgroups and uses independent knowledge about subpopulations. For example, you want to test the representative reliability of a questionnaire item that asks about a person's education. You conduct a subpopulation analysis to see whether the question works equally well for men and women. You ask men and women the question, then obtain independent information (e.g., check school records) and check to see whether the errors in answering the question are equal for men and women. The item has representative reliability if men and women have the same error rate.

Equivalence Reliability. *Equivalence reliability* applies when researchers use *multiple indicators*—that is, when multiple specific measures are used in the operationalization of a construct (e.g., several items in a questionnaire all measure the same construct). It addresses the question, "Does the measure yield consistent results across different indicators?" If several different indicators measure the same construct, then a reliable measure gives the same result with all indicators.

Researchers examine equivalence reliability on examinations and long questionnaires with the *split-half method.* This involves dividing the indicators of the same construct into two groups, usually by a random process, and determining whether both halves give the same results. For example, you have 14 items on a questionnaire. All measure political conservatism among college students. If your indicators (i.e., questionnaire items) have equivalence reliability, then you can randomly divide them into two groups of 7 and get the same results. For example, you use the first 7 questions and find that a class of 50 business majors is twice as conservative as a class of 50 education majors. You get the same results using the second 7 questions. There are also special statistical measures (e.g., Cronbach's alpha) to determine this type of reliability.

A special type of equivalence reliability, *intercoder reliability,* arises when there are several observers, raters, or coders of information. In a sense, each person who is observing is an indicator. A measure is reliable if the observers, raters, or coders agree with each other. It is a common type of reliability reported in content analysis studies, but it can be used whenever multiple raters or coders are involved. For example, you hire six students to observe student seating patterns in a cafeteria. If all six are equally skilled at observing and recording, you can combine the information from all six into a single reliable measure. But if one or two students are lazy, inattentive, or sloppy, then your measure will have lower reliability.

Intercoder reliability is tested by having several coders measure the same thing, then comparing the measures. For instance, you have three coders independently code the seating patterns during the same hour on three different days. You compare the recorded observations. If they agree, you can be confident of your measure's intercoder reliability. Special statistical techniques measure the degree of intercoder reliability.

How to Improve Reliability.   It is rare to have perfect reliability. There are four ways to increase the reliability of measures: (1) clearly conceptualize constructs, (2) use a precise level of measurement, (3) use multiple indicators, and (4) use pilot tests.

Clearly Conceptualize All Constructs.   Reliability increases when a single construct or subdimension of a construct is measured. This means developing unambiguous, clear theoretical definitions. Constructs should be specified to eliminate "noise" (i.e., distracting or interfering information) from other constructs. Each measure should indicate one and only one concept. Otherwise, it is impossible to determine which concept is being "indicated." For example, the indicator of a pure chemical compound is more reliable than one in which the chemical is mixed with other material or dirt. In the latter case it is difficult to separate the "noise" of other material from the pure chemical.

Let us return to teacher morale. You should separate morale from related concepts (e.g., mood, personality, spirit, job attitude). If you did not do this, you could not be sure what you were really measuring. You might develop an indicator for morale that also indicates personality; that is, the construct

of personality contaminates that of morale and produces a less reliable indicator. Bad measurement occurs when one indicator is used to operationalize different constructs (e.g., using the same questionnaire item to indicate morale and personality).

Increase the Level of Measurement.   Levels of measurement are discussed later. Indicators at higher or more precise levels of measurement are more likely to be reliable than less precise measures because the latter pick up less detailed information. If more specific information is measured, then it is less likely that anything other than the construct will be captured. The general principle is this: Try to measure at the most precise level possible. However, it is more difficult to measure at higher levels of measurement. For example, if you have a choice of measuring morale as either high or low, or in 10 categories from extremely low to extremely high, it would be better to measure it in 10 refined categories.

Use Multiple Indicators of a Variable.   A third way to increase reliability is to use *multiple indicators* because two (or more) indicators of the same construct are better than one.[7] Figure 7.2 illustrates the use of multiple indicators in hypothesis testing. Three indicators of the one independent variable construct are combined into an overall measure, *A,* and two indicators of a dependent variable are combined into a single measure, *B.* For example, you have three specific measures of *A,* which is

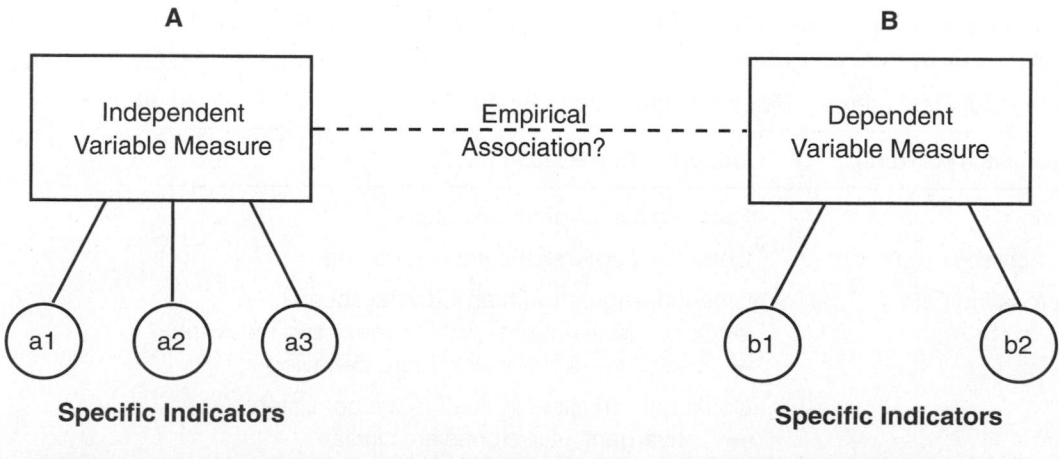

FIGURE 7.2   Measurement Using Multiple Indicators

teacher morale: answers to a survey question on attitudes about school, number of absences for reasons other than illness and requests for transfers, and number of complaints others heard a teacher voice. You also have two measures of your dependent variable, *B,* giving students extra attention: number of hours teacher spent staying after school hours to meet individually with students and whether the teacher inquires frequently about a student's progress in other classes.

Multiple indicators let a researcher take measurements from a wider range of the content of a conceptual definition. Some writers call this *sampling from the conceptual domain.* Different aspects of the construct can be measured, each with its own indicator. Also, one indicator (e.g., one question on a questionnaire) may be imperfect, but several measures are less likely to have the same (systematic) error. Multiple indicator measures tend to be more stable than measures with one item.

Use Pretests, Pilot Studies, and Replication. Reliability can be improved by using a pretest or pilot version of a measure first. Develop one or more draft or preliminary versions of a measure and try them before applying the final version in a hypothesis-testing situation. This takes more time and effort. For example, in your survey of teacher morale, you go through many drafts of a question before the final version. You test early versions by asking people the question and checking to see whether it is clear.

The principle of using pilot tests extends to replicating the measures other researchers have used. For example, you search the literature and find measures of morale from past research. You may want to build on and use a previous measure if it is a good one, citing the source, of course. In addition, you may want to add new indicators and compare them to the previous measure. In this way the quality of the measure can improve over time, as long as the same definition is used. See Table 7.1 for a summary of reliability types.

Validity. *Validity* is an overused term. Sometimes validity is used to mean "true" or "correct." There are several general types of validity. Here, we are concerned with *measurement validity.* There are also several types of measurement validity. Nonmeasurement types of validity are discussed later.

When a researcher says that an indicator is valid, it is valid for a particular purpose and definition. The same indicator can be valid for one purpose (i.e., a research question with its units of analysis and a universe of elements to be sampled) but less valid or invalid for others. The measure of morale discussed here (e.g., questions about feelings toward school) might be valid for measuring morale among teachers but invalid for measuring the morale of police officers.[8]

At its core, measurement validity refers to how well the conceptual and operational definitions mesh with each other. The better the fit, the greater the measurement validity. Validity is more difficult to achieve than reliability. We cannot have absolute confidence about validity, but some measures are *more valid* than others. The reason we can never achieve absolute validity is that constructs are

TABLE 7.1 Summary of Measurement Reliability and Validity Types

RELIABILITY (Dependable Measure)	VALIDITY (True Measure)
Stability—over time	Face—in the judgment of others
Representative—across subgroups	Content—captures the entire meaning
Equivalence—across indicators	Criterion—agrees with an external source
	▬ Concurrent—agrees with a preexisting measure
	▬ Predictive—agrees with future behavior
	Construct—multiple indicators are consistent
	▬ Convergent—alike ones are similar
	▬ Discriminant—different ones differ

abstract ideas, whereas indicators refer to concrete observation. This is the gap between our mental pictures about the world and the specific things we do at particular times and places. Bohrnstedt (1992b:2217) argued that validity cannot be determined directly. Validity is part of a dynamic process that grows by accumulating evidence over time, and without it, all measurement becomes meaningless.

Some researchers use rules of correspondence to reduce the gap between abstract ideas and specific indicators. (Rules of correspondence were discussed earlier.) They are logical statements about the fit between indicators and definitions. For example, here is a rule of correspondence: If a teacher agrees with statements that "things have gotten worse at this school in the past five years" and that "there is little hope for improvement," this indicates low morale on the part of the teacher. Another way of talking about measurement validity is the *epistemic correlation*. This refers to a hypothetical correlation between a specific indicator and the essence of the construct that the indicator measures. We cannot measure such correlations directly because correlations between a measure and an abstraction are impossible, but they can be estimated with advanced statistical techniques.[9]

Four Types of Measurement Validity

Face Validity. The easiest to achieve and the most basic kind of validity is *face validity*. It is a judgment by the scientific community that the indicator really measures the construct. It addresses the question, "On the face of it, do people believe that the definition and method of measurement fit?" It is a consensus method of measurement validity. For example, few people would accept a measure of college student math ability using a question that asked students, "2 + 2 = ?" This is not a valid measure of college-level math ability on the face of it. Recall that the principle of organized skepticism in the scientific community means that aspects of research are scrutinized by others.[10] See Table 7.1 for a summary of types of measurement validity. Figure 7.3 presents the types in pictorial form.

Content Validity. *Content validity* is a special type of face validity. It addresses the question, "Is the full content of a definition represented in a measure?" A conceptual definition holds ideas; it is a "space" containing ideas and concepts. Measures should sample or represent all ideas or areas in the conceptual space. Content validity involves three steps. First, specify the content in a construct's definition. Next, sample from all areas of the definition. Finally, develop an indicator that taps all of the parts of the definition.

An example of content validity is the definition of *feminism* as a person's commitment to a set of beliefs creating full equality between men and women in areas of the arts, intellectual pursuits, family, work, politics, and authority relations. You create a measure of feminism in which you ask two survey questions: (1) "Should men and women get equal pay for equal work?" and (2) "Should men and women share household tasks?" Your measure has low content validity because the two questions ask only about pay and household tasks. They ignore the other areas (intellectual pursuits, politics, authority relations, and other aspects of work and family). For a content-valid measure, you must either expand the measure or narrow the definition.[11]

Criterion Validity. *Criterion validity* uses some standard or criterion to indicate a construct accurately. The validity of an indicator is verified by comparing it with another measure of the same construct in which a researcher has confidence. There are two subtypes of this kind of validity.[12]

Concurrent. To have *concurrent validity*, an indicator must be associated with a preexisting indicator that is judged to be valid (i.e., it has face validity). For example, you create a new test to measure intelligence. For it to be concurrently valid, it should be highly associated with existing IQ tests (assuming the same definition of intelligence is used). This means that most people who score high on the old measure should also score high on the new one, and vice versa. The two measures may not be perfectly associated, but if they measure the same or a similar construct, it is logical for them to yield similar results.

Predictive. Criterion validity whereby an indicator predicts future events that are logically related to

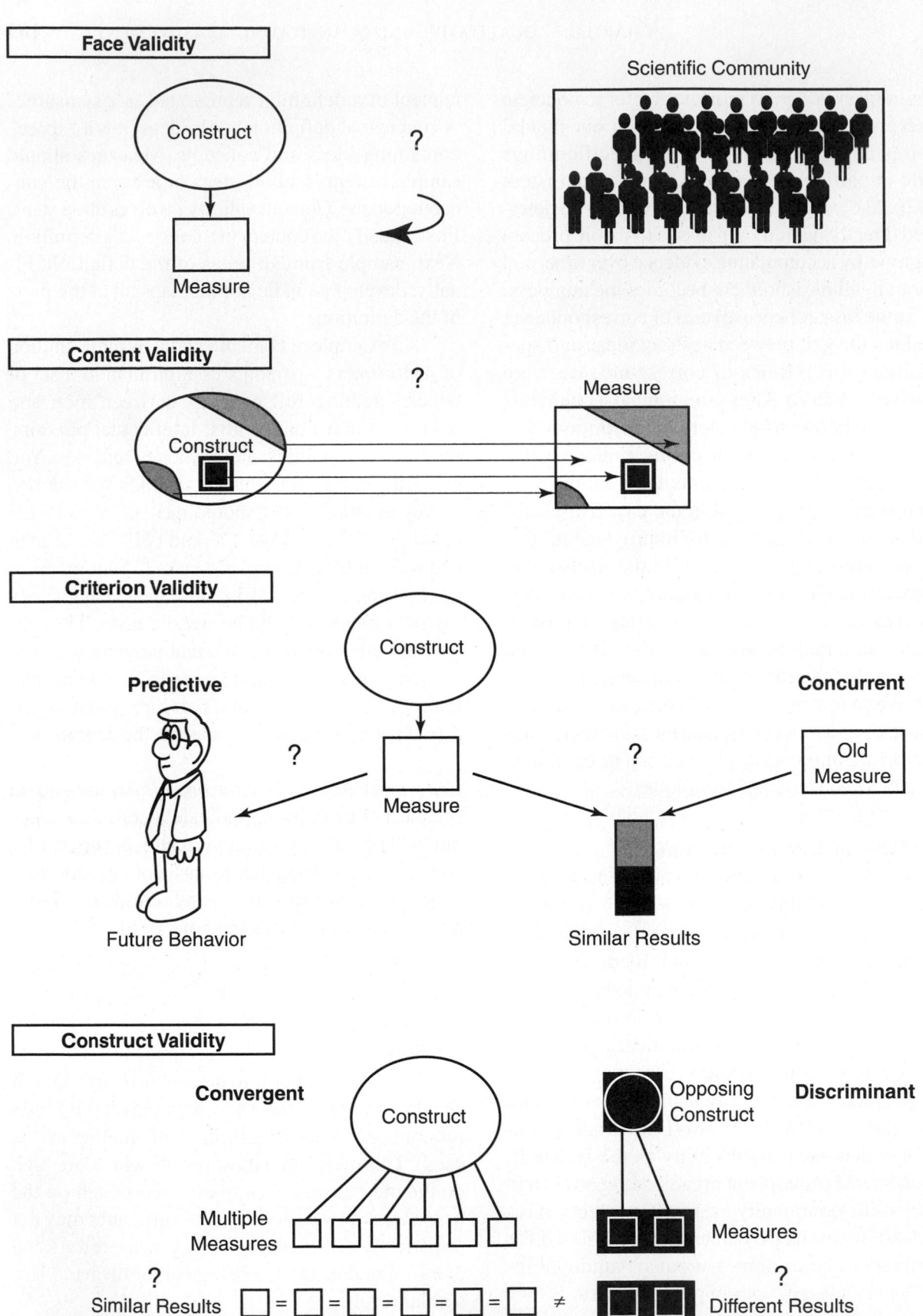

FIGURE 7.3 Types of Validity

a construct is called *predictive validity*. It cannot be used for all measures. The measure and the action predicted must be distinct from, but indicate, the same construct. Predictive measurement validity should not be confused with prediction in hypothesis testing, where one variable predicts a different variable in the future. For example, the SAT that many U.S. high school students take measures scholastic aptitude—the ability of a student to perform in college. If the SAT has high predictive validity, then students who get high SAT scores will subsequently do well in college. If students with high scores perform the same as students with average or low scores, then the SAT has low predictive validity.

Another way to test predictive validity is to select a group of people who have specific characteristics and predict how they will score (very high or very low) vis-à-vis the construct. For example, let's say you have a measure of political conservatism. You predict that members of conservative groups (e.g., John Birch Society, Conservative Caucus, Daughters of the American Revolution, Moral Majority) will score high on it, whereas members of liberal groups (e.g., Democratic Socialists, People for the American Way, Americans for Democratic Action) will score low. You "validate" the measure with the groups—that is, you pilot test it by using it on members of the groups. It can then be used as a measure of political conservatism for the general public.

Construct Validity.   *Construct validity* is for measures with multiple indicators. It addresses the question, "If the measure is valid, do the various indicators operate in a consistent manner?" It requires a definition with clearly specified conceptual boundaries.

Convergent validity.   This kind of validity applies when multiple indicators converge or are associated with one another. *Convergent validity* means that multiple measures of the same construct hang together or operate in similar ways. For example, you measure the construct "education" by asking people how much education they have completed, looking up school records, and asking the people to complete a test of school knowledge. If the measures do not converge (i.e., people who claim to have a college

degree have no records of attending college, or those with college degrees perform no better than high school dropouts on your tests), then your measure has weak convergent validity and you should not combine all three indicators into one measure.

Discriminant validity.   Also called divergent validity, *discriminant validity* is the opposite of convergent validity. It means that the indicators of one construct hang together or converge, but also diverge from or are negatively associated with, opposing constructs. It says that if two constructs *A* and *B* are very different, then measures of *A* and *B* should not be associated. For example, you have 10 items that measure political conservatism. People answer all 10 in similar ways. But you also put 5 questions on the same questionnaire that measure political liberalism. Your measure of conservatism has discriminant validity if the 10 conservatism items both hang together and are negatively associated with the 5 liberalism ones.

Reliability and Validity in Qualitative Social Work Research

Most qualitative social work researchers accept the principles of reliability and validity, but use the terms infrequently because of their close association with quantitative measurement. In addition, qualitative researchers apply the principles differently in practice.

Reliability.   *Reliability* means dependability or consistency. Qualitative social work researchers use a variety of techniques (e.g., interviews, participation, photographs, document studies, etc.) to record their observations consistently. Qualitative researchers want to be consistent (i.e., not vacillating and erratic) in how, over time, they make observations, similar to the idea of stability reliability. One difficulty is that they often study processes that are not stable over time. Moreover, they emphasize the value of a changing or developing interaction between the researcher and what he or she studies. Qualitative researchers believe that the subject matter and a researcher's relationship to it should be a growing, evolving process. The metaphor for the relationship between a researcher and the data is one of an evolving relationship or living organism (e.g., a plant) that naturally matures. Most qualitative social work researchers resist the quantitative approach to reliability, which they see as a cold, fixed mechanical instrument that one repeatedly injects into or applies to some static, lifeless material.

Qualitative researchers consider a range of data sources and employ multiple measurement methods. They question the quantitative–positivist ideas of replication, equivalence, and subpopulation reliability. They accept that different researchers or researchers using alternative measures will get distinctive results. This is because they see data collection as an interactive process in which particular researchers operate in an evolving setting, and the setting's context dictates using a unique mix of measures that cannot be repeated. The diverse measures and interactions with different researchers are beneficial because they can illuminate different facets or dimensions of a subject matter. Many qualitative researchers question the quantitative researcher's quest for standard, fixed measures. They fear such measures ignore benefits of having a variety of researchers with many approaches and may neglect key aspects of diversity that exist in the social world.

Validity.   *Validity* means truthfulness. It refers to the bridge between a construct and the data. Qualitative social work researchers are more interested in authenticity than validity. *Authenticity* means giving a fair, honest, and balanced account of social life from the viewpoint of someone who lives it every day. Qualitative researchers are less concerned with trying to match an abstract concept to empirical data and more concerned with giving a candid portrayal of social life that is true to the experiences of people being studied. Most qualitative researchers concentrate on ways to capture an inside view and provide a detailed account of how those being studied feel about and understand events.

Qualitative researchers have developed several methods that serve as substitutes for the quantitative approach to validity. Thus, field researchers discuss ecological validity or natural history methods (see Chapter 13). These emphasize conveying the insider's view to others. Historical researchers use internal and external criticisms to determine whether the evidence they have is real or they believe it to be. Qualitative researchers adhere to the core principle of validity, to be truthful (i.e., avoid false or distorted accounts). They try to create a tight fit between their understanding, ideas, and statements about the social world and what is actually occurring in it.

Relationship between Reliability and Validity

Reliability is necessary for validity and is easier to achieve than validity. Although reliability is necessary in order to have a valid measure of a concept, it does not guarantee that a measure will be valid. It is not a sufficient condition for validity. A measure can produce the same result over and over (i.e., it has reliability), but what it measures may not match the definition of the construct (i.e., validity).

A measure can be reliable but invalid. For example, you get on a scale and get weighed. The weight registered by the scale is the same each time you get on and off. But then you go to another scale—an "official" one that measures true weight—and it says that your weight is twice as great. The first scale yielded reliable (i.e., dependable and consistent) results, but it did not give a valid measure of your weight.

A diagram might help you see the relationship between reliability and validity. Figure 7.4 illustrates the relationship between the concepts by using the analogy of a target. The bull's-eye represents a fit between a measure and the definition of the construct.

Validity and *reliability* are usually complementary concepts, but in some special situations they conflict with each other. Sometimes, as validity increases, reliability is more difficult to attain, and vice versa. This occurs when the construct has a highly abstract and not easily observable definition. Reliability is easiest to achieve when the measure is precise and observable. Thus, there is a strain between the true essence of the highly abstract construct and measuring it in a concrete manner. For example, "alienation" is a very abstract, highly subjective construct, often defined as a deep inner sense of loss of one's humanity that diffuses across many aspects of one's life (e.g., social relations, sense of self, orientation toward nature). Highly precise

A Bull's-Eye = A Perfect Measure

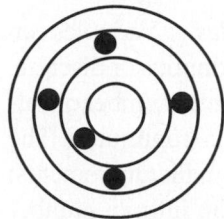
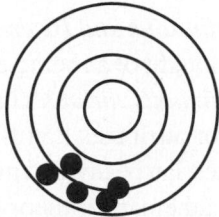
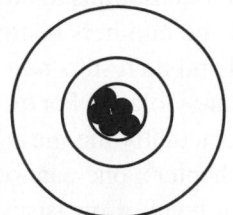

Low Reliability
and Low Validity

High Reliability
but Low Validity

High Reliability
and High Validity

FIGURE 7.4 Illustration of Relationship between Reliability and Validity

Source: From *Practice of Social Research,* 7th edition, by E.R. Babbie © 1995. Reprinted with permission of Wadsworth, an imprint of the Wadsworth Group, a division of Thomson Learning. Fax 800-730-2215.

questions in a questionnaire give reliable measures, but there is a danger of losing the subjective essence of the concept.

Some strongly positivist researchers argue that this means that alienation and constructs based on personal feelings and experiences are bad concepts and should be avoided. Others, who accept a more interpretive or critical approach to science, argue that these concepts should be retained. They say that measurement must be more flexible and less precise, using qualitative methods. Measurement issues ultimately return to assumptions about how to conduct research and how the concepts are defined.

Other Uses of the Terms *Reliable* and *Valid*

Many words have multiple definitions, including *reliability* and *validity*. This creates confusion unless we distinguish among alternative uses of the same word.

Reliability. We use *reliability* in everyday language. A reliable person is one who is dependable, stable, and responsible; a reliable car is dependable and trustworthy. This means the person responds in similar, predictable ways in different times and conditions; the same can be said for the car. In addition to measurement reliability, researchers sometimes say a study or its results are reliable (e.g., Yin, 1988). By this they mean that the method of conducting a

study or the results from it can be reproduced or replicated by other researchers.

Internal Validity. *Internal validity* means there are no errors internal to the design of the research project.[13] It is used primarily in experimental research to talk about possible errors or alternative explanations of results that arise despite attempts to institute controls. High internal validity means there are few such errors. Low internal validity means that such errors are likely.

External Validity. *External validity* is used primarily in experimental research. It is the ability to generalize findings from a specific setting and small group to a broad range of settings and people. It addresses the question, "If something happens in a laboratory or among a particular group of subjects (e.g., college students), can the findings be generalized to the "real" (nonlaboratory) world or to the general public (nonstudents)?" High external validity means that the results can be generalized to many situations and many groups of people. Low external validity means that the results apply only to a very specific setting.

Statistical Validity. *Statistical validity* means that the correct statistical procedure is chosen and its assumptions are fully met. Different statistical tests or procedures are appropriate for different conditions, which are discussed in textbooks that describe the statistical procedures.

All statistics are based on assumptions about the mathematical properties of the numbers being used. A statistic will be invalid and its results nonsense if the major assumptions are violated. For example, to compute an average (actually the mean, which is discussed in a later chapter), one cannot use information at the nominal level of measurement (to be discussed). For example, suppose you measure the race of a class of students. You give each race a number: White = 1, African American = 2, Asian = 3, others = 4. It makes no sense to say that the "mean" race of a class of students is 1.9 (almost African American?). This is a misuse of the statistical procedure, and the results are invalid even if the computation is correct. The degree to which statistical assumptions can be violated or bent (the technical term is *robustness*) is a topic in which professional statisticians take great interest.

A GUIDE TO QUANTITATIVE MEASUREMENT

Thus far, you have learned about the principles of measurement, including the principles of reliability and validity. Quantitative social work researchers have developed ideas and specialized measures to help them in the process of creating operational definitions that will be reliable and valid measures that yield numerical data for their variable constructs. This section of the chapter is a brief guide to these ideas and a few of the measures.

Levels of Measurement

Levels of measurement is an abstract but important and widely used idea. Basically, it says that some ways a researcher measures a construct are at a higher or more refined level, and others are crude or less precisely specified. The level of measurement depends on the way in which a construct is conceptualized— that is, assumptions about whether it has particular characteristics. The level of measurement affects the kinds of indicators chosen and is tied to basic assumptions in a construct's definition. The way in which a researcher conceptualizes a variable limits the levels of measurement that he or she can use and

has implications for how measurement and statistical analysis can proceed.

Continuous and Discrete Variables.   Variables can be thought of as being either continuous or discrete. *Continuous variables* have an infinite number of values or attributes that flow along a continuum. The values can be divided into many smaller increments; in mathematical theory there is an infinite number of increments. Examples of continuous variables include temperature, age, income, crime rate, and amount of schooling. *Discrete variables* have a relatively fixed set of separate values or variable attributes. Instead of a smooth continuum of values, discrete variables contain distinct categories. Examples of discrete variables include gender (male or female), religion (Protestant, Catholic, Jew, Muslim, atheist), and marital status (never married single, married, divorced or separated, widowed). Whether a variable is continuous or discrete affects its level of measurement.

Four Levels of Measurement

Precision and Levels.   The idea of levels of measurement expands on the difference between continuous and discrete variables and organizes types of variables for their use in statistics. The four levels of measurement categorize the degree of precision of measurement.[14]

Deciding on the appropriate level of measurement for a construct often creates confusion. The appropriate level of measurement for a variable depends on two things: (1) how a construct is conceptualized and (2) the type of indicator or measurement that a researcher uses.

The construct itself limits the level of precision. The way a researcher conceptualizes a construct can limit how precisely it can be measured. For example, some of the variables listed earlier as continuous can be reconceptualized as discrete. Temperature can be a continuous variable (e.g., degrees, fractions of degrees) or it can be crudely measured with discrete categories (e.g., hot or cold). Likewise, age can be continuous (how old a person is in years, months, days, hours, and minutes) or treated as discrete categories (infancy, childhood, adolescence, young adulthood, middle age, old age).

Yet, most discrete variables cannot be conceptualized as continuous variables. For example, sex, religion, and marital status cannot be conceptualized as continuous; however, related constructs *can* be conceptualized as continuous (e.g., femininity, degree of religiousness, commitment to a marital relationship, etc.).

The level of measurement limits the statistical measures that can be used. A wide range of powerful statistical procedures is available for the higher levels of measurement, but the types of statistics that can be used with the lowest levels are very limited.

There is a practical reason to conceptualize and measure variables at higher levels of measurement. You can collapse higher levels of measurement to lower levels, but the reverse is not true. In other words, it is possible to measure a construct very precisely, gather very specific information, and then ignore some of the precision. But it is not possible to measure a construct with less precision or with less specific information and then make it more precise later.

Distinguishing among the Four Levels.   The four levels from lowest to greatest or highest precision are nominal, ordinal, interval, and ratio. Each level gives a different type of information (see Table 7.2). *Nominal measures* indicate only that there is a difference among categories (e.g., religion: Protestant, Catholic, Jew, Muslim; racial heritage: African, Asian, Caucasian, Hispanic, other). *Ordinal measures* indicate a difference, *plus* the categories can be ordered or ranked (e.g., letter grades: A, B, C, D, F; opinion measures: Strongly Agree, Agree, Disagree, Strongly Disagree). *Interval measures* do everything the first two do, *plus* they can specify the amount of distance between categories (e.g., Fahrenheit or Celsius temperature: 5°, 45°, 90°; IQ scores: 95, 110, 125). Arbitrary zeros may be used in interval measures; they are there just to help keep score. *Ratio measures* do everything all the other levels do, *plus* there is a true zero, which makes it possible to state relations in terms of proportion or ratios (e.g., money income: $10, $100, $500; years of formal schooling: 1 year, 10 years, 13 years). In most practical situations the distinction between interval and ratio levels makes little difference. The arbitrary zeros of some interval measures can be confusing. For example, a rise in temperature from 30 to 60 degrees is not really a doubling of the temperature, although the numbers double, because zero degrees is not the absence of all heat.

Discrete variables are nominal and ordinal, whereas continuous variables can be measured at the interval or ratio level. A ratio-level measure can be turned into an interval, ordinal, or nominal level. The interval level can always be turned into an ordinal or nominal level, but the process does not work in the opposite way!

In general, if it is necessary to use ordinal measurement, use at least five ordinal categories and obtain many observations. This is because the distortion created by collapsing a continuous construct into a smaller number of ordered categories is minimized as the number of categories and the number of observations increase.[15]

The ratio level of measurement is rarely used in social work. For most purposes it is indistinguishable from interval measurement. The only difference is that ratio measurement has a "true zero."

TABLE 7.2   Characteristics of the Four Levels of Measurement

LEVEL	DIFFERENT CATEGORIES	RANKED	DISTANCE BETWEEN CATEGORIES MEASURED	TRUE ZERO
Nominal	Yes			
Ordinal	Yes	Yes		
Interval	Yes	Yes	Yes	
Ratio	Yes	Yes	Yes	Yes

This can be confusing because some measures, such as temperature, have zeros that are not true zeros. The temperature can be zero, or below zero, but zero is an arbitrary number when it is assigned to temperature. This can be illustrated by comparing zero degrees Celsius with zero degrees Fahrenheit—they are different temperatures. In addition, doubling the degrees in one system does not double the degrees in the other. Likewise, it does not make sense to say that it is "twice as warm," as is possible with ratio measurement, if the temperature rises from 2 to 4 degrees, from 15 to 30 degrees, or from 40 to 80 degrees. Another common example of arbitrary—not true—zeros occurs when measuring attitudes wherein numbers are assigned to statements (e.g., –1 = disagree, 0 = no opinion, +1 = agree). True zeros exist for variables such as income, age, or years of education. Examples of the four levels of measurement are shown in Table 7.3.

Specialized Measures: Scales and Indexes

In this last section of this chapter, we will look at a number of specialized measures, including scales and indexes. Researchers have created thousands of different scales and indexes to measure social variables.[16] For example, scales and indexes have been developed to measure the degree of formalization in bureaucratic organizations, the prestige of occupations, the adjustment of people to a marriage, the intensity of group interaction, the level of social activity in a community, the degree to which a state's sexual assault laws reflect feminist values, and the level of socioeconomic development of a nation. We cannot discuss the thousands of scales and indexes. Instead, we will focus on principles of scale and index construction and explore some major types.

Keep two things in mind. First, virtually every social phenomenon can be measured (Fischer, 1973). Some constructs can be measured directly and produce precise numerical values (e.g., family income). Other constructs require the use of surrogates or proxies that indirectly measure a variable and may not be as precise (e.g., predisposition to commit a crime). Second, a lot can be learned from measures used by other researchers. You are fortunate to have the work of thousands of researchers to draw upon. It is not always necessary to start from scratch. You can use a past scale or index, or you can modify it for your own purposes. Grosof and Sardy (1985:163) have warned that creating rating scales and attitude measures "is a particularly diffi-

---

TABLE 7.3 Example of Levels of Measurement

VARIABLE (Level of Measurement)	HOW VARIABLE IS MEASURED
Religion (nominal)	Different religious denominations (Jewish, Catholic, Lutheran, Baptist) are not ranked, just different (unless one belief is conceptualized as closer to heaven).
Attendance (ordinal)	"How often do you attend religious services? (0) Never, (1) less than once a year, (3) several times a year, (4) about once a month, (5) two or three times a week, or (8) several times a week?" This might have been measured at a ratio level if the exact number of times a person attended was asked instead.
IQ Score (interval)	Most intelligence tests are organized with 100 as average, middle, or normal. Scores higher or lower indicate distance from the average. Someone with a score of 115 has somewhat above average measured intelligence for people who took the test, while 90 is slightly below. Scores of below 65 or above 140 are rare.
Age (ratio)	Age is measured by years of age. There is a true zero (birth). Note that a 40-year-old has lived twice as long as a 20-year-old.

cult and delicate enterprise and requires a great deal of careful thought." The process of creating measures for a construct evolves over time. Measurement is an ongoing process with constant change; new concepts are developed, theoretical definitions are refined, and scales or indexes that measure old or new constructs are improved.

Indexes and Scales. You might find the terms *index* and *scale* confusing because they are often used interchangeably. One researcher's scale is another's index. Both produce ordinal- or interval-level measures of a variable. To add to the confusion, scale and index techniques can be combined in one measure. Scales and indexes give a researcher more information about variables and make it possible to assess the quality of measurement. Scales and indexes increase reliability and validity, and they aid in data reduction; that is, they condense and simplify the information that is collected (see Box 7.2).

Mutually Exclusive and Exhaustive Attributes. Before discussing scales and indexes, it is important to review features of good measurement. The attributes of all measures, including nominal-level measures, should be mutually exclusive and exhaustive.

Mutually exclusive attributes means that an individual or case fits into one and only one attribute of a variable. For example, a variable measuring type of religion—with the attributes Christian, non-Christian, and Jewish—is not mutually exclusive. Judaism is both a non-Christian religion and a Jewish religion, so a Jewish person fits into both the non-Christian and the Jewish category. Likewise, a variable measuring type of city, with the attributes river port city, state capital, and interstate exit, lacks mutually exclusive attributes. One city could be all three (a river port state capital with an interstate exit), any one or two of the three, or none of the three.

Exhaustive attributes means that all cases fit into one of the attributes of a variable. When measuring religion, a measure with the attributes Catholic, Protestant, and Jewish is not exclusive. The individual who is a Buddhist, a Muslim, or an agnostic does not fit anywhere. The attributes should be developed so that every possible situation is covered. For example, Catholic, Protestant, Jewish,

---

Box 7.2

Scales and Indexes: Are They Different?

For most purposes, you can treat scales and indexes as interchangeable. Social work researchers do not use a consistent nomenclature to distinguish between them.

A *scale* is a measure in which a researcher captures the intensity, direction, level, or potency of a variable construct. It arranges responses or observations on a continuum. A scale can use a single indicator or multiple indicators. Most are at the ordinal level of measurement.

An *index* is a measure in which a researcher adds or combines several distinct indicators of a construct into a single score. This composite score is often a simple sum of the multiple indicators. It is used for content and convergent validity. Indexes are often measured at the interval or ratio level.

Researchers sometimes combine the features of scales and indexes in a single measure. This is common when a researcher has several indicators that are scales (i.e., that measure intensity or direction). He or she then adds these indicators together to yield a single score, thereby creating an index.

---

or other is an exhaustive and mutually exclusive set of attributes.

Unidimensionality. In addition to being mutually exclusive and exhaustive, scales and indexes should also be unidimensional, or one dimensional. *Unidimensionality* means that all the items in a scale or index fit together, or measure a single construct. Unidimensionality was hinted at in the previous discussions of construct and content validity. Unidimensionality says, "If you combine several specific pieces of information into a single score or measure, have all the pieces measure the same thing." One of the more advanced techniques—factor analysis (see Appendix D)—is often used to test for the unidimensionality of data.

There is an apparent contradiction between using a scale or index to combine parts or subparts of a construct into one measure and the criteria of unidimensionality. It is only an apparent contradiction, however, because constructs are theoretically defined at different levels of abstraction. General, higher-level, or more abstract constructs can be defined as containing several subparts. Each subdimension is a part of the construct's overall content.

For example, we define the construct "feminist ideology" as a general ideology about gender. Feminist ideology is a highly abstract and general construct. It includes specific beliefs and attitudes towards social, economic, political, family, and sexual relations. The ideology's five belief areas are parts of the single general construct. The parts are mutually reinforcing and together form a system of beliefs about the dignity, strength, and power of women.

If feminist ideology is unidimensional, then there is a unified belief system that varies from very antifeminist to very profeminist. We can test the convergence validity of the measure that includes multiple indicators that tap the construct's subparts. If one belief area (e.g., sexual relations) is consistently distinct from the other areas in empirical tests, then we question its unidimensionality.

It is easy to become confused: A specific measure can be an indicator of a unidimensional construct in one situation and indicate a part of a different construct in another situation. This is possible because constructs can be used at different levels of abstraction.

For example, a person's attitude toward gender equality with regard to pay is more specific and less abstract than feminist ideology (i.e., beliefs about gender relations throughout society). An attitude toward equal pay can be both a unidimensional construct in its own right and a subpart of the more general and abstract unidimensional construct, *ideology toward gender relations.*

INDEX CONSTRUCTION

The Purpose

You hear about indexes all the time. For example, U.S. newspapers report the Federal Bureau of Investigation (FBI) crime index and the consumer price index (CPI). The FBI index is the sum of police reports on seven so-called index crimes (criminal homicide, aggravated assault, forcible rape, robbery, burglary, larceny of $50 or more, and auto theft). It

began with the Uniform Crime Report in 1930 (see Rosen, 1995). The CPI, which is a measure of inflation, is created by totaling the cost of buying a list of goods and services (e.g., food, rent, and utilities) and comparing the total to the cost of buying the same list in the previous year. The consumer price index has been used by the U.S. Bureau of Labor Statistics since 1919; wage increases, union contracts, and social security payments are based on it. An *index* is a collection of items combined into a single numerical score. Various components or subparts of a construct are each measured, then combined into one measure.

There are many types of indexes. For example, if you take an exam with 25 questions, the total number of questions answered correctly is a kind of index. It is a composite measure in which each question measures a small piece of knowledge, and all the answers scored correctly or incorrectly are totaled to produce a single measure.

Indexes measure the most desirable place to live (based on unemployment, commuting time, crime rate, recreation opportunities, weather, and so on), the degree of crime (based on combining the occurrence of different specific crimes), the mental health of a person (based on the person's adjustment in various areas of life), and the like.

One way to demonstrate that indexes are not very complicated is to use one. Answer yes or no to the seven questions that follow on the characteristics of an occupation. Base your answers on your thoughts regarding the following four occupations: long-distance truck driver, medical doctor, accountant, telephone operator. Score each answer 1 for yes and 0 for no.

1. Does it pay a good salary?
2. Is the job secure from layoffs or unemployment?
3. Is the work interesting and challenging?
4. Are its working conditions (e.g., hours, safety, time on the road) good?
5. Are there opportunities for career advancement and promotion?
6. Is it prestigious or looked up to by others?
7. Does it permit self-direction and the freedom to make decisions?

Total the seven answers for each of the four occupations. Which had the highest and which had the lowest score? The seven questions are the operational definition of the construct *good occupation*. Each question represents a subpart of a theoretical definition. A different theoretical definition would result in different questions, perhaps more than seven.

Creating indexes is so easy that it is important to be careful that every item in the index has face validity. Items without face validity should be excluded. Each part of the construct should be measured with at least one indicator. Of course, it is better to measure the parts of a construct with multiple indicators.

Another example of an index is a college-quality index (see Box 7.3). Our theoretical definition says that a high-quality college has six distinguishing characteristics: (1) fewer students per faculty member, (2) a highly educated faculty, (3) more books in the library, (4) fewer students dropping out of college, (5) more students who go on to advanced degrees, and (6) faculty members who publish books or scholarly articles. We score 100 colleges on each item, then add the scores for each to create an index score of college quality that can be used to compare colleges.

Box 7.3 _____

Example of Index

A quality-of-college index is based on the following six items:

1. Number of students per faculty member
2. Percentage of faculty members with Ph.D. degrees
3. Number of books in the library per student
4. Percentage of entering freshmen who fail to ever receive a degree
5. Percentage of students who go on to receive an advanced degree
6. Number of books and scholarly articles published by faculty members

In symbolic form, where

Q = overall college quality
R = number of students per faculty member
F = percentage of faculty with Ph.D.'s
B = number of books in library per student
D = percentage of freshmen who drop out or do not finish
A = percentage of graduates who go for an advanced degree
P = number of publications per faculty member

Unweighted formula: $(-1) R + (1) F + (1) B + (-1) D + (1) A + (1) P = Q$
Weighted formula: $(-2) R + (2) F + (1) B + (-3) D + (1) A + (3) P = Q$

Old Ivy College

Unweighted: $(-1) 13 + (1) 80 + (1) 334 + (-1) 14 + (1) 28 + (1) 4 = 419$
Weighted: $(-2) 13 + (2) 80 + (1) 334 + (-3) 14 + (1) 28 + (3) 4 = 466$

Local College

Unweighted: $(-1) 20 + (1) 82 + (1) 365 + (-1) 25 + (1) 15 + (1) 2 = 419$
Weighted: $(-2) 20 + (2) 82 + (1) 365 + (-3) 25 + (1) 15 + (3) 2 = 435$

Big University

Unweighted: $(-1) 38 + (1) 95 + (1) 380 + (-1) 48 + (1) 24 + (1) 6 = 419$
Weighted: $(-2) 38 + (2) 95 + (1) 380 + (-3) 48 + (1) 24 + (3) 6 = 392$

Indexes can be combined with one another. For example, in order to strengthen our college-quality index, we add a subindex on teaching quality. The index contains eight items: (1) average size of classes, (2) percentage of class time devoted to discussion, (3) number of different classes each faculty member teaches, (4) availability of faculty to students outside the classroom, (5) currency and amount of reading assigned, (6) degree to which assignments promote learning, (7) degree to which faculty get to know each student, and (8) student ratings of instruction. Similar subindex measures can be created for other parts of the college-quality index. They can be combined into a more global measure of college quality. This further elaborates the definition of the construct "quality of college."

Weighting

An important issue in index construction is whether to weight items. Unless it is otherwise stated, assume that an index is unweighted. Likewise, unless you have a good theoretical reason for assigning different weights, use equal weights. An *unweighted index* gives each item equal weight. It involves adding up the items without modification, as if each were multiplied by 1 (or –1 for items that are negative).

In a weighted index a researcher values or weights some items more than others. The size of weights can come from theoretical assumptions, the theoretical definition, or a statistical technique such as factor analysis (see Appendix D). Weighting changes the theoretical definition of the construct.

For example, we elaborate the theoretical definition of the college-quality index. We decide that the student/faculty ratio and number of faculty with Ph.D.'s are twice as important as the number of books in the library per student or the percentage of students pursuing advanced degrees. Also, the percentage of freshmen who drop out and the number of publications per faculty member are three times more important than books in the library or percentage pursuing an advanced degree. This is easier to see when it is expressed as a formula.

The number of students per faculty member and the percentage who drop out have negative signs because, as they get larger, the quality of the college

gets lower. The weighted and unweighted indexes can produce different results. Consider Old Ivy College, Local College, and Big University. All have identical unweighted index scores, but the colleges have different quality scores after weighting.

Weighting produces different index scores in this example, but in most cases, weighted and unweighted indexes yield similar results. Researchers are concerned with the relationships among variables, and weighted and unweighted indexes usually give similar results for these relationships.[17]

Missing Data

Missing data can be a serious problem when constructing an index. Validity and reliability are threatened whenever data for some cases are missing. There are four ways to attempt to resolve the problem (see Box 7.4), but none fully solves it.

For example, we construct an index of the degree of societal development in 1975 for 50 nations. The index contains four items: life expectancy, percentage of homes with indoor plumbing, percentage of population that is literate, and number of telephones per 100 people. We locate a source of United Nations statistics for this information. The values for Belgium are 68 + 87 + 97 + 28; for Turkey, the scores are 55 + 36 + 49 + 3; for Finland, however, we discover that literacy data are unavailable. We check other sources of information, but none has the data because they were not collected.

Rates and Standardization

You have heard of crime rates, rates of population growth, or the unemployment rate. Some indexes and single-indicator measures are expressed as rates. Rates involve standardizing the value of an item to make comparisons possible. The items in an index frequently need to be standardized before they can be combined.

Standardization involves selecting a base and dividing a raw measure by the base. For example, City A had 10 murders and City B had 30 murders in the same year. In order to compare murders in the two cities, the raw number of murders needs to be standardized by the city population. If the cities are

Box 7.4 _____

Ways to Deal with Missing Data

1. *Eliminate all cases for which any information is missing.* If Finland is removed from the study, the index will be reliable for the nations on which information is available. This is a problem if other nations have missing information. A study of 50 nations may become a study of 20 nations. Also, the cases with missing information may be similar in some respect (e.g., all are in eastern Europe or in the Third World), which limits the generalizability of findings.

2. *Substitute the average score for cases in which data are present.* The average literacy score from the other nations is substituted. This "solution" keeps Finland in the study but gives it an incorrect value. For an index with few items or for a case that is not "average," this creates serious validity problems.

3. *Insert data based on nonquantitative information about the case.* Other information about Finland (e.g., percentage of 13- to 18-year-olds in high school) is used to make an informed guess about the literacy rate. This "solution" is marginally acceptable in this situation. It is not as good as measuring Finland's literacy, and it relies on an untested assumption—that one can predict the literacy rate from other countries' high school attendance rate.

4. *Insert a random value.* This is unwise for the development index example. It might be acceptable if the index had a very large number of items and the number of cases was very large. If that were the situation, however, then eliminating the case is probably a better "solution" that produces a more reliable measure.

_____

the same size, City B is more dangerous. But City B may be safer if it is much larger. For example, if City A has 100,000 people and City B has 600,000, then the murder rate per 100,000 is 10 for City A and 5 for City B.

Standardization makes it possible to compare different units on a common base. The process of standardization, also called *norming,* removes the effect of relevant but different characteristics in order to make the important differences visible. For example, there are two classes of students. An art class has 12 smokers and a biology class has 22 smokers. A researcher can compare the rate or incidence of smokers by standardizing the number of smokers by the size of the classes. The art class has 32 students and the biology class has 143 students. One method of standardization that you already know is the use of percentages, whereby measures are standardized to a common base of 100. In terms of percentages, it is easy to see that the art class has more than twice the rate of smokers (37.5 percent) than the biology class (15.4 percent).

A critical question in standardization is deciding what base to use. In the examples given, how did we know to use city size or class size as the base? The choice is not always obvious; it depends on the theoretical definition of a construct.

Different bases can produce different rates. For example, the unemployment rate can be defined as the number of people in the work force who are out of work. The overall unemployment rate is

$$\text{Unemployment rate} = \frac{\text{Number of unemployed people}}{\text{Total number of people working}}$$

We can divide the total population into subgroups to get rates for subgroups in the population such as White males, African American females, African American males between the ages of 18 and 28, or people with college degrees. Rates for these subgroups may be more relevant to the theoretical definition or research problem. For example, a researcher believes that unemployment is an experience that affects an entire household or family and that the base should be households, not individuals. The rate will look like this:

$$\text{New unemployment rate} = \frac{\text{Number of households with at least one unemployed person}}{\text{Total number of households}}$$

Different conceptualizations suggest different bases and different ways to standardize. When combining several items into an index, it is best to standardize items on a common base (see Box 7.5).

Box 7.5 _____

Standardization and the Real Winners at the Olympics

U.S. sports fans were jubilant about "winning" at the 2000 Olympics by carrying off the most gold medals, but it is an illusion because they failed to standardize. Of course, the world's richest nation with the third largest population does well in one-on-one competition among all nations. To see what really happened, however, we must standardize on a base of the population and wealth. Standardization yields a more accurate picture by adjusting the results as if the nations had equal populations and wealth. The results show that the Bahamas, with less than 300,000 citizens (smaller than a medium-sized U.S. city), proportionately won the most gold. Adjusted for its population size or wealth, the U.S. is not even near the top, and it only appears to be the leader because of its great size and wealth. U.S. sports fans can perpetuate the illusion of being at the top only if they ignore the comparative advantage of the U.S.

Top Ten Gold Medal-Winning Countries at the 2000 Olympics in Sydney

Unstandardized Rank			*Standardized Rank*					
		TOTAL GOLD	**STANDARDIZED BY POPULATION SIZE**			**STANDARIZED BY NATIONAL WEALTH**		
RANK	**COUNTRY**	**MEDALS**	**RANK**	**COUNTRY**	**POPULATION***	**RANK**	**COUNTRY**	**GDP****
1	U.S.A.	40	1	Bahamas (1)	303	1	Ethiopia (4)	$ 1,598
2	Russia	32	2	Slovenia (2)	944	2	Cuba (11)	$ 1,745
3	China	28	3	Cuba (11)	1,017	3	Bulgaria (5)	$ 2,399
4	Australia	16	4	Norway (4)	1,123	4	Romania (11)	$ 3,338
5	Germany	14	5	Australia (16)	1,199	5	Bahamas (1)	$ 4,818
6	France	13	6	Hungary (6)	1,253	6	Estonia (1)	$ 4,969
7	Italy	13	7	Netherlands (12)	1,327	7	Lithuania (2)	$ 5,657
8	Netherlands	12	8	Estonia (1)	1,369	8	Hungary (6)	$ 5,704
9	Cuba	11	9	Bulgaria (5)	1,633	9	Latvia (1)	$ 7,150
10	Great Britain	11	10	Lithuania (2)	1,847	10	Russia (32)	$ 7,847
11	Romania	11	11	Romania (11)	2,039	11	Slovenia (2)	$ 9,065
12	S. Korea	8	12	Sweden (4)	2,217	12	Australia (16)	$ 24,382
				U.S.A. (40)	7,038		U.S.A. (40)	$245,935

Notes: Number in ( ) under standardized data columns = number of Gold Medals won. * = Number in population per gold medal won in 1000s. ** = GDP per gold medal won in $millions.

Source: From Horn, Robert V., *Statistical Indicators for the Economic and Social Sciences,* 1993, p, 45. Reprinted with permission of Cambridge University Press.

SCALES

The Purpose

Scaling, like index construction, creates an ordinal, interval, or ratio measure of a variable expressed as a numerical score. Scales are common in situations wherein a researcher wants to measure how an individual feels or thinks about something. Some call this the hardness or potency of feelings.

Scales are used for two related purposes. First, scales help in the conceptualization and operationalization processes. Scales show the fit between a set of indicators and a single construct. For example, a researcher believes that there is a single ideological dimension that underlies people's judgments about specific policies (e.g., housing, education, foreign affairs, etc.). Scaling can help determine whether a single construct—for instance, "conservative/liberal ideology"—underlies the positions people take on specific policies.

Second, scaling produces quantitative measures and can be used with other variables to test hypotheses. This second purpose of scaling is our primary focus because it involves scales as a technique for measuring a variable.

Logic of Scaling

As stated before, scaling is based on the idea of measuring the intensity, hardness, or potency of a variable. Graphic rating scales are an elementary form of scaling. People indicate a rating by checking a point on a line that runs from one extreme to another. This type of scale is easy to construct and use. It conveys the idea of a continuum, and assigning numbers helps people think about quantities. Scales assume that people with the same subjective feeling mark the graphic scale at the same place.

Figure 7.5 is an example of a "feeling thermometer" scale that is used to find out how people feel about various groups in society (e.g., the National Organization for Women, the Ku Klux Klan, labor unions, physicians, etc.). This type of measure has been used by political scientists in the National Election Study since 1964 to measure attitudes toward candidates, social groups, and issues.[18]

Commonly Used Scales

Likert Scale.   You have probably used *Likert scales;* they are widely used and very common in survey research. They were developed in the 1930s by Rensis Likert to provide an ordinal-level measure of a person's attitude.[19] Likert scales are called *summated-rating* or *additive scales* because a person's score on the scale is computed by summing the number of responses the person gives. Likert scales usually ask people to indicate whether they

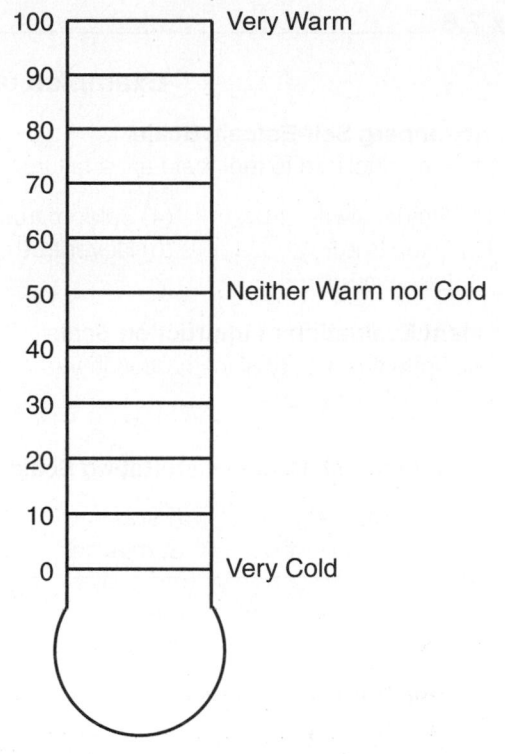

FIGURE 7.5   "Feeling Thermometer" Graphic Rating Scale

agree or disagree with a statement. Other modifications are possible; people might be asked whether they approve or disapprove, or whether they believe something is "almost always true." Box 7.6 presents several examples of Likert scales.

Likert scales need a minimum of two categories, such as "agree" and "disagree." Using only two choices creates a crude measure and forces distinctions into only two categories. It is usually better to use four to eight categories. A researcher can combine or collapse categories after the data are collected, but data collected with crude categories cannot be made more precise later.

You can increase the number of categories at the end of a scale by adding "strongly agree," "somewhat agree," "very strongly agree," and so forth. Keep the number of choices to eight or nine at most. More distinctions than that are probably not meaningful, and people will become confused. The choices should be evenly balanced (e.g., "strongly agree,"

Box 7.6 _____

Examples of Types of Likert Scales

The Rosenberg Self-Esteem Scale
All in all, I am inclined to feel that I am a failure:

(1) Almost always true   (4) Seldom true
(2) Often true   (5) Never true
(3) Sometimes true

A Student Evaluation of Instruction Scale
Overall, I rate the quality of instruction in this course as:

Excellent   Good   Average   Fair   Poor

A Market Research Mouthwash Rating Scale

Brand	Dislike Completely	Dislike Somewhat	Dislike a Little	Like a Little	Like Somewhat	Like Completely
X	____	____	____	____	____	____
Y	____	____	____	____	____	____

Work Group Supervisor Scale
My supervisor:

	Never	Seldom	Sometimes	Often	Always
Lets members know what is expected of them	1	2	3	4	5
Is friendly and approachable	1	2	3	4	5
Treats all unit members as equals	1	2	3	4	5

"agree" with "strongly disagree," "disagree"). Nunnally (1978:521) stated:

> As the number of scale steps is increased from 2 up through 20, the increase in reliability is very rapid at first. It tends to level off at about 7, and after about 11 steps, there is little gain in reliability from increasing the number of steps.

Researchers have debated about whether to offer a neutral category (e.g., "don't know," "undecided," "no opinion") in addition to the directional categories (e.g., "disagree," "agree"). A neutral category implies an odd number of categories.

A researcher can combine several Likert scale questions into a composite index if they all measure a single construct. Consider the Index of Equal Opportunity for Women and the Self-Esteem Index that Sniderman and Hagen (1985) created for their study (see Box 7.7). In the middle of larger surveys,

respondents were asked three questions about the position of women. The researchers later scored answers and combined items into an index that ranged from 3 to 15. Respondents also answered questions about self-esteem. Notice that when scoring these items, one item (question 2) is scored in reverse. The reason for switching directions in this way is to avoid the problem of the *response set*. The response set, also called *response style* and *response bias*, is the tendency of some people to answer a large number of items in the same way (usually agreeing) out of laziness or a psychological predisposition. For example, if items are worded so that saying "strongly agree" always indicates self-esteem, we would not know whether a person who always strongly agreed had high self-esteem or simply had a tendency to agree with questions. The person might be answering "strongly agree" out of habit or a tendency to agree. Researchers word statements in alternative

Box 7.7

Examples of Using the Likert Scale to Create Indexes

Sniderman and Hagen (1985) created indexes to measure beliefs about equal opportunity for women and self-esteem. For both indexes, scores were added to create an unweighted index.

Index of Equal Opportunity for Women

Questions

1. Women have less opportunity than men to get the education for top jobs.

Strongly Agree	Somewhat Agree	Somewhat Disagree	Disagree a Great Deal	Don't Know

2. Many qualified women cannot get good jobs; men with the same skills have less trouble.

Strongly Agree	Somewhat Agree	Somewhat Disagree	Disagree a Great Deal	Don't Know

3. Our society discriminates against women.

Strongly Agree	Somewhat Agree	Somewhat Disagree	Disagree a Great Deal	Don't Know

Scoring: For all items, Strongly Agree = 1, Somewhat Agree = 2, Somewhat Disagree = 4, Disagree a Great Deal = 5, Don't Know = 3.

Highest Possible Index Score = 15, respondent feels opportunities for women are equal
Lowest Possible Index Score = 3, respondent feels opportunities are not equal

Self-Esteem Index

Questions

1. On the whole, I am satisfied with myself.	Agree	Disagree	Don't Know
2. At times, I think I am no good at all.	Agree	Disagree	Don't Know
3. I sometimes feel that (other) men do not take my opinion seriously.	Agree	Disagree	Don't Know

Scoring: Items 1 and 3: 1 = Disagree, 2 = Don't Know, 3 = Agree, Item 2: 1 = Disagree, 2 = Don't Know, 1 = Agree.

Highest Possible Index Score = 9, high self-esteem
Lowest Possible Index Score = 3, low self-esteem

---

directions, so that anyone who agrees all the time appears to answer inconsistently or to have a contradictory opinion.

Researchers often combine many Likert-scaled attitude indicators into an index. The scale and indexes have properties that are associated with improving reliability and validity. An index uses multiple indicators, which improves reliability. The use of multiple indicators that measure several aspects of a construct or opinion improves content validity. Finally, the index scores give a more precise quantitative measure of a person's opinion. For example, each person's opinion can be measured with a number from 10 to 40, instead of in four categories: "strongly agree," "agree," "disagree," "strongly disagree."

Instead of scoring Likert items, as in the previous example, the scores –2, –1, +1, +2 could be used. This scoring has an advantage in that a zero implies neutrality or complete ambiguity, whereas a high negative number means an attitude that opposes the opinion represented by a high positive number.

The numbers assigned to the response categories are arbitrary. Remember that the use of a zero does not give the scale or index a ratio level of measurement. Likert-scale measures are at the ordinal level of measurement because responses indicate a ranking only. Instead of 1 to 4 or –2 to +2, the numbers 100, 70, 50, and 5 would have worked. Also, do not be fooled into thinking that the distances between the ordinal categories are intervals just because numbers are assigned. Although the number system has nice mathematical properties, the numbers are used for convenience only. The fundamental measurement is only ordinal.[20]

The simplicity and ease of use of the Likert scale is its real strength. When several items are combined, more comprehensive multiple-indicator measurement is possible. The scale has two limitations: Different combinations of several scale items can result in the same overall score or result, and the response set is a potential danger.

Thurstone Scaling.   Researchers sometimes want a measure with one numerical continuum, but the attitude variable in which they are interested has several characteristics or aspects. For example, a dry-cleaning business, Quick and Clean, wants to find out its image in Greentown compared to that of its major competitor, Friendly Cleaners. The researcher working for Quick and Clean conceptualizes a person's attitude toward the business as having four subparts or aspects: attitude toward location, hours, service, and cost. Quick and Clean is seen as having more convenient hours and locations, but higher costs and discourteous service, whereas Friendly Cleaners is seen as having low cost and friendly service, but inconvenient hours and locations. Unless the researcher knows how the four aspects relate to the core attitude—image of the dry cleaner—he or she cannot say which business is generally viewed more favorably. During the late 1920s Louis Thurstone developed scaling methods for assigning numerical values in such situations. These are now called *Thurstone scaling* or the *method of equal-appearing intervals.*[21]

Thurstone scaling is based on the *law of comparative judgment.* The law addresses the issue of measuring or comparing attitudes when each person makes a unique judgment. In other words, it anchors or fixes the position of one person's attitude relative to that of others as each makes an individual subjective judgment.

The law of comparative judgment states that it is possible to identify the "most common response" for each object or concept being judged. Although different people arrive at somewhat different judgments, the individual judgments cluster around a single most common response. The dispersion of individual judgments around the common response follows a general statistical pattern called the *normal distribution.* From the law it follows that, if many people agree that two objects differ, the most common responses for the two objects will be distant from each other. By contrast, if many people are confused or disagree about the differences between two objects, the common responses of the two objects will be closer to each other.

In Thurstone scaling, a researcher develops many statements (e.g., more than 100) regarding the object of interest, then uses many judges (e.g., 100) to reduce the number to a smaller set (e.g., 20) by eliminating ambiguous statements. Each judge rates the statements on an underlying continuum (e.g., favorable to unfavorable). The researcher examines the ratings and keeps those statements based on two factors: (1) agreement among the judges and (2) the statement's location on a range of possible values. The final set of statements is used to form a measurement scale that spans a range of values.

Thurstone scaling begins with a large number of evaluative statements that should be exhaustive and that cover all shades of opinion. Each should be clear and precise, and should express a single opinion. Good statements refer to the present and are not capable of being interpreted as facts. They are unlikely to be endorsed by everyone, are stated as simple sentences, and avoid words such as *always* and *never.* Researchers get ideas for writing the statements from reviewing the literature, from the mass media, from personal experience, and from asking others. For example, statements about the dry-cleaning business might include the four aspects listed before, plus the following:

— I think X Cleaners dry cleans clothing in a prompt and timely manner.
— In my opinion, X Cleaners keeps its stores looking neat and attractive.
— I do not think that X Cleaners does a good job of removing stains.
— I believe that X Cleaners charges reasonable prices for cleaning coats.
— I believe that X Cleaners returns clothing clean and neatly pressed.
— I think that X Cleaners has poor delivery service.

A researcher next locates 50 to 300 judges. The judges do not have to be experts on the topic, but they should be familiar with the object or concept in the statements. Each judge receives a set of statement cards and instructions. Each card has one statement on it, and the judges place each card in one of several piles. The number of piles is usually 7, 9, 11, or 13. The piles represent a range of values (e.g., favorable to neutral to unfavorable) with regard to the object or concept being evaluated. Each judge places cards in rating piles independently of the other judges.

After the judges place all cards in piles, the researcher creates a chart cross-classifying the piles and the statements. For example, 100 statements and 11 piles result in an 11 × 100 chart, or a chart with 11 × 100 = 1,100 boxes. The number of judges who assigned a rating to a given statement is written into each box of the chart. Statistical measures (beyond the present discussion) are used to compute the average rating of each statement and the degree to which the judges agree or disagree.

The researcher keeps the statements with the greatest among-judge agreement, or interrater reliability, as well as statements that represent the entire range of values. For example, suppose 100 statements were rated. The researcher computes the agreement score of each statement. Next, the location of the high-agreement scores across the continuum of 11 values (highly unfavorable, neutral, highly favorable) is examined. The researcher collapses the categories used by the judges into fewer

categories and selects the four statements with the greatest agreement among judges for each of five categories to identify 20 statements.

The researcher has 20 statements, 4 for each range of the value scale. The statements are randomly mixed. The 20 statements are next presented to people who are asked whether they agree or disagree with the statement. (See Box 7.8 for another example.)

With Thurstone scaling, a researcher can construct an attitude scale or select statements from a larger collection of attitude statements. The method is seldom used today because of its limitations:

1. It measures only agreement or disagreement with statements, not the intensity of agreement or disagreement.
2. It assumes that judges and others agree on where statements appear in a rating system.
3. It is time consuming and costly.
4. It is possible to get the same overall score in several ways because agreement or disagreement with different combinations of statements can produce the same average.

Nevertheless, Thurstone scaling selects attitude items that are relatively unambiguous. It can be combined with Likert or other methods to create ordinal-level measures.

Bogardus Social Distance Scale. The *Bogardus social distance scale* measures the social distance separating ethnic or other groups from each other. It is used with one group to determine how much distance it feels toward a target or "outgroup." It was developed in the 1920s by Emory Bogardus to measure the willingness of members of different ethnic groups to associate with each other. It can be used to see how close or distant people feel toward some other group (e.g., a religious minority or a deviant group).[22]

The scale has a simple logic. People respond to a series of ordered statements; those that are most threatening or most socially distant are at one end, and those that might be least threatening or socially intimate are at the other end. The logic of the scale assumes that a person who refuses contact or is uncomfortable with the socially distant items will refuse the socially closer items.

Box 7.8 _____

Example of Thurstone Scaling

Variable Measured: Opinion with regard to the death penalty.

Step 1:   Develop 120 statements about the death penalty using personal experience, the popular and professional literature, and listening to others.

Example Statements
1. I think that the death penalty is cruel and unnecessary punishment.
2. Without the death penalty, there would be many more violent crimes.
3. I believe that the death penalty should be used only for a few extremely violent crimes.
4. I do not think that anyone was ever deterred from committing a murder because of fear of the death penalty.
5. I do not think that people should be exempt from the death penalty if they committed a murder even if they are insane.
6. I believe that the Bible justifies the use of the death penalty.
7. The death penalty itself is not the problem for me, but I believe that electrocuting people is a cruel way to put them to death.

Step 2:   Place each statement on a separate card or sheet of paper and make 100 sets of the 120 statements.

Step 3:   Locate 100 persons who agree to serve as judges. Give each judge a set of the statement and instructions to place them in one of 11 piles, from 1 = highly unfavorable statement through 11 = highly favorable statement.

Step 4:   The judges place each statement into one of the 11 piles (e.g., Judge #1 puts statement 1 into pile #2; Judge #2 puts the same statement into pile #1; Judge #3 also puts it into pile #2; Judge #4 puts it into pile #3, and so on).

Step 5:   Collect piles from judges and create a chart summarizing their responses. See the example chart that follows.

CHART OF NUMBER OF JUDGES RATING EACH STATEMENT RATING PILE

Statement	Unfavorable					Neutral				Favorable		Total
	1	*2*	*3*	*4*	*5*	*6*	*7*	*8*	*9*	*10*	*11*	*Total*
1	23	60	12	5	0	0	0	0	0	0	0	100
2	0	0	0	0	2	12	18	41	19	8	0	100
3	2	8	7	13	31	19	12	6	2	0	0	100
4	9	11	62	10	4	4	0	0	0	0	0	100

Step 6:   Compute the average rating and degree of agreement by judges. For example, the average for question 1 is about 2, so there is high agreement; the average for question 3 is closer to 5, and there is much less agreement.

Step 7:   Choose the final 20 statements to include in the death penalty opinion scale. Choose statements if the judges showed agreement (most placed an item in the same or a nearby pile) and ones that reflect the entire range of opinion, from favorable to neutral to unfavorable.

Step 8:   Prepare a 20-statement questionnaire, and ask people in a study whether they agree or disagree with the statements.

Researchers use the scale in several ways. For example, people are given a series of statements: People from Group X are entering your country, are in your town, work at your place of employment, live in your neighborhood, become your personal friends, and marry your brother or sister. People are asked whether they feel comfortable with the statement or if the contact is acceptable. It is also possible to ask whether they feel uncomfortable with the relationship. People may be asked to respond to all statements, or they may keep reading statements until they are not comfortable with a relationship. There is no set number of statements required; the number usually ranges from five to nine.

A researcher can use the Bogardus scale to see how distant people feel from one outgroup versus another (see Box 7.9). The measure of social distance can be used as either an independent

---

Box 7.9 _____

Example of Bogardus Social Distance Scale

A researcher wants to find out how socially distant freshmen college students feel from exchange students from two different countries: Nigeria and Germany. She wants to see whether students feel more distant from students coming from Africa or from Europe. She uses the following series of questions in an interview:

Please give me your first reaction, yes or no, to whether you personally would feel comfortable having an exchange student from (name of country):

_____ As a visitor to your college for a week

_____ As a full-time student enrolled at your college

_____ Taking several of the same classes you are taking

_____ Sitting next to you in class and studying with you for exams

_____ Living a few doors down the hall on the same floor in your dormitory

_____ As a same-sex roommate sharing your dorm room

_____ As someone of the opposite sex who has asked you to go out on a date

Hypothetical Results

	Percentage of Freshmen Who Report Feeling Comfortable	
	Nigeria	*Germany*
Visitor	100%	100%
Enrolled	98%	100%
Same class	95%	98%
Study together	82%	88%
Same dorm	71%	83%
Roommate	50%	76%
Go on date	42%	64%

The results suggest that freshmen feel more distant from Nigerian students than from German students. Almost all feel comfortable having the international students as visitors, enrolled in the college, and taking classes. Feelings of distance increase as interpersonal contact increases, especially if the contact involves personal living settings or activities not directly related to the classroom.

or a dependent variable. For example, a researcher believes that social distance from a group is greatest for people who have some other characteristic. A hypothesis might be that feelings of social distance by Whites from Vietnamese boat people is negatively associated with education; that is, the least well-educated feel the most distant. Social distance from boat people is the dependent variable, and amount of education is the independent variable.

The social distance scale is a convenient way to determine how close a respondent feels toward a social group. It has two potential limitations. First, a researcher needs to tailor the categories to a specific outgroup and social setting. Second, it is not easy for a researcher to compare how a respondent feels toward several different groups unless the respondent completes a similar social distance scale for all outgroups at the same time. Of course, how a respondent completes the scale and the respondent's actual behavior in specific social situations may differ.

Semantic Differential. *Semantic Differential* was developed in the 1950s to provide an indirect measure of how a person feels about a concept, object, or other person. The technique measures subjective feelings toward something by using adjectives. This is because people communicate evaluations through adjectives in spoken and written language. Because most adjectives have polar opposites (e.g., *light/ dark, hard/soft, slow/fast*), it uses polar opposite adjectives to create a rating measure or scale. The Semantic Differential captures the connotations associated with whatever is being evaluated and provides an indirect measure of it.

The Semantic Differential has been used for many purposes. In marketing research it tells how consumers feel about a product; political advisers use it to discover what voters think about a candidate or issue; and therapists use it to determine how a client perceives himself or herself.

To use the Semantic Differential, a researcher presents subjects with a list of paired opposite adjectives with a continuum of 7 to 11 points between them. The subjects mark the spot on the continuum between the adjectives that expresses their feelings. The adjectives can be very diverse and should be well mixed (e.g., positive items should not be lo-

cated mostly on either the right or the left side). Studies of a wide variety of adjectives in English found that they fall into three major classes of meaning: evaluation *(good–bad),* potency *(strong–weak),* and activity *(active–passive).* Of the three classes of meaning, evaluation is usually the most significant. The analysis of results is difficult, and a researcher needs to use statistical procedures to analyze a subject's feelings toward the concept.

Results from a Semantic Differential tell a researcher how one person perceives different concepts or how different people view the same concept. For example, political analysts might discover that young voters perceive their candidate as traditional, weak, and slow, and as halfway between good and bad. Elderly voters perceive the candidate as leaning toward strong, fast, and good, and as halfway between traditional and modern. In the example in Box 7.10 a person rated two concepts. The pattern of responses for each concept illustrates how this individual feels about the concepts. This person views the two concepts differently and appears to feel rather negatively about the idea of divorce.

There are techniques for creating three-dimensional diagrams of results.[23] The three aspects are diagrammed in three-dimensional "semantic space." In the diagram, "good" is up and "bad" is down, "active" is left and "passive" is right, "strong" is away from the viewer and "weak" is close.

Guttman Scaling. *Guttman scaling,* or cumulative scaling, differs from the previous scales or indexes in that researchers use it to evaluate data after they are collected. This means that researchers must design a study with the Guttman scaling technique in mind. Louis Guttman developed the scale in the 1940s to determine whether a relationship existed among a set of indicators or measurement items. He used multiple indicators to document an underlying single dimension or cumulative intensity of a construct.[24]

Guttman scaling begins with measuring a set of indicators or items. These can be questionnaire items, votes, or observed characteristics. Guttman scaling measures many different phenomena (e.g., patterns of crime or drug use, characteristics of societies or organizations, voting or political partic-

Box 7.10

Example of Semantic Differential

Please read each pair of adjectives below, then place a mark on the blank space that comes closest to your first impression feeling. There are no right or wrong answers.

How do you feel about the idea of divorce?

Bad	x								Good
Deep							x		Shallow
Weak			x						Strong
Fair							x		Unfair
Quiet								x	Loud
Modern	x								Traditional
Simple					x				Complex
Fast		x							Slow
Dirty		x							Clean

How do you feel about the idea of marriage?

Bad								x	Good
Deep		x							Shallow
Weak							x		Strong
Fair		x							Unfair
Quiet			x						Loud
Modern								x	Traditional
Simple					x				Complex
Fast							x		Slow
Dirty					x				Clean

ipation, psychological disorders). The indicators are usually measured in a simple yes/no or present/absent fashion. From 3 to 20 indicators can be used. The researcher selects items on the belief that there is a logical relationship among them. He or she then places the results into a Guttman scale and determines whether the items form a pattern that corresponds to the relationship.

Once a set of items is measured, the researcher considers all possible combinations of responses for the items. For example, three items are measured: whether a child knows her age, her telephone number, and three local elected political officials. The little girl may know her age but no other answer, or all three, or only her age and telephone number. In fact, for three items there are eight possible combinations of answers or patterns of responses, from not knowing any through knowing all three. There

is a mathematical way to compute the number of combinations (e.g., 2^3), but you can write down all the combinations of yes or no for three questions and see the eight possibilities.

The logical relationship among items in Guttman scaling is hierarchical. Most people or cases have or agree to lower-order items. The smaller number of cases that have the higher-order items also have the lower-order ones, but not vice versa. In other words, the higher-order items build on the lower ones. The lower-order items are necessary for the appearance of the higher-order items.

An application of Guttman scaling, known as *scalogram analysis,* lets a researcher test whether a hierarchical relationship exists among the items. For example, it is easier for a child to know her age than her telephone number, and to know her telephone number than the names of political leaders. The items are called *scalable,* or capable of forming a Guttman scale, if a hierarchical pattern exists.

The patterns of responses can be divided into two groups: scaled and errors (or nonscalable). The scaled patterns for the child's knowledge example would be as follows: not knowing any item, knowing only age, knowing only age plus phone number, knowing all three. Other combinations of answers (e.g., knowing the political leaders but not her age) are possible but are nonscalable. If a hierarchical relationship exists among the items, then most answers fit into the scalable patterns.

The strength or degree to which items can be scaled is measured with statistics that measure whether the responses can be reproduced based on a hierarchical pattern. Most range from zero to 100 percent. A score of zero indicates a random pattern, or no hierarchical pattern. A score of 100 percent indicates that all responses to the answer fit the hierarchical or scaled pattern. Alternative statistics to measure scalability also have been suggested.[25] (See Box 7.11 for an example of a study using Guttman scaling.)

Clogg and Sawyer (1981) studied U.S. attitudes toward abortion using Guttman scaling by looking at different conditions under which people thought abortion was acceptable (e.g., mother's health in danger, pregnancy resulting from rape). They discovered that 84.2 percent of responses fit into a scaled response pattern. Another example of

---

Box 7.11 _____

Guttman Scale Example

Crozat (1998) examined public responses to various forms of political protest. He looked at survey data on the public's acceptance of forms of protest in Great Britain, Germany, Italy, Netherlands, and the United States in 1974 and 1990. He found that the pattern of the public's acceptance formed a Guttman scale. Those who accepted more intense forms of protest (e.g., strikes and sit-ins) almost always accepted more modest forms (e.g., petitions or demonstrations), but not all who accepted modest forms accepted the more intense forms. In addition to showing the usefulness of the Guttman scale, Crozat also found that people in different nations saw protest similarly and the degree of Guttman scalability increased over time. Thus, the pattern of acceptance of protest activities was Guttman "scalable" in both time periods, but it more closely followed the Guttman pattern in 1990 than 1974.

	FORM OF PROTEST				
	Petitions	*Demonstrations*	*Boycotts*	*Strike*	*Sit-In*
Guttman Patterns					
	N	N	N	N	N
	Y	N	N	N	N
	Y	Y	N	N	N
	Y	Y	Y	N	N
	Y	Y	Y	Y	N
	Y	Y	Y	Y	Y
Other Patterns (examples only)					
	N	Y	N	Y	N
	Y	N	Y	Y	N
	Y	N	Y	N	N
	N	Y	Y	N	N
	Y	N	N	Y	Y

the use of Guttman scaling is presented in McIver and Carmines (1981:55–58), who studied roll call votes of U.S. senators on a 1975 law to create a federal consumer protection agency. They examined votes on 12 substantive amendments to the law and discovered that the senators voted in a Guttman scalable pattern 92 percent of the time.

CONCLUSION

In this chapter you learned about the principles and processes of measurement in quantitative and qualitative research. All social work researchers conceptualize—or refine and clarify their ideas into conceptual definitions. All researchers operationalize—or develop a set of techniques or processes that will link their conceptual definitions to empirical reality. Qualitative and quantitative social work researchers differ in how they approach these processes, however. The quantitative researcher takes a more deductive path, whereas the qualitative researcher takes a more inductive path. The goal remains the same: to establish unambiguous links between a reseacher's abstract ideas and empirical data.

You also learned about the principles of reliability and validity that are shared by all researchers. Reliability refers to the dependability or consistency of a measure; validity refers to its truthfulness, or how well a construct and data for it fit together. Quantitative and qualitative styles of research significantly diverge in how they understand these principles. Nonetheless, both quantitative and qualitative social work researchers try to measure in a consistent way, and both seek a tight fit between the abstract ideas they use to understand *social world* and what occurs in the actual, empirical social world. In addition, you saw how quantitative researchers apply the principles of measurement when they create indexes and scales, and you read about some major scales they use.

Beyond the core ideas of reliability and validity, you now know principles of good measurement: Create clear definitions for concepts, use multiple indicators, and, as appropriate, weigh and standardize the data. These principles hold across all fields of study (e.g., family, criminology, inequality, race relations, etc.) and across the many research techniques (e.g., experiments, surveys, etc.).

As you are probably beginning to realize, a sound research project involves doing a good job in each phase of research. Serious mistakes or sloppiness in any one phase can do irreparable damage to the results, even if the other phases of the research project were conducted in a flawless manner.

KEY TERMS

auxiliary theory	external validity	predictive validity
Bogardus Social Distance Scale	face validity	ratio measures
	Guttman scaling	reliability
conceptual definition	index	representative reliability
conceptual hypothesis	intercoder reliability	response set
conceptualization	internal validity	rules of correspondence
concurrent validity	interval measures	scale
construct validity	law of comparative judgment	Semantic Differential
content validity	levels of measurement	split-half method
continuous variables	Likert scale	stability reliability
convergent validity	measurement validity	standardization
criterion validity	multiple indicators	statistical validity
discrete variables	mutually exclusive attributes	subpopulation analysis
discriminant validity	nominal measures	test–retest method
empirical hypothesis	operational definition	Thurstone scaling
equivalence reliability	operationalization	unidimensionality
exhaustive attributes	ordinal measures	validity

REVIEW QUESTIONS

1. What are the three basic parts of measurement, and how do they fit together?
2. What is the difference between reliability and validity, and how do they complement each other?
3. What are ways to improve the reliability of a measure?
4. How do the levels of measurement differ from each other?
5. What are the differences between convergent, content, and concurrent validity? Can you have all three at once? Explain your answer.
6. Why are multiple indicators usually better than one indicator?
7. What is the difference between the logic of a scale and that of an index?
8. Why is unidimensionality an important characteristic of a scale?
9. What are advantages and disadvantages of weighting indexes?
10. How does standardization make comparisons easier?

NOTES

1. Duncan (1984:220–239) presented some worthwhile cautions from a positivist approach on the issue of measuring anything.

2. The terms *concept, construct,* and *idea* are used more or less interchangeably, but there are differences in meaning among them. An *idea* is any mental image, belief, plan, or impression. It refers to any vague impression, opinion, or thought. A *concept* is a thought, a general notion, or a generalized idea about a class of objects. A *construct* is a thought that is systematically put together, an orderly arrangement of ideas, facts, and impressions. The term *construct* is used here because its emphasis is on taking vague concepts and turning them into systematically organized ideas.

3. See Grinnell (1987:5–18) for further discussion.

4. See Blalock (1982:25–27) and Costner (1985) on rules of correspondence or the auxiliary theories that connect abstract concept with empirical indicators. Also see Zeller and Carmines (1980:5) for a diagram that illustrates the place of the rules in the process of measurement.

5. See Bailey (1984, 1986) for a discussion of the three levels.

6. See Bohrnstedt (1992a) and Carmines and Zeller (1979) for discussions of reliability and various types of reliability.

7. See Sullivan and Feldman (1979) on multiple indicators. A more technical discussion can be found in Herting (1985), Herting and Costner (1985), and Scott (1968).

8. See Carmines and Zeller (1979:17). For a discussion of the many types of validity, see Brinberg and McGrath (1982).

9. The epistemic correlation is discussed in Costner (1985) and in Zeller and Carmines (1980:50–51, 137–139).

10. Kidder (1982) discussed the issue of disagreements over face validity, such as acceptance of a measure's meaning by the scientific community, but not the subjects being studied.

11. This was adapted from Carmines and Zeller (1979: 20–21).

12. For a discussion of types of criterion validity, see Carmines and Zeller (1979:17–19). See Fiske (1982) for construct validity.

13. See Cook and Campbell (1979) for elaboration.

14. See Borgatta and Bohrnstedt (1980) and Duncan (1984:119–155) for a discussion and critique of the topic of levels of measurement.

15. Johnson and Creech (1983) examined the measurement errors that occur when variables that are conceptualized as continuous are operationalized in a series of ordinal categories. They argued that errors caused by using categories (compared to a precise continuous measure) are not serious if more than four categories and large samples are used.

16. For compilations of indexes and scales used in social work research, see Brodsky and Smitherman (1983), Corcoran and Fischer (1994), Miller (1991), Nugent, Sieppert, and Hudson (2001), Robinson and colleagues

(1972), Robinson and Shaver (1969), Schuessler (1982), Sederer and Dickey (1996), and Wodarski (1997).

17. For a discussion of weighted and unweighted index scores, see Nunnally (1978:534).

18. Feeling thermometers are discussed in Wilcox and associates (1989).

19. For more information on Likert scales, see Anderson and associates (1983:252–255), Converse (1987:72–75), McIver and Carmines (1981:22–38), and Spector (1992).

20. Some researchers treat Likert scales as interval-level measures, but there is disagreement on this issue. Statistically, it makes little difference if the Likert scale has at least five response categories and an approximately even proportion of people answer in each category.

21. McIver and Carmines (1981:16–21) have an excellent discussion of Thurstone scaling. Also, see discussions in Anderson and colleagues (1983:248–252), Converse (1987:66–77), and Edwards (1957). The example used here is partially borrowed from Churchill (1983:249–254), who described the formula for scoring Thurstone scaling.

22. The social distance scale is described in Converse (1987:62–69). The most complete discussion can be found in Bogardus (1959).

23. The Semantic Differential is discussed in Nunnally (1978:535–543). Also, see Heise (1965, 1970) on the analysis of scaled data.

24. See Guttman (1950).

25. See Bailey (1987:349–351) for a discussion of an improved method for determining scalability called Minimal Marginal Reproducibility (from Edwards, 1957), which gives accurate measures of scalability. He also cited Mc-Conaghy (1975), who discussed techniques that improve upon the Minimal Marginal Reproducibility measure. Guttman scaling can involve more than yes/no choices and a large number of items, but the complexity increases quickly, and computers are needed for Guttman scalogram analysis. A more elaborate and sophisticated discussion of Guttman scaling can be found in Anderson and associates (1983:256–260), Converse (1987:189–195), McIver and Carmines (1981:40–71), and Nunnally (1978:63–66). Clogg and Sawyer (1981) presented alternatives to Guttman scaling.

QUALITATIVE AND QUANTITATIVE SAMPLING

*Sampling is a major problem for any type of research. We can't study every
case of whatever we're interested in, nor should we want to. Every scientific
enterprise tries to find out something that will apply to* everything *of a
certain kind by studying* a few examples, *the results of the study being,
as we say, "generalizable."*

—Howard Becker, *Tricks of the Trade*, p. 67.

INTRODUCTION

Qualitative and quantitative social work researchers approach sampling differently. Most discussions of sampling come from researchers who use the quantitative style. Their primary goal is to get a representative sample, or a small collection of units or cases from a much larger collection or population, such that the researcher can study the smaller group and produce accurate generalizations about the larger group. Researchers focus on the specific techniques that will yield highly representative *samples* (i.e., samples that are very much like the population). Quantitative researchers tend to use a type of sampling based on theories of probability from mathematics (called *probability sampling*).

Researchers have two motivations for using probability or random sampling. The first motivation is *time and cost*. If properly conducted, results from a sample may yield results at 1/100 the cost and time. For example, instead of gathering data from 20 million people, a researcher may draw a sample of 2,000; the data from those 2,000 are equal to the data from a sample of 20 million. The second purpose of probability sampling is *accuracy*. The results of a well-designed, carefully executed probability sample will produce results that are equally—if not more—accurate than trying to reach every single person in the whole population. A census is usually an attempt to count everyone. In 2000 the U.S. Census Bureau tried to count everyone in the nation, but it would have been more accurate if it had used very specialized statistical sampling.

Qualitative researchers focus less on a sample's representativeness or on detailed techniques for drawing a probability sample. Instead, they focus on how the sample or small collection of cases, units, or activities illuminates social life. The primary purpose of sampling is to collect specific cases, events, or actions that can clarify and deepen understanding. Qualitative social work researchers' concern is to find cases that will enhance what other researchers learn about the processes of social life in a specific context. For this reason, qualitative researchers tend to collect a second type of sampling: nonprobability sampling.

NONPROBABILITY SAMPLING

Qualitative researchers rarely draw a representative sample from a huge number of cases to intensely study the sampled cases—the goal in quantitative research. For qualitative researchers, "it is their relevance to the research topic rather than their representativeness which determines the way in which the people to be studied are selected" (Flick, 1998: 41). Qualitative researchers tend to use nonprobability or *nonrandom samples*. This means they rarely determine the sample size in advance and have limited knowledge about the larger group or population from which the sample is taken. Unlike the quantitative researcher, who uses a preplanned approach based on mathematical theory, the qualitative researcher selects cases gradually, with the specific content of a case determining whether it is chosen. Table 8.1 shows a variety of nonprobability sampling techniques.

Haphazard, Accidental, or Convenience Sampling

Haphazard sampling can produce ineffective, highly unrepresentative samples and is not recommended.

TABLE 8.1   Types of Nonprobability Samples

TYPE OF SAMPLE	PRINCIPLE
Haphazard	Get any cases in any manner that is convenient.
Quota	Get a preset number of cases in each of several predetermined categories that will reflect the diversity of the population, using haphazard methods.
Purposive	Get all possible cases that fit particular criteria, using various methods.
Snowball	Get cases using referrals from one or a few cases, and then referrals from those cases, and so forth.
Extreme Case	Get cases that substantially differ from the dominant pattern (a special type of purposive sample).
Sequential	Get cases until there is no additional information or new characteristics (often used with other sampling methods).
Theoretical	Get cases that will help reveal features that are theoretically important about a particular setting/topic.

When a researcher haphazardly selects cases that are convenient, he or she can easily get a sample that seriously misrepresents the population. Such samples are cheap and quick; however, the systematic errors that easily occur make them worse than no sample at all.[1] The person-on-the-street interview conducted by television programs is an example of a haphazard sample. Television interviewers go out on the street with a camera and microphone to talk to a few people who are convenient to interview. The people walking past a television studio in the middle of the day do not represent everyone (e.g., homemakers, people in rural areas, etc.). Likewise, television interviewers often select people who look "normal" to them and avoid people who are unattractive, poor, very old, or inarticulate.

Another example of a haphazard sample is that of a newspaper that asks readers to clip a questionnaire from the paper and mail it in. Not everyone reads the newspaper, has an interest in the topic, or will take the time to cut out the questionnaire and mail it. Some people will, and the number who do so may seem large (e.g., 5,000), but the sample cannot be used to generalize accurately to the population. Such haphazard samples may have entertainment value, but they can give a distorted view and seriously misrepresent the population.

Quota Sampling

Quota sampling is an improvement over haphazard sampling.[2] In quota sampling, a researcher first identifies relevant categories of people (e.g., male and female; or under age 30, ages 30 to 60, over age 60, etc.), then decides how many to get in each category. Thus, the number of people in various categories of the sample is fixed. For example, a researcher decides to select 5 males and 5 females under age 30, 10 males and 10 females aged 30 to 60, and 5 males and 5 females over age 60 for a 40-person sample. It is difficult to represent all population characteristics accurately (see Figure 8.1).

Quota sampling is an improvement because the researcher can ensure that some differences are in the sample. In haphazard sampling, all those interviewed might be of the same age, sex, or race. But once the quota sampler fixes the categories and number of cases in each category, he or she uses haphazard sampling. For example, the researcher interviews the first 5 males under age 30 he or she encounters, even if all 5 just walked out of the campaign headquarters of a political candidate.

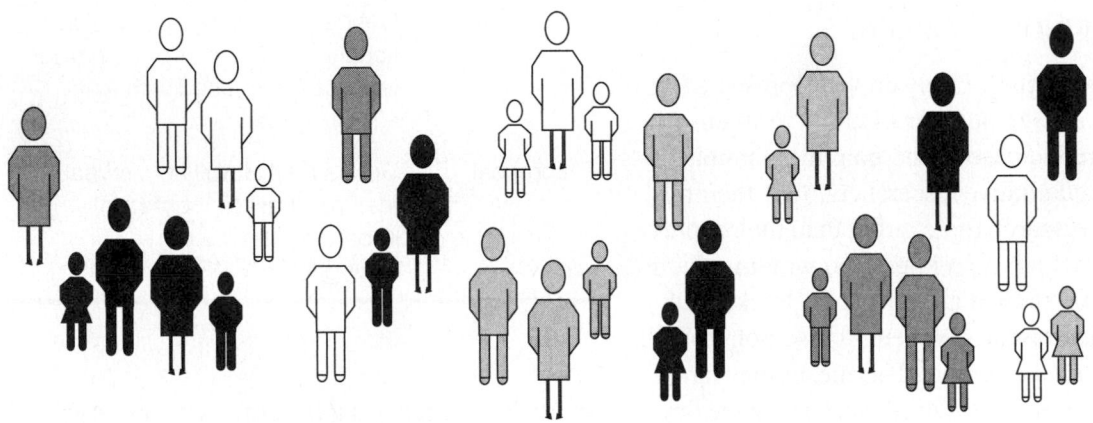

Of 32 adults and children in the street scene, select 10 for the sample:

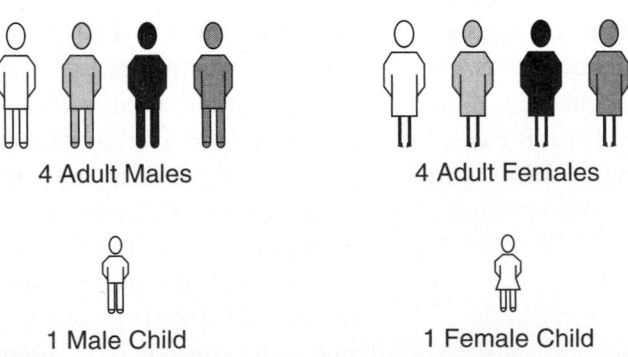

4 Adult Males   4 Adult Females

1 Male Child   1 Female Child

FIGURE 8.1   Quota Sampling

Not only is misrepresentation possible because haphazard sampling is used within the categories, but nothing prevents the researcher from selecting people who "act friendly" or who want to be interviewed.

Another case from the history of sampling illustrates the limitations of quota sampling. George Gallup's American Institute of Public Opinion, using quota sampling, successfully predicted the outcomes of the 1936, 1940, and 1944 U.S. presidential elections. But in 1948 Gallup predicted the wrong candidate. The incorrect prediction had several causes (e.g., many voters were undecided, interviewing stopped early), but a major reason was that the quota categories did not accurately represent all geographical areas and all people who actually cast a vote.

Purposive or Judgmental Sampling

Purposive sampling is an acceptable kind of sampling for special situations. It uses the judgment of an expert in selecting cases, or it selects cases with a specific purpose in mind. It is inappropriate if it is used to pick the "average householder" or the "typical school." With purposive sampling, the researcher never knows whether the cases selected represent the population. It is used in exploratory research or in field research.[3]

Purposive sampling is appropriate in three situations. First, a researcher uses it to select unique cases that are especially informative. For example, a researcher wants to use content analysis to study magazines to find cultural themes. He or she selects a specific popular women's magazine to study because it is trendsetting.

Second, a researcher may use purposive sampling to select members of a difficult-to-reach, specialized population. For example, the researcher wants to study abused women. It is impossible to list all abused women and sample randomly from the list. Instead, he or she uses subjective information and experts (e.g., social workers who work on domestic violence units, other sources, etc.) to identify a "sample" of abused women for inclusion in the research project. The researcher uses many different methods to identify the cases, because his or her goal is to locate as many cases as possible. For example, Harper (1982) formed the sample in his field research study of U.S. persons who were homeless in the 1970s by befriending and living with them on trains and in skid row areas. The special populations can be engaged in any activity. For example, McCall (1980) identified 31 female artists in St. Louis by asking a friend about other artists and by joining a local arts organization.

Another situation for purposive sampling occurs when a researcher wants to identify particular types of cases for in-depth investigation. The purpose is less to generalize to a larger population than it is to gain a deeper understanding of types. For example, Hochschild intensively interviewed 28 people about their beliefs. She selected some because they had low incomes and some because they had high incomes. Some were male and some were female.

Obviously, one cannot safely generalize from a sample of this kind to a national population: it would be worthless, for example, for me to point out what percentage of my sample sought more or fewer government services. . . . Intensive interviews are a device for generating insights, anomalies, and paradoxes, which later may be formalized into hypotheses that can be tested by quantitative social science methods. (1981:23–24)

In his study of the political influence of corporate elites, Useem (1984) used a type of quota and purposive sampling. He interviewed 72 directors of major British corporations and 57 officials from large U.S. firms. He chose the sample to include both U.S. and British firms and to include some directors who sat on the boards of more than one firm. In addition, he matched firms by industry and size, and limited geographical locations in order to reduce travel costs.

Gamson (1992) used purposive sampling in a focus group study of what working-class people think about politics. (Chapter 10 discusses focus groups.) Gamson wanted a total of 188 working-class people to participate in one of 37 focus groups. He sought respondents who had not completed college but who were diverse in terms of age, ethnicity, religion, interest in politics, and type of occupation. He recruited subjects from 35 neighborhoods in the

Boston area by going to festivals, picnics, fairs, and flea markets and by posting notices on many public bulletin boards. In addition to explaining the study, he paid respondents well so as to attract people who would not traditionally participate in a study.

Snowball Sampling

Social work researchers are often interested in an interconnected network of people or organizations.[4] The network could be scientists around the world investigating the same problem, the elites of a medium-sized city, the members of an organized crime family, persons who sit on the boards of directors of major banks and corporations, or people on a college campus who have had sexual relations with each other. The crucial feature is that each person or unit is connected with another through a direct or indirect linkage. This does not mean that each person directly knows, interacts with, or is influenced by every other person in the network. Rather, it means that, taken as a whole, with direct and indirect links, most are within an interconnected web of linkages.

For example, Sally and Tim do not know each other directly, but each has a good friend, Susan, so they have an indirect connection. All three are part of the same friendship network. Researchers represent such a network by drawing a *sociogram*—a diagram of circles connected with lines. The circles represent each person or case, and the lines represent friendship or other linkages (see Figure 8.2).

Snowball sampling (also called *network, chain referral,* or *reputational sampling*) is a method for identifying and sampling (or selecting) the cases in a network. It is based on an analogy to a snowball, which begins small but becomes larger as it is rolled on wet snow and picks up additional snow. Snowball sampling is a multistage technique. It begins with one or a few people or cases and spreads out on the basis of links to the initial cases.

For example, a researcher examines friendship networks among the teenagers in a community. He or she begins with three teenagers who do not know each other. Each teen names four close friends. The researcher then goes to the four friends and asks each to name four close friends, then goes to those four

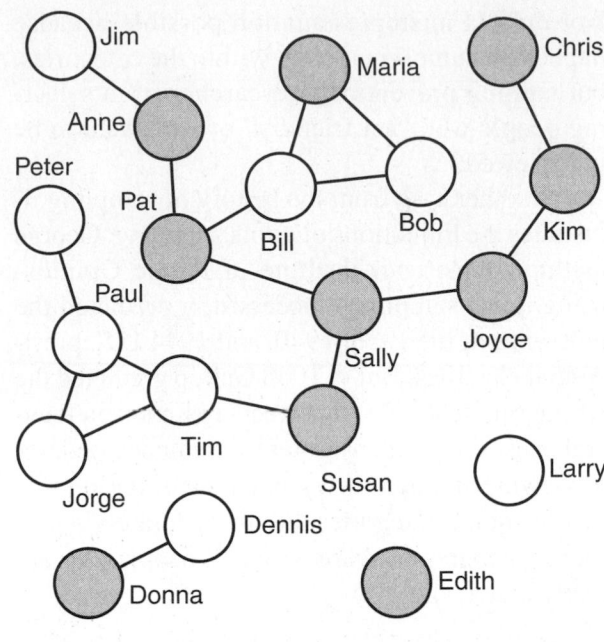

FIGURE 8.2 Sociogram of Friendship Relations

and does the same thing again, and so forth. Before long, a large number of people are involved. Each person in the sample is directly or indirectly tied to the original teenagers, and several people may have named the same person. The researcher eventually stops, either because no new names are given, indicating a closed network, or because the network is so large that it is at the limit of what he or she can study. The sample includes those named by at least one other person in the network as being a close friend. Ostrander's study of 36 upper-class women used snowball sampling.

> *At the conclusion of each interview, I asked the woman to "suggest another woman of your social group with a background like yours who might be willing to talk with me." This practical way of gaining access to respondents has theoretical as well as methodological advantages. . . . I was referred to women who were considered by their class peers to be representative of the class; thus, I did not speak with women who deviated significantly from the norms of upper class life. But I was most interested in "acceptable" people, since I wanted to learn the established norms and definitions of acceptable. (1984:9, 11)*

Extreme Case Sampling

A researcher uses *extreme case sampling* when he or she seeks cases that differ from the dominant pattern or that differ from the predominant characteristics of other cases. Similar to purposive sampling, a researcher uses a variety of techniques to locate cases with specific characteristics. Extreme case sampling differs from purposive sampling in that the goal is to locate a collection of unusual, different, or peculiar cases that are not representative of the whole. The extreme cases are selected because they are unusual, and a researcher hopes to learn more about the social life by considering cases that fall outside the general pattern or including what is beyond the main flow of events.

For example, a researcher is interested in studying high school dropouts. Let us say that previous research suggested that a majority of dropouts come from families that have low income, are single parent or unstable, have been geographically mobile, and are racial minorities. The family environment is one in which parents and/or siblings have low education or are themselves dropouts. In addition, dropouts are often engaged in illegal behavior and have a criminal record prior to dropping out. A researcher using extreme case sampling would seek majority-group dropouts who have no record of illegal activities and who are from stable two-parent, upper-middle-income families who are geographically stable and well educated.

Sequential Sampling

Sequential sampling is similar to purposive sampling with one difference. In purposive sampling, the researcher tries to find as many relevant cases as possible, until time, financial resources, or his or her energy is exhausted. The principle is to get every possible case. In sequential sampling, a researcher continues to gather cases until the amount of new information or diversity of cases is filled. The principle is to gather cases until a saturation point is reached. In economic terms information is gathered until the marginal utility, or incremental benefit for additional cases, levels off or drops significantly. It requires that a researcher continuously evaluate all the collected cases. For example, a researcher locates and plans in-depth interviews with 60 widows over 70 years old who have been living without a spouse for 10 or more years. Depending on the researcher's purposes, getting an additional 20 widows whose life experiences, social backgrounds, and worldviews differ little from the first 60 may be unnecessary.

Theoretical Sampling

In *theoretical sampling,* what the researcher is sampling (e.g., people, situations, events, time periods, etc.) are carefully selected, as the researcher develops grounded theory. A growing theoretical interest guides the selection of sample cases. The researcher selects cases based on new insights they may provide. For example, a field researcher may be observing a site and group of people during weekdays. Theoretically, the researcher may question whether the people act the same at other times or other aspects of the site change. He or she could then sample other time periods (e.g., nights and weekends) to get a larger picture and learn whether important conditions are the same.

PROBABILITY SAMPLING

A specialized vocabulary or jargon has developed around terms used in probability sampling. Before examining probability sampling, it is important to review its language.

Populations, Elements, and Sampling Frames

A researcher draws a sample from a larger pool of cases, or *elements*. A *sampling element* is the unit of analysis or case in a population. It can be a person, a group, an organization, a written document or symbolic message, or even a social action (e.g., an arrest, a divorce, or a kiss) that is being measured. The large pool is the *population,* which has an important role in sampling. Sometimes, the term *universe* (defined in Chapter 6) is used interchangeably with *population.* To define the population, a researcher specifies the unit being sampled, the geographical location, and the temporal boundaries of the population. Consider the examples of populations in Box 8.1. All the examples include the elements to be sampled (e.g.,

Box 8.1

Examples of Populations

1. All persons aged 16 or older living in Australia on December 2, 1989, who were not incarcerated in prison, asylums, and similar institutions
2. All business establishments employing more than 100 persons in Ontario Province, Canada, that operated in the month of July 1994
3. All admissions to public or private hospitals in the state of New Jersey between August 1, 1988, and July 31, 1993
4. All television commercials aired between 7:00 A.M. and 11:00 P.M. Eastern Standard Time on three major U.S. networks between November 1 and November 25, 1999
5. All currently practicing social workers in the United States who received degrees between January 1, 1950, and the present
6. All African American male heroin addicts in the Vancouver, British Columbia, or Seattle, Washington, metropolitan areas during 1992

people, businesses, hospital admissions, commercials, etc.) and geographical and time boundaries.

A researcher begins with an idea of the population (e.g., all people in a city) but defines it more precisely. The term *target population* refers to the specific pool of cases that he or she wants to study. The ratio of the size of the sample to the size of the target population is the *sampling ratio*. For example, the population has 50,000 people, and a researcher draws a sample of 150 from it. Thus, the sampling ratio is 150/50,000 = 0.003, or 0.3 percent. If the population is 500 and the researcher samples 100, then the sampling ratio is 100/500 = 0.20, or 20 percent.

A population is an abstract concept. How can population be an abstract concept, when there are a given number of people at a certain time? Except for specific small populations, one can never truly freeze a population to measure it. For example, in a city at any given moment, some people are dying, some are boarding or getting off airplanes, and some are in cars driving across city boundaries. The researcher must decide exactly who to count. Should he or she count a city resident who happens to be

on vacation when the time is fixed? What about the tourist staying at a hotel in the city when the time is fixed? Should he or she count adults, children, people in jails, those in hospitals? A population, even the population of all people over the age of 18 in the city limits of Milwaukee, Wisconsin, at 12:01 A.M. on March 1, 1999, is an abstract concept. It exists in the mind but is impossible to pinpoint concretely.

Because a population is an abstract concept, except for small specialized populations (e.g., all the students in a classroom), a researcher needs to estimate the population. As an abstract concept, the population needs an operational definition. This process is similar to developing operational definitions for constructs that are measured.

A researcher operationalizes a population by developing a specific list that closely approximates all the elements in the population. This list is a *sampling frame*. He or she can choose from many types of sampling frames: telephone directories, tax records, driver's license records, and so on. Listing the elements in a population sounds simple. It is often difficult because there may be no good list of elements in a population.

A good sampling frame is crucial to good sampling. A mismatch between the sampling frame and the conceptually defined population can be a major source of error. Just as a mismatch between the theoretical and operational definitions of a variable creates invalid measurement, so a mismatch between the sampling frame and the population causes invalid sampling. Researchers try to minimize mismatches. For example, you would like to sample all people in a region of the United States, so you decide to get a list of everyone with a driver's license. But some people do not have driver's licenses, and the lists of those with licenses, even if updated regularly, quickly go out of date. Next, you try income tax records. But not everyone pays taxes; some people cheat and do not pay, others have no income and do not have to file, others have died or have not begun to pay taxes, and still others have entered or left the area since the last time taxes were due. You try telephone directories, but they are not much better; some people are recent arrivals who are not listed in a telephone directory, some people have unlisted numbers, and others have recently moved.

With a few exceptions (e.g., a list of all students enrolled at a university), sampling frames are almost always inaccurate. A sampling frame can include some of those outside the target population (e.g., a telephone directory that lists people who have moved away) or might omit some of those inside it (e.g., those without telephones).

Any characteristic of a population (e.g., the percentage of city residents who smoke cigarettes, the average height of all women over the age of 21, the percentage of people who believe in UFOs) is a population *parameter.* It is the true characteristic of the population. Parameters are determined when all elements in a population are measured. The parameter is never known with absolute accuracy for large populations (e.g., an entire nation), so researchers must estimate it on the basis of samples. They use information from the sample, called a *statistic,* to estimate population parameters (see Figure 8.3).

A famous case in the history of sampling illustrates the limitations of the technique. The *Literary Digest,* a major U.S. magazine, sent postcards to people before the 1920, 1924, 1928, and 1932 U.S. presidential elections. The magazine took the names for the sample from automobile registrations and telephone directories—the sampling frame. People returned the postcards indicating whom they would vote for. The magazine correctly predicted all four election outcomes. The magazine's success with predictions was well known, and in 1936 it increased the sample to 10 million. The magazine predicted a huge victory for Alf Landon over Franklin D. Roosevelt. But the *Literary Digest* was wrong; Franklin D. Roosevelt won by a landslide.

The prediction was wrong for several reasons, but the most important were mistakes in sampling. Although the magazine sampled a large number of people, its sampling frame did not accurately represent the target population (i.e., all voters). It excluded people without telephones or automobiles, a sizable percentage of the population in 1936, during the worst of the Great Depression of the 1930s. The frame excluded as much as 65 percent of the population and a segment of the voting population (lower income) that tended to favor Roosevelt.[5] The magazine had been accurate in earlier elections because people with higher and lower incomes did not differ in how they voted. Also, during earlier elections, before the Depression, more lower-income people could afford to have telephones and automobiles.

You can learn two important lessons from the *Literary Digest* mistake. First, the sampling frame is crucial. Second, the size of a sample is less important than whether or not it accurately represents the population. A representative sample of 2,500 can give more accurate predications about the U.S. population than a nonrepresentative sample of 10 million or 50 million.

Why Random?

The area of applied mathematics called probability theory relies on random processes. The word *random* has a special meaning in mathematics. It refers

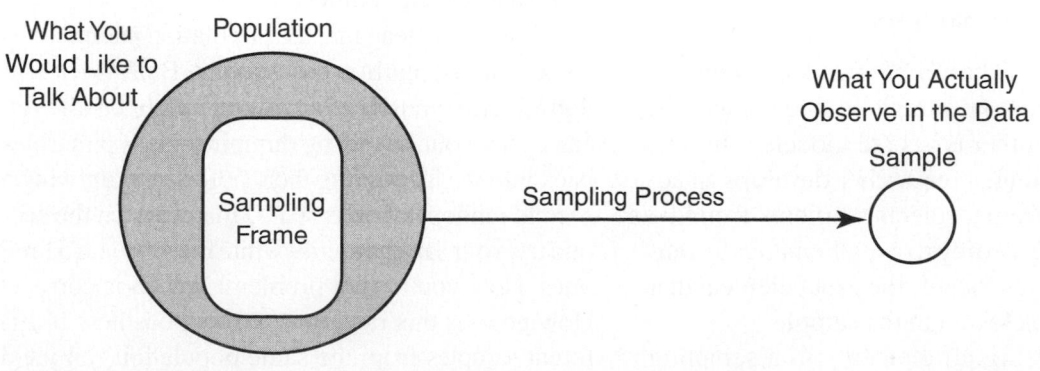

FIGURE 8.3 A Model of the Logic of Sampling

to a process that generates a mathematically random result; that is, the selection process operates in a truly random method (i.e., no pattern), and a researcher can calculate the probability of outcomes. In a true random process, each element has an equal probability of being selected.

Probability samples that rely on random processes require more work than nonrandom ones. A researcher must identify specific sampling elements (e.g., person) to include in the sample. For example, if conducting a telephone survey, the researcher needs to try to reach the specific sampled person, by calling back four or five times, to get an accurate *random sample.*[6]

Random samples are most likely to yield a sample that truly represents the population. In addition, random sampling lets a researcher statistically calculate the relationship between the sample and the population—that is, the size of the *sampling error.* A nonstatistical definition of the sampling error is the deviation between sample results and a population parameter due to random processes.

This chapter does not cover the technical and statistical details of random sampling. Instead, it focuses on the fundamentals of how sampling works, the differences between good and bad samples, how to draw a sample, and basic principles of sampling in social work research. This does not mean that random sampling is unimportant. It is essential to first master the fundamentals. If you plan to pursue a career using quantitative research, you should get more statistical background than space permits here.

Types of Probability Samples

Simple Random. The *simple random sample* is both the easiest random sample to understand and the one on which other types are modeled. In simple random sampling, a researcher develops an accurate sampling frame, selects elements from the sampling frame according to a mathematically random procedure, then locates the exact element that was selected for inclusion in the sample.

After numbering all elements in a sampling frame, a researcher uses a list of random numbers to decide which elements to select. He or she needs as many random numbers as there are elements to be sampled; for example, for a sample of 100, 100 random numbers are needed. The researcher can get random numbers from a *random-number table,* a table of numbers chosen in a mathematically random way. Random-number tables are available in most statistics and research methods books, including this one (see Appendix B). The numbers are generated by a pure random process so that any number has an equal probability of appearing in any position. Computer programs can also produce lists of random numbers.

You may ask, "Once I select an element from the sampling frame, do I then return it to the sampling frame, or do I keep it separate?" The common answer is that it is not returned. Unrestricted random sampling is random sampling with replacement—that is, replacing an element after sampling it so it can be selected again. In simple random sampling without replacement, the researcher ignores elements already selected into the sample.

The logic of simple random sampling can be illustrated with an elementary example—sampling marbles from a jar. You have a large jar full of 5,000 marbles, some red and some white. The 5,000 marbles are your population, and the parameter you want to estimate is the percentage of red marbles in it. You randomly select 100 marbles (you close your eyes, shake the jar, pick one marble, and repeat the procedure 99 times). You now have a random sample of marbles. You count the number of red marbles in your sample to estimate the percentage of red versus white marbles in the population. This is a lot easier than counting all 5,000 marbles. Your sample has 52 white and 48 red marbles.

Does this mean that the population parameter is 48 percent red marbles? Maybe not. Because of random chance, your specific sample might be off. You can check your results by dumping the 100 marbles back into the jar, mixing the marbles, and drawing a second random sample of 100 marbles. On the second try, your sample has 49 white marbles and 51 red ones. Now you have a problem. Which is correct? How good is this random sampling business if different samples from the same population can yield different results? You repeat the procedure over and over until you have drawn 130 different samples of

100 marbles each (see Box 8.2 for results). Most people might empty the jar and count all 5,000, but you want to see what is going on. The results of your 130 different samples reveal a clear pattern. The most common mix of red and white marbles is 50/50. Samples that are close to that split are more frequent than those with more uneven splits. The population parameter appears to be 50 percent white and 50 percent red marbles.

Mathematical proofs and empirical tests demonstrate that the pattern found in Box 8.2 always appears. The set of many different samples is your *sampling distribution.* It is a distribution of different samples that shows the frequency of different sample outcomes from many separate random samples. The pattern will appear if the sample size is 1,000 instead of 100; if there are ten colors of marbles instead of two; if the population has 100 marbles or 10 million marbles instead of 5,000; and if the population is people, automobiles, or colleges instead of marbles. In fact, the pattern will become clearer as more and more independent random samples are drawn from the population.

The pattern in the sampling distribution suggests that over many separate samples, the true population parameter (i.e., the 50/50 split in the preceding example) is more common than any other result. Some samples deviate from the population parameter, but they are less common. When many different random samples are plotted, as in the graph in Box 8.2, then the sampling distribution looks like a normal or bell-shaped curve. Such a curve is theoretically important and is used throughout statistics.

The *central limit theorem* from mathematics tells us that as the number of different random samples in a sampling distribution increases toward infinity, the pattern of samples and the population parameter become more predictable. With a huge number of random samples, the sampling distribution forms a normal curve, and the midpoint of the curve approaches the population parameter as the number of samples increases.

Perhaps you want only one sample because you do not have the time or energy to draw many different samples. You are not alone. A researcher rarely draws many samples. He or she usually draws only one random sample, but the central limit the-

orem lets him or her generalize from one sample to the population. The theorem is about many samples, but lets the researcher calculate the probability of a particular sample being off from the population parameter.

Random sampling does not guarantee that every random sample perfectly represents the population. Instead, it means that most random samples will be close to the population most of the time, and that one can calculate the probability of a particular sample being inaccurate. A researcher estimates the chance that a particular sample is off or unrepresentative (i.e., the size of the sampling error) by using information from the sample to estimate the sampling distribution. He or she combines this information with knowledge of the central limit theorem to construct *confidence intervals.*

The confidence interval is a relatively simple but powerful idea. When television or newspaper polls are reported, you may hear about something called the margin of error being plus or minus 2 percentage points. This is a version of confidence intervals. A confidence interval is a range around a specific point used to estimate a population parameter. A range is used because the statistics of random processes do not let a researcher predict an exact point, but they let the researcher say with a high level of confidence (e.g., 95 percent) that the true population parameter lies within a certain range.

The calculations for sampling errors or confidence intervals are beyond the level of this discussion. The sampling distribution is the key idea that lets a researcher calculate the sampling error and confidence interval. Thus, he or she cannot say, "This sample gives a perfect measure of the population parameter," but can say, "I am 95 percent certain that the true population parameter is no more than 2 percent different from what I have found in my sample."

For example, you cannot say, "There are precisely 2,500 red marbles in the jar based on a random sample." You can say, "I am 95 percent certain that the population parameter lies between 2,450 and 2,550." You can combine characteristics of the sample (e.g., its size, the variation in it) with the central limit theorem to predict specific ranges around the parameter with a great deal of confidence.

Box 8.2

Example of Sampling Distribution

Red	White	Number of Samples
42	58	1
43	57	1
45	55	2
46	54	4
47	53	8
48	52	12
49	51	21
50	50	31
51	49	20
52	48	13
53	47	9
54	46	5
55	45	2
57	43	1
	Total	130

Number of red and white marbles that were randomly drawn from a jar of 5,000 marbles with 100 drawn each time, repeated 129 times for 130 independent random samples.

Number of Samples

```
31                                      *
30                                      *
29                                      *
28                                      *
27                                      *
26                                      *
25                                      *
24                                      *
23                                      *
22                                      *
21                                  *   *
20                                  *   *   *
19                                  *   *   *
18                                  *   *   *
17                                  *   *   *
16                                  *   *   *
15                                  *   *   *
14                                  *   *   *
13                                  *   *   *   *
12                              *   *   *   *   *
11                              *   *   *   *   *
10                              *   *   *   *   *
 9                              *   *   *   *   *   *
 8                          *   *   *   *   *   *   *
 7                          *   *   *   *   *   *   *
 6                          *   *   *   *   *   *   *
 5                          *   *   *   *   *   *   *   *
 4                      *   *   *   *   *   *   *   *   *
 3                      *   *   *   *   *   *   *   *
 2                  *   *   *   *   *   *   *   *   *       *
 1          *   *       *   *   *   *   *   *   *   *   *       *
```

| | 42 | 43 | 44 | 45 | 46 | 47 | 48 | 49 | 50 | 51 | 52 | 53 | 54 | 55 | 56 | 57 |

Number of Red Marbles in a Sample

Systematic Sampling.   *Systematic sampling* is simple random sampling with a shortcut for random selection. Again, the first step is to number each element in the sampling frame. Instead of using a list of random numbers, a researcher calculates a *sampling interval,* and the interval becomes his or her quasi-random selection method. The sampling interval (i.e., 1 in *k,* where *k* is some number) tells the researcher how to select elements from a sampling frame by skipping elements in the frame before selecting one for the sample.

For instance, you want to sample 300 names from 900. After a random starting point, you select every third name of the 900 to get a sample of 300. Your sampling interval is 3. Sampling intervals are easy to compute. You need the sample size and the population size (or sampling frame size as a best estimate). You can think of the sampling interval as the inverse of the sampling ratio. The sampling ratio for 300 names out of 900 is 300/900 = .333 = 33.3 percent. The sampling interval is 900/300 = 3.

In most cases a simple random sample and a systematic sample yield virtually equivalent results. One important situation in which systematic sampling cannot be substituted for simple random sampling occurs when the elements in a sample are organized in some kind of cycle or pattern. For example, a researcher's sampling frame is organized by married couples with the male first and the female second (see Table 8.2). Such a pattern gives the researcher an unrepresentative sample if systematic sampling is used. His or her systematic sample can be nonrepresentative and include only wives because of how the cases are organized. When his or her sample frame is organized as couples, even-numbered sampling intervals result in samples with all husbands or all wives.

Table 8.3 illustrates simple random sampling and systematic sampling. Notice that different names were drawn in each sample. For example, H. Adams appears in both samples, but C. Droullard is only in the simple random sample. This is because it is rare for any two random samples to be identical.

The sampling frame contains 20 males and 20 females (gender is in parentheses after each name). The simple random sample yielded 3 males and 7 females, and the systematic sample yielded 5 males

TABLE 8.2   Problems with Systematic Sampling of Cyclical Data

CASE	
1	Husband
2[a]	Wife
3	Husband
4	Wife
5	Husband
6[a]	Wife
7	Husband
8	Wife
9	Husband
10[a]	Wife
11	Husband
12	Wife

Random start = 2; Sampling interval = 4.
[a]Selected into sample.

and 5 females. Does this mean that systematic sampling is more accurate? No. To check this, draw a new sample using different random numbers; try taking the first two digits and beginning at the end (e.g., 11 from 11,921, then 43 from 43,232). Also, draw a new systematic sample with a different random start. The last time the random start was 18. Try a random start of 11. What did you find? How many of each sex?[7]

Stratified Sampling.   In *stratified sampling* a researcher first divides the population into subpopulations (strata) on the basis of supplementary information.[8] After dividing the population into strata, the researcher draws a random sample from each subpopulation. He or she can sample randomly within strata using simple random or systematic sampling. In stratified sampling the researcher controls the relative size of each stratum, rather than letting random processes control it. This guarantees representativeness or fixes the proportion of different strata within a sample. Of course, the necessary supplemental information about strata is not always available.

In general, stratified sampling produces samples that are more representative of the population than simple random sampling if the stratum information is accurate. A simple example illustrates why

TABLE 8.3 How to Draw Simple Random and Systematic Samples

1. Number each case in the sampling frame in sequence. The list of 40 names is in alphabetical order, numbered from 1 to 40.
2. Decide on a sample size. We will draw two 25-percent (10-name) samples.
3. For a *simple random sample,* locate a random-number table (see excerpt; a fuller table appears in Appendix B). Before using a random-number table, count the largest number of digits needed for the sample (e.g., with 40 names, two digits are needed; for 100 to 999, three digits; for 1,000 to 9,999, four digits). Begin anywhere on the random-number table (we will begin in the upper left) and take a set of digits (we will take the last two). Mark the number on the sampling frame that corresponds to the chosen random number to indicate that the case is in the sample. If the number is too large (over 40), ignore it. If the number appears more than once (10 and 21 occurred twice in the example), ignore the second occurrence. Continue until the number of cases in the sample (10 in our example) is reached.
4. For a *systematic sample,* begin with a random start. The easiest way to do this is to point blindly at the random-number table, then take the closest number that appears on the sampling frame. In the example, 18 was chosen. Start with the random number, then count the sampling interval, or 4 in our example, to come to the first number. Mark it, and then count the sampling interval for the next number. Continue to the end of the list. Continue counting the sampling interval as if the beginning of the list was attached to the end of the list (like a circle). Keep counting until ending close to the start, or on the start if the sampling interval divides evenly into the total of the sampling frame.

No.	Name (Gender)	Simple Random	Systematic	No.	Name (Gender)	Simple Random	Systematic
01	Abrams, J. (M)			21	Hjelmhaug, N. (M)	Yes*	
02	Adams, H. (F)	Yes	Yes (6)	22	Huang, J. (F)	Yes	Yes (1)
03	Anderson, H. (M)			23	Ivono, V. (F)		
04	Arminond, L. (M)			24	Jaquees, J. (M)		
05	Boorstein, A. (M)			25	Johnson, A. (F)		
06	Breitsprecher, P. (M)	Yes	Yes (7)	26	Kennedy, M. (F)		Yes (2)
07	Brown, D. (F)			27	Koschoreck, L. (F)		
08	Cattelino, J. (F)			28	Koykkar, J. (M)		
09	Cidoni, S. (M)			29	Kozlowski, C. (F)	Yes	
10	Davis, L. (F)	Yes*	Yes (8)	30	Laurent, J. (M)		Yes (3)
11	Droullard, C. (M)	Yes		31	Lee, R. (F)		
12	Durette, R. (F)			32	Ling, C. (M)		
13	Elsnau, K. (F)	Yes		33	McKinnon, K. (F)		
14	Falconer, T. (M)		Yes (9)	34	Min, H. (F)	Yes	Yes (4)
15	Fuerstenberg, J. (M)			35	Moini, A. (F)		
16	Fulton, P. (F)			36	Navarre, H. (M)		
17	Gnewuch, S. (F)			37	O'Sullivan, C. (M)		
18	Green, C. (M)		START, Yes (10)	38	Oh, J. (M)		Yes (5)
19	Goodwanda, T. (F)	Yes		39	Olson, J. (M)		
20	Harris, B. (M)			40	Ortiz y Garcia, L. (F)		

Excerpt from a Random-Number Table (for Simple Random Sample)

150<u>10</u>	18590	001<u>02</u>	422<u>10</u>	94174	22099
901<u>22</u>	38221	215<u>29</u>	000<u>13</u>	047<u>34</u>	60457
67256	13887	941<u>19</u>	11077	01061	27779
13761	23390	12947	21280	445<u>06</u>	36457
81994	666<u>11</u>	16597	44457	076<u>21</u>	51949
79180	25992	46178	23992	62108	43232
07984	47169	88094	82752	15318	11921

*Numbers that appeared twice in random numbers selected.

220

this is so. Imagine a population that is 51 percent female and 49 percent male; the population parameter is a sex ratio of 51 to 49. With stratified sampling, a researcher draws random samples among females and among males so that the sample contains a 51 to 49 percent sex ratio. If the researcher had used simple random sampling, it would be possible for a random sample to be off from the true sex ratio in the population. Thus, he or she makes fewer errors representing the population and has a smaller sampling error with stratified sampling.

Researchers use stratified sampling when a stratum of interest is a small percentage of a population, and random processes could miss the stratum by chance. For example, a researcher draws a sample of 200 from 20,000 college students. He or she gets information from the college registrar indicating that 2 percent of the 20,000 students, or 400, are divorced women with children under the age of 5. This group is important to include in the sample. There would be 4 such students (2 percent of 200) in a represen-

tative sample, but the researcher could miss them by chance in one simple random sample. With stratified sampling, he or she obtains a list of the 400 such students from the registrar and randomly selects 4 from it. This guarantees that the sample represents the population with regard to the important strata (see Box 8.3).

In special situations a researcher may want the proportion of a stratum in a sample to differ from its true proportion in the population. For example, the population contains 0.5 percent Eskimos, but the researcher wants to examine Eskimos in particular. He or she oversamples so that Eskimos make up 10 percent of the sample. With this type of disproportionate stratified sample, the researcher cannot generalize directly from the sample to the population without special adjustments.

In some situations a researcher wants the proportion of a stratum or subgroup to differ from its true proportion in the population. For example, Davis and Smith (1992) reported that the 1987

Box 8.3 _____

Illustration of Stratified Sampling

Sample of 100 Staff of General Hospital, Stratified by Position

POSITION	POPULATION		SIMPLE RANDOM SAMPLE	STRATIFIED SAMPLE	ERRORS COMPARED TO THE POPULATION
	N	*Percent*	*n*	*n*	
Administrators	15	2.88	1	3	−2
Staff physicians	25	4.81	2	5	−3
Intern physicians	25	4.81	6	5	+1
Registered nurses	100	19.23	22	19	+3
Nurse assistants	100	19.23	21	19	+2
Social workers	75	14.42	9	14	+5
Orderlies	50	9.62	8	10	−2
Clerks	75	14.42	5	14	+1
Maintenance staff	30	5.77	3	6	−3
Cleaning staff	25	4.81	3	5	−2
Total	520	100.00	100	100	

Randomly select 3 of 15 administrators, 5 of 25 staff physicians, and so on.

Note: Traditionally, *N* symbolizes the number in the population and *n* represents the number in the sample.

The simple random sample overrepresents nurses, nursing assistants, and social workers, but underrepresents administrators, staff physicians, maintenance staff, and cleaning staff. The stratified sample gives an accurate representation of each type of position.

General Social Survey (explained in Chapter 11) oversampled African Americans. A random sample of the U.S. population yielded 191 Blacks. Davis and Smith conducted a separate sample of African Americans to increase the total number of Blacks to 544. The 191 Black respondents are about 13 percent of the random sample, roughly equal to the percentage of Blacks in the U.S. population. The 544 Blacks are 30 percent of the disproportionate sample. The researcher who wants to use the entire sample must adjust it to reduce the number of sampled African Americans before generalizing to the U.S. population. Disproportionate sampling helps the researcher who wants to focus on issues most relevant to a subpopulation. In this case he or she can more accurately generalize to African Americans using the 544 respondents than by using a sample of only 191. The larger sample is more likely to reflect the full diversity of the African American subpopulation.

Cluster Sampling. *Cluster sampling* addresses two problems: Researchers lack a good sampling frame for a dispersed population, and the cost to reach a sampled element is very high.[9] For example, there is no single list of all shelters serving homeless families in North America. Even if you got an accurate sampling frame, it would cost too much to reach the sampled shelters that are geographically spread out. Instead of using a single sampling frame, researchers use a sampling design that involves multiple stages and clusters.

A *cluster* is a unit that contains final sampling elements but can be treated temporarily as a sampling element itself. A researcher first samples clusters, each of which contains elements, then draws a second sample from within the clusters selected in the first stage of sampling. In other words, the researcher randomly samples clusters, then randomly samples elements from within the selected clusters. This has a big practical advantage. He or she can create a good sampling frame of clusters, even if it is impossible to create one for sampling elements. Once the researcher gets a sample of clusters, creating a sampling frame for elements within each cluster becomes more manageable. A second advantage for geographically dispersed populations is

that elements within each cluster are physically closer to one another. This may produce a savings in locating or reaching each element.

A researcher draws several samples in stages in cluster sampling. In a three-stage sample, stage 1 is random sampling of big clusters; stage 2 is random sampling of small clusters within each selected big cluster; and the last stage is sampling of elements from within the sampled small clusters. For example, a researcher wants a sample of individuals from Mapleville. First, he or she randomly samples city blocks, then households within blocks, then individuals within households (see Box 8.4). Although there is no accurate list of all residents of Mapleville, there is an accurate list of blocks in the city. After selecting a random sample of blocks, the researcher counts all households on the selected blocks to create a sample frame for each block. He or she then uses the list of households to draw a random sample at the stage of sampling households. Finally, the researcher chooses a specific individual within each sampled household.

Cluster sampling is usually less expensive than simple random sampling, but it is less accurate. Each stage in cluster sampling introduces sampling errors, so a multistage cluster sample has more sampling errors than a one-stage random sample.[10]

A researcher who uses cluster sampling must decide the number of clusters and the number of elements within clusters. For example, in a two-stage cluster sample of 240 people from Mapleville, the researcher could randomly select 120 clusters and select 2 elements from each, or randomly select 2 clusters and select 120 elements in each. Which is best? The general answer is that a design with more clusters is better because elements within clusters (e.g., people living on the same block) tend to be similar to each other (e.g., people on the same block tend to be more alike than those on different blocks). If few clusters are chosen, many similar elements could be selected, which would be less representative of the total population. For example, the researcher could select two blocks with relatively wealthy people and draw 120 people from each. This would be less representative than a sample with 120 different city blocks and 2 individuals chosen from each.

Box 8.4

Illustration of Cluster Sampling

Goal: Draw a random sample of 240 people in Mapleville.

Step 1: Mapleville has 55 districts. Randomly select 6 districts.

1 2 3* 4 5 6 7 8 9 10 11 12 13 14 15* 16 17 18 19 20 21 22 23 24 25 26
27* 28 29 30 31* 32 33 34 35 36 37 38 39 40* 41 42 43 44 45 46 47 48
49 50 51 52 53 54* 55

* = Randomly selected

Step 2: Divide the selected districts into blocks. Each district contains 20 blocks. Randomly select 4 blocks from the district.

Example of District 3 (selected in step 1):

1 2 3 4* 5 6 7 8 9 10* 11 12 13* 14 15 16 17* 18 19 20

* = Randomly selected

Step 3: Divide blocks into households. Randomly select households.

Example of Block 4 of District 3 (selected in step 2):

Block 4 contains a mix of single-family homes, duplexes, and four-unit apartment buildings. It is bounded by Oak Street, River Road, South Avenue, and Greenview Drive. There are 45 households on the block. Randomly select 10 households from the 45.

1	#1 Oak Street	16	"	31*	"	
2	#3 Oak Street	17*	#154 River Road	32*	"	
3*	#5 Oak Street	18	#156 River Road	33	"	
4	"	19*	#158 River Road	34	#156 Greenview Drive	
5	"	20*	"	35*	"	
6	"	21	#13 South Avenue	36	"	
7	#7 Oak Street	22	"	37	"	
8	"	23	#11 South Avenue	38	"	
9*	#150 River Road	24	#9 South Avenue	39	#158 Greenview Drive	
10*	"	25	#7 South Avenue	40	"	
11	"	26	#5 South Avenue	41	"	
12	"	27	#3 South Avenue	42	"	
13	#152 River Road	28	#1 South Avenue	43	#160 Greenview Drive	
14	"	29*	"	44	"	
15	"	30	#152 Greenview Drive	45	"	

* = Randomly selected

Step 4: Select a respondent within each household.

Summary of cluster sampling:
  1 person randomly selected per household
10 households randomly selected per block
  4 blocks randomly selected per district
  6 districts randomly selected in the city
  $1 \times 10 \times 4 \times 6 = 240$ people in sample

When a researcher samples from a large geographical area and must travel to each element, cluster sampling significantly reduces travel costs. As usual, there is a tradeoff between accuracy and cost.

For example, Alan, Ricardo, and Barbara each plan to visit and personally interview a sample of 1,500 students who represent the population of all college students in North America. Alan obtains an accurate sampling frame of all students and uses simple random sampling. He travels to 1,000 different locations to interview one or two students at each. Ricardo draws a random sample of three colleges from a list of all 3,000 colleges, then visits the three and selects 500 students from each. Barbara draws a random sample of 300 colleges. She visits the 300 and selects 5 students at each. If travel costs average $250 per location, Alan's travel bill is $250,000, Ricardo's is $750, and Barbara's is $75,000. Alan's sample is highly accurate, but Barbara's is only slightly less accurate for one-third the cost. Ricardo's sample is the cheapest, but it is not representative at all.

Within-Household Sampling. Once a researcher samples a household or similar unit (e.g., family or dwelling unit) in cluster sampling, the question arises, "Whom should the researcher choose?" A potential source of bias is introduced if the first person who answers the telephone, the door, or the mail is used in the sample. The first person who answers should be selected only if his or her answering is the result of a truly random process. This is rarely the case. Certain people are unlikely to be at home, and in some households one person (e.g., a husband) is more likely than another to answer the telephone or door. Researchers use within-household sampling to ensure that after a random household is chosen, the individual within the household is also selected randomly.

Researchers can randomly select a person within a household in several ways.[11] The most common method is to use a selection table specifying who is to be chosen (e.g., oldest male, youngest female, etc.) after the size and composition of the household are known (see Table 8.4). This removes any bias that might arise from choosing the first person to answer the door or telephone, or from the interviewer's selecting the person who appears to be friendliest.

Probability Proportionate to Size (PPS). There are two ways to cluster sample. The method just described is proportionate or unweighted cluster sampling. It is proportionate because the size of each cluster (or number of elements at each stage) is the same. Unfortunately, the more common situation is for the cluster groups to be of different sizes. When this is the case, the researcher must adjust the probability or sampling ratio at various stages in sampling.

The foregoing cluster sampling example with Alan, Barbara, and Ricardo illustrates the problem with unweighted cluster sampling. Barbara drew a simple random sample of 300 colleges from a list of all 3,000 colleges, but she made a mistake—unless every college has an identical number of students. Her method gave each college an equal chance of being selected—a 300/3,000 or 10 percent chance. But colleges have different numbers of students, so each student does not have an equal chance to end up in her sample.

Barbara listed every college and sampled from the list. A large university with 40,000 students and a small college with 400 students had an equal chance of being selected. But if she chose the large university, the chance of a given student at that college being selected was 5 in 40,000 ($5/40,000 = 0.0125$ percent), whereas a student at the small college had a 5 in 400 ($5/400 = 1.25$ percent) chance of being selected. The small-college student was 100 times more likely to be in her sample. The total probability of being selected for a student from the large university was 0.125 percent (10×0.0125), while it was 12.5 percent (10×1.25) for the small-college student. Barbara violated a principle of random sampling—that each element has an equal chance to be selected into the sample.

If Barbara uses *probability proportionate to size (PPS)* and samples correctly, then each final sampling element or student will have an equal probability of being selected. She does this by adjusting the chances of selecting a college in the first stage of sampling. She must give large colleges with more students a greater chance of being selected and small colleges a smaller chance. She adjusts the probability of selecting a college on the basis of the proportion of all students in the population who at-

TABLE 8.4 Within-Household Sampling

Selecting individuals within sampled households. Number selected is the household chosen in Box 8.4.

Number	Last Name	Adults (over Age 18)	Selected Respondent
3	Able	1 male, 1 female	Female
9	Bharadwaj	2 females	Youngest female
10	DiPiazza	1 male, 2 females	Oldest female
17	Wucivic	2 males, 1 female	Youngest male
19	Cseri	2 females	Youngest female
20	Taylor	1 male, 3 females	Second oldest female
29	Velu	2 males, 2 females	Oldest male
31	Wong	1 male, 1 female	Female
32	Gray	1 male	Male
35	Mall-Krinke	1 male, 2 females	Oldest female

Example Selection Table (Only Adults Counted)

Males	Females	Whom to Select	Males	Females	Whom to Select
1	0	Male	2	2	Oldest male
2	0	Oldest male	2	3	Youngest female
3	0	Youngest male	3	2	Second oldest male
4+	0	Second oldest male	3	3	Second oldest female
0	1	Female	3	4	Third oldest female
0	2	Youngest female	4	3	Second oldest male
0	3	Second oldest female	4	4	Third oldest male
0	4+	Oldest female	4	5+	Youngest female
1	1	Female	5+	4	Second oldest male
1	2	Oldest female	5+	5+	Fourth oldest female
1	3	Second oldest female			
2	1	Youngest male			
3	1	Second oldest male			

+ = or more

tend it. Thus, a college with 40,000 students will be 100 times more likely to be selected than one with 400 students. (See Box 8.5 for another example.)

Random-Digit Dialing. *Random-digit dialing (RDD)* is a special sampling technique used in research projects in which the general public is interviewed by telephone.[12] It differs from the traditional method of sampling for telephone interviews because a published telephone directory is not the sampling frame.

Three kinds of people are missed when the sampling frame is a telephone directory: people without telephones, people who have recently moved, and people with unlisted numbers. Those without phones (e.g., the poor, the uneducated, and transients) are missed in any telephone interview study, but the proportion of the general public with a telephone is nearly 95 percent in advanced industrialized nations. As the percentage of the public with telephones has increased, the percentage with unlisted numbers has also grown. Several kinds of people have unlisted numbers: people who want to avoid collection agencies; the very wealthy; and those who want privacy and want to avoid obscene calls, salespeople, and prank calls. In some urban areas

Box 8.5

Example of Probability Proportionate to Size (PPS) Sampling

Henry wants to conduct one-hour, in-person interviews with people living in the city of Riverdale. Riverdale is spread out over a large area; Henry wants to reduce his travel time and expenses, so he uses a *cluster sampling design.* The last census reported that the city had about 490,000 people. Henry can interview only about 220 people, or about 0.05 percent of the city population. He first gathers maps from the city tax office and fire department, and retrieves census information on city blocks. He learns that there are 2,182 city blocks. At first, he thinks he can randomly select 10 percent of the blocks (i.e., 218), go to a block and count housing units, then locate one person to interview in each housing unit (house, apartment, etc.), but the blocks are of unequal geographic and population size. He studies the population density of the blocks and estimated number of people in each, then develops a five-part classification based on the average size of a block:

Density	Number of Blocks	Average Number of People
Very high density	20	2,000
High density	200	800
Medium density	800	300
Low density	1,000	50
Semirural	162	10

Henry realizes that randomly selecting city blocks without adjustment will not give each person an equal chance of being selected. For example, 1 very high-density block has the same number of people as 40 low-density blocks. Henry adjusts proportionate to the block size. The easiest way to do this is to convert all city blocks to equal-sized units based on the smallest cluster, or the semirural city blocks. For example, there are 2,000/10 or 200 times more people in a high-density block than a semirural block, so Henry increases the odds of selecting such a block to make its probability 200 times greater than a semirural block. Essentially, Henry creates adjusted-cluster units of 10 persons each (because that is how many there are in the semirural blocks) and substitutes them for city blocks in the first stage of sampling. The 162 semirural blocks are unchanged, but after adjustment, he has $20 \times 200 = 4,000$ units for the very high-density blocks, $200 \times 80 = 16,000$ units for the high-density blocks, and so forth, for a total of 49,162 such units. Henry now numbers each block, using the adjusted-cluster units, with many blocks getting multiple numbers. For example, he assigns numbers 1 to 200 to the first very high-density block, and so forth, as follows:

1	Very high-density block #1
2	Very high-density block #1
3	Very high-density block #1

. . . and so forth

3,999	Very high-density block #20
4,000	Very high-density block #20
4,001	High-density block #1
4,002	High-density block #2

. . . and so forth

49,160	Semirural block #160
49,161	Semirural block #161
49,162	Semirural block #162

Henry still wants to interview about 220 people and wants to select one person from each adjusted-cluster unit. He uses simple random sampling methods to select 220 of the 49,162 adjusted-cluster units. He can then convert the cluster units back to city blocks. For example, if Henry randomly selected numbers 25 and 184, both are in very high-density block #1, telling him to select two people from that block. If the number 49,161 was randomly selected, he selects one person in semirural block #161. Henry now goes to each selected block, identifies all housing units in that block, and randomly selects housing units. Of course, Henry may use within-household sampling after he selects a housing unit.

---

the percentage of unlisted numbers is as high as 50 percent. In addition, people change their residences, so directories that are published annually or less often have numbers for people who have left and do not list those who have recently moved into an area. A researcher using RDD randomly selects telephone numbers, thereby avoiding the problems of telephone directories. The population is telephone numbers, not people with telephones. RDD is not difficult, but it takes time and can frustrate the person doing the calling.

Here is how RDD works in the United States. Telephone numbers have three parts: a three-digit area code, a three-digit exchange number or central office code, and a four-digit number. For example, the area code for Madison, Wisconsin, is 608, and there are many exchanges within the area code (e.g., 221, 993, 767, 455); but not all of the 999 possible three-digit exchanges (from 001 to 999) are active. Likewise, not all of the 9,999 possible four-digit numbers in an exchange (from 0001 to 9999) are being used. Some numbers are reserved for future expansion, are disconnected, or are temporarily withdrawn after someone moves. Thus, a possible U.S. telephone number consists of an active area code, an active exchange number, and a four-digit number in an exchange.

In RDD a researcher identifies active area codes and exchanges, then randomly selects four-digit numbers. A problem is that the researcher can select any number in an exchange. This means that some selected numbers are out of service, disconnected, pay phones, or numbers for businesses; only some numbers are what the researcher wants—working residential phone numbers. Until the researcher calls, it is not possible to know whether the number is a working residential number. This means spending a lot of time getting numbers that are disconnected, for businesses, and so forth. For example, Groves and Kahn (1979:45) found that only about 22 percent of the numbers called were working residential numbers. Research organizations often use computers to select random digits and dial the phone automatically. This speeds the process, but a human must still listen and find out whether the number is a working residential one.

Remember that the sampling element in RDD is the phone number, not the person or the household. Several families or individuals can share the same phone number, and in other situations each person may have a separate phone number or more than one phone number. This means that after a working residential phone is reached, a second stage of sampling is necessary, within-household sampling, to select the person to be interviewed.

Box 8.6 presents an example of how the many sampling terms and ideas can be used together in a specific real-life situation.

Hidden Populations

In contrast to sampling the general population or visible and accessible people, sampling *hidden populations* (i.e., people who engage in clandestine or concealed activities) is a recurrent issue in the studies of outsiders or stigmatized behavior. It illustrates the creative application of sampling principles, mixing qualitative and quantitative styles of research, and combining probability with nonprobability techniques. Three studies in which AIDS researchers drew samples of hidden populations are instructive.

Watters and Biernacki (1989) studied HIV-positive intravenous drug users in San Francisco and sought to evaluate a new AIDS prevention program. They adopted a procedure called *targeted sampling* in which they used a combination of chain referral (a kind of snowball sampling), stratified sampling, and quota sampling. They also used purposive sampling in carefully selected geographic districts with high concentrations of drug users. They remarked, "While they are not random samples, it is particularly important to emphasize that targeted samples are not convenience samples" (1989:420).

Martin and Dean (1993) wanted a sample of 700 gay men from New York City. The men had to live in the city, be over age 18, not be diagnosed as having AIDS, and engage in sex with other men. The sample was to represent all areas of the city, diverse lifestyles, and various ethnic backgrounds. The authors began with a purposive sample using five diverse sources to recruit 291 respondents. They first contacted 150 New York City organizations with predominately homosexual or bisexual members. They next screened these to 90 organizations that had eligible men for the study. From the 90, they drew a stratified random sample of 52 organizations by membership size. They randomly selected five members from each of the organizations. Reports of Martin and Dean's study appeared in local news sources. This brought calls from which they got 41 unsolicited volunteers. Another source of

Box 8.6

Example Sample

Sampling has many terms for the different parts of samples or types of samples. A complex sample illustrates how researchers use them. Look at the 1980 sample for the best-known national U.S. survey in sociology, the General Social Survey (discussed in Chapter 11).

The *population* is defined as all resident adults (18 years or older) in the U.S. for the *universe* of all Americans. The *target population* consists of all English-speaking adults who live in households, excluding those living in institutional settings such as college dormitories, nursing homes, or military quarters. The researchers estimated that 97.3 percent of all resident adults lived in households and that 97 percent of the household population spoke sufficient English to be interviewed.

The researchers used a complex multistage probability sample that is both a *cluster sample* and a *stratified sample*. First, they created a national *sampling frame* of all U.S. counties, independent cities, and Standard Metropolitan Statistical Areas (SMSAs), a Census Bureau designation for larger cities and surrounding areas. Each *sampling element* at this first level had about 4,000 households. They divided these elements into strata. The strata were the four major geographic regions as defined by the Census Bureau, divided into metropolitan and nonmetropolitan areas. They then sampled from each strata using *probability proportionate to size (PPS)* random selection, based on the number of housing units in each county or SMSA. This gave them a sample of 84 counties or SMSAs.

For the second stage the researchers identified city blocks, census tracts, or the rural equivalent in each county or SMSA. Each *sampling element* (e.g., city block) had a minimum of 50 housing units. In order to get an accurate count of the number of housing units for some counties, a researcher counted addresses in the field. The researchers selected 6 or more blocks within each county or SMSA, using PPS to yield 562 blocks.

In the third stage the researchers used the household as a *sampling element.* They randomly selected households from the addresses in the block. After selecting an address, an interviewer contacted the household and chose an eligible respondent from it. The interviewer looked at a selection table for possible respondents and interviewed a type of respondent (e.g., second oldest) based on the table. In total, 1,934 people were contacted for interviews and 75.9 percent of interviews were completed. This gave a final sample size of 1,468. We can calculate the *sampling ratio* by dividing 1,468 by the total number of adults living in households, which was about 150 million in 1980, which is 0.01 percent. To check the representativeness of their sample, the researchers also compared characteristics of the sample to census results (see Davis and Smith, 1992:31–44).

---

32 men were referrals from respondents who had participated in a small pilot study. In addition, 72 men were identified at an annual New York City Gay Pride Parade. And 15 eligible men were contacted at a New York City clinic and asked to participate.

The researchers next used snowball sampling. They asked each of the 291 respondents to give a recruitment packet to three gay male friends. Each friend who agreed to participate was also asked to give packets to three friends. This continued until it had gone five levels out from the initial 291 men. Eventually, 746 men were recruited into the study. Martin and Dean checked their sample against two random samples of gay men in San Francisco, a random-digit dialing sample of 500, and a cluster sample of 823 using San Francisco census tracts. Their sample paralleled those from San Francisco on race, age, and the percentage being "out of the closet."

Heckathorn (1997) used *respondent-drive sampling* to study 277 active drug injectors in two small Connecticut cities and the surrounding area. As of July 1996, 390 AIDS cases had been diagnosed in the towns; about half the cases involved drug injection. The sampling was purposive in that each sampled element had to meet certain criteria. Heckathorn also used a modified snowball sampling with a "dual reward system." He gave each person who completed an interview a monetary reward and a second monetary reward for recruiting a new respondent. The first person was asked not to identify the new person to the researcher, at times referred to as *masking* (i.e., protecting friends). This gets around the "snitching" issue and "war on drugs" stigma, especially strong in the U.S. context. This modified snowball sampling is like sequential sampling in that after a period of time, fewer and fewer new recruits are found, until the researcher comes to saturation or an equilibrium.

You are now familiar with several major types of probability samples (see Table 8.5) and supplementary techniques used with them (e.g., PPS, within-household, and RDD) that may be appropriate. In addition, you have seen how researchers combine nonprobability and probability sampling for special situations, such as hidden populations.

TABLE 8.5 Types of Probability Samples

TYPE OF SAMPLE	TECHNIQUE
Simple Random	Create a sampling frame for all cases, then select cases using a purely random process (e.g., random-number table or computer program).
Stratified	Create a sampling frame for each of several categories of cases, draw a random sample from each category, then combine the several samples.
Systematic	Create a sampling frame, calculate the sampling interval 1/*k*, choose a random starting place, then take every 1/*k* case.
Cluster	Create a sampling frame for larger cluster units, draw a random sample of the cluster units, create a sampling frame for cases within each selected cluster unit, then draw a random sample of cases, and so forth.

Next, we turn to determining a sample size for probability samples.

How Large Should a Sample Be?

Students and new researchers often ask, "How large does my sample have to be?" The best answer is, "It depends." It depends on the kind of data analysis the researcher plans, on how accurate the sample has to be for the researcher's purposes, and on population characteristics. As you have seen, a large sample size alone does not guarantee a representative sample. A large sample without random sampling or with a poor sampling frame is less representative than a smaller one with random sampling and an excellent sampling frame.

The question of sample size can be addressed in two ways. One is to make assumptions about the population and use statistical equations about random sampling processes. The calculation of sample size by this method requires a statistical discussion that goes beyond the level of this text.[13] The researcher must make assumptions about the degree of confidence (or number of errors) that is acceptable and the degree of variation in the population.

A second and more frequently used method is a rule of thumb—a conventional or commonly accepted amount. Researchers use it because they rarely have the information required by the statistical method and because it gives sample sizes close to those of the statistical method. Rules of thumb are not arbitrary but are based on past experience with samples that have met the requirements of the statistical method.

One principle of sample sizes is, the smaller the population, the bigger the sampling ratio has to be for an accurate sample (i.e., one with a high probability of yielding the same results as the entire population). Larger populations permit smaller sampling ratios for equally good samples. This is because as the population size grows, the returns in accuracy for sample size shrink.

For small populations (under 1,000), a researcher needs a large sampling ratio (about 30 percent). For example, a sample size of about 300 is required for a high degree of accuracy. For moderately large populations (10,000), a smaller sampling ratio (about 10 percent) is needed to be equally accurate, or a sample size of around 1,000. For large populations (over 150,000), smaller sampling ratios (1 percent) are possible, and samples of about 1,500 can be very accurate. To sample from very large populations (over 10 million), one can achieve accuracy using tiny sampling ratios (0.025 percent) or samples of about 2,500. The size of the population ceases to be relevant once the sampling ratio is very small, and samples of about 2,500 are as accurate for populations of 200 million as for those of 10 million. These are approximate sizes, and practical limitations (e.g., cost) also play a role in a researcher's decision.

A related principle is that for small samples, small increases in sample size produce big gains in accuracy. Equal increases in sample size produce more of an increase in accuracy for small than for large samples. For example, an increase in sample size from 50 to 100 reduces errors from 7.1 percent to 2.1 percent, but an increase from 1,000 to 2,000 decreases errors only from 1.6 percent to 1.1 percent (Sudman, 1976a:99).

A researcher's decision about the best sample size depends on three things: (1) the degree of accuracy required, (2) the degree of variability or diversity in the population, and (3) the number of different variables examined simultaneously in data analysis. Everything else being equal, larger samples are needed if one wants high accuracy, if the population has a great deal of variability or heterogeneity, or if one wants to examine many variables in the data analysis simultaneously. Smaller samples are sufficient when less accuracy is acceptable, when the population is homogeneous, or when only a few variables are examined at a time.

The analysis of data on subgroups also affects a researcher's decision about sample size. If the researcher wants to analyze subgroups in the population, he or she needs a larger sample. For example, you want to analyze four variables for males between the ages of 30 and 40 years old. If this sample is of the general public, then only a small proportion (e.g., 10 percent) of sample cases will be males in that age group. A rule of thumb is to have about 50 cases for each subgroup to be analyzed. Thus, if you want to analyze a group that is only 10 percent of the population, then you should have 10 × 50 or 500 cases in the sample to be sure you get enough for the subgroup analysis.

Drawing Inferences

A researcher samples so he or she can draw inferences from the sample to the population. In fact, a subfield of statistical data analysis that concerns drawing accurate inferences is called *inferential statistics.* The researcher directly observes variables, using units in the sample. The sample stands for or represents the population. Researchers are not interested in samples in themselves; they want to infer to the population. Thus, a gap exists between what the researcher concretely has (a sample) and what is of real interest (a population) (see Figure 8.4).

In the previous chapter you saw how the logic of measurement could be stated in terms of a gap between abstract constructs and concrete indicators. Measures of concrete, observable data are approximations for abstract constructs. Researchers use the approximations to estimate what is of real interest (i.e., constructs and causal laws). Conceptualization and operationalization bridge the gap in measurement just as the use of sampling frames, the sampling process, and inference bridge the gap in sampling.

Researchers put the logic of sampling and the logic of measurement together by directly observing measures of constructs and empirical relationships in samples (see Figure 8.4). They infer or generalize from what they can observe empirically in samples to the abstract causal laws and constructs in the population.

Validity and sampling error have similar functions, as can be illustrated by the analogy between the logic of sampling and the logic of measurement—that is, between what is observed and what is discussed. In measurement a researcher wants valid indicators of constructs—that is, concrete indicators that accurately represent abstract constructs. In sampling he or she wants samples that have little sampling error—concrete collections of cases that accurately represent unseen and abstract populations. A valid measure deviates little from the construct it represents. A sample with little sampling error permits estimates that deviate little from population parameters.

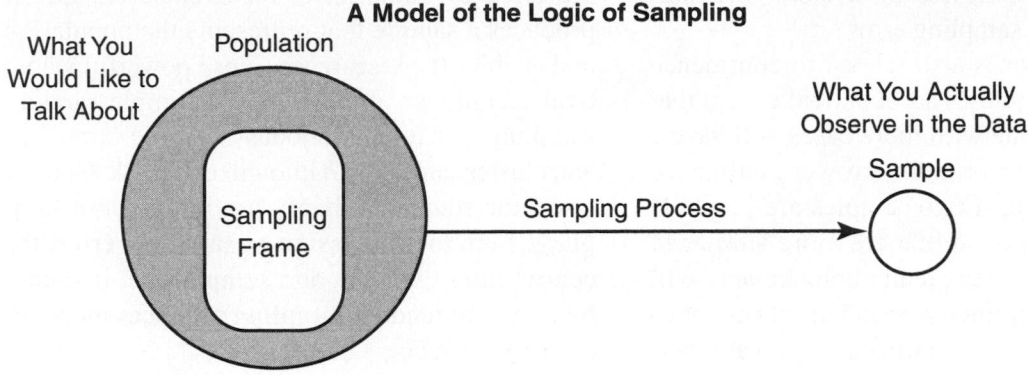

A Model of the Logic of Sampling

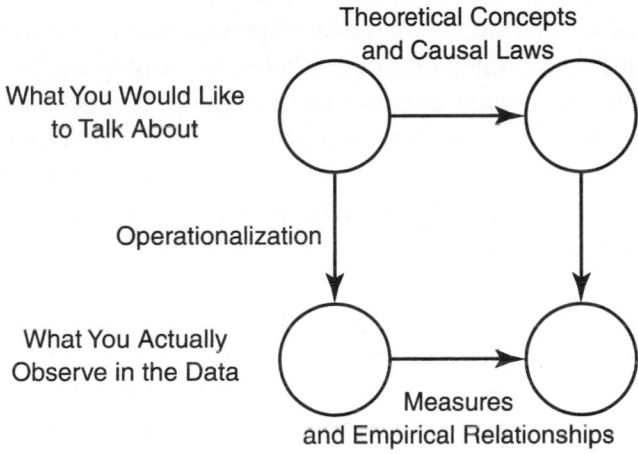

A Model of the Logic of Measurement

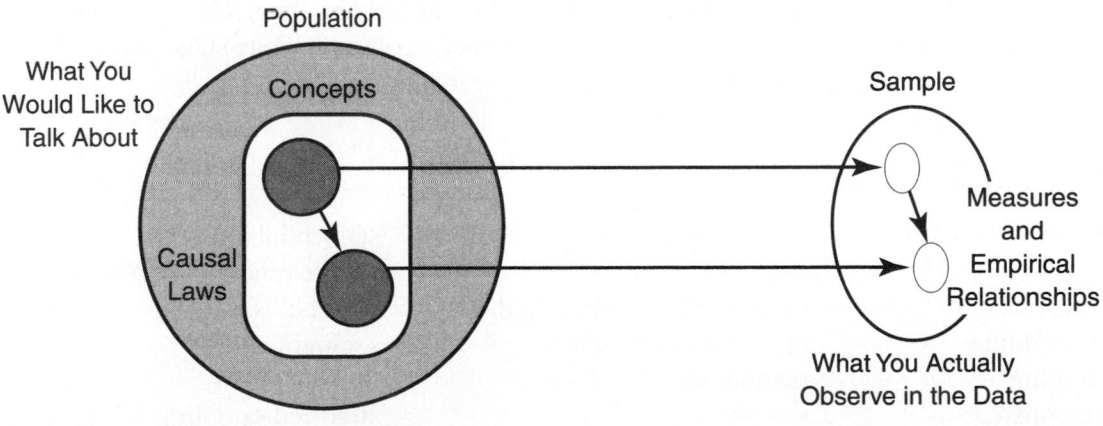

A Model Combining Logics of Sampling and Measurement

FIGURE 8.4   Model of the Logic of Sampling and of Measurement

Researchers try to reduce sampling errors. The calculation of the sampling error is not presented here, but it is based on two factors: the sample size and the amount of diversity in the sample. Everything else being equal, the larger the sample size, the smaller the sampling error. Likewise, the greater the homogeneity (or the less the diversity) in a sample, the smaller its sampling error.

Sampling error is also related to confidence intervals. If two samples are identical except that one is larger, the one with more cases will have a smaller sampling error and narrower confidence intervals. Likewise, if two samples are identical except that the cases in one are more similar to each other, the one with greater homogeneity will have a smaller sampling error and narrower confidence intervals. A narrow confidence interval means more precise estimates of the population parameter for a given level of confidence. For example, a researcher wants to estimate average annual family income. He or she has two samples. Sample 1 gives a confidence interval of $30,000 to $36,000 around the estimated population parameter of $33,000 for an 80-percent level of confidence. For a 95-percent level of confidence, the range is $23,000 to $43,000. A sample with a smaller sampling error (because it is larger or is more homogeneous) might give a $30,000 to $36,000 range for a 95-percent confidence level.

CONCLUSION

In this chapter you learned about sampling. Sampling is widely used in social work research. You learned about types of sampling that are not based on random processes. Only some are acceptable, and even then their use depends on special circumstances.[14] In general, probability sampling is preferred by quantitative researchers because it produces a sample that represents the population and enables the researcher to use powerful statistical techniques. In addition to simple random sampling, you learned about systematic, stratified, and cluster sampling. Although this book does not cover the statistical theory used in random sampling, from the discussion of sampling error, the central limit theorem, and sample size, it should be clear that random sampling produces more accurate and precise sampling.

Before moving on to the next chapter, it may be useful to restate a fundamental principle of social work research: Do not compartmentalize the steps of the research process; rather, learn to see the interconnections between the steps. Research design, measurement, sampling, and specific research techniques are interdependent. Unfortunately, the constraints of presenting information in a textbook necessitate presenting the parts separately, in sequence. In practice, social work researchers think about data collection when they design research and develop measures for variables. Likewise, sampling issues influence research design, measurement of variables, and data collection strategies. As you will see in future chapters, good social work research depends on simultaneously controlling quality at several different steps—research design, conceptualization, measurement, sampling, and data collection and handling. The researcher who makes major errors at any one stage may make an entire research project worthless.[15]

KEY TERMS

central limit theorem	purposive sampling	sequential sampling
cluster sampling	quota sampling	simple random sampling
confidence intervals	random-digit dialing (RDD)	snowball sampling
extreme case sampling	random-number table	sociogram
haphazard sampling	random sample	statistic
hidden populations	sample	stratified sampling
inferential statistics	sampling distribution	systematic sampling
nonrandom sample	sampling element	target population
parameter	sampling error	theoretical sampling
population	sampling frame	
probability proportionate to size (PPS)	sampling interval	
	sampling ratio	

REVIEW QUESTIONS

1. When is purposive sampling used?

2. When is the snowball sampling technique appropriate?

3. What is a sampling frame, and why is it important?

4. Which sampling method is best when the population has several groups and a researcher wants to ensure that each group is in the sample?

5. How can you get a sampling interval from a sampling ratio?

6. When should a researcher consider using probability proportionate to size?

7. What is the population in random-digit dialing? Are sampling frame problems avoided? Explain.

8. How do researchers decide how large a sample to use?

9. How are the logic of sampling and the logic of measurement related?

10. When is random-digit dialing used, and what are its advantages and disadvantages?

NOTES

1. See Stern (1979:77–81) on biased samples. He also discusses ways to identify problems with samples in published reports.

2. Quota sampling is discussed in Babbie (1998:196), Kalton (1983:91–93), and Sudman (1976a:191–200).

3. For further discussion on purposive sampling, see Babbie (1998:195), Grosof and Sardy (1985:172–173), and Singleton and associates (1988:153–154; 306). Bailey (1987:94–95) describes "dimensional" sampling, which is a variation of purposive sampling.

4. For additional discussion of snowball sampling, see Babbie (1998:194–196), Bailey (1987:97), and Sudman (1976a:210–211). Also, see Bailey (1987:366–367), Dooley (1984:86–87), Kidder and Judd (1986:240–241), Lindzey and Byrne (1968:452–525), and Singleton and associates (1988:372–373) for discussions of sociometry and sociograms. Network sampling issues are discussed in Galaskiewicz (1985), Granovetter (1976), and Hoffmann-Lange (1987).

5. For a discussion of the *Literary Digest* sampling mistake, see Babbie (1998:192–194), Dillman (1978:9–10), Frey (1983:18–19), and Singleton and colleagues (1988:132–133).

6. See Traugott (1987) on the importance of persistence in reaching sampled respondents for a representative sample. Also see Kalton (1983:63–69) on the importance of nonresponse.

7. Only one name appears in both. The stratified sample has 6 males and 4 females; the simple random sample has 5 males and 5 females. (Complete the lower block of numbers, then begin at the far right of the top block.)

8. Stratified sampling techniques are discussed in more detail in Frankel (1983:37–46), Kalton (1983:19–28), Mendenhall and associates (1971:53–88), Sudman (1976a:107–130), and Williams (1978:162–175).

9. Cluster sampling is discussed in Frankel (1983:47–57), Kalton (1983:28–38), Kish (1965), Mendenhall and associates (1971:121–141, 171–183), Sudman (1976a: 69–84), and Williams (1978:144–161).

10. For a discussion, see Frankel (1983:57–62), Kalton (1983:38–47), Sudman (1976a:131–170), and Williams (1978:239–241).

11. Within-household sampling is discussed in Czaja and associates (1982) and in Groves and Kahn (1979: 32–36).

12. For more on random-digit dialing issues, see Dillman (1978:238–242), Frey (1983:69–77), Glasser and Metzger (1972), Groves and Kahn (1979:20–21, 45–63), Kalton (1983:86–90), and Waksberg (1978). Kviz (1984) reported that telephone directories can produce relatively accurate sampling frames in rural areas, at least for mail questionnaire surveys. Also, see Keeter (1995).

13. See Kraemer and Thiemann (1987) for a technical discussion of selecting a sample size.

14. Berk (1983) argued that sampling that is nonrandom or a sampling process that excludes a nonrandom subset of cases can create seriously inaccurate estimates of causal relations.

15. For a further discussion of sample size calculation, see Grosof and Sardy (1985:181–185), Kalton (1983: 82–90), Sudman (1976a:85–105), and Williams (1978: 211–227).

EXPERIMENTAL RESEARCH

*Experimentation, the principal scientific method to be emphasized here,
involves at a simple level the comparison of groups or individuals who
have been differentially exposed to changes in their environment.*
—Leonard Saxe and Michelle Fine, *Social Experiments,* p. 45

INTRODUCTION

This chapter begins a new section of the book. In the previous three chapters, you learned about the foundations of qualitative and quantitative social work research design. This chapter and the three that follow it focus on quantitative research techniques. We begin with experimental research. It is the easiest to grasp, it is used across many fields of science, and it is most "pure" in terms of the standards of the positivist-oriented, quantitative style.

Experimental research builds on the principles of a positivist approach more directly than do the other research techniques.[1] Researchers in the natural sciences (e.g., chemistry and physics), related applied fields (e.g., agriculture, engineering, and medicine), and social work conduct experiments. The logic that guides an experiment on plant growth in biology or testing a metal in engineering is applied in experiments on human social behavior. Although it is most widely used in psychology, the experiment is found in education, criminal justice, journalism, marketing, nursing, political science, social work, and sociology. This chapter focuses first on the experiment conducted in a laboratory under controlled conditions, then looks at experiments conducted in the field.

The experiment's basic logic extends common-sense thinking. Commonsense experiments are less careful or systematic than scientifically based experiments. In commonsense language an *experiment* means modifying something in a situation, then comparing an outcome to what existed without the modification. For example, you try to start your car. To your surprise, it does not start. You "experiment" by cleaning off the battery connections, then try to start it again. You modified something (cleaned the connections) and compared the outcome (whether the car started) to the previous situation (it did not start). You began with an implicit "hypothesis"—a buildup of crud on the connections is the reason the car is not starting, and once the crud is cleaned off, the car will start. This illustrates three things researchers do in experiments: (1) begin with a hypothesis, (2) modify something in a situation, and (3) compare outcomes with and without the modification.

Compared to the other social work research techniques, experimental research is the strongest for testing causal relationships because the three conditions for causality (temporal order, association, and no alternative explanations) are clearly met in experimental designs.

Research Questions Appropriate for an Experiment

The Issue of an Appropriate Technique. Social work researchers use different research techniques (e.g., experiments and surveys) because some research questions can be addressed with certain techniques but not with others. New researchers often ask which research technique best fits which problem. This is difficult to answer because there is no fixed match between problem and technique. The answer is: Make an informed judgment.

General guidelines exist for fitting techniques to problems. Beyond guidelines, you can develop judgment from reading research reports, understanding the strengths and weaknesses of different techniques, assisting more experienced researchers with their research, and gaining practical experience.

Research Questions for Experimental Research. The logic of experimental design guides the types of research problems best addressed by experiments. A crucial factor is that in experimental design, a researcher changes a situation and has control over the setting in which the change is introduced. Only those research problems that let a researcher manipulate conditions are appropriate for experimental research. For example, experimental research cannot answer questions such as, "Do people who complete a college education increase their average annual income?" Researchers cannot randomly assign thousands of people across the country to a college or noncollege group. Even when a whole nation is not involved, many situations cannot be controlled. For example, do people who have younger siblings (brothers and sisters) have better leadership skills than only children? Researchers cannot assign couples to groups and then force them to produce or not produce children so that they can examine leadership skills.

Social work researchers are more limited than natural scientists in the degree to which they can intervene for research purposes. They are very creative in inventing treatments for independent variables (e.g., pressure to conform, anxiety, cooperation, high self-esteem, etc.), but they cannot manipulate many independent variables (e.g., sex, marital status, age, religious belief, level of income, parents' political affiliation, or size of community where raised). Researchers must decide which research design is most effective for answering the specific question, within practical and ethical limitations. For example, a research question is, "Does fear of crime affect the behaviors of elderly people by motivating them to seek self-protection and security?" An experimental researcher creates different levels of fear of crime among groups of elderly subjects. To create a fear of crime, he or she has subjects read about crimes, shows them films about crime, or places them in fear-inducing situations (e.g., in a locked room with a dangerous-looking person who makes threatening statements). Next, the researcher measures whether the subjects act in self-protective ways (e.g., push a button to create a physical barrier between themselves and the dangerous person) or answer questions about hypothetical situations involving security in certain ways (e.g., plan to buy new locks).

Other techniques (e.g., survey research) can address the same issue. A survey researcher asks elderly people questions about how much they fear crime and what they have done for self-protection and security. The researcher measures fear by asking subjects to tell how much they already fear crime on the basis of past experiences.

A source of confusion is that social work researchers can use a prior fixed condition (e.g., age or sex) as a variable in experiments. For example, Spillers (1982) asked whether age affected a child's decision to play with a child who is disabled. Her subjects were 32 preschool and 32 third-grade children. She showed each subject four pairs of photos, each pair showing one child in a wheelchair and the other standing. The children in the photographs were mixed for physical attractiveness, age, and sex. Each subject was asked, "Which child would you like to play with?" Spillers found that more third-graders than preschool children accepted the child with disabilities. Spillers did not modify the independent variable—age—to find its effect on the dependent variable—playmate choice—but she manipulated the decision process and controlled the setting in which it occurred.

A Short History of the Experiment in Social Work Research

The experimental method was borrowed by the social sciences from the natural sciences, and began in psychology. It was not widely accepted in psychology until after 1900.[2]

Wilhelm M. Wundt (1832–1920), a German psychologist and physiologist, introduced the experimental method into psychology. During the late 1800s Germany was the center of graduate education, and leading social scientists from around the world went to Germany to study. Wundt established a laboratory for experimentation in psychology that became a model for many other social work researchers. By 1900, researchers at many U.S. and other universities established psychology laboratories to conduct experimental social work research. The experiment replaced a more philosophical, introspective, integrative approach that was closer to interpretive social science. For example, William James (1842–1910), the foremost U.S. philosopher and psychologist of the 1890s, did not use or embrace the experimental method.

From the turn of the century to the time of World War II, the experimental method was elaborated and became entrenched in social work research. The method's widespread appeal was that it offered an objective, unbiased, scientific way to study human mental and social life at a time when the scientific study of social life was just gaining acceptance.

Four trends speeded the expansion of the experimental method in this period: the rise of behaviorism, the spread of quantification, various changes in research subjects, and practical applications.

Behaviorism is a school of psychology founded in the 1920s by the American John B. Watson (1878–1958) and extended by B. F. Skinner (1904–1990). It emphasized measuring observable behavior or outcomes of mental life and advocated the experimental method for conducting rigorous empirical tests of hypotheses. It became an influential, if not the dominant, school in American psychology.

Quantification, or measuring social phenomena with numbers, also grew between 1900 and 1940. Researchers reconceptualized social constructs so that they could be quantified, and other constructs (e.g., spirit, consciousness, will) were jettisoned from empirical research. An example is measuring mental ability by the IQ test. Originally developed by Alfred Binet (1857–1911), a Frenchman, the intelligence test was translated into English and revised by 1916. It was widely used, and the ability to express something as subjective as mental ability in a single score had public appeal as an objective way to rank and sort people. In fact, between the years of 1921 and 1936, over 5,000 articles were published on intelligence tests.[3] Many scaling and index techniques were developed in this period, and social work researchers began to use applied statistics.

Early reports of empirical social work research gave the names of the people who participated in research, and most early subjects were professional researchers. During the first half of the twentieth century, reports treated subjects anonymously and reported only the results of their actions. Subjects were primarily college students or school children.

These changes reflected an increasingly objective and distant relationship between the researcher and the people studied.

People increasingly used experimental methods for applied purposes. For example, intelligence testing was adopted by the U.S. Army during World War I to sort thousands of men into different positions. The leader of the "scientific management" movement, Frederick W. Taylor (1856–1915), advocated the use of the experimental method in factories and worked with management to modify factory conditions to increase worker productivity.

Through the 1950s and 1960s researchers continued to use the experimental method. They became concerned with artifacts, or sources of alternative explanations that could slip into experimental design. They discovered new artifacts and created ways to reduce these possible sources of systematic error in experiments with new research designs and statistical procedures. Experiments became more logically rigorous, and by the 1970s methodological criteria were increasingly used to evaluate research. A related trend that began in the 1960s was the increased use of deception and a concern with ethical issues. For example, a now common practice of debriefing did not come into use until the mid-1960s.[4] The experiment is still widely used because of its logical rigor and simplicity, consistency with positivist assumptions, and relatively low cost.

RANDOM ASSIGNMENT

Social work researchers frequently want to compare. For example, a researcher has two groups of 15 students and wants to compare the groups on the basis of a key difference between them (e.g., a course that one group completed). Or a researcher has five groups of customers and wants to compare the groups on the basis of one characteristic (e.g., geographic location). The cliché, "Compare apples to apples, don't compare apples to oranges," is not about fruit; it is about comparisons. It means that a valid comparison depends on comparing things that are fundamentally alike. Random assignment facilitates comparison in experiments by creating similar groups.

When making comparisons, researchers want to compare cases that do not differ with regard to variables that offer alternative explanations. For example, a researcher compares two groups of students to determine the impact of completing a course. In order to be compared, the two groups must be similar in most respects except for taking the course. If the group that completed the course is also older than the group that did not, for example, the researcher cannot determine whether completing the course or being older accounts for differences between the groups.

Why Randomly Assign?

Random assignment is a method for assigning cases (e.g., individuals, organizations, etc.) to groups for the purpose of making comparisons. It is a way to divide or sort a collection of cases into two or more groups in order to increase one's confidence that the groups do not differ in a systematic way. It is a mechanical method; the assignment is automatic, and the researcher cannot make assignments on the basis of personal preference or the features of specific cases.

Random assignment is random in a statistical or mathematical sense, not in an everyday sense. In everyday speech *random* means unplanned, haphazard, or accidental, but it has a specialized meaning in mathematics. In probability theory *random* describes a process in which each case has a known chance of being selected. Random selection lets a researcher calculate the odds that a specific case will be sorted into one group over another. Thus, the selection process obeys mathematical laws, which makes precise calculations possible. For example, a random process is one in which all cases have an exactly equal chance of ending up in one or the other group.

The wonderful thing about a random process is that over many separate random occurrences, predictable things happen. Although the process is entirely due to chance and it is impossible to predict a specific outcome at a specific time, very accurate predictions are possible over many situations.

Random assignment or randomization is unbiased because a researcher's desire to confirm a hypothesis or a research subject's personal interests do not enter into the selection process. *Unbiased* does not mean that groups with identical characteristics are selected in each specific situation of random assignment. Instead, it says something close to that: The probability of selecting a case can be mathematically determined, and, in the long run, the groups will be identical.

Sampling and random assignment are processes of systematically selecting cases for inclusion in a study. When a researcher randomly assigns, he or she sorts a collection of cases into two or more groups by using a random process. By contrast, in random sampling he or she selects a smaller subset of cases from a larger pool of cases (see Figure 9.1). A researcher can both sample and randomly assign. He or she can first sample to obtain

a smaller set of cases (e.g., 150 people out of 20,000) and then use random assignment to divide the smaller set into groups (e.g., divide the 150 people into three groups of 50).

How to Randomly Assign

Random assignment is very simple in practice. A researcher begins with a collection of cases (individuals, organizations, or whatever the unit of analysis is), then divides it into two or more groups by a random process, such as asking people to count off, tossing a coin, or throwing dice. For example, a researcher wants to divide 32 people into two groups of 16. A random method is writing each person's name on a slip of paper, putting the slips into a hat, mixing the slips with eyes closed, then draw-

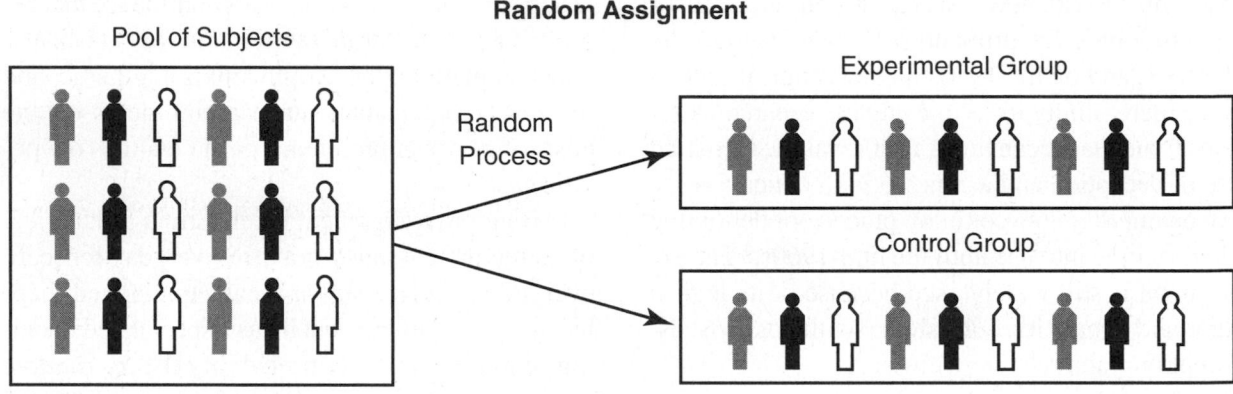

FIGURE 9.1   Random Assignment and Random Sampling

ing the first 16 names for group 1 and the second 16 for group 2.

Because random assignment for a specific situation gives only probabilities, a specific situation can be unusual and the groups can differ. For example, it is possible, though extremely unlikely, that all cases with one characteristic will end up in one group (see the example in Figure 9.2).

Matching versus Random Assignment

If the purpose of random assignment is to get two (or more) equivalent groups, would it not be simpler to match the characteristics of cases in each group? Some researchers match cases in groups on certain characteristics, such as age and sex. Matching is an alternative to random assignment, but it is an infrequently used one.

Matching presents a problem: What are the relevant characteristics to match on, and can one locate exact matches? Individual cases differ in thousands of ways, and the researcher cannot know which might be relevant. For example, a researcher compares two groups of 15 students. There are 8 males in one group, which means there should be 8 males in the other group. Two males in the first group are only children; one is from a divorced fam-

ily, one from an intact family. One is tall, slender, and Jewish; the other is short, heavy, and Methodist. In order to match groups, does the researcher have to find a tall Jewish male only child from a divorced home and a short Methodist male only child from an intact home? The tall, slender, Jewish male only child is 22 years old and is studying to become a physician. The short, heavy Methodist male is 20 years old and wants to be an accountant. Does the researcher also need to match the age and career aspirations of the two males? True matching soon becomes an impossible task.

EXPERIMENTAL DESIGN LOGIC

The Language of Experiments

Experimental research has its own language or set of terms and concepts. You already encountered the basic ideas: random assignment and independent and dependent variables. In experimental research the cases or people used in research projects and on whom variables are measured are called the *subjects*.

Parts of the Experiment.   We can divide the experiment into seven parts. Not all experiments have all these parts, and some have all seven parts plus

Step 1: Begin with a collection of subjects.

Step 2: Devise a method to randomize that is purely mechanical (e.g., flip a coin).

Step 3: Assign subjects with "Heads" to one group   and "Tails" to the other group.

Control Group

Experimental Group

FIGURE 9.2   How to Randomly Assign

others. The following seven, to be discussed here, make up a true experiment:

1. Treatment or independent variable
2. Dependent variable
3. Pretest
4. Posttest
5. Experimental group
6. Control group
7. Random assignment

In most experiments, a social work researcher creates a situation or enters into an ongoing situation, then modifies it. The *treatment* (or the stimulus or manipulation) is what the researcher modifies. The term comes from medicine, in which a physician administers a treatment to patients; the physician intervenes in a physical or psychological condition to change it. It is the independent variable or a combination of independent variables. In earlier examples of measurement, a researcher developed a measurement instrument or indicator (e.g., a survey question), then applied it to a person or case. In experiments, researchers "measure" independent variables by creating a condition or situation. For example, the independent variable is "degree of fear or anxiety"; the levels are high fear and low fear. Instead of asking subjects whether they are fearful, experimenters put subjects into either a high-fear or a low-fear situation. They measure the independent variable by manipulating conditions so that some subjects feel a lot of fear and others feel little.

Researchers go to great lengths to create treatments. Some are as minor as giving different groups of subjects different instructions. Others can be as complex as putting subjects into situations with elaborate equipment, staged physical settings, or contrived social situations to manipulate what the subjects see or feel. Researchers want the treatment to have an impact and produce specific reactions, feelings, or behaviors.

For example, a mock jury decision is one type of a treatment. Johnson (1985) asked subjects to watch a videotape of a child-abuse trial about a man who brought his 2-year-old son to an emergency room with a skull fracture. The videotapes were the same, except that in one the man's attorney argued that the father was a highly religious person who followed the word of God in the Bible in all family affairs. In the other videotape no such statement was made. The dependent variable was a decision of guilty or innocent and a recommended sentence for guilty decisions. Contrary to common sense, Johnson found that subjects were more likely to find the religious defendant guilty and to recommend longer sentences.

Dependent variables or outcomes in experimental research are the physical conditions, social behaviors, attitudes, feelings, or beliefs of subjects that change in response to a treatment. Dependent variables can be measured by paper-and-pencil indicators, observation, interviews, or physiological responses (e.g., heartbeat or sweating palms). An example is a study by Stephens and colleagues (1985) on helping people who have mobility limitations. In the experiment, subjects were 40 males and 40 females walking across a university campus, who encountered either a woman who was in a wheelchair or a woman who was not in a wheelchair. The woman asked for help in finding a lost earring in a hallway. The dependent variable was the number of minutes the subject spent helping find the earring, as measured by an observer a short distance away who appeared to be reading a book.

Frequently, a researcher measures the dependent variable more than once during an experiment. The *pretest* is the measurement of the dependent variable prior to introduction of the treatment. The *posttest* is the measurement of the dependent variable after the treatment has been introduced into the experimental situation.

Experimental social work researchers often divide subjects into two or more groups for purposes of comparison. A simple experiment has two groups, only one of which receives the treatment. The *experimental group* is the group that receives the treatment or in which the treatment is present. The group that does not receive the treatment is called the *control group*. When the independent variable takes on many different values, more than one experimental group is used.

Steps in Conducting an Experiment. Following the basic steps of the research process, experimenters decide on a topic, narrow it into a testable research problem or question, then develop a hypothesis with variables. Once a researcher has the hypothesis, the steps of experimental research are clear.

A crucial early step is to plan a specific experimental design (to be discussed). The researcher decides the number of groups to use, how and when to create treatment conditions, the number of times to measure the dependent variable, and what the groups of subjects will experience from beginning to end. He or she also develops measures of the dependent variable and pilot tests the experiment (see Box 9.1).

The experiment itself begins after a researcher locates subjects and randomly assigns them to groups. Subjects are given precise, preplanned instructions. Next, the researcher measures the dependent variable in a pretest before the treatment. One group is then exposed to the treatment. Finally, the researcher measures the dependent variable in a posttest. He or she also interviews subjects about the experiment before they leave. The researcher records measures of the dependent variable and examines the results for each group to see whether the hypothesis receives support.

Control in Experiments. Control is crucial in experimental research.[5] A researcher wants to control all aspects of the experimental situation to isolate the effects of the treatment and eliminate alternative explanations. Aspects of an experimental situation that are not controlled by the researcher are alternatives to the treatment for change in the dependent variable and undermine his or her attempt to establish causality.

Experimental researchers use deception to control the experimental setting. *Deception* occurs when the researcher intentionally misleads subjects through written or verbal instructions, the actions of others, or aspects of the setting. It may involve the use of *confederates* or stooges—people who pretend to be other subjects or bystanders but who actually work for the researcher and deliberately mislead subjects. Through deception the researcher tries to control what the subjects see and hear and what they believe is occurring. For example, a researcher's instructions falsely lead subjects to believe that they are participating in a study about group cooperation. In fact, the experiment

Box 9.1

Steps in Conducting an Experiment

1. Begin with a straightforward hypothesis that is appropriate for experimental research.
2. Decide on an experimental design that will test the hypothesis within practical limitations.
3. Decide how to introduce the treatment or create a situation that induces the independent variable.
4. Develop a valid and reliable measure of the dependent variable.
5. Set up an experimental setting and conduct a pilot test of the treatment and dependent variable measures.
6. Locate appropriate subjects or cases.
7. Randomly assign subjects to groups (if random assignment is used in the chosen research design) and give careful instructions.
8. Gather data for the pretest measure of the dependent variable for all groups (if a pretest is used in the chosen design).
9. Introduce the treatment to the experimental group only (or to relevant groups if there are multiple experimental groups) and monitor all groups.
10. Gather data for posttest measure of the dependent variable.
11. *Debrief* the subjects by informing them of the true purpose and reasons for the experiment. Ask subjects what they thought was occurring. Debriefing is crucial when subjects have been deceived about some aspect of the experiment.
12. Examine data collected and make comparisons between different groups. Where appropriate, use statistics and graphs to determine whether or not the hypothesis is supported.

is about male/female verbal interaction, and what subjects say is being secretly tape recorded. Deception lets the researcher control the subjects' definition of the situation. It prevents them from altering their cross-sex verbal behavior because they are unaware of the true research topic. By focusing their attention on a false topic, the researcher induces the unaware subjects to act "naturally." For realistic deception, researchers may invent false treatments and dependent variable measures to keep subjects unaware of the true ones. The use of deception in experiments raises ethical issues (to be discussed).

Design Notation

Experiments can be designed in many ways. *Design notation* is a shorthand system for symbolizing the parts of experimental design.[6] Once you learn design notation, you will find it easier to think about and compare designs. For example, design notation expresses a complex, paragraph-long description of the parts of an experiment in five or six symbols arranged in two lines. It uses the following symbols: O = observation of dependent variable; X = treatment, independent variable; R = random assignment.

The Os are numbered with subscripts from left to right based on time order. Pretests are O_1, posttests O_2. When the independent variable has more than two levels, the Xs are subscripted with letters to distinguish among them. Symbols are in time order from left to right. The R is first, followed by the pretest, the treatment, and then the posttest. Symbols are arranged in rows, with each row representing a group of subjects. For example, an experiment with three groups has an R (if random assignment is used), followed by three rows of Os and Xs. The rows are on top of each other because the pretests, treatment, and posttest occur in each group at about the same time. Table 9.1 gives the notation for many standard experimental designs.

TABLE 9.1   Summary of Experimental Designs with Notation

NAME OF DESIGN	DESIGN NOTATION
Classical experimental design	R $\quad$ O_1 $\qquad$ X $\qquad$ O_2 $\quad$ O_1 $\qquad\qquad$ O_2
Preexperimental Designs	
One-shot case study	X $\qquad$ O
One-group pretest–posttest	O_1 $\qquad$ X $\qquad$ O_2
Static group comparison	X $\qquad$ O $\qquad$ O
Quasi-Experimental Designs	
Two-group posttest only	R $\quad$ X $\qquad\qquad$ O $\qquad\qquad\qquad$ O
Interrupted time series	O_1 $\ O_2$ $\quad$ O_3 $\ O_4$ X $\ O_5 O_6 O_7$
Equivalent time series	O X $\quad$ O X $\quad$ O X O X O
Latin square designs	R $\quad$ $O_1\ X_a\ O_2\ X_b\ O_3\ X_c\ O_4$ $\quad O_1\ X_b\ O_2\ X_a\ O_3\ X_c\ O_4$ $\quad O_1\ X_c\ O_2\ X_b\ O_4\ X_a\ O_4$ $\quad O_1\ X_a\ O_2\ X_c\ O_4\ X_b\ O_4$ $\quad O_1\ X_b\ O_2\ X_c\ O_4\ X_a\ O_4$ $\quad O_1\ X_c\ O_2\ X_a\ O_4\ X_b\ O_4$
Solomon four-group design	$\quad$ O_1 $\qquad$ X $\qquad$ O_2 $\quad$ O_1 $\qquad\qquad$ O_2 R $\qquad\qquad$ X $\qquad$ O_2 $\qquad\qquad\qquad$ O_2
Factorial designs	$\quad$ X_1 $\quad$ Z_1 $\quad$ O R $\quad$ X_1 $\quad$ Z_2 $\quad$ O $\quad$ X_2 $\quad$ Z_1 $\quad$ O $\quad$ X_2 $\quad$ Z_2 $\quad$ O

Types of Design

Researchers combine parts of an experiment (e.g., pretests, control groups, etc.) into an *experimental design.* For example, some designs lack pretests, some do not have control groups, and others have many experimental groups. Certain widely used standard designs have names.

You should learn the standard designs for two reasons. First, in research reports social work researchers give the *name* of a standard design instead of *describing* it. When reading reports, you will be able to understand the design of the experiment if you know the standard designs. Second, the standard designs illustrate common ways to combine design parts. You can use them for experiments you conduct, or create your own variations.

The designs are illustrated with two examples. In the first a researcher wants to find out whether learning is faster if accompanied by quiet classical music or by silence. The experiment involves having rats run a maze. The treatment is classical music, and the dependent variable is the speed of completing the maze. In the second example the researcher wants to find out whether students are more accepting of violence after viewing a horror film. The treatment is a film with violence and gore, and the dependent variable is the subjects' attitudes toward violence.

Classical Experimental Design. All designs are variations of the *classical experimental design,* the type of design discussed so far, which has random assignment, a pretest and a posttest, an experimental group, and a control group. In example 1 the researcher randomly divides rats into two groups and measures their speed. Rats run the maze and the researcher records speeds; one group hears music and the other does not. In example 2 the researcher randomly divides students into two groups and measures their attitudes with a questionnaire. One group watches a violent horror film, the other a nonhorror film; the researcher then measures attitudes again.

Preexperimental Designs. Some designs lack random assignment and are compromises or shortcuts. These *preexperimental designs* are used in situations in which it is difficult to use the classical design. They have weaknesses that make inferring a causal relationship more difficult.

One-Shot Case Study Design. Also called the one-group posttest-only design, the *one-shot case study design* has only one group, a treatment, and a posttest. Because there is only one group, there is no random assignment. In example 1 the researcher puts a group of rats into a maze with classical music playing and records their speed. In example 2 the researcher shows a group of students a horror film, then measures their attitudes with a questionnaire. A weakness of this design is that it is difficult to say for sure that the treatment affected the dependent variable. If subjects were the same before and after the treatment, the researcher would not know it.

One-Group Pretest–Posttest Design. This design has one group, a pretest, a treatment, and a posttest. It lacks a control group and random assignment. In example 1 the researcher measures the speed of a group of rats, has them run a maze while he or she plays music, and measures their speed again. In example 2 the researcher gives a group of students an attitude questionnaire to complete, shows a horror film, then has them complete another questionnaire. This is an improvement over the one-shot case study because the researcher measures the dependent variable both before and after the treatment. But it lacks a control group. The researcher cannot know whether something other than the treatment occurred between the pretest and the posttest to cause the outcome.

Static Group Comparison. Also called the posttest-only nonequivalent group design, *static group comparison* has two groups, treatment, and a posttest. It lacks random assignment and a pretest. In example 1 the researcher has two groups of rats. One group runs a maze with music, the other without music. He or she measures each group's speed. In example 2 the researcher lets students form two groups themselves. He or she shows one group a horror film and the other a nonhorror film. Both groups then complete the questionnaire. A weakness is that any posttest outcome difference between the groups could be due to group differences prior to the experiment instead of to the treatment.

A static group comparison experiment is Shively's (1992) study on perceptions of Western films among Native Americans and Anglos. Her hypothesis was that a person's ethnically based cultural background influences what that person sees or enjoys in a film with relevant themes. Shively created matched samples of 20 Native American males and 20 Anglo males (European ancestry). The subjects lived in a town of about 1,200 on a Native American reservation in the western United States. The groups were matched on income, education, employment status, occupation, and age. They ranged in age from 36 to 64 years. Both groups watched *The Searchers,* a 1956 Western film starring John Wayne that was a top-grossing film in the 1950s. It shows the standard "cowboy and Indian" conflict. The film was watched in private homes with a group of five ethnically similar male friends.

Shively measured views on the film (the dependent variable) with a written questionnaire and group interview. She found that both groups liked the film, enjoyed its "action," and most identified with one of the lead "cowboy" characters. No one favored the Native Americans, who were portrayed in the film with negative stereotypes as violent savages. The Native American subjects identified with cowboys in the film and saw them as similar to contemporary Native Americans. A difference was that the Native American subjects enjoyed the landscape scenery and the portrayal of an idealized cowboy way of life, which they saw as a myth or fantasy. By contrast, the Anglos saw the film as authentic history; they took it to be reality. Another difference was that the Native American subjects rated bravery and toughness as making a good hero in a Western. Anglos did not rate these high, but rated honesty and intelligence as top characteristics. Shively indirectly manipulated the independent variable, which was the subject's ethnicity combined with viewing the film. She used two groups, but no pretest, and substituted matching for randomization.

Quasi-Experimental and Special Designs. These designs, just as the classical design, make identifying a causal relationship more certain than do pre-experimental designs. *Quasi-experimental designs* help researchers test for causal relationships in a variety of situations wherein the classical design is difficult or inappropriate. They are called *quasi* because they are variations of the classical experimental design. Some have randomization but lack a pretest, some use more than two groups, and others substitute many observations of one group over time for a control group. In general, the researcher has less control over the independent variable than in the classical design.

Two-Group Posttest-Only Design. This is identical to the static group comparison, with one exception: The groups are randomly assigned. It has all the parts of the classical design except a pretest. The random assignment reduces the chance that the groups differed before the treatment, but without a pretest, a researcher cannot be as certain that the groups began the same on the dependent variable. For example, Johnson and Johnson (1985) used a two-group posttest-only design. In the experiment sixth-grade students were randomly assigned to one of two conditions: work groups in which points were awarded for how well the entire class learned material, or groups in which each group competed against others for points. All groups were mixed by race, sex, and ability level. Several dependent variables were measured, including academic achievement, cooperation across racial groups, and attitude toward others. The dependent variables were measured only after working in groups on an instruction unit for 10 days. The main result was that cooperative groups were more likely to promote cooperation and friendship across racial lines.

Interrupted Time Series. In an *interrupted time series* design a researcher uses one group and makes multiple pretest measures before and after the treatment. For example, after remaining level for many years, in 1979 cigarette taxes jumped 35 percent. Taxes remained relatively constant for the next 10 years. The hypothesis is that increases in taxes lower cigarette consumption. A researcher plots the rate of cigarette consumption for 1970 through 1990. The researcher notes that cigarette consumption was level during the nine years prior to the new taxes, then dropped in 1979 and stayed about the same for the next 10 years.

Equivalent Time Series. An *equivalent time series* is another one-group design that extends over a time period. Instead of one treatment, it has a pretest, then a treatment and posttest, then treatment and posttest, then treatment and posttest, and so on. For example, people who drive motorcycles were not required to wear helmets before 1975, when a law was passed requiring helmets. In 1981 the law was repealed because of pressure from motorcycle clubs. The helmet law was reinstated in 1989. The researcher's hypothesis is that wearing protective helmets results in a lower number of head injury deaths in accidents. The researcher plots head injury death rates in motorcycle accidents over time. He or she finds the rate was very high prior to 1975, dropped sharply between 1975 and 1981, then rose to pre-1975 levels between 1981 and 1989, then dropped again from 1989 to the present.

Latin Square Design. For an example of *Latin square design,* consider a social work instructor who has three units to teach social work students in a practice class: understanding body language, using content-relevant conversational skills, and how to conduct an intake interview. The units can be taught in any order, but the teacher wants to know which order most helps students learn. In one class students first learn to read body language, then how to make content-relevant converational responses, and finally how to conduct an intake interview. In another class the content-relevant conversational skills are taught first, body language is second, and the intake interview is last. In a third class the instructor teaches intake interviews first, content-relevant conversation second, and body language last. The students take tests after each unit, and a comprehensive exam at the end of the term. The students were randomly assigned to classes, so the instructor can see whether presenting units in one sequence or another resulted in improved learning.

Solomon Four-Group Design. A researcher may believe that the pretest measure has an influence on the treatment or dependent variable. A pretest can sometimes sensitize subjects to the treatment or improve their performance on the posttest (see the discussion of testing effect to come). Richard L. Solomon developed the *Solomon four-group design*

to address the issue of pretest effects. It combines the classical experimental design with the two-group posttest-only design and randomly assigns subjects to one of four groups. For example, a mental health worker wants to determine whether a new training method improves clients' coping skills. The worker measures coping skills with a 20-minute test of reactions to stressful events. Because the clients might learn coping skills from taking the test itself, a Solomon four-group design is used. The mental health worker randomly divides clients into four groups. Two groups receive the pretest; one of them gets the new training method and the other gets the old method. Another two groups receive no pretest; one of them gets the new method and the other the old method. All four groups are given the same posttest, and the posttest results are compared. If the two treatment (new method) groups have similar results, and the two control (old method) groups have similar results, then the mental health worker knows pretest learning is not a problem. If the two groups with a pretest (one treatment, one control) differ from the two groups without a pretest, then the worker concludes that the pretest itself may have an effect on the dependent variable.

Factorial Design. Sometimes a research question suggests looking at the simultaneous effects of more than one independent variable. A *factorial design* uses two or more independent variables in combination. Every combination of the categories in variables (sometimes called *factors*) is examined. When each variable contains several categories, the number of combinations grows very quickly. The treatment or manipulation is not each independent variable; rather, it is each combination of the categories. For example, a researcher examines the productivity of work groups. The research question is, "Does productivity vary under different combinations of group cooperation and stress?" The independent variables are "level of cooperation" and "degree of stress," and the dependent variable is "productivity." The level of cooperation has two categories, cooperative and noncooperative; the degree of stress has three categories, high, medium, and low. There are six combinations of categories for the two variables (see Box 9.2).

Box 9.2

Example of Factorial Design with Two Variables

LEVEL OF COOPERATION	DEGREE OF STRESS		
	Low	*Medium*	*High*
Competitive	Group 1	Group 2	Group 3
Cooperative	Group 4	Group 5	Group 6

Group Number		*Design Notation*		
1		X_1	Z_1	O
2		X_1	Z_2	O
3	R	X_1	Z_3	O
4		X_2	Z_1	O
5		X_2	Z_2	O
6		X_2	Z_3	O

Where
X_1 = noncooperative group, X_2 = cooperative group
Z_1 = low stress, Z_2 = medium stress, Z_3 = high stress

GRAPHS PLOTTING HYPOTHETICAL RESULTS

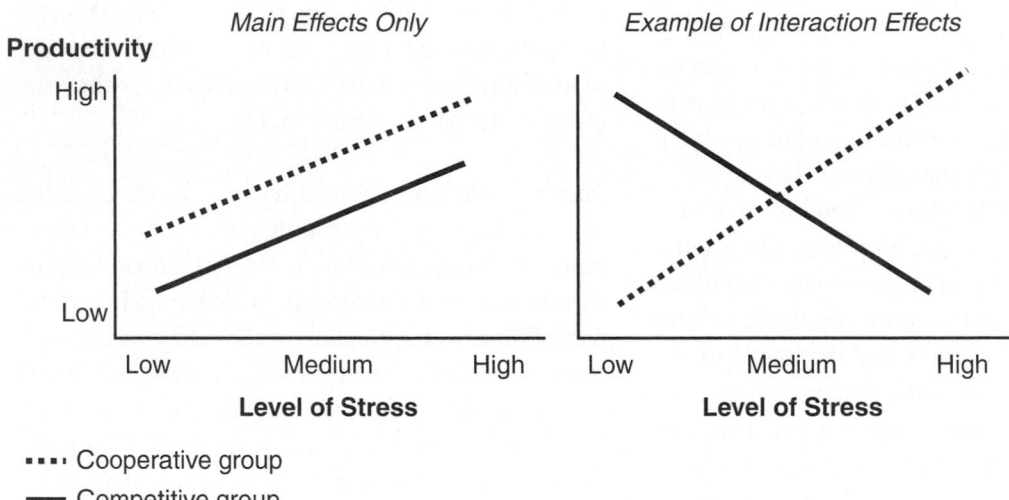

Main Effects Only   *Example of Interaction Effects*

···· Cooperative group
— Competitive group

The treatments in a factorial design can have two kinds of effects on the dependent variable: main effects and interaction effects. Only *main effects* are present in one-factor or single-treatment designs. In a factorial design specific combinations of independent variable categories can also have an effect. They are called *interaction effects* because the categories in a combination interact to produce an effect beyond that of each variable alone. For example, Bar-

dack and McAndrew (1985) wanted to determine the effects of physical attractiveness and appropriate dress on the decision to hire someone. They had six photographs of females with either high, average, or low attractiveness and appropriate or inappropriate clothing. Subjects saw one of the six photographs with identical resumés and were asked to decide whether to hire the person for an entry-level managerial position in a major corporation. Both variables affected the decision to hire; that is, subjects were more likely to hire attractive and appropriately dressed people. In addition to these main effects, the experimenters found interaction effects; attractive and well-dressed women were much more likely to be hired than would be expected as a result of either dress or appearance alone. Combined, the two factors gave an extra boost to the hiring decision, with physical attractiveness having a stronger effect.

The effects can be shown in the example of the impact of cooperation and stress on the productivity of five-person work groups. A social work researcher measures productivity by the percentage of a complicated jigsaw puzzle completed in two hours. There is a separate group for each combination, so the researcher computes the number of groups by multiplying the number of levels or categories in each variable. The stress variable has three levels and the cooperation variable two levels, so the researcher uses six groups, one for each combination (see Box 9.2).

The researcher pays subjects in the cooperative groups equally by dividing the reward by five. The subjects in competitive groups are paid a percentage of the group reward based on the number of pieces each one correctly places. In the low-stress situation, the researcher gives the group one dollar for each one percent of the puzzle completed in two hours, up to $100. In the medium-stress situation, he or she uses the same pay system but adds a $50 bonus if the puzzle is completed in one hour. In the high-stress condition, he or she pays the group $100 for a completed puzzle and nothing if it is incomplete, and he or she also doubles the reward to $200 if the group completes the puzzle in one hour.

The main effect for the cooperation factor is that cooperative groups (no matter what the stress level) have higher productivity than the competitive groups. The main effect for the stress factor is that productivity rises as stress increases, whether or not the groups are cooperative. The left-hand graph in Box 9.2 shows main effects. It suggests that for each level of stress, cooperative groups outperform competitive groups, and for both groups, productivity is higher as the level of stress goes up.

The researcher hypothesizes the presence of interaction effects—that is, that specific combina-

tions of the two factors produce specific effects on the dependent variable. For example, he or she finds that cooperative groups work best in high-stress situations, competitive groups work best in low-stress situations, and both types of groups work equally well under medium levels of stress (see the right-hand graph in Box 9.2).

Researchers discuss factorial design in a shorthand way. A "two-by-three factorial design" is written 2 × 3. It means that there are two treatments, with two categories in one and three categories in the other. A 2 × 3 × 3 design means that there are three independent variables, one with two categories and two with three categories each.

Valentine-French and Radtke (1989) used a 2 × 2 × 3 factorial design to study the effect of victim reaction to sexual harassment blame. The subjects were 120 male and 120 female undergraduate volunteers from the University of Calgary. The researchers operationalized the independent variable as an audiotaped vignette in which a professor guaranteed a good grade to a student if she or he was willing to cooperate, permitted caressing of the student's shoulder, and let the professor kiss her or him on the cheek. The experimenters varied the situation by having the student victim be male or female and by using one of three endings: The victim blamed his or her own behavior for the incident, blamed the professor, or gave no reaction. Thus, there were six combinations of victim gender and endings.

The subjects did not know the purpose of the study and listened to the vignette alone. The experimenters measured various background characteristics of the subjects with a questionnaire, as well as the main dependent variable—attribution of blame, or who was at fault. They operationalized the variable as an eight-item index measured with a seven-point Likert scale. Valentine-French and Radtke found that women were more likely to label the incident as sexual harassment and blame the professor. Male subjects, more than females, blamed the victim when the victim made a statement of self-blame. This was a 2 × 2 × 3 factorial design because three independent variables were examined: the subject's gender, the victim's gender, and the victim's reactions. (Also, see Box 9.3.)

Box 9.3 _____

What Did the "Willie Horton" Television Advertisement Do?

Willie Horton became well known in a political advertisement aired during the 1988 presidential campaign. He was a convicted murderer who, on a weekend leave from a Massachusetts state prison, committed rape and torture. Candidate George Bush ran the advertisement against his opponent Michael Dukakis, the governor of Massachusetts when Horton was released. Despite misleading information in it, observers felt the advertisement played on public fears of crime. Critics claimed it also contained a racial message because viewers were shown that Horton was an African American.

Mendelberg (1997) designed an experiment to test whether White viewers responded to the crime or the racist message. Experimental subjects were 77 White, non-Hispanic students from the University of Michigan with a median age of 18 years. Subjects completed a modern racism index with seven items using a five-point Likert scale and were classified as prejudiced or not, based on scores. The students were randomly assigned to two groups and viewed a 50-minute news program. They were told the study was on "horse race" versus "substantive issue" coverage in political campaigns. The experimental group saw a news segment on Willie Horton in the middle of the program, while the control group viewed a segment about pollution that also criticized candidate Dukakis.

In the posttest, subjects completed questionnaires on a range of public issues, including crime control and government programs to reduce racial inequality. After completing the posttest, they were debriefed. The experiment used a two-group posttest-only 2×2 factorial design (racial prejudice or not by Willie Horton advertisement or not). The results suggested that the advertisement was more about race than crime. Viewers of the Horton advertisement did not become greater proponents of anticrime, but prejudiced viewers of it became more opposed to racial equality. The author concluded, "When it is activated by a racially implicit symbol like the Horton story, prejudice will lead to perceptions that African Americans' position has improved and to a sense that Whites are losing their jobs to African Americans. . . . People who are prejudiced become even more resistant to racial equality with exposure to Horton."

INTERNAL AND EXTERNAL VALIDITY

The Logic of Internal Validity

Internal validity means the ability to eliminate alternative explanations of the dependent variable. Variables, other than the treatment, that affect the dependent variable are threats to internal validity. They threaten the researcher's ability to say that the treatment was the true causal factor producing change in the dependent variable. Thus, the logic of internal validity is to rule out variables other than the treatment by controlling experimental conditions and through experimental designs. Next, we examine major threats to internal validity.

Threats to Internal Validity

The following are ten common threats to internal validity.[7]

Selection Bias. _Selection bias_ is the threat that subjects will not form equivalent groups. It is a problem in designs without random assignment. It occurs when subjects in one experimental group have a characteristic that affects the dependent variable. For example, in an experiment on physical aggressiveness, the treatment group unintentionally contains subjects who are football, rugby, and hockey players, whereas the control group is made up of musicians, chess players, and painters. Another example is an experiment on the ability of people to dodge heavy traffic. All subjects assigned to one group come from rural areas, and all subjects in the other grew up in large cities. An examination of pretest scores helps a researcher detect this threat, because no group differences are expected.

History. This is the threat that an event unrelated to the treatment will occur during the experiment and influence the dependent variable. _History effects_ are more likely in experiments that continue over a long time period. For example, halfway through a two-week experiment to evaluate subject attitudes toward space travel, a spacecraft explodes on the launch pad, killing the astronauts. The history effect can occur in the cigarette tax example discussed earlier (see the discussion of interrupted time series design). If a public antismoking campaign or reduced cigarette advertising also began in 1979, it would be hard to say that higher taxes caused less smoking.

Maturation. This is the threat that some biological, psychological, or emotional process within the subjects and separate from the treatment will change over time. *Maturation* is more common in experiments over long time periods. For example, during an experiment on reasoning ability, subjects become bored and sleepy and, as a result, score lower. Another example is an experiment on the styles of children's play between grades 1 and 6. Play styles are affected by physical, emotional, and maturation changes that occur as the children grow older, instead of or in addition to the effects of a treatment. Designs with a pretest and control group help researchers determine whether maturation or history effects are present, because both experimental and control groups will show similar changes over time.

Testing. Sometimes the pretest measure itself affects an experiment. This *testing effect* threatens internal validity because more than the treatment alone affects the dependent variable. The Solomon four-group design helps a researcher detect testing effects. For example, a researcher gives students an examination on the first day of class. The course is the treatment. He or she tests learning by giving the same exam on the last day of class. If subjects remember the pretest questions and this affects what they learned (i.e., paid attention to) or how they answered questions on the posttest, a testing effect is present. If testing effects occur, a researcher cannot say that the treatment alone has affected the dependent variable.

Instrumentation. This threat is related to stability reliability. It occurs when the *instrument* or dependent variable measure changes during the experiment. For example, in a weight-loss experiment, the springs on the scale weaken during the experiment, giving lower readings in the posttest. Another example might have occurred in an experiment by Bond and Anderson (1987) on the reluc-

tance to transmit bad news. The experimenters asked subjects to tell another person the results of an intelligence test and varied the test results to be either well above or well below average. The dependent variable was the length of time it took to tell the test taker the results. Some subjects were told that the session was being videotaped. During the experiment, the video equipment failed to work for one subject. If it had failed to work for more than one subject or had worked for only part of the session, the experiment would have had instrumentation problems. (By the way, subjects took longer to deliver bad news only if they thought they were doing so publicly—that is, being videotaped.)

Mortality. *Mortality,* or attrition, arises when some subjects do not continue throughout the experiment. Although the word *mortality* means death, it does not necessarily mean that subjects have died. If a subset of subjects leaves partway through an experiment, a researcher cannot know whether the results would have been different had the subjects stayed. For example, a researcher begins a weight-loss program with 50 subjects. At the end of the program, 30 remain, each of whom lost 5 pounds with no side effects. The 20 who left could have differed from the 30 who stayed, changing the results. Maybe the program was effective for those who left, and they withdrew after losing 25 pounds. Or perhaps the program made subjects sick and forced them to quit. Researchers should notice and report the number of subjects in each group during pretests and posttests to detect this threat to internal validity.

Statistical Regression. *Statistical regression* is not easy to grasp intuitively. It is a problem of extreme values or a tendency for random errors to move group results toward the average. It can occur in two ways.

One situation arises when subjects are unusual with regard to the dependent variable. Because they begin as unusual or extreme, subjects are unlikely to respond further in the same direction. For example, a researcher wants to see whether violent films make people act violently. He or she chooses a group of violent criminals from a high-security prison, gives them a pretest, shows violent films, then administers a posttest. To the researcher's shock, the criminals are slightly less violent after the film, whereas a control group of nonprisoners who did not see the film are slightly more violent than before. Because the violent criminals began at an extreme, it is unlikely that a treatment could make them more violent; by random chance alone, they appear less extreme when measured a second time.[8]

A second situation involves a problem with the measurement instrument. If many subjects score very high (at the ceiling) or very low (at the floor) on a variable, random chance alone will produce a change between the pretest and the posttest. For example, a researcher gives 80 subjects a test, and 75 get perfect scores. He or she then gives a treatment to raise scores. Because so many subjects already had perfect scores, random errors will reduce the group average because those who got perfect scores can randomly move in only one direction—to get some answers wrong. An examination of scores on pretests will help researchers detect this threat to internal validity.

Diffusion of Treatment.   *Diffusion of treatment,* or *contamination,* is the threat that subjects in different groups will communicate with each other and learn about the other's treatment. Researchers avoid it by isolating groups or having subjects promise not to reveal anything to others who will become subjects. For example, subjects participate in a day-long experiment on a new way to memorize words. During a break, treatment group subjects tell those in the control group about the new way to memorize, which control group subjects then use. A researcher needs outside information such as postexperiment interviews with subjects to detect this threat.

Compensatory Behavior.   Some experiments provide something of value to one group of subjects but not to another, and the difference becomes known. The inequality may produce pressure to reduce differences, competitive rivalry between groups, or resentful demoralization. All these types of *compensatory behavior* can affect the dependent variable in addition to the treatment. For example, one school system receives a treatment (longer lunch breaks) to produce gains in learning. Once the inequality is known, subjects in the control group demand equal treatment and work extra hard to

learn and overcome the inequality. Smith and Glass (1987:136) called this the *John Henry effect.* Another group becomes demoralized by the unequal treatment and withdraws from learning. It is difficult to detect this threat unless outside information is used (see the earlier discussion of diffusion of treatment).

Experimenter Expectancy.   Although it is not always considered a traditional internal validity problem, the experimenter's behavior, too, can threaten causal logic.[9] A researcher may threaten internal validity, not by purposefully unethical behavior, but by indirectly communicating *experimenter expectancy* to subjects. Social work researchers may be highly committed to the hypothesis and indirectly communicate desired findings to subjects. For example, a researcher studying reactions toward the disabled deeply believes that females are more sensitive toward the disabled than males are. Through eye contact, tone of voice, pauses, and other nonverbal communication, the researcher unconsciously encourages female subjects to report positive feelings toward the disabled; the researcher's nonverbal behavior is the opposite for male subjects.

Here is a way to detect experimenter expectancy. A researcher hires assistants and teaches them experimental techniques. The assistants train subjects and test their learning ability. The researcher gives the assistants fake transcripts and records showing that subjects in one group are honor students and the others are failing, although in fact the subjects are identical. Experimenter expectancy is present if the fake honor students, as a group, do much better than the fake failing students.

The *double-blind experiment* is designed to control researcher expectancy. In it, people who have direct contact with subjects do not know the details of the hypothesis or the treatment. It is *double* blind because both the subjects and those in contact with them are blind to details of the experiment (see Figure 9.3). For example, a researcher wants to see if a new drug is effective. Using pills of three colors—green, yellow, and pink—the researcher puts the new drug in the yellow pill, puts an old drug in the pink one, and makes the green pill a *placebo*—a false treatment that appears to be real (e.g., a sugar pill without any physical effects). Assistants who give the pills and record the effects do not know which color

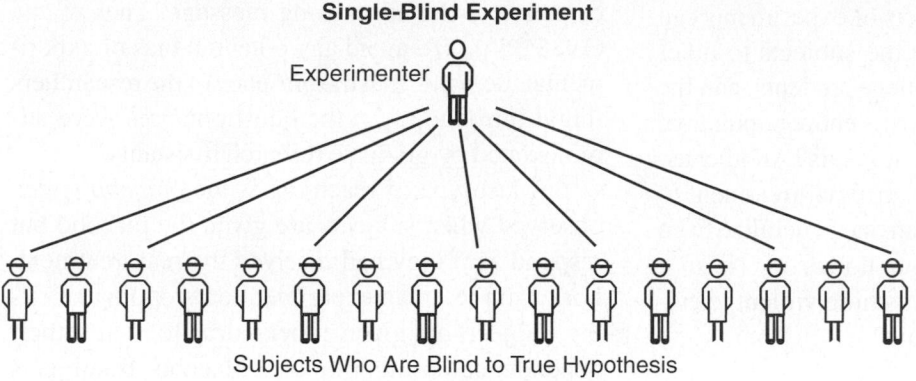

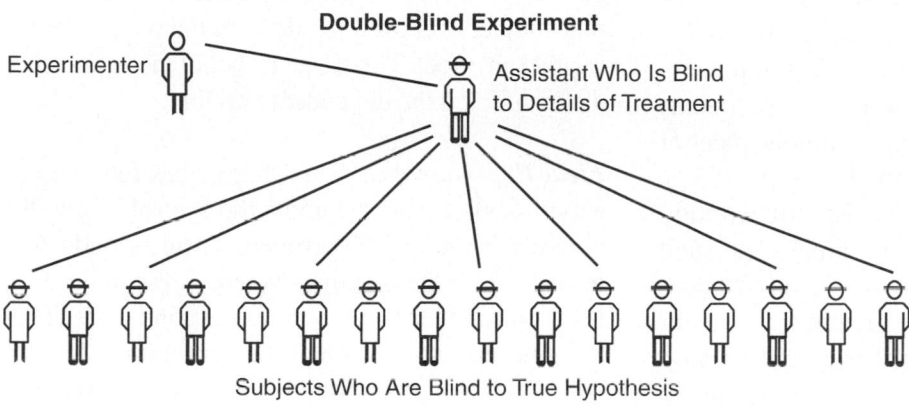

FIGURE 9.3   Double-Blind Experiments: An Illustration of Single-Blind, or Ordinary, and Double-Blind Experiments

contains the new drug. Only another person who does not deal with subjects directly knows which colored pill contains the drug and examines the results.

External Validity and Field Experiments

Even if an experimenter eliminates all concerns about internal validity, external validity remains a potential problem. *External validity* is the ability to generalize experimental findings to events and settings outside the experiment itself. If a study lacks external validity, its findings hold true only in experiments, making them useless to both basic and applied science.

Realism.   Are experiments realistic? There are two types of realism to consider.[10] *Experimental realism* is the impact of an experimental treatment or setting on subjects; it occurs when subjects are caught up in the experiment and are truly influenced by it. It is weak if subjects remain unaffected by the

treatment, which is why researchers go to great lengths to create realistic conditions. Aronson and Carlsmith (1968:25) noted:

All experimental procedures are "contrived" in the sense that they are invented. Indeed, it can be said that the art of experimentation rests primarily on the skill of the investigator to judge the procedure which is the more accurate realization of his conceptual variable and has the greatest impact and the more credibility for the subject.

Mundane realism asks, "Is the experiment like the real world?" For example, a researcher studying learning has subjects memorize four-letter nonsense syllables. Mundane realism would be stronger if he or she had subjects learn factual information used in real life instead of something invented for an experiment alone.

Mundane realism most directly affects external validity—the ability to generalize from experiments to the real world.[11] Two aspects of experiments can be generalized. One is from the subjects to other people. If the subjects are college students, can the researcher generalize results to the entire population, most of whom are not college students? Another aspect is generalizing from an artificial treatment to everyday life. For example, can one generalize from subjects watching a two-hour horror movie in a classroom to the impact of watching violent television programs over many years?

Reactivity. Subjects may react differently in an experiment than they would in real life because they know they are in a study; this is called *reactivity.* The *Hawthorne effect* is a specific kind of reactivity.[12] The name comes from a series of experiments by Elton Mayo at the Hawthorne, Illinois, plant of Westinghouse Electric during the 1920s and 1930s. Researchers modified many aspects of working conditions (e.g., lighting, time for breaks, etc.) and measured productivity. They discovered that productivity rose after each modification, no matter what it was. This curious result occurred because the workers did not respond to the treatment but to the additional attention they received from being part of the experiment and knowing that they were being watched. Later research questioned whether this occurred, but the name is used for an effect from the attention of researchers. A related effect is the effect of something new, which may wear off over time. Smith and Glass (1987:148) have called this the *novelty effect.*

Demand characteristics are another type of reactivity. Subjects may pick up clues about the hypothesis or goal of an experiment, and they may change their behavior to what they think is demanded of them (i.e., support the hypothesis) in order to please the researcher. For example, Chebat and Picard (1988) wanted to see whether people are more persuaded by one-sided (showing only positive features) versus two-sided (showing both positive features and limitations) advertisements. They created professional advertisements for a new soap and a car, with a one-sided and a two-sided advertisement for each. They presented the advertisements to 434 undergraduates at the University of Québec at Montréal who were asked to complete questionnaires with eight Likert-type questions on the ac-

ceptance of the advertising message. They stated (1988:356), "To avoid any potential bias or experimental 'demand' that the presence of the researchers might introduce . . . , the questionnaires were administered by graduate research assistants."

A last type of reactivity is the *placebo effect,* observed when subjects are given the placebo but respond as if they had received the real treatment. For example, in an experiment on stopping smoking, subjects are given either a drug to reduce their dependence on nicotine or a placebo. If subjects who received the placebo also stop smoking, then participating in an experiment and taking something that subjects believed would help them quit smoking had an effect. The subjects' belief in the placebo alone affected the dependent variable.

Field Experiments. This chapter has focused on experiments conducted under the controlled conditions of a laboratory. Experiments are also conducted in real-life or field settings where a researcher has less control over the experimental conditions. The amount of control varies on a continuum. At one end is the highly controlled *laboratory experiment,* which takes place in a specialized setting or laboratory; at the opposite end is the *field experiment,* which takes place in the "field"—in natural settings such as a subway car, a liquor store, or a public sidewalk. Subjects in field experiments are usually unaware that they are involved in an experiment and react in a natural way. For example, researchers have had a confederate fake a heart attack on a subway car to see how the bystanders react.[13]

A dramatic example is a field experiment by Harari and colleagues (1985) on whether a male passerby will attempt to stop an attempted rape. In this experiment, conducted at San Diego State University, an attempted rape was staged on a somewhat isolated campus path in the evening. The staged attack was clearly visible to unsuspecting male subjects who approached alone or in groups of two or three. In the attack, a female student was grabbed by a large man hiding in the bushes. As the man pulled her away and tried to cover her mouth, the woman dropped her books. She struggled and screamed. "No, no! Help, help, please help me!" and "Rape!" Hidden observers told the actors when to begin to stage the attack and noted the actions of subjects. Assistance was measured as movement toward the attack site or movement toward a police officer visible across a nearby parking lot. The study found that 85 percent of men in groups and 65 percent of men walking alone made a detectable move to assist the woman.

The amount of experimenter control is related to internal and external validity. Laboratory experiments tend to have greater internal validity but lower external validity; that is, they are logically tighter and better controlled, but less generalizable. Field experiments tend to have greater external validity but lower internal validity; that is, they are more generalizable but less controlled. Quasi-experimental designs are more common. For example, in the experiment involving the staged attempted rape, the experimenters recreated a very realistic situation with high external validity. It had more external validity than putting people in a laboratory setting and asking them what they would do hypothetically. Yet, subjects were not randomly assigned. Any man who happened to walk by became a subject. The experimenters could not precisely control what the subject heard or saw. The measurement of subject response was based on hidden observers who may have missed some subject responses.

PRACTICAL CONSIDERATIONS

Every research technique has informal tricks of the trade. They are pragmatic and based on common sense but account for the difference between the successful research projects of an experienced researcher and the difficulties a novice researcher faces. Three are discussed here.

Planning and Pilot Tests

All social work research requires planning, and most quantitative researchers use pilot tests. During the planning phase of experimental research, a researcher thinks of alternative explanations or threats to internal validity and how to avoid them. The researcher also develops a neat and well-organized system for recording data. In addition, he or she should devote serious effort to pilot testing any apparatus (e.g., computers, video cameras, tape recorders, etc.) that will be used in the treatment

situation, and he or she must train and pilot test confederates. After the pilot tests, the researcher should interview the pilot subjects to uncover aspects of the experiment that need refinement.

Instructions to Subjects

Most experiments involve giving instructions to subjects to set the stage. A researcher should word instructions carefully and follow a prepared script so that all subjects hear the same thing. This ensures reliability. The instructions are also important in creating a realistic cover story when deception is used. Aronson and Carlsmith (1968:46) noted, "One of the most common mistakes the novice experimenter makes is to present his instructions too briefly."

Postexperiment Interview

At the end of an experiment the researcher should interview subjects, for three reasons. First, if deception was used, the researcher needs to debrief the subjects, telling them the true purpose of the experiment and answering questions. Second, he or she can learn what the subjects thought and how their definitions of the situation affected their behavior. Finally, he or she can explain the importance of not revealing the true nature of the experiment to other potential subjects.

RESULTS OF EXPERIMENTAL SOCIAL WORK RESEARCH: MAKING COMPARISONS

Comparison is the key to all research. By carefully examining the results of experimental research, a researcher can learn a great deal about threats to internal validity, and whether the treatment has an impact on the dependent variable. For example, in the Bond and Anderson (1987) experiment on delivering bad news, discussed earlier, it took an average of 89.6 and 73.1 seconds to deliver favorable versus 72.5 and 147.2 seconds to deliver unfavorable test scores in private and public settings, respectively. A comparison shows that delivering bad news in public takes the longest, whereas good news takes a bit longer in private.

A more complex illustration of such comparisons is shown in Table 9.2 on the results of a series

TABLE 9.2   Comparisons of Results, Classical Experimental Design, Intervention Experiments

	ENRIQUE'S INTERVENTION				NATALIE'S INTERVENTION	
	Pretest	*Posttest*			*Pretest*	*Posttest*
Experimental	190 (30)	140 (29)		Experimental	190 (30)	188 (29)
Control group	189 (30)	189 (30)		Control group	192 (29)	189 (28)

	SUSAN'S INTERVENTION				PAULINE'S INTERVENTION	
	Pretest	*Posttest*			*Pretest*	*Posttest*
Experimental	190 (30)	141 (19)		Experimental	190 (30)	158 (30)
Control group	189 (30)	189 (28)		Control group	191 (29)	159 (28)

	CARL'S INTERVENTION				SYMBOLS FOR COMPARISON PURPOSES	
	Pretest	*Posttest*			*Pretest*	*Posttest*
Experimental	160 (30)	152 (29)		Experimental	A (A)	C (C)
Control group	191 (29)	189 (29)		Control group	B (B)	D (D)

COMPARISONS

	A–B	*C–D*	*A–C*	*B–D*	*(A)–(C)*	*(B)–(D)*
Enrique's	1	49	−50	0	−1	0
Susan's	1	48	−49	0	−11	0
Carl's	31	37	−8	−2	−1	0
Natalie's	2	1	−2	−3	−1	−1
Pauline's	1	1	−32	−32	0	−1

A–B   Do the two groups begin the same? If not, selection bias may be possibly occurring.

C–D   Do the two groups end the same? If not, the treatment may be ineffective, or there may be strong history, maturation, or diffusion of treatment effects.

A–C   Did the experimental group change? If not, treatment may be ineffective.

(A)–(C) and (B)–(D)   Did the number of subjects in the experimental group or control group change? If a large drop occurs, experimental mortality may be a threat to internal validity.

INTERPRETATION

Enrique's: No internal validity threats evident, treatment effects
Susan's: Experimental mortality threat likely problem
Carl's: Selection bias likely problem
Natalie's: No internal validity threat evident, no treatment effects
Pauline's: History, maturation, diffusion of treatment threats are a likely problem

Note: Numbers are average number of tardy days. Numbers in parentheses ( ) are number of mothers per group. Random assignment is made to the experimental or control group.

of five social workers using different interventions to help young mothers (each with one child) get their children to school on time, using the classical experimental design. In the example, the 30 mothers in the experimental group who were accompanied to a school by Enrique had an average of 190 tardy days for their children, whereas the thirty in the control group had an average of 189 tardy days. Only one mother dropped out during this experiment, and at the end of the study the experimental group had an average of only 140 tardy days, whereas the control group had not changed. Susan's telephone reminder intervention had equally dramatic results, but eleven mothers in her experimental group dropped out. This suggests a problem with experimental mortality. People in the experimental group that Carl directed who received free transportation, got an average of 152 tardy days, compared to an averaage of 189 tardy days for the control group, but the control group and the experimental group began with an average of 31 days difference at time 1. This suggests a problem with selection bias. Natalie's post card reminder intervention had no experimental mortality or selection bias problems, but those in the experimental group ended up with the same average number of tardy days as those in the control group. It appears that the treatment was not effective. Pauline's intervention (making home visits) also avoided selection bias and experimental mortality problems. Mothers in her group made an average of 158 tardy days at the conclusion of the study, but so did those in the control group. This suggests that the maturation, history or diffusion of intervention effects may have occurred. Thus, the intervention of Enrique (accompanying the mothers to school) appears to have been the most effective.

A WORD ON ETHICS

Ethical considerations are a significant issue in experimental social work research because experimental research is intrusive (i.e., it interferes). Treatments may involve placing people in contrived social settings and manipulating their feelings or behaviors. Dependent variables may be what subjects say or do. The amount and type of intrusion are limited by ethical standards. Researchers must be very careful not to place subjects in physical danger or in embarrassing or anxiety-inducing situations. They must painstakingly monitor events and control what occurs.

Deception used to be common in social work experiments, but it involves misleading or lying to subjects. Such dishonesty is not condoned as acceptable.

CONCLUSION

In this chapter you learned about random assignment and the methods of experimental research. Random assignment is an effective way to create two (or more) groups, which can be treated as equivalent and hence compared. In general, experimental research provides precise and relatively unambiguous evidence for a causal relationship. It follows the positivist approach and produces quantitative results that can be analyzed with statistics.

This chapter also examined the parts of an experiment and how they can be combined to produce different experimental designs (see Box 9.4). In addition to the classical experimental design, you learned about preexperimental and quasi-experimental designs. You also learned how to express them using design notation.

You learned that internal validity—the internal logical rigor of an experiment—is a key idea in experimental research. Threats to internal validity are possible alternative explanations to the treatment. You also learned about external validity and how field experiments maximize external validity.

The real strength of experimental research is its control and logical rigor in establishing evidence for causality. In general, experiments tend to be easier to replicate, less expensive, and less time consuming than the other techniques. Experimental research also has limitations. First, some questions in social work cannot be addressed using experimental methods because control and experimental manipulation are impossible. Another limitation is that experiments usually test one or a few hypotheses at a time. This fragments knowledge and makes it necessary to try to synthesize results across many research reports using a strategy known as meta-analysis. External validity is another potential problem because many experiments rely on small nonrandom samples.[14]

Box 9.4

Use of Experiments for Evaluation Research

In a study that you read about in Chapter 2, Wysong and colleagues (1994) used an experiment to evaluate the effectiveness of the D.A.R.E. (Drug Abuse Resistance Education) program. Now that you better understand experiments, let us review its design.

The authors examined two groups of students that were not randomly divided but were separated into groups without a pattern. The experimental group participated in the D.A.R.E. program in grade 7; the control group did not. The treatment was participation in D.A.R.E., a program of presentations and discussions led by trained police officers in schools.

The program claims to help students resist peer pressure to use alcohol and illegal drugs and to raise student self-esteem. The dependent variables included age of first drug use, frequency of drug use, and student's self-esteem. The authors measured the variables four years after the treatment to determine whether it had any lasting impact on student behavior in the high school years. When the authors compared measures of the dependent variables for the two groups, they found no difference between them. They failed to reject the null hypothesis that the program had no effect.

You learned how a careful examination and comparison of results can alert you to potential problems in research design. Finally, you saw some practical and ethical considerations in experiments.

In the next chapters you will examine survey research and other research techniques. The logic of the nonexperimental methods differs from that of the experiment. Experimenters focus narrowly on a few hypotheses. They usually have one or two independent variables, a single dependent variable, a few small groups of subjects, and an independent variable that the researcher induces. By contrast, other social work researchers test many hypotheses at once. They measure a large number of independent and dependent variables and use a larger number of randomly sampled subjects. Their independent variables are usually preexisting conditions in subjects.

KEY TERMS

classical experimental design	factorial design	placebo
compensatory behavior	field experiment	placebo effect
control group	Hawthorne effect	posttest
debrief	history effects	preexperimental designs
deception	interaction effect	pretest
demand characteristics	interrupted time series	quasi-experimental designs
design notation	laboratory experiment	random assignment
diffusion of treatment	Latin square design	reactivity
double-blind experiment	maturation	selection bias
equivalent time series	mortality	Solomon four-group design
experimental design	mundane realism	static group comparison
experimental group	novelty effect	subjects
experimental realism	one-shot case study design	treatment
experimenter expectancy		

REVIEW QUESTIONS_____

1. What are the seven elements or parts of an experiment?

2. What distinguishes preexperimental designs from the classical design?

3. Which design permits the testing of different sequences of several treatments?

4. A researcher says, "It was a three-by-two design, with the independent variables level of fear (low, medium, high) and ease of escape (easy/difficult) and the dependent variable anxiety." What does this mean? What is the design notation, assuming that random assignment with posttest only was used?

5. How do the interrupted and the equivalent time series designs differ?

6. What is the logic of internal validity and how does the use of a control group fit into that logic?

7. How does the Solomon four-group design show the testing effect?

8. What is the double-blind experiment and why is it used?

9. Do field or laboratory experiments have greater internal validity? External validity? Explain.

10. What is the difference between experimental and mundane realism?

NOTES_____

1. Cook and Campbell (1979:9–36, 91–94) argued for a modification of a more rigid positivist approach to causality for experimental research. They suggested a "critical–realist" approach, which shares some features of the critical approach outlined in Chapter 4.

2. For discussions of the history of the experiment, see Danziger (1988), Gillespie (1988), Hornstein (1988), O'Donnell (1985), and Schcibe (1988).

3. See Hornstein (1988:11).

4. For events after World War II, see Harris (1988) and Suls and Rosnow (1988). For a discussion of the increased use of deception, see Reynolds (1979:60).

5. For a discussion of control in experiments, see Cook and Campbell (1979:7–9) and Spector (1981:15–16).

6. The notation for research design is discussed in Cook and Campbell (1979:95–96), Dooley (1984: 132–137), and Spector (1981:27–28).

7. For additional discussions of threats to internal validity, see Cook and Campbell (1979:51–68), Kercher

(1992), Smith and Glass (1987), Spector (1981:24–27), and Suls and Rosnow (1988).

8. This example is borrowed from Mitchell and Jolley (1988:97).

9. Experimenter expectancy is discussed in Aronson and Carlsmith (1968:66–70), Dooley (1984:151–153), and Mitchell and Jolley (1988:327–329).

10. Also, see Aronson and Carlsmith (1968:22–25).

11. For a discussion of external validity, see Cook and Campbell (1979:70–80).

12. The Hawthorne effect is described in Franke and Kaul (1978), Lang (1992), and Roethlisberger and Dickenson (1939). Also, sec the discussion in Cook and Campbell (1979:123–125) and Dooley (1984:155–156). Gillespie (1988, 1991) discussed the political context of the experiments and how it shaped them.

13. See Piliavin and associates (1969).

14. See Graham (1992).

SURVEY RESEARCH

*Every method of data collection, including the survey, is only an
approximation to knowledge. Each provides a different glimpse of reality,
and all have limitations when used alone. Before undertaking a survey the
researcher would do well to ask if this is the most appropriate and fruitful
method for the problem at hand. The survey is highly valuable for studying
some problems, such as public opinion, and worthless for others.*

—Warwick and Lininger, *The Sample Survey,* pp. 5–6

INTRODUCTION

Someone hands you a sheet of paper full of questions. The first reads: "We would like to learn your opinion of the Neuman–Kreuger social work research methods textbook. Would you say it is (a) well organized, (b) adequately organized, or (c) poorly organized?" You probably would not be shocked by this. It is a kind of survey, and most of us are accustomed to surveys by the time we reach adulthood.

The survey is the most widely used data-gathering technique in social work, and it is used in many other fields, as well. In fact, surveys are almost too popular. People sometimes say, "Do a survey" to get information about the social world, when they should be asking, "What is the most appropriate research design?" Despite the popularity of surveys, it is easy to conduct a survey that yields misleading or worthless results. Good surveys require thought and effort. "Surveys, like other scientific and technical tools, can be well made or poorly made and can be used in appropriate or inappropriate ways" (Bradburn and Sudman, 1988:37).

All surveys are based on the professional social work research survey. In this chapter you will learn the main ingredients of good survey research, as well as the limitations of the survey method.

Research Questions Appropriate for a Survey

Survey research developed within the positivist approach to social science.[1] As Robert Groves, a leading expert on surveys, remarked, "Surveys produce information that is inherently statistical in nature. Surveys are quantitative beasts" (1996:389). The survey asks many people (called *respondents*) about their beliefs, opinions, characteristics, and past or present behavior.

Surveys are appropriate for research questions about self-reported beliefs or behaviors. They are strongest when the answers people give to questions measure variables. Researchers usually ask about many things at one time in surveys, measure many variables (often with multiple indicators), and test several hypotheses in a single survey.

Although the categories overlap, the following can be asked in a survey:

1. *Behavior.* How frequently do you brush your teeth? Did you vote in the last city election? When did you last visit a close relative?
2. *Attitudes/beliefs/opinions.* What kind of job do you think the mayor is doing? Do you think other people say many negative things about you when you are not there? What is the biggest problem facing the nation these days?

3. *Characteristics.* Are you married, never married, single, divorced, separated, or widowed? Do you belong to a union? What is your age?
4. *Expectations.* Do you plan to buy a new car in the next 12 months? How much schooling do you think your child will get? Do you think the population in this town will grow, shrink, or stay the same?
5. *Self-classification.* Do you consider yourself to be liberal, moderate, or conservative? Into which social class would you put your family? Would you say you are highly religious or not religious?
6. *Knowledge.* Who was elected mayor in the last election? About what percentage of the people in this city are non-White? Is it legal to own a personal copy of Karl Marx's *Communist Manifesto* in this country?

Scholars warn against using surveys to ask "why" questions (e.g., Why do you think crime occurs?).[2]

A History of Survey Research

The modern survey can be traced back to ancient forms of the census.[3] A *census* includes information on characteristics of the entire population in a territory. It is based on what people tell officials or what officials observe. For example, the *Domesday Book* was a famous census of England conducted from 1085 to 1086 by William the Conqueror. Early censuses assessed the property available for taxation or the young men available for military service. With the development of representative democracy, officials used the census to assign the number of elected representatives based on the population in a district.

The survey has a long and varied history. Its use for social work research in the United States and Great Britain began with social reform movements and social service professions documenting the conditions of urban poverty that followed early industrialization. At first, surveys were overviews of an area based on questionnaires and other data. Scientific sampling and statistics were absent. For example, between 1851 and 1864, Henry Mayhew published the four-volume *London Labour and the London Poor,* based on conversations with street people and observations of daily life. Charles Booth's 17-volume (1889–1902) *Labour and Life of the People of London* and B. Seebohm Rowntree's *Poverty: A Study of Town Life* (1906) also examined the extent of urban poverty. Similar work appeared in the United States in *Hull House Maps and Papers of 1895* and in W. E. B. DuBois's *Philadelphia Negro* (1899).

The *social survey* grew into both the modern quantitative survey research and qualitative field research in a community. From the 1890s to the 1930s, it was the major method of social work research practiced by the Social Survey Movement in Canada, Great Britain, and the United States. The Social Survey Movement used systematic empirical inquiry to support social–political reform goals. Today, the social survey would be called an action-oriented community survey. By the mid-1940s the modern quantitative survey had largely displaced it.

Early social surveys were detailed empirical studies of specific local areas based on many sources of quantitative and qualitative data. Most were exploratory and descriptive. Researchers wanted to inform the public of the problems of industrialism and provide information for democratic decison making by the people of a community. Some leaders of the early social survey—Florence Kelly and Jane Addams of the Hull House and settlement movement, and African American W. E. B. DuBois—were unable to secure regular work in universities because of gender and race discrimination. Social surveys provide impressive pictures of daily community life. For example, the six-volume *Pittsburgh Survey* published in 1914 was based on face-to-face interviews; existing statistical data on health, crime, and industrial injury; and direct observations.

Four forces greatly reshaped the social survey into modern quantitative survey research in the United States from 1920 to World War II. First, researchers applied statistically based sampling techniques and precise measurement to the survey, especially after the *Literary Digest* debacle. Second, researchers created scales and indexes to gather systematic quantitative data on attitudes, opinions, and subjective aspects of social life. Third, many others found uses for the survey and adapted it to a variety of applied areas. Market research emerged as a distinct field and adapted surveys to study con-

sumer behavior. Journalists used surveys to measure public opinion and the impact of the radio. Religious organizations and charities used surveys to identify areas of need. Government agencies used surveys to improve services for agricultural and social programs. Also, more social workers began to use the survey as a source of empirical data for their basic research.

In addition, most empirical social work research moved away from nonacademics using a mixture of methods to focus on local social problems. The reorientation created respectable, "scientific" methods modeled after the natural sciences. Social work research became more professional, objective, and nonpolitical. This reorientation was stimulated by (1) a competition among researchers and universities for status, prestige, and funds; (2) researchers turning away from social reform ideals after the end of the Progressive Era (1895–1915) in U.S. politics; and (3) a program of major private foundations (Carnegie, Rockefeller, and Sage) to fund the expansion of quantitative, positivist social research.[4]

Survey research expanded and matured during World War II, especially in the United States. Academic social work researchers and practitioners from industry converged in Washington, D.C., to work in the war effort. Survey researchers studied morale, consumer demand, production capacity, enemy propaganda, and the effectiveness of bombing. The wartime cooperation helped academic social work researchers and applied practitioners learn from each other and gain experience in conducting many large-scale surveys. Academic researchers helped practitioners appreciate precise measurement, sampling, and statistical analysis, while practitioners helped academics learn the practical side of organizing and conducting large-scale surveys.

After World War II, officials dismantled the extensive government survey research establishment. This was, in part, a cost-cutting move. Also, some members of the U.S. Congress feared that others might use survey results to advance social policies, such as helping the unemployed or promoting equal rights for African Americans who lived in racially segregated southern states.

Many researchers returned to universities and created new social work research organizations. At first, the universities were hesitant to embrace expanded survey research. Survey research was expensive and involved many people. In addition, traditional social researchers were wary of quantitative research and skeptical of a technique used in private industry. The culture of applied researchers and business-oriented poll takers clashed with that of traditional basic researchers who lacked statistical training. Yet, surveys grew in use. This growth was not limited to the United States. Within three years of the end of World War II, national survey research institutes had been established in France, Norway, Germany, Italy, the Netherlands, Czechoslovakia, and Britain (Scheuch, 1990).

Despite initial uncertainty, survey research grew through the 1970s. For example, about 18 percent of articles published in sociology journals used the survey method in 1939–1940; this rose to 55 percent by 1964–1965. A dramatic expansion of U.S. higher education and of the social science fields during the 1960s also spurred the growth of survey research. More people learned about survey research, and the method gained in popularity. Five factors contributed to the postwar growth of survey research:[5]

1. *Computers.* Computer technology that became available to social workers by the 1960s made the sophisticated statistical analysis of large-scale survey data sets feasible for the first time. Today, the computer is an indispensable tool for analyzing data from most surveys.

2. *Organizations.* New social work research centers with an expertise and interest in quantitative research were established at U.S. universities. About 50 such centers were created in the years after 1960.

3. *Data storage.* By the 1970s data archives were created to store, and permit the sharing of, the large-scale survey data for secondary analysis (discussed in Chapter 11). The collection, storage, and sharing of information on hundreds of variables for thousands of respondents expanded the use of surveys.

4. *Funding.* For about a decade (late 1960s to late 1970s), the U.S. federal government expanded funds for social work research. Total federal spending for research and development in the social sciences in-

creased nearly tenfold from 1960 to the mid-1970s before it declined.

5. *Methodology.* By the 1970s substantial research was being conducted on ways to improve the validity of surveys. The survey technique advanced as errors were identified and corrected.[6] In addition, researchers created improved statistics for analyzing quantitative data and taught them to a new generation of researchers. In the 1980s new cognitive psychology theories were applied to survey research (Sudman et al., 1996).

Today quantitative survey research is a major industry both within and outside universities. The professional survey industry probably employs over 60,000 people in the United States alone. Most of these are part-time workers, assistants, or semiprofessionals. About 6,000 full-time professional survey researchers design and analyze surveys.[7]

Researchers use surveys for basic research in universities and research centers. Researchers in many fields (communication, education, economics, political science, social psychology, and sociology) conduct and analyze surveys. Many U.S. universities have centers for survey research. Major centers include the Survey Research Center at the University of California at Berkeley, the National Opinion Research Center (NORC) at the University of Chicago, and the Institute for Social Research (ISR) at the University of Michigan.

Several applied areas rely heavily on the survey: government, marketing, private policy research, and mass media. Governments around the world at the national and local levels regularly conduct surveys to inform policy decisions. Private-sector survey research can be divided into three types of organizations: opinion polling organizations (e.g., Gallup, Harris, Roper, Yankelovich and Associates, etc.), marketing firms (e.g., Nielsen, Market Facts, Market Research Corporation, etc.), and nonprofit research organizations (e.g., Mathematica Policy Research, Rand Corporation, etc.).[8]

Major television and newspaper organizations regularly conduct surveys. Rossi and Associates, who (1983:14) found 174 polls sponsored by media organizations, stated, "Polling is as much a feature of the media as comics and the horoscope!" In addition, there are many ad hoc or in-house surveys. Businesses, schools, and other organizations conduct small-scale surveys of employees, clients, students, and the like to address specific applied questions.

Survey researchers have formed separate professional organizations. The American Association for Public Opinion Research, founded in 1947, sponsors a scholarly journal devoted to survey research called *Public Opinion Quarterly*. The Council of American Survey Research Organizations is an organization for commercial polling firms. There is also an international survey research organization—the World Association of Public Opinion Research.[9]

In the past three decades the quantitative survey has become a widely used technology for social work research both inside and outside universities. Although knowledge about how to conduct a good survey has grown significantly, the explosion of survey applications has outpaced developments in the survey technique as a method to quantitatively measure human social life.

THE LOGIC OF SURVEY RESEARCH

What Is a Survey?

In experiments, researchers place people in small groups and test one or two hypotheses with a few variables. Subjects respond to a treatment created by the researcher. Researchers show the timing of the treatment by observing associations between the treatment and the dependent variable, and by controlling for alternative explanations.

By contrast, survey researchers sample many respondents who answer the same questions. They measure many variables, test multiple hypotheses, and infer temporal order from questions about past behavior, experiences, or characteristics. For example, years of schooling or a respondent's race are prior to current attitudes. An association among variables is measured with statistical techniques.

Experimenters physically control for alternative explanations. Survey researchers think of alternative explanations when planning a survey, measure variables that represent alternative explanations (i.e., control variables), then statistically examine their effects to rule out alternative explanations.

Survey research is often called correlational. Survey researchers use control variables to approximate the rigorous test for causality that experimenters achieve with their physical control over temporal order and alternative explanations.

Steps in Conducting a Survey

The survey researcher follows a deductive approach. He or she begins with a theoretical or applied research problem and ends with empirical measurement and data analysis. Once a researcher decides that the survey is an appropriate method, basic steps in a research project can be divided into the substeps outlined in Figure 10.1.

In the first phase the researcher develops an instrument—a survey questionnaire or interview schedule—that he or she uses to measure variables. Respondents read the questions themselves and mark answers on a *questionnaire*. An *interview schedule* is a set of questions read to the respondent by an interviewer, who also records responses. To simplify the discussion, we will use only the term *questionnaire*.

A survey researcher conceptualizes and operationalizes variables as questions. He or she writes and rewrites questions for clarity and completeness, and organizes questions on the questionnaire based on the research question, the respondents, and the type of survey. (The types of surveys are discussed later.)

When preparing a questionnaire, the researcher thinks ahead to how he or she will record and organize data for analysis. He or she pilot tests the questionnaire with a small set of respondents similar to those in the final survey. If interviewers are used, the researcher trains them with the questionnaire. He or she asks respondents in the pilot test whether the questions were clear and explores their interpretations to see whether his or her intended meaning was clear.[10] The researcher also draws the sample during this phase.

After the planning phase, the researcher is ready to collect data. This phase is usually shorter than the planning phase. He or she locates sampled respondents in person, by telephone, or by mail. Respondents are given information and instructions on

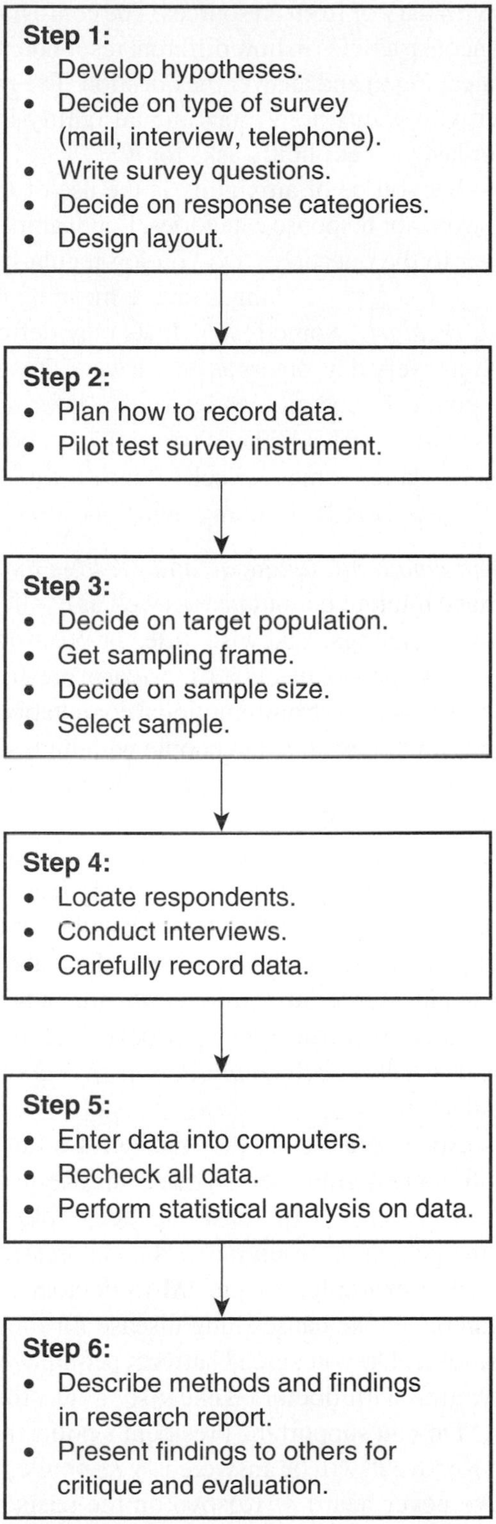

Step 1:
- Develop hypotheses.
- Decide on type of survey (mail, interview, telephone).
- Write survey questions.
- Decide on response categories.
- Design layout.

↓

Step 2:
- Plan how to record data.
- Pilot test survey instrument.

↓

Step 3:
- Decide on target population.
- Get sampling frame.
- Decide on sample size.
- Select sample.

↓

Step 4:
- Locate respondents.
- Conduct interviews.
- Carefully record data.

↓

Step 5:
- Enter data into computers.
- Recheck all data.
- Perform statistical analysis on data.

↓

Step 6:
- Describe methods and findings in research report.
- Present findings to others for critique and evaluation.

FIGURE 10.1 Steps in the Process of Survey Research

completing the questionnaire or interview. The questions follow, and there is a simple stimulus/response or question/answer pattern. The researcher accurately records answers or responses immediately after they are given. After all respondents complete the questionnaire and are thanked, he or she organizes the data and prepares them for statistical analysis.

Survey research can be complex and expensive and it can involve coordinating many people and steps. The administration of survey research requires organization and accurate record keeping.[11] The researcher keeps track of each respondent, questionnaire, and interviewer. For example, he or she gives each sampled respondent an identification number, which also appears on the questionnaire. He or she then checks completed questionnaires against a list of sampled respondents. Next, the researcher reviews responses on individual questionnaires, stores original questionnaires, and transfers information from questionnaires to a format for statistical analysis. Meticulous bookkeeping and labeling are essential. Otherwise, the researcher may find that valuable data and effort are lost through sloppiness.

CONSTRUCTING THE QUESTIONNAIRE

Principles of Good Question Writing

A good questionnaire forms an integrated whole. The researcher weaves questions together so they flow smoothly. He or she includes introductory remarks and instructions for clarification and measures each variable with one or more survey questions.

There are two key principles for good survey questions: Avoid confusion and keep the respondent's perspective in mind. Good survey questions give the researcher valid and reliable measures. They also help respondents feel that they understand the question and that their answers are meaningful. Questions that do not mesh with a respondent's viewpoint or that respondents find confusing are not good measures. A survey researcher exercises extra care if the respondents are heterogeneous or come from different life situations than his or her own.

Researchers face a dilemma. They want each respondent to hear exactly the same question, but will the questions be equally clear, relevant, and meaningful to all respondents? If respondents have diverse backgrounds and frames of reference, exactly the same wording may not have the same meaning. Yet, tailoring question wording to each respondent makes comparisons almost impossible. A researcher would not know whether the wording of the question or differences in respondents accounted for different answers.

Question writing is more of an art than a science. It takes skill, practice, patience, and creativity. The principles of question writing are illustrated in this list of 10 things to avoid when writing survey questions. The list does not include every possible error, only the more frequent problems.[12]

1. *Avoid jargon, slang, and abbreviations.* Jargon and technical terms come in many forms. Plumbers talk about *snakes,* lawyers about a contract of *uberrima fides,* psychologists about the *Oedipus complex.* Slang is a kind of jargon within a subculture. For example, homeless people may talk about a *snowbird* and skiers about a *hotdog.* Also avoid abbreviations. *NATO* usually means North Atlantic Treaty Organization, but for a respondent, it might mean something else (National Auto Tourist Organization, Native Alaskan Trade Orbit, or North African Tea Office). Avoid slang and jargon unless a specialized population is being surveyed. Target the vocabulary and grammar to the respondents sampled. For the general public this is the language used on television or in the newspaper (about an eighth-grade reading vocabulary). Survey researchers learned that respondents may not understand some basic terminology. For example, one-fourth of respondents who had less than a high school diploma (about 20 percent of the U.S. population) have difficulty understanding the meaning of sexual terms such as *vaginal intercourse* (Binson and Catania, 1998).

2. *Avoid ambiguity, confusion, and vagueness.* Ambiguity and vagueness plague most question writers. A researcher might make implicit assumptions without thinking of the respondents. For example, the question, "What is your income?" could mean weekly, monthly, or annual; family or personal; before taxes or after taxes; for this year or last

year; from salary or from all sources. The confusion causes inconsistencies in how different respondents assign meaning to and answer the question. The researcher who wants before-tax annual family income for last year explicitly asks for it.[13]

Another source of ambiguity is the use of indefinite words or response categories. For example, an answer to the question, "Do you jog regularly? Yes _____ No _____ ," hinges on the meaning of the word *regularly.* Some respondents may define *regularly* as every day, others as once a week. To reduce respondent confusion and get more information, be specific—ask whether a person jogs "about once a day," "a few times a week," "once a week," and so on. (See Box 10.1 on improving questions.)

3. *Avoid emotional language and prestige bias.* Words have implicit connotative as well as explicit denotative meanings. Likewise, titles or positions in society (e.g., president, expert, etc.) carry prestige or status. Words with strong emotional connotations and stands on issues linked to people with high social status can color how respondents hear and answer survey questions.

Use neutral language. Avoid words with emotional "baggage" because respondents may react to the emotionally laden words rather than to the issue. For example, the question, "What do you think about a policy to pay murderous terrorists who threaten to steal the freedoms of peace-loving people?" is full of emotional words—such as *murderous, freedoms, steal,* and *peace.*

Also, avoid *prestige bias*—associating a statement with a prestigious person or group. Respondents may answer on the basis of their feelings toward the person or group rather than addressing the issue. For example, saying, "Most doctors say that cigarette smoke causes lung disease for those near a smoker. Do you agree?" affects people who want to agree with doctors. Likewise, a question such as, "Do you support the president's policy regarding Kosovo?" will be answered by respondents who have never heard of Kosovo on the basis of their view of the president.

4. *Avoid double-barreled questions.* Make each question about one and only one topic. A *double-*

Box 10.1 _____

Improving Unclear Questions

Here are three survey questions written by experienced professional researchers. They revised the original wording after a pilot test revealed that 15 percent of respondents asked for clarification or gave inadequate answers (e.g., don't know). As you can see, question wording is an art that may improve with practice, patience, and pilot testing.

ORIGINAL QUESTION	PROBLEM	REVISED QUESTION
Do you exercise or play sports regularly?	What counts as exercise?	Do you do any sports or hobbies, physical activities, or exercise, including walking, on a regular basis?
What is the average number of days each week you have butter?	Does margarine count as butter?	The next question is just about butter—not including margarine. How many days a week do you have butter?
[Following question on eggs] What is the number of servings in a typical day?	How many eggs is a serving? What is a typical day?	On days when you eat eggs, how many eggs do you usually have?

	RESPONSES TO QUESTION		PERCENTAGE ASKING FOR CLARIFICATION	
	Original	*Revision*	*Original*	*Revision*
Exercise question (% saying "yes")	48%	60%	5%	0%
Butter question (% saying "none")	33%	55%	18%	13%
Egg question (% saying "one")	80%	33%	33%	0%

Source: From *Public Opinion Quarterly,* Volume 56: 218–231 by the American Association for Public Opinion Research. © 1992 All rights reserved. Reprinted by permission of The University of Chicago Press.

barreled question consists of two or more questions joined together. It makes a respondent's answer ambiguous. For example, if asked, "Does this company have pension and health insurance benefits?" a respondent at a company with health insurance benefits only might answer either yes or no. The response has an ambiguous meaning, and the researcher cannot be certain of the respondent's intention. Labaw (1980:154) noted, "Perhaps the most basic principle of question wording, and one very often ignored or simply unseen, is that only one concept or issue or meaning should be included in a question." A researcher who wants to ask about the joint occurrence of two things—for example, a company with both health insurance and pension benefits—should ask two separate questions.

Also, do not confuse a respondent's belief that a relationship exists between two variables with the empirical measurement of variables in a relationship. For example, a researcher wants to find out whether students rate teachers higher who tell many jokes in class. The two variables are "teacher tells jokes" and "rating the teacher." The *wrong* way to approach the issue is to ask students, "Do you rate a teacher higher if the teacher tells many jokes?" This measures whether or not students *believe* that they rate teachers based on joke telling; it does not measure the relationship. The *correct* way is to ask two separate questions: "How do you rate the teacher?" and "How many jokes does the teacher tell in class?" Then the researcher can examine answers to the two questions to see whether an association exists between them.

Beliefs about a relationship are distinct from an actual relationship.

5. *Avoid leading questions.* Make respondents feel that all responses are legitimate. Do not let them become aware of an answer that the researcher wants. A *leading* (or *loaded*) *question* is one that leads the respondent to choose one response over another by its wording. There are many kinds of leading questions. For example, the question, "You don't smoke, do you?" leads respondents to state that they do not smoke.

Loaded questions can be stated to get either positive or negative answers. For example, "Should the mayor spend even more tax money trying to keep the streets in top shape?" leads respondents to disagree, whereas "Should the mayor fix the pot-holed and dangerous streets in our city?" is loaded for agreement.

6. *Avoid asking questions that are beyond respondents' capabilities.* Asking something that few respondents know frustrates respondents and produces poor-quality responses. Respondents cannot always recall past details and may not know specific factual information. For example, asking an adult, "How did you feel about your brother when you were 6 years old?" is probably worthless. Asking respondents to make a choice about something they know nothing about (e.g., a technical issue in foreign affairs or an internal policy of an organization) may result in an answer, but one that is unreliable and meaningless. When many respondents are unlikely to know about an issue, use a full-filter question form (to be discussed).

Phrase questions in the terms in which respondents think. For example, few respondents will be able to answer, "How many gallons of gasoline did you buy last year for your car?" Yet, respondents may be able to answer a question about gasoline purchases for a typical week, which the researcher can multiply by 52 to estimate annual purchases (see Sudman et al., 1996:197–226).

7. *Avoid false premises.* Do not begin a question with a premise with which respondents may not agree, then ask about choices regarding it. Respondents who disagree with the premise will be frus-

trated and not know how to answer. For example, the question, "The post office is open too many hours. Do you want it to open four hours later or close four hours earlier each day?" leaves those who either oppose the premise or oppose both alternatives without a meaningful choice.

A better question explicitly asks the respondent to assume a premise is true, then asks for a preference. For example, "Assuming the post office has to cut back its operating hours, which would you find more convenient, opening four hours later or closing four hours earlier each day?" Answers to a hypothetical situation are not very reliable, but being explicit will reduce frustration.

8. *Avoid asking about future intentions.* Avoid asking people about what they might do under hypothetical circumstances. Responses are poor predictors of behavior. Questions such as, "Suppose a new grocery store opened down the road. Would you shop at it?" are usually a waste of time. It is better to ask about current or recent attitudes and behavior. In general, respondents answer specific, concrete questions that relate to their experiences

"We're still debating."

more reliably than they do those about abstractions that are beyond their immediate experiences.

9. *Avoid double negatives.* Double negatives in ordinary language are grammatically incorrect and confusing. For example, "I ain't got no job" logically means that the respondent does have a job, but the second negative is used in this way for emphasis. Such blatant errors are rare, but more subtle forms of the double negative are also confusing. They arise when respondents are asked to agree or disagree with a statement. For example, respondents who *dis*agree with the statement, "Students should not be required to take a comprehensive exam to graduate" are logically stating a double negative because they *disagree* with *not* doing something.

10. *Avoid overlapping or unbalanced response categories.* Make response categories or choices mutually exclusive, exhaustive, and balanced. *Mutually exclusive* means that response categories do not overlap. Overlapping categories that are numerical ranges (e.g., 5–10, 10–20, 20–30) can be easily corrected (e.g., 5–9, 10–19, 20–29). The ambiguous verbal choice is another type of overlapping response category—for example, "Are you satisfied with your job, or are there things you don't like about it?" *Exhaustive* means that every respondent has a choice—a place to go. For example, asking respondents, "Are you working or unemployed?" leaves out respondents who are not working but do not consider themselves unemployed (e.g., full-time homemakers, people on vacation, students, people with disabilities, retired people, etc.). A researcher first thinks about what he or she wants to measure and then considers the circumstances of respondents. For example, when asking about a respondent's employment, does the researcher want information on the primary job or on all jobs? On full-time work only or both full- and part-time work? On jobs for pay only or on unpaid or volunteer jobs as well?

Keep response categories *balanced.* A case of unbalanced choices is the question, "What kind of job is the mayor doing: outstanding, excellent, very good, or satisfactory?" Another type of unbalanced question omits information—for example, "Which of the five candidates running for mayor do you favor: Eugene Oswego or one of the others?"

Researchers can balance responses by offering bipolar opposites. It is easy to see that the terms *honesty* and *dishonesty* have different meanings and connotations. Asking respondents to rate whether a mayor is highly, somewhat, or not very *honest* is not the same as asking them to rate the mayor's level of *dishonesty.* Unless there is a specific purpose for doing otherwise, it is better to offer respondents equal polar opposites at each end of a continuum (Ostrom and Gannon, 1996)—for example, "Do you think the mayor is: very honest, somewhat honest, neither honest nor dishonest, somewhat dishonest, or very dishonest?" (See Box 10.2 on types of bias.)

Aiding Respondent Recall

Survey researchers have recently examined a respondent's ability to accurately recall past behavior and events when answering survey questions.[14] This always has been a critical issue in oral history and recollections for historical research, but it is also a significant issue for survey questions about recent events. Recalling events accurately takes more time and effort than the few seconds that respondents have to answer survey questions. Also, one's ability to recall accurately declines over time. Studies in hospitalization and crime victimization show that although most respondents can recall significant events that occurred in the past several weeks, half are inaccurate a year later.

Survey researchers recognize that memory is less trustworthy than was once assumed. It is affected by many factors—the topic (threatening or socially desirable), events occurring simultaneously and subsequently, the significance of an event for a person, situational conditions (question wording and interview style), and the respondent's need to have internal consistency. "Evidence now accumulating suggests that the task of recalling if and when events occur is far more difficult than survey researchers typically assumed. Real world events appear to be forgotten rapidly" (Turner and Martin, 1984:296).

The complexity of respondent recall does not mean that survey researchers cannot ask about past events; rather, they need to customize questions and interpret results cautiously. Researchers should provide respondents with special instructions and

Box 10.2 _____

Biased Survey Questions

The following questions are taken from mail questionnaires received at home. The first two questions came from a Congressman. Do you think they are unbiased?

1. Some advocate giving the President the power to strike out specific budget requests from large appropriations bills. They say the "line-item veto" will prevent Congress from passing wasteful pork-barrel spending bills. Do you believe that the line-item veto would help control wasteful government spending?

    a. Yes   b. No   c. Undecided

2. Farming is one of the most dangerous occupations in this country. However, in many rural agricultural states, access to basic health care services, including medical services, is severely restricted. Do you believe that rural Wisconsin residents need better access to health care services?

    a. Yes   b. No   c. Undecided

The next two questions are from a mail questionnaire from a U.S. political party in April 1998 called "1998 Election Year Critical Issues Survey." It was really political propaganda and a fund-raising appeal disguised as a survey questionnaire.

3. The average family of four today pays a whopping 24% of its annual income to the federal government. Add state and local taxes and the burden climbs to 40% . . . 50% . . . as much as 80% with estate taxes. And to make matters worse, taxpayers must deal with 17,000 pages of IRS regulations and laws—forcing millions of taxpayers to use professionals to prepare their taxes, at a cost of $2,000,000,000. Is moving forward with massive reform of our tax system and the IRS important to you?

    ○ Yes   ○ No   ○ Undecided

4. The respected Grace Commission documents that a staggering $350 *billion* of our tax dollars are being completely wasted through poor procurement procedures, bad management, sloppy bookkeeping, "defective" contract management, personnel abuses, and other wasteful practices and programs. Is cutting pork-barrel spending and eliminating government waste important to you?

    ○ Yes   ○ No   ○ Undecided

The preceding questions contain several survey question-writing practices to avoid:

Emotional language. Examples are "wasteful pork-barrel spending bills," "one of the most dangerous occupations in this country," "whopping," "burden climbs," "staggering $350 *billion,*" and "completely wasted."

Prestige bias. An example is "respected Grace Commission."

Leading or loaded. The items provide a lot of one-sided information on an issue before getting to the question itself, and it is presented in a manner that leads to one answer. For example, look at the actual question in number 2: "Do you believe that rural Wisconsin residents need better access to health care services?" Few would disagree with this statement, but it avoids the real policy questions: How should health care be delivered? What should be the level of health care provided? How should the services be paid for?

False premises. The questions give selective information. A reader who seriously questioned or disagreed with the alleged facts will have difficulty responding. For question 1, what if a respondent did not feel that Congress is "passing wasteful pork-barrel spending bills"?

Double-barreled. The last two questions ask respondents if they feel a problem is important; they implicitly, simultaneously ask whether respondents agree with a specific remedy to the problem (i.e., "massive reform" and "eliminating government waste").

Unbalanced responses. The last two questions use a yes/no format that implies one either thinks it is important or not, or is undecided. The format does not allow expressing a degree of importance for the issue, and support or opposition to a proposed remedy. A respondent who feels it is somewhat important or a minor problem has no response category to select.

extra thinking time. They should also provide aids to respondent recall, such as a fixed time frame or location references. Rather than ask, "How often did you attend a sporting event last winter?" they should say, "I want to know how many sporting events you attended last winter. Let's go month by month. Think back to December. Did you attend any sporting events for which you paid admission in December? Now, think back to January. Did you attend any sporting events in January?"

A study by Mooney and Gramling (1991) illustrates the importance of using recall aids. They asked students two types of questions about drinking behavior and found that standard questions, such as, "On the average, how many days a month have you had something to drink (wine, beer, liquor)?" and "On the average, how many drinks do you have each of these times?" yielded much lower results than asking the same question about 12 locations (e.g., bar, relative's home, fraternity/sorority house, etc.) and summing the total. Such aided recall reduces omissions and enhances accuracy, but it does not produce overestimating. Many respondents will *telescope*— compress time when asked about frequency and overreport recent events. Two techniques reduce telescoping: situational framing (e.g., ask the respondent to recall a specific situation and then ask about it) and decomposition (e.g., ask several specifics and add them up—such as how much one drank in a week then total for drinking in a year). Survey researchers who ask about past events or behavior, even within the past year, need to do so with care.

Types of Questions and Response Categories

Threatening versus Nonthreatening Questions. Researchers sometimes ask about sensitive issues or ones that respondents find threatening.[15] Many respondents find questions about sexual behavior, drug or alcohol use, deviant behavior, mental health, illegal activity, or controversial public issues to be threatening. Researchers who ask such questions must do so with extra care.

Threatening questions are part of a broader issue. Respondents may try to present a positive image of themselves to interviewers or researchers instead of giving true answers. Respondents may be ashamed, embarrassed, or afraid to give a truthful answer. Instead, they give what they believe to be the normative or socially desirable answer. This is the *social desirability bias.* This social pressure can cause an overreporting or underreporting of the true situation (see Table 10.1).

People are likely to overreport being a good citizen (e.g., voting, knowing about issues), being well informed and cultured (e.g., reading, going to cultural events), fulfilling moral responsibilities (e.g., having a job, giving to charity), or having a good family life (e.g., having a happy marriage and good relations with children). For example, Denver respondents were asked whether they gave to a charity. A check of charity records revealed that 34 percent who said they gave in fact did not.[16]

Because most people want to present positive self-images and merge a sense of self with normative expectations, "false claims or exaggerations of socially desirable behavior occur more frequently than untruthful denials, false claims, minimizations,

TABLE 10.1   Threatening Questions and Sensitive Issues

TOPIC	PERCENTAGE VERY UNEASY
Masturbation	56
Sexual intercourse	42
Use of marijuana or hashish	42
Use of stimulants and depressants	31
Getting drunk	29
Petting and kissing	20
Income	12
Gambling with friends	10
Drinking beer, wine, or liquor	10
Happiness and well-being	4
Education	3
Occupation	3
Social activities	2
General leisure	2
Sports activity	1

Source: From *Improving Interview Method and Question-naire Design* by Norman M. Bradburn and Seymour Sudman. Copyright © 1979, Jossey-Bass, Inc., Publishers. Reprinted by permission of Norman M. Bradburn.

or exaggerations of socially undesirable behavior" (Wentworth, 1993:180). When a researcher suspects social desirability, he or she may ask several more specific questions and use the techniques for aiding respondent recall.

People are likely to underreport having an illness or disability (e.g., cancer, mental illness, venereal disease), engaging in illegal or deviant behavior (e.g., evading taxes, taking drugs, consuming alcohol, engaging in uncommon sexual practices), or revealing their financial status (e.g., income, savings, debts) (see Table 10.2).

Survey researchers have created several techniques to increase truthful answers to threatening questions. Some techniques involve the context and wording of the question itself. Researchers should ask threatening questions only after a warm-up, when an interviewer has developed rapport and trust with the respondents, and they should tell respondents that they want honest answers. They can phrase the question in an "enhanced way" to provide a context that makes it easier for respondents to give honest answers. For example, the following enhanced question was asked of heterosexual males: "In past surveys, many men have reported that at some point in their lives they have had some type of sexual experience with another male. This could have happened before adolescence, during adolescence, or as an adult. Have you ever had sex with a male at some point in your life?" In contrast, a standard form of the question would have asked, "Have you ever had sex with another male?"

The interviewer's gender also affects answers. Catania and colleagues (1996) found that when asked by a man, 3.5 percent answered "yes" to the standard and 8.2 percent to the enhanced form of the question; when asked by a woman, the percentages were 3.2 and 4.0 percent, respectively. The authors also note, "With respect to age of coital onset and adolescent virginity, enhanced items were associated with an increase in the age of coital onset for men and a decrease for women, and increased reports of adolescent virginity for men and decrease in teen virginity for women" (Catania et al., 1996:367).

Also, by embedding a threatening response within more serious activities, it may be made to seem less deviant. For example, respondents may hesitate to admit shoplifting if it is asked first, but after being asked about armed robbery or burglary, they may admit to shoplifting because it appears less serious.

Another technique involves the setting or format in which questions are asked. Survey methods that permit the greatest anonymity are better for threatening questions. Thus, more honest answers may come from mail or self-administered questionnaires than from face-to-face or telephone interviews. One new technique that may be effective for threatening questions involves *computer-assisted self-administered interviews (CASAI)*. In it, a respondent is "interviewed" by responding via a keyboard or computer mouse to questions that appear on a computer screen (or also heard over ear-

TABLE 10.2 Over- and Underreporting Behavior on Surveys

	PERCENTAGE OF DISTORTED OR ERRONEOUS ANSWERS		
	Face-to-Face	*Phone*	*Self-Administered*
Low Threat/Normative			
Registered to vote	+15	+17	+12
Voted in primary	+39	+31	+36
Have own library card	+19	+21	+18
High Threat			
Bankruptcy	−32	−29	−32
Drunk driving	−47	−46	−54

Source: From *Improving Interview Method and Questionnaire Design* by Norman M. Bradburn and Seymour Sudman. Copyright © 1979, Jossey-Bass, Inc., Publishers. Reprinted by permission of Norman M. Bradburn.

phones) while sitting in front of a computer. One study found that from 44 to 66 percent of respondents reported they ever smoked marijuana, depending on the questioning format used, with CASAI yielding the highest (and most honest) levels. Studies also found that the effectiveness of the CASAI techniques varies depending on the respondent's age, race, and level of distrust.[17]

A complicated invention for asking threatening questions in face-to-face interview situations is the *randomized response technique (RRT)*. The technique uses statistics beyond the level of this book, but the basic idea is to use known probabilities to estimate unknown proportions. Here is how RRT works. An interviewer gives the respondent two questions: One is threatening (e.g., "Do you use heroin?"), the other not threatening (e.g., "Were you born in September?"). A random method (e.g., toss of coin) is used to select the question to answer. The interviewer does not see which question was chosen but records the respondent's answer. The researcher uses knowledge about the probability of the random outcome and the frequency of the nonthreatening behavior to estimate the frequency of the sensitive behavior.

Knowledge Questions. Studies suggest that a large majority of the public cannot correctly answer elementary geography questions or identify important political documents (e.g., the Declaration of Independence). Researchers sometimes want to find out whether respondents know about an issue or topic, but knowledge questions can be threatening because respondents do not want to appear ignorant.[18]

Surveys may measure opinions better if they first ask about factual information, because many people have inaccurate factual knowledge. For example, Nadeau and colleagues (1993) found that most Americans seriously overestimate the percentage of racial minorities in the population. Only 15 percent of U.S. adults accurately report (plus or minus 6 percent) that 12.1 percent of the U.S. population is African American. Over half believe it is above 30 percent. Similarly, Jews make up about 3 percent of the U.S. population, but a majority (60 percent) of Americans believe the proportion to be 10 percent. Others have found that many Americans oppose foreign aid spending. Their opposition is based on extremely high overestimates of the cost of the programs. When asked what they would prefer to spend on foreign aid, most give an amount much higher than what now is being spent.

In another example 65 percent of Americans said that covering college costs for their children is one of their major concerns, but most estimated the tuition at public universities to be double its true amount, overestimating it by $6,800 (Archibald, 1998). They also overestimated tuition for private colleges by $5,600 and vastly underestimated the availability of financial aid. Survey questions about the public's knowledge can reveal serious distortions, but researchers have to phrase them carefully.

First, a researcher pilot tests questions so that questions are at an appropriate level of difficulty. Little is gained if 99 percent of respondents cannot answer the question. Knowledge questions can be worded so that respondents feel comfortable saying they do not know the answer—for example, "How much, if anything, have you heard about . . . ."

Respondents may overstate their knowledge or recognition of people or events. One way to check this is to use a *sleeper question*—a question or response choice about which a respondent could not possibly know. For example, in a study to determine which U.S. civil rights leaders respondents recognized, the name of a fictitious person was added. The person was "recognized" by 15 percent of the respondents. This implies that actual leaders who were recognized by only 15 percent were probably actually unknown. Another method is to ask respondents to "tell me about the person" after they say they recognize a name in a list.

Skip or Contingency Questions. Researchers avoid asking questions that are irrelevant for a respondent. Yet, some questions apply only to specific respondents. A *contingency question* is a two- (or more) part question.[19] The answer to the first part of the question determines which of two different questions a respondent next receives. Contingency questions select respondents for whom a second question is relevant. Sometimes they are called *screen* or *skip questions*. On the basis of the answer to a first question, the respondent or an interviewer is instructed to go to another or to skip certain questions.

The following example is a contingency question, adapted from deVaus (1986:79).

1. Were you born in Australia?
   [ ] Yes (GO TO QUESTION 2)
   [ ] No _____
       (a) What country were you born in?
           _____
       (b) How many years have you lived in Australia? _____
       (c) Are you an Australian citizen?
           [ ] Yes   [ ] No
   NOW GO TO QUESTION 2

Open versus Closed Questions

There has been a long debate about open versus closed questions in survey research.[20] An *open-ended* (unstructured, free-response) *question* asks a question (e.g., "What is your favorite television program?") to which respondents can give any answer. A *closed-ended* (structured, fixed-response) *question* both asks a question and gives the respondent fixed responses from which to choose (e.g., "Is the president doing a very good, good, fair, or poor job, in your opinion?").

Each form has advantages and disadvantages (see Box 10.3). The crucial issue is not which form is best. Rather, it is under what conditions a form is most appropriate. A researcher's choice to use an open- or closed-ended question depends on the purpose and the practical limitations of a research project. The demands of using open-ended questions, with interviewers writing verbatim answers followed by time-consuming coding, may make them impractical for a specific project.

Large-scale surveys have closed-ended questions because they are quicker and easier for both respondents and researchers. Yet, something important may be lost when an individual's beliefs and feelings are forced into a few fixed categories that a researcher created. To learn how a respondent thinks, to discover what is really important to him or her, or to get an answer to a question with many possible answers (e.g., age), open questions may be best. In addition, sensitive topics (e.g., sexual behavior, liquor consumption) may be more accurately measured with closed questions.

The disadvantages of a question form can be reduced by mixing open-ended and closed-ended questions in a questionnaire. Mixing them also offers a change of pace and helps interviewers establish rapport. Periodic probes (i.e., follow-up questions by interviewers) with closed-ended questions can reveal a respondent's reasoning.

Having interviewers periodically use probes to ask about a respondent's thinking is a way to check whether respondents are understanding the questions as a researcher intended. However, probes are not substitutes for writing clear questions or creating a framework of understanding for the respondent. Unless carefully stated, probes might shape the respondent's answers or force answers when a respondent does not have an opinion or information. Yet, flexible or conversational interviewing, in which interviewers use many probes, can improve accuracy on questions about complex issues on which respondents do not clearly understand basic terms or about which they have difficulty expressing their thoughts.[21] For example, to the question, "Did you do any work for money last week?" a respondent might hesitate, then reply, "Yes." An interviewer probes, "Could you tell me exactly what work you did?" The respondent may reply, "On Tuesday and Wednesday, I spent a couple hours helping my buddy John move into his new apartment. For that he gave me $40, but I didn't have any other job or get paid for doing anything else." If the researcher's intention was only to get reports of regular employment, the probe revealed a misunderstanding. Researchers also use *partially open questions* (i.e., a set of fixed choices with a final open choice of "other"), which allow respondents to offer an answer that the researcher did not include.

A total reliance on closed questions can distort results. For example, a study compared open and closed versions of the question, "What is the major problem facing the nation?" Respondents ranked different problems as most important depending on the form of the question. As Schuman and Presser (1979:86) reported, "Almost all respondents work within the substantive framework of the priorities provided by the investigators, *whether or not it fits their own priorities*" (emphasis added). In another study, respondents were asked open and closed questions about what was important in a

Box 10.3 _____

Closed versus Open Questions

ADVANTAGES OF CLOSED

- It is easier and quicker for respondents to answer.
- The answers of different respondents are easier to compare.
- Answers are easier to code and statistically analyze.
- The response choices can clarify question meaning for respondents.
- Respondents are more likely to answer about sensitive topics.
- There are fewer irrelevant or confused answers to questions.
- Less articulate or less literate respondents are not at a disadvantage.
- Replication is easier.

DISADVANTAGES OF CLOSED

- They can suggest ideas that the respondent would not otherwise have.
- Respondents with no opinion or knowledge can answer anyway.
- Respondents can be frustrated because their desired answer is not a choice.
- It is confusing if many (e.g., 20) response choices are offered.
- Misinterpretation of a question can go unnoticed.
- Distinctions between respondent answers may be blurred.
- Clerical mistakes or marking the wrong response are possible.
- They force respondents to give simplistic responses to complex issues.
- They force people to make choices they would not make in the real world.

ADVANTAGES OF OPEN

- They permit an unlimited number of possible answers.
- Respondents can answer in detail and can qualify and clarify responses.
- Unanticipated findings can be discovered.
- They permit adequate answers to complex issues.
- They permit creativity, self-expression, and richness of detail.
- They reveal a respondent's logic, thinking process, and frame of reference.

DISADVANTAGES OF OPEN

- Different respondents give different degrees of detail in answers.
- Responses may be irrelevant or buried in useless detail.
- Comparisons and statistical analysis become very difficult.
- Coding responses is difficult.
- Articulate and highly literate respondents have an advantage.
- Questions may be too general for respondents who lose direction.
- Responses are written verbatim, which is difficult for interviewers.
- A greater amount of respondent time, thought, and effort is necessary.
- Respondents can be intimidated by questions.
- Answers take up a lot of space in the questionnaire.

---

job. Half of the respondents who answered the open-ended version gave answers that were outside closed-question responses.

Open-ended questions are especially valuable in early or exploratory stages of research. For large-scale surveys, researchers use open questions in pilot tests, then develop closed-question responses from the answers given to the open questions. Glock (1987:50) noted

> _A major source of data in survey research is the qualitative interview conducted during the planning phases of a project. Such interviews, with a small but roughly representative sample of the population to be surveyed subsequently, afford an indispensable_

way to learn about the nature of variation and how to go about operationalizing it.

Researchers writing closed questions have to make many decisions. How many response choices should be given? Should they offer a middle or neutral choice? What should be the order of responses? What types of response choices? How will the direction of a response be measured?

Answers to these questions are not easy. For example, two response choices are too few, but more than five response choices are rarely a benefit. Researchers want to measure meaningful distinctions and not collapse them. More specific responses yield more information, but too many specifics create confusion. For example, rephrasing the question, "Are you satisfied with your dentist?" (which has a yes/no answer) to "How satisfied are you with your dentist: very satisfied, somewhat satisfied, somewhat dissatisfied, or not satisfied at all?" gives the researcher more information and a respondent more choices.

Nonattitudes and the Middle Positions.   Survey researchers debate whether to include choices for neutral, middle, and nonattitudes (e.g., "not sure," "don't know," or "no opinion").[22] Two types of errors can be made: accepting a middle choice or "no attitude" response when respondents hold a nonneutral opinion, or forcing respondents to choose a position on an issue when they have no opinion about it. Researchers also try to avoid both false positives (falsely stating an opinion when one does not know) and false negatives (falsely stating "don't know" when one has an opinion) with more attention given to false positives (Gilljam and Granberg, 1993).

Many fear that respondents will choose nonattitude choices to avoid making a choice. Yet, it is usually best to offer a nonattitude choice, because people will express opinions on fictitious issues, objects, and events. By offering a nonattitude (middle or no opinion) choice, researchers identify those holding middle positions or those without opinions.

The issue of nonattitudes can be approached by distinguishing among three kinds of attitude questions: standard-format, quasi-filter, and full-filter questions (see Box 10.4). The *standard-format*

"Next question: I believe that life is a constant striving for balance, requiring frequent tradeoffs between morality and necessity, within a cyclic pattern of joy and sadness, forging a trail of bittersweet memories until one slips, inevitably, into the jaws of death. Agree or disagree?"

question does not offer a "don't know" choice; a respondent must volunteer it. A *quasi-filter question* offers respondents a "don't know" alternative. A *full-filter question* is a special type of contingency question. It first asks if respondents have an opinion, then asks for the opinion of those who state that they do have an opinion.

Many respondents will answer a question if a "no opinion" choice is missing, but they will choose "don't know" when it is offered, or say that they do not have an opinion if asked. Such respondents are called *floaters* because they "float" from giving a response to not knowing. Their responses are affected by minor wording changes, so researchers screen them out using quasi-filter or full-filter questions. Filtered questions do not eliminate all answers to nonexistent issues, but they reduce the problem.

Box 10.4 _____

Standard-Format, Quasi-Filter, and Full-Filter Questions

STANDARD-FORMAT

Here is a question about another country. Do you agree or disagree with this statement? "The Russian leaders are basically trying to get along with America."

QUASI-FILTER

Here is a statement about another country: "The Russian leaders are basically trying to get along with America." Do you agree, disagree, or have no opinion on that?

FULL-FILTER

Here is a statement about another country. Not everyone has an opinion on this. If you do not have an opinion, just say so. Here's the statement: "The Russian leaders are basically trying to get along with America." Do you have an opinion on that? If yes, do you agree or disagree?

Example of Results from Different Question Forms

	Standard-Format (%)	Quasi-Filter (%)	Full-Filter (%)
Agree	48.2	27.7	22.9
Disagree	38.2	29.5	20.9
No opinion	13.6*	42.8	56.3

*Volunteered

Source: Adapted from Schuman and Presser (1981:116–125). Standard-format is from Fall 1978; quasi- and full-filter are from February 1977.

Middle alternative floaters choose a middle position when it is offered, or another alternative if it is not. They have less intense feelings about an issue. There is also a slight *recency effect;* that is, respondents are more likely to choose the last alternative offered. The recency effect suggests that it is best to present responses on a continuum, with the middle or neutral position stated in the middle.

Researchers have two options: offering a middle position for those who are truly ambiguous or moderate, or omitting the middle choice and forcing respondents to choose a position but following it immediately with a question asking how strongly they feel about the choice. This latter choice is preferred because attitudes have two aspects: direction (for or against) and intensity (strongly held or weakly held). For example, two respondents both oppose abortion, but one holds the opinion fiercely, with a strong commitment, whereas the other holds it weakly.

Agree/Disagree, Rankings or Ratings? Survey researchers who measure values and attitudes have debated two issues about the responses offered.[23] Should questionnaire items make a statement and ask respondents whether they agree or disagree with it, or should items offer respondents specific alternatives? Should the questionnaire include a set of items and ask respondents to rate them (e.g., approve, disapprove), or should it give them a list of items and force them to rank-order items (e.g., from most favored to least favored)?

It is best to offer respondents explicit alternatives. For example, instead of asking, "Do you agree or disagree with the statement, 'Men are better suited to . . . ,' " instead ask, "Do you think men are better suited, women are better suited, or both are equally suited?" Less well-educated respondents are more likely to agree with a statement, whereas forced-choice alternatives encourage thought and avoid the *response set* bias—a tendency of some respondents to agree and not really decide (Narayan and Krosnick, 1996).

Researchers create bias if question wording gives respondents a reason for choosing one alternative. For example, respondents were asked whether they supported or opposed a law on energy conservation. The results changed when respondents heard, "Do you support the law or do you oppose it because the law would be difficult to enforce?" instead of simply, "Do you support or oppose the law?"

It is better to ask respondents to choose among alternatives by ranking instead of rating items along an imaginary continuum. Respondents can rate several items equally high, but will place them in a hierarchy if asked to rank them.[24]

Attaching numbers to a response scale can assist respondents and give them clues for understanding. Positive and negative numbers at the extremes (e.g., +5 to –5) are best when a researcher conceptualizes the variable as bipolar opposites, and a series of positive numbers (e.g., 0 to 10) is best if he or she conceptualizes the variable as a single continuum.[25]

Wording Issues

Survey researchers face two wording issues. The first, discussed earlier, is to use simple vocabulary and grammar to minimize confusion. The second issue involves effects of specific words or phrases. It is trickier because it is not possible to know in advance whether a word or phrase affects responses.[26]

The well-documented difference between *forbid* and *not allow* illustrates the problem of wording differences. Both terms have the same meaning, but many more people are willing to "not allow" something than to "forbid" it. In general, less well-educated respondents are most influenced by minor wording differences.

Certain words seem to trigger an emotional reaction, and researchers are just beginning to learn of them. For example, Smith (1987) found large differences (e.g., twice as much support) in U.S. survey responses depending on whether a question asked about spending "to help the poor" or "for welfare." He suggested that the word *welfare* has such strong negative connotations for Americans (lazy people, wasteful and expensive programs, etc.) that it is best to avoid it.

Possible *wording effects* are illustrated by what appears to be a noncontroversial question. Peterson (1984) examined four ways to ask about age: "How old are you?", "What is your age?", "In what year were you born?", and "Are you . . . 18–24, 25–34, . . . ?" He checked responses against birth certificate records and found that from 95.1 to 98.7 percent of respondents gave correct responses depending on the form of question used. He also found that the form of the question that had the fewest errors had the highest percentage of refusals to answer, and the form with the most errors had the lowest refusal rate. This example suggests that errors in a noncontroversial factual question vary with minor wording changes and that increasing the respondent's willingness to answer may increase errors in responses.

Many respondents are confused by words or their connotations. For example, respondents were asked whether they thought television news was impartial. Researchers later learned that large numbers of respondents had ignored the word *impartial*—a term the middle-class, educated researchers assumed everyone would know. Less than half the respondents had interpreted the word as intended with its proper meaning. Over one-fourth ignored it or had no idea of its meaning. Others gave it unusual meanings, and one-tenth thought it was directly opposite to its true meaning. Researchers need to be cautious, because some wording effects (e.g., the difference between *forbid* and *not allow*) remain the same for decades, while other effects may appear.[27]

Questionnaire Design Issues

Length of Survey or Questionnaire. How long should a questionnaire be or an interview last?[28] Researchers prefer long questionnaires or interviews because they are more cost-effective. The cost for extra questions—once a respondent has been sampled, has been contacted, and has completed other questions—is small. There is no absolute proper length. The length depends on the survey format (to be discussed) and on the respondent's characteristics. A 10-minute telephone interview is rarely a problem and can usually be extended to 20 minutes. A few researchers stretch this to beyond 30 minutes. Mail questionnaires are more variable. A short (3- or 4-page) questionnaire is appropriate for the general population. Some researchers have had success with questionnaires as long as 10 pages (about 100 items) with the general public, but responses drop significantly for longer questionnaires. For highly educated respondents and a salient topic, using questionnaires of 15 pages may be possible. Face-to-face interviews lasting an hour are not uncommon. In special situations face-to-face interviews as long as three to five hours have been conducted.

Question Order or Sequence.   A survey researcher faces two question-sequence issues.[29] The first is how to organize items in the overall questionnaire. The second involves context effects of answering specific questions before others.

In general, you should sequence questions to minimize the discomfort and confusion of respondents. A questionnaire has opening, middle, and ending questions. After an introduction explaining the survey, it is best to make opening questions pleasant, interesting, and easy to answer so that they help a respondent feel comfortable about the questionnaire. Avoid asking many boring background questions or threatening questions first. Organize questions in the middle into common topics. Mixing questions on different topics causes confusion. Orient respondents by placing questions on the same topic together and introduce the section with a short introductory statement (e.g., "Now I would like to ask you questions about housing"). Make question topics flow smoothly and logically, and organize them to assist respondents' memory or comfort levels. Do not end with highly threatening questions, and always end with a "thank you."

Researchers are concerned that the order in which questions are presented may influence respondents' answers. These *order effects* are strongest for respondents who lack strong opinions or who are less well educated. They use previous questions as a context to help them answer later questions (see Box 10.5). You can do two things about specific question-order effects: Use a *funnel sequence* of

---

Box 10.5 _____

Question-Order Effects

QUESTION 1

"Do you think that the United States should let Communist newspaper reporters from other countries come in here and send back to their papers the news as they see it?"

QUESTION 2

"Do you think a Communist country like Russia should let American newspaper reporters come in and send back to America the news as they see it?"

PERCENTAGE SAYING YES

Heard First	Yes to #1 (Communist Reporter)	Yes to #2 (American Reporter)
#1	54%	75%
#2	64%	82%

Here are two questions asked of Americans in a survey during the 1970s. The context created by answering the first question affects the answer to the second question.

_____

Source: Adapted from Schuman and Presser (1981:29).

questions—that is, ask more general questions before specific ones (e.g., ask about health in general before asking about specific diseases). Or divide the number of respondents in half and give one half questions in one order and the other half in the alternative order, then examine the results to see whether question order mattered. If question-order effects are found, which order tells you what the respondents really think? The answer is that you cannot know for sure.

For example, a few years ago, a class of our students conducted a telephone survey on two topics: concern about crime and attitudes toward a new drunk-driving law. A random half of the respondents heard questions about the drunk-driving law first; the other half heard about crime first. We examined the results to see whether there was any *context effect*—a difference by topic order. We found that respondents who were asked about the drunk-driving law first expressed less fear about crime than did those who were asked about crime first. Likewise, they were more supportive of the drunk-driving law than were those who first heard about crime. The first topic created a context within which respondents answered questions on the second topic. After they were asked about crime in general and thought about violent crime, drunk driving may have appeared to be a less important issue. By contrast, after they were asked about drunk driving and thought about drunk driving as a crime, they may have expressed less concern about crime in general.

Respondents answer all questions based on a context of preceding questions and the interview setting. A researcher needs to remember that the more ambiguous a question's meaning, the stronger the context effects, because respondents will draw on the context to interpret and understand the question. Previous questions on the same topic and heard just before a question can have a large context effect. For example, Sudman and associates (1996:90–91) contrasted three ways of asking how much a respondent followed politics. When they asked the question alone, about 21 percent of respondents said they followed politics "now and then" or "hardly at all." When they asked the question after asking what the respondent's elected representative recently did, the percentage who said they did not follow politics

nearly doubled, going to 39 percent. The knowledge question about the representative made many respondents feel that they did not really know much. When a question about the amount of "public relations work" the elected representative provided to the area came between the two questions, 29 percent of respondents said they did not follow politics. This question gave respondents an excuse for not knowing the answer to the first question—they could blame their representative for their ignorance. The context of a question can make a difference, and researchers need to be aware of it at all times: "Question comprehension is not merely a function of the wording of a question. Respondents use information provided by the context of the question to determine its intended meaning" (Sudman et al., 1996:69).

Nonresponse, Refusals, and Response Rates. Have you ever refused to answer a survey? The likelihood that people will agree to a request to complete a questionnaire varies for different types of contact. Charities expect a 1-percent response rate, whereas the government census expects a 95-percent rate. Response rates are a big concern in survey research. If a high proportion of the sampled respondents do not respond, researchers become cautious about generalizing from the results. If the nonresponders differ from those who respond (e.g., are less educated), low response rates can create bias and weaken validity.

Failure to get a response from a sampled respondent can take several forms: The respondent could not be contacted, he or she was contacted but was unable to complete the survey (e.g., spoke another language, had no time, was ill, etc.), he or she refused to complete a questionnaire or refused to be interviewed, or he or she refused to answer some questions.[30]

Mandatory appeals (e.g., a statement that says "Answering this is required by law") dramatically improve responses, even if it is on an envelope, but appeals such as, "Please answer; this will help you" (or your area) and promises of confidentiality have little effect on response rates. Many minor factors can affect responses or refusals. Small incentives (e.g., payments of $1) and comments by a respondent before an interview begins (e.g., "I'm too busy now" or "I'm not interested but okay I'll do it") are associated with how a respondent answers and the completeness of survey responses.[31]

Public participation in survey research has declined in the United States since the 1950s, especially in urban areas. One report notes that as many as 38 percent of Americans refuse to participate in surveys.[32] This is a disturbing trend for survey researchers. It is due to many factors—a fear of strangers and crime, social isolation, an overload of surveys, and, most important,

> *people who refuse to participate in surveys appear to be more negative about surveys in general, more withdrawn and isolated from their environment and more concerned about maintaining their privacy free of any intrusion by strangers. (Sudman and Bradburn, 1983:11)*

In addition to privacy concerns, an unfavorable past experience with surveys is a major cause of nonresponse. Legitimate survey research is impeded by misused survey techniques, insensitive interviewers, poorly designed or written questionnaires, and inadequate explanations of surveys to respondents.

Survey researchers disagree about what constitutes an adequate response rate. *Adequate* is a judgment call that depends on the population, practical limitations, the topic, and the response with which specific researchers feel comfortable. Most researchers consider anything below 50 percent to be poor and over 90 percent as excellent.

If response rates are below 75 percent, the survey results can differ significantly from what they would be if everyone responded. For example, a survey reports that a majority of respondents favor a product or a new policy, when in fact a majority of the population actually oppose it. This is likely when the response rate is low and those who do not respond have different views from those who do (see Box 10.6).

Researchers compute response rates using the following kinds of "nonresponse":

- Unable to locate a respondent
- Located the respondent, but could not make contact (no answer, never available, or incapable of answering)
- Located and contacted respondent, but respondent refused to participate

- Located and contacted respondent who agreed to participate, but respondent failed to answer most questions or ended before completing the questionnaire

A *location rate* is the number of located respondents out of all respondents. For example, we want to survey 600 alumni from a school, but we find addresses or phone numbers for 300. Our location rate is 300 of 600, or 50 percent. A *contact rate* is the number of respondents contacted out of those located. For example, of the 300 alumni we locate, we get a response from 200; the remaining 100 never answer phones, do not return mail questionnaires, or are incapable (e.g., very ill) of answering. Our contact rate is 200 of 300, or 66.7 percent. A *refusal rate* is the percentage of contacted respondents who refuse to participate. For example, we contact 200 alumni, but 20 refuse to participate. Our refusal rate is 20 of 200, or 10 percent. A *completion rate* is the proportion of respondents who begin a survey and complete all items. For example, of the 180 alumni who agreed to participate and began the questionnaire, 150 answer all questions. The other 30 stopped part-way through or skipped or refused to answer large blocks of questions. Our completion rate is 150 of 180, or 83.3 percent. Researchers should disclose each type of nonreponse.

Researchers report different response rates, or they mix them with location, contact, refusal, or completion rates. The *active response rate* is the number of completed questionnaires out of all located respondents. Using the preceding example, 150 alumni completed the questionnaire out of 300 who were located, so the active response rate is 50 percent. Nonresponse includes those who refuse to participate or fail to answer all questions. The *total response rate* is the number who completed the questions out of all possible respondents. Again, using the alumni example, the total response rate is 150 of 600, or 25 percent.

Response rates for self-administered questionnaires (e.g., those distributed to a class) or the government census are close to 100 percent and present little problem (see Box 10.7). Rates are high for face-to-face interviews (about 90 percent), followed by telephone interviews (about 80 percent).

Box 10.6

Example of Response-Rate Problems

Assuming 70 percent of the respondents respond, how far off could the observed results be from the true population parameter? A series of possible situations is illustrated below:

RESPONSE TO QUESTION	OBSERVED PERCENTAGE OF ANSWERING RESPONDENTS	HYPOTHETICAL RESPONSE OF THOSE NOT RESPONDING	TRUE RESPONSE OF WHOLE POPULATION (PARAMETER)[a]
Favor	50 (35)[b]	60 (18)	53%
Oppose	50 (35)	40 (12)	47%
Favor	50 (35)	90 (27)	62%
Oppose	50 (35)	10 (3)	38%
Favor	20 (14)	60 (18)	32%
Oppose	80 (56)	40 (12)	68%
Favor	20 (14)	90 (27)	41%
Oppose	80 (56)	10 (3)	59%
Favor	45 (31.5)	60 (18)	49.5%
Oppose	55 (38.5)	40 (12)	50.5%
Favor	45 (31.5)	90 (27)	58.5%
Oppose	55 (38.5)	10 (3)	41.5%

[a]This assumes a perfect sampling frame, with no sampling errors or measurement errors. Any such error could increase or decrease the difference between observed survey results and the population parameter.

[b]The number in parentheses is the actual percentage in the population choosing an answer. For example, 50 percent choosing an answer with a 70-percent response rate is 50% × 70% = 35% of the population choosing that answer. The estimate of population parameter is calculated by adding the actual percentage in the population for the observed and the hypothetical nonrespondent answers.

Response rates are a major concern for mail questionnaires. A response rate of 10 to 50 percent is common for a mail survey.

A researcher can increase response rates in several ways. In telephone interview surveys, interviewers can make five callbacks before dropping a respondent. They can keep a record of each call so that they do not always call back at the same time. Ideal times to call vary, but from 6:00 through 9:00 P.M. on Sunday through Thursday is usually a good period of time.

Even with several callbacks, noncontact rates of 20 percent are common. Once interviewers contact a respondent, he or she must be persuaded to cooperate. Refusal rates for telephone interviews are often about 20 percent. Although it is impossible with random-digit dialing, cooperation rates on telephone interviews are usually higher if the researcher sends a letter three to five days in advance telling the respondent to expect the interview call. Interviewers give their name, the organization conducting the survey, the general topic of the survey, and the approximate amount of time the interview will take—for example: "My name is Larry Neuman, I am calling for the Survey Research Corporation. I'd like to ask you some questions about your television viewing habits. The interview shouldn't last more than 10 minutes, and your answers will be kept confidential."

Face-to-face interviewers first have the task of locating a respondent. An advance letter or telephone call to arrange an appointment is wise, but

Box 10.7

Census Undercounts or Nonlocation Rates

The U.S. Census is a survey conducted by the U.S. government for various purposes (e.g., deciding the number of elected representatives for geographic areas, distributing funds to provide services, etc.). The U.S. government conducts a census every 10 years. So far, it has not used sampling but has tried to count everyone. This has resulted in miscounting and response rates of 93 to 100 percent, depending on the area. The greatest undercount in the 1990 census occured in South Bronx, New York City. An estimated 40,245 people were not located or asked census questions. The next to largest undercount was also in New York City, with an estimated 250,000 people not located or counted in the city. For example, each congressional district in the United States should have 550,000 people, but the South Bronx undercount missed 7.3 percent of the people in the 16th Congressional District of New York. Undercounts tend to occur in areas with large numbers of low-income people, racial minorities, transients, and recent immigrants. In contrast, people in some areas are counted twice, with an estimated 7,448 counted twice in one area. Overcounting tends to occur in upper-income, suburban areas with large numbers of well-educated people who own more than one house (see Holmes, 1998).

repeat visits may be necessary. Even with an appointment, respondents may hesitate or refuse. Interviewers should have a photo identification card and should explain who is interviewing the respondent and why. Once a respondent is contacted and a well-trained, pleasant interviewer is at the doorstep, most respondents cooperate.

Getting survey responses from some populations, such as low-income, inner-city minorities, poses a special challenge. Pottick and Lerman (1991) used a journalistic-style letter introducing the survey and a personal telephone call reminding respondents of an interview. They compared this approach with a standard method using an academic-style letter and a follow-up letter. Their approach produced a more rapid response and more respondents. For example, their technique resulted in 65 percent participation, compared to 39 percent for the standard method. Their approach also brought in respondents who were more generally pessimistic and those who felt less well understood by government and social service agencies.

There is a large body of literature on ways to increase response rates for mail questionnaires (see Box 10.8).[33] Heberlein and Baumgartner (1978) reported 71 factors affecting mail questionnaire response rates.

A meta-analysis (meta-analysis is explained in the last chapter) of 115 articles on mail survey responses taken from 25 journals published between 1940 and 1988 revealed that cover letters, questionnaires of four pages or fewer, a return envelope with postage, and a small monetary reward all increase returns (Yammarino et al., 1991). Many of the techniques suggested follow the Total Design Method (to be discussed) and help to make the task easy and interesting for respondents.

Format and Layout. There are two format or layout issues: the overall physical layout of the questionnaire and the format of questions and responses.

Questionnaire Layout. Layout is important, whether a questionnaire is for an interviewer or for the respondent.[34] Questionnaires should be clear, neat, and easy to follow. Give each question a number and put identifying information (e.g., name of organization) on questionnaires. Never cramp questions together or create a confusing appearance. A few cents saved in postage or printing will ultimately cost more in terms of lower validity due to a lower response rate or to confusion of interviewers and respondents. Make a *cover sheet* or face sheet for each interview, for administrative use. Put the time and date of interview, the interviewer, the respondent identification number, and the interviewer's comments and observations on it. A professional appearance with high-quality graphics, space between

Box 10.8 _____

Ten Ways to Increase Mail Questionnaire Response

1. Address the questionnaire to a specific person, not "Occupant," and send it via first-class mail.
2. Include a carefully written, dated cover letter on letterhead stationery. In it, request respondent cooperation, guarantee confidentiality, explain the purpose of the survey, and give the researcher's name and phone number.
3. *Always* include a postage-paid, addressed return envelope.
4. The questionnaire should have a neat, attractive layout and reasonable page length.
5. The questionnaire should be professionally printed and easy to read, with clear instructions.
6. Send two follow-up reminder letters to those not responding. The first should arrive about one week after sending the questionnaire, the second a week later. Gently ask for cooperation again and offer to send another questionnaire.
7. Do not send questionnaires during major holiday periods.
8. Do not put questions on the back page. Instead, leave a blank space and ask the respondent for general comments.
9. Sponsors that are local and are seen as legitimate (e.g., government agencies, universities, large firms, etc.) get a better response.
10. Include a small monetary inducement ($1) if possible.

---

questions, and good layout improves accuracy and completeness and helps the questionnaire flow.

Give interviewers or respondents instructions on the questionnaire. Print instructions in a different style from the questions (e.g., in a different color or font or in all capitals) to distinguish them. This is important for interview surveys so that an interviewer can distinguish between questions for respondents and instructions intended for the interviewer alone.

Layout is crucial for mail questionnaires because there is no friendly interviewer to interact with the respondent. Instead, the questionnaire's appearance persuades the respondent. In mail surveys include a polite, professional cover letter on letterhead stationery, identifying the researcher and offering a telephone number for questions. Details matter. Respondents will be turned off if they receive a bulky brown envelope with bulk postage addressed to Occupant or if the questionnaire does not fit into the return envelope. Always end with "Thank you for your participation." Interviewers and questionnaires should leave respondents with a positive feeling about the survey and a sense that their participation is appreciated.

Question Format.   Survey researchers decide on a format for questions and responses. Should respondents circle responses, check boxes, fill in dots, or put an × in a blank? The principle is to make responses unambiguous. Boxes or brackets to be checked and numbers to be circled are usually clearest. Also, listing responses down a page rather than across makes them easier to see (see Box 10.9). As mentioned before, use arrows and instructions for contingency questions. Visual aids are also helpful. For example, hand out thermometer-like drawings to respondents when asking about how warm or cool they feel toward someone. A *matrix question* (or grid question) is a compact way to present a series of questions using the same response categories. It saves space and makes it easier for the respondent or interviewer to note answers for the same response categories.

Sanchez (1992) examined the effect of two questionnaire layouts on questions about religion asked by experienced interviewers. She found that a clearer layout reduced "not ascertained" responses from 8.8 to 2.04 percent. In addition, when she changed the format for a contingency question to make it clearer, the percentage of interviewers who probed for specific religious denomination increased from about 91 percent to over 99 percent.

Total Design Method.   Dillman (1978) developed the *Total Design Method (TDM)* to improve mail and telephone surveys. The method has both theoretical and practical parts. The theory says that a survey is a social interaction in which respondents act on the basis of what they expect to receive in

Box 10.9

Question Format Examples

EXAMPLE OF HORIZONTAL VERSUS VERTICAL RESPONSE CHOICES

Do you think it is too easy or too difficult to get a divorce, or is it about right?
o Too Easy   o Too Difficult   o About Right

Do you think it is too easy or too difficult to get a divorce, or is it about right?
o Too Easy
o Too Difficult
o About Right

EXAMPLE OF A MATRIX QUESTION FORMAT

	Strongly Agree	Agree	Disagree	Strongly Disagree	Don't Know
The teacher talks too fast.	o	o	o	o	o
I learned a lot in this class.	o	o	o	o	o
The tests are very easy.	o	o	o	o	o
The teacher tells many jokes.	o	o	o	o	o
The teacher is organized.	o	o	o	o	o

EXAMPLES OF SOME RESPONSE CATEGORY CHOICES

Excellent, Good, Fair, Poor

Approve/Disapprove

Favor/Oppose

Strongly Agree, Agree, Somewhat Agree, Somewhat Disagree, Disagree, Strongly Disagree

Too Much, Too Little, About Right

Better, Worse, About the Same

Regularly, Often, Seldom, Never

Always, Most of Time, Some of Time, Rarely, Never

More Likely, Less Likely, No Difference

Very Interested, Interested, Not Interested

---

exchange for their cooperation. They cooperate when social costs are low, when the expected benefit exceeds the perceived costs, and when researchers create a feeling of trust. The practical part repeats the advice given here about good question wording and questionnaire design. Thus, a good survey design has pilot tests, minimizes personal costs to respondents, and requires minimal effort and time from respondents. It creates intangible rewards, such as a feeling of doing something of value or being important.

TYPES OF SURVEYS: ADVANTAGES AND DISADVANTAGES

Mail and Self-Administered Questionnaires

Advantages.   Researchers can give questionnaires directly to respondents or mail them to respondents who read instructions and questions, then record their answers. This type of survey is by far the cheapest, and it can be conducted by a single researcher. A researcher can send questionnaires to a wide geographical area. The respondent can complete the questionnaire when it is convenient and can check personal records if necessary. Mail questionnaires offer anonymity and avoid interviewer bias. They are very effective, and response rates may be high for a target population that is well educated or has a strong interest in the topic or the survey organization.

Disadvantages.   Since people do not always complete and return questionnaires, the biggest problem with mail questionnaires is a low response rate. Most questionnaires are returned within two weeks, but others trickle in up to two months later. Researchers can raise response rates by sending nonrespondents reminder letters, but this adds to the time and cost of data collection.

A researcher cannot control the conditions under which a mail questionnaire is completed. A questionnaire completed during a drinking party by a dozen laughing people may be returned along with one filled out by an earnest respondent. Also, no one is present to clarify questions or to probe for more information when respondents give incomplete answers. Someone other than the sampled respondent (e.g., spouse, new resident, etc.) may open the mail and complete the questionnaire without the researcher's knowledge. Different respondents can complete the questionnaire weeks apart or answer questions in a different order than that intended by researchers. Incomplete questionnaires can also be a serious problem.

Researchers cannot visually observe the respondent's reactions to questions, physical characteristics, or the setting. For example, an impoverished 70-year-old White woman living alone on a farm could falsely state that she is a prosperous 40-year-old Asian male doctor with three children living in a town. Such extreme lies are rare, but serious errors can go undetected.

The mail questionnaire format limits the kinds of questions that a researcher can use. Questions requiring visual aids (e.g., look at this picture and tell me what you see), open-ended questions, many contingency questions, and complex questions do poorly in mail questionnaires. Likewise, mail questionnaires are ill-suited for the illiterate or near-illiterate in English. Questionnaires mailed to illiterate respondents are not likely to be returned; if they are completed and returned, the questions were probably misunderstood, so the answers are meaningless (see Table 10.3).

Telephone Interviews

Advantages.   The telephone interview is a popular survey method because about 95 percent of the population can be reached by telephone. An interviewer calls a respondent (usually at home), asks questions, and records answers. Researchers sample respondents from lists, telephone directories, or use RDD, and can quickly reach many people across long distances. A staff of interviewers can interview 1,500 respondents across a nation within a few days and, with several callbacks, response rates can reach 90 percent. Although this method is more expensive than a mail questionnaire, special reduced long distance phone rates help. In general, the telephone interview is a flexible method with most of the strengths of face-to-face interviews but for about half the cost. Interviewers control the sequence of questions and can use some probes. A specific respondent is chosen and is likely to answer all the questions alone. The researcher knows when the questions were answered and can use contingency questions effectively, especially with computer-assisted telephone interviewing (CATI) (to be discussed).

Disadvantages.   Relatively high cost and limited interview length are disadvantages of telephone interviews. In addition, respondents without telephones are impossible to reach, and the call may come at an inconvenient time. The use of an interviewer reduces anonymity and introduces potential interviewer bias. Open-ended questions are difficult to use, and questions requiring visual aids are impossible. Interviewers can only note serious disruptions (e.g., background noise) and respondent tone of voice (e.g., anger or flippancy) or hesitancy.

Face-to-Face Interviews

Advantages.   Face-to-face interviews have the highest response rates and permit the longest questionnaires. They have the advantages of the telephone interview, and interviewers also can

TABLE 10.3   Types of Surveys and Their Features

FEATURES	TYPE OF SURVEY		
	Mail Questionnaire	Telephone Interview	Face-to-Face Interview
Administrative Issues			
Cost	Cheapest	Moderate	Expensive
Speed	Slowest	Fastest	Slow to moderate
Length (number of questions)	Moderate	Short	Longest
Response rate	Lowest	Moderate	Highest
Research Control			
Probes possible	No	Yes	Yes
Specific respondent	No	Yes	Yes
Question sequence	No	Yes	Yes
Only one respondent	No	Yes	Yes
Visual observation	No	No	Yes
Success with Different Questions			
Visual aids	Limited	None	Yes
Open-ended questions	Limited	Limited	Yes
Contingency questions	Limited	Yes	Yes
Complex questions	Limited	Limited	Yes
Sensitive questions	Some	Some	Some
Sources of Bias			
Social desirability	No	Some	Worse
Interviewer bias	No	Some	Worse
Respondent's reading skill	Yes	No	No

observe the surroundings and can use nonverbal communication and visual aids. Well-trained interviewers can ask all types of questions, can ask complex questions, and can use extensive probes.

Disadvantages.   High cost is the biggest disadvantage of face-to-face interviews. The training, travel, supervision, and personnel costs for interviews can be high. Interviewer bias is also greatest in face-to-face interviews. The appearance, tone of voice, question wording, and so forth of the interviewer may affect the respondent. In addition, interviewer supervision is less than for telephone interviews, which supervisors monitor by listening in.[35]

Special Situations

There are many kinds of special surveys. One is a survey of organizations (e.g., businesses, schools, etc.). Mail questionnaires are usually used, but other methods are possible. A researcher writes questions to ask about the organization. He or she learns who in the organization has the necessary information, because it is essential to contact someone capable of responding. He or she then makes the significance of the survey clear because officials receive many requests for information and do not answer all of them.

Surveying white-collar elites requires special techniques.[36] Powerful leaders in business, government, and so on are difficult to reach. Assistants may intercept mail questionnaires, and restricted access can present a formidable obstacle to face-to-face or telephone interviewing. Access is facilitated when a prestigious source calls or sends a letter of introduction. Once the researcher makes an appointment, the researcher, not a hired interviewer, conducts the interviews. Personal interviews with a high percentage of open-ended questions are usually more successful than all closed-ended questions. Confidentiality is a crucial issue and should be guaranteed, since elites often have information that few others do.

The focus group is a special kind of interview situation that is largely nonquantitative.[37] In *focus groups* a researcher gathers together 6 to 12 people in a room with a moderator to discuss one or more issues for one to two hours. The issue can be a public concern, a product, a television program, a political candidate, or a policy. The moderator introduces issues and ensures that no one person dominates. The moderator is flexible, keeps people on the topic, and encourages discussion. Responses are tape recorded or recorded by a secretary who assists the moderator. The group members should be homogeneous enough to reduce conflict but should not include friends or relatives. Focus groups are useful in exploratory research or to generate new ideas for hypotheses, questionnaire items, and the interpretation of results.

Costs

Professional-quality survey research can be expensive if all costs are considered. The cost varies according to the type of survey used. A simple formula is that for every $1 in cost for a mail survey, a telephone interview survey costs about $5 and a face-to-face interview about $15. For example, Dillman (1983) estimated that a 12-page mail survey of 450 respondents cost over $3,000 in 1980 dollars. This estimate is low because the labor to develop and pretest questions and costs associated with data analysis are not included.

Costs vary greatly.[38] Beyond modest supply costs, the biggest expenses are labor costs for professional staff who develop and pilot test a questionnaire, costs to train interviewers, and labor costs for clerical staff and interviewers. Beginning researchers and students tend to seriously underestimate the expenses and the amount of time required. In 1998 a two-page mail questionnaire sent to 300 respondents cost us $1,500, or about $5 each. This did not include pay for the 24 hours we spent writing and checking the questionnaire nor any costs to prepare the data for the

computer or to analyze the data. With a 70-percent response rate, the real cost was closer to $7.50 per respondent.

Professional survey organizations often charge $50 and up per completed 15-minute telephone interview. The costs for a face-to-face interview study are higher. Professionally completed face-to-face interviews can cost over $200 per completed interview, depending on the interview length and travel expenses. At one extreme, a face-to-face survey of 1,000 geographically dispersed respondents from the general public may cost over $250,000 and take over a year to complete. At the other extreme, a simple one-page, self-administered questionnaire that a teacher photocopies and distributes to 100 students in one school can cost very little, except for the teacher's time and effort. The teacher might be able to prepare and distribute the questionnaire, collect responses, and tabulate results in as little as one week.

INTERVIEWING

The Role of the Interviewer

Interviews to gather information occur in many settings. Employers interview prospective employees, medical personnel interview patients, mental health professionals interview clients, social service workers interview the needy, reporters interview politicians and others, police officers interview witnesses and crime victims, and talk-show hosts interview celebrities (see Box 10.10). Survey research interviewing is a specialized kind of interviewing. As with most interviewing, its goal is to obtain accurate information from another person.[39]

The survey interview is a social relationship. Like other social relationships, it involves social roles, norms, and expectations. The interview is a short-term, secondary social interaction between two strangers with the explicit purpose of one person's obtaining specific information from the other. The social roles are those of the interviewer and the interviewee or respondent. Information is obtained in a structured conversation in which the interviewer asks prearranged questions and records answers, and the respondent answers.

Box 10.10

Types of Nonresearch Interviews

1. *Job interview.* An employer asks open-ended questions to gather information about a candidate for a job and to observe how the candidate presents himself or herself. The candidate (respondent) initiates the contact and attempts to present a positive self-image. The employer (interviewer) tries to discover the candidate's true talents and flaws. A serious, judgmental tone exists, with the employer having the power to accept or reject the candidate. This often creates tension and limited trust. The parties may have conflicting goals and each may use some deception. The results are not confidential.

2. *Assistance interview.* A helping professional (counselor, lawyer, social worker, medical doctor, etc.) seeks information on a client's problem, including background and current conditions. The helping professional (interviewer) uses the information to understand and translate the client's (respondent's) problem into professional terms for problem resolution. The tone is serious and concerned. There is usually low tension and high mutual trust. The parties share the goal of resolving the client's problem, and deception is rare. The interview results are usually confidential.

3. *Journalistic interview.* A journalist gathers information from a celebrity, newsmaker, witness, or background person for later use in constructing a newsworthy story. The journalist (interviewer) uses various skills in attempting to get novel information, some of which may not be easily revealed, and "quotable quotes" from the news source (respondent). The journalist uses the interview information selectively in combination with other information, usually beyond the respondent's control. The tone and degree of trust and tension vary greatly. The

goals of the parties may diverge and each may use deception. The interview results are not confidential and they may get a lot of publicity.

4. *Interrogation or investigative interview.* A criminal justice official, auditor, or other person in authority seriously asks questions to obtain information from an accused person or others with information about wrongdoing. The official (interviewer) will use the information as evidence to construct a case against someone (possibly the respondent). The tension is often extreme with mutual distrust. The goals of the parties diverge sharply, and each often uses deception. Interview results are rarely confidential and may become part of an official, public record.

5. *Entertainment interview.* An emcee or show host offers comments and asks open-ended questions to a celebrity or other person who may digress in answers or begin a monologue. The primary goal is to stimulate interest, enjoyment, or gaiety among an audience. Often, the style displayed by each is more central than any information revealed. The host (interviewer) seeks an immediate response or reaction in the audience, while the celebrity (respondent) tries to increase his or her fame or reputation. The tone is light, tension is low, and trust is moderately high. The limited goals of each often converge. They may deceive each other or join in deceiving the audience. The situation is the opposite to one in which confidentiality can occur.

People can mix the types of interviews, and people often use several types. For example, the social worker in a social control role instead of a helping role may conduct an investigative interview. Or a police officer helping a crime victim may use an assistance interview instead of an interrogation.

It differs in several ways from ordinary conversation (see Table 10.4).

An important problem for interviewers is that many respondents are unfamiliar with the survey respondents' role and "respondents often do not have a clear conception of what is expected of them" (Turner and Martin, 1984:282). As a result, they

substitute another role that may affect their responses. Some believe the interview is an intimate conversation or therapy session, some see it as a bureaucratic exercise in completing forms, some view it as a citizen referendum on policy choices, some view it as a testing situation, and some see it as a form of deceit in which interviewers are trying to

TABLE 10.4   Differences between Ordinary Conversation and a Structured Survey Interview

ORDINARY CONVERSATION	THE SURVEY INTERVIEW
1. Questions and answers from each participant are relatively equally balanced.	1. Interviewer asks and respondent answers most of the time.
2. There is an open exchange of feelings and opinions.	2. Only the respondent reveals feelings and opinions.
3. Judgments are stated and attempts made to persuade the other toward a particular point of view.	3. Interviewer is nonjudgmental and does not try to change respondent's opinions or beliefs.
4. A person can reveal deep inner feelings to gain sympathy or as a therapeutic release.	4. Interviewer tries to obtain direct answers to specific questions.
5. Ritual responses are common (e.g., "Uh huh," shaking head, "How are you?" "Fine").	5. Interviewer avoids making ritual responses that influence a respondent and also seeks genuine answers, not ritual responses.
6. The participants exchange information and correct the factual errors that they are aware of.	6. Respondent provides almost all information. Interviewer does not correct a respondent's factual errors.
7. Topics rise and fall and either person can introduce new topics. The focus can shift directions or digress to less relevant issues.	7. Interviewer controls the topic, direction, and pace. He or she keeps the respondent "on task," and irrelevant diversions are contained.
8. The emotional tone can shift from humor, to joy, to affection, to sadness, to anger, and so on.	8. Interviewer attempts to maintain a consistently warm but serious and objective tone throughout.
9. People can evade or ignore questions and give flippant or noncommittal answers.	9. Respondent should not evade questions and should give truthful, thoughtful answers.

Source: Adapted from Gorden (1980:19–25) and Sudman and Bradburn (1983:5–10).

trick or entrap respondents (Turner and Martin, 1984:262–269). Even in a well-designed, professional survey, follow-up research found that only about half the respondents understand questions exactly as intended by researchers. Respondents reinterpreted questions to make them applicable to their ideosyncratic, personal situations or to make them easy to answer (Turner and Martin, 1984:282).

The role of interviewers is difficult. They obtain cooperation and build rapport, yet remain neutral and objective. They encroach on the respondents' time and privacy for information that may not directly benefit the respondents. They try to reduce embarrassment, fear, and suspicion so that respondents feel comfortable revealing information. They may explain the nature of survey research or give hints about social roles in an inter-

view. Good interviewers monitor the pace and direction of the social interaction as well as the content of answers and the behavior of respondents.

Survey interviewers are nonjudgmental and do not reveal their opinions, verbally or nonverbally (e.g., by a look of shock). If a respondent asks for an interviewer's opinion, he or she politely redirects the respondent and indicates that such questions are inappropriate. For example, if a respondent asks, "What do you think?" the interviewer may answer, "Here, we are interested in what *you* think; what I think doesn't matter." Likewise, if the respondent gives a shocking answer (e.g., "I was arrested three times for beating my infant daughter and burning her with cigarettes"), the interviewer does not show shock, surprise, or disdain but treats the answer in a matter-of-fact manner. He or she helps respondents feel that they can give any truthful answer.

You might ask, "If the survey interviewer must be neutral and objective, why not use a robot or machine?" Machine interviewing has not been successful because it lacks the human warmth, sense of trust, and rapport that an interviewer creates. An interviewer helps define the situation and ensures that respondents have the information sought, understand what is expected, give relevant answers, are motivated to cooperate, and give serious answers. The interview is a social interaction in which "the behavior of both interviewer and respondent stems from their attitudes, motives, expectations, and perceptions" (Cannell and Kahn, 1968:538).

Interviewers do more than interview respondents. For example, Moser and Kalton (1972:273) reported that face-to-face interviewers spend only about 35 percent of their time interviewing. About 40 percent is spent in locating the correct respondent, 15 percent in traveling, and 10 percent in studying survey materials and dealing with administrative and recording details.

Stages of an Interview

The interview proceeds through stages, beginning with an introduction and entry. The interviewer gets in the door, shows authorization, and reassures and secures cooperation from the respondent. He or she is prepared for reactions such as, "How did you pick me?" "What good will this do?" "I don't know about this." "What's this about, anyway?" The interviewer can explain why the specific respondent is interviewed and not a substitute.

The main part of the interview consists of asking questions and recording answers. The interviewer uses the exact wording on the questionnaire—no added or omitted words and no rephrasing. He or she asks all applicable questions in order, without returning to or skipping questions unless the directions specify this. He or she goes at a comfortable pace and gives nondirective feedback to maintain interest.

In addition to asking questions, the interviewer accurately records answers. This is easy for closed-ended questions, where interviewers just mark the correct box. For open-ended questions the interviewer's job is more difficult. He or she listens carefully, must have legible writing, and must record what is said verbatim without correcting grammar or slang. More importantly, the interviewer never summarizes or paraphrases. This causes a loss of information or distorts answers. For example, the respondent says, "I'm really concerned about my daughter's heart problem. She's only 10 years old and already she has trouble climbing stairs. I don't know what she'll do when she gets older. Heart surgery is too risky for her and it costs so much. She'll have to learn to live with it." If the interviewer writes, "concerned about daughter's health," much is lost.

The interviewer knows how and when to use probes. A *probe* is a neutral request to clarify an ambiguous answer, to complete an incomplete answer, or to obtain a relevant response. Interviewers recognize an irrelevant or inaccurate answer and use probes as needed.[40] There are many types of probes. A three- to five-second pause is often effective. Nonverbal communication (e.g., tilt of head, raised eyebrows, or eye contact) also works well. The interviewer can repeat the question or repeat the reply and then pause. She or he can ask a neutral question, such as, "Any other reasons?" "Can you tell me more about that?" "How do you mean?" "Could you explain more for me?" (see Box 10.11).

The last stage is the exit, when the interviewer thanks the respondent and leaves. He or she then goes to a quiet, private place to edit the questionnaire and record other details such as the date, time, and place of the interview; a thumbnail sketch of the respondent and interview situation; the respondent's attitude (e.g., serious, angry, or laughing); and any unusual circumstances (e.g., "Telephone rang at question 27 and respondent talked for four minutes before the interview started again"). He or she notes anything disruptive that happened during the interview (e.g., "Teenage son entered room, sat at opposite end, turned on television with the volume loud, and watched a baseball game"). The interviewer also records personal feelings and anything that was suspected (e.g., "Respondent became nervous and fidgeted when questioned about his marriage"). Converse and Schuman (1974) provided

Box 10.11 _____

Example of Probes and Recording Full Responses
to Closed Questions

Interviewer question: What is your occupation?

Respondent answer: I work at General Motors.
  Probe: What is your job at General Motors? What type of work do you do there?

Interviewer question: How long have you been unemployed?

Respondent answer: A long time.
  Probe: Could you tell me more specifically when your current period of unemployment began?

Interviewer question: Considering the country as a whole, do you think we will have good times during the next year, or bad times, or what?

Respondent answer: Maybe good, maybe bad, it depends, who knows?
  Probe: What do you expect to happen?

Record Response to a Closed Question
Interviewer question: On a scale of 1 to 7, how do you feel about capital punishment or the death penalty, where 1 is strongly in favor of the death penalty, and 7 is strongly opposed to it?
(Favor) 1 _   2 _   3 _   4 _   5 _   6 _   7 _ (Oppose)

Respondent's answer: About a 4. I think that all murderers, rapists, and violent criminals should get death, but I don't favor it for minor crimes like stealing a car.

---

examples of face-to-face interviewing events from such sketches.

Training Interviewers

A large-scale survey requires hiring several interviewers.[41] Few people other than professional survey researchers appreciate the difficulty of the interviewer's job. A professional-quality interview requires the careful selection of interviewers and good training. As with any employment situation, adequate pay and good supervision are important for consistent, high-quality performance.

Unfortunately, professional interviewing has not always paid well or provided regular employment. In the past, interviewers were largely drawn from a pool of middle-aged women willing to accept irregular part-time work. Good interviewers are pleasant, honest, accurate, mature, responsible,

moderately intelligent, stable, and motivated. They have a nonthreatening appearance, have experience with many types of people, and possess poise and tact. If the survey involves interviewing in high-crime areas, interviewers need extra protection. Researchers may consider interviewers' physical appearance, age, race, sex, languages spoken, and even the voice. For example, in a study using trained female telephone interviewers from homogeneous social backgrounds, Oksenberg and colleagues (1986) found fewer refusals for interviewers whose voices had higher pitch and greater pitch variation, and who spoke louder, faster, with clear pronunciation and sounded more pleasant and cheerful.

Researchers train professional interviewers in a one- to two-week training course, which usually includes lectures and reading, observation of expert interviewers, mock interviews in the office and in the field that are recorded and critiqued, many practice interviews, and role playing. The interviewers learn what survey research is about and the role of the interviewer. They become familiar with the questionnaire and the purpose of questions, although not with the answers expected.

Although interviewers largely work alone, researchers use an interviewer supervisor in large-scale surveys with several interviewers. Supervisors are familiar with the area, assist with problems, oversee the interviewers, and ensure that work is completed on time. For telephone interviewing, this includes helping with calls, checking when interviewers arrive and leave, and monitoring interview calls. In face-to-face interviews, supervisors check to find out whether the interview actually took place. This means calling back or sending a confirmation postcard to a sample of respondents. They can also check the response rate and incomplete questionnaires to see whether interviewers are obtaining cooperation, and they may reinterview a small subsample, analyze answers, or observe interviews to see whether interviewers are accurately asking questions and recording answers.

Interviewer Bias

Survey researchers prescribe interviewer behavior to reduce bias. Ideally, the actions of a particular interviewer will not affect how a respondent answers, and responses will not vary from what they would be if asked by any other interviewer. This goes beyond reading each question exactly as worded: "Strictly speaking, interviewer distortion exists whenever there is any deviation from the "true" response (defined in terms of the purpose of the study) in the response elicited and recorded by the interviewer" (Hyman, 1975:226).

Interview bias falls into six categories:

1. Errors by the respondent—forgetting, embarrassment, misunderstanding, or lying because of the presence of others
2. Unintentional errors or interviewer sloppiness—contacting the wrong respondent, misreading a question, omitting questions, reading questions in the wrong order, recording the wrong answer to a question, or misunderstanding the respondent
3. Intentional subversion by the interviewer—purposeful alteration of answers, omission or rewording of questions, or choice of an alternative respondent
4. Influence due to the interviewer's expectations about a respondent's answers based on the respondent's appearance, living situation, or other answers
5. Failure of an interviewer to probe or to probe properly
6. Influence on the answers due to the interviewer's appearance, tone, attitude, reactions to answers, or comments made outside of the interview schedule

Survey researchers are still learning about the factors that influence survey interviews. They know that interviewer expectations can create significant bias. Interviewers who expect difficult interviews have them, and those who expect certain answers are more likely to get them (see Box 10.12). Proper interviewer behavior and exact question reading may be difficult, but the issue is larger.

The social setting in which the interview occurs can affect answers, including the presence of other people. For example, students answer differently depending on whether they are asked questions at home or at school (Zane and Matsoukas, 1979). In general, survey researchers do not want others present because they may affect respondent answers. It may not always make a difference, however, especially if the others are small children.[42] For example, Aquilino (1993) found that when a spouse is present, respondents are more likely to indicate that a divorce or separation will make them worse off. Also, wives report greater husband contributions to housework when the husband is present.

An interviewer's visible characteristics, including race and gender, often affect interviews and respondent answers, especially for questions about issues related to race or gender. For example, African American and Hispanic respondents express different policy positions on race- or ethnic-related issues depending on the apparent race or ethnicity of the interviewer. This occurs even with

Box 10.12 _____

Interviewer Characteristics Can Affect Responses

EXAMPLE OF INTERVIEWER-EXPECTATION EFFECTS

Asked by Female Interviewer Whose Own	_Female Respondent Reports That_ _Husband Buys Most Furniture_
Husband buys most furniture	89%
Husband does not buy most furniture	15%

EXAMPLE OF RACE- OR ETHNIC-APPEARANCE EFFECTS

	PERCENTAGE ANSWERING YES TO:	
Interviewer	_"Do you think there are too many Jews in government jobs?"_	_"Do you think that Jews have too much power?"_
Looked Jewish with Jewish-sounding name	11.7	5.8
Looked Jewish only	15.4	15.6
Non-Jewish appearance	21.2	24.3
Non-Jewish appearance and non-Jewish-sounding name	19.5	21.4

Note: Racial stereotypes held by respondents can affect how they respond in interviews.

Source: From _Interviewing in Social Research_ by Herbert H. Hyman. © 1954, 1975 by the University of Chicago Press. Reprinted by permission of the The University of Chicago Press.

telephone interviews when a respondent has clues about the interviewer's race or ethnicity. In general, interviewers of the same ethnic/racial group get more accurate answers.[43] Gender also affects interviews both in terms of obvious issues, such as sexual behavior, as well as support for gender-related collective action or gender equality.[44] Survey researchers need to note the race and gender of both interviewers and respondents.

Interview characteristics can influence answers in many ways. For example, when the interviewer was a person with disabilities, respondents lowered their self-reported level of "happiness," compared to when they answered a self-administered questionnaire. Apparently, they did not want to sound too well-off compared to the interviewer. However, when the respondent completed a self-administered questionnaire while a disabled person was in the same room, they reported higher levels of happiness than if the respondent was alone. Apparently, respondents felt comparatively better off due to the

physical presence of the disabled person compared to when there was no immediate reminder of the life situations of others (see Sudman et al., 1996:74–76). When a respondent answers identical questions differently depending on the race, gender, or physical conditions of the person who asks it, it threatens representative reliability.

Cultural Meanings and Survey Interviews

Research into survey errors and interview bias has advanced thinking about larger issues of how people create social meaning and achieve cultural understanding.[45] Survey researchers are troubled when the same words have different meanings and implications depending on the social situation, who speaks them, how they are spoken, and the social distance between the speaker and listener. Also, respondents do not always understand the social situation of the survey interview, may misinterpret the nature of survey research, and may seek clues for how to answer in the wording of questions or subtle actions of the interviewer. Moreover, "it is important not to lose sight of the fact that the interview setting is itself distinct from other settings in which attitudes are expressed, and hence we should not expect to find complete congruence between attitudes expressed in interviews and in other social contexts" (Turner and Martin, 1984:276).

Initially, survey research was based on a "naive assumption model" (Foddy, 1993:13). Researchers try to improve survey research by reducing the gap between actual experience in conducting surveys and the ideal survey expressed as the model's assumptions. The model's assumptions include the following:

1. Researchers have clearly conceptualized all variables being measured.
2. Questionnaires have no wording, question order, or related effects.
3. Respondents are motivated and willing to answer all the questions asked.
4. Respondents possess complete information and can accurately recall events.
5. Respondents understand each question exactly as the reseacher intends it.
6. Respondents give more truthful answers if they do not know the hypotheses.
7. Respondents give more truthful answers if they receive no hints or suggestions.
8. The interview situation and specific interviewers have no effects on answers.
9. The process of the interview has no impact on the respondents' beliefs or attitudes.
10. Respondents' behaviors match perfectly their verbal responses in an interview.

Some survey researchers question the assumptions of this model. For example, as an interviewer strives to act in a more neutral and uniform way, he or she reduces the type of bias that causes unreliability because of individual interviewer behavior. Yet, such attempts cause other problems according to interpretive or critical social work researchers (see Box 10.13; also see Devault, 1990).[46] They argue that meaning is created in social context; therefore, standard wording will not produce the same meaning for all respondents. For example, some respon-

dents express their values and feelings by telling stories instead of answering straightforward questions with fixed answers.

In complex human interaction, people often add interpretive meaning to simple questions. For example, your neighbor asks you the simple question, "How often do you mow your lawn?" You could interpret her question in the following ways:

— How often do I personally mow the lawn (versus having someone else mow it for me)?

— How often do I mow it to cut grass (versus run my lawnmower over it to chop up leaves)?

— How often do I mow the entire lawn (versus cutting the quick-growing parts only)?

— How often do I mow it during an entire season, a month, a week?

— How often do I mow it most seasons (versus last year when my lawnmower was broken several times and it was very dry and the grass grew less tall, so I did not mow it as frequently)?

Within seconds, you make an interpretation and give an answer, but the open-ended, ongoing interaction between yourself and the neighbor permits you to ask for clarification and to ask several follow-up questions that help you arrive at mutual understanding.

The dilemma is that ordinary conversations contain organizational features that are designed to detect and correct misintepretation and build shared understanding. Many of these very features are controlled in the survey interview situation to ensure that each respondent is treated in a standard way. Standardizing words does not automatically produce standardized meaning. Paradoxically, "the validity of survey data is potentially undermined by the same prohibition against interaction that is intended to ensure reliability" (Suchman and Jordan, 1992:242).

Social meaning does not reside in the words alone. It resides in the social context and interaction among people, and in cultural frames (sometimes divided by gender, race, region, etc.) in which people live. For example, men and women think differently about their health, and they will report the same health status differently (Groves et al., 1992). Does this mean that far more men are in excellent health

Box 10.13 _____

Interviewing: Positivist and Feminist Approaches

In this chapter you have learned the positivist approach to survey-research interviewing. In the ideal survey interview, the interviewer withholds her or his own feelings and beliefs. The interviewer should be so objective and neutral that it should be possible to substitute another interviewer and obtain the same responses.

Feminist researchers approach interviewing very differently. Feminist interviewing is similar to qualitative interviewing (to be discussed in Chapter 14). Oakley (1981) criticized positivist-survey interviewing as being part of a masculine paradigm. It is a social situation in which the interviewer exercises control and dominance while suppressing the expression of personal feelings. It is manipulative and instrumental. The interviewer and the respondent become merely the vehicles for obtaining the objective data.

The goals of feminist research vary, but two common goals are to give greater visibility to the subjective experience of women and to increase the involvement of the respondent in the research process. Features of feminist interviewing include the following:

— A preference for an unstructured and open-ended format
— A preference for interviewing a person more than once
— Creation of social connections and building a trusting social relationship
— Disclosure of personal experiences by the interviewer
— Drawing on female skills of being open, receptive, and understanding
— Avoiding control and fostering equality by downplaying professional status
— Careful listening, interviewers become emotionally engaged with respondents
— Respondent-oriented direction, not researcher-oriented or questionnaire-oriented
— Encouragement of respondents to express themselves in ways they are most comfortable—for example, by telling stories or following digressions
— Creation of a sense of empowerment and an esprit de corps among women

---

than women? Even so-called objective categories in survey research, such as race or ethnicity, can vary greatly in how respondents think subjectively and answer (Smith, 1984). Human responses in interviews are more complex than outlined by the naive assumption model. For example, "Inaccurate reporting is not a response tendency or a predisposition to be untruthful. Individuals who are truthful on one occasion or in response to particular questions may not be truthful at other times or to other questions" (Wentworth, 1993:130).

Given this complexity and possible distortion, what should the diligent survey researcher do? Survey researchers should at least supplement closed-ended questionnaires with open-ended questions and probes. This takes more time, requires better-trained interviewers, and produces responses that may be less standardized and more difficult to quantify. Fixed-answer questionnaires based on the naive assumption model imply a more simple and mechanical way of responding than occurs in many sit-

uations. The inquiry into interviewer bias, cultural meanings, and the interview as a social situation provides a lesson in how qualitative and quantitative styles of social work research complement one another. As quantitative survey researchers strove to eliminate sources of interviewer bias and respondent confusion, they discovered that qualitative researchers offered valuable insights into how people construct meaning in various social settings.

Computer-Assisted Telephone Interviewing

Advances in computer technology and lower computer prices have enabled professional survey research organizations to install *computer-assisted telephone interviewing (CATI)* systems.[47] With CATI, the interviewer sits in front of a computer and makes calls. Wearing a headset and microphone, the interviewer reads the questions from a computer screen for the specific respondent who is called, then enters the answer via the keyboard. Once he or she enters an answer, the computer shows the next question on the screen.

CATI speeds interviewing and reduces interviewer errors. It also eliminates the separate step of entering information into a computer and speeds data processing. Of course, CATI requires an investment in computer equipment and some knowledge of computers. CATI is valuable for contingency questions because the computer can show the questions appropriate for a specific respondent; interviewers do not have to turn pages looking for the next question. In addition, the computer can check an answer immediately after the interviewer enters it. For example, if an interviewer enters an answer that is impossible or clearly an error (e.g., an *H* instead of an *M* for "Male"), the computer will request another answer.

Several companies have developed software programs for personal computers that help researchers develop questionnaires and analyze survey data. The programs provide guides for writing questions, recording responses, analyzing data, and producing reports. The programs may speed the more mechanical aspects of survey research—such as typing questionnaires, organizing layout, and recording responses—but they cannot substitute for a good understanding of the survey method or an appreciation of its limitations. The researcher must still clearly conceptualize variables, prepare well-worded questions, design the sequence and forms of questions and responses, and pilot test questionnaires. Communicating unambiguously with respondents and eliciting credible responses remain the most important parts of survey research. See Box 10.14 for an example of survey research.

THE ETHICAL SURVEY

Like all social work research, people can conduct surveys in ethical or unethical ways. A major ethical issue in survey research is the invasion of privacy.[48] Survey researchers can intrude into a respondent's privacy by asking about intimate actions and personal beliefs. People have a right to privacy. Respondents decide when and to whom to reveal personal information. They are likely to pro-

---

Box 10.14 _____

Example Survey

Hagan (1990) examined gender discrimination and income inequality among Canadian lawyers. He drew a stratified sample of lawyers in the Toronto area, stratifying by type of employment (large firm, small-to-medium firm, or nonfirm) and gender. In 1985 he mailed 1,609 questionnaires with two follow-up reminders. He received 1,051 back, for a 65.3 percent active return rate. The questionnaire asked respondents to put their 1984 before-tax income into one of 26 categories, ranging from under $10,000 to over $500,000. The average income for the 445 female lawyers who responded was $44,210, compared to $86,756 for the 396 male lawyers. The questionnaire also included questions on the following control variables: type of position (e.g., managing partner, solo practitioner), religious background, area of specialization (e.g., tax, family, criminal), years of experience, job history, and prestige of the law school attended. After a detailed statistical analysis, Hagan concluded that about one-fourth of the gender income gap, $10,636 per year, is caused by gender discrimination. Female lawyers gained income compared to previous years, but the men had larger gains. A man with career advantages, such as an elite education or many years of experience, can better translate the advantages into income than a woman with the same advantages. For example, a man who becomes a managing partner of a medium-to-large firm earns $84,000 more than a man who is a partner in a small firm. The comparable difference for women is $24,000.

---

vide such information when it is asked for in a comfortable context with mutual trust, when they believe serious answers are needed for legitimate research purposes, and when they believe answers will remain confidential. Researchers should treat all respondents with dignity and reduce anxiety or discomfort. They are also responsible for protecting the confidentiality of data.

A second issue involves voluntary participation by respondents. Respondents agree to answer questions and can refuse to participate at any time. They give "informed consent" to participate in research.

Researchers depend on respondents' voluntary cooperation, so researchers need to ask well-developed questions in a sensitive way, treat respondents with respect, and be very sensitive to confidentiality.

A third ethical issue is the exploitation of surveys and pseudosurveys. Because of its popularity, some people use surveys to mislead others. A *pseudosurvey* is someone's use of the survey format in an attempt to persuade someone else to do something and has little or no real interest in learning information from a respondent. Charlatans use the guise of conducting a survey to invade privacy, gain entry into homes, or "suggle" (sell in the guise of a survey). An example of a pseudosurvey occurred in the 1994 U.S. election campaign as "suppression polls." In this situation an unknown survey organization telephoned a potential voter and asked whether the voter supported a given candidate. If the voter supported the candidate, the interviewer asked whether the respondent would still support the candidate if he or she knew that the candidate had an unfavorable characteristic (e.g., had been arrested for drunk driving, used illegal drugs, raised the wages of convicted criminals in prison, etc.). The goal of the interview was not to measure candidate support; rather, it was to identify a candidate's supporters, then attempt to suppress voting. One of the authors of this book received such calls, as did an unsuccessful candidate for governor who was the object of the suppression poll. No one has been prosecuted for using this campaign tactic.

Another ethical issue is the misuse of survey results or use of poorly designed or purposely rigged surveys (see Box 10.15). People may demand answers from surveys that surveys cannot provide or may not understand a survey's limitations. Those who design and prepare surveys may lack sufficient training to conduct a legitimate survey. Policy decisions made, based on careless or poorly designed surveys, may result in waste and human hardship. Such misuse makes it important that legitimate researchers conduct methodologically rigorous survey research. Researchers should be aware of, and report, the limitations of survey results.

Mass media reporting of survey results and the quality of surveys being reported permits abuse.[49] Few people reading survey results may appreci-

Box 10.15 _____

Poll Finds That Most Oppose Regulations on Cigarettes, or Does It?

The lobbying arm of the tobacco industry released results from a poll showing "that a solid majority of Americans oppose expanding the Federal Government's regulation of cigarettes." Experts from several opinion-polling organizations called it a biased survey. Data came from a telephone survey of 1,000 randomly selected adults commissioned by the tobacco industry in December 1994. Respondents were asked if to "increase regulation on cigarettes" was their top priority, very important, somewhat important, or not important at all. It was unclear whether respondents compared this issue to others, such as taxes, crime, or schools. Another question asked whether respondents wanted more regulation, the same amount, or less. Because a majority of people did not rank tobacco regulation as highly important, industry officials interpreted the results to mean that they opposed regulation (Hilts, 1995).

ate it, but researchers should include details about the survey (see Table 10.5) to reduce the misuse of survey research and increase questions about surveys that lack such information. Survey researchers urge the media to include such information, but it is rarely included. Over 88 percent of reports on surveys in the mass media fail to reveal the researcher who conducted the survey, and only 18 percent provide details on how the survey was conducted (Singer, 1988). This occurs while the media report more surveys than other types of social work research.

Currently, there are no quality-control standards to regulate the opinion polls or surveys reported in the U.S. media (see Box 10.16). Researchers have made unsuccessful attempts since World War II to require adequate samples, interviewer training and supervision, satisfactory questionnaire design, public availability of results, and controls on the integrity of survey organizations (Turner and Martin, 1984:62). As a result, the mass media report both biased and misleading survey results and rigorous,

TABLE 10.5   Ten Items to Include When Reporting Survey Research

1. The sampling frame used (e.g., telephone directories)
2. The dates on which the survey was conducted
3. The population that the sample represents (e.g., U.S. adults, Australian college students)
4. The size of the sample for which information was collected
5. The sampling method (e.g., random)
6. The exact wording of the questions asked
7. The method of the survey (e.g., face-to-face, telephone)
8. The organizations that sponsored the survey (paid for it and conducted it)
9. The response rate or percentage of those contacted who actually completed the questionnaire
10. Any missing information or "don't know" responses when results on specific questions are reported

professional survey results without distinction. The media report "the commonly cited margins of error . . . [that] promote overconfidence in survey estimates. These figures commonly account only for sampling variations and do not take into account other sources of variation in survey estimates" (Turner and Martin, 1984:107). It is not surprising that public confusion and a distrust of all surveys occurs.

CONCLUSION

In this chapter you learned about survey research. Survey research is the most widely used social work research technique. It has a long history, but it has undergone dramatic expansion and maturation in the past three decades. You also learned some principles of writing good survey questions. There are many things to avoid and to include when writing questions. You also learned about the advantages and disadvantages of three types of survey research: mail, telephone interviews, and face-to-face interviews. You saw that interviewing, especially face-to-face interviewing, can be difficult.

Although this chapter focused on survey research, researchers use questionnaires to measure variables in other types of quantitative research (e.g.,

Box 10.16 _____

Problems with *Money* Magazine's "Best Places to Live" Poll

Each year since the late 1980s, *Money* magazine has published a list of the "Best Places to Live in America" that ranks 300 U.S. metropolitan areas. The results get widespread publicity. But a study by Gutterbock (1997) stated that the magazine "does an unfortunate misservice to the credibility of survey research" (p. 355). The *Money* data are based on an annual telephone interview survey of 250 subscribers to *Money* magazine, with a substantial oversampling of new subscribers. Respondents are asked to rate 40 characteristics (e.g., crime rate, sunny weather, property taxes, etc.) on a scale from 1 to 10. Little information on details of the methods is published, and Gutterbock could learn only a little more from the magazine officials. In the telephone surveys, there are few "callbacks" and within-household sampling is not used. The sampling frame is unclear, but it is apparently a list of subscribers who provide phone numbers. The estimated response rate is a low 36 percent. The magazine does not provide question wording but changes questions slightly over the years. A ranking index is created by combining responses, but the weights for the index are not made public. Of the 40 items included, a large number (10) involve the economy. Far fewer cover other issues (e.g., 3 on education, 4 on housing). Gutterbock argues that the "Best Places to Live" poll is based on inadequate survey methods, reports on methodology that is far below professional standards, and presents findings in a manner that "substantially misrepresents the public's views" (p. 535).

experiments). The survey, often called the sample survey because random sampling is usually used with it, is a distinct technique. It is a process of asking many people the same questions and examining their answers.

The survey is a process in which researchers translate a research problem into questionnaires, then use these with respondents to create data. Survey researchers involve other people—respondents—who answer the questions. From the answers the researcher creates quantitative data that he or she analyzes to address the research problem. Survey researchers try to minimize errors, but survey data often contain them. Errors in surveys can compound each other. For example, errors can arise in sampling frames, from nonresponse, from question wording or order, and from interviewer bias. Do not let the existence of errors discourage you from using the survey, however. Instead, learn to be very careful when designing survey research and cautious about generalizing from the results of surveys.

KEY TERMS

closed-ended question
computer-assisted telephone
  interviewing (CATI)
context effect
contingency question
cover sheet
double-barreled question
floaters
focus groups
full-filter question
funnel sequence

interview schedule
matrix question
open-ended question
order effects
partially open question
prestige bias
probe
quasi-filter question
questionnaire
randomized response technique
  (RRT)

recency effect
response set
sleeper question
social desirability bias
standard-format question
telescoping
threatening questions
Total Design Method (TDM)
wording effects

REVIEW QUESTIONS

1. What are the six types of things surveys often ask about? Give an example of each that is different from the examples in the book.

2. Why are surveys called *correlational,* and how do they differ from experiments?

3. What five changes occurred in the 1960s and 1970s that dramatically affected survey research?

4. Identify 5 of the 10 things to avoid in question writing.

5. What topics are threatening to respondents, and how can a researcher ask about them?

6. What are advantages and disadvantages of open-ended versus closed-ended questions?

7. What are filtered, quasi-filtered, and standard-format questions? How do they relate to floaters?

8. How does ordinary conversation differ from a survey interview?

9. Under what conditions are mail, telephone interviews, or face-to-face interviews best?

10. What is CATI, and when might it be useful?

NOTES

1. The use of a strict positivist approach within survey research is a source of criticism by those who adopt an interpretive approach. For such criticism see Denzin (1989), Mishler (1986), and Phillips (1971). Also, see Carr-Hill (1984b) for a similar criticism from the critical social work approach.

2. "Why" questions require special techniques, and such questions or intense questioning may alter respondent

beliefs or opinions. See Barton (1995) and Wilson and colleagues (1996).

3. The history of survey research is discussed in Converse (1987), Hyman (1991), Marsh (1982:9–47), Miller (1983:19–125), Moser and Kalton (1972:6–15), Rossi and colleagues (1983), Sudman (1976b), and Sudman and Bradburn (1987).

4. See Bannister (1987), Blumer (1991a, 1991b), Blumer and associates (1991), Camic and Xie (1994), Cohen (1991), Deegan (1988), Ross (1991), Sklar (1991), Turner (1991), and Yeo (1991).

5. See Converse (1987:383–385), *Statistical Abstract of the United States,* and Rossi and colleagues (1983:8).

6. As Hyman (1975:4) remarked, "Let it be noted that the demonstration of error marks an advanced stage of a science. All scientific inquiry is subject to error, and it is far better to be aware of what it is, to study the sources in an attempt to reduce it, and to estimate the magnitudes of errors in our findings, than to be ignorant of errors concealed in the data." Examples of research on survey methodology include Bishop and colleagues (1983, 1984, 1985), Bradburn (1983), Bradburn and Sudman (1980), Cannell and colleagues (1981), Converse and Presser (1986), Groves and Kahn (1979), Hyman (1991), Schuman and Presser (1981), Sudman and Bradburn (1983), and Tanur (1992).

7. See Rossi and associates (1983:10).

8. See Bayless (1981) on the Research Triangle Institute.

9. For a list of survey organizations, see Bradburn and Sudman (1988).

10. For a discussion of pilot-testing techniques, see Bolton and Bronkhorst (1996), Fowler and Cannell (1996), and Sudman and colleagues (1996).

11. The administration of survey research is discussed in Backstrom and Hursh-Cesar (1981:38–45), Dillman (1978:200–281;1983), Frey (1983:129–169), Groves and Kahn (1979:40–78, 186–212), Prewitt (1983), Tanur (1983), and Warwick and Lininger (1975:20–45, 220–264).

12. Similar lists of prohibitions can be found in Babbie (1990:127–132), Backstrom and Hursh-Cesar (1981: 140–153), Bailey (1987:110–115), Bradburn and Sudman (1988:145–153), Converse and Presser (1986:13–31), deVaus (1986:71–74), Dillman (1978:95–117), Frey (1983:116–127), Fowler (1984:75–86), Moser and Kalton (1972:318–341), Sheatsley (1983:216–217), Sudman and Bradburn (1983:132–136), and Warwick and Lininger (1975: 140–148).

13. Sudman and Bradburn (1983:39) suggest that even simple questions (e.g., "What brand of soft drink do you usually buy?") can cause problems. Respondents who are highly loyal to one brand of traditional carbonated sodas can answer the question easily. Other respondents must implicitly address the following questions to answer the question as it was asked: (a) What time period is involved—the past month, the past year, the last 10 years? (b) What conditions count—at home, at restaurants, at sporting events? (c) Buying for oneself alone or for other family members? (d) What is a "soft drink"? Do lemonade, iced tea, mineral water, or fruit juices count? (e) Does "usually" mean a brand purchased as 51 percent or more of all soft drink purchases, or the brand purchased more frequently than any other? Respondents rarely stop and ask for clarification; they make assumptions about what the researcher means.

14. See Abelson and associates (1992), Auriat (1993), Bernard and associates (1984), Croyle and Loftus (1992), Krosnick and Abelson (1992), Loftus and colleagues (1990), Loftus and colleagues (1992), Pearson and Dawes (1992), and Sudman and colleagues (1996).

15. See Bradburn (1983), Bradburn and Sudman (1980), and Sudman and Bradburn (1983) on threatening or sensitive questions. Backstrom and Hursh-Cesar (1981:219) and Warwick and Lininger (1975:150–151) provide useful suggestions as well. Fox and Tracy (1986) discuss the randomized response technique. Also, see DeLamater and MacCorquodale (1975) on measuring sexual behavior with survey research, and see Herzberger (1993) for general design issues when examining sensitive topics.

16. See DeMaio (1984) and Sudman and Bradburn (1983:59).

17. For more on surveys with threatening or sensitive topics and computer-assisted techniques, see Aquilino and Losciuto (1990), Couper and Rowe (1996), Johnson and associates (1989), Tourangeau and Smith (1996), and Wright and associates (1998).

18. For a discussion of knowledge questions, see Converse and Presser (1986:24–31), Backstrom and Hursh-Cesar (1981:124–126), Sudman and Bradburn (1983:88–118), and Warwick and Lininger (1975:158–160).

19. Contingency questions are discussed in Babbie (1990:136–138), Bailey (1987:135–137), deVaus (1986:78–80), Dillman (1978:144–146), and Sudman and Bradburn (1983:250–251).

20. For a further discussion of open and closed questions, see Bailey (1987:117–122), Converse (1984), Converse and Presser (1986:33–34), deVaus (1986:74–75), Geer (1988), Moser and Kalton (1972: 341–345), Sudman and Bradburn (1983:149–155), Schuman and Presser (1979;1981:79–111), and Warwick and Lininger (1975:132–140).

21. See Foddy (1995), Schober and Conrad (1997), and Smith (1989) for a discussion of probes.

22. For a discussion of the "don't know," "no opinion," and middle positions in response categories, see Backstrom and Hursh-Cesar (1981:148–149), Bishop (1987), Bradburn and Sudman (1988:154), Brody (1986), Converse and Presser (1986:35–37), Duncan and Stenbeck (1988), Poe and associates (1988), and Sudman and Bradburn (1983:140–141). The most extensive discussion is found in Schuman and Presser (1981:113–178). For more on filtered questions, see Bishop and colleagues (1983, 1984) and Bishop and colleagues (1986).

23. The disagree/agree versus specific alternatives debate is discussed in Bradburn and Sudman (1988:149–151), Converse and Presser (1986:38–39), Schuman and Presser (1981:179–223), and Sudman and Bradburn (1983:119–140). Backstrom and Hursh-Cesar (1981:136–140) discuss forms of asking Likert, agree/disagree questions.

24. The ranking versus ratings issue is discussed in Alwin and Krosnick (1985), Krosnick and Alwin (1988), and Presser (1984). Also see Backstrom and Hursh-Cesar (1981:132–134) and Sudman and Bradburn (1983:156–165) for formats of asking rating and ranking questions.

25. See Ostrom and Gannon (1996) and Schwarz and associates (1991).

26. For a discussion of wording effects in questionnaires, see Bradburn and Miles (1979), Peterson (1984), Schuman and Presser (1981:275–296), Sheatsley (1983), and Smith (1987). Hippler and Schwartz (1986) found the same difference between *forbid* and *not allow* in the Federal Republic of Germany, suggesting that the distinction is not unique to the United States or to the English language.

27. See Foddy (1993) and Presser (1990).

28. The length of questionnaires is discussed in Dillman (1978:51–57; 1983), Frey (1983:48–49), Herzog and Bachman (1981), and Sudman and Bradburn (1983:226–227).

29. For a discussion of the sequence of questions or question-order effects, see Backstrom and Hursh-Cesar (1981:154–176), Bishop and colleagues (1985), Bradburn (1983:302–304), Bradburn and Sudman (1988:153–154), Converse and Presser (1986:39–40), Dillman (1978:218–220), McFarland (1981), McKee and O'Brien (1988), Moser and Kalton (1972:346–347), Schuman and Ludwig (1983), Schuman and Presser (1981:23–74), Schwartz and Hippler (1995), and Sudman and Bradburn (1983:207–226).

30. For additional discussion of nonresponse and refusal rates, see Backstrom and Hursh-Cesar (1981:140–141, 274–275), DeMaio (1980), Frey (1983:38–41), Groves and Kahn (1979:218–223), Martin (1985:701–706), Nederhof (1986), Oksenberg and associates (1986), Schu-

man and Presser (1981:331–336), Sigelman (1982), Stech (1981), Sudman and Bradburn (1983), and Yu and Cooper (1983). Also, see Fowler (1984:46–52) on calculating response rates and bias due to nonresponse. For a discussion of methods for calculating response rates, see Bailey (1987:169), Dillman (1978:49–51), and Frey (1983:38). Bailar and Lanphier (1978:13) noted that improper calculation of response rates is not uncommon, and in a review of surveys found nonresponse rates of 4 to 75 percent.

31. Introductions and incentives are discussed in Brehm (1994), Couper (1997), and Singer and associates (1998). Dillman and colleagues (1996) discuss mandatory appeals.

32. See "Surveys Proliferate, but Answers Dwindle," *New York Times,* October 5, 1990, p. 1. Smith (1995) and Sudman (1976b:114–116) also discuss refusal rates.

33. More extensive discussions of how to increase mail questionnaire return rates can be found in Bailey (1987:153–168), Church (1993), Dillman (1978, 1983), Fox and colleagues (1988), Goyder (1982), Heberlein and Baumgartner (1978, 1981), Hubbard and Little (1988), Jones (1979), and Willimack and colleagues (1995). Bailey (1987) has given a useful summary of experiments on return rates. Dillman (1978) has given practical advice on sending out a mailing, including examples of follow-up letters and instructions on folding letters into envelopes with questionnaires.

34. For a discussion of general format and the physical layout of questionnaires, see Babbie (1990), Backstrom and Hursh-Cesar (1981:187–236), Dillman (1978, 1983), Mayer and Piper (1982), Sudman and Bradburn (1983:229–260), Survey Research Center (1976), and Warwick and Lininger (1975:151–157).

35. For additional discussion of comparing types of surveys, see Backstrom and Hursh-Cesar (1981:16–23), Bradburn and Sudman (1988:94–110), Dillman (1978:39–78), Fowler (1984:61–73), and Frey (1983:27–55). For specific details on telephone interviews, see Blankenship (1977), Frey (1983), and Groves and Kahn (1979).

36. Elite interviewing is discussed in Dexter (1970). Also, see Galaskiewicz (1987), Useem (1984), Verba and Orren (1985), and Zuckerman (1972). Also, see Chapter 13.

37. For additional discussion of focus groups, see Churchill (1983:179–184), Krueger (1988), and Labaw (1980:54–58).

38. A discussion of costs can be found in Dillman (1983) and Groves and Kahn (1979:188–212).

39. For more on survey research interviewing, see Brenner and colleagues (1985), Cannell and Kahn (1968), Converse and Schuman (1974), Dijkstra and van der Zouwen (1982), Foddy (1993), Gorden (1980), Hyman

(1975), Moser and Kalton (1972:270–302), and Survey Research Center (1976). For a discussion of telephone interviewing in particular, see Frey (1983), Groves and Mathiowetz (1984), Jordan and colleagues (1980), and Tucker (1983).

40. The use of probes is discussed in Backstrom and Hursh-Cesar (1981:266–273), Gorden (1980:368–390), and Hyman (1975:236–241).

41. For a discussion of interviewer training and interview expectations, see Backstrom and Hursh-Cesar (1981:237–307), Billiet and Loosveldt (1988), Bradburn and Sudman (1980), Oksenberg and associates (1986), Singer and Kohnke-Aguirre (1979), and Tucker (1983). Sudman (1976b:115) noted that middle-class women are less likely nowadays to want to work as interviewers.

42. See Bradburn and Sudman (1980) and Pollner and Adams (1997).

43. The race or ethnicity of interviewers is discussed in Anderson and colleagues (1988), Bradburn (1983), Cotter and colleagues (1982), Finkel and colleagues (1991), Gorden (1980:168–172), Reese and colleagues (1986), Schaffer (1980), Schuman and Converse (1971), and Weeks and Moore (1981).

44. See Catania and associates (1996) and Kane and MacAulay (1993).

45. See Bateson (1984), Clark and Schober (1992), Foddy (1993), Lessler (1984), and Turner (1984).

46. See Briggs (1986), Cicourel (1982), and Mishler (1986) for critiques of survey research interviewing.

47. CATI is discussed in Bailey (1987:201–202), Bradburn and Sudman (1988:100–101), Frey (1983: 24–25, 143–149), Groves and Kahn (1979:226), Groves and Mathiowetz (1984), and Karweit and Meyers (1983). Also, see Freeman and Shanks (1983).

48. For a discussion of ethical concerns specific to survey research, see Backstrom and Hursh-Cesar (1981:46–50), Fowler (1984:135–144), Frey (1983:177–185), Kelman (1982:79–81), and Reynolds (1982:48–57). Marsh (1982:125–146) and Miller (1983:47–96) provided useful discussions for and against the use of survey research. The use of informed consent is discussed in Singer and Frankel (1982) and in Sobal (1984).

49. On reporting survey results in the media, see Channels (1993) and MacKeun (1984).

CHAPTER 11

NONREACTIVE RESEARCH AND SECONDARY ANALYSIS

There are a number of research conditions in which the sole use of the interview or questionnaire leaves unanswerable rival explanations. The purpose of those less popular measurement classes emphasized here is to bolster these weak spots and provide intelligence to evaluate threats to validity. The payout for using these measures is high, but the approach is more demanding of the investigator.

—Eugene Webb et al., *Nonreactive Measures in the Social Sciences*, pp. 315–316

INTRODUCTION

Experiments and survey research are both *reactive;* that is, the people being studied are aware of that fact. The techniques in this chapter address a limitation of reactive measures. You will learn about four quantitative research techniques that are *nonreactive;* that is, those being studied are not aware that they are part of a research project. Nonreactive tech-niques are largely based on positivist principles but are also used by interpretive and critical researchers.

The first technique you will learn about is not really a distinct technique but a loose collection of inventive nonreactive measures. It is followed by content analysis, which builds on the fundamentals of quantitative research design and is a well-developed research technique in social work. Existing statistics and secondary analysis, the last two techniques, refer to the collection of existing information from government documents or previous surveys. Researchers examine the data in new ways to address new questions. Although the data may have been reactive when first collected, a researcher can address new questions without reactive effects.

NONREACTIVE MEASUREMENT

The Logic of Nonreactive Research

Nonreactive measurement begins when a researcher notices something that indicates a variable of interest. The critical thing about nonreactive or *unobtrusive measures* (i.e., measures that are not obtrusive or intrusive) is that the people being studied are not aware of it but leave evidence of their social behav-

ior or actions "naturally." The observant researcher infers from the evidence to behavior or attitudes without disrupting those being studied. Unnoticed observation is also a type of nonreactive measure. For example, McKelvie and Schamer (1988) unobtrusively observed whether drivers stopped at stop signs. They made observations during both daytime and nighttime. Observers noted whether the driver was male or female; whether the driver was alone or with passengers; whether other traffic was present; and whether the car came to a complete stop, a "rolling stop," or no stop.

Varieties of Nonreactive or Unobtrusive Observation

Nonreactive measures are varied, and researchers have been creative in inventing indirect ways to measure social behavior (see Box 11.1 for examples).

Box 11.1 _____

Examples of Nonreactive Measures

PHYSICAL TRACES

Erosion: Wear suggests greater use.
Example: A researcher examines children's toys at a day care that were purchased at the same time. Worn-out toys suggest greater interest by the children.

Accretion: Accumulation of physical evidence suggests behavior.
Example: A researcher examines the brands of aluminum beverage cans in trash or recycling bins in male and female dormitories. This indicates the brands and types of beverages favored by each sex.

ARCHIVES

Running Records: Regularly produced public records may reveal much.
Example: A researcher examines marriage records for the bride's and groom's ages. Regional differences suggest that the preference of males for marrying younger females is greater in certain areas of the country.

Other Records: Irregular or private records can reveal a lot.
Example: A researcher finds the number of reams of paper purchased by a college dean's office for 10

years when student enrollment was stable. A sizable increase suggests that bureaucratic paperwork has increased.

OBSERVATION

External Appearance: How people appear may indicate social factors.
Example: A researcher watches students to see whether they are more likely to wear their school's colors and symbols after the school team won or lost.

Count Behaviors: Counting how many people do something can be informative.
Example: A researcher counts the number of men and women who come to a full stop and those who come to a rolling stop at a stop sign. This suggests gender difference in driving behavior.

Time Duration: How long people take to do things may indicate their attention.
Example: A researcher measures how long men and women pause in front of the painting of a nude man and in front of a painting of a nude woman. Time may indicate embarrassment or interest in same- or cross-sex nudity by each sex.

Because the measures have little in common except being nonreactive, they are best learned through examples. Some are *erosion measures,* wherein selective wear is used as a measure, and some are *accretion measures,* wherein the measures are deposits of something left behind.[1]

Researchers have examined family portraits in different historical eras to see how gender relations within the family are reflected in seating patterns. Urban anthropologists have examined the contents of garbage dumps to learn about lifestyles from what is thrown away (e.g., liquor bottles indicate level of alcohol consumption). Based on garbage, people underreport their liquor consumption by 40 to 60 percent (Rathje and Murphy, 1992:71). Researchers have studied the listening habits of drivers by checking what stations their radios are tuned to when cars are repaired. They have measured interest in different exhibits by noting worn tiles on the floor in different parts of a museum. They have studied differences in graffiti in male versus female high school restrooms to show gender differences in themes. Some have examined high school yearbooks to compare the high school activities of those who had psychological problems in later life versus those who did not. Researchers have noted bumper stickers in support of different political candidates to see if one candidate's supporters are more likely than another's to obey traffic laws. Some have even measured television-watching habits by noting changes in water pressure due to the use of toilets during television commercials.[2] (Also, see Box 11.2.)

Recording and Documentation

Creating nonreactive measures follows the logic of quantitative measurement, although qualitative researchers also use nonreactive observation. A researcher first conceptualizes a construct, then links the construct to nonreactive empirical evidence, which is its measure. The operational definition of the variable includes how the researcher systematically notes and records observations.

Because nonreactive measures indicate a construct indirectly, the researcher needs to rule out reasons for the observation other than the construct of interest. For example, a researcher wants to mea-

sure customer walking traffic in a store. The researcher's measure is dirt and wear on floor tiles. He or she first clarifies what the customer traffic means (e.g., Is the floor a path to another department? Does it indicate a good location for a visual display?) Next, he or she systematically measures dirt or wear on the tiles, compares it to that in other locations, and records results on a regular basis (e.g., every month). Finally, the researcher rules out other reasons for the observations (e.g., the floor tile is of lower quality and wears faster, or the location is near an outside entrance).

CONTENT ANALYSIS

What Is Content Analysis?

Content analysis is a technique for gathering and analyzing the content of text. The *content* refers to words, meanings, pictures, symbols, ideas, themes, or any message that can be communicated. The *text* is anything written, visual, or spoken that serves as a medium for communication. It includes books, newspaper or magazine articles, advertisements, speeches, official documents, films or videotapes, musical lyrics, photographs, articles of clothing, or works of art. For example, Cerulo (1989) studied national anthems.

Content analysis goes back nearly a century and is used in many fields—literature, history, journalism, political science, education, psychology, and so on. At the first meeting of the German Sociological

Society, in 1910, Max Weber suggested using it to study newspapers.[3]

In content analysis, a researcher uses objective and systematic counting and recording procedures to produce a quantitative description of the symbolic content in a text.[4] In fact, Markoff and colleagues (1974) suggested that "textual coding" might be a better name than content analysis. There are qualitative or interpretive versions of content analysis. The emphasis here is on quantitative data about a text's content.

Content analysis is nonreactive because the process of placing words, messages, or symbols in a text to communicate to a reader or receiver occurs without influence from the researcher who analyzes its content. For example, we, as authors of this book, wrote words or drew diagrams to communicate research methods content to you, the student. The way the book was written and the way you read it are without any knowledge or intention of its ever being content analyzed.

Content analysis lets a researcher reveal the content (i.e., messages, meanings, symbols, etc.) in a source of communication (i.e., a book, article, movie, etc.). It lets him or her probe into and discover content in a different way from the ordinary way of reading a book or watching a television program.

With content analysis a researcher can compare content across many texts and analyze it with quantitative techniques (e.g., charts and tables). In addition, he or she can reveal aspects of the text's content that are difficult to see. For example, you might watch television commercials and feel that non-Whites rarely appear in commercials for expensive consumer goods (e.g., luxury cars, furs, jewelry, perfume, etc.). Content analysis can document—in objective, quantitative terms—whether your vague feelings based on unsystematic observation are true. It yields repeatable, precise results about the text.

Content analysis involves random sampling, precise measurement, and operational definitions for abstract constructs. *Coding* turns aspects of content that represent variables into numbers. After a content analysis researcher gathers the data, he or she enters them into computers and analyzes them with statistics in the same way that an experimenter or survey researcher would.

Topics Appropriate for Content Analysis

Researchers have used content analysis for many purposes: to study themes in popular songs and religious symbols in hymns, trends in the topics that newspapers cover and the ideological tone of newspaper editorials, sex-role stereotypes in textbooks or feature films, how often people of different races appear in television commercials and programs, answers to open-ended survey questions, enemy propaganda during wartime, the covers of popular magazines, personality characteristics from suicide notes, themes in advertising messages, gender differences in conversations, and so on. Seider (1974) content analyzed the public speeches of U.S. corporate executives. He discovered five ideological themes that executives emphasized more or less depending on the industry of their corporation. Woodrum (1984:1) noted

> *Content analysis remains an underutilized research method with great potential for studying beliefs, organizations, attitudes, and human relations. The limited application and development of content analysis is due more to unfamiliarity with the method and to its historic isolation from mainstream social science than to its inherent limitations.*

Generalizations that researchers make on the basis of content analysis are limited to the cultural communication itself. Content analysis cannot determine the truthfulness of an assertion or evaluate the aesthetic qualities of literature. It reveals the content in text but cannot interpret the content's significance. Researchers should examine the text directly. Holsti (1968:602) warned, "Content analysis may be considered as a supplement to, not as a substitute for, subjective examination of documents."

Content analysis is useful for three types of research problems. First, it is helpful for problems involving a large volume of text. A researcher can measure large amounts of text (e.g., years of newspaper articles) with sampling and multiple coders. Second, it is helpful when a topic must be studied "at a distance." For example, content analysis can be used to study historical documents, the writings of someone who has died, or broadcasts in a hostile foreign country. Finally, content analysis can reveal messages in a text that are difficult to see with casual observation. The creator of the text or those who read it may not be aware of all its themes, biases, or characteristics. For example, authors of preschool picture books may not consciously intend to portray children in traditional stereotyped sex roles, but a high degree of sex stereotyping has been revealed through content analysis.[5] Another example is that of conversations in all-male versus all-female groups. Although people may be unaware of it, in same-sex groups, women talk more about interpersonal matters and social relationships, whereas men talk more about achievement and aggressive themes.[6]

Measurement and Coding

General Issues.   Careful measurement is crucial in content analysis because a researcher takes diffuse and murky symbolic communication and turns it into precise, objective, quantitative data. He or she carefully designs and documents procedures for coding to make replication possible. For example, a researcher wants to determine how frequently television dramas portray elderly characters in terms of negative stereotypes. He or she develops a measure of the construct "negative stereotypes of the elderly." The conceptualization may result in a list of stereotypes or negative generalizations about older people (e.g., senile, forgetful, cranky, frail, hard of hearing, slow, ill, in nursing homes, inactive, conservative, etc.) that do not accurately reflect the elderly. For example, if 5 percent of people over age 65 are in nursing homes, yet 50 percent of those over age 65 on television are portrayed as being in nursing homes, it is evidence of negative stereotyping.[7]

Constructs in content analysis are operationalized with a *coding system,* a set of instructions or rules on how to systematically observe and record content from text. A researcher tailors it to the type of text or communication medium being studied (e.g., television drama, novels, photos in magazine advertisements, etc.). It also depends on the researcher's unit of analysis.

Units.   The unit of analysis can vary a great deal in content analysis. It can be a word, a phrase, a theme, a plot, a newspaper article, a character, and so forth.

In addition to units of analysis, researchers use other units in content analysis that may or may not be the same as units of analysis: recording units, context units, and enumeration units. There are few differences among them, and they are easily confused, but each has a distinct role. In simple projects, all three are the same.

What Is Measured?   Measurement in content analysis uses *structured observation:* systematic, careful observation based on written rules. The rules explain how to categorize and classify observations. As with other measurement, categories should be mutually exclusive and exhaustive. Written rules make replication possible and improve reliability. Although researchers begin with preliminary coding rules, they often conduct a pilot study and refine coding on the basis of it.

Coding systems identify four characteristics of text content: frequency, direction, intensity, and space. A researcher measures from one to all four characteristics in a content analysis research project.

Frequency.   *Frequency* simply means counting whether or not something occurs and, if it occurs, how often. For example, how many elderly people appear on a television program within a given week? What percentage of all characters are they, or in what percentage of programs do they appear?

Direction.   *Direction* is noting the direction of messages in the content along some continuum (e.g., positive or negative, supporting or opposed). For example, a social work researcher devises a list of ways an elderly television character can act. Some are positive (e.g., friendly, wise, considerate) and some are negative (e.g., nasty, dull, selfish).

Intensity.   *Intensity* is the strength or power of a message in a direction. For example, the characteristic of forgetfulness can be minor (e.g., not remembering to take your keys when leaving home, taking time to recall the name of someone whom you have not seen in years) or major (e.g., not remembering your name, not recognizing your children).

Space.   A researcher can record the size of a text message or the amount of space or volume allocated to it. *Space* in written text is measured by counting words, sentences, paragraphs, or space on a page (e.g., square inches). For video or audio text, space can be measured by the amount of time allocated. For example, a TV character may be present for a few seconds or continuously in every scene of a two-hour program.

Coding, Validity, and Reliability

Manifest Coding.   Coding the visible, surface content in a text is called *manifest coding.* For example, a researcher counts the number of times a phrase or word (e.g., *red*) appears in written text, or whether a specific action (e.g., a kiss) appears in a photograph or video scene. The coding system lists terms or actions that are then located in text. A researcher can use a computer program to search for words or phrases in text and have a computer do the counting work. To do this, he or she learns about the computer program, develops a comprehensive list

of relevant words or phrases, and puts the text into a form that computers can read.[8]

Manifest coding is highly reliable because the phrase or word either is or is not present. Unfortunately, manifest coding does not take the connotations of words or phrases into account. The same word can take on different meanings depending on the context. The possibility that there are multiple meanings of a word limits the measurement validity of manifest coding (see Figure 11.1).

For example, Tom read a book with a *red* cover that is a real *red* herring. Unfortunately, its publisher drowned in *red* ink because the editor could not deal with the *red* tape that occurs when a book is *red* hot. The book has a story about a *red* fire truck that stops at *red* lights only after the leaves turn *red.* There is also a group of *Reds* who carry *red* flags to the little *red* schoolhouse. They are opposed by *red*-blooded *red*necks who eat *red* meat and honor the *red,* white, and blue. The main character is a *red*-nosed

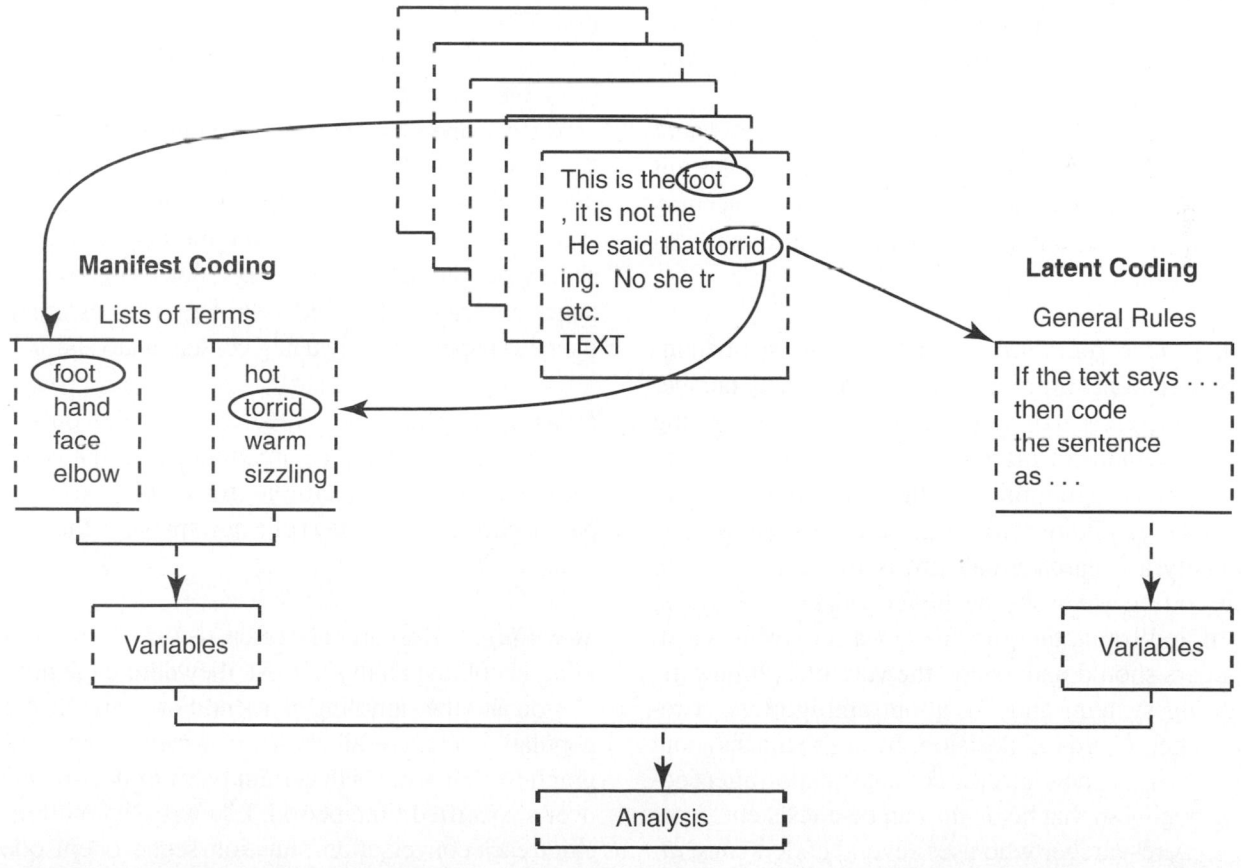

FIGURE 11.1   Manifest and Latent Coding

matador who fights *red* foxes, not bulls, with his *red* cape. *Red*-lipped little *Red* Riding Hood is also in the book. She develops *red* eyes and becomes *red*-faced after eating a lot of *red* peppers in the *red*-light district. She is given a *red* backside by her angry mother, a *red*head.

Latent Coding. A researcher using *latent coding* (also called *semantic analysis*) looks for the underlying, implicit meaning in the content of a text. For example, a researcher reads an entire paragraph and decides whether it contains erotic themes or a romantic mood. His or her coding system has general rules to guide his or her interpretation of the text and for determining whether particular themes or moods are present (see Figure 11.1).

Latent coding tends to be less reliable than manifest coding. It depends on a coder's knowledge of language and social meaning.[9] Training, practice, and written rules improve reliability, but still it is difficult to consistently identify themes, moods, and the like. Yet, the validity of latent coding can exceed that of manifest coding because people communicate meaning in many implicit ways that depend on context, not just in specific words.

A researcher can use both manifest and latent coding. If the two approaches agree, the final result is strengthened; if they disagree, the researcher may want to reexamine the operational and theoretical definitions.

Intercoder Reliability. Content analysis often involves coding information from a very large number of units. A research project might involve observing the content in dozens of books, hundreds of hours of television programming, or thousands of newspaper articles. In addition to coding the information personally, a researcher may hire assistants to help with the coding. He or she teaches coders the coding system and trains them to fill out a recording sheet. Coders should understand the variables, follow the coding system, and ask about ambiguities. A researcher records all decisions he or she makes about how to treat a new specific coding situation after coding begins so that he or she can be consistent.

A researcher who uses several coders must *always* check for consistency across coders. He or she does this by asking coders to code the same text in-dependently and then checks for consistency across coders. The researcher measures *intercoder reliability,* a type of equivalence reliability, with a statistical coefficient that tells the degree of consistency among coders.[10] The coefficient is *always* reported with the results of content analysis research.

When the coding process stretches over a considerable time period (e.g., more than three months), the researcher also checks stability reliability by having each coder independently code samples of text that were previously coded. He or she then checks to see whether the coding is stable or changing. For example, six hours of television episodes are coded in April and coded again in July without the coders looking at their original coding decisions. Large deviations in coding necessitate retraining and coding the text a second time.

How to Conduct Content Analysis Research

Question Formulation. As in most research, content analysis researchers begin with a research question. When the question involves variables that are messages or symbols, content analysis may be appropriate. For example. Dr. Neuman wanted to study how newspapers cover a political campaign. His construct "coverage" includes the amount of coverage, the prominence of the coverage, and whether the coverage favors one candidate over another. He could survey people about what they think of the newspaper coverage, but a better strategy is to examine the newspapers directly using content analysis.

Units of Analysis. A researcher decides on the units of analysis (i.e., the amount of text that is assigned a code). For example, for a political campaign, each issue (or day) of a newspaper is the unit of analysis.

Sampling. Researchers often use random sampling in content analysis. First, they define the population and the sampling element. For example, the population might be all words, all sentences, all paragraphs, or all articles in certain types of documents over a specified time period. Likewise, it could include each conversation, situation, scene, or episode of certain types of television programs over a specified time period. For example, you want to know how women and minorities are portrayed in U.S. weekly newsmagazines. Your unit of analysis is the article. Your population includes all articles published in *Time, Newsweek,* and *U.S. News and World Report* between 1979 and 1998. You first verify that the three magazines were published in those years and define precisely what is meant by an article. For example, do film reviews count as articles? Is there a minimum size (two sentences) for an article? Is a multipart article counted as one or as more articles?

You next examine the three magazines and find that the average issue of each contains 45 articles and that the magazines are published 52 weeks per year. With a 20-year time frame, your population contains over 140,000 articles ($3 \times 45 \times 52 \times 20 = 140,400$). Your sampling frame is a list of all the articles. Next, you decide on the sample size and design. After looking at your budget and time, you decide to limit the sample size to 1,400 articles.

Thus, the sampling ratio is 1 percent. You also choose a sampling design. You avoid systematic sampling because magazine issues are published cyclically according to the calendar (e.g., an interval of every 52nd issue results in the same week each year). Because issues from each magazine are important, you use stratified sampling. You stratify by magazine, sampling $1,400/3 = 467$ articles from each. You want to ensure that articles represent each of the 20 years, so you also stratify by year. This results in about 23 articles per magazine per year.

Finally, you draw the random sample using a random-number table to select 23 numbers for the 23 sample articles for each magazine for each year. You develop a sampling frame worksheet to keep track of your sampling procedure. See Table 11.1 for a sampling frame worksheet in which 1,398 sample articles are randomly selected from 140,401 articles.

TABLE 11.1 Excerpt from Sampling Frame Worksheet

MAGAZINE	ISSUE	ARTICLE	NUMBER	ARTICLE IN SAMPLE?[a]	SAMPLED ARTICLE ID
Time	January 1–7, 1979	pp. 2–3	000001	No	
Time	"	p. 4, bottom	000002	No	
Time	"	p. 4, top	000003	Yes—1	0001
.					
.					
Time	March 1–7, 1998	pp. 2–5	002101	Yes—10	0454
Time	"	p. 6, right column	002102	No	
Time	"	p. 6, left column	002103	No	
Time	"	p. 7	002104	No	
.					
.					
Time	December 24–31, 1998	pp. 4–5	002201	Yes—22	0467
Time	"	p. 5, bottom	002202	No	
Time	"	p. 5, top	002203	Yes—23	0468
Newsweek	January 1–7, 1979	pp. 1–2	010030	No	
Newsweek	"	p. 3	010031	Yes—1	0469
.					
.					
U.S. News	December 25–31, 1998	p. 62	140401	Yes—23	1389

[a]"Yes" means the number was chosen from a random-number table. The number after the dash is a count of the number of articles selected for a year.

Variables and Constructing Coding Categories. In this example you are interested in the construct of an African American or Hispanic woman portrayed in a significant leadership role. You must define "significant leadership role" in operational terms and express it as written rules for classifying people named in an article. For example, if an article discusses the achievements of someone who is now dead, does the dead person have a significant role? What is a significant role—a local Girl Scout leader or a corporate president?

You must also determine the race and sex of people named in the articles. What if the race and sex are not evident in the text or accompanying photographs? How do you decide on the person's race and sex?

Because you are interested in positive leadership roles, your measure indicates whether the role was positive or negative. You can do this with either latent or manifest coding. With manifest coding you create a list of adjectives and phrases. If someone in a sampled article is referred to with one of the adjectives, then the direction is decided. For example, the terms *brilliant* and *top performer* are positive, whereas *drug kingpin* and *uninspired* are negative. For latent coding you create rules to guide judgments. For example, you classify stories about a diplomat resolving a difficult world crisis, a business executive unable to make a firm profitable, or a lawyer winning a case into positive or negative terms. (Relevant questions for coding each article are in Box 11.3.)

In addition to written rules for coding decisions, a content analysis researcher creates a *recording sheet* (also called a *coding form* or *tally sheet*) on which to record information (see Box 11.4). Each unit should have a separate recording sheet. The sheets do not have to be pieces of paper; they can be 3" × 5" or 4" × 6" file cards, or lines in a computer record or file. When a lot of information is recorded for each recording unit, more than one sheet of paper can be used. When planning a project, researchers calculate the work required. For example, during your pilot test you find that it takes an average of 15 minutes to read and code an article. This does not include sampling or locating magazine articles. With approximately 1,400 articles, that is 350

Box 11.3

Example of Latent Coding Questions, Magazine Article Leadership Role Study

1. *Characteristics of the article.* What is the magazine? What is the date of the article? How large is the article? What was its topic area? Where did it appear in the issue? Were photographs used?
2. *People in the article.* How many people are named in the article? Of these, how many are significant in the article? What is the race and sex of each person named?
3. *Leadership roles.* For each significant person in the article, which ones have leadership roles? What is the field of leadership or profession of the person?
4. *Positive or negative roles.* For each leadership or professional role, rate how positively or negatively it is shown. For example, 5 = highly positive, 4 = positive, 3 = neutral, 2 = negative, 1 = highly negative, 0 = ambiguous.

hours of coding, not counting time to verify the accuracy of coding. Because 350 hours is about nine weeks of nonstop work at 40 hours a week, you should consider hiring assistants as coders.

Each recording sheet has a place to record the identification number of the unit and spaces for information about each variable. You also put identifying information about the research project on the sheet in case you misplace it or it looks similar to other sheets you have. Finally, if you use multiple coders, the sheet notes the coder to check intercoder reliability and, if necessary, makes it possible to recode information for inaccurate coders. After completing all recording sheets and checking for accuracy, you can begin data analysis.

Inferences

The inferences a researcher can or cannot make on the basis of results are critical in content analysis. Content analysis describes what is in the text. It cannot reveal the intentions of those who created the text or the effects that messages in the text have

Box 11.4 _____

Example of Recording Sheet

BLANK EXAMPLE

Coder:_____

Minority/Majority Group Representation in Newsmagazines Project

ARTICLE #_____   MAGAZINE:_____   DATE:_____   SIZE:_____ col. in.

Total number of people named_____   Number of Photos_____
No. people with significant roles:_____   Article Topic:_____

Person_____:	Race:_____	Gender:_____	Leader?:_____	Field?_____	Rating:_____
Person_____:	Race:_____	Gender:_____	Leader?:_____	Field?_____	Rating:_____
Person_____:	Race:_____	Gender:_____	Leader?:_____	Field?_____	Rating:_____
Person_____:	Race:_____	Gender:_____	Leader?:_____	Field?_____	Rating:_____
Person_____:	Race:_____	Gender:_____	Leader?:_____	Field?_____	Rating:_____
Person_____:	Race:_____	Gender:_____	Leader?:_____	Field?_____	Rating:_____
Person_____:	Race:_____	Gender:_____	Leader?:_____	Field?_____	Rating:_____
Person_____:	Race:_____	Gender:_____	Leader?:_____	Field?_____	Rating:_____

EXAMPLE OF COMPLETED RECORDING SHEET FOR ONE ARTICLE

Coder: Susan J.

Minority/Majority Group Representation in Newsmagazines Project

ARTICLE # 0454   MAGAZINE: Time   DATE: March 1–7, 1995   SIZE: 14 col. in.

Total number of people named 5   Number of Photos 0 _____
No. people with significant roles: 4   Article Topic: Foreign Affairs

Person 1 :	Race: White	Gender: M	Leader?: Y	Field? Banking	Rating: 5
Person 2 :	Race: White	Gender: M	Leader?: N	Field? Government	Rating: NA
Person 3 :	Race: Black	Gender: F	Leader?: Y	Field? Civil Rights	Rating: 2
Person 4 :	Race: White	Gender: F	Leader?: Y	Field? Government	Rating: 0
Person ___:	Race: _____	Gender: ___	Leader?: ___	Field? _____	Rating: ____
Person ___:	Race: _____	Gender: ___	Leader?: ___	Field? _____	Rating: ____
Person ___:	Race: _____	Gender: ___	Leader?: ___	Field? _____	Rating: ____
Person ___:	Race: _____	Gender: ___	Leader?: ___	Field? _____	Rating: ____

---

on those who receive them. For example, content analysis shows that children's books contain sex stereotypes. That does not necessarily mean that children's beliefs or behaviors are influenced by the stereotypes; such an inference requires a separate research project on children's perceptions.

Here is an example of a content analysis research project. (See Box 11.5 for another example.) Marshall (1986) studied women in a counter-movement that opposed granting women the right to vote in the United States during the early twentieth century. A *countermovement* is a conservative movement opposing social change. Some argue that countermovements are based in conflict over status and lifestyle. Others argue that they are a form of class conflict. Past research has documented that women both supported and opposed the suffrage movement. Marshall's research question was,

Box 11.5 _____

Social Science in the News

Evans and colleagues (1990) conducted a content analysis of science results reported in the print media. They examined every issue of the *New York Times,* the *Philadelphia Inquirer,* the *National Enquirer,* and the *Star* for the month of September 1987. The first two of these are prestigious daily urban newspapers, the other two are national weekly tabloid-style "scandal sheets." The authors identified all articles with applied or basic research findings on behavioral, biological, chemical, physical, or social work research. They included only articles that had the reporting of findings as a major focus. Thus, a mere mention of a scientist's name was not sufficient. The researchers coded the following items: field of research, type of employment of researcher (e.g., university, government, private firm), researcher's name, original format of research report (e.g., book, article, conference paper), research method used, context of research (i.e., context of prior research, limitations of findings), and length of article. They located 291 scientific research articles. Each article was coded by one member of a team of trained coders. In addition, a random selection of 10 percent of the articles was coded by all coders. Intercoder reliability was 82 percent.

The researchers found that the newspapers published more research (185 articles compared to 106 for the tabloids). Both published more social work research than other types (39 percent to 44 percent). The prestigious newspapers published more research conducted by government agencies, and tabloid weeklies published more university research—90 percent of the newspaper articles compared to 62 percent of those in the tabloids. Both types of media focused on the findings. Only a little over one-third of either publication described or discussed how the research was conducted. Both publication types rarely placed the research in a context of other findings. Almost none told readers about limitations of the findings (e.g., limits on the study's generalizability).

"Were antisuffrage arguments based on class or status differences?"

Marshall first consulted documents and historical studies on the countermovement. The heyday of the countermovement was between 1911 and 1916, and it was dominated by upper- and middle-class White women. She also content analyzed 68 issues of *The Women's Protest,* a publication of the National Association Opposed to Woman Suffrage published monthly between 1912 and 1918. Each article, letter, or report (recording or "theme unit") was coded. Some 57 percent of all theme units contained a rationale for opposing women's right to vote. In all, Marshall analyzed 2,078 units and found 21 different "rhetorical themes" against woman suffrage. She organized them into four categories: the negative consequences for society, for women, and for men, and the reasons woman suffrage was unnecessary.

Marshall found that a fear of status loss and class conflict were both evident in antisuffrage arguments, and they were mutually reinforcing. Status loss was evident in themes suggesting that women's voting would destroy the cultured, refined feminine sphere of society located in the home and centered around family and children. The countermovement wanted to keep a female home-based sphere distinct from the nasty, dirty, vulgar male world of politics. Class conflict themes were expressed in attacks on the poor, immigrants, and working-class women who had to work outside the home. Upper- and middle-class women feared that female voters might favor labor legislation, social welfare programs, rights for non-Whites or immigrants, and social equality.

Marshall's research makes the text's meaning accessible for analysis, but she cannot conclude that the articles represent the whole range of thinking on the issue, or even that those who read the magazine had their opinions shaped by what they read. Her study reveals only the content of published ideas about the issue within a particular politically active group. She can combine it with other data to address larger research questions.

EXISTING STATISTICS/DOCUMENTS AND SECONDARY ANALYSIS

Topics Appropriate for Existing Statistics Research

Many types of information about the social world have been collected and are available to the researcher. Some information is in the form of statistical documents (books, reports, etc.) that contain numerical information. Other information is in the form of published compilations available in a library or on computerized records. In either case the social work researcher can search through collections of information with a research question and variables in mind, and then reassemble the information in new ways to address the research question.

It is difficult to specify topics that are appropriate for existing statistics research because they are so varied. Any topic on which information has been collected and is publicly available can be studied. In fact, existing statistics projects may not fit neatly into a deductive model of research design. Rather, researchers creatively reorganize the existing information into the variables for a research question after first finding what data are available.

Experiments are best for topics wherein the researcher controls a situation and manipulates an independent variable. Survey research is best for topics wherein the researcher asks questions and learns about reported attitudes or behavior. Content analysis is for topics that involve the content of messages in cultural communication.

Existing statistics research is best for topics that involve information collected by large bureaucratic organizations. Public or private organizations systematically gather many types of information. Such information is gathered for policy decisions or as a public service. It is rarely collected for purposes directly related to a specific research question. Thus, existing statistics research is appropriate when a researcher wants to test hypotheses involving variables that are also in official reports of social, economic, and political conditions. These include descriptions

of organizations or the people in them. Often, such information is collected over long time periods. For example, existing statistics can be used by a researcher who wants to see whether unemployment and crime rates are associated in 150 cities across a 20-year period.

Existing statistics are valuable over time or across nations. Firebaugh and Chen (1995) studied the legacy of the Nineteenth Amendment to the U.S. Constitution, which gave women the right to vote. They wanted to see whether there was a cohort effect (discussed in Chapter 2) of an enduring gender gap in voting. Looking at time-series existing statistics on voter turnout by gender, they found that between 1952 and 1988, the women who grew up in an era before the amendment voted less often. In other words, cohorts from the pre-Nineteenth Amendment era never voted as much as women who grew up later.

Brinton and colleagues (1995) used cross-national existing government statistics to examine patterns of married women entering the paid labor force in rapidly industrializing nations. Looking at South Korea and Taiwan, they found many similarities. Both had strong patriarchal cultural values and similar education levels for women. Yet, they differed on the percentage of women in the labor force. Korean women were less likely to work outside the home than women in Taiwan. The authors found this was due to different government industrialization policies and differences in how industry grew in each nation.

SOCIAL INDICATORS

During the 1960s some social workers, dissatisfied with the information available to decision makers, spawned the "social indicators' movement" to develop indicators of social well-being. Many hoped that information about social well-being could be combined with widely used indicators of economic performance (e.g., gross national product) to better inform government and other policy-making officials. Thus, researchers wanted to measure the quality of social life so that such information could influence public policy.[11]

Today, there are many books, articles, and reports on social indicators, and even a scholarly journal, *Social Indicators Research,* devoted to the creation and evaluation of social indicators. The U.S. Census Bureau produced a report, *Social Indicators,* and the United Nations has many measures of social well-being in different nations.

A *social indicator* is any measure of social well-being used in policy. Many specific indicators are operationalizations of well-being. For example, social indicators have been developed for the following areas: population, family, housing, social security and welfare, health and nutrition, public safety, education and training, work, income, culture and leisure, social mobility, and participation.

A more specific example of a social indicator is the FBI's uniform crime index. It indicates the amount of crime in U.S. society. Social indicators can measure negative aspects of social life, such as the infant mortality rate (the death rate of infants during the first year of life) or alcoholism, or they can indicate positive aspects, such as job satisfaction or the percentage of housing units with indoor plumbing. Social indicators often involve implicit value judgments (e.g., which crimes are serious or what constitutes a good quality of life).

Researchers at the Institute for Innovation in Social Policy at Fordham University in New York created a social indicator called the "Index of Social Well-Being" for the United States. The index combines measures of 16 social problem areas (e.g., child abuse rates, teenage suicide rates, high school dropout rates, alcohol-related traffic accidents, percentage of population without health insurance, etc.) from various existing U.S. government statistics. The level in a year is compared to the best level recorded for an item since 1970, when the index began. It is placed on a scale of 0 to 100, with 100 being the best score. The United States reached its highest level of social well-being in 1973, when the index score was 77.5. It declined somewhat, then in the 1990s the index dropped sharply to about 38. This suggests that the current social well-being of Americans is sharply lower than in the recent past (Ravo, 1996).

Locating Data

Locating Existing Statistics.   The main sources of existing statistics are government or international agencies and private sources. An enormous volume and variety of information exists. If you plan to conduct existing statistics research, it is wise to discuss your interests with an information professional—in this case, a reference librarian, who can point you in the direction of possible sources.

Many existing documents are "free"—that is, publicly available at libraries—but the time and effort it takes to search for specific information can be substantial. Researchers who conduct existing statistics research spend many hours in libraries or on the Internet. After the information is located, it is recorded on cards, graphs, or recording sheets for later analysis. Often, it is already available in a format for computers to read. For example, instead of recording voting data from books, a researcher could use a social science data archive at the University of Michigan (to be discussed).

There are so many sources that only a sample of what is available is discussed here. The most valuable source of statistical information about the United States is the *Statistical Abstract of the United States,* which has been published annually (with a few exceptions) since 1878. The *Statistical Abstract* is available in all public libraries and on the Internet and can be purchased from the U.S. Superintendent of Documents. It is a selected compilation of the many official reports and statistical tables produced by U.S. government agencies. It contains statistical information from hundreds of more detailed government reports. You may want to examine more specific government documents. (The detail of what is available in government documents is mind boggling. For example, you can learn that there were two African American females over the age of 75 in Tucumcari City, New Mexico, in 1980.)

The *Statistical Abstract* has 1,400 charts, tables, and statistical lists from over 200 government and private agencies. It is hard to grasp all that it contains (see Figure 11.2) until you skim through the tables. A two-volume set summarizes similar information across many years; it is called *Historical Statistics of the U.S.: Colonial Times to 1970.*

Most governments publish similar statistical yearbooks. Australia's Bureau of Statistics produces *Yearbook Australia,* Statistics Canada produces *Canada Yearbook,* New Zealand's Department of Statistics publishes *New Zealand Official Yearbook,*

FIGURE 11.2 A Selected List of the Types of Information in the *Statistical Abstract of the United States* (represents only a tiny percentage of what is available)

Divorce rate by state by year

Number of burglary arrests resulting in a conviction

Deaths from motor vehicle accidents

State government expenditures for water pollution control

Average monthly temperature for cities of over 50,000 population

Number of votes for political candidates, by state

Tons of salt mined, by state

Number of employees in the farm machinery industry

Federal government spending for law enforcement

Number of aliens expelled from the country

Number of banks suspended or bankrupt per year

Average teacher salaries and spending per pupil in each state

Number of handguns legally imported per year

Housing units without indoor plumbing occupied by different races

Millions of feet of plywood imported and exported per year

Billions of dollars in profits for 170 largest corporations, by year

Number of new books published in history in a year

Number of hunting licenses in South Dakota or any other state

Party composition of each state legislature in the United States by year

Average dollars in sales per employee in motor vehicle companies

Number of overnight camping stays in Yosemite National Park

Number of master's degrees granted in social work in a year by gender

Military pay for a staff sergeant for various years

Death rates by race for different states

Number of public executions by state and race for different years

Millions of dollars in revenue for television networks

Number of hogs in Arkansas or in any other state

Average cost for a dozen eggs in various years

Number of submarines France or other nations have

Electricity production of Hungary or other nations

Number of juvenile delinquents per 1,000 population per year

Average net corporate profit for different sizes of firms

Percentage of city government revenue coming from liquor store taxes

Percentage of all retail sales that tobacco products represent

Number of square miles of water in each state

Acres of federally owned land in each state

Percentage of households with a color television, by family income

Average farm size and farm value by state

Average amount spent on newspaper advertising for real estate, by year

Average number of local telephone calls per day in various years

Total annual sales of vacuum cleaners per year

Average residential rent in selected major metropolitan areas

Number of physicians per 1,000 population in various nations

Number of barrels of oil imported to United States from Canada per year

Number of successful and unsuccessful spacecraft launches by United States and USSR (Russia) each year since 1957

---

and in the United Kingdom, the Central Statistics Office publishes *Annual Abstract of Statistics.*[12] Many nations publish books with historical statistics, as well.

Locating government statistical documents is an art in itself. Some publications exist solely to assist the researcher. For example, the *American Statistics Index: A Comprehensive Guide* and *Index to the Statistical Publications of the U.S. Government* and *Statistics Sources: A Subject Guide to Data on Industrial, Business, Social Education, Financial and Other Topics for the U.S. and Internationally* are two helpful guides for the United States.[13] The United Nations and international agencies such as the World Bank have their own publications with statistical information for various countries (e.g., literacy rates, percentage of the labor force working in agriculture, birth rates)—such as the *Demographic Yearbook, UNESCO Statistical Yearbook,* and *United Nations Statistical Yearbook.*

In addition to government statistical documents, there are dozens of other publications. Many are produced for business purposes and can be obtained only for a high cost. They include information on consumer spending, the location of high-income neighborhoods, trends in the economy, and the like.[14]

Over a dozen publications list characteristics of businesses or their executives. These are found in larger libraries. Three such publications are:

Dun and Bradstreet Principal Industrial Businesses is a guide to approximately 51,000 businesses in 135 countries with information on sales, number of employees, officers, and products.

Who Owns Whom comes in volumes for nations or regions (e.g., North America, the United Kingdom, Ireland, and Australia). It lists parent companies, subsidiaries, and associated companies.

Standard and Poor's Register of Corporations, Directors and Executives lists about 37,000 U.S. and Canadian companies. It has information on corporations, products, officers, industries, and sales figures.

Many biographical sources list famous people and provide background information on them. These are useful when a researcher wants to learn about the social background, career, or other characteristics of famous individuals. The publications are compiled by companies that send out questionnaires to people identified as "important" by some criteria. They are public sources of information, but they depend on the cooperation and accuracy of individuals who are selected.

The publications in Box 11.6 cover only famous Americans, but similar biographical publications exist for many countries. For example, a researcher interested in British banking executives would want to consult *Dictionary of Business Biography* and *Who's Who in British Finance,* whereas information on a famous Canadian would be found in *Canadian Who's Who, Who's Who in Canada,* and the *Dictionary of Canadian Biography.*

Politics has its own specialized publications. There are two basic types. One has biographical information on contemporary politicians. The other type has information on voting, laws enacted, and the like. Here are three examples of political information publications for the United States:

Almanac of American Politics is a biannual publication that includes photographs and short biographies of U.S. government officials. Committee appointments, voting records, and similar information are provided for members of Congress and leaders in the executive branch.

Box 11.6 _____

Sources of Biographic Information

Who's Who in America is a popular biographic source that has been published since 1908. It lists the name, birth date, occupation, honors, publications, memberships, education, positions held, spouse, and children's names for those included. Specialized editions are devoted to regions of the United States (e.g., *Who's Who in the East*), to specific occupations (e.g., *Who's Who in Finance and Industry*), and to specific subgroups (e.g., women, Jews, African Americans).

Dictionary of American Biography is a more detailed listing on fewer people than *Who's Who.* It began in 1928 and has supplements to update information. Each supplement lists about 550 people and devotes about a page to each. It has details about careers, travels, the titles of publications, and relations with other famous people.

Biographical Dictionaries Master Index is an index listing names in the various *Who's Who* publications and many other biographic sources (e.g., *Who's Who in Hockey*). If a researcher knows a name, the index tells where biographic information can be found for the person.

America Votes: A Handbook of Contemporary American Election Statistics contains detailed voting information by county for most statewide and national offices. Primary election results are included down to the county level.

Vital Statistics on American Politics provides dozens of tables on political behavior, such as the campaign spending of every candidate for Congress, their primary and final votes, ideological ratings by various political organizations, and a summary of voter registration regulations by state.

Another source of public information consists of lists of organizations (e.g., business, educational, etc.) produced for general information purposes. A researcher can sometimes obtain membership lists of organizations. There are also publications of public speeches given by famous people.

Secondary Survey Data. Secondary analysis is a special case of existing statistics; it is the reanalysis of previously collected survey or other data that were originally gathered by others. As opposed to primary research (e.g., experiments, surveys, and content analysis), the focus is on analyzing rather than collecting data. Secondary analysis is increasingly used by researchers. It is relatively inexpensive; it permits comparisons across groups, nations, or time; it facilitates replication; and it permits asking about issues not thought of by the original researchers. There are several questions the researcher interested in secondary research should ask (Dale, Arber, and Procter, 1988:27–31; Parcel, 1992): "Are the secondary data appropriate for the research question? What theory and hypothesis can a researcher use with the data? Is the researcher already familiar with the substantive area? Does the researcher understand how the data were originally gathered and coded?"

Large-scale data collection is expensive and difficult. The cost and time required for a major national survey that uses rigorous techniques are prohibitive for most researchers. Fortunately, the organization, preservation, and dissemination of major survey data sets have improved. Today, there are archives of past surveys that are open to researchers (see Appendix C).

The Inter-University Consortium for Political and Social Research (ICPSR) at the University of Michigan is the world's major archive of social science data. Over 17,000 survey research and related sets of information are stored and made available to researchers at modest costs. Other centers hold survey data in the United States and other nations.[15]

A widely used source of survey data for the United States is the *General Social Survey (GSS),* which has been conducted annually in most years by the National Opinion Research Center at the University of Chicago. In recent years it has covered other nations as well. The data are made publicly available for secondary analysis at a low cost[16] (see Box 11.7).

Reliability and Validity

Existing statistics and secondary data are not trouble free just because a government agency or other source gathered the original data. Researchers must be concerned with validity and reliability, as well as with some problems unique to this research technique (Maier, 1991).

A common error is the *fallacy of misplaced concreteness.* It occurs when someone gives a false impression of accuracy by quoting statistics in greater detail than is warranted by how the statistics are collected and by overloading detail (Horn, 1993:18). For example, in order to impress an audience of one's command of particulars, a politician might say that the population of South Africa is 36,075,861, when he or she should say it is about 36 million.

Units of Analysis and Variable Attributes. A common problem in existing statistics is finding the appropriate units of analysis. Many statistics are published for aggregates, not the individual. For example, a table in a government document has information (e.g., unemployment rate, crime rate, etc.) for a state, but the unit of analysis for the research question is the individual (e.g., "Are unemployed people more likely to commit property crimes?"). The potential for committing the ecological fallacy is very real in this situation. It is less of a problem

Box 11.7 _____

The General Social Survey

The General Social Survey (GSS) is the best-known set of survey data used by social work researchers for secondary analysis. The mission of the GSS is "to make timely, high quality, scientifically relevant data available to the social science research community" (Davis and Smith, 1992:1). It is available in many computer-readable formats and is widely accessible for a low cost. Neither datasets nor codebooks are copyrighted. Users may copy or disseminate them without obtaining permission. You can find results using the GSS in over 2,000 research articles and books.

The National Opinion Research Center (NORC) has conducted the GSS almost every year since 1972. A typical year's survey contains a random sample of about 1,500 adult U.S. residents. A team of researchers selects some questions for inclusion, and individual researchers can recommend questions. They repeat some questions and topics each year, include some on a four- to six-year cycle, and add other topics in specific years. For example, in 1988 the special topic was religion, and in 1990 it was intergroup relations.

Interviewers collect the data through face-to-face interviews. The NORC staff carefully selects interviewers and trains them in social science methodology and survey interviewing. About 120 to 140 interviewers work on the GSS each year. About 95 percent are women, and most are middle aged. The NORC recruits bilingual and minority interviewers. Interviewers are race-matched with respondents. Interviews are typically 90 minutes long and contain approximately 500 questions. The response rate has been 71 to 79 percent. The major reason for nonresponse is a refusal to participate.

The International Social Survey Program conducts similar surveys in other nations. Beginning with the German ALLBUS and British Social Attitudes Survey, participation has grown to include Australia, Austria, Italy, Hungary, Ireland, Israel, the Netherlands, Switzerland, and Poland. The goal is to conduct on a regular basis large-scale national general surveys in which some common questions are asked across cooperating nations.

---

for secondary survey analysis because researchers can obtain raw information on each respondent from archives.

A related problem involves the categories of variable attributes used in existing documents or survey questions. This is not a problem if the initial data were gathered in many highly refined categories. The problem arises when the original data were collected in broad categories or ones that do not match the needs of a researcher. For example, a researcher is interested in people of Asian heritage. If the racial and ethnic heritage categories in a document are "White," "Black," and "Other," the researcher has a problem. The "Other" category includes people of Asian and other heritages. Sometimes information was collected in refined categories but is published only in broad categories. It takes special effort to discover whether more refined information was collected or is publicly available.

Validity. Validity problems can occur when the researcher's theoretical definition does not match

that of the government agency or organization that collected the information. Official policies and procedures specify definitions for official statistics. For example, a researcher defines a *work injury* as including minor cuts, bruises, and sprains that occur on the job, but the official definition in government reports includes only injuries that require a visit to a physician or hospital. Many work injuries, as defined by the researcher, would not be in official statistics. Another example occurs when a researcher defines people as *unemployed* if they would work if a good job were available, if they have to work part time when they want full-time work, and if they have given up looking for work. The official definition, however, includes only those who are now actively seeking work (full or part time) as unemployed. The official statistics exclude those who stopped looking, who work part time out of necessity, or who do not look because they believe no work is available. In both cases the researcher's definition differs from that in official statistics (see Box 11.8).

Box 11.8

Official Unemployment Rates versus the Nonemployed

In most countries the official unemployment rate measures only the unemployed (see below) as a percentage of all working people. It would be 50 percent higher if two other categories of nonemployed people were added: involuntary part-time workers and discouraged workers (see below). In some countries (e.g., Sweden and United States), it would be nearly double if it included these people. This does not consider other nonworking people, transitional self-employed, or the underemployed (see below). What a country measures is a theoretical and conceptual definition issue: What construct should an unemployment rate measure and why measure it?

An economic policy or labor market perspective says the rate should measure those ready to enter the labor market immediately. It defines nonworking people as a supply of high-quality labor, an input for use in the economy available to employers. By contrast, a social policy or human resource perspective says the rate should measure those who are not currently working to their fullest potential. The rate should represent people who are not or cannot utilize their talents, skills, or time to the fullest. It defines nonworking people as a social problem of individuals unable to realize their capacity to be productive, contributing members of society.

CATEGORIES OF NONEMPLOYED/FULLY UTILIZED

Unemployed people	People who meet three conditions: lack a paying job outside the home, are taking active measures to find work, can begin work immediately if it is offered.
Involuntary part-time workers	People with a job, but who work irregularly or fewer hours than they are able and willing to do.
Discouraged workers	People able to work and who actively sought it for some time, but being unable to find it, have given up looking.
Other nonworking	Those not working because they are retired, on vacation, temporarily laid off, semidisabled, homemakers, full-time students, or in the process of moving.
Transitional self-employed	Self-employed who are not working full time because they are just starting a business or are going through bankruptcy.
Underemployed	People with a temporary full-time job for which they are seriously overqualified. They seek a permanent job in which they can fully apply their skills and experience.

Source: Adapted from *The Economist,* July 22, 1995, p. 74.

Another validity problem arises when official statistics are a surrogate or proxy for a construct in which a researcher is really interested. This is necessary because the researcher cannot collect original data. For example, the researcher wants to know how many people have been robbed, so he or she uses police statistics on robbery arrests as a proxy. But the measure is not entirely valid because many robberies are not reported to the police, and reported robberies do not always result in an arrest.

A researcher who wants to measure marriages "forced" by a premarital pregnancy serves as another example. The researcher can use the date of marriage and the date of the birth of a child in official records to estimate whether a marriage was "forced" by a pregnancy. This does not tell him or her that pregnancy was the motivation for the marriage, however. A couple may have planned to marry and the pregnancy was irrelevant, or the pregnancy may have been unknown at the date of marriage. Likewise, some marriages without a recorded birth could be forced by a false belief in pregnancy or a pregnancy that ended in a miscarriage or abortion instead of a birth. In addition, a child might be conceived after the date of marriage, but be born very prematurely. If a researcher measures forced marriages as those in which a child was born less than nine months after a marriage date, some will be mislabeled, thereby lowering validity.

A third validity problem arises because the researcher lacks control over how information is collected. All information, even that in official government reports, is originally gathered by people in bureaucracies as part of their jobs. A researcher depends on them for collecting, organizing, reporting, and publishing data accurately. Systematic errors in collecting the initial information (e.g., census people who avoid poor neighborhoods and make up information, or people who put a false age on a driver's license); errors in organizing and reporting information (e.g., a police department that is sloppy about filing crime reports and loses some); and errors in publishing information (e.g., a typographical error in a table) all reduce measurement validity.

This kind of problem happened in U.S. statistics on the number of people permanently laid off from their jobs. A university researcher reexamined the methods used to gather data by the U.S. Bureau of Labor Statistics and found an error. Data on permanent job losses came from a survey of 50,000 people, but the government agency failed to adjust for a much higher survey nonresponse rate. The corrected figures showed that instead of a 7-percent decline in the number of people laid off between 1993 and 1996, as had been first reported, there was no change (Stevenson, 1996).

Reliability.   Problems with reliability can plague existing statistics research. Stability reliability problems develop when official definitions or the method of collecting information changes over time. Official definitions of work injury, disability, unemployment, and the like change periodically. Even if a researcher learns of such changes, consistent measurement over time is impossible. For example, during the early 1980s the method for calculating the U.S. unemployment rate changed. Previously, the unemployment rate was calculated as the number of unemployed persons divided by the number in the civilian work force. The new method divided the number of unemployed by the civilian work force plus the number of people in the military. Likewise, when police departments computerize their records, there is an apparent increase in crimes reported, not because crime increases but due to improved record keeping.

Equivalence reliability can also be a problem. For example, a measure of crime across a nation depends on each police department's providing accurate information. If departments in one region of a country have sloppy bookkeeping, the measure loses equivalence reliability. Likewise, studies of police departments suggest that political pressures to increase arrests are closely related to the number of arrests. For example, political pressure in one city may increase arrests (e.g., a crackdown on crime), whereas pressures in another city may decrease arrests (e.g., to show a drop in crime shortly before an election in order to make officials look better).

Representative reliability can be a serious problem in official government statistics. This goes beyond recognized problems, such as the police stopping poorly dressed people more than well-dressed people, hence poorly dressed, lower-income people appear more often in arrest statistics. For example, the U.S. Bureau of Labor Statistics found a 0.6-percent increase in the female unemployment rate after it used gender-neutral measurement procedures. Until the mid-1990s, interviewers asked women only whether they had been "keeping house or something else?" The women who answered "keeping house" were categorized as housewives, and not unemployed. Because the women were not asked, this occurred even if the women had been seeking work. Once women were asked the same question as men, "Were you working or something else?" more women said they were not working but doing "something else" such as looking for work. This shows the importance of methodological details in how government statistics get created.

Social work researchers often use official statistics for international comparisons, but national governments collect data differently and the quality of data collection varies. For example, in 1994 the official unemployment rate reported for the United States was 7 percent, Japan's was 2.9 percent, and France's was 12 percent. If the nations defined and gathered data the same way, including rates for discouraged workers and involuntary part-time workers, the rates would have been 9.3 percent for the United States, 9.6 percent for Japan, and 13.7 percent for France. To evaluate the quality of official government statistics, *The Economist* magazine asked a team of 20 leading statisticians to evaluate the statistics of 13 nations based on freedom from political interference, reliability, statistical methodology, and coverage of topics. The top five nations in order were Canada, Australia, Holland, France, and Sweden. The United States was tied for sixth with Britain and Germany. The United States spent more per person gathering its statistics than all nations except Australia, and it released data the fastest. The quality of U.S. statistics suffered from being highly decentralized, from having fewer statisticians employed than any other nation, and from politically motivated cutbacks on the range of data collected.

Data collected internationally can be controversial. The International Labor Organization of the United Nations reported in 1998 that the official statistics of total economic activity for several nations are inaccurate because they exclude the sex industry. In some countries (especially Thailand and the Philippines) millions of workers (primarily young women) are employed and billions of dollars in revenue are generated from prostitution and the sex industry. This has a large impact on the economy, but it does not appear in any official reports or statistics.[17]

Missing Data. One problem that plagues researchers who use existing statistics and documents is that of missing data. Sometimes, the data were collected but have been lost. More frequently, the data were never collected. The decision to collect official information is made within government agencies. The decision to ask questions on a survey whose data are later made publicly available is made by a group of researchers. In both cases those who decide what to collect may not collect what another researcher needs in order to address a research question. Government agencies start or stop collecting information for political, budgetary, or other reasons. For example, during the early 1980s, cost-cutting measures by the U.S. federal government stopped the collection of information that social work researchers

found valuable. Missing information is especially a problem when researchers cover long time periods. For instance, a researcher interested in the number of work stoppages and strikes in the United States can obtain data from the 1890s to the present, except for a five-year period after 1911 when the federal government did not collect the data.

Example of Existing Statistics/Documents Research

Here is an example that shows how data from existing statistical sources and available documents can be used to address a research question from theories about gender inequality.

Tickamyer (1981) compared two theories of gender inequality that explain sex differences among the wealthy and powerful in the United States. Her research was nonreactive and based on publicly available data. Past research found unequal wealth and property ownership in the United States, with the very wealthy forming a distinct social group with power in society. One theory says that new technology and social organization since the 1920s have eliminated the ways that men gained control over wealth and power. Women's power has grown over time, and social class, not sex, is the primary source of inequality today. Another theory says that sex is an overriding factor. Patriarchal norms and structures take precedence over class inequality. Compared to men, fewer women are wealthy, their patterns of wealth ownership differ, and they are less able to use their wealth to achieve power. Tickamyer's hypotheses are that fewer women are wealthy, their wealth is more likely to be inherited or given as a gift, they have less control over their wealth (more often it is held by banks for them), and they use their wealth differently (more often for arts, civic affairs, and nonbusiness activities).

Tickamyer used two approaches. First, she used a formula to estimate the wealth of the living population from statistics from the U.S. Internal Revenue Service (IRS) on estates larger than $60,000. Second, she collected biographical materials on the wealthy. She found that between the 1920s and the 1970s, over half of all top wealth holders were men. The percentage of women who were top wealth holders increased very slightly over time. Women's wealth was likely to be in the form of trusts and personal property (jewelry, automobiles). Men's wealth was in the form of real estate and mortgages. She concluded that women own "passive" wealth, where few decisions are needed, whereas men own "active" wealth involving business transactions.

Her second approach was to examine business publications (e.g., *Fortune* magazine) to identify people owning at least $100 million. She found 18 women and a sample of 20 men. She then looked up each name in six biographical reference works (e.g., *Who's Who in America*). Six of the 18 women and all 20 of the men were listed in at least one source. Compared to the wealthy men, the women had less education and held fewer positions in government, business, or charity organizations. In addition, Tickamyer checked the membership lists of the boards of directors of the 25 largest U.S. corporations and found that 93 percent of the directors were men.

Tickamyer concluded that although the percentage of women among the wealthy increased slightly over time, men still dominate. Moreover, in contrast to women, men use their wealth to actively influence decisions in government, business, and elsewhere in society.

ISSUES OF INFERENCE AND THEORY TESTING

Inferences from Nonreactive Data

A researcher's ability to infer causality or test a theory on the basis of nonreactive data is limited. It is difficult to use unobtrusive measures to establish temporal order and eliminate alternative explanations. In content analysis a researcher cannot generalize from the content to its effects on those who read the text, but can only use the correlation logic of survey research to show an association among variables. Unlike the ease of survey research, a researcher does not ask respondents direct questions to measure variables, but relies on the information available in the text.

Ethical Concerns

Ethical concerns are not at the forefront of most nonreactive research because the people being studied are not directly involved. The primary ethical concern is the privacy and confidentiality of using information gathered by someone else. Another ethical issue is that official statistics are social and political products. Implicit theories and value assumptions guide which information is collected and the categories used when gathering it. Measures or statistics that are defined as official and collected on a regular basis are objects of political conflict and guide the direction of policy. By defining one measure as official, public policy is shaped to lead to outcomes that would be different if an alternative, but equally valid, measure had been used. For example, the collection of information on many social conditions (e.g., the number of patients who died while in public mental hospitals) was stimulated by political activity during the Great Depression of the 1930s. Previously, the conditions were not defined as sufficiently important to warrant public attention. Likewise, information on the percentage of non-White students enrolled in U.S. schools at various ages is available only since 1953, and for various non-White races only since the 1970s. Earlier, such information was not salient for public policy.

The collection of official statistics stimulates new attention to a problem, and public concern about a problem stimulates the collection of new official statistics. For example, drunk driving became an issue once statistics were collected on the number of automobile accidents and on whether alcohol was a factor in an accident.

Political and social values influence decisions about which existing statistics to collect. Most official statistics are designed for top-down bureaucratic or administrative planning purposes. They may not conform to a researcher's purposes or the purposes of those opposed to bureaucratic decision makers. For example, a government agency measures the number of tons of steel produced, miles of highway paved, and average number of people in a household. Information on other conditions such as drinking-water quality, time needed to commute to work, stress related to a job, or number of children needing child care may not be collected because officials say it is unimportant. In many countries the gross national product (GNP) is treated as a critical measure of societal progress. But the GNP ignores noneconomic aspects of social life (e.g., time spent playing with one's children) and types of work (e.g., housework) that are not paid. The information available reflects the outcome of political debate and the values of officials who decide which statistics to collect.[18]

CONCLUSION

In this chapter you have learned about several types of nonreactive research techniques. They are ways to measure or observe aspects of social life without affecting those who are being studied. They result in objective, numerical information that can be analyzed to address research questions. The techniques can be used in conjunction with other types of quantitative or qualitative social work research to address a large number of questions.

As with any form of quantitative data, researchers need to be concerned with measurement issues. It is easy to take available information from a survey or government document, but this does not mean that it measures the construct of interest to the researcher.

You should be aware of two potential problems in nonreactive research. First, the availability of existing information restricts the questions that a researcher can address. Second, the nonreactive variables often have weaker validity because they do not measure the construct of interest. Although existing statistics and secondary data analysis are low-cost research techniques, the researcher lacks control over, and substantial knowledge of, the data collection process. This potential source of errors means that researchers need to be especially vigilant and cautious.

In the next chapter we move from designing research projects and collecting data to analyzing data. The analysis techniques apply to the quantitative data you learned about in the previous chapters. So far, you have seen how to move from a topic, to a research design and measures, to collecting data. Next, you will learn how to look at data and see what they can tell you about a hypothesis or research question.

KEY TERMS

accretion measures
coding
coding system
erosion measures
fallacy of misplaced
  concreteness

General Social Survey (GSS)
latent coding
manifest coding
nonreactive
recording sheet

*Statistical Abstract of the
  United States*
structured observation
text
unobtrusive measures

REVIEW QUESTIONS

1. For what types of research questions is content analysis appropriate?

2. What are the four characteristics of content that are observed and recorded in coding systems?

3. Of what reliability problems should the researcher using existing statistical data be aware?

4. What are the advantages and disadvantages of secondary data analysis?

5. Why do content analysis researchers use multiple coders, and what is the possible problem with doing this?

6. How are inferences limited in content analysis?

7. What units of analysis are used in content analysis?

8. What is the aggregation problem in existing statistics?

9. What are the three validity problems in content analysis?

10. Of what limitations of using existing statistics should researchers be aware?

NOTES

1. See Webb and colleagues (1981:7–11).
2. For an inventory of nonreactive measures, see Bouchard (1976) and Webb and associates (1981).
3. See Krippendorff (1980:13).
4. For definitions of content analysis, see Holsti (1968:597), Krippendorff (1980:21–24), Markoff and associates (1974:5–6), Stone and Weber (1992), and Weber (1985:81, note 1).
5. Weitzman and colleagues (1972) is a classic in this type of research.
6. See Aries (1977) for an example.
7. Examples of content analysis studies can be found in Berelson (1952), Carney (1972), McDiarmid (1971), Myers and Margavio (1983), Namenwirth (1970), Sepstrup (1981), Stempel (1971), Stewart (1984), and Stone and colleagues (1966). Also, see Weber (1983) for a discussion of measurement issues in content analysis.
8. Weber (1984, 1985) and Stone and Weber (1992) provided a summary of computerized content analysis techniques.
9. See Andren (1981:58–66) for a discussion of reliability and latent or semantic analysis. Coding categorization in content analysis is discussed in Holsti (1968b:94–126).
10. See Krippendorff (1980) for various measures of intercoder reliability. Also, see Fiske (1982) for the related issue of convergent validity.
11. A discussion of social indicators can be found in Carley (1981). Also see Bauer (1966), Duncan (1984:233–235), Juster and Land (1981), Land (1992), Rossi and Gilmartin (1980), and Taylor (1980). Also, see Ferriss (1988) on the use of social indicators for planning and social forecasting.
12. Many other nations also produce yearbooks; for example, *Statistiches Jahrbuch* for the Federal Republic of Germany, *Annuaire Statistique de la France* for

France, *Year Book Australia* for Australia, and Denmark's *Statiskisk Ti Arsoversigt*. Japan produces an English version of its yearbook called the *Statistical Handbook of Japan*.
13. Guides exist for the publications of various governments—for example, the *Guide to British Government Publications, Australian Official Publications*, and *Irish Official Publications*. Similar publications exist for most nations. For example, *DOD's Parliamentary Companion for the United Kingdom* and the *Parliamentary Handbook of the Commonwealth of Australia* are both similar to the *Almanac of American Politics*.
14. See Churchill (1983:140–167) and Stewart (1984) for lists of business information sources.
15. Other major U.S. archives of survey data include the National Opinion Research Center, University of Chicago; the Survey Research Center, University of California–Berkeley; the Behavioral Sciences Laboratory, University of Cincinnati; Data and Program Library Service, University of Wisconsin–Madison; the Roper Center, University of Connecticut–Storrs; and the Institute for Research in Social Science, University of North Carolina–Chapel Hill. Also, see Kiecolt and Nathan (1985) and Parcel (1992).
16. The General Social Survey is described in Alwin (1988) and in Davis and Smith (1986).
17. See *The Economist*, "The Good Statistics Guide" (September 11, 1993), "The Overlooked Housekeeper" (February 5, 1994), and "Fewer Damned Lies?" (March 30, 1996). Also, see "U.N. Urges Fiscal Accounting to Include Sex Trade," *New York Times* (August 20, 1998).
18. See Block and Burns (1986), Carr-Hill (1984a), Hindess (1973), Horn (1993), Maier (1991), and Van den Berg and Van der Veer (1985). Discussions by Norris (1981) and Starr (1987) are also very helpful.

ANALYSIS OF QUANTITATIVE DATA

---

*Statistics may also be regarded as a method of dealing with data.
This definition stresses the view that statistics is a tool concerned
with the collection, organization, and analysis of numerical facts or
observations. . . . The major concern of descriptive statistics is to present
information in a convenient, usable, and understandable form.*

—Richard Runyon and Audry Haber, *Fundamentals of Behavioral Statistics*, p. 6

INTRODUCTION

If you read a research report or article in social work based on quantitative data, you will probably find it has charts, graphs, and tables full of numbers. Do not be intimidated by them. A researcher provides the charts, graphs, and tables to give you, the reader, a condensed picture of the data. The charts and tables allow you to see the evidence collected by the researcher and learn for yourself what is in it. When you collect your own quantitative data, you will have to use similar techniques to help you to see what is inside the data. You will need to organize and ma-

nipulate the quantitative data to get them to reveal things of interest about the social world. In this chapter you will learn the fundamentals of organizing and analyzing quantitative data. The analysis of quantitative data is a complex field of knowledge. This chapter cannot substitute for a course in social statistics. It covers only the basic statistical concepts and data-handling techniques necessary to understand social work research.

Data collected using the techniques in the past chapters are in the form of numbers. The numbers represent values of variables, which measure characteristics of subjects, respondents, or other cases. The numbers are in a raw form, on questionnaires, note pads, recording sheets, or paper.

Researchers do several things to the raw data in order to see what they can say about the hypotheses: Reorganize them into a form suitable for computers, present them in charts or graphs to summarize their features, and interpret or give theoretical meaning to the results.

DEALING WITH DATA

Coding Data

Before a researcher examines quantitative data to test hypotheses, he or she needs to put them into a different form. You encountered the idea of coding data in the previous chapter. Here data *coding* means systematically reorganizing raw data into a format that is machine readable (i.e., easy to analyze using computers). As with coding in content analysis, researchers create and consistently apply rules for transferring information from one form to another.[1]

Coding can be a simple clerical task when the data are recorded as numbers on well-organized recording sheets, but it is very difficult when, for example, a researcher wants to code answers to open-ended survey questions into numbers in a process similar to latent content analysis.

Researchers use a coding procedure and a codebook. The *coding procedure* is a set of rules stating that certain numbers are assigned to variable attributes. For example, a researcher codes males as 1 and females as 2. Each category of a variable and missing information needs a code. A *codebook* is a document (i.e., one or more pages) describing the coding procedure and the location of data for variables in a format that computers can use.

When you code data, it is very important to create a well-organized, detailed codebook and make multiple copies of it. If you do not write down the details of the coding procedure, or if you misplace the codebook, you have lost the key to the data and may have to recode the data again.

Researchers begin thinking about a coding procedure and codebook before they collect data. For example, a survey researcher precodes a questionnaire before collecting data. *Precoding* means placing the code categories (e.g., 1 for male, 2 for female) on the questionnaire. Sometimes, to reduce dependence on a codebook, researchers also place the location in the computer format on the questionnaire.

If a researcher does not precode, his or her first step after collecting data is to create a codebook. He or she also gives each case an identification number to keep track of the cases. Next, the researcher transfers the information from each questionnaire into a format that computers can read.

Entering Data

Most computer programs designed for data analysis need the data in a grid format. (See Appendix F for an overview of data entry and analysis using the SPSS software program for microcomputers.) In the grid each row represents a respondent, subject, or case. In computer terminology these are called *data records*. Each is the record of data for a single case. A column or set of columns represents specific variables. It is possible to go from a column and row location (e.g., row 7, column 5) back to the original source of data (e.g., a questionnaire item on marital status for respondent 8). A column or set of columns assigned to a variable is called a *data field* or just a *field*.

For example, a researcher codes survey data for three respondents in a format for computers like that presented in Figure 12.1. People cannot easily read it, and without the codebook, it is worthless. It condenses answers to 50 survey questions for three respondents into three lines or rows. The raw data for many research projects look like this, except that there may be over 1,000 rows, and the lines may be over 100 columns long. For example, a 15-minute telephone survey of 250 students produces a grid of data that is 250 rows by 240 columns.

The codebook in Figure 12.1 says that the first two numbers are identification numbers. Thus, the example data are for the first (01), second (02), and third (03) respondents. Notice that researchers use zeros as placeholders to reduce confusion between 1 and 01. The 1s are always in column 2; the 10s are in column 1. The codebook says that column 5 contains the variable "sex": Cases 1 and 2 are male

FIGURE 12.1   Coded Data for Three Cases and Codebook

EXCERPT OF CODED DATA

Column

```
00000000001111111111222222222233333333334444 ... etc. (tens)
1234567890123456789012345678901234567890012 ... etc. (ones)
01  212736302 182738274 10239 18.82 3947461 ... etc.
02  213334821 124988154 21242 18.21 3984123 ... etc.
03  420123982 113727263 12345 17.36 1487645 ... etc.
etc.
```
Raw data for first three cases, columns 1 through 42.

EXCERPT FROM CODEBOOK

Column	Variable Name	Description
1–2	ID	Respondent identification number
3	BLANK	
4	Interviewer	Interviewer who collected the data: 1 = Susan 2 = Carlos 3 = Juan 4 = Sophia 5 = Clarence
5	Sex	Interviewer report of respondent's sex 1 = Male, 2 = Female
6	PresJob	The president of the United States is doing a great job. 1 = Strongly agree 2 = Agree 3 = No opinion 4 = Disagree 5 = Strongly disagree Blank = missing information

and Case 3 is female. Column 4 tells us that Carlos interviewed Cases 1 and 2, and Sophia Case 3.

A researcher transfers information from questionnaires, recording sheets, or similar raw data forms into a format for computers in four ways: code sheets, direct entry, optical scan sheets, and computer-assisted telephone interviewing (CATI). First, he or she can use graph paper or special grid forms for computers (called *transfer* or *code sheets*) by writing code numbers in squares that correspond to a row and column location, then typing them into a computer. Second, the researcher can sit at a computer and directly type in the data. This *direct-entry method* is easiest if information is already in a sim-

ilar format, as with content analysis recording sheets. Otherwise, it can be very time consuming and error prone. Third, he or she can put data on an *optical scan sheet*. Special machines—optical scanners—read the information from the sheets into a computer. You may have used optical scan sheets, which are used for scoring multiple-choice tests. They are specially printed forms on which a person fills in boxes or circles using a pencil to indicate a response. The researcher can use the last method if his or her project involved telephone interviewing. Computer-assisted telephone interviewing was described in Chapter 10. Interviewers wearing telephone headsets sit at a computer keyboard and enter data directly as respondents answer questions during the interview.

Cleaning Data

Accuracy is extremely important when coding data. (See Box 12.1 for an example.) Errors made when coding or entering data into a computer threaten the validity of measures and cause misleading results. A researcher who has a perfect sample, perfect measures, and no errors in gathering data, but who makes errors in the coding process or in entering data into a computer, can ruin a whole social work research project.

After very careful coding, the researcher checks the accuracy of coding, or "cleans" the data. He or she may code a 10- to 15-percent random sample of the data a second time. If no coding errors appear, the researcher proceeds; if he or she finds errors, the researcher rechecks all coding.

Box 12.1 _____

Example of Dealing with Data

There is no good substitute for getting your hands dirty with the data. Here is an example of data preparation from a study conducted with one of the author's students. The university surveyed about one-third of the students to learn their thinking and experience with sexual harassment on campus. A research team drew a random sample, then developed and distributed a self-administered questionnaire. Respondents put answers on optical scan sheets that were similar to the answer sheets used for multiple-choice exams. The story begins with the delivery of over 3,000 optical scan sheets.

After the sheets arrived, we visually scanned each one for obvious errors. Despite instructions to use pencil and fill in each circle neatly and darkly, we found that about 200 respondents had used a pen, and another 200 were very sloppy or had used very light pencil marks. We cleaned up the sheets and redid them in pencil. We also found about 25 unusable sheets that were defaced or damaged, or were too incomplete (e.g., only the first 2 of 70 questions answered).

Next, we read the usable optical scan sheets into a computer. We had the computer produce the number of occurrences, or frequency, of the attributes for each variable. Looking at them, we discovered several kinds of errors. Some respondents had filled in two responses for a question to which only one answer was requested or possible. Some had filled in impossible response codes (e.g., the numeral 4 for sex, when the only legitimate codes were 1 for male and 2 for female), and some had filled in every answer in the same way, suggesting that they did not take the survey seriously. For each case with an error, we returned to the optical scan sheet to see whether we could recover any information. If we could not recover information, we reclassified the case as a nonresponse or recoded a response as missing information.

The questionnaire had two contingency questions. For each, a respondent who answered "No" to one question was to skip the next five questions. We created a table for each question. We looked to see whether all respondents who answered "No" to the first question skipped or left blank the next five. We found about 35 cases in which the respondent answered "No" but then went on to answer the next five questions. We returned to each sheet and tried to figure out which the respondent really intended. In most cases it appeared that the respondent meant the "No" but failed to read the instructions to skip questions.

Finally, we examined the frequency of attributes for each variable to see whether they made sense. We were very much surprised to learn that about 600 respondents had marked "Native American" for the racial heritage question. In addition, over half of those who had done so were freshmen. A check of official records revealed that the university enrolled a total of about 20 Native Americans or American Indians, and that over 90 percent of the students were White, non-Hispanic Caucasians. The percentage of respondents marking Black, African American, or Hispanic–Chicano matched the official records. We concluded that some White Caucasian respondents had been unfamiliar with the term "Native American" for "American Indian." Apparently, they had mistakenly marked it instead of "White, Caucasian." Since we expected about 7 Native Americans in the sample, we recoded the "Native American" responses as "White, Caucasian." This meant that we reclassified Native Americans in the sample as Caucasian. At this point we were ready to analyze the data.

Researchers verify coding after the data are in a computer in two ways. *Possible code cleaning* (or *wild code checking*) involves checking the categories of all variables for impossible codes. For example, respondent sex is coded 1 = Male, 2 = Female. Finding a 4 for a case in the field for the sex variable indicates a coding error. A second method, *contingency cleaning* (or *consistency checking*), involves cross-classifying two variables and looking for logically impossible combinations. For example, education is cross-classified by occupation. If a respondent is recorded as never having passed the eighth grade and also is recorded as being a legitimate medical doctor, the researcher checks for a coding error.

A researcher can modify data after they are in a computer. He or she may not use more refined categories than were used when collecting the original data, but may combine or group information. For example, the researcher may group ratio-level income data into five ordinal categories. Also, he or she can combine information from several indicators to create a new variable or add the responses to several questionnaire items into an index score.

RESULTS WITH ONE VARIABLE

Frequency Distributions

The word *statistics* has several meanings. It can mean a set of collected numbers (e.g., numbers telling how many people live in a city) as well as a branch of applied mathematics used to manipulate and summarize the features of numbers. Social work researchers use both types of statistics. Here, we focus on the second type—ways to manipulate and summarize numbers that represent data from a research project.

Descriptive statistics describe numerical data. They can be categorized by the number of variables involved: univariate, bivariate, or multivariate (for one, two, and three or more variables). *Univariate statistics* describe one variable (*uni-* refers to one; *-variate* refers to variable). The easiest way to describe the numerical data of one variable is with a *frequency distribution*. It can be used with nominal-, ordinal-, interval-, or ratio-level data and takes many forms. For example, we have data for 400 respondents. We can summarize the information on the gender of respondents at a glance with a raw count or a percentage frequency distribution (see Figure 12.2). We can present the same information in graphic form. Some common types of graphic representations are the *histogram, bar chart,* and *pie chart*. Bar charts or graphs are used for discrete variables. They can have a vertical or horizontal orientation with a small space between the bars. The terminology is not exact, but histograms are usually upright bar graphs for interval or ratio data.[2]

For interval- or ratio-level data a researcher often groups the information into categories. The grouped categories should be mutually exclusive. Interval- or ratio-level data are often plotted in a *frequency polygon*. In it the number of cases, or frequency, is along the vertical axis, and the values of the variable, or scores, are along the horizontal axis. A polygon appears when the dots are connected.

Measures of Central Tendency

Researchers often want to summarize the information about one variable into a single number. They use three measures of central tendency, or measures of the center of the frequency distribution: mean, median, and mode, which are often called *averages* (a less precise and less clear way of saying the same thing).

The *mode* is the easiest to use and can be used with nominal, ordinal, interval, or ratio data. It is simply the most common or frequently occurring number. For example, the mode of the following list is 5: 6 5 7 10 9 5 3 5. A distribution can have more than one mode. For example, the mode of this list is both 5 and 7: 5 6 1 2 5 7 4 7. If the list gets long, it is easy to spot the mode in a frequency distribution— just look for the most frequent score. There will always be at least one case with a score that is equal to the mode.

The *median* is the middle point. It is also the 50th percentile, or the point at which half the cases are above it and half below it. It can be used with ordinal-, interval-, or ratio-level data (but not nominal level). You can "eyeball" the mode, but computing a median requires a little more work. The easiest way is first to organize the scores from highest to lowest, then count to the middle. If there is an odd

FIGURE 12.2 Examples of Univariate Statistics

RAW COUNT FREQUENCY DISTRIBUTION		PERCENTAGE FREQUENCY DISTRIBUTION	
Gender	*Frequency*	*Gender*	*Percentage*
Male	100	Male	25%
Female	<u>300</u>	Female	<u>75%</u>
Total	400	Total	100%

BAR CHART OF SAME INFORMATION

Males

Females

EXAMPLE OF GROUPED DATA FREQUENCY DISTRIBUTION

First Job Annual Income	*N*
Under $5,000	25
$5,000 to $9,999	50
$10,000 to $15,999	100
$16,000 to $19,999	150
$20,000 to $29,999	50
$30,000 and over	<u>25</u>
Total	400

EXAMPLE OF FREQUENCY POLYGON

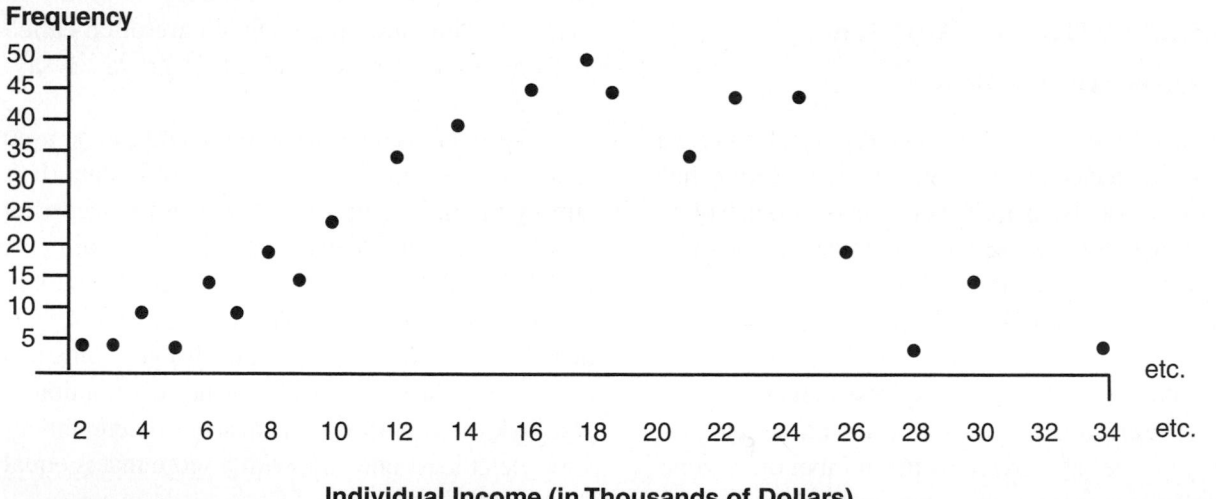

Individual Income (in Thousands of Dollars)

number of scores, it is simple. Seven people are waiting for a bus; their ages are: 12 17 20 27 30 55 80. The median age is 27. Note that the median does not change easily. If the 55-year-old and the 80-year-old both got on one bus, and the remaining people were joined by two 31-year-olds, the median remains un-changed. If there is an even number of scores, things are a bit more complicated. For example, six people at a bus stop have the following ages: 17 20 26 30 50 70. The median is somewhere between 26 and 30. Compute the median by adding the two middle scores together and dividing by 2, or 26 + 30 = 56/2

= 28. The median age is 28, even though no person is 28 years old. Note that there is no mode in the list of six ages because each person has a different age.

The *mean,* also called the arithmetic average, is the most widely used measure of central tendency. It can be used *only* with interval- or ratio-level data.[3] Compute the mean by adding up all scores, then dividing by the number of scores. For example, the mean age in the previous example is 17 + 20 + 26 + 30 + 50 + 70 = 213; 213/6 = 35.5. No one in the list is 35.5 years old, and the mean does not equal the median.

The mean is strongly affected by changes in extreme values (very large or very small). For example, the 50- and 70-year-old left and were replaced with two 31-year-olds. The distribution now looks like this: 17 20 26 30 31 31. The median is unchanged: 28. The mean is 17 + 20 + 26 + 30 + 31 + 31 = 155; 155/6 = 25.8. Thus, the mean dropped a great deal when a few extreme values were removed.

If the frequency distribution forms a *normal distribution,* or bell-shaped curve, the three mea-

sures of central tendency equal each other. If the distribution is a *skewed distribution* (i.e., more cases are in the upper or lower scores), then the three will not be equal. If most cases have lower scores with a few extreme high scores, the mean will be the highest, the median in the middle, and the mode the lowest. If most cases have higher scores with a few extreme low scores, the mean will be the lowest, the median in the middle, and the mode the highest. In general, the median is best for skewed distributions, although the mean is used in most other statistics (see Figure 12.3).

Measures of Variation

Measures of central tendency are a one-number summary of a distribution; however, they give only its *center.* Another characteristic of a distribution is its spread, dispersion, or variability around the center. Two distributions can have identical measures of central tendency but differ in their spread about the center. For example, seven people are at a bus stop

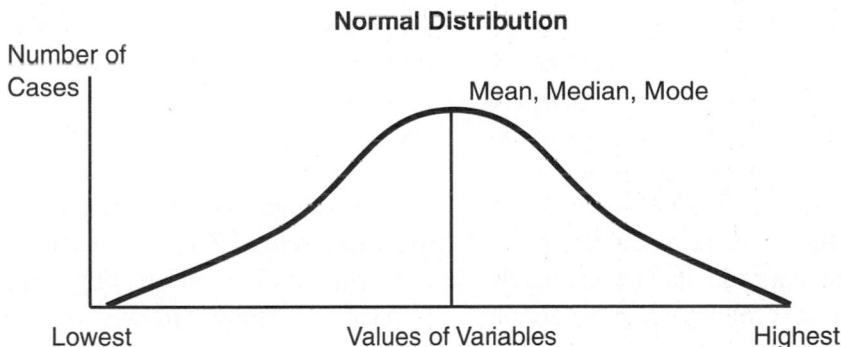

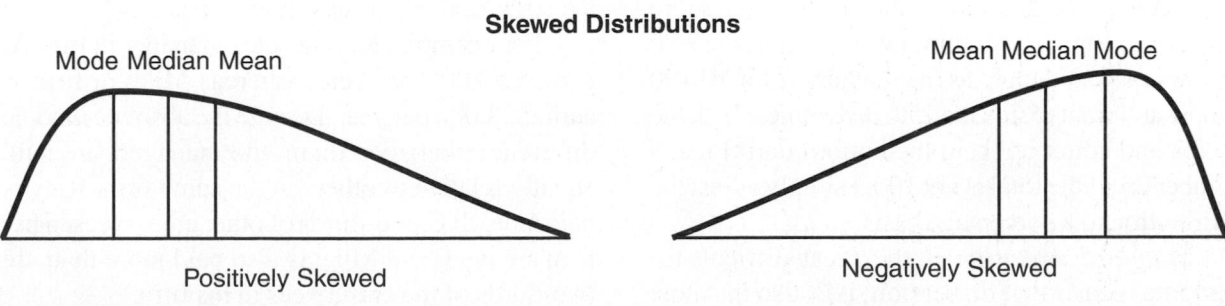

FIGURE 12.3 Measures of Central Tendency

in front of a bar. Their ages are 25 26 27 30 33 34 35. Both the median and the mean are 30. At a bus stop in front of an ice cream store, seven people have the identical median and mean, but their ages are 5 10 20 30 40 50 55. The ages of the group in front of the ice cream store are spread more from the center, or the distribution has more variability.

Variability has important social implications. For example, in city X, the median and mean family income is $25,600 per year, and it has zero variation. *Zero variation* means that every family has an income of exactly $25,600. City Y has the same median and mean family income, but 95 percent of its families have incomes of $8,000 per year and 5 percent have incomes of $300,000 per year. City X has perfect income equality, whereas there is great inequality in city Y. A social work researcher who does not know the variability of income in the two cities misses very important information.

Researchers measure variation in three ways: range, percentile, and standard deviation. *Range* is the simplest. It consists of the largest and smallest scores. For example, the range for the bus stop in front of the bar is from 25 to 35, or 35 − 25 = 10 years. If the 35-year-old got onto a bus and was replaced by a 60-year-old, the range would change to 60 − 25 = 45 years. Range has limitations. For example, here are two groups of six with a range of 35 years: 30 30 30 30 30 65 and 20 45 46 48 50 55.

Percentiles tell the score at a specific place within the distribution. One percentile you already learned is the median, the 50th percentile. Sometimes the 25th and 75th percentiles or the 10th and 90th percentiles are used to describe a distribution. For example, the 25th percentile is the score at which 25 percent of the distribution have either that score or a lower one. The computation of a percentile follows the same logic as the median. If I have 100 people and want to find the 25th percentile, I rank the scores and count up from the bottom until I reach number 25. If the total is not 100, I simply adjust the distribution to a percentage basis.

Standard deviation is the most difficult-to-compute measure of dispersion; it is also the most comprehensive and widely used. The range and percentile are for ordinal-, interval-, and ratio-level data, but the standard deviation requires an interval or ratio level of measurement. It is based on the mean and gives an "average distance" between all scores and the mean. People rarely compute the standard deviation by hand for more than a handful of cases because computers and calculators can do it in seconds.

Look at the calculation of the standard deviation in Figure 12.4. If you add up the absolute difference between each score and the mean (i.e., subtract each score from the mean), you get zero. This is because the mean is equally distant from all scores. Also, notice that the scores that differ the most from the mean have the largest effect on the sum of squares and on the standard deviation.

The standard deviation is of limited usefulness by itself. It is used for comparison purposes. For example, the standard deviation for the schooling of parents of children in class A is 3.317 years; for class B, it is 0.812; and for class C, it is 6.239. The standard deviation tells a researcher that the parents of children in class B are very similar, whereas those for class C are very different. In fact, in class B, the schooling of an "average" parent is less than a year above or below the mean for all parents, so the parents are very homogeneous. In class C, however, the "average" parent is more than six years above or below the mean, so the parents are very heterogeneous.

The standard deviation and the mean are used to create z-scores. *Z-scores* let a researcher compare two or more distributions or groups. The z-score, also called a *standardized score,* expresses points or scores on a frequency distribution in terms of a number of standard deviations from the mean. Scores are in terms of their relative position within a distribution, not as absolute values.

For example, Katy, a sales manager in firm A, earns $50,000 per year, whereas Mike in firm B earns $38,000 per year. Despite the absolute income differences between them, the managers are paid equally relative to others in the same firm. Katy is paid more than two-thirds of other employees in her firm are paid, and Mike is also paid more than are two-thirds of the employees in his firm.

Here is another example of how to use z-scores. Hans and Heidi are twin brother and sister, but Hans

FIGURE 12.4   The Standard Deviation

STEPS IN COMPUTING THE STANDARD DEVIATION
1. Compute the mean.
2. Subtract the mean from each score.
3. Square the resulting difference for each score.
4. Total up the squared differences to get the sum of squares.
5. Divide the sum of squares by the number of cases to get the variance.
6. Take the square root of the variance, which is the standard deviation.

EXAMPLE OF COMPUTING THE STANDARD DEVIATION

[8 respondents, variable = years of social work experience]

Score	Score – Mean	Squared (Score – Mean)
15	15 – 12.5 = 2.5	6.25
12	12 – 12.5 = –0.5	.25
12	12 – 12.5 = –0.5	.25
10	10 – 12.5 = –2.5	6.25
16	16 – 12.5 = 3.5	12.25
18	18 – 12.5 = 5.5	30.25
8	8 – 12.5 = 4.5	20.25
9	9 – 12.5 = –3.5	12.25

Mean = 15 + 12 + 12 + 10 + 16 + 18 + 8 + 9 = 100, 100/8 = 12.5
Sum of squares = 6.25 + .25 + .25 + 6.25 + 12.25 + 30.25 + 20.25 + 12.25 = 88
Variance = Sum of squares/Number of cases = 88/8 = 11
Standard deviation = Square root of variance = $\sqrt{11}$ = 3.317 years.
Here is the standard deviation in the form of a formula with symbols.

Symbols:
X = SCORE of case Σ = Sigma (Greek letter) for sum, add together
$\bar{X}$ = MEAN N = Number of cases

Formula:[a]

$$\text{Standard deviation} = \sqrt{\frac{\Sigma(X - \bar{X})^2}{N}}$$

[a] There is a slight difference in the formula depending on whether one is using data for the population or a sample to estimate the population parameter.

is shorter than Heidi. Compared to other girls her age, Heidi is at the mean height; she has a z-score of zero. Likewise, Hans is at the mean height among boys his age. Thus, within each comparison group, the twins are at the same z-score, so they have the same relative height.

Z-scores are easy to calculate from the mean and standard deviation (see Box 12.2). For example, an employer interviews students from Kings College and Queens College. She learns that the colleges are similar and that both grade on a 4.0 scale. Yet, the mean grade-point average at Kings College is 2.62 with a standard deviation of .50, whereas the mean grade-point average at Queens College is 3.24 with a standard deviation of .40. The employer suspects that grades at Queens College are inflated. Suzette from Kings College has a grade-point average of 3.62, while Jorge from Queens College has a grade-point average of 3.64. Both students took the same courses. The employer wants to adjust the grades for the grading practices of the two colleges (i.e., create standardized scores). She calculates z-scores by subtracting each student's score from the mean, then dividing by the standard deviation. For example, Suzette's z-score is 3.62 – 2.62 = 1.00/.50 = 2, whereas Jorge's z-score is 3.64 – 3.24 = .40/.40 = 1. Thus, the employer learns that Suzette is two standard deviations above the mean in her college, whereas Jorge is only one standard deviation above the mean for his college. Although Suzette's absolute grade-point average is lower than Jorge's, when considered relative to the students in each of their colleges, Suzette's grades are much higher than Jorge's.

RESULTS WITH TWO VARIABLES

A Bivariate Relationship

Univariate statistics describe a single variable in isolation. *Bivariate statistics* are much more valuable. They let a researcher consider two variables together and describe the relationship between variables. Even simple hypotheses require two variables.

Bivariate statistical analysis shows a *statistical relationship* between variables—that is, things that appear together. For example, a relationship exists between water pollution in a stream and the fact that people who drink the water get sick. It is a statistical relationship between two variables: pollution in the water and the health of the people who drink it.

Statistical relationships are based on two ideas: covariation and independence. *Covariation* means that things go together or are associated. To covary means to vary together; cases with certain values on one variable are likely to have certain values on the other one. For example, people with higher values on the income variable are likely to have higher values on the life expectancy variable. Likewise, those with lower incomes have lower life expectancy. This is usually stated in a shorthand way by saying that income and life expectancy are related to each other, or covary. We could also say that knowing one's income tells us one's probable life expectancy, or that life expectancy depends on income.

Independence is the opposite of covariation. It means there is no association or no relationship between variables. If two variables are independent,

Box 12.2 _____

Calculating *Z*-Scores

The formula for z-scores is

Z-score = (Score – Mean)/Standard deviation, or in symbols:

$$z = \frac{X - \overline{X}}{\delta}$$

where X = score, $\overline{X}$ = mean, δ = standard deviation.

A simple conceptual diagram does the same thing and shows what z-scores really do. Consider data on the ages of schoolchildren with a mean of 7 years and a standard deviation of 2 years. How do you compute the z-score of 5-year-old Miguel, or what if you know that Yashohda's z-score is a +2 and you need to know her age in years? First, you draw a little chart from –3 to +3 with zero in the middle. You will put the mean value at zero, because a z-score of zero is the mean, and z-scores measure distance above or below it. You stop at 3 because virtually all cases fall within 3 standard deviations of the mean in most situations. The chart looks like this:

```
|____|____|____|____|____|____|____|
 –3   –2   –1    0   +1   +2   +3
```

Now you label the values of the mean and add or subtract standard deviations from it. One standard deviation above the mean (+1)—when the mean is 7 and standard deviation is 2 years—is just 7 + 2, or 9 years. For a –2 z-score, you put 3 years. This is because it is 2 standard deviations, of 2 years each (or 4 years), lower than the mean of 7. Your diagram now looks like this:

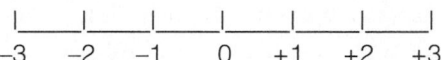

```
 1    3    5    7    9   11    13   age in years
|____|__|__|____|____|____|____|
 –3   –2  –1   0   +1   +2   +3
```

It is easy to see that Miguel, who is 5 years old, has a z-score of –1, whereas Yashohda's z-score of +2 corresponds to 11 years old. You can read from z-score to age, or age to z-score. For fractions, such as a z-score of –1.5, you just apply the same fraction to age to get 4 years. Likewise, an age of 12 is a z-score of +2.5.

cases with certain values on one variable do not have any particular value on the other variable. For example, Rita wants to know whether number of siblings is related to life expectancy. If the variables are independent, then people with many brothers and sisters have the same life expectancy as those who are only children. In other words, knowing how many brothers or sisters someone has tells Rita nothing about the person's life expectancy.

Most researchers state hypotheses in terms of a causal relationship or expected covariation; if they use the null hypothesis, the hypothesis is that there is independence. It is used in formal hypothesis testing and is frequently found in inferential statistics (to be discussed).

Three techniques help researchers decide whether a relationship exists between two variables: (1) a scattergram, or a graph or plot of the relationship; (2) cross-tabulation, or a percentaged table; and (3) measures of association, or statistical measures that express the amount of covariation by a single number (e.g., correlation coefficient). Also, see Box 12.3 on graphing data.

Seeing the Relationship: The Scattergram

What Is a Scattergram (or Scatterplot)?   A *scattergram* is a graph on which a researcher plots each case or observation, where each axis represents the value of one variable. It is used for variables measured at the interval or ratio level, rarely for ordinal variables, and never if either variable is nominal. There is no fixed rule for which variable (independent or dependent) to place on the horizontal or vertical axis, but usually the independent variable (symbolized by the letter X) goes on the horizontal axis and the dependent variable (symbolized by Y) on the vertical axis. The lowest value for each should be the lower left corner, and the highest value should be at the top or to the right.

How to Construct a Scattergram.   Begin with the range of the two variables. Draw an axis with the values of each variable marked and write numbers on each axis (graph paper is helpful). Next, label each axis with the variable name and put a title at the top.

You are now ready for the data. For each case find the value of each variable and mark the graph at a place corresponding to the two values. For example, a researcher makes a scattergram of years of schooling by number of children. He or she looks at the first case to see years of schooling (e.g., 12) and at the number of children (e.g., 3). Then he or she goes to the place on the graph where 12 for the "schooling" variable and 3 for the "number of children" variable intersect and puts a dot for the case.

The scattergram in Figure 12.5 is a plot of data for 33 women. It shows a negative relationship between the years of education the woman completed and the number of children she gave birth to.

What Can You Learn from the Scattergram?   A social work researcher can see three aspects of a bivariate relationship in a scattergram: form, direction, and precision.

Form.   Relationships can take three forms: independence, linear, and curvilinear. *Independence,* or no relationship, is the easiest to see. It looks like a random scatter with no pattern, or a straight line that is exactly parallel to the horizontal or vertical axis. A *linear relationship* means that a straight line can be visualized in the middle of a maze of cases running from one corner to another. A *curvilinear relationship* means that the center of a maze of cases would form a U curve, right side up or upside down, or an S curve.

Direction.   Linear relationships can have a positive or negative direction. The plot of a *positive* relationship looks like a diagonal line from the lower left to the upper right. Higher values on X tend to go with higher values on Y, and vice versa. The income and life expectancy example described a positive linear relationship.

A *negative* relationship looks like a line from the upper left to the lower right. It means that higher values on one variable go with lower values on the other. For example, people with more education are less likely to have been arrested. If we look at a scattergram of data on a group of males wherein years of schooling (X axis) are plotted by number of arrests (Y axis), we see that most cases (or men) with many arrests are in the lower right, because most of them completed few years of school. Most cases

Box 12.3 _____

Graphing Accurately

The pattern in graph A shows drastic change. A steep drop in 1980 is followed by rapid recovery and instability. The pattern in graph B is much more constant. The decline from 1978 to 1980 is smooth, and the other years are almost level. Both graphs are for identical data, the U.S. business failure rate from 1975 to 1992. The *X* axis (bottom) for years is the same. The scale of the *Y* axis is 60 to 160 in graph A and 0 to 400 in graph B. The pattern in graph A looks more dramatic only because of the *Y*-axis scale. When reading graphs, be careful to check the scale. Some people purposely choose a scale to minimize or dramatize a pattern in the data.

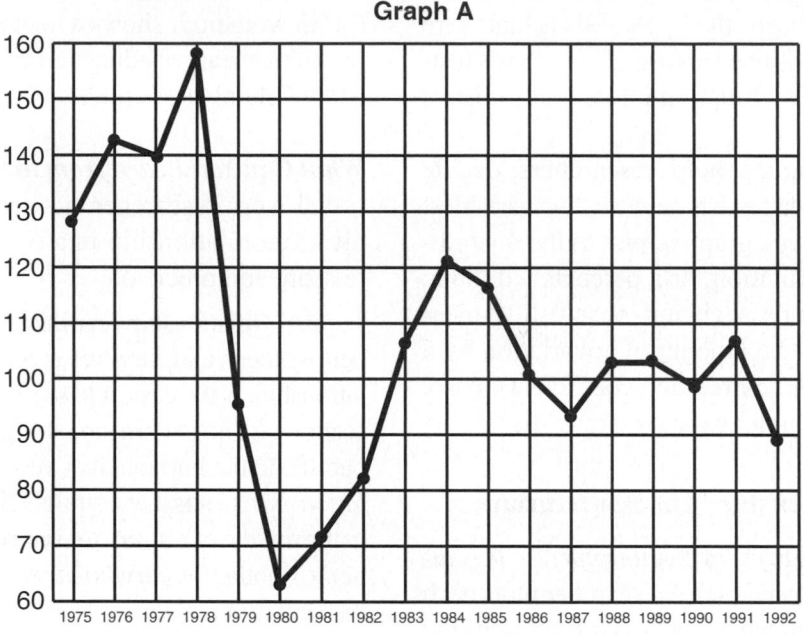

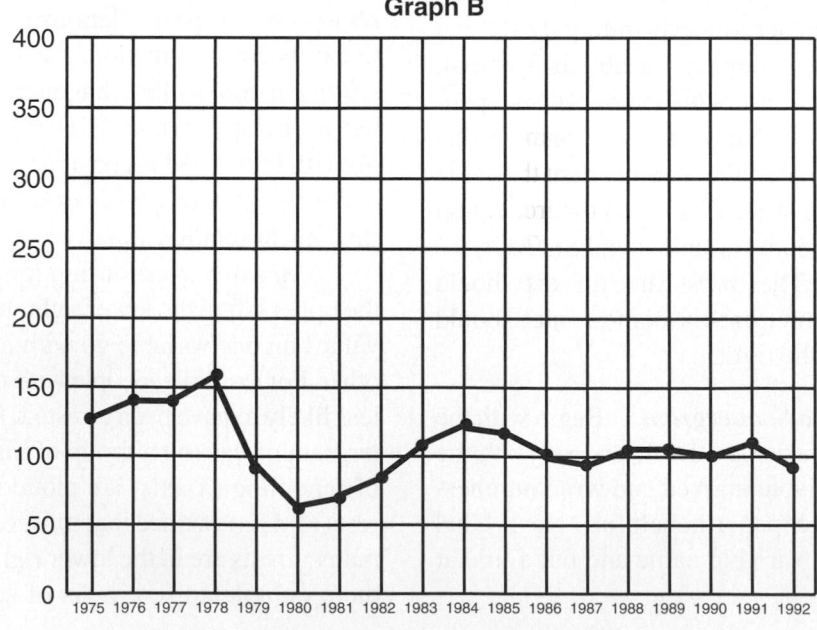

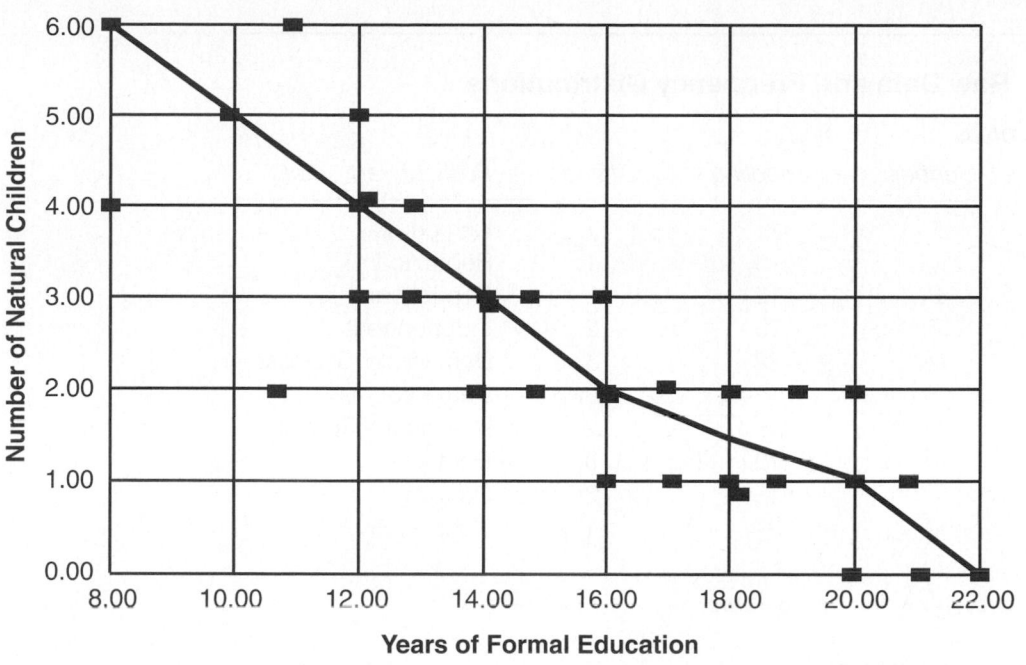

FIGURE 12.5 Example of a Scattergram: Years of Education by Number of Natural Children for 33 Women

with few arrests are in the upper left because most have had more schooling. The imaginary line for the relationship can have a shallow or a steep slope. More advanced statistics provide precise numerical measures of the line's slope.

Precision. Bivariate relationships differ in their degree of precision. *Precision* is the amount of spread in the points on the graph. A high level of precision occurs when the points hug the line that summarizes the relationship. A low level occurs when the points are widely spread around the line. Researchers can "eyeball" a highly precise relationship. They can also use advanced statistics to measure the precision of a relationship in a way that is analogous to the standard deviation for univariate statistics.

Bivariate Tables

What Is a Bivariate Table? The bivariate contingency table is widely used. It presents the same information as a scattergram in a more condensed form. The data can be measured at any level of measurement, although interval and ratio data must be grouped if there are many different values. The table is based on *cross-tabulation;* that is, the cases are organized in the table on the basis of two variables at the same time.

A *contingency table* is formed by cross-tabulating two or more variables. It is contingent because the cases in each category of a variable get distributed into each category of a second (or additional) variable. The table distributes cases into the categories of multiple variables at the same time and shows how the cases, by category of one variable, are "contingent upon" the categories of other variables.

Constructing Percentaged Tables. It is easy to construct a percentaged table, but there are ways to make it look professional. We will first review the steps for constructing a table by hand. The same principles apply if a computer makes the table. We begin with the raw data, which can be organized into a format for computers. They might look like data from an imaginary survey in Box 12.4.

If creating a table by hand, the next step is to create a *compound frequency distribution (CFD).* This is similar to the frequency distribution, except

Box 12.4 _____

Raw Data and Frequency Distributions

EXAMPLE OF RAW DATA

Case	Age	Gender	Schooling	Attitude	Political Party, etc. . . .
01	21	F	14	1	Democrat
02	36	M	8	1	Republican
03	77	F	12	2	Republican
04	41	F	20	2	Independent
05	29	M	22	3	Democratic Socialist
06	45	F	12	3	Democrat
07	19	M	13	2	Missing information
08	64	M	12	3	Democrat
09	53	F	10	3	Democrat
10	44	M	21	1	Conservative

etc.

(Attitude scoring, 1 = Agree, 2 = No opinion, 3 = Disagree)

TWO FREQUENCY DISTRIBUTIONS:
AGE AND ATTITUDE TOWARD CHANGING THE DRINKING AGE

Age Group	Number of Cases	Attitude	Number of Cases
Under 30	26		
30–45	30	Agree	38
46–60	35	No opinion	26
61 and older	15	Disagree	40
Missing	3	Missing	5
Total	109	Total	109

COMPOUND FREQUENCY DISTRIBUTION:
AGE GROUP AND ATTITUDE TOWARD CHANGING THE DRINKING AGE

Age	Attitude	Number of Cases
Under 30	Agree	20
Under 30	No opinion	3
Under 30	Disagree	3
30–45	Agree	10
30–45	No opinion	10
30–45	Disagree	5
46–60	Agree	4
46–60	No opinion	10
46–60	Disagree	21
61 and older	Agree	3
61 and older	No opinion	2
61 and older	Disagree	10
	Subtotal	101
Missing on either variable		8
Total		109

that it is for each combination of the values of two variables. For example, a researcher wants to see the relationship between age and attitude. Age is a ratio measure, so it is grouped to treat the ratio-level variable as if it were ordinal. Ratio- or interval-level data are converted to the ordinal level for percentaged tables. Otherwise, there could be 50 categories for a variable and a table that was impossible to read.

The CFD is an intermediate step that makes table construction easier. Computer programs give you the completed table right away.

The CFD has every combination of categories. Age has four categories and Attitude three, so there are 3 × 4 = 12 rows. The steps to create a CFD are as follows:

1. Figure all possible combinations of variable categories.
2. Make a mark next to the combination category into which each case falls.

3. Add up the marks for the number of cases in a combination category.

If there is no missing information problem, add up the numbers of categories (e.g., all the "Agree"s, or all the "61 and Older"s). In the example, missing data are an issue. The four "Agree" categories in the CFD add up to 37 (20 + 10 + 4 + 3), not 38, as in the univariate frequency distribution, because one of the 38 cases has missing information for age.

The next step is to set up the parts of a table (see Figure 12.6) by labeling the rows and columns. The independent variable usually is placed in the columns, but this convention is not always followed. Next, each number from the CFD is placed into a cell in the table that corresponds to the combination of variable categories. For example, the CFD shows that 20 of the under-30-year-olds agree (top number), and so does Figure 12.6 (upper left cell).

FIGURE 12.6 Age Group by Attitude about Changing the Drinking Age, Raw Count Table

RAW COUNT TABLE (a)

ATTITUDE (b)	AGE GROUP (b)				TOTAL (c)
	Under 30	30–45	46–60	61 and Older	
Agree	20	10	4	3	37
No opinion	3 (d)	10	10	2	25
Disagree	3	5	21	10	39
Total (c)	26	25	35	15	101
Missing cases (f) = 8.			(e)▲		

THE PARTS OF A TABLE

(a) Give each table a *title,* which names variables and provides background information.

(b) Label the row and column variable and give a name to each of the variable categories.

(c) Include the totals of the columns and rows. These are called the *marginals.* They equal the univariate frequency distribution for the variable.

(d) Each number or place that corresponds to the intersection of a category for each variable is a *cell of a table.*

(e) The numbers with the labeled variable categories and the totals are called the *body of a table.*

(f) If there is missing information (cases in which a respondent refused to answer, ended interview, said "don't know," etc.), report the number of missing cases near the table to account for all original cases.

Figure 12.6 is a raw count or frequency table. Its cells contain a count of the cases. It is easy to make, but interpreting a raw count table is difficult because the rows or columns can have different totals, and what is of real interest is the relative size of cells compared to others.

Researchers convert raw count tables into percentaged tables to see bivariate relationships. There are three ways to percentage a table: by row, by column, and for the total. The first two are often used and show relationships.

Is it best to percentage by row or by column? Either can be appropriate. Let us first review the mechanics of percentaging a table. When calculating column percentages, compute the percentage each cell is of the column total. This includes the total column or marginal for the column variable. For example, the first column total is 26 (there are 26 people under age 30), and the first cell of that col-

umn is 20 (there are 20 people under age 30 who agree). The percentage is 20/26 = 0.769 or 76.9 percent. Or, for the first number in the marginal, 37/101 = 0.366 = 36.6 percent (see Table 12.1). Except for rounding, the total should equal 100 percent.

Computing row percentages is similar. Compute the percentage of each cell as a percentage of the row total. For example, using the same cell with 20 in it, we now want to know what percentage it is of the row total of 37, or 20/37 = 0.541 = 54.1 percent. Percentaging by row or column gives different percentages for a cell unless the marginals are the same.

The row and column percentages let a researcher address different questions. The row percentage table answers the question, "Among those who hold an attitude, what percentage come from each age group?" It says of respondents who agree, 54.1 percent are in the under-30 age group. The

TABLE 12.1 Age Group by Attitude about Changing the Drinking Age, Percentaged Tables

COLUMN-PERCENTAGED TABLE

ATTITUDE	Under 30	30–45	46–60	61 and Older	TOTAL
Agree	76.9%	40%	11.4%	20%	36.6%
No opinion	11.5	40	28.6	13.3	24.8
Disagree	11.5	20	60	66.7	38.6
Total	99.9	100	100	100	100
(N)	(26)*	(25)*	(35)*	(15)*	(101)*

Missing cases = 8

ROW-PERCENTAGED TABLE

ATTITUDE	Under 30	30–45	46–60	61 and Older	TOTAL	(N)
Agree	54.1%	27%	10.8%	8.1%	100%	(37)*
No opinion	12	40	40	8	100	(25)*
Disagree	7.7	12.8	53.8	25.6	99.9	(39)*
Total	25.7	24.8	34.7	14.9	100.1	(101)*

Missing cases = 8

*For percentaged tables, provide the number of cases or N on which percentages are computed in parentheses near the total of 100%. This makes it possible to go back and forth from a percentaged table to a raw count table and vice versa.

column percentage table addresses the question, "Among those in each age group, what percentage hold different attitudes?" It says that among those who are under 30, 76.9 percent agree. From the row percentages, a researcher learns that a little over half of those who agree are under 30 years old, whereas from column percentages, the researcher learns that among the under-30 people, over three-quarters agree. One way of percentaging tells about people who have specific attitudes; the other tells about people in specific age groups.

A social work researcher's hypothesis may imply looking at row percentages or column percentages. When beginning, calculate percentages each way and practice interpreting, or figuring out, what each says. For example, a hypothesis is that age affects attitude, so column percentages are most helpful. However, if our interest were in describing the age makeup of groups of people with different attitudes, then row percentages are appropriate. As Zeisel (1985:34) noted, whenever one factor in a cross-tabulation can be considered the cause of the other, percentage will be most illuminating if they are computed in the direction of the causal factor.

Reading a Percentaged Table.   Once you understand how a table is made, reading it and figuring out what it says are much easier. To read a table, first look at the title, the variable labels, and any background information. Next, look at the direction in which percentages have been computed—in rows or columns. Notice that the percentaged tables in Table 12.1 have the same title. This is because the same variables are used. It would have helped to note how the data were percentaged in the title, but this is rarely done. Sometimes, researchers present abbreviated tables and omit the 100-percent total or the marginals, which adds to the confusion. It is best to include all the parts of a table and clear labels.

Researchers read percentaged tables to make comparisons. Comparisons are made in the opposite direction from that in which percentages are computed. A rule of thumb is to compare across rows if the table is percentaged down (i.e., by column) and to compare up and down in columns if the table is percentaged across (i.e., by row).

For example, in row-percentaged Table 12.1, compare columns or age groups. Most of those who agree are in the youngest group, with the proportion declining as age increases. Most no-opinion people are in the middle-age groups, whereas those who disagree are older, especially in the 46-to-60 group. When reading column-percentaged Table 12.1, compare across rows. For example, a majority of the youngest group agree, and they are the only group in which most people agree. Only 11.5 percent disagree, compared to a majority in the two oldest groups.

It takes practice to see a relationship in a percentaged table. If there is no relationship in a table, the cell percentages look approximately equal across rows or columns. A linear relationship looks like larger percentages in the diagonal cells. If there is a curvilinear relationship, the largest percentages form a pattern across cells. For example, the largest cells might be the upper right, the bottom middle, and the upper left. It is easiest to see a relationship in a moderate-sized table (9 to 16 cells) wherein most cells have some cases (at least five cases are recommended) and the relationship is strong and precise.

Principles of reading a scattergram can help you see a relationship in a percentaged table. Imagine a scattergram that has been divided into 12 equal-sized sections. The cases in each section correspond to the number of cases in the cells of a table that is superimposed onto the scattergram. The table is a condensed form of the scattergram. The bivariate relationship line in a scattergram corresponds to the diagonal cells in a percentaged table. Thus, a simple way to see strong relationships is to circle the largest percentage in each row (for row-percentaged tables) or column (for column-percentaged tables) and see if a line appears.

The circle-the-largest-cell rule works—with one important caveat. The categories in the percentages table *must* be ordinal or interval and in the same order as in a scattergram. In scattergrams the lowest variable categories begin at the bottom left. If the categories in a table are not ordered the same way, the rule does not work.

For example, Table 12.2a looks like a positive relationship and Table 12.2b like a negative

TABLE 12.2a   Age by Schooling

AGE	YEARS OF SCHOOLING				TOTAL
	0–11	12	13–14	16+	
Under 30	5%	25	30	40	100
30–45	15	25	40	20	100
46–60	35	45	12	8	100
61 +	45	35	15	5	100

TABLE 12.2b   Age by Schooling

AGE	YEARS OF SCHOOLING				TOTAL
	0–11	12	13–14	16+	
61 +	45%	35	15	5	100
46–60	35	45	12	8	100
30–45	15	25	40	20	100
Under 30	5	25	30	40	100

TABLE 12.3   Attitude about Changing the Drinking Age by Mean Age of Respondent

DRINKING AGE ATTITUDE	MEAN AGE	(N)
Agree	26.2	(37)
No opinion	44.5	(25)
Disagree	61.9	(39)

Missing cases = 8

relationship. Both use the same data and are percentaged by row. The actual relationship is negative. Look closely—Table 12.2b has age categories ordered as in a scattergram. When in doubt, return to the basic difference between positive and negative relationships. A positive relationship means that as one variable increases, so does the other. A negative relationship means that as one variable increases, the other decreases.

Bivariate Tables without Percentages. Researchers condense information in another kind of bivariate table with a measure of central tendency (usually the mean) instead of percentages. It is used when one variable is nominal or ordinal and another is measured at the interval or ratio level. The mean (or a similar measure) of the interval or ratio variable is presented for each category of the nominal or ordinal variable. Such tables are not constructed from the CFD. Instead, all cases are divided into the ordinal or nominal variable categories; then the mean is calculated for the cases in each variable category from the raw data.

Table 12.3 shows the mean age of people in each of the attitude categories. The results suggest that the mean age of those who disagree is much higher than for those who agree or have no opinion.

Measures of Association

A measure of association is a single number that expresses the strength, and often the direction, of a relationship. It condenses information about a bivariate relationship into a single number.

There are many measures of association. The correct one depends on the level of measurement. Many measures are called by letters of the Greek alphabet. Lambda, gamma, tau, chi (squared), and rho are commonly used measures. The emphasis here is on interpreting the measures, not on their calculation. In order to understand each measure, you will need to complete a beginning statistics course. See Box 12.5 on the correlation.

Most of the elementary measures discussed here follow a *proportionate reduction in error (PRE)* logic. The logic asks: How much does knowledge of one variable reduce the errors that are made when guessing the values of the other variable? Independence means that knowledge of one variable does not reduce the chance of errors on the other variable. Measures of association equal zero if the variables are independent.

If there is a strong association or relationship, then few errors are made predicting a second variable on the basis of knowledge of the first, or the proportion of errors reduced is large. A large number of correct guesses suggests that the measure of association is a nonzero number if an association exists between the variables. Table 12.4 describes five

Box 12.5 _____

Correlation

The formula for a correlation coefficient (rho) looks awesome to most people. Calculating it by hand, especially if the data have multiple digits, can be a very long and arduous task. Nowadays, computers do the calculation. However, the problem with relying on computers to do the work is that a researcher may not understand what the coefficient means. Here is a short, simplified example to show how it is done.

The purpose of a correlation coefficient is to show how much two variables "go together" or covary. Ideally, the variables have a ratio level of measurement (some use variables at the interval level). To calculate the coefficient, we first convert each score on a variable into its z-score. This "standardizes" the variable based on its mean and standard deviation. Next, we multiply the z-scores for each case together. This tells us how much the variables for a case vary together—cases with high z-scores on both variables get much bigger, while those low on both are much smaller. Finally, we divide the sum of the multiplied z-scores by the number of cases. It yields a type of "average" co-variation that has been standardized. In short, a correlation coefficient is the product of z-scores added together, then divided by the number of cases. It is always between +1.0 and −1.0 and summarizes scattergram information about a relationship into a single number.

Let us look at the correlation between the years of social work experience and hourly wage for five social workers. First, anyone who is brave or lacks math-symbol phobia can look at one of the frequently used formulas for a correlation coefficient:

$$(\Sigma\,[z\text{-score}_1][z\text{-score}_2])/N$$

where Σ = sum, $z\text{-score}_1$ = z-score for 1st variable (see Box 12.2), $z\text{-score}_2$ = z-score for 2nd variable, N = number of cases

Here is how to calculate a correlation coefficient without directly using the formula:

SOCIAL WORKER	YEARS OF SOCIAL WORK EXPERIENCE	HOURLY WAGE	(DIFFERENCE) Age	(DIFFERENCE) Price	SQUARED DIFF. Age	SQUARED DIFF. Price	Z-SCORES Age	Z-SCORES Price	Z-SCORE Product
A	2	$10	−2	−5	4	25	−1.43	−0.70	1.0
B	3	$ 5	−1	−10	1	100	−0.71	−1.41	1.0
C	5	$20	+1	+5	1	25	+0.71	+0.70	0.50
D	6	$25	+2	+10	4	100	+1.43	+1.41	2.0
E	4	$15	0	0	0	0	0	0	0
Total	20	$75			10	250			4.50

Mean: Experience = 4; Wage = $15
Variance: Experience = 10/5 = 2; Wage = 250/5 = 50.
Stnd. Dev.: Experience = square root of 2 = 1.4; Wage = square root of 50 = 7.1
Correlation: 4.50/5 = .90

Step 1: Calculate the mean and standard deviation for each variable. (For the standard deviation, first subtract each score from its mean, next square the difference, now sum squared differences, then divide the sum by the number of cases for the variance. Then take the square root of the variance.)

Step 2: Convert each score for the variables into their z-scores. (Just subtract each score from its mean and divide by its standard deviation.)

Step 3: Multiply the z-scores together for each case.

Step 4: Sum the products of z-scores, then divide by the number of cases.

TABLE 12.4   Five Measures of Association

Lambda is used for nominal-level data. It is based on a reduction in errors based on the mode and ranges between 0 (independence) and 1.0 (perfect prediction or the strongest possible relationship).

Gamma is used for ordinal-level data. It is based on comparing pairs of variable categories and seeing whether a case has the same rank on each. Gamma ranges from –1.0 to +1.0, with 0 meaning no association.

Tau is also used for ordinal-level data. It is based on a different approach than gamma and takes care of a few problems that can occur with gamma. Actually, there are several statistics named tau (it is a popular Greek letter), and the one here is Kendall's tau. Kendall's tau ranges from –1.0 to +1.0, with 0 meaning no association.

Rho is also called Pearson's product moment correlation coefficient (named after the famous statistician Karl Pearson and based on a product moment statistical procedure). It is the most commonly used measure of correlation, the correlation statistic people mean if they use the term *correlation* without identifying it further. It can be used only for data measured at the interval or ratio level. Rho is used for the mean and standard deviation of the variables and tells how far cases are from a relationship (or regression) line in a scatterplot. Rho ranges from –1.0 to +1.0, with 0 meaning no association. If the value of rho is squared, sometimes called *R*-squared, it has a unique proportion reduction in error meaning. *R*-squared tells how the percentage in one variable (e.g., the dependent) is accounted for, or explained by, the other variable (e.g., the independent). Rho measures linear relationships only. It cannot measure nonlinear or curvilnear relationships. For example, a rho of zero can indicate either no relationship or a curvilinear relationship (see Box 12.5).

The *chi-square* has two different uses. It can be used as a measure of association in descriptive statistics such as the others listed here, or in inferential statistics. Inferential statistics are briefly described next. As a measure of association, the chi-square can be used for nominal and ordinal data. It has an upper limit of infinity and a lower limit of zero, meaning no association (see Box 12.8).

SUMMARY OF MEASURES OF ASSOCIATION

Measure	Greek Symbol	Type of Data	High Association	Independence
Lambda	λ	Nominal	1.0	0
Gamma	γ	Ordinal	+1.0, –1.0	0
Tau (Kendall's)	τ	Ordinal	+1.0, –1.0	0
Rho	ρ	Interval, ratio	+1.0, –1.0	0
Chi-square	χ^2	Nominal, ordinal	Infinity	0

commonly used bivariate measures of association. Notice that most range from –1 to +1, with negative numbers indicating a negative relationship and positive numbers a positive relationship. A measure of 1.0 means a 100-percent reduction in errors, or perfect prediction.

MORE THAN TWO VARIABLES

Statistical Control

Showing an association or relationship between two variables is not sufficient to say that an independent variable *causes* a dependent variable. In addition to temporal order and association, a researcher must eliminate alternative explanations—explanations that can make the hypothesized relationship spurious. Experimental researchers do this by choosing a research design that physically controls potential alternative explanations for results (i.e., that threaten internal validity).

In nonexperimental research a researcher controls for alternative explanations with statistics. He or she measures possible alternative explanations with *control variables,* then examines the control variables with multivariate tables and statistics that help him or her decide whether a bivariate relationship is spurious. They also show the relative size of the effect of multiple independent variables on a dependent variable.

A researcher controls for alternative explanations in multivariate (more than two variables) analysis by introducing a third (or sometimes a fourth or fifth) variable. For example, a bivariate table shows that taller teenagers like baseball more than shorter ones do. But the bivariate relationship between height and attitude toward baseball may be spurious because teenage males are taller than females, and males tend to like baseball more than females. To test whether the relationship is actually due to sex, a researcher must *control for* gender; in other words, effects of sex are statistically *removed.* Once this is done, a researcher can see whether the bivariate relationship between height and attitude toward baseball remains.

A researcher controls for a third variable by seeing whether the bivariate relationship persists within categories of the control variable. For example, a researcher controls for sex, and the relationship between height and baseball attitude persists. This means that tall males and tall females both like baseball more than short males and short females do. In other words, the control variable has no effect. When this is so, the bivariate relationship is not spurious.

If the bivariate relationship weakens or disappears after the control variable is considered, it means that tall males are no more likely than short males to like baseball, and tall females are no more likely than short females to like baseball. It indicates that the initial bivariate relationship is spurious and suggests that

the third variable, sex, and not height, is the true cause of differences in attitudes toward baseball.

Statistical control is a key idea in advanced statistical techniques. A measure of association such as the correlation coefficient only suggests a relationship. Until a researcher considers control variables, the bivariate relationship could be spurious. Researchers are cautious in interpreting bivariate relationships until they have considered control variables.

After they introduce control variables, researchers talk about the *net effect* of an independent variable—the effect of the independent variable "net of," or in spite of, the control variable. There are two ways to introduce control variables: trivariate percentaged tables and multiple regression analysis. Each will be briefly discussed next.

The Elaboration Model of Percentaged Tables

Constructing Trivariate Tables. In order to meet all the conditions needed for causality, researchers want to "control for" or see whether an alternative explanation explains away a causal relationship. If an alternative explanation explains a relationship, then the bivariate relationship is spurious. Alternative explanations are operationalized as third variables, which are called *control variables* because they control for alternative explanation.

One way to take such third variables into consideration and see whether they influence the bivariate relationship is to statistically introduce control variables using trivariate or three-variable tables. Trivariate tables differ slightly from bivariate tables; they consist of multiple bivariate tables.

A trivariate table has a bivariate table of the independent and dependent variable for each category of the control variable. These new tables are called *partials.* The number of partials depends on the number of categories in the control variable. Partial tables look like bivariate tables, but they use a subset of the cases. Only cases with a specific value on the control variable are in the partial. Thus, it is possible to break apart a bivariate table to form partials, or combine the partials to restore the initial bivariate table.

Trivariate tables have three limitations. First, they are difficult to interpret if a control variable has more than four categories. Second, control variables can be at any level of measurement, but interval or ratio control variables must be grouped (i.e., converted to an ordinal level), and how cases are grouped can affect the interpretation of effects. Finally, the total number of cases is a limiting factor because the cases are divided among cells in partials. The number of cells in the partials equals the number of cells in the bivariate relationship multiplied by the number of categories in the control variable. For example, a control variable has three categories, and a bivariate table has 12 cells, so the partials have $3 \times 12 = 36$ cells. An average of five cases per cell is recommended, so the researcher will need $5 \times 36 = 180$ cases at minimum.

Like bivariate table construction, a trivariate table begins with a compound frequency distribution (CFD), but it is a three-way instead of a two-way CFD. An example of a trivariate table with "gender" as a control variable for the bivariate table in Figure 12.6 is shown in Table 12.5.

As with the bivariate tables, each combination in the CFD represents a cell in the final (here the partial) table. Each partial table has the variables in an initial bivariate table.

For three variables, three bivariate tables are logically possible. In the example the combinations are (1) gender by attitude, (2) age group by attitude, and (3) gender by age group. The partials are set up on the basis of the initial bivariate relationship. The independent variable in each is "age group" and the dependent variable is "attitude." "Gender" is the control variable. Thus, the trivariate table consists of a pair of partials, each showing the age/attitude relationship for a given gender.

A researcher's theory suggests the hypothesis in the initial bivariate relationship; it also tells him or her which variables provide alternative explanations (i.e., the control variables). Thus, the choice of the control variable is based on theory.

As with bivariate tables, the CFD provides the raw count for cells (partials here). A researcher converts them into percentages in the same way as for a bivariate table (i.e., divide cells by the row or column total). For example, in the partial table for females, the upper left cell has a 10. The row percentage for that cell is $10/17 = 58$ percent.

The *elaboration paradigm* is a system for reading percentaged trivariate tables.[4] It describes the

pattern that emerges when a control variable is introduced. Five terms describe how the partial tables compare to the initial bivariate table, or how the original bivariate relationship changes after the control variable is considered (see Box 12.6). The examples of patterns presented here show strong cases. More advanced statistics are needed when the differences are not as obvious.

The *replication pattern* is the easiest to understand. It occurs when the partials replicate or reproduce the same relationship that existed in the bivariate table before considering the control variable. It means that the control variable has no effect.

The *specification pattern* is the next easiest pattern. It occurs when one partial replicates the initial bivariate relationship but other partials do not. For example, you find a strong (negative) bivariate relationship between automobile accidents and college grades. You control for gender and discover that the relationship holds only for males (i.e., the strong negative relationship was in the partial for males, but not for females). This is specification because a researcher can specify the category of the control variable in which the initial relationship persists.

The control variable has a large impact in both the interpretation and explanation patterns. In both, the bivariate table shows a relationship that disappears in the partials. In other words, the relationship appears to have independence in the partials. The two patterns cannot be distinguished by looking at the tables alone. The difference between them depends on the location of the control variable in the causal order of variables. Theoretically, a control variable can be in one of two places, either between the original independent and dependent variables (i.e., the control variable is intervening), or before the original independent variable.

The *interpretation pattern* describes the situation in which the control variable intervenes between the original independent and dependent variables. For example, you examine a relationship between religious upbringing and abortion attitude. Political ideology is a control variable. You reason that religious upbringing affects current political ideology and abortion attitude. You theorize that political ideology is logically prior to an attitude about a specific issue, such as abortion. Thus,

TABLE 12.5   CFD and Tables for a Trivariate Analysis

COMPOUND FREQUENCY DISTRIBUTION FOR TRIVARIATE TABLE

MALES			FEMALES		
Age	*Attitude*	*Number of Cases*	*Age*	*Attitude*	*Number of Cases*
Under 30	Agree	10	Under 30	Agree	10
Under 30	No opinion	1	Under 30	No opinion	2
Under 30	Disagree	2	Under 30	Disagree	1
30–45	Agree	5	30–45	Agree	5
30–45	No opinion	5	30–45	No opinion	5
30–45	Disagree	2	30–45	Disagree	3
46–60	Agree	2	46–60	Agree	2
46–60	No opinion	5	46–60	No opinion	5
46–60	Disagree	11	46–60	Disagree	10
61 and older	Agree	3	61 and older	Agree	0
61 and older	No opinion	0	61 and older	No opinion	2
61 and older	Disagree	5	61 and older	Disagree	5
	Subtotal	51		Subtotal	50
Missing on either variable		4	Missing on either variable		4
Number of males		55	Number of females		54

PARTIAL TABLE FOR MALES

ATTITUDE	AGE GROUP				TOTAL
	Under 30	*30–45*	*46–60*	*61 and Older*	
Agree	10	5	2	3	20
No opinion	1	5	5	0	11
Disagree	2	2	11	5	20
Total	13	12	18	8	51

Missing cases = 4

PARTIAL TABLE FOR FEMALES

ATTITUDE	AGE GROUP				TOTAL
	Under 30	*30–45*	*46–60*	*61 and Older*	
Agree	10	5	2	0	17
No opinion	2	5	5	2	14
Disagree	1	3	10	5	19
Total	13	13	17	7	50

Missing cases = 4

religious upbringing causes political ideology, which in turn has an impact on abortion attitude. The control variable is an intervening variable, which helps you interpret the meaning of the complete relationship.

The *explanation pattern* looks the same as interpretation. The difference is the temporal order of the control variable. In this pattern a control variable comes before the independent variable in the initial bivariate relationship. For example, the original

Box 12.6

Summary of the Elaboration Paradigm

Pattern Name	Pattern Seen When Comparing Partials to the Original Bivariate Table
Replication	Same relationship in both partials as in bivariate table.
Specification	Bivariate relationship is seen in only one of the partial tables.
Interpretation	Bivariate relationship weakens greatly or disappears in the partial tables (control variable is intervening).
Explanation	Bivariate relationship weakens greatly or disappears in the partial tables (control variable is before independent variable).
Suppressor variable	No bivariate relationship; relationship appears in partial tables only.

EXAMPLES OF ELABORATION PATTERNS

Replication

	BIVARIATE TABLE			PARTIALS			
				Control = Low		Control = High	
	Low	*High*		*Low*	*High*	*Low*	*High*
Low	85%	15%	Low	84%	16%	86%	14%
High	15%	85%	High	16%	84%	14%	86%

Interpretation or Explanation

	BIVARIATE TABLE			PARTIALS			
				Control = Low		Control = High	
	Low	*High*		*Low*	*High*	*Low*	*High*
Low	85%	15%	Low	45%	55%	55%	45%
High	15%	85%	High	55%	45%	45%	55%

Specification

	BIVARIATE TABLE			PARTIALS			
				Control = Low		Control = High	
	Low	*High*		*Low*	*High*	*Low*	*High*
Low	85%	85%	Low	95%	5%	50%	50%
High	15%	15%	High	5%	95%	50%	50%

Suppressor Variable

	BIVARIATE TABLE			PARTIALS			
				Control = Low		Control = High	
	Low	*High*		*Low*	*High*	*Low*	*High*
Low	54%	46%	Low	84%	16%	14%	86%
High	46%	54%	High	16%	84%	86%	14%

relationship is between religious upbringing and abortion attitude, but now gender is the control variable. Gender comes before religious upbringing because one's sex is fixed at birth. The explanation pattern changes how a researcher explains the results. It implies that the initial bivariate relationship is spurious (see the discussion of spuriousness in Chapter 6).

The *suppressor variable pattern* occurs when the bivariate tables suggest independence but a relationship appears in one or both of the partials. For example, religious upbringing and abortion attitude are independent in a bivariate table. Once the control variable "region of the country" is introduced, religious upbringing is associated with abortion attitude in the partial tables. The control variable is a suppressor variable because it suppressed the true relationship. The true relationship appears in the partials.

Multiple Regression Analysis

Multiple regression is a statistical technique whose calculation is beyond the level of this book. Although it is quickly computed by the appropriate statistics software, a background in statistics is needed to prevent making errors in its calculation and interpretation. It requires interval- or ratio-level data. It is discussed here for two reasons. First, it controls for many alternative explanations and variables simultaneously (it is rarely possible to use more than one control variable at a time using percentaged tables). Second, it is widely used in social work, and you are likely to encounter it when reading research reports or articles.

Multiple regression results tell the reader two things. First, the results have a measure called *R* squared (R^2), which tells how well a set of variables explains a dependent variable. *Explain* means reduced errors when predicting the dependent variable scores on the basis of information about the independent variables. A good model with several independent variables might account for, or explain, a large percentage of variation in a dependent variable. For example, an R^2 of .50 means that knowing the independent and control variables improves the accuracy of predicting the dependent variable by 50 percent, or half as many errors are made as would be made without knowing about the variables.

Second, the regression results measure the direction and size of the effect of each variable on a dependent variable. The effect is measured precisely and given a numerical value. For example, a researcher can see how five independent or control variables simultaneously affect a dependent variable, with all variables controlling for the effects of one another. This is especially valuable for testing theories that state that multiple independent variables cause one dependent variable. (See Chapter 3 for examples of causal diagrams.)

The effect on the dependent variable is measured by a standardized regression coefficient or the Greek letter beta (ß). It is similar to a correlation coefficient. In fact, the beta coefficient for two variables equals the *r* correlation coefficient.

Researchers use the beta regression coefficient to determine whether control variables have an effect. For example, the bivariate correlation between *X* and *Y* is .75. Next, the researcher statistically considers four control variables. If the beta remains at .75, then the four control variables have no effect. However, if the beta for *X* and *Y* gets smaller (e.g., drops to .20), it indicates that the control variables have an effect.

Consider an example of regression analysis with age, income, education, religious attendance, and region as independent variables. The dependent variable is a score on a political ideology index. The multiple regression results show that income and religious attendance have large effects, education and region minor effects, and age no effect. All the independent variables together have a 38-percent accuracy in predicting a person's political ideology (see Box 12.7).[5] The example suggests that high income, frequent religious attendance, and a southern

---

Box 12.7 _____

Example of Multiple Regression Results

DEPENDENT VARIABLE IS POLITICAL IDEOLOGY INDEX (HIGH SCORE MEANS VERY LIBERAL)

Independent Variable	Standardized Regression Coefficients
Region = South	−.19
Age	.01
Income	−.44
Years of education	.23
Religious attendance	−.39
R^2 = .38	

residence are positively associated with conservative opinions, whereas having more education is associated with liberal opinions. The impact of income is more than twice the size of the impact of living in a southern region.

INFERENTIAL STATISTICS

The Purpose of Inferential Statistics

The statistics discussed so far in this chapter are descriptive statistics. But researchers often want to do more than describe; they want to test hypotheses, know whether sample results hold true in a population, and decide whether differences in results (e.g., between the mean scores of two groups) are big enough to indicate that a relationship really exists. Inferential statistics use probability theory to test hypotheses formally, permit inferences from a sample to a population, and test whether descriptive results are likely to be due to random factors or to a real relationship.

This section explains the basic ideas of inferential statistics but does not deal with inferential statistics in any detail. This area is more complex than descriptive statistics and requires a background in statistics.

Inferential statistics rely on principles from probability sampling, wherein a researcher uses a random process (e.g., a random-number table) to select cases from the entire population. Inferential statistics are a precise way to talk about how confident a researcher can be when inferring from the results in a sample to the population.

You have already encountered inferential statistics if you have read or heard about "statistical significance" or results "significant at the .05 level." Researchers use them to conduct various statistical tests (e.g., a *t*-test or an *F*-test). Statistical significance is also used in formal hypothesis testing, which is a precise way to decide whether to accept or to reject a null hypothesis.[6]

Statistical Significance

Statistical significance means that results are not likely to be due to chance factors. It indicates the probability of finding a relationship in the sample when there is none in the population. Because probability samples involve a random process, it is always possible that sample results will differ from a population parameter. A researcher wants to estimate the odds that sample results are due to a true population parameter or to chance factors of random sampling. Statistical significance uses probability theory and specific statistical tests to tell a researcher whether the results (e.g., an association, a difference between two means, a regression coefficient) are produced by random error in random sampling.

Statistical significance only tells what is likely. It cannot prove anything with absolute certainty. It states that particular outcomes are more or less probable. Statistical significance is *not* the same as practical, substantive, or theoretical significance. Results can be statistically significant but theoretically meaningless or trivial. For example, two variables can have a statistically significant association due to coincidence, with no logical connection between them (e.g., length of fingernails and ability to speak French).

Levels of Significance

Researchers usually express statistical significance in terms of levels (e.g., a test is statistically significant at a specific level) rather than giving the specific probability. The *level of statistical significance* (usually .05, .01, or .001) is a way of talking about the likelihood that results are due to chance factors—that is, that a relationship appears in the sample when there is none in the population. If a researcher says that results are significant at the .05 level, this means the following:

- Results like these are due to chance factors only 5 in 100 times.
- There is a 95-percent chance that the sample results are not due to chance factors alone, but reflect the population accurately.
- The odds of such results based on chance alone are .05, or 5 percent.
- One can be 95-percent confident that the results are due to a real relationship in the population, not chance factors.

These all say the same thing in different ways. This may sound like the discussion of sampling distributions and the central limit theorem in the chapter on sampling. It is not an accident. Both are based on probability theory, which researchers use to link sample data to a population. Probability theory lets us predict what happens in the long run over many events when a random process is used. In other words, it allows precise prediction over many situations in the long run, but not for a specific situation. Since we have one sample and we want to infer to the population, probability theory helps us estimate the odds that our particular sample represents the population. We cannot know for certain unless we have the whole population, but probability theory lets us state our confidence—how likely it is that the sample shows something that is also true in the population. For example, a sample shows that college men and women differ in how many hours they study. Is the result due to an unusual sample, and there is really no difference in the population, or does it reflect a true difference between the sexes in the population? (See Box 12.8 on chi-square.)

Type I and Type II Errors

If the logic of statistical significance is based on stating whether chance factors produce results, why use the .05 level? It means a 5-percent chance that randomness could cause the results. Why not use a more certain standard—for example, a 1 in 1,000 probability of random chance? This gives a smaller chance that randomness versus a true relationship caused the results.

There are two answers to this way of thinking. The simple answer is that the scientific community has informally agreed to use .05 as a rule of thumb for most purposes. Being 95-percent confident of results is the accepted standard for explaining the social world.

A second, more complex answer involves a tradeoff between making Type I and Type II errors. A researcher can make two kinds of logical errors. A *Type I error* occurs when the researcher says that a relationship exists when in fact none exists. It means falsely rejecting a null hypothesis. A *Type II error* occurs when a researcher says that a rela-

tionship does not exist, when in fact it does. It means falsely accepting a null hypothesis (see Table 12.6). Of course, researchers want to avoid both errors. They want to say that there is a relationship in the data only when it does exist and that there is no relationship only when there really is none, but they face a dilemma: As the odds of making one type of error decline, the odds of making the opposite error increase.

The idea of Type I and Type II errors may seem difficult at first, but the same logical dilemma appears outside research settings. For example, a jury can err by deciding that an accused person is guilty when in fact he or she is innocent. Or the jury can err by deciding that a person is innocent when in fact he or she is guilty. The jury does not want to make either error. It does not want to jail the innocent or to free the guilty, but the jury must make a judgment using limited information. Likewise, a pharmaceutical company has to decide whether to sell a new drug. The company can err by stating that the drug has no side effects when, in fact, it has the side effect of causing blindness. Or it can err by holding back a drug because of fear of serious side effects when in fact there are none. The company does not want to make either error. If it makes the first error, the company will face lawsuits and injure people. The second error will prevent the company from selling a drug that may cure illness and produce profits.

Let us put the ideas of statistical significance and the two types of error together. An overly cautious researcher sets a high level of significance and is likely to make one kind of error. For example, the researcher might use the .0001 level. He or she attributes the results to chance unless they are so rare that they would occur by chance only 1 in 10,000 times. Such a high standard means that the researcher is most likely to err by saying results are due to chance when in fact they are not. He or she may falsely accept the null hypothesis when there is a causal relationship (a Type II error). By contrast, a risk-taking researcher sets a low level of significance, such as .10. His or her results indicate a relationship would occur by chance 1 in 10 times. He or she is likely to err by saying that a causal relationship exists, when in fact random factors (e.g., random-sampling error) actually cause the results.

Box 12.8

Chi-Square

The chi-square (χ^2) is used in two ways. This creates confusion. As a *descriptive statistic*, it tells us the strength of the association between two variables; as an *inferential statistic*, it tells us the probability that any association we find is likely to be due to chance factors. The chi-square is a widely used and powerful way to look at variables measured at the ordinal level. It is a more precise way to tell whether there is an association in a bivariate percent-aged table than by just "eyeballing" it.

Logically, we first figure out "expected values" in a table. We do this based on information from the marginals alone. Recall that marginals are frequency distributions of each variable alone. An expected value can be thought of as our "best guess" without looking at the body of the table. Next, we look at the data to see how much they differ from the "expected value." If they differ by a lot, then there may be an association between the variables. If the data in a table are identical or very close to the expected values, then the variables are not associated; they are independent. In other words, *independence* means "what is going on" in a table is what we would expect based on the marginals alone. The chi-square is zero if there is independence and gets bigger as the association gets stronger. If the data in the table greatly differ from the expected values, then we know something is "going on" beyond what we would expect from the marginals alone (i.e., an association between the variables). See the example of an association between height and grade.

Raw or Observed Data Table

STUDENT HEIGHT	GRADE IN RESEARCH METHODS			TOTAL
	C	B	A	
Tall	30	10	10	50
Medium	10	30	10	50
Short	30	20	50	100
Total	70	60	70	200

Expected Values Table

Expected value = (Column total × Row total)/Grand total. EXAMPLE (70 × 50)/200 = 17.5

STUDENT HEIGHT	GRADE IN RESEARCH METHODS			TOTAL
	C	B	A	
Tall	17.5	15	17.5	50
Medium	17.5	15	17.5	50
Short	35	30	35	100
Total	70	60	70	200

Difference Table

Difference = (Observed – Expected). EXAMPLE (30 – 17.5) = 12.5

STUDENT HEIGHT	GRADE IN RESEARCH METHODS			TOTAL
	C	B	A	
Tall	12.5	–5	–7.5	0
Medium	–7.5	15	–7.5	0
Short	–5	–10	15	0
Total	0	0	0	0

(continued)

Box 12.8   (Continued)_____

Chi-square = Sum of each difference squared, then divided by the expected value of the cell. Example: 12.5 squared = 156.25, divided by 17.5 = 8.93.

Chi-square = 1st row (8.93 + 1.67 + 3.21) +
           2nd row (3.21 + 15 + 3.21) +
           3rd row (.71 + 3.33 + 6.43) = 45.7

Since the chi-square is not zero, the data are not independent; there is an association. The chi-square coefficient cannot tell us the direction (e.g., negative) of the association. For inferential statistics we need to use a chi-square table or computer program to evaluate the association (i.e., to see how likely such a large chi-square is to occur by chance alone). Without going into all the details about the chi-square table, this association is rare; it occurs by chance less than 1 in 1,000 times. For a table with nine cells, a chi-square of 45.7 is significant at the .001 level.

TABLE 12.6   Type I and Type II Errors

WHAT THE RESEARCHER SAYS	TRUE SITUATION IN THE WORLD	
	No Relationship	*Causal Relationship*
No relationship	No error	Type II error
Causal relationship	Type I error	No error

The researcher is likely to falsely reject the null hypothesis (Type I error). In sum, the .05 level is a compromise between Type I and Type II errors.

This section outlines the basics of inferential statistics. The statistical techniques are precise and rely on the relationship between sampling error, sample size, and central limit theorem. The power of inferential statistics is their ability to let a researcher state, with specific degrees of certainty, that specific sample results are likely to be true in a population. For example, a researcher conducts statistical tests and finds that a relationship is statistically significant at the .05 level. He or she can state that the sample results are probably not due to chance factors. Indeed, there is a 95-percent chance that a true relationship exists in the social world.

Tests for inferential statistics are useful but limited. The data must come from a random sample, and tests take into account only sampling errors. Nonsampling errors (e.g., a poor sampling frame or a poorly designed measure) are not considered. Do not be fooled into thinking that such tests offer easy, final answers.

CONCLUSION

You learned about organizing quantitative data to prepare them for analysis, and analyzing them (organizing data into charts or tables, or summarizing them with statistical measures). Researchers use statistical analysis to test hypotheses and answer research questions. You saw how data must first be coded and then analyzed using univariate or bivariate statistics. Bivariate relationships might be spurious, so control variables and multivariate analysis are often necessary. You also learned some basics about inferential statistics.

Beginning researchers sometimes feel they have done something wrong if their results do not support a hypothesis. *There is nothing wrong with rejecting a hypothesis.* The goal of scientific research is to produce knowledge that truly reflects the social world, not to defend pet ideas or hypotheses. Hypotheses are theoretical guesses based on limited knowledge; they need to be tested. Excellent-quality research can find that a hypothesis is wrong, and poor-quality research can support a hypothesis. Good research depends on high-quality methodology, not on supporting a specific hypothesis.

Good research means guarding against possible errors or obstacles to true inferences from data to the social world. Errors can enter into the research process and affect results at many places: research design, measurement, data collection, coding, calculating statistics and constructing tables, or interpreting results. Even if a researcher can design, measure, collect, code, and calculate without error, another step in the research process remains. It is to interpret the tables, charts, and statistics, and to answer the question, "What does it all mean?" The only way to assign meaning to facts, charts, tables, or statistics is to use theory.

Data, tables, or computer output cannot answer research questions. The facts do not speak for themselves. As a researcher, you must return to your theory (i.e., concepts, relationships among concepts, assumptions, theoretical definitions) and give the results meaning. Do not lock yourself into the ideas with which you began. There is room for creativity, and new ideas are generated by trying to figure out what results really say. It is important to be careful in designing and conducting research so that you can look at the results as a reflection of something in the social world and not worry about whether they are due to an error or an artifact of the research process itself.

Before we leave quantitative research, there is one last issue. Journalists, politicians, and others increasingly use statistical results to make a point or bolster an argument. This has not produced greater accuracy and information in public debate. More often, it has increased confusion and made it more important to know what statistics can and cannot do. The cliché that you can prove anything with statistics is false; however, people can and do *misuse* statistics. Through ignorance or conscious deceit, some people use statistics to manipulate others. The way to protect yourself from being misled by statistics is not to ignore them or hide from the numbers. Rather, it is to understand the research process and statistics, think about what you hear, and ask questions.

We turn next to qualitative research. The logic and purpose of qualitative research differ from those of the quantitative, positivist approach of the past chapters. It is less concerned with numbers, hypotheses, and causality and more concerned with words, norms and values, and meaning.

KEY TERMS

bar chart	elaboration paradigm	percentile
bivariate statistics	explanation pattern	pie chart
body of a table	frequency distribution	possible code cleaning
cell of a table	frequency polygon	range
code sheets	independence	replication pattern
codebook	interpretation pattern	scattergram
coding procedure	level of statistical significance	skewed distribution
contingency cleaning	linear relationship	specification pattern
contigency table	marginals	standard deviation
control variable	mean	statistical relationship
covariation	median	statistical significance
cross-tabulation	mode	suppressor-variable pattern
curvilinear relationship	net effect	Type I error
data field	normal distribution	Type II error
data records	optical scan sheet	univariate statistics
descriptive statistics	partials	z-score
direct-entry method		

REVIEW QUESTIONS

1. What is a codebook, and how is it used in research?

2. How do researchers clean data and check their coding?

3. Describe how researchers used the IBM card in data analysis.

4. In what ways can a researcher display frequency distribution information?

5. Describe the differences among mean, median, and mode.

6. What three features of a relationship can be seen from a scattergram?

7. What is a covariation, and how is it used?

8. When can a researcher generalize from a scattergram to a percentaged table to find a relationship among variables?

9. Discuss the concept of control as it is used in trivariate analysis.

10. What does it mean to say "statistically significant at the .001 level," and what type of error is more likely: Type I or Type II?

NOTES

1. Some of the best practical advice on coding and handling quantitative data comes from survey research. See discussions in Babbie (1998:363–367), Backstrom and Hursh-Cesar (1981:309–400), Fowler (1984:127–133), Sonquist and Dunkelberg (1977:210–215), and Warwick and Lininger (1975:234–291).

2. For discussions of many different ways to display quantitative data, see Fox (1992), Henry (1995), Tufte (1983, 1991), and Zeisel (1985:14–33).

3. There are other statistics to measure a special kind of mean for ordinal data and for other special situations, which are beyond the level of discussion in this book.

4. For a discussion of the elaboration paradigm and its history, see Babbie (1998:388–400) and Rosenberg (1968).

5. Beginning students and people outside the social sciences are sometimes surprised at the low (10- to 50-percent) predictive accuracy in multiple regression re-

sults. There are three responses to this. First, a 10- to 50-percent reduction in errors is really not bad compared to purely random guessing. Second, positivist social science is still developing. Although the levels of accuracy may not be as high as those of the physical sciences, they are much higher than for any explanation of the social world possible 10 or 20 years ago. Finally, the theoretically important issue in most multiple regression models is less the accuracy of overall prediction than the effects of specific variables. Most hypotheses involve the effects of specific independent variables on dependent variables.

6. In formal hypothesis testing, researchers test the *null hypothesis*. They usually want to reject the null because rejection of the null indirectly supports the alternative hypothesis to the null, the one they deduced from theory as a tentative explanation. The null hypothesis was discussed in Chapter 6.

CHAPTER 13

FIELD RESEARCH

*Field research is the study of people acting in the natural courses of their
daily lives. The fieldworker ventures into the worlds of others in order to
learn firsthand about how they live, how they talk and behave, and what
captivates and distresses them. . . . It is also seen as a method of study
whose practitioners try to understand the meanings that activities
observed have for those engaging in them.*

—Robert Emerson, *Contemporary Field Research*, p. 1

INTRODUCTION

This chapter and the two that follow represent a
major shift away from the quantitative style of the
past several chapters to the qualitative research
style. You may recall from Chapter 6 that the qualitative and the quantitative styles can differ a great
deal, and from Chapter 4, that the nonpositivist
approaches to social work differ from the qualitative
research style. This chapter describes field research,

also called *ethnography* or *participant-observation research*. It is a qualitative style in which a researcher directly observes and participates in small-scale social settings in the present time and in the researcher's home culture. Chapter 15 will discuss the analysis of qualitative data.

Many students are excited by field research because it involves hanging out with some exotic group of people. There are no cold mathematics or complicated statistics, no abstract deductive hypotheses. Instead, there is direct, face-to-face social interaction with "real people" in a natural setting.

In field research the individual researcher directly talks with and observes the people being studied. Through interaction over months or years, the researcher learns about them, their life histories, their hobbies and interests, and their habits, hopes, fears, and dreams. Meeting new people, developing friendships, and discovering new social worlds can be fun. It is also time consuming, emotionally draining, and sometimes physically dangerous.

Research Questions Appropriate for Field Research

When should you use field research? Field research is appropriate when the research question involves learning about, understanding, or describing a group of interacting people. It is usually best when the question is, "How do people do Y in the social world?" or "What is the social world of X like?" It can be used when other methods (e.g., survey, experiments) are not practical, as in studying street gangs. Douglas (1976:xii) stated that most of what social researchers really want to learn about can be studied only through the direct involvement of a researcher in the field.

Field researchers study people in a location or setting. It has been used to study entire communities. Beginning field researchers should start with a relatively small group (30 or fewer) who interact with each other on a regular basis in a relatively fixed setting (e.g., a street corner, church, barroom, beauty parlor, baseball field, etc.). Field research is also used to study amorphous social experiences that are not fixed in place, but where intensive in-terviewing and observation are the only way to gain access to the experience—for example, the feelings of a person who has been mugged, or who is the widow of someone who committed suicide.[1]

In order to use consistent terminology, we can call the people who are studied in a field setting *members*. They are insiders or natives in the field and belong to a group, subculture, or social setting that the "outsider" field researcher wants to penetrate and learn about.

Field researchers have explored a wide variety of social settings, subcultures, and aspects of social life, as illustrated by the examples of settings and subcultures listed here: laundromats (Kenen, 1982), camera clubs (Schwartz, 1986), waiting rooms (Gross, 1986; Goodsell, 1983; Lofland, 1972), battered women's shelters (Wharton, 1987), social movements (Downey, 1986; Snow and Associates, 1986b), social welfare offices (G. Miller, 1983), television stations (Altheide, 1976), airplane passengers (Zurcher, 1979), and bars (Byrne, 1978; LeMasters, 1975). In addition, field researchers have studied larger settings such as small towns (Vidich and Bensman, 1968), retirement communities (Hochschild, 1978; Jacobs, 1974; Marshall, 1975), working-class communities (Kornblum, 1974), and urban ethnic neighborhoods (Whyte, 1955). Additional studies can be found in two scholarly journals that specialize in field research: *Journal of Contemporary Ethnography* and *Qualitative Sociology*.

Field research is valuable for examining the culture of children's social worlds. Researchers have studied Little League baseball (Fine, 1979, 1987), children's playgrounds (Lever, 1978), and school children (Corsaro, 1988; Eder, 1981, 1985; Maynard, 1985; Thorne and Luria, 1986). Many occupations have been studied by field researchers, including medical students (Becker et al., 1961), cab drivers (Davis, 1959), cocktail waitresses (Hearn and Stoll, 1976; Spradley and Mann, 1975), dogcatchers (Palmer, 1978), police officers (Hunt, 1984; Pepinsky, 1980; Van Maanen, 1973; Waegel, 1984), door-to-door salespeople (Bogdan and Taylor, 1975:174–186), social workers (Johnson, 1975), jazz musicians (Sudnow, 1978), factory workers (Burawoy, 1979; Burawoy and Lukacs, 1985), milkmen (Bigus, 1972), airline attendants (Hochschild,

1983), and artists (Basirico, 1986; McCall, 1980; Sharon, 1979; Sinha, 1979).

Field researchers have contributed to medical sociology by examining intensive care units (Coombs and Goldman, 1973) and emergency rooms (Kurz, 1987), and important life events such as pregnancy/birth (Annandale, 1988; Danziger, 1979; Weitz and Sullivan, 1986), abortion (Ball, 1967), and death (Glaser and Strauss, 1968). Field research is especially valuable for studying deviant behavior. Field researchers have studied nude beaches (Douglas and Rasmussen, 1977), gambling (Hayano, 1982; Lesiuer and Sheley, 1987), big-time drug dealing (Adler, 1985; Adler and Adler, 1983), drug addicts (Faupel and Klockars, 1987), street gangs (Moore et al., 1983), street people, tramps, or hoboes (Liebow, 1967; Polsky, 1967; Snow et al., 1986a; Spradley, 1970), prostitutes (Bryan, 1965; Prus and Vassilakopoulos, 1979), hippie communes (Cavan, 1974), pornographic bookstores (Karp, 1973; Sudholm, 1973), the occult (Jorgensen and Jorgensen, 1982), and cults (Bromley and Shupe, 1979; Gordon, 1987; Lofland, 1966).

A Short History of Field Research

Early Beginnings. Field research can be traced back to the reports of travelers to distant lands.[2] In the 1200s European explorers and missionaries wrote descriptions of the strange cultures and peoples they encountered. Others read these descriptions to learn about foreign cultures. Later, in the nineteenth century, when European trade and empires rapidly expanded and there were more literate, educated travelers, the number of reports grew.

Academic field research began in the late nineteenth century with anthropology. The first anthropologists only read the reports of explorers, government officials, or missionaries but lacked direct contact with the people they studied. The reports focused on the exotic and were highly racist and ethnocentric. Travelers rarely spoke the local language and had to rely on interpreters. Not until the 1890s did European anthropologists begin to travel to faraway lands to learn about other cultures.

British social anthropologist Bronislaw Malinoski (1844–1942) was the first researcher to live

with a group of people for a long period of time and write about collecting data. In the 1920s he presented intensive fieldwork as a new method and argued for separating direct observation and native statements from the observer's inferences. He said that social researchers should directly interact with and live among the native peoples and learn their customs, beliefs, and social processes.

Researchers also used field research to study their own society. The observations of the London poor by Charles Booth and Beatrice Webb in the 1890s began both survey research and field research outside of anthropology. Booth and Webb directly observed people in natural settings and used an inductive data-gathering approach. Participant observation may have originated in Germany in 1890. Paul Gohre worked and lived as a factory apprentice for three months and took detailed notes each night at home in order to study factory life. His published work influenced scholars in the universities, including the sociologist Max Weber.

Chicago School. Field research in the United States began at the University of Chicago Department of Sociology in what is known as the Chicago school of sociology. The Chicago school's influence on field research had two phases. In the first phase, from the 1910s to 1930s, the school used a variety of methods based on the case-study or life-history approach, including direct observation, informal interviews, and reading documents or official records. Important influences came from Booker T. Washington, William James, and John Dewey. In 1916 Robert E. Park (1864–1944) drew up a research program for the social investigation of the city of Chicago. Influenced by his background as a newspaper reporter, he said that social researchers should leave the libraries and "get their hands dirty" through direct observations and conversations on street corners, in barrooms, and in luxury hotel lobbies. Early studies such as *The Hobo* (Anderson, 1923), *The Jack Roller* (Shaw, 1930), and *The Gang* (Thrasher, 1927) established early Chicago school sociology as the descriptive study of street life with little analysis.

Journalistic and anthropological models of research were combined in the first phase. The journalistic model has a researcher get behind fronts, use informants, look for conflict, and expose what is "really happening." In the anthropological model, a researcher attaches himself or herself to a small group for an extended period of time and reports on the members' views of the world.

In the second phase, from the 1940s to the 1960s, the Chicago school developed participant observation as a distinct technique. It applied an expanded anthropological model to groups and settings in the researcher's society. Three principles emerged:

1. Study people in their natural settings, or in situ.
2. Study people by directly interacting with them.
3. Gain an understanding of the social world and make theoretical statements about the members' perspectives.

Over time, the method moved from strict description to theoretical analyses based on involvement by the researcher in the field.

After World War II, field research faced increased competition from survey and quantitative research. Field research declined as a proportion of all social work research from World War II to the 1970s. In the 1970s and 1980s, however, several changes rejuvenated field research. First, field researchers borrowed ideas and techniques from cognitive psychology, cultural anthropology, folklore, and linguistics. Second, researchers reexamined the epistemological roots and philosophical assumptions of social work (see Chapter 4) that justified their method. Finally, field researchers became more self-conscious about their techniques and methods. They wrote about methodology and became more systematic about it as a research technique.

Today field research has a distinct set of methodologies. Field researchers directly observe and interact with members in natural settings to get inside their perspective. They embrace an activist or social constructionist perspective on social life. They do not see people as a neutral medium through which social forces operate, nor do they see social meanings as something "out there" to observe. Instead, they hold that people create and define the social world through their interactions.

Human experiences are filtered through a subjective sense of reality, which affects how people see and act on events. Thus, they replace the positivist emphasis on "objective facts" with a focus on the everyday, face-to-face social processes of negotiation, discussion, and bargaining to construct social meaning.

Field researchers see research as simultaneously a description of the social world and a part of it. As part of a socially created setting, a researcher's presence in the field cannot be just neutral data gathering.

Ethnography and Ethnomethodology. Two modern extensions of field research, ethnography and ethnomethodology, build on the social constructionist perspective. Each is redefining how field research is conducted. They are not yet the core of field research, so they are discussed only briefly here.

Ethnography comes from cultural anthropology.[3] *Ethno* means people or folk, and *graphy* refers to describing something. Thus, *ethnography* means describing a culture and understanding another way of life from the native point of view. As Franke (1983:61) stated, "Culture, the object of our description, resides within the thinking of natives." Ethnography assumes that people make inferences—that is, go beyond what is explicitly seen or said to what is meant or implied. People display their culture (what people think, ponder, or believe) through behavior (e.g., speech and actions) in specific social contexts. Displays of behavior do not give meaning; rather, meaning is inferred, or someone figures out meaning. Moving from what is heard or observed to what is actually meant is at the center of ethnography. For example, when a student is invited to a "kegger," the student infers that it is an informal party with other student-aged people at which beer will be served, based on his or her cultural knowledge. Cultural knowledge includes symbols, songs, sayings, facts, ways of behaving, and objects (e.g., telephones, newspapers, etc.). We learn the culture by watching television, listening to parents, observing others, and the like.

Cultural knowledge includes both explicit knowledge, what we know and talk about, and tacit knowledge, what we rarely acknowledge. For example, *explicit knowledge* includes the social event (e.g., a "kegger"). Most people can easily describe what happens at one. *Tacit knowledge* includes the unspoken cultural norm for the proper distance to stand from others. People are generally unaware that they use this norm. They feel unease or discomfort when the norm is violated, but it is difficult to pinpoint the source of discomfort. Ethnographers describe the explicit and tacit cultural knowledge that members use. Their detailed descriptions and careful analysis take what is described apart and put it back together.

Anthropologist Clifford Geertz stated that a critical part of ethnography is *thick description,*[4] a rich, detailed description of specifics (as opposed to summary, standardization, generalization, or variables). A thick description of a three-minute event may go on for pages. It captures the sense of what occurred and the drama of events, thereby permitting multiple interpretations. It places events into a context so that the reader of an ethnographic report can infer cultural meaning.

Ethnomethodology is a distinct approach developed in the 1960s, with its own unique terminology.[5] It combines theory, philosophy, and method. Some do not consider it a part of social work. Mehan and Wood (1975:3, 5) argued that

> *ethnomethodology is not a body of findings, nor a method, nor a theory, nor a world view. I view ethnomethodology as a form of life. . . . Ethnomethodology is an attempt to display the reality of a level which exists beyond the sociological level. . . . It differs from sociology much as sociology differs from psychology.*

A simple definition of *ethnomethodology* is the study of commonsense knowledge. Ethnomethodologists study common sense by observing its creation and use in ongoing social interaction in natural settings. Ethnomethodology is a radical or extreme form of field research, based on phenomenological philosophy and a social constructionist approach. It involves the specialized, highly detailed analysis of micro-situations (e.g., transcripts of short conversations or videotapes of social interactions). Com-

pared to Chicago school field research, it is more concerned about method and argues that research findings result as much from the method used as from the social life studied.

Ethnomethodology assumes that social meaning is fragile and fluid, not fixed, stable, or solid. Meaning is constantly being created and re-created in an ongoing process. For this reason ethnomethodologists analyze language, including pauses and the context of speech. They assume that people "accomplish" commonsense understanding by using tacit social–cultural rules, and social interaction is a process of reality construction. People interpret everyday events by using cultural knowledge and clues from the social context. Ethnomethodologists examine how ordinary people in everyday settings apply tacit rules to make sense of social life (e.g., to know whether or not someone is joking).

Ethnomethodologists examine ordinary social interaction in great detail to identify the rules for constructing social reality and common sense, how these rules are applied, and how new rules are created. For example, they argue that standardized tests or survey interviews measure a person's ability to pick up implicit clues and apply common sense more than measuring objective facts.

Ethnomethodologists sometimes use *breaching* experiments to demonstrate the simple tacit rules that people rely on to create a sense of reality in everyday life (also, see the discussion of breakdown later). The researchers purposefully violate a tacit social norm. The breach usually creates a powerful social response, which verifies the rule's existence, shows the fragility of social reality, and demonstrates that such tacit rules are essential for the flow of ordinary life. For example, ethnomethodology's founder, Harold Garfinkel, sent students to stores where they were told to "mistake" customers for salesclerks. At first, the customers were confused and stammered explanations. But as the students persisted in the misinterpretation, the bewildered customers either reluctantly accepted the new definition of the situation and awkwardly filled the salesclerk role, or "blew up" and "lost their cool." The breach illustrated how the operation of social reality depended on tacit knowledge (e.g., distinguishing salesclerks from customers). Filmmakers use similar situations for comic effect when people from a different culture who do not share the same tacit rules or who are unaware of the unspoken rules of proper behavior are seen as humorous.[6]

THE LOGIC OF FIELD RESEARCH

What Is Field Research?

It is difficult to pin down a specific definition of *field research* because it is more of an orientation toward research than a fixed set of techniques to apply.[7] A field researcher uses various methods to obtain information. As Schatzman and Strauss (1973:14) said, "Field method is more like an umbrella of activity beneath which any technique may be used for gaining the desired knowledge, and for processes of thinking about this information." A *field researcher* is a "methodological pragmatist" (Schatzman and Strauss, 1973:7), a resourceful, talented individual who has ingenuity, and an ability to think on her or his feet while in the field.

Field research is based on naturalism, which is also used to study other phenomena (e.g., oceans, animals, plants, etc.). *Naturalism* involves observing ordinary events in natural settings, not in contrived, invented, or researcher-created settings. Social work research occurs in the field and outside the safe settings of an office, laboratory, or classroom. Reiss (1992) has said that a researcher's direct observation of events in natural settings is central to sociology's status as a science, and that this status is threatened if sociology turns from naturalism.

A field researcher examines social meanings and grasps multiple perspectives in natural social settings. He or she gets inside the meaning system of members and then goes back to an outside or research viewpoint. As Van Maanen (1982:139) noted, "Fieldwork means involvement and detachment, both loyalty and betrayal, both openness and secrecy, and most likely love and hate." The researcher switches perspectives and sees the setting from multiple points of view simultane-

ously: "Researchers maintain membership in the culture in which they were reared while establishing membership in the groups which they are studying; they are socialized into another culture" (Burgess, 1982a:1).

Let us look at what practicing field researchers do (see Box 13.1). Research is usually conducted by a single individual, although small teams have been effective. A researcher is directly involved in and part of the social world studied, so his or her personal characteristics are relevant in research. Wax (1979:509) noted

In formal and quantitative methods, the peculiarities of the individual tend to go unnoticed. Electronic data processing pays no heed to the age, gender, or ethnicity of the research director or programmer. But, in fieldwork, these basic aspects of personal identity become salient; they drastically affect the process of field research.

The researcher's direct involvement in the field often has an emotional impact. Field research can be fun and exciting, but it can also disrupt one's personal life, physical security, or mental well-being. More than other types of social work research, it reshapes friendships, family life, self-identity, or personal values:

The price of doing fieldwork is very high, not in dollars (fieldwork is less expensive than most other kinds of research) but in physical and mental effort. It is very hard work. It is exhausting to live two lives simultaneously. (Bogdan and Taylor, 1975:vi)

Steps in a Field Research Project

Naturalism and direct involvement mean that field research is more flexible or less structured than quantitative research. This makes it essential for a researcher to be well organized and prepared for the field. It also means that the steps of a project are not entirely predetermined but serve as an approximate guide or road map (see Figure 13.1).

Flexibility.   Field researchers rarely follow fixed steps. In fact, flexibility is a key advantage of field research, which lets a researcher shift direction and follow leads. Good field researchers recognize and

Box 13.1 _____

What Do Field Researchers Do?

A field researcher does the following:

1. Observes ordinary events and everyday activities as they happen in natural settings, in addition to any unusual occurrences
2. Becomes directly involved with the people being studied and personally experiences the process of daily social life in the field setting
3. Acquires an insider's point of view while maintaining the analytic perspective or distance of an outsider
4. Uses a variety of techniques and social skills in a flexible manner as the situation demands
5. Produces data in the form of extensive written notes, as well as diagrams, maps, or pictures to provide very detailed descriptions
6. Sees events holistically (e.g., as a whole unit, not in pieces) and individually in their social context
7. Understands and develops empathy for members in a field setting, and does not just record "cold" objective facts
8. Notices both explicit (recognized, conscious, spoken) and tacit (less recognized, implicit, unspoken) aspects of culture
9. Observes ongoing social processes without upsetting, disrupting, or imposing an outside point of view
10. Copes with high levels of personal stress, uncertainty, ethical dilemmas, and ambiguity

_____

seize opportunities, "play it by ear," and rapidly adjust to fluid social situations. Douglas (1976:14–16) argued that the techniques of field research share much in common with those of other types of investigative inquiry such as investigative journalism and detective work.

A field researcher does not begin with a set of methods to apply or explicit hypotheses to test. Rather, he or she chooses techniques on the basis of their value for providing information. In the beginning the researcher expects little control over data and little focus. Once socialized to the setting, however, he or she focuses the inquiry and asserts control over the data.

FIGURE 13.1 Steps in Field Research

_____

1. Prepare oneself, read the literature, and defocus.
2. Select a field site and gain access to it.
3. Enter the field and establish social relations with members.
4. Adopt a social role, learn the ropes, and get along with members.
5. Watch, listen, and collect quality data.
6. Begin to analyze data and to generate and evaluate working hypotheses.
7. Focus on specific aspects of the setting and use theoretical sampling.
8. Conduct field interviews with member informants.
9. Disengage and physically leave the setting.
10. Complete the analyses and write the research report.

_____

Note: There is no fixed percentage of time needed for each step. For a rough approximation, Junker (1960:12) suggested that, once in the field, the researcher should expect to spend approximately one-sixth of his or her time observing, one-third recording data, one-third of the time analyzing data, and one-sixth reporting results. Also, see Denzin (1989:176) for eight steps of field research.

Getting Organized in the Beginning. Human and personal factors can play a role in any research project, but they are crucial in field research. Field projects often begin with chance occurrences or a personal interest. Field researchers can begin with their own experiences, such as working at a job, having a hobby, or being a patient or an activist.[8]

Field researchers use the skills of careful looking and listening, short-term memory, and regular writing. Before entering the field, a new researcher practices observing the ordinary details of situations and writing them down. Attention to details and short-term memory can improve with practice. Likewise, keeping a daily diary or personal journal is good practice for writing field notes.

As with all social work research, reading the scholarly literature helps the researcher learn concepts, potential pitfalls, data collection methods, and techniques for resolving conflicts. In addition, a field researcher finds diaries, novels, journalistic accounts, and autobiographies useful for gaining familiarity and preparing emotionally for the field.

Field research begins with a general topic, not specific hypotheses. A researcher does not get locked into any initial misconceptions. He or she needs to be well informed but open to discovering new ideas. Finding the right questions to ask about the field takes time.

A researcher first empties his or her mind of preconceptions and defocuses. There are two types of *defocusing*.[9] The first is casting a wide net in order to witness a broad range of situations, people, and settings—getting a feel for the overall setting before deciding what to include or exclude. The second type of defocusing means not focusing exclusively on the role of researcher. As Douglas (1976:122) noted, it is important to extend one's experience beyond a strictly professional role. The researcher should move outside his or her comfortable social niche to experience as much as possible in the field without betraying a primary commitment to being a researcher.

Another preparation for field research is self-knowledge. A field researcher needs to know himself or herself and reflect on personal experiences. He or she can expect anxiety, self-doubt, frustration, and uncertainty in the field. Especially in the beginning, the researcher may feel that he or she is collecting the wrong data and may suffer emotional turmoil, isolation, and confusion. He or she often feels doubly marginal: an outsider in the field setting and also distant from friends, family, and other researchers.[10] The relevance of a researcher's emotional makeup, personal biography, and cultural experiences makes it important to be aware of his or her personal commitments and inner conflicts (see the later section on stress; see also Box 13.2).

Fieldwork can have a strong impact on a researcher's identity and outlook. Researchers may be personally transformed by the field experience.

Box 13.2 _____

Field Research at a Country and Western Bar

Eliasoph (1998) conducted field research on several groups in a California community to understand how Americans avoid political expression. One was a social club. Eliasoph described herself as an "urban, bi-coastal, bespectacled, Jewish, Ph.D. candidate from a long line of communists, atheists, liberals, book-readers, ideologues, and arguers" (p. 270). The social club world was very foreign to her. The social club, the Buffalos, centered on country/western music at a bar, the Silverado Club. She described it:

The Silverado huddled on a vast, rutted parking lot on what was once wetlands and now was a truck stop, a mile and a half from Amargo's [town name] nuclear battleship station. Occasional gulleys of salt water cattails poked through the wide flat miles of paved malls and gas stations. Giant four-wheeled-drive vehicles filled the parking lot, making my miniature Honda look like a toy. . . . Inside the windowless Silverado, initial blinding darkness gave way to a huge Confederate flag pinned up behind the bandstand, the standard collection of neon beer signs

and beer mirrors, men in cowboys hats, cowboys shirts and jeans, women in curly perms and tiered flounces of lace or denim skirts, or jeans, and belts with their names embroidered in glitter on the back. (1998:92)

Eliasoph introduced herself as a student. During her two years of research, she endured smoke-filled rooms as well as expensive beer and bottled-water prices; attended a wedding and many dance lessons; and participated in countless conversations and heard many abusive sexist/racist jokes. She listened, asked questions, observed, and took notes in the bathroom. When she returned home after hours with club members, it was to a university crowd who had little understanding of the world she was studying. For them, witty conversation was central and being bored was to be avoided. The club members used more nonverbal than verbal communication and being bored, or sitting and doing nothing, was just fine. The research forced Eliasoph to reexamine her own views and tastes, which she had taken for granted.

Some adopt new values, interests, and moral commitments, or change their religion or political ideology.[11] Hayano (1982:148) remarked from his study on gambling:

> By this time I felt more comfortable sitting at a poker table than I did at faculty meetings and in my classes. Most of my social life focused on poker playing, and often, especially after a big win, I felt the desire to give up my job as a university professor in order to spend more time in the cardroom.

CHOOSING A SITE AND GAINING ACCESS

Although a field research project does not proceed by fixed steps, some common concerns arise in the early stages. These include selecting a site, gaining access to the site, entering the field, and developing rapport with members in the field.

Selecting a Site

Where to Observe.   Field researchers talk about doing research in a setting, or *field site,* but this term is misleading. A site is the context in which events or activities occur, a socially defined territory with shifting boundaries. A social group may interact across several physical sites. For example, a college football team may interact on the playing field, in the locker room, in a dormitory, at a training camp, or at a local hangout. The team's field site includes all five locations.

The field site and research question are bound up together, but choosing a site is not the same as focusing on a *case* for study. A case is a social relationship or activity; it can extend beyond the boundaries of the site and have links to other social settings. A researcher selects a site, then identifies cases to examine within it—for example, how football team members relate to authority figures.

Selecting a field site is an important decision, and researchers take notes on the site selection processes. Three factors are relevant when choosing a field research site: richness of data, unfamiliarity, and suitability.[12] Some sites are more likely than others to provide rich data. Sites that present a web of social relations, a variety of activities, and diverse events over time provide richer, more interesting

data. Beginning field researchers should choose an unfamiliar setting. It is easier to see cultural events and social relations in a new site. Bodgan and Taylor (1975: 28) noted, *"We would recommend that researchers choose settings in which the subjects are strangers and in which they have no particular professional knowledge or expertise"* (emphasis in original). When "casing" possible field sites, one must consider such practical issues as the researcher's time and skills, serious conflicts among people in the site, the researcher's personal characteristics and feelings, and access to parts of a site.

A researcher's ascriptive characteristics can limit access. For example, an African American researcher cannot hope to study the Ku Klux Klan or neo-Nazis, although some researchers have successfully crossed some ascriptive lines.[13] Sometimes "insider" and "outsider" teams can work together. For example, the outsider Douglas teamed up with a member insider, Flanagan, for a study of nude beaches (Douglas and Rasmussen, 1977), and a White (Rainwater) collaborated with a Black (Yancey) to study a Black housing project (Yancey and Rainwater, 1970).

Physical access to a site can be an issue. Sites are on a continuum, with open and public areas (e.g., public restaurants, airport waiting areas, etc.) at one end and closed and private settings (e.g., private firms, clubs, activities in a person's home, etc.) at the other. A researcher may find that he or she is not welcome or not allowed on the site, or there are legal and political barriers to access. Laws and regulations in institutions (e.g., public schools, hospitals, prisons, etc.) restrict access. In addition, institutional review boards may limit field research on ethical grounds.

Gatekeepers.   A *gatekeeper* is someone with the formal or informal authority to control access to a site.[14] It can be anyone on a street corner, an administrator of a hospital, or the owner of a business. Informal public areas (e.g., sidewalks, public waiting rooms, etc.) rarely have gatekeepers; formal organizations have authorities from whom permission must be obtained.

Field researchers expect to negotiate with gatekeepers and bargain for access. The gatekeepers may not appreciate the need for conceptual distance or ethical balance. The researcher must set non-negotiable limits to protect research integrity. If there are many restrictions initially, a researcher can often reopen negotiations later, and gatekeepers may forget their initial demands as trust develops. It is ethically and politically astute to call on gatekeepers. Researchers do not expect them to listen to research concerns or care about the findings, except insofar as these findings might provide evidence for someone to criticize them.

Dealing with gatekeepers is a recurrent issue as a researcher enters new levels or areas. In addition, a gatekeeper can shape the direction of research:

> Even the most friendly and cooperative gatekeepers or sponsors will shape the conduct and development of research. To one degree or another, the ethnographer will be channeled in line with existing networks of friendship and enmity, territory, and equivalent boundaries. (Hammersley and Atkinson, 1983:73)

In some sites gatekeeper approval creates a stigma that inhibits the cooperation of members. For example, prisoners may not be cooperative if they know that the prison warden gave approval to the researcher. As West (1980:35) remarked regarding juvenile delinquents, "I am convinced that such access routes almost always retard—or in some cases prevent—the establishment of rapport with delinquents."

Strategy for Entering

Entering a field site requires having a flexible strategy or plan of action, negotiating access and relations with members, and deciding how much to disclose about the research to field members or gatekeepers.

Planning. Entering and gaining access to a field site is a process that depends on commonsense judgment and social skills. Field sites usually have different levels or areas, and entry is an issue for each. Entry is more analogous to peeling the layers of an onion than to opening a door. Moreover, bargains and promises of entry may not remain stable over time. A researcher needs fallback plans or may have to return later for renegotiation. Because the spe-

cific focus of research may not emerge until later in the research process or may change, it is best to avoid being locked into specifics by gatekeepers.

Entry and access can be visualized as an *access ladder* (see Figure 13.2). A researcher begins at the bottom rung, where access is easy and where he or she is an outsider looking for public information. The next rung requires increased access. Once close on-site observation begins, he or she becomes a passive observer, not questioning what members say. With time in the field, the researcher observes specific activities that are potentially sensitive or seeks clarification of what he or she sees or hears. Reaching this access rung is more difficult. Finally, the researcher may try to shape interaction so that it reveals specific information, or he or she may want to see highly sensitive material. This highest rung of the access ladder is rarely attained and requires deep trust.[15]

Negotiation. Social relations are negotiated and formed throughout the process of fieldwork.[16] Negotiation occurs with each new member until a stable relationship develops to gain access, develop trust, obtain information, and reduce hostile

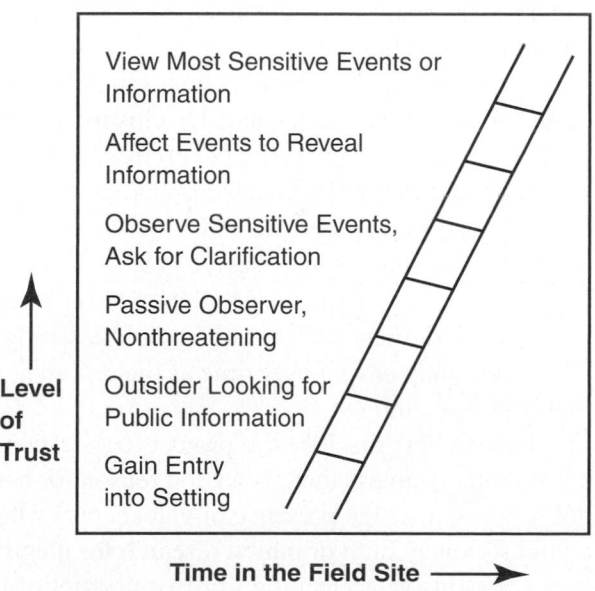

FIGURE 13.2 The Access Ladder

reactions. The researcher expects to negotiate and explain what he or she is doing over and over in the field (see the discussion of normalizing social work research, to follow).

Bart (1987) argued that her background as a feminist activist and her nonprofessional demeanor were essential for gaining access to a feminist abortion clinic.[17]

Access to elites and professionals often depends on luck or personal ties (see Lofland and Lofland, 1995:12). Hoffman-Lange (1980) gained access to wealthy individuals on the boards of directors by using her family ties and including personal references in letters requesting interviews. Ostrander's (1984) access into a network of upper-class women depended on a chance meeting with a prominent upper-class woman through an academic colleague. Danziger (1979) gained access to physicians' activities because her father was a doctor. Johnson's (1975) access to a social work agency was aided by mentioning that someone in the agency was a friend of his wife.

Disclosure. A researcher must decide how much to reveal about himself or herself and the research project. Disclosing one's personal life, hobbies, interests, and background can build trust and close relationships, but the researcher will also lose privacy, and he or she needs to ensure that the focus remains on events in the field.

A researcher also decides how much to disclose about the research project. Disclosure ranges on a continuum from fully covert research, in which no one in the field is aware that research is taking place, to the opposite end, where everyone knows the specifics of the research project. The degree and timing of disclosure depends on a researcher's judgment and particulars in the setting. Disclosure may unfold over time as the researcher feels more secure.

Researchers disclose the project to gatekeepers and others unless there is a good reason for not doing so, such as the presence of gatekeepers who would seriously limit or inhibit research for illegitimate reasons (e.g., to hide graft or corruption). Even in these cases, a researcher may disclose his or her identity as a researcher, but may pose as one who seems submissive, harmless, and interested in nonthreatening issues.

Entering the Field

After a field site is selected and access obtained, researchers must learn the ropes, develop rapport with members, adopt a role in the setting, and maintain social relations. Before confronting such issues, the researcher should ask: How will I present myself? What does it mean for me to be a "measurement instrument"? How can I assume an "attitude of strangeness"?

Presentation of Self. People explicitly and implicitly present themselves to others. We display who we are—the type of person we are or would like to be—through our physical appearance, what we say, and how we act. The presentation of self sends a symbolic message. It may be, "I'm a serious, hard-working student," "I'm a warm and caring person," "I'm a cool jock," or "I'm a rebel and party animal." Many selves are possible, and presentations of selves can differ depending on the occasion.

A field researcher is conscious of the presentation of self in the field. For example, how should he or she dress in the field? The best guide is to respect both oneself and those being studied. Do not overdress so as to offend or stand out, but copying the dress of those being studied is not always necessary. A professor who studies street people does not have to dress or act like one; dressing and acting informally is sufficient. Likewise, more formal dress and professional demeanor are required when studying corporate executives or top officials.[18]

A researcher must be aware that self-presentation will influence field relations to some degree. It is difficult to present a highly deceptive front or to present oneself in a way that deviates sharply from the person one is ordinarily.

Being herself and revealing her personal background as a Jewish woman helped Myerhoff (1989) gain access and develop rapport in a field site of elderly residents in a Jewish senior citizen home. At the same time, her understanding and awareness of her identity changed as a result of her field interactions. Stack (1989) began as an outsider—a White woman studying a low-income Black industrial community. Eventually, she was accepted into a kin-like relationship with the women she studied. Assigned nickname "White Caroline" was a signal of acceptance and endearment. She performed many small favors, such as driving people to the hospital or welfare office, shopping, and visiting sick children. She achieved this by how she interacted with others—her openness and willingness to share personal feelings. Although he was an African American man in an inner-city bar, Anderson (1989) found social class to be a barrier. The setting was a corner bar and liquor store on the south side of Chicago in a poor African American neighborhood. Anderson developed a social relationship of trust and was "sponsored." This occurred when he befriended "Herman," a witty, easy-going person who was street smart and socially well connected in the setting. Anderson succeeded by "the low-key, nonassertive role I assumed . . . not to disrupt the consensual definition of the social order in this type of setting" (Anderson, 1989:19).

Researcher as Instrument.   The researcher is the instrument for measuring field data. This has two implications. First, it puts pressure on the researcher to be alert and sensitive to what happens in the field and to be disciplined about recording data. Second, it has personal consequences. Fieldwork involves social relationships and personal feelings. Field researchers are flexible about what to include as data and admit their own subjective insights and feelings, or "experiential data."[19] Personal, subjective experiences are part of field data. They are valuable both in themselves and for interpreting events in the field. Instead of trying to be objective and eliminate personal reactions, field researchers treat their feelings toward field events as data. For example, Karp's (1973, 1980) personal feelings of tension in his study of pornographic bookstores were a critical part of the data. His personal discomfort in the field revealed some dynamics of the setting. "If we avoid writing about our reactions, we cannot examine them. We cannot achieve immersion without

bringing our subjectivity into play" (Kleinman and Copp, 1993:19).

Field research can heighten a researcher's awareness of personal feelings. For example, a researcher may not be fully aware of personal feelings about nudity until he or she is in a nudist colony, or about personal possessions until he or she is in a setting where others "borrow" many items. The researcher's own surprise, indignation, or questioning then may become an opportunity for reflection and insight.[20]

An Attitude of Strangeness.   It is hard to recognize what we are very close to. The everyday world we inhabit is filled with thousands of details. If we paid attention to everything all the time, we would suffer from severe information overload. We manage by ignoring much of what is around us and by engaging in habitual thinking. Unfortunately, we fail to see the familiar as distinctive, and assume that others experience reality just as we do. We tend to treat our own way of living as natural or normal.

Field research in familiar surroundings is difficult because of a tendency to be blinded by the familiar. In fact, "intimate acquaintance with one's own culture can create as much blindness as insight" (McCracken, 1988:12). By studying other cultures, researchers encounter dramatically different assumptions about what is important and how things are done. This confrontation of cultures, or culture shock, has two benefits: It makes it easier to see cultural elements, and it facilitates self-discovery. Researchers adopt the attitude of strangeness to gain these benefits. The *attitude of strangeness* means questioning and noticing ordinary details or looking at the ordinary through the eyes of a stranger. Strangeness helps a researcher overcome the boredom of observing ordinary details. It helps him or her see the ordinary in a new way, one that reveals aspects of the setting of which members are not consciously aware.

People rarely recognize customs they take for granted. For example, when someone gives us a gift, we say thank you and praise the gift. By contrast, gift-giving customs in many cultures include complaining that the gift is inadequate. The attitude of strangeness helps make the tacit culture visible—for example, that gift givers expect to hear "thank you" and "the gift is nice," and become upset otherwise. A field researcher adopts both a stranger's and an insider's point of view. The stranger sees events as specific social processes, whereas to an insider, they seem natural. Davis (1973) called this the Martian and the convert: The Martian sees everything as strange and questions assumptions, whereas the convert accepts everything and wants to become a believer. Researchers need both views, as well as the ability to switch back and forth.[21]

Strangeness also encourages a researcher to reconsider his or her own social world. Immersion in a different setting breaks old habits of thought and action. He or she finds reflection and introspection easier and more intense when encountering the unfamiliar, whether it is a different culture or a familiar culture seen through a stranger's eyes.

Building Rapport

A field researcher builds rapport by getting along with members in the field. He or she forges a friendly relationship, shares the same language, and laughs and cries with members. This is a step toward obtaining an understanding of members and moving beyond understanding to empathy—that is, seeing and feeling events from another's perspective.

It is not always easy to build rapport. The social world is not all in harmony, with warm, friendly people. A setting may contain fear, tension, and conflict. Members may be unpleasant, untrustworthy, or untruthful; they may do things that disturb or disgust a researcher. An experienced researcher is prepared for a range of events and relationships. He or she may find, however, that it is impossible to penetrate a setting or get really close to members. Settings where cooperation, sympathy, and collaboration are impossible require different techniques.[22] Also, the researcher accepts what he or she hears or sees at face value, but without being gullible. As Schatzman and Strauss (1973:69) remarked, "The researcher believes 'everything' and 'nothing' simultaneously."

Charm and Trust. A field researcher needs social skills and personal charm to build rapport. Trust,

friendly feelings, and being well liked facilitate communication and help him or her to understand the inner feelings of others. There is no magical way to do this. Showing a genuine concern for and interest in others, being honest, and sharing feelings are good strategies, but they are not foolproof. It depends on the specific setting and members.

Many factors affect trust and rapport—how a researcher presents himself or herself; the role he or she chooses for the field; and the events that encourage, limit, or make it impossible to achieve trust. Trust is not gained once and for all. It is a developmental process built up over time through many social nuances (e.g., sharing of personal experiences, storytelling, gestures, hints, facial expressions). It is constantly re-created and seems easier to lose once it has been built up than to gain in the first place.

Establishing trust is important, but it does not ensure that all information will be revealed. It may be limited to specific areas. For example, trust can be built up regarding financial matters but not to disclose intimate dating behavior. Trust may have to be created anew in each area of inquiry; it requires constant reaffirmation.

Freeze Outs. Some members may not be open and cooperative. *Freeze outs* are members who express an uncooperative attitude or an overt unwillingness to participate. Field researchers may never gain the cooperation of everyone, or a warm relationship may develop only after prolonged persistence.

Understanding. Rapport helps field researchers understand members, but understanding is a precondition for greater depth, not an end in itself. It slowly develops in the field as the researcher overcomes an initial bewilderment with a new or unusual language and system of social meaning. Once he or she attains an understanding of the member's point of view, the next step is to learn how to think and act within a member's perspective. This is *empathy,* or adopting another's perspective. Empathy does not necessarily mean sympathy, agreement, or approval; it means feeling things as another does.[23]

Rapport helps create understanding and ultimately empathy, and the development of empathy facilitates greater rapport. The novel *To Kill a Mock-*

ingbird notes the link between rapport and empathic understanding in the following passage:

> *"First of all," he said, "if you can learn a simple trick, Scout, you'll get along a lot better with all kinds of folks. You never really understand a person until you consider things from his point of view."*
>
> *"Sir?"*
>
> *"—until you climb into his skin and walk around in it." (Lee, 1960:34)*

RELATIONS IN THE FIELD

You play many social roles in daily life—daughter/son, student, customer, sports fan—and maintain social relations with others. You choose some roles, and others are structured for you. Few have a choice but to play the role of son or daughter. Some roles are formal (e.g., bank teller, police chief, etc.), others are informal (flirt, elder statesperson, buddy, etc.). You can switch roles, play multiple roles, and play a role in a particular way. Field researchers play roles in the field. In addition, they learn the ropes and maintain relations with members.

Roles in the Field

Preexisting versus Created Roles.   At times a researcher adopts an existing role. Some existing roles provide access to all areas of the site, the ability to observe and interact with all members, the freedom to move around, and a way to balance the requirements of researcher and member. At other times a researcher creates a new role or modifies an existing one. For example, Fine (1987) created a role of the "adult friend" and performed it with little adult authority when studying preadolescent boys. He was able to observe parts of their culture and behavior that were otherwise inaccessible to adults. The adoption of a field role takes time, and a researcher may adopt several different field roles over time.

Limits on the Role Chosen.   The field roles open to a researcher are affected by ascriptive factors and physical appearance. He or she can change some aspects of appearance, such as dress or hairstyle, but not ascriptive features such as age, race, gender, and attractiveness. Nevertheless, such factors can be important in gaining access and can restrict the available roles. For example, Gurney (1985) reported that being a female in a male-dominated setting required extra negotiations and "hassles." Nevertheless, her gender provided insights and created situations that would have been absent with a male researcher.

Since many roles are sex-typed, gender is an important consideration. Female researchers often have more difficulty when the setting is perceived as dangerous or seamy and where males are in control (e.g., police work, fire fighting, etc.). They may be shunned or pushed into limiting gender stereotypes (e.g., "sweet kid," "mascot," "loud mouth," etc.). Male researchers have more problems in routine and administrative sites where males are in control (e.g., courts, large offices, etc.). They may not be accepted in female-dominated territory. In sites where both males and females are involved, both sexes may be able to enter and gain acceptance.[24]

Level of Involvement.   Field roles can be arranged on a continuum by the degree of detachment or involvement a researcher has with members. At one extreme are roles of a detached outsider; at the other extreme are roles of an intimately involved insider. The range of field roles is described in three systems developed by Junker, Gans, and the Adlers.

Junker (1960, but also see Denzin, 1989, Gold, 1969, and Roy, 1970) describes a range of four roles. The range is from *complete observer* (e.g., researcher is behind a one-way mirror or taking on an "invisible role" such as an eavesdropping janitor), to *observer as participant* (e.g., researcher is known from the beginning but has limited contact), to *participant as observer* (e.g., researcher is overt and is an intimate friend of participants), and finally to *complete participant* (e.g., researcher acts as member and shares secret information of insiders). This range is similar to that of Gans (1982), who collapses the two middle categories into *researcher participant*. He emphasizes the degree of attachment/emotional involvement or detachment of the research at each level.

Adler and Adler (1987) suggest three roles. *Peripheral membership* means maintaining distance between self and those studied, or setting limits by the researcher's beliefs or discomfort with the members' activities. *Active membership* is when the researcher assumes a membership role and goes through a similar induction into membership and participates like a member. The researcher maintains high levels of trust and can withdraw from the field periodically. *Complete membership* is when the researcher converts and "goes native." As a fully committed member, the researcher experiences the same emotions as others and must leave the field to return to being a researcher.

The field researcher's level of involvement depends on negotiations with members, specifics of the field setting, the researcher's personal comfort, and the particular role adopted in the field. Many move from outsider to insider levels with more time in the field. Each level has its advantages and disadvantages. Different field researchers advocate different levels of involvement. For example, the Adlers's complete member role is criticized by some for overinvolvement and loss of a researcher's perspective. Others argue that it is the only way to really understand a member's social world.

Roles at the outsider end of the continuum reduce the time needed for acceptance, make over-rapport less of an issue, and can sometimes help members open up. They facilitate detachment and protect the researcher's self-identity. A researcher feels marginal. Although there is less risk of "going native," he or she is also less likely to know an insider's experience, and misinterpretation is more likely.

By contrast, roles at the insider end of the continuum facilitate empathy and sharing of a member's experience. The goal of fully experiencing the intimate social world of a member is achieved. Nevertheless, a lack of distance from, too much sympathy for, or overinvolvement with members is likely. A researcher's reports may be questioned, data gathering is difficult, there can be a dramatic impact on the researcher's self, and the distance needed for analysis may be hard to attain.[25]

To really understand social meaning for those being studied, the field researcher must participate in the setting, as others do. Holy (1984:29–30) observed

> *The researcher does not participate in the lives of subjects in order to observe them, but rather ob-*

> *serves while participating fully in their lives . . . through living with the people being studied. . . . She comes to share the same meanings with them in the process of active participation in their social life. . . . Research means, in this sense, socialization to the culture being studied.*

Other Considerations.   Almost any role limits access to some parts of a field site. For example, the role of a bartender in a bar limits knowledge of intimate customer behavior or presence at customer gatherings in other locations. A field researcher takes care when choosing roles but recognizes that all roles involve tradeoffs.

Most social settings contain cliques, informal groups, hierarchies, and rivalries. A role can help a researcher gain acceptance into or be excluded from a clique, be treated as a person in authority or as an underling, and be a friend or an enemy of some members. A researcher is aware that by adopting a role, he or she may be forming allies and enemies who can assist or limit research.

Learning the Ropes

As a researcher learns the ropes on the field site, he or she learns how to cope with personal stress, how to normalize the social research, and how to act like an "acceptable incompetent."

Stress.   Fieldwork can be highly rewarding, exciting, and fulfilling, but it also can be difficult:

> *Fieldwork must certainly rank with the more disagreeable activities that humanity has fashioned for itself. It is usually inconvenient, to say the least, sometimes physically uncomfortable, frequently embarrassing, and, to a degree, always tense. (Shaffir et al., 1980:3)*

New researchers face embarrassment, experience discomfort, and are overwhelmed by the details in the field. For example, in her study of U.S. relocation camps for Japanese Americans during World War II, respected field researcher Rosalie Wax (1971) reported that she endured the discomfort of 120-degree Fahrenheit temperatures, filthy and dilapidated living conditions, dysentery, and mosquitoes. She felt isolated, she cried a lot, and she gained

30 pounds from compulsive eating. After months in the field, she thought she was a total failure; she was distrusted by members and got into fights with the camp administration.

Maintaining a "marginal" status is stressful; it is difficult to be an outsider who is not fully involved, especially when studying settings full of intense feelings (e.g., political campaigns, religious conversions, etc.). The loneliness and isolation of fieldwork may combine with the desire to develop rapport and empathy to cause overinvolvement. A researcher may *go native* and drop the professional researcher's role to become a full member of the group being studied. Or the researcher may feel guilt about learning intimate details as members drop their guard, and may come to overidentify with members.[26]

Some emotional stress is inevitable in field research. Instead of suppressing emotional responses, the field researcher is sensitive to emotional reactions. He or she copes in the field by keeping a personal diary, emotional journal, or written record of inner feelings, or by having sympathetic people outside the field site with whom to confide.[27]

Normalizing Social Research. A field researcher not only observes and investigates members in the field but is observed and investigated by members as well: "While the fieldworker is undertaking a study of others, others are undertaking a study of the fieldworker" (Van Maanen, 1982:110). As Wax (1979:363) argued, fieldwork is not performed by an isolated individual but is created by everyone in the field setting.

In overt field research, members are usually initially uncomfortable with the presence of a researcher. Most are unfamiliar with field research and fail to distinguish between sociologists, psychologists, counselors, and social workers. They may see the researcher as an outside critic or spy, or as a savior or all-knowing expert.

An overt field researcher must *normalize social research*—that is, help members redefine social research from something unknown and threatening to something normal and predictable. He or she can help members manage research by presenting his or her own biography, explaining field research a little at a time, appearing nonthreatening, or ac-

cepting minor deviance in the setting (e.g., minor violations of official rules).[28]

Another way to normalize research is to explain it in terms members understand. Sometimes members' excitement about being written up in a book is useful, as Fine and Glassner (1979) and LeMasters (1975) found. In his study of a neighborhood tavern in Wisconsin, LeMasters became a regular over a five-year period, going to the bar several nights a week. He (1975:7) stated how he explained to members what he was doing:

> *I initially assumed the role of patron—just another person who liked to drink beer and shoot some pool. This finally became difficult because the amount of time I spent in the tavern began to raise questions. Some of the regular customers, I learned later, had decided I must be an undercover agent from the state liquor commission. . . . I adopted the following stance when queried about being in the tavern: that sociologists have to have some knowledge of various aspects of American society to be effective teachers, that I found The Oasis men and women to be helpful in understanding how blue-collar people feel about American society, and, further, that I became bored by constant association with white-collar people and that the tavern contacts were refreshing. All of the above statements were true.*

Acceptable Incompetent. A researcher is in the field to learn, not to be an expert. Depending on the setting, he or she appears to be a friendly but naive outsider, an acceptable incompetent who is interested in learning about the social life of the field. An *acceptable incompetent* is someone who is partially competent (skilled or knowledgeable) in the setting but who is accepted as a nonthreatening person who needs to be taught.[29] As Schatzman and Strauss (1973:25) noted, "The researcher should play down any expertise or profound knowledge he may have on the subject on which the hosts may claim to be expert; the researcher is and should act as the learner, indicating no inclination to evaluate the host's activities."

A field researcher may know little about the setting or subculture at first. He or she may be seen as a fool who is hoodwinked or shortchanged, and may be the butt of jokes for his or her lack of adeptness in the setting. Even when the researcher is knowledgeable, he or she displays less than full information to draw out a member's knowledge. Of course, the researcher can overdo this and appear so ignorant that he or she is not taken seriously.

Maintaining Relations

Social Relations. With time, a field researcher develops and modifies social relationships. Members who are cool at first may warm up later. Or they may put on a front of initial friendliness, and their fears and suspicions surface only later. A researcher is in a delicate position. Early in a project, when not yet fully aware of everything about a field site, the researcher does not form close relationships because circumstances may change. Yet, if he or she does develop close friends, they can become allies who will defend the researcher's presence and help him or her gain access.

A field researcher monitors how his or her actions or appearance affect members. For example, a physically attractive researcher who interacts with members of the opposite sex may encounter crushes, flirting, and jealousy. He or she develops an awareness of these field relations and learns to manage them.[30]

In addition to developing social relationships, a field researcher must be able to break or withdraw from relationships as well. Ties with one member may have to be broken in order to forge ties with others or to explore other aspects of the setting. As with the end of any friendly relationship, the emotional pain of social withdrawal can affect both the researcher and the member. The researcher must balance social sensitivity and the research goals.

Small Favors. *Exchange relationships* develop in the field, in which small tokens or favors, including deference and respect, are exchanged.[31] A researcher may gain acceptance by helping out in small ways. Exchange helps when access to sensitive issues is limited. A researcher may offer small favors but not burden members by asking for return favors. As the researcher and members share experiences and see each other again, members recall the favors and reciprocate by allowing access. For example, Fine (1987:242) learned a lot when he was providing small favors (e.g., driving the boys to the movies) as part of his "adult friend" role.

Conflicts in the Field. Fights, conflict, and disagreements can erupt in the field, or a researcher may study groups with opposing positions. In such situations the researcher will feel pressure to take sides and will be tested to see if he or she can be trusted. In such occasions a researcher usually stays on the neutral sidelines and walks a tightrope between opposing sides. This is because once he or she becomes aligned with one side, the researcher will cut off access to the other side.[32] In addition, he or she will see the situation from only one point of view. Nevertheless, some (e.g., Van Maanen, 1982:115) argue that true neutrality is illusory. As a researcher becomes involved with members and embroiled in webs of relationships and commitments, neutrality becomes almost impossible.

Appearing Interested. Field researchers maintain an *appearance of interest* in the field. An experienced researcher appears to be interested in and involved with field events by statements and behaviors (e.g., facial expression, going for coffee, organizing a party, etc.) even if he or she is not truly interested. This is because field relations may be disrupted if the researcher appears to be bored or distracted. Putting up such a temporary front of involvement is a common small deception in daily life and is part of being polite.[33]

Of course, selective inattention (i.e., not staring or appearing not to notice) is also part of acting polite. If a person makes a social mistake (e.g., accidentally uses an incorrect word, passes gas, etc.), the polite thing to do is to ignore it. Selective inattention is used in fieldwork, as well. It gives an alert researcher an opportunity to learn by casually eavesdropping on conversations or observing events not meant to be public.

Social Breakdowns. A social breakdown occurs when two cultural traditions or social assumptions fail to mesh. *Breakdowns* highlight social meaning because hidden routine expectations and assumptions become explicit in a breakdown. They appear as misunderstandings or confusion over which of several implicit social rules to apply. For example, you go to a restaurant and sit down and wait for a server to appear. Twenty minutes later, having gotten no service, you become angry. You look around and notice that you have not seen any servers. You see customers enter from a doorway carrying their own food and realize your misunderstanding. Your implicit expectation was that the restaurant had table service; in fact, it is one where patrons go to a counter, order, and pick up their own food. Once you recognize which rules to apply in the context, you can resolve the breakdown.

Breakdowns produce embarrassment because the mismatch of cultural meanings often causes a person to look foolish, ignorant, or uninformed. For example, you are invited to a party that begins at 8:00. You show up in your usual attire, old jeans and a wrinkled sweater, and arrive at your usual time for an 8:00 party—8:30. The door opens and you enter. Shocked, you see that everyone else is formally dressed and sitting at a formal dinner, which was served about 30 minutes ago. People stare at you, and you feel out of place. Your cultural expectation (this is an informal student party with loud music, dancing, beer, and informal dress) does not match the setting (this is a formal dinner party, where people expect to eat, engage in polite conversation, and act professional). The breakdown makes explicit the unspoken social rules that "everyone knows" or assumes.

Breakdowns can be unexpected or can be purposefully created to test working hypotheses. As with an ethnomethodologist's breaching experiments, a researcher may violate social rules to illustrate the existence of tacit rules and their importance. Researchers observe unplanned breakdowns, or they create breakdowns and watch reactions in order to pinpoint implicit social expectations.

OBSERVING AND COLLECTING DATA

This section looks at how to get good qualitative field data. Field data are what the researcher experiences and remembers, and what are recorded in field notes and become available for systematic analysis.

Watching and Listening

Observing. A great deal of what social work researchers do in the field is to pay attention, watch, and listen carefully. They use all the senses, noticing what is seen, heard, smelled, tasted, or touched. The researcher becomes an instrument that absorbs all sources of information.

A field researcher carefully scrutinizes the physical setting to capture its atmosphere. He or she asks, "What are the colors of the floor, walls, ceiling? How large is a room? Where are the windows and doors? How is the furniture arranged, and what is its condition (e.g., new or old and worn, dirty or clean)? What type of lighting is there? Are there signs, paintings, plants? What are the sounds or smells?"

Why bother with such details? You may have noticed that stores and restaurants often plan lighting, colors, and piped-in music to create a certain atmosphere. Maybe you know that used-car sales people spray a new-car scent into cars or that shops in shopping malls intentionally send out the odor of freshly made cookies. These subtle, unconscious signals influence human behavior.

Observing in field research is often detailed, tedious work. Silverman (1993:30) noted, "If you go to the cinema to see action [car chases, hold-ups, etc.], then it is unlikely that you will find it easy to be a good observer." Instead of the quick flash, motivation arises out of a deep curiosity about the details. Good field researchers are intrigued about details that reveal "what's going on here" through careful listening and watching. Field researchers believe that the core of social life is communicated through the mundane, trival, everyday minutia. This is what people often overlook, but field researchers need to learn how to notice.

In addition to physical surroundings, a field researcher observes people and their actions, noting each person's observable physical characteristics: age, sex, race, and stature. People socially interact differently depending on whether another person is

18, 40, or 70 years old; male or female; White or non-White; short and frail or tall, heavyset, and muscular. When noting such characteristics, the researcher is included. For example, an attitude of strangeness heightens sensitivity to a group's racial composition. A researcher who ignores the racial composition of a group of Whites in a multiracial society because he or she too is White is being racially insensitive. Likewise, "Gender insensitivity occurs when the sex of participants in the research process is neglected" (Eichler, 1988:51). The researcher records such details because something of significance *might* be revealed. It is better to err by including everything than to ignore potentially significant details.

A field researcher notes aspects of physical appearance such as neatness, dress, and hairstyle because they express messages that can affect social interactions. People spend a great deal of time and money selecting clothes, styling and combing hair, grooming with makeup, shaving, ironing clothes, and using deodorant or perfumes. These are part of their presentation of self. Even people who do not groom, shave, or wear deodorant present themselves and send a symbolic message by their appearance. No one dresses or looks "normal." Such a statement suggests that a researcher is not seeing the social world through the eyes of a stranger or is insensitive to social signals.

What people do is also significant. A field researcher notices where people sit or stand, the pace at which they walk, and their nonverbal communication. People express social information, feelings, and attitudes through nonverbal communication, including gestures, facial expressions, and how one stands or sits (standing stiffly, sitting in a slouched position, etc.). People express relationships by how they position themselves in a group and through eye contact. A researcher may read the social communication of people by noting that they are standing close together, looking relaxed, and making eye contact.

A field researcher also notices the context in which events occur: Who was present? Who just arrived or left the scene? Was the room hot and stuffy? Such details may help the researcher assign mean-

ing and understand why an event occurred. If they are not noticed, the details are lost, as is a full understanding of the event.

Listening. A field researcher listens carefully to phrases, accents, and incorrect grammar, listening to both *what* is said and *how* it is said or what was implied. For example, people often use phrases such as "you know" or "of course" or "et cetera." A field researcher knows the meaning behind such phrases. He or she can try to hear everything, but listening is difficult when many conversations occur at once or when eavesdropping. Luckily, significant events and themes usually recur.

Argot. People who interact with each other over a time period develop shared symbols and terminology. They create new words or assign new meanings to ordinary words. New words develop out of specific events, assumptions, or relations. Knowing and using the language can signal membership in a distinct subculture. A field researcher learns the specialized language, or *argot*.[34]

> Researchers must start with the premise that words and symbols used in their world may have different meaning in the world of their subjects. They must also be attuned to new words and words used in contexts other than those with which they are familiar. (Bogdan and Taylor, 1975:53)

A field researcher discovers how the argot fits into social relations or meanings. The argot gives a researcher clues to what is important to members and how they see the world. For example, Douglas (1976:125) discovered the term *vultching* in a study of nude beaches. It was a member's label for the practice of some males who sat around an attractive nude woman on the beach.

In their study of sales practices of a vacation condominium ownership firm, Katovich and Diamond (1986) conducted observations and informal interviews over six months when one researcher was employed and the other was a trainee. They analyzed the salesroom as a stage in which a series of events are presented to prospective buyers, and they discussed the argot used. For example, "drops" occur when the finance manager enters and "drops" information during a discussion between the sales-person and potential buyers. The purpose of such staged events is to stimulate sales. Common reve-lations were: A major corporation that bought 20 units just decided it only needed 15, so 5 are sud-denly available at a special price; a previous client was denied financing, so a property can be offered at a reduced price; or only a few charter members can qualify for a special deal.

Taking Notes

Most field research data are in the form of field notes. Good notes are the bricks and mortar of field re-search (Fetterman, 1989). Full field notes can con-tain maps, diagrams, photographs, interviews, tape recordings, videotapes, memos, objects from the field, notes jotted in the field, and detailed notes writ-ten away from the field. A field researcher expects to fill many notebooks, or the equivalent in computer memory. He or she may spend more time writing notes than being in the field. Some researchers pro-duce 40 single-spaced pages of notes for three hours of observation. With practice, even a new field re-searcher can produce several pages of notes for each hour in the field.

Writing notes is often boring, tedious work that requires self-discipline. The notes contain extensive descriptive detail drawn from memory. A researcher makes it a daily habit or compulsion to write notes immediately after leaving the field. The notes must be neat and organized because the researcher will return to them over and over again. Once written, the notes are private and valuable. A researcher treats them with care and protects confidentiality. Members have the right to remain anonymous, and researchers often use *pseudonyms* (false names) in notes. Field notes may be of interest to hostile par-ties, blackmailers, or legal officials, so some re-searchers write field notes in code.

A researcher's state of mind, level of attention, and conditions in the field affect note taking. He or she will usually begin with relatively short one- to three-hour periods in the field before writing notes. Johnson (1975:187) remarked

The quantity and quality of the observational records vary with the field worker's feelings of rest-edness or exhaustion, reactions to particular events, relations with others, consumption of alcoholic beverages, the number of discrete observations, and so forth.

Types of Field Notes. Field researchers take notes in many ways.[35] The recommendations here (also, see Box 13.3) are suggestions. Full field notes have several types or levels. Five levels will be described. It is usually best to keep all the notes for an obser-vation period together and to distinguish types of notes by separate pages. Some researchers include inferences with direct observations if they are set off by a visible device such as brackets or colored ink. The quantity of notes varies across types. For ex-ample, six hours in the field might result in one page of jotted notes, 40 pages of direct observation, five pages of researcher inference, and two pages total for methodological, theoretical, and personal notes.

Jotted Notes. It is nearly impossible to take good notes in the field. Even a known observer in a pub-lic setting looks strange when furiously writing. More important, when looking down and writing, the researcher cannot see and hear what is happen-ing. The attention given to note writing is taken from field observation where it belongs. The specific set-ting determines whether any notes in the field can be taken. The researcher may be able to write, and members may expect it, or he or she may have to be secretive (e.g., go to the restroom).

Jotted notes are written in the field. They are short, temporary memory triggers such as words, phrases, or drawings taken inconspicuously, often scribbled on any convenient item (e.g., napkin, matchbook). They are incorporated into direct ob-servation notes but are never substituted for them.

Direct Observation Notes. The basic source of field data is notes a researcher writes immediately after leaving the field, which he or she can add to later. The notes should be ordered chronologically with the date, time, and place on each entry. They serve as a detailed description of what the researcher heard and saw in concrete, specific terms. To the

Box 13.3

Recommendations for Taking Field Notes

1. Record notes as soon as possible after each period in the field, and do not talk with others until observations are recorded.
2. Begin the record of each field visit with a new page, with the date and time noted.
3. Use jotted notes only as a temporary memory aid, with key words or terms, or the first and last things said.
4. Use wide margins to make it easy to add to notes at any time. Go back and add to the notes if you remember something later.
5. Plan to type notes and keep each level of notes separate so it will be easy to go back to them later.
6. Record events in the order in which they occurred, and note how long they last (e.g., a 15-minute wait, a one-hour ride).
7. Make notes as concrete, complete, and comprehensible as possible.
8. Use frequent paragraph breaks and quotation marks. Exact recall of phrases is best, with double quotes; use single quotes for paraphrasing.
9. Record small talk or routines that do not appear to be significant at the time; they may become important later.
10. "Let your feelings flow" and write quickly without worrying about spelling or "wild ideas." Assume that no one else will see the notes, but use pseudonyms.
11. Never substitute tape recordings completely for field notes.
12. Include diagrams or maps of the setting, and outline your own movements and those of others during the period of observation.
13. Include the researcher's own words and behavior in the notes. Also, record emotional feelings and private thoughts in a separate section.
14. Avoid evaluative summarizing words. Instead of "The sink looked disgusting," say, "The sink was rust-stained and looked as if it had not been cleaned in a long time. Pieces of food and dirty dishes looked as if they had been piled in it for several days."
15. Reread notes periodically and record ideas generated by the rereading.
16. Always make one or more backup copies, keep them in a locked location, and store the copies in different places in case of fire.

---

extent possible, they are an exact recording of the particular words, phrases, or actions.

A researcher's memory improves with practice. A new researcher can soon remember exact phrases from the field. Verbatim statements should be written with double quote marks to distinguish them from paraphrases. Dialogue accessories (nonverbal communication, props, tone, speed, volume, gestures) should be recorded as well. A researcher records what was actually said and does not clean it up; notes include ungrammatical speech, slang, and misstatements (e.g., write, "Uh, I'm goin' home, Sal," not "I am going home, Sally").

A researcher puts concrete details in notes, not summaries. For example, instead of, "We talked about sports," he or she writes, "Anthony argued with Sam and Jason. He said that the Cubs would win next week because they traded for a new shortstop, Chiappetta. He also said that the team was better than the Mets, who he thought had inferior infielders. He cited last week's game where the Cubs won against Boston by 8 to 3." A researcher notes who was present, what happened, where it occurred, when, and under what circumstances. New researchers may not take notes because "nothing important happened." An experienced researcher knows that events when "nothing happened" can reveal a lot. For example, members may express feelings and organize experience into folk categories even in trivial conversations.

A field researcher listens to members in order to "climb into their skin" or "walk in their shoes."[36] This involves a three-step process. The researcher listens without applying analytical categories; he or she compares what is heard to what was heard at other times and to what others say; then the researcher applies his or her own interpretation to infer or figure out what it means. In ordinary interaction, we do all three steps simultaneously and jump quickly to our own inferences. A field researcher learns to look and listen without inferring or imposing an interpretation. His or her observations without inferences go into *direct observation notes*.

Researcher Inference Notes. A researcher records inferences in a separate section that is keyed to direct observations. People never see social relationships, emotions, or meaning. They see specific physical actions and hear words; then they use background cultural knowledge, clues from the context, and what is done or said to assign social meaning. For example, one does not see *love* or *anger;* one sees and hears specific actions (red face, loud voice, wild gestures, obscenities) and draws inferences from them (the person is angry).

A researcher keeps inferred meaning separate from direct observation because the meaning of actions is not always self-evident. Sometimes people try to deceive others. For example, an unrelated couple register at a motel as Mr. and Mrs. Smith. More frequently, social behavior is ambiguous, or multiple meanings are possible. For example, you see a White male and female, both in their late twenties, get out of a car and enter a restaurant together. They sit at a table, order a meal, and talk with serious expressions in hushed tones, sometimes leaning forward to hear each other. As they get up to leave, the woman, who has a sad facial expression and appears ready to cry, is briefly hugged by the male. They then leave together. Did you witness a couple breaking up, two friends discussing a third, two people trying to decide what to do because they have discovered that their spouses are having an affair with each other, or a brother and sister whose father just died? The *separation of inference* allows multiple meanings to arise upon rereading direct observation notes. If a researcher records inferred meaning without separation, he or she loses other possible meanings.

Analytic Notes. Researchers make many decisions about how to proceed while in the field. Some acts are planned (e.g., to conduct an interview, to observe a particular activity, etc.), and others seem to occur almost out of thin air. Field researchers keep methodological ideas in analytic notes to record their plans, tactics, ethical and procedural decisions, and self-critiques of tactics.

Theory emerges in field research during data collection and is clarified when a researcher reviews field notes. Analytic notes have a running account of a researcher's attempts to give meaning to field events. He or she thinks out loud in the notes by suggesting links between ideas, creating hypotheses, proposing conjectures, and developing new concepts.

Analytic memos are part of the theoretical notes. They are systematic digressions into theory, wherein a researcher elaborates on ideas in depth, expands on ideas while still in the field, and modifies or develops more complex theory by rereading and thinking about the memos.

Personal Notes. As discussed earlier, personal feelings and emotional reactions become part of the data; they color what a researcher sees or hears in the field. A researcher keeps a section of notes that is like a personal diary. He or she records personal life events and feelings in it ("I'm tense today, I wonder if it's because of the fight I had yesterday with . . ."; "I've got a headache on this gloomy, overcast day").

Personal notes serve three functions: They provide an outlet for a researcher and a way to cope with stress; they are a source of data about personal reactions; and they give him or her a way to evaluate direct observation or inference notes when the notes are later reread. For example, if the researcher was in a good mood during observations, it might color what he or she observed (see Figure 13.3).

Maps and Diagrams. Field researchers often make maps and draw diagrams or pictures of the features of a field site.[37] This serves two purposes: It helps a researcher organize events in the field and it helps convey a field site to others. For example, a researcher observing a bar with 15 stools may draw and number 15 circles to simplify recording

Direct Observation	Inference	Analytic	Personal Journal
Sunday, October 4. Kay's Kafe 3:00 pm. Large Caucasian male in mid-40s, overweight, enters. He wears worn brown suit. He is alone; sits at booth #2. Kay comes by, asks, "What'll it be?" Man says, "Coffee, black for now." She leaves and he lights cigarette and reads menu. 3:15 pm. Kay turns on radio.	Kay seems friendly today, humming. She becomes solemn and watchful. I think she puts on the radio when nervous.	Women are afraid of men who come in alone since the robbery.	It is raining. I am feeling comfortable with Kay but am bored today.

FIGURE 13.3   Types of Field Notes

(e.g., "Yosuke came in and sat on stool 12; Phoebe was already on stool 10"). Field researchers find three types of maps helpful: spatial, social, and temporal. The first helps orient the data; the latter two are preliminary forms of data analysis. A *spatial map* locates people, equipment, and the like in terms of geographical physical space to show where activities occur (Figure 13.4A). A *social map* shows the number or variety of people and the arrangements among them of power, influence, friendship, division of labor, and so on (Figure 13.4B). A *temporal map* shows the ebb and flow of people, goods, services, and communications, or schedules (Figure 13.4C).

Machine Recordings to Supplement Memory.
Tape recorders and videotapes can be helpful supplements in field research. They never substitute for field notes or a researcher's presence in the field. They cannot be introduced into all field sites, and can be used only after a researcher develops rapport. Recorders and videotapes provide a close approximation to what occurred and a permanent record that others can review. They help a researcher recall events and observe what does not happen, or nonresponses, which are easy to miss. Nevertheless, these items create disruption and an increased awareness of surveillance. Researchers who rely on

them must address associated problems (e.g., ensure that batteries are fresh and there are enough blank tapes). Also, relistening to or viewing tapes can be time consuming. For example, it may take over 100 hours to listen to 50 hours recorded in the field. Transcriptions of tape are expensive and not always accurate; they do not always convey subtle contextual meanings or mumbled words.[38]

Interview Notes.   If a researcher conducts field interviews (to be discussed), he or she keeps the interview notes separate.[39] In addition to recording questions and answers, he or she creates a *face sheet*. This is a page at the beginning of the notes with information such as the date, place of interview, characteristics of interviewee, content of the interview, and so on. It helps the interviewer when rereading and making sense of the notes.

Data Quality

The Meaning of Quality.   What does the term *high-quality data* mean in field research, and what does a researcher do to get such data?[40] For a quantitative researcher, high-quality data are reliable and valid; they give precise, consistent measures of the same "objective" truth for all researchers. An interpretive approach suggests a different kind of data

A Spatial Map

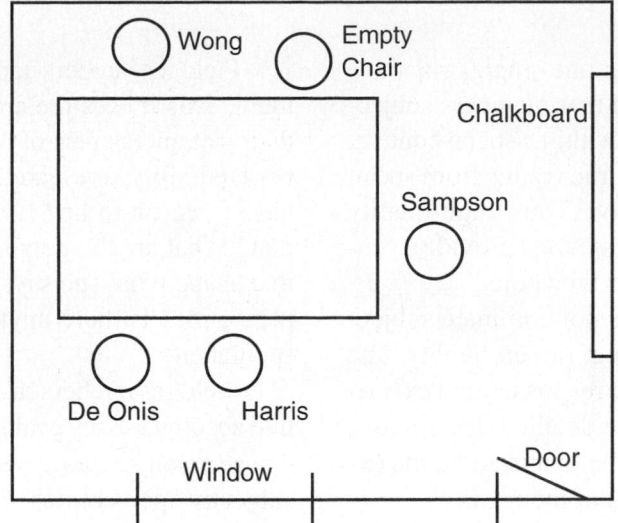

B Social Map

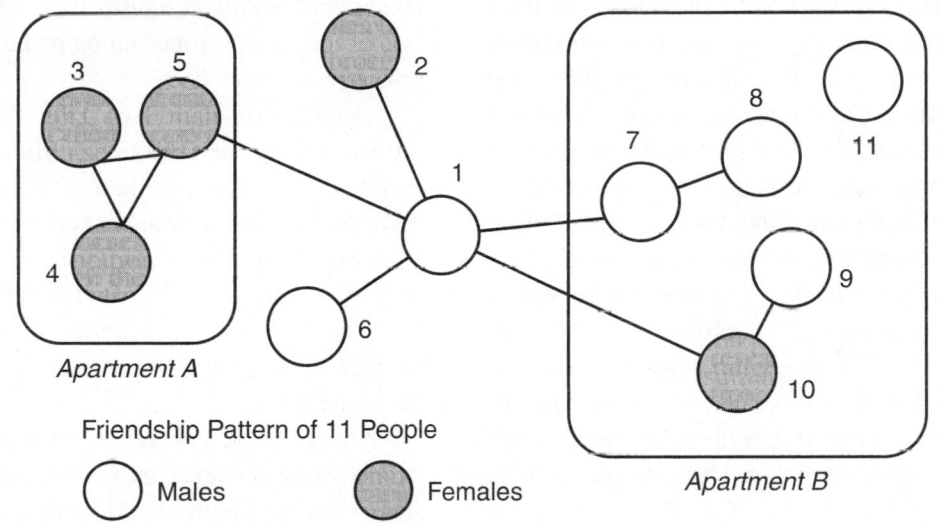

Friendship Pattern of 11 People

○ Males   ● Females

Apartment A

Apartment B

C Temporal Map

Day of Week, Buzz's Bar

	Mon	Tue	Wed	Thr	Fri	Sat
Open 10:00	Old Drinkers	Old Drinkers	Old Drinkers	Old Drinkers	Skip Work or Leave Early	Going to Fish
5:00	Football Watchers	Neighbors and Bridge Players	Softball Team (All-Male Night)	Young Crowd	Loud Music, Mixed Crowd	Loners and No Dates
Close 1:00						

FIGURE 13.4 Types of Maps Used in Field Research

quality. Instead of assuming one single, objective truth, field researchers hold that members subjectively interpret experiences within a social context. What a member takes to be true results from social interaction and interpretation. Thus, high-quality field data capture such processes and provide an understanding of the member's viewpoint.

A field researcher does not eliminate subjective views to get quality data; rather, quality data include his or her subjective responses and experiences. Quality field data are detailed descriptions from the researcher's immersion and authentic experiences in the social world of members.[41]

Reliability in Field Research. The reliability of field data addresses the question, "Are researcher observations about a member or field event internally and externally consistent?" *Internal consistency* refers to whether the data are plausible, given all that is known about a person or event, eliminating common forms of human deception. In other words, do the pieces fit together into a coherent picture? For example, are a member's actions consistent over time and in different social contexts?

External consistency is achieved by verifying or cross-checking observations with other, divergent sources of data. In other words, does it all fit into the overall context? For example, can others verify what a researcher observed about a person? Does other evidence confirm the researcher's observations?

Reliability in field research also includes what is not said or done, but is expected or anticipated. Such omissions or null data can be significant but are difficult to detect. For example, when observing a cashier end her shift, a researcher notices that the money in a drawer is not counted. He or she may notice the omission only if other cashiers always count money at the end of the shift.

Reliability in field research depends on a researcher's insight, awareness, suspicions, and questions. He or she looks at members and events from different angles (legal, economic, political, personal) and mentally asks questions: "Where does the money come from for that? What do those people do all day?"

Field researchers depend on what members tell them. This makes the credibility of members and their statements part of reliability. To check member credibility, a researcher asks, "Does the person have a reason to lie? Is she in a position to know that? What are the person's values and how might that shape what she says? Is he just saying that to please me? Is there anything that might limit his spontaneity?"

Field researchers take subjectivity and context into account as they evaluate credibility. They know that a person's statements or actions are affected by subjective perceptions. Statements are made from a particular point of view and colored by an individual's experiences. Instead of evaluating each statement to see if it is true, a field researcher finds statements useful in themselves. Even inaccurate statements and actions can be revealing from a researcher's perspective.

As mentioned before, actions and statements are shaped by the context in which they appear. What is said in one setting may differ in other contexts. For example, when asked, "Do you dance?" a member may say no in a public setting full of excellent dancers, but yes in a semiprivate setting with few good dancers and different music. It is not that the member is lying but that the answer is shaped by the context.

Other obstacles to reliability include behaviors that can mislead a researcher: misinformation, evasions, lies, and fronts.[42] *Misinformation* is an unintended falsehood caused by the uncertainty and complexity of life. For example, nurses in a hospital state something as "official hospital policy" when, in fact, there is no such written policy.

Evasions are intentional acts of avoiding or not revealing information. Common evasions include not answering questions, answering a different question than was asked, switching topics, or answering in a purposefully vague and ambiguous manner. For example, a salesman appears uncomfortable when the topic of using call girls to get customers comes up at a dinner party. He says, "Yes, a lot of people use them." But later, alone, after careful questioning, the salesman is drawn out and reveals that he himself uses the practice.

Lies are untruths intended to mislead or to give a false view. For example, a gang member gives the researcher a false name and address, or a church minister gives an inflated membership figure in order to look more successful. Douglas (1976:73) noted, "In all other research settings I've known about in any detail, lying was common, both among members and to researchers, especially about the things that were really important to the members."

Fronts are shared and learned lies and deceptions. They can include the use of physical props and collaborators. For example, a bar is really a place to make illegal bets. The bar appears legitimate and sells drinks, but its true business is revealed only by careful investigation. A common example is that of Santa Claus—a "front" put on for small children.

Validity in Field Research.

Validity in field research is the confidence placed in a researcher's analysis and data as accurately representing the social world in the field. Replicability is not a criterion because field research is virtually impossible to replicate. Essential aspects of the field change: The social events and context change, the members are different, the individual researcher differs, and so on. There are four kinds of validity or tests of research accuracy: ecological validity, natural history, member validation, and competent insider performance.

Ecological validity is the degree to which the social world described by a researcher matches the world of members. It asks, "Is the natural setting described relatively undisturbed by the researcher's presence or procedures?" A project has ecological validity if events would have occurred without a researcher's presence.

Natural history is a detailed description of how the project was conducted. It is a full and candid disclosure of a researcher's actions, assumptions, and procedures for others to evaluate. A project is valid in terms of natural history if outsiders see and accept the field site and the researcher's actions.

Member validation occurs when a researcher takes field results back to members, who judge their adequacy. A project is member valid if members recognize and understand the researcher's description as reflecting their intimate social world. Member validation has limitations because conflicting perspectives in a setting produce disagreement with the researcher's observations, and members may object when results do not portray their group in a favorable light. In addition, members may not recognize the description because it is not from their perspective or does not fit with their purposes.[43]

Competent insider performance is the ability of a nonmember to interact effectively as a member or pass as one. This includes the ability to tell and understand insider jokes. A valid field project gives enough of a flavor of the social life in the field, and sufficient detail so that an outsider can act as a member. Its limitation is that it is not possible to know the social rules for every situation. Also, an outsider might be able to pass simply because members are being polite and do not want to point out social mistakes.[44]

Focusing and Sampling

Focusing.

The field researcher first gets a general picture, then focuses on a few specific problems or issues (see Figure 13.5).[45] A researcher decides on specific research questions and develops hypotheses only after being in the field and experiencing it firsthand. At first, everything seems relevant; later, however, selective attention focuses on specific questions and themes.

Sampling.

Field research sampling differs from survey research sampling, although both sometimes use snowball sampling (see Chapter 8).[46] A field researcher samples by taking a smaller, selective set of observations from all possible observations. It is called *theoretical sampling* because it is guided by the researcher's developing theory. Field researchers sample times, situations, types of events, locations, types of people, or contexts of interest.

For example, a researcher samples time by observing a setting at different times. He or she observes at all times of the day, on every day of the week, and in all seasons to get a full sense of how the field site stays the same or changes. It is often best

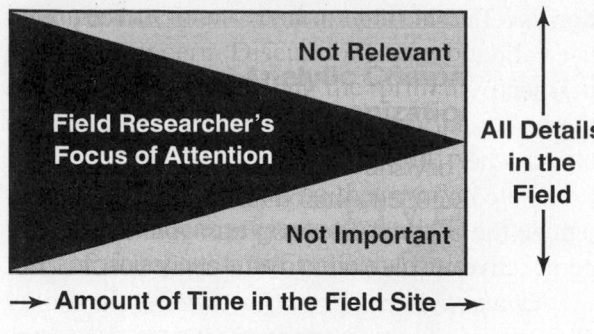

FIGURE 13.5 Focusing in Field Research

to overlap when sampling (e.g., to have sampling times from 7:00 A.M. to 9:00 A.M., from 8:00 A.M. to 10:00 A.M., from 9:00 A.M. to 11:00 A.M., etc.).

A researcher samples locations because one location may give depth, but a narrow perspective. Sitting or standing in different locations helps the researcher get a sense of the whole site. For example, the peer-to-peer behavior of school teachers usually occurs in a faculty lounge, but it also occurs at a local bar when teachers gather or in a classroom temporarily used for a teacher meeting. In addition, researchers trace the paths of members to various field locations.

Field researchers sample people by focusing their attention or interaction on different kinds of people (old-timers and newcomers, old and young, males and females, leaders and followers). As a researcher identifies types of people, or people with opposing outlooks, he or she tries to interact with and learn about all types.

For example, a researcher samples three kinds of field events: routine, special, and unanticipated. Routine events (e.g., opening up a store for business) happen every day and should not be considered unimportant simply because they are routine. Special events (e.g., annual office party) are announced and planned in advance. They focus member attention and reveal aspects of social life not otherwise visible. Unanticipated events are those that just happen to occur while a researcher is present (e.g., unsupervised workers when the manager gets sick and cannot oversee workers at a store for a day). In this

case the researcher sees—by chance—something unusual, unplanned, or rare.

THE FIELD RESEARCH INTERVIEW

So far you have learned how field researchers observe and take notes. They also interview members, but field interviews differ from survey research interviews. This section introduces the field interview.

The Field Interview

Field researchers use unstructured, nondirective, in-depth interviews, which differ from formal survey research interviews in many ways (see Table 13.1).[47] The field interview involves asking questions, listening, expressing interest, and recording what is said.

The field interview is a joint production of a researcher and a member. Members are active participants whose insights, feelings, and cooperation are essential parts of a discussion process that reveals subjective meanings. "The interviewer's presence and form of involvement—how she or he listens, attends, encourages, interrupts, digresses, initiates topics, and terminates responses—is integral to the respondent's account" (Mishler, 1986:82).

Field research interviews go by many names: unstructured, depth, ethnographic, open-ended, informal, and long. Generally, they involve one or more people being present, occur in the field, and are informal and nondirective (i.e., the respondent may take the interview in various directions) (see Fontana and Frey, 1994).

A field interview involves a mutual sharing of experiences. A researcher might share his or her background to build trust and encourage the informant to open up, but does not force answers or use leading questions. She or he encourages and guides a process of mutual discovery.

In field interviews members express themselves in the forms in which they normally speak, think, and organize reality. A researcher retains members' jokes and narrative stories in their natural form and does not repackage them into a standardized format. The focus is on the member's perspec-

TABLE 13.1 Survey Interviews versus Field Research Interviews

TYPICAL SURVEY INTERVIEW	TYPICAL FIELD INTERVIEW
1. It has a clear beginning and end.	1. The beginning and end are not clear. The interview can be picked up later.
2. The same standard questions are asked of all respondents in the same sequence.	2. The questions and the order in which they are asked are tailored to specific people and situations.
3. The interviewer appears neutral at all times.	3. The interviewer shows interest in responses, encourages elaboration.
4. The interviewer asks questions, and the respondent answers.	4. It is like a friendly conversational exchange, but with more interviewer questions.
5. It is almost always with one respondent alone.	5. It can occur in a group setting or with others in the area, but varies.
6. It has a professional tone and businesslike focus; diversions are ignored.	6. It is interspersed with jokes, asides, stories, diversions, and anecdotes, which are recorded.
7. Closed-ended questions are common, with rare probes.	7. Open-ended questions are common, and probes are frequent.
8. The interviewer alone controls the pace and direction of the interview.	8. The interviewer and member jointly control the pace and direction of the interview.
9. The social context in which the interview occurs is ignored and assumed to make little difference.	9. The social context of the interview is noted and seen as important for interpreting the meaning of responses.
10. The interviewer attempts to mold the communication pattern into a standard framework.	10. The interviewer adjusts to the member's norms and language usage.

Source: Adapted from Briggs (1986), Denzin (1989), Douglas (1985), Mishler (1986), and Spradley (1979a).

tive and experiences. In order to stay close to the member's experience, the researcher asks questions in terms of concrete examples or situations—for example, "Could you tell me things that led up to your quitting in June?" instead of "Why did you quit your job?"

Field interviews occur in a series over time. A researcher begins by building rapport and steering conversation away from evaluative or highly sensitive topics. He or she avoids probing inner feelings until intimacy is established, and even then, the researcher expects apprehension. After several meetings he or she may be able to probe more deeply into sensitive issues and seek clarification of less sensitive issues. In later interviews he or she may return to topics and check past an-

swers by restating them in a nonjudgmental tone and asking for verification—for example, "The last time we talked, you said that you started taking things from the store after they reduced your pay. Is that right?"

The field interview is a "speech event," closer to a friendly conversation than the stimulus–response model found in a survey research interview (see Chapter 10). You are familiar with a friendly conversation, which has its own informal rules and the following elements: (1) a greeting ("Hi, it's good to see you again"); (2) the absence of an explicit goal or purpose (we don't say, "Let's now discuss what we did last weekend"); (3) avoidance of repetition (we don't say, "Could you clarify what you said about . . ."); (4) question asking ("Did you see the race yesterday?"); (5) expressions of interest ("Really? I wish I could have been there!"); (6) expressions of ignorance ("No, I missed it. What happened?"); (7) turn taking, so the encounter is balanced (one person does not always ask questions and the other only answer); (8) abbreviations ("I missed the Derby, but I'm going to the Indy," not "I missed the Kentucky Derby horse race but I will go to the Indianapolis 500 automotive race"); (9) a pause or brief silence when neither person talks is acceptable; (10) a closing (we don't say, "Let's end this conversation"; instead, we give a verbal indicator before physically leaving—"I've got to get back to work now. See ya tomorrow.").

The field interview differs from a friendly conversation. It has an explicit purpose—to learn about the informant and setting. A researcher includes explanations or requests that diverge from friendly conversations. For example, he or she may say, "I'd like to ask you about . . . ," or "Could you look at this and see if I've written it down right?" The field interview is less balanced. A higher proportion of questions come from the researcher, who expresses more ignorance and interest. Also, it includes repetition, and a researcher asks the member to elaborate on unclear abbreviations.[48]

Field research interviewers watch for markers. A *marker* in a field interview is "a passing reference made by a respondent to an important event or feeling state" (Weiss, 1994:77). For example, during an interview with a 45-year-old physician, the interviewee mentions casually, while describing having difficulty in a high school class, "It was about that time that my sister was seriously injured in a car accident." Maybe the person never said anything about the sister or the accident before. By dropping it in, the respondent is indicating it was an important event at the time. A researcher should pick up on the marker and later may ask, "Earlier, you mentioned that your sister was seriously injured in a car accident. Could you tell me more about that?" Most importantly, the interviewer listens. He or she does not interrupt frequently, repeatedly finish the respondent's sentences, offer associations (e.g., "Oh, that is just like X"), insist on finishing asking a question that the respondent has begun to answer, fight for control over

the interview process, or stay with a line of thought and ignore new leads (see Weiss, 1994:78).

Life History

A life-history, life-story, or biographical interview is a special type of field interviewing. It overlaps with oral history.[49] There are multiple purposes for stories of the past, and these may shape the forms of interview (see Smith, 1994). In a *life-history interview,* researchers interview and gather documentary material about a particular individual's life, usually someone who is old. "The concept of *life story* is used to designate the retrospective information itself without the corroborative evidence often implied by the term *life history*" (Tagg, 1985:163). Researchers ask open-ended questions to capture how the person understands his or her own past. Exact accuracy in the story is less critical than the story itself. Researchers recognize that the person may reconstruct or add present interpretations to the past; the person may "rewrite" his or her story. The main purpose is to get at how the respondent sees or remembers the past, not just some kind of objective truth (see Box 13.4).

Researchers sometimes use a life-story grid in which they ask the person what happened at various dates and in several areas of life. A grid may consist of categories such as migration, occupation, education, or family events for each of a dozen ages in the person's life. Researchers often supplement the interview information with artifacts (e.g., old photos) and may present them during the interview to stimulate discussion or recollection. "Life writing as an empirical exercise feeds on data: letters, documents, interviews" (Smith, 1994:290). McCracken (1988: 20) gave an example of how objects aided the interview by helping him understand how the person being interviewed saw things. When interviewing a 75-year-old woman in her living room, McCracken initially thought the room contained just a lot of cluttered physical objects. After having the woman explain the meaning of each item, it was clear that she saw each as a memorial or a memento. The room was a museum to key events in her life. Only after the author looked at the objects in this new way, did

Box 13.4

The Life-History or Life-Story Interview

Life-history or life-story interviews usually involve two to six open-ended interviews, usually recorded, of 60 to 90 minutes. These interviews serve several purposes. First, they can assist the informant being interviewed in reconstructing his or her life memories. Retelling and remembering one's life events as a narrative story can have therapeutic benefits and pass on personal wisdom to a new generation. Second, these interviews can create new qualitative data on the life cycle, the development of self, and how people experience events that can be archived and added to similar data (e.g., The Center for Life Stories at University of Southern Maine is such an archive). Third, life-story interviews can provide the interviewer with an in-depth look at another's life. This is often an enriching experience that creates a close personal relationship and encourages self-reflection in ways that enhance personal integrity. Steps in the process are as follows:

1. The researcher prepares with background reading, refines his or her interview skills, contacts the informant, gets permission for the interview, and promises anonymity.

2. The researcher conducts a series of interviews, audio- or video-recording them. The interviewer suspends any prior history with an informant and gives his or her total respect, always showing sincere interest in what another says. He or she asks open-ended questions, but is flexible and never forces a question. The interviewer acts as a guide, knowing when to ask a question that will open up stories; gives intense attentiveness, and is completely nonjudgmental and supportive. Often, the interviewer offers photographs or objects to help spark memories and past feelings.

3. The researcher transcribes the recorded interviews in four stages: (a) prepares a summary of each tape; (b) makes a verbatim transcription, with minor editing (e.g., adds sentences, paragraphs, etc.) and stage directions (e.g., laughter, coughing, etc.); (c) reviews the whole transcript for clarity of meaning and does further editing and minor rearranging; and (d) has the informant review the transcript for any corrections and modifications.

4. The researcher sends a note of appreciation to the informant and prepares a commentary on major themes and/or sends it to an archive.

Source: Adapted from Atkinson, 1998.

he begin to see the furniture and objects not as inanimate things but as objects that radiated meaning.

Sometimes researchers find an existing archive with a person; other times they must search out the documents and create an archive. Locating such documentary data can be a tremendous task, followed by that of carefully reviewing, cataloging, and organizing the information. The interview and documentary data together form the basis of the life story.

Types of Questions in Field Interviews

Field researchers ask three types of questions in a field interview: descriptive, structural, and contrast questions. All are asked concurrently, but each type is more frequent at a different stage in the research process (see Figure 13.6). During the early stage a researcher primarily asks descriptive questions. He or she gradually adds structural questions until, in the middle stage after analysis has begun, they make up a majority of the questions. Contrast questions appear in the middle of a field research study and increase until, by the end, they are asked more than any other type.[50]

A researcher asks a *descriptive question* to explore the setting and learn about members. Descriptive questions can be about time and space—for example, "Where is the bathroom?" "When does the delivery truck arrive?" "What happened Monday night?" They can also be about people and activities: "Who is sitting by the window?" "What is your uncle like?" "What happens during the initiation ceremony?" They can be about objects: "When do you use a saber saw?" "Which tools do you carry

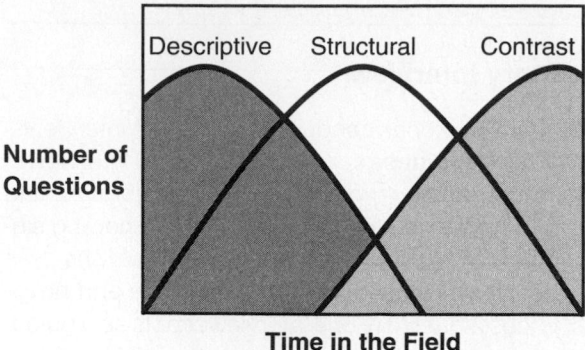

FIGURE 13.6   Types of Questions in Field Research Interviews

with you on an emergency water leak job?" Questions asking for examples or experiences are descriptive questions—for example, "Could you give me an example of a great date?" "What were your experiences as a postal clerk?" Descriptive questions may ask about hypothetical situations: "If a student opened her book during the exam, how would you deal with it?" Another type of descriptive question asks members about the argot of the setting: "What do you call a deputy sheriff?" (The answer is a "county mounty.")

A researcher uses a *structural question* after spending time in the field and starting to analyze data, especially with a domain analysis (to be discussed in Chapter 15). It begins after a researcher organizes specific field events, situations, and conversations into conceptual categories. For example, a researcher's observations of a highway truck-stop restaurant revealed that the employees informally classify customers who patronize the truck stop. In a preliminary analysis the researcher creates a conceptual category of kinds of customers and has members verify the categories with structural questions.

One way to pose a structural question is to ask the members whether a category includes elements in addition to those already identified by a researcher —for example, "Are there any types of customers other than regulars, greasers, pit stoppers, and long haulers?" In addition, a researcher asks for confirmation: "Is a greaser a type of customer that you serve?" "Would you call a customer who . . . a

greaser?" "Would a pit stopper ever eat a three-course dinner?"

The *contrast question* builds on the analysis that has been verified by structural questions. Questions focus on similarities or differences between elements in categories or between categories as the researcher asks members to verify similarities and differences: "You seem to have a number of different kinds of customers come in here. I've heard you call some customers 'regulars' and others 'pit stoppers.' How are a regular and a pit stopper alike?" or "Is the difference between a long hauler and a greaser that the greaser doesn't tip?" or "Two types of customers just stop to use the restroom—entire families and a lone male. Do you call both pit stoppers?"

Informants

An informant or key actor in field research is a member with whom a field researcher develops a relationship and who tells about, or informs on, the field.[51] Who makes a good informant? The ideal informant has four characteristics:

1. The informant who is totally familiar with the culture and is in position to witness significant events makes a good informant. He or she lives and breathes the culture and engages in routines in the setting without thinking about them. The individual has years of intimate experience in the culture; he or she is not a novice.
2. The individual is currently involved in the field. Ex-members who have reflected on the field may provide useful insights, but the longer they have been away from direct involvement, the more likely it is that they have reconstructed their recollections.
3. The person can spend time with the researcher. Interviewing may take many hours, and some members are simply not available for extensive interviewing.
4. Nonanalytic individuals make better informants. A nonanalytic informant is familiar with and uses native folk theory or pragmatic common sense. This is in contrast to the analytic member, who preanalyzes the setting, using categories from the media or education.

Even members educated in the social sciences can learn to respond in a nonanalytic manner, but only if they set aside their education and use the member perspective.

A field researcher may interview several types of informants. Contrasting types of informants who provide useful perspectives include rookies and old-timers, people in the center of events and those on the fringes of activity, people who recently changed status (e.g., through promotion) and those who are static, frustrated or needy people and happy or secure people, the leader in charge and the subordinate who follows. A field researcher expects mixed messages when he or she interviews a range of informants.

Interview Context

Field researchers recognize that a conversation in a private office may not occur in a crowded lunchroom.[52] Often, interviews take place in the member's home environment so that he or she is comfortable. This is not always best. If a member is preoccupied or there is no privacy, a researcher will move to another setting (e.g., restaurant or university office).

The interview's meaning is shaped by its Gestalt, or the whole interaction of a researcher and a member in a specific context. A researcher notes nonverbal forms of communication (e.g., shrugs, gestures, etc.) that add meaning:

> *The investigator should note important facts that will not appear on the record of the interview itself, be it a tape recording or a video recording or a set of notes. Detailed notes on the setting, the participants, time of day, ongoing social or ritual events, and so forth should be complemented by the researcher's perceptions of the interaction. (Briggs, 1986:104)*

LEAVING THE FIELD

Work in the field can last for a few weeks to a dozen years.[53] In either case, at some point work in the field ends. Some researchers (e.g., Schatzman and Strauss) suggest that the end comes naturally when theory building ceases or reaches a closure; others (e.g., Bogdan and Taylor) feel that fieldwork could go on without end and that a firm decision to cut off relations is needed.

Experienced field researchers anticipate a process of disengaging and exiting the field. Depending on the intensity of involvement and the length of time in the field, the process can be disruptive or emotionally painful for both the researcher and the members. A researcher may experience the emotional pain of breaking intimate friendships when leaving the field. He or she may feel guilty and depressed immediately before and after leaving. He or she may find it difficult to let go because of personal and emotional entanglements. If the involvement in the field was intense and long, and the field site differed from his or her native culture, the researcher may need months of adjustment before feeling at home with his or her original cultural surroundings.

Once a researcher decides to leave—because the project reaches a natural end and little new information is being learned, or because external factors force it to end (e.g., end of a job, gatekeepers order the researcher out, etc.)—he or she chooses a method of exiting. The researcher can leave by a quick exit (simply not return one day) or slowly withdraw, reducing his or her involvement over weeks. He or she also needs to decide how to tell members and how much advance warning to give.

The exit process depends on the specific field setting and the relationships developed. In general, a researcher lets members know a short period ahead of time. He or she fulfills any bargains or commitments that were built up and leaves with a clean slate. Sometimes, a ritual or ceremony, such as a going-away party or shaking hands with everyone, helps signal the break for members. Maintaining friendships with members is also possible and is preferred by feminist researchers.

A field researcher is aware that leaving affects members. Some members may feel hurt or rejected because a close social relationship is ending. They may react by trying to pull a researcher back into the field and make him or her more of a member, or they may become angry and resentful. They may grow cool and distant because of an awareness that the researcher is really an outsider. In any case, fieldwork is not finished until the process of disengagement and exiting is complete.

ETHICAL DILEMMAS OF FIELD RESEARCH

The direct personal involvement of a field researcher in the social lives of other people raises many ethical dilemmas. The dilemmas arise when a researcher is alone in the field and has little time to make a moral decision. Although he or she may be aware of general ethical issues before entering the field, they arise unexpectedly in the course of observing and interacting in the field. We will look at five ethical issues in field research: deception, confidentiality, involvement with illegal subcultures, the powerful, and publishing field reports.[54]

Deception

Deception arises in several ways in field research: The research may be covert, may assume a false role, name, or identity, or may mislead members in some way. The most hotly debated of the ethical issues arising from deception is that of covert versus overt field research.[55] Some support it (Douglas, 1976; Johnson, 1975) and see it as necessary for entering into and gaining full knowledge of many areas of social life. Others oppose it (Erikson, 1970) and argue that it undermines a trust between researchers and society. Although its moral status is questionable, there are some field sites or activities that can be studied only covertly.

Covert research is never preferable and never easier than overt research because of the difficulties of maintaining a front and the constant fear of getting caught. As Lofland and Lofland (1995:35) noted, "As in all other ethical dilemmas of naturalistic research, we believe that the ethically sensitive, thoughtful and knowledgeable investigator is the best judge of whether covert research is justified."

Confidentiality

A researcher learns intimate knowledge that is given in confidence. He or she has a moral obligation to uphold the confidentiality of data. This includes keeping information confidential from others in the field and disguising members' names in field notes.

Involvement with Illegal Subcultures

Researchers who conduct field research on individuals who engage in illegal behavior face additional dilemmas. They know of and are sometimes involved in illegal activity. Fetterman (1989) called this *guilty knowledge.* Such knowledge is of interest not only to law enforcement officials but also to other subculture members. The researcher faces a dilemma of building trust and rapport with such individuals, yet not becoming so involved as to violate his or her basic personal moral standards. Usually, the researcher makes an explicit arrangement with the subculture members. West (1980:38) remarked

> *I indicated my desire not to participate actively in the relatively risk-prone crimes with victims (e.g., theft, assault) explaining how such behavior was not worth the risk to me or was personally repugnant: I turned down invitations for "cuts in jobs." Although the few occasions when I was accidentally present at the commission of such victim crimes presented invaluable data, my wishes were generally respected and my obvious discomfort resulted in subjects warning me on subsequent occasions.*

The Powerful

Field researchers tend to study those without power in society (e.g., street people, the poor, children, and lower-level workers in bureaucracies). Powerful elites can block access and have effective gatekeepers. Researchers are criticized for ignoring the powerful, and they are also criticized by the powerful for being biased toward the less powerful. Becker (1970c) explained this by the *hierarchy of credibility,* which says that those who study the poor or low-level subordinates in an organization are viewed as biased, whereas those with authority are assumed to be credible. In groups with hierarchies or organizations, most people assume that those at or near the top have the right to define the way things are going to be, that they have a broader view, and are in a position to do something. When field researchers become immersed in the world of the less powerful and understand that point of view, they are expressing a rarely heard perspective. They may be accused of bias because they give a voice to parts of society that are not otherwise heard.

Publishing Field Reports

The intimate knowledge that a researcher obtains and reports creates a dilemma between the right of privacy and the right to know. A researcher does not publicize member secrets, violate privacy, or harm reputations. Yet, if he or she cannot publish anything that might offend or harm someone, some of what the researcher learned will remain hidden, and it may be difficult for others to believe the report if critical details are omitted.

Some researchers suggest asking members to look at a report to verify its accuracy and to approve of their portrayal in print. For marginal groups (e.g., addicts, prostitutes, crack users) this may not be possible, but researchers must always respect member privacy. On the other hand, censorship or self-censorship can be a danger. A compromise position is that truthful but unflattering material may be published only if it is essential to the researchers' larger arguments.[56]

CONCLUSION

In this chapter you learned about field research and the field research process (choosing a site and gaining access, relations in the field, observing and collecting data, and the field interview). Field researchers begin data analysis and theorizing during the data collection phase.

You can now appreciate the implications of saying that in field research, the researcher is directly involved with those being studied and is immersed in a natural setting. Doing field research usually has a greater impact on the researcher's emotions, personal life, and sense of self than doing other types of research. Field research is difficult to conduct, but it is a way to study parts of the social world that otherwise could not be studied.

Field research is strongest when a researcher studies a small group of people interacting in the present. It is valuable for micro-level or small-group face-to-face interaction. It is less effective when the concern is macro-level processes and social structures. It is nearly useless for events that occurred in the distant past or processes that stretch across decades.

KEY TERMS

acceptable incompetent
access ladder
analytic memos
appearance of interest
argot
attitude of strangeness
breakdown
competent insider performance
contrast question
defocusing
descriptive question
direct observation notes

ecological validity
ethnography
ethnomethodology
external consistency
face sheet
field site
freeze outs
fronts
gatekeeper
go native
guilty knowledge
hierarchy of credibility

jotted notes
life-history interview
marker
member validation
natural history
naturalism
normalize social research
pseudonyms
separation of inference
structural question
thick description

REVIEW QUESTIONS

1. What were the two major phases in the development of the Chicago school, and what are the journalistic and anthropological models?

2. List 5 of the 10 things the "methodological pragmatist" field researcher does.

3. Why is it important for a field researcher to read the literature before beginning fieldwork? How does this relate to defocusing?

4. Identify the characteristics of a field site that make it a good one for a beginning field researcher.

5. How does the "presentation of self" affect a field researcher's work?

6. What is the "attitude of strangeness," and why is it important?

7. What are relevant considerations when choosing roles in the field, and how can the degree of researcher involvement vary?

8. Identify three ways to ensure quality field research data.

9. Compare differences between a field research and a survey research interview, and between a field interview and a friendly conversation.

10. What are the different types or levels of field notes, and what purpose does each serve?

NOTES

1. See Lofland and Lofland (1995:6,18–19).

2. For a background in the history of field research, see Adler and Adler (1987:8–35), Burgess (1982a), Douglas (1976:39–54), Holy (1984), and Wax (1971:21–41). For additional discussion of the Chicago school, see Blumer (1984) and Faris (1967).

3. Ethnography is described in Agar (1986), Franke (1983), Hammersley and Atkinson (1983), Sanday (1983), and Spradley (1979a:3–12; 1979b:3–16).

4. See Geertz (1973, 1979) on "thick description." Also, see Denzin (1989:159–160) for additional discussion.

5. For more on ethnomethodology, see Cicourel (1964), Denzin (1970), Leiter (1980), Mehan and Wood (1975), and Turner (1974). Also, see Emerson (1981: 357–359) and Lester and Hadden (1980) on the relationship between field research and ethnomethodology. Garfinkel (1974a) discussed the origins of the term *ethnomethodology.*

6. The misunderstandings of people resulting from the disjuncture of different cultures is a common theme. The disjuncture of class cultures is also a common theme. The most famous example is George Bernard Shaw's play *Pygmalion,* which was later made into the musical *My Fair Lady.*

7. For a general discussion of field research and naturalism, see Adler and Adler (1994), Georges and Jones (1980), Holy (1984), and Pearsall (1970). For discussions of contrasting types of field research, see Clammer (1984), Gonor (1977), Holstein and Gubrium (1994), Morse (1994), Schwandt (1994), and Strauss and Corbin (1994).

8. See Georges and Jones (1980:21–42) and Lofland and Lofland (1995:11–15).

9. Johnson (1975:65–66) has discussed defocusing.

10. See Lofland (1976:13–23) and Shaffir and colleagues (1980:18–20) on feeling marginal.

11. See Adler and Adler (1987:67–78).

12. See Hammersley and Atkinson (1983:42–45) and Lofland and Lofland (1995:16–30).

13. Jewish researchers have studied Christians (Kleinman, 1980), Whites have studied African Americans (Liebow, 1967), and adult researchers have become intimate with youngsters (Fine, 1987; Fine and Glassner, 1979; Thorne and Luria, 1986). Also, see Eichler (1988), Hunt (1984), and Wax (1979) on the role of race, sex, and age in field research.

14. For more on gatekeepers and access, see Beck (1970:11–29), Bogdan and Taylor (1975:30–32), and Wax (1971:367).

15. Adapted from Gray (1980:311). See also Hicks (1984) and Schatzman and Strauss (1973:58–63).

16. Negotiation in the field is discussed in Gans (1982), Johnson (1975:58–59, 76–77), and Schatzman and Strauss (1973:22–23).

17. Entering and gaining access to field sites is discussed in Becker (1970a:31–38), Lofland and Lofland (1995: 31–41), and West (1980). Elite access is discussed by Hoffman (1980) and Spencer (1982). Also, see Hammersley and Atkinson (1983:54–76).

18. For more on roles in field settings, see Barnes (1970:241–244), Emerson (1981:364), Hammersley and Atkinson (1983:88–104), Warren and Rasmussen (1977), and Wax (1979). On dress, see Bogdan and Taylor (1975:45) and Douglas (1976).

19. See Strauss (1987:10–11).

20. See Georges and Jones (1980:105–133) and Johnson (1975:159). Clarke (1975) noted that it is not necessarily "subjectivism" to recognize this in field research.

21. See Gurevitch (1988), Hammersley and Atkinson (1983), and Schatzman and Strauss (1973:53) on "strangeness" in field research.

22. See Douglas (1976), Emerson (1981:367–368), and Johnson (1975:124–129) on the question of whether the researcher should always be patient, polite, and considerate.

23. See Wax (1971:13) for a discussion of understanding in field research.

24. For discussions of ascribed status (and, in particular, gender) in field research, see Adler and Adler (1987), Ardener (1984), Ayella (1993), Denzin (1989: 116–118), Douglas (1976), Easterday and associates (1982), Edwards (1993), Lofland and Lofland (1995:23), and Van Maanen (1982).

25. Roy (1970) argued for the "Ernie Pyle" role based on his study of union organizing in the southern United States. In this role, named after a World War II battle journalist, the researcher "goes with the troops" as a type of participant observer. Trice (1970) discussed the advantages of an outsider role. Schwartz and Schwartz (1969) gave a valuable discussion of roles in participant observation and the effects of various roles.

26. See Gans (1982), Goward (1984b), and Van Maanen (1983b:282–286).

27. See Douglas (1976:216) and Corsino (1987).

28. For discussion of "normalizing," see Gans (1982: 57–59), Georges and Jones (1980:43–164), Hammersley and Atkinson (1983:70–76), Harkens and Warren (1993), Johnson (1975), and Wax (1971). Mann (1970) discussed how to teach members about a researcher's role.

29. The acceptable incompetent or learner role is discussed in Bogdan and Taylor (1975:46), Douglas (1976), Hammersley and Atkinson (1983:92–94), and Lofland and Lofland (1995:56).

30. See Warren and Rasmussen (1977) for a discussion of cross-sex tension.

31. Also, see Adler and Adler (1987:40–42), Bogdan and Taylor (1975:35–37), Douglas (1976), and Gray (1980:321).

32. See Bogdan and Taylor (1975:50–51), Lofland and Lofland (1995:57–58), Shupe and Bromley (1980), and Wax (1971).

33. See Johnson (1975:105–108).

34. See Becker and Geer (1970), Schatzman and Strauss (1973), and Spradley (1979a, 1979b) on argot.

35. For more on ways to record and organize field data, see Bogdan and Taylor (1975:60–73), Hammersley and Atkinson (1983:144–173), and Kirk and Miller (1986: 49–59).

36. See Schatzman and Strauss (1973:69) on inference.

37. See Denzin (1989:87), Lofland and Lofland (1995: 197–201), Schatzman and Strauss (1973:34–36), and Stimson (1986) for discussions of maps in field research.

38. See Albrecht (1985), Bogdan and Taylor (1975:109), Denzin (1989:210–233), and Jackson (1987) for more on taping in field research.

39. See Burgess (1982b), Lofland and Lofland (1995: 89–98), and Spradley (1979a, 1979b) on notes for field interviews.

40. For additional discussion of data quality, see Becker (1970b), Dean and Whyte (1969), Douglas (1976:7), Kirk and Miller (1986), and McCall (1969).

41. Douglas (1976:115) argued that it is easier to "lie" with "hard numbers" than with detailed observations of natural settings, especially if the field data were collected with others and have extensive quotes presented in context.

42. Adapted from Douglas (1976:56–104).

43. See Bloor (1983) and Douglas (1976:126).

44. For more on validity in field research, see Bogdan and Taylor (1975), Briggs (1986:24), Douglas (1976), Emerson (1981:361–363), and Sanjek (1990).

45. See Lofland (1976) and Lofland and Lofland (1995:99–116) for an especially valuable discussion of focusing. Spradley (1979b:100–111) also provides helpful discussion.

46. See Denzin (1989:71–73, 86–92), Glaser and Strauss (1967), Hammersley and Atkinson (1983: 45–53), Honigmann (1982), and Weiss (1994:25–29) on sampling in field research.

47. Discussion of field interviewing can be found in Banaka (1971), Bogdan and Taylor (1975:95–124), Briggs (1986), Burgess (1982c), Denzin (1989: 103–120), Douglas (1985), Lofland and Lofland (1995:78–88), Spradley (1979a), and Whyte (1982).

48. For more on comparisons with conversations, see Briggs (1986:11), Spradley (1979a:56–68), and Weiss (1994:8).

49. See Atkinson (1988), Denzin (1989:182–209), Nash and McCurdy (1989), Smith (1994), and Tagg (1985) on life-history interviews.

50. The types of questions are adapted from Spradley (1979a, 1979b).

51. Field research informants are discussed in Dean and associates (1969), Kemp and Ellen (1984), Schatzman and Strauss (1973), Spradley (1979a:46–54), and Whyte (1982).

52. Interview contexts are discussed in Hammersley and Atkinson (1983:112–126) and in Schatzman and

Strauss (1973:83–87). Briggs (1986) argued that non-traditional populations and females communicate better in unstructured interviews than with standardized forms of expression.

53. Altheide (1980), Bogdan and Taylor (1975:75–76), Lofland and Lofland (1995:61), Maines and colleagues (1980), and Roadburg (1980) discuss leaving the field.

54. See Lofland and Lofland (1995:26, 63, 75, 168–177), Miles and Huberman (1994:288–297), and Punch (1986).

55. Covert, sensitive study is discussed in Ayella (1993), Edwards (1993), and Mitchell (1993).

56. See Barnes (1970), Becker (1969), Fichter and Kolb (1970), Goward (1984a), Lofland and Lofland (1995:204–230), Miles and Huberman (1994:298–307), and Wolcott (1994) on publishing field research results.

CHAPTER 14

EVALUATION RESEARCH

> "Evaluations are undertaken for a variety of reasons: to judge the worth of ongoing programs and to estimate the usefulness of attempts to improve them; to assess the utility of innovative programs and initiatives; to increase the effectiveness of program management and administration; and to satisfy the accountability requirements of program sponsors."
> —Rossi, P., Freeman, H., and Lipsey, M. (1999) p. 13.

INTRODUCTION

When you visit a health care provider, you will very likely be asked to step on a scale to have your weight taken, and your temperature, heart rate, and blood pressure will also commonly be recorded. Why? The answer should be obvious to most of us; namely, health care providers want to obtain basic measurements of our overall health status. They want to be able to compare, from one visit to the next, how our health has changed. This will give health care providers and patients a way to tell if different types of interventions have been successful. As social workers we are interested in the "health" of our clients, and we are professionally obligated to conduct *evaluations* to determine how well our programs, treatments, and efforts to strengthen and help others are indeed working. We would be remiss as professionals if we did not hold ourselves to high standards of assessing how our clients are doing, of selecting alternative treatment regimes if necessary, of monitoring our interventions, and of understanding the relationships between our efforts and various outcomes for clients or client systems.[1] Section 5.02 of the *NASW Code*

of Ethics (NASW Press, 1996) calls for us to evaluate the effectiveness of our interventions requiring knowledge and skills in research and an understanding of practice interventions, programs, and policies, as seen in Box 14.1.

Box 14.1 _____

NASW Code of Ethics: Section 5.02 on Evaluation and Research

(a) Social workers should monitor and evaluate policies, the implementation of programs, and practice interventions.

(b) Social workers should promote and facilitate evaluation and research to contribute to the development of knowledge.

(c) Social workers should critically examine and keep current with emerging knowledge relevant to social work and fully use evaluation and research evidence in their professional practice.

(d) Social workers engaged in evaluation or research should carefully consider possible consequences and should follow guidelines developed for the protection of evaluation and research participants. Appropriate institutional review boards should be consulted.

(e) Social workers engaged in evaluation or research should obtain voluntary and written informed consent from participants, when appropriate, without any implied or actual deprivation or penalty for refusal to participate; without undue inducement to participate; and with due regard for participants' well-being, privacy, and dignity. Informed consent should include information about the nature, extent, and duration of the participation requested and disclosure of the risks and benefits of participation in the research.

(f) When evaluation or research participants are incapable of giving informed consent, social workers should provide an appropriate explanation to the participants, obtain the participants' assent to the extent they are able, and obtain written consent from an appropriate proxy.

(g) Social workers should never design or conduct evaluation or research that does not use consent procedures, such as certain forms of naturalistic observation and archival research, unless rigorous and responsible review of the research has found it to be justified because of its prospective scientific, educational, or applied value and unless equally effective alternative procedures that do not involve waiver of consent are not feasible.

(h) Social workers should inform participants of their right to withdraw from evaluation and research at any time without penalty.

(i) Social workers should take appropriate steps to ensure that participants in evaluation and research have access to appropriate supportive services.

(j) Social workers engaged in evaluation or research should protect participants from unwarranted physical or mental distress, harm, danger, or deprivation.

(k) Social workers engaged in the evaluation of services should discuss collected information only for professional purposes and only with people professionally concerned with this information.

(l) Social workers engaged in evaluation or research should ensure the anonymity or confidentiality of participants and of the data obtained from them. Social workers should inform participants of any limits of confidentiality, the measures that will be taken to ensure confidentiality, and when any records containing research data will be destroyed.

(m) Social workers who report evaluation and research results should protect participants' confidentiality by omitting identifying information unless proper consent has been obtained authorizing disclosure.

(n) Social workers should report evaluation and research findings accurately. They should not fabricate or falsify results and should take steps to correct any errors later found in published data using standard publication methods.

(o) Social workers engaged in evaluation or research should be alert to and avoid conflicts of interest and dual relationships with participants, should inform participants when a real or potential conflict of interest arises, and should take steps to resolve the issue in a manner that makes participants' interests primary.

(p) Social workers should educate themselves, their students, and their colleagues about responsible research practices.

WHAT IS EVALUATION?

Why Evaluate an Agency?

Social workers should be interested in how effective services are for particular programs or clients. The recent movement in social work and related professions toward evidence-based practice, or EBP (Gambrill, 1999; Geyman, Deyo, and Ramsey, 2000; Katz, 2001; and Webb, 2001), for instance, focuses our attention as a profession on using the best available evidence to support our interventions (Witkin and Harrison, 2001). Funders or sponsors may wonder whether resources used for programs or projects are being well spent. Administrators may want to know the extent to which services are efficient or cost-effective and reach their specified target populations. Clients and consumers may be interested in how well their needs are being met. Evaluators may be able to identify problems as early as possible and to make comparisons within and between programs so that stakeholders will have the opportunity to celebrate their successes, help to empower clients and strengthen areas that may need resources, and replace programs that are found to be ineffective.[2]

Why Not Evaluate an Agency?

If an organization's or program's goals are unrealistic or the intervention strategies are not well-grounded in practice wisdom, theory, and/or prior evidence, then evaluation at the present time may not be wise. We need to know what data are already available and what kinds of information will be needed, and from how many clients? (Logan and Royse, 2001). Where possible, we should try to maximize the use of existing client records or agency files, as long as such records contain valid (accurate) indicators of important concepts, and the indicators are reliable (consistent over time). If crucial information about clients or programs is not available, decisions will then need to be made about how much time and energy will be needed to generate such data.

According to Tripodi (2001), if an evaluation is to be used as a means to secure only positive information about an organization's or agency's practices or only as a political device to delay making decisions, then an evaluation might better be de-

layed or put off altogether. In addition, if there are insufficient resources to provide a comprehensive evaluation, it might be better to delay. Finally, if a program is not sufficiently developed or if clients have not received sufficient services so as to be able to demonstrate program effectiveness, an evaluation may not be warranted. In other words, it may be too early in the program's cycle to tell whether or not an intervention is working as anticipated.

When Is an Agency Ready for an Evaluation?

An *evaluability assessment* is a set of procedures for determining an organization's readiness for evaluation, whether evaluation is possible and likely to offer helpful information. Issues to be considered in the assessment of evaluability include whether the organization's or program's mission, goals, and objectives are plausible, given the resources available and knowledge base of the profession. Related to this is the question of the extent to which information already exists in various agency documents, reports, or the social work literature or online sources, on the same or a closely related organization's programs or interventions. Two key questions of concern to evaluators is whether previous attempts by other social work agencies may yield promising models for replication in practice and whether previous unsuccessful attempts may inform the current evaluation (Weiss, 1972).

Whether to provide preliminary evaluation reports to staff for use in improving program operations and developing additional services is an issue that needs to be faced early in the planning process (Beck and Rossi, 1990). Preliminary results can be effectively used to identify operational problems and develop the capacity of program staff to conduct their own ongoing evaluation and monitoring activities. But this use of ongoing evaluation findings, called formative evaluation in Chapter 2 (Herman, Lyons-Morris, and Fitz-Gibbon 1987), presents a challenge to evaluators who are faced with the much more difficult task of estimating the impact of an evolving intervention. When the program itself is continuing to change, measuring impact requires ongoing measurement of the types and level of service provided (Mohr, 1992). The danger in some evaluations is that the line between program operations and assessment will be blurred. The extra effort and resources that are required for impact analysis in formative evaluations have to be measured against the potential gains to the program from ongoing improvements and the greater usefulness of the final evaluation findings.

A critical question in the assessment of evaluability is whether there are adequate resources and assets such as staff time and expertise; incidentals such as supplies, access to equipment, hardware, and software; and the capability of these systems to provide support. A final question raised during the assessment of evaluability is whether the evaluation will be achieved in a time frame that will permit findings to be useful in making program and policy decisions.[3]

Should an Agency Use Internal or External Evaluators?

Agencies need to decide whether to use their own staff (internal evaluators), outsiders (external evaluators), or both. Internal evaluators have the advantage of having more familiarity with the organization. It may be easier for them to facilitate program improvement as they are already part of the organization, they may have more credibility, they may develop an institutional memory that can aid hunting for records and remembering why decisions were made, and many of them may be better positioned to monitor and follow up recommendations because they have an investment in the agency. The disadvantages of using internal evaluators include possible lack of independence, perceived organization bias, possible ethical dilemmas because they know many of the clients and likely all of the staff, whom they may have intimate knowledge of, additional tasks may add to their usual workloads, and they may lack power (Sonnichsen, 1999). Advantages of external evaluators include the fact that they may have superior skills, the possibility of fresh ideas and new perspectives, they may have more independence and objectivity, and they may be in a position to facilitate program accountability. Disadvantages, on the other hand, include less knowledge of the organization, limited access to information and stakeholders, they may be more ex-

pensive, and they may lack the capacity to perform follow-up (Sonnichsen, 1999).

What Should Be the Scope of an Agency Evaluation?

According to Boyle, Lemaire, and Rist (1999), a critical question facing agency evaluators involves the *range* of the study. That is, should the evaluation be centralized with one authority system making all of the decisions in a hierarchical fashion? Or should each department or unit in an agency be responsible for its own decentralized evaluation? Centralization may save on resources; it may serve to unify people and processes across many different departments; and it may be able to provide a conceptual umbrella to help all departments find common definitions of success. However, centralization may increase the power of one set of people over others; it may stifle creativity in smaller subunits and increase dependence of some people on others. Decentralization, on the other hand, may increase competition between subunits; it may have greater costs; and it may serve to marginalize select groups who lack power.

Another key issue is *coverage*. That is, what kinds of activities, efforts, and alternatives should be included or excluded? Should an evaluation be global in coverage, trying to see how everything functions and fits together, or directed to a more limited set of local inputs, throughputs, and outputs in one part of a larger organizational system? A newly emerging emphasis in social work, called *translational research* (Hudgins and Allen-Meares, 2000), attempts to bring evaluators and practitioners together so that research findings can be more easily incorporated into practice.

Another issue in scope is the *time frame* to be covered. Should the evaluation look at interventions and outcomes in the near term, for some intermediate period of time, or over the long run? The important concern here is that the evaluation provides the maximal opportunity for the intervention to take effect. For example, there may be a considerable lag in time before a particular intervention is able to take hold, or have an impact. If evaluators attempt to measure program success too soon, it is possible that an intervention or program may appear ineffective simply because there has not been enough time for the treatment to work. If you have a headache, take two aspirin, and a friend asks you two minutes later if you are feeling any better, you will likely report that your head still hurts. Wait fifteen or twenty minutes, on the other hand, and you are much more likely to report feeling better.

Another concern in the scope of the evaluation is the *target population* to be included. One simple measure of the effectiveness of an intervention (Rosen and Proctor, 1978) is the extent to which all those intended to receive an intervention actually received it. A second question involves whether there might have been other persons who received part or all of an intervention who were not originally included in a target population, a spillover effect. A final question involves the *gap effectiveness* issue. That is, what is the relationship, or gap, between where clients started out before an intervention or program and what would have been an ideal position or condition for the clients after the intervention, and how much did the intervention close the gap, as shown in Figure 14.1?

Evaluators also have to engage the issue of participation by decision makers and professionals, consumers and clients, and other stakeholders. Who will be involved in planning, executing, and assessing the evaluation? According to Mayne, Divorski, and Lemaire (1999), program users will be primarily interested in the extent to which an intervention solves a problem, reduces suffering, or closes a gap. Social workers and those delivering services and interventions will likely want to know how well clients were served and how satisfied clients are. Managers will be interested in how effectively and efficiently services were delivered. Executives and CEOs will wonder whether a long-range plan is being implemented properly and whether strategic goals are being achieved. Various external audiences, such as accreditation and licensing boards, may ask about whether policies and procedures are being followed and whether they are ethical, equitable, and reasonable. The social work profession will ask about whether the intervention is working and what research is available to document program effectiveness.

Should an Evaluation Look at Existing Information or Start Fresh?

Herman, Lyons-Morris, and Fitz-Gibbon (1987), describe two fundamental ways to organize an agency evaluation. One way, deemed *summative evaluation* (which we encountered in Chapter 2), looks at existing information across a number of areas to ask how well an existent system has functioned. How effective has the program been to date? What did the program accomplish? Summative evaluation looks back from the present into the past in a retrospective fashion. It asks if the planned program actually occurred. How costly was the program? Who were the program funders, implementers, and policymakers? Summative evaluators want to know what kinds of information are available to document intervention or program outcomes. Summative evaluations are necessarily limited in scope, able to focus only on what has already happened. Summative evaluations are often carried out by external evaluators. They are likely to be quantitative in their measures and assessments, and will likely involve formal reports to stakeholders.

The other way to organize an evaluation, according to Herman, Lyons-Morris, and Fitz-Gibbon (1987), is to do so more prospectively—that is, from the present into the future—in a *formative evaluation*. This type of evaluation is focused on the question of improving existing services to become more effective or efficient, which asks, "What can be done differently?" Formative evaluations ask, "What are

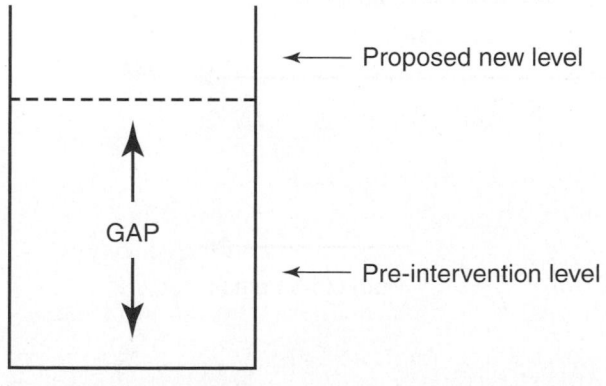

FIGURE 14.1 Gap Effectiveness

the most important aspects of a program or intervention? What problems are there? How are problems being solved?" Formative evaluators want to know what kinds of information are available to document intervention or program outcomes. Formative evaluations are more open in scope and able to focus on any of a number of planned activities. Such evaluations are often carried out by both internal and external evaluators; they are likely to involve more qualitative and developmental measures and assessments, and will likely involve more informal feedback to a range of consumers, professionals, and stakeholders than will summative evaluations.

Developing a Logic Model

A good way to think about program evaluation is with a graphic presentation of program goals and program sequencing that demonstrates the links between program efforts and expected program outcomes. A program *logic model* helps to specify relationships between program components (Unrau, 1993). Often logic models are conjointly developed between and within social agencies and funders through discussions about the mission, goals, and objectives of the agency. Figure 14.2 is a simple graphic presentation of the flow of clients through a program of local health care for the homeless in St. Louis, Missouri. Logic models move from left to right, showing the progression of program activities through boxes or picture icons representing various program locations and efforts.

Logic models provide a graphic description of the *program,* the intended *outputs,* and the intended *outcomes.* Program characteristics include the population, the resources to be used, and identification of the types and levels of service elements. Normally, outputs are immediate program products resulting from the internal operations of the program, such as the delivery of planned services. Examples

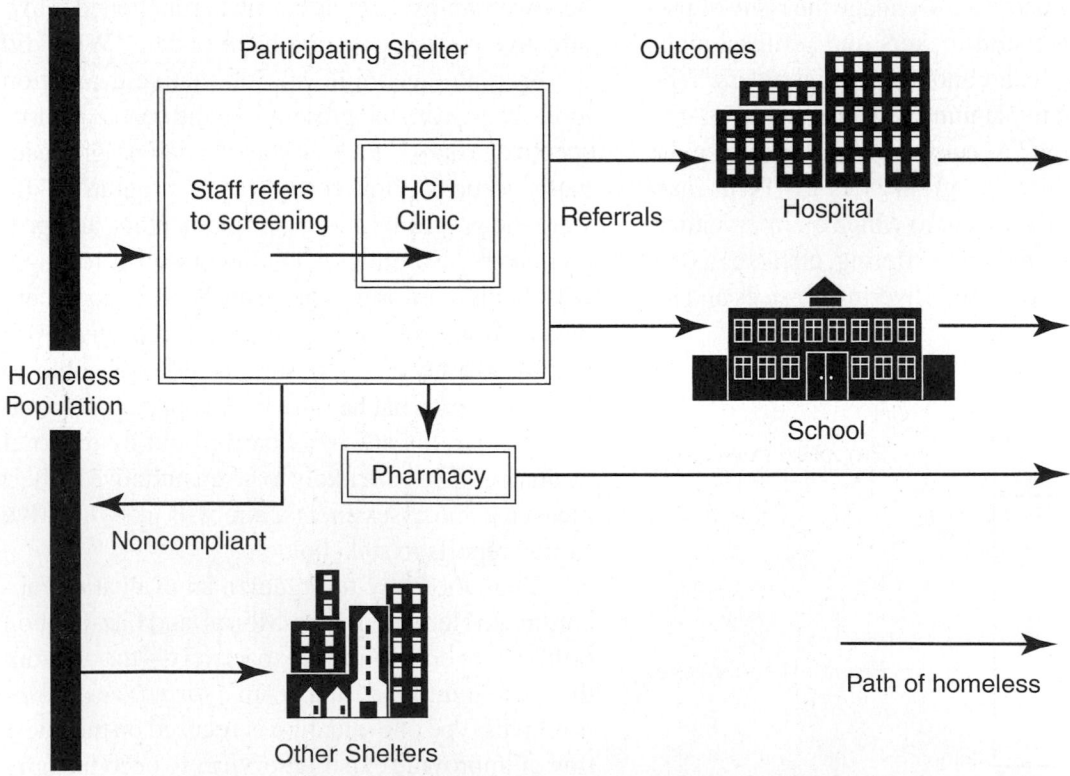

St. Louis HCH Model

FIGURE 14.2   Flow of Clients through Health Care for the Homeless Coalition in St. Louis, MO

of output indicators in the area of programs for vulnerable children and adolescents who are homeless might include the numbers of children screened, adolescents successfully placed into school programs, or children provided with needed reading glasses. These outputs are, in turn, the vehicle for producing the desired program outcomes—for example, decreases in communicable diseases and lice among children and adolescents living in shelters. Concern must be given to the expected outcomes with regard to their sequencing. For example, shorter-term outcomes are easier to track and may be easier to measure, and therefore also may be used to demonstrate program effectiveness in the near term.

The second example is a logic model that was developed by program evaluators in a not-for-profit child welfare setting for a program designed to work with young mothers and their children. The model shows inputs, intervenient activities, outputs, and three levels of outcomes: initial, intermediate, and long term. Logic models serve as a

visual method of presenting program activities. They also help *stakeholders* to understand how a set of program activities are related, how efforts are directed toward outputs, and how these in turn are intended to lead to various levels of outcomes, as noted in Figure 14.3.

MAJOR TYPES OF EVALUATION IN SOCIAL WORK

Evaluations begin by determining which clients, stakeholders, and constituencies will review the evaluation findings, what they need to know, and when. These questions go hand in hand with the type(s) of evaluation to be implemented. There are five general categories of evaluation in social work.

Impact/Outcome Evaluation

A major type of evaluation in social work is *impact evaluation,* sometimes also known as outcome

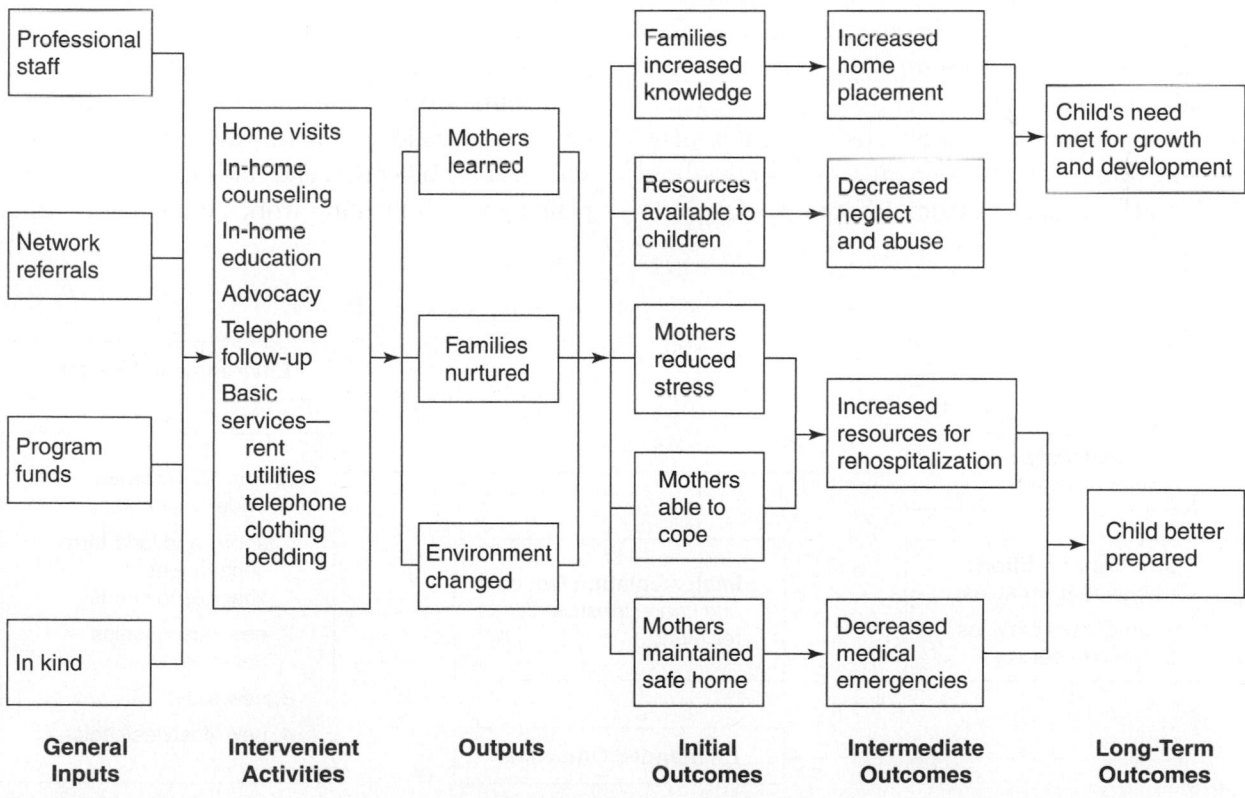

FIGURE 14.3 Logic Model for Not-for-Profit Child Welfare Program

evaluation. It focuses on the major explanatory issues concerning whether a program or set of interventions can be shown to provide intended benefits or outcomes. How well did the program have its intended effects? Who was helped, and what activities or characteristics of the program created or produced the impact? Did the program have any unintended consequences, positive or negative, short or long term? What other programs and environmental factors may have influenced the outcomes and impacts in addition to the main program efforts? Programs and interventions have to be implemented through some sort of delivery mechanism. This necessarily includes the interface between the intervention efforts or activities and the clients or program recipients, as noted in Figure 14.4.

According to Tripodi (2001), the critical question in program evaluation is, "Who does what to, for, or with whom with what expected change or changes?" (pp. 27–29). **Who** refers to the number and qualifications and personal characteristics of the social work staff who are providing services to clientele. **What** refers to the contents of staff contacts with clients, the site of contacts, and their frequency and duration. **Whom** is the intended target population, that is, a person or persons to whom the social work intervention is directed. Typically, there are likely to be eligibility requirements regarding who receives services from different social work

agencies or programs. **Expected change** can be considered in relation to four interrelated questions: What are the contents of the expected change? What is the degree of change? Where is the change expected to occur? And, if expected changes occur, how long will they last?

Impact/Outcome Evaluation Designs

Three general designs are available for impact evaluations: experimental, quasi-experimental, and nonexperimental. They all share the strategy of comparing program outcomes with some measure of what would have happened without the program. Explanatory (experimental) designs are the most powerful and produce the strongest evidence. These are not always possible, however, in which case one of the two other alternatives (quasi-experimental or nonexperimental) must be chosen.

Experimental (Explanatory) Evaluations. In Chapter 8 you learned the basics of experimental design. Experimental (explanatory) program evaluation designs provide answers to basic "why" questions (Campbell and Cook, 1963). Determining *if* something works is a relatively straightforward empirical question, ordinarily addressed with measurements of outcomes and statistical analysis. Explaining *why* something works, on the other hand,

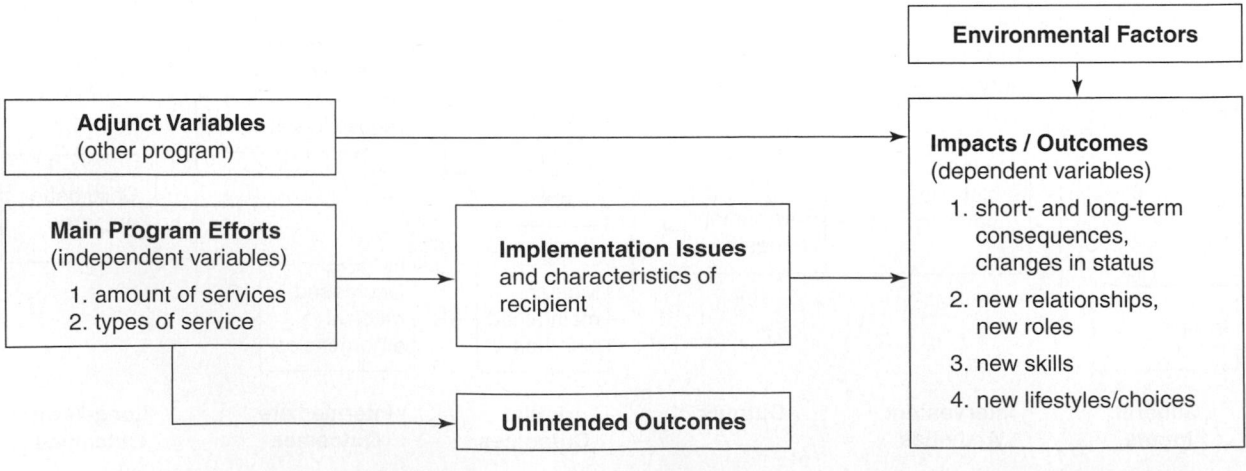

FIGURE 14.4   Basic Program Evaluation Impact/Outcome Model

uses a branch of reasoning called "erotetics." Three questions must be addressed in *erotetic reasoning* (Haack, 1980). The first question is fairly simple; it asks, "What is the *topic?*" Let us say we are interested in the question, "Why did Adam eat the apple?" Before answering fully, we need to establish the topic. That is, are we talking here about original sin? Are we talking about good versus evil? Let us say that in order to keep things simple, we are talking about eating fruits.

After establishing the topic, the second question is, "What is the *contrast class?*" That is, did Adam eat the apple (in contrast to, or instead of, what?) in order to satisfy his hunger? Did he eat the apple because it was the only thing available? Did he eat the apple because he was tired of eating oranges? The question of the contrast class asks us to specify what we are comparing things to. Let us decide that for this example the contrast class is oranges, and we conclude that Adam ate the apple instead of an orange.

The third and final question in erotetic reasoning is, "What is the *relevance relation?*" That is, what do the answers to the first two questions (the topic and the contrast class) tell us about the larger world that might be relevant now? Are there any lessons to be learned? Can we generalize from what we've discovered here to some other place or time? Did Adam's eating of the apple as a piece of fruit, in contrast to oranges, satisfy his hunger, and would we recommend others may find this result helpful? These are questions having to do with the relevance relation.

In principle, in experimental program evaluation designs the treatment group or groups are designated to receive particular services that have been chosen to achieve clearly specified outcomes. If multiple treatment groups are designated, the outcomes for the treatment groups may be compared to one another (the contrast class) to estimate the relative impact of the different services or the impact relative to a control group. A control group (contrast class) receives either the old intervention or treatment, or perhaps no services at all. The treatment group outcomes are compared to control group outcomes to estimate impact. If random assignment and random division are used, then evaluators as-sume chance alone determines who receives the program services. The two groups can be assumed to be similar on all characteristics that might affect the outcome measures other than the program itself. In principle, any differences between treatment and control (contrast) groups should be attributed to the effectiveness of the program.

Experimental program evaluation designs, while often considered to be the most powerful types of evaluation design in the human services, are nonetheless difficult to implement in human service settings. Experiments require that clients or groups of clients, such as families residing in a shelter for homeless persons or patients in a state hospital program, be assigned at random to one or more groups prior to the introduction of the intervention. But this can be difficult to do in human services settings due to the need for careful delivery of services and the assumption of a considerable amount of self-determination for clients or patients. How can we designate some clients to receive treatment A and others treatment B, when much of our effort to help people focuses on clients participating in these decisions? How can we randomly assign clients to different programs when ordinarily we don't have that much control in an agency or community setting? That is, as social workers we are not likely to be in a position to decide between intervention A or B as a matter of experimental manipulation. Rather, we will have to make our treatment decisions based on the best interests of the clients.

One design variation is based on a random selection of time periods during which services are provided. For example, new services may be offered on randomly chosen weeks or days. A version of this approach is to use "day on/day off" assignment procedures. Although not random, this approach approximates random assignment if client characteristics do not vary systematically from day to day. It has the major advantage that program staff often find it easier to implement, rather than making decisions on program entry by the flip of a coin on a case-by-case basis. A second design variation is a staggered start approach. In this case some members of the target group are randomly selected to receive services with the understanding that the remainder will receive services at a later time (in the case of families in shelters or persons in the hospital, the next week or month).

A second consideration is whether random assignment is ethical and acceptable to the profession. The *NASW Code of Ethics* resists treating similar clients on the basis of a coin flip, and it may view random assignment as exploiting vulnerable clients. Carefully designed procedures for randomization may be able to overcome such resistance. One strategy is random selection of those who receive services from a list of those who meet eligibility requirements when resources are not available to serve everyone who is eligible. One of the authors was involved in an Aid to Victims of Crime Project in which services were made available to persons who were victimized by crimes against person or property. Persons were eligible for services within a few days after being victimized. Counseling and other supportive services were offered. Those on the waiting list who had not yet received services were considered as a control group. This form of drawing lots, loosely based on a "first come, first served" principle, may be seen as fair in many situations. Providing services for some clients at a later time (the next month or as soon as possible) may satisfy some concerns about fairness and be consistent with available program resources. The *NASW Code of Ethics* recommends a formal review of the research design by a human subjects review team who follow guidelines developed to protect research participants.

Another potential concern is that information for treatment and control group members may not make a good contrast. Caseworkers readily collect data and provide contact information for treatment group members because they have continuing contacts with clients. Collecting comparable data and contact information on control group members who may not be receiving services may be problematic as such clients may be less likely to be available (Royse and Thyer, 1996). Another concern is the constancy of the program over time. That is, it may be difficult to determine what level or type of interventions produced the measured improvements if too much time has passed. One strategy is for social workers to keep track of key changes in their program as part of routine operating procedures and

use this information to define "types of program" variations in the experience of different participants for the impact/outcome analysis.[4]

Example of an Experimental Impact/Outcome Evaluation: Medication Monitoring Evaluation Project.   The Medication Compliance Monitoring Evaluation Project of the Veterans Administration (VA) was an eighteen-month-long program for the purpose of assessing whether clients who carried a small electronic medication dispensing device would have improved health outcomes compared to those who received their medicine in traditional plastic containers. Three hundred veterans who attended an outpatient hypertension clinic in an urban hospital were randomly selected and asked to volunteer for the eighteen-month study. After a six-month baseline period in which blood pressure (the dependent variable) and other questions about health care behavior were measured, patients were divided into three groups: (1) those in the control group who were to continue to receive their hypertension medication in traditional plastic pill bottles, (2) those who received their medication in an electronic medication dispensing device (about the size of a pocket calculator) along with a printout that was put into their medical chart for examination by VA physicians and nurses, and (3) a second experimental group who received their medication in an electronic medication dispenser but did not receive a printout (Eisen, Hanpeter, and Kreuger, 1983). The purpose for the second experimental group was to ascertain the importance of the printout. That is, if carrying the electronic medication monitor throughout their daily activities was sufficient to help clients remember to take their medication on time, and if the additional information gleaned from the printout (that showed how many pills were removed at what time over the last month) was not needed, then the impact of the program intervention would be considerably less expensive than it would be if the printout were necessary. Evaluators must be very careful to determine exactly what the contrast class is to consist of, as noted in Figure 14.5.

Quasi-Experimental Evaluation Designs.   As with experiments, quasi-experimental designs com-

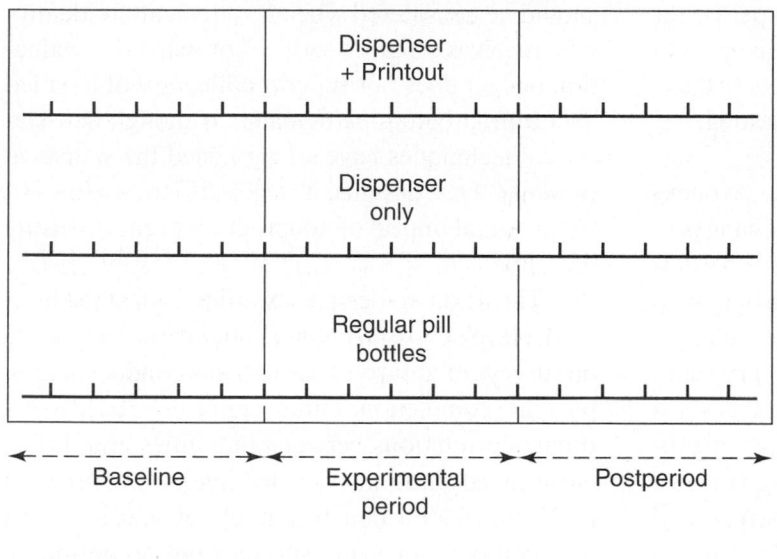

VA Medication Monitor Study
Program Evaluation Experiment

Dispenser
+ Printout

Dispenser
only

Regular pill
bottles

Baseline   Experimental   Postperiod
period

⊥ Monthly measures of blood pressure

FIGURE 14.5   Example of an Experimental Impact/Outcome
Evaluation

pare outcomes from program participants or those receiving an intervention to outcomes for comparison groups that do not receive program or intervenient services. The critical difference between experimental and nonexperimental designs is that the decision regarding who receives the intervention or treatment is not random. When random assignment is not possible, comparison groups should be made up of members of the target population who are as similar as possible to program participants on factors that could affect the selected outcomes to be observed. More complex multivariate statistical techniques are then used to control for remaining differences between the groups.

Usually, evaluators will use existing population groups for comparison purposes, such as those who live in a similar area, or those who are receiving the same service from a different but similar agency, or those who received the same services in the previous time period. Sometimes evaluators do not have a comparison group of people, who are different from the original target population. In such cases evaluators have to be creative in thinking of a group that can reasonably be compared. For example, researchers have used those clients on a waiting list as a comparison group to be compared to those who are already enrolled in a working treatment group.

Quasi-experimental designs vary in the number and timing of the collection of data on program outcome measures. The selection of the number and timing of measurements is based on an assessment of the potential threats posed by competing hypotheses that cannot be ruled out by the comparison methodology. In many situations the strongest designs are those that collect preprogram measures of outcomes and risk factors and use these in the analysis to focus on within-individual changes that occur during the program period. These variables are also used to identify groups of participants who benefit most from the services. One design variation involves more measurement points (in addition to simple before and after) to measure trends more precisely. Another variation is useful when preprogram data collection (such as administering a test on knowledge or attitudes) might "teach" recipients about the questions to be asked after the program to measure change, and thus distort the measurement of program impact. This variation involves limiting data collection to the end of the program period for some groups, allowing their postprogram answers to be compared with the postprogram answers of those who also participated in the preprogram testing.

Nonexperimental Evaluation Designs.   Nonexperimental impact evaluations examine changes in levels of risk or outcomes among program participants, or groups including program participants, but do not include comparison groups of other individuals or groups not exposed to the program. The four primary types of nonexperimental designs include (1) before-and-after comparisons of program participants; (2) time-series designs based on repeated measures of outcomes before and after the program for groups that include program participants; (3) panel studies based on repeated measurement of outcomes on the same group of participants; and (4) postprogram comparisons among groups of participants.

The first two designs are based on analysis of aggregate data. In *before-and-after comparisons,* outcomes for groups of participants (program groups that enter the program at a specific time and progress through it over the same time frame) are measured before and after an intervention, and an assessment of impact is inferred from the differences. This simple design is often used to assess whether knowledge, attitudes, or behavior of the group changed after exposure to the program. A *time-series design* is an extension of the before-and-after design that uses multiple measures of the outcome variables before an intervention begins and continues to take multiple measures after intervention is in place. If a change in the trend (direction or level) in the outcome occurs at, or shortly after, the time of the intervention, the significance of the observed change is tested statistically. Time-series measures may be based on larger groups or units that include, but are not restricted to, program participants. For example, crime rates for neighborhoods in which most or all youth participate in a delinquency prevention program might be used to assess reductions in illegal activity. Evaluation of a series of dropout-prevention activities offered across the school year could ex-

amine the percentages of entering classes that graduate over a period of years. Time-series designs should be considered when it is difficult to identify who receives program services or when the evaluation budget does not support collection of detailed data from program participants. Although new statistical techniques have strengthened the statistical power of these designs, it is still difficult to rule out the potential impact of nonprogram events by using this approach.

The next two designs examine data at the individual level. *Cross-sectional comparisons* are based on surveys of groups of participants conducted after program completion. This design can be used to estimate correlations between outcomes and differences in the duration, type, and intensity of services received, yielding conclusions about plausible links between outcomes and services but no definitive conclusions about what caused what. *Panel designs* use repeated measures of the outcome variables for each individual. In this design, outcomes are measured for the same group of program participants, often starting at the time they enter the program and continuing at intervals over time. For example, the evaluation of Health Planning and Promotion: Life Planning Education used pre–post data from participants to measure gains in understanding the best combinations of contraceptive methods and the consequences of early childbearing. This design allows the characteristics of individual participants to be used in the analysis to identify different patterns of change associated with individual characteristics of participants and to control for other events to which they were exposed.

When individual program records are not available, aggregate statistics may be obtained from the program or from other community agencies with information on the outcomes among groups of participants. For example, crime rates, average promotion rates, and rates of births to teen mothers can be collected from existing records. The primary problem encountered in using such statistics for assessing impacts is that they may not be available for the specific population or geographic area targeted by the program. Often these routinely collected statistics are based on the general population or geographic areas served by the agency (e.g., the police precinct or the clinic catchment area). The rates of negative outcomes for the entire set of cases included may well differ from rates for the targeted group of vulnerable children and youth; this risk is greater for larger rather than smaller statistical areas.

A more expensive form of data collection for nonexperimental evaluations is a survey of participants some time after the end of the program. These surveys can provide much-needed information on longer-term outcomes such as rates of employment or earnings or high school graduation. As in any survey research, the quality of the results is determined by response rate rather than overall sample size, and by careful attention to the validity and reliability of the questionnaire items.

Example of a Nonexperimental Impact/Outcome Evaluation: The Evaluation of Shelter-Based Services for Families Who Are Homeless.   One of the first tasks facing social work program evaluators is the definition of what to count as success in outcome. One strategy is to determine what an ideal outcome would be, and then work backward in thinking about what is actually achieved. If the topic is homelessness, the logical place to look is in the area of what it means to have a home, what the risks might be in losing a place of residence, and what the consequences are. Box 14.2 presents the basic

functions of a home and the risks and consequences of losing the place of residence.

A second concern in program evaluation is to determine the reasons why current services are offered. That is, what is the purpose of the existing set of programs or services in terms of the stated rationale for offering services? What is supposed to happen as a result of the delivery of a particular set of interventions? The rationale for shelter-based services (Stretch and Kreuger, 1993) included

1. Shelter-based nightly quarters are preferable to sleeping in harsh conditions under bridges or in cardboard houses.
2. Shelters provide emergency living quarters on a temporary substitute basis for low-income, often minority, families who cannot afford other living arrangements and who suffer from random and unpredictable natural events such as fires and disasters or from largely unpredictable political or economic events such as foreclosures, evictions, and condemnations.
3. Shelters provide short-term solutions to immediate survival needs for food, clothing, and bedding for people who have lost their place of residence.
4. Shelters offer some protection for potential victims of crimes of street violence such as rape or

---

Box 14.2 _____

The Meaning of a Home, Risks and Consequences of Losing Their Place of Residence*

FUNCTIONS OF HOME	RISKS DUE TO LOSS	CONSEQUENCES
Physical shelter	Hydration/Sustenance	Exposure, heat stroke
Place for belongings	Security	Need to carry possessions, health risks
Recovery	Comfort, healing	Fatigue, poor judgment
Haven/Protection	Privacy	Crimes against person/property
Primary relationships	Affection, stability	Stress, separation anxiety
Autonomy	Control over environment	Anxiety, angst, depression
Privacy	Control of personal space	Dehumanization, prejudice/discrimination
Growth/Development	Family interaction	Delayed development, separation anxiety
Recreation	Physical well-being	Fatigue, sleep disorders
Dignity	Self-esteem	Difficulty making decisions, poor judgment

*Sources: Huttman (1993) and Jahiel (1992).

drive-by shooting and other environmental trauma.

5. Shelters offer security as stopping-off havens for low-income persons passing through and transients who would otherwise be sleeping on park benches.

6. Shelters provide safe destinations for abused women and abused or neglected adolescents who are contemplating seeking help.

7. Shelters sometimes offer a mechanism for getting better housing through placements, subsidies, and vouchers.

8. Shelters offer a minimal last line of defense against the harsh economic and political reality of mean-spirited politicians whose economic policies cause gentrification and the subsequent loss of low-income housing, as well as the various economies of greed.

9. Shelters provide collateral support for law enforcement officers who are able to drop off intoxicated persons who need a place to sleep it off rather than using inappropriate hospital or jail space.

10. Shelters offer a last line of defense for persons of color who have been systematically discriminated against in the search for apartment rentals, in mortgage and home repair loans, and through redlining by banks.

The Setting. This 54-bed shelter utilized a 60-day program aimed at preventing, ameliorating, and correcting the undesirable effects of displacement on homeless families through an intensive case-management approach. For a five-year period the authors tracked services provided and selected outcomes on 875 families who were homeless. One data set, existing agency records, provided information on services rendered, length of stay, and feedback from 30-,60-, and 90-day follow-up tracking. A second set of data needed to be constructed: namely, what were the long-term outcomes associated with these families up to five years after leaving the shelter? For this second data set a search would be needed.

Target Population and Sample. Out of 875 total families served during the period of interest, 450 families who had resided at the shelter were selected

as eligible members of the initial target population to be located and interviewed. The population deemed eligible for the evaluation was narrowed to the study population of 450 cases because these families had received housing placements considered by staff to be relatively permanent (Section 8, other public housing, rented or purchased housing, and other permanent arrangements). To this extent the 450 out of the 875 total families were considered as the likely best-served families. Searches through state databases, city and county housing offices, and telephone directories produced a pool of 256 out of 450 families in the general metropolitan area deemed eligible for contact for interviewing. Of these 256 families, 201 (78.5%) were extensively interviewed at their place of current residence.

These search procedures and the contact and interview process, in addition to selecting from among likely best-served formerly homeless families, resulted in some systematic biases in the final data set of 201 cases. The final 201 interviewed families were by necessity selected by nonprobability (availability) sampling procedures; thus, generalizations to the entire 450 best-served formerly homeless families in the target population, and inferences beyond that to the 875 total served, were guarded.

Findings. Data from the 201 field interviews showed an average time since leaving the shelter of 1294 days (median 1331 days), or about 3.5 years. Approximately 37 percent (76) reported that they were living in permanent residences, which the shelter had located for them upon termination of shelter residence. Approximately one-third (37%) of those interviewed reported living in only one residence since staying at the shelter.

1. **Where were formerly homeless families, who once received intensive shelter-based services, living up to 5 years later?**
   Data from a study of 201 formerly homeless families who had once resided in an intensively case-managed family shelter showed that approximately 64 percent (129) of the former shelter families resided in federally subsidized (Section 8) housing; 17 percent (35) were found in private rental or purchased units; 2 percent

(4) were found in homeless shelters in the city; and the remainder were located in other public-assistance settings.

2. **How many recipients of intensive shelter-based services experienced additional homeless episodes since leaving the shelter?**

   In these data about one-sixth (33/201) of former shelter residents suffered from additional homeless episodes.

3. **Did the families who rerooted and maintained stable residences receive more shelter-based services than those who become homeless again?**

   No, there was no empirical relationship between amount of shelter-based service and additional homeless episodes ($t = .859$, $df = 187$, $p = .39$).

4. **Did amount of time elapsed since receiving shelter-based services have any impact on whether families became homeless again?**

   Yes, families who had become homeless again had received services an average of 3.5 years earlier, compared to those who had not been homeless again, who averaged 1.5 years since services ($t = 4.23$, $df = 199$, $p = .004$).

5. **Did any one factor distinguish those who became homeless again from those who did not?**

   Yes, data show that those who received a Federal Housing Subsidy (Section 8 certificate) housing placement at termination from the shelter were much less likely to become homeless again (6%), compared to those families who did not receive a Section 8 certificate (33%), as shown in Figure 14.6.

6. **What other factors were empirically related to successful rerooting by formerly homeless families?**

   Family supports included amount of education, employment status, participation in job training, and amounts of income and AFDC/Food Stamps. These were all unrelated to the likelihood of additional homeless episodes. Poor families who were residentially stable, however, were much less likely to ever be homeless again, compared to those who experienced multiple residential episodes (chi-square 11.45, $df = 1$, $p < .001$).

7. **If residential instability was highly correlated with homelessness, did housing subsidies have any impact on residential stability?**

   Yes, those receiving Federal Housing Subsidy placements were much less likely to have ever moved than those not receiving such placements (chi-square 10.94, $df = 1$, $p < .001$). In addition, those receiving subsidies moved less often than those who did not receive such a placement ($t = 4.98$, $df = 199$, $p < .001$).

This nonexperimental impact evaluation project was one of the early attempts to look at the long-term impacts of shelter-based services on homeless families (Kreuger and Stretch, 1994). The study found that while many formerly homeless families had successfully rerooted, those who had become homeless again suffered from general residential instability that was empirically related to lack of a housing subsidy, as noted in Figure 14.7.

Contrary to initial expectations, the amount of overall shelter-based services was unrelated to

FIGURE 14.6   Correlation of Factors Tested against Key Variable of Successful Placement

	SUCCESSFUL PLACEMENT	NUMBER OF MOVES	PRIOR HOMELESS	AMOUNT OF SERVICE	SUBSIDY RECEIVED?
Number of Moves	.453*				
Prior Homeless	.054	−.093			
Amount of Service	−.072	−.161	.045		
Subsidy Received?	−.363*	−.333*	−.074	.212	
Time Since Shelter Stay	.202	.344*	.061	−.434	−.499

* = significant at .05 level

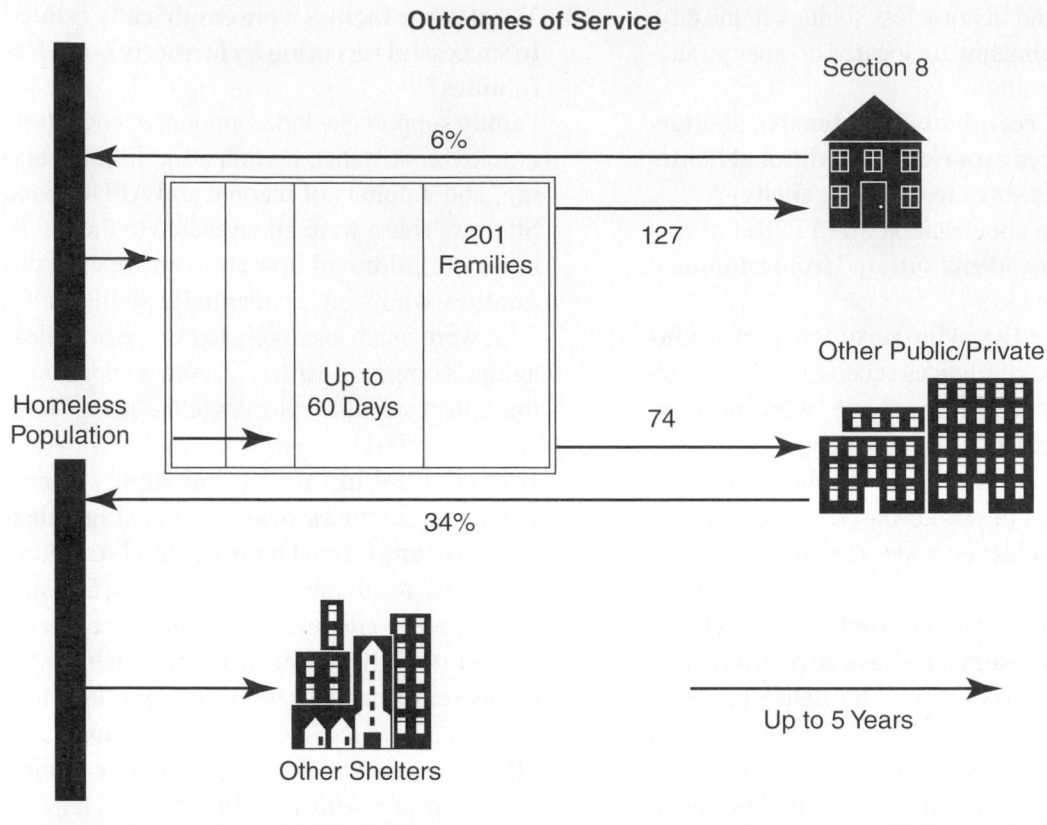

FIGURE 14.7   Logic Model for Shelter-Based Services for Homeless Families

rerooting, but type of housing placement was crucial (specifically, Section 8 subsidies) in preventing additional homelessness. Finally, it was found that shelter-based services apparently work in the short run (very few families immediately became homeless again), but the impacts of service were unlikely to last long term (Fogel 1997). These data pointed to the need for housing supports both to reroot those once homeless and to prevent additional homeless episodes (Schmitz, Wagner and Menke, 2001). These data did not empirically support the use of intensive shelter services, however, as a way to prevent additional homeless episodes.

Monitoring Program Performance

Performance monitoring provides feedback on how a program or series of interventions is operating and to what extent intended objectives are being attained. Results may be utilized by providers, policymakers, and stakeholders to measure the success of the intervention or program performance. Indicators can also be developed to monitor program quality by collecting data on client satisfaction or caseworker perceptions to assess program efficiency, effectiveness, and the relationship between the resources and output. According to Royse and Thyer (1996), the first step in monitoring program performance is deciding what to count, be it interventions, clients served, days of treatment, number of telephone calls—the list goes on and on. But Royse and Thyer also caution that counting something is not the same as ensuring quality of program performance.

Performance monitoring can provide social agency managers and social workers with regular feedback that will allow them to identify problems in program or intervention delivery, take action as needed, and subsequently determine whether improvements were made. Performance monitoring can move social workers and managers, clients and program recipients, and other stakeholders to take action to maintain a successful program, make modifications, or totally scrap an unworkable or out-of-date program.

Performance monitoring may be utilized by social workers to provide information on how a system or program is operating; the extent to which program objectives are being attained (e.g., numbers of homeless families served in comparison to target goals; number of families who obtained jobs after leaving welfare rolls); and recognition of possible failures to attain program outputs. Performance indicators can also be developed to monitor intervention quality by collecting data on the conditions of those served, and to assess program effectiveness by assessing the relationship between the resources used (program inputs) and the output and outcome indicators.

If conducted frequently enough and in a timely way, performance monitoring can provide human services managers with regular feedback that will allow them to identify problems, take timely action, and subsequently assess whether their actions have led to the improvements in services or interventions sought. Performance measures can also stimulate communication about program goals, progress, obstacles, and results among social workers and managers, the public, and other stakeholders. They focus attention on the specific outcomes desired and better ways to achieve them, and can promote credibility by highlighting the accomplishments and value of the interventions and programs.

In selecting performance indicators, the evaluators and service providers need to consider the relevance of potential measures to the mission, goals, and objectives of the local program or intervention. Do the various indicators measure intervention strategies/activities identified in mission statements? Do outcomes cover objectives identified in mission statements? Do indicators capture the priorities at different levels of intervention?

Another question is whether the performance measures cover inputs, outputs, and service quality as well as outcomes, and whether they include issues important to stakeholders and clients. Does the agency or program control the outputs or outcomes measured by the indicator? If the program has only limited influence over the outputs or outcomes being measured, the indicator may not fairly reflect program performance. Do the proposed indicators adequately measure the range of outcomes the intervention or program hopes to bring about? Are the measures valid (measure what they are intended to measure) and reliable (consistent over time)? Generally speaking, measures known to be reliable may or may not be valid. For example, a bathroom scale may consistently (reliably) report the same weight time after time, but not an accurate weight (it may "reliably" show you weighing five pounds too heavy). On the other hand, measures known to be valid must be at least as much reliable. A scale that accurately measures your weight will be very likely to do so one minute later or soon thereafter (hence, to "validly" report your weight, the scale must also do so consistently, i.e., reliably).

Finally, we need to ask about how much energy and resources are required to generate each measure. Should a particularly costly measure be retained because it is perceived as critically important? A set of performance indicators should be straightforward and relate to priority outcomes. Too many indicators will slow down the data collection and analysis process and make it less likely that social work managers will understand and use the collected information.

As noted in the example, most performance monitoring data come from records maintained by social workers. Today, microcomputers are used to collect and analyze these records, thus saving time and energy. An external consultant may be required for a well-designed assessment of previous clients; alternatively, a self-administered exit questionnaire can be given to clients at the end of services and during follow-up periods.

Example of An Evaluation Using Performance Monitoring: A Performance Evaluation of the CARE Program.   CARE (Career Awareness Related Experience) was a job-readiness program aimed at providing high-risk youth with meaningful work experience, job-skill training, and a career orientation over the summer months. The program was designed to combine the development of job skills and career interests among socially, economically, and academically disadvantaged youth with additional incentives to receive educational credit, and perhaps stay in school, through an educational program component. Funding for the CARE program was provided by local city government, with supporting services from public schools, the Chamber of Commerce, and others. Funders for the program wanted to know (1) To what extent were selected CARE program goals being achieved?; (2) How available, accessible, acceptable, and adequate were existing CARE program components in terms of two primary data sources, (a) trainees and (b) employers?; and (3) What changes, additions, or deletions (if any) in the existing CARE program components were warranted by the *performance evaluation?*

Discussions in initial meetings with planners and administrators from funders and city officials, CARE program directors, and staff—that included a review of written program descriptions, goal statements, prior assessments, and existing trainee and employer data formats from the CARE program—led to an agreement to review the following four sources of performance evaluation data: (a) existing records on all cases operating during the current program cycle, (b) confidential interviews with a limited random sample of trainees and their supervisors, (c) confidential discussions with CARE management and staff, and (d) observations from an external evaluator.

The Setting. The city Parks and Recreation Department administered the CARE program through its Neighborhood Services Division with program facilities located in what was considered to be a high-program-impact section of the city. An oversight advisory board, consisting of professionals from both public and private sectors, provided additional feedback and oversight.

Applications to the CARE program were accepted during the late winter and early spring of each school year. An intensive screening process limited applicants to those deemed by CARE program staff to be most likely to receive maximal benefit from various CARE program components.

In addition to summer employment and career experience, trainees are also required to attend a one-day program orientation workshop and a six-day

educational/training component. The component introduces disadvantaged, at-risk trainees to job-skill training, career exploration, and life-planning instruction. The curriculum was developed and designed by an educational coordinator who was certified by a local public school district. In addition, the curriculum was reviewed and approved by authorities from the state Department of Education and specialists from the local public school system.

At the conclusion of the program cycle a banquet provided closure for the participants to the CARE program for the summer. Annual in-house program evaluation data were collected from employers and trainees and distributed by the CARE program director to relevant oversight and funding audiences.

Program funders and oversight groups wanted to evaluate performance in a summative end-of-program-year performance evaluation that would focus on the relationships between selected programmatic inputs or efforts and selected aspects of the program. One disadvantage of such procedures was the restricted scope of conclusions that could be drawn. The primary advantage of such short-term outside evaluations, on the other hand, is their relatively low cost and potential for objectively answering a few key performance questions about current program operation.

The type of evaluation conducted was a one-shot, after-only review of the existing program inputs and outcomes. In cases such as this, where evaluation takes place toward the completion of a program cycle, data collection procedures tend to focus on existing records and self-report data from those who deliver program services and those who receive them.

Target Population and Sample. Due to a limited time available for contacting trainees and their supervisors, arranging for appointments, and scheduling interviews, the study focused on analysis of data on 20 trainees and their corresponding supervisors. The final data set was to consist of 40 interviews in all.

An initial population of 131 CARE cases was examined with the aim of restricting the sample selected for study to those trainees who fully participated in the CARE program through one program cycle. After removing records of trainees who resigned from the program (15), those who were dropped due to rule violations (8), and those who had signed up but did not actually begin the program (10), a final sampling frame of 98 names was utilized. Thus, the final sample study was to entail examination of slightly over 20 percent (20/98) of the trainees active during that period.

The sample selection procedures involved a simple random sample without replacement; thus, the probability for selection of any similarly randomly selected set of 20 cases was approximately .2014. This type of sample selection procedure tends to minimize bias in the data collection stages and ensures that inferences to the remaining 78 cases who were not selected can be made within known margins of error.

Examination of existing CARE office records and discussions with CARE management and staff produced three data sets. First, demographic and basic programmatic information were available from CARE office files on all 98 continuing cases. Second, after consultation with CARE program managers, two field instruments, to be employed in face-to-face interviews, were constructed for the field interview phase. The data-collection instrument for the trainees queried recipients about amount of participation in the CARE program, types of skills learned, transportation and access to the job site, self-assessment of a number of indicators of individual effort, assessments of the job supervisor and Job Coach, and educational components. Additional indicators of both self-reported work habits and judgments about various aspects of the CARE program were also elicited. Third, a data-collection instrument for job supervisors was designed. It paralleled the trainee interview format, asking many of the same questions from the point of view of job supervisors. In addition, supervisors were asked to rate the trainees on a number of attitude and performance scales.

By combining data from parallel interview questions of 20 trainees with 20 supervisors, a final data set of 40 observations were to be available for the analysis. Two trained field interviewers were hired to conduct the field study, after pretesting ear-

lier versions of the interview instruments on one trainee and one supervisor. An interview notification letter, mailed to trainees and supervisors by the CARE director, described the purposes of the study and requested participation from all those randomly selected.

Excluded from consideration as relevant evaluation sources were other data not included in the initial summary review proposal. For example, the evaluation team did not meet with CARE board members, policymakers and planners from the Department of Parks and Recreation, its Neighborhood Services Division, nor others who may have offered additional insights on this summary review evaluation project. The evaluator's decision to exclude additional data sources was based on both the limited time frame proposed for the study and the expressed interest in an outside review driven by data generated by an external evaluator.

Findings. Demographic data examined showed that approximately 40 percent (40) of the trainees had Juvenile Offender status before entering the CARE program. A little less than half, 49 percent of the trainees (48), were eligible for high school credit, and females (51) outnumbered males (47) by about 4 percent. Trainees ranged in age from 14 through 18, with a mean age of 15.65 years. Approximately one-fifth (20) of the trainees were participating in the CARE program for the second time, and the remaining 80 percent (78) were first-time trainees. About 55 percent of the trainees were African American (54), 39 percent were Caucasian (39), and the remainder (5) were Asian American, Hispanic or Latino American, and "Other" in racial background.

Trainees reported a wide variety of more specific job tasks, which included cleaning, sweeping, lawn mowing, boxing and loading/unloading, stock work, filing and billing, working with food setup, telephone receptionist work, and interpersonal work with children, including physical supervision. Also noted were teaching and playground supervision, word processing, data entry and retrieval, carpentry, photocopying, and related office activity.

Asked to grade their supervisors on the same performance scales as applied to themselves, trainees tended to give their supervisors highest grades for

Treating Trainees With Respect, and next highest for Helping Trainees Learn About Work in General. Lower grades were given for Teaching Specific Job Skills and for Giving Instructions. Overall grades for the supervisors as assigned by the trainees included 58 percent grade of A, 23 percent grade of B, 11 percent C, and 6 percent a grade of D. Approximately 70 percent of the trainees rated their job placement as Very Satisfactory, 17 percent rated their placement in the Middle, and 6 percent rated it as Unsatisfactory. Asked if they would rather have had a different job, 64 percent reported being satisfied with the job they had, and the remaining 36 percent mentioned jobs they would rather have had. About 40 percent said they attended special group sessions as part of their job placement, and of those who attended, trainees were evenly split as to the helpfulness of these group meetings.

Overall, the trainees reported experiencing a wide variety of types of employment with positions that varied in level of physical, interpersonal, and technical skill required. Trainees had little difficulty gaining access to their work site and experienced few direct transportation costs. They worked an average of 30 hours per week (6.7 hours per day), and reported earning an average of $594 per week. Most of the trainees reported saving at least some portion of their summer wages.

Nearly one-half of the trainees indicated that they would be looking for a part-time job after the CARE program ended, and most felt that they were ready to succeed on a job. Overall, trainees felt that the CARE job experience helped to keep them out of trouble, they were satisfied with their supervisors, and they said they would recommend the program to a friend.

The supervisors represented a wide variety of public and private job placements and described an equally varied set of available job skills. Almost all of the supervisors rated the trainees as increasing in skills over the summer employment period. Supervisors felt trainees had little trouble getting to work, were late or missed work for what were seen for the most part as acceptable reasons, and felt that the few unexcused absences were resolved by the Job Coaches. Those interviewed gave high marks to the trainees for ability to work with others and some-

what lower grades for working independently, dealing with criticism, and following instructions. Supervisors gave themselves high marks for treating the trainees with respect and teaching them about work in general, while somewhat lower grades were assigned for giving constructive criticism and teaching specific job skills. Supervisors rated the Job Coaches as easy to contact, quite helpful both routinely and on an as-needed basis, and able to resolve most of the problems they were confronted with. Asked about CARE personnel in general, supervisors felt they had good access, were satisfied with the program operation, and would not recommend changes in personnel.

Overall, the supervisors were satisfied with their assigned trainees. Some expressed an interest in working with trainees who had higher skills to begin with and some felt their trainees were quite young or otherwise lacking in maturity. Almost all of the supervisors felt that the CARE program helped trainees stay out of trouble. In addition, trainees received positive ratings for Manners/politeness, Attitude on the job, Grooming/self-care, and Maturity. They received more average ratings for Concentration and Job readiness, while Verbal communication and Reading/literacy received relatively lower ratings. Approximately 80 percent of the supervisors said they would recommend hiring their trainee should a position become available, and 24 percent said they thought their organization or business would help pay wages next summer.

An examination of the 131 adolescents who initially applied to the CARE program, with special emphasis on those who did not remain with the program to completion, provides some insight on the overall condition of the target population at the beginning of the program year. Of the 15 adolescents who resigned from the program, several dropped out because of learning disabilities, some changed residences due to joint custody decisions, some were required by the Court to withdraw, some had health problems, and a few had parents who demanded withdrawal from the program. Of those 8 applicants who were dismissed from the CARE program, probation violations, excessive unexcused absences, and employer terminations accounted for this set. Finally, of those 10 applicants who had signed up but failed to complete the program, several were detained for acting-out behavior during the training sessions, or failed to show up altogether.

Process Evaluations

Process evaluations answer questions about how the program operates and document the procedures and activities undertaken in service delivery. Such evaluations help identify problems faced in delivering services, and strategies for overcoming these problems. They are useful to practitioners and service providers in replicating or adapting program strategies.

The key element in process evaluation is a systematic, focused plan for collecting data to (1) determine whether the program model is being implemented as specified and, if not, how operations differ from those initially planned; (2) identify unintended consequences and unanticipated outcomes; and (3) understand how the program operates from the perspectives of various stakeholders.

Case Studies.   A *case study* involves the detailed analysis of selected program sites or clients to determine how the interventions or programs are operating, what obstacles to implementation have been experienced, what strategies, if any, have been the most successful in overcoming obstacles, and what capabilities and resources are still needed. Case studies may be useful in providing guidance to stakeholders, funders, and program planners to help them identify key program elements and to generate hypotheses about program impact that can be further investigated. Case studies are also utilized to compare rival hypotheses concerning differences in the outcome of services.

Clients or sites chosen for case studies should represent wide variation in settings, program models, and clients. Identification of sample members within sites, interview topics, and key data elements begins with the logic model as a guide. In a case study, qualitative data—collected using semi-structured interviews and observations of program operations—are often supplemented and verified by quantitative data on program operations and performance, collected from records and reports. Case

studies may use several different approaches for collecting qualitative data for program evaluation. The most frequently used are semi-structured interviews, focus groups, and researcher observations while on-site. Semi-structured interviews allow for the discovery of unanticipated factors associated with program interpretation and outcomes. Protocols for semi-structured interviews contain specific questions about particular issues or program practices. The "semi" aspect of these discussion guides refers to the fact that a respondent may give as long, detailed, and complex a response as he or she desires to the question—whatever conveys the full reality of the program's experience with the issue at hand. If some issues have typical categories associated with them, the protocols will usually contain probes to make sure the researcher learns about each category of interest.

In case studies, observations at program sites provide an important method of validating information from interviews. The observations are often guided by structured or semi-structured protocols. The protocols ensure that key items reported in interviews are verified and that consistent procedures for rating program performance are used across time and across sites.

Focus Groups.   We briefly looked at *focus groups* in Chapter 10. Focus groups in social work are hardly novel as a form of program evaluation because group formation and group practice comprise an integral type of social work treatment. Focus groups have been used extensively in the business world to address consumer interest, to try out different types of commercials, and for other reasons (see Krueger and Casey, 2000). They may be generally aimed at understanding the beliefs and feelings of clients and/or other stakeholders through a series of discussions guided by one social worker acting as a group discussion specialist, something social workers ordinarily excel at. Sometimes another social work researcher serves as a note taker. A number of questions are selected to guide open-ended discussions lasting anywhere from a few minutes to perhaps two hours. The goals of the evaluation discussions may vary from achieving consensus to emphasizing points of divergence among participants regarding an intervention or program concern. Discussions may be video- or audiotape recorded, but the primary data are recorded by the social worker note taker. Sometimes facilitators use an overhead projector or chalkboard or flip chart so that everyone participates in the ideas presented for all. The key feature of focus groups is the narrative of what develops around group issues deemed by the members to be significant, whether issues are ones of agreement or of disagreement.

Ethnography. You read about *ethnographic* studies in the previous chapter. They rely almost exclusively on observation and unstructured interviews to study natural settings (Guba, 1987). Ethnographic evaluators are commonly interested in agency and organizational dynamics occurring at a particular program site. Typically, ethnographic evaluators examine the larger community context in which the program is taking place and the relationship between program activities and other activities in the community; they are especially interested in who has and uses power.

Ethnography tries to learn about the program from the perspective of program participants and stakeholders at the agency or in the task environment. They are particularly interested in the perspective of local cultures and subcultures. Ethnographers may assess a program or series of interventions unobtrusively in the role of overt or covert participant observer. Qualitative research skills are helpful in taking notes that can be transcribed and coded to identify emerging themes and trends, or entered into a qualitatively oriented software program. The evaluative goal is to capture personal insights and narratives of clients and stakeholders and to ascertain if the program goals are being achieved.

Ethnography uses procedures that are deliberately flexible. As a result, ethnography is helpful in gathering information on unintended consequences and unanticipated outcomes. These unexpected observations may lead to an entirely new concept of program delivery. In a recent project examining service integration programs for at-risk youth, observations helped clarify that service integration

needed to go beyond formal links and on-paper agreements, and provided insights into how informal processes bonded services together in their efforts to make a difference for high-risk youth in the community. Observations from ethnographic studies are perhaps the hardest type of qualitative information to analyze, since they generate volumes of information, much of which may not be directly related to evaluation goals and may not be comparable across sites.

Collecting qualitative data requires skilled researchers who are experienced with the techniques being used (Denzin, 1993). To analyze these data, careful notes must be taken to ensure that responses are correctly recorded and to aid in interpreting them (Miles and Huberman, 1994). Interviewers must be trained to understand the intent of each question, the possible variety of answers that respondents might give, and ways to probe to ensure that full information about the issues under investigation is obtained.

Analysis of qualitative data requires an in-depth understanding of programs, respondents and responses, and especially the context in which they are evaluated. Ultimately, the analyst makes judgments regarding the relative importance or significance of various responses. This requires an unbiased assessment of whether responses support or refute hypotheses about the way the program works and the effects it has.

One way to handle qualitative data is to treat one's interview and observational notes as text, and to conduct a textual analysis using specialized computer software that can search for the presence of specific themes or content. Qualitative software is available to facilitate the location and retrieval of information from massive textual files (Richards and Richards, 1991). This kind of software is expensive to use because huge amounts of text must be entered into a computer. Further, either the exact words one wants to search for must appear in the text, or the text must be marked for the presence of any theme or topic that the researcher wants to retrieve. Often researchers can achieve equal or better results with carefully constructed interview or data-collection guides or structured focus groups, and with systematic recording of responses or coding of data encountered in the field (Silverman, 1993).

Cost Studies and Productivity

Recall cost–benefit analysis from Chapter 2. Cost evaluations address how much the program or program components cost, preferably in relation to alternative uses of the same resources and to the benefits being produced by the program. In periods of fiscal restraint, programs must expect to defend their costs against alternative uses. According to Yates, Delany, and Dillard (2001), *cost analysis* involves a thorough description of the type and amount of all resources used to produce program services. Cost analysis examines data on investments in programs by collecting information on such things that Brinkerhoff and Dressler (1990) argue amount to various types of productivity.

Productivity assessment may include something very straightforward, such as program results compared to program effort, or something as simple as outputs divided by inputs. For example, one measure of productivity might be number of families helped in a shelter serving families who are homeless divided by the number of casework encounters between social workers and sheltered family members. As noted by Brinkerhoff and Dressler (1990), increasing productivity in human services organizations is not simply a matter of working harder, rather it may mean working "smarter" (p. 20).

For example, one of the critical concerns facing agency evaluators is how to conceptualize and define success. Sometimes busy agency administrators lose sight of the need to focus on ways to conceive of human services so as to maximize the possibility of finding success, no matter how difficult it may be to locate and measure. One useful strategy entails expanding definitions. For example, instead of measuring miles per gallon in an agency van used to transport elderly clients back and forth from a health care facility, we might be better off measuring the number of clients safely transported in miles per gallon of fuel. Costs therefore might be better seen as costs per unit of successful service.

Productivity can be measured for a number of reasons. First, it may serve as a way of evaluating the effectiveness or efficiency of the organization. According to Tripodi (1983), "*Effectiveness* is the extent to which the social work objectives are realized," "*efficiency* is assessed by relating the achievement of objectives to the expenditure of the social worker's time, energy, and resources," and "*effort* refers to those program or practice activities carried out for the purpose of attaining objectives for that stage" (pp. 34–35).

Brinkerhoff and Dressler (1990) define productivity in a number of ways that can be useful for social workers. Productivity may include something very simple, such as the results of an intervention or program divided by the effort it takes, or outputs compared to (divided by) inputs. For example, we might look at the number of families helped by a given program compared to the number of casework visits made. The assessment of productivity may be able to help spot problem areas or warn of early deficiencies in an intervention or a program. Productivity studies may help managers make decisions about staffing and might help program planners evaluate new methods.[5]

Inputs. Inputs generally refer to resources that can be consumed (material, supplies), services that support production (heat, light, space, rentals, computer time), and effort and labor of social workers and staff who use these resources to produce outputs (secretarial time, labor hours, capital equipment, services of consultants, and management time). Evaluators are often concerned about the relationship between inputs and outputs, particularly if there is a decline in inputs followed by the same amount of outputs. A second possibility is the same amount of inputs and an increase in outputs. A third possibility involves an increase in inputs and an increase in outputs, and finally, a decrease in inputs and an increase in outputs.

Outputs. Output normally expresses units in quantifiable terms, such as the number or amount of families who successfully resettle in neighborhoods after receiving services from shelters serving families who are homeless. Sometimes a more important concern involves the quality of an output, rather than quantity. We need to be concerned about high-quality services delivered to individuals, families, and communities without making mistakes. In other words, services may vary from only a little intervention (one phone call or one follow-up visit) to a large number of phone calls or visits. We sometimes are called upon to count visits or services "as if" they are delivered in their entirety, when in fact perhaps only a small part of the actual intervention or service is delivered. Sometimes we may measure the wrong thing, or more than one thing at a time. Measuring reading readiness in school children may also be a measure of parental involvement, general intelligence, and vocabulary, in addition to the actual score a child achieves on a standardized reading readiness inventory.

Typical Outputs.

(1) number of intake summaries successfully completed
(2) number of social histories successfully completed
(3) number of home visits made
(4) number of student weekly reports completed
(5) number of new client experiences correctly understood
(6) number of satisfied client relatives and family members
(7) number of special education referrals correctly filled
(8) number of families successfully placed

Single-Case Designs

An important development in the last quarter of the twentieth century is a blending of clinical social work and variations of experimental design in social work research methodology (Bloom, Fischer, and Orme, 1999). This blending occurred in clinical psychology, counseling, and social work at about the same time (Herson and Barlow, 1976). It provides social work with a research program to apply to clinical social work called single-subject or *single-case design*. The basic plan of single-case design is to combine the best thinking available in clinical practice with some of the basic elements of the experimental method to derive a research-practice strategy that allows clinical practitioners to perform their interventions. At the same time, they make observations that may then inform their judgments about clinical effectiveness, one case (subject or client) at a time (Blythe and Briar, 1985).

The Basic Single-Case Design.   There are numerous ways to implement a single-case design (Thyer, 1998). The most basic plan calls for a period of baseline observation of the client's agreed-upon targeted behaviors, called the A or baseline period. Here the client's targeted behavior (the dependent variable) is clearly specified (Nelsen, 1984), and then repeated measures of the targeted behavior are taken throughout a baseline (A) period, so that the naturally occurring frequency of the target behavior can be accurately measured, prior to intervention. No intervention is introduced during this stage, as the A period is analogous to the control group in a classic experimental design.

During the second phase of this design, called the B or treatment period, the intervention or treatment (experimental variable, x) is introduced, and again the target behavior (the dependent variable, y) is observed. This is analogous to the experimental condition introduced in an experimental research design (Berlin, 1983), as noted in Figure 14.8.

In this example the client's problem or targeted behavior during the baseline varies slightly over a seven-week baseline (A) period, prior to the introduction of the treatment. We plot the frequency of targeted behavior prior to the intervention. Usually, simple counts are made of the behavior that is targeted for change. In this case we will use an example of someone who smokes cigarettes. The asterisk represents a count of the number of packs of cigarettes smoked each week. This period is analogous to a control group, where the experimental condition or treatment has not been introduced or has been withheld. During the treatment phase (B) the client is introduced to the treatment (experimental condition), and the targeted behavior (number of packs of cigarettes smoked) is again observed and plotted. We note in this example that fewer packs of cigarettes are consumed during the B period, and the client seems to be responding to treatment, as

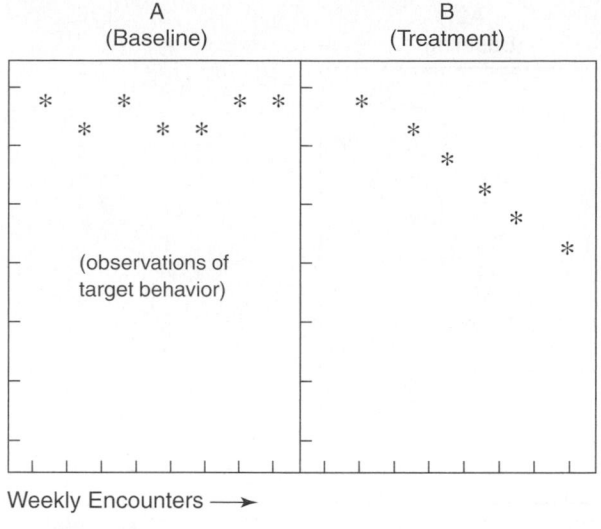

A (Baseline)   B (Treatment)

(observations of target behavior)

Weekly Encounters ⟶

FIGURE 14.8 A–B Single-Case Design

we notice a steady reduction in the client's targeted behavior over the treatment period.

Now, as you may be thinking, isn't it possible that changes in the number of cigarettes smoked during the seven-week experiment (B) period might have been due to something other than the treatment? Also, how do we know what will happen if the treatment were to end at the conclusion of the treatment (B) period? Isn't is possible that the client's targeted behavior may increase if the intervention is withdrawn? The answer to all of these questions is yes, these explanations are possible; and, indeed, it might be important to find out if rival explanations account for what appears to be changes in the client's targeted behavior over time. It is not possible to tell for sure whether the observed reduction in cigarette consumption is due to the treatment, some other factor, or some combination of the treatment and other factors. Nonetheless, those who advocate single-case designs can certainly make a case that two of the three criteria of causation (the presumed cause should precede the effect in time, and the establishing of an empirical relationship between the presumed cause and effect) seem to be supported in this example. The third criterion of causation, that rival explanations for the changes in the dependent variable have been ruled out, has not been done, as is the case in almost all research and

evaluation in the human services. There are reasons why methodologists have developed alternatives to the A–B *design*.

A–B–A Design (a withdrawal design).   In the *A–B–A design* a treatment variable is introduced and then withdrawn. If after the baseline measurement during A, the application of treatment during B leads to improvement, and conversely results in deterioration if withdrawn during A2, one can make a stronger case that the treatment variable is the agent responsible for observed changes in target behavior, as noted in Figure 14.9.

One problem with the A–B–A design is that the program finishes during a measurement period and the client may still be in need of intervention. It is also not possible to tell strictly what has happened here as the initial A period was not preceded by treatment, whereas the second A period was, so that what was being measured in the first A period may have been very different from what is measured after, during A2.

A–B–A–B (equivalent time-samples design).   In the *A–B–A–B design* the program ends after a treatment phase that can be continued beyond the basic design, thus providing the clinician with more options. Two separate treatment phases give the clinician more opportunity to demonstrate effectiveness, thus providing for more firm conclusions about effectiveness, as noted in Figure 14.10.

B–A–B (no baseline period).   Sometimes in clinical practice it is not possible to measure the dependent variable (target behavior) at the beginning or all throughout a set of clinical encounters with a client, because treatment must begin immediately, as in a crisis situation, and a baseline measurement period is precluded. In such cases, when a concurrent or prospective baseline (Bloom, Fischer, and Orme, 1999) is impossible, the social worker may still be in a position to approximate these measures by using retrospective or reconstructed baselines. In such cases, clients may be asked to report from memory the frequency, intensity, or duration of the behavior in question over a specified period of time. It must be remembered that memory fades quickly; hence,

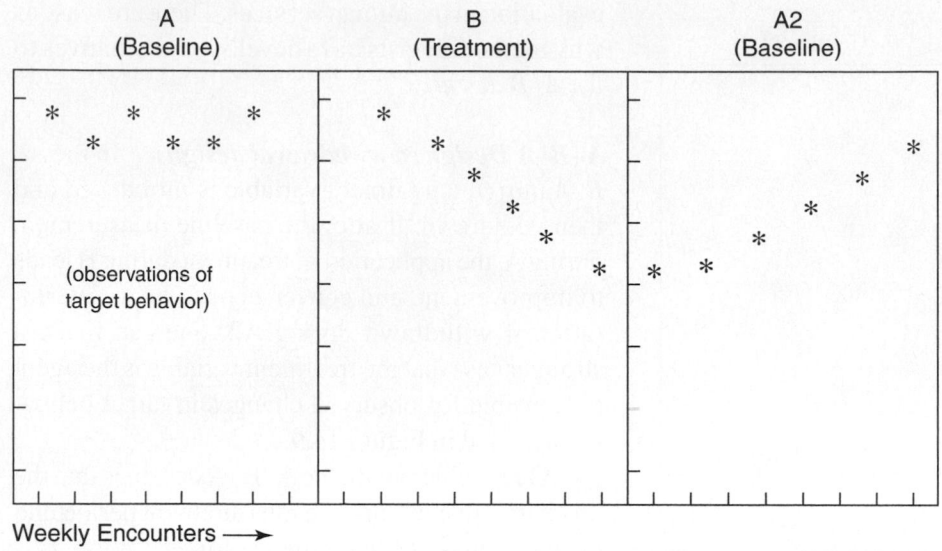

FIGURE 14.9   A–B–A Single-Case Design

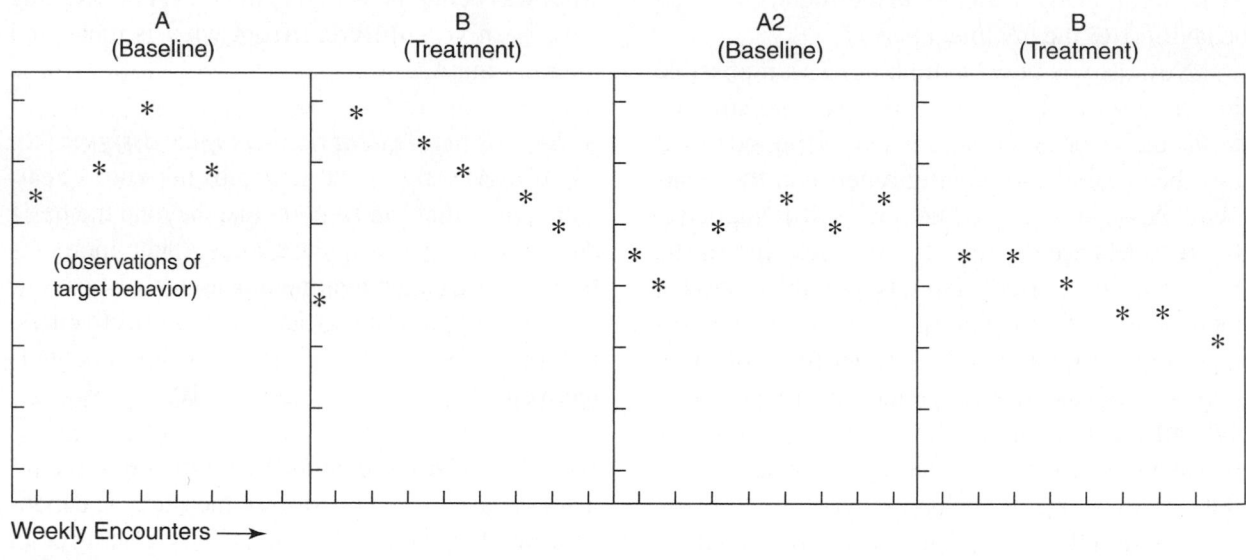

FIGURE 14.10   A–B–A–B Single-Case Design

it is recommended that a reconstructed baseline that depends upon memory should extend back only a few weeks (Bloom, Fischer, and Orme, 1999).

In the *B–A–B design,* the baseline is skipped altogether, and the process begins with the treatment (B) period, as noted in Figure 14.11.

The B–A–B design, which has no baseline measures taken at time 1, can be used when inter-

vention must begin immediately as might be needed in a crisis situation. Here the analogous measure of the control condition (when the control group does not receive the experimental condition) is not taken at the beginning. It is often not possible to delay a treatment or intervention while measures are made regarding a target behavior, as in the standard A–B or A–B–A–B designs. It may be much more realis-

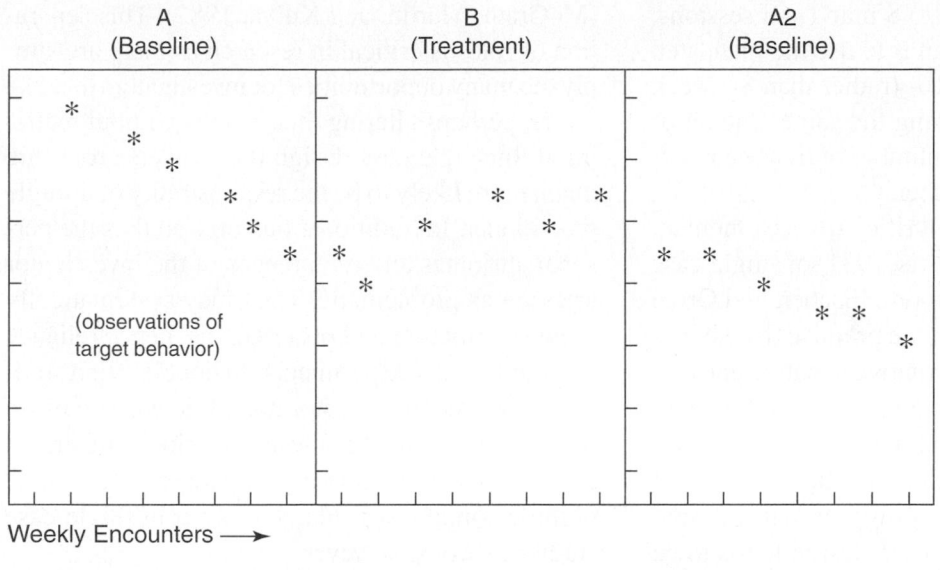

A
(Baseline)

B
(Treatment)

A2
(Baseline)

(observations of
target behavior)

Weekly Encounters ⟶

FIGURE 14.11   B–A–B Single-Case Design

tic to assume your treatment regimen with clients will be more likely to fit the B–A–B model.

Traditional quantitative analysis in social work ordinarily involves the assessment of a group of clients or participants so that comparisons usually involve a much larger number of people than is the case in single-case design. Hence, it can be difficult to compare single-case designs to large research designs because of the discrepancy in the number of cases. However, statistical analysis in single-case design, while beyond the scope of this book, may still be quite useful (Marsh and Shibano, 1984). There are a number of excellent personal computer software programs for setting up single-case designs, entering and analyzing data, and generating graphical and other reports.[6]

Advantages of Single-Case Designs.   According to Grinnell (1999), single-case designs can be used in practice with minimal disruption of service or intervenient efforts. Single-case designs offer one tool for evaluating effectiveness by providing continuous information about how the client is changing (hopefully benefiting) in regard to treatment. While it may be difficult to draw inferences or generalizations one case at a time, advocates feel that this form of clinical evaluation is critically

important to social work because it can be highly integrated into practice while it generally avoids the use of outside evaluators, and it is reasonably easy to use (Slonim-Nevo and Anson, 1998). Also, according to Bloom, Fischer, and Orme (1999), single-case designs provide a great deal of useful information to practitioners about clients and treatment progress that might not otherwise have been available.[7]

Disadvantages of Single-Case Designs.   The push to move much of the health- and mental health-related clinical practice work into the managed care movement (Corcoran and Gingerich, 1994), where speed of treatment is of the essence, may make single-case design more difficult to apply (Balassone and Ruckdeschel, 1994). The need to begin an interventive program quickly and end it within a comparatively short period of time may make single-case design (as other forms of clinical evaluation) difficult to implement. Bloom, Fischer, and Orme (1999) recommend a single-case design *stretch* procedure as one way to accommodate truncated periods of treatment and evaluation. Say, for example, that a traditional treatment plan called for 16 treatment sessions over 16 weeks. However, due to managed care requirements to limit treatments, an intervenient program must be reduced to 8 mandated sessions. The single-case *stretch* plan is to use the mandated 8 sessions over an entire 16- (rather than 8-) week time period, thus maintaining the same amount of total time but limiting the number of treatment sessions to the mandated number.

More philosophical criticisms (Heineman, 1981; Ruckdeschel and Farris, 1981) of single-case designs are outlined by Bloom, Fischer, and Orme (1999). Some are based on the premise that single-case design is heavily quantitative in nature and carries the same excess baggage as positivism in general. The concern is that the scientific methods tied to positivism may not have the best interests of clients in mind. Critics also suggest that information gathered from single-case design tends to be shallow and lacks the strength of more in-depth qualitative encounters. A related critique involves the requirement of single-case design to make behavioral observations. This leads to a behavioralist theoretical orientation that, while important in some circles in social work (Thyer, 2001), is nonetheless viewed less favorably elsewhere.[8]

Finally, we have the larger issue of dangers researchers face when they try to introduce quantitative research agendas into their clinical practices. These dangers are not meant to be applied to single-case design alone; they are also valid concerns in any clinical evaluation strategy. Nonetheless, clinical single-case evaluation is subject to same set of concerns facing traditional researchers, namely, that researchers should not be intimately familiar with their clients or participants. For example, in traditional clinical outcome studies, investigators must be aware of how their underlying paradigm (theory) may influence their observations in sometimes very subtle ways. Isolated scientists may be more easily fooled into making inferences that are unjustified (Pickering, 1995). Hence, there is a need for evaluation teams to have access to a great deal of outside opinion that may not be readily available to the single-case design practitioner.

Another concern is that the lead investigator in traditional research should not also have primary responsibility for designing the investigation, collecting data, and performing statistical analysis

(McGrath, Martin, and Kulka, 1982). This separation of roles is critical in research as there are simply too many opportunities for investigators to make errors, perhaps altering their results without realizing it. In single-case design these diverse roles are much more likely to be the responsibility of a single practitioner. In traditional outcome studies the personal attributes and preferences of the investigator are seen as problematic. They may systematically skew information and observations, hence reliance on double-blind experiments. In double-blind studies neither the investigator nor clinicians are aware of who is receiving the new intervention or treatment and who is in the control or comparison group. None of these conditions is likely to occur in single-case study situations, however.

These criticisms are not sufficient to recommend against the use of any one strategy for evaluating clinical practice. Rather, we need to be aware of both the strengths and weaknesses of a variety of methods. We should never be satisfied that we have found the one golden rule or preferred strategy for demonstrating the effectiveness of our efforts to help others.

Empowerment Evaluation

Empowerment evaluation is a trend in social work evaluation that incorporates the values of diversity (Rodgers-Farmer and Potocky-Tripodi, 2001), the strengths perspective (Saleebey, 2002), and postmodernism (Chambron and Irving, 1994).

The *empowerment* approach in general in social work (Holmes, 1992; Lee, 1994; Gutierrez, Parsons, and Cox, 1998) merges many of the strategies of constructivist (Fisher, 1991; Dean, 1993; Rodwell, 1998), ecological (Germain and Gitterman, 1996), feminist, and critical perspectives into a research orientation that blends the concepts of helping others with social and economic justice (Flynn, 1995; Gil, 1998; Appleby, Colon, and Hamilton, 2000; Pelton, 2001; Longres and Scanlon, 2001). Empowerment evaluators believe that there is no such thing as completely objective, disinterested assessment. Green (1997) explained that, "Program evaluators are inevitably on somebody's side and not on somebody else's side. The sides chosen by evaluators are most importantly expressed in whose questions are being addressed and, therefore, what criteria are used to make judgments about program quality" (p. 25).

Empowerment evaluators feel they are especially well adapted to working with social work clients who are marginalized from mainstream and traditional "Euro-centered" societies. Lee (1994) suggests five concerns when working with non-"Euro-centered" groups: evaluators must (1) include a historical understanding of the kinds of oppression suffered by those they are evaluating; (2) have knowledge of the ecological perspective, especially the adaptive functioning capacities and stress reactions of those who have been oppressed; (3) acknowledge unequal power arrangements and how oppression is often internalized (oppressed people often blame themselves for their own circumstances); (4) focus on the effects of socioeconomic class, race, and gender; and (5) have a critical perspective that analyzes the link between individual pain and strategies for change.[9]

Rodgers-Farmer and Potocky-Tripodi (2001) contend that within the empowerment framework the worker and the client must share power and that clients should become "co-researchers." Further, evaluation tasks should be mutual. That is, the evaluation activities should be made to cycle back and forth so that more power will come to reside in the client (Lee, 1996). According to Appleby, et al. (2000), sharing responsibility between client and evaluator involves three steps: Both must (1) acknowledge and honor their own personal sense of self, involving their self-esteem, self-direction, and competence; (2) work to facilitate the interpersonal problem-solving potential; and (3) be concerned about their environment, as it is in the environment that resources can be brought to bear to reach goals (Gutierrez, Parsons, and Cox, 1998; Lee, 1996).

Rodwell (1998) combines, in what she calls *constructivist research,* many of the traditional strategies found in qualitative methods, particularly in much of the social constructionists' work, with basically an empowering method. The constructivist (empowerment-oriented) evaluator, according to Rodwell, begins in the natural setting, using the human being as the primary data-gathering instrument. The constructivist evaluator employs tacit or intuitive/felt knowledge derived from qualitative research methods. The constructivist evaluator uses purposive sampling, grounded theory, case studies, and tentative application of findings, and depends on her or his trustworthiness and authenticity.

According to Rodwell, verbal and nonverbal data are not the only way of knowing in constructive evaluation. Intuition and other instinctive ways of knowing are central. *Intuition* operates when the inquirer knows what the next questions are and what next steps need to be taken to enhance co-construction. The major role of tacit knowledge occurs in reflexivity. It is in the doing of the data collection that the understanding of the subject is achieved.[10]

Special attention in social work needs to be directed toward making evaluation both accessible and available to subjugated populations and others who have traditionally been left out of research and evaluation activities in social work. Illustrative sources are provided in Box 14.4.

IS THERE A ROLE FOR INTUITION?

Have you ever wondered about those special moments when you have the feeling that something special is going on without knowing why or how? Have you ever felt that someone was lying even through she or he professed to be telling the truth? Have you ever had an inkling that something was about to happen, and then it did (or didn't)? Have you ever recognized a pattern without knowing how? These may be instances of intuition (Roberts, 1989). The philosophical issues that underlie intuitive social work knowledge and the question of what constitutes reliable and valid knowledge in social work research are both closely related to the advocacy of differing research methods. They also have something to do with questions that have been raised about the adequacy of knowledge based solely on "Euro-male" paradigms that have guided the development of traditional quantitative (nonintuitive) research perspectives.

Box 14.4 _____

Illustrative Sources on Empowerment, Diversity, and Social Justice in Social Work Research and Practice

Balgopol, P. (2000). *Social work practice with immigrants and refugees.* New York: Columbia University Press.

Blount, M. (1996). Social work practice with Native Americans. In D. Harrison, et al., *Cultural Diversity and Social Work Practice.* Springfield, IL: Charles C. Thomas.

Bullis, R. (1996). *Spirituality in social work practice.* Washington, D.C.: Taylor and Francis.

Chow, J. (1999). Multiservice centers in Chinese American immigrant communities: Practice principles and challenges. *Social Work, 44*(1), 70–81.

Coe, A., and D. Elliott. (1999). An evaluation of teaching direct practice courses in a distance education program for rural settings. *Journal of Social Work Education, 35*(3), 353–365.

Cowger, C. D., and C. A. Snively. (2002). Assessing client strengths: Individual, family and community empowerment. In *The Strengths Perspective in Social Work Practice,* 3rd ed., edited by D. Saleebey, pp. 106–123. NY: Addison-Wesley Longman.

Devore, W., and E. Schlesinger. (1996). *Ethnicsensitive social work practice,* 4th ed. Boston: Allyn and Bacon.

Dungee-Anderson, D., and J. Beckett. (1995). A process model for multicultural social work practice. *Families in Society, 78,* 459–468.

Flynn, J. (1995). Social justice and social agencies. In *Encyclopedia of Social Work,* 19th ed., edited by R. L. Edwards, pp. 2173–2179. Washington, DC: NASW Press.

Fogel, S. (1998). Sexual harassment in BSW field placement students: Is it a problem? *Journal of Baccalaureate Social Work, 3*(2), 17–29.

Freire, P. (1991). Pedagogy of the oppressed: New revised 20th anniversary edition. New York: Continuum.

Gil, D. (1998). *Confronting injustice and oppression: Concepts and strategies for social workers.* New York: Columbia University Press.

Gitterman, A. (Ed.) (2001). *Handbook of social work practice with vulnerable and resilient populations.* New York: Columbia University Press.

Green, J. (1999). *Cultural awareness in the human services: A multi-ethnic approach,* 3rd ed. Boston: Allyn and Bacon.

Gross, E. (1995). Deconstructing politically correct practice literature: The American Indian case. *Social Work, 40*(2), 206–214.

Ho, M. (1976). Social work with Asian Americans. *Social Casework, 57,* 195–201.

Holmes, G. (1992). Social work research and the empowerment paradigm. In *The Strengths Perspective in Social Work Practice,* edited by D. Saleebey, pp. 158–168. New York: Longman.

Imrie, R. (1996). Disability and the city: International perspectives. New York: St. Martin's Press.

Kelly, M., and M. Lauderdale. (1999). Globalization, technology and continued professional education. *Professional Development: The International Journal of Continuing Social Work Education, 2*(1), 4–9.

Kim, Y. O. (1995). Cultural pluralism and Asian Americans: Culturally sensitive social work practice. *International Social Work, 38,* 69–78.

Lee, J. (2000). The empowerment approach to social work practice. New York: Columbia University Press.

Levine, J. (2001). Working with victims of persecution: Lessons from Holocaust survivors. *Social Work, 46*(4), 350–360.

Lieberman, A. (1990). Culturally sensitive intervention with children and families. *Child and Adolescent Social Work, 7,* 101–120.

Longres, J. (1997). The impact and implications of multiculturalism, pp. 38–47. In M. Reisch and H. Gambrill, *Social work in the 21st century.* Thousand Oaks, CA: Pine Forge Press.

Longres, J., and E. Scanlon. (2001). Social justice and the research curriculum. *Journal of Social Work Education, 37*(3), 447–463.

Lum, D. (2000). Social work practice and people of color: A process-stage approach. Belmont, CA: Brooks/Cole.

McMahon, A., and P. Meares. (1992). Is social work racist? A content analysis of recent literature. *Social Work, 37,* 533–539.

Mills, L. (1996). Empowering battered women transnationally: The case for postmodern interventions. *Social Work, 41*(3), 261–268.

Mokuau, N., and J. Matsuoka. (1995). Turbulence among a native people: Social work practice with Hawaiians. *Social Work, 40*(4), 465–472.

Mondros, J., and S. Wilson. (1994). Organizing for power and enhancement. New York: Columbia University Press.

Morales, A. (1981). Social work with third world people. *Social Work,* 26, 45–51.

National Association of Social Workers (1997). Lesbian, gay and bisexual issues. Social Work Speaks: NASW Policy Statements. Washington, DC: NASW.

Normal, A. E., ed. (2000). *Resiliency enhancement: Putting the strengths perspective into social work practice.* New York: Columbia University Press.

Pelton, L. (2001). Social justice and social work. *Journal of Social Work Education,* 37(3), 433–439.

Pinderhughes, E. (1989). Understanding race, ethnicity and power: Key efficacy in clinical practice. New York: Free Press.

Reinharz, S. (1996). Feminist methods for social research. New York: Oxford University Press.

Rooney, R. (1992). Strategies for work with involuntary clients. New York: Columbia University Press.

Saleebey, D. (1990). Philosophical disputes in social work: Social justice denied. *Journal of Sociology and Social Welfare,* 17, 29–40.

Saleebey, D. (2001). The diagnostic strengths manual? *Social Work,* 46(2), 183–187.

Saleebey, D., ed. (2002). *The strengths perspective in social work practice.* New York: Allyn and Bacon.

Schiele, J. (1996). Afrocentricity: An emerging paradigm in social work practice. *Social Work,* 41(3), 284–294.

Simon, R., and R. Rhodes. (2000). In their own voices: Transracial adoptees tell their stories. New York: Columbia University Press.

Tully, C. (2000). Lesbians, gays and the empowerment perspective. New York: Columbia University Press.

Vacc, N., S. DeVaney, and J. Wittmer. (1995). Experiencing and counseling multicultural and diverse populations, 3rd ed. Bristol, PA: Taylor and Francis.

Van Warmer, K., J. Wells, and M. Boes. (2000). *Social work with lesbians, gays and bisexuals: A strengths perspective.* Boston: Allyn and Bacon.

Wares, D., K. Wedel, J. Rosenthal, and A. Dolbrec. (1994). Indian child welfare: A multicultural challenge. *Journal of Multicultural Social Work,* 3(3), 1–15.

Weaver, H. (1999). Indigenous people and the social work profession: Defining culturally competent services. *Social Work,* 44(3), 217–225.

According to Heineman-Piper (1985), Ruckdeschel (1981), and Imre (1984), mainstream quantitative social work researchers informed by the philosophies of logical positivism (as noted in Chapter 4) tend to mistrust intuitive experience as the basis for research findings. Qualitative methodologists, on the other hand, have argued that some degree of involvement of the researcher in the "life world" of those being studied is essential to the gathering and interpreting of data. According to Lofland (1984), this is particularly true of participant observation in the field, where researchers participate with and interact with those whom they are studying. We believe that field-based research has close parallels in social work practice as social workers and clients meet in numerous face-to-face situations, (Moustakas, 1990). Hence, social workers are candidates for a more qualitative attitude toward the use of intuitive information in research practices.

Lofland (1984) and Patton (1990) have argued that the recording of the observer's own impressions, attitudes, and feelings is an important part of the data-gathering process. In a similar vein Denzin (1990) contended that we must use multiple data sources, one of which should include the investigator's own experiences. Imre (1984) maintained that knowledge in social work practice need not be confined to information available through traditional methods of positivist science. Subjective knowledge as seen by Imre is both implicit and explicit in the interpersonal activities that constitute social work practice. It therefore makes sense to use that knowledge in research methods as well.

Rein and White (1981) suggested that the traditional dependence of researchers on objective, generalized knowledge in social work is misplaced. They propose that the profession has a need for context-specific knowledge that includes the observer–practitioner–researcher as part of the content. Heineman-Piper (1985) criticized what she refers to as the traditional models of science in social work for being prescriptive and ruling out subjective, intuitive data. She further maintained that the traditional view of science is outmoded and has inhibited the development of our profession. Finally, Heineman-Piper advocated a methodological stance she termed "heuristics," which does not regard one method as superior to another but rather views methods in light of their problem-solving pragmatic utility (see also Siegel, 1994).

We believe that social work practice and research both contain intuitive data, and this must be so as social workers and researchers both engage in the same process of reflection. The social work profession is characterized by person–environment interface; thus, it seems that social workers have to be sensitive to the multi-faceted nature of knowledge, including intuition, rather than insisting upon formal "objective" knowledge as the only basis for engaging in or evaluating practice.[11]

What Does an Intuition-Based Social Work Evaluator Do?

From an intuition-accepting perspective (Carew, 1987; Allen-Meares and DeRoos, 1994) a social work researcher necessarily includes the experiences of the researcher looking inward as much as it involves the collection of information about others. While intuition-accepting researchers recognize the importance of traditional, mainstream, and quantitative analysis, they live also in the everyday world of friends and acquaintances, clients, and colleagues who are part and parcel of our profession and, therefore, also of our research agendas.

The intuitive researcher is poised to look beyond rigid adherence to external, universal research constants and focuses on internal (cognitive, affective) components of consciousness during the research experience. The intuitive researcher remains ready to step out of the traditional quantitative research roles and remains free to meet the world in its fullness and richness.

The intuitive researcher focuses internal attention upon idealizations and characterizations within

his or her own stream of consciousness. From this perspective there are no such things as facts pure and simple. Facts are instead selections the researcher's consciousness make by the activities of the researcher's own mind. Facts, therefore, are always interpreted features of consciousness, and hence must rely to a certain extent upon intuition.

The intuitive researcher rejects the "Mathesis Universalis" principle of traditional logical positivist science that asserts that the world is knowable and predictable only mathematically. The intuitive researcher temporarily suspends belief or doubts the substance of the world in order to obtain a condition of reflexivity critical to intuition. This may happen in one or more of the following ways.

1. Learn to absorb research experience as it actually unfolds; make sense out of experience only after it has happened. According to phenomenologists, it is not possible to understand something until after it has been experienced. In the meantime learn to pay attention to your stomach and to your heart.

2. Do not draw hard and fast boundaries around what counts as "research" experience. You may not know, at least in the short run, whether an experience, happening, or event is something that should be considered incidental or whether it may have consequences that turn out to be very important to a research agenda. Therefore, you must have patience.

3. Learn to engage in reflective note taking on thoughts, feelings, and experiences. Carry a small notebook, voice recorder, or Palm Pilot so that you always have access to a way to keep records.

4. There are no set rules or procedures regarding intuition; your experiences should be your only guide.

5. Tape-record thoughts and reflections at intervals throughout your experience. Listen to your own voice. As you hear yourself speak about your experience, you can interrogate you own consciousness. Ask yourself what you were feeling, what you had in mind at that earlier time.

6. Maintain lists or records of personal biographical events and life experiences that may help (or hinder) your current ability to intuitively focus.

7. Engage in your work in the company of others. Collective investigation and analysis may provide insights missed by the solitary mind.

According to Braud and Anderson (1998), intuitive researchers work to improve in many areas. First is the important skill of community building and sharing of possibilities among three participants in every research process: the researcher, the participants or subjects, and the anticipated audience or consumers—all of whom, according to Braud and Anderson, should have the opportunity to impact the gradual unfolding of the research inquiry. It is important therefore to pay attention to your own feelings and values, as well as to those of participants or clients, other researchers, and those who will consume whatever findings may be generated.

The second area that needs work, according to Braud and Anderson, involves learning to explore thoroughly the landscape of each particular facet of human experience. Not only do researchers have the responsibility to use their five senses, but they also need to be sensitive to subtle insights that may occur due to changes in consciousness itself (Ballenger, 2000). Everything may become raw material for scrutiny: relationships, dreams, bumper stickers, newspaper articles, chance encounters, casual conversations, and synchronistic events such as a drop-in visit from a least favorite relative.

A final skill, called *trickstering* by Braud and Anderson, involves presenting contradictions, paradoxes, and confusion. The idea of being deliberately nonrational and exaggerating differences may seem unusual to most people, but this is exactly what the trickster does. In addition, recording dreams, drawing, storytelling, and other expressions of one's imagination may help a researcher expand his or her understanding in new ways. For example, let us say that an authority figure, such as a professor, tells you that the most important thing to know about getting along with others is your ability to empathize. The trickster might take this idea and instead of applying it as directed, do the exact opposite, and try for a time not being empathetic. See what difference it makes if you try to do exactly the opposite of what is proposed by the authority figure. See if you have a different understanding of authority figures if you assume (for the time being at least) that they are dead wrong.

STUDYING YOUR COMMUNITY: NEEDS ASSESSMENT AND BEYOND

A key question facing social workers beyond the effectiveness of agency-based services is the extent to which there are individuals or families in a community, region, or catchment area who are in need of services but have not been receiving them (Gregoire and Snively, 2001). *Needs assessment* gathers information to help social workers answer this question.[12]

Kuh (1982) lists five general reasons social workers might want to evaluate a community via a needs assessment: to *determine* whether needs have been met; to *assess* client satisfaction with services; to *monitor* stakeholders' perceptions of various issues that can guide the development of new programs or policies; to *justify* existing policies and programs; and to *select* the most desirable program or policy from among several different alternatives.

Defining Need

Lenning (1980) defined *met needs* as necessary or desirable conditions that already exist in actuality. *Unmet needs,* on the other hand, were defined by Lenning as arising when there was a discrepancy between desirable conditions and current actuality. Both met and unmet needs may be the focus of needs assessment. Witkin and Altschuld (1995) saw need as a discrepancy or gap between what is—or the present state of affairs—and what should be, or a desired state of affairs.

Bradshaw (1972) defined four different ways to ascertain need. First, a *normative need* is a circumstance, condition, or situation that is identified by a social worker, key informant, or other community expert who has been able to determine that there is a gap in existing services relative to some subpopulation's need. For example, a community organizer may know, by examining information from a central clearinghouse on services to families who are homeless, that there are far more families with children who need educational resources than there are children from area shelters enrolled in community schools. The social worker might recommend that transportation services be increased to make sure children residing in shelters for families who are homeless receive support.

A second definition of need, according to Bradshaw, is *felt need*. This involves the traditional notion of ascertaining need by examining actual clients. Much of the literature on needs assessment provides methodological strategies to conceptualize and gather data pertaining to the opinions and beliefs (felt need) of clients in a particular community (Davenport and Davenport, 1999).

Bradshaw called the demand for services *expressed need*. Expressed need may refer to those actual clients or potential clients who have applied for services or those who have already received services. It might refer to those on a waiting list.

The final need identified by Bradshaw is called *comparative need*. This type of need is actually an estimation of the amount of need that may be ascertained by finding out characteristics of those who have already obtained services and then determining how many of those in the larger population are likely to share the same characteristics and hence be likely to benefit from service.

Who Should Be Involved?

Needs assessments gather information about gaps between real and ideal conditions, the reasons these gaps exist, and what can be done about them, all within the context of the beliefs of the community and available resources for change. Needs assessments have traditionally looked at three groups as sources of data. The *target group or population* (clients, potential clients) are the very individuals whose needs we wish to assess (Danis, 1999). How-

ever, hard-to-reach groups and individuals may not be accustomed to having their needs assessed and may lack the verbal or other skills needed. A second group consists of *key informants* (community leaders, service providers): These may be opportunistically connected individuals with a knowledge of, and ability to report on, community needs. Often they are ministers, minority group leaders, newspaper editors and reporters—individuals who may have broad knowledge of community affairs. However, the danger is that these key informants may also overestimate the target population's interest in a program and overestimate the felt need for change in the community.[13]

Community members comprise the third group, which includes all of the members of the entire community; this includes members of the target population as well as unaffected individuals and families. Approaching everyone for information has the advantage of potentially showing how broadly based needs are, rather than assuming they are restricted to the target population. A problem, however, is that the entire population may not be aware of the extent of the needs of more marginalized members of the community.

Methods for Assessing Needs

Survey and Standardized Needs Assessment Measures.   These are cross-sectional special-purpose questionnaires (mailed or distributed, telephone), gathering primarily quantitative data. The key questions here include deciding whom to survey; selecting a sampling method; determining the content of items to be asked; choosing what type of questionnaire to use (open ended, multiple choice, scaled with respect to extent of agreement); and selecting a method of distribution (mail, telephone).

Surveys are standardized, relatively inexpensive and allow for a considerable amount of data to be collected. A disadvantage of surveys involves their possible lack of flexibility regarding the types of information respondents are able to offer. That is, the advantage of using published standardized instruments is ease of use. But, specialized instruments created elsewhere (for example, a standardized instrument measuring the needs of homeless persons living in shelters in an inner city) may lack locality-relevance for clients living in your community.

Examining Existing Statistics and Secondary Information.

Existing records, statistics, and secondary information may be available from service providers, agency files, libraries, and government offices, thus saving the researcher time in gathering primary (new) data. A disadvantage is that secondary data may limit the kinds of information to the pre-existing categories, offering only limited help. Also, existing information may reflect political decisions/compromises of prior administrations for which the current evaluators may have little insight or understanding.

According to Payne (1999), there are six questions to ask when using existing information: *What geographical areas are covered?* Often public and private agencies and providers have different boundaries and coverage areas. *Have existing boundaries changed?* Often information may not be compara ble over time as boundaries and catchment area definitions may change. *How old is the information?* Is it up to date? Many calculations are based on data from censuses that may be as many as 10 years old. Often information gathered between the decennial census is more up-to-date information but likely from estimates, perhaps using samples. If so, how accurate are the estimates? Are you able to estimate a range for likely sampling errors? *Have definitions changed over time?* Are there any common or disparate elements in definitions that vary? *Is the information complete?* If information is categorical, how much specificity may have been lost due to grouping of data? If averages are reported, are they appropriate; for example, is using the mean most appropriate, or would the median or mode be a better measure of central tendency? Researchers reporting on average incomes often use the median instead of the mean, as one or two very large (or very small) incomes will skew a distribution if the mean is calculated. *What information is missing?* Quite often there may be holes or gaps in data gathered in the past. A look at the literature of those also working in your interest area may provide insights as to what is missing.

Individual Interviews. Face-to-face and telephone interviews can provide rich information about a range of human needs, primarily because of the evaluator's ability to elicit information through follow-up and probe questions. Good rapport between evaluator and respondent can provide extremely valid and reliable data.

Focus Groups. These are relatively unstructured exercises with small groups (8–12 participants). Membership is usually homogeneous in that members share a particular experience or interest; these sessions usually last from one to two hours (Morgan, 1988). Initially, members hear a general statement of the purpose of the session and are given a question pertinent to eliciting information about their needs. Often participants are asked to write down their ideas or thoughts and share these with the rest of the group. The leader usually tracks ideas, writes up summaries, and makes sure there is agreement as to what is being recorded. The advantage (that individuals may offer ideas they would not ordinarily have thought of) can also be a disadvantage (they may not feel comfortable saying what they actually feel).

Nominal Groups. These are more structured than focus groups and often larger. Individuals may list problems or needs in a round-robin format, adding to a list. The items on the list are then ranked, and sums or weightings may be used to generate a final listing.

Community Forums. These consist of large open public meetings or community gatherings that can be used to obtain information about diverse individuals who make up a community. They are similar to town hall meetings lasting several hours with large numbers of participants. Special leadership skills are needed to manage the information gathering at such meetings. One key disadvantage is that there is no assurance of representativeness of participants, and often those who are most vocal are well represented while those less verbal may be left behind.

Other Information-Gathering Strategies. Community researchers have found that it can be very helpful in studying a community to map the community, neighborhood, or area of interest. You can do this by selecting geographic maps from city agencies, libraries, or online map-making services and then drawing boundaries around areas you wish to study. Another method is called "cognitive mapping." This can be a very useful source of information in and of itself, in that this method asks local residents to "draw a map" on a blank piece of paper. You might ask residents to draw a map of where they drive or ride a bus to do their shopping. You might ask adolescents to draw a map of their neighborhood and where they play or where they meet friends. Such freehand maps are often very helpful in stimulating ideas and information that might not otherwise come to mind, especially when residents are responding to your questions about unmet needs.

Another handy source of information is the local newspaper. Newspaper publishers almost always retain copies of their various publications, stored away as hard copy, on microfilm, or on computer disk. Depending on the size of the newspaper and community under study, it may be possible to gather information not otherwise available from newspaper files in this way. Newspaper reporters and editors can also be quite valuable sources of information, not only about historical events but also about ongoing issues and controversies. Other helpful sources include librarians, local school teachers, members of the clergy, museum staff, local college personnel, and long-time community residents.

Another strategy for gathering information on your community is to photograph it and/or examine photographs taken by others. Again, newspapers, libraries, schools, churches, temples, synagogues, museums, and historical associations are likely to be excellent sources for this kind of information. You may find it helpful to ask residents to photograph their favorite (or least favorite) locations, such as streets, alleys, parks, and business districts. A wealth of information can be transmitted by the use of photographs that can tell us a great deal about a community. Figure 14.12 provides exam-

FIGURE 14.12 Websites for Studying Your Community

Sustainable Communities Network	www.sustainable.org
Asset Based Community Development	www.nwu.edu/IPR/abcd.html
Center for Excellence on Sustainable Development	www.sustainable.doe.gov
Community Health Status Indicators (CHSI)	www.communityhealth.hrsa.gov
Community Indicators on the Web	www.rprogress.org/resources/cip/links/cips_web.html
National Civic League (NCL)	www.ncl.org
National Neighborhood Indicators Partnership	www.urban.org/nnip
Redefining Progress	www.rprogress.org
Sustainable Measures	www.sustainablemeasures.com
U.S. Interagency Working Group on Sustainable Development Indicators	www.sdi.gov/reports.htm
Measuring Community Success	www.ncrcrd.iastate.edu
The Resource Guide to Indicators	www.gmied.org/PUBS/papers/inddocs/irguide.html
Building Neighborhood Indicators	www.urban.org/nnip/pdf/guidebk.pdf
Building Healthy Rural Communities	www.ruralaction.org/build_indicators.html

ples of websites that may give you more ideas for studying your community.

THE ROLE OF DIVERSITY IN EVALUATION

In keeping with the *NASW Code of Ethics* and the Council on Social Work Education guidelines concerning diversity and multicultural awareness, we need to be especially concerned in evaluation research with being sensitive to the viewpoints of differing cultures. Robinson and Howard-Hamilton (2000) have developed a series of characteristics that differentiate dominant group orientations in the United States from those that reflect more traditional cultures in the United States and elsewhere. We have expanded somewhat their analysis to represent what we consider to be a Euro-male and non-Euro-male orientation to research and evaluation in general. As shown in Figure 14.13, a Euro-male orientation to research and evaluation includes more emphasis on individualism and personal autonomy while the non-Euro-male orientation focuses more on the entire group or community. The Euro-male

orientation places an emphasis on positivist science, empiricism, and masculine images of the sacred, whereas the non-Euro-male orientation shows more concern for naturalism and a multi-gendered view of spirituality. The Euro-male viewpoint reflects the role of capitalism in Western civilization with its emphasis on products, competition, performance, and achievement, whereas the non-Euro-male viewpoint looks more to process, cooperation, and extended family obligations that include benevolence and sharing. These capitalist values may provide the foundation for the Euro-male orientation to monochronic time, that is, the institutionalization of one universal time frame that is heavily dependent upon market cycles. In contrast, the non-Euro-male orientation may be more polychonic (involving many diverse times) and may reflect more of a concern about the pace of life. Finally, the Euro-male orientation is more likely to involve formal codes and emphasis on the written word, which support authority systems and control centers, whereas the non-Euro-male orientation is more comfortable using the more informal communications involving oral traditions and the spoken

FIGURE 14.13 Comparison of Two Cultural Orientations

EURO-MALE ORIENTATION	NON-EURO-MALE ORIENTATION
Individualism (Self-Reference)	Tribalism (Group-Reference)
Autonomy	Community
Empiricism: Respect for Science	Naturalism: Respect for the Earth
Masculine Spirituality	Mother Earth–Father Sky Spirituality
Product Orientation	Process Orientation
Competition	Cooperation
Performance Teams	Extended Family
Achievement–Affluence	Benevolence–Sharing
Monochronic Time (Pace of Market)	Polychronic Time (Pace of Life)
Formal codes	Oral traditions
Written word	Spoken language
Authority–Control	Deference–Giving Voice

Adapted from Robinson, T. and Howard-Hamilton, M. (2000). *The convergence of race, ethnicity and gender: Multiple identities in counseling.* Upper Saddle River, NJ: Prentice-Hall.

word, which tend to lead more to showing deference to those who are revered and to giving voice to those who are otherwise shut out.

Tran and Aroian (2000) suggest that evaluators use in-depth qualitative interviews instead of standardized quantitative scales or indices to gather evaluative information in cross-cultural settings. They further recommend a process of developing evaluation and assessment measuring devices that use local and indigenous people, either separately or in focus groups, to pretest an instrument for peer validation. This may help facilitate the correct conceptualization of problem questions and help evaluators in rewriting questions that, while easily asked in one culture, may be difficult to ask in another. Tran and Aroian (2000:46) are particularly concerned about the role of language in multicultural evaluation:

> Researchers should be mindful of cross-cultural issues when planning and conducting cross-cultural research. There is a need to develop systematic, valid and reliable procedures for translating research instruments from one language to another. Evaluation studies are needed on the appropriateness, efficacy, and outcomes of social, psycho-

logical and health interventions in different cultural groups.

CONCLUSION

In this chapter you learned the basic processes for evaluation practice from the point of view of agency-based program evaluation and from the perspective of the evaluation of clinical practice. You learned that agency evaluation entails a number of questions about whether the agency is ready for an evaluation, whether to use external or internal evaluators, the scope of the evaluation, whether it should be formative or summative, and the importance of having a logic model.

You can now appreciate different types of evaluation strategies in social work practice settings, including impact evaluation using an experimental, quasi-experimental, or nonexperimental design. You learned about the importance of monitoring program performance, process analysis, cost–benefit and productivity assessment, single-case designs, empowerment evaluation, the role of intuition, and the basics of how to study your own community.

KEY TERMS

A–B design	evaluability assessment	normative need
A–B–A–B design	expressed need	output
case study	felt need	performance evaluation
comparative need	focus group	productivity assessment
contrast class	formative evaluation	relevance relation
cost analysis	gap effectiveness	single-case design
effectiveness	impact evaluation	stakeholders
empowerment	inputs	summative evaluation
erotetic reasoning	intuition	target population
ethnographic	logic model	trickstering
evaluation	needs assessment	

REVIEW QUESTIONS

1. Why is it important for social workers to evaluate their interventions and services, and what does the *NASW Code of Ethics* say about this?

2. What do social workers typically decide on during evaluability assessment?

3. Make up an example of a "why" question that might be decided by erotetic reasoning. In your example what are the topic, contrast class, and relevance relation?

4. What are the advantages and disadvantages of using internal and external evaluators?

5. What are the differences between formative and summative evaluation?

6. Make up a logic model for a program or set of interventions in a hypothetical social work setting.

7. Briefly describe the three types of impact evaluations; give an example of each.

8. Why is it important in the human services to monitor performance?

9. Using a hypothetical example, how would you set up a single-case design?

10. What are the advantages and disadvantages of using a single-case design?

11. In what ways is empowerment evaluation different from traditional evaluation methods?

12. How might social workers use their intuition to help them understand and evaluate a social services setting?

13. Briefly describe the major differences between expressed need, felt need, comparative need, and normative need.

NOTES

1. For more background on both clinical and program evaluation in social work and the human services see Chelminski and Shadish (1997), Chen and Rossi (1992), Herman, Lyons-Morris, and Fitz-Gibbon (1987), Jordan and Franklin (1995), Logan and Royse (2001), Patton (1990), Rossi, Freeman, and Lipsey (1999), Slonim-Nevo and Anson (1998), Tripodi (2001), and Weiss (1972).

2. For a discussion of a variety of issues regarding science and social work evaluation of practice see Alter and Evens (1990), Beck and Rossi (1990), Bloom, Fischer, and Orme (1999), Blythe and Tripodi (1989), Fink (1993), Fischer (1973, 1978a, 1978b), Grinnell (1999), Thyer (1986), and Wodarski and Thyer (1998). For more on the advantages of evidence-based practice see Gambrill (1999), Katz (2001), and Webb (2001). For a review and critique of evidence-based practice see Trinder and Reynolds (2000) and Witkin and Harrison (2001). Finally, evidence-based medicine is discussed in Geyman, Deyo, and Ramsey (2000) and Sackett, Straus, Richardson, Rosenberg, and Haynes (2000).

3. For more discussion of the readiness of an agency for evaluation see Boyle and Lemaire (1999), Herman, Lyons-Morris, and Fitz-gibbon (1987), and Smith (1989).

4. Impact evaluation and experimental design methods in the human services are discussed in Auslander, Haire-Joshe, Houston, Williams, and Krebill (2000), House (1993), and Mohr (1992).

5. Cost studies and productivity in social work are reviewed by Edgar, Friedman, and Zimmer (1990), Ell (1996), Jackson, Olsen, and Schafer (1986), Robertson and Knapp (1988), Yates (1996), and Yates, Delany, and Dillard (2001); find discussions of managed care in Bloom, Fischer and Orme (1999), Corcoran and Gingerich (1994), and Watt and Kallmann (1998).

6. See, for example, the Computer Assisted Social Services [CASS] program (Hudson, 1996) and SINGWIN program (Bloom, 1999).

7. Examples of single-case designs can be found in Berlin (1983), Bloom, Fischer, and Orme (1999), Blythe (1999), Carrillo, DeWeaver, Kilpatrick, and Smith (1993), Corcoran (1993), Downs and Rubin (1994), Gambrill and Barth (1980), Herson and Barlow (1976), Howe (1974), Kagle (1983), Kazdin (1982), Nelson (1993, 1994), Nugent (1991, 1993a,1993b), Rabin (1981), Robinson, Bronson, and Blythe (1988), Thyer (1993, 1998), and Tripodi (1994).

8. For more on the debate about single-case design from its critics see Balassone and Ruckdeschel (1994), Heineman-Piper (1985), Mattaini (1996), and Ruckdeschel and Farris (1981).

9. For more on empowerment evaluation and related social justice issues see Braud and Anderson (1998), Cowger (1994), Cowger and Snively (2002), Fetterman (2001), Florin and Wandersman (1990), Green (1997), Gutierrez, Parsons, and Cox (1998), Holmes (1992), Lather (1991), Lee (1994, 1996, 2000), Markward (1999), Mermelstein (1999), Newman and Brown (1996), Normal (2000), Pollio, McDonald, and North (1996), Pomeroy, Demeter, and Tyler (1995), Stufflebean (1994), and Zimmerman (1990).

10. Constructivist issues and qualitative evaluation methods are discussed by Appleby, Colon and Hamilton (2000), Carpenter (1996), Cowger and Menon (2000), Germain and Gitterman (1996), Imre (1984), Moustakas (1990), Parker-Oliver (2000), Reid (1994), Rodwell (1998), Saleebey (2002), and Scott (1989).

11. For more on intuition in research and evaluation see Allen-Meares and DeRoos (1994), Braud and Anderson (1998), Carew (1987), Denzin (1990), Goldstein (1992), Kahneman and Tversky (1979), Ruckdeschel (1981), and Siegel (1994).

12. For more on needs assessment in social work and related fields see Burke, Dannerbeck, and Watt (1999), Chen and Marks (1998), Davidson (1997), Gregoire and Snively (2001), Hall, Amodeo, Shaffer, and Bilt (2000), Neuber (1983), Payne (1999), Percy-Smith (1996), Tutty and Rothery (2001), Weiner (1996), and Witkin and Altschuld (1995).

13. See for example, Hardcastle, Wenocur, and Powers (1997) on special skills needed to study your community. Hardcastle, D., Wenocur, S., and Powers, P. (1997). *Community Practice. Theories and skills for social workers.* New York: Oxford University Press.

ANALYSIS OF QUALITATIVE DATA

> *Much of the best work in sociology has been carried out using qualitative
> methods without statistical tests. This has been true of research areas
> ranging from organization and community studies to microstudies
> of face to face interaction and macrostudies of the world system. Nor
> should such work be regarded as weak or initial "exploratory"
> approaches to those topics.*
>
> —Randall Collins, "Statistics versus Words," p. 340

INTRODUCTION

Qualitative data are in the form of text, written words, phrases, or symbols describing or representing people, actions, and events in social life. Except for the occasional content analysis study, qualitative researchers rarely use statistical analysis. This does not mean that qualitative data analysis is based on speculation or on vague impressions. It can be systematic and logically rigorous, although in a different way from quantitative or statistical analysis.

In the past, few qualitative researchers explained how they analyzed data. In fact, a common criticism of qualitative research was that data analysis was not made explicit or open to inspection. Qualitative data analysis has moved to a more explicit and systematic step-by-step approach.[1]

Nevertheless, no single qualitative data analysis approach is widely accepted. In this chapter you will learn about a few qualitative analysis techniques. Some of the approaches are used more often in historical–comparative research and others more in field research.

QUANTITATIVE AND QUALITATIVE ANALYSIS

Qualitative and quantitative forms of data analysis have similarities and differences.

Similarities

First, the form of analysis for both types of data in both styles of research involves inference. Researchers infer from the empirical details of social life. To *infer* means to pass a judgment, to use reasoning, and to reach a conclusion based on evidence. In both forms of data analysis, the researcher carefully examines empirical information to reach a conclusion. The conclusion is reached by reasoning and simplifies the complexity in the data. There is some abstraction or distance from the data, but this varies by the style of research. Both forms of data analysis anchor statements about the social world in an inquiry that has adequacy (i.e., it is faithful to the data). "In qualitative research *adequacy* refers to the amount of data collected, rather than to the number of subjects as in quantitative research. Adequacy is attained when sufficient data has been collected that saturation occurs" (Morse, 1994:230, emphasis in original).

A second similarity is that both forms of analysis involve a public method or process. Researchers systematically record or gather data and in doing so make accessible to others what they did. Both types of researchers collect large amounts of data. They describe the data and document how they collected and examined it. The degree to which the method is standardized and visible may vary, but all researchers reveal their study design in some way. "Research designs in qualitative research are not always made explicit, but they are at least implicit in every piece of research" (King et al., 1994:118).

Next, comparison is a central process to all data analysis, qualitative or quantitative. All social work researchers compare features of the evidence they have gathered internally or with related evidence. Researchers identify multiple processes, causes, properties, or mechanisms within the evidence. They then look for patterns—similarities and differences, aspects that are alike and unlike:

> *[Qualitative] researchers examine patterns of similarities and differences across cases and try to come to terms with their diversity. . . . Quantitative researchers also examine differences among cases, but with a different emphasis; the goal is to explain the covariation of one variable with another, usually across many cases. . . . The quantitative researcher typically has only broad familiarity with the cases. (Ragin, 1994:107)*

Fourth, in both qualitative and quantitative forms of data analysis, researchers strive to avoid errors, false conclusions, and misleading inferences. Researchers are also alert for possible fallacies or illusions. They sort through various explanations, discussions, and descriptions, and evaluate merits of rivals, seeking the more authentic, valid, true, or worthy among them.

Differences

Qualitative data analysis differs from quantitative analysis in four ways. First, quantitative social work researchers choose from a specialized, standardized set of data analysis techniques. Hypothesis testing and statistical methods vary little across different social work research projects or across the natural and social sciences. Quantitative analysis is highly developed and builds on applied mathematics. By contrast, qualitative data analysis is less standardized. The wide variety in possible approaches to qualitative research is matched by the many approaches to data analysis. Qualitative social work research is often inductive. Researchers rarely know the specifics of data analysis when they begin a project. Schatzman and Strauss (1973:108) remarked, "Qualitative analysts do not often enjoy the operational advantages of their quantitative cousins in being able to predict their own analytic processes; consequently, they cannot refine and order their raw data by operations built initially into the design of research."

A second difference is that quantitative social work researchers do not begin data analysis until they have collected all of the data and condensed them into numbers. They then manipulate the numbers in order to see patterns or relationships. Qualitative social work researchers can look for patterns or relationships, but they begin analysis early in a research project, while they are still collecting data. The results of early data analysis guide subsequent data collection. Thus, analysis is less a distinct final stage of research than a dimension of research that stretches across all stages.

Another difference is the relation to social theory. Quantitative social work researchers manipulate numbers that represent empirical facts in order to test an abstract hypothesis with variable constructs. By contrast, qualitative social work researchers create new concepts and theory by blending together empirical evidence and abstract concepts. Instead of testing a hypothesis, a qualitative analyst may illustrate or color in evidence showing that a theory, generalization, or interpretation is plausible.

The fourth difference is the degree of abstraction or distance from the details of social life. In all data analysis a researcher places raw data into categories that he or she manipulates in order to identify patterns and arrive at generalizations. In quantitative analysis this process is clothed in statistics, hypotheses, and variables. Quantitative social work researchers use the symbolic language of statistical relationships between variables to discuss causal relations. They assume that social life can be measured by using numbers. When they manipulate the numbers according to the laws of statistics, the numbers reveal features of social life.

Qualitative analysis is less abstract than statistical analysis and closer to raw data. Qualitative analysis does not draw on a large, well-established body of formal knowledge from mathematics and statistics. The data are in the form of words, which are relatively imprecise, diffuse, and context-based, and can have more than one meaning:

Words are not only more fundamental intellectually; one may also say that they are necessarily superior to mathematics in the social structure of the discipline. For words are a mode of expression with greater open-endedness, more capacity for connecting various realms of argument and experience, and more capacity for reaching intellectual audiences. (Collins, 1984:353)

Explanations and Qualitative Data

Qualitative explanations take many forms. A qualitative social work researcher does not have to choose between a rigid ideographic/nomothetic dichotomy—that is, between describing specifics and verifying universal laws. Instead, a researcher develops explanations or generalizations that are close to concrete data and contexts but are more than simple descriptions. He or she usually uses a lower-level, less abstract theory, which is grounded in concrete details. He or she may build new theory to create a realistic picture of social life and stimulate understanding more than to test a causal hypothesis. Explanations tend to be rich in detail, sensitive to context, and capable of showing the complex processes or sequences of social life. The explanations may be causal, but this is not always the case. The researcher's goal is to organize a large quantity of specific details into a coherent picture, model, or set of interlocked concepts.

A qualitative social work researcher rarely tries to document universal laws; rather, he or she divides explanations into two categories: highly unlikely and plausible. The researcher is satisfied by building a case or supplying supportive evidence. He or she may eliminate some theoretical explanations from consideration while increasing the plausibility of others, because only a few explanations will be consistent with a pattern in the data. Qualitative analysis can eliminate an explanation by showing that a wide array of evidence contradicts it. The data might support more than one explanation, but not *all* explanations will be consistent with it. In addition to eliminating less plausible explanations, qualitative data analysis helps to verify a sequence of events or the steps of a process. This temporal ordering is the basis of finding associations among variables, and it is useful in supporting causal arguments.

The form of analysis and theorizing in qualitative research sometimes makes it difficult to see generalizations. Some qualitative social work researchers are almost entirely descriptive and avoid theoretical analysis. In general, it is best to make theories and concepts explicit. Without an analytic interpretation or theory provided by the researcher, the readers of qualitative research may use their own everyday, taken-for-granted ideas. Their common-sense framework is likely to contain implicit assumptions, biases, ethnocentrism, and ill-defined concepts from dominant cultural values.[2]

CONCEPT FORMATION

In this section you will learn about themes or concepts, coding qualitative data, and analytic memo writing. Qualitative researchers sometimes use variables, but more often they use general ideas, themes, or concepts as analytic tools for making generalizations. Qualitative analysis often uses nonvariable concepts or simple nominal-level variables.

Conceptualization in Qualitative Social Work Research

Quantitative researchers conceptualize variables and refine concepts as part of the process of measuring variables that comes before data collection or analysis. By contrast, qualitative researchers form new concepts or refine concepts that are grounded in the data. Concept formation is an integral part of data analysis and begins during data collection. Thus, conceptualization is one way that a qualitative researcher organizes and makes sense of data.

A qualitative researcher analyzes data by organizing it into categories on the basis of themes, concepts, or similar features. He or she develops new concepts, formulates conceptual definitions, and examines the relationships among concepts. Eventually, he or she links concepts to each other in terms of a sequence, as oppositional sets (X is the opposite of Y), or as sets of similar categories that he or she interweaves into theoretical statements. Qualitative researchers conceptualize or form concepts as they

read through and ask critical questions of data (e.g., field notes, historical documents, secondary sources, etc.). The questions can come from the abstract vocabulary of a discipline such as sociology—for example: Is this a case of class conflict? Was role conflict present in that situation? Is this a social movement? Questions can also be logical—for example: What was the sequence of events? How does the way it happened here compare to over there? Are these the same or different, general or specific cases?[3] Researchers often conceptualize as they code qualitative data.

In qualitative social work research, ideas and evidence are mutually interdependent. This applies particularly to case study analysis. Cases are not given preestablished empirical units or theoretical categories apart from data; they are defined by data and theory. By analyzing a situation, the researcher organizes data and applies ideas simultaneously to create or specify a case. Making or creating a case, called *casing,* brings the data and theory together. Determining what to treat as a case resolves a tension or strain between what the researcher observes and his or her ideas about it. "Casing viewed as a methodological step, can occur at any phase of the research process, but occurs especially at the beginning of the project and at the end" (Ragin, 1992b:218).

Coding Qualitative Data

A quantitative social work researcher codes after all the data have been collected. He or she arranges measures of variables, which are in the form of numbers, into a machine-readable form for statistical analysis.

Coding data has a different meaning and role in qualitative research. A researcher organizes the raw data into conceptual categories and creates themes or concepts, which he or she then uses to analyze data. Instead of a simple clerical task, qualitative coding is an integral part of data analysis. It is guided by the research question and leads to new questions. It frees a researcher from entanglement in the details of the raw data and encourages higher-level thinking about them. It also moves him or her toward theory and generalizations:

Codes are tags or labels for assigning units of meaning to the descriptive or inferential information compiled during a study. Codes usually are attached to "chunks" of varying size—words, phases, sentences or whole paragraphs, connected or unconnected to a specific setting. (Miles and Huberman, 1994:56)

Coding is two simultaneous activities: mechanical data reduction and analytic categorization of data into themes. The researcher imposes order on the data (see Box 15.1). "Contrasted with the weeks and weeks in which she will be engaged in mechanical processing, the truly analytic moments will occur during bursts of insight or pattern recognition" (Wolcott, 1994:24). Coding data is the hard work of reducing mountains of raw data into manageable piles. In addition to making a large mass of data manageable, coding allows a researcher to quickly retrieve relevant parts of it. Between the moments of thrill and inspiration, a great deal of coding qualitative data, or filework, can be wearisome and tedious. Plath (1990:375) remarked, it has "all the dramatic tension of watching paint dry." She also stated:

The task of shifting through much material can become daunting. For weeks, even months, you may have nothing to show as proof of effort expended. . . . Filework is the outward manifestation of an inward pledge that most of us make to continue striving to understand a particular people. (Plath, 1990:374)

Strauss (1987) defined three kinds of qualitative data coding, which are described next. The researcher reviews the data on three occasions, using a different coding each time, and codes the same raw data in three passes. Strauss (1987:55) warned, "Coding is the most difficult operation for inexperienced researchers to understand and to master."[4]

Box 15.1

Themes and Coding Qualitative Data

"A good thematic code is one that captures the qualitative richness of the phenomenon. It is usable in the analysis, the interpretation, and the presentation of research" (Boyatzis, 1998:31). To code data into themes, a researcher first needs to learn how "to see" or recognize themes in the data. Seeing themes rests on four abilities: (1) recognizing patterns in the data, (2) thinking in terms of systems and concepts, (3) having tacit knowledge or in-depth background knowledge (e.g., it helps to know Greek myths to understand Shakespeare's plays), and (4) possessing relevant information (e.g., one needs to know a lot about rock musicians and music to code themes about a rock music concert) (see Boyatzis, 1998:7–8). Codes have five parts: a one- to three-word label or name, a definition with a main characteristic, a "flag" description of how to recognize the code in the data, any exclusions or qualification, and an example, as shown here:

Label.   Gender-role disputes are an example.

Definition.   Interpersonal verbal disagreements are an example, as are conflicts or disputes over what is proper or acceptable behavior for males and females in their interactions together or separately because they are male or female.

Flag.   An example would be sarcastic remarks, jokes, or disagreements (very mild to angry arguments) over what a male or female should do because they are male or female.

Qualifications.   Disputes among only same-gendered persons are considered. Any type of behavior (verbal or nonverbal) can be the target of a dispute. Interactions among overtly homosexual and transgendered persons are not included.

Example.   Outside a classroom, Sara and Jessica, 16 years old, discuss their dates last night. Sara says, "We went out for pizza—of course he paid." Jessica remarks, "Of course? You mean you *expect* the guy to pay?" Sara answers, "Oh, forget it."

Three errors to avoid when coding (see Schwandt, 1997:17) are staying at a descriptive level only (not being analytic), treating coding as a purely mechanical process, and keeping codes fixed and inflexible.

Open Coding. *Open coding* is performed during a first pass through recently collected data. The researcher locates themes and assigns initial codes or labels in a first attempt to condense the mass of data into categories. He or she slowly reads field notes, historical sources, or other data, looking for critical terms, key events, or themes, which are then noted. Next, he or she writes a preliminary concept or label at the edge of a note card or computer record and highlights it with brightly colored ink or in some similar way. The researcher is open to creating new themes and to changing these initial codes in subsequent analysis. A theoretical framework helps if it is used in a flexible manner.

Open coding brings themes to the surface from deep inside the data. The themes are at a low level of abstraction and come from the researcher's initial research question, concepts in the literature, terms used by members in the social setting, or new thoughts stimulated by immersion in the data. As Schatzman and Strauss (1973:121) warned, it is important for researchers to see abstract concepts in concrete data and to move back and forth between abstract concepts and specific details:

> *Novices occasionally, if not characteristically, bog down in their attempts to utilize substantive levers [i.e., concepts of a discipline] because they view them as real forms. Experienced researchers and scholars more often see through these abstract devices to the ordinary, empirical realities they represent; they are thereby capable of considerable conceptual mobility. Thus, we urge the novice in analysis to convert relatively inert abstractions into stories—even with plots.*

An example of this is found in LeMasters's (1975) field research study of a working-class tavern when he found that marriage came up in many conversations. If he open coded field notes, he might have coded a block of field notes with the theme *marriage.* Following is an example of hypothetical field notes that can be open coded with the theme *marriage:*

> *I wore a tie to the bar on Thursday because I had been at a late meeting. Sam noticed it immediately and said, "Damn it, Doc. I wore one of them things once—when I got married—and look what happened to me! By God, the undertaker will have to put the next one on." I ordered a beer, then asked*

> *him, "Why did you get married?" He replied, "What the hell you goin' to do? You just can't go on shacking up with girls all your life—I did plenty of that when I was single," with a smile and wink. He paused to order another beer and light a cigarette, then continued, "A man, sooner or later, likes to have a home of his own, and some kids, and to have that you have to get married. There's no way out of it—they got you hooked." I said, "Helen [his wife] seems like a nice person." He returned, "Oh, hell, she's not a bad kid, but she's a goddamn woman and they get under my skin. They piss me off. If you go to a party, just when you start having fun, the wife says 'let's go home.' " (Adapted from LeMasters, 1975:36–37)*

Historical–comparative researchers also use open coding. For example, a researcher studying the Knights of Labor, an American nineteenth-century movement for economic and political reform, reads a secondary source about the activities of a local branch of the movement in a specific town. When reading and taking notes, the researcher notices that the Prohibition party was important in local elections and that temperance was debated by members of the local branch. The researcher's primary interest is in the internal structure, ideology, and growth of the Knights movement. Temperance is a new and unexpected category. The researcher codes the notes with the label "temperance" and includes it as a possible theme.

Although some researchers (e.g., Miles and Huberman, 1994:58) suggest that a researcher begins coding with a list of concepts, researchers generate most coding themes while reading data notes. Regardless of whether he or she begins with a list of themes, a researcher makes a list of themes *after* open coding. Such a list serves three purposes:

1. It helps the researcher see the emerging themes at a glance.
2. It stimulates the researcher to find themes in future open coding.
3. The researcher uses the list to build a universe of all themes in the study, which he or she reorganizes, sorts, combines, discards, or extends in further analysis.

Qualitative social work researchers vary in how completely and in how much detail they code. Some code every line or every few words; others code paragraphs and argue that much of the data are not coded and are dross or left over. The degree of detail in coding depends on the research question, the "richness" of the data, and the researcher's purposes.

Open-ended coding extends to analytic notes or memos that a researcher writes to himself or herself while collecting data. Researchers should write memos on their codes (see the later discussion of analytic memo writing).

Axial Coding. This is a "second pass" through the data. During open coding, a researcher focuses on the actual data and assigns code labels for themes. There is no concern about making connections among themes or elaborating the concepts that the themes represent. By contrast, in *axial coding,* the researcher begins with an organized set of initial codes or preliminary concepts. In this second pass he or she focuses on the initial coded themes more than on the data. Additional codes or new ideas may emerge during this pass, and the researcher notes them; but his or her primary task is to review and examine initial codes. He or she moves toward organizing ideas or themes and identifies the axis of key concepts in analysis.

Miles and Huberman (1994:62) have warned:

Whether codes are created and revised early or late is basically less important than whether they have some conceptual and structural order. Codes should relate to one another in coherent, study-important ways; they should be part of a governing structure.

During axial coding, a researcher asks about causes and consequences, conditions and interactions, strategies and processes, and looks for categories or concepts that cluster together. He or she asks questions such as, "Can I divide existing concepts into subdimensions or subcategories? Can I combine several closely related concepts into one more general one? Can I organize categories into a sequence (i.e., A, then B, then C), or by their physical location (i.e., where they occur), or their relationship to a major topic of interest?" A field researcher studying working-class life may divide the general issue of marriage into subparts (e.g., engagement, weddings). He or she marks all notes involving parts of marriage and then relates marriage to themes of sexuality, division of labor in household tasks, views on children,

and so on. When the theme reappears in different places, the researcher makes comparisons so he or she can see new themes (e.g., men and women have different attitudes toward marriage).

In the example of historical research on the Knights of Labor, a researcher looks for themes related to temperance. He or she looks for discussions of saloons, drinking or drunkenness, and relations between the movement and political parties that support or oppose temperance. Themes that cluster around temperance could also include drinking as a form of recreation, drinking as part of ethnic culture, and differences between men and women regarding drinking.

Axial coding not only stimulates thinking about linkages between concepts or themes but it also raises new questions. It can suggest dropping some themes or examining others in more depth. In addition, it reinforces the connections between evidence and concepts. As a researcher consolidates codes and locates evidences, he or she finds evidence in many places for core themes and builds a dense web of support in the qualitative data for them. This is analogous to the idea of multiple indicators described with regard to reliability and measuring variables. The connection between a theme and data is strengthened by multiple instances of empirical evidence.[5]

Selective Coding. By the time a researcher is ready for this last pass through the data, he or she has identified the major themes of the research project. *Selective coding* involves scanning data and previous codes. Social work researchers look selectively for cases that illustrate themes and make comparisons and contrasts after most or all data collection is complete. They begin after they have well-developed concepts and have started to organize their overall analysis around several core generalizations or ideas. For example, a researcher studying working-class life in a tavern decides to make gender relations a major theme. In selective coding the researcher goes through his or her field notes, looking for differences in how men and women talk about dating, engagements, weddings, divorce, extramarital affairs, or husband/wife relations. He or she then compares male and female attitudes on each part of the theme of marriage.

Likewise, the researcher studying the Knights of Labor decides to make the movement's failure to form alliances with other political groups a major theme. The researcher goes through his or her notes looking for compromise and conflict between the Knights and other political parties, including temperance groups and the Prohibition party. The array of concepts and themes that are related to temperance in axial coding helps him or her discover how the temperance issue facilitated or inhibited alliances.

During selective coding, major themes or concepts ultimately guide the researcher's search. He or she reorganizes specific themes identified in earlier coding and elaborates more than one major theme. For example, in the working-class tavern study, the researcher examines opinions on marriage to understand both the theme of gender relations and the theme of different stages of the life cycle. He or she does this because marriage can be looked at both ways. Likewise, in the Knights of Labor study, the researcher can use temperance to understand the major theme of failed alliances and also to understand another theme, sources of division within the movement

that were based on ethnic or religious differences among members.

Analytic Memo Writing

Qualitative researchers are always writing notes. Their data are recorded in notes, they write comments on their method or research strategy in notes, and so on. They are compulsive note takers, keep their notes organized in files, and often have many files with different kinds of notes: a file on methodological issues (e.g., locations of sources or ethical issues), a file of maps or diagrams, a file on possible overall outlines of a final report or chapter, a file on specific people or events, and so on.

The *analytic memo* is a special type of note.[6] It is a memo or discussion of thoughts and ideas about the coding process that a researcher writes to himself or herself. Each coded theme or concept forms the basis of a separate memo, and the memo contains a discussion of the concept or theme. The rough theoretical notes form the beginning of analytic memos.

The analytic memo forges a link between the concrete data or raw evidence and more abstract, theoretical thinking (see Figure 15.1). It contains a

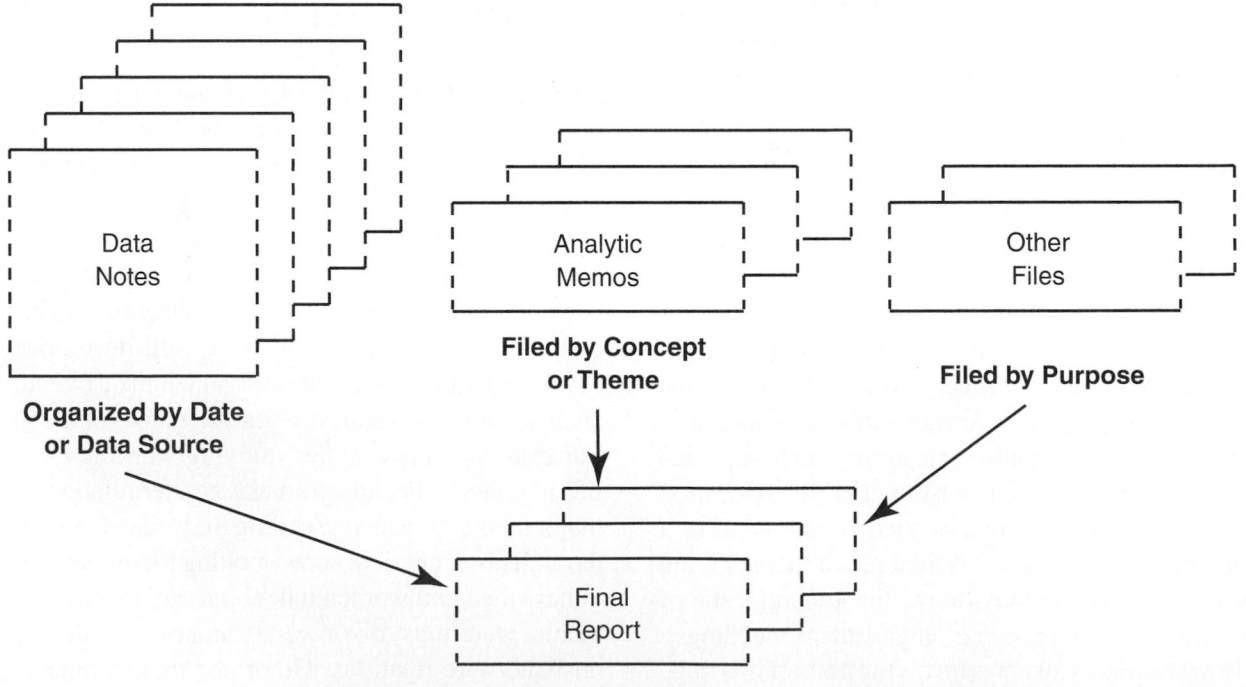

FIGURE 15.1 Analytic Memos and Other Files

researcher's reflections on and thinking about the data and coding. The researcher adds to the memo and uses it as he or she passes through the data with each type of coding. The memos form the basis for analyzing data in the research report. In fact, rewritten sections from good-quality analytic memos can become sections of the final report.

The technology involved in writing analytic memos is simple: pen and paper, a few notebooks, a stack of file folders, and photocopies of notes. Some researchers use computers, but it is not necessary. There are many ways to write analytic memos; each researcher develops his or her own style or method. Some concrete suggestions based on the experience of other researchers are provided in Box 15.2. Some researchers make multiple copies of notes, then cut them and place parts of a copy into an analytic memo file. This works well if the physical files are large and analytic memos are kept distinct within the file (e.g., on different-colored paper or placed at the beginning). Other researchers list— within the analytic memo—file locations in the data notes where a theme appears. Then it is easy to move between the analytic memo and the data. Because data notes contain highlighted or marked themes, it is easy to find specific sections in the data. An intermediate strategy is to keep a running list of locations where a major theme appears in the data, but also include copies of a few key sections of the notes for easy reference.[7]

As a researcher reviews and modifies analytic memos, he or she discusses ideas with colleagues and returns to the literature with a focus on new issues. Analytic memos may help to generate

---

Box 15.2

Suggestions for Analytic Memo Writing

1. Start to write memos shortly after you begin data collection, and continue memo writing until just before the final research report is completed.
2. Put the date on memo entries so that you can see progress and the development of thinking. This will be helpful when rereading long, complicated memos, since you will periodically modify memos as research progresses and add to them.
3. Interrupt coding or data recording to write a memo. Do not wait and let a creative spark or new insight fade away—write it down.
4. Periodically read memos and compare memos on similar codes to see whether they can be combined, or whether differences between codes can be made clearer.
5. Keep a separate file for memos on each concept or theme. All memo writing on that theme or concept is kept together in one file, folder, or notebook. Label it with the name of the concept or theme so it can be located easily. It is important to be able to sort or reorganize memos physically as analysis progresses, so you should be able to sort the memos in some way.
6. Keep analytic memos and data notes separate because they have different purposes. The data are evidence. The analytic memos have a conceptual, theory-building intent. They do not report data, but comment on how data are tied together or how a cluster of data is an instance of a general theme or concept.
7. Refer to other concepts within an analytic memo. When writing a memo, think of similarities to, differences between, or causal relationships to other concepts. Note these in the analytic memo to facilitate later integration, synthesis, and analysis.
8. If two ideas arise at once, put each in a separate memo. Try to keep each distinct theme or concept in a separate memo and file.
9. If nothing new can be added to a memo and you have reached a point of saturation in getting any further data on a theme or concept, indicate that in the memo.
10. Keep a list of codes or labels for the memos that will let you look down the list and see all the memos. When you periodically sort and regroup memos, reorganize this list of memo labels to correspond to the sorting.

Source: Adapted from Miles and Huberman (1994:72–76), Lofland and Lofland (1995:193–194), and Strauss (1987:127–129). Also, see Lester and Hadden (1980).

potential hypotheses, which can be added and dropped as needed, and to develop new themes or coding systems.

METHODS OF QUALITATIVE DATA ANALYSIS

The coding and memo-writing techniques discussed in the previous section are generic and can be used in most types of analyses. There are also more specific methods of qualitative data analysis. In this section you will learn about six such methods selected from all possible methods: successive approximation, the illustrative method, analytic comparison, domain analysis, ideal types, and event-structure analysis. Qualitative researchers sometimes combine the methods or use them with quantitative analysis.

In general, *data analysis* means a search for patterns in data—recurrent behaviors, objects, or a body of knowledge. Once a pattern is identified, it is interpreted in terms of a social theory or the setting in which it occurred. The qualitative researcher moves from the description of a historical event or social setting to a more general interpretation of its meaning.

A potential source of confusion is the multiple forms that data take in various stages of qualitative research. For example, field research data are raw sense data that a researcher experiences, recorded data in field notes, and selected or processed data that appear in a final report (see Figure 15.2). Data analysis involves examining, sorting, categorizing, evaluating, comparing, synthesizing, and contemplating the coded data as well as reviewing the raw and recorded data.

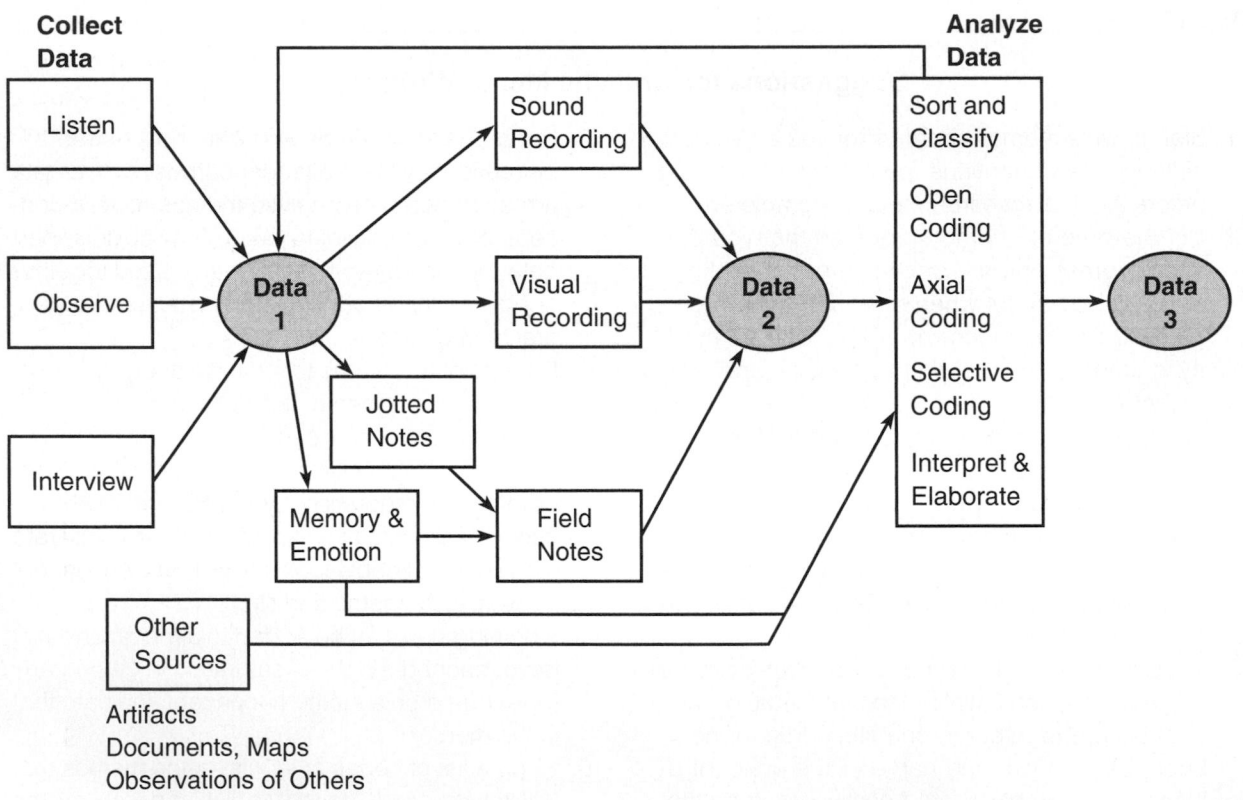

FIGURE 15.2   Data in Field Research (Data 1 = Raw sense data, experiences of researcher; Data 2 = Recorded data, physical record of experiences; Data 3 = Selected, processed data in a final report)

Source: Adapted from Ellen (1984a:214).

Successive Approximation

This method involves repeated iterations or cycling through steps, moving toward a final analysis. Over time, or after several iterations, a researcher moves from vague ideas and concrete details in the data toward a comprehensive analysis with generalizations. This is similar to three kinds of coding discussed earlier.

A social work researcher begins with research questions and a framework of assumptions and concepts. He or she then probes into the data, asking questions of the evidence to see how well the concepts fit the evidence and reveal features of the data. He or she also creates new concepts by abstracting from the evidence and adjusts concepts to fit the evidence better. The researcher then collects additional evidence to address unresolved issues that appeared in the first stage, and repeats the process. At each stage, the evidence and the theory shape each other. This is called *successive approximation* because the modified concepts and the model approximate the full evidence and are modified over and over to become successively more accurate.

Each pass through the evidence is provisional or incomplete. The concepts are abstract, but they are rooted in the concrete evidence and reflect the context. As the analysis moves toward generalizations that are subject to conditions and contingencies, the researcher refines generalizations and linkages to reflect the evidence better.[8] For example, a historical–comparative researcher believes that historical reality is not even or linear; rather, it has discontinuous stages or steps. He or she may divide 100 years of history into periods by breaking continuous time into discrete units or periods and define the periods theoretically. Theory helps him or her identify what is significant and what is common within periods or between different periods. As Carr (1961:76) remarked, "The division of history into periods is not a fact, but a necessary hypothesis." The breaks between periods are artificial; they are not natural in history, but they are not arbitrary.

The researcher cannot determine the number and size of periods and the breaks between them until after the evidence has been examined. He or she may begin with a general idea of how many periods to create and what distinguishes them, but will adjust the number and size of the periods and the location of the breaks after reviewing the evidence. He or she then reexamines the evidence with added data, readjusts the periodization, and so forth. After several cycles, he or she approximates a set of periods in 100 years on the basis of successively theorizing and looking at evidence.

The Illustrative Method

Another method of analysis uses empirical evidence to illustrate or anchor a theory. With the *illustrative method*, a researcher applies theory to a concrete historical situation or social setting, or organizes data on the basis of prior theory. Preexisting theory provides the *empty boxes*. The researcher sees whether evidence can be gathered to fill them.[9] The evidence in the boxes confirms or rejects the theory, which he or she treats as a useful device for interpreting the social world. The theory can be in the form of a general model, an analogy, or a sequence of steps.[10]

There are two variations of the illustrative method. One is to show that the theoretical model illuminates or clarifies a specific case or single situation. The second is the parallel demonstration of a model in which a researcher juxtaposes multiple cases (i.e., units or time periods) to show that the theory can be applied in multiple cases. In other cases the researcher illustrates theory with specific material from multiple cases. An example of parallel demonstration is found in Paige's (1975) study of rural class conflict. Paige first developed an elaborate model of conditions that cause class conflict, and then provided evidence to illustrate it from Peru, Angola, and Vietnam. This demonstrated the applicability of the model in several cases.

Analytic Comparison

British philosopher and social thinker John Stuart Mill (1806–1873) developed logical methods for making comparisons that are still used today. His *method of agreement* and *method of difference* form the basis of *analytic comparison* in qualitative data analysis.[11] Aspects of this logic are also used when making comparisons in experimental research. This differs from the illustrative method in that a researcher does not begin with an overall model consisting of empty boxes to fill with details. Instead, he or she develops ideas about regularities or patterned relations from preexisting theories or induction. The researcher then focuses on a few regularities and makes contrasts with alternative explanations, then looks for regularities that are not limited to a specific setting (time, place, group, etc.). He or she is not seeking universal laws, only regularities within a social context. For example, the researcher looks for a pattern within all late twentieth-century U.S. urban public schools, not a causal law that applies to all educational organizations or all bureaucracies.

Method of Agreement.   The method of agreement focuses a researcher's attention on what is common across cases. The researcher establishes that cases have a common outcome, then tries to locate a common cause, although other features of the cases may differ. The method proceeds by a process of elimination. He or she eliminates features as possible causes if they are not shared across cases that have a common outcome. For example, a researcher looks at four cases, all of them either small social groups or entire societies. All four share two common features, but they also differ in many respects. He or she looks for one or more common causes to explain the common outcome in all cases. At the same time, alternative possibilities are eliminated and a few primary causal factors are identified. The researcher can argue that, despite the differences, the critical similarities exist.

Method of Difference.   Researchers can use the method of difference alone or in conjunction with the method of agreement. The method of difference is usually stronger and is a "double application" of the method of agreement. A researcher first locates cases that are similar in many respects but differ in a few crucial ways. He or she pinpoints features whereby a set of cases is similar with regard to an outcome and causal features, and another set whereby the cases differ on outcomes and causal features. The method of difference reinforces information from positive cases (e.g., cases that have common causal features and outcomes) with negative cases

(e.g., cases lacking the outcome and causal features). Thus, a researcher looks for cases that have many of the causal features of positive cases but lack a few key features and have a different outcome.

An Example.   The method of agreement and method of difference are difficult to grasp in the abstract. Ragin (1987) provided a system for using the methods of agreement and difference. Look at Box 15.3 for an example of each method. In the method of agreement chart, note that a and b are common in all four cases and are crucial similarities despite the many differences (c–q).

Suppose cases 1 through 4 represent four communities and the letters represent features of the communities. Thus, a is a very active client's rights group, b is a socioeconomic structure with several equally large social classes, c is a small set of not-for-profit human services providers, d is a strong and effective network of committed not-for-profit community human services agencies; e is a large state-run public welfare office, f is a public/private shared substance abuse treatment system, and so on. Using the method of agreement, a social work researcher interested in explaining outcome a (active client's rights group) notes the regularity of b (several equally strong socioeconomic classes) across all four cases where an active client's rights group has developed. She or he hypothesizes that b is a critical causal factor for the development of a.

Now consider the second half of Box 15.3, the method of difference. Note that cases 1 and 2 are similar on five features. They differ from either case 5 or case 6 or both on all other features except f. A researcher who wants to explain conditions causing a (active client's rights group) without cases 5 and 6 may have difficulty. He or she could not separate out how important b, c, o, or f are for the client's rights group. Using the method of difference and including cases 4 and 5, he or she notes that x (very active interfaith council) develops despite the presence of some characteristics common to client's rights groups. Thus, the researcher concludes that some features such as c (a small number of not-for-profit community human services providers), o (vocal school board), and f (public/private shared

Box 15.3

Example of Method of Agreement and Method of Difference

METHOD OF AGREEMENT

Case 1	Case 2	Case 3	Case 4
a	a	a	a
b	b	b	b
c	c	d	e
f	f	g	h
i	j	k	k
l	m	l	n
o	o	p	q

METHOD OF DIFFERENCE

Case 1	Case 2	Case 5	Case 6
a	a	x	x
b	b	z	q
c	c	d	c
f	f	f	f
i	j	k	k
l	m	l	n
o	o	o	q

Key: Each letter represents a characteristic that a community has.

a = an active client's rights group
b = a socioeconomic structure with several equally strong social classes
c = a small set of not-for-profit community human services providers
d = a strong and effective network of committed not-for-profit human services agencies
e = a large state-run public welfare county office
f = a public/private shared substance abuse treatment system
g = a large number of recreational facilities
h = a history of housing discrimination against minorities
i = a history of housing rehabilitation
j = a problem locating qualified social workers
k = high personal property taxes
l = active labor unions
m = a large state-run university
n = a small private college
o = a vocal school board
p = an active Ku Klux Klan
q = an inadequate public transportation system
x = a very active interfaith council

substance abuse treatment system) probably are not critical to *a*. Again, it appears that *b* is the key causal feature, in that it is a crucial difference between the set of cases 1 and 2 and the set of cases 5 and 6. (See also another example in Box 15.4.)

Domain Analysis

Ethnographer James Spradley (1979a, 1979b) developed *domain analysis,* an innovative and comprehensive approach for analyzing qualitative data. A key part of his system, which is an orga-

nized structure for qualitative data analysis, is described here.

Spradley defined the basic unit in a cultural setting as a *domain,* an organizing idea or concept. His system is built on analyzing domains. Domains are later combined into taxonomies and broader themes to provide an overall interpretation of a cultural scene or social setting. Domains have three parts: a cover term or phrase, a semantic relationship, and included terms. The cover term is simply the domain's name. Included terms are the subtypes or parts of the domain. A semantic relationship tells

Box 15.4

Analytic Comparison to Study the Success and Failure of Organizations Serving People Who Are Homeless

Cress and Snow (1996) used analytic comparison to analyze field research data (1,500 pages of field notes) that they had gathered on 15 social movement organizations to help people who were homeless in eight U.S. cities. They identified four general types of resources—moral, material, information, and human—that the movements could have. They measured a movement organization's resources by whether it had 14 specific resources, at least two for each of the four types. For example, a specific moral resource was a public statement of support by an external organization, material support included supplies such as paper or telephone service, information support included

people who were experienced at running meetings, and human support included individuals who volunteered time on a regular basis and followed orders.

The researchers classified whether the movement organizations were *viable* (seven were and eight were not), meaning that the organization had survived for one year or more during which meetings were held at least twice a month. They found that nine specific resources were necessary, or the organization would fail, as well as combinations of the five other resources. The development of the 15 organizations followed one of three "paths" based on the combination of the nine necessary and the five "other" resources.

---

how the included terms fit logically within the domain. For example, in the domain of a witness in a judicial setting, the cover term is "witness." Two subtypes or included terms are "defense witness" and "expert witness." The semantic relationship is "is a kind of." Thus, an expert witness and a defense witness are kinds of witnesses. Other semantic relationships are listed in Table 15.1.

Spradley's system was developed by analyzing the argot of members in ethnographic field research, but it can be extended to other qualitative research. For example, Zelizer (1985) studied the changing social value of children by examining documents on attitudes and behaviors toward a child's death in the late nineteenth century. She could have used a domain analysis in which "attitude toward child's death" was a domain, and the statements of various attitudes she discovered in documents were included terms. The attitudes could be organized by the semantic relationship "is a kind of."

Spradley identified three types of domains: folk domains, mixed domains, and analytic domains. *Folk domains* contain terms from the argot of the members in a social setting. To use them, a researcher pays close attention to language and usage. The domain uses the relationship among terms from a subculture's argot or in the language of historical actors to identify cultural meaning:

Mixed domains contain folk terms, but the researcher adds his or her own concepts. For example, kinds of runners are named by the terminology of runners (e.g., long-distance runner, track people, etc.), but a researcher observes other types of people for whom no term exists in the argot. He or she gives them labels (e.g., infrequent visitors, newcomers, amateurs, etc.).

Analytic domains contain terms from the researcher and social theory. They are most helpful when the meanings in a setting are tacit, implicit, or unrecognized by participants. The researcher infers meaningful categories and identifies patterns from observations and artifacts, then assigns terms to them.

Domains are constructed from data notes and are embedded in the notes. A researcher reads his or her notes, looking for common semantic relationships (e.g., is a kind of place, is a kind of person, is a kind of feeling, etc.) in order to find them. He or she proceeds by identifying a list of cover terms. In the examples a witness in a judicial setting or an attitude toward a child's death are cover terms for the domain. Once he or she has a list of cover terms, the researcher next organizes the information from the notes as included terms. He or she prepares a worksheet for each domain relationship. The worksheet contains the cover

TABLE 15.1   Forms of Relationships in Domains

SEMANTIC RELATIONSHIP	EXAMPLE OF USE
is a kind of	A bus *is a kind of* motor vehicle [kinds of vehicles].
is a part of/is a place in	A tire *is a part of* a car [parts of cars].
is a way to	Cheating *is a way to* get high grades in school [ways students get high grades].
is used for	A train *is used for* transporting goods [ways to transport goods].
is a reason for	High unemployment *is a reason for* public unrest [reasons for public unrest].
is a stage of	The charge *is a stage of* a battle [stages of battle].
is a result of/is a cause of	A coal power plant *is a cause of* acid rain [causes of acid rain].
is a place for	A town square *is a place for* a mob to gather [places where mobs gather].
is a characteristic of	Wearing spiked, colored hair *is a characteristic of* punks [characteristics of punks].

term, the list of included terms, and the semantic relationship. An example worksheet is shown in Box 15.5.

Next, the researcher locates examples of the domain relationship from his or her notes. The analysis proceeds until all relevant domains have been identified. He or she then organizes the domains by comparing their differences and similarities. Finally, the researcher reorganizes domains into typologies or taxonomies and reexamines the domains to create new, broader domains that include other domains as included terms.

Spradley's domain analysis formalizes six steps common to most forms of qualitative data analysis. A researcher (1) rereads data notes full of details, (2) mentally repackages details into organizing ideas, (3) constructs new ideas from notes on the subjective meanings or from the researcher's organizing ideas, (4) looks for relationships among ideas and puts them into sets on the basis of logical similarity, (5) organizes them into larger groups by comparing and contrasting the sets of ideas, and (6) reorganizes and links the groups together with broader integrating themes. The process builds up from specifics in the notes to an overall set of logical relationships.

Ideal Types

Max Weber's *ideal type* is used by many qualitative social work researchers. Ideal types are models or mental abstractions of social relations or processes. They are pure standards against which the data or "reality" can be compared. An ideal type is a device used for comparison because no reality ever fits an ideal type. For example, a researcher develops a mental model of the ideal democracy or an ideal college beer party. These abstractions, with lists of characteristics, do not describe any specific democracy or beer party; nevertheless, they are useful when applied to many specific cases to see how well each case measures up to the ideal. This stage can be used with the illustrative method described earlier.

Weber's method of ideal types also complements Mills's method of agreement. Recall that with the method of agreement, a researcher's attention is focused on what is common across cases, and he or she looks for common causes in cases

Box 15.5 _____

Example of Domain Analysis Worksheet

1. Semantic relationship: <u>Strict inclusion</u>
2. Form: <u>_X_ (is a kind of) _Y_</u>
3. Example: <u>An oak (is a kind of) tree</u>

INCLUDED TERMS	SEMANTIC RELATIONSHIP	COVER TERM
<u>laundromat</u> <u>hotel lobby</u> <u>motor box</u> <u>orchard</u>	is a kind of ⟶	
<u>flophouse</u> <u>under bridge</u> <u>box car</u> <u>alley</u> <u>public toilet</u> <u>steam grate</u>		<u>flop</u>

Structural questions: <u>Would you call an alley a flop?</u>

INCLUDED TERMS	SEMANTIC RELATIONSHIP	COVER TERM
<u>trusty</u> <u>ranger</u> <u>bull cook</u> <u>mopper</u>	is a kind of ⟶	
<u>head trusty</u> <u>lockup</u> <u>bullet man</u> <u>sweeper</u> <u>lawn man</u> <u>inmate's barber</u>		<u>jail inmate</u>

Structural questions: <u>Would you call a trusty a type of jail inmate?</u>

with a common outcome. By itself, the method of agreement implies a comparison against actual cases. This comparison of cases could also be made against an idealized model. A researcher could develop an ideal type of a social process or relationship, then compare specific cases to it.

Qualitative researchers have used ideal types in two ways: to contrast the impact of contexts and as analogy.

Contrast Contexts.   Researchers who adopt a strongly interpretive approach may use ideal types to interpret data in a way that is sensitive to the context and cultural meanings of members. They do not test hypotheses or create a generalizable theory, but use the ideal type to bring out the specifics of each case and to emphasize the impact of the unique context.[12]

Researchers making contrasts between contexts often choose cases with dramatic contrasts or distinctive features. For example, in _Work and Author-_

ity in Industry, Reinhard Bendix (1956) compared management relations in very different contexts, Czarist Russia and industrializing England.

When comparing contexts, researchers do not use the ideal type to illustrate a theory in different cases or to discover regularities. Instead, they accentuate the specific and the unique. Other methods of analysis focus on the general and ignore peculiarities. By contrast, a researcher who uses ideal types can show how unique features shape the operation of general processes. As Skocpol and Somers (1980:178) explained:

> _Above all, contrasts are drawn between or among individual cases. Usually such contrasts are developed with the aid of references to broad themes or orienting questions or ideal type concepts. Themes and questions may serve as frameworks for pointing out differences among cases. Ideal types may be used as sensitized devices—benchmarks against which to establish the particular features of each case._

Thus, one use of the ideal type is to show how specific circumstances, cultural meanings, and the perspectives of specific individuals are central for understanding a social setting or process. The ideal type becomes a foil against which unique contextual features can be more easily seen.

Analogies. Ideal types are used as analogies to organize qualitative data. An *analogy* is a statement that two objects, processes, or events are similar to each other. Researchers use them to communicate ideas and to facilitate logical comparisons. Analogies transmit information about patterns in data by referring to something that is already known or an experience familiar to the reader. Analogies can describe relationships buried deep within many details and are a shorthand method for seeing patterns in a maze of specific events. They make it easier to compare social processes across different cases or settings.[13] For example, a researcher says that a room went silent after person X spoke and "a chill like a cold gust of air" spread through it. This does not mean that the room temperature dropped or that a breeze was felt, but it succinctly expresses a rapid change in emotional tone. Likewise, a researcher reports that gender relations in society Y were such that women were "viewed like property and treated like slaves." This does not mean that the legal and social relations between genders were identical to those of slave owner and slave. It implies that an ideal type of a slave-and-master relationship would show major similarities to the evidence on relations between men and women if applied to society Y.

The use of analogies to analyze qualitative data serves as a heuristic device (i.e., a device that helps one learn or see). It can represent something that is unknown and is especially valuable when researchers attempt to make sense of or explain data by referring to a deep structure or an underlying mechanism.[14] Ideal types do not provide a definitive test of an explanation. Rather, they guide the conceptual reconstruction of the mass of details into a systematic format.

Event-Structure Analysis

Many qualitative researchers organize data chronologically in a narrative form to tell a story. *Event-structure analysis (ESA)* is a new type of data analysis method to help researchers organize the sequence of events in ways that facilitate seeing causal relations. The method and a computer program used with it (called ETHNO) were first used for field research data, but it can be used for historical data as well. In ESA the researcher first organizes the data into events, then places the events into a temporal sequence.[15]

ESA differs from a narrative in that the researcher does not just repeat a story, but outlines a set of links between events that happened. He or she separates what had to happen before other events from what could have happened. The computer program forces the researcher to answer questions about the logical relationships among events. For example, a situation has events A, B, C, X, and Y. The researcher is asked, "Must event A occur prior to X causing Y (i.e., Is A a necessary precondition for the X:Y causal relationship?), or would X affect Y without A?" If it is required, A must recur before X will affect Y again. This process forces a researcher to explain whether the causal relation between two events is a unique and one-time relation or a recurring relationship that can be repeated either indefinitely or for a limited number of cycles.

Event-structure analysis has limitations. It does not provide the theory or causal logic; the researcher must supply that. It only creates maps or diagrams (with the computer program) that make it easier to see relationships. When the researcher makes a decision about logically possible relations, ESA clarifies a chain of events and highlights those that might have been different. ESA does not have a place for enduring social structures that frame the action of event sequences: The researcher adds more traditional analysis.

Griffin's (1993) analysis of a lynching illustrates ESA. Based on many oral histories, a book, and newspaper reports, he reconstructed the sequence of events surrounding the lynching of David Harris in Bolivar County, Mississippi in April 1930. After answering many yes/no questions about possible linkages among a long series of events and analyzing the linkages, Griffin was able to conclude that the critical factor was the inaction of the local deputy who could have stopped the process. An abbreviated summary of the ESA diagram is presented in Figure 15.3.

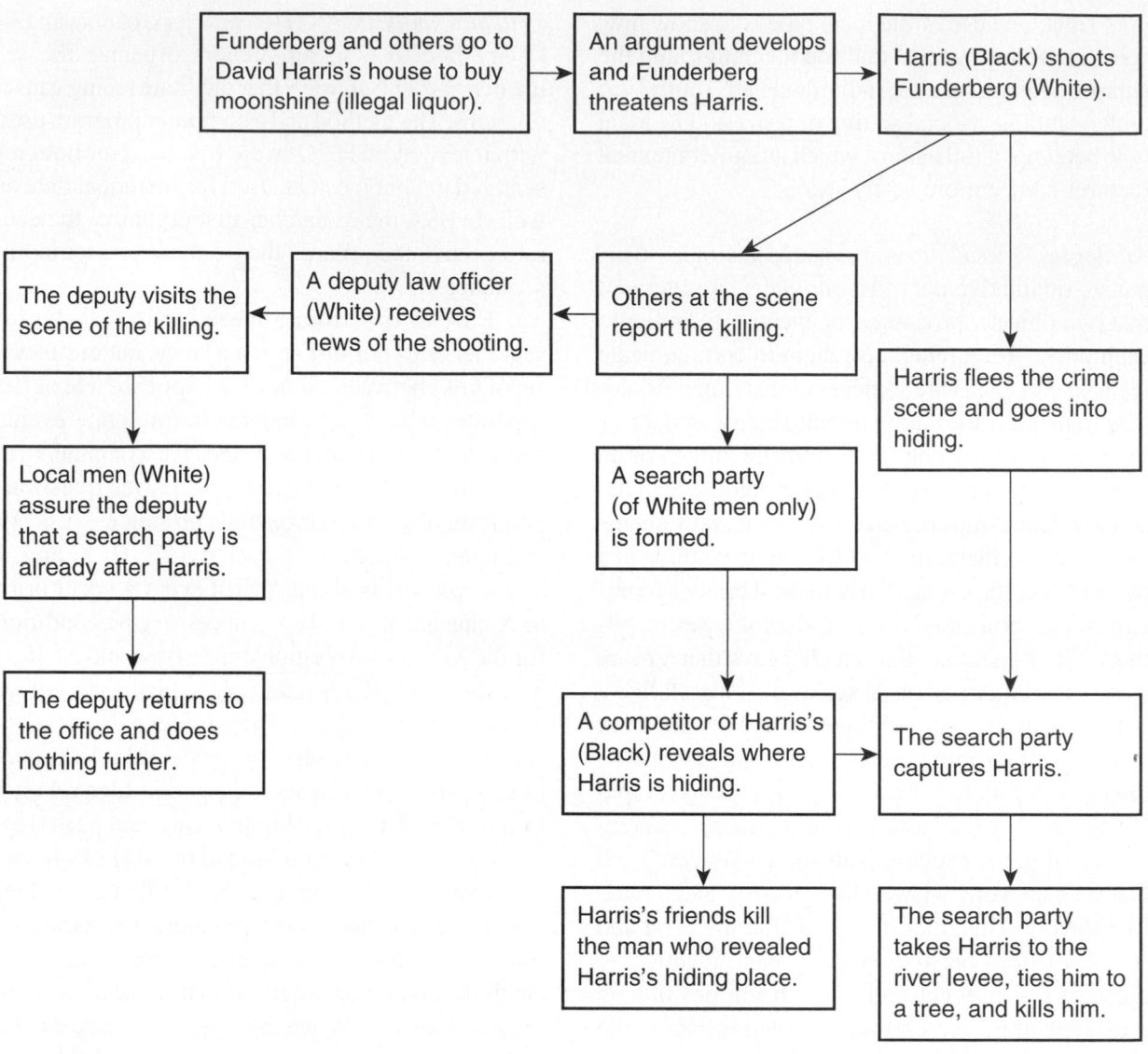

FIGURE 15.3   Example of Event-Structure Analysis of the Lynching of David Harris
Source: Adapted from Griffin (1993).

Other Techniques

Qualitative social work researchers use many other analysis techniques. Here we briefly look at four of the many other techniques to illustrate the variety.

Network Analysis.   The idea of social networks was discussed in Chapter 3 with network theory and in Chapter 8 with snowball sampling. Qualitative researchers often "map" the connections among a set of people, organizations, events, or places. Using sociograms and similar mapping techniques,

they can discover, analyze, and display sets of relations. For example, in a company, Harry gives Sue orders, Sue and Sam consult and help one another. Sam gets materials from Sandra. Sandra socializes with Mary. Researchers find that networks help them see and understand the structure of complex social relations.[16]

Time Allocation Analysis.   Time is an important resource. Researchers examine the way people or organizations spend or invest time to reveal implicit rules of conduct or priorities. Researchers document the duration or amount of time devoted to various activities. Often, people are unaware of (or do not explicitly acknowledge the importance of) an activity on which they spent time. For example, a researcher notices that certain people are required to wait before seeing a person, while others do not wait. The researcher may analyze the amount of time, who waits, what they do while waiting, and whether they feel waiting is just. Or the researcher documents that people say that a certain celebration in a corporation is not important. Yet, everyone attends and spends two hours at the event. The collective allocation of two hours during a busy week for the celebration signals its latent or implicit importance in the culture of the corporation.[17]

Flowchart and Time Sequence.   In addition to the amount of time devoted to various activities, researchers analyze the order of events or decisions. Historical researchers have traditionally focused on documenting the sequence of events, but comparative and field researchers also look at flow or sequence. In addition to when events occur, researchers use the idea of a decision tree or flowchart to outline the order of decisions, to understand how

one event or decision is related to others. For example, an activity as simple as making a cake can be outlined (see Figure 15.4). The idea of mapping out steps, decisions, or events and looking at their interrelationship has been applied to many settings. For example, Brown and Canter (1985) developed a detailed flowchart for house-buying behavior. They divided it into 50 steps, with a time line and many actors (e.g., involved buyer, financial official, surveyor, buyer's attorney, advertising firm/realtor, seller, seller's attorney).[18]

Multiple Sorting Procedure.   Multiple sorting is a technique similar to domain analysis that a researcher can use in field research or oral history. Its purpose is to discover how people categorize their experiences or classify items into systems of similar or different. Multiple sorting procedure has been adopted by cognitive anthropologists and psychologists. It can be used to collect, verify, or analyze data. Here is how it works. The researcher gives those being studied a list of terms, photos, places, names of people, and so on, and asks them to organize the lists into categories or piles. The subjects or members use categories of their own

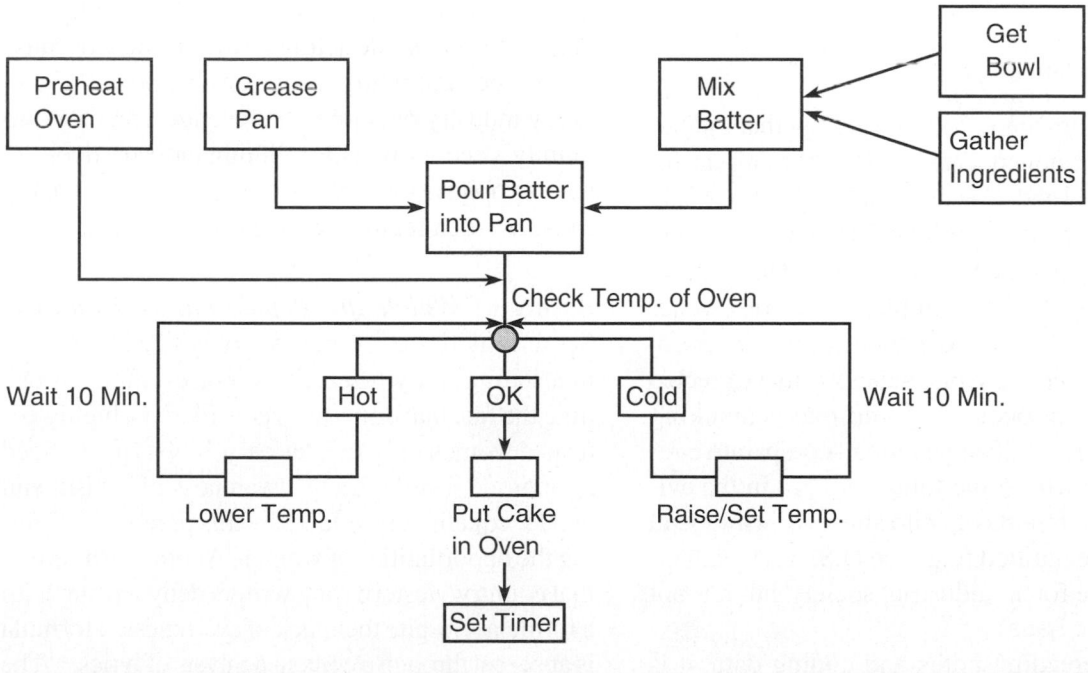

FIGURE 15.4 Partial Flowchart of Cake Making

devising. Once sorted, the researcher asks about the criteria used. The subjects are then given the items again and asked to sort them in other ways they may think of them. There is a similarity to Thurstone scaling in that people sort items, but here, the number of piles and types of items differ. More significantly, the purpose of the sorting is not to create a uniform scale but to discover the variety of ways people understand the world. For example (see Canter et al., 1985:90), a gambler sorts a list of eight gambling establishments five times. Each sort had three to four categories. One of the sorts organized them based on "class of casino" (high to low). Other sorts were based on "frills," "size of stake," "make me money," and "personal preference." By examining the sorts, the researcher sees how others organize their worlds.[19]

WHAT IS MISSING, OR THE IMPORTANCE OF NEGATIVE EVIDENCE

You have seen some of the ways that qualitative researchers analyze data. The emphasis has been on finding patterns, analyzing events, and using models to present what is found in the data. In this section we look at how things that are *not* in the data can be important for analysis.

Negative Evidence

It may seem strange to look for things that did not happen, but the nonappearance of something can reveal a great deal and provide valuable insights. Many researchers emphasize positive data and ignore what is not explicitly in the data, but being alert to absences is also important. For example, a field researcher notices that certain types of people are not present in a setting (e.g., older people, males) or that expected activities do not occur (e.g., no one is smoking cigarettes in a bar). The historical–comparative researcher asks why some things are not in the evidence (e.g., no reports of child abuse) or why social conditions are ignored (e.g., the U.S. has a high infant death rate for an industrial society, but it is not a major public issue).

When rereading notes and coding data, it is easy to forget about things that do not appear, and it is hard to learn how to think about things that are not evident in the data but are important. One technique is to conduct a mind experiment. For example, how might things be different today if the South had won the American Civil War? Another technique is to consider nonevents when analyzing data. For example, why did the person not pick up the five-dollar bill lying on the floor when no one was looking? Comparison also helps. For example, many lower-class youths are arrested for a particular crime. Does this mean that middle-class youths do not engage in it? If not, why not?

Lewis and Lewis (1980) provided seven kinds of *negative evidence* to consider.

Events That Do Not Occur. Some events are expected to occur on the basis of past experience, but do not. For example, research on the Progressive Era of U.S. history found that large corporations did not veto moderate labor reform legislation. Such a veto was expected after they had showed hostility toward labor for years. Instead, they actually encouraged the reform because it would quiet growing labor unrest.

Likewise, nondecisions may occur when powerful groups do not participate directly in events, because their powerful positions shape which issues arise. For example, a city has terrible air pollution, but there is no public action on the problem because "everyone" implicitly recognizes the power of polluting industry over jobs, tax revenue, and the community's economy. The polluting industry does not have to oppose local regulations over pollution, because no such regulations are ever proposed.

Events of Which the Population Is Unaware. Some activities or events are not noticed by people in a setting or by researchers. For example, at one time the fact that employers considered a highly educated woman only for clerical jobs was not noticed as an issue. Until societal awareness of sexism and gender equality grew, few saw this practice as limiting the opportunities of women. Another example is that country/western song writers deny writing with a formula. Despite their lack of awareness, a formula is apparent through a content analysis of lyrics.[20] The fact that members or participants in a setting are unaware of an issue does not mean that a researcher should ignore it or fail to look for its influence.

Events the Population Wants to Hide.   People may misrepresent events to protect themselves or others. For example, elites often refuse to discuss unethical behavior and may have documents destroyed or held from public access for a long period. Likewise, for many years, cases of incest went unreported in part because they violated such a serious taboo that incest was simply hushed up.

Overlooked Commonplace Events.   Everyday, routine events set expectations and create a taken-for-granted attitude. For example, television programs appear so often in conversations that they are rarely noticed. Because most people have a television set and watch TV regularly, only someone who rarely watches television or who is a careful analyst may notice the topic. Or a researcher observes a historical period in which cigarette smoking is common. He or she may become aware only if he or she is a nonsmoker or lives in a period when smoking has become a public health issue.

Effects of a Researcher's Preconceived Notions.   Researchers must take care not to let their prior theoretical framework or preconceived notions blind them to contrary events in a social setting. Strong prior notions of where to look and what data are relevant may inhibit a researcher from noticing other relevant or disconfirming evidence. For example, a researcher expects violent conflict between drug addicts and their children and notices it immediately, but fails to see that they also attempt to form a loving relationship.[21]

Unconscious Nonreporting.   Some events appear (in the mind of a researcher) to be insignificant and not worthy of being reported. Yet, if detailed observations are recorded, a critical rereading of notes looking for negative cases may reveal overlooked events. For example, at first a researcher does not consider company picnics to be important. However, after rereading data notes and careful consideration, he or she realizes that they play an important symbolic role in building a sense of community.

Conscious Nonreporting.   Researchers may omit aspects of the setting or events to protect individuals or relations in the setting. For example, a researcher discovers an extramarital affair involving a prominent person but wishes to protect the person's good name and image. A more serious problem is a breach of ethics. This occurs when a researcher fails to present evidence that does not support his or her argument or interpretation of data. Researchers should present evidence that both supports and fails to confirm an interpretation. Readers can then weigh both types of evidence and judge their support for the researcher's interpretation.

Limitation by Omission

Qualitative researchers need to be sensitive to distinctions of race, sex, age, and other social divisions. For example, a White field or historical–comparative researcher who includes only Whites in a study of a multiracial society needs to recognize that his or her analysis is limited. Had the researcher included all perspectives, his or her interpretations might have been different. When engaged in data analysis, a researcher needs to ask, "What points of view are not being considered? What do events look like from the standpoint of all parts of society?"

Likewise, gender is a salient social category in most social situations. For example, in the past it was not uncommon for historical researchers to study "leaders," all of whom were males, and then make statements about social life in general. The same event (e.g., marriage, leisure, or work) may have very different meanings and implications for each sex. Eichler (1988:160) warned: "Gender insensitivity in data interpretation takes two basic forms: ignoring sex as a socially significant variable, and ignoring a relevant sex-differentiated social context." This does not imply that single-sex or single-race studies are not valuable. Rather, when researchers interpret data, they need to be aware of alternative perspectives and not let the limits of the specific social group to which they belong, or which they studied, blind them to a broader view.

Closely related to negative evidence is the *negative case method* (Becker and Geer, 1982; Emigh, 1997). It blends extreme case analysis with analytic comparison. In field research it highlights the complexity of a setting and shows how alternative meaning systems can operate in one setting. In historical–comparative research the researcher focuses on the one case (or a few) that does not fit a broad empirical pattern or a theoretical prediction. This forces him or her to reexamine why the case does not fit and it expands theoretical understanding. Negative case method adds the method of difference from analytic comparison, which focuses attention on differences among cases. Focusing on why one or a few cases differs helps to identify critical contributing factors that might be overlooked otherwise. For example, Italy did not industrialize at the same time as the rest of Western Europe, although it had all the same preconditions. A careful examination of what specific factor differed in the Italian situation helps to explain the negative case (i.e., failure to industrialize at the same time). This enables researchers to better understand the general causal process.

OTHER TOOLS

The ancestors of today's computer were huge mechanical devices of the late 1880s that sorted cardboard cards with holes punched in them. Such machines proved to be fast and reliable, and quickly replaced paper-and-pencil methods. For example, in the 1890s the new technology allowed the U.S. Census Bureau to cut the time for processing returns from nine years to six weeks![22] U.S. military and space technology spinoffs spurred dramatic advances in computer technology in the 1950s and 1960s. Quantitative social work researchers quickly adopted computers, and, by the late 1960s, computers were used for statistical analysis. More rapid advances in the 1970s and the microcomputer revolution in the 1980s greatly reduced the size and cost of computers. What took up an entire building and cost millions of dollars in the 1960s fits into a briefcase and costs $1,000 today.

Software for Qualitative Data

Quantitative researchers have used computers for over three decades to generate tables, graphs, and charts to analyze and present numerical data. By contrast, qualitative researchers moved to computers and diagrams only in the past 5 to 10 years.[23] A researcher who enters notes into a word-processing program may quickly search for words and phrases that can be adapted to coding data and linking codes to analytic memos. Word processing can also help a researcher revise and move codes and parts of field notes.

Here we will consider software specifically created for qualitative data analysis. Many are new and are quickly changing. Weitzman and Miles (1995:4) noted, "Things have happened so fast that many qualitative researchers are bewildered and uncertain." This review of software covers only some of the major approaches at this time.

Text Retrieval. Some programs perform searches of text documents. What they do is similar to the searching function available in most word-processing software. The specialized text retrieval programs are faster and have the capability of finding close matches, slight misspellings, similar sounding words, or synonyms. For example, when a researcher looks for the keyword *boat,* the program might also tell whether any of the following appeared: *ship, battleship, frigate, rowboat, schooner, vessel, yacht, steamer, ocean liner, tug, canoe, skiff, cutter, aircraft carrier, dinghy, scow, galley, ark, cruiser, destroyer, flagship,* and *submarine.* In addition, some programs permit the combination of words or phases using logical terms *(and, or, not)* in what are called *Boolean searches.* For example, a researcher may search long documents for the keywords *college student* and *drinking* and *smoking* occurring within four sentences of one another, but only when the word *fraternity* is not present in the block of text. This Boolean search uses *and* to seek the intersection of *college student* with either of two behaviors that are connected by the logical term *or,* whereas the logical search word *not* excludes situations in which the term *fraternity* appears.

Most programs show the keyword or phrase and the surrounding text. The programs may also permit a researcher to write separate memos or add short notes to the text. Some programs count the keywords found and give their location. Most programs create a very specific index for the text, based only on the terms of interest to the researcher. Examples of such programs include Metamorph and ZyIndex.

Textbase Managers.   Textbase managers are similar to text retrieval programs. The key difference is their ability to organize or sort information about search results. Many programs create subsets of text data that help a researcher make comparisons and contrasts. They allow researchers to sort notes by a key idea or to add factual information. For example, when the data are detailed notes on interviews, a researcher can add information on the date and length of the interview, gender of interviewee, location of interview, and so on. The researcher can then sort and organize each interview or part of the interview notes by using a combination of key words and added information.

In addition, some programs have *Hypertext* capability. Hypertext is a way of linking terms to other information. It works such that clicking the mouse on one term causes a new screen (one that has related information) to appear. The researcher can identify keywords or topics and link them together in the text. For example, a field researcher wants to examine the person Susan and the topic of hair (including haircuts, hairstyles, hair coloring, and hats or hair covering). The researcher can use Hypertext to connect all places Susan's name appears to discussions of hair. By mouse clicking on Susan's name, one block of text quickly jumps to another in the notes to allow the researcher to see all places where Susan and the hair topic appear together.

Some textbase manager software creates cross-tabulation or scatterplot cross-classifications from information in text documents. For example, students keep journals on a course. They write their feelings about each day, using one of four categories (boring, stimulating, challenging, or creative). The students also describe the major activities of each day (e.g., group work, discussion, watch videotape, lecture, or demonstration). A researcher can cross-classify student feelings by activity. By adding other information (e.g., male or female), the researcher can see how students with different characteristics felt about various activities and examine whether the feelings changed with the topic being presented or the time during

the academic year. Two example programs are askSam and Folio VIEWS.

Code-and-Retrieve Programs.   Researchers often assign codes or abstract terms to qualitative data (text field notes, interview records, and video or audiotape transcripts). Code-and-retrieve programs allow a researcher to attach codes to lines, sentences, paragraphs, or blocks of text. The programs may permit multiple codes for the same data. In addition to attaching codes, most programs also allow the researcher to organize the codes. For example, a program can help a researcher make outlines or "trees" of connections (e.g., trunks, branches, and twigs) among the codes, and among the data to which the codes refer. The qualitative data are rearranged in the program based on the researcher's codes and the relations among codes that a researcher specifies. Two example programs are Kwalitan and Ethnograph.

Code-Based Theory Builders.   Qualitative researchers are often interested in the evaluation and generation of theory. Code-based theory builders require that a researcher first assign codes to the data. The programs provide ways for manipulating or drawing contrasts and comparisons among the codes. The relationships among the codes then become the basis for a researcher to test or generate theory.

The types of relations created among the codes may vary by program. A program may permit *if-then* types of logical relations used in event-structure analysis. For example, Corsaro and Heise (1990) described how they coded field research data on young children into separate events. They then examined the logical sequence and relations among the events to search for principles or a "grammar" of implicit rules. They looked for rules that guided the sequencing, combination, or disconnection among events. The computer software ETHNO asks for logical connections among the events (e.g., time order, necessary precondition, co-occurrence, etc.), then shows the pattern among events.

In contrast to other qualitative programs, code-based theory builders have a powerful ability to manipulate codes to reveal patterns or show relations in data that are not immediately evident. It becomes easier for researchers to compare and classify categories of data. The program QCA (Qualitative Comparative Analysis) uses Boolean logic or algebra to help a researcher analyze the characteristics of several cases and apply the method of difference and method of agreement. It performs algebraic computations to identify common and unique characteristics among a set of cases. The algebra is not difficult, but it can be time consuming and subject to human error without the program. NUD*IST is another program of this type.

Conceptual Network Builders. This category of programs helps a researcher build and test theory by presenting graphic displays or networks. The displays do more than diagram data; they help organize a researcher's concepts or thinking about the data. The programs use nodes, or key concepts, that the researcher identifies in data. They then show links or relationships among the nodes. Most programs give graphic presentations with boxes or circles and connected by lines with arrows. The output looks similar to a flowchart diagram, with a web or network of connections among concepts. For example, the data might be a family tree in which the relationships among several generations of family members are presented. Relations among family members (X is a sibling of Y, Z is married to Y, G is an offspring of X) can be used to discuss and analyze features of the network. Example programs include MetaDesign and SemNet.

Diagrams and Qualitative Data

Qualitative researchers have moved toward presenting summaries of their data analysis in the form of diagrams and charts. They have many ways to present data analysis. Diagrams and charts help them organize ideas and systematically investigate relations in the data, as well as communicate results to readers. Researchers first use spatial or temporal maps (see Chapter 13), typology (see Chapter 3), or sociograms. For example, in his study of Little League baseball, Fine (1987) used sociograms to present the social relations among players. Likewise,

Spradley's (1979a, 1979b) domain analysis makes extensive use of taxonomies.

Quantitative researchers have developed many graphs, tables, charts, and pictorial devices to present information. Event-structure analysis is just one example. Miles and Huberman (1994) argued that data display is a critical part of qualitative analysis. In addition to taxonomies, maps, and lists, they suggested the use of flowcharts, organizational charts, causal diagrams, and various lists and grids to illustrate analysis (see Figure 15.5). An example of a diagram to assist qualitative analysis is found in Broadbent's (1989a, 1989b) study of Japanese environmental politics. He created a set of 24 small boxes in a table to analyze and present his results. Six different political groups (e.g., political party, union, business interests, the legislature) are named across the top, and four levels or arenas of political conflict (national, prefectural, town, neighborhood) are listed up and down the side of the table to form the 24 boxes. Thus, each box represents the actions of a political group at a particular level or in one arena of politics. Broadbent drew arrows between the boxes to indicate a sequence of coalition formation, political conflict, or attempts at political influence among the groups at the different levels, based on specific events and political actions.

Outcroppings

Many qualitative social work researchers operate on an assumption that the empirical evidence they gather is related to both their theoretical ideas and structures beneath observable reality. The relationship, modeled in Figure 15.6, suggests that a reseacher's data from the observable, surface reality are only samples of what happens on the visible, surface level. The researcher uses the data to generate and evaluate theories and generalizations. At the same time, he or she assumes that beneath the outer surface of reality lie deeper social structures or relationships.

The surface reality that we see only partially reflects what goes on unseen, beneath the surface. Events on the surface are *outcroppings,* to use a term from geology (see Fetterman, 1989:68). In geology

EXAMPLE 1

Person	Worked Before College	Part-Time Job in College	Pregnant Now	Had Own Car
John	Yes	Yes	N/A	No
Mary	Yes	DK	No	Yes
Martin	No	Yes	N/A	Yes
Yoshi	Yes	No	Yes	Yes

DK = don't know, N/A = not applicable

EXAMPLE 2

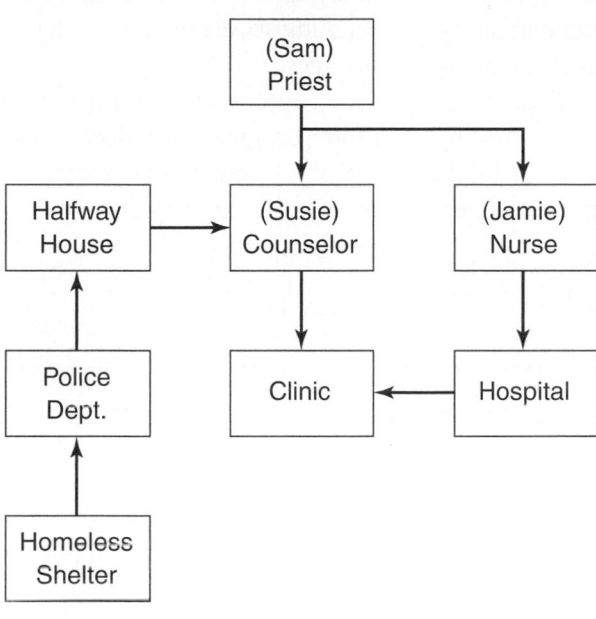

FIGURE 15.5   Examples of the Use of Diagrams in Qualitative Analysis

an outcropping is the part of bedrock that is exposed on the surface for people to see. It is the outward manifestation of central, solid features of the land. Geologists study outcroppings to get clues about what lies beneath the surface.

There are many things we cannot directly observe in the social world. We cannot observe a deep loving relationship between two people. We can see its outward manifestation in a kiss, specific deeds of affection, and acts of kindness. Likewise, we cannot directly observe a social structure such as social class. We can see its outward signs in differences in how people act, their career assumptions, their material possessions, and so forth. Sometimes we are misled by outward observation. Researchers use qualitative data analysis to examine and organize the observable data so that their ideas and theories about the social world reflect not only the

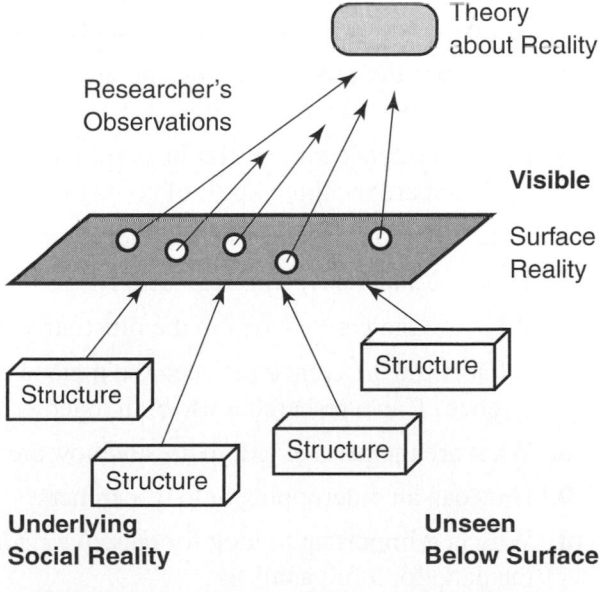

FIGURE 15.6   Theory, Surface Reality, and Underlying Structures

surface level of reality but, more importantly, the deeper structures and forces that may lie unseen beneath the surface.

CONCLUSION

In this chapter you have learned how researchers analyze qualitative data. In many respects qualitative data are more difficult to deal with than data in the form of numbers. Numbers have mathematical properties that let a researcher use statistical procedures. Qualitative analysis requires more effort by an individual researcher to read and reread data notes, reflect on what is read, and make comparisons based on logic and judgment.

Most forms of qualitative data analysis involve coding and writing analytic memos. Both are labor-intensive efforts by the researcher to read over data carefully and think about them seriously. In addition, you learned about methods that researchers have used for the analysis of qualitative data. They are a sample of the many methods of qualitative data analysis. You also learned about the importance of thinking about negative evidence and events that are not present in the data.

This chapter ends the section of the book on research design, data collection, and data analysis. Social work research also involves preparing reports on a research project, which is addressed in the next chapter.

KEY TERMS

analytic comparison	event-structure analysis (ESA)	negative evidence
analytic domain	folk domain	open coding
axial coding	illustrative method	outcropping
domain	method of agreement	selective coding
domain analysis	method of difference	successive approximation
empty boxes	mixed domains	

REVIEW QUESTIONS

1. Identify four differences between quantitative and qualitative data analysis.

2. How does the process of conceptualization differ in qualitative and quantitative social work research?

3. How does data coding differ in quantitative and qualitative social work research, and what are the three kinds of coding used by a qualitative researcher?

4. What is the purpose of analytic memo writing in qualitative data analysis?

5. Describe *successive approximation.*

6. What are the *empty boxes* in the illustrative method, and how are they used?

7. What is the difference between the method of agreement and the method of difference? Can a researcher use both together? Explain why or why not.

8. What are the parts of a domain, and how are they used in domain analysis?

9. How can an outcropping help researchers?

10. Why is it important to look for *negative evidence,* or things that do not appear in the data, for a full analysis?

NOTES

1. See Miles and Huberman (1994) and Ragin (1987). These should not be confused with statistical techniques for "qualitative" data (see Haberman, 1978). These are sophisticated statistical techniques (e.g., logit and log linear) for quantitative variables where the data are at the nominal or ordinal level. They are better labeled as techniques for categorical data.

2. Sprague and Zimmerman (1989) discuss the importance of an explicit theory.

3. See Hammersley and Atkinson (1983:174–206) for a discussion of questions.

4. See Boyatzis (1998), Lofland and Lofland (1995: 192–193), Miles and Huberman (1994:57–71), Sanjek (1990:388–392), and Wolcott (1994) for additional discussions of coding.

5. See also Horan (1987) and Strauss (1987:25) for multiple indicator measurement models with qualitative data.

6. For more on memoing, see Lester and Hadden (1980), Lofland and Lofland (1995:193–197), Miles and Huberman (1994:72–77), and Strauss (1987:107–129).

7. Also, see Barzun and Graff (1970:255–274), Bogdan and Taylor (1975), Lofland and Lofland (1984:131–140), Shafer (1980:171–200), Spradley (1979a, 1979b), and Schatzman and Strauss (1973:104–120) on notes and codes.

8. For more on successive approximation and a debate over it, see Applebaum (1978a), McQuaire (1978, 1979), Paul Thompson (1978), Wardell (1979), and Young (1980).

9. For a discussion of empty boxes, see Bonnell (1980) and Smelser (1976).

10. For a discussion of the illustrative method, see Bonnell (1980) and Skocpol (1984). Bogdan and Taylor (1975:79) describe a similar method.

11. For a discussion of methods of difference and agreement, see Ragin (1987:36–42), Skocpol (1984), Skocpol and Somers (1980), and Stinchcombe (1978:25–29).

12. See Skocpol (1984) and Skocpol and Somers (1980).

13. For a discussion of analogies and models, see Barry (1975), Glucksmann (1974), Harré (1972), Hesse (1970), and Kaplan (1964).

14. For a discussion of the importance of analogies in social theory, see Lloyd (1986:127–132) and Stinchcombe (1978).

15. For a more in-depth discussion of event-structure analysis, see Abbott (1992), Griffin (1993), Griffin and Ragin (1994), Heise (1991), and Issac and colleagues (1994).

16. See Sanjek (1978) and Werner and Schoepfle (1987a).

17. See Gross (1984) and Miles and Huberman (1994: 85, 119–126).

18. See Lofland and Lofland (1995:199–200) and Werner and Schoepfle (1987a:130–146).

19. See Canter and associates (1985) and Werner and Schoepfle (1987a:180–181).

20. See Blee and Billings (1986) for a discussion of analyzing "silences" and unnoticed features in ethnographic or historical text.

21. See Becker and Geer (1982) for a discussion of negative cases and preconceived notions.

22. For a discussion of computer use in social work research, see Cozby (1984), Grosof and Sardy (1985: 191–206), Heise (1981), Karweit and Meyers (1983), and Norusis (1986).

23. See Weitzman and Miles (1995) for a comprehensive review of 24 software programs for qualitative data analysis. Also, see Fielding and Lee (1991) and Richards and Richards (1994).

REVIEWING THE LITERATURE AND WRITING A REPORT

But that's our business: to arrange ideas in so rational an order that another person can make sense of them. We have to deal with that problem on two levels. We have to arrange the ideas in a theory or narrative, to describe causes and conditions that lead to the effects that we want to explain, and do it in an order that is logically and empirically correct. . . . Finally, we want our prose to make the order we have constructed clear. We don't want imperfection in our prose to interfere with our readers' understanding. These two jobs converge and cannot be separated.

—Howard Becker, *Writing for Social Scientists*, p. 133

INTRODUCTION: WHY WRITE A REPORT?

Social work research is a communal activity. It involves communicating with others, usually in a written form. As you learned in Chapter 1, the norm of communalism emphasizes that researchers are obligated to make public how they conducted the research and their findings or results. A research project is not completed until it is shared with others. In this chapter you will learn the format for reporting on a study and the system of storing, retrieving, and referencing the research reports of others.

Good research practice requires that you read numerous reports before beginning research. The reports will provide you with ideas for topics and issues to study, are an invaluable source of concepts and theories, will guide you on how to focus a research project, and will supply specific data-gathering or analysis techniques that you might want to borrow. A beginning researcher should read many published reports before and during the research process to learn about the substantive topic, to discover techniques that he or she might apply, and to see models of how to report research. Good research practice means thinking about the final report throughout the research process. This chapter discusses the research report, how to locate and read the research literature and related sources, use of the Internet for research purposes, and how to write a research report.

THE LITERATURE REVIEW

A literature review is based on the assumption that knowledge accumulates and that we learn from and build on what others have done. Scientific research is a collective effort of many researchers who share their results with one another and who pursue knowledge as a community. Although some studies may be especially important and individual researchers may become famous, a specific research project is just a tiny part of the overall process of creating knowledge. Today's studies build on those of yesterday. Researchers read studies to compare, replicate, or criticize them for weaknesses.

Reviews vary in scope and depth. Different kinds of reviews are stronger at fulfilling one or another of four goals (see Box 16.1). It may take a researcher over a year to complete an extensive professional summary review of all the literature on a broad question. The same researcher might complete a highly focused review in a very specialized area in a few weeks. When beginning a review, a researcher decides on a topic or field of knowledge to examine, how much depth to go into, and the kind of review to conduct. The six kinds listed in Box 16.2 are ideal types. A specific review often combines features of several kinds.

All reviews follow the first goal—to show familiarity and establish credibility—to some degree. It is one reason teachers ask students to write library

---

Box 16.1

Goals of a Literature Review

1. *To demonstrate a familiarity with a body of knowledge and establish credibility.* A review tells a reader that the researcher knows the research in an area and knows the major issues. A good review increases a reader's confidence in the researcher's professional competence, ability, and background.

2. *To show the path of prior research and how a current project is linked to it.* A review outlines the direction of research on a question and shows the development of knowledge. A good review places a research project in a context and demonstrates its relevance by making connections to a body of knowledge.

3. *To integrate and summarize what is known in an area.* A review pulls together and synthesizes different results. A good review points out areas where prior studies agree, where they disagree, and where major questions remain. It collects what is known up to a point in time and indicates the direction for future research.

4. *To learn from others and stimulate new ideas.* A review tells what others have found so that a researcher can benefit from the efforts of others. A good review identifies blind alleys and suggests hypotheses for replication. It divulges procedures, techniques, and research designs worth copying so that a researcher can better focus hypotheses and gain new insights.

Box 16.2 _____

Six Types of Reviews

1. *Self-study reviews* increase the reader's confidence.
2. *Context reviews* place a specific project in the big picture.
3. *Historical reviews* trace the development of an issue over time.
4. *Theoretical reviews* compare how different theories address an issue.
5. *Integrative reviews* summarize what is known at a point in time.
6. *Methodological reviews* point out how methodology varies by study.

_____

research term papers. A review that demonstrates only familiarity with an area is rarely published, but it often is part of an educational program. When this goal is combined with the fourth goal, it is a *self-study review.* In addition to giving others confidence in a reviewer's command of a field, it has the side benefit of building the reviewer's self-confidence.

The most common reason for writing a literature review is the second goal: creating links to a developing body of knowledge. This is a background or *context review.* It usually appears at the beginning of a report or article. It introduces the rest of a research report and establishes the significance and relevance of a research question. It tells the reader how a project fits into the big picture and its implications for a field of knowledge. The review can emphasize how the current research continues a developing line of thought, or it can point to a question or unresolved conflict in prior research to be addressed.

Another kind of review combines the second and third goals. The *historical review* traces the development of an idea or shows how a particular issue or theory has evolved over time. Researchers conduct historical reviews only on the most important ideas in a field. These reviews are also used in studies of the history of thought. Sometimes they are helpful, when students are introduced to an area, to show how we got to where we are today. They may show how, during the advance of knowledge,

a single past idea split into different parts or separate ideas combined into broad thought.

The *theoretical review* primarily follows the third goal. It presents different theories that purport to explain the same thing, then evaluates how well each accounts for findings. In addition to examining the consistency of predictions with findings, a theoretical review may compare theories for the soundness of their assumptions, logical consistency, and scope of explanation. Researchers also use it to integrate two theories or extend a theory to new issues. It sometimes forms a hybrid—the historical–theoretical review.

The *integrative review* presents the current state of knowledge and pulls together disparate research reports in a fast-growing area of knowledge. Researchers may publish such valuable reviews as an article to provide a service to other researchers.

The *methodological review* is a specialized type of the integrative review. In it, a researcher evaluates the methodological strength of past studies. It describes conflicting results and shows how different research designs, samples, measures, and so on account for different results. For example, a researcher may discover that all experiments that relied on males yielded different results than those that used both sexes.

A *meta-analysis* is a special technique researchers use in an integrative review, or more often, in a methodological review.[1] The researcher gathers the details about a large number of research projects (e.g., sample size, when published, size of the effects of variables) and then statistically analyzes this information. For example, Armstrong and Lusk (1987) conducted a meta-analysis on return postage in mail surveys. They searched the literature extensively and found 34 studies that examined the effects of including postage, of first-class versus business-reply postage, and of commemorative versus standard stamps. They examined the type of postage that is most likely to get respondents to return a questionnaire. For each study, they looked at the number of questionnaires mailed out, the percentage returned, and the types of postage used. The researchers found that when first-class postage was used instead of business reply, the questionnaire return rate was consistently higher by about 9 percent.

Cox and Davidson (1995) used meta-analysis to examine findings on whether alternative education programs help juvenile delinquents. These nontraditional programs are designed specifically for troubled youths, using low student/teacher ratios, an unstructured environment, and individualized learning. The authors first conducted a computerized search of three sources: ERIC (Educational Resources Information Circuit), PSYCHLIT, and NCJRS (National Criminal Justice Reference Service) for the years 1966 to 1993. They looked for all citations that mentioned alternative education programs for youth and found 241 citations. They next read each to see whether the article met three criteria: (1) mentioned a separate curriculum, (2) was held in a separate location or building, (3) included quantitative measures of program outcomes. Of the 241 studies, only 87 met all three criteria. The researchers then checked whether the studies used specific statistical measures or tests; they found that 57 studies had the statistics. After statistically analyzing the results of the 57 studies, the authors learned that such programs slightly improve school performance and self-esteem but do not directly reduce delinquent behavior.

WHERE TO FIND SOCIAL WORK RESEARCH LITERATURE

Researchers present reports of their research projects in several written forms. For the most part you can find them only in a college or university library. Researchers publish studies as books, scholarly journal articles, dissertations, government documents, or policy reports. They also present them as papers at the meetings of professional societies. This section briefly discusses each type and gives you a simple road map on how to access them.

You can find the results of research in textbooks, newspapers, popular magazines (e.g., *Time, New Statesman,* and *The Economist*), and radio or television news, but these are not true reports of scientific research. Rather, they are condensed summaries of true reports. Authors or journalists selected them for their popular appeal or teaching usefulness and rewrote them for a general audience. Such popularizations lack essential details that the scientific community requires for a serious evaluation of the research and for use in building the knowledge base.

Scholarly Journals

A researcher who conducts a complete literature review will examine all research outlets. Different types of reports require different search strategies. Let us begin with scholarly journals because they are the place in which most reports appear and are the most crucial outlet. As you saw in Chapter 1, they are central to the communication system of science.

Critics charge that numerous journals have sprung up that permit any study, no matter how flawed or trivial, to be published, and that no one reads the articles. The evidence does not support this view. Hargens (1988) found that rejection rates were higher in the social than in the natural sciences, and that rejection rates are higher now than 20 years ago.

Your college library has a section for scholarly journals and magazines, or, in some cases, they may be mixed with books. Look at a map of library facilities or ask a librarian to find this section. The most recent issues, which look like thin paperbacks or thick magazines, are often physically separate in a "current periodicals" section. This is done to store them temporarily and make them available until the library receives all the issues of a volume. Most often, libraries bind all issues of a volume together as a book before adding it to their permanent collection.

Scholarly journals from many different fields are placed together with popular magazines. All are periodicals, or *serials* in the jargon of librarians. Thus, you will find popular magazines (e.g., *Time, Road and Track, Cosmopolitan,* and *Atlantic Monthly*) next to journals for astronomy, chemistry, mathematics, literature, and philosophy as well as sociology, psychology, social work, and education. Some fields have more scholarly journals than others. The "pure" academic fields usually have more than the "applied" or practical fields such as marketing or social work. The journals are listed by title in a card catalog or a computerized catalog system. Libraries can provide you with a list of the periodicals to which they subscribe. (See Figure 16.1 for a list of journals.)

Many libraries do not retain physical, paper copies of older journals. To save space and costs,

FIGURE 16.1 Scholarly Journals in the Social Work and Allied Fields

Addictive Behaviors

Administration in Social Work

Adolescence

Advances in Behavior Research and Therapy

Affilia: The Journal of Women and Social Work

Aggression and Violent Behavior

AIDS Education and Prevention: An Interdisciplinary Journal

Alcohol Health and Research World

Alcoholism Treatment Quarterly

American Journal of Community Psychology

American Journal of Drug and Alcohol Abuse

American Journal of Family Therapy

American Journal of Mental Deficiency

American Journal of Orthopsychiatry

Areté

Asia Pacific Journal of Social Work

Behavior Modification

Behavior Therapy

Behaviour Research and Therapy

British Journal of Social Work

Canadian Social Work Review

Child Abuse and Neglect: The International Journal

Child and Adolescent Social Work Journal

Child and Family Social Work

Child and Youth Services

Child Care Health and Development

Child Maltreatment

Child Welfare

Children and Society

Children and Youth Services Review

Children Today

Clinical Social Work Journal

Crime and Delinquency

Crisis Intervention and Time-Limited Treatment

Drug and Alcohol Dependence

Ethnic and Racial Studies

Evaluation and Program Planning: An International Journal

Families in Society (Social Casework)

Families in Society: The Journal of Contemporary Human Services

Family Planning Perspectives

Family Process

Family Relations: Interdisciplinary Journal of Applied Family Studies

The Gerontologist

The Hastings Center Report

Health and Social Care in Community

Health and Social Work

Hispanic Journal of Behavioral Sciences

Hospice Journal

Human Services in the Rural Environment

Indian Journal of Social Work

Information and Referral: The Journal of the Alliance of Information and Referral Systems

International Journal of Aging and Human Development

International Journal of the Addictions

International Social Work

Journal of Aging and Social Policy

Journal of Analytic Social Work

Journal of Applied Gerontology

Journal of Applied Psychology

Journal of Applied Social Psychology

Journal of Child and Adolescent Substance Abuse

Journal of Community Psychology

Journal of Criminal Justice

Journal of Divorce and Remarriage

Journal of Family Issues

Journal of Family Social Work

Journal of Family Therapy

Journal of Family Violence

Journal of Gay and Lesbian Social Services

Journal of Gerontological Social Work

Journal of Gerontology

Journal of Homosexuality

Journal of Independent Social Work

Journal of Marital and Family Therapy

Journal of Marriage and the Family

Journal of Multicultural Social Work

Journal of Progressive Human Services

Journal of Research in Crime and Delinquency

Journal of School Psychology

Journal of Social Policy

Journal of Social Service Research

Journal of Social Work Education

Journal of Social Work Practice

Journal of Sociology and Social Welfare

Journal of Studies on Alcohol

Journal of Substance Abuse Treatment

Journal of Teaching in Social Work

Journal of Women and Aging

Journal of Youth and Adolescence

Marriage and Family Review

Mediation Quarterly: Journal of the Academy of Family Mediators

Omega: Journal of Death and Dying

Personality and Individual Differences

Policy and Practice (formerly *Public Welfare*)

Professional Development: The Journal of Continuing Social Work Education

Public Administration Review

Qualitative Social Work

Research on Social Work Practice
Research, Policy and Planning: The Journal of the
   Social Services Research Group
Residential Treatment for Children and Youth
School Social Work Journal
Smith College Studies in Social Work
Social Forces
Social Policy
Social Problems
Social Psychology Quarterly

Social Service Review
Social Work
Social Work Abstracts
Social Work in Education
Social Work in Health Care
Social Work Research
Social Work with Groups
Suicide and Life Threatening Behavior
Youth and Society

---

they retain only microfilm or online versions. There are hundreds of scholarly journals in most academic fields, with each costing $50 to $1,500 per year. Only the large research libraries subscribe to all of them. You may have to borrow a journal or photocopy of an article from a distant library through an *interlibrary loan service,* a system by which libraries lend books or materials to other libraries. Few libraries allow people to check out recent issues of scholarly journals. You should plan to use these in the library. More and more scholarly journals are available in an electronic form, to be read using computers and the Internet.

Once you find the periodicals section, wander down the aisles and skim what is on the shelves. You will see volumes containing many research reports. Each title of a scholarly journal has a call number like that of a regular library book. Libraries often arrange them alphabetically by title. Because journals change titles, it may create confusion if the journal is shelved under its original title.

Scholarly journals differ by field and by type. Most contain articles that report on research in an academic field. Thus, most mathematics journals contain reports on new mathematical studies or proofs, literature journals contain commentary and literary criticism on works of literature, and social work journals contain reports of social work research. Some journals cover a broad field (e.g., social work, psychology, education, political science) and contain reports from the entire field. Others specialize in a subfield (e.g., the family, criminology, early childhood education, comparative politics). There are also a few hybrids or "crossover" publications that try to bridge the gap between academic scholarly journals and popular magazines (e.g., *Psychology Today* and

Society). Another hybrid focuses on how to teach or use knowledge in an area. Some journals contain a mix of research reports, book reviews, and so on, whereas others contain only research reports. A few journals specialize in book review articles, literature reviews, policy analysis, and theoretical essays.

Scholarly journals are published as rarely as once a year or as frequently as weekly. Most appear four to six times a year. To assist in locating articles, librarians and scholars have developed a system for tracking scholarly journals and the articles in them. Each issue is assigned a date, volume number, and issue number. This information makes it easier to locate an article. Such information—along with details such as author, title, and page number—is called an article's *citation* and is used in bibliographies. When a journal is first published, it begins with volume 1, number 1, and continues increasing the numbers thereafter. Although most journals follow a similar system, there are enough exceptions that you have to pay close attention to citation information. For most journals each volume is one year. If you see a journal issue with volume 52, it probably means that the journal has been in existence for 52 years. Most, but not all, journals begin their publishing cycle in January.

Most journals number pages by volume, not by issue. The first issue of a volume usually begins with page 1, and page numbering continues throughout the entire volume. For example, the first page of volume 52, issue 4, may be page 547. Most journals have an index for each volume and a table of contents for each issue that lists the title, the author's or authors' names, and the page on which the article begins. Issues contain as few as 1 or 2 articles or as many as 50. Most have 8 to 18 articles, which may be 5 to 50 pages long. The articles often have *abstracts,* short summaries on the first page of the article or grouped together at the beginning of the issue.

An article's citation is the key to locating it. Suppose you want to read the study on skin tone and stratification among African Americans. If you go to the bibliography of this textbook, you will read its citation as follows:

> Keith, Verna M., and Cedric Herring. (1991). Skin tone and stratification in the black community. *American Journal of Sociology,* 97:760–778.

This tells you that you can find the article in an issue of *American Journal of Sociology* published in 1991. The citation does not give you the month or the issue, but it provides the volume number, 97, and the page numbers, 760–778.

There are many ways to cite the literature. Formats for citing literature in the text itself vary, with the internal citation format of using an author's last name and date of publication in parentheses being very popular. The full citation appears in a separate bibliography or reference section. There are many styles for full citations of journal articles, with books and other types of works each having a separate style. When citing articles, it is best to check with an instructor, journal, or other outlet for the desired format. Almost all include the names of authors, article title, journal name, and volume and page numbers. Beyond these basic elements, there is great variety. Some include the authors' first names, others use initials only. Some include all authors, others give only the first one. Some include information on the issue or month of publication, others do not.

Citation formats can get complex. Two major reference tools on the topic in social work are the *Chicago Manual of Style,* which has nearly 80 pages on bibliographies and reference formats, and the *American Psychological Association (APA) Publication Manual,* which devotes about 60 pages to the topic. In social work the APA style is widely followed.

Books

Books communicate many types of information, provoke thought, and entertain. There are many types of books: picture books, textbooks, short story books, novels, popular fiction or nonfiction, reli-

gious books, children's books, and others. Our concern here is with those books containing reports of original research or collections of research articles. Libraries shelve these books and assign call numbers to them, as they do with other types of books. You can find citation information on them (e.g., title, author, publisher) in the library's catalog system.

It is not easy to distinguish a book that reports on research from other books. You are more likely to find such books in a college or university library. Some publishers, such as university presses, specialize in publishing them. Nevertheless, there is no guaranteed method for identifying one without reading it.

Some types of social research are more likely to appear in book form than others. For example, studies by anthropologists and historians are more likely to appear in book-length reports than are those of economists or psychologists. Yet, some anthropological and historical studies are articles, and some economic and psychological studies appear as books. In education, social work, sociology, and political science, the results of long, complex studies may appear both in two or three articles and in book form. Studies that involve detailed clinical or ethnographic descriptions and complex theoretical or philosophical discussions usually appear as books. Finally, an author who wants to communicate to scholarly peers and to the educated public may write a book that bridges the scholarly, academic style and a popular nonfiction style, such as James Hunter's *Culture Wars* (1991).

Locating original research articles in books can be difficult because there is no single source listing them. Three types of books contain collections of articles or research reports. The first is designed for teaching purposes. Such books, called *readers,* may include original research reports. Usually, articles on a topic from scholarly journals are gathered and edited to be easier for nonspecialists to read and understand.

The second type of collection is designed for scholars and may gather journal articles or may contain original research or theoretical essays on a specific topic. Some collections contain articles from journals that are difficult to locate. They may include original research reports organized around a specialized topic. The table of contents lists the titles and authors. Libraries shelve these collections with other books, and some library catalog systems include them.

Finally, there are annual research books that contain reports on studies that are not found elsewhere. These are hybrids between scholarly journals and collections of articles: They appear year after year, with volume numbers for each year, but they are not journals. These volumes, such as the *Review of Research in Political Sociology* and *Comparative Social Research,* are shelved with books. There is no comprehensive list of these books as there is for scholarly journals. The only way someone new to an area can find out about them is by spending a lot of time in the library or asking a researcher who is already familiar with a topic area.

Citations or references to books are shorter than article citations. They include the author's name, book title, year and place of publication, and publisher's name.

Dissertations

All graduate students who receive the Ph.D. degree are required to complete a work of original research, which they write up as a dissertation thesis. The dissertation is bound and shelved in the library of the university that granted the Ph.D. About half of all dissertations are eventually published as books or articles. Because dissertations report on original research, they can be valuable sources of information. Some students who receive the master's degree conduct original research and write a master's thesis, but fewer master's theses involve serious research, and they are much more difficult to locate than unpublished dissertations.

Specialized indexes list dissertations completed by students at accredited universities. For example, *Social Work Abstracts* lists dissertations with their authors, titles, and universities. This index is organized by topic and contains an abstract of each dissertation. You can borrow most dissertations via interlibrary loan from the degree-granting university if the university permits this. An alternative is to purchase a copy from a national dissertation microfilm/photocopy center such as the one at the University of Michigan, Ann Arbor, for U.S. universities. Some large research libraries

contain copies of dissertations from other libraries if others have previously requested them.

Government Documents

The federal government of the United States, the governments of other nations, state or provincial-level governments, the United Nations, and other international agencies such as the World Bank, all sponsor studies and publish reports of the research. Many college and university libraries have these documents in their holdings, usually in a special "government documents" section. These reports are rarely found in the catalog system. You must use specialized lists of publications and indexes, usually with the help of a librarian, to locate these reports. Most college and university libraries hold only the most frequently requested documents and reports.

Policy Reports and Presented Papers

A researcher conducting a thorough review of the literature will examine these two sources, which are difficult for all but the trained specialist to obtain. Research institutes and policy centers (e.g., Brookings Institute, Institute for Research on Poverty, Rand Corporation, etc.) publish papers and reports. Some major research libraries purchase these and shelve them with books. The only way to be sure of what has been published is to write directly to the institute or center and request a list of reports.

Each year, the professional associations in academic fields (e.g., social work, political science, psychology) hold annual meetings. Hundreds of researchers assemble to give, listen to, or discuss oral reports of recent research. Most of these oral reports are available as written papers to those attending the meeting. People who do not attend the meetings but who are members of the association receive a program of the meeting, listing each paper to be presented with its title, author, and author's place of employment. They can write directly to the author and request a copy of the paper. Many, but not all, of the papers are later published as articles. The papers may be listed in indexes or abstract services (to be discussed).

HOW TO CONDUCT A SYSTEMATIC LITERATURE REVIEW

Define and Refine a Topic

Just as a researcher must plan and clearly define a topic and research question when beginning a research project, you need to begin a literature review with a clearly defined, well-focused research question and a plan. A good review topic should be as focused as a research question. For example, "divorce" or "crime" is much too broad. A more appropriate review topic might be "the stability of families with stepchildren" or "economic inequality and crime rates across nations." If you conduct a context review for a research project, it should be slightly broader than the specific research question being tested. Often, a researcher will not finalize a specific research question for a study until he or she has reviewed the literature. The review helps bring greater focus to the research question.

Design a Search

After choosing a focused research question for the review, the next step is to plan a search strategy. The reviewer needs to decide on the type of review, its extensiveness, and the types of materials to include. The key is to be careful, systematic, and organized. Set parameters on your search: how much time you will devote to it, how far back in time you will look, the minimum number of research reports you will examine, how many libraries you will visit, and so forth.

Also, decide how to record the bibliographic citation for each reference you find and how to take notes (e.g., in a notebook, on 3 × 5 cards, in a computer file). Develop a schedule, because several visits are usually necessary. You should begin a file folder or computer file in which you can place possible sources and ideas for new sources. As the review proceeds, it should become more focused.

Locate Research Reports

Locating research reports depends on the type of report or "outlet" of research being searched. As a general rule, use multiple search strategies in order to counteract the limitations of a single search method.

Articles in Scholarly Journals.   As discussed earlier, most social work research is likely published in scholarly journals. These journals are the vehicles of communication in science. Before beginning a search, pick up a journal in an area with which you are somewhat familiar and skim its contents. There are dozens of journals, many going back decades, each containing many articles. The task of searching for articles can be formidable. Luckily, specialized publications make the task easier.

You may have used an index for general publications such as the *Reader's Guide to Periodical Literature.* Many academic fields have "abstracts" or "indexes" for the scholarly literature (e.g., *Social Work Abstracts, Psychological Abstracts, Social Sciences Index, Sociological Abstracts,* and *Gerontological Abstracts*). For education-related topics, the Educational Resources Information Center (ERIC) system is especially valuable. There are over 100 such publications. You can usually find them in the reference section of a library. Many abstracts or index services as well as ERIC are available via computer access, which speeds the search process.

Abstracts or indexes are published on a regular basis (monthly, six times a year, etc.) and allow a reader to look up articles by author name or subject. The journals covered by the abstract or index are listed in it, often in the front. An index, such as the *Social Sciences Index,* lists only the citation, whereas an abstract such as *Social Work Abstracts* lists the citation and has a copy of the article's abstract. Abstracts do not give you all the findings and details of a research project. Researchers use abstracts to screen articles for relevance, then locate the more relevant articles. Abstracts may also include papers presented at professional meetings.

It may sound as if all you have to do is to go find the index in the reference section of the library and look up a topic. Unfortunately, things are more complicated than that. In order to cover the studies across many years, you may have to look through many issues of the abstracts or indexes. Also, the subjects or topics listed in the abstracts or indexes are broad. The specific research question that interests you may fit into several subject areas. You should check each one. For example, for the topic of illegal drugs in high schools, you might look up these subjects: drug addiction, drug abuse, substance abuse, drug laws, illegal drugs, high schools, and secondary schools. Many of the articles under a subject area will not be relevant for your literature review. Also, there is a 3- to 12-month time lag between the publication of an article and its appearance in the abstracts or indexes. Unless you are at a major research library, the most useful article may not be available in your library. You can obtain it only by using an interlibrary loan service, or it may be in a foreign language that you do not read.

Most research-oriented libraries subscribe to the *Social Science Citation Index (SSCI)* of the Institute for Scientific Information, and many libraries carry SSCI online. This is a valuable resource with information on over 1,400 journals. It is similar to other indexes and abstracts, but it takes time to learn how to use it. The hard copy of the SSCI comes in four books. One is a source index, which provides complete citation information on journal articles. The other three books refer to articles in the source book. They are organized by subject, by the university or research center for which the researcher works, or by authors who are cited in the reference sections of other articles.

You can begin an SSCI search in one of three ways: (1) with a subject (e.g., alcohol use among children), (2) with a known research center (e.g., the Center for Alcohol Studies at Rutgers, the State University of New Jersey), or (3) with an earlier article (e.g., Kandel's "Drug and Drinking Behavior among Youth" in the 1980 *Annual Review of Sociology*). The first search directs you to the authors of current research reports. The second search identifies all authors from the same research center who published articles. The third search directs you to all citations included in earlier articles' reference sections. This last type of search is important when a researcher wants to trace research that influenced other research. For example, you find a 1980 article relevant. The SSCI tells you all articles published since 1980 that listed it in their reference section. Even if your library does not have hard-copy or online access to the *Social Science Citation Index,* a good search principle is to examine the bibliography of articles to find additional articles or books on a topic.

Another resource for locating articles is the computerized literature search, which works on the same principle as an abstract or an index. Researchers organize computerized searches in several ways—by author, by article title, by subject, or by keyword. A *keyword* is an important term for a topic that is likely to be found in a title. You will want to use six to eight keywords in most computer-based searches and consider several synonyms. The computer's searching method can vary and most look for a keyword only in a title or abstract. If you choose too few words or very narrow terms, you will miss a lot of relevant articles. If you choose too many words or very broad terms, you will get a huge number of irrelevant articles. The best way to learn the appropriate breadth and number of keywords is by trial and error.

In a study on how college students define *sexual harassment* (Neuman, 1992), the following keywords were used: *sexual harassment, sexual assault, harassment, gender equity, gender fairness,* and *sex discrimination.* It was later discovered that a few important studies lacked any of these keywords in their titles. Also tried were the keywords *college student* and *rape,* but this search yielded huge numbers of unrelated articles that could not even be skimmed due to lack of time.

There are numerous computer-assisted search databases or systems. Some may be online at your library, some are on CD-ROM, and others are available through the Internet or another long-distance connection (to be discussed later). A person with a computer and an Internet hook-up can search some article index collections, the catalogs of libraries, and other information sources around the globe if they are available on the Internet.

Often the same articles will appear in multiple scholarly literature databases, but each database may identify a few new articles not found in the others. This points to a critical lesson: "Do not rely exclusively on computerized literature searches, on abstracting services, [or] on the literature in a single discipline, or on an arbitrarily defined time period" (Bausell, 1994:24).

Scholarly Books.   Finding scholarly books on a subject can be difficult. The subject topics of library catalog systems are usually incomplete and too broad to be useful. Moreover, they list only books that are in a particular library system, although you may be able to search other libraries for interlibrary loan books. Libraries organize books by call numbers based on subject matter. Again, the subject matter classifications may not reflect the subjects of interest to you or all the subjects discussed in a book. Once you learn the system for your library, you will find that most books on a topic will share the main parts of the call number. In addition, librarians can help you locate books from other libraries. For example, the *Library of Congress National Union Catalog* lists all books in the U.S. Library of Congress. Librarians have access to sources that list books at other libraries, or you can use the Internet. There is no sure-fire way to locate relevant books. Use multiple search methods, including a look at journals that have book reviews and the bibliographies of articles.

Dissertations. A publication called *Dissertation Abstracts International* lists most dissertations. Just as the indexes and abstracts for journal articles do, it organizes dissertations by broad subject category, author, and date. Researchers look up all titles in the subject areas that include a topic. Unfortunately, after you have located the dissertation title and abstract, you may find that obtaining a copy of it takes time and involves added costs.

Government Documents. The "government documents" sections of libraries contain specialized lists of government documents. A useful index for documents issued by the U.S. federal government is the *Monthly Catalog of Government Documents,* which is often available on computer. It has been issued since 1885, but other supplemental sources should be used for research into documents more than a decade old. The catalog has an annual index, and monthly issues have subject, title, and author indexes. *Indexes to Congressional Hearings,* another useful source, lists committees and subjects going back to the late 1930s. The *Congressional Record* contains debate of the U.S. Congress with synopses of bills, voting records, and changes in bills. *United States Statutes* lists each individual U.S. federal law by year and subject. The *Federal Register,* a daily publication of the U.S. government, contains all rules, regulations, and announcements of federal agencies. It has both monthly and annual indexes. There are other indexes that cover treaties, technical announcements, and so forth.

Other governments have similar lists. For example, the British government's *Government Publications Index* lists government publications issued during a year. *Parliamentary Papers* lists official social and economic studies going back 200 years. It is usually best to rely on the expertise of librarians for assistance in using these specialized indexes. The topics used by index makers may not be the best ones for your specific research question.

Policy Reports and Presented Papers. The most difficult sources to locate are policy reports and presented papers. They are listed in some bibliographies of published studies; some are listed in the abstracts or indexes. To locate these studies, try several methods: email online centers and ask for lists of publications, obtain lists of papers presented at professional meetings, and so forth. Once you locate a research report, try writing to the relevant author or institute.

What to Record

After you locate a source, you should write down all details of the reference (full names of authors, titles, volume, issue, pages, etc.). It is usually best to record more than the minimum needed to form a citation. Most researchers create one set of cards or a computer file with the full references and another with notes on the research report. Create a code or indicator to link unambiguously the reference or source of the notes to each note card or file. For example, put the last name of the first author and the year of the book or article on each note card or record. You can quickly look up the complete reference in a set of reference cards or file organized by author's last name and date. You will find it much easier to take all notes on the same type and size of paper or card, rather than having some notes on sheets of paper, others on cards, and so on. Researchers have to decide what to record about an article, book, or other source. It is better to err in the direction of recording too much rather than too little. In general, record the hypotheses tested, how major concepts were measured, the main findings, the basic design of the research, the group or sample used, and ideas for future study (see Box 16.3). It is wise to examine the report's bibliography and note sources that you can add to your search.

How to Read Journal Articles

1. Read with a clear purpose or goal in mind. Are you reading for basic knowledge or to apply it to a specific question?
2. Skim the article before reading it all. What can you learn from the title, abstract, summary and conclusions, and headings? What are the topic, major findings, method, and main conclusion?
3. Consider your own orientation. What is your bias toward the topic, the method, the publication source, and so on, that may color your reading?
4. Marshal external knowledge. What do you already know about the topic and the methods used? How credible is the publication source?
5. Evaluate as you read the article. What errors are present? Do findings follow the data? Is the article consistent with assumptions of the approach it takes?
6. Summarize information as an abstract with the topic, the methods used, and the findings. Assess the factual accuracy of findings and cite questions about the article.

Source: Adapted from Katzer, Cook, and Crouch (1998: 190–196).

Photocopying all relevant articles or reports will save you time recording notes and will ensure that you will have an entire report. You can make notes on the photocopy. There are several warnings about this practice. First, photocopying can be expensive for a large literature search. Second, be aware of and obey copyright laws. U.S. copyright laws permit photocopying for personal research use. Third, remember to record or photocopy the entire article, including all citation information. Fourth, organizing entire articles can be cumbersome, especially if several different parts of a single article are being used. Finally, unless you highlight carefully or take good notes, you may have to reread the entire article later.

Organize Notes

After gathering a large number of references and notes, you need an organizing scheme. One approach is to group studies or specific findings by skimming notes and creating a mental map of how they fit together. Try several organizing schemes before setting on a final one. Organizing is a skill that improves with practice. For example, place notes into piles representing common themes, or draw charts comparing what different reports state about the same question, noting agreements and disagreements.

In the process of organizing notes, you will find that some references and notes do not fit and should be discarded as irrelevant. Also, you may discover gaps or areas and topics that are relevant but that you did not examine. This necessitates return visits to the library.

There are many organizing schemes. The best one depends on the purpose of the review. A context review implies organizing recent reports around a specific research question. A historical review implies organizing studies by major theme and by the date of publication. An integrative review implies organizing studies around core common findings of a field and the main hypotheses tested. A methodological review implies organizing studies by the topic and, within topic, by the design or method used. A theoretical review implies organizing studies by the theories and major thinkers being examined.

Write the Review

A literature review requires planning and good, clear writing, which requires a lot of rewriting. This step is often merged with organizing notes. All the rules of good writing (e.g., clear organizational structure, an introduction and conclusion, transitions between sections, etc.) apply to writing a literature review. Keep your purposes in mind when you write, and communicate clearly and effectively.

To prepare a good review, read articles and other literature critically. Recall that skepticism is a norm of science. It means that you should not accept what is written simply on the basis of the authority of its having been published. Question what you read, and evaluate it. The first hurdle to overcome is thinking something must be perfect just because it has been published.

Critically reading research reports requires skills that take time and practice to develop. Despite a peer review procedure and high rejection rates, errors and sloppy logic slip in. When reading an article, read carefully to see whether the introduction and title really fit with the rest of the article. Sometimes, titles, abstracts, or the introduction are misleading. They may not fully explain the research project's method and results. An article should be logically tight, and all the parts should fit together. Strong logical links should exist between parts of the argument. Weak articles make leaps in logic or omit transitional steps. Likewise, articles do not always make their theory or approach to research explicit. Be prepared to read the article more than once to determine its underlying theory or approach. (See Box 16.4 on taking notes on an article.)

The most critical areas of an article to read are the methods and results sections. Few studies are perfect. Researchers do not always describe the methods they used as fully as they should. Sometimes, the results presented in tables or charts do not match what the researcher says. For example, an author might overlook an important result in a table, while giving minor results too much attention. The careful reader evaluates how the research project was done and reads the data that are presented. Too frequently, authors give one interpretation and ignore equally possible interpretations.

Box 16.4 _____

Example of Notes on an Article

FULL CITATION ON BIBLIOGRAPHY CARD

Pierce, John C., M. A. E. Steger, N. P. Lovrich, B. S. Steel, 1988. "Public Information on Acid Rain in Canada and the United States." *Social Science Quarterly,* 69:193–202.

NOTE CARD

Pierce et al. 1988	**Topics** Factors that shape people's knowledge about public issues. Acid Rain. Self-interest. U.S. and Canada

Based on a prior study, the researchers note that education alone does not lead to knowledge about a public policy issue. Knowledge can be based on characteristics of the individual (e.g., gender, income, education), which works in general regardless of a specific policy, or on motivation due to the relevance of a policy for individual self-interest. They are interested in how knowledge on a public issue results from a person's motivation to acquire information. They looked at one policy, acid rain, and asked: Does motivation affect knowledge in different settings—Canadian culture, which is more collectivistic and where people are the victims of U.S. policy and the individualistic U.S. culture?

Hypotheses People acquire knowledge about a public issue when they perceive it as affecting their self-interest.

Method The authors mailed questionnaires to samples of 1,000 people living in Michigan and 1,000 in Ontario. A little over half were completed and returned. They measured knowledge about the issue in four ways. They also looked at motivational variables, including general characteristics and the personal sensitivity or relevance of the issue.

Findings Using statistics and percentaged tables, they found that motivational factors (e.g., personal sensitivity and relevance) led to greater knowledge of the acid rain issue than did general characteristics, although both had some effect. Motivation or personal relevance was stronger in Canada, where the national context heightened sensitivity.

Also be careful when reading conclusions. Do not assume that they are entirely consistent with all the data; check the data for yourself.

WHAT DOES A GOOD REVIEW LOOK LIKE?

An author should communicate a review's purpose to the reader by its organization. The *wrong* way to write a review is to list a series of research reports with a summary of the findings of each. This fails to communicate a sense of purpose. It reads as a set of notes strung together. Perhaps the reviewer got sloppy and skipped over the important organizing step in writing the review. The *right* way to write a review is to organize common findings or arguments together. A well-accepted approach is to address the most important ideas first, to logically link statements or findings, and to note discrepancies or weaknesses in the research (see Box 16.5 for an example).

Box 16.5

Examples of Bad and Good Reviews

EXAMPLE OF BAD REVIEW

Sexual harassment has many consequences. Adams, Kottke, and Padgitt (1983) found that some women students said they avoided taking a class or working with certain professors because of the risk of harassment. They also found that men and women students reacted differently. Their research was a survey of 1,000 men and women graduate and undergraduate students. Benson and Thomson's study in *Social Problems* (1982) lists many problems created by sexual harassment. In their excellent book, *The Lecherous Professor,* Dziech and Weiner (1990) give a long list of difficulties that victims have suffered.

Researchers study the topic in different ways. Hunter and McClelland (1991) conducted a study of undergraduates at a small liberal arts college. They had a sample of 300 students, and students were given multiple vignettes that varied by the reaction of the victim and the situation. Jaschik and Fretz (1991) showed 90 women students at a mideastern university a videotape with a classic example of sexual harassment by a teaching assistant. Before it was labeled as *sexual harassment,* few women called it that. When asked whether it was sexual harassment, 98 percent agreed. Weber-Burdin and Rossi (1982) replicated a previous study on sexual harassment, only they used students at the University of Massachusetts. They had 59 students rate 40 hypothetical situations. Reilley, Carpenter, Dull, and Bartlett (1982) conducted a study of 250 female and 150 male undergraduates at the University of California at Santa Barbara. They also had a sample of 52 faculty. Both samples completed a questionnaire in which respondents were presented vignettes of sexual-harassing situations that they were to rate. Popovich et al. (1987) created a nine-item scale of sexual harassment. They studied 209 undergraduates at a medium-sized university in groups of 15 to 25. They found disagreement and confusion among students.

EXAMPLE OF GOOD REVIEW

The victims of sexual harassment suffer a range of consequences, from lowered self-esteem and loss of self-confidence to withdrawal from social interaction, changed career goals, and depression (Adams, Kottke, and Padgitt, 1983; Benson and Thomson, 1982; Dziech and Weiner, 1990). For example, Adams, Kottke, and Padgitt (1983) noted that 13 percent of women students said they avoided taking a class or working with certain professors because of the risk of harassment.

Research into campus sexual harassment has taken several approaches. In addition to survey research, many have experimented with vignettes or presented hypothetical scenarios (Hunter and McClelland, 1991; Jaschik and Fretz, 1991; Popovich et al., 1987; Reilley, Carpenter, Dull, and Bartlett, 1982; Rossi and Anderson, 1982; Valentine-French and Radtke, 1989; Weber-Burdin and Rossi, 1982). Victim verbal responses and situational factors appear to affect whether observers label a behavior as harassment. There is confusion over the application of a sexual harassment label for inappropriate behavior. For example, Jaschik and Fretz (1991) found that only 3 percent of the women students shown a videotape with a classic example of sexual harassment by a teaching assistant initially labeled it as *sexual harassment.* Instead, they called it "sexist," "rude," "unprofessional," or "demeaning." When asked whether it was sexual harassment, 98 percent agreed. Roscoe et al. (1987) reported similar labeling difficulties.

USING THE INTERNET FOR SOCIAL WORK RESEARCH

The Internet (see Box 16.6) has revolutionized how social work researchers work. Just five years ago, it was rarely used; today, most social work researchers use the Internet regularly to help them review the literature, to communicate with other researchers, and to search for other information sources. The Internet continues to expand and change at an explosive rate.

The Internet has been a mixed blessing for social work research, but it has not proved to be the panacea that some people first thought it might be. It provides new and important ways to find information, but it remains one tool among others. It can quickly make some specific pieces of information accessible. For example, from a home computer, one author was able to go to the U.S. Federal Bureau of Prisons and in less than three minutes locate a table showing that in 1970, 16.3 percent of prisoners were incarcerated for drug offenses, whereas in 1997 (the most recent data available), it was 60.3 percent. The Internet is best thought of as a supplement rather than as a replacement for traditional library research. There are "up" and "down" sides to using the Internet for social work research.

The Up Side.

1. The Internet is easy, fast, and inexpensive. It is widely accessible and can be used from many locations. This low-cost resource allows people to find source material from almost anywhere—local public libraries, homes, labs or classrooms, or anywhere a computer is connected to the Internet system. Also, the Internet does not close; it operates 24 hours a day, 7 days a week. With minimal training, most people can quickly perform searches and get information on their computer screens that would have required them to take a major trip to large research libraries a few years ago. Searching a vast quantity of information electronically has always been easier and faster than a manual search, and the Internet greatly expands the amount and variety of source material. More and more information (e.g., *Statistical Abstract of the United States*) is becoming available on the Internet. In addition, once the information is located, a researcher can often store it electronically or print it at a local site.

Box 16.6

The Internet

The Internet is not a single thing in one place. Rather, the Internet is a system or interconnected web of computers around the world. It is changing very rapidly. We cannot describe everything on the Internet; many large books attempt to do that. Plus, even if we tried, it would be out of date in six months. The Internet is changing, in a powerful way, how many people communicate and share information. During the past few years, the number of people using the Internet has been doubling every six months.

The Internet provides low-cost (often free), worldwide, fast communication among people with computers or between people with computers and information in the computers of organizations (e.g., universities, government agencies, businesses). There are special hardware and software requirements, but the Internet potentially can transmit electronic versions of text material, up to entire books, as well as photos, music, video, and other information.

To get onto the Internet, a person needs an account in a computer that is connected to the Internet. Most college mainframe computers are connected, many business or government computers are connected, and individuals with modems can purchase a connection in some areas from private companies that provide access over telephone lines. In addition to a microcomputer, the person needs only a little knowledge about using computers. As more people learn to use computers, as computers become more powerful, and as the Internet expands to more people, it has the potential to accelerate significantly the exchange of various types of information around the globe.

2. The Internet has "links" that provide additional ways to find and connect to many other sources of information. Many websites, home pages, and other Internet resource pages have "hot links" that can call up information from related sites or sources simply by clicking on the link indicator (usually a button or a highlighted word or phrase). This connects people to more information and provides "instant" access to cross-referenced material. Links make embedding one source within a network of related sources easy.

3. The Internet speeds the flow of information around the globe and has a "democratizing" effect. It provides rapid transmission of information (e.g., text, news, data, and photos) across long distances and international borders. Instead of waiting a week for a report or having to send off for a foreign publication and wait for a month, the information is often available in seconds at no cost. There are virtually no restrictions on who can put material on the Internet or what appears on it, so many people who had difficulty publishing or disseminating their materials can now do so with ease. Because of its openness, the Internet reinforces the norm of universalism.

4. The Internet is the provider of a very wide range of information sources, some in formats that are more dynamic and interesting. It can send and be a resource for more than straight black and white text, as in traditional academic journals and sources. It transmits information in the form of bright colors, graphics, "action" images, audio (e.g., music, voices, sounds), photos, and even video clips. Authors and other creators of information can be creative in their presentations.

The Down Side.

1. There is no quality control over what gets on the Internet. Unlike standard academic publications, there is no peer review process or any review. Anyone can put almost anything on a website. It may be of poor quality, undocumented, highly biased, totally made up, or plain fraudulent. There is a lot of real "trash" out there! Once a person finds material, the real work is to distinguish the "trash" from valid information. One needs to treat a webpage with the same caution that one applies to a paper flyer someone hands out on the street; it could contain the drivel of a "nut" or be really valuable information. A less serious problem is that the "glitz" of bright colors, music, or moving images found in sites can distract unsophisticated users. The "glitz" may attract them more than serious content, and they may confuse glitz for high-caliber information. The Internet is better designed for a quick look and short attention spans rather than the slow, deliberative, careful reading and study of content.

2. Many excellent sources and some of the most important resource materials (research studies and data) for social work research are *not* available on the Internet (e.g., *Sociofile,* GSS datafiles, and recent journal articles). Much information is available only through special subscription services that can be expensive. Contrary to popular belief, the Internet has *not* made all information free and accessible to everyone. Often, what is free is limited, and more detailed information is available only to those who pay. In fact, because some libraries redirected funds to buy computers for the Internet and cut the purchases for books and paper copies of documents, the Internet's overall impact may have actually reduced what is available for some users.

3. Finding sources on the Internet can be very difficult and time consuming. It is not easy to locate specific source materials. Also, different "search engines" can produce very different results. It is wise to use multiple *search engines* (e.g., Yahoo, Excite, and Alta Vista), since they work differently. Most search engines simply look for specific words in a short description of the webpage. This description may not reveal the full content of the source, just as a title does not fully tell what a book or article is about. In addition, search engines often come up with tens of thousands of sources, far too many for anyone to examine. The ones at the "top" may be there because they were recently added to the Internet or because their short description had several versions of the search word. The "best" or most relevant source might be buried as the 150th item found in a search. Also, one must often wade through a lot of commercials and advertisements to locate "real" information.

4. Internet sources can be "unstable" and difficult to document. After one conducts a search on

the Internet and locates webpages with information, it is important to note the specific "address" (usually it starts with www.) where it resides. This address refers to an electronic file sitting in a computer somewhere. If the computer file is moved, it may not be at the same address six months later. Unlike a journal article that will be stored on a shelf or on microfiche in hundreds of libraries for many decades to come and available for anyone to read, webpages can quickly vanish. This means it may not be possible to check someone's web references easily, verify a quote in a document, or go back to original materials and read them for ideas or to build on them. Also, it is easy to copy, modify, or distort, then reproduce copies of a source. For example, a person could alter a text passage or a photo image, then create a new webpage to disseminate the false information. This raises issues about copyright protection and the authenticity of source material.

Understanding the Internet, its jargon (see Box 16.7), and how to identity a worthwhile site takes time and practice. There are few rules for locating the best sites on the Internet—ones that have useful and truthful information. Sources that originate at universities, research institutes, or government agencies usually are more trustworthy for research purposes than ones that are individual home pages of unspecified origin or location, or that a commercial organization or a political/social issue advocacy group sponsors. In addition to moving or disappearing, many webpages or sources fail to provide complete information to make citation easy. Better sources provide more information about the author, date, location, and so on. Box 16.8 lists selected websites that contain information on social work in general, government, and writing and style references.

THE WRITING PROCESS

Your Audience

Professional writers say: Always know for whom you are writing. This is because communication is more effective when it is tailored to a specific audience. You should write a research report differently depending on whether the primary audience is an instructor, students, professional social scientists, practitioners, or the general public. It goes without saying that the writing should be clear, accurate, and organized.

Instructors assign a report for different reasons and may place requirements on how it is written. In general, instructors want to see writing and an organization that reflect clear, logical thinking. Student reports should demonstrate a solid grasp of substantive and methodological concepts. A good way to do this is to use technical terms explicitly *when appropriate;* they should not be used excessively or incorrectly.

When writing for students, it is best to define technical terms and label each part of the report. The discussion should proceed in a logical, step-by-step manner with many specific examples. Use straightforward language to explain how and why you conducted the various steps of the research project. One strategy is to begin with the research question, then structure the report as an answer.

Scholars do not need definitions of technical terms or explanations of why standard procedures (e.g., random sampling) were used. They are interested in how the research is linked to abstract theory or previous findings in the literature. They want a condensed, detailed description of research design. They pay close attention to how variables are measured and the methods of data collection. Scholars like a compact, tightly written, but extensive section on data analysis, with a meticulous discussion of results.

Practitioners prefer a short summary of how the study was conducted and results presented in a few simple charts and graphs. They like to see an outline of alternative paths of action implied by results with the practical outcomes of pursuing each path. Practitioners must be cautioned not to overgeneralize from the results of one study. It is best to place the details of research design and results in an appendix.

When writing for the general public, use simple language, provide concrete examples, and focus on the practical implications of findings for social problems. Do not include details of research design or of results, and be careful not to make unsupported claims when writing for the public. Informing the public is an important service, which can

Box 16.7 _____

Some Useful Internet Jargon

Like many areas, a specialized language or jargon has developed around the Internet. It can be intimidating at first. To put the jargon in perspective, recall that you know and use telephone jargon (e.g., *dial tone, busy signal, phone number, area code, directory assistance, touch tone,* etc.) that frightened people when telephone technology first began. The terms refer to one another, so it is easier to learn the set than each term separately.

Broken Link is a Hyperlink that has an incorrect URL or that points to a site that no longer exists. It prevents a user from moving from one site to another on the Internet.

Download is a verb that means transferring a computer file from a distant or source computer (usually a server) to a local computer.

Email is a system, technically separate from the Internet, that allows people to quickly send and receive messages, documents, and visual images electronically. It requires that the receiver have an electronic address and electronic storage space.

FTP (file transfer protocol) is a system for rapidly uploading or downloading files (numerical data or text) to or from a large computer to another (local) computer. Access to files residing on the large computer may be restricted, or it may be open to the public (called *Anonymous FTP*).

HTML (Hypertext markup language) is a system of instructions for assigning formatting, font styles, colors, graphic images, and so forth to a webpage, but it is not seen or shown on the page itself.

HTTP (Hypertext transfer protocol) is a format identification system for URLs.

Hyperlink is a marked location on a webpage (usually a visual button or a highlighted word) that takes the user to another site on the Internet quickly by clicking on it.

Hypertext is text or other material written with embedded hyperlink references that, once activated, enable the user to jump to another location (e.g., a footnote, another chapter, a different document, a webpage, etc.).

LAN (local area network) is a localized network (see **Network**).

Link is shorthand for a connection (see **Hyperlink**) to another webpage or Internet source.

LISTSERV is an electronic information distribution system. Users "sign up" to receive messages on a topic by email. The message can be newsletter-type information or email messages that are shared with all subscribers.

MetaSearch Engine is searching software with multiple individual search engines for conducting a more intensive and extensive search (e.g., Dogpile, Metacrawler, Debriefing, and Hotbot).

Modem is a piece of equipment (separate or inside a computer) for transferring electronic information over telephone or similar lines. It is capable of different information transfer speeds.

Network is a system of electronic communication that permits shared resources (e.g., software) and quick communication among a set of ports, or connections, to microcomputers. Networks can be limited to one room, one building, a large campus, or many locations (e.g., all offices of a large corporation). The communication is coordinated by one or more servers.

Network Card is a piece of equipment placed inside a microcomputer that permits rapid communication within a network. It often substitutes for a modem.

Search Engine is specialized software that works within web browsers to search the web for keywords and return a list of possible pages or sites with URLs (e.g., Yahoo, Excite, and Lycos).

Server is a fast, powerful computer that permits access from outside users and on which webpages reside. It can be the center of a network.

Telnet is a system for remote access to a large computer that is connected to the Internet or a telephone line. It allows a person with a computer at one location to operate a computer at a distant location.

Upload is a verb that means transferring a computer file from a local computer to a distant computer (usually a server).

URL (uniform resource locator) is an "address" of an Internet site (it usually begins with www.).

Web is a shortened version of World Wide Web or WWW (see **WWW**).

Web Browser is a "navigational" tool for the WWW; a specialized software that interprets URLs (e.g., Netscape and Explorer).

Webpage is the main unit, site, or node of the WWW. A page is a computer file that appears to the user as one or more screens full of information on a computer.

WWW (World Wide Web) is a hypertext-based distribution system for sharing information on webpages located on various servers around the world.

Box 16.8

Selected Websites and Addresses

WEBSITES CONTAINING INFORMATION ON SOCIAL WORK IN GENERAL

Child Welfare League of America	www.cwla.org/default.htm
Council on Social Work Education	www.cswe.org
Federal Interagency Forum on Child and Family Statistics (ChildStats)	www.childstats.gov
International Federation of Social Workers	www.ifsw.org
National Association of Social Workers	www.socialworkers.org
National Center for PTSD	www.dartmouth.edu/dms/ptsd/pilots.html
National Coalition for the Homeless	www.nationalhomeless.org
National Data Archive on Child Abuse and Neglect	www.ndacan.cornell.edu
Research Forum on Children, Families, and the New Federalism	www.researchforum.org
Social Work Action Network (SWAN)	www.sc.edu/swan
Social Work Examination Services, Inc.	www.swes.net
World Wide Web Resources for Social Workers	www.nyu.edu/socialwork/wwwrsw

WEBSITES CONTAINING GOVERNMENT INFORMATION

Bureau of Justice Statistics, U.S. Department of Justice	www.ojp.usdoj.gov/bjs
Catalog of Federal Domestic Assistance	http://aspe.hhs.gov/cfda/index.htm
Federal Government Agencies Directory	www.lib.lsu.edu/gov/fedgov.html
Federal Web Locator	www.inforctr.edu/fwl
FedStats (Federal Statistics)	www.fedstats.gov
Office of the Assistant Secretary for Planning and Evaluation, U.S. Department of Health and Human Services	http://aspe.hhs.gov
State and Local Governments	www.lcweb.loc.gov/global/state
U.S. Census Bureau	www.census.gov
U.S. Congress	http://thomas.loc.gov
U.S. Department of Health and Human Services	www.hhs.gov
U.S. Department of Housing and Urban Development	www.hud.gov
U.S. Depository Libraries	www.lib.uidaho.edu/govdoc/otherdep.html
U.S. Government Information Locator Service	www.access.gpo.gov/su_docs/gils/index.html
U.S. Government Printing Office	www.access.gpo.gov/sudocs
U.S. House Committee on Ways and Means	http://waysandmeans.house.gov
U.S. House of Representatives	www.house.gov
U.S. Senate	www.senate.gov
U.S. White House	www.whitehouse.gov

WEBSITES CONTAINING WRITING AND STYLE INFORMATION

APA Publication Manual	www.apastyle.org
Center for Democracy and Technology	www.cdt.org
Critical Evaluation of Resources on the Internet	www.library.ualberta.ca/guides/criticalevaluation/index.cfm
Educational Resources Information Center (ERIC)	www.eric.ed.gov
Electronic Privacy Information Center	www.epic.org
Encyclopedia Britannica	www.britannica.com
How to Search the Internet	www.brightplanet.com/deepcontent/index.asp

Merriam-Webster Dictionary — www.m-w.com/cgi-bin/netdict
Online Writing Lab — http://owl.english.purdue.edu
Reference Desk — www.refdesk.com
Roget's Thesaurus — http://humanities.uchicago.edu/forms_unrest/ROGET.html

WEBSITES CONTAINING RESEARCH AND EVALUATION INFORMATION

Annie E. Casey Foundation Family to Family Tools — www.aecf.org/familytofamily/tools.htm
Bureau of Justice Assistance Evaluation Web Site — www.bja.evaluationwebsite.org/index.html
Inter-University Consortium for Political and Social Research — www.icpsr.umich.edu
Fetterman: Collaboration, Participatory, and Empowerment Evaluation — www.stanford.edu/~davidf/empowermentevaluation.html
Fetterman: Web Resources — www.stanford.edu/~davidf/webresources.html
Innovation Network (InnoNet) Participatory Evaluation Resources — www.innonet.org
Inter-University Consortium for International Social Development — www.iucisd.org
Kellogg Foundation Evaluation Handbook — www.wkkf.org/pubs/Pub770.pdf
Knowing Your Community / Showing Your Community — www.communityresources.org/knowshowpresenta.html
Walmyr Assessment Scales — www.walmyr.com/scales.html
National Academy of Sciences — www4.nationalacademies.org/nas/nashome.nsf
National Association for Welfare Research and Statistics — www.nawrs.org
NSF Handbook for Mixed Methods Evaluation — www.nsf.gov/cgi-bin/getpub?nsf97153
NSF User-Friendly Handbook for Project Evaluation — www.ehr.nsf.gov/ehr/red/eval/handbook/handbook.htm
NWU Asset-Based Community Development Institute — www.nwu.edu/ipr/abcd.html
NWU Mapping Community Capacity — www.nwu.edu/ipr/publications/community/mcc.html
Pitfalls of Data Analysis — www.execpc.com/~helberg/pitfalls
Research Methods Knowledge Base — http://trochim.human.cornell.edu/kb
Social Justice Research — www.kluweronline.com/issn//0885-7466
Social Research Update — www.soc.surrey.ac.uk/sru/sru.html
Society for Social Work and Research — www.sswr.org
StatSoft Electronic Statistics Textbook — www.statsoftinc.com/textbook/stathome.html
The Qualitative Report Online — www.nova.edu/ssss/QR

---

help nonspecialists make better judgments about public issues.

Style and Tone

Research reports are written in a narrow range of styles and have a distinct tone. Their purpose is to communicate clearly the research method and findings.

Style refers to the types of words chosen by the writer and the length and form of sentences or paragraphs used. *Tone* is the writer's attitude or relation toward the subject matter. An informal, conversational style (e.g., colloquial words, idioms, clichés, and incomplete sentences) with a personal tone (e.g., these are my feelings) is appropriate for writing a letter to a close friend, but not for research reports. Research reports have a formal and succinct (saying a lot in few words) style. The tone expresses distance from the subject matter; it is professional and serious. Field researchers sometimes use an informal style and a personal tone, but this is the exception. Avoid moralizing and flowery language. The goal is to inform, not to advocate a position or to entertain.

A research report should be objective, accurate, and clear. Check and recheck details (e.g., page references in citations) and fully disclose how you conducted the research project. If readers detect carelessness in writing, they may question the research itself. The details of a research project can be complex, and such complexity means that confusion is always a danger. It makes clear writing essential. Clear writing can be achieved by thinking and rethinking the research problem and design, explicitly defining terms, writing with short declarative sentences, and limiting conclusions to what is supported by the evidence.

Organizing Thoughts

Writing does not happen magically or simply flow out of a person when he or she puts pen to paper (or fingers to keyboard) although many people have such an illusion. Rather, it is hard work, involving a sequence of steps and separate activities that result in a final product. Writing a research report is not radically different from other types of writing. Although some steps differ and the level of complexity may be greater, most of what a good writer does when writing a long letter, a poem, a set of instructions, or a short story applies to writing a research report.

First, a writer needs something about which to write. The "something" in the research report includes the topic, research question, design and measures, data collection techniques, results, and implications. With so many parts to write about, organization is essential. The most basic tool for organizing writing is the outline. Outlines help a writer ensure that all ideas are included and that the relationship between them is clear. Outlines are made up of topics (words or phrases) or sentences. Most of us are familiar with the basic form of an outline (see Figure 16.2).

Outlines can help the writer, but they can also become a barrier if they are used improperly. An outline is simply a tool to help the writer organize ideas. It helps (1) put ideas into a sequence (e.g., what will be said first, second, and third); (2) group related ideas together (e.g., these are similar to each other, but differ from those); and (3) separate the more general, or higher-level, ideas from more specific ideas, and the specific ideas from very specific details.

Some students feel that they need a complete outline before writing, and that once an outline is prepared, deviations from it are impossible. Few writers begin with a complete outline. The initial outline is sketchy because until you write everything down, it is impossible to put all ideas into a sequence, group them together, or separate the general from the specific. For most writers, new ideas develop or become clearer in the process of writing itself.

A beginning outline may differ from the final outline by more than degree of completeness. The

FIGURE 16.2   Form of Outline

I. First major topic	One of the most important
A. Subtopic of topic I	Second level of importance
1. Subtopic of A	Third level of importance
a. Subtopic of 1	Fourth level of importance
b. Subtopic of 1	"
(1) Subtopic of b	Fifth level of importance
(2) Subtopic of b	"
(a) Subtopic of (2)	Sixth level of importance
(b) Subtopic of (2)	"
i. Subtopic of (b)	Seventh level of importance
ii. Subtopic of (b)	"
2. Subtopic of A	Third level of importance
B. Subtopic of topic I	Second level of importance
II. Second major topic	One of the most important

process of writing may not only reveal or clarify ideas for the writer, but also stimulate new ideas, new connections between ideas, a different sequence, or new relations between the general and the specific. In addition, the process of writing may stimulate re-analysis or a reexamination of the literature or findings. This does not mean beginning all over again. Rather, it means keeping an open mind to new insights and being candid about the research project.

Back to the Library

Few researchers finish their literature review before completing a research project. The researcher should be familiar with the literature before beginning a project, but will need to return to the literature after completing data collection and analysis, for several reasons. First, time has passed between the beginning and the end of a research project, and new studies may have been published. Second, after completing a research project, a researcher will know better what is or is not central to the study and may have new questions in mind when rereading studies in the literature. Finally, when writing the report, researchers may find that notes are not complete enough or a detail is missing in the citation of a reference source (see Box 16.9). The visit to the library after data collection is less extensive and more selective or focused than that conducted at the beginning of research.

When writing a research report, researchers frequently discard some of the notes and sources that were gathered prior to completing the research project. This does not mean that the initial library work and literature review were a waste of time and effort. Researchers expect that some of the notes (e.g., 25 percent) taken before completing the project will become irrelevant as the project gains focus. They do not include notes or references in a report that are no longer relevant, for they distract from the flow of ideas and reduce clarity.

Returning to the library to verify and expand references focuses ideas. It also helps avoid plagiarism. *Plagiarism* is a serious form of cheating, and many universities expel students caught engaging in it. If a professional ever plagiarizes in a scholarly journal, it is treated as a very serious offense.[2] Take careful notes and identify the exact source of phrases or ideas to avoid unintentional plagiarism. Cite the sources of both directly quoted words and paraphrased ideas. For direct quotes, include the location of the quote with page numbers in the citation.

Using another's written words and failing to give credit is wrong, but *paraphrasing* is not using another's exact words; it is restating another's ideas in your own words, condensing at the same time. Researchers regularly paraphrase, and good paraphrasing requires a solid understanding of what is being paraphrased. It means more than replacing another's words with synonyms; paraphrasing is borrowing an idea, boiling it down to its essence, and giving credit to the source.[3]

The Process

Writing is a process. The way to learn to write is by writing.[4] It takes time and effort, and it improves with practice. There is no single correct way to write, but some methods are associated with good writing. The process has three steps:

1. *Prewriting.* Prepare to write by arranging notes on the literature, making lists of ideas, outlining, completing bibliographic citations, and organizing comments on data analysis.
2. *Composing.* Get your ideas onto paper as a first draft by freewriting, drawing up the bibliography and footnotes, preparing data for presentation, and forming an introduction and conclusion.
3. *Rewriting.* Evaluate and polish the report by improving coherence, proofreading for mechanical errors, checking citations, and reviewing voice and usage.

Many people find that getting started is difficult. Beginning writers often jump to the second step and end there, which results in poor-quality writing. *Prewriting* means that a writer begins with a file folder full of notes, outlines, and lists. You must think about the form of the report and audience. Thinking time is important. It often occurs in spurts over a period of time before the bulk of composing begins.

Some people become afflicted with a strange ailment when they sit down to compose writing. It is known as *writer's block*—a temporary inability to write. It comes when the mind goes blank, the fingers

Box 16.9 _____

Citation Components

The American Psychological Association (APA) *Manual of Style* requires the following basic citation components. For a complete listing and explanations of this protocol, consult the *Publication Manual* of the American Psychological Association. This publication is normally available in college and university bookstores, libraries, and can be ordered online at www.apa.org.

Journal article	Baker, D., and Wilson, M. (1972). An evaluation of the scholarly productivity of doctoral graduates. *Journal of Social Work Education, (28)2,* 204–213.
Book (one author)	Dean, R. (1993). *Constructivism: An approach to clinical practice.* New York: Harper and Row.
Two or more book authors	Alter, C., and Evans, W. (1990). *Evaluating your practice: A guide to self-assessment.* New York: Springer.
Corporate author	Everyday Corporation. (1999). *Title of Document.* New York: Betty Warren.
Editor	Barker, R. (Ed.) (1999). *The social work dictionary (3rd Ed.).* Silver Spring, MD: The National Association of Social Workers.
Chapter in an edited work	Bellack, A., and Herson, M. (1977). Self-report inventories in behavioral assessment. In J. D. Cone and R. P. Hawkins (Eds.). *Behavioral assessment: New directions in clincial psychology* (pp. 52–76). New York: Bruner/Mazel.
Article in a magazine	Public, J. (1999, April). Title of the article. *Magazine Name,* 5, 15–25.
Article in a journal paginated by issue	Blakely, T. (1992). Strategies for distance learning. *Journal of Continuing Social Work Education, 6(1),* 4–7.
Article in a journal paginated by volume	Blakely, T. (1994). A model for distance education delivery. *Journal of Social Work Education, 28,* 214–221.
Article in press	Public, J. (in press). Title of article. *Title of Journal.*
Letter to the editor	Ephross, P. (1995). [Letter to the editor]. *Journal of Social Work Education, 31(1),* 130.
Personal communication	J. Q. Public (personal communication, March 2, 1999).
Diagnostic and Statistical Manual	American Psychiatric Association (200X). *Diagnostic and statistical manual of mental disorders* (xxth ed.). Washington, D.C. Author.
Encyclopedia or Dictionary	Barker, R. (2001). *The social work dictionary* (3rd ed.). Silver Spring, MD: The National Association of Social Workers.
Entry by an author in an Encyclopedia	Gillespie, D. (1999). Ethical issues in research. In R. Edwards (Editor-in-Chief), *Encyclopedia of Social Work, (19th ed., Vol. 1, pp. 884–893).* Washington, D.C.: National Association of Social Workers
Article in an Internet-only journal	Public, J. (2001, April 15). Title of the article. Title of the Periodical, Volume, Retrieved June 15, 2001 from: http://www.journals.website/organization/xxxx.html

A stand-alone Internet article or document, no author identified, no date	Title of the document. (n.d.). Retrieved June 20, 2001 from: http://www.website/organization/xxxx.html
Documents available from school or university websites	Public, J. (1998). Title of the document. Retrieved July 12, 2001, from University of Missouri, School of Social Work website: http://www.missouri.edu/publications/document.html

INTERNET SOURCES

[*Note:* The date retrieved is the date that the reader located and read the work on the Internet.]

Announcement or Personal Home Page	American Sociological Association 1999. Journals and Newsletters. Retrieved January 16, 1999. http://www.asanet.org/Pubs/publicat.html
Online Journal Article	Sosteric, Mike, Mike Gismondi and Gina Ratkovic. 1998. "The University, Accountability, and Market Discipline in the Late 1990s." *Electronic Journal of Sociology* April 1988, Vol. 3. Retrieved January 16, 1999. http://www.sociology.org/content/vol003.003/sosteric.html
Newspaper Article	Lee, Don. 1999. "State's Job Growth Hits Unexpected Cold Spell." *Los Angeles Times* (January 16). Retrieved January 16, 1999. http://www.latimes.com/HOME/BUSINESS/topstory.html
Journal Abstract or Book Review	Grills, Steven. 1999. Review of *Missing Persons: A Critique of Personhood in the Social Science* by Mary Douglas and Steven Ney. *Canadian Journal of Sociology* on line. Retrieved January 16, 1999. http://www.alberta.ca/~cjscopy/reviews/persons.html

---

freeze, and panic sets in. Writers from beginners through experts occasionally experience it. If you experience it, calm down and work on overcoming it (see Figure 16.3).

Numerous writers begin to compose by *freewriting,* a process of sitting down and writing down everything you can as quickly as it enters into your mind. Freewriting establishes a link between a rapid flow of ideas in the mind and writing. When you freewrite, you do not stop to reread what you wrote, you do not ponder the best word, you do not worry about correct grammar, spelling, or punctuation. You just put ideas on paper as quickly as possible to get and keep the creative juices or ideas flowing. You can later clean up what you wrote.

Writing and thinking are so intertwined that it is impossible to know where one ends and the other begins. This means that if you plan to sit and stare at the wall, the computer output, the sky, or whatever until all thoughts become totally clear before beginning, you will rarely get anything written. The thinking process can be ignited during the writing itself.

Rewriting

Perhaps one in a million writers is a creative genius who can produce a first draft that communicates with astounding accuracy and clarity. For the rest of us mortals, writing means that rewriting—and rewriting again—is necessary. For example, Ernest Hemingway is reported to have rewritten the end of *Farewell to Arms* 39 times.[5] It is not unusual for a professional researcher to rewrite a report a dozen times. Do not become discouraged. If anything, rewriting reduces the pressure; it means you can start writing soon and get out a rough draft that you can polish later. Plan to rewrite a draft

FIGURE 16.3   Suggestions for Ending Writer's Block

1. *Begin early.* Do not procrastinate or wait until the last minute. This not only gives you time to come back to the task but it also reduces the tension because you have time to write a poor-quality first draft that can be improved upon. Shafer (1980:205) chided, "Writing is hard work, and the excuses authors find for postponing it are legendary." Set yourself a deadline for a first draft that is at least a week before the final deadline, and keep it!

2. *Take a break, then return.* Some writers find that if they take a walk, get a snack, read a newspaper, and come back to the task a half hour later, the block is gone. Small diversions, if they remain small and short term, can help on occasion.

3. *Begin in the middle.* You do not have to begin at the beginning. Begin in the middle and just start writing, even if does not seem to be directly relevant. It may be easier to get to your topic once the writing/thinking process is moving.

4. *Engage in personal magic rituals.* Some people have unusual habits or rituals that they engage in before writing (e.g., washing dishes, clearing a desk, sharpening pencils). These can serve as mental triggers to help you get started. Do what gets you started writing.

5. *Break it into small parts.* Do not feel that you have to sit down and complete the writing task as a whole. Begin with pieces that come easily to you and stitch together the pieces later.

6. *Do not expect perfection.* Write a draft, which means that you can throw away, revise, and change what you wrote. It is always easier to revise a rough draft than to create perfect writing the first time.

---

at least three or four times. A draft is a complete report, from beginning to end, not a few rough notes or an outline.

Rewriting helps a writer express himself or herself with greater clarity, smoothness, precision, and economy of words. When rewriting, the focus is on clear communication, not pompous or complicated language. As Leggett and colleagues (1965:330) stated, "Never be ashamed to express a simple idea in simple language. Remember that the use of complicated language is not in itself a sign of intelligence."

Rewriting means slowly reading what you have written and, if necessary, out loud to see whether it sounds right. It is a good idea to share your writing with others. Professional writers have others read and criticize their writing. New writers soon learn that friendly, constructive criticism is very valuable. Sharing your writing with others may be difficult at first. It means exposing your written thoughts and encouraging criticism. Yet, the purpose of the criticism is to clarify writing, and the critic is doing you a favor.

Rewriting involves two processes: revising and editing. *Revising* is inserting new ideas, adding supporting evidence, deleting or changing ideas, moving sentences around to clarify meaning, or strengthening transitions and links between ideas. *Editing* means cleaning up and tightening the more mechanical aspects of writing, such as spelling, grammar, usage, verb tense, sentence length, and paragraph organization. When you rewrite, go over a draft and revise it brutally to improve it. This is easier if some time passes between a draft and rewriting. Phrases that seemed satisfactory in a draft may look fuzzy or poorly connected after a week or two (see Figure 16.4).

Even if you have not acquired typing skills, it is a good idea to type, or print out if you use a word processor, at least one draft before the final draft. This is because it is easier to see errors and organization problems in a clean, typed draft. Feel free to cut and paste, cross out words, or move phrases on the printed copy.

Good typing skills and an ability to use a word processor are extremely valuable when writing reports and other documents. Serious professionals find that the time they invest into building typing skills and learning to use a word processor pays huge dividends later. Word processors not only make editing much easier but they also check spelling and offer synonyms. In addition, there are programs that check grammar. You cannot rely on the computer program to do all the work, but it

FIGURE 16.4   Suggestions for Rewriting

1. *Mechanics*. Check grammar, spelling, punctuation, verb agreement, verb tense, and verb/subject separation with each rewrite. Remember that each time new text is added, new errors can creep in. Mistakes are not only distracting but they also weaken the confidence readers place in the ideas you express.

2. *Usage*. Reexamine terms, especially key terms, when rewriting to see whether you are using the exact word that expresses your intended meaning. Do not use technical terms or long words unnecessarily. Use the plain word that best expresses meaning. Get a thesaurus and use it. A *thesaurus* is an essential reference tool, like a dictionary, that contains words of similar meaning and can help you locate the exact word for a meaning you want to express. Precise thinking and expression require precise language. Do not say *average* if you use the *mean*. Do not say *mankind* or *policeman* when you intend *people* or *police officer*. Do not use *principal* for *principle*.

3. *Voice*. Writers of research reports often make the mistake of using the passive instead of the active voice. It may appear more authoritative, but passive voice obscures the actor or subject of action. For example, the passive, *The relationship between grade in school and more definite career plans was confirmed by the data* is better stated as the active, *The data confirm the relationship between grade in school and more definite career plans*. The passive, *Respondent attitude toward abortion was recorded by an interviewer* reads easier in the active voice: *An interviewer recorded respondent attitude toward abortion*. Also, avoid unnecessary qualifying language, such as *seems to* or *appears to*.

4. *Coherence*. Sequence, steps, and transitions should be logically tight. Try reading the entire report one paragraph at a time. Does the paragraph contain a unified idea? A topic sentence?

Is there a transition between paragraphs within the report?

5. *Repetition*. Remove repeated ideas, wordiness, and unnecessary phrases. Ideas are best stated once, forcefully, instead of repeatedly in an unclear way. When revising, eliminate deadwood (words that add nothing) and circumlocution (the use of several words when one more precise word will do). Directness is preferable to wordiness. The wordy phrase, *To summarize the above, it is our conclusion in light of the data that X has a positive effect of considerable magnitude on the occurrence of Y, notwithstanding the fact that Y occurs only on rare occasions,* is better stated, *In sum, we conclude that X has a large positive effect on Y, but Y occurs infrequently.* As Selvin and Wilson (1984) warned, verbose and excessive words or qualifiers make it difficult to understand what is written.

6. *Structure*. Research reports should have a transparent organization. Move sections around as necessary to fit the organization better, and use headings and subheadings. A reader should be able to follow the logical structure of a report.

7. *Abstraction*. A good research report mixes abstract ideas and concrete examples. A long string of abstractions without the specifics is difficult to read. Likewise, a mass of specific concrete details without periodic generalization also loses readers.

8. *Metaphors*. Many writers use metaphors to express ideas. Phrases like *the cutting edge, the bottom line,* and *penetrating to the heart* are used to express ideas by borrowing images from other contexts. Metaphors can be an effective method of communication, but they need to be used sparingly and with care. A few well-chosen, consistently used, fresh metaphors can communicate ideas quickly and effectively; however, the excessive use of metaphors, especially overused metaphors (e.g., *the bottom line*), is a sloppy, unimaginative method of expression.

makes writing easier. The speed and ease that a word processor offers is so dramatic that few people who become skilled at using one ever go back to writing by hand or typing.

One last suggestion: Rewrite the introduction and title after completing a draft so that they accurately reflect what is said.[6] Titles should be short and descriptive. They should communicate the topic and the major variables to readers. They can describe the type of research (e.g., "An experiment on . . .") but should not have unnecessary words or phrases (e.g., "An investigation into the . . .").

THE QUANTITATIVE RESEARCH REPORT

The principles of good writing apply to all reports, but the parts of a report differ depending on whether the research is quantitative or qualitative. Before writing any report, read reports on the same kind of research for models.

We begin with the quantitative social work research report. The sections of the report roughly follow the sequence of steps of a research project.[7]

Abstract or Executive Summary

Quantitative research reports usually begin with a short summary or abstract. The size of an abstract varies; it can be as few as 50 words (this paragraph has 75 words) or as long as a full page. Most scholarly journal articles have abstracts that are printed on the first page of the article. The abstract has information on the topic, the research problem, the basic findings, and any unusual research design or data collection features.

Reports of applied research that are written for practitioners have a longer summary called the *executive summary*. It contains more detail than an article abstract and includes the implications of research and major recommendations made in the report. Although it is longer than an abstract, an executive summary rarely exceeds four or five pages.

Abstracts and executive summaries serve several functions: For the less interested reader, they tell what is in a report; for readers looking for specific information, they help the reader determine whether the full report contains important information. Readers use the abstract or summary to screen information and decide whether the entire report should be read. It gives serious readers who intend to read the full report a quick mental picture of the report, which makes reading the report easier and faster.

Presenting the Problem

The first section of the report defines the research problem. It can be placed in one or more sections with titles such as "Introduction," "Problem Definition," "Literature Review," "Hypotheses," or "Background Assumptions." Although the subheadings vary, the contents include a statement of the research problem and a rationale for what is being examined. Here researchers explain the significance of, and provide a background to, the research question. They explain the significance of the research by showing how different solutions to the problem lead to different applications or theoretical conclusions. Introductory sections frequently include a context literature review and link the problem to theory. Introductory sections also define key concepts and present conceptual hypotheses.

Describing the Methods

The next section of the report describes how the researcher designed the study and collected the data. It goes by several names (e.g., "Methods," "Research Design," or "Data") and may be subdivided into other parts (e.g., "Measures," "Sampling," or "Manipulations"). It is the most important section for evaluating the methodology of the project. The section answers several questions for the reader:

1. What type of study (e.g., experiment, survey) was conducted?
2. Exactly how were data collected (e.g., study design, type of survey, time and location of data collection, experimental design used)?
3. How were variables measured? Are the measures reliable and valid?
4. What is the sample? How many subjects or respondents are involved in the study? How were they selected?
5. How were ethical issues and specific concerns of the design dealt with?

Results and Tables

After describing how data were collected, methods of sampling, and measurement, you then present the data. This section presents—it does not discuss, analyze, or interpret the data. Researchers sometimes combine the "Results" section with the next section, called "Discussion" or "Findings."

Researchers make choices in how to present the data.[8] When analyzing the data, they look at dozens of univariate, bivariate, and multivariate tables and statistics to get a feel for the data. This does not mean that every statistic or table is in a final report. Rather, the researcher selects the minimum number of charts or tables that fully inform the reader and rarely present the raw data itself. Data analysis techniques should summarize the data and test hypotheses (e.g., frequency distributions, tables with means and standard deviations, correlations, and other statistics).

A researcher wants to give a complete picture of the data without overwhelming the reader—not provide data in excessive detail nor present irrelevant data. Readers can make their own interpretations. Detailed summary statistics belong in appendixes.

Discussion

In the discussion section, researchers give the reader a concise, unambiguous interpretation of the research results. The discussion is not a selective emphasis or partisan interpretation; rather, it is a candid discussion of what is in the results section. The discussion section is separated from the results so that a reader can examine the data and arrive at different interpretations. Grosof and Sardy (1985: 386) warned, "The arrangement of your presentation should reflect a strict separation between data (the record of your observations) and their summary and analysis on one hand, and your interpretations, conclusion, and comment on the other."

Beginning researchers often find it difficult to organize a discussion section. One approach is to organize the discussion according to hypotheses, discussing how the data relate to each hypothesis. In addition, researchers should discuss unanticipated findings, possible alternative explanations of results, and weaknesses or limitations.

Drawing Conclusions

Researchers restate the research question and summarize findings in the conclusion. Its purpose is to summarize the report, and it is sometimes titled "Summary."

The only sections after the conclusion are the references and appendixes. The references section contains only sources that were referred to in the text or notes of the report. Appendixes, if used, usually contain additional information on methods of data collection (e.g., questionnaire wording) or results (e.g., descriptive statistics). The footnotes or endnotes in quantitative research reports expand or elaborate on information in the text. Researchers use them sparingly to provide secondary information that clarifies the text but might distract from the flow of the reading.

THE QUALITATIVE RESEARCH REPORT

Compared to quantitative research, it is more difficult to write a report on qualitative social work research. It has fewer rules and less structure. Nevertheless, the purpose is the same: to clearly communicate the research process and the data collected through the process. As Bogdan and Taylor (1975:142) remarked, "A report, article, or monograph based on qualitative research is not, or should not be, an individual's off-the-cuff view of a situation. Rather, it should be a descriptive and analytic presentation of data that have been laboriously and systematically collected and interpreted."

Quantitative reports present hypotheses and evidence in a logically tight and condensed style. By contrast, qualitative reports tend to be longer, and book-length reports are common. The greater length is for five reasons:

1. The data in a qualitative report are more difficult to condense. Data are in the form of words, pictures, or sentences and include many quotes and examples.

2. Qualitative researchers may want to create a subjective sense of empathy and understanding among readers in addition to presenting factual evidence and analytic interpretations. Detailed descriptions of specific settings and situations help readers better understand or get a feel for settings. Researchers attempt to transport the reader into the subjective world view and meaning system of a social setting.

3. Qualitative researchers use less standardized techniques of gathering data, creating analytic categories, and organizing evidence. The techniques applied may be particular to individual researchers

or unique settings. Thus, researchers explain what they did and why, because it has not been done before.

4. Exploring new settings or constructing new theory is a common goal in qualitative research. The development of new concepts and examination of relationships among them adds to the length of reports. Theory flows out of evidence, and detailed descriptions demonstrate how the researcher created interpretations.

5. Qualitative researchers may use more varied and literary writing styles, which increases length. They have greater freedom to employ literary devices to tell a story or recount a tale.

Field research reports rarely follow a fixed format with standard sections, and theoretical generalizations and data are not separated into distinct sections.[9] Generalizations are intertwined with the evidence, which takes the form of detailed description with frequent quotes.

Researchers balance the presentation of data and analysis to avoid an excessive separation of data from analysis, called the *error of segregation*. This occurs when researchers separate data from analysis so much that readers cannot see the connection.[10]

The tone of field research reports is less objective and formal, and more personal. Field research reports may be written in the first person (i.e., using the pronoun *I*) because the researcher was directly involved in the setting, interacted with the people studied, and was the measurement "instrument." The decisions or indecisions, feelings, reactions, and personal experiences of the researcher are parts of the field research process.

Field research reports often face more skepticism than quantitative reports do. This makes it essential to assess an audience's demands for evidence and to establish credibility. The key is to provide readers with enough evidence so that they believe the recounted events and accept the interpretations as plausible. A degree of selective observation is accepted in field research, so the critical issue is whether other observers could reach the same conclusion if they examined the same data.[11] Schatzman and Strauss (1973:133) stressed the issue of establishing credibility:

An essential prerequisite to establishing credibility with any audience is the researcher's conviction that what he is saying or writing is so. And this conviction rests upon necessary and credible procedures performed, as well as upon the sense of certainty that the observer did in fact see what he says he saw.

Field researchers face a data reduction dilemma when presenting evidence. Most data are in the form of an enormous volume of field notes, but a researcher cannot directly share all the observations or recorded conversations with the readers. For example, in their study of medical students, *Boys in White,* Becker and Geer (1961) had about 5,000 pages of single-spaced field notes. Field researchers include only about 5 percent of their field notes in a report as quotes. The remaining 95 percent is not wasted; there is just no room for it. Thus, writers select quotes and indirectly convey the rest of the data to readers.

There is no fixed organization for a field research report, although a literature review often appears near the beginning. There are many acceptable organizational forms. Lofland (1976) suggests the following:

1. Introduction
   a. Most general aspects of situation
   b. Main contours of the general situation
   c. How materials were collected
   d. Details about the setting
   e. How the report is organized
2. The situation
   a. Analytic categories
   b. Contrast between situation and other situations
   c. Development of situation over time
3. Strategies
4. Summary and implications

Devices for organizing evidence and analysis also vary a great deal.[12] For example, writers can organize the report in terms of a *natural history,* an unfolding of events as you discovered them, or as a *chronology,* following the developmental cycle or career of an aspect of the setting or people in it. Another possibility is to organize the report as a *zoom lens,* beginning broadly and then focusing increasingly narrowly on a specific topic. Statements can move from universal statements about all cultures, to general statements about a specific cultures, to statements about a specific cultural scene, to specific statements about an aspect of culture, to specific statements about specific incidents.[13]

Field researchers also organize reports by themes. A writer chooses between using abstract analytic themes and using themes from the categories used by the people who were studied. The latter gives readers a vivid description of the setting and displays knowledge of the language, concepts, categories, and beliefs of those being written about.[14]

Field researchers discuss the methods used in the report, but the location and form of this discussion vary. One technique is to interweave a description of the setting, the means of gaining access, the role of the researcher, and the subject/researcher relationship into the discussion of evidence and analysis. This is intensified if the writer adopts what Van Maanen (1988:73) called a "confessional" style of writing. A chronological, zoom lens, or theme-based organization allows placing the data collection method near the beginning or the end. In book-length reports, methodological issues are usually discussed in a separate appendix.

Field research reports can contain transcriptions of tape recordings, maps, photographs, or charts illustrating analytic categories. They supplement the discussion and are placed near the discussion they complement. Qualitative field research can use creative formats that differ from the usual written text with examples from field notes. Harper's (1982) book contains many photographs with text. The photographs give a visual inventory of the settings described in the text and present the meanings of settings in the terms of those being studied. For example, field research articles have appeared in the form of all photographs (Jackson, 1978) or as a script for a play (Becker et al., 1989). A documentary film on a setting is another form of data presentation.[15]

Direct, personal involvement in the intimate details of a social setting heightens ethical concerns. Ethical concerns are discussed with methodological issues or as a separate topic. Researchers write in a manner that protects the privacy of those being studied and helps prevent the publication of a report from harming those who were studied.[16] They usually change the names of members and exact locations in field reports. Personal involvement in field research sometimes leads researchers to include a short autobiography. For example, in the appendix to *Street Corner Society* the author, William Foote Whyte (1982), gave a detailed account of the occupations of his father and grandfather, his hobbies and interests, the jobs he held, how he ended up going to graduate school, and how his research was affected by his getting married.

THE RESEARCH PROPOSAL

What Is the Proposal?

A research *proposal* is a document that presents a plan for a project to reviewers for evaluation. It can be a supervised project submitted to instructors as part of an educational degree (e.g., a master's thesis or a Ph.D. dissertation), or it can be a research project proposed to a funding agency. Its purpose is to convince reviewers that you, the researcher, are capable of successfully conducting the proposed research project. Reviewers have more confidence that a planned project will be successfully completed if the proposal is well written and organized, and if you demonstrate careful planning.

The proposal is similar to a research report, but it is written before the research project begins. A proposal describes the research problem and its importance, and gives a detailed account of the methods that will be used and why they are appropriate.

The proposal for quantitative social work research has most of the parts of a research report: a title, an abstract, a problem statement, a literature review, a methods or design section, and a bibliography. It lacks results, discussion, and conclusion sections. The proposal has a plan for data collection and analysis (e.g., types of statistics). It frequently includes a schedule of the steps to be undertaken and an estimate of the time required for each step.

Proposals for qualitative social work research are more difficult to write because the research process itself is less structured and preplanned.

The researcher prepares a problem statement, literature review, and bibliography. He or she demonstrates an ability to complete a proposed qualitative project in two ways. First, the proposal is well written, with an extensive discussion of the literature, significance of the problem, and sources. This shows reviewers familiarity with qualitative research and the appropriateness of the method for studying the problem. Second, the proposal describes a qualitative pilot study. This demonstrates motivation, familiarity with research techniques, and ability to complete a report about unstructured research.

Proposals to Fund Research

The purpose of a research grant is to provide the resources needed to help complete a worthy project. Researchers whose primary goal is to use funding for personal benefit or prestige, to escape from other activities, or to build an "empire" are less successful. The strategies of proposal writing and getting grants has become an industry called *grantsmanship*.

There are many sources of funding for research proposals. Colleges, private foundations, and government agencies have programs to award grants to researchers. Funds may be used to purchase equipment, to pay your salary or that of others, for research supplies, for travel to collect data, or for help with the publication of results. The degree of competition for a grant varies a great deal, depending on the source. Some sources fund more than 3 out of 4 proposals they receive; others fund fewer than 1 in 20.

There are many sources of funding for social research, but there may be no source willing to fund a specific project. The researcher needs to investigate funding sources and ask questions: What types of projects are funded—applied versus basic research, specific topics, or specific research techniques? What are the deadlines? What kind (e.g., length, degree of detail, etc.) of proposal is necessary? How large are most grants? What aspects (e.g., equipment, personnel, travel, etc.) of a project are or are not funded? There are many sources of information on funding sources. Librarians or officials who are responsible for research grants at a college are good resource people. For example, private foundations are listed in an annual publication, *The Foundation Directory. The Guide to Federal Funding for Social Scientists* lists sources in the U.S. government. In the United States there are many newsletters on funding sources and two national computerized databases (SPIN and IRIS), which subscribers can search for funding sources. Some agencies periodically issue *requests for proposals (RFPs)* that ask for proposals to conduct research on a specific issue. Researchers need to learn about funding sources, because it is essential to send the proposal to an appropriate source in order to be successful.[17]

Researchers need to show a track record of past success in the proposal, especially if they are going to be in charge of the project. The researcher in charge of a research project is the *principal investigator (PI)* or project director. Proposals usually include a curriculum vitae or academic resumé, letters of support from other researchers, and a record of past research. Reviewers feel safer investing funds in a project headed by someone who already has research experience than in a novice. One can build a track record with small research projects or by assisting an experienced researcher before seeking funding as a principal investigator.

The reviewers who evaluate a proposal judge whether the proposal project is appropriate to the funding source's goals. Most funding sources have guidelines stating the kinds of projects they fund. For example, programs that fund basic research have the advancement of knowledge as a goal. Programs to fund applied research often have improvements in the delivery of services as a goal. Instructions specify page length, number of copies, deadlines, and the like. Follow all instructions exactly. Why would reviewers give thousands of dollars to a researcher to carry out a complicated research project if he or she cannot even follow instructions on the page length of a proposal?

Proposals should be neat and professional in appearance. The instructions usually ask for a detailed plan for the use of time, services, and personnel. These should be clearly stated and realistic for the project. Excessively high or low estimates, unnecessary add-ons, or omitted essentials will lower how reviewers evaluate a proposal. Creating a budget for a proposed project is complicated and usually requires technical assistance. For example, pay rates, fringe benefit rates, and so on that must be charged may not be easy to obtain. It is best to consult a grants officer at a college or an experienced proposal writer. In addition, endorsements or clearances of regulations are often necessary (e.g., IRB approval; see Chapter 5). Proposals should also include specific plans for disseminating results (e.g., publications, presentations before professional groups, etc.) and a plan for evaluating whether the project met its objectives.

The proposal is a kind of contract between researcher and the funding source to complete the project. Funding agencies often require a final report, including details on how funds were spent, the findings, and an evaluation of whether the project met its objectives. Failure to spend funds properly, complete the project described in the proposal, or file a final report may result in a researcher facing legal action or being barred from receiving future funding. A serious misuse of funds may result in the banning of others at the same institution from receiving future funding.

The process of reviewing proposals after they are submitted to a funding source takes anywhere from a few weeks to almost a year, depending on the funding source. In most cases reviewers rank a large group of proposals, and only highly ranked proposals receive funding. A proposal often undergoes a blind peer review in which the reviewers are other researchers who know the proposer from the vitae in the proposal, but the proposer does not know the reviewers. Sometimes a proposal is reviewed by nonspecialists or nonresearchers. Instructions on preparing a proposal indicate whether to write for specialists in a field or for an educated general audience. A proposal may be evaluated by more than one group of reviewers. In general, proposals that ask for larger amounts of money receive closer review.

If a proposal is funded, celebrate, but only for a short time. If the proposal is rejected, which is more likely, do not despair. Most proposals are rejected the first—and even the second—time they are submitted. Many funding sources provide written reviewer evaluations of the proposal. Always request them if they are provided. Sometimes, a courteous talk on the telephone with a person at the funding source will reveal the reasons for rejection.

Strengthen and resubmit a proposal on the basis of the reviewer's comments. Most funding sources accept repeated resubmissions of revised proposals, and proposals that have been revised may be stronger in subsequent competitions.

If a proposal has been submitted to an appropriate funding source and all instructions are followed, reviewers are more likely to rate it high when

1. It addresses an important research question. It builds on prior knowledge and represents a substantial advance of knowledge for basic research. It documents a major social problem and holds promise for solutions for applied research.
2. It follows all instructions, is well written, and is easy to follow, with clearly stated objectives.
3. It completely describes research procedures that include high standards of research methodology, and it applies research techniques that are appropriate to the research question.
4. It includes specific plans for disseminating the results and evaluating whether the project has met its objectives.
5. The project is well designed and shows serious planning. It has realistic budgets and schedules.
6. The researcher has the necessary experience or background to complete the project successfully.

CONCLUSION

This chapter has two major themes: Communication is central to the process of social work research, and social work research is a collective activity that builds on the work of many people. These were also themes in Chapter 1, but their significance should be clearer now. The knowledge social work researchers produce advances only by building on the work of many individuals. This is why the literature review is so important and why researchers prize a library full of scholarly journals with tools to locate articles in them. The Internet has wrought changes in how researchers work, but it has not altered the fundamentals.

The other side of studying and reading reports on research conducted by others is to write about the research that one personally conducts. This chapter contained many suggestions for writing—ones that differ little from basic writing principles found in most other fields. The most important suggestion, and one that applies to doing research itself, pertains to the importance of practice. The best way to become a good researcher and the way one learns to write a quality research report are the same. It is to become directly involved in the processes of research and writing and to repeat the processes over and over again. The first steps for the beginning researcher are to embrace the scientific attitude, to adopt ethical responsibilities, and to read the details of how others conducted research. The second steps are to design and conduct a research project and to communicate what was done in a research report. At that point, the researcher crosses the invisible line from being an observer on the sidelines to become a participant in the ongoing enterprise of social work research.

KEY TERMS

abstract	integrative review	search engine
citation	keyword	self-study review
context review	meta-analysis	theoretical review
download	methodological review	Uniform Resource Locator
error of segregation	paraphrasing	(URL)
executive summary	principal investigator (PI)	upload
freewriting	request for proposals (RFP)	web browser
historical review	rewriting	writer's block

REVIEW QUESTIONS

1. What are the four major goals of a literature review?

2. Which outlets of research are easiest to locate and which the most difficult?

3. How would you go about locating a Ph.D. dissertation?

4. What are the first steps in beginning a systematic literature review?

5. What distinguishes a strong from a weak literature review?

6. What are the major strengths and weaknesses of using the Internet for social research?

7. What can you do if you experience writer's block?

8. Where is the methods section in a report on quantitative research?

9. Why are qualitative research reports usually longer than quantitative reports?

10. What is an RFP, and what is its purpose?

NOTES

1. See Hunter and associates (1982).
2. See "Plagiarism Case Documented," in American Sociological Association *Footnotes,* 17(2) (February 1989), p. 2, or "Noted Harvard Psychiatrist Resigns Post after Faculty Group Finds He Plagiarized," in *Chronicle of Higher Education,* 35(15) (December 7, 1989), p. 1.
3. From Sociology Writing Group (1991).

4. For suggestions on writing, see Donald and colleagues (1983) and Leggett and colleagues (1965).
5. From Sociology Writing Group (1991:40).
6. See Fine (1988) for this and other suggestions on writing.
7. See Mullins (1977:11–30) for a discussion of outlines and the organization of quantitative research reports.

Also, see Williams and Wolfe (1979:85–116) for good hints on how to organize ideas in a paper.

8. Grosof and Sardy (1985:386–389) have provided suggestions on how to explain quantitative findings.

9. Lofland (1974) inductively discovered what he identifies as five major writing styles for reporting field research (generic, novel, elaborated, eventful, and interpenetrated) and discusses how they are evaluated.

10. The error of segregation is discussed in Lofland and Lofland (1984:146).

11. See Becker and Geer (1982:244) and Schatzman and Strauss (1973:130) for a discussion of this and related issues.

12. See Hammersley and Atkinson (1983) and Van Maanen (1988).

13. Discussed in Spradley (1970:162–167).

14. See Van Maanen (1988:13).

15. See Dabbs (1982) for a discussion of graphic and other visual forms of analyzing and presenting qualitative data.

16. For a discussion of ethical concerns in writing field research reports, see Becker (1969), Punch (1986), and Wax (1971).

17. For more on writing proposals to fund research projects, see Bauer (1988), Locke and associates (1987), and Quarles (1986). A somewhat dated but useful short introduction to proposal writing is Krathwohl (1965).

CODE OF ETHICS OF THE NATIONAL ASSOCIATION OF SOCIAL WORKERS

*Approved by the 1996 NASW Delegate Assembly
and revised by the 1999 NASW Delegate Assembly.*

PREAMBLE

The primary mission of the social work profession is to enhance human well-being and help meet the basic human needs of all people, with particular attention to the needs and empowermentof people who are vulnerable, oppressed, and living in poverty. A historic and defining feature of social work is the profession's focus on individual well-being in a social context and the well-being of society. Fundamental to social work is attention to the environmental forces that create, contribute to, and address problems in living.

Social workers promote social justice and social change with and on behalf of clients. "Clients" is used inclusively to refer to individuals, families, groups, organizations, and communities. Social workers are sensitive to cultural and ethnic diversity and strive to end discrimination, oppression, poverty, and other forms of social injustice. These activities may be in the form of direct practice, community organizing, supervision, consultation, administration, advocacy, social and political action, policy development and implementation, education, and research and evaluation. Social workers seek to enhance the capacity of people to address their own needs. Social workers also seek to promote the responsiveness of organizations, communities, and other social institutions to individuals' needs and social problems.

The mission of the social work profession is rooted in a set of core values. These core values, embraced by social workers throughout the profession's history, are the foundation of social work's unique purpose and perspective:

- service
- social justice
- dignity and worth of the person
- importance of human relationships
- integrity
- competence

This constellation of core values reflects what is unique to the social work profession. Core values, and the principles that flow from them, must be balanced within the context and complexity of the human experience.

PURPOSE OF THE NASW CODE OF ETHICS

Professional ethics are at the core of social work. The profession has an obligation to articulate its basic values, ethical principles, and ethical standards. The *NASW Code of Ethics* sets forth these values, principles, and standards to guide social workers' conduct. The *Code* is relevant to all social workers and social work students, regardless of their professional functions, the settings in which they work, or the populations they serve.

The *NASW Code of Ethics* serves six purposes:

1. The *Code* identifies core values on which social work's mission is based.
2. The *Code* summarizes broad ethical principles that reflect the profession's core values and

establishes a set of specific ethical standards that should be used to guide social work practice.

3. The *Code* is designed to help social workers identify relevant considerations when professional obligations conflict or ethical uncertainties arise.

4. The *Code* provides ethical standards to which the general public can hold the social work profession accountable.

5. The *Code* socializes practitioners new to the field to social work's mission, values, ethical principles, and ethical standards.

6. The *Code* articulates standards that the social work profession itself can use to assess whether social workers have engaged in unethical conduct. NASW has formal procedures to adjudicate ethics complaints filed against its members.* In subscribing to this *Code*, social workers are required to cooperate in its implementation, participate in NASW adjudication proceedings, and abide by any NASW disciplinary rulings or sanctions based on it.

*For information on NASW adjudication procedures, see *NASW Procedures for the Adjudication of Grievances.*

The *Code* offers a set of values, principles, and standards to guide decision making and conduct when ethical issues arise. It does not provide a set of rules that prescribe how social workers should act in all situations. Specific applications of the *Code* must take into account the context in which it is being considered and the possibility of conflicts among the *Code*'s values, principles, and standards. Ethical responsibilities flow from all human relationships, from the personal and familial to the social and professional.

Further, the *NASW Code of Ethics* does not specify which values, principles, and standards are most important and ought to outweigh others in instances when they conflict. Reasonable differences of opinion can and do exist among social workers with respect to the ways in which values, ethical principles, and ethical standards should be rank ordered when they conflict. Ethical decision making in a given situation must apply the informed judgment of the individual social worker and should also consider how the issues would be judged in a peer review process where the ethical standards of the profession would be applied.

Ethical decision making is a process. There are many instances in social work where simple answers are not available to resolve complex ethical issues. Social workers should take into consideration all the values, principles, and standards in this *Code* that are relevant to any situation in which ethical judgment is warranted. Social workers' decisions and actions should be consistent with the spirit as well as the letter of this *Code*.

In addition to this *Code,* there are many other sources of information about ethical thinking that may be useful. Social workers should consider ethical theory and principles generally, social work theory and research, laws, regulations, agency policies, and other relevant codes of ethics, recognizing that among codes of ethics social workers should consider the *NASW Code of Ethics* as their primary source. Social workers also should be aware of the impact on ethical decision making of their clients' and their own personal values and cultural and religious beliefs and practices. They should be aware of any conflicts between personal and professional values and deal with them responsibly. For additional guidance social workers should consult the relevant literature on professional ethics and ethical decision making and seek appropriate consultation when faced with ethical dilemmas. This may involve consultation with an agency-based or social work organization's ethics committee, a regulatory body, knowledgeable colleagues, supervisors, or legal counsel.

Instances may arise when social workers' ethical obligations conflict with agency policies or relevant laws or regulations. When such conflicts occur, social workers must make a responsible effort to resolve the conflict in a manner that is consistent with the values, principles, and standards expressed in this *Code*. If a reasonable resolution of the conflict does not appear possible, social workers should seek proper consultation before making a decision.

The *NASW Code of Ethics* is to be used by NASW and by individuals, agencies, organizations, and bodies (such as licensing and regulatory boards, professional liability insurance providers, courts of law, agency boards of directors, government agencies, and other professional groups) that choose to adopt it or use it as a frame of reference. Violation of standards in this *Code* does not automatically imply legal liability or violation of the law. Such determination can only be made in the context of legal and judicial proceedings. Alleged violations of the *Code* would be subject to a peer review process. Such processes are generally separate from legal or administrative procedures and insulated from legal review or proceedings to allow the profession to counsel and discipline its own members.

A code of ethics cannot guarantee ethical behavior. Moreover, a code of ethics cannot resolve all ethical issues or disputes or capture the richness and complexity involved in striving to make responsible choices within a moral community. Rather, a code of ethics sets forth values, ethical principles, and ethical standards to which professionals aspire and by which their actions can be judged. Social workers' ethical behavior should result from their personal commitment to engage in ethical practice. The *NASW Code of Ethics* reflects the commitment of all social workers to uphold the profession's values and to act ethically. Principles and standards must be applied by individuals of good character who discern moral questions and, in good faith, seek to make reliable ethical judgments.

ETHICAL PRINCIPLES

The following broad ethical principles are based on social work's core values of service, social justice, dignity and worth of the person, importance of human relationships, integrity, and competence. These principles set forth ideals to which all social workers should aspire.

Value: *Service*

Ethical Principle: *Social workers' primary goal is to help people in need and to address social problems.*

Social workers elevate service to others above self-interest. Social workers draw on their knowledge, values, and skills to help people in need and to address social problems. Social workers are encouraged to volunteer some portion of their professional skills with no expectation of significant financial return (pro bono service).

Value: *Social Justice*

Ethical Principle: *Social workers challenge social injustice.*

Social workers pursue social change, particularly with and on behalf of vulnerable and oppressed individuals and groups of people. Social workers' social change efforts are focused primarily on issues of poverty, unemployment, discrimination, and other forms of social injustice. These activities seek to promote sensitivity to and knowledge about oppression and cultural and ethnic diversity. Social workers strive to ensure access to needed information, services, and resources; equality of opportunity; and meaningful participation in decision making for all people.

Value: *Dignity and Worth of the Person*

Ethical Principle: *Social workers respect the inherent dignity and worth of the person.*

Social workers treat each person in a caring and respectful fashion, mindful of individual differences and cultural and ethnic diversity. Social workers promote clients' socially responsible self-determination. Social workers seek to enhance clients' capacity and opportunity to change and to address their own needs. Social workers are cognizant of their dual responsibility to clients and to the broader society. They seek to resolve conflicts between clients' interests and the broader society's interests in a socially responsible manner consistent with the values, ethical principles, and ethical standards of the profession.

Value: *Importance of Human Relationships*

Ethical Principle: *Social workers recognize the central importance of human relationships.*

Social workers understand that relationships between and among people are an important vehicle for change. Social workers engage people as partners in the helping process. Social workers seek to strengthen relationships among people in a purposeful effort to promote, restore, maintain, and enhance the well-being of individuals, families, social groups, organizations, and communities.

Value: *Integrity*

Ethical Principle: *Social workers behave in a trustworthy manner.*

Social workers are continually aware of the profession's mission, values, ethical principles, and ethical standards and practice in a manner consistent with them. Social workers act honestly and responsibly and promote ethical practices on the part of the organizations with which they are affiliated.

Value: *Competence*

Ethical Principle: *Social workers practice within their areas of competence and develop and enhance their professional expertise.*

Social workers continually strive to increase their professional knowledge and skills and to apply them in practice. Social workers should aspire to contribute to the knowledge base of the profession.

ETHICAL STANDARDS

The following ethical standards are relevant to the professional activities of all social workers. These standards concern (1) social workers' ethical responsibilities to clients, (2) social workers' ethical responsibilities to colleagues, (3) social workers' ethical responsibilities in practice settings, (4) social workers' ethical responsibilities as professionals, (5) social workers' ethical responsibilities to the social work profession, and (6) social workers' ethical responsibilities to the broader society.

Some of the standards that follow are enforceable guidelines for professional conduct, and some are aspirational. The extent to which each standard is enforceable is a matter of professional judgment to be exercised by those responsible for reviewing alleged violations of ethical standards.

1. Social Workers' Ethical Responsibilities to Clients

1.01 Commitment to Clients

Social workers' primary responsibility is to promote the well-being of clients. In general, clients' interests are primary. However, social workers' responsibility to the larger society or specific legal obligations may on limited occasions supersede the loyalty owed clients, and clients should be so advised. (Examples include when a social worker is required by law to report that a client has abused a child or has threatened to harm self or others.)

1.02 Self-Determination

Social workers respect and promote the right of clients to self-determination and assist clients in their efforts to identify and clarify their goals. Social workers may limit clients' right to self-determination when, in the social workers' professional judgment, clients' actions or potential actions pose a serious, foreseeable, and imminent risk to themselves or others.

1.03 Informed Consent

(a) Social workers should provide services to clients only in the context of a professional relationship based, when appropriate, on valid informed consent. Social workers should use clear and understandable language to inform clients of the purpose of the services, risks related to the services, limits to services because of the requirements of a third-party payer, relevant costs, reasonable alternatives, clients' right to refuse or withdraw consent, and the time frame covered by the consent. Social workers should provide clients with an opportunity to ask questions.

(b) In instances when clients are not literate or have difficulty understanding the primary language used in the practice setting, social workers should take steps to ensure clients' comprehension. This may include providing clients with a detailed verbal explanation or arranging for a qualified interpreter or translator whenever possible.

(c) In instances when clients lack the capacity to provide informed consent, social workers should protect clients' interests by seeking permission from an appropriate third party, informing clients consistent with the clients' level of understanding. In such instances social workers should seek to ensure that the third party acts in a manner consistent with clients' wishes and interests. Social workers should take reasonable steps to enhance such clients' ability to give informed consent.

(d) In instances when clients are receiving services involuntarily, social workers should provide information about the nature and extent of services and about the extent of clients' right to refuse service.

(e) Social workers who provide services via electronic media (such as computer, telephone, radio, and television) should inform recipients of the limitations and risks associated with such services.

(f) Social workers should obtain clients' informed consent before audiotaping or videotaping clients or permitting observation of services to clients by a third party.

1.04 Competence

(a) Social workers should provide services and represent themselves as competent only within the boundaries of their education, training, license, certification, consultation received, supervised experience, or other relevant professional experience.

(b) Social workers should provide services in substantive areas or use intervention techniques or approaches that are new to them only after engaging in appropriate study, training, consultation, and supervision from people who are competent in those interventions or techniques.

(c) When generally recognized standards do not exist with respect to an emerging area of practice, social workers should exercise careful judgment and take responsible steps (including appropriate education, research, training, consultation, and supervision) to ensure the competence of their work and to protect clients from harm.

1.05 Cultural Competence and Social Diversity

(a) Social workers should understand culture and its function in human behavior and society, recognizing the strengths that exist in all cultures.

(b) Social workers should have a knowledge base of their clients' cultures and be able to demonstrate competence in the provision of services that are sensitive to clients' cultures and to differences among people and cultural groups.

(c) Social workers should obtain education about and seek to understand the nature of social diversity and oppression with respect to race, ethnicity, national origin, color, sex, sexual orientation, age, marital status, political belief, religion, and mental or physical disability.

1.06 Conflicts of Interest

(a) Social workers should be alert to and avoid conflicts of interest that interfere with the exercise of professional discretion and impartial judgment. Social workers should inform clients when a real or potential conflict of interest arises and take reasonable steps to resolve the issue in a manner that makes the clients' interests primary and protects clients' interests to the greatest extent possible. In some cases, protecting clients' interests may require termination of the professional relationship with proper referral of the client.

(b) Social workers should not take unfair advantage of any professional relationship or exploit others to further their personal, religious, political, or business interests.

(c) Social workers should not engage in dual or multiple relationships with clients or former clients in which there is a risk of exploitation or potential harm to the client. In instances when dual or multiple relationships are unavoidable, social workers should take steps to protect clients and are responsible for setting clear, appropriate, and culturally sensitive boundaries. (Dual or multiple relationships occur when social workers relate to clients in more than one relationship, whether professional, social, or business. Dual or multiple relationships can occur simultaneously or consecutively.)

(d) When social workers provide services to two or more people who have a relationship with each other (for example, couples, family members), social workers should clarify with all parties which individuals will be considered clients and the nature of social workers' professional obligations to the various individuals who are receiving services. Social workers who anticipate a conflict of interest among the individuals receiving services or who anticipate having to perform in potentially conflicting roles (for example, when a social worker is asked to testify in a child custody dispute or divorce proceedings involving clients) should clarify their role with the parties involved and take appropriate action to minimize any conflict of interest.

1.07 Privacy and Confidentiality

(a) Social workers should respect clients' right to privacy. Social workers should not solicit private information from clients unless it is essential to providing services or conducting social work evaluation or research. Once private information is shared, standards of confidentiality apply.

(b) Social workers may disclose confidential information when appropriate with valid consent from a client or a person legally authorized to consent on behalf of a client.

(c) Social workers should protect the confidentiality of all information obtained in the course of professional service, except for compelling professional reasons. The general expectation that social workers will keep information confidential does not apply when disclosure is necessary to prevent serious, foreseeable, and imminent harm to a client or other identifiable person. In all instances, social workers should disclose the least amount of confidential information necessary to achieve the desired purpose; only information that is directly relevant to the purpose for which the disclosure is made should be revealed.

(d) Social workers should inform clients, to the extent possible, about the disclosure of confidential information and the potential consequences, when feasible before the disclosure is made. This applies whether social workers disclose confidential information on the basis of a legal requirement or client consent.

(e) Social workers should discuss with clients and other interested parties the nature of confidentiality and limitations of clients' right to confidentiality. Social workers should review with clients circumstances where confidential information may be requested and where disclosure of confidential information may be legally required. This discussion should occur as soon as possible in the social worker–client relationship and as needed throughout the course of the relationship.

(f) When social workers provide counseling services to families, couples, or groups, social workers should seek agreement among the parties involved concerning each individual's right to confidentiality and obligation to preserve the confidentiality of information shared by others. Social workers should inform participants in family, couples, or group counseling that social workers cannot guarantee that all participants will honor such agreements.

(g) Social workers should inform clients involved in family, couples, marital, or group counseling of the social worker's, employer's, and agency's policy concerning the social worker's disclosure of confidential information among the parties involved in the counseling.

(h) Social workers should not disclose confidential information to third-party payers unless clients have authorized such disclosure.

(i) Social workers should not discuss confidential information in any setting unless privacy can be ensured. Social workers should not discuss confidential information in public or semipublic areas such as hallways, waiting rooms, elevators, and restaurants.

(j) Social workers should protect the confidentiality of clients during legal proceedings to the extent permitted by law. When a court of law or other legally authorized body orders social workers to disclose confidential or privileged information without a client's consent and such disclosure could cause harm to the client, social workers should request that the court withdraw the order or limit the order as narrowly as possible or maintain the records under seal, unavailable for public inspection.

(k) Social workers should protect the confidentiality of clients when responding to requests from members of the media.

(l) Social workers should protect the confidentiality of clients' written and electronic records and other sensitive information. Social workers should take reasonable steps to ensure that clients' records are stored in a secure location and that clients' records are not available to others who are not authorized to have access.

(m) Social workers should take precautions to ensure and maintain the confidentiality of information transmitted to other parties through the use of computers, electronic mail, facsimile machines, telephones and telephone answering machines, and other electronic or computer technology. Disclosure of identifying information should be avoided whenever possible.

(n) Social workers should transfer or dispose of clients' records in a manner that protects clients' confidentiality and is consistent with state statutes governing records and social work licensure.

(o) Social workers should take reasonable precautions to protect client confidentiality in the event of the social worker's termination of practice, incapacitation, or death.

(p) Social workers should not disclose identifying information when discussing clients for teaching or training purposes unless the client has consented to disclosure of confidential information.

(q) Social workers should not disclose identifying information when discussing clients with consultants unless the client has consented to disclosure of confidential information or there is a compelling need for such disclosure.

(r) Social workers should protect the confidentiality of deceased clients consistent with the preceding standards.

1.08 Access to Records

(a) Social workers should provide clients with reasonable access to records concerning the clients. Social workers who are concerned that clients' access to their records could cause serious misunderstanding or harm to the client should provide assistance in interpreting the records and consultation with the client regarding the records. Social workers should limit clients' access to their records, or portions of their records, only in exceptional circumstances when there is compelling evidence that such access would cause serious harm to the client. Both clients' requests and the rationale for withholding some or all of the record should be documented in clients' files.

(b) When providing clients with access to their records, social workers should take steps to protect the confidentiality of other individuals identified or discussed in such records.

1.09 Sexual Relationships

(a) Social workers should under no circumstances engage in sexual activities or sexual contact with current clients, whether such contact is consensual or forced.

(b) Social workers should not engage in sexual activities or sexual contact with clients' relatives or other individuals with whom clients maintain a close personal relationship when there is a risk of exploitation or potential harm to the client. Sexual activity or sexual contact with clients' relatives or other individuals with whom clients maintain a personal relationship has the potential to be harmful to the client and may make it difficult for the social worker and client to maintain appropriate professional boundaries. Social workers—not their clients, their clients' relatives, or other individuals with whom the client maintains a personal relationship—assume the full burden for setting clear, appropriate, and culturally sensitive boundaries.

(c) Social workers should not engage in sexual activities or sexual contact with former clients because of the potential for harm to the client. If social workers engage in conduct contrary to this prohibition or claim that an exception to this prohibition is warranted because of extraordinary circumstances, it is social workers—not their clients—who assume the full burden of demonstrating that the former client has not been exploited, coerced, or manipulated, intentionally or unintentionally.

(d) Social workers should not provide clinical services to individuals with whom they have had a prior sexual relationship. Providing clinical services to a former sexual partner has the potential to be harmful to the individual and is likely to make it difficult for the social worker and individual to maintain appropriate professional boundaries.

1.10 Physical Contact

Social workers should not engage in physical contact with clients when there is a possibility of psychological harm to the client as a result of the contact (such as cradling or caressing clients). Social workers who engage in appropriate physical contact with clients are responsible for setting clear, appropriate, and culturally sensitive boundaries that govern such physical contact.

1.11 Sexual Harassment

Social workers should not sexually harass clients. Sexual harassment includes sexual advances, sexual solicitation, requests for sexual favors, and other verbal or physical conduct of a sexual nature.

1.12 Derogatory Language

Social workers should not use derogatory language in their written or verbal communications to or about clients. Social workers should use accurate and respectful language in all communications to and about clients.

1.13 Payment for Services

(a) When setting fees, social workers should ensure that the fees are fair, reasonable, and commensurate with the services performed. Consideration should be given to clients' ability to pay.

(b) Social workers should avoid accepting goods or services from clients as payment for professional services. Bartering arrangements, particularly involving services, create the potential for conflicts of interest, exploitation, and inappropriate boundaries in social workers' relationships with clients. Social workers should explore and may participate in bartering only in very limited circumstances when it can be demonstrated that such arrangements are an accepted practice among professionals in the local community, considered to be essential for the provision of services, negotiated without coercion, and entered into at the client's initiative and with the client's informed consent. Social workers who accept goods or services from clients as payment for professional services assume the full burden of demonstrating that this arrangement will not be detrimental to the client or the professional relationship.

(c) Social workers should not solicit a private fee or other remuneration for providing services to clients who are entitled to such available services through the social workers' employer or agency.

1.14 Clients Who Lack Decision-Making Capacity

When social workers act on behalf of clients who lack the capacity to make informed decisions, social workers should take reasonable steps to safeguard the interests and rights of those clients.

1.15 Interruption of Services

Social workers should make reasonable efforts to ensure continuity of services in the event that services are interrupted by factors such as unavailability, relocation, illness, disability, or death.

1.16 Termination of Services

(a) Social workers should terminate services to clients and professional relationships with them when such services and relationships are no longer required or no longer serve the clients' needs or interests.

(b) Social workers should take reasonable steps to avoid abandoning clients who are still in need of services. Social workers should withdraw services precipitously only under unusual circumstances, giving careful consideration to all factors in the situation and taking care to minimize possible adverse effects. Social workers should assist in making appropriate arrangements for continuation of services when necessary.

(c) Social workers in fee-for-service settings may terminate services to clients who are not paying an overdue balance if the financial contractual arrangements have been made clear to the client, if the client does not pose an imminent danger to self or others, and if the clinical and other consequences of the current nonpayment have been addressed and discussed with the client.

(d) Social workers should not terminate services to pursue a social, financial, or sexual relationship with a client.

(e) Social workers who anticipate the termination or interruption of services to clients should notify clients promptly and seek the transfer, referral, or continuation of services in relation to the clients' needs and preferences.

(f) Social workers who are leaving an employment setting should inform clients of appropriate options for the continuation of services and of the benefits and risks of the options.

2. Social Workers' Ethical Responsibilities to Colleagues

2.01 Respect

(a) Social workers should treat colleagues with respect and should represent accurately and fairly the qualifications, views, and obligations of colleagues.

(b) Social workers should avoid unwarranted negative criticism of colleagues in communications with clients or with other professionals. Unwarranted negative criticism may include demeaning comments that refer to colleagues' level of competence or to individuals' attributes such as race, ethnicity, national origin, color, sex, sexual orientation, age, marital status, political belief, religion, and mental or physical disability.

(c) Social workers should cooperate with social work colleagues and with colleagues of other professions when such cooperation serves the well-being of clients.

2.02 Confidentiality

Social workers should respect confidential information shared by colleagues in the course of their professional relationships and transactions. Social workers should ensure that such colleagues understand social workers' obligation to respect confidentiality and any exceptions related to it.

2.03 Interdisciplinary Collaboration

(a) Social workers who are members of an interdisciplinary team should participate in and contribute to decisions that affect the well-being of clients by drawing on the perspectives, values, and experiences of the social work profession. Professional and ethical obligations of the interdisciplinary team as a whole and of its individual members should be clearly established.

(b) Social workers for whom a team decision raises ethical concerns should attempt to resolve the disagreement through appropriate channels. If the disagreement cannot be resolved, social workers should pursue other avenues to address their concerns consistent with client well-being.

2.04 Disputes Involving Colleagues

(a) Social workers should not take advantage of a dispute between a colleague and an employer to obtain a position or otherwise advance the social workers' own interests.

(b) Social workers should not exploit clients in disputes with colleagues or engage clients in any inappropriate discussion of conflicts between social workers and their colleagues.

2.05 Consultation

(a) Social workers should seek the advice and counsel of colleagues whenever such consultation is in the best interests of clients.

(b) Social workers should keep themselves informed about colleagues' areas of expertise and competencies. Social workers should seek consultation only from colleagues who have demonstrated knowledge, expertise, and competence related to the subject of the consultation.

(c) When consulting with colleagues about clients, social workers should disclose the least amount of information necessary to achieve the purposes of the consultation.

2.06 Referral for Services

(a) Social workers should refer clients to other professionals when the other professionals' specialized knowledge or expertise is needed to serve clients fully or when social workers believe that they are not being effective or making reasonable progress with clients and that additional service is required.

(b) Social workers who refer clients to other professionals should take appropriate steps to facilitate an orderly transfer of responsibility. Social workers who refer clients to other professionals should disclose, with clients' consent, all pertinent information to the new service providers.

(c) Social workers are prohibited from giving or receiving payment for a referral when no professional service is provided by the referring social worker.

2.07 Sexual Relationships

(a) Social workers who function as supervisors or educators should not engage in sexual activities or contact with supervisees, students, trainees, or other colleagues over whom they exercise professional authority.

(b) Social workers should avoid engaging in sexual relationships with colleagues when there is potential for a conflict of interest. Social workers who become involved in, or anticipate becoming involved in, a sexual relationship with a colleague have a duty to transfer professional responsibilities, when necessary, to avoid a conflict of interest.

2.08 Sexual Harassment

Social workers should not sexually harass supervisees, students, trainees, or colleagues. Sexual harassment includes sexual advances, sexual solicitation, requests for sexual favors, and other verbal or physical conduct of a sexual nature.

2.09 Impairment of Colleagues

(a) Social workers who have direct knowledge of a social work colleague's impairment that is due to personal problems, psychosocial distress, substance abuse, or mental health difficulties and that interferes with practice effectiveness should consult with that colleague when feasible and assist the colleague in taking remedial action.

(b) Social workers who believe that a social work colleague's impairment interferes with practice effectiveness and that the colleague has not taken adequate steps to address the impairment should take action through appropriate channels established by employers, agencies, NASW, licensing and regulatory bodies, and other professional organizations.

2.10 Incompetence of Colleagues

(a) Social workers who have direct knowledge of a social work colleague's incompetence should consult with that colleague when feasible and assist the colleague in taking remedial action.

(b) Social workers who believe that a social work colleague is incompetent and has not taken adequate steps to address the incompetence should take action through appropriate channels established by employers, agencies, NASW, licensing and regulatory bodies, and other professional organizations.

2.11 Unethical Conduct of Colleagues

(a) Social workers should take adequate measures to discourage, prevent, expose, and correct the unethical conduct of colleagues.

(b) Social workers should be knowledgeable about established policies and procedures for handling concerns about colleagues' unethical behavior. Social workers should be familiar with national, state, and local procedures for handling ethics complaints. These include policies and procedures created by NASW, licensing and regulatory bodies, employers, agencies, and other professional organizations.

(c) Social workers who believe that a colleague has acted unethically should seek resolution by discussing their concerns with the colleague when feasible and when such discussion is likely to be productive.

(d) When necessary, social workers who believe that a colleague has acted unethically should take action through appropriate formal channels (such as contacting a state licensing board or regulatory body, an NASW committee on inquiry, or other professional ethics committees).

(e) Social workers should defend and assist colleagues who are unjustly charged with unethical conduct.

3. Social Workers' Ethical Responsibilities in Practice Settings

3.01 Supervision and Consultation

(a) Social workers who provide supervision or consultation should have the necessary knowledge and skill to supervise or consult appropriately and should do so only within their areas of knowledge and competence.

(b) Social workers who provide supervision or consultation are responsible for setting clear, appropriate, and culturally sensitive boundaries.

(c) Social workers should not engage in any dual or multiple relationships with supervisees in which there is a risk of exploitation of or potential harm to the supervisee.

(d) Social workers who provide supervision should evaluate supervisees' performance in a manner that is fair and respectful.

3.02 Education and Training

(a) Social workers who function as educators, field instructors for students, or trainers should provide instruction only within their areas of knowledge and competence and should provide instruction based on the most current information and knowledge available in the profession.

(b) Social workers who function as educators or field instructors for students should evaluate students' performance in a manner that is fair and respectful.

(c) Social workers who function as educators or field instructors for students should take reasonable steps to ensure that clients are routinely informed when services are being provided by students.

(d) Social workers who function as educators or field instructors for students should not engage in any dual or multiple relationships with students in which there is a risk of exploitation or potential harm to the student. Social work educators and field instructors are responsible for setting clear, appropriate, and culturally sensitive boundaries.

3.03 Performance Evaluation

Social workers who have responsibility for evaluating the performance of others should fulfill such responsibility in a fair and considerate manner and on the basis of clearly stated criteria.

3.04 Client Records

(a) Social workers should take reasonable steps to ensure that documentation in records is accurate and reflects the services provided.

(b) Social workers should include sufficient and timely documentation in records to facilitate the delivery of services and to ensure continuity of services provided to clients in the future.

(c) Social workers' documentation should protect clients' privacy to the extent that is possible and appropriate and should include only information that is directly relevant to the delivery of services.

(d) Social workers should store records following the termination of services to ensure reasonable future access. Records should be maintained for the number of years required by state statutes or relevant contracts.

3.05 Billing

Social workers should establish and maintain billing practices that accurately reflect the nature and extent of services provided and that identify who provided the service in the practice setting.

3.06 Client Transfer

(a) When an individual who is receiving services from another agency or colleague contacts a social worker for services, the social worker should carefully consider the client's needs before agreeing to provide services. To minimize possible confusion and conflict, social workers should discuss with potential clients the nature of the clients' current relationship with other service providers and the implications, including possible benefits or risks, of entering into a relationship with a new service provider.

(b) If a new client has been served by another agency or colleague, social workers should discuss with the client whether consultation with the previous service provider is in the client's best interest.

3.07 Administration

(a) Social work administrators should advocate within and outside their agencies for adequate resources to meet clients' needs.

(b) Social workers should advocate for resource allocation procedures that are open and fair. When not all clients' needs can be met, an allocation procedure should be developed that is nondiscriminatory and based on appropriate and consistently applied principles.

(c) Social workers who are administrators should take reasonable steps to ensure that adequate agency or organizational resources are available to provide appropriate staff supervision.

(d) Social work administrators should take reasonable steps to ensure that the working environment for which they are responsible is consistent with and encourages compliance with the *NASW Code of Ethics.* Social work administrators should take reasonable steps to eliminate any conditions in their organizations that violate, interfere with, or discourage compliance with the *Code.*

3.08 Continuing Education and Staff Development

Social work administrators and supervisors should take reasonable steps to provide or arrange for continuing education and staff development for all staff for whom they are responsible. Continuing education and staff development should address current knowledge and emerging developments related to social work practice and ethics.

3.09 Commitments to Employers

(a) Social workers generally should adhere to commitments made to employers and employing organizations.

(b) Social workers should work to improve employing agencies' policies and procedures and the efficiency and effectiveness of their services.

(c) Social workers should take reasonable steps to ensure that employers are aware of social workers' ethical obligations as set forth in the *NASW Code of Ethics* and of the implications of those obligations for social work practice.

(d) Social workers should not allow an employing organization's policies, procedures, regulations, or administrative orders to interfere with their ethical practice of social work. Social workers should take reasonable steps to ensure that their employing organizations' practices are consistent with the *NASW Code of Ethics*.

(e) Social workers should act to prevent and eliminate discrimination in the employing organization's work assignments and in its employment policies and practices.

(f) Social workers should accept employment or arrange student field placements only in organizations that exercise fair personnel practices.

(g) Social workers should be diligent stewards of the resources of their employing organizations, wisely conserving funds where appropriate and never misappropriating funds or using them for unintended purposes.

3.10 Labor–Management Disputes

(a) Social workers may engage in organized action, including the formation of and participation in labor unions, to improve services to clients and working conditions.

(b) The actions of social workers who are involved in labor–management disputes, job actions, or labor strikes should be guided by the profession's values, ethical principles, and ethical standards. Reasonable differences of opinion exist among social workers concerning their primary obligation as professionals during an actual or threatened labor strike or job action. Social workers should carefully examine relevant issues and their possible impact on clients before deciding on a course of action.

4. Social Workers' Ethical Responsibilities as Professionals

4.01 Competence

(a) Social workers should accept responsibility or employment only on the basis of existing competence or the intention to acquire the necessary competence.

(b) Social workers should strive to become and remain proficient in professional practice and the performance of professional functions. Social workers should critically examine and keep current with emerging knowledge relevant to social work. Social workers should routinely review the professional literature and participate in continuing education relevant to social work practice and social work ethics.

(c) Social workers should base practice on recognized knowledge, including empirically based knowledge, relevant to social work and social work ethics.

4.02 Discrimination

Social workers should not practice, condone, facilitate, or collaborate with any form of discrimination on the basis of race, ethnicity, national origin, color, sex, sexual orientation, age, marital status, political belief, religion, or mental or physical disability.

4.03 Private Conduct

Social workers should not permit their private conduct to interfere with their ability to fulfill their professional responsibilities.

4.04 Dishonesty, Fraud, and Deception

Social workers should not participate in, condone, or be associated with dishonesty, fraud, or deception.

4.05 Impairment

(a) Social workers should not allow their own personal problems, psychosocial distress, legal problems, substance abuse, or mental health difficulties to interfere with their professional judgment and performance or to jeopardize the best interests of people for whom they have a professional responsibility.

(b) Social workers whose personal problems, psychosocial distress, legal problems, substance abuse, or mental health difficulties interfere with their professional judgment and performance should immediately seek consultation and take appropriate remedial action by seeking professional help, making adjustments in workload, terminating practice, or taking any other steps necessary to protect clients and others.

4.06 Misrepresentation

(a) Social workers should make clear distinctions between statements made and actions engaged in as a private individual and as a representative of the social work profession, a professional social work organization, or the social worker's employing agency.

(b) Social workers who speak on behalf of professional social work organizations should accurately represent the official and authorized positions of the organizations.

(c) Social workers should ensure that their representations to clients, agencies, and the public of professional qualifications, credentials, education, competence, affiliations, services provided, or results to be achieved are accurate. Social workers should claim only those relevant professional credentials they actually possess and take steps to correct any inaccuracies or misrepresentations of their credentials by others.

4.07 Solicitations

(a) Social workers should not engage in uninvited solicitation of potential clients who, because of their circumstances, are vulnerable to undue influence, manipulation, or coercion.

(b) Social workers should not engage in solicitation of testimonial endorsements (including solicitation of consent to use a client's prior statement as a testimonial endorsement) from current clients or from other people who, because of their particular circumstances, are vulnerable to undue influence.

4.08 Acknowledging Credit

(a) Social workers should take responsibility and credit, including authorship credit, only for work they have actually performed and to which they have contributed.

(b) Social workers should honestly acknowledge the work of and the contributions made by others.

5. Social Workers' Ethical Responsibilities to the Social Work Profession

5.01 Integrity of the Profession

(a) Social workers should work toward the maintenance and promotion of high standards of practice.

(b) Social workers should uphold and advance the values, ethics, knowledge, and mission of the profession. Social workers should protect, enhance, and improve the integrity of the profession through appropriate study and research, active discussion, and responsible criticism of the profession.

(c) Social workers should contribute time and professional expertise to activities that promote respect for the value, integrity, and competence of the social work profession. These activities may include teaching, research, consultation, service, legislative testimony, presentations in the community, and participation in their professional organizations.

(d) Social workers should contribute to the knowledge base of social work and share with colleagues their knowledge related to practice, research, and ethics. Social workers should seek to contribute to the profession's literature and to share their knowledge at professional meetings and conferences.

(e) Social workers should act to prevent the unauthorized and unqualified practice of social work.

5.02 Evaluation and Research

(a) Social workers should monitor and evaluate policies, the implementation of programs, and practice interventions.

(b) Social workers should promote and facilitate evaluation and research to contribute to the development of knowledge.

(c) Social workers should critically examine and keep current with emerging knowledge relevant to social work and fully use evaluation and research evidence in their professional practice.

(d) Social workers engaged in evaluation or research should carefully consider possible consequences and should follow guidelines developed for the protection of evaluation and research participants. Appropriate institutional review boards should be consulted.

(e) Social workers engaged in evaluation or research should obtain voluntary and written informed consent from participants, when appropriate, without any implied or actual deprivation or penalty for refusal to participate; without undue inducement to participate; and with due regard for participants' well-being, privacy, and dignity. Informed consent should include information about the nature, extent, and duration of the participation requested and disclosure of the risks and benefits of participation in the research.

(f) When evaluation or research participants are incapable of giving informed consent, social workers should provide an appropriate explanation to the participants, obtain the participants' assent to the extent they are able, and obtain written consent from an appropriate proxy.

(g) Social workers should never design or conduct evaluation or research that does not use consent procedures, such as certain forms of naturalistic observation and archival research, unless rigorous and responsible review of the research has found it to be justified because of its prospective scientific, educational, or applied value and unless equally effective alternative procedures that do not involve waiver of consent are not feasible.

(h) Social workers should inform participants of their right to withdraw from evaluation and research at any time without penalty.

(i) Social workers should take appropriate steps to ensure that participants in evaluation and research have access to appropriate supportive services.

(j) Social workers engaged in evaluation or research should protect participants from unwarranted physical or mental distress, harm, danger, or deprivation.

(k) Social workers engaged in the evaluation of services should discuss collected information only for professional purposes and only with people professionally concerned with this information.

(l) Social workers engaged in evaluation or research should ensure the anonymity or confidentiality of participants and of the data obtained from them. Social workers should inform participants of any limits of confidentiality, the measures that will be taken to ensure confidentiality, and when any records containing research data will be destroyed.

(m) Social workers who report evaluation and research results should protect participants' confidentiality by omitting identifying information unless proper consent has been obtained authorizing disclosure.

(n) Social workers should report evaluation and research findings accurately. They should not fab-

ricate or falsify results and should take steps to correct any errors later found in published data using standard publication methods.

(o) Social workers engaged in evaluation or research should be alert to and avoid conflicts of interest and dual relationships with participants, should inform participants when a real or potential conflict of interest arises, and should take steps to resolve the issue in a manner that makes participants' interests primary.

(p) Social workers should educate themselves, their students, and their colleagues about responsible research practices.

6. Social Workers' Ethical Responsibilities to the Broader Society

6.01 Social Welfare

Social workers should promote the general welfare of society, from local to global levels, and the development of people, their communities, and their environments. Social workers should advocate for living conditions conducive to the fulfillment of basic human needs and should promote social, economic, political, and cultural values and institutions that are compatible with the realization of social justice.

6.02 Public Participation

Social workers should facilitate informed participation by the public in shaping social policies and institutions.

6.03 Public Emergencies

Social workers should provide appropriate professional services in public emergencies to the greatest extent possible.

6.04 Social and Political Action

(a) Social workers should engage in social and political action that seeks to ensure that all people have equal access to the resources, employment, services, and opportunities they require to meet their basic human needs and to develop fully. Social workers should be aware of the impact of the political arena on practice and should advocate for changes in policy and legislation to improve social conditions in order to meet basic human needs and promote social justice.

(b) Social workers should act to expand choice and opportunity for all people, with special regard for vulnerable, disadvantaged, oppressed, and exploited people and groups.

(c) Social workers should promote conditions that encourage respect for cultural and social diversity within the United States and globally. Social workers should promote policies and practices that demonstrate respect for difference, support the expansion of cultural knowledge and resources, advocate for programs and institutions that demonstrate cultural competence, and promote policies that safeguard the rights of and confirm equity and social justice for all people.

(d) Social workers should act to prevent and eliminate domination of, exploitation of, and discrimination against any person, group, or class on the basis of race, ethnicity, national origin, color, sex, sexual orientation, age, marital status, political belief, religion, or mental or physical disability.

TABLE OF RANDOMLY SELECTED FIVE-DIGIT NUMBERS

10819	85717	64540	95692	44985	88504	50298	20830	67124	20557
28459	13687	50699	62110	49307	84465	66518	08290	96957	45050
19105	52686	51336	53101	81842	20323	71091	78598	60969	74898
35376	72734	13951	27528	36140	42195	25942	70835	45825	49277
93818	84972	66048	83361	56465	65449	87748	95405	98712	97183
35859	82675	87301	71211	78007	99316	25591	63995	40577	78894
66241	89679	04843	96407	01970	06913	19259	72929	82868	50457
44222	37633	85262	65308	03252	36770	51640	18333	33971	49352
54966	75662	80544	48943	87983	62759	55698	41068	35558	60870
43351	15285	38157	45261	50114	35934	05950	11735	51769	07389
11208	80818	78325	14807	19325	41500	01263	09211	56005	44250
71379	53517	15553	04774	63452	50294	06332	69926	20592	06305
63162	41154	78345	23645	74235	72054	84152	27889	76881	58652
17457	68490	19878	04981	83667	00053	12003	84614	14842	29462
28042	42748	55801	94527	21926	07901	89855	21070	80320	91153
32240	24201	24202	45025	07664	11503	97375	83178	26731	45568
87288	22996	67529	38344	29757	74161	16834	40238	48789	99995
39052	23696	42858	85695	50783	51790	80882	97015	81331	76819
71528	74553	32294	86652	15224	07119	45327	69072	64572	07658
76921	04502	78240	89519	02621	40829	88841	66178	01266	10906
45889	22839	77794	94068	85709	96902	19646	40614	03169	45434
10486	79308	75231	33615	42194	49397	91324	79553	66976	83861
42051	14719	80056	74811	58453	04526	90724	36151	09168	04291
47919	11314	80282	09297	02824	59530	31237	26311	62168	46591
19634	40589	28985	40577	33213	52852	17556	85342	66881	18944
10265	45549	38771	38740	48104	63990	73234	19398	33740	97345
74975	33526	36190	25201	19239	06254	02198	99109	01005	20983
37677	76778	15736	57675	81153	59651	69262	89250	75156	59164
18774	15979	26466	80236	65400	24272	02088	09307	33426	11230
93728	14965	85141	27821	53791	38728	66369	29415	55330	99228
34212	15590	41336	23614	26153	19466	44176	80885	00015	40077
81984	54478	45226	97338	14064	45768	13538	49093	05691	69720
72755	15743	00552	89374	85400	37392	26598	71917	64275	16125
13162	57044	75982	15819	23385	40860	51585	44542	39656	91139
64686	62224	34124	79171	73909	26196	54057	63264	72089	06658
00157	64594	03178	75774	32315	34443	37224	85593	55251	42666
84194	83591	82152	24311	22414	43244	81542	31491	42075	17275
05776	60399	65218	89299	20273	30071	53077	18853	56652	63896
33365	18314	81074	49433	10884	75467	56085	14731	98085	60895
67928	38976	38480	59980	23156	72335	33489	59420	67819	51874

64394	45154	81851	54228	73095	97217	16908	90242	92869	17311
73000	20948	57065	70195	87563	41590	85047	71743	94916	50534
63555	03388	96638	16591	13641	73342	59131	63144	63587	62084
84005	02035	08182	16395	44928	08897	44750	71378	67522	20180
42593	35102	14577	38102	60403	04540	53992	27069	69574	76682
49519	49517	88147	83375	87045	57466	91259	06680	45586	36257
42149	01579	83056	19423	28165	25620	68035	17919	09120	59078
66192	98427	10152	96970	89990	34604	49632	46533	63362	43151
16124	88620	87074	37851	77131	73855	03740	10306	63858	04349
35492	47334	57189	26465	70078	14477	00881	00929	86907	73764
54503	40155	94734	20689	32475	62851	13216	21419	95502	36783
88063	53451	15642	67345	06935	70644	68570	79176	31975	83082
83689	14426	40357	34906	56282	96104	83796	57663	88627	17521
40393	72810	00681	15351	28858	72086	99090	39741	17914	27385
76648	61322	06817	64674	50317	52373	78223	84222	14021	43432
42091	27088	37686	88033	68007	71009	24018	49568	64351	94130
78925	41509	14319	92389	85492	40880	01487	85509	48316	62618
61915	98081	87996	53798	51485	38912	85858	43392	64678	44458
29504	66960	42645	54547	20615	77035	79942	33972	46112	78290
90170	97643	46284	34591	42692	72933	66166	98389	37460	14545
96439	06806	76714	80084	57685	37447	44901	64699	89142	64657
98365	28725	84376	50634	79289	31106	71351	10533	57545	27399
74794	91013	89791	54236	02369	35317	31103	82481	52256	94510
37499	85907	16293	17673	13373	06599	50138	19860	46716	36928
77530	25960	33671	54383	25144	82627	99266	75134	96539	47242
67990	35106	05214	82928	39824	11128	31390	76293	52809	54881
07355	29187	09357	94498	69697	92515	89812	90794	44738	46806
40716	05787	68975	38937	44033	50064	25582	09428	10220	42455
97748	64395	13937	60406	99182	92720	80805	26242	81943	40341
83682	18775	60095	78600	03994	30313	21418	58563	47258	75582
73506	30672	18213	37887	26698	87700	75784	86878	74004	88636
36274	02333	43132	93725	87912	90341	74601	77001	30717	60002
73508	00852	94044	98474	12621	91655	55258	85551	76122	68052
06488	12362	60020	66902	90734	73689	22382	40896	09028	72925
20201	31560	98885	32275	46818	76114	07959	65639	33267	98595
49947	13114	06773	06454	95070	26564	08974	11640	76202	86105
79928	50600	06586	72129	37233	02564	83265	32579	21234	83535
76360	86412	36240	20210	17692	80482	67007	15474	23198	74250
54601	84643	66759	57661	16434	61708	93185	75957	61056	90678
23441	63863	95238	59665	55789	26180	12566	58645	15125	76707
47093	90509	48767	09874	23363	84954	09789	30178	28804	93294
93603	11580	94163	85561	71328	88735	69859	84563	25579	52858
68812	15299	99296	45906	37303	49507	70680	74412	96425	38134
69023	84343	36736	52659	90751	20115	89920	44995	17109	96613
76913	03158	83461	27842	03903	34683	89761	80564	45806	88009
99426	99643	00749	79376	44910	27490	59668	93907	73112	46365
59429	08121	06954	28120	17606	22482	91924	00401	16459	15570
38121	05358	01205	00662	73934	97834	56917	64058	05148	87599
97781	32170	99914	75565	79802	38905	17167	08196	46043	72094
79068	21760	78832	93795	67798	54968	87328	46494	74338	89805
46601	04015	00484	39366	56233	22622	90706	02327	60807	39009

(continued)

64821	72859	83471	60448	49159	38242	84473	05512	20200	91109
49216	15978	76313	82040	79322	53190	99705	86694	39000	59173
85909	77399	56836	38084	24480	16180	58023	20122	78348	36906
72284	62418	84313	85377	00039	90894	72976	19553	22917	58585
20210	90083	06608	43380	76224	87362	81200	91427	34115	36488
63659	42186	61396	94269	58196	42997	96272	02004	63365	75665
60022	62412	97267	13525	36794	68402	10902	87223	95682	18000
32399	18357	80684	50976	28717	95782	31227	99800	62642	33563
88488	73641	06447	51771	17572	68734	75964	54434	21852	80662
87642	39726	67296	75473	82899	06689	09402	18953	07418	89659
89586	59644	02486	95252	57771	97979	44761	10361	99589	57982
72544	38997	64243	04873	97006	55074	63062	06692	69940	94364
50807	84525	33191	49539	51414	87457	36296	68915	78902	60245
59490	00996	40795	05159	14215	72282	99887	93436	73440	57270
38626	50552	71131	69450	00534	26851	63155	61856	31104	52773
51982	59414	61762	30549	38914	30613	48661	47104	84319	71299
37747	69944	81040	53066	72265	63828	33559	21167	44864	91959
35752	01162	55189	98224	83276	35108	65759	47387	78381	53662
39473	21252	53693	49359	00691	82273	87378	90967	06356	77705
55572	52235	46693	87891	13626	50676	16806	23052	49743	44683
86396	26942	31794	03215	14813	07506	40853	79461	69114	32357
33555	56824	39948	35309	27279	78587	02790	98720	57920	30931
23433	11441	30625	68538	85671	78168	60754	37067	99579	76294
08339	60862	33225	85288	47812	89681	04184	87755	59664	46025
12952	73728	73346	54435	12067	18137	24559	99949	29504	82736
31065	41220	40348	71545	27046	95290	38752	13456	16147	20025
38062	29620	11459	24800	99422	31514	42673	62254	50236	52802
22365	00954	49547	16844	04006	09907	87626	60601	21891	14980
86779	89664	29030	91894	73718	73392	65469	79340	90014	00229
43233	48154	74284	65921	63641	00481	08578	22188	38029	68894
74503	33076	28357	23271	05919	12247	65814	51837	17689	67065
80697	09861	44996	94438	79742	44904	43997	30676	47959	91749
66890	59837	08731	62577	45661	40331	20461	40292	58324	50957
65029	71853	28424	48445	86207	05328	12631	18104	56863	84071
03322	46034	72527	42011	69919	00090	04986	06121	81888	04985
37951	98690	60776	79282	17148	79300	67391	53561	46702	99623
36747	35157	67719	81282	86592	21054	10617	10464	79204	16241
49340	44927	10914	17275	58227	91974	75268	28733	43893	17837
92271	64437	96956	18631	88405	96753	81024	21948	63478	73161
92299	36704	68944	92681	77662	54685	48356	21081	76717	47337
48344	93928	34136	47466	72646	18566	96759	31149	74706	37745
61726	51613	52816	33027	24383	07647	95883	28605	62283	18197
54433	70788	83880	31335	21145	16946	98191	37417	11780	41066
58541	72719	59340	60681	11593	06237	94809	58680	87392	55946
61516	65817	41065	83854	15993	83786	78324	06439	17050	62552
29215	08513	25460	52439	15219	69991	59623	35029	02632	33829
50164	57477	50446	22847	43803	56626	88506	88224	84080	29224
46923	73217	29155	22288	27172	09824	49339	80134	53208	89901
39385	54156	74135	82779	58336	79663	26502	78853	95172	24059
75334	79987	15894	18571	81773	50842	49946	04147	92224	41201
41285	32053	40984	90635	22067	11948	11443	99064	14675	16826

27423	31830	04828	05954	38820	94218	32586	04261	80975	47008
35906	67533	20585	21162	75252	73296	37607	92368	10867	69657
08554	70414	77644	99739	27390	80574	80240	19485	45190	36046
70966	52860	29353	41888	80187	97313	32440	08527	47081	17205
34154	79907	00949	54009	49291	48157	17375	13343	44727	36956
86436	46594	80734	80081	02314	42041	67591	78793	15440	21127
06339	10486	48944	44373	78872	90269	36662	40163	95780	06374
17715	18488	29772	86669	12401	86000	78660	00923	77884	44633
39611	02846	95861	49731	95395	26893	13314	07928	77911	53123
87271	46990	77790	79885	68909	54505	83646	78409	72846	28686
11996	29733	05629	93964	14193	83846	99389	50959	31927	79226
46940	09460	89582	17701	60658	71768	45426	93490	35636	70854
03412	41860	78660	76735	61981	37962	16512	87707	27622	17311
25077	14423	76933	16748	00741	62390	43843	80842	10219	54622
36495	82476	90894	71327	38924	07373	84495	31424	21285	08333
58500	55613	12395	00199	57097	24914	01779	02403	93251	44807
75248	35900	97246	15383	43870	60826	54130	63156	50504	52135
92175	62718	99616	61643	26886	14107	90719	47074	91737	97462
32463	69375	39095	36324	78594	57722	23596	36217	96947	44887
03693	77597	35029	70206	04705	91187	18602	86022	87337	23965
06721	33386	12162	55884	10420	30100	28445	77620	05067	10724
98591	40854	94023	57651	02409	76108	19790	48544	26777	42597
82535	71772	85767	76266	29140	47778	73492	53870	45014	08608
20105	25926	56710	14862	44589	57022	17734	38841	92896	40737
01749	78458	35863	82790	02427	87027	40106	94542	70051	68439
66826	49905	97602	26543	32418	22873	58878	34287	98272	00311
19242	91018	31082	73167	82661	20369	22976	86145	11196	51282
07788	16036	93946	83038	33324	79508	15514	84539	76833	02366
10238	51425	12133	60556	66023	78920	45286	79512	93581	56294
70278	45813	02647	70584	58543	31479	69235	12031	72235	67157
68633	59965	98891	65043	20653	78122	38989	65198	18659	79978
45164	32766	09525	49788	28780	54551	09208	91609	28711	97751
44701	18094	65320	24871	03285	61221	76401	81827	52742	90754
51254	38946	10820	30486	43737	91703	54377	04192	24354	21605
84819	68816	08575	93437	41898	71419	69327	00712	64283	82111
18122	52721	39067	33039	57890	71647	29730	09964	42192	59661
74518	17688	24087	59431	94219	31903	31093	95252	78310	29618
29507	76366	37600	35446	66362	17595	37560	14716	94629	39897
17615	22514	51864	04371	67231	61647	94074	24199	35525	69556
10735	07934	13585	35967	14790	78730	59122	01989	95596	05732
27515	94008	99354	12854	19839	02870	09161	52671	74303	58650
87240	67750	02552	56223	09496	21435	43859	17700	55974	93075
30474	21865	41837	44887	38330	51929	92959	72672	65078	33986
81033	89276	51464	63498	12766	55494	86208	16462	55022	56727
03550	49560	71142	85413	90974	88062	52135	84299	37041	88678
91516	90902	16387	47167	06377	86048	97771	53715	57709	61076
60915	35579	76264	72403	02744	52525	70804	28840	15504	80628
20281	63058	68322	36364	88444	68667	48877	28781	98458	05481

SAMPLE OF DATA ARCHIVES AND RESOURCES FOR SECONDARY ANALYSIS

Dozens of social science data archives around the world provide researchers free or inexpensive access to quantitative data. The Inter-University Consortium for Political and Social Research (University of Michigan) and the Social Sciences Data Collection (University of California at San Diego) are good starting places. Social science data archives and other sources in the following list are generally available in English and have Internet sites. The list is not comprehensive, because new archives and sources are being created or changing location.

Social Science Data Archives
and Sources

Archivio Dati e Programmi per le Scienze Sociali, ADPSS (Italy)

Australian Consortium for Social and Political Research Incorporated

Behavioral Risk Factor Surveillance System (U.S.A.)

Belgian Archives for the Social Sciences, BASS

Centers for Disease Control and Prevention and Health Promotion (U.S.A.)

Central Archive for Empirical Social Research (Cologne, Germany)

Central Intelligence Agency (U.S.A.)

Centre d'Informatisation des Données Socio-Politiques/Banque de Données Socio-Politiques, CIDSP/BDSP (France)

Centre for Applied Social Surveys (University of Southhampton, U.K.)

Centre for Ethnic Studies (University of Montreal, Canada)

Centre for International Statistics at the Canadian Council on Social Development

Children of the National Longitudinal Survey of Youth (U.S.A.)

Council of European Social Sciences Data Archives, CESSDA

Danish Data Archives, DDA

Data and Program Library Service, DPLS (University of Wisconsin at Madison)

Data Archive (University of Essex, U.K.)

Estonian Social Science Data Archive

European Centre for Analysis in the Social Sciences (University of Essex, U.K.)

European Research Centre on Migration and Ethnic Relations (ERCOMER)

General Social Survey (National Opinion Research Center, University of Chicago)

Health Retirement Study and Survey of Asset and Health Dynamics among the Oldest Old (U.S.A.)

Indian Social Science Research Center Data Archive, SSDA-IND (India)

Institute for Social Development and Policy Research (Seoul National University, South Korea)

Institute for Social Research in Social Science and Louis Harris Data Center (University of North Carolina)

Institute for Social Science Research, Social Science Data Archive (University of California at Los Angeles)

Inter-University Consortium for Political and Social Research, ICPSR (University of Michigan)

Israel Social Sciences Data Archive

Jerusalem Social Sciences Data Archive, SSDA-IL (Israel)

Lijphart Elections Archive (University of California at San Diego)

Luxembourg Income Study

Mexican Migration Project (U.S.A.)

National Election Studies (University of Michigan)

National Institute of Child Health and Human Development (U.S.A.)

National Institute on Aging (U.S.A.)

National Longitudinal Study of Adolescent Health (U.S.A.)

National Survey of Families and Households (U.S.A.)

Netherlands Historical Data Archive, NHDA

New Zealand Social Science Research Data and Information Services Centre

Norwegian Social Sciences Data Archive, NSD

Panel Study of Income Dynamics (U.S.A.)

Population Studies Center (University of Michigan)

Roper Center for Public Opinion Research (University of Connecticut)

Scandinavian Research Council for Criminology (University of Iceland)

Social Indicators of Development (University of North Carolina at Charlotte)

Social Science Data Archives (Australian National University)

Social Science Data Archives (Norway)

Social Science Data Services (Brown University)

Social Science Japan Data Archive (Institute of Social Science, University of Tokyo)

Social Science Research Centre (University of Hong Kong)

Social Sciences Data Collection (University of California at San Diego)

Social Stratification and Social Mobility survey (Japan)

Sociology of Development Research Centre (University of Bielefeld, Germany)

South African Data Archive

State of the Nation's Cities (Center for Urban Policy Research, Rutgers University)

Statistical Data Locators (Nanyang Technological University, Singapore)

Statistics Canada

Supreme Court Decisions (U.S.A.)

Swedish Social Science Data Service (Goteborg University, Sweden)

Swiss Information and Data Archive Service for the Social Sciences, SIDOS

United Nations Crime and Justice Information Network

United Nations Statistics

United States Department of Justice, Bureau of Justice Statistics

United States Department of Labor, Bureau of Labor Statistics, National Longitudinal Surveys

Wiener Institut für Sozialwissenschaftliche Dokumentation und Metodik, WISDOM (Austria)

Wisconsin Longitudinal Study (University of Wisconsin at Madison)

World Bank Statistics

World-Systems Archive (University of Colorado at Boulder)

Zentralarchiv für Empirische Sozialforschung an der Universität zu Köln (Germany)

MEASUREMENT THEORY AND SPECIALIZED TECHNIQUES FOR INDEX AND SCALE CONSTRUCTION

This appendix covers two more technical topics in quantitative measurement, although at an elementary level. The first is a general approach to measurement based on logical or mathematical-type theory. The second is a set of advanced statistical techniques that require the use of computer programs. Although the topics themselves are advanced for the beginning student of social work research, the presentation here lays a foundation for further study, and it provides a basis for understanding if the techniques appear in scholarly journal articles.

Introduction to Measurement Theory

Measurement theory is the name for a body of mathematical and methodological theory on reliability, validity, and related topics.[1] Measurement theory gets quite technical, but a general introductory summary of its core assumptions can help you understand the principles of good measurement. Measurement theory is based on the idea that an empirical measure of a concept reflects three components: (1) the true construct or an absolutely perfect measure of it, (2) systematic error, and (3) random error. People can see only the empirical measure; the three components are unobserved, hypothetical ideas about what measurement involves. The parts of measurement can be symbolically expressed as follows:

X *Observation:* The empirical indicator or observation

T *True measure:* Ideal, pure construct

S *Systematic error:* Bias; any error that is not random

R *Random error:* Nonsystematic, unavoidable, chance errors

Thus, measurement theory assumes that a specific observation is made up of the construct and of two components that are called errors because they represent deviations from the true construct. If this is put in the form of an equation, it becomes

$$X = T + S + R$$

This equation is the core of measurement theory. In plain English, it says that an empirical observation by a researcher actually comprises three unseen sources: the construct plus two kinds of potential errors or possible sources of deviation from the true construct.

In Chapter 7 you saw that perfect measurement validity is a perfect match between an empirical indicator and the construct it indicates (or its theoretical definition). The measurement theory equation says that an empirical observation and the construct are equal when there are no measurement errors—that is, when the two components that represent potential errors equal zero. Thus, using the equation and measurement theory, we can restate the definition of perfect measurement validity as $X = T$. Researchers use the equation to think about and improve validity by focusing their attention on the two possible types of errors, S and R, and how to get them to equal zero.

Let us focus on the R, or random error, part of the equation first. Probability theory from mathematics says that in the long run, over enough cases, the R becomes zero and drops out of the equation. In the language of statistical theory, the random error has an *expected value* of zero. Without getting into complex probability theory, this happens because errors that are truly random cancel each other out in the long run. Various mathematical proofs and empirical tests show that over a very large number of separate events (e.g., several million), truly random processes stabilize around a true value and errors become zero. For example, you flip a perfectly balanced coin in a truly random way 10 million times. The "errors"—or in this situation, getting more heads than tails or vice versa—will disappear. You can be extremely certain that your flipping will result in 50 percent heads and 50 percent tails. Another example is that of driving a car at a constant speed. Assume that you have a valid and reliable speedometer and you try to drive exactly 50 kilometers per hour, no more and no less. You will be slightly above this speed at some times and slightly below it at other times. If your errors are truly random, the speeds over and under 50 kilometers per hour will cancel each other out, or the expected value of the deviations above and below the speed will be zero and your speed will be 50 kilometers per hour. Researchers do not worry a lot about random error. They assume that there is always some random error, but that, over enough replications or cases, it can be safely ignored.

Once we ignore random error, an observation *(X)* equals the true construct *(T)* and systematic or nonrandom error *(S)*. Systematic error is a potentially avoidable error that distorts results in a systematic manner. An example of a systematic error can be a poorly worded question that causes most respondents to answer in a particular way, or an interviewer's attempts to get respondents to answer in a particular way. Systematic error is at the heart of validity and reliability. It prevents indicators from measuring what they claim to measure (i.e., the true construct). Thus, another way to think about improving measurement is to eliminate systematic error or *bias*.[2]

Systematic error shows how causal inferences from empirical data can be in error. What was said earlier about measurement validity can be restated as validity when the observed measure *(X)* equals

the true measure *(T)*. $X = T$ when the systematic error *(S)* is zero.

There are many possible sources of systematic errors. For example, a lack of stability reliability is a type of systematic error. A bathroom scale may lack stability reliability because the spring in it is getting weaker, so the user appears to be getting lighter with each successive measurement. This error in measuring weight is a type of systematic error that undermines validity. In the example of driving 50 kilometers per hour, random errors may cancel each other out, but if your speedometer was systematically showing a lower speed, your observation would not be a valid measure. The measurement theory equation is a way to show that any measurement bias or deviation (i.e., nonzero value for systematic error) reduces measurement validity.

Specialized Techniques. Researchers can choose from numerous advanced statistical techniques to help them in constructing quantitative indexes and scales. Some techniques help researchers test for unidimensionality among indicators, some provide researchers with weight for indicators that are being combined into an index, and some help researchers sort and divide a very large number of indicators. The three briefly summarized in this appendix are examples of the powerful techniques available. You will need to acquire a background in statistics and learn to use computer programs before you will be able to use these techniques.

The purpose of introducing you to the techniques is twofold. First, you may encounter them in the methods, analysis, or results sections of scholarly journal articles. This introduction will help you understand why they are being used. Second, the logic of the techniques reinforces the basic principles of measurement and index or scale construction that you have already learned. The logic illustrates how the principles are extended to complex, sophisticated applications. Although the three techniques use advanced statistics, their logic is consistent with basic measurement principles.

Factor Analysis. *Factor analysis* is a group of sophisticated statistical techniques that require a computer to conduct.[3] Statistical training is necessary to use factor analysis properly. Improperly used, it creates nonsense. Factor analysis helps researchers construct indexes, test the unidimensionality of scales, assign weights to items in an index, and statistically reduce a large number of indicators to a smaller set. The statistical theory and algebra on which factor analysis is based are beyond the level of this book, but its conceptual principles are not difficult to grasp. The fundamental logic of factor analysis is based on the idea that it is possible to manipulate statistically the empirical relationships among several indicators to reveal a common unobserved factor or hypothetical construct.

When conducting factor analysis, a researcher begins with a number of items he or she believes to measure a single construct. At least five indicators are recommended. The indicators should be measured at the ordinal, interval, or ratio level. The interval or ratio level is preferred, and extra caution is necessary for ordinal-level measurement. The researcher gives the factor analysis computer program characteristics of the variables and technical information. The factor analysis results tell a researcher how well the items or indicators relate to an underlying factor or hypothetical construct. For example, factor analysis results tell the researcher whether the items all load, or are associated with, one or more than one factor.

Factor analysis also produces factor scores, which can be used as weights in creating an index. These scores represent how strongly each indicator is associated with the unobserved factor. For example, you conduct an Australian survey in which there are 16 Likert-scale items that measure attitudes toward Japan. You use factor analysis to tell you whether the 16 items are explained by two factors. For example, 5 attitude items load on a factor that indicates a fear of military conflict construct. The other 11 items load on a factor that indicates antagonism toward a different racial group. The meaning of a factor comes from looking at the items that load on it. You can combine each set of items into two separate indexes of attitudes toward Japan.

Q-Sort Analysis. *Q-sort analysis* is a close relative of factor analysis.[4] As with factor analysis, the technique requires statistical background beyond the scope of this book. It illustrates an interesting scaling logic as well.

Q-sort methodology uses *ipsative scoring,* as opposed to *normative scoring,* which is used in most scaling or index techniques. With normative scoring, a person rates each item in an index or scale independently. With ipsative scoring, a person is forced to decide between the items, so a decision on one item affects other items.

For example, you rank movie stars. When you choose an actor as number one, it means that no other actor can be number one. The decision about one item (i.e., the number-one actor) affects or limits your decision about other items. This is ipsative scoring. By contrast, with normative scoring, you rate a list of actors from "highly like" to "highly dislike," as with a Likert scale. You could rate several actors "highly like." Your decision to rate one actor does not limit your decisions about rating others.

Q-sort analysis begins with people ranking statements about a concept or object. In a manner somewhat like Thurstone scaling, people are given a large number of statements (e.g., 30 to 50) and asked to sort them. The statements are taken from popular writings on a topic, everyday conversations, television programs, and the like, and should represent diverse ways people think about a topic.

Instead of piles along one continuum, the Q-sort technique has people place statements into boxes in a grid that varies along two continua. There are as many boxes in the grid as there are statements. Each statement goes into one box. One continuum (e.g., right to left) indicates how positively or negatively a person feels about the statement. The other continuum (e.g., up and down) indicates the strength of commitment to the positive or negative feelings about statements. The decision to place a statement into a box excludes placing any other statements in the same location. The raw data for Q-sort analysis are the statements as they are organized in the grid.

In factor analysis the researcher enters the data from many indicators, and the computer program produces a small number of factors. In Q-sort analysis the researcher enters the grid location of statements, and the computer program identifies clusters or sets of people. Thus, Q-sort analysis shows which people organize statements in similar ways.

Q-sort analysis identifies how people organize their thinking on a topic on the basis of how they organized statements in the grid. It gives a researcher a map of major positions on an issue held by people. For example, 20 people place 45 statements about Arab–Israeli relations into a grid. The results of Q-sort analysis show a researcher that the 20 people think about Arab–Israeli relations in one of three main ways: (1) a concern for Israeli security and fear of Arabs, (2) frustration with U.S. support for Israel and resentment toward Israel, or (3) a feeling that the world balance of power depends on what happens with Israel and its neighbors.

Cluster Analysis. As with factor and Q-sort analysis, cluster analysis is a sophisticated statistical technique that will be described only briefly and in general terms.[5]

Cluster analysis is a technique for organizing information or items measuring a variable. It statistically organizes relationships among a large number of items and places them into groups. The grouping or classification procedure uses statistical techniques such as those in factor analysis and Q-sort analysis. The technique groups items by similarity and difference.

Factor analysis results tell a researcher how each item relates to one or more unobserved factors. Results appear as a list of items with a number next to each; the number is the association between an item and a factor. Results from Q-sort analysis tell a researcher how people organize statements and show that people organize statements in a small number of ways. Results consist of the list of people with a number next to each person representing the degree to which a person followed one of a few patterns for organizing statements.

Cluster analysis results, by contrast, are in the form of a graph or picture, which resembles a tree diagram because it looks like the branches of a tree. Lines extend from a trunk, to large branches, to smaller branches, and so forth to tiny twigs. There are several levels of branching. The branching diagram shows a researcher which items are similar to each other and which are different. Each item in the cluster analysis represents a tiny twig, and the pattern of connections illustrates similarity and differences. Two items that share connections to a common nearby branch are more similar than two items that share no common branch until they reach the trunk.

For example, a researcher asks mental patients 556 true/false statements in a personality test. Cluster analysis organizes the 566 items into "twigs" of a tree diagram. There are four major levels of branching: twigs to small branches, small branches to medium branches, medium branches to large branches, and large branches to the trunk. At each level, the branching shows groups of items that represent psychological disorders, or shows how sets of psychological disorders form common psychotic types. A researcher examines the pattern of branching to see how the answers to items form groups and how the groups can, in turn, be grouped.

NOTES

1. See Blalock (1982) and Zeller and Carmines (1980) for more in-depth discussions of measurement theory in the social sciences.
2. See Carmines and Zeller (1979:13–15) and Nunally (1978).
3. Factor analysis is discussed in Kim and Mueller (1978). For more technical discussions see Bohrnstedt and Borgatta (1981) and Jackson and Borgatta (1981). Duncan (1984:209–216) offers a critique of factor analysis.
4. Q-sort analysis is discussed in Brown (1980, 1986), Nunnally (1978:544–558), and McKeown (1988).

5. Cluster analysis is introduced in Aldenderfer and Blashfield (1984). Also, see Bailey (1975, 1983) and Lorr (1983) for social science applications.

SOURCES FOR MEASUREMENT SCALES IN SOCIAL WORK AND RELATED FIELDS

Bearden, W., R. Netemeyer, and M. Mobley. (1993). *Handbook of marketing scales: Multi-item measure for marketing and consumer behavior research.* Newbury Park, CA: Sage.

Blythe, B., and T. Tripodi. (1989). *Measurement in direct practice.* Newbury Park: Sage.

Cautela, J. (1988). *Behavior analysis forms for clinical intervention.* Champaign, IL: Research Press.

Cowger, C. (1994). Assessing client strengths: Clinical assessment for client empowerment. *Social Work, 39,* 262–268.

Drew, C., M. Hardman, and A. Hart. (1996). *Designing and conducting research: Inquiry in education and social science.* Boston: Allyn and Bacon.

Fischer, J., and K. Corcoran. (1994). *Measures for clinical practice: A source book,* Vol. 1 & 2. New York: Free Press.

Goldman, B., and J. Bausch. (1997). *Directory of unpublished experimental mental measures.* Washington, DC: American Psychological Association.

Herson, M., and D. Barlow. (1976). *Single case experimental design: Strategies for studying behavior change.* New York: Pergamon Press.

Hudson, W. (1982). *The clinical measurement package: A field manual.* Newbury Park, CA: Wadsworth.

Hudson, W., and A. Faul. (1998). *The clinical measurement package: A field manual* (2nd ed.). Tallahassee, FL: WALMYR Publishing Co.

Hudson, W., and B. Thyer. (1987). Research measurements and indices in direct practice. In *Encyclopedia of Social Work,* 18th ed., edited by A. Minahan, pp. 487–498. Silver Spring, MD: National Association of Social Workers.

Isaac, S., and W. Michael. (1971). *Handbook in research and evaluation.* San Diego, CA: EDITS Publishers.

Jordan, C., and C. Franklin. (1995). *Clinical assessment for social workers.* Chicago: Lyceum.

Jordan, C., C. Franklin, and K. Corcoran. (1993). Standardized measuring instruments. In *Social work research and evaluation,* 4th ed., edited by R. Grinnell, pp. 198–220. Itasca, IL: F. E. Peacock Publishers.

Laufer, A. (1982). *Assessment tools.* Newbury Park, CA: Sage.

Lukas, S. (1993). *Where to start and what to ask: An assessment handbook.* New York: Norton.

Lyons, J., K. Howard, M. O'Mahoney, and J. Lish. (1997). *The measurement and management of clinical outcomes in mental health.* New York: John Wiley and Sons.

Mash, E., and L. Terdal. (Eds.). (1976). *Behavior therapy assessment.* New York: Springer.

Neuber, K. (1983). *Needs assessment: A model for community planning.* Newbury Park, CA: Sage.

Nurius, P., and W. Hudson. (1993a). *Human services: Practice, evaluation and computers.* Pacific Grove, CA: Brooks/Cole.

Nurius, P., and W. Hudson. (1993b). *Computer assisted practice: Theory, methods and software.* Belmont, CA: Wadsworth.

Pecora, P., M. Frazer, K. Nelson, J. McCrosky, and W. Meezan. (1990). *Evaluating family-based services.* New York: Aldine De Gruyter.

Sederer, L., and B. Dickey. (Eds.). (1996). *Outcomes assessment in clinical practice.* Baltimore: Williams and Wilkins Scales.

Shin, H., and N. Abell. (1999). The homesickness and contentment scales: Developing a culturally sensitive measure of adjustment for Asians. *Research on Social Work Practice, 9,* 45–60.

Wodarski, J., and B. Thyer. (1998). *Handbook of empirical practice: Social problems and practice issues.* New York: John Wiley and Sons.

WALMYR AND RELATED SOCIAL WORK SCALES

The following social work assessment scales are available at www.walmyr.com/wp01002.htm

Unless otherwise noted, each of these scales has a published reliability of .90 or higher and a validity of .60 or higher.

Personal Adjustment Scales

Generalized Contentment Scale (GCS)
The GCS is designed to measure the severity of nonpsychotic depression.
Author: Walter W. Hudson.

Index of Self-Esteem (ISE)
The ISE is designed to measure the severity of problems with self-esteem.
Author: Walter W. Hudson.

Index of Clinical Stress (ICS)
The ICS is designed to measure the severity of problems with personal stress.
Authors: Walter W. Hudson and J. Neil Abell.

Clinical Anxiety Scale (CAS)
The CAS is designed to measure the severity of problems with phobic anxiety.
Author: Bruce A. Thyer.

Index of Peer Relations (IPR)
The IPR is designed to measure the severity of problems in peer relationships.
Author: Walter W. Hudson.

Index of Alcohol Involvement (IAI)
The IAI is designed to measure the severity of problems with alcohol abuse.
Authors: Walter W. Hudson and James W. Garner.

Index of Drug Involvement (IDI)
The IDI is designed to measure the severity of problems with drug abuse.
Author: Walter W. Hudson.

Sexual Attitude Scale (SAS)
The SAS is designed to measure a liberal or conservative orientation toward human sexual expression.
Authors: Walter W. Hudson and Gerald J. Murphy.

Index of Homophobia (IHP)
The SAS is designed to measure the level of homophobia.
Authors: Wendell A. Ricketts and Walter W. Hudson.

Dyadic Adjustment Scales

Several short-form assessment scales focus on problems in dyadic relationships.

Index of Marital Satisfaction (IMS)
The IMS is designed to measure the severity of problems in a dyadic relationship.
Author: Walter W. Hudson.

Index of Sexual Satisfaction (ISS)
The ISS is designed to measure the severity of problems in the sexual component of a dyadic relationship.
Author: Walter W. Hudson.

Partner Abuse Scale: Non-Physical (PASNP)
The PASNP is completed by the abuse victim and is designed to measure the severity of problems with nonphysical abuse in a dyadic relationship.
Author: Walter W. Hudson.

Partner Abuse Scale: Physical (PASPH)
The PASPH is completed by the abuse victim and is designed to measure the severity of problems with physical abuse in a dyadic relationship.
Author: Walter W. Hudson.

Non-Physical Abuse of Partner Scale (NPAPS)
The NPAPS is completed by the abuser and is designed to measure the severity of problems with nonphysical abuse in a dyadic relationship.
Authors: Walter W. Hudson and James W. Garner.

Physical Abuse of Partner Scale (PAPS)
The PAPS is completed by the abuser and is designed to measure the severity of problems with physical abuse in a dyadic relationship. It has a reliability of .90 and a validity of .60.
Authors: Walter W. Hudson and James W. Garner.

Family Adjustment Scales

Several short-form assessment scales focus on problems in family relationships.

Index of Family Relations (IFR)
The IFR is designed to measure the severity of family relationship problems as seen by the respondent.
Author: Walter W. Hudson.

Index of Parental Attitudes (IPA)
The IPA is designed to measure the severity of problems in a parent–child relationship as seen by the parent.
Author: Walter W. Hudson.

Child's Attitude toward Mother (CAM)
Child's Attitude toward Father (CAF)
The CAM and CAF scales are designed to measure the severity of problems in a parent–child relationship as seen by the child.
Author: Walter W. Hudson.

Index of Brother Relations (IBR)
Index of Sister Relations (ISR)
The IBR and ISR scales are designed to measure the severity of problems with sibling relationships. Author: Walter W. Hudson.

Children's Behavior Rating Scale (CBRS)
The CBRS is designed for use by a parent or guardian as a scaled checklist to reflect the type and degree of behavioral problems that are exhibited by a child. Reliability and validity are not available. Author: Walter W. Hudson.

Organizational Assessment Scales

Several short-form assessment scales focus on problems in organizational settings or environments.

Index of Sexual Harassment (ISH)
The ISH is designed to measure the severity of sexual harassment as seen by the respondent. Author: Adrienne L. Decker.

Client Satisfaction Inventory (CSI)
The CSI is designed to measure the degree of satisfaction clients experience with respect to services provided to them by human services agencies and practitioners. Author: Steven L. McMurtry.

Index of Managerial Effectiveness (IME)
The IME scale is designed to measure the severity of problems in managerial ability as seen by the respondent. Author: Walter W. Hudson.

Index of Job Satisfaction (IJS)
The IJS scale is designed to measure the degree of satisfaction an employee feels in relationship to her or his current employment situation. Authors: Walter W. Hudson and Cathy King Pike.

Educational Assessment Scales

The following short-form assessment scales focus on evaluating educational settings or environments.

Classroom Teacher Evaluation Scale (CTES)
The CTES is used to evaluate teacher performance in the classroom. It has a reliability of .97. Author: Walter W. Hudson.

Practicum Instructors Evaluation Form (PIEF)
The PIEF is used to evaluate field practicum instructor performance as a teacher. It has a reliability of .96. Author: Walter W. Hudson.

Brief Adult Assessment Scale

The *Brief Adult Assessment Scale* or BAAS is a self-report measure that attempts to assess the severity or magnitude of adult client problems across 16 different areas of personal and social functioning.

> Depression
> Self-Esteem Problems
> Partner Problems
> Sexual Discord
> Problems With a Child
> Personal Stress
> Problems with Friends
> Aggression
> Problems with Work Associates
> Family Problems
> Suicide
> Nonphysical Abuse
> Physical Abuse
> Problems at Work
> Alcohol Abuse
> Drug Use

Brief Family Assessment Scale

The *Brief Family Assessment Scale* or BFAS is a self-report measure that attempts to assess the severity or magnitude of seven different family problems.

> Personal Stress
> Family Supports for Members
> Familial Economic Stress
> Family Member Aggressive Behavior
> Problems with Children
> Drug Use in the Family
> Alcohol Use in the Family

Family Assessment Screening Inventory

The *Family Assessment Screening Inventory* or FASI scale is a multidimensional self-report measure that attempts to assess and understand the severity or magnitude of family problems across 25 different areas of personal and social functioning.

Inner Interaction Scale of Social Functioning

The *Inner Interaction Scale of Social Functioning* or IISSF is a multidimensional self-report measure that attempts to assess the severity or magnitude of social functioning problems across three different areas of social functioning—namely, achievement, satisfaction, and expectation—and three areas of social dysfunctioning—namely, frustration, stress, and helplessness.

Multidimensional Adolescent Adjustment Scale

The *Multidimensional Adolescent Assessment Scale* or MAAS is a self-report measure that attempts to assess the severity or magnitude of adolescent client problems across 16 different areas of personal and social functioning.

> Depression
> Self-Esteem Problems

Problems with Mother
Problems with Father
Personal Stress
Problems with Friends
Problems with School
Aggression
Family Problems
Suicide
Guilt
Confused Thinking
Disturbing Thoughts
Memory Loss
Alcohol Abuse
Drug Use

Multi-Problem Screening Inventory

The *Multi-Problem Screening Inventory* or MPSI scale is a multidimensional self-report measure that attempts to assess the severity or magnitude of client problems across 27 different areas of personal and social functioning.

Multi-Problem Screening Questionnaire

The *Multi-Problem Screening Questionnaire* or MPSQ scale is a brief multidimensional self-report measure that provides a rapid client assessment across eight areas of personal and social functioning.

SAMPLE IRB PROPOSAL

**SAMPLE APPLICATION
TO AN INSTITUTIONAL REVIEW BOARD FOR THE
PROTECTION OF HUMAN SUBJECTS IN RESEARCH**

Review Requested: __X__ **Exemption** _____ **Expedited** _____ **Full Board**

1a. Primary Investigator: _John Q. Public_ **Daytime Phone Number:** _123-4567_

     Mailing Address: _100 Main Hall_ **City/State/Zip:** _Anytown USA 00000_

     E-Mail Address: _professorjq@university.edu_ **Department:** _School of Social Work_

1b. Additional Applicant(s): _____

1c. Advisor: _____NA_____ **Daytime Phone Number:** _____NA_____

     Advisor's E-Mail Address: _NA_ **Department:** _NA_

     Campus Mailing Address: _NA_

2. Project Period: From _Feb, xxxx_ **to** _May, xxxx_

3. Funding Source(s): _____NA_____

4. Site of Work: _University_

5a. Title of Project: _Class Project Learning Survey Research Methods_

5b. Brief description of its general purpose:

Students in class are required to gain experience collecting and analyzing survey data. A class of 45 students breaks into groups, selects a survey topic, designs an instrument, and each group member requests 10 other students, selected in a purposive fashion, to consent to complete the questionnaire and place completed instruments in a large envelope. No identifying information is requested. Instruments contain 15–20 attitude/opinion questions plus 10–15 demographic items. Data for each group are entered into SPSS and analyses of univariate and bivariate relationships are performed to produce a final paper.

6. Give details of the procedures that relate to the subjects' participation, including at a minimum the following information (append additional page(s) if necessary):

a) **How will the subjects be selected and recruited? (Append copy of letter, ad, or transcript of verbal announcement.)**

Each student group member selects respondent in a purposive fashion among fellow students. Instruments take approximately 15 minutes to complete.

b) **What inducement is offered?**

None

c) **Number and salient characteristics of subjects, i.e., age range, sex, institutional affiliation, other pertinent characterizations.**

Approximately 450 graduate and undergraduate students attending the University

d) **If a cooperating institution (school, hospital, prison, etc.) is involved, has written permission been obtained? (Append letters.)**

NA

e) **Number of times observations will be made?**

Each participating subject will self-administer one survey once, covering answers by a blank attached sheet of paper, and then place the instrument in a large envelope and return it to the student distributing it.

f) **What do the subjects do, or what is done to them, in the study? (Append copy of questionnaires or test instruments, description of procedure to be conducted on the subject.)**

The proposed study is descriptive. Respondents complete a 25–40 item survey instrument containing closed-ended attitude, opinion, and demographic questions. Survey instruments will be submitted as soon as prepared. No experimental manipulation is proposed. The instrument will be submitted to the IRB for approval when complete.

g) **Is it clear to the subject that their participation is voluntary, that they may withdraw at any time, and that they may refuse to answer any specific question that they may be asked?**

Yes

h) **Number of subjects to be used in the project:** _____Approximately 450_____

i) **Please indicate below if any of your proposed subjects might fit into the following categories:**

Minors? _____ **Yes** __X__ **No** __18+__ **Age**

Incompetent Persons? _____ **Yes** __X__ **No**

Pregnant Women? _____ **Yes** __X__ **No**   **Students?** __X__ **Yes** _____ **No**

Women of Child-Bearing Age?   _X_ Yes   ____ No

Low-Income Persons?   _X_ Yes   ____ No

Institutionalized Persons?   ____ Yes   _X_ No

Minorities?   _X_ Yes   ____ No

j) **Cite your experience with this type of research.**

Fifteen years supervising student projects of this general type.

7. **How do you intend to obtain the subjects' informed consent? If in writing, attach a copy of the consent form. If not in writing, include a written summary of what is to be said to the subject(s), and justify the reason that oral, rather than written, consent is being used. Also, explain how you will ascertain that the subjects understand what they are agreeing to.**

Respondents will be provided oral information about the nature of these class projects, risk and benefits, and assurance of voluntary participation, no identifying information, withdrawal and informed consent (although signed consent forms will not be solicited in order to protect anonymity).

8. **In your view, would benefits result from the study that would justify asking the subjects to participate?**

Yes, class projects designing data collection instruments, gathering data and analyzing findings should prove valuable to students involved in the class.

9a. **Do you see any chance that subjects might be harmed in any way? Do you deceive them in any way? Are there any physical risks? Psychological? (Might a subject feel demeaned or embarrassed or worried or upset?) Social? (Is there a possible loss of status, privacy, reputation?)**

No, there is very little likelihood of risk or harm. No deception is involved, respondents are free to look over the instrument prior to agreeing to participate and place their responses in a large envelope upon finishing a 10–15 minute task. It is possible that being asked questions on ____ may be mildly disconcerting. Referral information and the instructor's phone number will be included with the instructions handed out.

9b. **How do you ensure confidentiality of information collected? (Consider 9a and 9b from the point of view of the subject.)**

Respondents will complete the instrument on their own and place it into a large envelope. No identifying information is requested.

Applicant's Name (Please Print)	**Faculty Advisor's Name (Please Print)**	**Date**
John Q. Professor	NA	

Applicant Signature	**Faculty Advisor Signature**	**Date**

OFFICIAL LETTERHEAD

Sample Solicitation Script

Class participants, read the following to each potential participant.

My name is _____ (class participant's name), and I am a student in a Research Methods class at the University. For a class project, we are conducting a study so that by practicing we can learn more about how to do research. We created a survey in our class, and it has been approved by the University's Internal Review Board. Now we are asking students across campus to participate in our study. There is no specific reason why we are asking you to complete the survey. If you choose to participate, your answers will be completely anonymous. We have no way to identify who completed the surveys. No one will know which survey is yours or even if you chose to fill the survey out. Your participation is completely voluntary, and you can decide at any time to not participate. The survey takes about 15 minutes to complete. When it is completed, you can place it into a large envelope and return it to me.

Are there any questions?

Answer any questions the potential subject may have. If you do not know how to answer the question, ask the subject to anonymously contact Dr. Professor at xxx-xxxx. If the potential subject has a question about participating in research at the University, please ask her/him to call the Campus IRB office at xxx-xxxx.

Has anyone else asked you to complete this survey?

If the potential subject states she has already been approached by a classmate, discontinue the script and walk away.

Thank you very much.

Hand the potential subject an instrument and pen or pencil and ask her or him to place the instrument into a large envelope. If at any point, the potential subject states she or he does not wish to participate, discontinue the script and walk away.

OFFICIAL LETTERHEAD

Dear Student:

For a class project, we are conducting a study to help social work students learn how to do research. The class chose to study about _____ among students at the University. The title of our project is _____. We created a survey, and it has been approved by the University Internal Review Board. Now we are asking students across campus to participate in our study. There is no specific reason why we are asking you to complete the survey. If you choose to participate, your answers will be completely anonymous. We have no way to identify who completed the surveys. There is no way of knowing which survey is yours or even if you chose to fill the survey out. Your participation is completely voluntary. The survey takes about 15 minutes to complete. Please know that

Your participation is completely voluntary.

You may stop participating at any time without prejudice to you.

You do not have to answer any questions that may be asked.

If at any time, you have questions or want more information, please contact Dr. Professor at xxx-xxxx. You do not need to identify yourself when you call. For more information about human participation in research at the University, please contact the Campus IRB Office at xxx-xxxx.

When it is completed, you can place the survey into the large envelope provided by the class member. By placing the completed survey in the envelope, you have consented to participate in our project. By your consenting to participate, we will believe that you understand the purposes, procedures, and duration of the study; that you have consented to participate in our project; and that you acknowledge that all concerns regarding this project have been directed to the researchers or the Campus IRB.

Thank you in advance for considering participation in this very important learning experience!

J. Q. Public, Ph.D.
Associate Professor
100 Main Hall
School of Social Work

STATISTICAL PACKAGE FOR THE SOCIAL SCIENCES (SPSS)

1. Data Entry Using SPSS
2. Doing Univariate Analysis Using SPSS
3. Doing Bivariate Analysis Using SPSS

DATA ENTRY USING SPSS

The Statistical Package for the Social Sciences (SPSS) software program is one of the most widely used software programs in the social sciences, including social work. It has been available on mainframe computers on university and college campuses since the 1970s. The SPSS program is likely available on personal computers accessible to you on campus. There are also several student versions of the SPSS program that can be purchased at a reasonable cost. (See www.spss.com for more information.)

When you load the SPSS program, your screen will look the one in Figure 1. Earlier versions of the SPSS software program may have used slightly different looking icons or different names for some of these menu choices. You should have no problem following along with these instructions, however, as the steps are basically identical. Figure 1 shows the database design data editor, where you enter data, assign names to your columns (variables), insert labels as desired, and enter and edit your data. When you first load SPSS your cursor will be resting on the first column (var) and the first row, as noted in Figure 1.

If you enter the numeral 1 in the first cell and press return or enter, SPSS will enter 1.00 into this cell, and give your column (variable) the name var00001. This was done three times, using the right arrow key to move to the right, as you see in Figure 2. Generally, each row will be a case or record (usually referring to a person, client, or other unit of analysis), and each column will contain one piece of information (one variable) such as an answer to a questionnaire item, for each row in the database.

Let us set up a database with three columns and five records (rows) for each. We will also use the SPSS Variable View to give our columns (variables) names, and we will use the Labels feature of the Variable View so that it will be easier to understand our printouts. In this hypothetical example our first three columns will be CaseID, Gender, and Age. Move

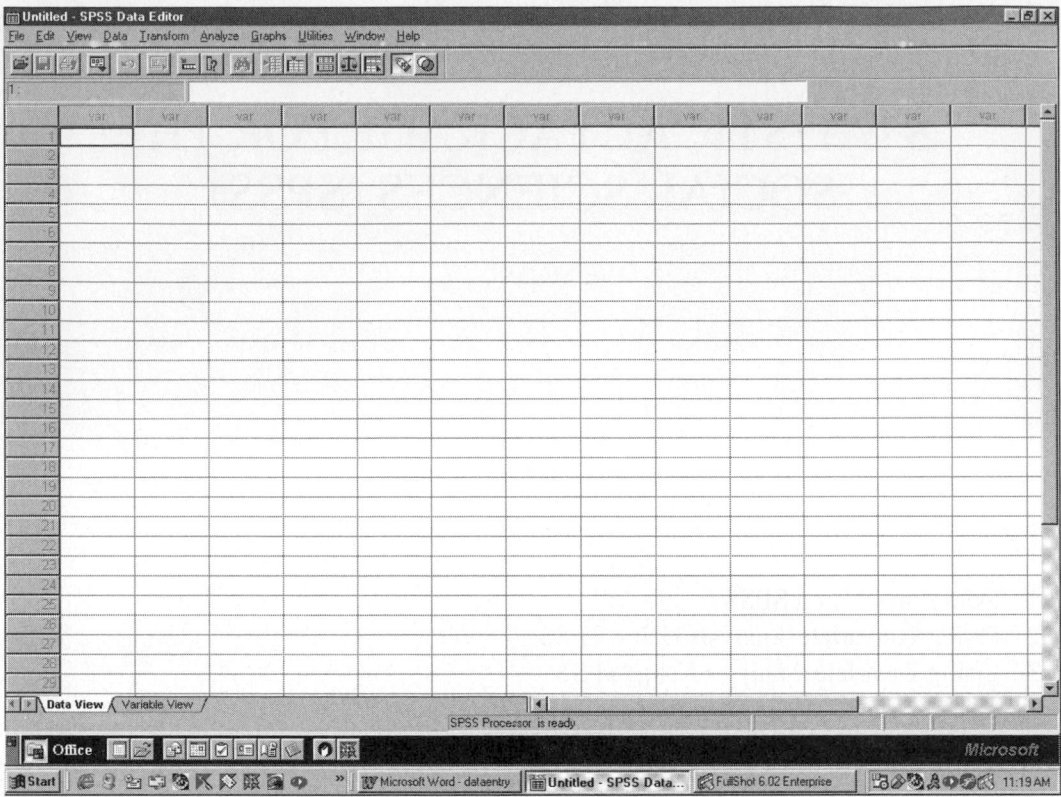

FIGURE 1

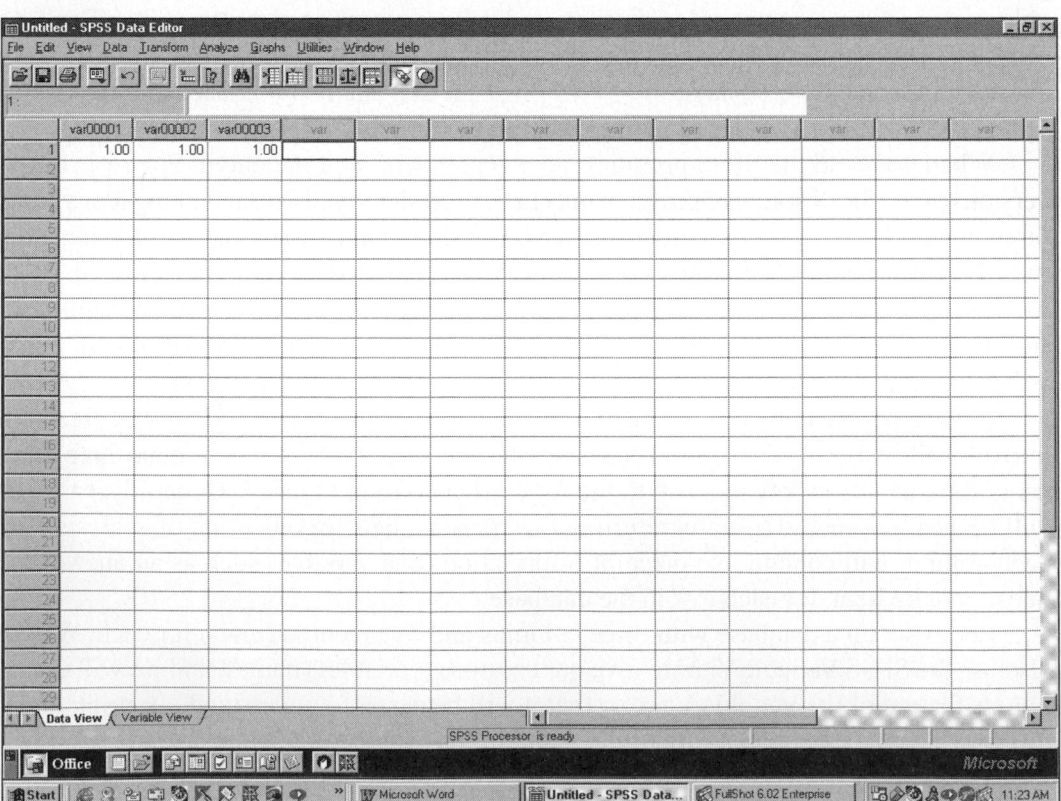

FIGURE 2

the cursor into the tab on the bottom left of the data editor labeled "Variable View" to retrieve the variable view editor, as seen in Figure 3.

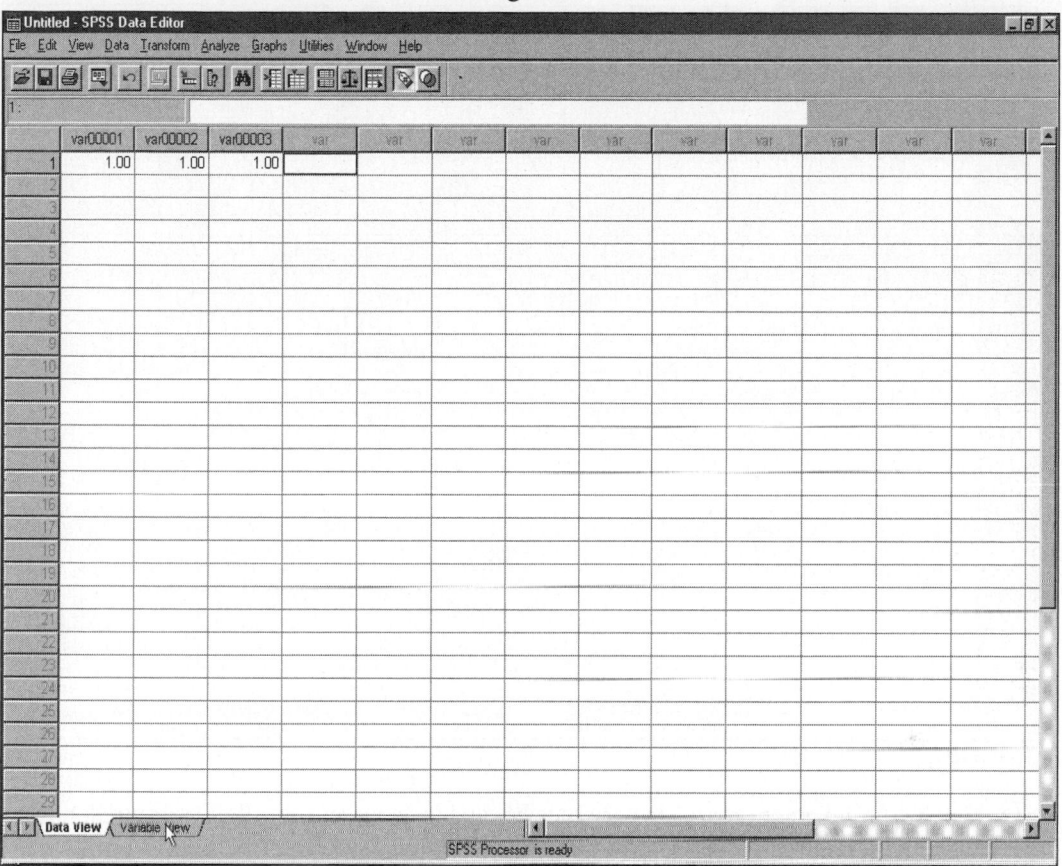

FIGURE 3

Now let us enter the Variable Name CaseID, for the first column, as shown in Figure 4.

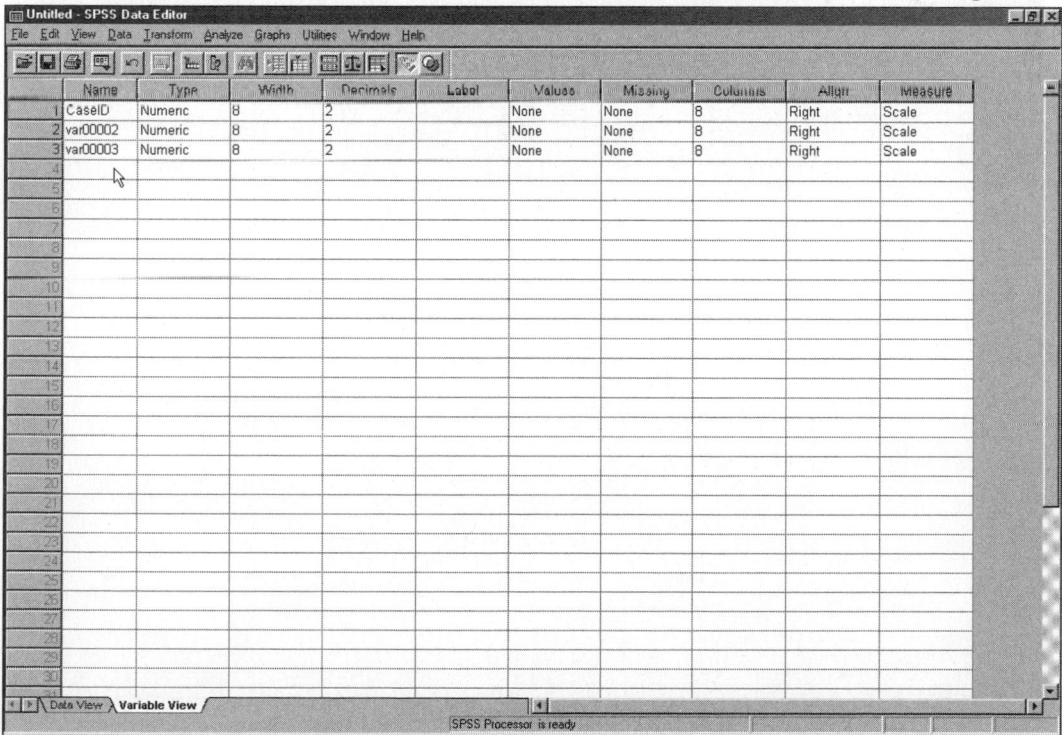

FIGURE 4

Notice SPSS has changed the column name from var00001 to CaseID. Let us name the second column Gender, and the third column Age, as shown in Figure 5.

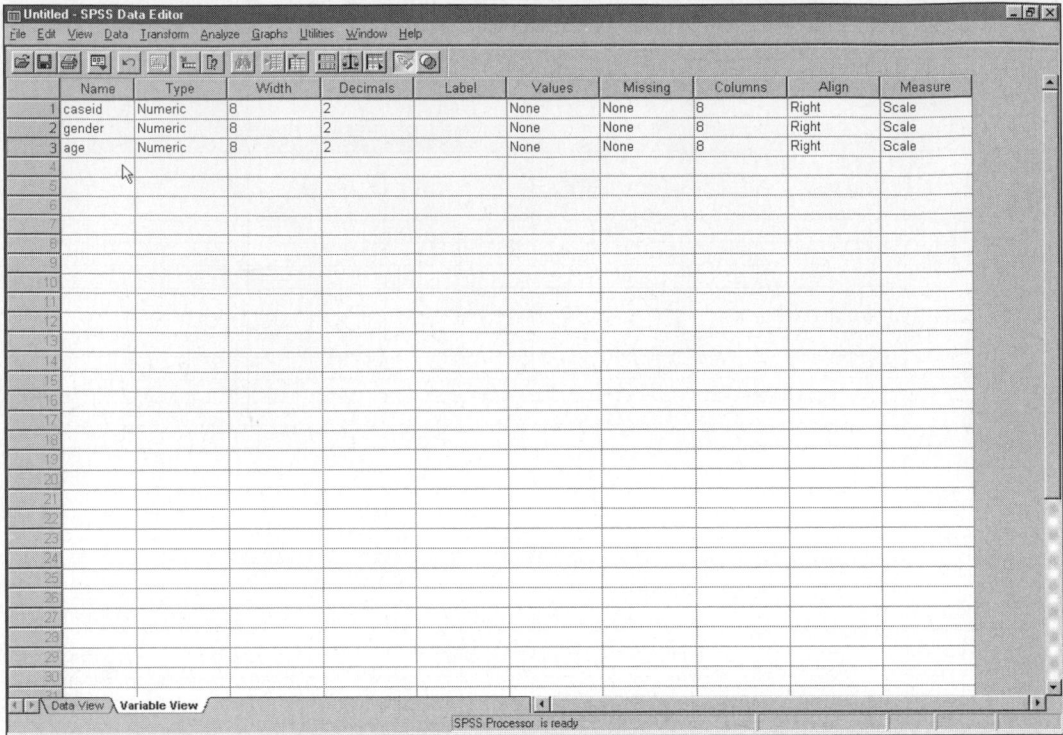

FIGURE 5

CaseID and Age are numeric variables because we can use numbers to represent the ID information and each person's age. The Gender variable, on the other hand, can receive either numerals such as 1 and 2 or text labels such as "Male" and "Female" as well. By clicking on the Values column, as in Figure 6, you will be able to add labels to your database.

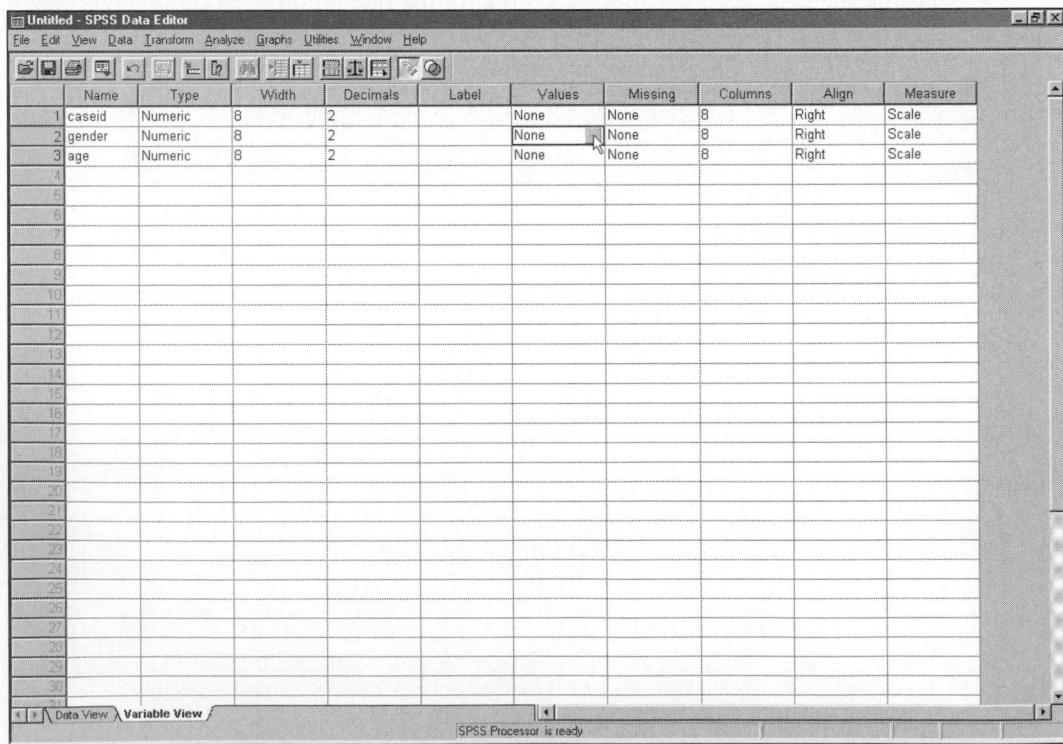

FIGURE 6

In the Value Labels insert box, you can add both your values (in this case, we have decided that 1 = Male, 2 = Female) and value labels. Be sure to click Add to enter your labels for both values, as shown in Figure 7.

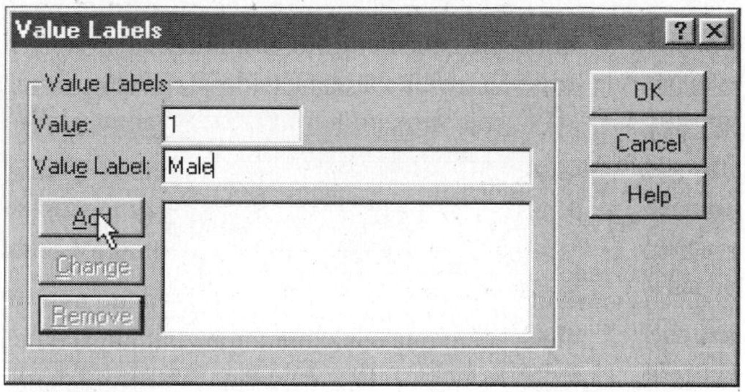

FIGURE 7

Next, be sure to click on OK, to set your value labels into your data file, as seen in Figure 8.

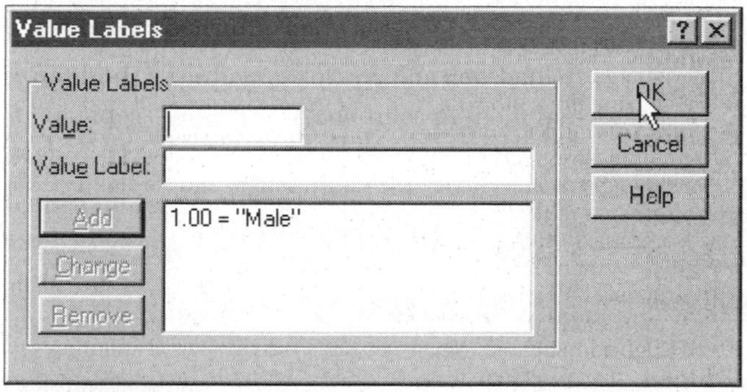

FIGURE 8

Next, we will add labels for Female = 2, as shown in Figure 9.

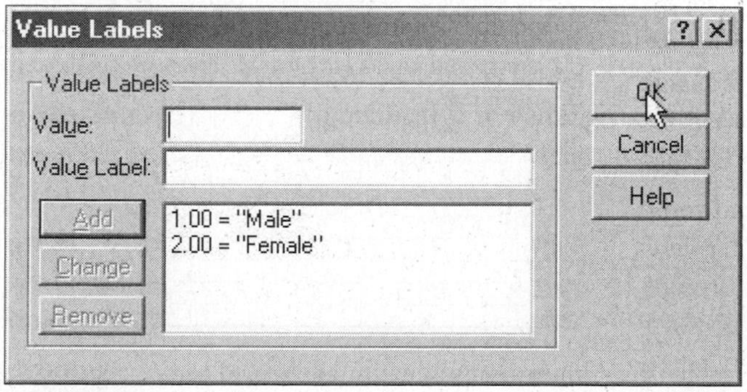

FIGURE 9

Now we are ready to return to the data editor, so click on the tab at the bottom left called Data View, to switch back and forth between the Data Editor and the Variable View, as shown in Figure 10.

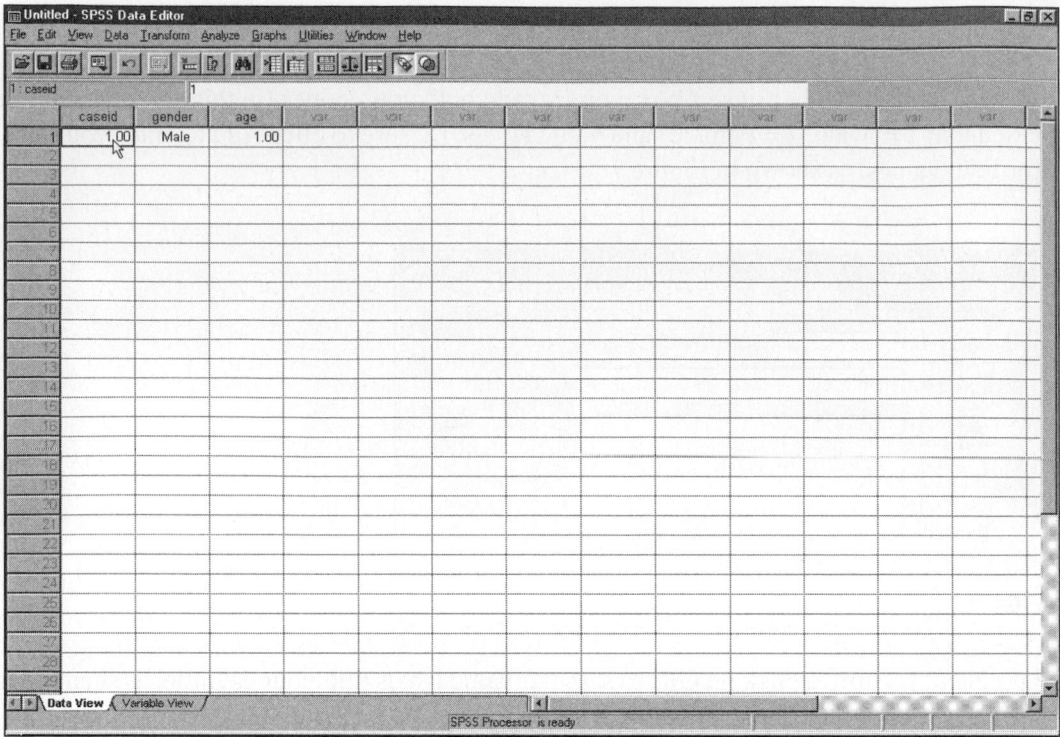

FIGURE 10

Now we are ready to save this data file, so click on the File button and then on Save As, as shown in Figure 11.

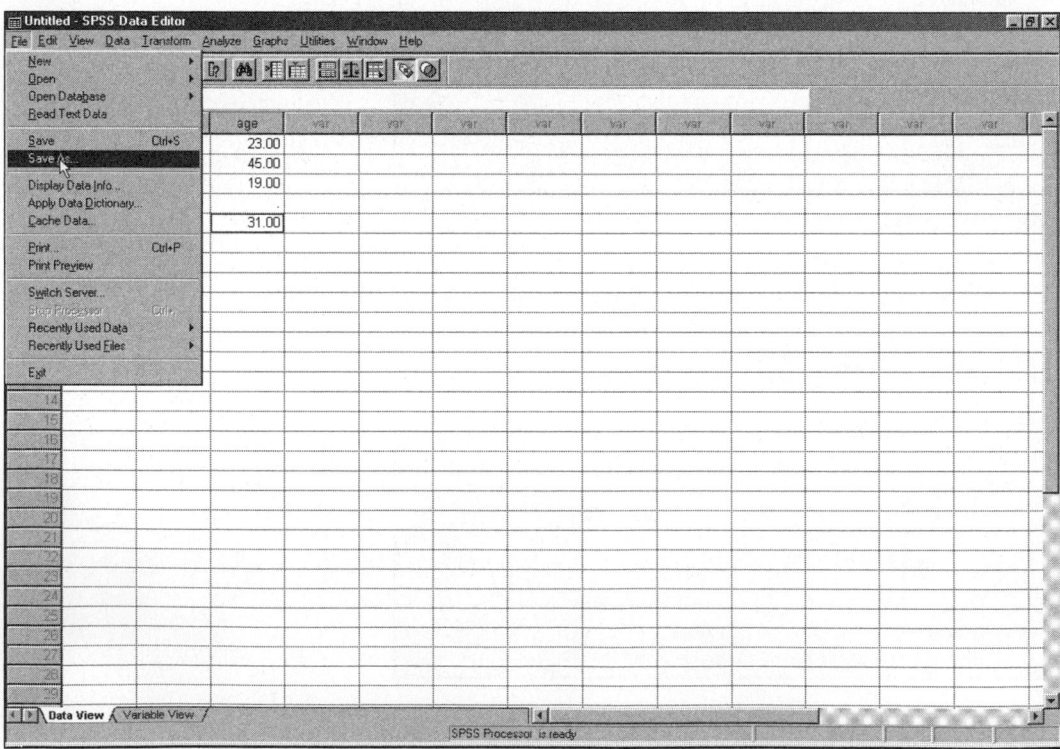

FIGURE 11

Next, you will need to decide where to store your data. It is always a good idea to store your data on a floppy disk as well as your hard drive. In Figure 12 we show our data being saved to Drive A.

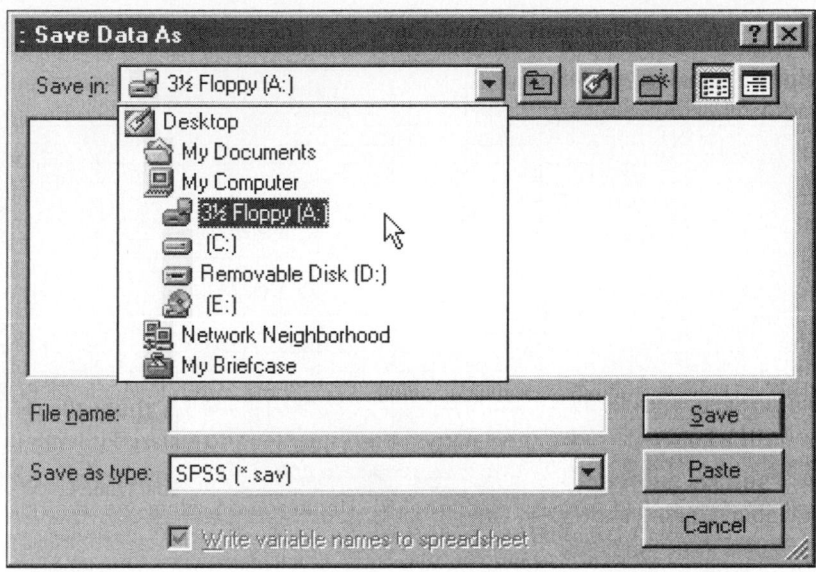

FIGURE 12

As seen in Figure 13, we have saved our data file as datafile1.

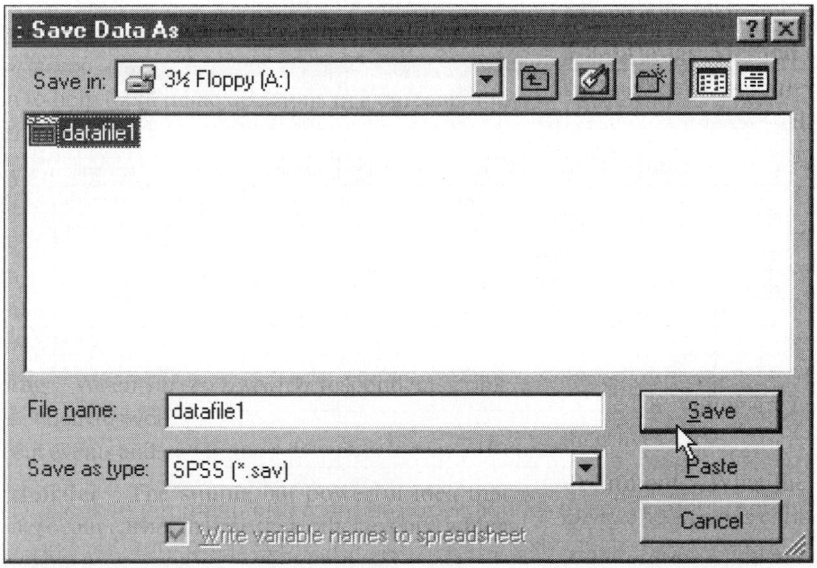

FIGURE 13

Now you may exit from the SPSS program if you are finished entering data and labeling your variables. Click on the File button, then Exit, to exit from SPSS and return to your Windows program, as seen in Figure 14.

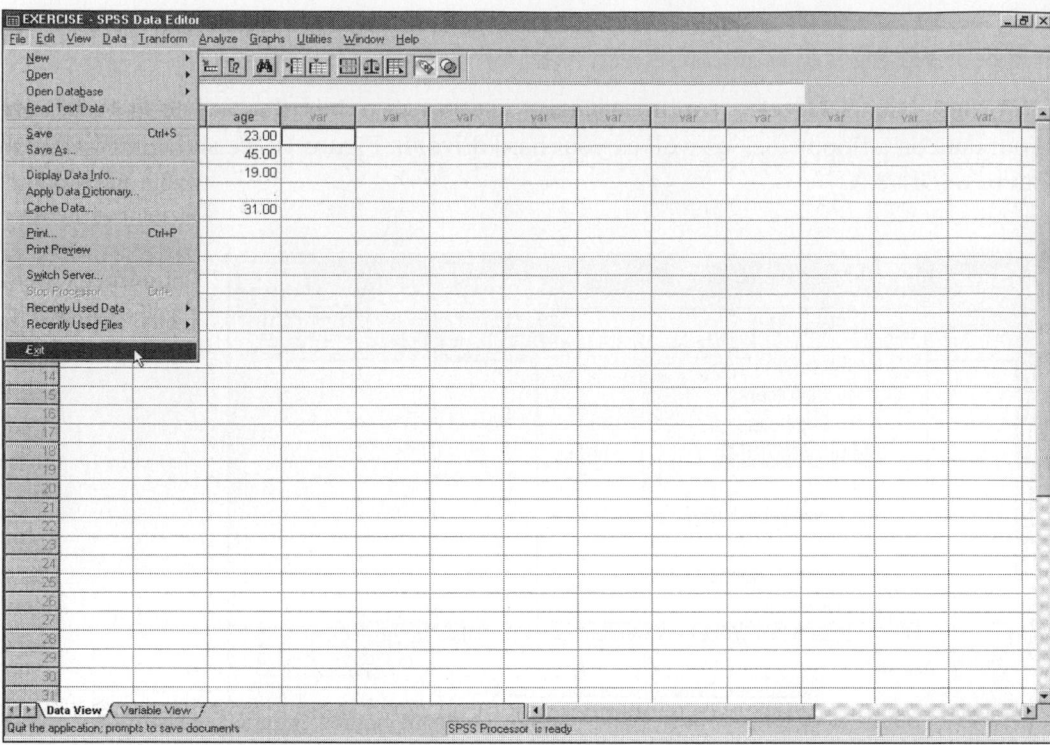

FIGURE 14

DOING UNIVARIATE ANALYSIS USING SPSS

Load your data file as usual; you should have a data file that looks something like Figure 15. Notice in this example we have toggled View to Label, so that our columns show up as labels rather than numbers, in the SPSS Data Editor.

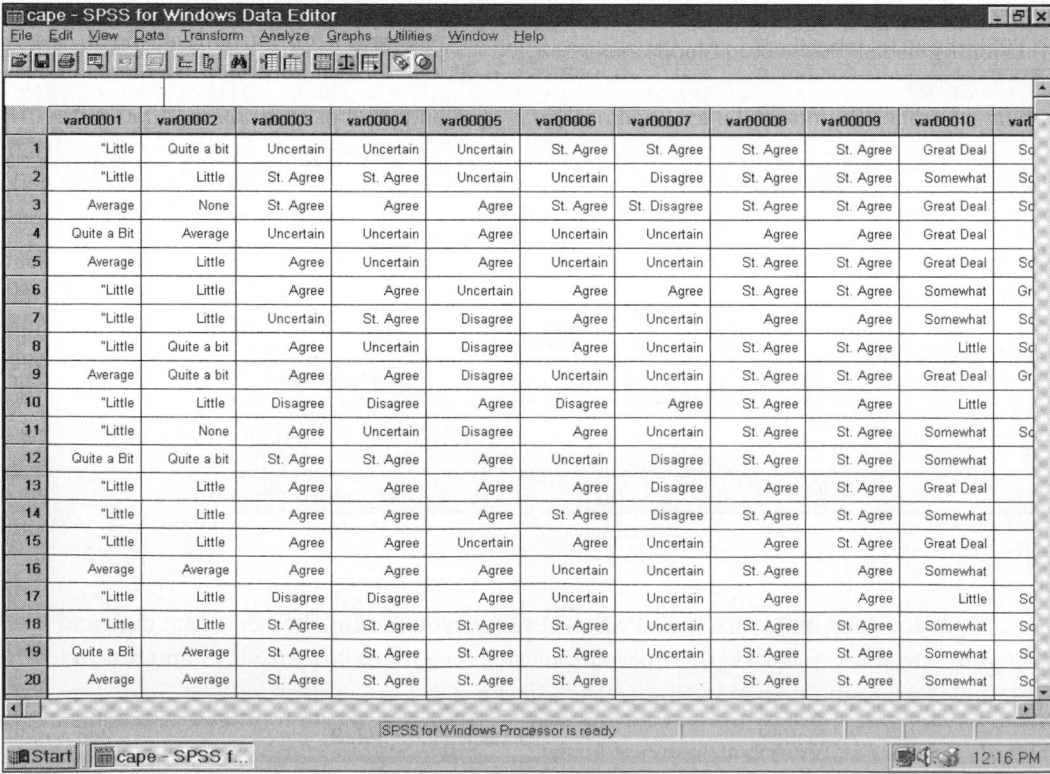

FIGURE 15

Univariate analysis involves the retrieval of basic descriptive and summary statistics such as measures of central tendency and variability, frequency counts and percentages, and graphic printout. To obtain univariate information, click on Analyze, Descriptive Statistics, and Frequencies, as shown in Figure 16.

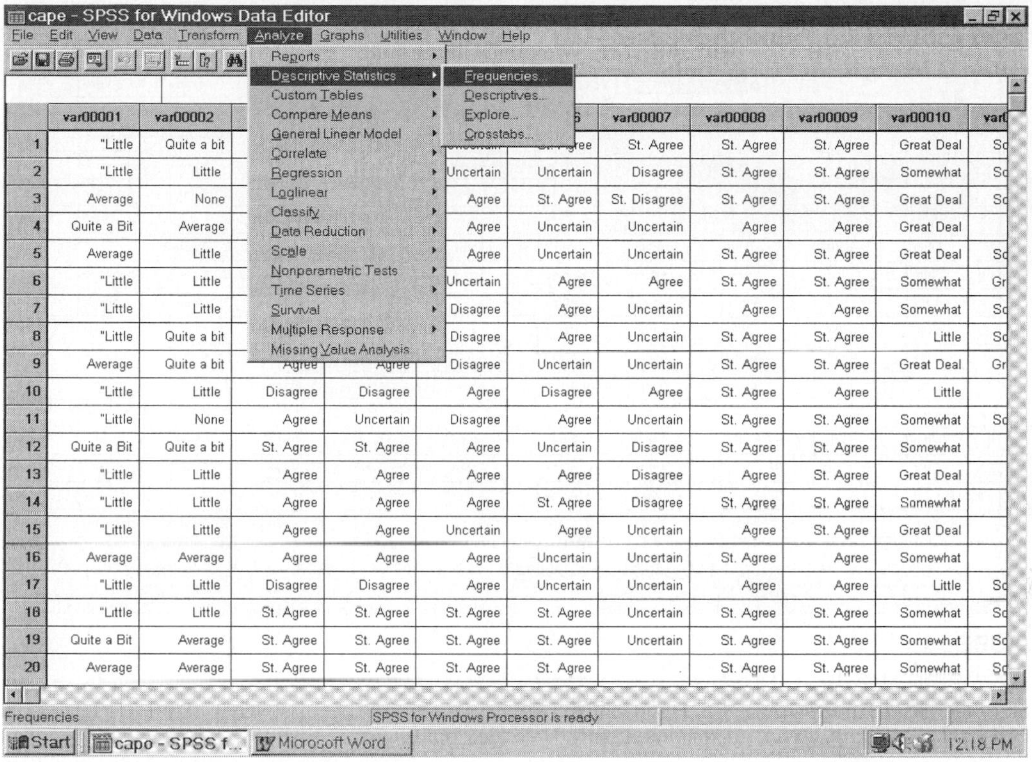

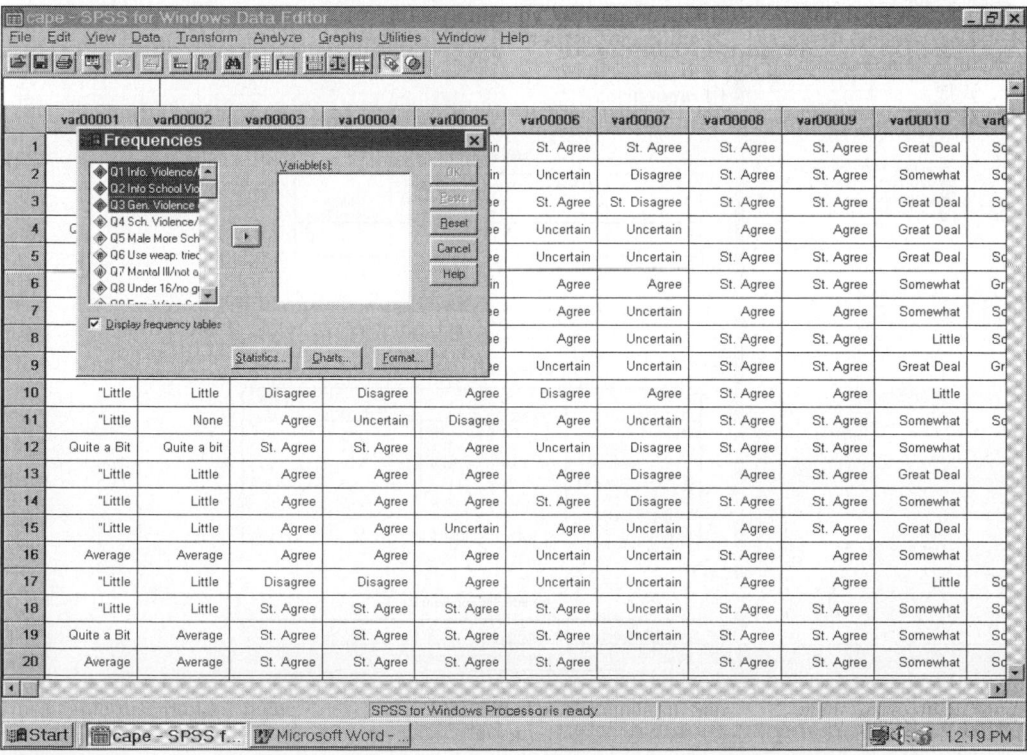

FIGURE 16

Highlight the variables you want to select for your univariate analysis, and use the arrow key to move these into the variables window, as shown in Figures 17 and 18 . . . then click OK.

FIGURE 17

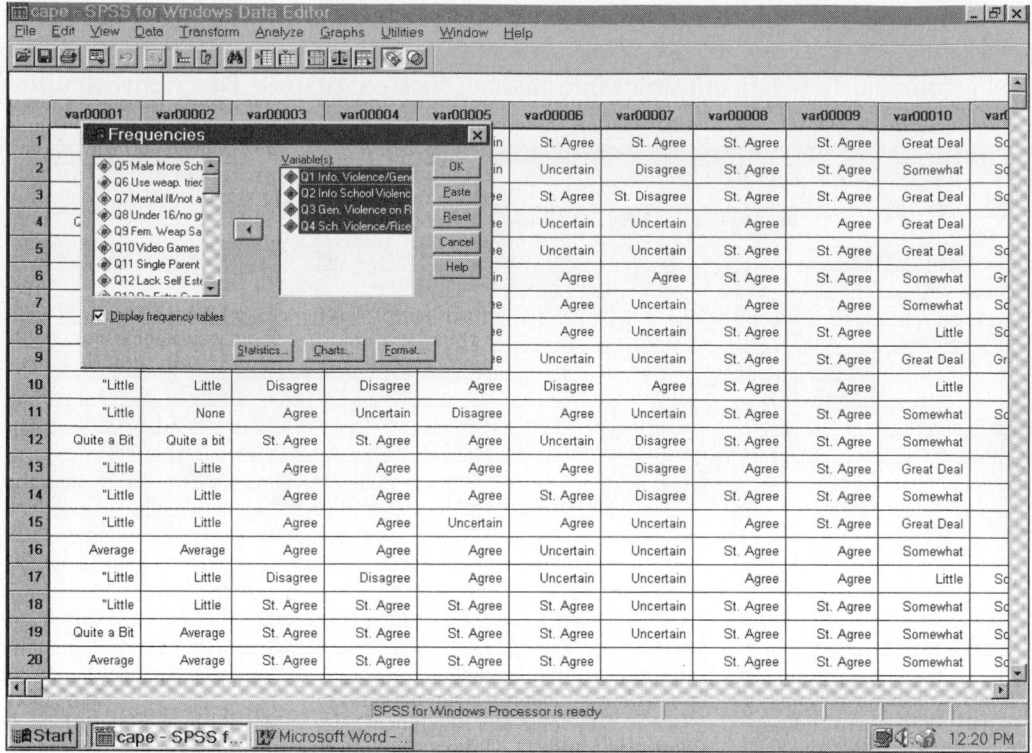

FIGURE 18

You will obtain an output screen that looks like the one in Figure 19. Usually, you will need to save this output to use in your analysis and in reports or documentation of your findings. You may choose to print your output now or save it as a text file and print it from your word processor. You may also save your printouts onto disk and later import them into your

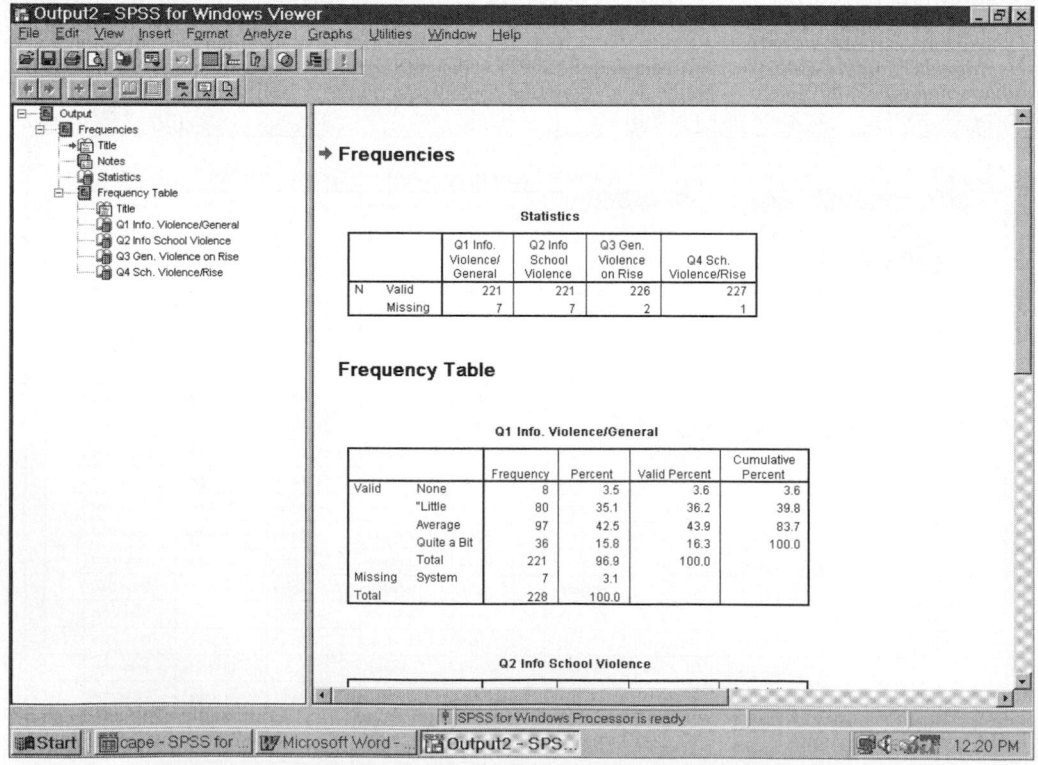

FIGURE 19

word processor and fold them into your report. See the SPSS help feature on saving output to disk and using your output in a word processor or other software program.

Next, if you are using interval-level data you will want to also examine your variables using the Analyze, Descriptive Statistics, Descriptives option, as shown in Figures 20 and 21.

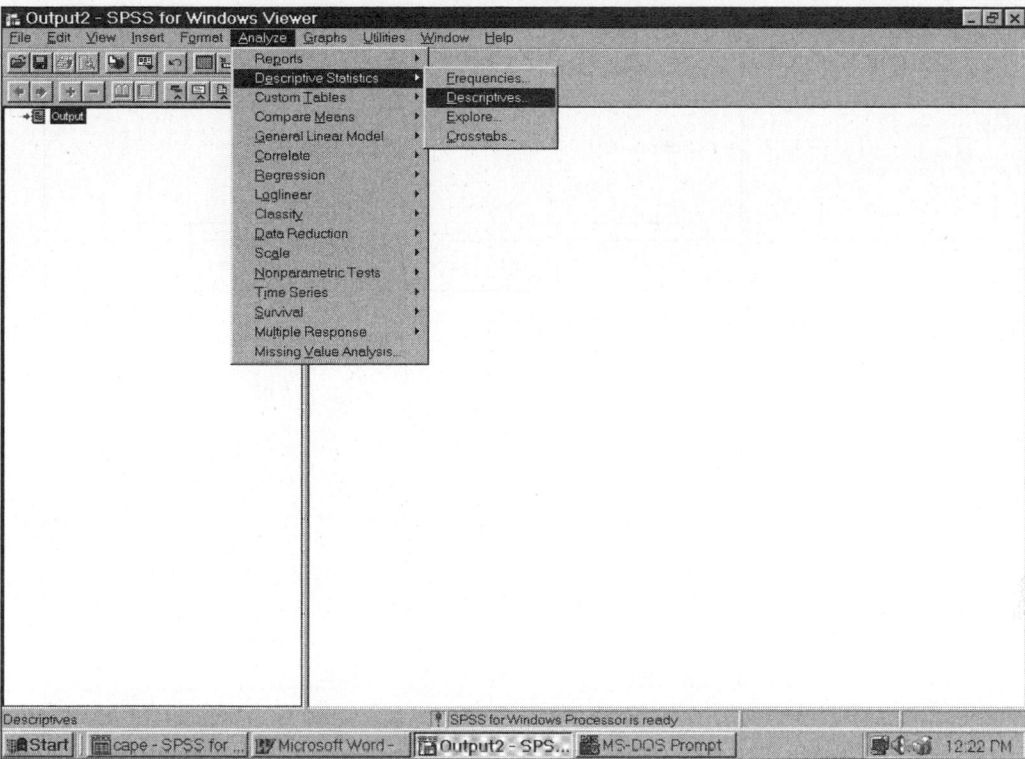

FIGURE 20

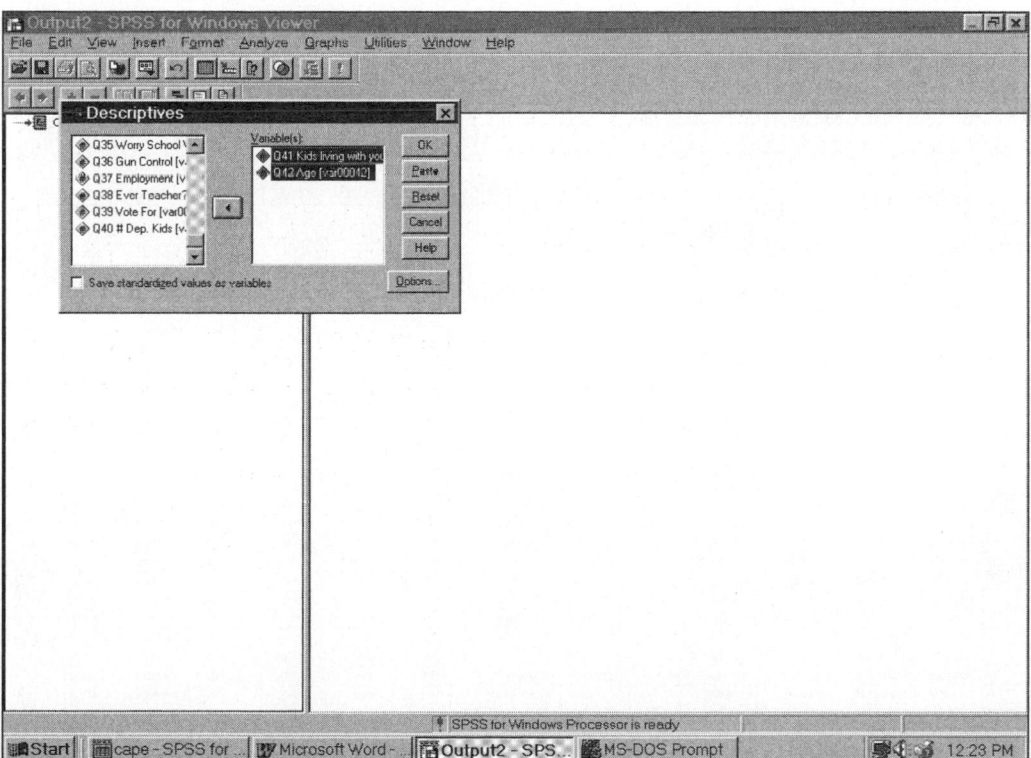

FIGURE 21

In this instance we selected two questions from our hypothetical survey: How many dependent children do you have living with you? and, current Age. Notice in Figure 22 the Descriptive statistics include minimum, maximum, the mean, and a measure of variability (the standard deviation).

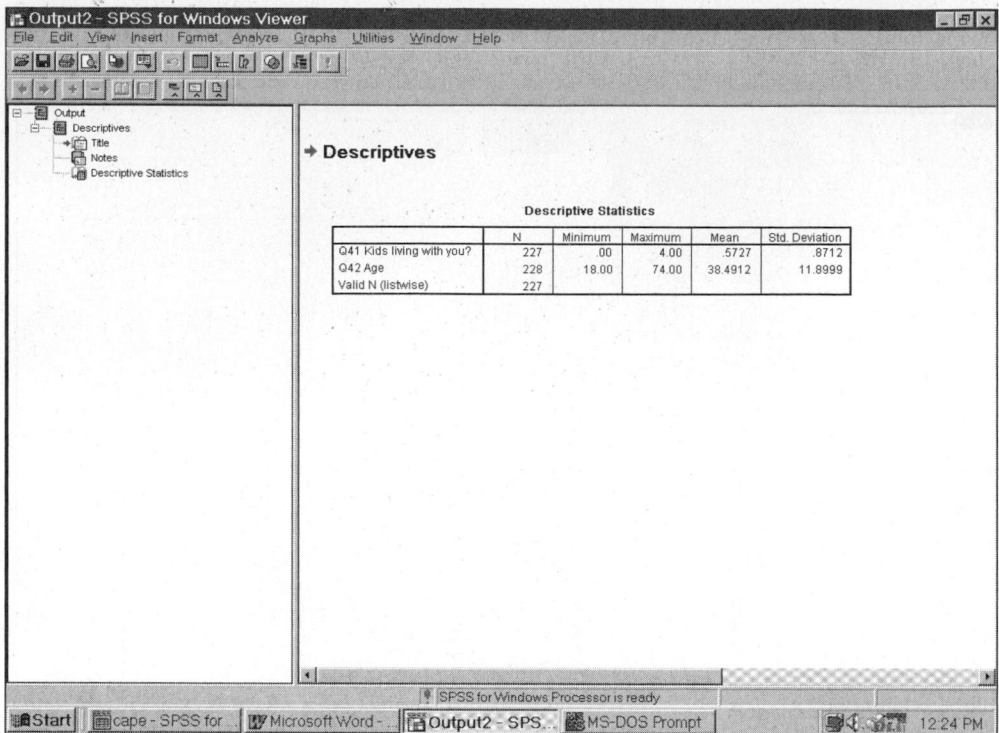

FIGURE 22

Next, we optionally want to generate SPSS graphics to enhance our presentation of findings. To do this, select Graphs, Pie, as shown in Figure 23, and Define (Summaries for groups of cases), as shown in Figure 24.

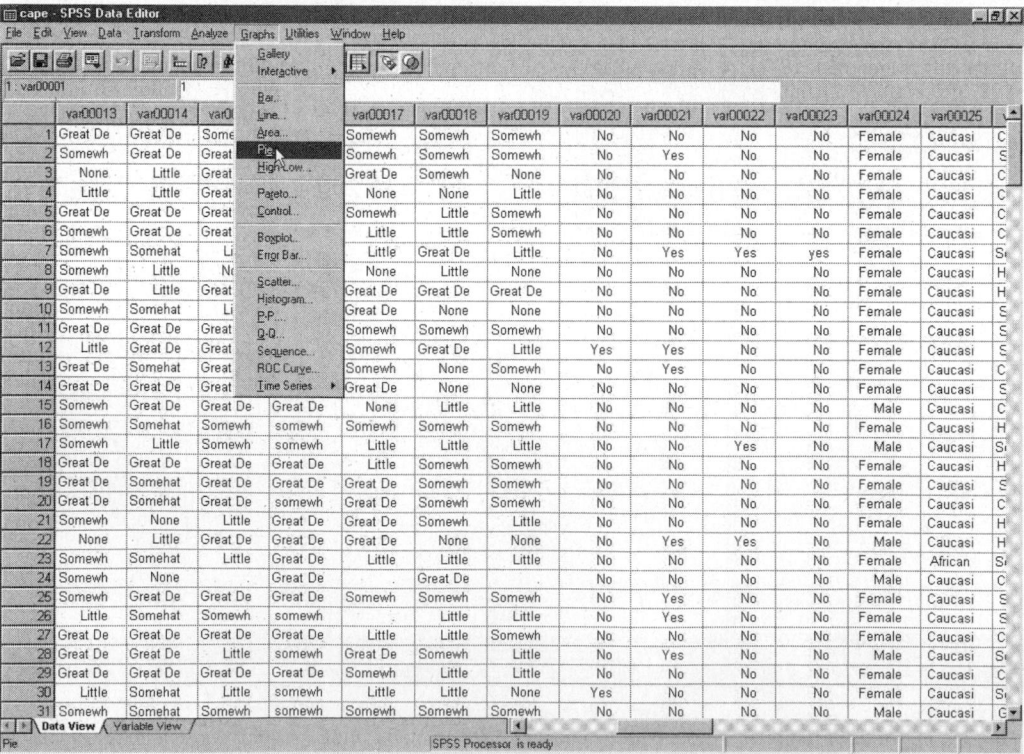

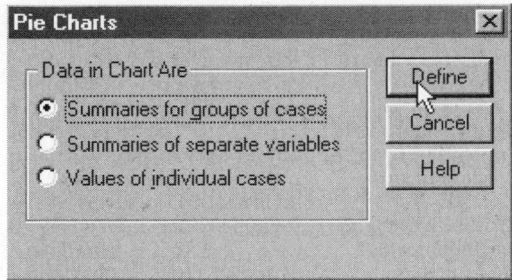

FIGURE 24

Next, move the variable you want to graph into the "Define Slices by" box, as shown in Figure 25, then click OK.

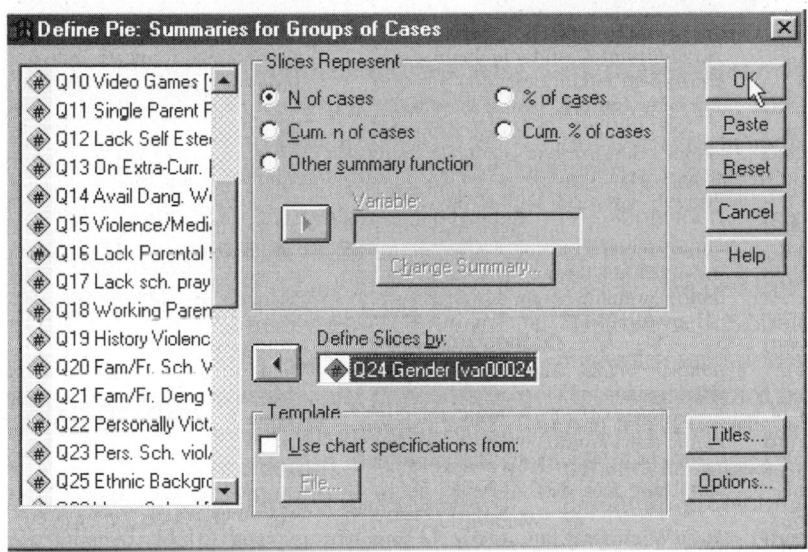

FIGURE 25

Here we note SPSS has generated a pie chart of our var24 Gender, showing proportions of females and males in our data file, as seen in Figure 26.

Next, we are going to generate a bar graph for our question on marital status. First, select Bar from the Graphs pull-down menu, as shown in Figure 27.

Next, from the graphs bar charts options pull-down menu select Simple, and in the Define Simple Bar menu move the variable you are interested in into the Category Axis slot, as we have done for Q28 Marital Status in Figure 28.

Notice in Figure 29 the bar graph that we generated shows the actual counts for each category of marital status, including those few cases where no marital status was selected (Missing), as well as those indicating Never Married, Separated, and so on.

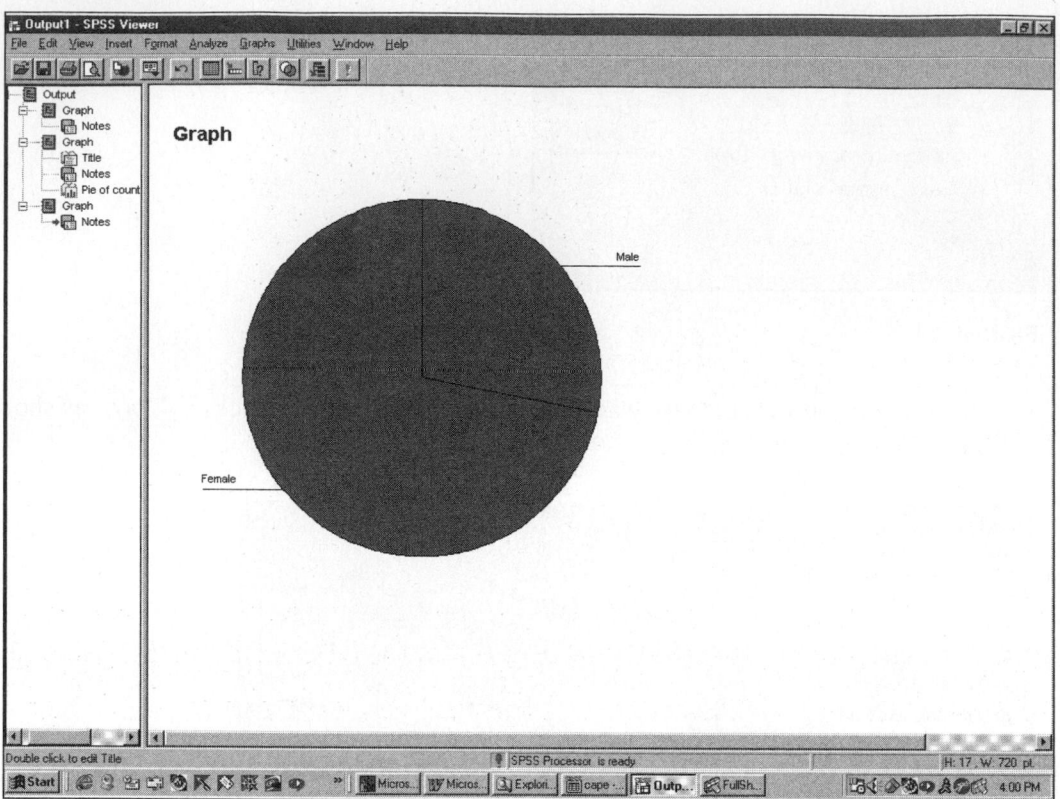

FIGURE 26

FIGURE 27

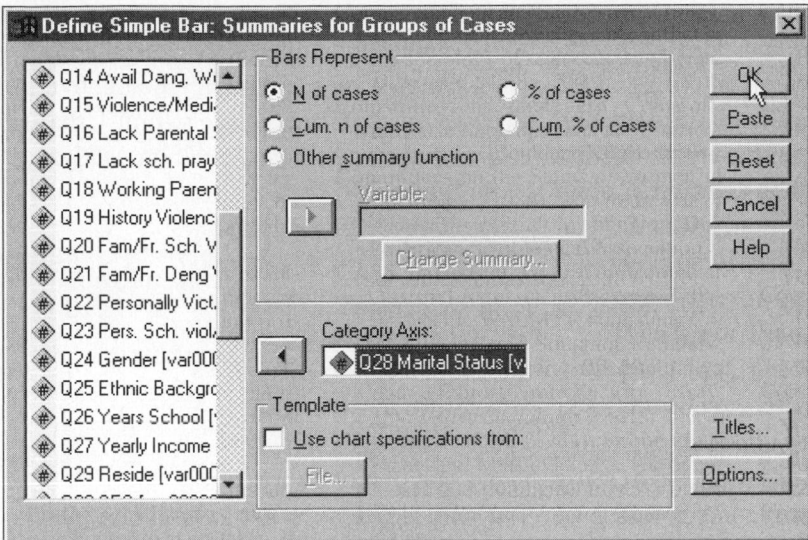

FIGURE 28

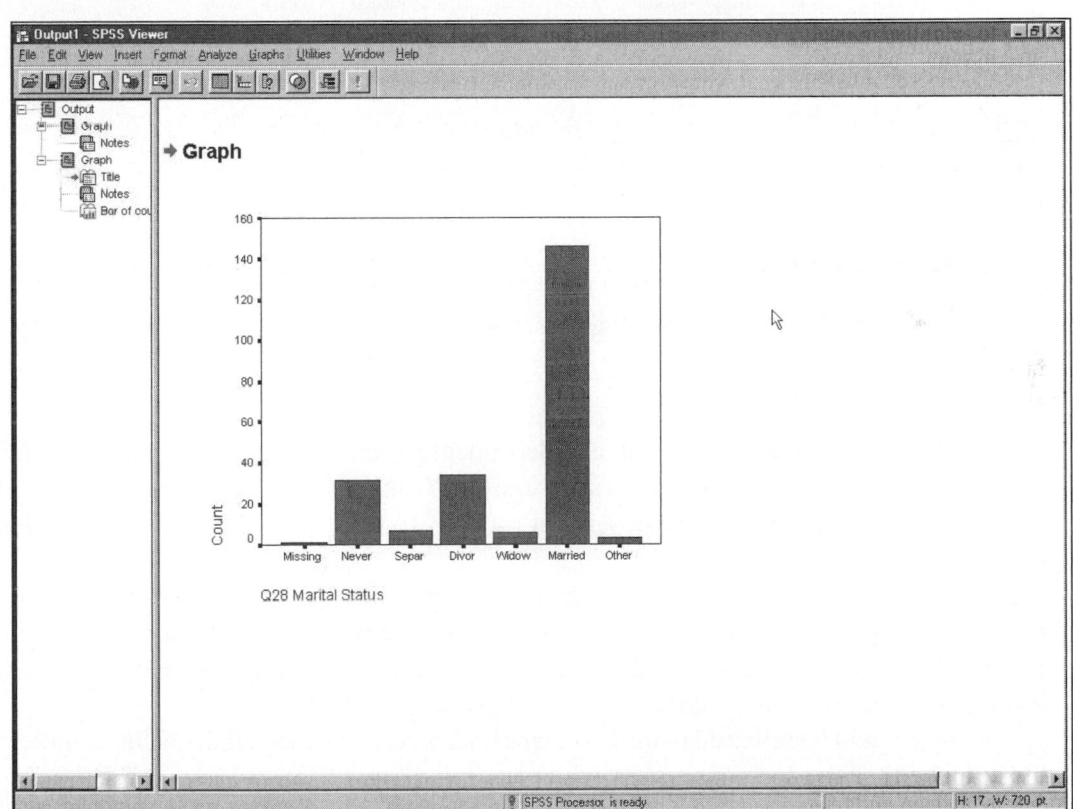

FIGURE 29

DOING BIVARIATE ANALYSIS USING SPSS

Below are several examples of printouts from an SPSS data file of 362 cases. Load your SPSS data file as usual. In this example we are going to test a hypothesis that people who say they are from more urban places of residence will also say they are more liberal in political orientation. Our independent variable (Rural-Urban) is item #26 on our questionnaire, while our dependent variable (Conservative-Liberal) is item #28 on our questionnaire. We believe these questionnaire items are both ordinal level, our sample was nonprobability purposive, and thus we feel confident using a nonparametric measure—Chi-square, to test the null hypothesis, H_0: There is no relationship between place of residence (Rural-Urban) and political orientation (Conservative-Liberal). To test this hypothesis, click on Analyze, Descriptive Statistics, then Crosstabs, as shown in Figure 30.

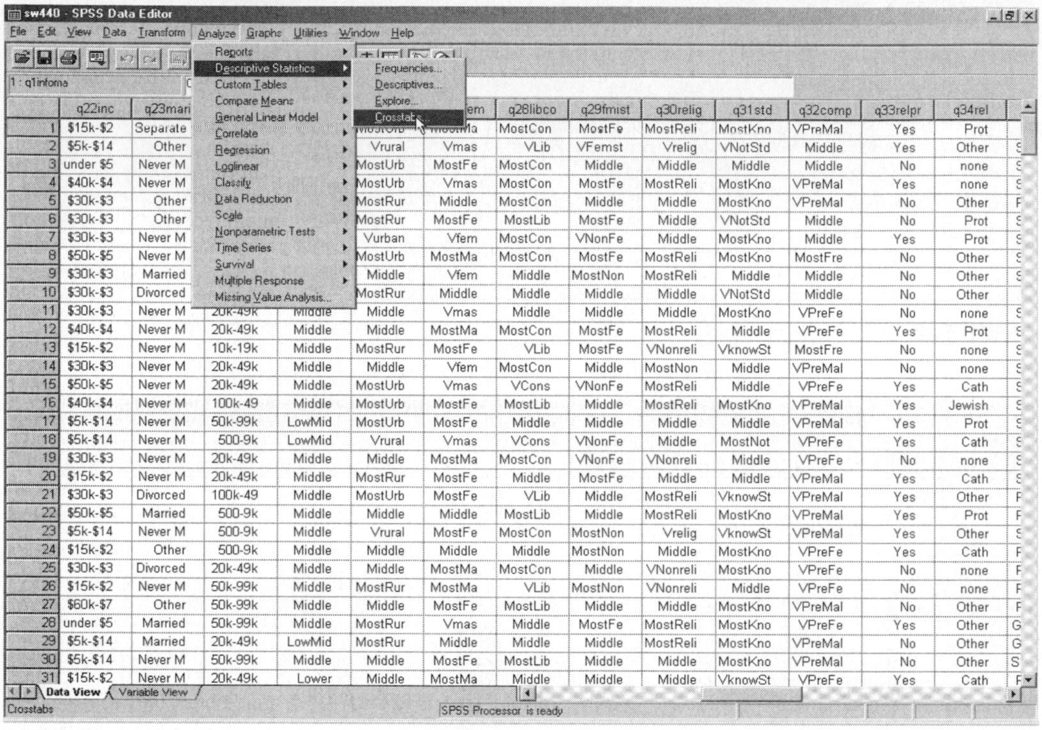

FIGURE 30

Next, highlight the independent and dependent variables from the listing on the left, and click to move the independent variable into the "Columns" box, as shown in Figure 31.

Then highlight and move the dependent variable into the "Rows" box, as shown in Figure 32.

Next, click on the Statistics button at the bottom of the Crosstabs box to select appropriate statistics to test the null hypothesis. In this case we will use Chi-square as our test of H_0, and Gamma as a measure of the size of the reltionship (as both variables are ordinal level). Click on Continue when finished, as shown in Figure 33.

Now you will be returned to the Crosstabs box, where you may click on OK to move to the output editor and see your results, which we will discuss in H_1 below.

Here we present a formal description of our findings, as you will likely do in writing up your research or evaluation report. First, we write out our research hypothesis and the null, we list the independent and dependent variables, indicate our planned cutoff for the associated probability (significance level or Alpha of .05), and finally, we print the actual

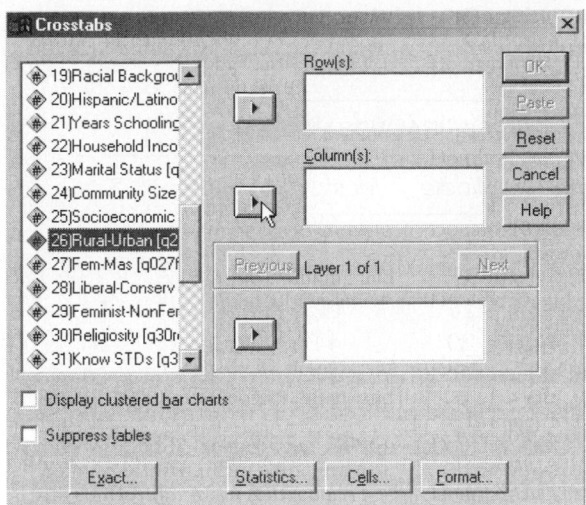

FIGURE 31

FIGURE 32

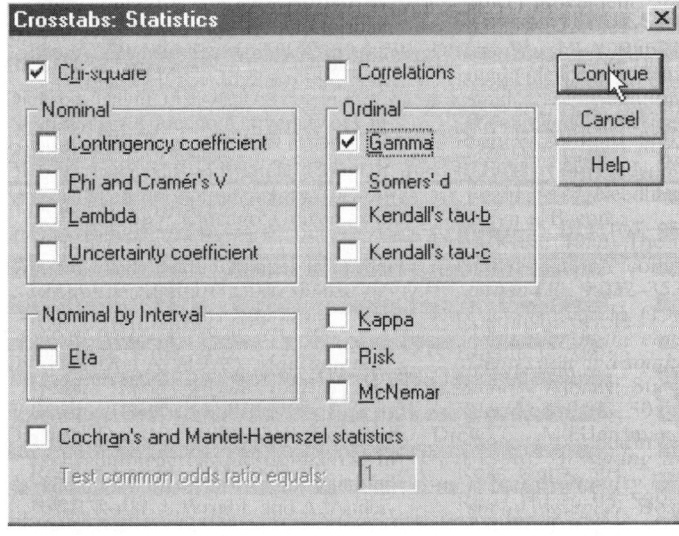

FIGURE 33

table as generated by SPSS. Below we copied the SPSS printout from the SPSS output editor into our word processing program. Simply click on the table you want to copy, select Copy Objects from the Edit toolbar, open your word processing program, locate the area where you want your output to go, and select Paste Special from your Edit toolbar.

H₁: Persons who report themselves as having a more urban place of residence will say they are more liberal compared to those who report themselves as rural.

H₀: There is no difference between urban and rural place of residence in reporting liberal-conservativism.

Independent Variable: Q26 Rural-Urban   Ordinal level

Dependent Variable: Q28 Liberal-Conservative   Ordinal level

Type I Error Level: Significance level set to .05

28)Liberal-Conserv * 26)Rural-Urban Cross-tabulation

Count

		26)RURAL-URBAN					
		Vrural	MostRur	Middle	MostUrb	Vurban	Total
28)Liberal-Conserv	VCons	10	10	3	8	5	36
	MostCon	8	10	17	17	21	73
	Middle	12	22	28	22	13	97
	MostLib	3	12	20	44	15	94
	VLib	1	9	14	24	13	61
Total		34	63	82	115	67	361

Chi-Square Tests

	Value	df	Asymp. Sig. (2-sided)
Pearson Chi-Square	51.961[a]	16	.000
Likelihood Ratio	50.738	16	.000
Linear-by-Linear Association	12.687	1	.000
N of Valid Cases	361		

[a]1 cell (4.0%) has expected count less than 5. The minimum expected count is 3.39.

Symmetric Measures

		Value	Asymp. Std. Error[a]	Approx. T[b]	Approx. Sig.
Ordinal by Ordinal	Gamma	.174	.056	3.074	.002
N of Valid Cases		361			

[a]Not assuming the null hypothesis.

[b]Using the asymptotic standard error assuming the null hypothesis.

Interpretation

First, look at Pearson Chi-Square; note that it equals 51.961 with 16 degrees of freedom and the associated probability = .000 (we round up in this case to .001). This means that, in roughly 1 out of 1000 times over the long run, findings as big as ours would be due to chance. This associated probability is smaller than our preselected significance (Type 1 Error Level) of .05, so our null hypothesis falls at the .05 level. Some alternative hypothesis stands by default. Note that there are differing opinions on how to talk about the meaning of associated probability of .001 (Oakes, 1986). You can't go wrong, however, if you say that the Asymp. Sig. [Asymptotic Significance] of 0.001 is the long-run relative probability (frequency) of obtaining a statistic (Chi-Square in this case) as large as ours (given the same-sized sample) when (pick one): (1) there is no relationship in the data, (2) the null hypothesis is true, or (3) the data came from a table of random numbers. Note that we are in a position to have possibly made a Type I error at this point, as we toppled the null hypothesis and it is possible that we have fooled ourselves in claiming to have found a pattern in these data.

Now that we have decided H_0 falls, we should examine a measure of the strength of the relationship as well. Because both variables were measured at the ordinal level, we will use Gamma. In this case Gamma is $-.174$. On a scale from 0.00 to 1.00, .174 would be considered a small-sized relationship. We use the following rough guidelines for assessing strength:

0.0 to .20 = weak
.20 to .40 = moderate
.40 to 1.00 = strong

Next, we examine the direction of the relationship. Note that Gamma of $-.174$ is negative, as there is a minus (–) sign. A negative relationship means that as one variable increases, the other decreases. To understand how this fits our data, we have to look at the two variables in our table (questions 26 and 28). On Q28 we note that higher numbers are at the more liberal end of our coding, and lower numbers are at the conservative end. On Q26 note that high numbers mean more urban, and lower numbers mean more rural. So a negative Gamma would indicate that less rural tend to go with (be correlated with) those who say they are more liberal, etc. Hence, there is support for our research hypothesis in these data, showing that people who rate themselves as more urban are more likely to rate themselves as liberal.

Here we have additional examples of printouts already generated in SPSS and copied into our word processing program, using the Copy Objects and Paste Special commands in the Edit tool. We have included our interpretation of the findings to help you learn to read and interpret SPSS output.

H_2: Males are more likely than females to say they are in better overall health.

H_0: There is no difference between males and females in attitudes toward their own health.

Independent Variable: Q 23 Gender   Nominal level

Dependent Variable: Q16 Overall Health   Ordinal level

Type I Error Level: Significance level set to .05

Q16HEALT * GENDER Cross-tabulation

Count

		GENDER		
		Female	Male	Total
Q16HEALT	VeryPoor	1		1
	SomePoor	4	3	7
	Middle	24	17	41
	SomeGood	88	49	137
	VeryGood	63	39	102
Total		180	108	288

Chi-Square Tests

	Value	df	Asymp. Sig. (2-sided)
Pearson Chi-Square	1.160[a]	4	.885
Likelihood Ratio	1.496	4	.827
N of Valid Cases	288		

[a]4 cells (40.0%) have expected count less than 5. The minimum expected count is .38.

Interpretation

There is no relationship in these data as the Asymptotic Significance probability of .885 is greater than .05. The null hypothesis (H_0) stands—there is no relationship in these data—so measures of the size of the relationship are irrelevant. We are in a position to have possibly made a Type II error at this point, as we were unable to topple the null hypothesis. It is possible that we should have toppled the null; thus, we may be in error in claiming to have found nothing.

H_3 Younger persons will more likely rate themselves as liberal compared to older persons.

H_0: There is no relationship between age and liberal-conservative political orientation.

Independent Variable: AGE Measured at interval level

Dependent Variable: LIBERAL-CONSERVATIVE preference measured at interval level where (5 = Conservative 1 = Liberal) the higher the score, the more conservative the response.

Type I Error Level: Significance level set to .05

Correlations

		AGE	LIBERAL
AGE	Pearson Correlation	1.000	.227**
	Sig. (2-tailed)		.000
	N	287	284
LIBERAL	Pearson Correlation	.227**	1.000
	Sig. (2-tailed)	.000	
	N	284	285

**Correlation is significant at the 0.01 level (2-tailed).

Interpretation

Here we note that the Pearson's r is called Multiple R in this printout ($r = 0.227$), and under the Asymp. Sig. (2-tailed) section, we notice the associated probability is 0.000 (or 0.001, as we rounded up here). Note that we are in a position to have possibly made a Type I error at this point, as we toppled the null hypothesis, and it is possible that we have fooled ourselves in claiming to have found a pattern in these data.

This associated probability is smaller than .05, so the H_0 falls. Now we have to examine r of .227 to see if it corroborates our H_3. We note that because there is no minus sign (–) on the printout next to the actual correlation, the correlation is positive. A positive correlation means that as one variable increases, the other increases (or as one decreases, the other decreases). We have a positive correlation, so in this case we say that as age increases, conservatism increases. Following our usual criteria we can comment on the size of the correlation on a scale between 0.0 and 1.0; here we see that we have a moderately sized relationship. Finally, in the case of Pearson's r we can square the actual correlation of .227 to get R squared as the measure of the proportion of variability in the dependent variable that is "explained" by, or accounted for by, the independent variable. Thus (.227 * .227 = .0515), we can say that a little more than 5 percent (.0515) of political orientation was accounted for by age in these data. This is a fairly common finding regarding the size of the relationship we have uncovered. That is, while researchers often find something in their data, what they find isn't necessarily very big.

Below is an example of an independent groups t-test with a boxplot generated in SPSS to help visualize the comparisons.

H_4: Males are more likely to be homophobic (have a higher IAH score)[1] than females.

H_0: There is no relationship between HOMOPHOBIA score and GENDER.

Independent Variable: Gender (coded 1 & 2)

Dependent Variable: Index of Homophobia measured at interval level as a score from 0–100.

Type I Error Level: Significance level set to .05

Group Statistics

	GENDER	N	Mean	Std. Deviation	Std. Error Mean
IAH	1	108	55.70	25.94	2.50
	2	178	43.84	22.36	1.68

Independent Samples Test

IAH	LEVENE'S TEST FOR EQUALITY OF VARIANCES		T-TEST FOR EQUALITY OF MEANS						95% Confidence Interval of the Difference	
	F	Sig.	t	df	Sig. (2-tailed)	Mean Difference	Std. Error Difference		Lower	Upper
Equal variances assumed	3.858	.050	4.090	284	.000	11.86	2.90		6.15	17.57
Equal variances not assumed			3.945	200.585	.000	11.86	3.01		5.93	17.79

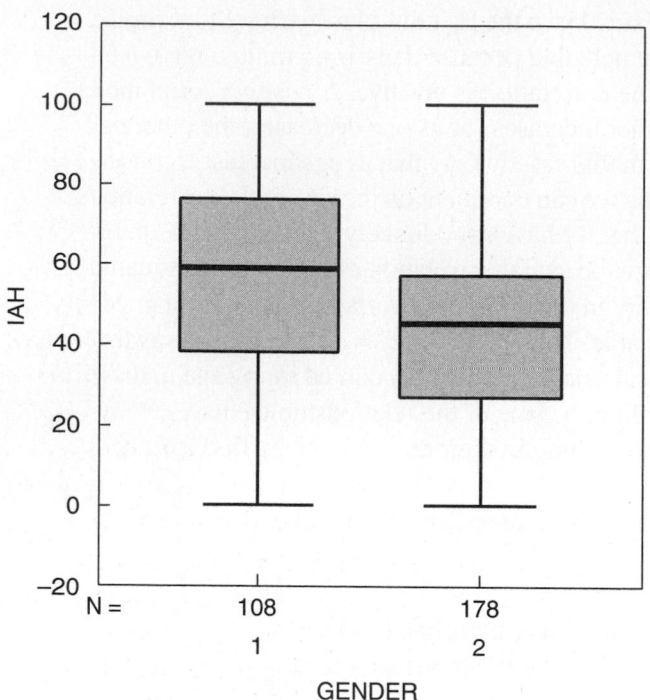

Interpretation

Here we note that, for the *t*-test, $t = 4.090$, and under the Sig. (2-tailed) we notice the associated probability is 0.000 (or, 0.001, as we rounded down here). Note that we are in a position to have possibly made a Type I error at this point, as we toppled the null hypothesis and it is possible that we have fooled ourselves in claiming to have found a pattern in these data.

This associated probability is smaller than .05, so H_0 falls. Now we have to examine the data to see if it corroborates our H_4. We note from the Group Statistics printout that the mean IAH score for Females = 43.84, and the mean IAH score for Males = 55.7. The *t*-test compares these two means to see how often over the long run this difference would occur by chance in a sample the same size as ours. Here the average score for males (55.7) is larger (more homophobic) than the average score for females (43.8), which tends to corroborate our H_4. The boxplots we generated provide a visual comparison of the average IAH scores for group 1 (Males) and group 2 (Females).

SOURCES FOR MORE HELP USING SPSS

Brace, N., R. Kemp, and R. Snelgar. (2000). *SPSS for psychologists: A guide to data analysis using SPSS for Windows versions 8, 9 and 10.* Basingstoke: Palgrave.

Corston, R., and A. Coleman. (2000). *A crash course in SPSS for Windows.* London: Blackwell Publishers.

Kinnear, P., and C. Gray. (1997). *SPSS for Windows made simple,* 2nd ed. Hove, East Sussex, UK: Psychology Press.

Norusis, M. (2000). *SPSS 10.0 guide to data analysis.* Upper Saddle River, NJ: Prentice Hall.

Weinberg, S. (2001). *Data analysis for the behavioral sciences using SPSS.* Cambridge: Cambridge University Press.

NOTES

1. Hudson, W., and W. Ricketts. (1980). A strategy for the measurement of homophobia. *Journal of Homosexuality,* 5, 357–372.

GLOSSARY

Following the definition, the number in parentheses is the chapter in which the term first appears in the text and is in the Key Terms section. Italicized terms in a definition refer to terms defined elsewhere in this glossary.

A–B design The most basic type of *single-case design* that compares measured progress of a client for a selected target behavior prior to an intervention (the A or baseline phase, logically equivalent to a control period), to progress during the intervention (B or *treatment* phase, logically equivalent to an experimental period). (14)

Abstract A term with two meanings in literature reviews: a short summary of a *scholarly journal article* that usually appears at its beginning, and a reference tool for locating *scholarly journal articles*. (16)

Academic freedom A guarantee that researchers and/or teachers are free to examine all topics and discuss all ideas without any restrictions, threats, or interference from people or authorities outside the community of teachers, scholars, and scientists. (5)

Acceptable incompetent When a researcher conducting *field research* pretends to be less skilled or knowledgeable in order to learn more about a *field site*. (13)

Access ladder The idea that a field researcher may only be able to see and learn about public, noncontroversial events at first, but, with time and effort, may gain entry to more hidden, intimate, and controversial information and thoughts. (13)

Accretion measures *Nonreactive* measures of the residue of the activity of people or what they leave behind. (11)

Action-oriented research A type of *applied research* in which the purpose is to facilitate social change or a political–social goal. (2)

Alternative hypothesis A *hypothesis* paired with a *null hypothesis* stating that the *independent variable* has an effect on a *dependent variable*. (6)

Analytic comparison A type of *qualitative data* analysis in which a researcher uses the *method of agreement* and the *method of difference* to discover causal factors that affect an outcome among a set of cases. (15)

Analytic domain A type of *domain* in which a researcher uses categories or terms he or she developed to understand a social setting. (15)

Analytic memo The written notes a qualitative researcher takes during data collection and afterwards to develop concepts, themes, or preliminary generalizations. (13)

Anonymity The ethical protection that the people who are studied remain nameless; their identity is protected from disclosure and remains unknown. (5)

Appearance of interest A technique in *field research* in which researchers maintain relations in a *field site* by pretending to be interested and excited by the activities of those studied, even though they are actually uninterested or very bored. (13)

Applied research Research that attempts to solve a concrete problem or address a specific policy question and that has a direct, practical application. (2)

Argot The special language or terminology of a subculture or group that interacts regularly. (13)

Association A co-occurrence of two events, factors, characteristics, or activities, such that when one happens, the other is likely to occur as well. Many *statistics* measure this. (3)

Assumption Parts of *social theories* that are not tested, but act as starting points or basic beliefs about the world. They are necessary to make other theoretical statements and to build *social theory*. (3)

Asynchronous A type of communication that occurs at different times from the same place(s). (2)

Attitude of strangeness A technique in *field research* in which researchers study a *field site* by mentally adjusting to "see" it for the first time or as an outsider. (13)

Attributes The categories or levels of a variable. (6)

Auxiliary theory A supplemental theory that researchers use to reduce the gap between the abstract constructs and specific measurement operations they use. (7)

Axial coding A second *coding* of *qualitative data* after *open coding*. The researcher organizes the codes, develops links among them, and discovers key analytic categories. (15)

Bad blood   A name for the study by the U.S. Public Health Service that highlighted a failure to protect subjects from physical harm and a failure to obtain *informed consent*. In the study, researchers withheld medical treatment for syphilis for many years from poor African American males who were *subjects* so they could study the disease. *Subjects* were never told they had syphilis. (5)

Bandwidth   The range of frequencies a communication channel can transmit. The higher the frequency, the wider the bandwidth and the more data or information a channel can carry. (2)

Bar chart   A display of *quantitative data* for one variable in the form of rectangles where longer rectangles indicate more cases in a variable category. Usually, it is used with discrete data and there is a small space between rectangles. They can have a horizonal or vertical orientation. Also called bar graphs. (12)

Basic research   Research that advances knowledge of the fundamentals of how the social world works and develops general theoretical explanations. (2)

BBSs   Bulletin Board Systems: online meeting places for discussions, *uploading* and *downloading* of files, and obtaining services. (2)

Bivariate statistics   Statistical measures that involve two variables only. (12)

Blind review   The process of evaluating a research report for possible publication in which evaluators do not know the name of the researcher and the researcher does not know who serves as evaluators. (1)

Body of a table   The center part of a *contingency table*. It contains all the cells, but not the totals or labels. (12)

Bogardus social distance scale   A *scale* that measures the distance between two or more social groups by having members of one group express the point at which they feel comfortable with various types of social interaction or closeness with members of the other group(s). (7)

Breakdown   When social rules and patterns of behavior in a *field site* do not operate as expected, or are purposely disrupted or broken by a researcher. The disruptions often reveal a great deal about social meanings and relationships. (13)

Bricolage   A characteristic of the qualitative style in which a researcher creatively works with his or her hands and pragmatically combines diverse odds and ends to accomplish a specific task. (6)

Case study   Research in which one studies a few people or cases in great detail over time. (2)

Causal explanation   A statement in *social theory* about why events occur that is expressed in terms of causes and effects. They correspond to *associations* in the *empirical world*. (3)

Causal laws   Basic rules outlined in *social theory* that identify *associations* in *empirical* social reality. They are used by the *positivist social science* approach to talk about how events in the social world operate (i.e., in terms of regular, systematic cause–effect relations). (4)

Cell of a table   A part of the *body of a table*. In a *contingency table* it shows the distribution of cases into categories of variables as a specific number or percentage. (12)

Central limit theorem   A lawlike mathematical relationship that states: Whenever many *random samples* are drawn from a *population* and plotted, a *normal distribution* is formed, and the center of such a distribution for a variable is equal to its *population parameter*. (8)

Citation   Details of a *scholarly journal article's* location that helps people to find it quickly. (16)

Classical experimental design   An *experimental design* that has *random assignment*, a *control group*, an *experimental group*, and *pretests* and *posttests* for each group. (9)

Classification   Complex, multidimensional concepts that have subtypes. They are parts of *social theories* between one simple concept and a full theoretical explanation. (3)

Closed-ended question   A type of *survey research* question in which respondents must choose from a fixed set of answers. (10)

Cluster sampling   A type of *random sampling* that uses multiple stages and is often used to cover wide geographic areas in which aggregated units are randomly selected, then *samples* are drawn from the sampled aggregated units, or clusters. (8)

Code of ethics   A list of principles and guidelines offered by professional organizations to guide research practice and to clarify behaviors that are ethical. (5)

Code sheets   Paper with a printed grid on which a researcher records information so that it can be easily entered into a computer. It is an alternative to the *direct-entry method* and using *optical-scan sheets*. (12)

Codebook   A document that describes the procedure for *coding variables* and their location in a format for computers. (12)

Coding   The process of converting raw information or data into another form for analysis. In *content analysis* it is a means for determining how to convert symbolic meanings in *text* into another form, usually numbers (see *Coding system*); in *quantitative data* analysis it is a means for assigning numbers (see *Coding procedure*); and in *qualitative data* analysis it is a series of steps for reading raw notes and assigning codes or conceptual terms (see *Open coding, Axial coding, Selective coding*). (11)

Coding procedure   A set of rules created by a quantitative researcher for assigning numbers to specific variable *attributes,* usually in preparation for statistical analysis and carefully recorded in a *codebook.* (12)

Coding system   A set of instructions or rules used in *content analysis* to explain how to systematically convert the symbolic content from *text* into *quantitative data.* (11)

Cohort analysis   Research on a set of people who share a common experience across time. (2)

Communalism   A norm of the *scientific community* that creating scientific knowledge is a public act, that the knowledge belongs to everyone and should be communicated. (1)

Comparative need   An examination that uses information from those who have already obtained services to estimate how many of those in the larger *population* are likely to share the same characteristics and hence likely to benefit from additional services if offered. (14)

Compensatory behavior   A threat to *internal validity* that occurs when *subjects* in the *control group* modify their behavior to make up for not getting the *treatment.* (9)

Competent insider performance   Demonstrating the authenticity and trustworthiness of a *field research* study by the researcher "passing" as a member of the group under study. (13)

Computer-assisted telephone interviewing (CATI)   *Survey research* in which the interviewer sits before a computer screen and keyboard and uses the computer to read questions that are asked in a telephone interview, then enters answers directly into the computer. (10)

Concept cluster   A collection of interrelated ideas that share common *assumptions,* belong to the same larger *social theory,* and refer to one another. (3)

Conceptual definition   A careful, systematic definition of a construct that is explicitly written to clarify one's thinking. It is often linked to other concepts or theoretical statements. (7)

Conceptual hypothesis   A type of *hypothesis* in which the researcher expresses variables in abstract, conceptual terms and expresses the relationship among variables in a theoretical way. (7)

Conceptualization   The process of developing clear, rigorous, systematic *conceptual definitions* for abstract ideas/concepts. (7)

Concurrent validity   *Measurement validity* that relies on a preexisting and already accepted measure to verify the indicator of a construct. (7)

Confidence interval   A range of values, usually a little higher and lower than a specific value found in a *sample,* within which a researcher has a specified and high degree of confidence that the *population parameter* lies. (8)

Confidentiality   The ethical protection of *subjects* by holding research data in confidence or keeping them secret from the public; not releasing information in a way that permits linking specific individuals to specific responses. Researchers do this by presenting data only in an aggregate form (e.g., percentages, means, etc.). (5)

Construct validity   A type of *measurement validity* that uses *multiple indicators.* It has two subtypes. One looks at how well similar indicators converge, the other looks at how well different indicators diverge or distinguish differences. (7)

Content analysis   Research in which one examines patterns of symbolic meaning within written text, audio, visual, or other communication media. (2)

Content validity   *Measurement validity* that requires that a measure represent all the aspects of the conceptual definition of a construct. (7)

Context effect   An effect in *survey research* when an overall tone or set topics heard by a respondent affects how they interpret the meaning of subsequent questions. (10)

Context review   A type of literature review in which the writer places a specific study in a web of previous research and shows the connections from one study to related studies. (16)

Contingency cleaning   Cleaning data using a computer in which the researcher looks at the combination of categories for two variables for logically impossible cases. (12)

Contingency question   A type of *survey research* question in which the respondent next goes to one or another question based on his or her answer. (10)

Contingency table   A table that shows the *cross-tabulation* of two or more variables. It usually shows *bivariate quantitative data* for variables in the form of percentages across rows or down columns for the categories of one variable. (12)

Continuous variable   Variables measured on a continuum in which an infinite number of finer gradations between variable *attributes* are possible. (7)

Contract research   A type of *applied research* that is sponsored (i.e., paid for by a government agency, foundation, company, or similar organization). The researcher agrees to conduct a study on the sponsor's research question and finish the study by a set deadline for a fixed price. (5)

Contrast class In *erotetic reasoning,* the category or group that is being compared to the original "instead of" group. A student studied (the original category) instead of going out with friends (the contrast class). (14)

Contrast question A type of interview question asked late in *field research* in which the researcher verifies the correctness of distinctions found among categories in the meaning system of people being studied. (13)

Control group The group that does not get the *treatment* in *experimental research.* (9)

Control variable A "third" variable that shows whether a *bivariate relationship* holds up to alternative explanations. It can occur before or between other variables. (12)

Convergent validity A type of *measurement validity* that uses *multiple indicators* and looks at how well similar indicators converge . (7)

Cost analysis An evaluation that assesses how much a program or its components cost. (415)

Cost–benefit analysis A technique economists developed in which one assigns events or conditions a monetary value, then estimates the positive and negative consequences. (2)

Covariation The idea that two variables vary together, such that knowing the values in one variable provides information about values found in another variable. (12)

Cover sheet One or more pages at the beginning of a *questionnaire* with information about an interview or respondent. (10)

Criterion validity *Measurement validity* that relies on some independent, outside verification. (7)

Critical social science An approach to social science that goes beyond surface illusions to reveal underlying structures and conflicts of social relations as a way to empower people to improve the social world. (4)

Cross-over design A type of *experimental design* in which all groups receive the *treatment* so that discomfort or benefits are shared and inequality is not created. (5)

Cross-sectional research Research that is like a "snapshot"; it looks at a single point in time. (2)

Cross-tabulation Placing data for two variables in a *contingency table* to show the number or percentage of cases at the intersection of categories of the two variables. (12)

Crucial experiment A rare test of two or more competing explanations of the same phenomenon. The test results will clearly show that one *social theory* is correct and the other(s) is (are) false. (6)

Curvilinear relationship A relationship between two variables such that as the values of one variable increase, the values of the second show a changing pattern (e.g., first decrease, then increase, then decrease). It is not a *linear relationship.* (12)

Cyberspace A term coined by author William Gibson for the digital world linked by computer networks. (5)

Data Numerical and nonnumerical forms of information and evidence that have been carefully gathered according to rules or established procedures. (1)

Data field One or more columns of data already organized for a computer representing the location of information on a specific variable. (12)

Data records A name for the units that computers read that contain quantitative information on variables for one case or person. (12)

Debrief When a researcher gives a true explanation of the experiment to *subjects* after using *deception.* (9)

Deception When an experimenter lies to *subjects* about the true nature of an experiment or creates a false impression through his or her actions or the setting. (9)

Deductive approach An approach to inquiry or *social theory* in which one begins with abstract ideas and principles, then works toward concrete, *empirical* details to test the ideas. (3)

Defocusing A technique used early in *field research* when a researcher removes his or her past *assumptions* and preconceptions to become more open to events in a *field site.* (13)

Demand characteristics A type of *reactivity* in which the *subjects* in *experimental research* pick up clues about the *hypothesis* and alter their behavior accordingly. (9)

Dependent variable The effect variable that is last and results from the causal variable(s) in a *causal explanation.* Also, the variable that is measured in the *pretest* and *posttest* and that is the result of the *treatment* in *experimental research.* (6)

Descriptive question A type of question asked early in *field research.* The researcher seeks basic information (e.g., who, what, when, where) about the *field site.* (13)

Descriptive research Research in which one "paints a picture" with words or numbers, presents a profile, outlines stages, or classifies types. (2)

Descriptive statistics A general type of simple statistics used by researchers to describe basic patterns in the data. (12)

Design notation The name of a symbol system used to discuss the parts of an experiment and to make diagrams of them. (9)

Determinism   The *assumption* that individuals have little freedom to decide and act. People are greatly affected by external social pressure or forces. (4)

Dialectic   A pattern of change emphasized by *critical social science*. Over time, the very makeup and organization of a society, social institution or organization, or social relationship contains internal contradictions and deep-seated tensions. The contradictions trigger the destruction of one form of society, institution, or organization and propel its transformation into a new, qualitatively distinct form or stage. (4)

Diffusion of treatment   A threat to *internal validity* that occurs when the *treatment* "spills over" from the *experimental group,* and *control group subjects* modify their behavior because they learn of the *treatment*. (9)

Direct-entry method   A method of entering data into a computer by typing data without *code sheets* or *optical-scan sheets*. (12)

Direct observation notes   Notes taken in *field research* that attempt to include all details and specifics of what the researcher heard or saw in a *field site*. They are written in a way that permits multiple interpretations later. (13)

Discrete variables   Variables in which the *attributes* can be measured only with a limited number of distinct, separate categories. (7)

Discriminant validity   A type of *construct validity* in which multiple indicators of one construct "hang together." At the same time, indicators of a different construct operate differently. (7)

Disinterestedness   A norm of the *scientific community* to be neutral, impartial, receptive, and open-minded to new ideas and not rigidly wedded to a particular point of view. (1)

Domain   Used in *domain analysis,* a cultural setting or site in which people regularly interact and develop a set of shared understandings or "mini-culture." (15)

Domain analysis   A method of *qualitative data* analysis in which a researcher describes a *domain* or sphere of cultural activities, using the ideas and *argot* of people in a *field site,* or creates his or her own ideas. The general categories in the domain are cover terms, and more specific observations in it are included terms. (15)

Double-barreled hypothesis   A *hypothesis* that has more than one *independent variable* and is stated in a confusing way that makes it unclear whether each *independent variable* separately has an effect or only the combination of both together has an effect on the *dependent variable*. (6)

Double-barreled question   A problem in *survey research* question wording that occurs when two ideas are combined into one question, and it is unclear whether the answer is for the combination of both or one or the other question. (10)

Double-blind experiment   A type of *experimental research* in which neither the *subjects* nor the person who directly deals with the *subjects* for the experimenter knows the specifics of the experiment. (9)

Download   A verb that means transferring a computer file from a distant or source computer to a local computer. (16)

Ecological fallacy   Something that appears to be a *causal explanation* but is not. It occurs because of a confusion about *units of analysis*. A researcher has *empirical* evidence about an *association* for large-scale units or huge aggregates, but *overgeneralizes* to make theoretical statements about an *association* among small-scale units or individuals. (6)

Ecological validity   A way to demonstrate the authenticity and trustworthiness of a *field research* study by showing that the researcher's descriptions of the *field site* match those of the members from the site and that the researcher was not a major disturbance. (13)

Effectiveness   Pertaining to how well programs achieve their stated objectives, how well these achieved objectives in turn actually solve problems or improve conditions for some designated target population. (14)

Elaboration paradigm   A system for describing patterns evident among tables when a *bivariate contingency table* is compared with *partials* after the *control variable* has been added. (12)

Empirical   Events and things that are observable and can be experienced through the human senses (e.g., touch, sight, hearing, smell, taste). (1)

Empirical generalization   A quasi-theoretical statement that summarizes findings or *empirical* regularities. It uses few if any abstract concepts and only makes a statement about a recurring pattern that researchers observe. (3)

Empirical hypothesis   A type of *hypothesis* in which the researcher expresses variables in specific *empirical* terms and expresses the *association* among the measured indicators in observable, *empirical* terms. (7)

Empowerment evaluation   A type of assessment that involves individuals, families, groups, and communities in the evaluation of their circumstances in regard to some intended interventions, programs, or policies with the goal of improving their life chances. (14)

Empty boxes A name for conceptual categories in an explanation that a researcher uses as part of the *illustrative method* of *qualitative data* analysis. (15)

Equivalence reliability *Reliability* across indicators; a measure that yields consistent results over multiple observers or indicators, assuming that all measure the same construct. (7)

Equivalent time-series design An *experimental design* in which there are several repeated *pretests, posttests,* and *treatments* for one group often over a period of time. (9)

Erosion measures *Nonreactive* measures of the wear or deterioration on surfaces due to the activity of people. (11)

Erotetic reasoning The logical process (sometimes also called preference logic) that decides exactly what is being evaluated (the topic), what is being compared (the *contrast class*) and what the implications are (what the *relevance relation* is). (14)

Error of segregation A mistake that can occur when writing qualitative research in which a writer separates concrete *empirical* details from abstract ideas too much. (16)

Ethnography An approach to *field research* that emphasizes providing a very detailed description of a different culture from the viewpoint of an insider in that culture in order to permit a greater understanding of it. (13) (14)

Ethnomethodology An approach to social science that combines philosophy, *social theory,* and method to study commonsense knowledge. Researchers using it study ordinary social interaction in small-scale settings to reveal the rules that people use to construct and maintain their everyday social reality. (13)

Evaluability assessment An organization's readiness for evaluation as determined by a set of procedures for deciding whether assessment is possible and likely to offer helpful information. (14)

Evaluation research A type of *applied research* in which one tries to determine how well a program or policy is working or reaching its goals and objectives. (2)

Event–structure analysis (ESA) A type of *qualitative data* analysis that forces a researcher to specify the links among a sequence of many events. It clarifies causal relationships by asking whether one event logically had to follow another, or it just happened to follow. (15)

Executive summary A summary of a research project's findings placed at the beginning of a report for an applied, nonspecialist audience. Usually, a little longer than an *abstract*. (16)

Exhaustive attributes The principle that response categories in a *scale* or other measure should provide a cat-

egory for all possible responses (i.e., every possible response fits into some category). (7)

Existing statistics research Research in which one examines numerical information from government documents or official reports to address new research questions. (2)

Experimental design Arranging the parts of an experiment and putting them together. (9)

Experimental group The group that receives the *treatment* in *experimental research*. (9)

Experimental realism *External validity* in which the experiment is made to feel realistic, so that experimental events have a real impact on *subjects*. (9)

Experimental research Research in which one intervenes or does something to one group of people but not to another, then compares results for the two groups. (2)

Experimenter expectancy A type of *reactivity* and threat to *internal validity* due to the experimenter indirectly making *subjects* aware of the *hypothesis* or desired results. (9)

Explanation pattern A pattern in the *elaboration paradigm* in which the *bivariate contingency table* shows a relationship, but the *partials* show no relationship and the *control variable* occurs prior to the *independent variable*. (12)

Explanatory research Research that focuses on why events occur or tries to test and build *social theory*. (2)

Exploratory research Research into an area that has not been studied and in which a researcher wants to develop initial ideas and a more focused research question. (2)

Expressed need The responses individual community or *target population* members make when they are asked to describe what their needs are. (14)

External consistency A way to achieve *reliability* of data in *field research* in which the researcher cross-checks and verifies *qualitative data* using multiple sources of information. (13)

External validity The ability to generalize from *experimental research* to settings or people that differ from the specific conditions of the study. (7)

Extreme case sampling A type of *nonrandom sample*, especially used by qualitative researchers, in which a researcher selects unusual or nonconforming cases purposely as a way to provide greater insight into social processes or a setting. (8)

Face sheet A page at the beginning of interview or field notes with information on the date, place of observations, interviews, the context, and so forth. (13)

Face validity A type of *measurement validity* in which an indicator "makes sense" as a measure of a construct in the judgment of others, especially those in the scientific community. (7)

Factorial design A type of *experimental design* that considers the impact of several *independent variables* simultaneously. (9)

Fallacy of misplaced concreteness When a person uses too many digits in a quantitative measure in an attempt to create the impression that the data are accurate or the researcher is highly capable. (11)

Felt need The individual subjective feelings people have about what they perceive to be a gap in expectations related to performance. (14)

Feminist research A type of *critical social science* that advocates *action-oriented research*. It views the social world as a web of social relations based on mutual obligations, and it rejects *positivism* as having many *assumptions* that are male oriented. (4)

Field experiment *Experimental research* that takes place in a natural setting. (9)

Field research A type of qualitative research in which a researcher directly observes the people being studied in a natural setting for an extended period. Often the researcher combines intense observing with participation in the people's social activities. (2)

Field site The one or more natural locations where a researcher conducts *field research*. (13)

First-order interpretation In qualitative research, what the people who are being studied actually feel and think. (6)

Floaters Respondents who lack a belief or opinion, but who give an answer anyway if asked in a *survey research* question. Often, their answers are inconsistent. (10)

Focus group A type of group interview in which an interviewer asks questions to the group, and answers are given in an open discussion among the group members. (10)

Folk domain A type of *domain* based on the *argot* and categories used by the people being studied in a *field site*. (15)

Formative evaluation research *Evaluation research* that occurs throughout the process of a program or policy being evaluated. (2) (14)

Freewriting A very early step in the writing process in which the writer tries to get his or her ideas down on paper as quickly as possible, not worrying about grammar or spelling. (16)

Freeze outs When one or more people being studied in *field research* refuse to cooperate with the researcher or to become involved in the study. (13)

Frequency distribution A table that shows the distribution of cases into the categories of one variable (i.e., the number or percentage of cases in each category). (12)

Frequency polygon A graph of connected points showing the distribution of how many cases fall into each category of a variable. (12)

Fronts When one or more people in a *field site* engage in actions and say things that give an impression or appearance that differs from what is actually occurring. (13)

Full-filter question A type of *survey research* question in which respondents are first asked whether they have an opinion or know about a topic, then only the respondents with an opinion or knowledge are asked a specific question on the topic. (10)

Functional theory A type of *social theory* based on biological analogies, in which the social world or its parts are seen as systems, with its parts serving the needs of the system. (3)

Funnel sequence A way to order *survey research* questions in a *questionnaire* from general to specific ones. (10)

Gap effectiveness How well a social work intervention or program closes the distance between a pre-intervention level and a targeted amount of improvement in the condition targeted for change. (14)

Gatekeeper A person in an official or unofficial role who controls access to a setting. (13)

General Social Survey (GSS) A survey of a *random sample* of about 1,500 U.S. adults that has been conducted in most years between 1972 and the present and is available for many researchers to analyze. (11)

Go native What happens when a researcher in *field research* gets overly involved and loses all distance or objectivity and becomes like the people being studied. (13)

Grounded theory *Social theory* that is rooted in observations of specific, concrete details. (3)

Guilty knowledge When a researcher in *field research* learns of illegal, unethical, or immoral actions by the people in the *field site* that are not widely known. (13)

Guttman scaling A *scale* that researchers use after data are collected to reveal whether a hierarchical pattern exists among responses, such that people who give responses at a "higher level" also tend to give "lower-level" ones. (7)

Halo effect   A tendency to allow the positive reputation of people, places, or things to "rub off" or color thinking and judgments instead of remaining neutral. (1)

Haphazard sampling   A type of *nonrandom sampling* in which the researcher selects anyone he or she happens to come across. (8)

Hawthorne effect   An effect of *reactivity* named after a famous case in which *subjects* reacted to the fact that they were in an experiment more than they reacted to the *treatment.* (9)

Hermeneutics   An approach that was originally used to study a written text both in detail and as a whole to enable people to see the deeper meanings contained within it. The approach was expanded in *interpretive social science* to be a method for developing a deeper understanding of events in the social world. (4)

Hidden populations   People who engage in clandestine, deviant, or concealed activities and who are difficult to locate and study. (8)

Hierarchy of credibility   In *field research,* a researcher who learns much about weaker members of society whose views are rarely heard often gets accused of "bias" when presenting findings. At the same time, opposing views presented by powerful people are accepted as "unbiased" simply because of their high social status. (13)

Historical–comparative research   Research in which one examines different cultures or periods to better understand the social world. (2)

Historical review   A literature review in which the writer traces the development of a concept, *social theory,* or set of findings over time. (16)

History effect   A threat to *internal validity* due to something that occurs and affects the *dependent variable* during an experiment, but which is unplanned and outside the control of the experimenter. (9)

Hypothesis   The statement from a *causal explanation* or a *proposition* that has at least one *independent* and one *dependent variable,* but it has yet to be *empirically* tested. (6)

Ideal type   A pure model about an idea, process, or event. One develops it to think about it more clearly and systematically. It is used both as a method of *qualitative data* analysis and in *social theory* building. (3)

Ideographic   An approach that focuses on creating detailed descriptions of specific events in particular time periods and settings. It rarely goes beyond *empirical generalizations* to abstract *social theory* or *causal laws.* (4)

Illustrative method   A method of *qualitative data* analysis in which a researcher takes the concepts of a *social theory* or explanation and treats them as *empty boxes* to be filled with *empirical* examples and descriptions. (15)

Impact evaluation   The assessment used by agency administrators or policymakers in determining the effect of a social work program, law, or policy on the relevant *target population.* (14)

Independence   The absence of a *statistical relationship* between two variables (i.e., when knowing the values on one variable provides no information about the values that will be found on another variable). There is no *association* between them. (12)

Independent variable   The first variable that causes or produces the effect in a *causal explanation.* (6)

Index   The summing or combining of many separate measures of a construct or variable. (7)

Inductive approach   An approach to inquiry or *social theory* in which one begins with concrete *empirical* details, then works toward abstract ideas or general principles. (3)

Inferential statistics   A branch of applied mathematics or statistics based on a *random sample.* It lets a researcher make precise statements about the level of confidence he or she has in the results of a *sample* being equal to the *population parameter.* (8)

Informed consent   A statement, usually written, in which people in a research project learn basic aspects about the project and formally agree to participate. (5)

Input   Resources that can be consumed (such as material and supplies), services that support production (heat, light, space, rentals, computer time), and the effort and labor of social workers and staff who use these resources to produce outputs. (14)

Institutional Review Board (IRB)   A committee at U.S. colleges, hospitals, and research institutes that is required by federal law to ensure that research involving humans is conducted in a responsible, ethical manner. (5)

Instrumental orientation   A view of the world that is "means–ends" oriented. In it, the value of an activity, event, or object primarily depends on whether a person can use it to accomplish some other purpose or goal; it has little intrinsic value in itself. (4)

Integrative review   A type of literature review in which the writer blends together several past lines of inquiry into a coherent whole. (16)

Interaction effect   The effect of two *independent variables* that operate simultaneously together. The effect of the variables together is greater than what would occur from a simple addition of the effects from each. The variables operate together on one another to create an extra "boost." (9)

Intercoder reliability   The agreement among or dependability of several different *content analysis* coders. A type of *equivalence reliability.* (7)

Internal validity   The ability of experimenters to strengthen a *causal explanation's* logical rigor by eliminating potential alternative explanations for an *association* between the *treatment* and the *dependent variable* through an *experimental design.* (7)

Interpretation pattern   A pattern in the *elaboration paradigm* in which the *bivariate contingency table* shows a relationship, but the *partials* show no relationship and the *control variable* is intervening in the *causal explanation.* (12)

Interpretive social science (ISS)   An approach to social science that focuses on achieving an understanding of how people create and maintain their social worlds. (4)

Interrupted time series   An *experimental design* in which the *dependent variable* is measured periodically across many time points, and the *treatment* occurs in the midst of such measures, often only once. (9)

Intersubjectivity   The idea that different people will agree on what they observe in the *empirical* world through careful use of their senses (e.g., touch, sight, hearing, etc.). (4)

Interval level of measurement   A *level of measurement* that identifies differences among variable *attributes,* ranks, and categories, and that measures distance between categories, but there is no true zero. (7)

Intervening variable   A variable that is between the initial causal variable and the final effect variable in a *causal explanation.* (6)

Interview schedule   The name of a *survey research questionnaire* when a telephone or face-to-face interview is used. (10)

Jargon   A language and set of terms used by a group of people with specialized knowledge or expertise to communicate more quickly and effectively with one another. It may be used inappropriately when experts fail to translate their ideas into ordinary terms for nonspecialists or when people are trying to give an impression that they are experts. (3)

Jotted notes   In *field research,* what a researcher inconspicuously writes while in the *field site* on whatever is convenient in order to "jog the memory" later. (13)

Keyword   A term or word with substantive meaning in a title or about a topic that a researcher uses to locate literature or sources related to a topic. (16)

Laboratory experiment   *Experimental research* that takes place in an artificial setting over which the experimenter has great control. (9)

Latent coding   A type of *content analysis* coding in which a researcher identifies subjective meaning such as general themes or motifs in a communication medium. (11)

Latin square design   An *experimental design* used to examine whether the order or sequence in which *subjects* receive multiple versions of the *treatment* has an effect. (9)

Law of comparative judgment   A "law" used in *Thurstone scaling* that says if many people independently compare and rank a set of items, researchers can treat the items on which most people subjectively agree and give a similar rank as being at an *interval level of measurement.* (7)

Level of abstraction   A characteristic of concepts or thoughts about social reality. They range from the very concrete and *empirical* to the very abstract. (3)

Level of analysis   A way to talk about the scope of a *social theory, causal explanation, proposition, hypothesis,* or theoretical statement. The range of phenomena it covers, or to which it applies, goes from social–psychological (*micro level*) to organizational (*meso level*) to large-scale social structure (*macro level*). (6)

Level of measurement   A system that organizes the information in the measurement of variables into four general levels, from *nominal level* to *ratio level.* (7)

Level of statistical significance   A set of numbers researchers use as a simple way to measure the degree to which a *statistical relationship* results from random factors rather than the existence of a true relationship among variables. (12)

Life-history interview   An open-ended interview, usually recorded, with one person who describes his or her entire life. It often has therapeutic benefits for the person interviewed and creates *qualitative data* on the life cycle. It can be considered a subtype of oral history. (13)

Likert scale   A *scale* often used in *survey research* in which people express attitudes or other responses in terms of several *ordinal-level* categories (e.g., agree, disagree) that are ranked along a continuum. (7)

Linear relationship   An *association* between two variables that is positive or negative across the *attributes* or levels of the variables. When plotted in a *scattergram,* the basic pattern of the *association* forms a straight line, not a curve or other pattern. (12)

Linear research path   Research that proceeds in a clear, logical, step-by-step straight line. It is more characteristic of a quantitative than a qualitative approach to social research. (6)

Logic of disconfirming hypothesis   The basis of the *null hypothesis*. It is the idea that it is easier to find *empirical* evidence that supports an *association* than evidence against it. It means that when testing a *causal explanation,* researchers try to find evidence that fails to support an association, and not just evidence that supports it. (6)

Logic in practice   A logic of doing social work research based on having informal discussions among active researchers about how to do social work research. It grows from how the researchers addressed practical problems in specific studies they conducted, it is taught largely by an apprenticeship method, and it is most used in a qualitative style of research. (6)

Logic model   A graphic presentation using boxes and arrows to show basic program components and linkages between program efforts (or inputs) and outputs or outcomes. (14)

Longitudinal research   Any research that examines more than one time point. (2)

Macro level   *Social theories* and explanations about more abstract, large-scale, and broad-scope aspects of social reality, such as social change in major institutions (e.g., the family, education, etc.) in a whole nation across several decades. (3)

Manifest coding   A type of *content analysis coding* in which a researcher first develops a list of specific words, phrases, or symbols, then finds them in a communication medium. (11)

Marginals   The totals in a *contingency table,* outside the *body of a table.* (12)

Marker   A passing reference made by a person in a *field site* that actually indicates a very important event or feeling. (13)

Matrix question   A type of *survey research* question in which a set of questions is listed in a compact form together, all questions sharing the same set of answer categories. (10)

Maturation   A threat to *internal validity* in *experimental research* due to natural processes of growth, boredom, and so on, that occur among *subjects* during the experiment and affect the *dependent variable.* (9)

Mean   A measure of central tendency for one variable that indicates the arithmetic average (i.e., the sum of all scores divided by the total number of scores). (12)

Meaningful social action   The type of actions that people engage in for subjective reasons or to which other people in a social setting attach significance. (4)

Measurement validity   How well an *empirical* indicator and the *conceptual definition* of the construct that the indicator is supposed to measure "fit" together. (7)

Mechanical model of man   A view of people embraced by some *positivists* in which researchers can develop *social theories* and explanations that are based on careful observations of people's external behaviors and their responses to outside forces alone (i.e., without any reference to a mind or consciousness). (4)

Median   A measure of central tendency for one variable indicating the point or score at which half the cases are higher and half are lower. (12)

Member validation   A way to demonstrate the authenticity and trustworthiness of a *field research* study by having the people who were studied (i.e., members) read and confirm as being true that which the researcher has reported. (13)

Meso level   *Social theories* and explanations about the middle level of social reality between a broad and narrow scope, such as the development and operation of social organizations, communities, or social movements over a five-year period. (3)

Meta-analysis   A special type of literature review in which a writer organizes the results from many studies and uses statistical techniques to identify common findings in them. (16)

Method of agreement   A method of *qualitative data* analysis in which a researcher compares characteristics that are similar across a group of cases, and where the cases share a significant outcome. (15)

Method of difference   A method of *qualitative data* analysis in which a researcher compares the characteristics among cases, and where only some cases share a significant outcome, while others do not. (15)

Methodological review   A type of literature review in which the writer shows how the research design and techniques used to study a topic differ and accounts for discrepancies in findings due to the method used in studies. (16)

Micro level   *Social theories* and explanations about the concrete, small-scale, and narrow level of reality, such as face-to-face interaction in small groups during a two-month period. (3)

Milgram's obedience study   A famous experiment that highlighted the issue of protecting *subjects* from psychological harm. In the study, the experimenter instructed *subjects* to administer increasingly intense electric shocks to another person for failing to learn. Many *subjects* became upset and falsely believed that they had caused severe physical harm to an innocent person. (5)

Mixed domain   A type of *domain* that combines the *argot* and categories of members under study and the categories developed by a researcher for analysis. (15)

Mode   A measure of central tendency for one variable that indicates the most frequent or common score. (12)

Models of relevance   A set of *ideal type* ways that social researchers understand the purpose for conducting research and the proper use of research results. (5)

Mortality   Threats to *internal validity* due to *subjects* failing to participate through the entire experiment. (9)

Multiple indicators   Many procedures or instruments that indicate, or provide evidence of, the presence or level of a variable in *empirical* reality. Researchers use the combination of several together to measure a variable. (7)

Mundane realism   A type of *external validity* in which the experiment is real, such as settings or situations outside a lab setting. (9)

Mutually exclusive attributes   The principle that response categories in a *scale* or other measure should be organized so that a person's responses fit into only one category (i.e., categories should not overlap). (7)

Natural history   A way a researcher can demonstrate the authenticity and trustworthiness of a *field research* study by fully disclosing his or her actions and procedures in depth as they occurred over time. (13)

Naturalism   The principle that researchers should examine events as they occur in natural, everyday ongoing social settings. (13)

Needs assessment   *Applied research* in which one collects data to identify problems that require attention and considers the extent and severity of the problems. (2)

Negative evidence   In the analysis of *qualitative data,* when a researcher fails to find *empirical* data on a specific issue, but logically expects such evidence based on all other evidence and the *social theory* that the researcher is using. (15)

Negative relationship   An *association* between two variables such that as values on one variable increase, values on the other variable fall or decrease. (3)

Net effect   The effect of one variable (usually *independent*) on another (usually *dependent*) after the impact of one or more *control variables* that affects both has been taken into consideration and statistically removed. (12)

Network theory   A type of *social theory* in which the logic of explanation is not a *causal explanation* with *linear relationships*. Instead, the logic is one of branching out or a set of interlocked linkages around a central core, as a spider web. (3)

Nominal-level measurement   The lowest, least precise *level of measurement* for which there is a difference only in type among the categories of a variable. (7)

Nomothetic   An approach based on laws or one that operates according to a system of laws. (4)

Nonlinear research path   Research that proceeds in a circular, back-and-forth manner. It is more characteristic of a qualitative than a quantitative style to social research. (6)

Nonrandom sample   A type of *sample* in which the *sampling elements* are selected using something other than a mathematically random process. (8)

Nonreactive   Measures in which people being studied are unaware that they are in a study. (11)

Normal distribution   A "bell-shaped" frequency polygon for a distribution of cases, with a peak in the center and identical curving slopes on either side of the center. It is the distribution of many naturally occurring phenomena and is a basis of much statistical theory. (12)

Normalize social research   Techniques in *field research* used by researchers to make the people being studied feel more comfortable with the research process and to help them accept the researcher's presence. (13)

Normative need   A specified amount of well being for some *target population* that is described according to an acceptable standard or benchmark. (14)

Novelty effect   An effect that occurs when *subjects* respond because something is new, different, or surprising. (9)

Null hypothesis   A *hypothesis* that says there is no relationship or *association* between two variables, or no effect. (6)

Nuremberg code   An international code of what constitutes moral, ethical behavior that was the beginning of *codes of ethics* for human research. It was adopted after the war crime trials of World War II in response to inhumane Nazi medical experiments. (5)

One-shot case study   An *experimental design* with only an *experimental group* and a *posttest,* no *pretest.* (9)

Open coding   A first *coding* of *qualitative data* in which a researcher examines the data to condense them into preliminary analytic categories or codes for analyzing the data. (15)

Open-ended question   A type of *survey research* question in which respondents are free to offer any answer they wish to the question. (10)

Operational definition   The definition of a variable in terms of the specific activities to measure or indicate it in the *empirical* world. (7)

Operationalization   The process of moving from the *conceptual definition* of a construct to a set of specific activities or measures that allow a researcher to observe it *empirically* (i.e., its *operational definition*). (7)

Optical scan sheet   A sheet with organized spaces or dots that one can fill in, usually with a pencil. A special machine can read information from it into a computer. (12)

Order effects   An effect in *survey research* in which respondents hear some specific questions before others, and the earlier questions affect their answers to later questions. (10)

Ordinal-level measurement   A *level of measurement* that identifies a difference among categories of a variable and allows the categories to be rank ordered. (7)

Organized skepticism   A norm of the *scientific community* not to accept a new idea or evidence in a carefree, uncritical manner, but to question and subject it to intense scrutiny. (1)

Outcropping   An aspect of *qualitative data* a researcher recognizes as representing some part of the underlying social structure. (15)

Output   The intended consequences of interventions or programs expressed in quantifiable units such as the number or amount of families who successfully resettle in neighborhoods after receiving services from shelters serving families who are homeless. (14)

Overgeneralization   The acceptance of broad statements about the social world based on a narrow perspective or very few cases. (1)

Panel study   *Longitudinal research* in which the same cases or people are observed at multiple points in time. (2)

Paradigm   A general organizing framework for *social theory* and *empirical* research. It includes basic *assumptions,* major questions to be answered, models of good research practice and theory, and methods for finding the answers to questions. (4)

Parameter   A characteristic of the entire *population* that is estimated from a *sample.* (8)

Paraphrasing   When a writer restates or rewords the ideas of another person, giving proper credit to the original source. (16)

Parsimony   The idea that simple is better. Everything else being equal, a *social theory* or argument that can explain more with less complexity is best. (3)

Partially open question   A type of *survey research* question in which respondents are given a fixed set of answers to choose from, but in addition, an "other" category is offered so that they can specify a different answer. (10)

Partials   In *contingency tables* for three variables, tables that show the *association* between the *independent* and *dependent variables* for each category of a *control variable.* (12)

Percentile   A measure of dispersion for one variable that indicates the percentage of cases at or below a score or point. (12)

Performance evaluation   An evaluative strategy that provides feedback on how a program or series of interventions is operating and to what extent intended objectives are being attained. (14)

Pie chart   A display of numerical information on one variable that divides a circle into fractions by lines representing the proportion of cases in the variable's *attributes.* (12)

Placebo   A false *treatment* or one that has no effect in an experiment. It is sometimes called a "sugar pill" that a *subject* mistakes for a true *treatment.* (9)

Placebo effect   A type of *reactivity* that occurs when *subjects* do not receive the real *treatment.* Instead, they receive a *placebo,* but they respond as if they had received the real *treatment.* (9)

Plagiarism   A type of unethical behavior in which one uses the writings or ideas of another without giving proper credit. It is "stealing ideas." (5)

Planning, Programming, and Budgeting System (PPBS)   A type of *evaluation research* first used by the U.S. Department of Defense, which measures program success based on its costs and efficiency at reaching preset goals and objectives. (2)

Population   The name for the large general group of many cases from which a researcher draws a *sample* and which is usually stated in theoretical terms. (8)

Positive relationship   An *association* between two variables such that as values on one increase, values on the other also increase. (3)

Positivism   See *Positivist social science.*

Positivist social science   An approach to social science that combines a *deductive approach* with precise measurement of *quantitative data* so researchers can discover and confirm *causal laws* that will permit *predictions* about human behavior. (4)

Possible code cleaning   Cleaning data using a computer in which the researcher looks for responses or answer categories that cannot have cases. (12)

Postmodern research   A very radical approach to social research that eliminates the distinction between artistic expression or subjective experience and science. It deconstructs or takes apart surface appearances; rejects logical reasoning and the ideal that a universal truth exists; and denies the idea of progress or a movement toward more knowledge. (4)

Posttest   The measurement of the *dependent variable* in *experimental research* after the *treatment*. (9)

Postulate of adequacy   An idea from *interpretive social science* that for an explanation to be true, the people being studied can understand it, and it "makes sense" to them. (4)

Practical orientation   An approach to *social theory* that focuses on getting ordinary things accomplished in the "real" world of common, everyday affairs. (4)

Praxis   An idea in *critical social science* that *social theory* and everyday practice interact or work together, mutually affecting one another. This interaction can promote social change. (4)

Prediction   A statement about something that is likely to occur in the future. (3)

Predictive validity   *Measurement validity* that relies on the occurrence of a future event or behavior that is logically consistent to verify the indicator of a construct. (7)

Preexperimental designs   *Experimental designs* that lack *random assignment* or use shortcuts and are much weaker than the *classical experimental design*. They may be substituted in situations wherein an experimenter cannot use all the features of a *classical experimental design*, but they have weaker *internal validity*. (9)

Premature closure   A tendency to accept information quickly, failing to investigate it to the degree of depth demanded by scientific standards. (1)

Prestige bias   A problem in *survey research* question writing that occurs when a highly respected group or individual is linked to one of the answers. (10)

Pretest   The measurement of the *dependent variable* of an experiment prior to the *treatment*. (9)

Principal investigator (PI)   The person who is primarily in charge of research on a project that is sponsored or funded by an organization. (16)

Principle of voluntary consent   An ethical principle of social research that people should never participate in research unless they first explicitly agree to do so. (5)

Probability proportionate to size (PPS)   An adjustment made in *cluster sampling* when each cluster does not have the same number of *sampling elements*. (8)

Probe   A follow-up question or action in *survey research* used by an interviewer to have a respondent clarify or elaborate on an incomplete or inappropriate answer. (10)

Productivity assessment   An evaluative analysis that looks at the effort it takes, or outputs compared to (divided by) inputs, to help spot problem areas or warn of early deficiencies in an intervention or program. (14)

Project Camelot   A controversial research project funded by the U.S. Army in the 1960s that highlights a violation of the *principle of voluntary consent* and of a principle to show respect for people in a host country in comparative research. In the study, American researchers secretly studied political protest by peasants and the poor in Chile. (5)

Proposition   A basic statement in *social theory* that two ideas or variables are related to one another. It can be true or false (e.g., most sex offenders were themselves sexually abused when growing up), conditional (e.g., if a foreign enemy threatens, then the people of a nation will feel much stronger social solidarity), and/or causal (e.g., poverty causes crime). (3)

Pseudonyms   In *field research*, false or made-up names researchers put in field notes to protect the identity of the people they study. (13)

Pseudoscience   Ideas or information presented with the *jargon* and outward appearance of science to win acceptance, but which lacks the systematic rigor of the scientific method. (1)

Purposive sampling   A type of *nonrandom sample* in which the researcher uses a wide range of methods to locate all possible cases of a highly specific and difficult-to-reach *population*. (8)

Qualitative data   Information in the form of words, pictures, sounds, visual images, or objects. (1)

Quantitative data   Information in the form of numbers. (1)

Quasi-experimental designs   *Experimental designs* that are stronger than *preexperimental designs*. They are variations on the *classical experimental design* that an experimenter uses in special situations or when an experimenter has limited control over the *independent variable*. (9)

Quasi-filter question   A type of *survey research* question including the answer choice "no opinion" or "don't know." (10)

Questionnaire   A written document in *survey research* that has a set of questions given to respondents or used by an interviewer to ask questions and record the answers. (10)

Quota sampling   A type of *nonrandom sample* in which the researcher first identifies general categories into which cases or people will be selected, then he or she selects a predetermined number of cases in each category. (8)

Random assignment Dividing *subjects* into groups at the beginning of *experimental research* using a random process, so the experimenter can treat the groups as equivalent. (9)

Random-digit dialing (RDD) A method of randomly selecting cases for telephone interviews that uses all possible telephone numbers as a *sampling frame.* (8)

Random-number table A list of numbers that has no pattern in it and that is used to create a random process for selecting cases and other randomization purposes. (8)

Random sample A type of *sample* in which the researcher uses a *random-number table* or similar mathematical random process so that each *sampling element* in the *population* will have an equal probability of being selected. (8)

Randomized response technique (RRT) A specialized technique in *survey research* that is used for very sensitive topics. With it, a respondent randomly receives a question without the interviewer being aware of the question the respondent is answering. (10)

Range A measure of dispersion for one variable indicating the highest and lowest scores. (12)

Ratio-level measurement The highest, most precise *level of measurement* for which variable *attributes* can be rank ordered, the distance between the *attributes* can be precisely measured, and an absolute zero exists. (7)

Reactivity The general threat to *external validity* that arises because *subjects* are aware that they are in an experiment and being studied. (9)

Recency effect An effect in *survey research* that occurs when respondents tend to choose the last answer response offered. (10)

Reconstructed logic A logic of doing research based on reorganizing the practices and ideas for doing good research into a set of coherent, systematic, formal rules and techniques. Researchers standardize the rules and techniques, codify them in textbooks, and teach them by formal instruction. It is used more often in the quantitative research style. (6)

Recording sheet Pages on which a researcher writes down what is coded in *content analysis.* (11)

Reductionism Something that appears to be a *causal explanation,* but is not, because of a confusion about *units of analysis.* A researcher has *empirical* evidence for an association at the level of individual behavior or very small-scale units, but *overgeneralizes* to make theoretical statements about very large-scale units. (6)

Relational position An idea proposed by Karl Mannheim that professional academic researchers and free intellectuals occupy a unique social position. They are detached from the major groups in society, which puts them in the best position to develop unbiased knowledge about all social groups and issues. (5)

Relativism The idea that there is no single correct way to do things or correct values; rather, every value or point of view is valid for those who hold it. (4)

Relevance relation In erotetic reasoning, the decision as to what the topic and contrast class refer to. (401)

Reliability The dependability or consistency of the measure of a variable. (7)

Replication pattern A pattern in the *elaboration paradigm* in which the *partials* show the same relationship as in a *bivariate contingency table* of the *independent* and *dependent variable* alone. (12)

Representative reliability *Reliability* across groups or subpopulations; a measure that yields consistent results across different social groups. (7)

Request for proposal (RFP) An announcement by a funding organization that it is willing to fund research and it is soliciting written plans of research projects. (16)

Research fraud A type of unethical behavior in which a researcher fakes or creates false data, or falsely reports on the research procedure. (5)

Response set An effect in *survey research* when respondents tend to agree with every question in a series rather than thinking through their answer to each question. (10)

Rewriting A step in the writing process in which the writer goes over a previous draft to improve communication of ideas and clarity of expression. (16)

Rules of correspondence Rules that researchers use to reduce the gap between the abstract constructs and the specific measurement operations they use in concrete social reality. (7)

Sample A smaller set of cases a researcher selects from a larger pool and generalizes to the *population.* (8)

Sampling distribution A distribution created by drawing many *random samples* from the same *population.* (8)

Sampling element The name for a case or single unit to be selected. (8)

Sampling error How much a *sample* deviates from being representative of the *population.* (8)

Sampling frame A list of cases in a *population,* or the best approximation of it. (8)

Sampling interval The inverse of the *sampling ratio,* which is used in *systematic sampling* to select cases. (8)

Sampling ratio   The number of cases in the *sample* divided by the number of cases in the *population* or the *sampling frame,* or the proportion of the *population* in the *sample.* (8)

Scale   A type of *quantitative data* measure often used in *survey research* that captures the intensity, direction, level, or potency of a variable construct along a continuum. Most are at the *ordinal level* of measurement. (7)

Scattergram   A diagram to display the *statistical relationship* between two variables based on plotting each case's values for both of the variables. (12)

Scholarly journal article   The primary form in which new research is publicly communicated and made available within the *scientific community.* (1)

Scientific attitude   A way of thinking about and looking at the world that reflects a commitment to the norms and values of the *scientific community.* (1)

Scientific community   A collection of people who share a system of rules and attitudes that sustain the process of producing scientific knowledge. (1)

Scientific method   The process of creating new knowledge using the ideas, techniques, and rules of the *scientific community.* (1)

Scientific misconduct   When someone engages in *research fraud, plagiarism,* or other unethical conduct that significantly deviates from the accepted practice for conducting and reporting research within the *scientific community.* (5)

Search engine   Specialized software to search the Internet using *keywords* or other information. They return a list of possible web pages or matching sites. (16)

Secondary analysis research   Research in which one does not gather data oneself, but reexamines data previously gathered by someone else and asks new questions. (2)

Second-order interpretation   In qualitative research, what a researcher believes the people being studied feel and think. (6)

Selection bias   A threat to *internal validity* when groups in an experiment are not equivalent at the beginning of the experiment. (9)

Selective coding   A last pass at *coding qualitative data* in which a researcher examines previous codes to identify and select illustrative data that will support the conceptual *coding* categories that he or she developed. (15)

Selective observation   The tendency to take notice of certain people or events, based on past experience or attitudes. (1)

Self-study review   A type of literature review in which a student demonstrates his or her familiarity with past research to other people, usually teachers. (16)

Semantic differential   A *scale* in which people are presented with a topic or object and a list of many polar opposite adjectives or adverbs. They are to indicate their feelings by marking one of several spaces between two adjectives or adverbs. (7)

Separation of inference   In *field research,* the researcher writes *direct observation notes* in a way that keeps what he or she actually observed separate from what he or she infers or believes occurred. (13)

Sequential sampling   A type of *nonrandom sampling* in which a researcher tries to find as many relevant cases as possible, until time, financial resources, or his/her energy are exhausted, or until there is no new information or diversity from the cases. (8)

Serendipity   The idea that chance occurrences or unexpected things can happen that reveal much about the social world. (2)

Simple random sampling   A type of *random sampling* in which a researcher creates a *sampling frame* and uses a pure random process to select cases. Each *sampling element* in the *population* will have an equal probability of being selected. (8)

Single-case design   A clinical evaluative strategy that uses the logic of experimental design to assess improvement for one person in regard to a targeted behavior over a relatively short period of time. (14)

Skewed distribution   A distribution of cases among the categories of a variable that is not *normal* (i.e., not a "bell shape"). Instead of an equal number of cases on both ends, more are at one of the extremes. (12)

Sleeper questions   *Survey research* questions about nonexistent people or events to check whether respondents are being truthful, or questions that appear more than once and are used to check a respondent's consistency. (10)

Snowball sampling   A type of *nonrandom sampling* in which the researcher begins with one case, then, based on information about interrelationships from that case, identifies other cases, and then repeats the process again and again. (8)

Social desirability bias   A bias in *survey research* in which respondents give a "normative" response or a socially acceptable answer rather than give a truthful answer. (10)

Social impact assessment   *Applied research* that documents the consequences for various areas of social life that are likely to result from introducing a major change in a community. (2)

Social theory A set of interconnected ideas that condense, systematize, and organize knowledge about the social world. (1)

Sociogram A diagram or "map" that shows the network of social relationships, influence patterns, or communication paths among a group of people or units. (8)

Solomon four-group design An *experimental design* in which *subjects* are randomly assigned to two *control groups* and two *experimental groups*. Only one *experimental group* and one *control group* receive a *pretest*. All four groups receive a *posttest*. (9)

Specification pattern A pattern in the *elaboration paradigm* in which the *bivariate contingency table* shows a relationship. One of the *partial tables* shows the relationship, but other tables do not. (12)

Split-half method A method for examining *equivalence reliability* that compares subsets of indicators. (7)

Spuriousness What a statement has when it appears to be a *causal explanation*, but is not because of a hidden, unmeasured, or initially unseen variable. The unseen variable comes earlier in the *temporal order*, and it has a causal impact on what was initially posited to be the *independent* variable as well as the *dependent variable*. (6)

Stability reliability *Reliability* across time; a measure that yields consistent results over different time points, assuming what one is measuring does not itself change. (7)

Stakeholders All those whose interests are affected by a program or policy decision, including clients, caseworkers, administrators, funders, policymakers, and community members. (14)

Standard deviation A measure of dispersion for one variable that indicates an average distance between the scores and the *mean*. (12)

Standard-format question A type of *survey research* question in which the answer categories fail to include "no opinion" or "don't know." (10)

Standardization The procedure to statistically adjust measures to permit making an honest comparison by giving a common basis to measures of different units. (7)

Static group comparison An *experimental design* with two groups, no *random assignment*, and only a *posttest*. (9)

Statistic A numerical estimate of a *population parameter* computed from a *sample*. (8)

Statistical Abstract of the United States A U.S. government publication that appears annually and con-tains an extensive compilation of statistical tables and information. (11)

Statistical relationship Expressing whether two or more variables affect one another based on the use of elementary applied mathematics (i.e., whether there is an *association* between them or *independence*). (12)

Statistical significance A way to discuss the likelihood that a finding or *statistical relationship* in a *sample* is due to random factors rather than due to the existence of an actual relationship in the entire *population*. (12)

Statistical validity Proper use of statistical techniques. This includes meeting all *assumptions* of the technique, selecting the appropriate technique for a purpose, performing all calculations correctly, and interpreting results in a manner that is fully consistent with the strengths and weaknesses of the technique. (7)

Stratified sampling A type of *random sampling* in which the researcher first identifies a set of *mutually exclusive* and *exhaustive* categories, then uses a random selection method to select cases for each category. (8)

Structural question A type of question in *field research* interviews in which the researcher attempts to verify the correctness of placing terms or events into the categories of the meaning system used by people being studied. (13)

Structured observation A method of watching what is happening in a social setting that is highly organized and that follows systematic rules for observation and documentation. (11)

Subjects The name for people who are studied and participate in *experimental research*. (9)

Subpopulation analysis A method for examining the *representative reliability* of a measure that compares measurements across different groups. (7)

Successive approximation A method of *qualitative data* analysis in which the researcher repeatedly moves back and forth between the *empirical data* and the abstract concepts, theories, or models. (15)

Summative evaluation research A type of *evaluation research* that occurs after a program or policy being evaluated ends. (2) (14)

Suppressor-variable pattern A pattern in the *elaboration paradigm* in which no relationship appears in a *bivariate contingency table*, but the *partials* show a relationship between the variables. (12)

Survey research Quantitative social work research in which one systematically asks many people the same questions, then records and analyzes their answers. (2)

Synchronous   A type of communication that occurs at the same time and in the same place (live). (2)

Systematic sampling   A type of *random sampling* in which a researcher selects every *k*th (e.g., 12th) case in the *sampling frame* using a *sampling interval*. (8)

Target population (A)   The name for the large general group of many cases from which a *sample* is drawn and which is specified in very concrete terms. (8)

Target population (B)   All those who are intended to receive benefits or intervention services from a program or policy. (8)

Tautology   A statement that appears to be a *causal explanation*, but is not, because the *dependent variable* is really only a restatement of the *independent variable;* it is true "by definition." (6)

Tearoom Trade study   A famous *field research* study that highlighted the issues of *anonymity* and *confidentiality*. In the study, the researcher covertly observed sexual contact among male homosexuals in a public restroom. Later, the researcher located the men at home and interviewed them in a disguise. (5)

Technocratic perspective   An orientation toward social work research in which the researcher accepts with little or no question the research questions as government officials, corporate leaders, or bureaucratic superiors formulate them. The researcher then conducts studies, often *applied research,* that will provide the officials with information to help them make decisions in a bureaucratic organization. (6)

Teleology   A statement that appears to be a *causal explanation*, but is not, because it cannot be tested *empirically*. The *independent variable* is an amorphous idea, a long-term goal, a future intention, or characteristic of an entire system. It usually lacks a clear *temporal order* prior to the *dependent variable*. (6)

Telescoping   When *survey research* respondents compress time when answering about past events. They overreport recent events and underreport distant past ones. (10)

Temporal order   The simple but powerful idea that some events occur earlier in time than other events, which is used in evaluating a *causal explanation*. (3)

Test–retest method   A method for examining *stability reliability* that compares measurements taken at different times. (7)

Text   A general name for symbolic meaning within a communication medium measured in *content analysis*. (11)

Theoretical review   A type of literature review in which the writer traces the development and elaboration of a concept, *social theory,* or theoretical framework. (16)

Theoretical sampling   A type of *nonrandom sampling* in which the researcher selects specific times, locations, or events to observe in order to develop a *social theory* or evaluate theoretical ideas. (8)

Thick description   In *qualitative data* collection, the researcher's attempt to capture all the details of a social setting in a highly detailed description to capture and convey an intimate feel for the setting and the inner lives of people in it. (13)

Third-order interpretation   In qualitative research, what a researcher tells the reader of a research report that the people he or she studied felt and thought. (6)

Threatening question   A type of *survey research* question in which respondents are likely to cover up or lie about their true behavior or beliefs because they fear a loss of self-image or that they may appear to be undesirable or deviant. (10)

Thurstone scaling   A *scale* in which the researcher gives a group of judges many items and asks them to sort the items into categories along a continuum, then looks at sorting results to select items on which the judges are in agreement. (7)

Time-series research   Any research that takes place over time, in which different people or cases may be looked at in each time point. (2)

Total Design Method (TDM)   An overall approach to writing *survey research* questions and interviewing in which a researcher makes participation as easy as possible and increases the response rate by giving respondents a feeling of importance. (10)

Transcendent perspective   An orientation toward research in which the researcher develops research questions based on independent judgment or the concerns of the people being studied. The researcher moves beyond current arrangements and tries to assist the people being studied in gaining greater understanding and control over their lives. (6)

Treatment   What the *independent variable* in *experimental research* is called. (9)

Triangulation   A term borrowed from surveying the land that says looking at an object from several different points gives a more accurate view of it. (6)

Trickstering   A strategy used by qualitative or intuitive evaluators to deliberately think nonrationally, perhaps by exaggerating differences in order to tease out new or innovative ways of seeing and understanding. (14)

Type I error   The logical error of falsely rejecting the *null hypothesis*. (12)

Type II error   The logical error of falsely accepting the *null hypothesis*. (12)

Typology   A type of *classification* with two or more concepts in which the intersection of the concepts creates a set of subtypes or lower-level concepts. Often it is the basis of a *concept cluster* in *social theory*. (3)

Unidimensionality   The principle that when using *multiple indicators* to measure a construct, all the indicators should consistently fit together and indicate a single construct. (7)

Uniform resource locator (URL)   An "address" of an Internet site. It usually begins with www. (16)

Unit of analysis   The kind of *empirical* case or unit that a researcher observes, measures, and analyzes in a study. (6)

Univariate statistics   Statistical measures that deal with one variable only. (12)

Universalism   A norm of the *scientific community* that, irrespective of who conducts research or where it was conducted, it should be judged on its merits alone. (1)

Universe   The broad class of units that are covered in a *hypothesis*. All the units to which the findings of a specific study might be generalized. (6)

Unobtrusive measures   Another name for *nonreactive* measures. It emphasizes that the people being studied are not aware of it because the measures do not intrude. (11)

Upload   A verb that means transferring a computer file from a local computer to a distant computer. (16)

Validity   A term meaning truth that can be applied to the logical tightness of *experimental design*, the ability to generalize findings outside a study, the quality of measurement, and the proper use of procedures. (7)

Value-free science   The ideal in which science must be totally objective and based on *empirical* evidence alone. There is no place for a culture's values or a researcher's personal values or beliefs. (4)

Value neutrality   See *Value-free science*. (5)

Variable   A concept or its *empirical* measure that can take on multiple values. (6)

Verstehen   A German word that translates as understanding; specifically, it means an empathic understanding of another's worldview. (4)

Volunteerism   The *assumption* that individuals have great freedom to decide and act, that people are little affected by external social pressure or forces. (4)

Web browser   A "navigational" tool that provides access to the Internet. It is able to interpret various software codes and addresses, and it provides screens of information. (16)

Wichita Jury Study   A study in the 1950s that highlights violation of the *principle of voluntary consent,* a lack of *informed consent,* and government interference in social work research. In the study, researchers tape recorded jury deliberations without consent from jury members. Afterward, a law was passed that prohibited research on juries. (5)

Wording effect   An effect that occurs when a specific term or word used in a *survey research* question affects how respondents answer the question. (10)

Writer's block   A writer's temporary inability to write. It is usually psychologically based. (16)

Zimbardo prison experiment   A famous experiment of the 1970s that highlights the ethical principle that researchers should protect people being studied from possible physical or psychological harm. In the study, the researcher created prisonlike conditions and assigned *subjects* to play the role of guards or prisoners. The experiment ended early because of the violent realism of *subject* behavior. (5)

Z-score   A way to locate a score in a distribution of scores by determining the number of *standard deviations* it is above or below the *mean* or arithmetic average. (12)

Abbott, Andrew. (1988). *The system of professions: An essay on the division of expert labor.* Chicago: University of Chicago Press.

Abbott, Andrew. (1992). From causes to events: Notes on narrative positivism. *Sociological Methods and Research,* 20:428–455.

Abelson, Robert P., Elizabeth F. Loftus, and Anthony G. Greenwald. (1992). Attempts to improve the accuracy of self-reports of voting. In *Questions about questions: Inquiries into the cognitive bases of surveys,* edited by J. Turner, pp. 138–153. New York: Russell Sage Foundation.

Abrams, Philip. (1982). *Historical sociology.* Ithaca, NY: Cornell University Press.

Abt, Charles. (1979). Government constraints on evaluation quality. In *Improving evaluation,* edited by L. Datta and R. Perloff. Beverly Hills, CA: Sage.

Achen, Christopher H. (1982). *Interpreting and using regression.* Beverly Hills, CA: Sage.

Adams, Gerald R., and Jay D. Schvaneveldt. (1985). *Understanding research methods.* New York: Longman.

Adler, Patricia A. (1985). *Wheeling and dealing.* New York: Columbia University Press.

Adler, Patricia A., and Peter Adler. (1983). Shifts and oscillations in deviant careers: The case of upper-level drug dealers and smugglers. *Social Problems,* 31:195–207.

Adler, Patricia A., and Peter Adler. (1987). *Membership roles in field research.* Beverly Hills, CA: Sage.

Adler, Patricia A., and Peter Adler. (1993). Ethical issues in self-censorship: Ethnographic research on sensitive topics. In *Research on Sensitive Topics,* edited by C. Renzetti and R. Lee, pp. 249–266. Thousand Oaks, CA: Sage.

Adler, Patricia A., and Peter Adler. (1994). Observational techniques. In *Handbook of qualitative research,* edited by N. Denzin and Y. Lincoln, pp. 377–392. Thousand Oaks, CA: Sage.

Adorno, Theodor W. (1976). The logic of the social sciences. In *The positivist dispute in German sociology,* edited by T. Adorno et al., trans. Glyn Adey and David Frisby, pp. 87–104. New York: Harper and Row.

Agar, Michael. (1980). Getting better quality stuff: Methodological competition in an interdisciplinary niche. *Urban Life,* 9:34–50.

Agar, Michael. (1986). *Speaking of ethnography.* Beverly Hills, CA: Sage.

Agger, Ben. (1991). Critical theory, poststructuralism, postmodernism: Their sociological relevance. *Annual Review of Sociology,* 17:105–131.

Agnew, Neil McK., and Sandra W. Pyke. (1991). *The science game: An introduction to research in the social sciences,* 5th ed. Englewood Cliffs, NJ: Prentice-Hall.

Albrecht, Gary L. (1985). Videotape safaris: Entering the field with a camera. *Qualitative Sociology,* 8:325–344.

Aldenderfer, Mark S., and Roger K. Blashfield. (1984). *Cluster analysis.* Beverly Hills, CA: Sage.

Alford, Robert R. (1998). *The craft of inquiry: Theories, method, evidence.* New York: Oxford University Press.

Allen, Michael Patrick. (1974). Construction of composite measures by the canonical-factor-regression method. In *Sociological methodology, 1973–74,* edited by H. L. Costner, pp. 51–78. San Francisco: Jossey-Bass.

Allen-Meares, P., and Y. DeRoos. (1994). Are practitioner intuition and empirical evidence equally valid sources of professional knowledge? Yes. In *Controversial Issues in Social Work Research,* edited by W. Hudson and P. Nurius, pp. 37–49. Boston: Allyn & Bacon.

Almgren, Gunnar, Avery Guest, George Imerwahr, and Michael Spittel. (1998). Joblessness, family disruption, and violent death in Chicago, 1970–1990. *Social Forces,* 76:1465–1494.

Alter, C., and W. Evens. (1990). *Evaluating your practice: A guide to self-assessment.* New York: Springer.

Altheide, David L. (1976). *Creating reality.* Beverly Hills, CA: Sage.

Altheide, David L. (1980). Leaving the newsroom. In *Fieldwork experience,* edited by W. B. Shaffir, R. Stebbins, and A. Turowetz, pp. 301–310. New York: St. Martin's Press.

Alwin, Duane F. (1977). Making errors in surveys. *Sociological Methods and Research,* 6:131–150.

Alwin, Duane F. (1988). The general social survey: A national data resource for the social sciences. *PS: Political Science and Politics,* 21:90–94.

Alwin, Duane F., and David J. Jackson. (1980). Measurement models for response errors in surveys: Issues and applications. In *Sociological methodology, 1980,* edited by S. Leinhardt. San Francisco: Jossey-Bass.

Alwin, Duane F., and Jon A. Krosnick. (1985). The measurement of values in surveys: A comparison of ratings and rankings. *Public Opinion Quarterly,* 49:535–552.

American Sociological Association. (1997). *American Sociological Association style guide, 2nd ed.* Washington, DC: American Sociological Association.

Anderson, Andy B., Alexander Basilevsky, and Derek P. J. Hum. (1983). Measurement: Theory and techniques. In *Handbook of survey research,* edited by P. Rossi, J. D. Wright, and A. Anderson, pp. 231–287. New York: Academic Press.

Anderson, Barbara A., Brian D. Silver, and Paul R. Abramson. (1988). The effects of the race of interviewer on race-related attitudes of black respondents in SRC/CPS national election studies. *Public Opinion Quarterly,* 52:289–324.

Anderson, Elijah. (1989). Jelly's place. In *In the field,* edited by C. Smith and W. Kornblum, pp. 9–20. New York: Praeger.

Anderson, N. (1923). *The hobo.* Chicago: University of Chicago Press.

Anderson, Perry. (1974). *Passages from antiquity to feudalism.* London: New Left Books.

Andren, Gunnar. (1981). Reliability and content analysis. In *Advances in content analysis,* edited by K. Rosengren, pp. 43–67. Beverly Hills, CA: Sage.

Andrews, Frank M., Laura Klem, Terrence Davidson, Patrick O'Malley, and Willard Rodgers. (1981). *A guide for selecting statistical techniques for analyzing social science data.* Ann Arbor: Institute for Social Research, University of Michigan.

Annandale, Ellen C. (1988). How midwives accomplish natural birth: Managing risk and balancing expectations. *Social Problems,* 35:95–110.

Appadurai, A. (1990). Disjuncture and difference in global cultural economy. *Public Culture,* 2(2):10.

Applebaum, Richard. (1978a). Marxist method: Structural constraints and social praxis. *American Sociologist,* 13:73–81.

Applebaum, Richard. (1978b). Marx's theory of the falling rate of profit. *American Sociological Review,* 43:67–80.

Appleby, G. A., E. Colon, and J. Hamilton, eds. (2000). *Diversity, oppression, and social functioning: Person-in-environment assessment and intervention.* Boston: Allyn & Bacon.

Appleby, G., and J. Anastas. (1998). *Not just a passing phase: Social work with gay, lesbian and bisexual people.* New York: Columbia University Press.

Aquilino, William S. (1993). Effects of spouse presence during the interview on survey response concerning marriage. *Public Opinion Quarterly,* 57:358–376.

Aquilino, William S., and Leonard Losciuto. (1990). Effects of interview mode on self-reported drug use. *Public Opinion Quarterly,* 54:362–395.

Archibald, Randall C. (May 25, 1998). Knowledge scare on cost of college study finds. *The New York Times.*

Ardener, Shirley. (1984). Gender orientations in fieldwork. In *Ethnographic research: A guide to general conduct,* edited by R. F. Ellen, pp. 118–129. Orlando, FL: Academic Press.

Ariès, E. (1977). Male-female interpersonal styles in all male, all female, and mixed groups. In *Beyond sex roles,* edited by A. Sargent, pp. 292–299. Boulder, CO: West.

Armstrong, J. Scott, and Edward J. Lusk. (1987). Return postage in mail surveys: A meta-analysis. *Public Opinion Quarterly,* 51:233–248.

Aronson, Elliot, and J. Merrill Carlsmith. (1968). Experimentation in social psychology. In *The handbook of social psychology, Vol. 2: Research methods,* edited by G. Lindzey and E. Aronson, pp. 1–78. Reading, MA: Addison-Wesley.

Asamoah, Y., L. Healy, and N. Mayadas. (1997). Ending the international/domestic dichotomy: New approaches to a global curriculum for the millenium. *Journal of Social Work Education,* 33:389–401.

Askonas, P., and A. Stewart, eds. (2000). *Social inclusion: Possibilities and tensions.* New York: St. Martin's Press.

Atkinson, Robert. (1998). *The life story interview.* Thousand Oaks, CA: Sage.

Auriat, Nadia. (1993). My wife knows best: A comparison of event dating accuracy between the wife, the husband, the couple, and the Belgium population register. *Public Opinion Quarterly,* 57:165–190.

Auslander, W., R. Haire-Joshe, C. Houston, J. Williams, and H. Krebill. (2000). The short-term impact of health promotion program for low-income African American women. *Research on Social Work Practice,* 10:78–97.

Auster, Carol J. (1985). Manual for socialization: Examples from Girl Scout handbooks, 1913–1984. *Qualitative Sociology,* 8:359–367.

Ayella, Marybeth. (1993). "They must be crazy:" Some of the difficulties in researching cults. In *Research on Sensitive Topics,* edited by C. Renzetti and R. Lee, pp. 108–124. Thousand Oaks, CA: Sage.

Babbie, Earl. (1989). *The practice of social research,* 5th ed. Belmont, CA: Wadsworth.

Babbie, Earl. (1990). *Survey research methods,* 2nd ed. Belmont, CA: Wadsworth.

Babbie, Earl. (1998). *The practice of social research,* 8th ed. Belmont, CA: Wadsworth.

Backstrom, Charles H., and Gerald Hursh-Cesar. (1981). *Survey research,* 2nd ed. New York: Wiley.

Bailar, Barbara A., and C. Michael Lanphier. (1978). *Development of survey methods to access survey practices.* Washington, DC: American Statistical Association.

Bailey, Kenneth D. (1975). Cluster analysis. In *Sociological methodology, 1975,* edited by D. Heise, pp. 59–128. San Francisco: Jossey-Bass.

Bailey, Kenneth D. (1983). Sociological classification and cluster analysis. *Quality and Quantity,* 17:251–268.

Bailey, Kenneth D. (1984). A three-level measurement model. *Quality and Quantity,* 18:225–245.

Bailey, Kenneth D. (1986). Philosophical foundations of sociological measurement: Notes on the three-level model. *Quality and Quantity,* 20:327–337.

Bailey, Kenneth D. (1987). *Methods of social research,* 3rd ed. New York: Free Press.

Bailey, Kenneth D. (1988). Ethical dilemmas in social problems research: A theoretical framework. *American Sociologist,* 19:121–137.

Bailey, Kenneth D. (1992). Typologies. *Encyclopedia of Sociology,* Vol. 4, edited by E. and M. Borgatta, pp. 2188–2194. New York: Macmillan.

Bakanic, Von, Clark McPhail, and Rita Simon. (1987). The manuscript review and decision-making process. *American Sociological Review,* 52:631–642.

Bakanic, Von, Clark McPhail, and Rita Simon. (1989). Mixed messages: Referees' comments on the manuscripts they review. *Sociological Quarterly,* 30:639–654.

Baker, D., and M. Wilson. (1992). An evaluation of the scholarly productivity of doctoral graduates. *Journal of Social Work Education,* (28)2:204–213.

Balassone, M., and R. Ruckdeschel. (1994). Does emphasizing accountability and evidence dilute service delivery and the helping role? In *Controversial issues in social work research,* edited by W. Hudson and P. Nurius, pp. 9–21. Needham Heights, MA: Allyn & Bacon.

Balgopol, P. (2000). *Social work practice with immigrants and refugees.* New York: Columbia University Press.

Ball, Donald. (1967). An abortion clinic ethnography. *Social Problems,* 14:293–301.

Ball, Michael, and Gregory W. H. Smith. (1992). *Analyzing visual data.* Thousand Oaks, CA: Sage.

Ball, Richard A., and G. David Curry. (1995). The logic of definition in criminology: Purposes and methods for defining "gangs." *Criminology,* 33:225–245.

Ballenger, E. (April/June, 2000). Breaking generational curses: A family systems and biblical perspective: Part I. *The Christian Counselor,* 5:36–37.

Banaka, William H. (1971). *Training in depth interviewing.* New York: Harper & Row.

Banks, H., and J. Pandiani. (2001). Probabilistic population estimation of the size and overlap of data sets based on date of birth. *Statistics in Medicine,* 20:1421–1430.

Bankston, William B., and Carol Y. Thompson. (1989). Carrying firearms for protection. *Sociological Inquiry,* 59:75–87.

Bannister, Robert C. (1987). *Sociology and scientism: The American quest for objectivity, 1880–1940.* Chapel Hill: University of North Carolina Press.

Barber, Jennifer S., and William G. Axinn. (1998). Gender attitudes and marriage among young women. *Sociological Quarterly,* 39:11–31.

Bardack, Nadia R., and Francis T. McAndrew. (1985). The influence of physical attractiveness and manner of dress on success in a simulated personnel decision. *Journal of Social Psychology,* 125:777–778.

Barlow, Melissa Hickman, David E. Barlow, and Theodore G. Chiricos. (1995). Economic conditions and ideologies of crime in the media: A content analysis of crime news. *Crime and Deliquency,* 41:3–19.

Barnes, Barry. (1974). *Scientific knowledge and sociological theory.* Boston: Routledge and Kegan Paul.

Barnes, J. A. (1970). Some ethical problems in modern fieldwork. In *Qualitative methodology,* edited by W. J. Filstead, pp. 235–251. Chicago: Markham.

Barnes, J. A. (1979). *Who should know what? Social science, privacy and ethics.* New York: Cambridge University Press.

Barry, Brian. (1975). On analogy. *Political Studies,* 23:208–224.

Bart, Pauline. (1987). Seizing the means of reproduction: An illegal feminist abortion collective—How and why it worked. *Qualitative Sociology,* 10:339–357.

Bart, Pauline, and Linda Frankel. (1986). *The student sociologist's handbook,* 4th ed. New York: Random House.

Bartiz, Loren. (1960). *Servants of power: A history of the use of social science in American industry.* Middletown, CT: Wesleyan University Press.

Barton, Allen H. (1995). Asking why about social problems: Ideology and causal models in the public mind. *International Journal of Public Opinion Research,* 7:299–327.

Barton, J. (1998). Culturally competent research protocols. In *Cultural awareness in the human services: A multiethnic approach,* edited by J. Green, pp. 285–303. Boston: Allyn & Bacon.

Barzun, Jacques, and Henry F. Graff. (1970). *The modern researcher,* rev. ed. New York: Harcourt, Brace and World.

Basirico, Laurence A. (1986). The art and craft fair: An institution in an old art world. *Qualitative Sociology,* 9:339–353.

Bateson, Nicholas. (1984). *Data construction in social surveys.* Boston: George Allen and Unwin.

Bauer, David G. (1988). *The "how to" grants manual,* 2nd ed. New York: Macmillan.

Bauer, Raymond, ed. (1966). *Social indicators.* Cambridge, MA: MIT Press.

Bausell, R. Barker. (1994). *Conducting meaningful experiments: Forty steps to becoming a scientist.* Thousand Oaks, CA: Sage.

Bayless, David L. (1981). Twenty-two years of survey research at the Research Triangle: 1959–1980. In *Current topics in survey sampling,* edited by D. Krewski, R. Platek, and J. N. K. Rao, pp. 87–103. New York: Academic Press.

Bearden, W., R. Netemeyer, and M. Mobley. (1993). *Handbook of marketing scales: Multi item measure for marketing and consumer behavior research.* Newbury Park, CA: Sage.

Beasley, David. (1988). *How to use a research library.* New York: Oxford University Press.

Beck, Bernard. (1970). Cooking welfare stew. In *Pathways to data,* edited by R. W. Habenstein, pp. 7–29. Chicago: Aldine.

Beck, E. M., and Stewart Tolnay (1990). The killing fields of the Deep South: The market for cotton and the lynching of blacks, 1882–1930. *American Sociological Review,* 55:526–539.

Beck, R., and P. Rossi. (1990). *Thinking about program evaluation.* Thousand Oaks, CA: Sage.

Becker, Howard. (1967). Whose side are we on? *Social Problems,* 14:239–247.

Becker, Howard S. (1969). Problems in the publication of field studies. In *Issues in participant observation,* edited by G. McCall and J. L. Simmons, pp. 260–275. Reading, MA: Addison-Wesley.

Becker, Howard S. (1970a). Practitioners of vice and crime. In *Pathways to data,* edited by R. W. Habenstein, pp. 30–49. Chicago: Aldine.

Becker, Howard S. (1970b). Problems of inference and proof in participant observation. In *Qualitative methodology: Firsthand involvement with the social world,* edited by W. J. Filstead, pp. 189–201. Chicago: Markham.

Becker, Howard S. (1970c). Whose side are we on? In *Qualitative methodology,* edited by W. J. Filstead, pp. 15–26. Chicago: Markham.

Becker, Howard S. (1986). *Writing for social scientists: How to start and finish your thesis, book or article.* Chicago: University of Chicago Press.

Becker, Howard S. (1993). How I learned what a crock was. *Journal of Contemporary Ethnography,* 22:28–35.

Becker, Howard S. (1998). *Tricks of the trade: How to think about your research while you're doing it.* Chicago: University of Chicago Press.

Becker, Howard S., and Blanche Geer. (1970). Participant observation and interviewing: A comparison. In *Qualitative methodology,* edited by W. J. Filstead, pp. 133–142. Chicago: Markham.

Becker, Howard S., and Blanche Geer. (1982). Participant observation: The analysis of qualitative field data. In *Field research: A sourcebook and field manual,* edited by R. G. Burgess, pp. 239–250. Boston: George Allen and Unwin.

Becker, Howard S., Blanche Geer, Everett C. Hughes, and Anselm Strauss. (1961). *Boys in white: Student culture in medical school.* Chicago: University of Chicago Press.

Becker, Howard S., Michal M. McCall, and Lori V. Morris. (1989). Theatres and communities: Three scenes. *Social Problems,* 36:93–116.

Beecher, H. K. (1970). *Research and the individual: Human studies.* Boston: Little, Brown.

Beisel, Nicola. (1990). Class, culture, and campaigns against vice in three American cities, 1872–1892. *American Sociological Review,* 55:44–62.

Belenky, Mary Field, Blythe McVicker Clinchy, Nancy Rule Goldberger, and Jill Mattuck Tarule. (1986). *Women's ways of knowing: The development of self, voice and mind.* New York: Basic Books.

Ben-David, Joseph. (1971). *The scientist's role in society.* Englewood Cliffs, NJ: Prentice-Hall.

Bendix, Reinhard. (1956). *Work and authority in industry.* New York: Wiley.

Bendix, Reinhard. (1963). Concepts and generalizations in comparative sociological studies. *American Sociological Review,* 28:91–116.

Bendix, Reinhard. (1978). *Kings or people: Power and the mandate to rule.* Berkeley: University of California Press.

Benton, Ted. (1977). *Philosophical foundations of the three sociologies.* Boston: Routledge and Kegan Paul.

Berelson, B. (1952). *Content analysis in communication research.* Glencoe, IL: Free Press.

Berg, Bruce L. (1989). *Qualitative research methods.* Boston: Allyn and Bacon.

Berger, Peter. (1963). *An invitation to sociology: A humanistic perspective.* Garden City, NY: Anchor.

Berger, Peter, and Thomas Luckman. (1967). *The social construction of reality: A treatise in the sociology of knowledge.* Garden City, NY: Anchor.

Berk, Richard A. (1983). An introduction to sample selection bias in sociological data. *American Sociological Review,* 48:386–397.

Berlin, S. B. (1983). Single-case evaluation: Another version. *Social Work Research & Abstracts,* 19(1):3–11.

Bermant, Gordon. (1982). Justifying social science research in terms of social benefit. In *Ethical issues in social science research,* edited by T. Beauchamp, R. Faden, R. J. Wallace, and L. Walters, pp. 125–142. Baltimore: Johns Hopkins University Press.

Bernard, H. Russell. (1988). *Research methods in cultural anthropology.* Newbury Park, CA: Sage.

Bernard, H. Russell, Peter Killworth, David Kronenfeld, and Lee Sailer. (1984). The problem of information accuracy: The validity of retrospective data. *Annual Review of Anthropology,* 13:495–517.

Bhaskar, Roy. (1975). *A realist theory of science.* Atlantic Highlands, NJ: Humanities.

Bigus, Odis. (1972). The milkman and his customer: A cultivated relationship. *Urban Life and Culture,* 1:131–165.

Billiet, Jacques, and Geert Loosveldt. (1988). Improvement of the quality of responses to faculty survey questions by interviewer training. *Public Opinion Quarterly,* 52:190–211.

Binson, Diane, and Joseph Catania. (1998). Respondents' understanding of the words in sexual behavior questions. *Public Opinion Quarterly,* 62: 190–208.

Birkerts, S. (1996). The electronic hive: Refuse it. In *Computerization and controversy: Value conflicts and social choices,* edited by R. Kling, pp. 79–82. San Diego, CA: Academic Press.

Bishop, George F. (1987). Experiments with the middle response alternative in survey questions. *Public Opinion Quarterly,* 51:220–232.

Bishop, George F., Robert W. Oldendick, and Alfred J. Tuchfarber. (1983). Effects of filter questions in public opinion surveys. *Public Opinion Quarterly,* 47:528–546.

Bishop, George F., Robert W. Oldendick, and Alfred J. Tuchfarber. (1984). What must my interest in politics be if I just told you "I don't know?" *Public Opinion Quarterly,* 48:510–519.

Bishop, George F., Robert W. Oldendick, and Alfred J. Tuchfarber. (1985). The importance of replicating a failure to replicate: Order effects on abortion items. *Public Opinion Quarterly,* 49:105–114.

Bishop, George F., Alfred J. Tuchfarber, and Robert W. Oldendick. (1986). Opinions on fictitious issues: The pressure to answer survey questions. *Public Opinion Quarterly,* 50:240–251.

Blaikie, Norman. (1993). *Approaches to social enquiry.* Cambridge, MA: Polity.

Blalock, Hubert M., Jr. (1968). The measurement problem: A gap between the language of theory and research. In *Methodology in social research,* edited by H. Blalock and A. Blalock, pp. 5–27. New York: McGraw-Hill.

Blalock, Hubert M., Jr. (1969). *Theory construction: From verbal to mathematical formulations.* Englewood Cliffs, NJ: Prentice-Hall.

Blalock, Hubert M., Jr. (1979a). Measurement and conceptualization problems: The major obstacle to integrating theory and research. *American Sociological Review,* 44:881–894.

Blalock, Hubert M., Jr. (1979b). *Social statistics,* 2nd ed. New York: McGraw-Hill.

Blalock, Hubert M., Jr. (1982). *Conceptualization and measurement in the social sciences.* Beverly Hills, CA: Sage.

Blalock, Hubert M., Jr., and Ann B. Blalock, eds. (1968). *Methodology in social research.* New York: McGraw-Hill.

Blankenship, Albert B. (1977). *Professional telephone surveys.* New York: McGraw-Hill.

Blaskett, B. (1998). Arguing for a social work role in the promotion of ethical social research. *Australian Social Work,* 51(4):19–25.

Blau, Judith R. (1978). Sociometric structure of a scientific discipline. *Research in Sociology of Knowledge, Sciences and Art,* 1:191–206.

Blee, Kathleen M., and Dwight B. Billings. (1986). Reconstructing daily life in the past: An hermeneutical approach to ethnographic data. *Sociological Quarterly,* 27:443–462.

Bleicher, Josef. (1980). *Contemporary hermeneutics.* Boston: Routledge and Kegan Paul.

Block, Fred, and Gene A. Burns. (1986). Productivity as a social problem: The uses and misuses of social indicators. *American Sociological Review,* 51:767–780.

Bloom, M. (1978). Challenges to helping professions and the response of scientific practice. *Social Service Review,* 52:584–595.

Bloom, M. (1995). The great philosophy of science war. *Social Work Research,* 19(1):19–23.

Bloom, M., J. Fischer, and J. Orme. (1999). *Evaluating practice: Guidelines for the accountable professional.* New York: Allyn & Bacon.

Bloor, Michael J. (1983). Notes on member validation. In *Contemporary field research,* edited by R. M. Emerson, pp. 156–171. Boston: Little, Brown.

Blount, M. (1996). Social work practice with native Americans. In *Cultural Diversity and Social Work Practice,* edited by D. Harrison, et al. Springfield, IL: Charles C. Thomas.

Blum, Debra E. (1989). A dean is charged with plagiarizing a dissertation for his book on Muzak. *Chronicle of Higher Education,* 35:A17.

Blume, Stuart S. (1974). *Toward a political sociology of science.* New York: Free Press.

Blumer, M. (1984). *The Chicago school of sociology.* Chicago: University of Chicago Press.

Blumer, Martin. (1991a). W. E. B. DuBois as a social investigator: The Philadelphia Negro 1889. In *The social survey in historical perspective, 1880–1940,* edited by M. Blumer, K. Bales, and K. Sklar, pp. 170–188. New York: Cambridge University Press.

Blumer, Martin. (1991b). The decline of the social survey movement and the rise of American empirical sociology. In *The social survey in historical perspective, 1880–1940,* edited by M. Blumer, K. Bales, and K. Sklar, pp. 271–315. New York: Cambridge University Press.

Blumer, Martin. (1992). The growth of applied sociology after 1945: The prewar establishment of the postwar infrastructure. *Sociology and its publics: The forms and fates of disciplinary organization,* edited by T. C. Halliday and M. Janowitz, pp. 317–346. Chicago: University of Chicago Press.

Blumer, Martin, K. Bales, and K. Sklar. (1991). The social survey in historical perspective. In *The social survey in historical perspective, 1880–1940,* edited by M. Blumer, K. Bales, and K. Sklar, pp. 1–48. New York: Cambridge University Press.

Blumstein, Alfred. (1974). Seriousness weights in an index of crime. *American Sociological Review,* 39:854–864.

Blythe, B. (1999). Single-system design. In *Encyclopedia of Social Work,* 19th ed., Vol. 2, edited by R. Edwards (Editor-in-chief), pp. 2164–2168. Washington, DC: NASW Press.

Blythe, B., and J., and S. Briar. (1985). Developing empirically based models of practice. *Social Work,* 30(6): 483–488.

Blythe, B., and T. Tripodi. (1989). *Measurement in direct practice.* Newbury Park, CA: Sage.

Bogardus, Emory S. (1959). *Social distance.* Yellow Springs, OH: Antioch Press.

Bogdan, Robert, and Steven J. Taylor. (1975). *Introduction to qualitative research methods: A phenomenological approach to the social sciences.* New York: Wiley.

Bohm, Robert M. (1990). Death penalty opinions: A classroom experience and public commitment. *Sociological Inquiry,* 60:285–297.

Bohrnstedt, George. (1992a). Reliability. *Encyclopedia of Sociology,* Vol. 3, edited by E. and M. Borgatta, pp. 1626–1632. New York: Macmillan.

Bohrnstedt, George. (1992b). Validity. *Encyclopedia of Sociology,* Vol. 4, edited by E. and M. Borgatta, pp. 2217–2222. New York: Macmillan.

Bohrnstedt, George W., and Edgar F. Borgatta, eds. (1981). *Social measurement: Current issues.* Beverly Hills, CA: Sage.

Bohrnstedt, George, and David Knoke. (1994). *Statistics for social data analysis,* 3rd ed. Itasca, IL: Peacock.

Bolton, Ruth N., and Tina Bronkhorst. (1996). Questionnaire pretesting: Computer-assisting coding of concurrent protocols. In *Answering questions,* edited by N. Schwarz and S. Sudman, pp. 37–64. San Francisco: Jossey-Bass.

Bond, Charles F., Jr., and Evan L. Anderson. (1987). The reluctance to transmit bad news: Private discomfort or public display? *Journal of Experimental Social Psychology,* 23:176–187.

Bonnell, Victoria E. (1980). The uses of theory, concepts and comparison in historical sociology. *Comparative Studies in Society and History,* 22:156–173.

Borgatta, Edgar F., and George W. Bohrnstedt. (1980). Level of measurement: Once over again. *Sociological Methods and Research,* 9:147–160.

Boruch, Robert F. (1982). Methods for revolving privacy problems in social research. In *Ethical issues in social science research,* edited by T. Beauchamp, R. Faden, R. J. Wallace, and L. Walters, pp. 292–313. Baltimore: Johns Hopkins University Press.

Bottomore, Thomas. (1984). *The Frankfurt School.* New York: Travistock.

Bouchard, Thomas J., Jr. (1976). Unobtrusive measures: An inventory of uses. *Sociological Methods and Research,* 4:267–300.

Boyatzis, Richard E. (1998). *Transforming qualitative information: Thematic analysis and code development.* Thousand Oaks, CA: Sage.

Boyle, R., D. Lemaire, and R. Rist. (1999). Building evaluation capacity within organizations. In *Building Effective Evaluation Capacity: Lessons from Practice,* edited by R. Boyle and D. Lemaire, pp. 1–23. New Brunswick, NJ: Transaction Publishers.

Bradburn, Norman M. (1983). Response effects. In *Handbook of survey research,* edited by P. Rossi, J. Wright, and A. Anderson, pp. 289–328. Orlando, FL: Academic.

Bradburn, Norman M., and Carrie Miles. (1979). Vague qualifiers. *Public Opinion Quarterly,* 43:92–101.

Bradburn, Norman M., and Seymour Sudman. (1980). *Improving interview method and questionnaire design.* San Francisco: Jossey-Bass.

Bradburn, Norman M., and Seymour Sudman. (1988). *Polls and surveys: Understanding what they tell us.* San Francisco: Jossey-Bass.

Bradshaw, J. (1972). A taxonomy of social need. In *Problems and progress in medical care,* edited by G. McIachlan, pp. 214–234. Oxford: Nuffield Provincial Hospital Trust.

Brandell, J., and Varkas. (2001). Narrative case studies. In *The handbook of social work research methods* edited by B. Thyer, pp. 293–308. Thousand Oaks, CA: Sage.

Brannigan, Augustine. (1992). Postmodernism. *Encyclopedia of Sociology,* Vol. 3, edited by E. and M. Borgatta, pp. 1522–1525. New York: Macmillan.

Braud, W., and R. Anderson. (1998). *Transpersonal research methods for the social sciences,* pp. 83–84. Thousand Oaks, CA: Sage.

Bredo, Eric, and Walter Feinberg, eds. (1982). *Knowledge and values in social and educational research.* Philadelphia: Temple University Press.

Brehm, John. (1994). Stubbing our toes for a foot in the door? Prior contact, incentives and survey response. *International Journal of Public Opinion Research,* 6:45–63.

Brenner, Michael. (1985). Survey interviewing. In *The research interview: Uses and approaches,* edited by M. Brenner, J. Brown, and D. Canter, pp. 9–36. New York: Academic Press.

Brenner, Michael, Jennifer Brown, and David Canter, eds. (1985). *The research interview: Uses and approaches.* Orlando, FL: Academic Press.

Briggs, Charles L. (1986). *Learning how to ask: A sociolinguist appraisal of the role of the interview in social science research.* New York: Cambridge University Press.

Brinberg, David, and Joseph E. McGrath. (1982). A network of validity concepts. In *Forms of validity in research,* edited by D. Brinberg and L. Kidder, pp. 5–21. San Francisco: Jossey-Bass.

Brinkerhoff, R., and D. Dressler. (1990). *Productivity measurement: A guide for managers and evaluators.* Newbury Park, CA: Sage Publications.

Brint, Steven. (1994). *In an Age of Experts: The changing role of professionals in politics and public life.* Princeton, NJ: Princeton University Press.

Brinton, Mary C., Yean-Ju Lee, and William L. Parish. (1995). Married women's employment in rapidly industrializing societies: Examples from East Asia. *American Journal of Sociology,* 100:1009–1130.

Britton, Dana M. (1990). Homophobia and homosociality: An analysis of boundary maintenance. *Sociological Quarterly,* 31:423–440.

Broad, W. J., and N. Wade. (1982). *Betrayers of the truth.* New York: Simon and Schuster.

Broadbent, Jeffrey. (1989a). Environmental politics in Japan: An integrated structural analysis. *Sociological Forum,* 4:179–202.

Broadbent, Jeffrey. (1989b). Strategies and structural contractions: Growth coalition politics in Japan. *American Sociological Review,* 54:707–721.

Broadhead, Robert, and Ray Rist. (1976). Gatekeepers and the social control of social research. *Social Problems,* 23:325–336.

Brodsky, Stanley L., and H. O'Neal Smitherman. (1983). *Handbook of scales for research in crime and delinquency.* New York: Plenum.

Brody, Charles J. (1986). Things are rarely black or white: Admitting gray into the converse model of attitude stability. *American Journal of Sociology,* 92:657–677.

Bromley, David G., and Anson D. Shupe, Jr. (1979). *Moonies in America: Culture, church and crusade.* Beverly Hills, CA: Sage.

Brown, E. (1981). Selection and formulation of a research problem. In *Social work research and evaluation,* edited by R. Grinnell, pp. 35–45. Itasca, IL: Peacock.

Brown, Jennifer, and David Canter. (1985). The uses of explanation in the research interview. In *The research interview: Uses and approaches,* edited by M. Brenner, J. Brown, and D. Canter, pp. 217–245. New York: Academic Press.

Brown, M. Craig, and Barbara Warner. (1992). Immigrants, urban politics, and policing in 1900. *American Sociological Review,* 57:293–305.

Brown, Richard Harvey. (1989). *Social science as civic discourse: Essays on the invention, legitimation and uses of social theory.* Chicago: University of Chicago Press.

Brown, Steven R. (1980). *Political subjectivity: Applications of Q methodology in political science.* New Haven, CT: Yale University Press.

Brown, Steven R. (1986). Q technique and method: Principles and procedures. In *New tools for social scientists: Advances and applications in research methods,* edited by W. D. Berry and M. Lewis-Beck, pp. 57–76. Beverly Hills, CA: Sage.

Bryan, James H. (1965). Apprenticeships in prostitution. *Social Problems,* 12:287–297.

Brym, Robert J. (1980). *Intellectuals and politics.* Boston: George Allen and Unwin.

Bucher, R. (2000). *Diversity consciousness: Opening our minds to people, cultures and opportunities.* Upper Saddle River, NJ: Prentice-Hall.

Bullis, R. (1996). *Spirituality in social work practice.* Washington, DC: Taylor and Francis.

Burawoy, Michael. (1979). *Manufacturing consent.* Chicago: University of Chicago Press.

Burawoy, Michael. (1985). Karl Marx and the satanic mills: Factory politics under early capitalism in England, the United States, and Russia. *American Journal of Sociology,* 90: 247–282.

Burawoy, Michael. (1989). Two methods in search of science: Skocpol versus Troksky. *Theory and Society,* 18:759–806.

Burawoy, Michael. (1990). Marxism as science: Historical challenges and theoretical growth. *American Sociological Review,* 55:775–793.

Burawoy, Michael. (1991). The extended case method. In *Ethnography unbound: Power and resistance in the modern metropolis,* edited by M. Burawoy et al., pp. 271–287. Berkeley: University of California Press.

Burawoy, Michael. (1998). The extended case method. *Sociological Theory,* 16:4–33.

Burawoy, Michael, and Janos Lukacs. (1985). Mythologies of work: A comparison of firms in state socialism and advanced capitalism. *American Sociological Review,* 50:723–737.

Burgess, Robert G. (1982a). Approaches to field research. In *Field research,* edited by R. G. Burgess, pp. 1–11. Boston: George Allen and Unwin.

Burgess, Robert G. (1982b). Keeping field notes. In *Field research,* edited by R. G. Burgess, pp. 191–194. Boston: George Allen and Unwin.

Burgess, Robert G. (1982c). The unstructured interview as a conversation. In *Field research,* edited by R. G. Burgess, pp. 107–110. Boston: George Allen and Unwin.

Burke, J. L., A. M. Dannerbeck, and J. W. Watt. (1999). Meeting the parenting skill needs of neglectful families by training child welfare workers as educators. *Journal of Children & Poverty,* 5(1):75–89.

Burke, Peter. (1992). *History and social theory.* Ithaca, NY: Cornell University Press.

Burnstein, Leigh, Howard E. Freeman, and Peter H. Rossi, eds. (1985). *Collecting evaluation data: Problems and solutions.* Beverly Hills, CA: Sage.

Byrne, Noel. (1978). Sociotemporal considerations of everyday life suggested by an empirical study of the bar milieu. *Urban Life,* 6:417–438.

Camic, Charles. (1980). The institutionalization of the role of scientist: England in the seventeenth century and ancient Greece. *Comparative Social Research,* 3:271–285.

Camic, Charles, and Yu Xie. (1994). The statistical turn in American social science: Columbia University, 1890–1915. *American Sociological Review,* 59:773–805.

Campbell, D., and J. Stanley. (1963). *Experimental and quasi-experimental designs for research.* Skokie, IL: Rand McNally.

Campbell, Donald T., and D. W. Fiske. (1959). Convergent and discriminant validation by the multitrait-multimethod matrix. *Psychological Bulletin,* 56:81–105.

Campbell, Donald T., and Julian C. Stanley. (1963). *Experimental and quasi-experimental designs for research.* Chicago: Rand McNally.

Campbell, John P., Richard L. Daft, and Charles L. Hulin. (1982). *What to study: Generating and developing research questions.* Beverly Hills, CA: Sage.

Cancian, Francesca M., and Cathleen Armstead. (1992). Participatory research. *Encyclopedia of Sociology,* Vol. 3, edited by E. and M. Borgatta, pp. 1427–1432. New York: Macmillan.

Cannell, Charles F., and Robert L. Kahn. (1968). Interviewing. In *The handbook of social psychology,* 2nd ed., Vol. 2, edited by G. Lindzey and E. Aronson, pp. 526–595. Reading, MA: Addison-Wesley.

Cannell, Charles F., Peter V. Miller, and Lois Oksenberg. (1981). Research on interviewing techniques. In *Sociological methodology, 1981,* edited by S. Leinhardt, pp. 389–436. San Francisco: Jossey-Bass.

Canter, David, Jennifer Brown, and Linda Goat. (1985). Multiple sorting procedure for studying conceptual systems. In *The research interview: Uses and approaches,* edited by M. Brenner, J. Brown, and D. Canter, pp. 79–114. New York: Academic Press.

Caplan, Arthur L. (1982). On privacy and confidentiality in social science research. In *Ethical issues in social science research,* edited by T. Beauchamp, R. Faden, R. J. Wallace, and L. Walters, pp. 315–327. Baltimore: Johns Hopkins University Press.

Capron, Alexander Morgan. (1982). Is consent always necessary in social science research? In *Ethical issues in social science research,* edited by T. Beauchamp, R. Faden, R. J. Wallace, and L. Walters, pp. 215–231. Baltimore: Johns Hopkins University Press.

Carew, R. (1987). The place of intuition in social work activity. *Australian Social Work,* 40(3):5–10.

Carl, Jim. (1994). Parental choice as national policy in England and the United States. *Comparative Education Review,* 38:294–322.

Carley, Michael. (1981). *Social measurement and social indicators: Issues of policy and theory.* London: George Allen and Unwin.

Carmines, E., and R. Zeller. (1979). *Reliability and validity assessment.* Beverly Hills, CA: Sage.

Carney, Thomas F. (1972). *Content analysis: A technique for systematic inference from communications.* Winnipeg: University of Manitoba Press.

Carpenter, D. (1996). Constructivism and social work treatment. In *Social work treatment: Interlocking theoretical approaches,* 4th ed., edited by F. Turner, pp. 146–167. New York: Free Press.

Carr, Edward Hallett. (1961). *What is history?* New York: Vintage.

Carr-Hill, Roy A. (1984a). The political choice of social indicators. *Quality and Quantity,* 18:173–191.

Carr-Hill, Roy A. (1984b). Radicalising survey methodology. *Quantity and Quality,* 18:275–292.

Carrillo, D., K. DeWeaver, A. Kilpatrick, and M. Smith. (1993). Single system design content in the doctoral curriculum. *Research on Social Work Practice,* 3(4):414–419.

Catania, Joseph, D. Dinson, J. Canahola, L. Pollack, W. Hauck, and T. Coates. (1996). Effects of interviewer gender, interviewer choice and item wording on responses to questions concerning sexual behavior. *Public Opinion Quarterly,* 60:345–375.

Caute, David. (1978). *The great fear.* New York: Touchstone.

Cautela, J. (1988). *Behavior analysis forms for clinical intervention.* Champaign, IL: Research Press SCALES.

Cavan, Sherri. (1974). Seeing social structure in a rural setting. *Urban Life,* 3:329–361.

Cerulo, Karen A. (1989). Sociopolitical control and the structure of national symbols: An empirical analysis of anthems. *Social Forces,* 68:76–99.

Chadwick, Bruce A., Howard M. Bahr, and Stan L. Albrecht. (1984). *Social science research methods.* Englewood Cliffs, NJ: Prentice-Hall.

Chafetz, Janet Saltzman. (1978). *A primer on the construction and testing of theories in sociology.* Itasca, IL: Peacock.

Chambers, D., Wedel, K., and Rodwell, M. (1992). *Evaluating social problems.* Boston: Allyn & Bacon.

Chambers, Marcia. (October 22, 1986). Jesuit priest standing by the survey that Vatican attempted to suppress. *The New York Times.*

Chambron, A., and A. Irving. (1994). *Essays on postmodernism and social work.* Toronto: Canadian Scholar's Press.

Channels, Noreen L. (1993). Anticipating media coverage: Methodological decisions regarding criminal justice research. In *Research on Sensitive Topics,* edited by C. Renzetti and R. Lee, pp. 267–280. Thousand Oaks, CA: Sage.

Chebat, Jean-Charles, and Jacques Picard. (1988). Receivers' self-acceptance and the effectiveness of two-sided messages. *Journal of Social Psychology,* 128:353–362.

Chelminski, E., and W. Shadish, eds. (1997). *Evaluation for the 21st century: A handbook.* Thousand Oaks, CA: Sage.

Chen, H., and P. Rossi, eds. (1992). *Using theory to improve program and policy evaluations.* New York: Greenwood Press.

Chen, J., and M. Marks. (1998). Assessing the needs of inner city youth: Beyond needs identification and prioritization. *Children and Youth Services Review,* 20:819–838.

Chicago manual of style for authors, editors and copywriters, 13th ed., revised and expanded. (1982). Chicago: University of Chicago Press.

Chow, J. (1999). Multiservice centers in Chinese American immigrant communities: Practice principles and challenges. *Social Work,* 44(1): 70–81.

Christodoulou, C. (1991). Racism—a challenge to social work education and practice: The British experience. *Journal of Multicultural Social Work,* 1:99–107.

Church, Allan H. (1993). Estimating the effect of incentives on mail survey response rates: A meta analysis. *Public Opinion Quarterly,* 57:62–80.

Churchill, Gilbert A., Jr. (1983). *Marketing research: Methodological foundations,* 3rd ed. New York: Dryden.

Cicourel, Aaron. (1964). *Method and measurement in sociology.* Glencoe, IL: Free Press.

Cicourel, Aaron. (1973). *Cognitive sociology.* London: Macmillan.

Cicourel, Aaron. (1982). Interviews, surveys, and the problem of ecological validity. *American Sociologist,* 17:11–20.

Clammer, John. (1984). Approaches to ethnographic research. In *Ethnographic research: A guide to general conduct,* edited by R. F. Ellen, pp. 63–85. Orlando, FL: Academic Press.

Clark, Herbert H., and Michael F. Schober. (1992). Asking questions and influencing answers. In *Questions about questions: Inquiries into the cognitive bases of surveys,* edited by J. Turner, pp. 15–48. New York: Russell Sage Foundation.

Clarke, Michael. (1975). Survival in the field: Implications of personal experience in field work. *Theory and Society,* 2:95–123.

Clemens, Elizabeth, and Walter Powell. (1995). Careers in print: Books, journals, and scholarly reputations. *American Journal of Sociology,* 101:433–497.

Clogg, Clifford C., and D. O. Sawyer. (1981). A comparison of alternative models for analyzing the scalability of response patterns. In *Sociological methodology, 1981,* edited by S. Leinhardt, pp. 240–280. San Francisco: Jossey-Bass.

Clubb, Jerome M., E. Austin, C. Geda, and M. Traugott. (1985). Sharing research data in the social sciences. In *Sharing research data,* edited by S. Fineberg, M. Martin, and M. Straf, pp. 39–88. Washington, DC: National Academy Press.

Cnaan, R., and Parsloe, P. (1989). *The impact of information technology on social work practice.* New York: Haworth Press.

Coe, A., and D. Elliott. (1999). An evaluation of teaching direct practice courses in a distance education program for rural settings. *Journal of Social Work Education,* 35(3):353–365.

Cohen, Patricia Cline. (1982). *A calculating people: The spread of numeracy in early America.* Chicago: University of Chicago Press.

Cohen, Stephen R. (1991). The Pittsburg survey and the social survey movement: A sociological road not taken. In *The social survey in historical perspective, 1880–1940,* edited by M. Blumer, K. Bales, and K. Sklar, pp. 245–268. New York: Cambridge University Press.

Cole, Jonathan R., and Stephen Cole. (1973). *Social stratification in science.* Chicago: University of Chicago Press.

Cole, Stephen. (1978). Scientific reward systems: A comparative analysis. *Research in the Sociology of Knowledge, Science and Art,* 1:167–190.

Cole, Stephen. (1983). The hierarchy of the sciences? *American Journal of Sociology,* 89:111–139.

Cole, Stephen. (1994). Why sociology doesn't make progress like the natural sciences. *Sociological Forum,* 9:133–154.

Cole, Stephen, Jonathan Cole, and Gary A. Simon. (1981). Chance and consensus in peer review. *Science,* 214:881–885.

Coleman, James, and Thomas Hoffer. (1987). *Public and private schools: The impact of community.* New York: Basic Books.

Collins, B. (1986). Defining feminist social work. *Social Work,* 31(3):214–219.

Collins, H. M. (1983). The sociology of scientific knowledge: Studies of contemporary science. *American Review of Sociology,* 9:265–285.

Collins, Randall. (1984). Statistics versus words. *Sociological Theory,* 2: 329–362.

Collins, Randall. (1986). Is 1980s sociology in the doldrums? *American Journal of Sociology,* 91:1336–1355.

Collins, Randall. (1988). *Theoretical sociology.* New York: Harcourt Brace Jovanovich.

Collins, Randall. (1989). Sociology: Proscience or anti-science? *American Sociological Review,* 54:124–139.

Collins, Randall. (1994). Why the social sciences won't become high-consensus, rapid-discovery science. *Sociological Forum,* 9:155–177.

Collins, Randall, and Sal Restivo. (1983). Development, diversity and conflict in the sociology of science. *Sociological Quarterly,* 24:185–200.

Comaroff, John, and Jean Comaroff. (1992). *Ethnography and the historical imagination.* Boulder, CO: Westview.

Committees on the Status of Women in Sociology. (1986). *The treatment of gender in research.* Washington, DC: American Sociological Association.

CASS, in Hudson, W. (1996). Computer Assisted Assessment Package. Tallahassee, FL. WALMYR Publishing Co.

Contrad, Peter, and Shulamit Reinharz. (1984). Computers and qualitative data: Editors' introductory essay. *Qualitative Sociology,* 7:3–15.

Converse, Jean M. (1984). Strong arguments and weak evidence: The open/closed questioning controversy of the 1940s. *Public Opinion Quarterly,* 48:267–282.

Converse, Jean M. (1987). *Survey research in the United States: Roots and emergence, 1890–1960.* Berkeley: University of California Press.

Converse, Jean M., and Stanley Presser. (1986). *Survey questions: Handcrafting the standardized questionnaire.* Beverly Hills, CA: Sage.

Converse, Jean M., and Howard Schuman. (1974). *Conversations at random: Survey research as interviewers see it.* New York: Wiley.

Cook, Judith A., and Mary Margaret Fonow. (1990). Knowledge and women's interests: Issues of epistemology and methodology in feminist sociological research. In *Feminist research methods,* edited by J. McCarl Nielsen, pp. 69–93. Boulder, CO: Westview.

Cook, Thomas D., and Donald T. Campbell. (1979). *Quasi-experimentation: Design and analysis issues for field settings.* Chicago: Rand McNally.

Coombs, R. H., and L. J. Goldman. (1973). Maintenance and discontinuity of coping mechanisms in an intensive care unit. *Social Problems,* 20:342–355.

Cooper, Harris M. (1984). *The integrative research review: A systematic approach.* Beverly Hills, CA: Sage.

Corcoran, K. (1993). Practice evaluation: Problems and promises of single-system designs in clinical practice. *Journal of Social Service Research,* 18(1/2):147–159.

Corcoran, K., and J. Fischer. (1994). *Measures for clinical practice,* Vol. 1 & 2, 2nd ed. New York: Free Press.

Corcoran, K., and W. Gingerich. (1994). Practice evaluation in the context of managed care: Case-recording methods for quality assurance reviews. *Research on Social Work Practice,* 4(3): 326–327.

Cordes, Colleen. (June 19, 1998). The academic pork barrel begins to fill up again. *Chronicle of Higher Education,* pp. A30–32.

Cordes, Colleen. (Dec. 14, 1988). Legacy of "Golden Fleece" awards to survive Proxmire's retirement. *Chronicle of Higher Education.*

Corsaro, William A. (1988). Routines in the peer culture of American and Italian nursery school children. *Sociology of Education,* 61:1–14.

Corsaro, William A. (1992). Cross-cultural analysis. In *Encyclopedia of Sociology,* Vol. 1, edited by E. and M. Borgatta, pp. 390–395. New York: Macmillan.

Corsaro, William A., and David Heise. (1990). Event structure models from ethnographic data. *Sociological Methodology,* 20:1–57.

Corsino, Louis. (1987). Fieldworkers blues: Emotional stress and research underinvolvement in fieldwork settings. *Social Science Journal,* 24: 275–285.

Coser, Lewis. (1981). The uses of classical sociological theory. *The future of the sociological classics,* edited by B. Rhea, pp. 170–182. Boston: George Allen and Unwin.

Costner, Herbert L. (1969). Theory, deduction and rules of correspondence. *American Journal of Sociology,* 75:245–263.

Costner, Herbert L. (1985). Theory, deduction and rules of correspondence. In *Causal models in the social sciences,* 2nd ed., edited by H. M. Blalock, Jr., pp. 229–250. New York: Aldine.

Cotter, Patrick R., Jeffrey Cohen, and Philip B. Coulter. (1982). Race of interview effects in telephone interviews. *Public Opinion Quarterly,* 46: 278–286.

Couch, Carl J. (1987). Objectivity: A crutch and club for bureaucrats/subjectivity: A haven for lost souls. *Sociological Quarterly,* 28:105–118.

Couper, Mick. (1997). Survey introductions and data quality. *Public Opinion Quarterly,* 61:317–338.

Couper, Mick, and Benjamin Rowe. (1996). Evaluation of a computer assisted self-interview component in a computer-assisted personal interview survey. *Public Opinion Quarterly,* 60:89–105.

Cowger, C. (1994). Assessing client strengths: Clinical assessment for client empowerment. *Social Work,* 39: 262–268.

Cowger, C. D., and G. Menon. (2000). Integrating qualitative and quantitative research methods. In *The handbook of social work research methods,* edited by B. Thyer, pp. 473–484. Thousand Oaks, CA: Sage.

Cowger, C. D., and C. A. Snively. (2002). Assessing client strengths: Individual, family and community empowerment. In *The strengths perspective in social work practice,* 3rd ed., edited by D. Saleebey, pp. 106–123. New York: Addison-Wesley Longman.

Cox, Stephen, and William Davidson. (1995). A meta-analysis of alternative education programs. *Crime and Delinquency,* 41:219–230.

Cozby, Paul C. (1984). *Using computers in the behavioral sciences.* Palo Alto, CA: Mayfield.

Craib, Ian. (1984). *Modern social theory: From Parsons to Habermas.* New York: St. Martin's Press.

Crane, Diana. (1967). The gatekeepers of science: Some factors affecting the selection of articles for scientific journals. *American Sociologist,* 2:195–201.

Crane, Diana. (1972). *Invisible colleges.* Chicago: University of Chicago Press.

Cress, Daniel M., and David A. Snow. (1996). Mobilization at the margins: Resources, benefactors, and the viability of homeless social movement organizations. *American Sociological Review,* 61:1089–1109.

Creswell, John W. (1994). *Research design: Qualitative and quantitative approaches.* Thousand Oaks, CA: Sage.

Croyle, Robert T., and Elizabeth Loftus. (1992). Improving episodic memory performance of survey respondents. In *Questions about questions: Inquiries into the cognitive bases of surveys,* edited by J. Turner, pp. 95–101. New York: Russell Sage Foundation.

Crozat, Matthew. (1998). Are the times a-changin'? Assessing the acceptance of protest in Western democracies. In *The Movement Society,* edited by D. Meyer and S. Tarrow, pp. 59–81. Totowa, NJ: Rowman and Littlefield.

Cullen, Francis T., Bruce Link, and Craig Polanzi. (1982). The seriousness of crime revisited: Have attitudes toward white collar crime changed? *Criminology,* 20:83–102.

Cummings, Scott. (1984). The political economy of funding for social science research. *Sociological Inquiry,* 54:154–170.

Curran, Daniel J., and Sandra Cook. (1993). Doing research in post-Tiananmen China. In *Research on Sensitive Topics,* edited by C. Renzetti and R. Lee, pp. 71–81. Thousand Oaks, CA: Sage.

Czaja, Ronald, Johnny Blair, and Jutta P. Sebestik. (1982). Respondent selection in a telephone survey: A comparison of three techniques. *Journal of Marketing Research,* 19:381–385.

Dabbs, James M., Jr. (1982). Making things visible. In *Varieties of qualitative research,* edited by J. Van Maanen, J. Dabbs, Jr., and R. R. Faulkner, pp. 31–64. Beverly Hills, CA: Sage.

Dale, Angela, S. Arber, and Michael Procter. (1988). *Doing secondary analysis.* Boston: Unwin Hyman.

Danis, F. (1999). Battered women and their families: Intervention strategies and treatment programs, edited by Albert R. Roberts. *Affilia: Journal of Women and Social Work,* 14(1): 130–132.

Dannefer, Dale. (1981). Neither socialization nor recruitment: The avocational careers of old car enthusiasts. *Social Forces,* 60:395–413.

D'Antonio, William V. (Aug. 1989). Executive office report: Sociology on the move. *ASA Footnotes,* 17, p. 2.

Danziger, Kurt. (1988). The question of identity: Who participated in psychological experiments? In *The rise of experimentation in American psychology,* edited by J. Morawski, pp. 35–52. New Haven, CT: Yale University Press.

Danziger, Sandra K. (1979). On doctor watching: Fieldwork in medical settings. *Urban Life,* 7:513–532.

Davenport, J. A., and J. Davenport. (1999). The corporatization of agriculture and the "browning" of Missouri. *NASW Missouri News,* 25(3):3.

Davidson, B. (1997). Service needs of relative caregivers: A qualitative analysis. *Families in Society,* 78:502–510.

Davis, Fred. (1959). The cabdriver and his fare: Facets of a fleeting relationship. *American Journal of Sociology,* 65:158–165.

Davis, Fred. (1973). The Martian and the convert: Ontological polarities in social research. *Urban Life,* 2:333–343.

Davis, James A. (1985). *The logic of causal order.* Beverly Hills, CA: Sage.

Davis, James A., and Tom W. Smith. (1986). *General social surveys 1972–1986 cumulative codebook.* Chicago: National Opinion Research Center, University of Chicago.

Davis, James A., and Tom W. Smith. (1992). *The NORC General Social Survey: A user's guide.* Newbury Park, CA: Sage.

Davis, L. (1985). Female and male voices in social work. *Social Work,* 30(2): 106–113.

Davis, L., and J. Marsh. (1994). Is feminist researach inherently qualitative, and is it a fundamentally different approach to research? In *Controversial issues in social work research,* edited by W. Hudson and P. Nurius, pp. 63–74. Needham Heights, MA: Allyn & Bacon.

Davis, L., and E. Proctor. (1989). *Race, gender and class. Guidelines for practice with individuals, families and groups.* Englewood Cliffs, NJ: Prentice-Hall.

Dawes, R. M., and T. W. Smith. (1985). Attitude and opinion measurement. In *The handbook of social psychology,* 3rd ed., Vol. 1, edited by G. Lindzey and E. Aronson, pp. 509–566. New York: Random House.

Dean, John P., Robert L. Eichhorn, and Lois R. Dean. (1969). Fruitful informants for intensive interviewing. In *Issues in participant observation,* edited by G. McCall and J. L. Simmons, pp. 142–144. Reading, MA: Addison-Wesley.

Dean, John P., and William Foote Whyte. (1969). How do you know if the informant is telling the truth? In *Issues in participant observation,* edited by G. McCall and J. L. Simmons, pp. 105–115. Reading, MA: Addison-Wesley.

Dean, R. (1993). *Constructivism: An approach to clinical practice.* New York: Harper and Row.

Dean, R., and B. Fendby. (1989). Exploring epistemologies: Social work action as a reflection of philosophical assumptions. *Journal of Social Work Education,* 5(1):46–54.

de Anda, D., ed. (1997). *Controversial issues in multiculturalism.* Needham Heights, MA: Allyn & Bacon.

Deegan, Mary Jo. (1988). *Jane Adams and the men of the Chicago School, 1892–1918.* New Brunswick, NJ: Transaction.

DeJong, P., and S. Miller. (1995). How to interview for client strengths. *Social Work,* 40(6):729–736.

DeLamater, John, and Pat MacCorquodale. (1975). The effects of interview schedule variations on reported sexual behavior. *Sociological Methods and Research,* 4:215–236.

DeMaio, Theresa J. (1980). Refusals: Who, where and why? *Public Opinion Quarterly,* 44:223–233.

DeMaio, Theresa J. (1984). Social desirability and survey measurement: A review. In *Surveying Subjective Phenomena,* Vol. 2, edited by C. Turner and E. Martin, pp. 257–282. New York: Russell Sage Foundation.

Denzin, Norman K. (1970). Symbolic interactionism and ethnomethodology. In *Understanding everyday life,* edited by J. Douglas, pp. 261–286. Chicago: Aldine.

Denzin, Norman K. (1989). *The research act: A theoretical introduction to sociological methods,* 3rd ed. Englewood Cliffs, NJ: Prentice-Hall.

Denzin, N. (1990). *The research act: A theoretical introduction to sociological methods.* New York: Aldine.

Denzin, N. (1993). The art and politics of interpretation. In *Handbook of qualitative research,* edited by N. Denzin and Y. Lincoln, pp. 500–515. Thousand Oaks, CA: Sage.

Denzin, Norman K., and Kai Erikson. (1982). On the ethics of disguised observation: An exchange. In *Social research ethics,* edited by M. Blume. New York: Macmillan.

Denzin, Norman K., and Yvonna S. Lincoln, eds. (1994). Introduction: Entering the field of qualitative research. In *Handbook of qualitative research,* pp. 1–18. Thousand Oaks, CA: Sage.

DePoy, E., A. Hartman, and D. Haslett. (1999). Critical action research: A model for social work knowing. *Social Work,* 44(6):560–569.

Derksen, Linda, and John Gartrell. (1992). Scientific explanation. In *Encyclopedia of sociology,* Vol. 4, edited by E. and M. Borgatta, pp. 1711–1720. New York: Macmillan.

Devaney, B., and Rossi, P. (1997). Thinking through evaluation design options. *Children and Youth Services Review,* 19:587–606.

Devault, Marjorie L. (1990). Talking and listening from women's standpoint: Feminist strategies for interviewing and analysis. *Social Problems,* 37:96–116.

deVaus, D. A. (1986). *Surveys in social research.* Boston: George Allen and Unwin.

Devore, W., and E. Schlesinger. (1996). *Ethnic-sensitive social work practice,* 4th ed. Boston: Allyn & Bacon.

Dexter, Lewis A. (1970). *Elite and specialized interviewing.* Evanston, IL: Northwestern University Press.

Diamond, Sigmund. (1988). Informed consent and survey research: The FBI and the University of Michigan Survey Research Center. In *Surveying social life: Papers in honor of Herbert H. Hyman,* edited by H. O'Gorman, pp. 72–99. Middletown, CT: Wesleyan University Press.

Dickson, David. (1984). *The new politics of science.* Chicago: University of Chicago Press.

Diener, Edward, and Rick Crandall. (1978). *Ethics in social and behavioral research.* Chicago: University of Chicago Press.

Dijkstra, Wil, and Johannes van der Zouwen, eds. (1982). *Response behavior in the survey interview.* New York: Academic Press.

Dillman, Don A. (1978). *Mail and telephone surveys: The total design method.* New York: Wiley.

Dillman, Don A. (1983). Mail and other self-administered questionnaires. In *Handbook of survey research,* edited by P. Rossi, J. Wright, and A. Anderson, pp. 359–377. Orlando, FL: Academic Press.

Dillman, Don A. (1991). The design and administration of mail surveys. *Annual Review of Sociology,* 17:225–249.

Dillman, Don A., Eleanor Singer, Jon Clark, and James Treat. (1996). Effects of benefits, appeals, mandatory appeals and variations in statements of confidentiality on completion rates for census questionnaires. *Public Opinion Quarterly,* 60:376–389.

Dixon, D., and Thyer, B. (1997). A multidisciplinary team treatment of Vietnam veterans with post traumatic stress disorder. *Social Work and Social Services Review,* 6(3):163–174.

Dixon, E., and L. Taylor. (March 1994). Workshop on cultural diversity in the workplace. The Center for Human Services Training and Development,

University Extension, University of California, Davis.

Dodgshon, R. (1998). *Society in time and space: A geographical perspective on change.* Cambridge: Cambridge University Press.

Domhoff, G. William. (1974). *The Bohemian Grove and other retreats.* New York: Harper and Row.

Donald, Robert B. et al. (1983). *Writing clear paragraphs,* 2nd ed. Englewood Cliffs, NJ: Prentice-Hall.

Dooley, David. (1984). *Social research methods.* Englewood Cliffs, NJ: Prentice-Hall.

Dorfman, R. (1996). *Paradigms of clinical social work,* Vol 2. New York: Brunner/Mazel Publishers.

Douglas, Jack D. (1976). *Investigative social research.* Beverly Hills, CA: Sage.

Douglas, Jack D. (1985). *Creative interviewing.* Beverly Hills, CA: Sage.

Douglas, Jack D., and Paul K. Rasmussen. (1977). *The nude beach.* Beverly Hills, CA: Sage.

Downey, Gary L. (1986). Ideology and the Clamshell identity: Organizational dilemmas in the anti-nuclear power movement. *Social Problems,* 33:357–373.

Downs, W., and A. Rubin. (1994). Lacking evidence of effectiveness, should single-case evaluation techniques be encouraged in practice? In *Controversial issues in social work research,* edited by W. Hudson and P. Nurius, pp. 113–127. Needham Heights, MA: Allyn & Bacon.

Drass, Kriss. (1980). The analysis of qualitative data: A computer program. *Urban Life,* 9:332–353.

Dressler, William H. (1991). *Stress and adaptation in the context of culture: Depression in a southern black community.* Albany: State University of New York Press.

Drew, C., M. Hardman, and A. Hart. (1996). *Designing and conducting research: Inquiry in education and social science.* Boston: Allyn & Bacon.

Drucker, P. (1993). *Post-capitalist society.* New York: Harper-Collins.

DuBois, W. E. Burghardt. (1899). *The Philadelphia Negro.* New York: Benjamin Bloom.

Duncan, Otis Dudley. (1975). *Introduction to structural equation models.* New York: Academic Press.

Duncan, Otis Dudley. (1984). *Notes on social measurement: Historical and critical.* New York: Russell Sage Foundation.

Duncan, Otis Dudley, and Magnus Stenbeck. (1988). No opinion or not sure? *Public Opinion Quarterly,* 52:513–525.

Dungee-Anderson, D., and J. Beckett. (1995). A process model for multicultural social work practice. *Families in Society,* 78:459–468.

Durkheim, Emile. (1938). *Rules of the sociological method,* trans. Sarah Solovay and John Mueller, edited by G. Catlin. Chicago: University of Chicago Press.

Dynes, Russell R. (1984). The institutionalization of COSSA. *Sociological Inquiry,* 54:211–229.

Easterday, Lois, Diana Papademas, Laura Schorr, and Catherine Valentine. (1982). The making of a female researcher: Role problems in fieldwork. In *Field research,* edited by R. G. Burgess, pp. 62–67. Boston: George Allen and Unwin.

Eastrope, Gary. (1974). *History of social research methods.* London: Longman.

Eckberg, Douglas Lee, and Lester Hill, Jr. (1979). The paradigm concept and sociology. *American Sociological Review,* 44:937–947.

Eder, Donna. (1981). Ability grouping as a self-fulfilling prophecy: A micro-analysis of teacher-student interaction. *Sociology of Education,* 54:151–162.

Eder, Donna. (1985). The cycle of popularity: Interpersonal relations among female adolescents. *Sociology of Education,* 58:154–165.

Edgar, G., B. Friedman, and J. Zimmer. (1990). Models of intensive case management. *Journal of Gerontological Social Work,* 15:75–101.

Edward, G. Franklin. (1974). E. Franklin Frazier. In *Black sociologists: Historical and contemporary perspectives,* edited by J. Blackwell and M. Janowitz, pp. 85–117. Chicago: University of Chicago Press.

Edwards, Allen L. (1957). *Techniques of attitude scale construction.* New York: Appleton-Century-Crofts.

Edwards, Rosalind. (1993). An education in interviewing: Placing the researcher and research. In *Research on sensitive topics,* edited by C. Renzetti and R. Lee, pp. 181–196. Thousand Oaks, CA: Sage.

Eichler, Margrit. (1988). *Nonsexist research methods: A practical guide.* Boston: George Allen and Unwin.

Eisen, S., J. Hanpeter, and L. Kreuger. (1983). Monitoring medication compliance: Discussion of a new device. *Journal of Compliance in Health Care,* 2(2):110–119.

Eliasoph, Nina. (1998). *Avoiding politics: How Americans produce apathy in everyday life.* New York: Cambridge University Press.

Ell, K. (1996). Social work and health care practice and policy: A psychosocial research agenda. *Social Work,* 41:583–592.

Ellen, R. F., ed. (1984a). *Ethnographic research: A guide to general conduct.* Orlando, FL: Academic Press.

Ellen, R. F. (1984b). Some other interactionist methods. In *Ethnographic research: A guide to general conduct,* edited by R. F. Ellen, pp. 273–293. Orlando, FL: Academic Press.

Emerson, Robert M. (1981). Observational field work. *Annual Review of Sociology,* 7:351–378.

Emerson, Robert M. (1983). Introduction. In *Contemporary field research,* edited by R. M. Emerson, pp. 1–16. Boston: Little, Brown.

Emigh, Rebecca Jean. (1997). The power of negative thinking: The use of negative case methodology in the development of sociological theory. *Theory and Society,* 26:649–684.

Epstein, W. (1990). Confirmation of bias among social work journals. *Science, Technology, and Human Values,* 15(1): 244–247.

Erikson, Kai T. (1970). A comment on disguised observation in sociology. In *Qualitative methodology,* edited by W. J. Filstead, pp. 252–260. Chicago: Markham.

Erikson, Kai T. (1978). *Everything in its path.* New York: Touchstone.

Evans, Peter, and John D. Stephens. (1989). Studying development since the sixties: The emergence of a new comparative political economy. *Theory and Society,* 17:713–746.

Evans, William A., Michael Krippendorf, Jae Yoon, Paulette Posluszny, and Sari Thomas. (1990). Science in the prestige and national tabloid press. *Social Science Quarterly,* 71:105–117.

Ewalt, P., and N. Mokuau. (1995). Self-determination from a Pacific perspective. *Social Work,* 40(2):168–176.

Fantasia, Rick. (1988). *Cultures of solidarity: Consciousness, action and contemporary American workers.* Berkeley: University of California Press.

Faris, R. E. L. (1967). *Chicago sociology, 1920–1932.* San Francisco: Chandler.

Faupel, Charles E., and Carl B. Klockars. (1987). Drugs-crime connections: Elaborations from the life history of hard-core heroin addicts. *Social Problems,* 34:54–68.

Fay, Brian. (1975). *Social theory and political practice.* London: George Allen and Unwin.

Fay, Brian. (1987). *Critical social science: Liberation and its limits.* Ithaca, NY: Cornell University Press.

Featherman, David L., and Richard C. Rockwell. (1992). Social science research council. *Encyclopedia of Sociology,* Vol. 4, edited by E. and M. Borgatta, pp. 1942–1945. New York: Macmillan.

Ferriss, Abbott L. (1988). The uses of social indicators. *Social Forces,* 66: 601–617.

Fetterman, David M. (1989). *Ethnography: Step by step.* Newbury Park, CA: Sage.

Fetterman, D. (2001). *Foundations of empowerment evaluation.* Thousand Oaks, CA: Sage.

Fichter, Joseph H., and William L. Kolb. (1970). Ethical limitations on socio-logical reporting. In *Qualitative methodology,* edited by W. J. Filstead, pp. 261–270. Chicago: Markham.

Fielding, Nigel G., and Raymond M. Lee, eds. (1991). *Using computers in qualitative research.* Newbury Park, CA: Sage.

Fine, Gary Alan. (1979). Small groups and culture creation: The idioculture of Little League baseball teams. *American Sociological Review,* 44: 733–745.

Fine, Gary Alan. (1987). *With the boys: Little League baseball and preadolescent culture.* Chicago: University of Chicago Press.

Fine, Gary Alan. (1988). The ten commandments of writing. *The American Sociologist,* 19:152–157.

Fine, Gary Alan. (1990). Organizational time: The temporal experience of restaurant kitchens. *Social Forces,* 69: 95–114.

Fine, Gary Alan. (1992). The culture of production: Aesthetic choices and constraints in culinary work. *American Journal of Sociology,* 97:1268–1294.

Fine, Gary Alan, and Barry Glassner. (1979). Participant observation with children: Promise and problems. *Urban Life,* 8:153–174.

Fink, A. (1993). *Evaluation fundamentals: Guiding health programs, research and policy.* Thousand Oaks, CA: Sage.

Finkel, Steven E., Thomas M. Guterbock, and Marian J. Borg. (1991). Race-of-interviewer effects in a preelection poll: Virginia 1989. *Public Opinion Quarterly,* 55:313–330.

Finsterbusch, Kurt, and Annabelle Bender Motz. (1980). *Social research for policy decisions.* Belmont, CA: Wadsworth.

Finsterbusch, Kurt, and C. P. Wolf. (1981). *Methodology of social impact assessment.* Stroudsburg, PA: Hutchinson Ross.

Firebaugh, Glenn, and Kevin Chen. (1995). Vote turnout of nineteenth amendment women: The enduring effect of disenfranchisement. *American Journal of Sociology,* 100:972–996.

Fischer, Claude S. (1992). *America calling: A social history of the telephone to 1940.* Berkeley: University of California Press.

Fischer, Claude S. et al. (1996). *Inequality by Design: Cracking the Bell Curve Myth.* Princeton, NJ: Princeton University Press.

Fischer, Frank. (1985). Critical evaluation of public policy: A methodological case study. In *Critical theory and public life,* edited by J. Forester, pp. 231–257. Cambridge, MA: MIT Press.

Fischer, J. (January 1973). Is casework effective? A review. *Social Work,* 1:5–20.

Fischer, J. (1978a). Does anything work? *Journal of Social Service Research,* 1:215–243.

Fischer, J. (1978b). *Effective casework practice: An eclectic approach.* New York: McGraw-Hill.

Fischer, J. (1983). Evaluation of social work effectiveness: Is positive evidence always good evidence? *Social Work,* 28(1):74–77.

Fischer, J., and K. Corcoran. (1994). *Measures for clinical practice: A source book,* Vol. 1 & 2. New York: Free Press.

Fisher, D. (1991). *An introduction to constructivism for social workers.* New York: Praeger.

Fiske, Donald W. (1982). Convergent-discriminant validation in measurements and research strategies. In *Forms of validation in research,* edited by D. Brinberg and L. H. Kidder, pp. 72–92. San Francisco: Jossey-Bass.

Fiske, Edward B. (July 12, 1989). The misleading concept of "average" on reading tests changes, and more students fall below it. *New York Times.*

Fitchen, Janet M. (1991). *Endangered spaces, enduring places: Change, identity and survival in rural America.* Boulder, CO: Westview.

Fletcher, Colin. (1974). *Beneath the surface: An account of three styles of sociological research.* Boston: Routledge and Kegan Paul.

Flick, Uwe. (1998). *An introduction to qualitative research.* Thousand Oaks, CA: Sage.

Flora, Cornelia Butler. (1979). Changes in women's status in women's magazine fiction: Differences by social class. *Social Problems,* 26:558–569.

Florin, P., and A. Wandersman. (1990). An introduction to citizen particpation, voluntary organizations and community development: Insights for empowerment research. *American Journal of Community Psychology,* 18(1):41–50.

Flynn, J. (1995). Social justice and social agencies. In *Encyclopedia of Social Work,* 19th ed., edited by R. L. Edwards, pp. 2173–2179. Washington, DC: NASW Press.

Foddy, William. (1993). *Constructing questions for interviews and questionnaires: Theory and practice in social research.* New York: Cambridge University Press.

Foddy, William. (1995). Probing: A dangerous practice in social surveys? *Quality and Quantity,* 29:73–86.

Fogel, S. (1997). Moving along: An exploratory study of homeless women with children using a transitional housing program. *Journal of Sociology and Social Welfare,* 24(3):113–133.

Fogel, S. (1998). Sexual harassment in BSW field placement students: Is it a problem? *Journal of Baccalaureate Social Work,* 3(2):17–29.

Fontana, Andrea, and James H. Frey. (1994). Interviewing: The art of science. In *Handbook of qualitative research,* edited by N. Denzin and

Y. Lincoln, pp. 361–376. Thousand Oaks, CA: Sage.

Fook, J. (1993). *Radical casework: A theory of practice.* St. Leonards, NSW: George Allen and Unwin.

Forest, Kay B., Phyllis Moen, and Donna Dempster-McClain. (1995). Cohort differences in the transition to motherhood: The variable effects of education and employment before marriage. *Sociological Quarterly,* 36:315–336.

Foster, Gary S., Richard L. Hummel, and Donald J. Adamchak. (1998). Patterns of conception, natality and mortality from midwestern cemeteries: A sociological analysis of historical data. *Sociological Quarterly,* 39:473–490.

Fowler, Edward. (1996). *San'ya blues: Laboring life in contemporary Tokyo.* Ithaca, NY: Cornell University Press.

Fowler, Floyd J., Jr. (1984). *Survey research methods.* Beverly Hills, CA: Sage.

Fowler, Floyd J., Jr. (1992). How unclear terms can affect survey data. *Public Opinion Quarterly,* 56:218–231.

Fowler, Floyd Jackson, and Charles Cannell. (1996). Using behavioral coding to identify cognitive problems with survey questions. In *Answering Questions,* edited by N. Schwarz and S. Sudman, pp. 15–36. San Francisco: Jossey-Bass.

Fox, James Alan, and Paul E. Tracy. (1986). *Randomized response: A method for sensitive surveys.* Beverly Hills, CA: Sage.

Fox, John. (1992). Statistical graphics. In *Encyclopedia of Sociology,* Vol 4, edited by E. and M. Borgatta, pp. 2054–2073. New York: Macmillan.

Fox, Richard, Melvin R. Crask, and Jonghoon Kim. (1988). Mail survey response rate: A meta-analysis of selected techniques for inducing response. *Public Opinion Quarterly,* 52:467–491.

Franke, Charles O. (1983). Ethnography. In *Contemporary field research,* edited by R. M. Emerson, pp. 60–67. Boston: Little, Brown.

Franke, Richard H., and James D. Kaul. (1978). The Hawthorne experiments: First statistical interpretation. *American Sociological Review,* 43:623–643.

Frankel, Martin. (1983). Sampling theory. In *Handbook of survey research,* edited by P. Rossi, J. Wright, and A. Anderson, pp. 21–67. Orlando, FL: Academic Press.

Franklin, D. (1985). Differential clinical assessments: The influence of class and race. *Social Service Review,* 59: 44–61.

Frazier, E. Franklin. (1957). *The black bourgeoisie.* Glencoe, IL: Free Press.

Frechette-Schrader, Kristin. (1994). *Ethics of scientific research.* Lanham, MD: Rowland and Littlefield.

Fredrickson, George. (1981). *White supremacy.* New York: Oxford University Press.

Freeman, Howard. (1983). *Applied sociology.* San Francisco: Jossey-Bass.

Freeman, Howard. (1992). Evaluation research. In *Encyclopedia of Sociology,* Vol. 2, edited by E. and M. Borgatta, pp. 594–598. New York: Macmillan.

Freeman, Howard, and Peter H. Rossi. (1984). Furthering the applied side of sociology. *American Sociological Review,* 49:571–580.

Freeman, Howard, and Merrill J. Shanks, eds. (1983). The emergence of computer assisted survey research. *Sociological Methods and Research,* 23: 115–230.

Freidson, Eliot. (1986). *Professional powers: A study of the institutionalization of formal knowledge.* Chicago: University of Chicago Press.

Freidson, Eliot. (1994). *Professionalism reborn: Theory, prophecy and policy.* Chicago: University of Chicago Press.

Freire, Paulo. (1970). *Pedagogy of the oppressed,* trans. Myra Bergman Ramos. New York: Seabury.

Freire, P. (1991). *Pedagogy of the oppressed: New revised 20th anniversary edition.* New York: Continuum.

Freitag, Peter. (1983). The myth of corporate capture. *Social Problems,* 30: 480–491.

Frey, James H. (1983). *Survey research by telephone.* Beverly Hills, CA: Sage.

Friedrichs, Robert W. (1970). *A sociology of sociology.* New York: Free Press.

Frost, Peter, and Ralph Stablein, eds. (1992). *Doing exemplary research.* Newbury Park, CA: Sage.

Fuchs, Stephan, and Jonathan H. Turner. (1986). What makes a science "mature"? Patterns of organizational control in scientific production. *Sociological Theory,* 4:143–150.

Fuller, Linda. (1988). Fieldwork in forbidden terrain: The U.S. state and the case of Cuba. *American Sociologist,* 19:99–120.

Gabor, P., Y. Unrau, and R. Grinnell, Jr. (1999). *Evaluation for social workers: A quality improvement approach for the social services.* New York: Allyn & Bacon.

Galaskiewicz, Joseph. (1985). Professional networks and the institutionalization of a single mind set. *American Sociological Review,* 50:639–658.

Galaskiewicz, Joseph. (1987). The study of a business elite and corporate philanthropy in a United States metropolitan area. In *Research methods for elite studies,* edited by G. Moyser and M. Wagstaffe, pp. 147–165. Boston: George Allen and Unwin.

Galaskiewicz, Joseph, and Stanley Wasserman. (1993). Social network analysis: Concepts, methodology and directions for the 1990s. *Sociological Methods and Research,* 22:3–22.

Galliher, John F., and James L. McCartney. (1973). The influence of funding agencies on juvenile delinquency research. *Social Problems,* 21:77–90.

Gambrill, E. (1999). Evidence-based practice: An alternative to authority-based practice. *Families in Society,* 80: 341–350.

Gambrill, E., and R. Barth. (1980). Single-case study designs revisited. *Social Work Research and Abstracts,* 16(3): 15–20.

Gamson, William A. (1992). *Talking politics.* Cambridge: Cambridge University Press.

Gans, Herbert J. (1982). The participant observer as a human being: Observations on the personal aspects of fieldwork. In *Field research,* edited by R. G. Burgess, pp. 53–61. Boston: George Allen and Unwin.

Garfinkel, Harold. (1967). *Studies in ethnomethodology.* Englewood Cliffs, NJ: Prentice-Hall.

Garfinkel, Harold. (1974a). The origins of the term "ethnomethodology." In *Ethnomethodology,* edited by R. Turner, pp. 15–18. Middlesex: Penguin.

Garfinkel, Harold. (1974b). The rational properties of scientific and common sense activities. In *Positivism and sociology,* edited by A. Giddens, pp. 53–74. London: Heinemann.

Gaston, Jerry. (1978). *The reward system in British and American science.* New York: Wiley.

Geer, John G. (1988). What do open-ended questions measure? *Public Opinion Quarterly,* 52:365–371.

Geertz, Clifford. (1973). *The interpretation of cultures.* New York: Basic Books.

Geertz, Clifford. (1979). From the native's point of view: On the nature of anthropological understanding. In *Interpretative social science: A reader,* edited by P. Rabinow and W. Sullivan, pp. 225–242. Berkeley: University of California Press.

Geiger, Roger L. (1986). *To advance knowledge: The growth of American research universities, 1900–1940.* New York: Oxford University Press.

Gelman, S., D. Pollack, and A. Little Soldier. (1999). Confidentiality of social work records in the computer age. *Social Work,* 44(3):243–252.

Georges, Robert A., and Michael O. Jones. (1980). *People studying people.* Berkeley: University of California Press.

Gephart, Robert P., Jr. (1988). *Ethnostatistics: Qualitative foundations for quantitative research.* Newbury Park, CA: Sage.

Germain, C. B., and A. Gitterman. (1996). *The life model of social work practice: Advanced theory and practice.* New York: McGraw-Hill.

Geyman, J., R. Deyo, and S. Ramsey, eds. (2000). *Evidence-based clinical practice: Concepts and approaches.* Boston: Butterworth-Heinemann.

Ghali, S. B. (1977). Cultural sensitivity and the Puerto Rican client. *Social Casework,* 58:459–468.

Gibbs, Jack. (1989). Conceptualization of terrorism. *American Sociological Review,* 54:329–340.

Gibelman, M., S. Gelman, and J. Fast. (1999). The downside of cyberspace: Cheating made easy. *Journal of Social Work Education,* 35(3):367–376.

Giddens, Anthony. (1976). *New rules of sociological method: Positivist critique of interpretative sociologies.* New York: Basic Books.

Giddens, Anthony. (1978). Positivism and its critics. In *A history of sociological analysis,* edited by T. Bottomore and R. Nisbet. New York: Basic Books.

Giddens, Anthony. (1994). Elites and power. In *Social stratification: Class, race & gender in sociological perspective,* edited by D. Grusky, pp. 170–174. Boulder, CO: Westview.

Gieryn, Thomas F. (1978). Problem retention and problem change in science. In *The sociology of science,* edited by J. Gaston. San Francisco: Jossey-Bass.

Gil, D. (1998). *Confronting injustice and oppression: Concepts and strategies for social workers.* New York: Columbia University Press.

Gilbert, Margaret. (1992). *On social facts.* Princeton, NJ: Princeton University Press.

Gilgun, J. (1994). A case for case studies in social work research. *Social Work,* 39(4):371–380.

Gillespie, D. (1999). Ethical issues in research. In *Encyclopedia of Social Work,* 19th ed., pp. 884–893. Washington, DC: NASW Press.

Gillespie, Richard. (1988). The Hawthorne experiments and the politics of experimentation. In *The rise of experimentation in American psychology,* edited by J. Morawski, pp. 114–137. New Haven, CT: Yale University Press.

Gillespie, Richard. (1991). *Manufacturing knowledge: A history of the Hawthorne experiments.* New York: Cambridge University Press.

Gilljam, Mikael, and David Granberg. (1993). Should we take Don't Know for an answer? *Public Opinion Quarterly,* 57:348–357.

Gitterman, A., ed. (2001). *Handbook of social work practice with vulnerable and resilient populations.* New York: Columbia University Press.

Glaser, Barney, and Anselm Strauss. (1967). *The discovery of grounded theory.* Chicago: Aldine.

Glaser, Barney, and Anselm Strauss. (1968). *A time for dying.* Chicago: Aldine.

Glasser, Gerald J., and Gale O. Metzger. (1972). Random digit dialing as a method of telephone sampling. *Journal of Marketing Research,* 9:59–64.

Glock, Charles Y. (1987). Reflections on doing survey research. In *Surveying social life: Papers in honor of Herbert H. Hyman,* edited by H. O'Gorman, pp. 31–59. Middletown, CT: Wesleyan University Press.

Glucksmann, Miriam. (1974). *Structuralist analysis in contemporary social thought: A comparison of the theories of Claude Levi-Strauss and Louis Althusser.* Boston: Routledge and Kegan Paul.

Gold, Raymond L. (1969). Roles in sociological field observation. In *Issues in participant observation,* edited by G. J. McCall and J. L. Simmons, pp. 30–38. Reading, MA: Addison-Wesley.

Golden, Tim. (December 9, 1996). Universities find donors sometimes impose a price. *The New York Times.*

Goldman, B., and J. Bausch. (1997). *Directory of unpublished experimental mental measures.* Washington, DC: American Psychological Association.

Goldstein, H. (1992). If social work hasn't made progress as a science, might it be an art? *Families in Society,* 73:48–55.

Goldstein, Robert Justin. (1978). *Political repression in modern America.* New York: Schenckman.

Gonor, George. (1977). "Situation" versus "frame": The "interactionist" and the "structuralist" analysis of everyday life. *American Sociological Review,* 42:854–867.

Goodsell, Charles B. (1983). Welfare waiting rooms. *Urban Life,* 12:464–477.

Gorden, Raymond. (1980). *Interviewing: Strategy, techniques and tactics,* 3rd ed. Homewood, IL: Dorsey Press.

Gorden, Raymond. (1992). *Basic interviewing skills.* Itasca, IL: Peacock.

Gordon, David F. (1987). Getting close by staying distant: Fieldwork with proselytizing groups. *Qualitative Sociology,* 10:267–287.

Gordon, Randall A., T. A. Bindrim, M. L. McNicholas, and T. L. Walden. (1988). Perceptions of blue-collar and white-collar crime: The effect of defendant race on simulated juror decisions. *Journal of Social Psychology,* 128:191–197.

Gorelick, Sherry. (1991). Contradictions of feminist methodology. *Gender and Society,* 5:459–477.

Gould, Roger V. (1991). Multiple networks and mobilization in the Paris Commune, 1871. *American Sociological Review,* 56:716–729.

Gouldner, Alvin. (1970). *The coming crisis of Western sociology.* New York: Basic Books.

Gouldner, Alvin W. (1976). The dark side of the dialectic: Toward a new objectivity. *Sociological Inquiry,* 46:3–16.

Goward, Nicola. (1984a). Publications on fieldwork experiences. In *Ethnographic research: A guide to general conduct,* edited by R. F. Ellen, pp. 88–100. Orlando, FL: Academic Press.

Goward, Nicola. (1984b). Personal interaction and adjustment. In *Ethnographic research: A guide to general conduct,* edited by R. F. Ellen, pp. 100–118. Orlando, FL: Academic Press.

Goyder, John C. (1982). Factors affecting response rates to mailed questionnaires. *American Sociological Review,* 47:550–554.

Graham, Sandra. (1992). Most of the subjects were white and middle class: Trends in published research on African Americans in selected APA journals, 1970–1989. *American Psychologist,* 47:629–639.

Granovetter, Mark. (1976). Network sampling: Some first steps. *American Journal of Sociology,* 81:1287–1303.

Grant, Linda, Kathryn B. Ward, and Xue Lan Rong. (1987). Is there an association between gender and methods of sociological research? *American Sociological Review,* 52:856–862.

Gray, Bradford H. (1982). The regulatory context of social and behavioral research. In *Ethical issues in social science research,* edited by T. Beauchamp, R. Faden, R. J. Wallace, and L. Walters, pp. 329–354. Baltimore: Johns Hopkins University Press.

Gray, Paul S. (1980). Exchange and access in field work. *Urban Life,* 9:309–331.

Green, J. (1999). *Cultural awareness in the human services: A multi-ethnic approach,* 3rd ed. Boston: Allyn & Bacon.

Green, J. C. (1997). Evaluation as advocacy. *Evaluation Practice,* 18(1): 25–35.

Green, R. (1994). *Human behavior theory: A diversity framework.* New York: Aldyne De Gruyger.

Green, R., and L. McGuire. (1998). Ecological perspective: Meeting the challenge of practice with diverse populations. In *Cultural awareness in the human services: A multi-ethnic approach,* edited by J. Green, pp. 1–27. Boston: Allyn & Bacon.

Greenberg, Daniel S. (1967). *The politics of pure science.* New York: New American Library.

Greenwald, Howard P. (1992). Ethics in social research. In *Encyclopedia of sociology,* Vol. 2., edited by E. and M. Borgatta, pp. 584–588. New York: Macmillan.

Gregoire, T., and C. Snively. (2001). The relationship of social support and economic self-sufficiency to substance abuse outcomes in a long-term recovery program for women. *Journal of Drug Education,* 31(3):221–237.

Griffin, Larry J. (1992). Comparative-historical analysis. In *Encyclopedia of sociology,* Vol. 1, edited by E. and M. Borgatta, pp. 263–271. New York: Macmillan.

Griffin, Larry J. (1993). Narrative, event structure analysis and causal interpretation in historical sociology. *American Journal of Sociology,* 98:1094–1133.

Griffin, Larry J., and Charles Ragin. (1994). Some observations on formal methods of qualitative analysis. *Sociological Methods and Research,* 23:4–22.

Griffin, Larry J., Michael E. Wallace, and Beth A. Rubin. (1986). Capitalist resistance to the organization of labor before the New Deal: Why? How? Success? *American Sociological Review,* 51:147–167.

Grinnell, Frederick. (1987). *The scientific attitude.* Boulder, CO: Westview.

Grinnell, R., ed. (1999). *Social work research and evaluation: Quantitative and qualitative approaches,* 5th ed. New York: Peacock.

Griswold, Wendy. (1987). A methodological framework for the sociology of culture. In *Sociological methodology, 1987,* edited by C. Clogg, pp. 1–35. San Francisco: Jossey-Bass.

Griswold, Wendy. (1994). *Cultures and societies in a changing world.* Thousand Oaks, CA: Pine Forge Press.

Grosof, Miriam Schapiro, and Hyman Sardy. (1985). *A research primer for the social and behavioral sciences.* Orlando, FL: Academic Press.

Gross, Daniel R. (1984). Time allocation: A tool for the study of cultural behavior. *Annual Review of Anthropology,* 13:519–558.

Gross, Edward. (1986). Waiting at Mayo. *Urban Life,* 15:139–164.

Gross, E. (1995). Deconstructing politically correct practice literature: The American Indian case. *Social Work,* 40(2):206–214.

Groves, Robert M. (1996). How do we know what we think they think is really what they think? In *Answering Questions,* edited by N. Schwarz and S. Sudman, pp. 389–402. San Francisco: Jossey Bass.

Groves, Robert M., Nancy H. Fultz, and Elizabeth Martin. (1992). Direct questioning about comprehension in a survey setting. In *Questions about questions: Inquiries into the cognitive bases of surveys,* edited by J. Turner, pp. 49–61. New York: Russell Sage Foundation.

Groves, Robert M., and Robert L. Kahn. (1979). *Surveys by telephone: A national comparison with personal interviews.* New York: Academic Press.

Groves, Robert M., and Nancy Mathiowetz. (1984). Computer assisted telephone interviewing: Effects on interviewers and respondents. *Public Opinion Quarterly,* 48:356–369.

Guba, E. (1987). *Naturalistic evaluation: New directions for program evaluation.* San Francisco: Jossey-Bass.

Guba, Egon G., and Yvonna S. Lincoln. (1994). Competing paradigms in qualitative research. In *Handbook of qualitative research,* edited by N. Denzin and Y. Lincoln, pp. 105–117. Thousand Oaks, CA: Sage.

Gubrium, Jaber F., and James A. Holstein. (1992). Qualitative methods. In *Encyclopedia of sociology,* Vol. 3, edited by E. and M. Borgatta, pp. 1577–1582. New York: Macmillan.

Gurevitch, Z. D. (1988). The other side of the dialogue: On making the other strange and the experience of otherness. *American Journal of Sociology,* 93:1179–1199.

Gurney, Joan Neff. (1985). Not one of the guys: The female researcher in a male-

dominated setting. *Qualitative Sociology,* 8:42–62.

Gusfield, Joseph. (1976). The literary rhetoric of science: Comedy and pathos in drinking driver research. *American Sociological Review,* 41: 16–34.

Gustavsen, Bjørn. (1986). Social research as participatory dialogue. In *The use and abuse of social science,* edited by F. Heller, pp. 143–156. Beverly Hills, CA: Sage.

Gustin, Bernard H. (1973). Charisma, recognition and the motivation of scientists. *American Journal of Sociology,* 86:1119–1134.

Gutierrez, L. M., R. J. Parsons, and E. O. Cox, eds. (1998). *Empowerment in social work practice: A sourcebook.* Pacific Grove, CA: Brooks/Cole.

Gutterbock, Thomas M. (1997). Review: Why *Money* magazine's "Best Places" keep changing. *Public Opinion Quarterly,* 61:339–355.

Guttman, Louis. (1950). The basis for scalogram analysis. In *Measurement and prediction,* edited by S. A. Stouffer, L. Buttman, E. A. Suchman, P. F. Lazarfeld, S. A. Star, and J. A. Clausen, pp. 60–90. Princeton, NJ: Princeton University Press.

Guttman, Louis. (1970). A basis for scaling qualitative data. In *Attitude measurement,* edited by G. Summers, pp. 174–186. Chicago: Rand McNally.

Guy, Rebecca F., Charles E. Edgley, Ibtihaj Arafat, and Donald E. Allan. (1987). *Social research methods: Puzzles and solutions.* Boston: Allyn and Bacon.

Haack, S. (1980). *Philosophy of logics.* London: Cambridge University Press.

Haberman, Shelby J. (1978). *Analysis of qualitative data.* New York: Academic Press.

Habermas, Jurgen. (1971). *Knowledge and human interests.* Boston: Beacon.

Habermas, Jurgen. (1973). *Theory and practice.* Boston: Beacon.

Habermas, Jurgen. (1976). *Legitimation crisis.* Boston: Beacon.

Habermas, Jurgen. (1979). *Communication and the evolution of society.* Boston: Beacon.

Habermas, Jurgen. (1988). *On the logic of the social sciences.* Oxford: Polity.

Hagan, John. (1990). The gender stratification of income inequality among lawyers. *Social Forces,* 63:835–855.

Hage, Jerald. (1972). *Techniques and problems of theory construction in sociology.* New York: Wiley.

Hagstrom, Warren. (1965). *The scientific community.* New York: Basic Books.

Haj-Yakia, M. (1997). Culturally sensitive supervision of Arab social work students in western universities. *Social Work,* 42(2):166–174.

Hakim, Catherine. (1987). *Research design: Strategies and choices in the design of social research.* Boston: George Allen and Unwin.

Halfpenny, Peter. (1979). The analysis of qualitative data. *Sociological Review,* 27:799–823.

Halfpenny, Peter. (1982). *Positivism and sociology: Explaining social life.* London: George Allen and Unwin.

Hall, E. (1959). *The silent language.* Garden City, NY: Anchor.

Hall, M., M. Amodeo, U. Shaffer, and J. Bilt. (2000). Social workers employed in substance abuse treatment agencies: A training needs assessment. *Social Work,* 45:141–154.

Hallin, Daniel C. (1985). The American news media: A critical theory perspective. In *Critical theory and public life,* edited by J. Forester, pp. 121–146. Cambridge, MA: MIT Press.

Hallowell, Lyle. (1985). *Ethical and legal problems of research: Professional workshop.* Presentation at the American Sociological Association annual meeting, Washington, DC, August 26.

Hammersley, Martyn. (1992). *What's wrong with ethnography? Methodological explorations.* New York: Routledge.

Hammersley, Martyn. (1995). Theory and evidence in qualitative research. *Quality and Quantity,* 29:55–66.

Hammersley, Martyn, and Paul Atkinson. (1983). *Ethnography: Principles in practice.* London: Tavistock.

Hannan, Michael T. (1985). Problems of aggregation. In *Causal models in the social sciences,* 2nd ed., edited by H. Blalock, Jr., pp. 403–439. Chicago: Aldine.

Harari, Herbert, Oren Harari, and Robert V. White. (1985). The reaction to rape by American bystanders. *Journal of Social Psychology,* 125: 653–658.

Harding, Sandra. (1986). *The science question in feminism.* Ithaca, NY: Cornell University Press.

Hargens, Lowell L. (1988). Scholarly consensus and journal rejection rates. *American Sociological Review,* 53:139–151.

Harkens, Shirley, and Carol Warren. (1993). The social relations of intensive interviewing: Constellations of strangeness and science. *Sociological Methods and Research,* 21:317–339.

Harper, Douglas. (1982). *Good company.* Chicago: University of Chicago Press.

Harper, Douglas. (1987). *Working knowledge.* Chicago: University of Chicago Press.

Harper, Douglas. (1994). On the authority of the image: Visual methods at the crossroads. In *Handbook of qualitative research,* edited by N. Denzin and Y. Lincoln, pp. 403–412. Thousand Oaks, CA: Sage.

Harré, Rom. (1972). *The philosophies of science.* London: Oxford University Press.

Harré, R., and P. F. Secord. (1979). *The explanation of social behavior.* Totowa, NJ: Littlefield, Adams.

Harris, Benjamin. (1988). Key words: A history of debriefing in social psychology. In *The rise of experimentation in American psychology,* edited by J. Morawski, pp. 188–212. New Haven, CT: Yale University Press.

Harrison, R. (1974). *Beyond words: An introduction to nonverbal communication.* Englewood Cliffs, NJ: Prentice-Hall.

Hartman, A. (1990). Many ways of knowing. *Social Work,* 35(1):3–5.

Harvey, Lee. (1990). *Critical social research.* London: Urwin Hyman.

Hastings, Philip K., and Dean R. Hodge. (1986). Religious and moral attitude trends among college students, 1948–84. *Social Forces,* 65:370–377.

Hauck, Matthew, and Michael Cox. (1974). Locating a sample by random digit dialing: Some hypotheses and a random sample. *Public Opinion Quarterly,* 38: 253–260.

Haworth, G. (1991). My paradigm can be your paradigm: Some reflections on knowledge conflicts. *Journal of Sociology and Social Welfare,* 19(4): 35–50.

Hayano, David M. (1982). *Poker faces: The life and work of professional card players.* Berkeley: University of California Press.

Hearn, H. L., and P. Stoll. (1976). The continuance of commitment in low status occupations: The cocktail waitress. *Sociological Quarterly,* 16:105–114.

Hearnshaw, L. S. (1979). *Cyril Burt: Psychologist.* London: Holder and Stoughten.

Heberlein, Thomas A., and Robert Baumgartner. (1978). Factors affecting response rates to mailed questionnaires: A quantitative analysis of the published literature. *American Sociological Review,* 43:447–462.

Heberlein, Thomas A., and Robert Baumgartner. (1981). Is a questionnaire necessary in a second mailing? *Public Opinion Quarterly,* 45:102–107.

Heckathorn, Douglas D. (1997). Respondent-driven sampling: A new approach to the study of hidden populations. *Social Problems,* 44:174–199.

Hegtvedt, Karen A. (1992). Replication. In *Encyclopedia of sociology,* Vol. 3, edited by E. and M. Borgatta, pp. 1661–1663. New York: Macmillan.

Heineman, M. (1981). The obsolete scientific paradigm in social work research. *Social Service Review,* 55 (3): 371–397.

Heineman-Piper, M. (1985). The future of social work research. *Social Research and Abstracts,* 21:3–11.

Heineman-Piper, M. (1989). The heuristic paradigm: A unifying and comprehensive approach to social work research. *Smith College Studies in Social Work,* 60:8–31.

Heise, David. (1965). Semantic differential profiles for 1,000 most frequent English words. *Psychological Monographs,* 70, No. 8.

Heise, David. (1970). The semantic differential and attitude research. In *Attitude measurement,* edited by G. Summers, pp. 235–253. Chicago: Rand McNally.

Heise, David. (1974). Some issues in sociological measurement. In *Sociological methodology, 1973–74,* edited by H. L. Costner, pp. 1–16. San Francisco: Jossey-Bass.

Heise, David, ed. (1981). *Microcomputers in social research.* Beverly Hills, CA: Sage.

Heise, David. (1991). Event structure analysis. In *Using computers in qualitative research,* edited by N. Fielding and R. Lee, pp. 136–163. Newbury Park, CA: Sage.

Held, David. (1980). *Introduction to critical theory: Horkheimer to Habermas.* Berkeley: University of California Press.

Heller, Nelson B., and J. Thomas McEwen. (1973). Applications of crime seriousness information in police departments. *Journal of Criminal Justice,* 1: 241–253.

Henry, Gary T. (1990). *Practical sampling.* Newbury Park, CA: Sage.

Henry, Gary T. (1995). *Graphing data: Techniques for display and analysis.* Thousand Oaks, CA: Sage.

Herman, J., L. Lyons-Morris, and C. Fitz-gibbon. (1987). *Evaluators handbook,* pp. 17–18. Newbury Park, CA: Sage.

Herrnstein, Richard, and Charles Murray. (1994). *The Bell Curve: Intelligence and class structure in American life.* New York: Free Press.

Herson, M., and D. Barlow. (1976). *Single case experimental design: Strategies for studying behavior change.* New York: Pergamon Press.

Herting, Jerald R. (1985). Multiple indicator models using LISREL. In *Causal models in the social sciences,* 2nd ed., edited by H. Blalock, Jr., pp. 263–320. New York: Aldine.

Herting, Jerald R., and Herbert L. Costner. (1985). Re-specification in multiple indicator models. In *Causal models in the social sciences,* 2nd ed., edited by H. Blalock, Jr., pp. 321–394. Chicago: Aldine.

Hertz, Rosanna, and Jonathan B. Imber. (1993). Fieldwork in elite settings. *Journal of Contemporary Ethnography,* 22:3–6.

Herzberger, Sharon D. (1993). The cyclical pattern of child abuse: A study of research methodology. In *Research on sensitive topics,* edited by C. Renzetti and R. Lee, pp. 33–51. Thousand Oaks, CA: Sage.

Herzog, A. Regula, and Jerald G. Bachman. (1981). Effects of questionnaire length on response quality. *Public Opinion Quarterly,* 45:549–559.

Hesse, Mary B. (1970). *Models and analogies in science.* Notre Dame, IN: Notre Dame Press.

Hicks, David. (1984). Getting into the field and establishing routines. In *Ethnographic research: A guide to general conduct,* edited by R. F. Ellen, pp. 192–199. Orlando, FL: Academic Press.

Hilts, Philip J. (Jan. 11, 1995). Majority backs cigarette rules, poll by tobacco industry finds. *New York Times.*

Himmelstein, Jerome L., and Mayer Zald. (1984). American conservatism and government funding of the social sciences and arts. *Sociological Inquiry,* 54:171–187.

Hindess, Barry. (1973). *The use of official statistics in sociology: A critique of positivism and ethnomethodology.* New York: Macmillan.

Hippler, Hans J., and Norbert Schwartz. (1986). Not forbidding isn't allowing: The cognitive basis of the forbid-allow asymmetry. *Public Opinion Quarterly,* 50:87–96.

Hirschman, Albert O. (1970). *Exit, voice, and loyalty: Response to decline in firms, organizations and states.* Cambridge, MA: Harvard University Press.

Ho, M. (1976). Social work with Asian Americans. *Social Casework,* 57: 195–201.

Hochschild, Arlie. (1978). *The unexpected community: Portrait of an old age subculture.* Berkeley: University of California Press.

Hochschild, Arlie. (1983). *The managed heart.* Berkeley: University of California Press.

Hochschild, Jennifer L. (1981). *What's fair? American beliefs about distributive justice.* Cambridge, MA: Harvard University Press.

Hoffman, K., and A. Salee. (1994). *Social work practice: Bridges to change.* Boston: Allyn & Bacon.

Hoffman-Lange, Ursula. (1980). Surveying national elites in the Federal Republic of Germany. In *Research methods for elite studies,* edited by G. Moyser and M. Wagstaffe, pp. 27–47. Boston: Allen and Unwin.

Hoffman-Lange, Ursula. (1987). Surveying national elites in the Federal Republic of Germany. In *Research methods for elite studies,* edited by G. Moyser and M. Wagstaffe, pp. 27–47. Boston: Allen and Unwin.

Hoffmann, Joan Eakin. (1980). Problems of access in the study of social elites and boards of directors. In *Fieldwork experience,* edited by W. B. Shaffir, R. A. Stebbins, and A. Turowetz, pp. 45–56. New York: St. Martin's Press.

Hollander, Myles, and Frank Proschan. (1984). *The statistical exorcist: Dispelling statistics anxiety.* New York: Marcel Decker.

Hollis, Martin. (1977). *Models of man: Philosophical thoughts on social ac-*

tion. New York: Cambridge University Press.

Holmes, G. (1992). Social work research and the empowerment paradigm. In *The strengths perspective in social work practice,* edited by D. Saleebey, pp. 158–168. New York: Longman.

Holmes, Steven A. (Sept. 18, 1998). Worst census undercount found in New York. *New York Times.*

Holstein, James A., and Jaber F. Gubrium. (1994). Phenomenology, ethnomethodology and interpretative practice. In *Handbook of qualitative research,* edited by N. Denzin and Y. Lincoln, pp. 262–272. Thousand Oaks, CA: Sage.

Holsti, Ole R. (1968a). Content analysis. In *The handbook of social psychology,* 2nd ed., Vol. 2, edited by G. Lindzey and E. Aronson, pp. 596–692. Reading, MA: Addison-Wesley.

Holsti, Ole R. (1968b). *Content analysis for the social sciences and humanities.* Reading, MA: Addison-Wesley.

Holub, Robert C. (1991). *Jürgen Habermas: Critic in the public sphere.* New York: Routledge.

Holy, Ladislav. (1984). Theory, methodology and the research process. In *Ethnographic research: A guide to general conduct,* edited by R. F. Ellen, pp. 13–34. Orlando, FL: Academic Press.

Homan, Roger. (1980). The ethics of covert methods. *British Journal of Sociology,* 31:46–57.

Honan, William H. (Jan. 22, 1997). Scholars attack public school TV program. *New York Times.*

Honigmann, John J. (1982). Sampling in ethnographic fieldwork. In *Field research,* edited by R. G. Burgess, pp. 79–90. Boston: Allen and Unwin.

Horan, Patrick. (1987). Theoretical models in social history research. *Social Science History,* 11:379–400.

Horn, Robert V. (1993). *Statistical indicators for the economic and social sciences.* Cambridge: Cambridge University Press.

Hornstein, Gail A. (1988). Quantifying psychological phenomena: Debates, dilemmas and implications. In *The rise of experimentation in American psychology,* edited by J. Morawski, pp. 1–34. New Haven, CT: Yale University Press.

Horowitz, Irving Louis. (1965). The life and death of Project Camelot. *Transaction,* 3:3–7, 44–47.

House, Ernest R. (1980). *Evaluating with validity.* Beverly Hills, CA: Sage.

House, E. (1993). *Professional evaluation: Social impact and political consequences.* Thousand Oaks, CA: Sage.

Howard, M. (1995). From oral tradition to computerization: A case study of a social work department. *Computers in Human Services,* 12(3-4): 203–219.

Howe, M. (1974). Casework self-evaluation: A single-subject approach. *Social Service Review,* 48(1):1–23.

Hoy, David Couzens. (1994). *Critical theory.* Cambridge, MA: Blackwell.

Hoynes, William. (May/June 1997). News for a captive audience extra. <http://www.fair.org/extra/9705/ch1-hoynes.html> November 2, 1998.

Hubbard, Raymond, and Eldon Little. (1988). Promised contributions to charity and mail survey responses: Replication with extension. *Public Opinion Quarterly,* 52:223–230.

Huck, Schuyler W., and Howard M. Sandler. (1979). *Rival hypotheses: Alternative interpretations of data based conclusions.* New York: Harper & Row.

Hudgins, C., and P. Allen-Meares. (2000). Translational research: A new solution to an old problem? *Journal of Social Work Education,* 36(1):2–4.

Hudson, W. (1982a). *The clinical measurement package: A field manual.* Newbury Park, CA: Wadsworth.

Hudson, W. (1982b). Scientific imperatives for social work research and practice. *Social Service Review,* 56(2): 258–264.

Hudson, W. (1996). *Computer Assisted Assessment Package.* Tallahassee, FL: WALMYR Publishing Co.

Hudson, W., and A. Faul. (1998). *The clinical measurement package: A field manual,* 2nd ed. Tallahassee, FL: WALMYR Publishing Co.

Hudson, W., and W. Ricketts. (1980). A strategy for the measurement of homophobia. *Journal of Homosexuality,* 5:357–372.

Hudson, W., and B. Thyer, eds. (1987). Research measurements and indices in direct practice. *Encyclopedia of Social Work,* 18th ed., p. 487. Silver Spring, MD: National Association of Social Workers.

Hughes, M. (1998). Turning points in the lives of young inner-city men forgoing destructive criminal behaviors: A qualitative study. *Social Work Research,* 22:143–151.

Humphreys, Laud. (1975). *Tearoom trade: Impersonal sex in public places,* enlarged ed. Chicago: Aldine.

Hunt, Jennifer. (1984). The development of rapport through the negotiation of gender in field work among police. *Human Organization,* 45:283–296.

Hunter, Albert. (1993). Local knowledge and local power: Notes on the ethnography of local community elites. *Journal of Contemporary Ethnography,* 22:36–58.

Hunter, James Davidson. (1991). *Culture wars: The struggle to define America.* New York: Basic Books.

Hunter, John E., Frank L. Schmidt, and Gregg B. Jackson. (1982). *Meta-analysis: Cumulating research findings across studies.* Beverly Hills, CA: Sage.

Huttman, E. (1993). The homeless and "doubled-up" households. In *The new housing shortage: Housing affordability in Europe and the USA,* edited by G. Hallett. New York: Routledge.

Hyman, Herbert H. (1975). *Interviewing in social research.* Chicago: University of Chicago Press.

Hyman, Herbert H. (1991). *Taking society's measure: A personal history of survey research.* New York: Russell Sage Foundation.

Hymes, Dell. (1983). *Essays in the history of linguistic anthropology.* Philadelphia: John Benjamins Publishers.

Imre, H. (1984). The nature of knowledge in social work. *Social Work,* 29(1): 41–45.

Imrie, R. (1996). *Disability and the city: International perspectives.* New York: St. Martin's Press.

Ing, Carol. (2001). Culturally appropriate evaluations. In *Evaluation in the human services,* edited by Y. Unrau, P. Gabor, and R. Grinnell, pp. 285–303. Boston: Peacock.

Inglehart, A., and R. Becerra. (1995). *Social services and the ethnic community.* Boston: Allyn & Bacon.

Inverarity, James M. (1976). Populism and lynching in Louisiana, 1889–1896: A test of Erikson's theory of the relationship between boundary crisis and repressive justice. *American Sociological Review,* 41:262–280.

Isaac, Larry W., and Larry J. Griffin. (1989). A historicism in time series analysis of historical process: Critique, redirection, and illustrations from U.S. labor history. *American Sociological Review,* 54:873–890.

Isaac, Larry W., Debra A. Street, and Stan J. Knapp. (1994). Analyzing historical contingency with formal methods: The case of the 'relief explosion' and 1968. *Sociological Methods and Research,* 23:114–141.

Isaac, S., and W. Michael. (1971). *Handbook in research and evaluation.* San Diego, CA: EDITS Publishers.

Jackson, Bruce. (1978). Killing time: Life in the Arkansas penitentiary. *Qualitative Sociology,* 1:21–32.

Jackson, Bruce. (1987). *Fieldwork.* Urbana, IL: University of Illinois Press.

Jackson, David J., and Edgar F. Borgatta, eds. (1981). *Factor analysis and measurement in sociological research.* Beverly Hills, CA: Sage.

Jackson, N., L. Olsen, and C. Schafer. (1986). Evaluating the treatment of emotionally disturbed adolescents. *Social Work,* 31:182–185.

Jacob, Herbert. (1984). *Using published data: Errors and remedies.* Beverly Hills, CA: Sage.

Jacobs, Jerry. (1974). *Fun City: An ethnographic study of a retirement community.* New York: Holt, Rinehart and Winston.

Jaeger, Richard M. (1983). *Statistics as a spectator sport.* Beverly Hills, CA: Sage.

Jahiel, R., ed. (1992). *Homelessness: A prevention-oriented approach.* Baltimore: The Johns Hopkins University Press.

Johnson, A., and L. Kreuger. (1988). Toward a better understanding of homeless women. *Social Work,* 34(6): 134–138.

Johnson, David Richard, and James C. Creech. (1983). Ordinal measures in multiple indicator models: A simulation study of categorization error. *American Sociological Review,* 48: 398–407.

Johnson, David W., and Roger T. Johnson. (1985). Relationships between black and white students in intergroup cooperation and competition. *Journal of Social Psychology,* 125:421–428.

Johnson, John M. (1975). *Doing field research.* New York: Free Press.

Johnson, P. Timonty, James G. Hougland, Jr., and Richard R. Clayton. (1989). Obtaining reports of sensitive behavior: A comparison of substance-use reports from telephone and face-to-face interviews. *Social Science Quarterly,* 70:173–183.

Johnson, Stephen D. (1985). Religion as a defense in a mock-jury trial. *Journal of Social Psychology,* 125:213–220.

Jones, J. H. (1981). *Bad blood: The Tuskegee syphilis experiment.* New York: Free Press.

Jones, Wesley H. (1979). Generalizing mail survey inducement methods: Populations' interactions with anonymity and sponsorship. *Public Opinion Quarterly,* 43:102–111.

Jordan, C., and C. Franklin. (1995). *Clinical assessment for social workers.* Chicago: Lyceum.

Jordan, C., C. Franklin, and K. Corcoran. (1993). Standardized measuring instruments. In *Social work research and evaluation,* 4th ed., edited by R. Grinnell, pp. 198–220. Itasca, IL: Peacock.

Jordan, Lawrence A., Alfred C. Marcus, and Leo G. Reeder. (1980). Response styles in telephone and household interviewing: A field experiment. *Public Opinion Quarterly,* 44:210–222.

Jorgensen, Danny L., and Lin Jorgensen. (1982). Social meanings of the occult. *Sociological Quarterly,* 23:373–389.

Josephson, Paul R. (Nov. 1, 1988). The FBI menaces academic freedom. *New York Times.*

Junker, Buford H. (1960). *Field work.* Chicago: University of Chicago Press.

Juster, F. Thomas, and Kenneth C. Land, eds. (1981). *Social accounting systems: Essays on the state of the art.* New York: Academic Press.

Kagle, J. (1983). Using single-subject measures in practice decisions: Systematic documentation or distortion? *Areté,* 2(Winter):1–10.

Kahneman, D., and A. Tversky. (1979). Intuitive prediction: Biases and corrective procedures. *TIMS Studies in Management Science,* 12:313–327.

Kalmijn, Matthijus. (1991). Shifting boundaries: Trends in religious and educational homogamy. *American Sociological Review,* 56:786–801.

Kalton, Graham. (1983). *Introduction to survey sampling.* Beverly Hills, CA: Sage.

Kandel, Denise B. (1980). Drug and drinking behavior among youth. *Annual Review of Sociology,* 6:235–265.

Kane, Emily W., and Laura J. MacAulay. (1993). Interview gender and gender attitudes. *Public Opinion Quarterly,* 57:1–28.

Kaplan, Abraham. (1964). *The conduct of inquiry: Methodology for behavioral science.* New York: Harper & Row.

Karger, H. (1986). Science, research and social work: Who controls the profession? *Social Work,* 28(3):200–205.

Karp, David A. (1973). Hiding in pornographic bookstores: A reconsideration of the nature of urban anonymity. *Urban Life,* 1:427–452.

Karp, David A. (1980). Observing behavior in public places: Problems and strategies. In *Fieldwork experience,* edited by W. B. Shaffir, R. A. Stebbins, and A. Turowetz, pp. 82–97. New York: St. Martin's Press.

Karweit, Nancy, and Edmund D. Meyers, Jr. (1983). Computers in survey research. In *Handbook of survey research,* edited by P. Rossi, J. Wright, and A. Anderson, pp. 379–414. Orlando, FL: Academic Press.

Katovich, Michael A., and Ron L. Diamond. (1986). Selling time: Situated transactions in a noninstitutional setting. *Sociological Quarterly,* 27: 253–271.

Katz, D. (2001). *Clinical epidemiology and evidence-based medicine: Fundamental principles of clinical reasoning and research.* Thousand Oaks, CA: Sage.

Katz, Jay. (1972). *Experimentation with human beings.* New York: Russell Sage Foundation.

Katzer, Jeffrey, Kenneth H. Cook, and Wayne W. Crouch. (1982). *Evaluating information: A guide for users of social science research,* 2nd ed. Reading, MA: Addison-Wesley.

Katzer, Jeffrey, Kenneth H. Cook, and Wayne W. Crouch. (1998). *Evaluating information: A guide for users of social science research,* 4th ed. New York: McGraw-Hill.

Kazdin, A. (1982). *Single case research designs: Methods for clinical and applied settings.* New York: Oxford University Press.

Keat, Russell. (1981). *The politics of social theory: Habermas, Freud and the critique of positivism.* Chicago: University of Chicago Press.

Keeter, Scott. (1995). Estimating telephone noncoverage bias with a telephone survey. *Public Opinion Quarterly,* 59: 196–217.

Keith, Verna M., and Cedric Herring. (1991). Skin tone and stratification in the black community. *American Journal of Sociology,* 97:760–778.

Keller, Bill. (May 27, 1988). Ups and downs of conducting the poll. *New York Times.*

Keller, Bill. (Jan. 19, 1989). Prying where it counts: Into census. *New York Times.*

Keller, Evelyn Fox. (1983). *A feeling for the organism: The life and work of Barbara McClintock.* New York: W. H. Freeman.

Keller, Evelyn Fox. (1985). *Reflections on gender and science.* New Haven, CT: Yale University Press.

Keller, Evelyn Fox. (1990). Gender and science. In *Feminist research methods,* edited by J. McCarl Nielsen, pp. 41–57. Boulder, CO: Westview.

Kelly, M., and M. Lauderdale. (1999). Globalization, technology and continued professional education. *Professional Development: The International Journal of Continuing Social Work Education,* 2(1):4–9.

Kelman, Herbert. (1982). Ethical issues in different social science methods. In *Ethical issues in social science research,* edited by T. Beauchamp, R. Faden, R. J. Wallace, and L. Walters, pp. 40–99. Baltimore: Johns Hopkins University Press.

Kemp, Jeremy, and R. F. Ellen. (1984). Informants. In *Ethnographic research: A guide to general conduct,* edited by R. F. Ellen, pp. 224–236. Orlando, FL: Academic Press.

Kenen, Regina. (1982). Soapsuds, space and sociability: A participant observation of a laundromat. *Urban Life,* 11:163–184.

Kent, Stephen A. (1992). Historical sociology. In *Encyclopedia of sociology,* Vol. 2, edited by E. and M. Borgatta, pp. 837–843. New York: Macmillan.

Kercher, Kyle. (1992). Quasi-experimental research designs. In *Encyclopedia of sociology,* Vol. 3, edited by E. and M. Borgatta, pp. 1595–1613. New York: Macmillan.

Kerlinger, Fred N. (1979). *Behavioral research: A conceptual approach.* New York: Holt, Rinehart and Winston.

Kidder, Louise H. (1982). Face validity from multiple perspectives. In *Forms of validity in research,* edited by D. Brinberg and L. Kidder, pp. 41–57. San Francisco: Jossey-Bass.

Kidder, Louise H., and Charles M. Judd. (1986). *Research methods in social relations,* 5th ed. New York: Holt, Rinehart and Winston.

Kiecolt, K. Jill, and Laura E. Nathan. (1985). *Secondary analysis of survey data.* Beverly Hills, CA: Sage.

Kim, Jae-On, and Charles W. Mueller. (1978). *Introduction to factor analysis: What it is and how to do it.* Beverly Hills, CA: Sage.

Kim, Y. O. (1995). Cultural pluralism and Asian Americans: Culturally sensitive social work practice. *International Social Work,* 38:69–78.

Kimmel, Allan J. (1988). *Ethics and values in applied social research.* Newbury Park, CA: Sage.

Kincheloe, Joe L., and Peter L. McLaren. (1994). Rethinking critical theory and qualitative research. In *Handbook of qualitative research,* edited by N. Denzin and Y. Lincoln, pp. 138–157. Thousand Oaks, CA: Sage.

King, Desmond. (1998). The politics of social research: Institutionalizing public funding regimes in the United States and Britain. *British Journal of Political Science,* 28:415–444.

King, Gary, Robert O. Keohane, and Sidney Verba. (1994). *Designing social inquiry: Scientific inference in qualitative research.* Princeton, NJ: Princeton University Press.

Kirk, Jerome, and Marc L. Miller. (1986). *Reliability and validity in qualitative research.* Beverly Hills, CA: Sage.

Kish, L. (1965). *Survey sampling.* New York: Wiley.

Klein, W., M. Bloom, and S. Chandler. (1994). Is there an ethical responsibility to use practice methods with the best empirical evidence of effectiveness? In *Controversial issues in social work research,* edited by W. Hudson and P. Nurius, pp. 100–112. Needham Heights, MA: Allyn & Bacon.

Kleinman, Sherry. (1980). Learning the ropes as fieldwork analysis. In *Fieldwork experience,* edited by W. B. Shaffir, R. A. Stebbins, and A. Turowetz, pp. 171–183. New York: St. Martin's Press.

Kleinman, Sherry, and Martha A. Copp. (1993). *Emotions and field work.* Thousand Oaks, CA: Sage.

Knapp, Peter. (1990). The revival of macrosociology: Methodological issues of discontiuity in comparative-historical theory. *Sociological Forum,* 5:545–567.

Knoke, David. (1993). Networks of elite structure and decision-making. *Sociological Methods and Research,* 22: 23–45.

Kohn, Melvin L., ed. (1989). *Cross-national research in sociology.* Newbury Park, CA: Sage.

Koretz, Daniel. (Summer 1988). Arriving in Lake Wobegon: Are standardized tests exaggerating achievement and distorting instruction? *American Educator,* 12:8–15.

Kornblum, William. (1974). *Blue collar community.* Chicago: University of Chicago Press.

Kraemer, Helena Chmura, and Sue Thiemann. (1987). *How many subjects? Statistical power analysis in research.* Newbury Park, CA: Sage.

Krathwohl, D. R. (1965). *How to prepare a research proposal.* Syracuse, NY: Syracuse University Bookstore.

Kreuger, L. (1997). The end of social work. *Journal of Social Work Education,* 33(1):19–27.

Kreuger, L., and J. Stretch. (1994). Are shelters for the homeless doing the job? In *Controversial issues in social policy,* edited by Karger and Midgley, pp. 131–140. Boston: Allyn & Bacon.

Kreuger, L., and J. Stretch. (2000a). How hypermodern technology in social work education bites back. *Journal of Social Work Education,* 36(1): 103–114.

Kreuger, L., and J. Stretch. (2000b). What is the role of hypertechnology in social work today?: A commentary. *Social Work,* 45(5):457–462.

Krippendorff, Klaus. (1980). *Content analysis: An introduction to its methodology.* Beverly Hills, CA: Sage.

Krosnick, Jon A., and Robert P. Abelson. (1992). The case for measuring attitude strength in surveys. In *Questions about questions: Inquiries into the cognitive bases of surveys,* edited by J. Turner, pp. 177–203. New York: Russell Sage Foundation.

Krosnick, Jon A., and Duane F. Alwin. (1988). A test of the form-resistant correlation hypothesis: Ratings, rankings and the measurement of values. *Public Opinion Quarterly,* 52:526–538.

Krueger, Richard A. (1988). *Focus groups: A practical guide for applied research.* Beverly Hills, CA: Sage.

Krueger, R., and M. Casey. (2000). *Focus groups: A practical guide for applied resesarch.* Newbury Park, CA: Sage.

Kuh, G. (1982). Purposes and principles for needs assessment in student affairs. *Journal of College Student Personnel,* 23:203–209.

Kuhn, Thomas S. (1970). *The structure of scientific revolutions,* 2nd ed. Chicago: University of Chicago Press.

Kuhn, Thomas S. (1979). The relations between history and the history of science. In *Interpretive social science: A reader,* edited by P. Rabinow and W. Sullivan. Berkeley: University of California Press.

Kurz, Demie. (1987). Emergency department responses to battered women: Resistance to medicalization. *Social Problems,* 34:69–81.

Kusserow, Richard P. (March 1989). *Misconduct in scientific research.* Report of the Inspector General of the U.S. Department of Health and Human Services. Washington, DC: Department of Health and Human Services.

Kviz, Frederick J. (1984). Bias in a directory sample for mail survey of rural households. *Public Opinion Quarterly,* 48:801–806.

Labaw, Patricia J. (1980). *Advanced questionnaire design.* Cambridge, MA: Abt Books.

Lachmann, Richard. (1988). Graffiti as career and ideology. *American Journal of Sociology,* 94:251–272.

Lagemann, Ellen Condliffe. (1989). *The politics of knowledge: The Carnegie Corporation, philanthropy and public policy.* Chicago: University of Chicago Press.

Land, Kenneth. (1992). Social indicators. *Encyclopedia of sociology,* Vol. 4, edited by E. and M. Borgatta, pp. 1844–1850. New York: Macmillan.

Lane, Michael. (1970). *Structuralism.* London: Jonathan Cape.

Lang, Eric. (1992). Hawthorne effect. *Encyclopedia of sociology,* Vol. 2, edited by E. and M. Borgatta, pp. 793–794. New York: Macmillan.

Laslett, Barbara. (1992). Gender in/and social history. *Social Science History,* 16:177–196.

Lather, P. (1991). *Getting smart: Feminist research and pedagogy within the postmodern.* New York: Routledge and Kegan Paul.

Laufer, A. (1982). *Assessment tools.* Newbury Park, CA: Sage.

Laxer, Gordon. (1989). *Open for business: The roots of foreign ownership in Canada.* New York: Oxford University Press.

Layder, Derek. (1993). *New strategies in social research.* Cambridge, MA: Polity.

Lazarsfeld, Paul F., and Jeffrey G. Reitz. (1975). *An introduction to applied sociology.* Amsterdam: Elsevier.

Lazere, Donald, ed. (1987). *American media and mass culture: Left perspectives.* Berkeley: University of California Press.

Lederman, Douglas. (Aug. 7, 1998). House votes to increase support for the NSF and to eliminate AmeriCorps. *Chronicle of Higher Education,* p. A31.

Lee, Alfred McClung. (1978). *Sociology for whom?* New York: Oxford University Press.

Lee, Harper. (1960). *To Kill a Mockingbird.* New York: Warner Books.

Lee, J. (1994). *The empowerment approach to social work practice.* New York: Columbia University Press.

Lee, J. (2000). *The empowerment approach to social work practice.* New York: Columbia University Press.

Lee, J. A. B. (1996). The empowerment approach to social work practice. In *Social work treatment interlocking theoretical approaches,* 4th ed., edited by F. J. Turner, pp. 219–249. New York: Free Press/Simon & Schuster.

Legge, Jerome S., and Joonghoon Park. (1994). Policies to reduce alcohol-impaired driving: Evaluating elements of deterrence. *Social Science Quarterly,* 75:594–606.

Leggett, Glenn, C. David Mean, and William Charvat. (1965). *Prentice-Hall handbook for writers,* 4th ed. Englewood Cliffs, NJ: Prentice-Hall.

Leiter, Kenneth. (1980). *A primer on ethnomethodology.* New York: Oxford University Press.

LeMasters, E. E. (1975). *Blue collar aristocrats.* Madison: University of Wisconsin Press.

Lemert, Charles. (1979). Science, religion and secularization. *Sociological Quarterly,* 20:445–461.

Lemert, Charles, ed. (1981). *French sociology: Rupture and renewal since 1968.* New York: Columbia University Press.

Lenning, O. (1980). Assessment and evaluation. In *Student services: A handbook for the profession,* edited by U. Delworth and G. Hanson, pp. 232–266. San Francisco: Jossey-Bass.

Lenski, Gerhard E. (1966). *Power and privilege.* New York: McGraw-Hill.

Lenzer, Gertrud, ed. (1975). *Auguste Comte and positivism: Essential writings.* New York: Harper & Row.

Leonard, P. (1997). *Postmodern welfare: Reconstructing an emancipatory project.* London: Sage.

Lesiuer, Henry R., and Joseph F. Sheley. (1987). Illegal appended enterprises: Selling the lines. *Social Problems,* 34:249–260.

Lessler, Judith T. (1984). Measurement error in surveys. In *Surveying subjective phenomena,* Vol. 2, edited by C. Turner and E. Martin, pp. 405–440. New York: Russell Sage Foundation.

Lester, Marilyn, and Stuart C. Hadden. (1980). Ethnomethodology and grounded theory methodology: An integration of perspective and method. *Urban Life,* 9:3–33.

Lever, Janet. (1978). Sex differences in the complexity of children's play and games. *American Sociological Review,* 43:471–483.

Lever, Janet. (1981). Multiple methods of data collection: A note on divergence. *Urban Life,* 10:199–213.

Levi, C. (1976). *Social work ethics.* New York: Human Service Press.

Levine, Joel H. (1993). *Exceptions are the rule: An inquiry into methods in the social sciences.* Boulder, CO: Westview.

Levine, J. (2001). Working with victims of persecution: Lessons from Holocaust survivors. *Social Work,* 46(4): 350–360.

Lewis, George H., and Jonathan F. Lewis. (1980). The dog in the night-time: Negative evidence in social research. *British Journal of Sociology,* 31: 544–558.

Lieberman, A. (1990). Culturally sensitive intervention with children and families. *Child and Adolescent Social Work,* 7:101–120.

Lieberson, Stanley. (1985). *Making it count: The improvement of social research and theory.* Berkeley: University of California Press.

Liebetrau, Albert M. (1983). *Measures of association.* Beverly Hills, CA: Sage.

Liebman, Robert, John R. Sutton, and Robert Wuthnow. (1988). Exploring social sources of denominationalism: Schisms in American Protestant denominations, 1890–1980. *American Sociological Review,* 53:343–352.

Liebow, Elliot. (1967). *Talley's corner.* Boston: Little, Brown.

Lifton, Robert J. (1986). *Nazi doctors.* New York: Basic Books.

Light, Ivan, and Edna Bonacich. (1988). *Immigrant entrepreneurs: Koreans in Los Angeles, 1965–1982.* Berkeley: University of California Press.

Light, Richard J., and David B. Pillemer. (1984). *Summing up: The science of reviewing research.* Cambridge, MA: Harvard University Press.

Likert, Rensis. (1970). A technique for the measurement of attitudes. In *Attitude measurement,* edited by G. Summers, pp. 149–158. Chicago: Rand McNally.

Lindblom, Charles E., and David K. Cohen. (1979). *Usable knowledge: Social science and social problem solving.* New Haven, CT: Yale University Press.

Lindsey, D. (1999). Ensuring standards in social work research. *Research on Social Work Practice,* 9(1):115–120.

Lindzey, Gardner, and Donn Byrne. (1968). Measurement of social choice and interpersonal attractiveness. In *The handbook of social psychology,* Vol. 2: Research methods, edited by G. Lindzey and E. Aronson, pp. 452–525. Reading, MA: Addison-Wesley.

Little, Daniel. (1991). *Varieties of social explanation: An introduction to the philosophy of science.* Boulder, CO: Westview.

Lloyd, Christopher. (1986). *Explanation in social history.* New York: Basil Blackwell.

Locke, Lawrence F., Warren Wyrick Spirduso, and Stephen J. Silverman. (1987). *Proposals that work: A guide for planning dissertations and grant proposals,* 2nd ed. Beverly Hills, CA: Sage.

Loewenstein, Gaither. (1985). The new underclass: A contemporary sociological dilemma. *Sociological Quarterly,* 26:35–48.

Lofland, John. (1966). *Doomsday cult.* Englewood Cliffs, NJ: Prentice-Hall.

Lofland, John. (1974). Styles of reporting qualitative field research. *American Sociologist,* 9:101–111.

Lofland, John. (1976). *Doing social life: The qualitative study of human interaction in natural settings.* New York: Wiley.

Lofland, J. (1984). *Analyzing social settings. A guide to qualitative observation and analysis.* Belmont, CA: Sage.

Lofland, John, and Lyn H. Lofland. (1984). *Analyzing social settings,* 2nd ed. Belmont, CA: Wadsworth.

Lofland, John, and Lyn H. Lofland. (1995). *Analyzing social settings,* 3rd ed. Belmont, CA: Wadsworth.

Lofland, Lyn H. (1972). Self management in public settings: Parts I and II. *Urban Life,* 1:93–108, 217–231.

Loftus, Elizabeth, Mark Klinger, Kyle Smith, and Judith Fiedler. (1990). A tale of two questions: Benefit of asking more than one question. *Public Opinion Quarterly,* 54:330–345.

Loftus, Elizabeth, Kyle D. Smith, Mark R. Klinger, and Judith Fiedler. (1992). Memory and mismemory of health events. In *Questions about questions: Inquiries into the cognitive bases of surveys,* edited by J. Turner, pp. 102–137. New York: Russell Sage Foundation.

Logan, T., and D. Royse. (2001). Program evaluation. In *The handbook of social work research methods,* edited by B. Thyer, pp. 193–206. Thousand Oaks, CA: Sage.

Long, J. Scott. (1976). Estimation and hypothesis testing in linear models containing measurement error: A review of Joreskog's model for the analysis of covariance structures. *Sociological Methods and Research,* 5:157–206.

Long, J. Scott. (1978). Productivity and academic positions in a scientific career. *American Sociological Review,* 43:889–908.

Longino, Helen E. (1990). *Science as social knowledge: Values and objectivity in scientific inquiry.* Princeton, NJ: Princeton University Press.

Longres, J. (1997). The impact and implications of multiculturalism. In *Social work in the 21st century,* edited by M. Reisch and E. Gambrill, pp. 38–47. Thousand Oaks, CA: Pine Forge Press.

Longres, J., and E. Scanlon. (2001). Social justice and the research curriculum. *Journal of Social Work Education,* 37(3):447–463.

Lorr, Maurice. (1983). *Cluster analysis for social scientists: Techniques for analyzing and simplifying complex blocks of data.* San Francisco: Jossey-Bass.

Lovdal, Lynn T. (1989). Sex role messages in television commercials: An update. *Sex Roles,* 20:715–724.

Lovin-Smith, Lynn, and Charles Brody. (1989). Interruptions in group discussions: The effects of gender and group composition. *American Sociological Review,* 54:424–435.

Luebke, Barbara F. (1989). Out of focus: Images of men and women in newspaper photographs. *Sex Roles,* 20: 121–133.

Lukas, S. (1993). *Where to start and what to ask: An assessment handbook.* New York: Norton.

Lum, D. (2000). *Social work practice and people of color: A process-stage approach.* Belmont, CA: Brooks/Cole.

Lynd, Robert S. (1964). *Knowledge for what? The place of social science in American culture.* New York: Grove.

(Originally published in 1939 by Princeton University Press.)

MacFarlane, Alan. (1977). *Reconstructing historical communities.* New York: Cambridge University Press.

MacKeun, Michael B. (1984). Reality, the press and citizens' political agendas. In *Surveying subjective phenomena,* Vol. 2, edited by C. Turner and E. Martin, pp. 443–473. New York: Russell Sage Foundation.

Maier, Mark H. (1991). *The data game: Controversies in social science statistics.* Armonk, NY: M. E. Sharpe.

Maines, David R., William Shaffir, and Allan Turowetz. (1980). Leaving the field in ethnographic research. In *The fieldwork experience: Qualitative approaches to social research,* edited by W. B. Shaffir, R. Stebbins, and A. Turowetz, pp. 261–280. New York: St. Martin's Press.

Maloney, Dennis M. (1984). *Protection of human research subjects: A practical guide to federal laws and regulations.* New York: Plenum.

Mann, Floyd C. (1970). Human relations skills in social research. In *Qualitative methodology,* edited by W. J. Filstead. Chicago: Markham.

Mannheim, Karl. (1936). *Ideology and utopia.* New York: Harcourt, Brace and World.

Markoff, John, Gilbert Shapiro, and Sasha R. Weitman. (1974). Toward the integration of content analysis and general methodology. In *Sociological methodology, 1974,* edited by D. Heise, pp. 1–58. San Francisco: Jossey-Bass.

Markward, M. (1999). Social development in social work practice: Enhancing human rights for children in the Czech Republic. *Social Development,* 21(1):57–61.

Marradi, Alberto. (1981). Factor analysis as an aid in the formation and refinement of empirically useful concepts. In *Factor analysis and measurement in social research: A multi-dimensional perspective,* edited by D. Jackson and E. Borgatta, pp. 11–50. Beverly Hills, CA: Sage.

Marsh, Catherine. (1982). *The survey method: The contribution of surveys to sociological explanation.* Boston: George Allen and Unwin.

Marsh, Catherine. (1984). Do polls affect what people think? In *Surveying subjective phenomena,* Vol. 2, edited by C. Turner and E. Martin, pp. 565–592. New York: Russell Sage Foundation.

Marsh, J., and M. Shibano. (1984). Issues in the statistical analysis of clinical time-series data. *Social Work Research & Abstracts,* 20(4):7–12.

Marshall, Catherine. (1985). Appropriate criteria of trustworthiness and goodness for qualitative research on educational organizations. *Quality and Quantity,* 19:353–373.

Marshall, Catherine, and Gretchen B. Rossman. (1989). *Designing qualitative research.* Beverly Hills, CA: Sage.

Marshall, Susan E. (1986). In defense of separate spheres: Class and politics in the antisuffrage movement. *Social Forces,* 65:327–351.

Marshall, Victor W. (1975). Socialization for impending death in a retirement village. *American Journal of Sociology,* 80:1124–1144.

Martin, Elizabeth. (1985). Surveys as social indicators: Problems of monitoring trends. In *Handbook of survey research,* edited by P. Rossi, J. Wright, and A. Anderson, pp. 677–743. Orlando, FL: Academic Press.

Martin, Jay. (1973). *The dialectical imagination.* Boston: Little, Brown.

Martin, John L., and Laura Dean. (1993). Developing a community sample of gay men for an epidemiological study of AIDS. In *Research on sensitive topics,* edited by C. Renzetti and R. Lee, pp. 82–100. Thousand Oaks, CA: Sage.

Marvell, Thomas R., and Carlisle E. Moody. (1995). The impact of enhanced prison terms for felonies committed with guns. *Criminology,* 33: 247–281.

Marx, Karl, and Friedrich Engels. (1947). *The German ideology, Parts I & III,* edited with introduction by R. Pascal. New York: International Publishers.

Mash, E., and L. Terdal, eds. (1976). *Behavior therapy assessment.* New York: Springer.

Masterman, Margaret. (1970). The nature of a paradigm. In *Criticism and the growth of knowledge,* edited by I. Lakatos and A. Musgrove, pp. 59–90. Cambridge: Cambridge University Press.

Matsouka, J., and D. Ryujin. (1991). Asian American immigrants: A comparison of the Chinese, Japanese, and Filipinos. *Journal of Sociology and Social Welfare,* 18(3):123–133.

Mattaini, M. (1996). The abuse and neglect of single-case designs. *Research on Social Work Practice,* 6(1): 83–90.

Mayer, Charles S., and Cindy Piper. (1982). A note on the importance of layout in self-administered questionnaires. *Journal of Marketing Research,* 19:390–391.

Mayhew, Bruce H. (1980). Structuralism versus individualism, Part I: Shadowboxing in the dark. *Social Forces,* 59:335–375.

Mayhew, Bruce H. (1981). Structuralism versus individualism, Part II: Ideological and other obfuscations. *Social Forces,* 59:627–648.

Maynard, Douglas W. (1985). On the functions of conflict among children. *American Sociological Review,* 50:207–223.

Mayne, J., S. Divorski, and D. Lemaire. (1999). Locating evaluation: Anchoring evaluation in the executive or legislature, or both, or elsewhere? In *Building Effective Evaluation Capacity: Lessons from Practice,* edited by R. Boyle and D. Lemaire, pp. 23–53. New Brunswick, NJ: Transaction Publishers.

McCabe, Donald L. (1992). The influence of situational ethics on cheating among college students. *Sociological Inquiry,* 62:365–374.

McCall, George. (1969). Quality control in participant observation. In *Issues in participant observation,* edited by G. McCall and J. L. Simmons, pp. 128–141. Reading, MA: Addison-Wesley.

McCall, George. (1984). Systematic field observation. *Annual Review of Sociology,* 10:263–282.

McCall, Michal. (1980). Who and where are the artists? In *The fieldwork experience: Qualitative approaches to social research,* edited by W. B. Shaffir, R. Stebbins, and A. Turowetz, pp. 145–158. New York: St. Martin's Press.

McCarthy, Thomas. (1978). *The critical theory of Jurgen Habermas.* Cambridge, MA: MIT Press.

McCartney, James L. (1984). Setting priorities for research: New politics for the social sciences. *Sociological Quarterly,* 25:437–455.

McConaghy, Maureen. (1975). Maximum possible error in Guttman scales. *Public Opinion Quarterly,* 39: 343–357.

McCracken, Grant. (1988). *The long interview.* Thousand Oaks, CA: Sage.

McDiarmid, Garnet. (1971). *Teaching prejudice: A content analysis of social studies textbooks authorized for use in Ontario.* Ontario: Ontario Institute for Studies in Education.

McFall, J. P., and P. P. Freddolio. (2000). The impact of distance education programs on community agencies. *Research on Social Work Practice,* 10(4): 438–453.

McFarland, Sam G. (1981). Effects of question order on survey responses. *Public Opinion Quarterly,* 45:208–215.

McGrath, Joseph, Joanne Martin, and Richard A. Kulka. (1982). *Judgment calls in research.* Beverly Hills, CA: Sage.

McIver, John P., and Edward G. Carmines. (1981). *Unidimensional scaling.* Beverly Hills, CA: Sage.

McKee, J. McClendon, and David J. O'Brien. (1988). Question order effects on the determinants of subjective well-being. *Public Opinion Quarterly,* 52:351–364.

McKelvie, Stuart J., and Linda A. Schamer. (1988). Effects of night, passengers and sex on driver behavior at stop signs. *Journal of Social Psychology,* 128:658–690.

McKeown, Bruce. (1988). *Q methodology.* Thousand Oaks, CA: Sage.

McMahon, A., and P. Meares. (1992). Is social work racist? A content analysis of recent literature. *Social Work,* 37: 533–539.

McMurtry, John. (1978). *The structure of Marx's world view.* Princeton, NJ: Princeton University Press.

McQuaire, Donald. (1978). Marx and the method of successive approximations. *Sociological Quarterly,* 20:431–435.

McQuaire, Donald. (1979). Reply to Wardell. *Sociological Quarterly,* 20: 431–435.

Meadows, A. J. (1974). *Communication in science.* Toronto: Butterworths.

Mehan, Hugh, and Houston Wood. (1975). *The reality of ethnomethodology.* New York: Wiley.

Meinert, R. (1998). Consequences for professional social work under conditions of postmodernity. *Social Thought,* 18(3):41–54.

Meinert, R., T. Pardeck, and L. Kreuger. (2000). *Social work: Seeking relevancy in the twenty-first century.* New York: The Haworth Press.

Melbin, Murray. (1978). Night as frontier. *American Sociological Review,* 43:3–22.

Mendelberg, Tali. (1997). Executing Hortons: Racial crime and the 1988 presidential campaign. *Public Opinion Quarterly,* 61:134–157.

Mendenhall, William, Lyman Ott, and Richard L. Scheaffer. (1971). *Elementary survey sampling.* Belmont, CA: Duxbury Press.

Mermelstein, J. (1999). Empowering rural women human service administrators. In *25th Anniversary Collection of the National Association for Rural Mental Health,* edited by M. Van Hook. Minneapolis, MN: National Association for Rural Mental Health.

Merton, Robert K. (1967). *On theoretical sociology: Five essays, old and new.* New York: Free Press.

Merton, Robert K. (1973). *The sociology of science.* Chicago: University of Chicago Press.

Midgley, J. (1990). International social work: Learning from the third world. *Social Work,* 35:295–301.

Midgley, J. (1997). From social casework to social development: Reflections on an international, intellectual journey. *Reflections,* 3(3):81–88.

Miles, Matthew B., and A. Michael Huberman. (1994). *Qualitative data analysis,* 2nd ed. Thousand Oaks, CA: Sage.

Milgram, Stanley. (1963). Behavioral study of obedience. *Journal of Abnormal and Social Psychology,* 6:371–378.

Milgram, Stanley. (1965). Some conditions of obedience and disobedience to authority. *Human Relations,* 18: 57–76.

Milgram, Stanley. (1974). *Obedience to authority.* New York: Harper & Row.

Miller, Delbert C. (1991). *Handbook of research design and social measurement,* 5th ed. Newbury Park, CA: Sage.

Miller, Gale. (1983). Holding clients accountable: The micro-politics of trouble in a work incentive program. *Social Problems,* 31:139–151.

Miller, Gale. (1992). Case studies. In *Encyclopedia of sociology,* Vol. 1, edited by E. and M. Borgatta, pp. 167–172. New York: Macmillan.

Miller, Mark Crispin. (May/June 1997). How to be stupid. *Extra.* <http://www.fair.org/extra/9705/ch1-miller.html> November 2, 1998.

Miller, Richard. (1987). *Fact and method: Explanation, confirmation and reality in the natural and social sciences.* Princeton, NJ: Princeton University Press.

Miller, William L. (1983). *The survey method in the social and political sciences: Achievements, failures and prospects.* London: Frances Pinter.

Mills, C. Wright. (1959). *The sociological imagination.* New York: Oxford University Press.

Mills, L. (1996). Empowering battered women transnationally: The case for postmodern interventions. *Social Work,* 41(3):261–268.

Mishler, Elliot G. (1986). *Research interviewing: Context and narrative.* Cambridge, MA: Harvard University Press.

Mitchell, Alison. (May 17, 1997). Survivors of Tuskegee study get apology from Clinton. *New York Times.*

Mitchell, C., and K. Weiler, eds. (1991). *Rewriting literacy: Culture and the discourse of the other.* New York: Bergin and Garvey.

Mitchell, J. Clyde. (1984). Case studies. In *Ethnographic research: A guide to general conduct,* edited by R. F. Ellen, pp. 237–241. Orlando, FL: Academic Press.

Mitchell, Mark, and Janina Jolley. (1988). *Research design explained.* New York: Holt, Rinehart and Winston.

Mitchell, Richard G., Jr. (1993). *Secrecy and fieldwork.* Thousand Oaks, CA: Sage.

Mitroff, Ian. (1974). Norms and counternorms in a select group of the Apollo moon scientists: A case study of ambivalence of scientists. *American Sociological Review,* 39:579–595.

Mohr, L. (1992). *Impact analysis for program evaluation.* Newbury Park, CA: Sage.

Mokuau, N., and J. Matsouka. (1995). Turbulence among a native people: Social work practice with Hawaiians. *Social Work,* 40(4):465–472.

Monaghan, Peter. (Apr. 7, 1993a). Facing jail, a sociologist raises question about a scholar's right to protect sources. *Chronicle of Higher Education,* p. A10.

Monaghan, Peter. (May 26, 1993b). Sociologist is jailed for refusing to testify about research subject. *Chronicle of Higher Education,* p. A10.

Monaghan, Peter. (Sept. 1, 1993c). Sociologist jailed because he "wouldn't snitch" ponders the way research ought to be done. *Chronicle of Higher Education,* pp. A8–A9.

Mondros, J., and S. Wilson. (1994). *Organizing for power and enhancement.* New York: Columbia University Press.

Mooney, Linda, and Robert B. Gramling. (1991). Asking threatening questions and situational framing: The effects of decomposing survey items. *Sociological Quarterly,* 32:277–288.

Moore, Joan. (1973). Social constraints on sociological knowledge: Academic and research concerning minorities. *Social Problems,* 21:65–77.

Moore, Joan, Diego Vigil, and Robert Garcia. (1983). Residence and territoriality in Chicago gangs. *Social Problems,* 31:182–194.

Morales, A. (1981). Social work with third world people. *Social Work,* 26: 45–51.

Morgan, D. (1988). *Focus groups as qualitative research.* Newbury Park, CA: Sage.

Morgan, Laurie A. (1998). Glass-ceiling effect or cohort effect? A longitudinal study of the gender gap earnings for engineers, 1982–1989. *American Sociological Review,* 63:479–483.

Morrow, Raymond Allan. (1994). *Critical theory and methodology.* Thousand Oaks, CA: Sage.

Morse, Janice M. (1994). Designing funded qualitative research. In *Handbook of qualitative research,* edited by N. Denzin and Y. Lincoln, pp. 220–235. Thousand Oaks, CA: Sage.

Moser, C. A., and G. Kalton. (1972). *Survey methods in social investigation.* New York: Basic Books.

Mostyn, Barbara. (1985). The content analysis of qualitative research data: A dynamic approach. In *The research interview: Uses and approaches,* edited by M. Brenner, J. Brown, and D. Canter, pp. 115–145. New York: Academic Press.

Moustakas, C. (1990). *Heuristic research: Design, methodology and applications.* Newbury Park, CA: Sage.

Mulford, Matthew, John Orbell, Catherine Shatto, and Jean Stockard. (1998). Physical attractiveness, opportunity and success in everyday exchange. *American Journal of Sociology,* 103:1565–1592.

Mulkay, Michael. (1979). *Science and the sociology of knowledge.* London: George Allen and Unwin.

Mullins, Carolyn J. (1977). *A guide to writing and publishing in the social and behavioral sciences.* New York: Wiley.

Mullins, Nicholas C. (1971). *The art of theory: Construction and use.* New York: Harper & Row.

Mullins, Nicholas C. (1973). *Theory and theory groups in American sociology.* New York: Harper & Row.

Murdock, George P. (1967). Ethnographic atlas. *Ethnology,* 6:109–236.

Murray, Shoon. (1992). Turning an elite cross-sectional survey into a panel study while protecting anonymity. *Journal of Conflict Resolution,* 36:586–595.

Myerhoff, Barbara. (1989). So what do you want from us here? In *In the field,* edited by C. Smith and W. Kornblum, pp. 83–90. New York: Praeger.

Myers, Gloria, and A. V. Margavio. (1983). The black bourgeoisie and reference group change: A content analysis of *Ebony. Qualitative Sociology,* 6:291–307.

Nadeau, Richard, Richard Miemi, and Jeffrey Levine. (1993). Innumeracy about minority population. *Public Opinion Quarterly,* 57:332–347.

Nafziger, E. Wayne. (1988). *Inequality in Africa: Political elites, proletariat, peasants and the poor.* New York: Cambridge University Press.

Nagin, Daniel S., David P. Farrington, and Terrie E. Moffitt. (1995). Life course trajectories of different types of offenders. *Criminology,* 33:111–139.

Nakanishi, M., and B. Rittner. (1992). The inclusionary cultural model. *Journal of Social Work Education,* 28:27–35.

Namenwirth, J. Z. (1970). Prestige newspapers and assessment of elite opinions. *Journalism Quarterly,* 47:318–323.

Narayan, Sowmya, and John A. Krosnick. (1996). Education moderates some response effects in attitude measurement. *Public Opinion Quarterly,* 60:58–88.

Nash, Jeffrey E., and David W. McCurdy. (1989). Cultural knowledge and systems of knowing. *Sociological Inquiry,* 59:117–126.

National Association of Social Workers. (1996). *Code of Ethics.* Washington, DC: NASW.

National Association of Social Workers. (1997). *Lesbian, gay and bisexual issues: Social Work Speaks: NASW Policy Statements.* Washington, DC: NASW.

Neapolitan, Jerry. (1988). The effects of different types of praise and criticism on performance. *Sociological Focus,* 21:223–232.

Nederhof, Anton J. (1986). Effects of research experiences of respondents. *Quality and Quantity,* 20:277–284.

Nelkin, Dorothy. (1982a). Forbidden research: Limits on inquiry in the social sciences. In *Ethical issues in social science research,* edited by T. L. Beauchamp, R. Faden, R. J. Wallace, and L. Walters, pp. 163–174. Baltimore: Johns Hopkins University Press.

Nelkin, Dorothy. (May 1982b). Intellectual property: The control of scientific information. *Science,* 216: 704–708.

Nelsen, J. C. (1984). Intermediate treatment goals as variables in single-case research. *Social Work Research and Abstracts,* 20(3):3–10.

Nelson, J. (1993). Testing practice wisdom: Another use for single-system research. *Journal of Social Service Research,* 18(3/4):139–152.

Neuber, K. (1983). *Needs assessment: A model for community planning.* Newbury Park, CA: Sage.

Neuberg, Leland Gerson. (1988). Distorted transmission: A case study in the diffusion of "social scientific" research. *Theory and Society,* 17: 487–526.

Neuman, W. Lawrence. (1992). Gender, race and age differences in student definitions of sexual harassment. *Wisconsin Sociologist,* 29:63–75.

Neuman, W. Russell, Marion R. Just, and Ann N. Crigler. (1992). *Common knowledge: News and the construction of political meaning.* Chicago: University of Chicago Press.

Newman, D., and R. Brown. (1996). *Applied ethics for program evaluation.* Thousand Oaks, CA: Sage.

Noelle-Neumann, Elisabeth. (1974). Spiral of silence: A theory of public opinion. *Journal of Communication,* 24:43–51.

Noelle-Neumann, Elisabeth. (1984). *The spiral of silence: Public opinion our social skin.* Chicago: University of Chicago Press.

Normal, A. E., ed. (2000). *Resiliency enhancement: Putting the strengths perspective into social work practice.* New York: Columbia University Press.

Norris, M. (1981). Problems in the analysis of soft data and some suggested solutions. *Sociology,* 15:337–351.

Norusis, Marija J. (1986). *The SPSS-X guide to data analysis.* Chicago: SPSS, Inc.

Nowotny, Helga, and Hilary Rose, eds. (1979). *Counter-movements in the sciences.* Boston: D. Reidel.

Nugent, W. (1991). A mathematical model for analyzing single-subject design replication series. *Journal of Social Service Research,* 15:93–129.

Nugent, W. (1993a). A series of single case design clinical evaluations of an Ericksonian hypnotic intervention used with clinical anxiety. *Journal of Social Service Research,* 17(3/4):41–69.

Nugent, W. (1993b). A vector model of single case design data and its use in analyzing large single case design replication series. *Journal of Social Service Research,* 12(1/2):49–82.

Nugent, W., J. Sieppert, and W. Hudson. (2001). *Practice evaluation for the 21st century.* Belmont, CA: Wadsworth.

Nunnally, Jum C. (1978). *Psychometric theory.* New York: McGraw-Hill.

Nurius, P., and W. Hudson. (1993a). *Computer assisted practice: Theory, methods and software.* Belmont, CA: Wadsworth.

Nurius, P., and W. Hudson. (1993b). *Human services: Practice, evaluation and computers.* Pacific Grove, CA: Brooks/Cole.

Oakes, M. (1986). *Statistical Inference: A commentary for the social and behavioral sciences.* New York: John Wiley & Sons.

Oakley, Ann. (1981). Interviewing women: A contradiction in terms. In *Doing feminist research,* edited by H. Roberts, pp. 30–61. London: Routledge.

O'Brien, Robert M. (1992). Levels of analysis. *Encyclopedia of sociology,* Vol. 3, edited by E. and M. Borgatta, pp. 1107–1112. New York: Macmillan.

O'Donnell, John M. (1985). *The origins of behaviorism: American psychology, 1870–1920.* New York: New York University Press.

Offe, Claus. (1981). The social sciences: Contract research or social movements? *Current Perspectives on Social Theory,* 2:31–37.

Ogles, B., and Masters, K. (1996). *Outcome assessment in clinical practice.* Boston: Allyn & Bacon.

Ohmae, K. (1995). *The end of the nation state: The rise of regional economies.* New York: Free Press.

Oksenberg, Lois, Lerita Coleman, and Charles F. Cannell. (1986). Interviewers' voices and refusal rates in telephone surveys. *Public Opinion Quarterly,* 50:97–111.

Oliker, Stacey J. (1994). Does workfare work? Evaluation research and workfare policy. *Social Problems,* 41:195–211.

Olsen, Marvin E., and Michael Micklin, eds. (1981). *Handbook of applied sociology.* New York: Praeger.

Olsen, Virginia. (1994). Feminism and models of qualitative research. In *Handbook of qualitative research,* edited by N. Denzin and Y. Lincoln, pp. 158–174. Thousand Oaks, CA: Sage.

Orbuch, Terri, and Sandra L. Eyster. (1997). Divison of labor among black couples and white couples. *Social Forces,* 76:301–332.

Orloff, Ann Shola. (1993). *The politics of pensions: A comparative analysis of Britain, Canada and the United States, 1880–1940.* Madison: University of Wisconsin Press.

Osgood, C. E., G. Suci, and H. Tannenbaum. (1957). *The measurement of meaning.* Urbana, IL: University of Illinois Press.

Ostrander, Susan. (1984). *Women of the upper class.* Philadelphia: Temple University Press.

Ostrander, Susan. (1993). "Surely you're not in this just to be helpful": Access, rapport and interview in three studies of elites. *Journal of Contemporary Ethnography*, 22:7–27.

Ostrom, Thomas M., and Katherine M. Gannon. (1996). Exemplar generation: Assessing how respondents give meaning to rating scales. In *Answering Questions*, edited by N. Schwarz and S. Sudman, pp. 293–318. San Francisco: Jossey-Bass.

O'Sullivan, Katherine. (1986). *First world nationalisms*. Chicago: University of Chicago Press.

Paige, Jeffrey M. (1975). *Agrarian revolution*. New York: Free Press.

Palmer, C. Eddie. (1978). Dog catchers: A descriptive study. *Qualitative Sociology*, 1:19–104.

Parcel, Toby L. (1992). Secondary data analysis and data archives. *Encyclopedia of sociology*, Vol. 4, edited by E. and M. Borgatta, pp. 1720–1728. New York: Macmillan.

Pardeck, J. (1992). Are social work journal editorial boards competent? Some disquieting data with implications for research on social work practice. *Research on Social Work Practice*, 2(4): 487–496.

Parker-Oliver, D. (2000). The social construction of the "dying role" and the hospice drama. *Omega Journal of Death and Dying*, 40(4):493–512.

Patton, M. (1990). *Qualitative evaluation and research methods*. Newbury Park, CA: Sage.

Payne, J. (1999). *Researching health needs*. Thousand Oaks, CA: Sage.

Peacock, Walter Gillis, Greg A. Hoover, and Charles D. Killian. (1988). Divergence and convergence in international development. *American Sociological Review*, 53:838–852.

Pearsall, Marion. (1970). Participant observation as role and method in behavioral research. In *Qualitative methodology*, edited by W. J. Filstead, pp. 340–352. Chicago: Markham.

Pearson, Michael Ross, and Robyn M. Dawes. (1992). Personal recall and the limits of retrospective questions in surveys. In *Questions about questions: Inquiries into the cognitive bases of surveys*, edited by J. Turner, pp. 65–94. New York: Russell Sage Foundation.

Pecora, P., M. Frazer, K. Nelson, J. McCrosky, and W. Meezan. (1990). *Evaluating family-based services*. New York: Aldine De Gruyter.

Pelton, L. (2001). Social justice and social work. *Journal of Social Work Education*, 37(3):433–439.

Pepinsky, Harold E. (1980). A sociologist on police control. In *Fieldwork experience*, edited by W. B. Shaffir, R. Stebbins, and A. Turowetz, pp. 223–234. New York: St. Martin's Press.

Percy-Smith, J., ed. (1996). *Needs assessments in public policy*. Philadelphia: Open University Press.

Peterson, Robert A. (1984). Asking the age question: A research note. *Public Opinion Quarterly*, 48:379–383.

Pfohl, Stephen. (1990). Welcome to the parasite cafe: Postmodernity as a social problem. *Social Problems*, 37: 421–442.

Phillips, Bernard. (1985). *Sociological research methods: An introduction*. Homewood, IL: Dorsey.

Phillips, D. C. (1987). *Philosophy, science and social inquiry: Contemporary methodological controversies in social science and related applied fields of research*. New York: Pergamon.

Phillips, Derek. (1971). *Knowledge from what?* Chicago: Rand McNally.

Pickering, A. (1995). *The mangle of practice: Time, agency and science*. Chicago: University of Chicago Press.

Piliavin, Irving M., J. Rodin, and Jane A. Piliavin. (1969). Good samaritanism: An underground phenomenon? *Journal of Personality and Social Psychology*, 13:289–299.

Pinderhughes, E. (1989). *Understanding race, ethnicity and power: Key efficacy in clinical practice*. New York: Free Press.

Plath, David W. (1990). Field notes, filed notes and the conferring of note. In *Field notes: The makings of anthropology*, edited by R. Sanjek, pp. 371–384. Ithaca, NY: Cornell University Press.

Poe, Gail S., et al. (1988). "Don't know" boxes in factual questions in a mail questionnaire: Effects on level and quality of response. *Public Opinion Quarterly*, 52:212–222.

Pollio, D., S. McDonald, and C. North. (1996). Combining a strengths-based approach and feminist theory in group work with persons "on the streets." *Social Work with Groups*, 19(4):5–20.

Pollner, Melvin, and Richard Adams. (1997). The effect of spouse presence on appraisals of emotional support and household strain. *Public Opinion Quarterly*, 61:615–626.

Polsky, Ned. (1967). *Hustlers, beats and others*. Chicago: Aldine.

Pomeroy, E., S. Demeter, and D. Tyler. (1995). Help book: A case study in empowerment research. *Prevention in the Human Services*, 12(1):89–102.

Popper, Karl. (1959/1934). *The logic of scientific discovery*. New York: Basic Books.

Porter, Theodore M. (1995). *Trust in numbers: The pursuit of objectivity in science and the public life*. Princeton, NJ: Princeton University Press.

Pottick, Kathleen, and Paul Lerman. (1991). Maximizing survey response rates for hard-to-reach inner-city populations. *Social Science Quarterly*, 72:172–180.

Presser, Stanley. (1984). Is inaccuracy on factual survey items item-specific or respondent-specific? *Public Opinion Quarterly*, 48:344–355.

Presser, Stanley. (1990). Measurement issues in the study of social change. *Social Forces*, 68:856–868.

Presser, Stanley, Johnny Blair, and Timothy Triplett. (1992). Survey sponsorship, response rates and response effects. *Social Science Quarterly*, 73: 699–702.

Prewitt, Kenneth. (1983). Management of survey organizations. In *Handbook of social research*, edited by P. Rossi, J. Wright, and A. Anderson, pp. 123–143. Orlando, FL: Academic Press.

Price, Vincent. (1989). Social identification and public opinion: Effects of communicating group conflict. *Public Opinion Quarterly*, 53: 197–224.

Proctor, E. (1990). Evaluating clinical practice: Issues of purpose and design. *Social Work Research and Abstracts*, 26:32–40.

Proctor, R., and L. Davis. (1994). The challenge of racial difference: Skills for clinical practice. *Social Work*, 39(3):314–323.

Prus, Robert C., and Steve Vassilakopoulos. (1979). Desk clerks and hookers. *Urban Life*, 8:52–71.

Przeworski, Adam, and Henry Teune. (1973). Equivalence in cross-national research. In *Comparative research methods*, edited by D. Warwick and S. Osherson, pp. 119–137. Englewood Cliffs, NJ: Prentice-Hall.

Punch, Maurice. (1986). *The politics and ethics of fieldwork*. Beverly Hills, CA: Sage.

Pusey, Michael. (1987). *Jügen Habermas*. New York: Tavistock.

Pyke, Sandra W., and Neil McK. Agnew. (1991). *The science game*, 5th ed. Englewood Cliffs, NJ: Prentice-Hall.

Quadagno, Jill S. (1984). Welfare capitalism and the Social Security Act of 1935. *American Sociological Review*, 49:632–648.

Quarles, Susan D., ed. (1986). *Guide to federal funding for social scientists*. New York: Russell Sage Foundation.

Rabinow, Paul, and William M. Sullivan. (1979). The interpretative turn: Emergence of an approach. In *Interpretative social science: A reader*, edited by P. Rabinow and W. Sullivan, pp. 1–24. Berkeley: University of California Press.

Rabin, C. (1981). The single-case design in family therapy evaluation research. *Family Processes*, 20(3):351–366.

Ragin, Charles C. (1987). *The comparative method*. Berkeley: University of California Press.

Ragin, Charles C. (1992a). Introduction: Cases of "what is a case?" In *What is a case: Exploring the foundations of social inquiry*, edited by C. Ragin and H. Becker, pp. 1–18. New York: Cambridge University Press.

Ragin, Charles C. (1992b). Casing and the process of social inquiry. In *What is a case: Exploring the foundations of social inquiry*, edited by C. Ragin and H. Becker, pp. 217–226. New York: Cambridge University Press.

Ragin, Charles C. (1994). *Constructing social research*. Thousand Oaks, CA: Pine Forge Press.

Ragin, Charles C., and David Zaret. (1983). Theory and method in comparative research. *Social Forces,* 61:731–754.

Rapp, C., W. Shera, and W. Kisthardt. (1993). Research strategies for consumer empowerment of people with severe mental illness. *Social Work,* 38(6):727–735.

Rathje, W. L., and W. W. Hughes. (1976). The garbage project as nonreactive approach: Garbage in-garbage out. In *Perspective on attitude assessment: Surveys and their alternatives,* edited by H. W. Sinaiko and L. A. Broeding. Champaign, IL: Pendleton Publications.

Rathje, William, and Cullen Murphy. (1992). *Rubbish: The archaeology of garbage.* New York: Vintage.

Ravo, Nick. (Oct. 14, 1996). Index of Social Well-Being is at the lowest in 25 years. *New York Times.*

Reamer, F. (1993). *The philosophical foundations of social work.* New York: Columbia University Press.

Reamer, F. (1998). The evolution of social work ethics. *Social Work,* 43(6): 488–500.

Reamer, F., and M. Abranson. (1982). *The teaching of social work ethics.* Hastings-on-Hudson, NY: The Hastings Center.

Reason, Peter. (1994). Three approaches to participative inquiry. In *Handbook of qualitative research,* edited by N. Denzin and Y. Lincoln, pp. 324–339. Thousand Oaks, CA: Sage.

Reese, Stephen, W. Danielson, P. Shoemaker, T. Chang, and H. Hsu. (1986). Ethnicity of interview effects among Mexican Americans and Anglos. *Public Opinion Quarterly,* 50:563–572.

Reid, W. (1994a). Reframing the epistemological debate. In *Qualitative research in social work,* edited by E. Sherman and W. Reid, pp. 464–481. New York: Columbia University Press.

Reid, W. (1994b). The empirical practice movement. *Social Service Review,* 68(2):165–184.

Reid, W. (1999). Research overview. In *Encyclopedia of Social Work,* 19th ed., Vol. 2, edited by R. Edwards (Editor-in-chief), pp. 2040–2054. Washington, DC: NASW Press.

Rein, M., and S. White. (1981). Knowledge in practice. *Social Service Review,* 55(1):1–41.

Reingold, Beth, and Richard Wike. (1998). Confederate symbols, southern identity, and racial attitudes: The case of the Georgia state flag. *Social Science Quarterly,* 79:568–580.

Reinharz, Shulamit. (1979). *On becoming a social scientist.* San Francisco: Jossey-Bass.

Reinharz, S. (1996). *Feminist methods for social research.* New York: Oxford University Press.

Reisch, M., and E. Gambrill, eds. (1997). *Social work in the 21st century.* Thousand Oaks, CA: Pine Forge Press.

Reiss, Albert J., Jr. (1992). Training incapacities of sociologists. In *Sociology and its publics: The forms and fates of disciplinary organization,* edited by T. Halliday and M. Janowitz, pp. 297–315. Chicago: University of Chicago Press.

Reskin, Barbara. (1977). Scientific productivity and the reward structure of science. *American Sociological Review,* 42:491–504.

Reynolds, Paul Davidson. (1971). *A primer in theory construction.* Indianapolis: Bobbs-Merrill.

Reynolds, Paul Davidson. (1979). *Ethical dilemmas and social science research.* San Francisco: Jossey-Bass.

Reynolds, Paul Davidson. (1982). *Ethics and social science research.* Englewood Cliffs, NJ: Prentice-Hall.

Richards, L., and T. Richards. (1991). Computing in qualitative analysis: A health development? *Qualitative Health Research,* 1:234–262.

Richards, Thomas J., and Lyn Richards. (1994). Using computers in qualitative research. In *Handbook of qualitative research,* edited by N. Denzin and Y. Lincoln, pp. 445–462. Thousand Oaks, CA: Sage.

Ricoeur, Paul. (1970). The model of the text: Meaningful action considered as a text. In *Interpretative social science: A reader,* edited by P. Rabinow and W. Sullivan, pp. 73–102. Berkeley: University of California Press.

Rippey-Massat, C., and M. Lundy. (1997). Empowering research participants. *Affilia—Journal of Women and Social Work,* 12(1):33–56.

Ritzer, George. (1975). *Sociology: A multi-paradigm science.* Boston: Allyn and Bacon.

Roadburg, Alan. (1980). Breaking relationships with field subjects: Some problems and suggestions. In *Fieldwork experience,* edited by W. B. Shaffir, R. Stebbins, and A. Turowetz, pp. 281–291. New York: St. Martin's Press.

Roberts, Carl W. (1989). Other than counting words: A linguistic approach to content analysis. *Social Forces,* 68: 147–177.

Roberts, R. (1989). *Serendipity: Accidental discoveries in science.* New York: John Wiley and Sons.

Robertson, E., and M. Knapp. (1988). Promoting intermediate treatment: A problem of excess demand or excess supply? *British Journal of Social Work,* 8:131–147.

Robertson, John A. (1982). The social scientist's right to research and the IRB system. In *Ethical issues in social science research,* edited by T. L. Beauchamp, R. Faden, R. J. Wallace, and L. Walters, pp. 356–372. Baltimore: Johns Hopkins University Press.

Robinson, E., D. Bronson, and B. Blythe. (1988). An analysis of the implementation of single case evaluation by practitioners. *Social Service Review,* 82(2):285–301.

Robinson, John P., Jerrold G. Rusk, and Kendra B. Head. (1972). *Measures of political attitudes.* Ann Arbor: Center for Political Studies, Institute for Social Research, University of Michigan.

Robinson, John P., and Philip R. Shaver. (1969). *Measures of social psychological attitudes.* Ann Arbor: Survey Research Center, Institute for Social Research, University of Michigan.

Robinson, T. (1999). The intersections of dominant discourses across race, gender and other identities. *Journal of Counseling and Development,* 77: 73–79. Copyright 1999 by the American Counseling Association.

Robinson, T., and M. Howard-Hamilton. (2000). *The convergence of race, ethnicity and gender: Multiple identities in counseling.* Upper Saddle River, NJ: Prentice-Hall.

Roderick, Rick. (1986). *Habermas and the foundations of critical theory.* New York: St. Martin's Press.

Rodgers-Farmer, A., and M. Potocky-Tripodi. (2001). Gender, ethnicity and race matters. In *The handbook of social work research methods,* edited by B. Thyer, pp. 445–454. Thousand Oaks, CA: Sage.

Rodwell, M. (1998). *Social work constructivist research.* New York: Garland Publishing.

Rodwell, M., and A. Blankebaker. (1992). Strategies for developing cross-cultural sensitivity: Wounding as a metaphor. *Journal of Social Work Education,* 28:153–165.

Roethlisberger, F. J., and W. J. Dickenson. (1939). *Management and the worker.* Cambridge, MA: Harvard University Press.

Rogers, M., ed. (1996). *Multicultural experiences: Multicultural theories.* New York: McGraw-Hill.

Rooney, R. (1992). *Strategies for work with involuntary clients.* New York: Columbia University Press.

Rose, Gerry. (1982). *Deciphering social research.* Beverly Hills, CA: Sage.

Rosen, A., and E. Proctor. (1978). Specifying the treatment process: The basis for effectiveness research. *Journal of Social Service Research,* 2(1):25–44.

Rosen, Lawrence. (1995). The creation of the Uniform Crime Report: The role of social science. *Social Science History,* 19:215–238.

Rosenau, Pauline Marie. (1992). *Post-modernism and the social sciences.* Princeton, NJ: Princeton University Press.

Rosenberg, Morris. (1968). *The logic of survey analysis.* New York: Basic Books.

Rosenthal, Robert. (1984). *Meta-analytic procedures for social research.* Beverly Hills, CA: Sage.

Rosnow, Ralph L. (1981). *Paradigms in transition: The methodology of social inquiry.* New York: Oxford University Press.

Ross, Dorothy. (1991). *The origins of American social science.* New York: Cambridge University Press.

Rossi, Peter H., ed. (1982). *Standards for evaluation practice.* San Francisco: Jossey-Bass.

Rossi, Peter H., and Howard E. Freeman. (1985). *Evaluation: A systematic approach,* 3rd ed. Beverly Hills, CA: Sage.

Rossi, P., H. Freeman, and M. Lipsey. (1999). *Evaluation: A systematic approach,* 6th ed. Beverly Hills, CA: Sage.

Rossi, Peter H., James D. Wright, and Andy Anderson. (1983). Sample surveys: History, current practice and future prospects. In *Handbook of social research,* edited by P. Rossi, J. Wright, and A. Anderson, pp. 1–20. Orlando, FL: Academic Press.

Rossi, Peter H., James D. Wright, and Eleanor Weber-Burdin. (1982). *Natural hazards and public choice.* New York: Academic Press.

Rossi, Robert J., and Kevin J. Gilmartin. (1980). *The handbook of social indicators: Sources, characteristics and analysis.* New York: Garland STPM Press.

Rounds, K., M. Weil, and K. Bishop. (1994). Practice with culturally diverse families of young children with disabilities. *Families in Society: The Journal of Contemporary Human Services,* 75(1):3–15.

Roy, Donald. (1970). The study of southern labor union organizing campaigns. In *Pathways to data,* edited by R. W. Habenstein, pp. 216–244. Chicago: Aldine.

Roy, William G. (1984). Class conflict and social change in historical perspective. *Annual Review of Sociology,* 10:483–506.

Royse, D., and B. Thyer. (1996). *Program evaluation: An introduction,* 2nd ed. Chicago: Nelson-Hall Publishers.

Rubin, A., and E. Babbie. (2001). *Research methods for social work,* 4th ed. Belmont, CA: Wadsworth.

Rubin, Herbert J. (1983). *Applied social research.* Columbus, OH: Charles E. Merrill.

Ruckdeschel, R. (1981). Qualitative research as a perspective. *Social Work Research and Abstracts,* 21(2):17–21.

Ruckdeschel, R., and B. Faris. (1981). Assessing practice: A critical look at the single-case design. *Social Casework,* 62:413–419.

Rueschemeyer, Dietrich, Evelyne Huber Stephens, and John D. Stephens. (1992). *Capitalist development and democracy.* Chicago: University of Chicago Press.

Rule, James. (1978a). *Insight and social betterment: A preface to applied social science.* New York: Oxford University Press.

Rule, James. (1978b). Models of relevance: The social effects of sociology.

American Journal of Sociology, 84: 78–98.

Runyon, Richard P., and Audry Haber. (1980). *Fundamentals of behavioral statistics.* Reading, MA: Addison-Wesley.

Russo, R. J. (1999). Applying a strengths-based practice approach in working with people with developmental disabilities and their families. *Families in Society,* January–February, 25–33.

Ryder, Norman B. (1992). Cohort analysis. In *Encyclopedia of sociology,* Vol. 1, edited by E. and M. Borgatta, pp. 227–231. New York: Macmillan.

Sabia, Daniel R., Jr., and Jerald T. Wallulis. (1983). *Changing social science: Changing theory and other critical perspectives.* Albany: State University of New York at Albany.

Sackett, D., S. Straus, W. Richardson, W. Rosenberg, and R. Haynes. (2000). *Evidence-based medicine: How to practice and teach EBM,* 2nd ed. New York: Churchill Livingstone.

Sagarin, Edward. (1973). The research setting and the right not to be researched. *Social Problems,* 21:52–64.

Saleebey, D. (1990). Philosophical disputes in social work: Social justice denied. *Journal of Sociology and Social Welfare,* 17:29–40.

Saleebey, D., ed. (1997). *The strengths perspective in social work practice,* 2nd ed. New York: Addison-Wesley Longman.

Saleebey, D. (2001). The diagnostic strengths manual. *Social Work,* 46(2): 183–187.

Saleebey, D., ed. (2002). *The strengths perspective in social work practice.* New York: Allyn & Bacon.

Sanchez, Maria Elena. (1992). Effects of questionnaire design on the quality of survey data. *Public Opinion Quarterly,* 56:206–217.

Sanday, Peggy Reeves. (1983). The ethnographic paradigm(s). In *Qualitative methodology,* edited by J. Van Maanen, pp. 19–36. Beverly Hills, CA: Sage.

Sanjek, Roger. (1978). A network method and its uses in urban anthropology. *Human Organization,* 37:257–268.

Sanjek, Roger. (1990). On ethnographic validity. In *Field notes: The makings of anthropology,* edited by R. Sanjek, pp. 385–418. Ithaca, NY: Cornell University Press.

Sarri, R. (1997). International social work at the millennium. In *Social work in the 21st century,* edited by M. Reisch and E. Gambrill, pp. 387–395. Thousand Oaks, CA: Pine Forge Press.

Saxe, Leonard, and Michelle Fine. (1981). *Social experiments: Methods for design and evaluation.* Beverly Hills, CA: Sage.

Sayer, Andrew. (1992). *Method in social science: A realist approach,* 2nd ed. New York: Routledge.

Schaefer, David, and Don A. Dillman. (1998). Development of a standard e-mail methodology. *Public Opinion Quarterly,* 62:378–397.

Schaffer, Nora Cate. (1980). Evaluating race-of-interviewer effects in a national survey. *Sociological Methods and Research,* 8:400–419.

Schatzman, Leonard, and Anselm L. Strauss. (1973). *Field research: Strategies for a natural sociology.* Englewood Cliffs, NJ: Prentice-Hall.

Scheibe, Karl E. (1988). Metamorphosis in the psychologist's advantage. In *The rise of experimentation in American psychology,* edited by J. Morawski, pp. 53–71. New Haven, CT: Yale University Press.

Scheuch, Erwin K. (1990). The development of comparative research: Towards causal explanations. In *Comparative methodology,* edited by E. Øyen, pp. 19–37. Newbury Park, CA: Sage.

Schiele, J. (1996). Afrocentricity: An emerging paradigm in social work practice. *Social Work,* 41(3):284–294.

Schiffman, Josepha. (1991). Fight the power: Two groups mobilize for peace. In *Ethnography unbound: Power and resistance in the modern metropolis,* edited by M. Burawoy et al., pp. 58–79. Berkeley: University of California Press.

Schlesinger, E., and W. Devore. (1995). Ethnic sensitive social work practice: The state of the art. *Journal of Sociology and Social Welfare,* 22: 29–58.

Schmeling, Sharon L., and Mike Miller. (Aug. 11, 1988). Whistleblower wins suit against UW. *Capital Times* (Madison, Wisconsin).

Schmitt, Eric. (June 27, 1997). Army criticized on survey on harrassment. *New York Times.*

Schmitz, C., J. Wagner, and E. Menke. (2001). The interconnection between childhood poverty and homelessness: Negative impact/point of access. *Families in Society,* 82(1):69–77.

Schneider, Mark A. (1987). Culture-as-text in the work of Clifford Geertz. *Theory and Society,* 16:809–883.

Schober, Michael, and Frederick G. Conrad. (1997). Does conversational interviewing reduce survey measurement error? *Public Opinion Quarterly,* 61:576–602.

Schrager, Laura, and James Short. (1980). How serious a crime? Perceptions of organizational and common crimes. In *White collar crime,* edited by G. Geis and E. Stotland, pp. 14–31. Beverly Hills, CA: Sage.

Schrecker, Ellen. (1986). *No ivory tower: McCarthyism and the university.* New York: Oxford University Press.

Schuessler, Karl. (1982). *Measuring social life feelings.* San Francisco: Jossey-Bass.

Schuman, Howard, and Lawrence Bobo. (1988). Survey-based experiments on white racial attitudes towards racial integration. *American Journal of Sociology,* 94:273–299.

Schuman, Howard, and Jean M. Converse. (1971). Effects of black and white interviewers on black response in 1968. *Public Opinion Quarterly,* 65:44–68.

Schuman, Howard, and Otis Dudley Duncan. (1974). Questions about attitude survey questions. In *Sociological methodology, 1973–1974,* edited by H. Costner, pp. 232–251. San Francisco: Jossey-Bass.

Schuman, Howard, and Jacob Ludwig. (1983). The norm of even-handedness in surveys as in life. *American Sociological Review,* 48:112–120.

Schuman, Howard, and Stanley Presser. (1977). Question wording as an independent variable in survey analysis. *Sociological Methods and Research,* 6:151–170.

Schuman, Howard, and Stanley Presser. (1979). The open and closed question. *American Sociological Review,* 44: 692–712.

Schuman, Howard, and Stanley Presser. (1981). *Questions and answers in attitude surveys: Experiments on question form, wording and content.* New York: Academic Press.

Schwandt, Thomas A. (1994). Constructivist, interpretivist approaches to human inquiry. In *Handbook of qualitative research,* edited by N. Denzin and Y. Lincoln, pp. 118–137. Thousand Oaks, CA: Sage.

Schwandt, Thomas A. (1997). *Qualitative inquiry: A dictionary of terms.* Thousand Oaks, CA: Sage.

Schwartz, David. (1997). *Culture and power: The sociology of Pierre Bourdieu.* Chicago: University of Chicago Press.

Schwartz, Dona. (1986). Camera clubs and fine art photography: The social construction of an elite code. *Urban Life,* 15:165–196.

Schwartz, Howard, and Jerry Jacobs. (1979). *Qualitative sociology: A method to the madness.* New York: Free Press.

Schwartz, Morris, and Charolotte Green Schwartz. (1969). Problems in field observation. In *Issues in participant observation,* edited by G. J. McCall and J. L. Simmons, pp. 89–105. Reading, MA: Addison-Wesley.

Schwarz, Norbert, and Hans-J. Hippler. (1995). Subsequent questions may influence answers to preceding questions in mail surveys. *Public Opinion Quarterly,* 59:93–97.

Schwarz, Norbert, Bäurbel Knäuper, Hans-J. Hippler, Elizabeth Noelle-Neumann, and Leslie Clark. (1991). Rating scales:

Numeric values may change the meaning of scale labels. *Public Opinion Quarterly,* 55:570–582.

Schwendinger, H., and J. Schwendinger. (1974). *Sociologists of the chair.* New York: Basic Books.

Scott, D. (1989). Meaning construction and social work practice. *Social Service Review,* 63:39–52.

Scott, William A. (1968). Attitude measurement. In *The handbook of social psychology, Vol. 2: Research methods,* edited by G. Lindzey and E. Aronson, pp. 204–273. Reading, MA: Addison-Wesley.

Scriven, M. (1991). *Evaluation thesaurus,* 4th ed. Newbury Park, CA: Sage.

Secret, M., Jordan, A., and Ford, J. (1999). Empowerment evaluation as a social work strategy. *Health and Social Work,* 24:120–127.

Sederer, L., and B. Dickey. (1996). *Outcomes assessment in clinical practice.* Baltimore: Williams & Wilkins.

Seeman, Melvin, and Carolyn S. Anderson. (1983). Alienation and alcohol: The role of work, mastery and community in drinking behavior. *American Sociological Review,* 48:60–77.

Seider, Maynard S. (1974). American big business ideology: A content analysis of executive speeches. *American Sociological Review,* 39:802–815.

Sellin, Thorsten, and Marvin E. Wolfgang. (1964). *The measurement of delinquency.* New York: Wiley.

Selvin, Hanan C., and Everett K. Wilson. (1984). On sharpening sociologists' prose. *Sociological Quarterly,* 25:205–223.

Sepstrup, P. (1981). Methodological developments in content analysis. In *Advances in content analysis,* edited by K. Rosengren, pp. 133–158. Beverly Hills, CA: Sage.

Seybold, Peter. (1987). The Ford Foundation and the transformation of political science. In *The structure of power in America,* edited by M. Schwartz, pp. 185–198. New York: Holmes and Meier.

Shafer, Robert Jones. (1980). *A guide to historical method,* 3rd ed. Homewood, IL: Dorsey.

Shaffir, William B., Robert A. Stebbins, and Allan Turowetz. (1980). Introduction. In *Fieldwork experience,* edited by W. B. Shaffir, R. Stebbins, and A. Turowetz, pp. 3–22. New York: St. Martin's Press.

Shands, K. (1999). *Embracing space: Spatial metaphors in feminist discourse.* Westport, CT: Greenwood Press.

Sharon, Batia. (1979). Artist-run galleries: A contemporary institutional change in the visual arts. *Qualitative Sociology,* 2:3–28.

Shattuck, John, and Muriel Morisey Spence. (1988). *Government information controls: Implications for scholarship, science and technology.*

Washington, DC: Association of American Universities.

Shaw, C. (1930). *The jack roller.* Chicago: University of Chicago Press.

Sheatsley, Paul B. (1983). Questionnaire construction and item writing. In *Handbook of social research,* edited by P. Rossi, J. Wright, and A. Anderson, pp. 195–230. Orlando, FL: Academic Press.

Sheflen, A., and A. Sheflen. (1974). *Body language and the social order: Communication as behavioral control.* Englewood Cliffs, NJ: Prentice-Hall.

Shihadeh, Edward S., and Graham Ousey. (1998). Industrial restructuring and violence: The link between entry-level jobs, economic deprivation, and black and white homicide. *Social Forces,* 77:185–206.

Shin, H., and N. Abell. (1999). The homesickness and contentment scales: Developing a culturally sensitive measure of adjustment for Asians. *Research on Social Work Practice,* 9:45–60.

Shively, JoEllen. (1992). Cowboys and Indians: Perceptions of western films among American Indians and Anglos. *American Sociological Review,* 57:725–734.

Shupe, Anston D., Jr., and David G. Bromley. (1980). Walking a tightrope: Dilemmas of participation observation of groups in conflict. *Qualitative Sociology,* 2:3–21.

Sieber, Joan, ed. (1982). *The ethics of social research: Fieldwork, regulation, and publication.* New York: Springer-Verlag.

Sieber, Joan E. (1992). *Planning ethically responsible research: A guide for students and internal review boards.* Thousand Oaks, CA: Sage.

Sieber, Joan E. (1993). The ethics and politics of sensitive research. In *Research on Sensitive Topics,* edited by C. Renzetti and R. Lee, pp. 14–26. Thousand Oaks, CA: Sage.

Sieber, Sam D. (1973). The integration of fieldwork and survey methods. *American Journal of Sociology,* 78: 1335–1359.

Siegel, D. (1994). Are practitioner intuition and empirical evidence equally valid sources of professional knowledge? No. In *Controversial issues in social work research,* edited by W. Hudson and P. Nurius, pp. 37–49. Boston: Allyn & Bacon.

Siegel, E., J. Jennings, J. Conklin, and S. Flynn. (1998). Distance learning in social work education: Results and implications of a national survey. *Journal of Social Work Education,* 34(1):71–80.

Sigelman, Lee. (1982). The uncooperative interviewee. *Quality and Quantity,* 16:345–353.

Silva, Edward T., and Sheila Slaughter. (1980). Prometheus bound: Limits of social science professionalization. *Theory and Society,* 9:781–819.

Silverman, David. (1972). Some neglected questions about social reality. In *New directions in sociological theory,* edited by P. Filmer et al. Cambridge, MA: MIT Press.

Silverman, David. (1993). *Interpreting qualitative data.* Thousand Oaks, CA: Sage.

Simon, R., and R. Rhodes. (2000). *In their own voices: Transracial adoptees tell their stories.* New York: Columbia University Press.

Singer, Benjamin D. (1989). The criterial crisis of the academic world. *Sociological Inquiry,* 59:127–143.

Singer, Eleanor. (1978). Informed consent: Consequences for response rate and response quality in social survey. *American Sociological Review,* 43:144–162.

Singer, Eleanor. (1988). Surveys in the mass media. In *Surveying social life: Papers in honor of Herbert H. Hyman,* edited by H. O'Gorman, pp. 413–436. Middletown, CT: Wesleyan University Press.

Singer, Eleanor, and Martin R. Frankel. (1982). Informed consent procedures in telephone interviews. *American Sociological Review,* 47:416–426.

Singer, Eleanor, and Luane Kohnke-Aguirre. (1979). Interviewer expectation effects: A replication and extension. *Public Opinion Quarterly,* 43:245–260.

Singer, Eleanor, John Van Hoewyk, and Mary Maher. (1998). Does the payment of incentives create expectation effects? *Public Opinion Quarterly,* 62:152–164.

Singer, Eleanor, Dawn R. Von Thurn, and Ester R. Miller. (1995). Confidentiality assurances and response: A quantitative review of the experimental literature. *Public Opinion Quarterly,* 59:66–77.

Singleton, Royce, Jr., B. Straits, Margaret Straits, and Ronald McAllister. (1988). *Approaches to social research.* New York: Oxford University Press.

Sinha, Anita. (1979). Control in craft work: The case of production potters. *Qualitative Sociology,* 2:3–25.

Siu, Paul C. P. (1987). *The Chinese laundryman: A study of social isolation,* edited by J. K. W. Tchen. New York: New York University Press.

Skidmore, William. (1979). *Theoretical thinking in sociology,* 2nd ed. New York: Cambridge University Press.

Sklar, Kathryn Kish. (1991). Hull House maps and papers: Social science as women's work in the 1890s. In *The social survey in historical perspective, 1880–1940,* edited by M. Blumer, K. Bales, and K. Sklar, pp. 111–147. New York: Cambridge University Press.

Skocpol, Theda. (1979). *States and social revolutions.* New York: Cambridge University Press.

Skocpol, Theda. (1984). Emerging agendas and recurrent strategies in historical sociology. In *Vision and method in historical sociology,* edited by T. Skocpol, pp. 356–392. Cambridge: Cambridge University Press.

Skocpol, Theda. (1988). The "uppity generation" and the revitalization of macroscopic sociology: Reflections at mid-career of a woman from the sixties. *Theory and Society,* 17:627–644.

Skocpol, Theda, and Margaret Somers. (1980). The uses of comparative history in macrosocial inquiry. *Comparative Studies in Society and History,* 22:174–197.

Slater, Phil. (1977). *Origin and significance of the Frankfurt School.* Boston: Routledge and Kegan Paul.

Slonim-Nevo, V., and Y. Anson. (1998). Evaluating practice: Does it improve treatment outcome? *Social Work Research,* 22(2):66–74.

Smart, Barry. (1976). *Sociology, phenomenology, and Marxian analysis: A critical discussion of the theory and practice of a science of society.* Boston: Routledge and Kegan Paul.

Smelser, Neil J. (1959). *Social change in the industrial revolution.* Chicago: University of Chicago Press.

Smelser, Neil J. (1976). *Comparative methods in the social sciences.* Englewood Cliffs, NJ: Prentice-Hall.

Smith, Christopher. (1995). Asian New York: The geography and politics of diversity. *International Migration Review,* 29:59–84.

Smith, D. (1987). The limits of positivism in social work research. *British Journal of Social Work,* 17(4):401–416.

Smith, Dennis. (1991). *The rise of historical sociology.* Philadelphia: Temple University Press.

Smith, George W., and Dorothy E. Smith. (1998). The ideology of "fag": The high school experience of gay students. *Sociological Quarterly,* 39:289–308.

Smith, Louis M. (1994). Biographical method. In *Handbook of qualitative research,* edited by N. Denzin and Y. Lincoln, pp. 286–305. Thousand Oaks, CA: Sage.

Smith, M. (1989). *Evaluability assessment: A practical approach.* Boston: Kluwer Academic Publishers.

Smith, Mary Lee, and Gene V. Glass. (1987). *Research and evaluation in education and the social sciences.* Englewood Cliffs, NJ: Prentice-Hall.

Smith, Robert B. (1987). Linking quality and quantity; Part I: Understanding and explanation. *Quantity and Quality,* 21:291–311.

Smith, Robert B. (1988). Linking quality and quantity, Part II: Surveys as formalizations. *Quantity and Quality,* 22:3–30.

Smith, Tom W. (1984). The subjectivity of ethnicity. In *Surveying subjective phenoemona,* Vol. 2, edited by C. Turner and E. Martin, pp. 117–128. New York: Russell Sage Foundation.

Smith, Tom W. (1987). That which we call welfare by any other name would smell sweeter: An analysis of the impact of question wording on response patterns. *Public Opinion Quarterly,* 51:75–83.

Smith, Tom W. (1989). Random probes of GSS questions. *International Journal of Public Opinion Research,* 1:305–325.

Smith, Tom W. (1995). Trends in non-response rates. *International Journal of Public Opinion Research,* 7:156–171.

Sniderman, Paul M., and Michael Gray Hagen. (1985). *Race and inequality: A study in American values.* Chatham, NJ: Chatham House.

Snow, David A., Susan G. Baker, Leon Anderson, and Michael Martin. (1986b). The myth of pervasive mental illness among the homeless. *Social Problems,* 33:407–423.

Snow, David A., E. Burke Bochford, Jr., Steven K. Worden, and Robert D. Benford. (1986a). Frame alignment process, micromobilization and movement participation. *American Sociological Review,* 51:464–481.

Sobal, Jeffery. (1984). The content of survey introductions and the provision of informed consent. *Public Opinion Quarterly,* 48:788–793.

Sociology Writing Group, UCLA. (1991). *A guide to writing sociology papers,* 2nd ed. New York: St. Martin's Press.

Sohn-Rethel, Alfred. (1978). *Intellectual and manual labor: A critique of epistemology.* New York: Macmillan.

Sonnichsen, L. (1999). Building evaluation capacity within organizations. In *Building effective evaluation capacity: Lessons from practice,* edited by R. Boyle and D. Lemaire, pp. 53–73. New Brunswick, NJ: Transaction Publishers.

Sonquist, J. A., and C. Dunkelberg. (1977). *Survey and opinion research: Procedures for processing and analysis.* Englewood Cliffs, NJ: Prentice-Hall.

South, Scott, and Kim Lloyd. (1995). Spousal alternatives and marital dissolution. *American Sociological Review,* 60:126–140.

Spector, Paul E. (1981). *Research designs.* Beverly Hills, CA: Sage.

Spector, Paul E. (1992). *Summated rating scale construction.* Newbury Park, CA: Sage.

Spencer, Gary. (1982). Methodological issues in the study of bureaucratic elites: A case study of West Point. In *Field research,* edited by R. G. Burgess, pp. 23–30. Boston: Allen and Unwin.

Spillers, Cindy S. (1982). An investigation of children's attitudes towards physically disabled peers. *Mid-American Review of Sociology,* 7:55–69.

Spradley, James P. (1970). *You owe yourself a drunk.* Boston: Little, Brown.

Spradley, James P. (1979a). *The ethnographic interview.* New York: Holt, Rinehart and Winston.

Spradley, James P. (1979b). *Participant observation.* New York: Holt, Rinehart and Winston.

Spradley, James P., and B. J. Mann. (1975). *The cocktail waitress.* New York: Wiley.

Sprague, Joey, and Mary K. Zimmerman. (1989). Quality and quantity: Reconstructing feminist methodology. *American Sociologist,* 20:71–86.

Stack, Carol. (1989). Doing research in the flats. In *In the field,* edited by C. Smith and W. Kornblum, pp. 21–26. New York: Praeger.

Stack, Steven. (1987). Celebrities and suicide: A taxonomy and analysis, 1948–1983. *American Sociological Review,* 52:401–412.

Staggenborg, Susan. (1988). "Hired hand research" revised. *American Sociologist,* 19:260–269.

Stake, Robert E. (1994). Case studies. In *Handbook of qualitative research,* edited by N. Denzin and Y. Lincoln, pp. 236–247. Thousand Oaks, CA: Sage.

Starr, Paul. (1987). The sociology of official statistics. In *The politics of numbers,* edited by W. Alonso and P. Starr, pp. 7–58. New York: Russell Sage Foundation.

Starr, Paul, and Ross Corson. (1987). Who will have the numbers? The rise of the statistical services industry and the politics of public data. In *The politics of numbers,* edited by W. Alonso and P. Starr, pp. 415–447. New York: Russell Sage Foundation.

Stech, Charlotte G. (1981). Trends in nonresponse rates, 1952–1979. *Public Opinion Quarterly,* 45:40–57.

Stempel, G., III. (1971). Visibility of blacks in news and news-picture magazines. *Journalism Quarterly,* 48:337–339.

Stephens, Mary Ann Parris, N. S. Cooper, and J. M. Kinney. (1985). The effects of effort on helping the physically disabled. *Journal of Social Psychology,* 125:495–503.

Stephenson, Richard M. (1978). The CIA and the professor: A personal account. *American Sociologist,* 13:128–133.

Stern, Paul C. (1979). *Evaluating social science research.* New York: Oxford University Press.

Stevens, Carla, and Micah Dial, Eds. (1994). Preventing the misuse of evaluation. *New Directions for Program Evaluation, 64.* San Francisco: Jossey-Bass.

Stevenson, Richard W. (Oct. 16, 1996). U.S. to revise its estimate of layoffs. *New York Times.*

Stewart, David W. (1984). *Secondary research: Information sources and methods.* Beverly Hills, CA: Sage.

Stewart, Donald E. (1983). *The television family.* Melborne: Institute of Family Studies.

Stimson, Gerry B. (1986). Place and space in sociological fieldwork. *The Sociological Review,* 34:641–656.

Stinchcombe, Arthur L. (1968). *Constructing social theories.* New York: Harcourt, Brace and World.

Stinchcombe, Arthur L. (1973). Theoretical domains and measurement, Part 1. *Acta Sociologica,* 16:3–12.

Stinchcombe, Arthur L. (1978). *Theoretical methods in social history.* New York: Academic Press.

Stoeker, Randy. (1993). The federated frontstage structure and localized social movements: A case study of the Ceder-Riverside neighborhood movement. *Social Science Quarterly,* 74:169–184.

Stoesz, D. (1997). The end of social work. In *Social work in the 21st century,* edited by M. Reisch and E. Gambrill, pp. 368–375. Thousand Oaks, CA: Pine Forge Press.

Stoianovich, Traian. (1976). *French historical method.* Ithaca, NY: Cornell University Press.

Stone, John. (1985). *Racial conflict in contemporary society.* Cambridge, MA: Harvard University Press.

Stone, Philip, et al. (1966). *The general inquirer: A computer approach to content analysis in the behavioral sciences.* Cambridge, MA: MIT Press.

Stone, Philip J., and Robert P. Weber. (1992). Content analysis. In *Encyclopedia of sociology,* Vol. 1, edited by E. and M. Borgatta, pp. 290–295. New York: Macmillan.

Stoner, Norman W. (1966). *The social system of science.* New York: Holt, Rinehart and Winston.

Strauss, Anselm. (1987). *Qualitative analysis for social scientists.* New York: Cambridge University Press.

Strauss, Anselm, and Juliet Corbin. (1990). *Basics of qualitative research: Grounded theory procedures and techniques.* Newbury Park, CA: Sage.

Strauss, Anselm, and Juliet Corbin. (1994). Grounding theory methodology: An overview. In *Handbook of qualitative research,* edited by N. Denzin and Y. Lincoln, pp. 273–285. Thousand Oaks, CA: Sage.

Stretch, J. (1967). Existentialism: A proposed philosophical orientation for social work. *Social Work,* 12(4):97–102.

Stretch, J., and L. Kreuger. (1993). Five year cohort study of homeless families: A joint policy research venture. *Journal of Sociology and Social Welfare,* 19(1): 73–88.

Stufflebean, D. L. (1994). Empowerment evaluation, objectivist evaluation, and evaluation standards: Where the future of evaluation should not go and where it needs to go. *Evaluation Practice,* 15(3):321–338.

Suchman, Luch, and Brigitte Jordan. (1992). Validity and the collaborative construction of meaning in face-to-face surveys. In *Questions about questions: Inquiries into the cognitive bases of surveys,* edited by J. Turner, pp. 241–267. New York: Russell Sage Foundation.

Sudholm, Charles A. (1973). The pornographic arcade: Ethnographic notes on moral men in immoral places. *Urban Life,* 2:85–104.

Sudman, Seymour. (1976a). *Applied sampling.* New York: Academic Press.

Sudman, Seymour. (1976b). Sample surveys. *Annual Review of Sociology,* 2:107–120.

Sudman, Seymour. (1983). Applied sampling. In *Handbook of survey research,* edited by P. Rossi, J. Wright, and A. Anderson, pp. 145–194. Orlando, FL: Academic Press.

Sudman, Seymour, and Norman M. Bradburn. (1983). *Asking questions: A practical guide to questionnaire design.* San Francisco: Jossey-Bass.

Sudman, Seymour, and Norman M. Bradburn. (1987). The organizational growth of public opinion research in the United States. *Public Opinion Quarterly,* 51:S67-S78.

Sudman, Seymour, Norman M. Bradburn, and Norbert Schwarz. (1996). *Thinking about answers: The application of cognitive processes to survey research.* San Francisco: Jossey-Bass.

Sudnow, David. (1978). *Ways of the hand: The organization of improvised conduct.* Cambridge, MA: Harvard University Press.

Sullivan, John L., and Stanley Feldman. (1979). *Multiple indicators: An introduction.* Beverly Hills, CA: Sage.

Suls, Jerry M., and Ralph L. Rosnow. (1988). Concerns about artifacts in psychological experiments. In *The rise of experimentation in American psychology,* edited by J. Morawski, pp. 153–187. New Haven, CT: Yale University Press.

Sundet, P., and J. Mermelstein. (2000). Sustainability of rural communities: Lessons from natural disaster. In *Tulane studies in social welfare,* Vol. 21–22: *Disaster and traumatic stress research and intervention,* edited by M. J. Zakour, pp. 25–40. New Orleans, LA: Tulane University.

Suppe, Frederick, ed. (1977). *The structure of scientific theories,* 2nd ed. Urbana, IL: University of Illinois Press.

Survey Research Center, Institute for Social Research. (1976). *Interviewer's manual,* rev. ed. Ann Arbor: University of Michigan.

Sutton, John R. (1991). The political economy of madness: The expansion of the asylum in progressive America. *American Sociological Review,* 56:665–678.

Swafford, Michael. (Nov. 1987). Soviet, U.S. sociologists work together. American Sociological Association *Footnotes,* 15:9.

Swanborn, Peter G. (1996). A common base for quality control criteria in quantitative and qualitative research. *Quality and Quantity,* 30:19–35.

Swanson, Guy E. (1971). Frameworks for comparative research. In *Comparative methods in sociology,* edited by I. Vallier, pp. 141–203. Berkeley: University of California Press.

Swidler, Ann. (1986). Culture in action: Symbols and strategies. *American Sociological Review,* 51: 273–286.

Swigonski, M. (1994). The logic of feminist standpoint theory for social work research. *Social Work,* 39:737–741.

Tagg, Stephen K. (1985). Life story interviews and their interpretation. In *The research interview: Uses and approaches,* edited by M. Brenner, J. Brown, and D. Canter, pp. 163–199. New York: Academic Press.

Tanur, Judith H., ed. (1992). *Questions about questions: Inquiries into the cognitive bases of surveys.* New York: Russell Sage Foundation.

Tanur, Judith M. (1983). Methods for large scale surveys and experiments. In *Sociological Methodology, 1983–1984,* edited by S. Leinhardt, pp. 1–71. San Francisco: Jossey-Bass.

Tashakkori, Abbas, and Charles Teddlie. (1998). *Mixed methodology: Combining qualitative and quantitative approaches.* Thousand Oaks, CA: Sage.

Taylor, Charles. (1979). Interpretation and the sciences of man. In *Interpretative social science: A reader,* edited by P. Rabinow and W. Sullivan, pp. 25–72. Berkeley: University of California Press.

Taylor, Charles Lewis, ed. (1980). *Indicator systems for political, economic and social analysis.* Cambridge, MA: Oelgeschlager, Gunn and Hain.

Taylor, Charles R., and Barbara B. Stern. (1997). Asian Americans: Television advertising and the "model minority" stereotype. *Journal of Advertising,* 26:47–62.

Taylor, Steven. (1987). Observing abuse: Professional ethics and personal morality in field research. *Qualitative Sociology,* 10:288–302.

The 1999 Peter Hodge Memorial Lecture, Hong Kong. (2000). *Journal of Social Work Research and Evaluation,* 1(1): 5–16.

Thomas, Robert J. (1993). Interviewing important people in big companies. *Journal of Contemporary Ethnography,* 22:80–96.

Thompson, E. P. (1967). Time, work-discipline, and industrial capitalism. *Past and Present,* 38:56–97.

Thompson, E. P. (1978). *The poverty of theory and other essays.* New York: Monthly Review Press.

Thompson, Paul. (1978). *The voice of the past: Oral history.* New York: Oxford University Press.

Thorne, Barrie, and Zella Luria. (1986). Sexuality and gender in children's daily world. *Social Problems,* 33:176–190.

Thrasher, F. M. (1927). *The gang.* Chicago: University of Chicago Press.

Thurow, L. (1996). *The future of capitalism: How today's economic forces shape tomorrow's world.* New York: William Morrow and Company.

Thurstone, L. L. (1970). Attitudes can be measured. In *Attitude measurement,* edited by G. Summers, pp. 127–141. Chicago: Rand McNally.

Thyer, B. (1986). On pseudoscience and pseudoreasoning. *Social Work Research and Abstracts,* 22(2):371–372.

Thyer, B. (1989). Exploring epistemologies: The debate continues. *Journal of Social Work Education,* 25(2):174–176.

Thyer, B. (1993a). Single-system designs. In *Social work research and evalution,* 4th ed., edited by R. M. Grinnell, Jr., pp. 92–117. Itasca, IL: Peacock.

Thyer, B. (1993b). Social work theory and practice research: The approach of logical positivism. *Social Work and Social Sciences Review,* 4(1):5–26.

Thyer, B. (1998). Promoting research on community practice: Using single-system designs. In *Research strategies in community practice,* edited by R. H. MacNair, pp. 47–61. New York: Haworth.

Thyer, B., ed. (2001). *The handbook of social work research methods,* pp. 193–206. Thousand Oaks, CA: Sage.

Tickamyer, Ann R. (1981). Wealth and power: A comparison of men and women in the property elite. *Social Forces,* 60:463–481.

Tilly, Charles, Louise Tilly, and Richard Tilly. (1975). *The rebellious century, 1830–1930.* Cambridge, MA: Harvard University Press.

Toulmin, Stephen. (1953). *The philosophy of science: An introduction.* New York: Harper & Row.

Tourangeau, Roger, and Tom Smith. (1996). Asking sensitive questions: The impact of data collection mode, question format and question context. *Public Opinion Quarterly,* 60:275–304.

Tran, T., and K. Aroian. (2000). Developing cross cultural research instruments. *Journal of Social Work Research and Evaluation: An International Publication,* 1(1):35–48.

Traugott, Michael W. (1987). The importance of persistence in respondent selection for preelection surveys. *Public Opinion Quarterly,* 51:48–57.

Trice, H. M. (1970). The "outsider's" role in field study. In *Qualitative methodology,* edited by W. J. Filstead, pp. 77–82. Chicago: Markham.

Trinder, L., and S. Reynolds. (2000). *Evidence-based practice: A critical appraisal.* London: Blackwell Science.

Tripodi, T. (1983). *Evaluation research for social workers.* Englewood Cliffs, NJ: Prentice-Hall.

Tripodi, T. (1994). A primer on single-subject design for social workers. Washington, DC: NASW Press.

Tripodi, T. (2001). The contemporary challenge in evaluating social services. An international perspective. The 1999 Peter Hodge Memorial Lecture, Hong Kong. *Journal of Social Work Research and Evaluation,* 1(1):5–16.

Tropp, Richard A. (1982). A regulatory perspective on social science research. In *Ethical issues in social science research,* edited by T. Beauchamp, R. Faden, R. J. Wallace, and L. Walters, pp. 391–415. Baltimore: Johns Hopkins University Press.

Trovato, Frank. (1998). The Stanley cup of hockey and suicide in Quebec, 1951–1992. *Social Forces,* 77:105–126.

Tucker, Clyde. (1983). Interviewer effects in telephone interviewing. *Public Opinion Quarterly,* 47:84–95.

Tufte, Edward. (1983). *The visual display of quantitative information.* Cheshire, CT: Graphics Press.

Tufte, Edward. (1991). *Envisioning information,* rev. ed. Cheshire, CT: Graphics Press.

Tully, C. (2000). *Lesbians, gays and the empowerment perspective.* New York: Columbia University Press.

Tuma, Nancy B., and Andrew Grimes. (1981). A comparison of models of role orientations of professionals in a research oriented university. *Administrative Science Quarterly,* 21:187–206.

Turner, Charles. (1984). Why do surveys disagree? Some preliminary hypotheses and some disagreeable examples. In *Surveying subjective phenomena,* Vol. 2, edited by C. Turner and E. Martin, pp. 157–214. New York: Russell Sage Foundation.

Turner, Charles, and Elizabeth Martin, eds. (1984). *Surveying subjective phenomena,* Vol. 1. New York: Russell Sage Foundation.

Turner, Jonathan H. (1985). In defense of positivism. *Sociological Theory,* 3:24–30.

Turner, Jonathan H. (1992). Positivism. In *Encylopedia of sociology,* Vol. 3, edited by E. and M. Borgatta, pp. 1509–1512. New York: Macmillan.

Turner, Roy. (1974). *Ethnomethodology.* Middlesex: Penguin.

Turner, Stephen P. (1980). *Sociological explanation as translation.* New York: Cambridge University Press.

Turner, Stephen P. (1991). The world of academic quantifiers: The Columbia

University family and its connections. In *The social survey in historical perspective, 1880–1940,* edited by M. Blumer, K. Bales, and K. Sklar, pp. 269–290. New York: Cambridge University Press.

Turner, Stephen Park, and Jonathan H. Turner. (1991). *The impossible science: An institutional analysis of American sociology.* Newbury Park, CA: Sage.

Tutty, L., and M. Rothery. (2001). Needs assessments. In *The handbook of social work research methods,* edited by B. Thyer, pp. 161–176. Thousand Oaks, CA: Sage.

Umberson, Debra, and Meichu D. Chen. (1994). Effects of a parent's death on adult children: Relationship salience and reaction to loss. *American Sociological Review,* 59:152–168.

Unrau, Y. (1993). A program logic model approach to conceptualizing social services programs. *Canadian Journal of Program Evaluation,* 8:33–42.

U.S. Department of Health, Education, and Welfare Publication (OS)78-0012. (1978). *The Belmont report: Ethical principles and guidelines for the protection of human subjects of research,* pp. 1–97.

Useem, Michael. (1976a). Government influence on the social science paradigm. *Sociological Quarterly,* 17:146–161.

Useem, Michael. (1976b). State production of social knowledge: Patterns of government financing of academic social research. *American Sociological Review,* 41:613–629.

Useem, Michael. (1984). *The inner circle: Large corporations and the rise of business political activity in the U.S. and the U. K.* New York: Oxford University Press.

Vacc, N., S. DeVaney, and J. Wittmer. (1995). *Experiencing and counseling multicultural and diverse populations,* 3rd ed. Bristol, PA: Taylor and Francis.

Valentine-French, Suzanne, and H. Lorraine Radtke. (1989). Attributions of responsibility for an incident of sexual harassment in a university setting. *Sex Roles,* 21:545–555.

Vallier, Ivan. (1971). Empirical comparisons of social structure. In *Comparative methods in sociology,* edited by I. Vallier, pp. 203–263. Berkeley: University of California Press.

Van den Berg, Harry, and Cees Van der Veer. (1985). Measuring ideological frames of references. *Quality and Quantity,* 19:105–118.

Van den Berge, Pierre L. (1967). Research in South Africa: The story of my experiences with tyranny. In *Ethics, politics and social research,* edited by G. Sjøberg. New York: Schenckman.

Van Maanen, John. (1973). Observations on the making of policemen. *Human Organization,* 32:407–418.

Van Maanen, John. (1982). Fieldwork on the beat. In *Varieties of qualitative research,* edited by J. Van Maanen, J. Dabbs, Jr., and R. Faulkner, pp. 103–151. Beverly Hills, CA: Sage.

Van Maanen, John. (1983a). Epilogue: Qualitative methods reclaimed. In *Qualitative methodology,* edited by J. Van Maanen, pp. 247–268. Beverly Hills, CA: Sage.

Van Maanen, John. (1983b). The moral fix: On the ethics of fieldwork. In *Contemporary field research,* edited by R. M. Emerson, pp. 269–287. Boston: Little, Brown.

Van Maanen, John. (1988). *Tales of the field: On writing ethnography.* Chicago: University of Chicago Press.

Van Warmer, K., J. Wells, and M. Boes. (2000). *Social work with lesbians, gays and bisexuals: A strengths perspective.* Boston: Allyn & Bacon.

Vaughan, Diane. (1992). Theory elaboration: The heuristics of case analysis. In *What is a case? Exploring the foundations of social inquiry,* edited by C. Ragin and H. Becker, pp. 173–202. Cambridge: Cambridge University Press.

Vaughan, Ted R. (1967). Government intervention in social research: Political and ethical dimensions of the Wichita jury recordings. In *Ethics, politics and social research,* edited by G. Sjøberg. New York: Schenckman.

Veltmeyer, Henry. (1978). Marx's two methods of sociological analysis. *Sociological Inquiry,* 48:101–112.

Verba, Sidney, and Gary R. Orren. (1985). *Equality in America: The view from the top.* Cambridge, MA: Harvard University Press.

Vidich, Arthur Joseph, and Joseph Bensman. (1968). *Small town in mass society,* rev. ed. Princeton, NJ: Princeton University Press.

Wade, Nicholas. (1976). IQ and heredity: Suspicion of fraud beclouds classic experiment. *Science,* 194: 916–919.

Waegel, William B. (1984). How police justify the use of deadly force. *Social Problems,* 32:133–143.

Waksberg, J. (1978). Sampling methods for random digit dialing. *Journal of the American Statistical Association,* 73:40–46.

Wallace, Walter. (1971). *The logic of science in sociology.* Chicago: Aldine.

Walsh, David. (1972). Varieties of positivism. In *New directions in sociological theory,* edited by P. Filmer et al. Cambridge, MA: MIT Press.

Walster, Elaine. (1965). The effect of self-esteem on romantic liking. *Journal of Experimental Social Psychology,* 1:194–197.

Walton, John. (1992a). *Western times and water wars: State, culture and rebellion in California.* Berkeley: University of California Press.

Walton, John. (1992b). Making the theoretical case. In *What is a case? Exploring the foundations of social inquiry,* edited by C. Ragin and H. Becker, pp. 121–138. Cambridge: Cambridge University Press.

Walz, T., and H. Ritchie. (2000). Gandhian principles in social work practice: Ethics revisited. *Social Work,* 45(3): 213–222.

Ward, Benjamin. (1972). *What's wrong with economics.* New York: Basic Books.

Ward, Kathryn B., and Linda Grant. (1985). The feminist critique and a decade of published research in sociology journals. *Sociological Quarterly,* 26:139–158.

Wardell, Mark L. (1979). Marx and his method: A commentary. *Sociological Quarterly,* 20:425–436.

Wares, D., K. Wedel, J. Rosenthal, and A. Dolbrec. (1994). Indian child welfare: A multicultural challenge. *Journal of Multicultural Social Work,* 3(3):1–15.

Warner, R. Stephen. (1971). The methodology of Marx's comparative analysis of modes of production. In *Comparative methods in sociology,* edited by I. Vallier, pp. 49–74. Berkeley: University of California Press.

Warren, Carol A. B., and Paul K. Rasmussen. (1977). Sex and gender in field research. *Urban Life,* 6:349–369.

Warwick, Donald P. (1982). Types of harm in social science research. In *Ethical issues in social science research,* edited by T. Beauchamp, R. Faden, R. J. Wallace, and L. Walters, pp. 101–123. Baltimore: Johns Hopkins University Press.

Warwick, Donald P., and Charles A. Lininger. (1975). *The sample survey: Theory and practice.* New York: McGraw-Hill.

Watt, J. W., and G. L. Kallmann. (1998). Managing professional obligations under managed care: A social work perspective. *Family and Community Health,* 21(2):40–49.

Watters, John K., and Patrick Biernacki. (1989). Targeted sampling: Options for the study of hidden populations. *Social Problems,* 36:416–430.

Wax, Rosalie H. (1971). *Doing fieldwork: Warnings and advice.* Chicago: University of Chicago Press.

Wax, Rosalie H. (1979). Gender and age in fieldwork and fieldwork education: No good thing is done by any man alone. *Social Problems,* 26: 509–522.

Weaver, H. (1999). Indigenous people and the social work profession: Defining culturally competent services. *Social Work,* 44(3):217–225.

Webb, Eugene J., Donald T. Campbell, Richard D. Schwartz, Lee Sechrest, and Janet Belew Grove. (1981). *Nonreactive measures in the social sciences,* 2nd ed. Boston: Houghton Mifflin.

Webb, S. (2001). Some considerations on the validity of evidence-based practice in social work. *British Journal of Social Work,* 31:57–79.

Weber, Max. (1949). *The methodology of the social sciences,* trans. and edited by E. Shils and H. Finch. New York: Free Press.

Weber, Max. (1974). Subjectivity and determinism. In *Positivism and sociology,* edited by A. Giddens, pp. 23–32. London: Heinemann.

Weber, Max. (1978). *Economy and society,* Vol. 1, edited by G. Roth and C. Wittich. Berkeley: University of California Press.

Weber, Max. (1981). Some categories of interpretative sociology. *Sociological Quarterly,* 22:151–180.

Weber, Robert P. (1983). Measurement models for content analysis. *Quality and Quantity,* 17:127–149.

Weber, Robert P. (1984). Computer assisted content analysis: A short primer. *Qualitative Sociology,* 7:126–149.

Weber, Robert P. (1985). *Basic content analysis.* Beverly Hills, CA: Sage.

Weeks, M. F., and R. P. Moore. (1981). Ethnicity of interviewer effects on ethnic respondents. *Public Opinion Quarterly,* 45:245–249.

Weiner, A. (1996). Understanding the social needs of streetwalking prostitutes. *Social Work,* 47:97–105.

Weinstein, Deena. (1979). Fraud in science. *Social Science Quarterly,* 59:639–652.

Weiss, Carol H. (1972). *Evaluation research: Methods of assessing program effectiveness.* Englewood Cliffs, NJ: Prentice-Hall.

Weiss, Janet A., and Judith E. Gruber. (1987). The managed irrelevance of educational statistics. In *The politics of numbers,* edited by W. Alonso and P. Starr, pp. 363–391. New York: Russell Sage Foundation.

Weiss, Robert S. (1994). *Learning from strangers: The arts and method of qualitative interview studies.* New York: Free Press.

Weitz, Rose, and Deborah A. Sullivan. (1986). The politics of childbirth: The re-emergence of midwifery in Arizona. *Social Problems,* 33:163–175.

Weitzman, Eben, and Matthew Miles. (1995). *Computer programs for qualitative data analysis.* Thousand Oaks, CA: Sage.

Weitzman, Lenore, D. Eifler, E. Hokada, and C. Ross. (1972). Sex role socialization in picture books for preschool children. *American Journal of Sociology,* 77:1125–1150.

Welch, Michael, and Melissa Fenwick. (1997). Primary definitions of crime and moral panic: A content analysis of expert's quotes in feature stories. *Journal of Research in Crime and Delinquency,* 34:474–495.

Wenger, G. Clare, ed. (1987). *The research relationship: Practice and politics in social policy research.* Boston: Allen and Unwin.

Wentworth, Ellen J. (1993). *Survey responses: An evaluation of their validity.* New York: Academic Press.

Werner, Oswald, and G. Mark Schoepfle. (1987a). *Systematic fieldwork, Vol. 1: Foundations of ethnography and interviewing.* Beverly Hills, CA: Sage.

Werner, Oswald, and G. Mark Schoepfle. (1987b). *Systematic fieldwork, Vol. 2: Ethnographic analysis and data management.* Beverly Hills, CA: Sage.

West, W. Gordon. (1980). Access to adolescent deviants and deviance. In *Fieldwork experience,* edited by W. B. Shaffir, R. A. Stebbins, and A. Turowetz, pp. 31–44. New York: St. Martin's Press.

Whalley, Peter. (1984). Deskilling engineers? The labor process, labor markets, and labor segmentation. *Social Problems,* 32:117–132.

Wharton, Carol S. (1987). Establishing shelters for battered women. *Qualitative Sociology,* 10:146–163.

Whitfield, G. W. (1999). Validating school social work: An evaluation of a cognitive–behavioral approach to reduce school violence. *Research on Social Work Practice,* 9(4):399–426.

Whyte, William Foote. (1955). *Street corner society: The social structure of an Italian slum,* 2nd ed. Chicago: University of Chicago Press.

Whyte, William Foote. (1982). Interviewing in field research. In *Field research,* edited by R. G. Burgess, pp. 111–122. Boston: George Allen and Unwin.

Whyte, William Foote. (1984). *Learning from the field: A guide from experience.* Beverly Hills, CA: Sage.

Whyte, William Foote. (1986). On the uses of social science research. *American Sociological Review,* 51:555–563.

Whyte, William F. (1989). Advancing scientific knowledge through participatory action research. *Sociological Forum,* 4:367–385.

Wieder, D. Lawrence. (1977). Ethnomethodology and ethnosociology. *Mid-American Review of Sociology,* 2:1–18.

Wilcox, Clyde, Lee Sigelman, and Elizabeth Cook. (1989). Some like it hot: Individual differences in responses to group feeling thermometers. *Public Opinion Quarterly,* 53:246–257.

Wilhelm, Brenda. (1998). Changes in cohabitation across cohorts: The influence of political activism. *Social Forces,* 77:289–310.

Williams, Bill. (1978). *A sampler on sampling.* New York: Wiley.

Williams, Carol I., and Gary K. Wolfe. (1979). *Elements of research: A guide for writers.* Palo Alto, CA: Mayfield.

Williams, E., and F. Ellison. (1996). Culturally informed social work practice with American Indians clients: Guidelines for non-Indian social workers. *Social Work,* 41:147–151.

Willimack, Diane K., Howard Schuman, Beth-Ellen Pennell, and James M. Lepkowski. (1995). Effects of prepaid non-monetary incentives on response rates and response quality in face-to-face survey. *Public Opinion Quarterly,* 59:78–92.

Willis, Paul. (1977). *Learning to labor: How working class kids get working class jobs.* New York: Columbia University Press.

Wilson, John. (1982). Realist philosophy as a foundation for Marx's social theory. *Current Perspectives in Social Theory,* 3:243–263.

Wilson, Thomas P. (1970). Normative and interpretative paradigms in sociology. In *Understanding everyday life: Toward the reconstruction of sociological knowledge,* edited by J. Douglas, pp. 57–79. New York: Aldine.

Wilson, Timothy, Suzzane J. LaFleur, and D. Eric Anderson. (1996). The validity and consequence of verbal reports about attitudes. In *Answering questions,* edited by N. Schwarz and S. Sudman, pp. 91–114. San Francisco: Jossey-Bass.

Winston, Chester. (1974). *Theory and measurement in sociology.* New York: Wiley.

Witkin, B., and J. Altschuld. (1995). *Planning and conducting needs assessments: A practical guide.* Thousand Oaks, CA: Sage.

Witkin, S. (2000). Ethics-r-us. *Social Work,* 45(3):197–200.

Witkin, S., and W. Harrison. (2001). Whose evidence and for what purpose? *Social Work,* 46(4):293–296.

Wodarski, J. (1997). *Research methods for clinical social workers: Empirical practice.* New York: Springer.

Wodarski, J., and B. Thyer. (1998). *Handbook of empirical practice: Social problems and practice issues.* New York: Wiley.

Wolcott, Harry F. (1994). *Transforming qualitative data: Description, analysis and interpretation.* Thousand Oaks, CA: Sage.

Woodrum, Eric. (1984). "Mainstreaming" content analysis in social science: Methodological advantages, obstacles, and solutions. *Social Science Research,* 13:1–19.

Wright, Debra L., William S. Aquilino, and Andrew J. Supple. (1998). A comparison of computer-assisted and paper-and-pencil administered questionnaires in a survey on smoking, alcohol and drug use. *Public Opinion Quarterly,* 62:311–353.

Wright, Erik O. (1978). *Class, crisis and state.* London: New Left Books.

Wright, James D., and Peter H. Rossi, eds. (1981). *Social science and natural hazards.* Cambridge, MA: Abt Books.

Wuthnow, Robert. (1979). The emergence of modern science and world system theory. *Theory and Society,* 8:215–243.

Wuthnow, Robert. (1987). *Meaning and moral order: Explorations in cultural analysis.* Berkeley: University of California Press.

Wysong, Earl, Richard Aniskiewicz, and David Right. (1994). Truth and DARE: Tracking drug education from graduation and symbolic politics. *Social Problems,* 41:448–468.

Yammarino, Francis, Steven Skiner, and Terry Childers. (1991). Understanding mail survey response behavior: A meta-analysis. *Public Opinion Quarterly,* 55:613–640.

Yancey, William L., and Lee Rainwater. (1970). Problems in the ethnography of the urban underclasses. In *Pathways to data,* edited by R. W. Habenstein, pp. 245–269. Chicago: Aldine.

Yates, B. (1996). *Analyzing costs, procedures, processes and outcomes in human services.* Thousand Oaks, CA: Sage.

Yates, B., P. Delany, and D. Dillard. (2001). Using cost-procedure-process-outcome analysis. In *The handbook of social work research methods,* edited by B. Thyer, pp. 207–238. Thousand Oaks, CA: Sage.

Yeo, Eileen James. (1991). The social survey in social perspective, 1830–1930. In *The social survey in historical perspective, 1880–1940,* edited by M. Blumer, K. Bales, and K. Sklar, pp. 49–65. New York: Cambridge University Press.

Yin, Robert K. (1988). *Case study research,* rev. ed. Newbury Park, CA: Sage.

Young, T. R. (1980). Comment on the McQuaire-Wardell debate. *Sociological Quarterly,* 21:459–462.

Yow, Valerie Raleigh. (1994). *Recording oral history: A practical guide for social scientists.* Thousand Oaks, CA: Sage.

Yu, J., and H. Cooper. (1983). A quantitative review of research design effects on response rates to questionnaires. *Journal of Marketing Research,* 20:36–44.

Zaller, John, and Stanley Feldman. (1992). A simple theory of survey responses: Answering questions versus revealing preferences. *American Journal of Political Science,* 36:579–616.

Zane, Anne, and Euthemia Matsoukas. (1979). Different settings, different results? A comparison of school and home responses. *Public Opinion Quarterly,* 43:550–557.

Zeisel, Hans. (1985). *Say it with figures,* 6th ed. New York: Harper & Row.

Zelizer, Viviana A. (1985). *Pricing the priceless child.* New York: Basic Books.

Zeller, Richard, and Edward G. Carmines. (1980). *Measurement in the social sciences: The link between theory and data.* New York: Cambridge University Press.

Ziman, John. (1968). *Public knowledge: An essay concerning the social dimension of science.* New York: Cambridge University Press.

Ziman, John. (1976). *The force of knowledge: The scientific dimension of society.* New York: Cambridge University Press.

Zimbardo, Philip G. (1972). Pathology of imprisonment. *Society,* 9:4–6.

Zimbardo, Philip G. (1973). On the ethics of intervention in human psychological research. *Cognition,* 2:243–256.

Zimbardo, Philip G., et al. (Apr. 8, 1973). The mind is a formidable jailer: A pirandellian prison. *New York Times Magazine,* 122:38–60.

Zimbardo, Philip G., et al. (1974). The psychology of imprisonment: Privation, power and pathology. In *Doing unto others,* edited by Z. Rubin. Englewood Cliffs, NJ: Prentice-Hall.

Zimmerman, M. (1990). Taking aim on empowerment research: On the distinction between individual and psychological conceptions. *American Journal of Community Psychology,* 18(1):169–181.

Zuckerman, Harriet. (1972). Interviewing an ultra-elite. *Public Opinion Quarterly,* 36:159–175.

Zuckerman, Harriet. (1978). Theory choice and problem choice in science. In *Sociology of science,* edited by J. Gaston, pp. 65–95. San Francisco: Jossey-Bass.

Zuiches, James J. (1984). The organization and funding of social science in the NSF. *Sociological Inquiry,* 54:188–210.

Zurcher, Louis A. (1979). The airline passenger: Protection of self in an encapsulated group. *Qualitative Sociology,* 1:77–99.

NAME INDEX